TEACHER'S EDITION

collections

Houghton
Mifflin
Harcourt

GRADE 6

Program Consultants:

Kylene Beers

Martha Hougen

Carol Jago

William L. McBride

Erik Palmer

Lydia Stack

HISTORY

bio.

Printed in the U.S.A.

ISBN 978-0-544-56956-0

4 5 6 7 0690 19 18 17 16

4500608123   B C D E F G

Houghton
Mifflin
Harcourt

collections

Teacher's Edition Table of Contents

Kylene Beers Nationally known lecturer and author on reading and literacy; 2011 recipient of the Conference on English Leadership Exemplary Leader Award; coauthor of *Notice and Note: Strategies for Close Reading*; former president of the National Council of Teachers of English. Dr. Beers is the nationally known author of *When Kids Can't Read: What Teachers Can Do* and coeditor of *Adolescent Literacy: Turning Promise into Practice*, as well as articles in the *Journal of Adolescent and Adult Literacy*. Former editor of *Voices from the Middle*, she is the 2001 recipient of NCTE's Richard W. Halley Award, given for outstanding contributions to middle school literacy. She recently served as Senior Reading Researcher at the Comer School Development Program at Yale University as well as Senior Reading Advisor to Secondary Schools for the Reading and Writing Project at Teachers College.

Martha Hougen National consultant, presenter, researcher, and author. Areas of expertise include differentiating instruction for students with learning difficulties, including those with learning disabilities and dyslexia; and teacher and leader preparation improvement. Dr. Hougen has taught at the middle school through graduate levels. Recently her focus has been on working with teacher educators to enhance teacher and leader preparation to better meet the needs of all students. Currently she is working with the University of Florida at the Collaboration for Effective Educator Development, Accountability, and Reform Center (CEEDAR Center) to improve the achievement of students with disabilities by reforming teacher and leader licensure, evaluation, and preparation. She has led similar efforts in Texas with the Higher Education Collaborative and the College & Career Readiness Initiative Faculty Collaboratives. In addition to peer-reviewed articles, curricular documents, and presentations, Dr. Hougen has published two college textbooks: *The Fundamentals of Literacy Assessment and Instruction Pre-K–6* (2012) and *The Fundamentals of Literacy Assessment and Instruction 6–12* (2014).

Carol Jago Teacher of English with 32 years of experience at Santa Monica High School in California; author and nationally known lecturer; and former president of the National Council of Teachers of English. Currently serves as Associate Director of the California Reading and Literature Project at UCLA. With expertise in standards assessment and secondary education, Ms. Jago is the author of numerous books on education, including *With Rigor for All* and *Papers, Papers, Papers*, and is active with the California Association of Teachers of English, editing its scholarly journal *California English* since 1996. Ms. Jago also served on the planning committee for the 2009 NAEP Framework and the 2011 NAEP Writing Framework.

William L. McBride Curriculum specialist. Dr. McBride is a nationally known speaker, educator, and author who now trains teachers in instructional methodologies. He is coauthor of *What's Happening?*, an innovative, high-interest text for middle-grade readers, and author of *If They Can Argue Well, They Can Write Well*. A former reading specialist, English teacher, and social studies teacher, he holds a master's degree in reading and a doctorate in curriculum and instruction from the University of North Carolina at Chapel Hill. Dr. McBride has contributed to the development of textbook series in language arts, social studies, science, and vocabulary. He is also known for his novel *Entertaining an Elephant*, which tells the story of a veteran teacher who becomes reinspired with both his profession and his life.

Erik Palmer Veteran teacher and education consultant based in Denver, Colorado. Author of *Well Spoken: Teaching Speaking to All Students* and *Digitally Speaking: How to Improve Student Presentations*. His areas of focus include improving oral communication, promoting technology in classroom presentations, and updating instruction through the use of digital tools. He holds a bachelor's degree from Oberlin College and a master's degree in curriculum and instruction from the University of Colorado.

Lydia Stack Internationally known teacher educator and author. She is involved in a Stanford University project to support English Language Learners, *Understanding Language*. The goal of this project is to enrich academic content and language instruction for English Language Learners (ELLs) in grades K-12 by making explicit the language and literacy skills necessary to meet the Common Core State Standards (CCSS) and Next Generation Science Standards. Her teaching experience includes twenty-five years as an elementary and high school ESL teacher, and she is a past president of Teachers of English to Speakers of Other Languages (TESOL). Her awards include the TESOL James E. Alatis Award and the San Francisco STAR Teacher Award. Her publications include *On Our Way to English, Visions: Language, Literature, Content,* and *American Themes*, a literature anthology for high school students in the ACCESS program of the U.S. State Department's Office of English Language Programs.

Additional thanks to the following Program Reviewers

Rosemary Asquino	Carol M. Gibby	Linda Beck Pieplow
Sylvia B. Bennett	Angie Gill	Molly Pieplow
Yvonne Bradley	Mary K. Goff	Mary-Sarah Proctor
Leslie Brown	Saira Haas	Jessica A. Stith
Haley Carroll	Lisa M. Janeway	Peter Swartley
Caitlin Chalmers	Robert V. Kidd Jr.	Pamela Thomas
Emily Colley-King	Kim Lilley	Linda A. Tobias
Stacy Collins	John C. Lowe	Rachel Ukleja
Denise DeBonis	Taryn Curtis MacGee	Lauren Vint
Courtney Dickerson	Meredith S. Maddox	Heather Lynn York
Sarah Easley	Cynthia Martin	Leigh Ann Zerr
Phyllis J. Everette	Kelli M. McDonough	
Peter J. Foy Sr.	Megan Pankiewicz	

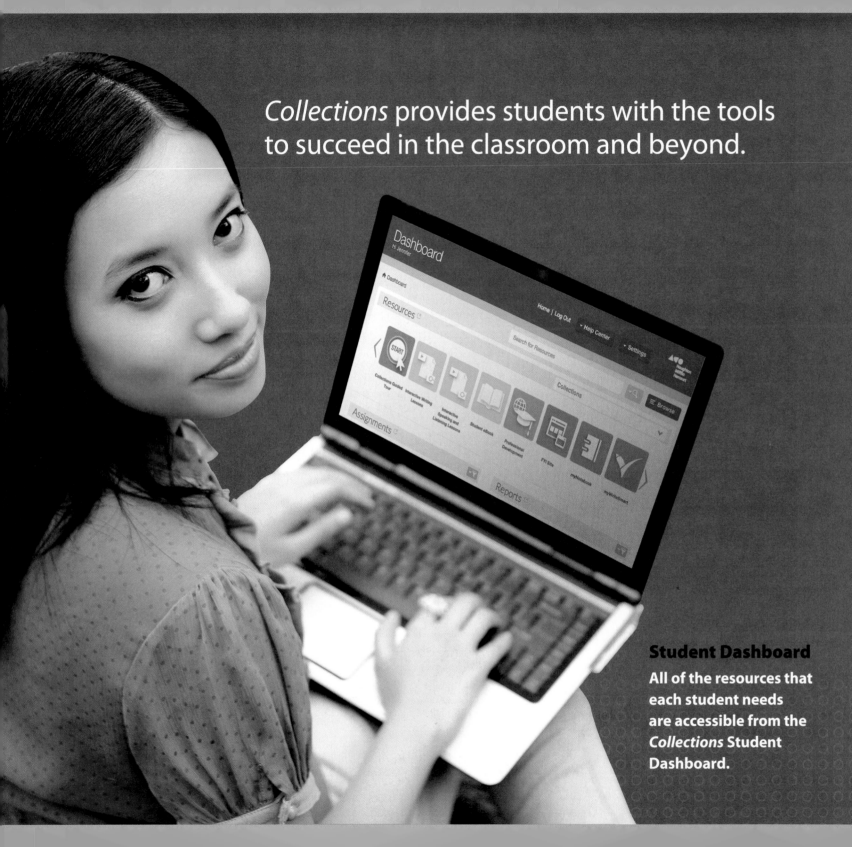

Collections provides students with the tools to succeed in the classroom and beyond.

Student Dashboard

All of the resources that each student needs are accessible from the *Collections* Student Dashboard.

in the 21st Century

HMH Player App provides innovative features supporting instruction both in class and outside of class, synchronizing online and offline work.
available in iOS® and Google Chrome™ formats

Teachers can plan lessons, customize content, present instruction, assign assessments and activities, and review student progress.

Students can download content to their devices and fully use *Collections* without an Internet connection. When back online, all student work is saved and available.

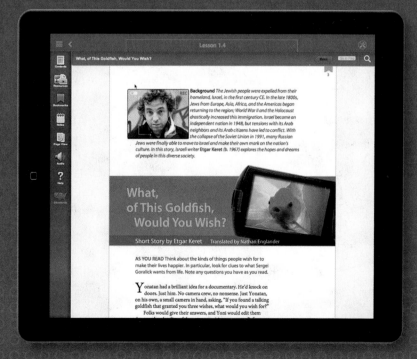

Teaching Every Student

Supporting students' individual strengths, *Collections* integrates scaffolds that build competencies.

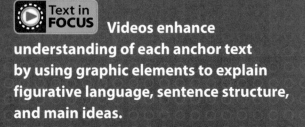 **Videos enhance understanding of each anchor text by using graphic elements to explain figurative language, sentence structure, and main ideas.**

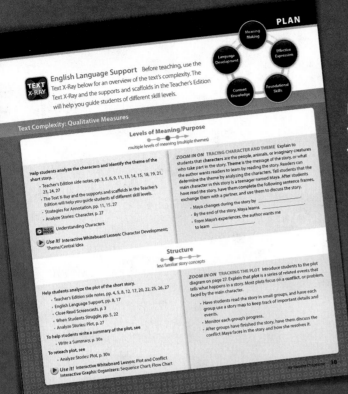

Integrated English Language Development

Integrated ELD instruction is woven seamlessly throughout *Collections*, providing directions for teachers and scaffolding for students.

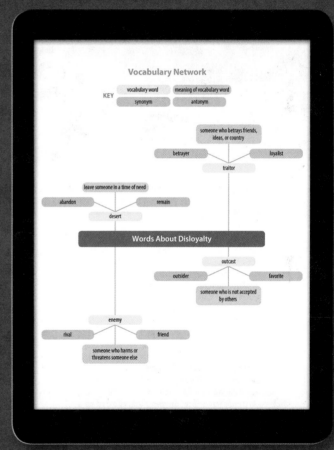

Designated English Language Development

Language Workshop provides instruction and the opportunity for students to master collaboration, interaction, and language production as they develop English language skills.

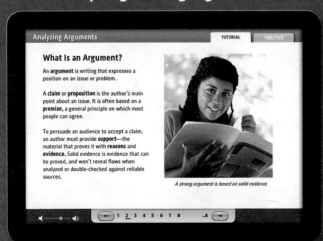

Level Up Interactive Tutorials

Tutorials escalate learning with new digital instruction and feedback for critical learning objectives.

Collections' digital annotation and note-taking tools are essential for text analysis and for writing to sources.

Online Annotation Tools allow students to make meaning and draw conclusions supported by text evidence.

myNotebook stores students' annotations and notes for use in Performance Tasks.

Close Read Screencasts provide modeled conversations about text at point of use in your eBook.

Does love
look with the eyes. . .

Stream to Start

Stream to Start Videos delight and instruct with engaging digital explanations of each collection's theme.

Close Reader allows students to apply standards and practice close-reading strategies in a digital or consumable print format.

Background *A member of the Standing Rock Sioux, Susan Power was born in 1961 and grew up in Chicago. She spent her childhood listening to her mother tell stories about their American Indian heritage. These stories later served as inspiration for Power's writing. As a young girl, Power made frequent visits with her mother to local museums—trips that inspired her memoir "Museum Indians."*

Museum Indians

Memoir by Susan Power

CLOSE READ
Notes

1. **READE** ▶ As you read lines 1–16, begin to cite text evidence.
   - Underline a metaphor in the first paragraph that describes the mother's braid.
   - Underline a metaphor in the second paragraph that describes the mother's braid differently.
   - In the margin, note the adjectives the narrator uses to describe the

...n't cut my hair, will you?" I'm sure this is a whine.
...t a little trim now and then to even the ends."
..."the dark snake to its nest among my mother's slips,
...g so that its thin tail hides beneath the wide mouth sheared

coils in my mother's dresser drawer; it is thick and black,
...as sequins. My mother cut her hair several years ago,
... born, but she kept one heavy braid. It is the three-foot
...from its nest and handle as if it were alive.
...why did you cut your hair?" I ask. I am a little girl lifting a
...river into the light that streams through the kitchen
...om turns to me.
...me headaches. Now put that away and wash your hands

thick
black
glossy

13

Anchor Texts drive each collection and have related selections in the **Close Reader.**

Background *A member of the Standing Rock Sioux, Susan Power was born in 1961 and grew up in Chicago. She spent her childhood listening to her mother tell stories about their American Indian heritage. These stories later served as inspiration for Power's writing. As a young girl, Power made frequent visits with her mother to local museums—trips that inspired her memoir "Museum Indians."*

Museum Indians

Memoir by Susan Power

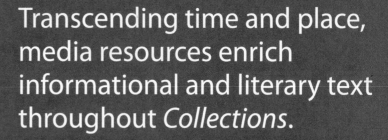

COMPARE ANCHOR TEXTS AND MEDIA

HISTORY VIDEO

The March on Washington

I Have a Dream
Speech by Martin Luther King Jr.

from Nobody Turn Me Around:
A History of the 1963 March on Washington
History Writing by Charles Euchner

MEDIA
AMERICA The Story of Us:
March on Washington
Video by HISTORY®

Background *On August 28, 1963, thousands of Americans marched on Washington, D.C., to urge Congress to pass a civil rights bill. Martin Luther King Jr. delivered his "I Have a Dream" speech on the steps of the Lincoln Memorial before more than 250,000 people. After you read and analyze the speech, you will read an excerpt from a history text which describes the historic speech in detail and includes first-hand accounts from people who were on the National Mall that day. Then you will watch a short video about the march and compare the two accounts.*

Martin Luther King Jr. *(1929–1968) became a catalyst for social change in the 1950s and 1960s. Preaching a philosophy of nonviolence, he galvanized people of all races to participate in boycotts, marches, and demonstrations against racial injustice. His moral leadership stirred the conscience of the nation and helped bring about the passage of the Civil Rights Act of 1964. In that same year, he was awarded the Nobel Peace Prize. King continued his work for justice and equality until he was assassinated in 1968.*

Compare Anchor Texts

Transcending time and place, media resources enrich informational and literary text throughout *Collections*.

Voices and images from A&E®, Bio®, and HISTORY® transport students to different times and places.

Informational text on *FYI* is linked to each collection topic and is curated and updated monthly.

Channel One News®

Channel One helps students become global citizens in a digital world.

Media Lessons prompt students to read news reports, literary adaptations, ads, and websites as complex texts.

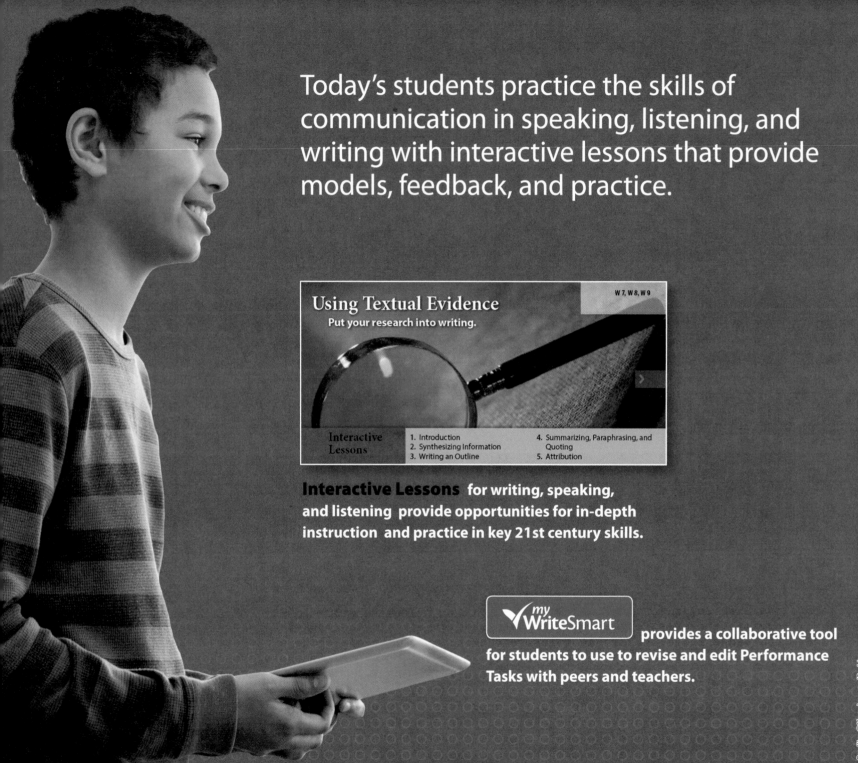

Today's students practice the skills of communication in speaking, listening, and writing with interactive lessons that provide models, feedback, and practice.

Using Textual Evidence
Put your research into writing.

W 7, W 8, W 9

Interactive Lessons

1. Introduction
2. Synthesizing Information
3. Writing an Outline
4. Summarizing, Paraphrasing, and Quoting
5. Attribution

Interactive Lessons for writing, speaking, and listening provide opportunities for in-depth instruction and practice in key 21st century skills.

my **WriteSmart** provides a collaborative tool for students to use to revise and edit Performance Tasks with peers and teachers.

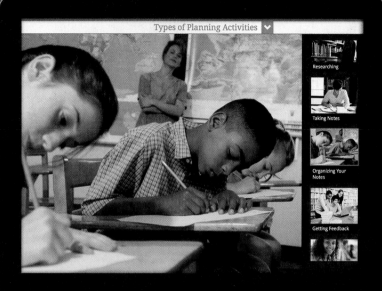

Types of Planning Activities ⌄

Using Precise and Descriptive Language

Good morning, _____! Are you ready _____ the day? This is Zoey here, _____ announcements for Principal Powers wh_____ Let's begin with today's campus _____

_____, the math club will host a mee_____ classroom #221. In addition, all _____ reviews for exam week. And after school _____ skies for the baseball game.

Finally, here's a thought for the day: Wh_____ than ours? Nooooobody! And that's bec_____ one of you. Now _____ with it!

Researching
Taking Notes
Organizing Your Notes
Getting Feedback

Speaking and Listening

Interactive lessons provide audio and video speeches and class discussions for students to critique using rubrics for each activity.

Writing

Models, rubrics, direct instruction, and ongoing feedback provide quality interactive instruction in each of the primary writing types.

Performance Tasks for each collection provide explicit writing process instruction and links to *my*Notebook and to related Interactive Lessons.

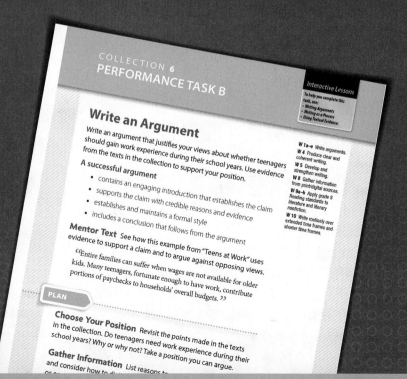

COLLECTION 6
PERFORMANCE TASK B

Interactive Lessons
To help you complete this task, use:
• *Writing Arguments*
• *Writing as a Process*
• *Using Textual Evidence*

Write an Argument

Write an argument that justifies your views about whether teenagers should gain work experience during their school years. Use evidence from the texts in the collection to support your position.

A successful argument

• contains an engaging introduction that establishes the claim
• supports the claim with credible reasons and evidence
• establishes and maintains a formal style
• includes a conclusion that follows from the argument

W 1a–e Write arguments.
W 4 Produce clear and coherent writing.
W 5 Develop and strengthen writing.
W 8 Gather information from print/digital sources.
W 9a–b Apply grade 8 Reading standards to literature and literary nonfiction.
W 10 Write routinely over extended time frames and shorter time frames.

Mentor Text See how this example from "Teens at Work" uses evidence to support a claim and to argue against opposing views.

"Entire families can suffer when wages are not available for older kids. Many teenagers, fortunate enough to have work, contribute portions of paychecks to households' overall budgets. "

PLAN

Choose Your Position Revisit the points made in the texts in the collection. Do teenagers need work experience during their school years? Why or why not? Take a position you can argue.

Gather Information List reasons to _____ and consider how to d_____

Achieving Success

Collections provides 21st century resources supporting teachers and students in achieving their learning goals.

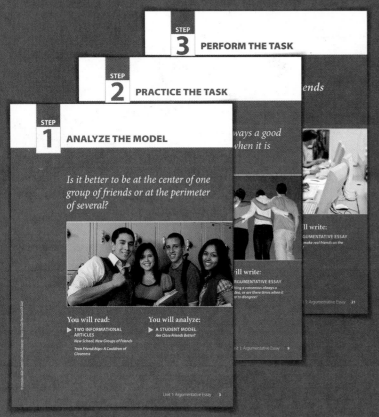

Performance Assessment

Guided instruction and practice performance tasks prepare students for reading and writing tasks in state and national assessments. Three detailed steps—Analyze the Model, Practice the Task, and Perform the Task—lead students to confidence and success.

HMH Close Reads App engages learners with appealing digital instruction in close reading, informing learning with instant feedback as students practice.

Professional Development for Language Arts

The world around us is constantly changing. Current and timely on-going professional development can help you prepare your students for whatever comes their way.

Close Reading

Choosing Complex Texts

Writing & Language

Vocabulary

Speaking & Listening

Media Literacy & Technology

Differentiation

Reading Support

Engagement & Motivation

Performance Task Assessments

HMH Professional Development Website provides teachers with instructional videos by our authors and with podcasts, teaching resources, and more to enhance classroom success.

Assessment Drives Informed Instruction

- **Diagnostic tests with Lexile® scores**
- **Selection and collection tests**
- **ExamView® customization**
- **Selection and collection performance tasks**
- **Benchmark tests**
- **Summative evaluation**

Foundational Skills and Intervention

System 44 provides intensive intervention and support to help students master foundational reading skills through explicit instruction in phonics, comprehension, and writing.

READ 180 provides a personalized learning experience for students reading two or more years below grade level.

COLLECTION 1
Facing Fear

Collection Overviews

Each collection provides overviews of digital resources, key learning objectives, instructional topics for selections, and student support.

COLLECTION PERFORMANCE TASKS

Image Credit: ©Corbis

Annotated Student Edition Table of Contents

Topical Organization

Each collection reflects an engaging topic that connects selections for discussion and analysis so students can integrate and synthesize evidence as they explore several dimensions of the topic.

COLLECTION **1**

Facing Fear

Close Reader

KEY LEARNING OBJECTIVES
Make inferences.
Describe characters and setting.
Describe plot.
Identify repetition and rhyme scheme.
Analyze structure of lyric poems.
Analyze point of view.
Cite evidence.
Determine central ideas and details.
Analyze text features and structure.
Analyze purpose in media.
Understand visual and sound elements.

Image credit: © Corbis

eBook *Explore It!*

 Video Links   **Visit hmhfyi.com** for current articles and informational texts.

Standards Coverage

Each collection addresses a range of standards, ensuring coverage of Reading Literature and Reading Informational Texts standards.

Close Reader

The **Close Reader** provides selections related to the collection topic for additional practice and application of close reading skills and annotation strategies.

COLLECTION **2**
Animal Intelligence

Student Edition + Close Reader

In each collection, the collection topic is explored in both the **Student Edition** and **Close Reader** selections. This page shows how the two components are integrated.

COLLECTION PERFORMANCE TASKS

Image Credit: ©Doug Norman/Alamy

Annotated Student Edition Table of Contents

Anchor Texts

Complex and intellectually challenging, the anchor texts provide a cornerstone for exploring the collection topic and completing the Collection Performance Task. Close Reader selections relate to the Student Edition anchor texts.

Variety of Genres

Both the Student Edition and the Close Reader include a variety of genres of literary texts, informational texts, and media. The genre of each selection is clearly labeled.

COLLECTION **2**

Animal Intelligence

Close Reader

KEY LEARNING OBJECTIVES

Paraphrase ideas.
Describe character responses.
Identify and analyze imagery.
Identify and analyze personification.
Analyze point of view.
Summarize central ideas and details.

Analyze anecdotes.
Identify persuasive techniques.
Analyze text features and structure.
Determine author's purpose.
Integrate information in different media.
Trace and evaluate an argument.

Image credits: ©Doug Norman/Alamy

eBook *Explore It!*

 Video Links

Visit hmhfyi.com
for current articles and informational texts.

Collection Performance Tasks

One or two Collection Performance Tasks present a cumulative task in which students draw on their reading and analysis of the collection's selections as well as on additional research.

INTEGRATED PROGRAM CONTENTS

Cultural Diversity
To enrich students' perspectives, writers from diverse cultures are featured.

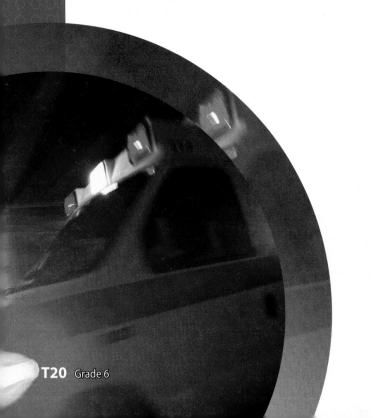

Annotated Student Edition Table of Contents

Compare Texts

To enrich the analysis and discussion of each text, students compare and contrast selections, evaluating elements such as authors' choices, themes, and the structure of arguments.

COLLECTION 3
Dealing with Disaster

Close Reader

KEY LEARNING OBJECTIVES
Identify alliteration.
Identify figurative language.
Identify dialect.
Understand tone.
Compare and contrast poetic forms.
Analyze elements of narrative nonfiction.

Determine meanings of technical language.
Analyze author's style.
Analyze cause-and-effect organization.
Interpret elements of a documentary.
Integrate information in media.

Image credits: ©13/Corbis

eBook *Explore It!*

▶ Video Links   **Visit hmhfyi.com** for current articles and informational texts.

x   Grade 6

Contents   **xi**

Media Analysis

Lessons based on media provide opportunities for students to apply analysis and techniques of close reading to other kinds of texts.

eBook

The eBook, both Student Edition and Teacher's Edition, is your entryway to a full complement of digital resources that promote 21st century skills.

Focus on Argument

Through a range of content-rich informational texts—including editorials and commentaries—students analyze claims and supporting evidence.

Image Credit: ©Fred de Noyelle/Godong/Corbis

Annotated Student Edition Table of Contents

Complex Texts

Complex texts from a variety of genres and content areas include rich themes, sophisticated concepts, and high knowledge demands that challenge students to make meaning as readers and thinkers.

COLLECTION **4**

Making Your Voice Heard

Close Reader

KEY LEARNING OBJECTIVES	
Determine theme.	Analyze author's style.
Identify internal and external conflicts.	Analyze persuasive techniques.
Describe characterization.	Trace and evaluate an argument.
Identify figurative language.	Compare and contrast arguments.
Analyze tone.	

Image credits: © Fred de Noyelle/Godong/Corbis

eBook *Explore It!*

▶ Video Links   Visit **hmhfyi.com** for current articles and informational texts.

Digital Resources

From video links to additional selections and informational texts, a range of digital resources in the eBook enriches students' reading and supports technology skills.

INTEGRATED PROGRAM CONTENTS

Biography and Autobiography

Students analyze literary nonfiction by comparing and contrasting the characteristics of biography and autobiography of the same person.

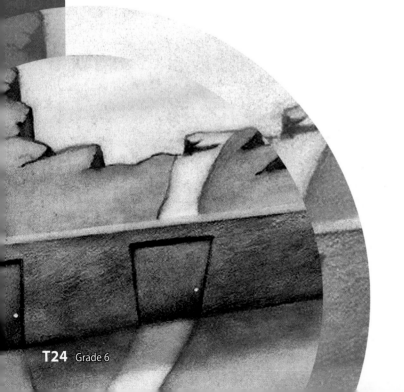

Image Credit: ©images.com/Corbis

Annotated Student Edition Table of Contents

COLLECTION 5

Decisions That Matter

KEY LEARNING OBJECTIVES
Determine theme in poetry.
Describe flashback.
Determine and analyze mood.
Analyze poetic structure.
Analyze narrative poetry.
Analyze elements of a news report.
Identify elements of a memoir.
Identify elements of a biography.
Compare and contrast genres.
Analyze primary and secondary sources.
Integrate information in different media.

Close Reader

Image credits: © Images.com/Corbis

eBook *Explore It!*

▶ **Video Links**   Channel One News® **Visit hmhfyi.com** for current articles and informational texts.

Compare Text and Media

To underscore that textual analysis applies to media as well as print, a rich variety of media is compared to other texts for close reading, analysis, and meaning making.

INTEGRATED PROGRAM CONTENTS

Canonical and Contemporary Texts

Students analyze and compare several versions of a classic story presented in different genres.

Annotated Student Edition Table of Contents

Text-Dependent Questions

Both the Student Edition and the Close Reader include a range of text-dependent questions that require students to engage with the text, make inferences, and cite text evidence to support their claims.

COLLECTION **6**

What Tales Tell

KEY LEARNING OBJECTIVES	Determine theme.	Describe elements of drama.
	Describe foreshadowing.	Compare and contrast genres.
	Describe elements of myths.	Cite textual evidence.
	Describe elements of folk tales.	Analyze structure.
	Determine elements of parody.	

Close Reader

eBook *Explore It!*

 Video Links   **Visit hmhfyi.com** for current articles and informational texts.

Image credits: ©Robert Llewellyn/Corbis

Collection Performance Tasks

Collection Performance Tasks require students to develop a variety of writing and speaking products, working through the process of planning, producing, revising, and presenting for each task.

fyi

The fyi website at hmhfyi.com provides additional contemporary informational texts to enhance each collection. Updated regularly, this site expands background knowledge, discussion, and research.

Student Resources

Information, Please

When students have questions, they can turn to Student Resources for answers. This section includes information about Performance Tasks, the nature of argument, vocabulary and spelling, and grammar, usage, and mechanics.

Word Knowledge

The Glossaries provide definitions for selection, academic, and domain-specific vocabulary, conveniently compiled in a single location.

Connecting to Your World

Every time you read something, view something, write to someone, or react to what you've read or seen, you're participating in a world of ideas. You do this every day, inside the classroom and out. These skills will serve you not only at home and at school but eventually in your career.

The digital tools in this program will tap into the skills you already use and help you sharpen those skills for the future.

Start your exploration at my.hrw.com

Start with the Dashboard

Get one-stop access to the complete digital program for *Collections* and to management and assessment tools.

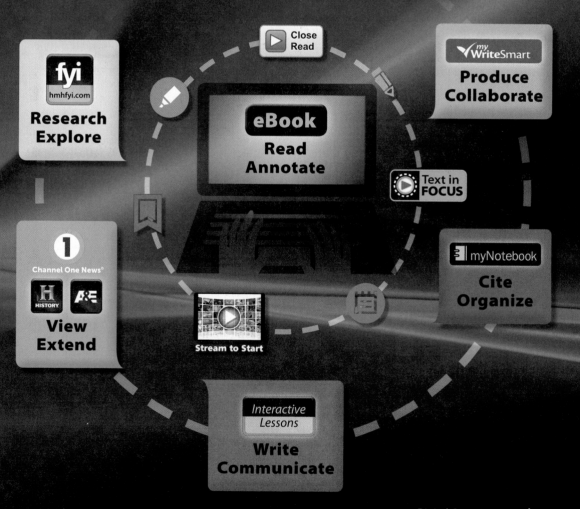

Close Read

my WriteSmart
Produce Collaborate

fyi hmhfyi.com
Research Explore

eBook
Read Annotate

Text in **FOCUS**

1 Channel One News®
HISTORY **A&E**
View Extend

myNotebook
Cite Organize

Stream to Start

Interactive Lessons
Write Communicate

Writing and Speaking & Listening

Communication in today's world requires quite a variety of skills. To express yourself and win people over, you have to be able to write for print, for online media, and for spoken presentations. To collaborate, you have to work with people who might be sitting right next to you or at the other end of an Internet connection.

Comprehensive Standards Coverage

Twelve interactive lessons provide thorough coverage of all Writing standards and Speaking and Listening standards.

Available Only in Your eBook

Interactive Lessons

These interactive lessons will help you master the skills needed to become an expert communicator.

Choosing Relevant Evidence

Choose the pieces of evidence that support the reason shown and drag them into the box.

Tip

Reality stars are often placed in situations that cause them to grow or change in a positive way.

> One contestant who participated in a fashion reality show remarked, "The show made me a better designer." ✓

The winner of one cooking show won a million dollars.

According to Nielsen ratings for this season, 17 of the top 50 most popular TV shows for viewers between the ages of 18-49 were reality shows.

68% of former contestants on a popular weight-loss show have maintained their goal weight for five years post-show.

You've got it! This quotation shows how one contestant experienced personal growth.

xx   Grade 6

Writing Arguments
Learn how to build a strong argument.

W 1, W 10

Interactive Lessons

1. Introduction
2. What Is a Claim?
3. Support: Reasons and Evidence
4. Building Effective Support
5. Creating a Coherent Argument
6. Persuasive Techniques
7. Formal Style
8. Concluding Your Argument

Student-Directed Lessons

Though primarily intended for individual student use, these interactive lessons also offer opportunities for whole-class and small-group instruction and practice.

Writing Informative Texts
Shed light on complex ideas and topics.

W 2, W 10

Interactive Lessons

1. Introduction
2. Developing a Topic
3. Organizing Ideas
4. Introductions and Conclusions
5. Elaboration
6. Using Graphics and Multimedia
7. Precise Language and Vocabulary
8. Formal Style

Writing Narratives
A good storyteller can always capture an audience.

W 3, W 10

Interactive Lessons

1. Introduction
2. Narrative Context
3. Point of View and Characters
4. Narrative Structure
5. Narrative Techniques
6. The Language of Narrative

Writing as a Process

W 4, W 5, W 10

Get from the first twinkle of an idea to a sparkling final draft.

Interactive Lessons	
1. Introduction	4. Revising and Editing
2. Task, Purpose, and Audience	5. Trying a New Approach
3. Planning and Drafting	

Teacher Support

Each lesson in your teacher eBook includes

- support for English language learners and less-proficient writers
- instructional and management tips for every screen
- a rubric
- additional writing applications

Producing and Publishing with Technology

W 6

Learn how to write for an online audience.

SUBMIT

Interactive Lessons	
1. Introduction	3. Interacting with Your Online Audience
2. Writing for the Internet	4. Using Technology to Collaborate

Conducting Research

W 6, W 7, W 8

There's a world of information out there. How do you find it?

Interactive Lessons	
1. Introduction	5. Conducting Field Research
2. Starting Your Research	6. Using the Internet for Research
3. Types of Sources	7. Taking Notes
4. Using the Library for Research	8. Refocusing Your Inquiry

Image Credits: (t) ©JUPITERIMAGES/Bananastock/Alamy; (c) ©Tan Kian Khoon/Shutterstock; (b) ©oliy/Shutterstock

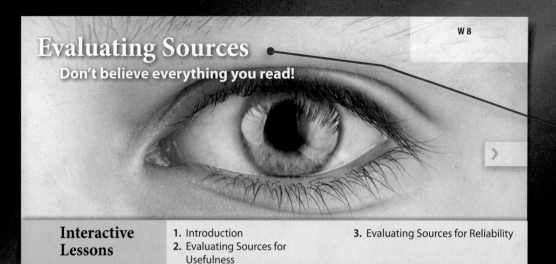

Evaluating Sources
Don't believe everything you read!

W 8

Interactive Lessons	1. Introduction 2. Evaluating Sources for Usefulness	3. Evaluating Sources for Reliability

Authentic Practice of 21st Century Skills

Students have ample opportunities to evaluate real websites, engage in digital collaboration, conduct Web research, and critique student discussions.

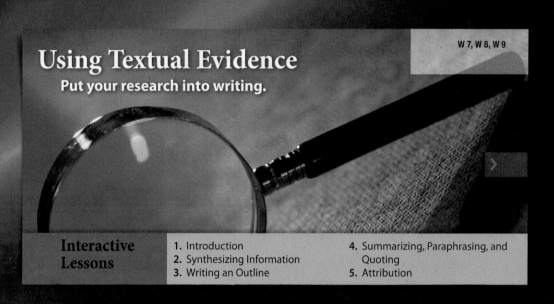

Using Textual Evidence
Put your research into writing.

W 7, W 8, W 9

Interactive Lessons	1. Introduction 2. Synthesizing Information 3. Writing an Outline	4. Summarizing, Paraphrasing, and Quoting 5. Attribution

Participating in Collaborative Discussions

There's power in putting your heads together.

SL 1

Interactive Lessons	1. Introduction 2. Preparing for Discussion 3. Establishing and Following Procedure	4. Speaking Constructively 5. Listening and Responding 6. Wrapping Up Your Discussion

Image Credits: (t) ©Bo Valentino/Shutterstock; (b) ©Getty Images RF; (c) ©Corbis

Analyzing and Evaluating Presentations

SL 2, SL 3, SL 6

Media-makers all want your attention. What are they trying to tell you?

Interactive Lessons		
1. Introduction	4. Tracing a Speaker's Argument	
2. Analyzing a Presentation	5. Rhetoric and Delivery	
3. Evaluating a Speaker's Reliability	6. Synthesizing Media Sources	

Giving a Presentation

SL 4, SL 6

Learn how to talk to a roomful of people.

Interactive Lessons		
1. Introduction	3. The Content of Your Presentation	
2. Knowing Your Audience	4. Style in Presentation	
	5. Delivering Your Presentation	

Using Media in a Presentation

SL 5

If a picture is worth a thousand words, just think what you can do with a video.

Interactive Lessons		
1. Introduction	3. Using Presentation Software	
2. Types of Media: Audio, Video, and Images	4. Practicing Your Presentation	

DIGITAL SPOTLIGHT

| eBook | myNotebook | fyi
hmhfyi.com | my WriteSmart |

Supporting 21st Century Skills

The amount of information people encounter each day keeps increasing. Whether you're working alone or collaborating with others, it takes effort to analyze the complex texts and competing ideas that bombard us in this fast-paced world. What can allow you to succeed? Staying engaged and organized. The digital tools in this program will help you to think critically and take charge of your learning.

Integrated Digital Suite

The digital resources and tools in *Collections* are designed to support students in grappling with complex text and formulating interpretations from text evidence.

Stream to Start

Ignite your Investigation

You learn best when you're engaged. The **Stream to Start** video at the beginning of each collection is designed to inspire interest in the topics being explored. Watch it and then let your curiosity lead your investigations.

Videos to Motivate and Engage

Spark student curiosity and conversation by viewing short, engaging videos at the start of each collection.

Digital Spotlight   **xxv**

Close Read Screencasts

For each anchor text, students can access modeled conversations in which readers analyze and annotate key passages.

Text in Focus Videos

These engaging videos will help students better comprehend the anchor texts. Each video targets a particular passage or element of the text and then provides students with concrete tips for fixing their comprehension.

Close Read

Learn How to Do a Close Read

An effective close read is all about the details; you have to examine the language and ideas a writer includes. See how it's done by accessing the **Close Read Screencasts** in your eBook. Hear modeled conversations about anchor texts.

Contents
Resources
Bookmarks
Notes
Page View
Audio
? Help
Standards

Close Read

long after we got here, Papa got a job driving a cab, and Mama worked cleaning people's houses. It was hard for them not to have the respect they were used to from holding government
60 teaching jobs, but they had high regard for the food they could now easily buy at the store.

Six months after we got here, the Boeing Company moved to Chicago and Mr. Bob Campbell got transferred there. When Aunt Madina left with him, it broke Mama's heart. Aunt Madina was the only person we knew from Kazakhstan, and it felt like our family just huddled together on a tiny island in the middle of a great American sea.

I looked at the permission slip, wishing there were some special words I could say to get Mama and Papa to sign it.
70 Around me, everyone in my homeroom was talking excitedly about the Spring Fling. Mama says she thinks the school is

Text in FOCUS

Increase Your Understanding

TEXT IN FOCUS helps you dig deeper into complex texts by offering visual explanations of potential stumbling blocks. Look for **TEXT IN FOCUS** videos in anchor texts.

"sank our roots"

Annotate the Texts

Practice close reading by utilizing the powerful annotation tools in your eBook. Mark up key ideas and observations using highlighters and sticky notes. Tag unfamiliar words to create a personal word list in *my*Notebook.

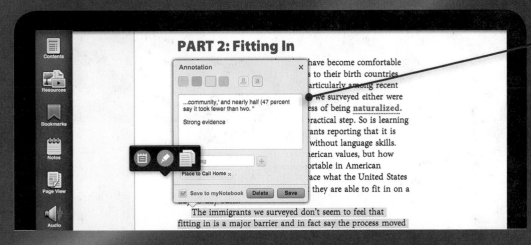

Digital Tools for Close Reading

Annotation tools allow students to note central ideas and details as they gather evidence from the text.

Find More Text Evidence on the Web

Tap into the *fyi* website for links to high-interest informational texts about collection topics. Synthesize information and connect notes and text evidence from any Web source by including it in *my*Notebook

High-Interest Informational Text

Updated monthly, *FYI* features links to reputable sources of informational text.

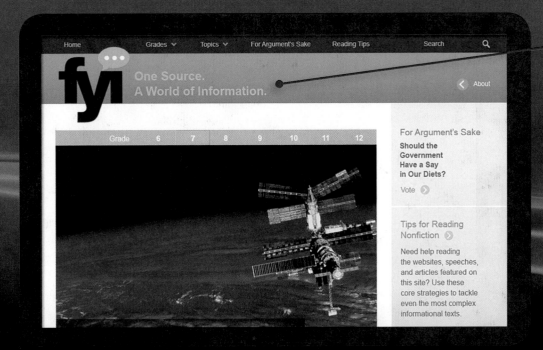

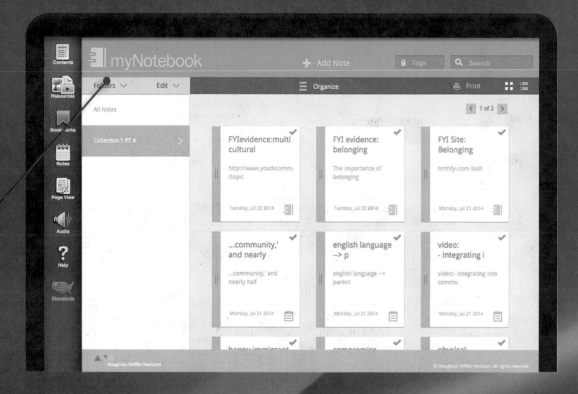

🔲 myNotebook

Save and Organize Your Notes

Save your annotations to *my*Notebook, where you can organize them to use as text evidence in performance tasks and other writing assignments. You can also organize the unfamiliar words you tagged by creating word lists, which will help you grow your vocabulary.

Digital Notebook

Students can save their annotations to *my*Notebook, tag them to particular performance tasks, and create word lists for vocabulary development.

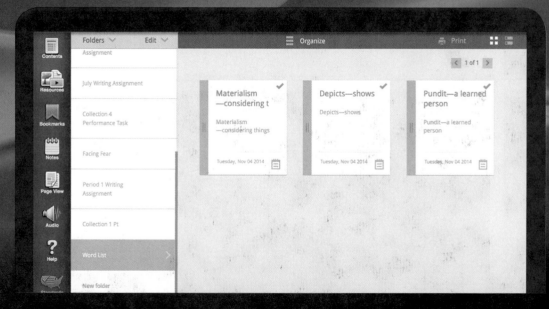

Create, Communicate, and Collaborate

Use the technology provided by the *myWriteSmart* tool to keep track of your writing assignments, create drafts, and collaborate and communicate with peers and your teacher. Use the evidence you've gathered in *my*Notebook to support your ideas.

Tools for Writing

Assign and manage performance tasks in *my*WriteSmart. Students can use the annotations they've gathered and tools for writing and collaboration to complete each task.

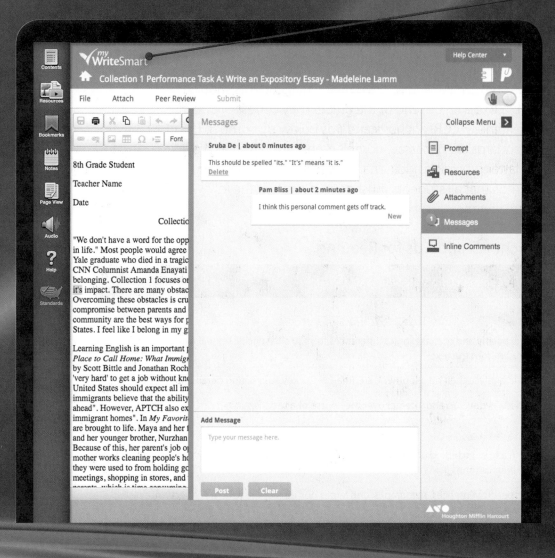

Correlation of *Collections*, Grade 6, to the English Language Arts Common Core State Standards

The grade 6 standards on the following pages define what students should understand and be able to do by the end of the grade. They correspond to the College and Career Readiness (CCR) anchor standards below by number. The CCR and grade-specific standards are necessary complements—the former providing broad standards, the latter providing additional specificity—that together define the skills and understandings that all students must demonstrate. In the following pages, Teacher's Edition page references are boldfaced.

College and Career Readiness Anchor Standards for Reading

Common Core State Standards
KEY IDEAS AND DETAILS
1. Read closely to determine what the text says explicitly and to make logical inferences from it; cite specific textual evidence when writing or speaking to support conclusions drawn from the text.
2. Determine central ideas or themes of a text and analyze their development; summarize the key supporting details and ideas.
3. Analyze how and why individuals, events, and ideas develop and interact over the course of a text.
CRAFT AND STRUCTURE
4. Interpret words and phrases as they are used in a text, including determining technical, connotative, and figurative meanings, and analyze how specific word choices shape meaning or tone.
5. Analyze the structure of texts, including how specific sentences, paragraphs, and larger portions of the text (e.g., a section, chapter, scene, or stanza) relate to each other and the whole.
6. Assess how point of view or purpose shapes the content and style of a text.
INTEGRATION OF KNOWLEDGE AND IDEAS
7. Integrate and evaluate content presented in diverse media and formats, including visually and quantitatively as well as in words.
8. Delineate and evaluate the argument and specific claims in a text, including the validity of the reasoning as well as the relevance and sufficiency of the evidence.
9. Analyze how two or more texts address similar themes or topics in order to build knowledge or to compare the approaches the authors take.
RANGE OF READING AND LEVEL OF TEXT COMPLEXITY
10. Read and comprehend complex literary and informational texts independently and proficiently.

Reading Standards for Literature

Standard	Where Taught

KEY IDEAS AND DETAILS

RL 1
Cite textual evidence to support analysis of what the text says explicitly as well as inferences drawn from the text.

INSTRUCTION
Student Edition/**Teacher's Edition:**
3, **4**, **5**, 6, **7**, **8**, **9**, 10, **11**, **12**, 13, **13**, 17, 18, 19, 21, 22, 23, 25, 26, 27, 28, 29, 30, **31**, **32**, **37**, **73**, **74**, **75**, **76**, 78, 79, **80**, **81**, **82**, **83**, **84**, **85**, 86, 88, **89**, 89, **100**, **101**, **102**, 103, **103**, 158, **159**, **160**, **161**, 162, **163**, **164**, 166, **167**, **171**, **173**, **174**, **175**, **176**, **177**, **178**, **179**, **180**, **184a**, **211**, **212**, **213**, **214**, 215, 216, 219, **233**, **234**, **235**, **236**, **237**, **242**, **243**, **244**, **245**, **271**, **272**, **273**, **274**, **275**, **276**, **280a**, **281**, **285**, **286**, **287**, **288**, **289**, **313**, **314**, **315**, 317, **318**, **320**, **321**, **322**, **323**, **324**, **326**, **331**, **332**, **333**, **335**, **336**, **337**, **338**, **339**, **346**, **347**, **348**, **349**, **350**, **351**, **352**, **353**, **354**, 356, **357**, **358**, **359**, 362, **362a**, **373–376**

APPLICATION
Student Edition/**Teacher's Edition:**
3–12, **3–12**, 17–32, **17–32**, 37–38, **37–38**, 73–88, **73–88**, 99–102, **99–102**, 157–164, **157–164**, 166–167, **166–167**, 171–180, **171–180**, 184a, 211–218, **211–218**, 233–236, **233–236**, 241–244, **241–244**, 271–276, **271–276**, 280a, 285–290, **285–290**, 313–326, **313–326**, 331–332, **331–332**, 335–340, **335–340**, 345–360, **345–360**, 373–376, **373–376**

Close Reader/**Teacher's Edition:**
3–8, **16b–16g**, 19–24, **92b–92g**, 43–52, **184b–184i**, 69–84, **240b–240k**, 97–98, **292b–292e**, 101–114, **330b–330k**, 115–128, **362b–362k**

ASSESSMENT
Student Edition/**Teacher's Edition:**
14, **14**, 34, **34**, 37, **37**, 40, **40**, 90, **90**, 104, **104**, 165, **165**, 168, **168**, 170, **170**, 182, **182**, 220, **220**, 238, **238**, 246, **246**, 278, **278**, 284, **284**, 292, **292**, 328, **328**, 334, **334**, 342, **342**, 362, **362**, 373–376, **373–376**

RL 2
Determine a theme or central idea of a text and how it is conveyed through particular details; provide a summary of the text distinct from personal opinions or judgments.

INSTRUCTION
Student Edition/**Teacher's Edition:**
9, **19**, **27**, **29**, **31**, **211**, **213**, **218**, 219, **219**, **222a**, **246b**, **282**, **283**, 283, **284a**, **316**, **319**, **320**, **323**, **325**, 327, **327**, **344a**, 357

APPLICATION
Student Edition/**Teacher's Edition:**
37–38, **37–38**, 99–102, **99–102**, 157–164, **157–164**, 166–167, **166–167**, 171–180, **171–180**, 211–218, **211–218**, 222a, 246b, 285–290, **285–290**, 313–326, **313–326**, 331–332, **331–332**, 335–340, **335–340**, **344a**, 345–360, **345–360**

Close Reader/**Teacher's Edition:**
43–52, **184b–184i**, 101–114, **330b–330k**

ASSESSMENT
Student Edition/**Teacher's Edition:**
40, **40**, 104, **104**, 165, **165**, 168, **168**, 182, **182**, 220, **220**, 246, **246**, 284, **284**, 292, **292**, 328, **328**, 334, **334**, 342, **342**, 362, **362**

Standard	Where Taught
RL 3 Describe how a particular story's or drama's plot unfolds in a series of episodes as well as how the characters respond or change as the plot moves towards a resolution.	**INSTRUCTION** Student Edition/**Teacher's Edition:** 3, **4, 5, 6, 7, 8, 9, 10, 11**, 13, **13, 16a, 17, 18, 19, 20, 21**, 24, **25, 26, 28, 29, 30, 31, 32**, 33, **33, 36a, 73, 74, 76, 78, 80, 81, 82, 84, 86, 88**, 89, **89, 212, 213, 214, 215, 216**, 219, **219, 233, 234, 235**, 237, **237, 240a, 274, 276, 277**, 277, **280a, 287, 289, 290, 313, 314, 315, 317, 318, 321, 322, 323, 324**, 327, **327, 330a, 335, 336, 337, 339, 340**, 341, **341, 346, 347, 348, 349, 350, 351, 352, 353, 354, 355, 356, 357, 358, 359**, 361, **361, 362a** **APPLICATION** Student Edition/**Teacher's Edition:** 3–12, **3–12, 16a**, 17–32, **17–32, 36a**, 73–88, **73–88**, 211–218, **211–218**, 233–236, **233–236, 240a**, 241–244, **241–244**, 271–276, **271–276, 280a**, 285–290, **285–290**, 313–326, **313–326, 330a**, 335–340, **335–340**, 345–360, **345–360, 362a** Close Reader/**Teacher's Edition:** 3–8, **16b–16g**, 19–24, **92b–92g**, 69–84, **240b–240k**, 101–114, **330b–330k**, 115–128, **362b–362k** **ASSESSMENT** Student Edition/**Teacher's Edition:** 14, **14**, 34, **34**, 90, **90**, 220, **220**, 238, **238**, 246, **246**, 278, **278**, 292, **292**, 328, **328**, 342, **342**, 362, **362**

Standard	Where Taught

CRAFT AND STRUCTURE

RL 4
Determine the meaning of words and phrases as they are used in a text, including figurative and connotative meanings; analyze the impact of a specific word choice on meaning and tone.

INSTRUCTION
Student Edition/**Teacher's Edition:**
4, 6, 7, 9, 25, 31, 37, 38, 39, **39**, **40a**, **92a**, 100, **101**, **102**, 103, **103**, **104a**, **159**, **160**, **164**, **166**, 169, **169**, **170a**, **171**, **172**, **173**, **174**, **175**, **176**, **177**, **178**, **179**, 180, 181, **181**, **184a**, **213**, **214**, **233**, **234**, **235**, **236**, 237, **237**, **240a**, **242**, **243**, **244**, 245, **245**, **246a**, **270a**, **271**, **272**, **273**, **274**, **275**, 277, **277**, **280a**, **281**, **282**, 283, **283**, **284a**, **286**, **292a**, **326**, **330a**, **332**, 333, **333**, **334a**, **347**, **350**

APPLICATION
Student Edition/**Teacher's Edition:**
37–38, **37–38**, **40a**, **92a**, 99–102, **99–102**, 104, **104**, **104a**, 157–164, **157–164**, **170a**, 171–180, **171–180**, **184a**, 211–218, **211–218**, 221, 233–236, **233–236**, **240a**, 241–244, **241–244**, **246a**, **270a**, **280a**, 281–282, **281–282**, **284a**, 285–290, **285–290**, **292a**, **330a**, 331–332, **331–332**, **334a**, 345–360, **345–360**

Close Reader/**Teacher's Edition:**
43–52, **184b–184i**, 69–84, **240b–240k**, 97–98, **292b–292e**

ASSESSMENT
Student Edition/**Teacher's Edition:**
40, **40**, 104, **104**, 165, **165**, 168, **168**, 170, **170**, 182, **182**, 220, **220**, 238, **238**, 246, **246**, 278, **278**, 284, **284**, 292, **292**, 334, **334**, 362, **362**

RL 5
Analyze how a particular sentence, chapter, scene, or stanza fits into the overall structure of a text and contributes to the development of the theme, setting, or plot.

INSTRUCTION
Student Edition/**Teacher's Edition:**
17, **18**, **19**, **21**, **23**, **24**, **25**, **28**, **30**, **31**, **32**, 33, **33**, **37**, **38**, 39, **39**, **40a**, **104a**, **158**, **160**, **161**, **163**, 165, **165**, **166**, **167**, 168, **168**, **170a**, **215**, **216**, 219, **219**, **274**, 277, **277**, **280a**, **281**, **282**, 283, **283**, **285**, **286**, **287**, **289**, **290**, 291, **291**, **292a**, **334a**, **337**, **338**, **340**, 341, **341**, **346**, **348**, **349**, **350**, **351**, **352**, **354**, **355**, **358**, **359**, 361, **361**, **362a**

APPLICATION
Student Edition/**Teacher's Edition:**
3–12, **3–12**, 37–38, **37–38**, **40a**, 73–88, **73–88**, **104a**, 157–164, **157–164**, 166–167, **166–167**, **170a**, 171–180, **171–180**, 211–218, **211–218**, 271–276, **271–276**, **280a**, 281–282, **281–282**, 285–290, **285–290**, **292a**, 313–326, **313–326**, 331–332, **331–332**, **334a**, 335–340, **335–340**, 345–360, **345–360**, **362a**

Close Reader/**Teacher's Edition:**
97–98, **292b–292e**

ASSESSMENT
Student Edition/**Teacher's Edition:**
14, **14**, 34, **34**, 40, **40**, 90, **90**, 165, **165**, 168, **168**, 170, **170**, 182, **182**, 220, **220**, 278, **278**, 284, **284**, 292, **292**, 328, **328**, 334, **334**, 342, **342**, 362, **362**

Standard	Where Taught
RL 6 Explain how an author develops the point of view of the narrator or speaker in a text.	**INSTRUCTION** Student Edition/**Teacher's Edition:** **18, 19, 20, 22, 26, 27, 28,** 33, **33, 36a, 37,** 39, **39, 40a, 73, 74, 75, 76, 77, 78, 79, 81, 82, 83, 85, 87,** 89, **89, 92a, 158, 162, 164, 222a, 242, 243,** 245, **245** **APPLICATION** Student Edition/**Teacher's Edition:** 17–32, **17–32, 36a,** 37–38, **37–38, 40a,** 73–88, **73–88, 92a,** 157–164, **157–164,** 166–167, **166–167, 222a,** 331–332, **331–332** Close Reader/**Teacher's Edition:** 19–24, **92b–92g** **ASSESSMENT** Student Edition/**Teacher's Edition:** 34, **34,** 40, **40,** 90, **90,** 165, **165,** 170, **170,** 246, **246,** 334, **334**

INTEGRATION OF KNOWLEDGE AND IDEAS

Standard	Where Taught
RL 7 Compare and contrast the experience of reading a story, drama, or poem to listening to or viewing an audio, video, or live version of the text, including contrasting what they "see" and "hear" when reading the text to what they perceive when they listen or watch.	**INSTRUCTION** Student Edition/**Teacher's Edition:** 292, **292, 292a,** 361, **361, 362a** **APPLICATION** Student Edition/**Teacher's Edition:** 285–290, **285–290, 292a,** 345–360, **345–360, 362a,** 377–380, **377–380** Close Reader/**Teacher's Edition:** 115–128, **362b–362k** **ASSESSMENT** Student Edition/**Teacher's Edition:** 292, **292,** 362, **362,** 377–380, **377–380**
RL 8 (Not applicable to literature)	

Standard	Where Taught
RL 9 Compare and contrast texts in different forms or genres (e.g., stories and poems; historical novels and fantasy stories) in terms of their approaches to similar themes and topics.	**INSTRUCTION** Student Edition/**Teacher's Edition:** 169, **169, 288, 331, 332,** 333, **333** **APPLICATION** Student Edition/**Teacher's Edition:** 157–164, 166–167, 241–244, **241–244,** 285–290, 313–326, 331–332, 335–340, **335–340** Close Reader/**Teacher's Edition:** 115–128, **362b–362k** **ASSESSMENT** Student Edition/**Teacher's Edition:** 170, **170,** 246, **246,** 334, **334,** 342, **342**

RANGE OF READING AND LEVEL OF TEXT COMPLEXITY

Standard	Where Taught
RL 10 By the end of the year, read and comprehend literature, including stories, dramas, and poems, in the grades 6–8 text complexity band proficiently, with scaffolding as needed at the high end of the range.	**APPLICATION** Student Edition/**Teacher's Edition:** **37A,** 37–40, **37–40,** 73–88, **73–88,** 90, **90, 99A, 99–102,** 104, **104, 171A,** 171–180, **171–180,** 182, **182, 233A,** 233–236, **233–236,** 284, **284, 285A,** 285–290, **285–290, 331A,** 331–332, **331–332,** 334, **334, 335A,** 335–342, **335–342, 345A,** 345–362, **345–362** Close Reader/**Teacher's Edition:** 43–52, **184b–184i,** 97–98, **292b–292e,** 101–114, **330b–330k,** 115–128, **362b–362k**

Reading Standards for Informational Text

Standard	Where Taught

KEY IDEAS AND DETAILS

RI 1
Cite textual evidence to support analysis of what the text says explicitly as well as inferences drawn from the text.

INSTRUCTION
Student Edition/**Teacher's Edition:**
41, 43, 44, 45, 46, 47, 47, 50a, 51, 52, 53, 54, 59, 60, 93, 94, 105, 106, 107, 108, 109, 110, 111, 112, 116a, 117, 118, 119, 120, 123, 124, 128a, 139, 140, 142, 143, 144, 145, 146, 147, 149, 150, 152, 185, 188, 189, 190, 191, 192, 193, 200b, 223, 224, 225, 227, 228, 230, 230, 253, 254, 256, 257, 260, 262, 263, 264, 265, 266, 266, 270a, 294, 295, 296, 298, 302a, 363, 364, 365, 366, 367, 368, 369, 369, 372b

APPLICATION
Student Edition/**Teacher's Edition:**
41–46, **41–46**, 50a, 51–54, **51–54**, 59–60, **59–60**, 93–94, **93–94**, 105–112, **105–112**, 116a, 117–124, **117–124**, 128a, 139–152, **139–152**, 185–192, **185–192**, 223–228, **223–228**, 253–258, **253–258**, 260–265, **260–265**, 270a, 302a, 363–368, **363–368**

Close Reader/**Teacher's Edition:**
9–12, **50b–50e**, 13–16, **58b–58e**, 25–28, **116b–116e**, 29–34, **128b–128g**, 37–42, **156b–156g**, 53–60, **196b–196g**, 63–68, **232b–232g**, 87–96, **270b–270i**

ASSESSMENT
Student Edition/**Teacher's Edition:**
48, **48**, 56, **56**, 62, **62**, 96, **96**, 114, **114**, 126, **126**, 154, **154**, 194, **194**, 226, **226**, 229, **229**, 230, **230**, 259, **259**, 266, **266**, 370, **370**

RI 2
Determine a central idea of a text and how it is conveyed through particular details; provide a summary of the text distinct from personal opinions or judgments.

INSTRUCTION
Student Edition/**Teacher's Edition:**
51, 52, 53, 54, 55, **55**, 58a, 106, 107, 108, 109, 110, 111, 113, **113**, 116a, 141, 232a, 255, **256, 364, 365, 366, 367, 368, 369, 372a**, R16–R21, **R16, R17**, R22–R27, **R22, R27**

APPLICATION
Student Edition/**Teacher's Edition:**
50a, 51–54, **51–54**, 58a, 59–60, **59–60**, 93–94, **93–94**, 105–112, **105–112**, 117–124, **117–124**, 139–152, **139–152**, 197–198, **197–198**, 223–235, **223–235**, 227–228, **227–228**, 259, **259**, 293–298, **293–298**, 363–368, **363–368**, R16–R21, **R16, R17**, R22–R27, **R22, R27**

Close Reader/**Teacher's Edition:**
9–12, **50b–50e**, 13–16, **58b–58e**, 25–28, **116b–116e**, 37–42, **156b–156g**, 87–96, **270b–270i**

ASSESSMENT
Student Edition/**Teacher's Edition:**
56, **56**, 62, **62**, 96, **96**, 114, **114**, 126, **126**, 154, **154**, 200, **200**, 226, **226**, 229, **229**, 230, **230**, 299, **299**, 370, **370**

Standard	Where Taught

RI 3
Analyze in detail how a key individual, event, or idea is introduced, illustrated, and elaborated in a text (e.g., through examples or anecdotes).

INSTRUCTION
Student Edition/**Teacher's Edition:**
44, **52**, **53**, **54**, 55, **55**, **117**, **118**, **119**, **120**, **121**, **122**, **123**, **124**, 125, **125**, **128a**, **185**, **188**, **189**, **190**, **192**, 193, **193**, 229, **229**, **253**, **254**, **255**, **256**, **257**, **258**, 259, **259**, **260**, **261**, **262**, **263**, **264**, 266, **266**, 267, **267**, **294**, **295**, 297, **298**, 299, **299**, R16–R21, **R16**, **R17**, **R18**, **R19**, **R21**

APPLICATION
Student Edition/**Teacher's Edition:**
41–46, **41–46**, 51–54, **51–54**, 59–60, **59–60**, 105–112, **105–112**, 117–124, **117–124**, **128a**, 185–192, **185–192**, 253–258, **253–258**, 260–265, **260–265**, 293–298, **293–298**, 363–368, **363–368**

Close Reader/**Teacher's Edition:**
9–12, **50b–50e**, 29–34, **128b–128g**, 53–60, **196b–196g**, 87–96, **270b–270i**

ASSESSMENT
Student Edition/**Teacher's Edition:**
48, **48**, 56, **56**, 62, **62**, 114, **114**, 126, **126**, 194, **194**, 266, **266**, 268, **268**, 299, **299**, 370, **370**, R16–R21, **R16**, **R17**, **R18**, **R19**, **R20**, **R21**

CRAFT AND STRUCTURE

RI 4
Determine the meaning of words and phrases as they are used in a text, including figurative, connotative, and technical meanings.

INSTRUCTION
Student Edition/**Teacher's Edition:**
42, **44**, **45**, **53**, **55**, **58a**, **59**, **60**, 61, **61**, **62b**, **94**, 95, **95**, **98a**, **121**, **123**, **128a**, **139**, **140**, **142**, **144**, **149**, **152**, 153, **153**, **185**, **186**, **187**, **189**, **190**, **191**, 193, **193**, **196a**, **227**, **228**, 229, **229**, **270a**, **295**, R22–R27, **R22**, **R23**, **R26**, **R27**

APPLICATION
Student Edition/**Teacher's Edition:**
51–54, **51–54**, 59–60, **59–60**, **62b**, 93–94, **93–94**, **98a**, 117–124, **117–124**, **128a**, 139–152, **139–152**, **196a**, 227–228, **227–228**, 253–258, **253–258**, 270a, R22–R27, **R22**, **R23**, **R26**, **R27**

Close Reader/**Teacher's Edition:**
37–42, **156b–156g**, 53–60, **196b–196g**

ASSESSMENT
Student Edition/**Teacher's Edition:**
56, **56**, 62, **62**, 96, **96**, 126, **126**, 154, **154**, 194, **194**, 229, **229**, 230, **230**, 259, **259**

Standard	Where Taught
RI 5 Analyze how a particular sentence, paragraph, chapter, or section fits into the overall structure of a text and contributes to the development of the ideas.	**INSTRUCTION** Student Edition/**Teacher's Edition:** **41, 42, 43, 46,** 47, **47, 51, 93, 94,** 95, **95, 117, 118, 119, 120,** 125, **125, 140, 141, 143, 144, 145, 146, 147, 148, 149, 150, 151,** 153, **153, 156a, 261,** 266, **266, 294, 297,** 299, **299, 363, 365, 367, 368,** 369, **369, 372b,** R16–R21, R22–R27 **APPLICATION** Student Edition/**Teacher's Edition:** 41–46, **41–46,** 51–54, **51–54,** 59–60, **59–60,** 93–94, **93–94,** 106–112, **106–112,** 117–124, **117–124,** 139–152, **139–152,** 185–192, **185–192,** 223–225, **223–225,** 253–258, **253–258,** 260–265, **260–265,** 293–298, **293–298,** 363–368, **363–368,** R16–R21, **R16, R17, R18, R19, R20, R21,** R22–R27, **R22, R23, R24, R26, R27** Close Reader/**Teacher's Edition:** 37–42, **156b–156g** **ASSESSMENT** Student Edition/**Teacher's Edition:** 48, **48,** 56, **56,** 62, **62,** 96, **96,** 114, **114,** 126, **126,** 154, **154,** 194, **194,** 226, **226,** 259, **259,** 266, **266,** 299, **299,** 370, **370**
RI 6 Determine an author's point of view or purpose in a text and explain how it is conveyed in the text.	**INSTRUCTION** Student Edition/**Teacher's Edition:** **60, 105, 107, 108, 109, 112,** 113, **113, 363** **APPLICATION** Student Edition/**Teacher's Edition:** 41–46, **41–46,** 51–54, **51–54,** 105–112, **105–112,** 223–225, **223–225,** 227–228, **227–228,** 253–258, **253–258,** 260–265, **260–265,** R22–R27, **R22, R24, R27** Close Reader/**Teacher's Edition:** 25–28, **116b–116e,** 63–68, **232b–232g** **ASSESSMENT** Student Edition/**Teacher's Edition:** 48, **48,** 56, **56,** 62, **62,** 114, **114,** 230, **230,** 259, **259,** 266, **266,** 268, **268**

Standard	Where Taught

INTEGRATION OF KNOWLEDGE AND IDEAS

RI 7
Integrate information presented in different media or formats (e.g., visually, quantitatively) as well as in words to develop a coherent understanding of a topic or issue.

INSTRUCTION
Student Edition/**Teacher's Edition:**
62a, 117, 119, 120, 121, 125, **125, 142, 153, 197, 198,** 199, **199, 200a, 200b, 296,** 299, **299,** 302, **302, 302a, 366**

APPLICATION
Student Edition/**Teacher's Edition:**
59–60, **59–60, 62a,** 117–124, **117–124,** 139–152, **139–152,** 197–198, **197–198, 200a, 200b,** 253–266, **253–266,** 293–298, **293–298,** 300, **300, 302a**

Close Reader/**Teacher's Edition:**
29–34, **128b–128g,** 37–42, **156b–156g,** 53–60, **196b–196g**

ASSESSMENT
Student Edition/**Teacher's Edition:**
62, **62,** 126, **126,** 154, **154,** 200, **200,** 268, **268,** 302, **302**

RI 8
Trace and evaluate the argument and specific claims in a text, distinguishing claims that are supported by reasons and evidence from claims that are not.

INSTRUCTION
Student Edition/**Teacher's Edition:**
93, 94, 95, **95, 98a, 223, 224, 225, 226, 227, 232a,** R22, **R22,** R24, **R24,** R26, **R26,** R27, **R27**

APPLICATION
Student Edition/**Teacher's Edition:**
93–94, **93–94,** 223–225, **223–225,** 227–228, **227–228**

Close Reader/**Teacher's Edition:**
63–68, **232b–232g**

ASSESSMENT
Student Edition/**Teacher's Edition:**
96, **96,** 226, **226,** 229, **229,** 230, **230**

Standard	Where Taught
RI 9 Compare and contrast one author's presentation of events with that of another (e.g., a memoir written by and a biography on the same person).	**INSTRUCTION** Student Edition/**Teacher's Edition:** 230, **230, 232a, 263, 265,** 267, **267, 270a** **APPLICATION** Student Edition/**Teacher's Edition:** 223–228, **223–228, 232a,** 253–266, **253–266, 270a** Close Reader/**Teacher's Edition:** 63–68, **232b–232g,** 87–96, **270b–270i** **ASSESSMENT** Student Edition/**Teacher's Edition:** 230, **230,** 268, **268**

RANGE OF READING AND LEVEL OF TEXT COMPLEXITY

Standard	Where Taught
RI 10 By the end of the year, read and comprehend literary nonfiction in the grades 6–8 text complexity band proficiently, with scaffolding as needed at the high end of the range.	**APPLICATION** Student Edition/**Teacher's Edition:** **41A,** 41–48, **41–48, 105A,** 105–113, **105–113,** 114, **114, 139A,** 139–153, **139–153,** 154, **154, 185A,** 185–193, **185–193,** 194, **194, 253A,** 253–258, **253–258,** 259, **259, 363A,** 363–370, **363–370** Close Reader/**Teacher's Edition:** 13–16, **58b–58e,** 25–28, **116b–116e,** 29–34, **128b–128g,** 37–42, **156b–156g,** 53–60, **196b–196g,** 87–96, **270b–270i**

College and Career Readiness Anchor Standards for Writing

Common Core State Standards

TEXT TYPES AND PURPOSES

1. Write arguments to support claims in an analysis of substantive topics or texts, using valid reasoning and relevant and sufficient evidence.

2. Write informative/explanatory texts to examine and convey complex ideas and information clearly and accurately through the effective selection, organization, and analysis of content.

3. Write narratives to develop real or imagined experiences or events using effective technique, well-chosen details, and well-structured event sequences.

PRODUCTION AND DISTRIBUTION OF WRITING

4. Produce clear and coherent writing in which the development, organization, and style are appropriate to task, purpose, and audience.

5. Develop and strengthen writing as needed by planning, revising, editing, rewriting, or trying a new approach.

6. Use technology, including the Internet, to produce and publish writing and to interact and collaborate with others.

RESEARCH TO BUILD AND PRESENT KNOWLEDGE

7. Conduct short as well as more sustained research projects based on focused questions, demonstrating understanding of the subject under investigation.

8. Gather relevant information from multiple print and digital sources, assess the credibility and accuracy of each source, and integrate the information while avoiding plagiarism.

9. Draw evidence from literary and/or informational texts to support analysis, reflection, and research.

RANGE OF WRITING

10. Write routinely over extended time frames (time for research, reflection, and revision) and shorter time frames (a single sitting or a day or two) for a range of tasks, purposes, and audiences.

Writing Standards

Standard	Where Taught
TEXT TYPES AND PURPOSES	

W 1
Write arguments to support claims with clear reasons and relevant evidence.

INSTRUCTION/APPLICATION
Interactive Lessons:
Writing Arguments
- Introduction
- What Is a Claim?
- Support: Reasons and Evidence
- Building Effective Support
- Creating a Coherent Argument
- Persuasive Techniques
- Formal Style
- Concluding Your Argument

Student Edition/**Teacher's Edition:**
230, **230,** 247–250, **247–250,** 307–310, **307–310,** R2–R3

ASSESSMENT
Student Edition/**Teacher's Edition:**
230, **230,** 247–250, **247–250,** 307–310, **307–310**

---

a. Introduce claim(s) and organize the reasons and evidence clearly.

INSTRUCTION/APPLICATION
Interactive Lessons:
Writing Arguments
- What Is a Claim?
- Creating a Coherent Argument

Student Edition/**Teacher's Edition:**
230, **230,** 247–250, **247–250,** 307–310, **307–310,** R2–R3

ASSESSMENT
Student Edition/**Teacher's Edition:**
230, **230,** 247–250, **247–250,** 307–310, **307–310**

---

b. Support claim(s) with clear reasons and relevant evidence, using credible sources and demonstrating an understanding of the topic or text.

INSTRUCTION/APPLICATION
Interactive Lessons:
Writing Arguments
- Support: Reasons and Evidence
- Building Effective Support

Student Edition/**Teacher's Edition:**
230, **230,** 247–250, **247–250,** 307–310, **307–310,** R2–R3

ASSESSMENT
Student Edition/**Teacher's Edition:**
230, **230,** 247–250, **247–250,** 307–310, **307–310**

Standard	Where Taught
c. Use words, phrases, and clauses to clarify the relationships among claim(s) and reasons.	**INSTRUCTION/APPLICATION** **Interactive Lessons:** Writing Arguments • Creating a Coherent Argument Student Edition/**Teacher's Edition:** 230, **230,** 247–250, **247–250,** 307–310, **307–310,** R2–R3 **ASSESSMENT** Student Edition/**Teacher's Edition:** 230, **230,** 247–250, **247–250,** 307–310, **307–310**
d. Establish and maintain a formal style.	**INSTRUCTION/APPLICATION** **Interactive Lessons:** Writing Arguments • Formal Style Student Edition/**Teacher's Edition:** 247–250, **247–250,** 307–310, **307–310,** R2–R3 **ASSESSMENT** Student Edition/**Teacher's Edition:** 247–250, **247–250,** 307–310, **307–310**
e. Provide a concluding statement or section that follows from the argument presented.	**INSTRUCTION/APPLICATION** **Interactive Lessons:** Writing Arguments • Concluding Your Argument Student Edition/**Teacher's Edition:** 230, **230,** 247–250, **247–250,** 307–310, **307–310,** R2–R3 **ASSESSMENT** Student Edition/**Teacher's Edition:** 247–250, **247–250,** 307–310, **307–310**

Standard	Where Taught
W 2 Write informative/explanatory texts to examine a topic and convey ideas, concepts, and information through the selection, organization, and analysis of relevant content.	**INSTRUCTION/APPLICATION** **Interactive Lessons:** Writing Informative Texts • Introduction • Developing a Topic • Organizing Ideas • Introductions and Conclusions • Elaboration • Using Graphics and Multimedia • Precise Language and Vocabulary • Formal Style Using Textual Evidence • Writing an Outline Student Edition/**Teacher's Edition:** 14, **14**, 48, **48, 50a**, 56, **56**, 63–66, **63–66**, 67–70, **67–70**, 90, 104, **104**, 114, **114**, 126, **126**, 129–132, **129–132**, 133–136, **133–136**, 220, **220**, 278, **278**, 292, **292**, 328, **328**, 373–376, **373–376**, R4–R5 **ASSESSMENT** Student Edition/**Teacher's Edition:** 14, **14**, 48, **48, 50a**, 56, **56**, 63–66, **63–66**, 67–70, **67–70**, 90, 104, **104**, 114, **114**, 126, **126**, 129–132, **129–132**, 133–136, **133–136**, 220, **220**, 278, **278**, 292, **292**, 328, **328**, 373–376, **373–376**
a. Introduce a topic; organize ideas, concepts, and information, using strategies such as definition, classification, comparison/ contrast, and cause/effect; include formatting (e.g., headings), graphics (e.g., charts, tables), and multimedia when useful to aiding comprehension.	**INSTRUCTION/APPLICATION** **Interactive Lessons:** Writing Informative Texts • Developing a Topic • Organizing Ideas • Introductions and Conclusions • Using Graphics and Multimedia Student Edition/**Teacher's Edition:** 14, **14**, 56, **56**, 67–70, **67–70**, 90, **90**, 104, **104**, 129–132, **129–132**, 133–136, **133–136**, 278, **278**, 292, **292**, 328, **328**, 373–376, **373–376**, R4–R5 **ASSESSMENT** Student Edition/**Teacher's Edition:** 14, **14**, 56, **56**, 67–70, **67–70**, 90, **90**, 104, **104**, 129–132, **129–132**, 133–136, **133–136**, 278, **278**, 292, **292**, 328, **328**, 373–376, **373–376**
b. Develop the topic with relevant facts, definitions, concrete details, quotations, or other information and examples.	**INSTRUCTION/APPLICATION** **Interactive Lessons:** Writing Informative Texts • Elaboration Student Edition/**Teacher's Edition:** 14, **14**, 56, **56**, 67–70, **67–70**, 90, **90**, 104, **104**, 129–132, **129–132**, 133–136, **133–136**, 278, **278**, 292, **292**, 328, **328**, 373–376, **373–376**, R4–R5 **ASSESSMENT** Student Edition/**Teacher's Edition:** 14, **14**, 56, **56**, 67–70, **67–70**, 90, **90**, 104, **104**, 129–132, **129–132**, 133–136, **133–136**, 278, **278**, 292, **292**, 328, **328**, 373–376, **373–376**

Standard	Where Taught
c. Use appropriate transitions to clarify the relationships among ideas and concepts.	**INSTRUCTION/APPLICATION** **Interactive Lessons:** Writing Informative Texts • Organizing Ideas Student Edition/**Teacher's Edition:** 14, **14**, 56, **56**, 67–70, **67–70**, 90, **90**, 104, **104**, 129–132, **129–132**, 133–136, **133–136**, 278, **278**, 292, **292**, 328, **328**, 373–376, **373–376**, R4–R5 **ASSESSMENT** Student Edition/**Teacher's Edition:** 14, **14**, 56, **56**, 67–70, **67–70**, 90, **90**, 104, **104**, 129–132, **129–132**, 133–136, **133–136**, 278, **278**, 292, **292**, 328, **328**, 373–376, **373–376**
d. Use precise language and domain-specific vocabulary to inform about or explain the topic.	**INSTRUCTION/APPLICATION** **Interactive Lessons:** Writing Informative Texts • Precise Language and Vocabulary Student Edition/**Teacher's Edition:** 14, **14**, 56, **56**, 67–70, **67–70**, 90, **90**, 104, **104**, 129–132, **129–132**, 133–136, **133–136**, 278, **278**, 292, **292**, 328, **328**, 373–376, **373–376**, R4–R5 **ASSESSMENT** Student Edition/**Teacher's Edition:** 14, **14**, 56, **56**, 67–70, **67–70**, 90, **90**, 104, **104**, 129–132, **129–132**, 133–136, **133–136**, 278, **278**, 292, **292**, 328, **328**, 373–376, **373–376**
e. Establish and maintain a formal style.	**INSTRUCTION/APPLICATION** **Interactive Lessons:** Writing Informative Texts • Formal Style Student Edition/**Teacher's Edition:** 14, **14**, 56, **56**, 67–70, **67–70**, 90, **90**, 104, **104**, 129–132, **129–132**, 133–136, **133–136**, 278, **278**, 292, **292**, 328, **328**, 373–376, **373–376**, R4–R5 **ASSESSMENT** Student Edition/**Teacher's Edition:** 14, **14**, 56, **56**, 67–70, **67–70**, 90, **90**, 104, **104**, 129–132, **129–132**, 133–136, **133–136**, 278, **278**, 292, **292**, 328, **328**, 373–376, **373–376**
f. Provide a concluding statement or section that follows from the information or explanation presented.	**INSTRUCTION/APPLICATION** **Interactive Lessons:** Writing Informative Texts • Introductions and Conclusions Student Edition/**Teacher's Edition:** 14, **14**, 56, **56**, 67–70, **67–70**, 90, **90**, 104, **104**, 129–132, **129–132**, 133–136, **133–136**, 278, **278**, 292, **292**, 328, **328**, 373–376, **373–376**, R4–R5 **ASSESSMENT** Student Edition/**Teacher's Edition:** 14, **14**, 56, **56**, 67–70, **67–70**, 90, **90**, 104, **104**, 129–132, **129–132**, 133–136, **133–136**, 278, **278**, 292, **292**, 328, **328**, 373–376, **373–376**, R4

Standard	Where Taught
W 3 Write narratives to develop real or imagined experiences or events using effective technique, relevant descriptive details, and well-structured event sequences.	**INSTRUCTION/APPLICATION** **Interactive Lessons:** **Writing Narratives** • Introductions • Narrative Context • Point of View and Characters • Narrative Structure • Narrative Techniques • The Language of Narrative Student Edition/**Teacher's Edition:** 34, **34**, 170, **170**, 182, **182**, 205–208, **205–208**, 246, **246**, 303–306, **303–306**, **334a**, 342, **342**, 377–380, **377–380**, R6–R7 **ASSESSMENT** Student Edition/**Teacher's Edition:** 34, **34**, 170, **170**, 182, **182**, 205–208, **205–208**, 246, **246**, 303–306, **303–306**, **334a**, 342, **342**, 377–380, **377–380**
a. Engage and orient the reader by establishing a context and introducing a narrator and/or characters; organize an event sequence that unfolds naturally and logically.	**INSTRUCTION/APPLICATION** **Interactive Lessons:** **Writing Narratives** • Narrative Context • Point of View and Characters • Narrative Structure Student Edition/**Teacher's Edition:** 34, **34**, 205–208, **205–208**, 303–306, **303–306**, **334a**, 342, **342**, 377–380, **377–380**, R6–R7 **ASSESSMENT** Student Edition/**Teacher's Edition:** 34, **34**, 205–208, **205–208**, 303–306, **303–306**, **334a**, 342, **342**, 377–380, **377–380**
b. Use narrative techniques, such as dialogue, pacing, and description, to develop experiences, events, and/or characters.	**INSTRUCTION/APPLICATION** **Interactive Lessons:** Writing Narratives • Narrative Techniques • The Language of Narrative Student Edition/**Teacher's Edition:** 34, **34**, 205–208, **205–208**, 303–306, **303–306**, 342, **342**, 377–380, **377–380**, R6–R7 **ASSESSMENT** Student Edition/**Teacher's Edition:** 34, **34**, 205–208, **205–208**, 303–306, **303–306**, 342, **342**, 377–380, **377–380**

Standard	Where Taught
c. Use a variety of transition words, phrases, and clauses to convey sequence and signal shifts from one time frame or setting to another.	**INSTRUCTION/APPLICATION** **Interactive Lessons:** Writing Narratives • Narrative Structure Student Edition/**Teacher's Edition:** 34, **34**, 205–208, **205–208**, 303–306, **303–306**, 334a, 342, **342**, 377–380, **377–380**, R6–R7 **ASSESSMENT** Student Edition/**Teacher's Edition:** 34, **34**, 205–208, **205–208**, 303–306, **303–306**, 334a, 342, **342**, 377–380, **377–380**
d. Use precise words and phrases, relevant descriptive details, and sensory language to convey experiences and events.	**INSTRUCTION/APPLICATION** **Interactive Lessons:** Writing Narratives • The Language of Narrative Student Edition/**Teacher's Edition:** 34, **34**, 170, **170**, 182, **182**, 205–208, **205–208**, 246, **246**, 303–306, **303–306**, 342, **342**, 377–380, **377–380**, R6–R7 **ASSESSMENT** Student Edition/**Teacher's Edition:** 34, **34**, 170, **170**, 182, **182**, 205–208, **205–208**, 246, **246**, 303–306, **303–306**, 342, **342**, 377–380, **377–380**
e. Provide a conclusion that follows from the narrated experiences or events.	**INSTRUCTION/APPLICATION** **Interactive Lessons:** Writing Narratives • Narrative Structure Student Edition/**Teacher's Edition:** 34, **34**, 205–208, **205–208**, 303–306, **303–306**, 342, **342**, 377–380, **377–380**, R6–R7 **ASSESSMENT** Student Edition/**Teacher's Edition:** 34, **34**, 205–208, **205–208**, 303–306, **303–306**, 342, **342**, 377–380, **377–380**

Standard	Where Taught

PRODUCTION AND DISTRIBUTION OF WRITING

W 4
Produce clear and coherent writing in which the development, organization, and style are appropriate to task, purpose, and audience.
(Grade-specific expectations for writing types are defined in Standards 1–3 above.)

INSTRUCTION/APPLICATION
Interactive Lessons:
Writing as a Process
• Task, Purpose, and Audience

Student Edition/**Teacher's Edition:**
48, **48**, **50a**, 67–70, **67–70**, 104, **104**, 129–132, **129–132**, 133–136, **133–136**, 200, **200**, 205–208, **205–208**, 292, **292**, 303–306, **303–306**, 307–310, **307–310**, **334a**, 377–380, **377–380**, R2–R3, R4–R5, R6–R7

ASSESSMENT
Student Edition/**Teacher's Edition:**
48, **48**, **50a**, 67–70, **67–70**, 104, **104**, 129–132, **129–132**, 133–136, **133–136**, 200, **200**, 205–208, **205–208**, 292, **292**, 303–306, **303–306**, 307–310, **307–310**, **334a**, 377–380, **377–380**

W 5
With some guidance and support from peers and adults, develop and strengthen writing as needed by planning, revising, editing, rewriting, or trying a new approach. (Editing for conventions should demonstrate command of Language standards 1–3 up to and including grade 6.)

INSTRUCTION/APPLICATION
Interactive Lessons:
Writing as a Process
• Introduction
• Planning and Drafting
• Revising and Editing
• Trying a New Approach

Student Edition/**Teacher's Edition:**
67–70, **67–70**, 129–132, **129–132**, 133–136, **133–136**, 205–208, **205–208**, 247–250, **247–250**, 303–306, **303–306**, 307–310, **307–310**, 377–380, **377–380**

ASSESSMENT
Student Edition/**Teacher's Edition:**
67–70, **67–70**, 129–132, **129–132**, 133–136, **133–136**, 205–208, **205–208**, 247–250, **247–250**, 303–306, **303–306**, 307–310, **307–310**, 377–380, **377–380**

W 6
Use technology, including the Internet, to produce and publish writing as well as to interact and collaborate with others; demonstrate sufficient command of keyboarding skills to type a minimum of three pages in a single sitting.

INSTRUCTION/APPLICATION
Interactive Lessons:
Producing and Publishing with Technology
• Introduction
• Writing for the Internet
• Interacting with Your Online Audience
• Using Technology to Collaborate

Student Edition/**Teacher's Edition:**
62, **62**, 126, **126**, 129–132, **129–132**, 133–136, **133–136**, 205–208, **205–208**, 247–250, **247–250**, 302, **302**, 377–380, **377–380**

ASSESSMENT
Student Edition/**Teacher's Edition:**
62, **62**, 126, **126**, 129–132, **129–132**, 133–136, **133–136**, 205–208, **205–208**, 247–250, **247–250**, 302, **302**, 377–380, **377–380**

Standard	Where Taught

RESEARCH TO BUILD AND PRESENT KNOWLEDGE

W 7
Conduct short research projects to answer a question, drawing on several sources and refocusing the inquiry when appropriate.

INSTRUCTION/APPLICATION
Interactive Lessons:
Conducting Research
- Introduction
- Starting Your Research
- Types of Sources
- Using the Library for Research
- Conducting Field Research
- Using the Internet for Research
- Refocusing Your Inquiry
Using Textual Evidence
- Synthesizing Information

Student Edition/**Teacher's Edition:**
126, **126,** 133–136, **133–136,** 194, **194,** 220, **220,** 230, **230,** R8–R11

ASSESSMENT
Student Edition/**Teacher's Edition:**
126, **126,** 133–136, **133–136,** 194, **194,** 220, **220,** 230, **230**

W 8
Gather relevant information from multiple print and digital sources; assess the credibility of each source; and quote or paraphrase the data and conclusions of others while avoiding plagiarism and providing basic bibliographic information for sources.

INSTRUCTION/APPLICATION
Interactive Lessons:
Conducting Research
- Types of Sources
- Using the Library for Research
- Using the Internet for Research
Evaluating Sources
- Introduction
- Evaluating Sources for Usefulness
- Evaluating Sources for Reliability
Using Textual Evidence
- Summarizing, Paraphrasing, and Quoting
- Attribution

Student Edition/**Teacher's Edition:**
67–70, **67–70,** 133–136, **133–136,** 201–204, **201–204,** 247–250, **247–250,** 302, **302,** 302a, R8–R11

ASSESSMENT
Student Edition/**Teacher's Edition:**
67–70, **67–70,** 133–136, **133–136,** 201–204, **201–204,** 247–250, **247–250,** 302, **302,** 302a

Standard	Where Taught
W 9 Draw evidence from literary or informational texts to support analysis, reflection, and research.	**INSTRUCTION/APPLICATION** **Interactive Lessons:** Writing Informative Texts • Elaboration Conducting Research • Taking Notes Using Textual Evidence • Introduction • Synthesizing Information • Writing an Outline • Summarizing, Paraphrasing, and Quoting Student Edition/**Teacher's Edition:** 14, **14**, 56, **56**, 63–66, **63–66,** 114, **114**, 129–132, **129–132**, 133–136, **133–136**, 268, **268**, 278, **278**, 292, **292**, 307–310, **307–310**, 328, 373–376, **373–376** **ASSESSMENT** Student Edition/**Teacher's Edition:** 14, **14**, 56, **56**, 63–66, **63–66,** 114, **114**, 129–132, **129–132**, 133–136, **133–136**, 268, **268**, 278, **278**, 292, **292**, 307–310, **307–310**, 328, 373–376, **373–376**
a. Apply *grade 6 Reading Standards* to literature (e.g., "Compare and contrast texts in different forms or genres [e.g., stories and poems; historical novels and fantasy stories] in terms of their approaches to similar themes and topics").	**INSTRUCTION/APPLICATION** Student Edition/**Teacher's Edition:** 104, **104**, 129–132, **129–132**, 278, **278**, 292, **292**, 307–310, **307–310**, 373–376, **373–376** **ASSESSMENT** Student Edition/**Teacher's Edition:** 104, **104**, 129–132, **129–132**, 278, **278**, 292, **292**, 307–310, **307–310**, 373–376, **373–376**
b. Apply *grade 6 Reading Standards* to literary nonfiction (e.g., "Trace and evaluate the argument and specific claims in a text, distinguishing claims that are supported by reasons and evidence from claims that are not").	**INSTRUCTION/APPLICATION** Student Edition/**Teacher's Edition:** 56, **56**, 133–136, **133–136**, 307–310, **307–310** **ASSESSMENT** Student Edition/**Teacher's Edition:** 56, **56**, 133–136, **133–136**, 307–310, **307–310**

Standard	Where Taught

RANGE OF WRITING

W 10
Write routinely over extended time frames (time for research, reflection, and revision) and shorter time frames (a single sitting or a day or two) for a range of discipline-specific tasks, purposes, and audiences.

INSTRUCTION/APPLICATION
Interactive Lessons:
Writing as a Process
• Task, Purpose, and Audience
Writing Arguments
Writing Informative Texts
Writing Narratives
Using Textual Evidence

Student Edition/**Teacher's Edition:**
129–132, **129–132**, 133–136, **133–136**, 247–250, **247–250**, 278, **278**, 292, **292**, 303–306, **303–306**, 307–310, **307–310**, 328, **328**, 373–376, **373–376**

ASSESSMENT
Student Edition/**Teacher's Edition:**
14, **14**, 34, **34**, 48, **48**, 56, **56**, 90, **90**, 104, **104**, 114, **114**, 129–132, **129–132**, 133–136, **133–136**, 170, **170**, 182, **182**, 194, **194**, 220, **220**, 246, **246**, 247–250, **247–250**, 278, **278**, 292, **292**, 303–306, **303–306**, 307–310, **307–310**, 328, **328**, 342, **342**

College and Career Readiness Anchor Standards for Speaking and Listening

Common Core State Standards

COMPREHENSION AND COLLABORATION

1. Prepare for and participate effectively in a range of conversations and collaborations with diverse partners, building on others' ideas and expressing their own clearly and persuasively.

2. Integrate and evaluate information presented in diverse media and formats, including visually, quantitatively, and orally.

3. Evaluate a speaker's point of view, reasoning, and use of evidence and rhetoric.

PRESENTATION OF KNOWLEDGE AND IDEAS

4. Present information, findings, and supporting evidence such that listeners can follow the line of reasoning and the organization, development, and style are appropriate to task, purpose, and audience.

5. Make strategic use of digital media and visual displays of data to express information and enhance understanding of presentations.

6. Adapt speech to a variety of contexts and communicative tasks, demonstrating command of formal English when indicated or appropriate.

Speaking and Listening Standards

Standard	Where Taught

COMPREHENSION AND COLLABORATION

SL 1
Engage effectively in a range of collaborative discussions (one-on-one, in groups, and teacher-led) with diverse partners on *grade 6 topics, texts, and issues,* building on others' ideas and expressing their own clearly.

INSTRUCTION/APPLICATION
Interactive Lessons:
Participating in Collaborative Discussions
- Introduction
- Preparing for Discussion
- Establishing and Following Procedure
- Speaking Constructively
- Listening and Responding
- Wrapping Up Your Discussion

Student Edition/Teacher's Edition:
12, **12**, 32, **32**, 38, **38**, **40a**, 46, **46**, 54, **54**, 60, **60**, **62a**, 88, **88**, 96, **96**, 102, **102**, **104a**, 112, **112**, 154, **154**, **156a**, 167, **167**, **170a**, 180, **180**, 198, **198**, 218, **218**, **222a**, 236, **236**, 238, **238**, **240a**, 244, **244**, **246a**, **246b**, 265, **265**, **270a**, 276, **276**, 282, **282**, 284, **284**, **284a**, 290, **290**, 292, **292**, **292a**, 300, **300**, 302, **302**, **302a**, 332, **332**, **344a**, 362, **362**, 368, **368**, 370, **370**, **372b**, 373–376, **373–376**, R12–R13

Close Reader/Teacher's Edition:
25–28, **116b–116e**, 87–96, **270b–270i**, 101–114, **330b–330k**

ASSESSMENT
Student Edition/Teacher's Edition:
96, **96**, 154, **154**, 238, **238**, 284, **284**, 292, **292**, 302, **302**, 362, **362**, 370, **370**, 373–376, **373–376**

---

a. Come to discussions prepared, having read or studied required material; explicitly draw on that preparation by referring to evidence on the topic, text, or issue to probe and reflect on ideas under discussion.

INSTRUCTION/APPLICATION
Interactive Lessons:
Participating in Collaborative Discussions
- Preparing for Discussion

Student Edition/Teacher's Edition:
12, **12**, 46, **46**, 96, **96**, 112, **112**, 154, **154**, **156a**, 167, **167**, 180, **180**, 198, **198**, 218, **218**, 236, **236**, 238, **238**, 244, **244**, 265, **265**, 276, **276**, 282, **282**, 290, **290**, 284, **284**, 300, **300**, 332, **332**, 368, **368**, 370, **370**, 373–376, **373–376**, R12–R13

Close Reader/Teacher's Edition:
87–96, **270b–270i**, 101–114, **330b–330k**

ASSESSMENT
Student Edition/Teacher's Edition:
96, **96**, 154, **154**, 238, **238**, 284, **284**, 370, **370**, 373–376, **373–376**

Standard	Where Taught
b. Follow rules for collegial discussions, set specific goals and deadlines, and define individual roles as needed.	**INSTRUCTION/APPLICATION** **Interactive Lessons:** Participating in Collaborative Discussions • Establishing and Following Procedure Student Edition/**Teacher's Edition:** 154, **154, 156a,** 238, **238,** 284, **284,** 370, **370,** 373–376, **373–376,** R12–R13 **ASSESSMENT** Student Edition/**Teacher's Edition:** 154, **154, 156a,** 238, **238,** 284, **284,** 370, **370,** 373–376, **373–376**
c. Pose and respond to specific questions with elaboration and detail by making comments that contribute to the topic, text, or issue under discussion.	**INSTRUCTION/APPLICATION** **Interactive Lessons:** Participating in Collaborative Discussions • Speaking Constructively • Listening and Responding Student Edition/**Teacher's Edition:** 154, **154, 156a,** 238, **238,** 370, **370, 372b,** 373–376, **373–376,** R12–R13 **ASSESSMENT** Student Edition/**Teacher's Edition:** 154, **154, 156a,** 238, **238,** 370, **370,** 373–376, **373–376**
d. Review the key ideas expressed and demonstrate understanding of multiple perspectives through reflection and paraphrasing.	**INSTRUCTION/APPLICATION** **Interactive Lessons:** Participating in Collaborative Discussions • Wrapping Up Your Discussion Student Edition/**Teacher's Edition:** 154, **154, 156a,** 238, **238,** 284, **284,** 370, **370,** 373–376, **373–376,** R12–R13 Close Reader/**Teacher's Edition:** 87–96, **270b–270i,** 101–114, **330b–330k** **ASSESSMENT** Student Edition/**Teacher's Edition:**
SL 2 Interpret information presented in diverse media and formats (e.g., visually, quantitatively, orally) and explain how it contributes to a topic, text, or issue under study.	**INSTRUCTION/APPLICATION** **Interactive Lessons:** Analyzing and Evaluating Presentations • Introduction • Analyzing a Presentation Student Edition/**Teacher's Edition:** 59–60, **59–60,** 61, **61, 62b,** 197–198, **197–198,** 199, **199, 200a,** 300, **300,** 301, **301, 302a** **ASSESSMENT** Student Edition/**Teacher's Edition:** 62, **62,** 200, **200,** 302, **302**

Standard	Where Taught
SL 3 Delineate a speaker's argument and specific claims, distinguishing claims that are supported by reasons and evidence from claims that are not.	**INSTRUCTION/APPLICATION** **Interactive Lessons:** Analyzing and Evaluating Presentations • Identifying a Speaker's Claim • Tracing a Speaker's Argument Student Edition/**Teacher's Edition:** 93–94, **93–94,** 95, **95,** 373–376, **373–376,** R14–R15 **ASSESSMENT** Student Edition/**Teacher's Edition:** 96, **96,** 373–376, **373–376**

PRESENTATION OF KNOWLEDGE AND IDEAS

Standard	Where Taught
SL 4 Present claims and findings, sequencing ideas logically and using pertinent descriptions, facts, and details to accentuate main ideas or themes; use appropriate eye contact, adequate volume, and clear pronunciation.	**INSTRUCTION/APPLICATION** **Interactive Lessons:** Giving a Presentation • Introduction • The Content of Your Presentation • Style in Presentation • Delivering Your Presentation Student Edition/**Teacher's Edition:** 40, **40, 62a,** 63–66, **63–66,** 96, **96,** 201–204, **201–204,** 247–250, **247–250,** 268, **268,** 302, **302,** 334, **334,** 362, **362,** 377–380, **377–380,** R14–R15 **ASSESSMENT** Student Edition/**Teacher's Edition:** 40, **40,** 63–66, **63–66,** 96, **96,** 201–204, **201–204,** 247–250, **247–250,** 268, **268,** 302, **302,** 334, **334,** 362, **362,** 377–380, **377–380**
SL 5 Include multimedia components (e.g., graphics, images, music, sound) and visual displays in presentations to clarify information.	**INSTRUCTION/APPLICATION** **Interactive Lessons:** Using Media in a Presentation • Introduction • Types of Media: Audio, Video, and Images • Using Presentation Software • Building and Practicing Your Presentation Student Edition/**Teacher's Edition:** 62, **62, 62a,** 126, **126,** 154, **154,** 200, **200,** 201–204, **201–204,** 302, **302** **ASSESSMENT** Student Edition/**Teacher's Edition:** 62, **62,** 126, **126,** 154, **154,** 200, **200,** 201–204, **201–204,** 302, **302**

Standard	Where Taught
SL 6 Adapt speech to a variety of contexts and tasks, demonstrating command of formal English when indicated or appropriate. (See grade 6 Language standards 1 and 3 for specific expectations.)	**INSTRUCTION/APPLICATION** **Interactive Lessons:** Participating in Collaborative Discussions • Speaking Constructively Giving a Presentation • Style in Presentation **Student Edition/Teacher's Edition:** 40, **40,** 63–66, **63–66,** 201–204, **201–204,** 268, **268,** 334, **334,** 362, **362,** 377–380, **377–380** **Standards Support and Enrichment** • Using Standard English **ASSESSMENT** **Student Edition/Teacher's Edition:** 40, **40,** 63–66, **63–66,** 201–204, **201–204,** 268, **268,** 334, **334,** 362, **362,** 377–380, **377–380**

College and Career Readiness Anchor Standards for Language

Common Core State Standards

CONVENTIONS OF STANDARD ENGLISH

1. Demonstrate command of the conventions of standard English grammar and usage when writing or speaking.

2. Demonstrate command of the conventions of standard English capitalization, punctuation, and spelling when writing.

KNOWLEDGE OF LANGUAGE

3. Apply knowledge of language to understand how language functions in different contexts, to make effective choices for meaning or style, and to comprehend more fully when reading or listening.

VOCABULARY ACQUISITION AND USE

4. Determine or clarify the meaning of unknown and multiple-meaning words and phrases by using context clues, analyzing meaningful word parts, and consulting general and specialized reference materials, as appropriate.

5. Demonstrate understanding of figurative language, word relationships, and nuances in word meanings.

6. Acquire and use accurately a range of general academic and domain-specific words and phrases sufficient for reading, writing, speaking, and listening at the college- and career-readiness; demonstrate independence in gathering vocabulary knowledge when encountering an unknown term important to comprehension or expression.

Language Standards

Standard	Where Taught
CONVENTIONS OF STANDARD ENGLISH	
L 1 Demonstrate command of the conventions of standard English grammar and usage when writing or speaking.	**INSTRUCTION/APPLICATION** Student Edition/**Teacher's Edition:** **4**, 16, **16**, 50, **50**, 58, **58**, 63–66, **63–66**, 92, **92**, 98, **98**, 116, **116**, 156, **156**, 222, **222**, 270, **270**, R28–R51, **R28, R36, R38, R40, R42, R43, R45, R46, R47, R51**
a. Ensure that pronouns are in the proper case (subjective, objective, possessive).	**INSTRUCTION/APPLICATION** Student Edition/**Teacher's Edition:** 50, **50**, 58, **58**, 98, **98**, R28, R36, **R36**
b. Use intensive pronouns (e.g., *myself, ourselves*).	**INSTRUCTION/APPLICATION** Student Edition/**Teacher's Edition:** 92, **92**, R28, R36–R37
c. Recognize and correct inappropriate shifts in pronoun number and person.	**INSTRUCTION/APPLICATION** Student Edition/**Teacher's Edition:** 116, **116**, 156, **156**, R28, R35–R38, **R36**
d. Recognize and correct vague pronouns (i.e., ones with unclear or ambiguous antecedents).	**INSTRUCTION/APPLICATION** Student Edition/**Teacher's Edition:** 270, **270**, R28, R38, **R38**
e. Recognize variations from standard English in their own and others' writing and speaking, and identify and use strategies to improve expression in conventional language.	**INSTRUCTION/APPLICATION** Student Edition/**Teacher's Edition:** **4**, 16, **16**, 222, **222**, R28

Standard	Where Taught
L 2 Demonstrate command of the conventions of standard English capitalization, punctuation, and spelling when writing.	**INSTRUCTION/APPLICATION** Student Edition/**Teacher's Edition:** 36, **36,** 128, **128,** 184, **184,** 232, **232,** 240, **240,** 330, **330,** 344, 372, R28, R31–R34, R52, R57–R60
a. Use punctuation (commas, parentheses, dashes) to set off nonrestrictive/parenthetical elements.	**INSTRUCTION/APPLICATION** Student Edition/**Teacher's Edition:** 36, **36,** 372, **372,** R28, R31–32
b. Spell correctly.	**INSTRUCTION/APPLICATION** Student Edition/**Teacher's Edition:** 232, **232,** 330, **330,** 344, **344,** R52, R57–R60

KNOWLEDGE OF LANGUAGE

Standard	Where Taught
L 3 Use knowledge of language and its conventions when writing, speaking, reading, or listening.	**INSTRUCTION/APPLICATION** Student Edition/**Teacher's Edition:** **6, 7,** 196, **196, 273,** 280, **280,** R28–51, **R28-51**
a. Vary sentence patterns for meaning, reader/listener interest, and style.	**INSTRUCTION/APPLICATION** Student Edition/**Teacher's Edition:** **6, 7, 273,** 280, **280,** R28, R46–47, **R46–R47**
b. Maintain consistency in style and tone.	**INSTRUCTION/APPLICATION** Student Edition/**Teacher's Edition:** 63–66, **63–66,** 196, **196,** R28

VOCABULARY ACQUISITION AND USE

Standard	Where Taught
L 4 Determine or clarify the meaning of unknown and multiple-meaning words and phrases based on *grade 6 reading and content,* choosing flexibly from a range of strategies.	**INSTRUCTION/APPLICATION** Student Edition/**Teacher's Edition:** 15, **15,** 35, **35,** 49, **49,** 57, **57, 62b,** 91, **91,** 97, **97,** 115, **115,** 127, **127,** 155, **155,** 183, **183,** 195, **195,** 221, **221,** 231, **231,** 239, **239,** 269, **269,** 279, **279,** 329, **329,** 343, **343,** 371, **371,** R52–R60, **R52**
a. Use context (e.g., the overall meaning of a sentence or paragraph; a word's position or function in a sentence) as a clue to the meaning of a word or phrase.	**INSTRUCTION/APPLICATION** Student Edition/**Teacher's Edition:** 15, **15,** 35, 49, **49,** 57, **57, 62b, 97,** 115, **115,** 155, **155,** 183, **183,** 195, **195,** 221, **221,** 231, **231,** 269, **269,** 279, **279,** 329, **329,** 343, **343,** 371, **371,** R52–R53, **R52**
b. Use common, grade-appropriate Greek or Latin affixes and roots as clues to the meaning of a word (e.g., *audience, auditory, audible*).	**INSTRUCTION/APPLICATION** Student Edition/**Teacher's Edition:** 35, **35,** 49, **49,** 57, **57,** 91, **91,** 155, **155,** 371, **371, R52,** R53–R54

Standard	Where Taught
c. Consult reference materials (e.g., dictionaries, glossaries, thesauruses), both print and digital, to find the pronunciation of a word or determine or clarify its precise meaning or its part of speech.	**INSTRUCTION/APPLICATION** Student Edition/**Teacher's Edition:** 15, **15,** 57, **57, 62b,** 97, **97,** 115, **115,** 127, **127,** 195, **195,** 239, **239,** 279, **279,** 343, **343, R52,** R56
d. Verify the preliminary determination of the meaning of a word or phrase (e.g., by checking the inferred meaning in context or in a dictionary).	**INSTRUCTION/APPLICATION** Student Edition/**Teacher's Edition:** 15, **15,** 49, **49,** 57, **57, 62b,** 115, **115,** 195, **195,** 221, **221**
L 5 Demonstrate understanding of figurative language, word relationships, and nuances in word meanings.	**INSTRUCTION/APPLICATION** Student Edition/**Teacher's Edition:** **100, 102, 103,** 127, **127, 171, 174, 175, 176, 178, 179, 180, 181, 184a, 214,** 221, **221, 231, 231,** 239, **239,** 269, **239,** 329, **329,** R52
a. Interpret figures of speech (e.g., personification) in context.	**INSTRUCTION/APPLICATION** Student Edition/**Teacher's Edition:** **100, 102, 103, 171, 174, 175, 176, 178, 179, 180, 181, 184a, 214,** 221, **221,** R52
b. Use the relationship between particular words (e.g., cause/effect, part/whole, item/category) to better understand each of the words.	**INSTRUCTION/APPLICATION** Student Edition/**Teacher's Edition:** 231, **231,** 269, **269,** 329, **329,** R52, R55
c. Distinguish among the connotations (associations) of words with similar denotations (definitions) (e.g., *stingy, scrimping, economical, unwasteful, thrifty*).	**INSTRUCTION/APPLICATION** Student Edition/**Teacher's Edition:** 239, **239,** R52, R55
L 6 Acquire and use accurately grade-appropriate general academic and domain-specific words and phrases; gather vocabulary knowledge when considering a word or phrase important to comprehension or expression.	**INSTRUCTION/APPLICATION** Student Edition/**Teacher's Edition:** 2, **2, 5,** 15, **15, 18,** 35, **35, 38,** 43, 49, **49, 52,** 57, **57, 60,** 63, **63,** 67, **67,** 72, **72, 75,** 91, **91, 94,** 97, **97, 100,** 107, 115, **115, 118,** 127, **127,** 129, **129,** 133, **133,** 138, **138, 141,** 155, **155, 159,** 172, 183, **183, 187,** 195, **195, 198,** 201, **201,** 205, **205,** 210, **210, 213,** 221, **221, 225,** 231, **231, 234,** 239, **239, 242,** 247, **247,** 252, **252, 255, 264,** 269, **269, 273,** 279, **279, 282, 287, 294, 300,** 303, **303,** 307, **307,** 312, **312, 315,** 329, **329, 337,** 343, **343, 347, 358, 364,** 371, **371,** 373, **373,** 377, **377,** R52–R56, **R54**

Making Meaning
in the 21ˢᵗ Century ... or Don't Let Complex Texts Get You Down

By Carol Jago

Do you sometimes think that what your teacher asks you to read is too hard? Let me tell you a secret. Those poems and passages can be tough for your teacher as well. Just because a text isn't easy doesn't mean there is something wrong with it or something wrong with the reader. It means you need to do more than skim across the words on the page or screen. You will need to think critically at every turn. Problem solving isn't only needed for math. Complex texts demand the same kind of effort and focused attention. Do you sometimes wish writers would just say what they have to say simply? I assure you that writers don't use long sentences and unfamiliar words to annoy their readers or make readers feel dumb. They employ complex syntax and rich language in order to express complex ideas.

Excellent literature and nonfiction—the kind you will be reading over the course of the year—challenges readers in various ways. Sometimes the background of a story or the content of an essay is so unfamiliar that it is difficult to understand why characters are behaving as they do or to follow the argument a writer is making. By persevering, reading like a detective, and following clues in the text, you will find that your store of background knowledge grows. As a result, the next time you read about global issues, financial matters, political events, environmental news (like the California drought) or health research, the text won't seem nearly as hard. The more you read, the better a reader you will become.

Good readers aren't put off by challenging text. When the going gets rough, they know what to do. Let's take vocabulary, a common measure of text complexity, as an example. Learning new words is the business of a lifetime. Rather than shutting down when you meet a word you don't know, take a moment to think about the word. Is any part of the word familiar to you? Is there something in the context of the sentence or paragraph that can help you figure out its meaning? Is there someone or something that can provide you with a definition? When reading literature or nonfiction from a time period other than our own, the text is often full of words we don't know. Each time you meet those words in succeeding readings you will be adding to your understanding of the word and its use. Your brain is a natural word-learning machine. The more you feed it complex text, the larger a vocabulary you'll have.

Have you ever been reading a long, complicated sentence and discovered that by the time you reached the end you had forgotten the beginning? Unlike the sentences we speak or dash off in a note to a friend, complex text is often full of sentences that are not only lengthy but also constructed in intricate ways. Such sentences require readers to slow down and figure out how phrases relate to one another as well as who is doing what to whom. Remember, rereading isn't cheating. It is exactly what experienced readers know to do when they meet dense text on the page. On the pages that follow you will find stories and articles that challenge you at the sentence level. Don't be intimidated. With careful attention to how those sentences are constructed, their meaning will unfold right before your eyes.

> "Your brain is a natural word-learning machine. The more you feed it complex text, the larger a vocabulary you'll have."

That same kind of attention is required for reading the media. Every day you are bombarded with messages—online, offline, everywhere you look. These, too, are complex texts that you want to be able to see through; that is, to be able to recognize the message's source, purpose, context, intended audience, and appeals. This is what it takes to be a 21st century reader.

Another way text can be complex involves the density of the ideas in a passage. Sometimes a writer piles on so much information that you think your head might explode if you read one more detail or one more qualification. At times like this talking with a friend can really help. Sharing questions and ideas, exploring a difficult passage together, can help you tease out the meaning of even the most difficult text. Poetry is often particularly dense and for that reason it poses particular challenges. A seemingly simple poem in terms of vocabulary and length may express extremely complex feelings and insights. Poets also love to use mythological and Biblical allusions which contemporary readers are not always familiar with. The only way to read text this complex is to read it again and again.

You are going to notice a range of complexity within each collection of readings. This spectrum reflects the range of texts that surround us: some easy, some hard, some seemingly easy but in fact hard, some seemingly hard but actually easy. Whatever their complexity, I think you will enjoy these readings tremendously. Remember, read for your life!

Understanding the Common Core State Standards

What are the English Language Arts Common Core State Standards?

The Common Core State Standards for English Language Arts indicate what you should know and be able to do by the end of your grade level. These understandings and skills will help you be better prepared for future classes, college courses, and a career. For this reason, the standards for each strand in English Language Arts (such as reading informational text or writing) directly relate to the College and Career Readiness Anchor Standards for each strand. The Anchor Standards broadly outline the understandings and skills you should master by the end of high school so that you are well-prepared for college or for a career.

How do I learn the English Language Arts Common Core State Standards?

Your textbook is closely aligned to the English Language Arts Common Core State Standards. Every time you learn a concept or practice a skill, you are working on mastering one of the standards. Each collection, each selection, and each performance task in your textbook connects to one or more of the standards for English Language Arts listed on the following pages.

The English Language Arts Common Core State Standards are divided into five strands: Reading Literature, Reading Informational Text, Writing, Speaking and Listening, and Language.

©Jose Luis Pelaez Inc/Getty Images

Strand	What It Means to You
Reading Literature (RL)	This strand concerns the literary texts you will read at this grade level: stories, drama, and poetry. The Common Core State Standards stress that you should read a range of texts of increasing complexity as you progress through high school.
Reading Informational Text (RI)	Informational text encompasses a broad range of literary nonfiction, including exposition, argument, and functional text, in such genres as personal essays, speeches, opinion pieces, memoirs, and historical and technical accounts. The Common Core State Standards stress that you will read a range of informational texts of increasing complexity as you progress from grade to grade.
Writing (W)	For the Writing strand you will focus on generating three types of texts—arguments, informative or explanatory texts, and narratives—while using the writing process and technology to develop and share your writing. The Common Core State Standards also emphasize research and specify that you should write routinely for both short and extended time frames.
Speaking and Listening (SL)	The Common Core State Standards focus on comprehending information presented in a variety of media and formats, on participating in collaborative discussions, and on presenting knowledge and ideas clearly.
Language (L)	The standards in the Language strand address the conventions of standard English grammar, usage, and mechanics; knowledge of language; and vocabulary acquisition and use.

Common Core Code Decoder

The codes you find on the pages of your textbook identify the specific knowledge or skill for the standard addressed in the text.

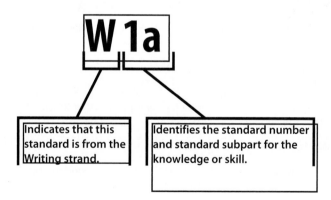

W 1a

Indicates that this standard is from the Writing strand.

Identifies the standard number and standard subpart for the knowledge or skill.

English Language Arts
Common Core State Standards

Listed below are the English Language Arts Common Core State Standards that you are required to master by the end of grade 6. To help you understand what is required of you, we have provided a summary of the concepts you will learn on your way to mastering each standard.

College and Career Readiness Anchor Standards for Reading

Common Core State Standards

KEY IDEAS AND DETAILS

1. Read closely to determine what the text says explicitly and to make logical inferences from it; cite specific textual evidence when writing or speaking to support conclusions drawn from the text.

2. Determine central ideas or themes of a text and analyze their development; summarize the key supporting details and ideas.

3. Analyze how and why individuals, events, and ideas develop and interact over the course of a text.

CRAFT AND STRUCTURE

4. Interpret words and phrases as they are used in a text, including determining technical, connotative, and figurative meanings, and analyze how specific word choices shape meaning or tone.

5. Analyze the structure of texts, including how specific sentences, paragraphs, and larger portions of the text (e.g., a section, chapter, scene, or stanza) relate to each other and the whole.

6. Assess how point of view or purpose shapes the content and style of a text.

INTEGRATION OF KNOWLEDGE AND IDEAS

7. Integrate and evaluate content presented in diverse media and formats, including visually and quantitatively, as well as in words.

8. Delineate and evaluate the argument and specific claims in a text, including the validity of the reasoning as well as the relevance and sufficiency of the evidence.

9. Analyze how two or more texts address similar themes or topics in order to build knowledge or to compare the approaches the authors take.

RANGE OF READING AND LEVEL OF TEXT COMPLEXITY

10. Read and comprehend complex literary and informational texts independently and proficiently.

Reading Standards for Literature, Grade 6 Students

The College and Career Readiness Anchor Standards for Reading apply to both literature and informational text.

Common Core State Standards	What It Means to You
KEY IDEAS AND DETAILS	
1. Cite textual evidence to support analysis of what the text says explicitly as well as inferences drawn from the text.	You will use information from the text to support its main ideas—both those that are stated directly and those that are suggested.
2. Determine a theme or central idea of a text and how it is conveyed through particular details; provide a summary of the text distinct from personal opinions or judgments.	You will analyze a text's main idea or theme by showing how it unfolds throughout the text. You will also summarize the main idea of the text as a whole without adding your own ideas or opinions.
3. Describe how a particular story's or drama's plot unfolds in a series of episodes as well as how the characters respond or change as the plot moves toward a resolution.	You will describe the events that make up a story or drama's plot and how those events affect the characters.
CRAFT AND STRUCTURE	
4. Determine the meaning of words and phrases as they are used in a text, including figurative and connotative meanings; analyze the impact of a specific word choice on meaning and tone.	You will analyze specific words, phrases, and patterns of sound in the text to determine what they mean and how they contribute to the text's larger meaning.
5. Analyze how a particular sentence, chapter, scene, or stanza fits into the overall structure of a text and contributes to the development of the theme, setting, or plot.	You will analyze how a specific section of a text contributes to its larger meaning.
6. Explain how an author develops the point of view of the narrator or speaker in a text.	You will analyze how an author shapes the narrator's point of view in a text.

Common Core State Standards	What It Means to You
INTEGRATION OF KNOWLEDGE AND IDEAS	
7. Compare and contrast the experience of reading a story, drama, or poem to listening to or viewing an audio, video, or live version of the text, including contrasting what they "see" and "hear" when reading the text to what they perceive when they listen or watch.	You will compare and contrast how events and information are presented in visual and non-visual texts.
8. (Not applicable to literature)	
9. Compare and contrast texts in different forms or genres (e.g., stories and poems; historical novels and fantasy stories) in terms of their approaches to similar themes and topics.	You will analyze how different forms of texts treat the same themes and topics.
RANGE OF READING AND LEVEL OF TEXT COMPLEXITY	
10. By the end of the year, read and comprehend literature, including stories, dramas, and poems, in the grades 6–8 text complexity band proficiently, with scaffolding as needed at the high end of the range.	You will read and understand grade-level appropriate literary texts by the end of grade 6.

Reading Standards for Informational Text, Grade 6 Students

Common Core State Standards	What It Means to You
KEY IDEAS AND DETAILS	
1. Cite textual evidence to support analysis of what the text says explicitly as well as inferences drawn from the text.	You will cite information from the text to support its main ideas—both those that are stated directly and those that are suggested.
2. Determine a central idea of a text and how it is conveyed through particular details; provide a summary of the text distinct from personal opinions or judgments.	You will analyze the development of a text's main idea. You will also summarize the text without adding your own ideas or opinions.
3. Analyze in detail how a key individual, event, or idea is introduced, illustrated, and elaborated in a text (e.g., through examples or anecdotes).	You will analyze how an author treats a key person, event, or idea throughout a text.

Common Core State Standards	What It Means to You
CRAFT AND STRUCTURE	
4. Determine the meaning of words and phrases as they are used in a text, including figurative, connotative, and technical meanings.	You will discover the meaning of specific words and phrases in the text.
5. Analyze how a particular sentence, paragraph, chapter, or section fits into the overall structure of a text and contributes to the development of the ideas.	You will examine the major sections of a text and analyze how each one adds to the whole.
6. Determine an author's point of view or purpose in a text and explain how it is conveyed in the text.	You will understand the author's point of view and explain how the author gets his or her point of view across.
INTEGRATION OF KNOWLEDGE AND IDEAS	
7. Integrate information presented in different media or formats (e.g., visually, quantitatively) as well as in words to develop a coherent understanding of a topic or issue.	You will use information from visual and non-visual sources to understand a topic or issue.
8. Trace and evaluate the argument and specific claims in a text, distinguishing claims that are supported by reasons and evidence from claims that are not.	You will evaluate the author's claims and reasoning and identify any weaknesses in them.
9. Compare and contrast one author's presentation of events with that of another (e.g., a memoir written by and a biography on the same person).	You will compare and contrast two different authors' treatments of the same subject.
RANGE OF READING AND LEVEL OF TEXT COMPLEXITY	
10. By the end of the year, read and comprehend literary nonfiction in the grades 6–8 text complexity band proficiently, with scaffolding as needed at the high end of the range.	You will demonstrate the ability to read and understand grade-level appropriate literary nonfiction texts by the end of grade 6.

College and Career Readiness Anchor Standards for Writing

TEXT TYPES AND PURPOSES

1. Write arguments to support claims in an analysis of substantive topics or texts, using valid reasoning and relevant and sufficient evidence.

2. Write informative/explanatory texts to examine and convey complex ideas and information clearly and accurately through the effective selection, organization, and analysis of content.

3. Write narratives to develop real or imagined experiences or events using effective technique, well-chosen details, and well-structured event sequences.

PRODUCTION AND DISTRIBUTION OF WRITING

4. Produce clear and coherent writing in which the development, organization, and style are appropriate to task, purpose, and audience.

5. Develop and strengthen writing as needed by planning, revising, editing, rewriting, or trying a new approach.

6. Use technology, including the Internet, to produce and publish writing and to interact and collaborate with others.

RESEARCH TO BUILD AND PRESENT KNOWLEDGE

7. Conduct short as well as more sustained research projects based on focused questions, demonstrating understanding of the subject under investigation.

8. Gather relevant information from multiple print and digital sources, assess the credibility and accuracy of each source, and integrate the information while avoiding plagiarism.

9. Draw evidence from literary and/or informational texts to support analysis, reflection, and research.

RANGE OF WRITING

10. Write routinely over extended time frames (time for research, reflection, and revision) and shorter time frames (a single sitting or a day or two) for a range of tasks, purposes, and audiences.

Writing Standards, Grade 6 Students

Common Core State Standards	What It Means to You
TEXT TYPES AND PURPOSES	
1. Write arguments to support claims with clear reasons and relevant evidence.	You will write and develop arguments with clear reasons and strong evidence that include
a. Introduce claim(s) and organize the reasons and evidence clearly.	a clear introduction and organization of claims
b. Support claim(s) with clear reasons and relevant evidence, using credible sources and demonstrating an understanding of the topic or text.	clear, accurate support for claims
c. Use words, phrases, and clauses to clarify the relationships among claim(s) and reasons.	use of clear words, phrases, and clauses to link information
d. Establish and maintain a formal style.	a formal style
e. Provide a concluding statement or section that follows from the argument presented.	a strong concluding statement that connects to the argument
2. Write informative/explanatory texts to examine a topic and convey ideas, concepts, and information through the selection, organization, and analysis of relevant content.	You will write clear, well-organized, and thoughtful informative and explanatory texts with
a. Introduce a topic; organize ideas, concepts, and information, using strategies such as definition, classification, comparison/contrast, and cause/effect; include formatting (e.g., headings), graphics (e.g., charts, tables), and multimedia when useful to aiding comprehension.	a clear introduction and organization, including headings and visuals (when appropriate)
b. Develop the topic with relevant facts, definitions, concrete details, quotations, or other information and examples.	strong supporting details and background information
c. Use appropriate transitions to clarify the relationships among ideas and concepts.	clear transitions to link ideas
d. Use precise language and domain-specific vocabulary to inform about or explain the topic.	precise language and vocabulary

Common Core State Standards	What It Means to You
e. Establish and maintain a formal style.	a formal style
f. Provide a concluding statement or section that follows from the information or explanation presented.	a strong conclusion that connects to the topic
3. Write narratives to develop real or imagined experiences or events using effective technique, relevant descriptive details, and well-structured event sequences.	You will write clear, well-structured, detailed narrative texts that
a. Engage and orient the reader by establishing a context and introducing a narrator and/or characters; organize an event sequence that unfolds naturally and logically.	draw your readers in with a clear topic that unfolds logically
b. Use narrative techniques, such as dialogue, pacing, and description, to develop experiences, events, and/or characters.	use narrative techniques to develop and expand on events and/or characters
c. Use a variety of transition words, phrases, and clauses to convey sequence and signal shifts from one time frame or setting to another.	use a variety of transition words to clearly signal shifts between time frames or settings
d. Use precise words and phrases, relevant descriptive details, and sensory language to convey experiences and events.	use precise words and sensory details that keep readers interested
e. Provide a conclusion that follows from the narrated experiences or events.	have a strong conclusion that connects to the topic

PRODUCTION AND DISTRIBUTION OF WRITING

4. Produce clear and coherent writing in which the development, organization, and style are appropriate to task, purpose, and audience. (Grade-specific expectations for writing types are defined in standards 1–3 above.)	You will produce writing that is appropriate to the task, purpose, and audience for whom you are writing.
5. With some guidance and support from peers and adults, develop and strengthen writing as needed by planning, revising, editing, rewriting, or trying a new approach.	With help from peers and adults, you will revise and refine your writing to address what is most important for your purpose and audience.

Common Core State Standards	What It Means to You
6. Use technology, including the Internet, to produce and publish writing as well as to interact and collaborate with others; demonstrate sufficient command of keyboarding skills to type a minimum of three pages in a single setting.	You will use technology to share your writing and to provide more information on your topic. You will also develop keyboarding skills to type at least three pages in a single setting.

RESEARCH TO BUILD AND PRESENT KNOWLEDGE

7. Conduct short research projects to answer a question, drawing on several sources and refocusing the inquiry when appropriate.	You will conduct short research projects to answer a question using multiple sources and altering your topic when needed.
8. Gather relevant information from multiple print and digital sources; assess the credibility of each source; and quote or paraphrase the data and conclusions of others while avoiding plagiarism and providing basic bibliographic information for sources.	You will gather, quote, or restate information from different sources, and assess the strength of each source. You will also provide information for a bibliography.
9. Draw evidence from literary or informational texts to support analysis, reflection, and research. a. Apply *grade 6 Reading standards* to literature (e.g., "Compare and contrast texts in different forms or genres [e.g., stories and poems; historical novels and fantasy stories] in terms of their approaches to similar themes and topics"). b. Apply *grade 6 Reading standards* to literary nonfiction (e.g., "Trace and evaluate the argument and specific claims in a text, distinguishing claims that are supported by reasons and evidence from claims that are not").	You will paraphrase, summarize, quote, and cite primary and secondary sources to support your analysis, reflection, and research.

RANGE OF WRITING

10. Write routinely over extended time frames (time for research, reflection, and revision) and shorter time frames (a single sitting or a day or two) for a range of discipline-specific tasks, purposes, and audiences.	You will write for many different purposes and audiences both over short and longer periods of time.

College and Career Readiness Anchor Standards for Speaking and Listening

Common Core State Standards

COMPREHENSION AND COLLABORATION

1. Prepare for and participate effectively in a range of conversations and collaborations with diverse partners, building on others' ideas and expressing their own clearly and persuasively.

2. Integrate and evaluate information presented in diverse media and formats, including visually, quantitatively, and orally.

3. Evaluate a speaker's point of view, reasoning, and use of evidence and rhetoric.

PRESENTATION OF KNOWLEDGE AND IDEAS

4. Present information, findings, and supporting evidence such that listeners can follow the line of reasoning and the organization, development, and style are appropriate to task, purpose, and audience.

5. Make strategic use of digital media and visual displays of data to express information and enhance understanding of presentations.

6. Adapt speech to a variety of contexts and communicative tasks, demonstrating command of formal English when indicated or appropriate.

Speaking and Listening Standards, Grade 6 Students

Common Core State Standards	What It Means to You
COMPREHENSION AND COLLABORATION	
1. Engage effectively in a range of collaborative discussions (one-on-one, in groups, and teacher-led) with diverse partners on grade 6 topics, texts, and issues, building on others' ideas and expressing their own clearly.	You will actively participate in a variety of discussions in which you
a. Come to discussions prepared, having read or studied required material; explicitly draw on that preparation by referring to evidence on the topic, text, or issue to probe and reflect on ideas under discussion.	have read any required material beforehand and have come to the discussion prepared
b. Follow rules for collegial discussions, set specific goals and deadlines, and define individual roles as needed.	work with others to set goals and processes within the group
c. Pose and respond to specific questions with elaboration and detail by making comments that contribute to the topic, text, or issue under discussion.	ask and respond to questions that relate to the topic

Common Core State Standards	What It Means to You
d. Review the key ideas expressed and demonstrate understanding of multiple perspectives through reflection and paraphrasing.	review and restate different points of view
2. Interpret information presented in diverse media and formats (e.g., visually, quantitatively, orally) and explain how it contributes to a topic, text, or issue under study.	You will analyze main ideas and details of various media and relate them to a topic under study.
3. Delineate a speaker's argument and specific claims, distinguishing claims that are supported by reasons and evidence from claims that are not.	You will evaluate a speaker's argument and identify any false reasoning or evidence.

PRESENTATION OF KNOWLEDGE AND IDEAS

Common Core State Standards	What It Means to You
4. Present claims and findings, sequencing ideas logically and using pertinent descriptions, facts, and details to accentuate main ideas or themes; use appropriate eye contact, adequate volume, and clear pronunciation.	You will organize and present information to your listeners in a logical sequence and style that is appropriate to your task and audience.
5. Include multimedia components (e.g., graphics, images, music, sound) and visual displays in presentations to clarify information.	You will use audio and/or visual materials to clarify and add to presentations.
6. Adapt speech to a variety of contexts and tasks, demonstrating command of formal English when indicated or appropriate.	You will adapt the formality of your speech appropriately.

College and Career Readiness Anchor Standards for Language

Common Core State Standards

CONVENTIONS OF STANDARD ENGLISH

1. Demonstrate command of the conventions of standard English grammar and usage when writing or speaking.

2. Demonstrate command of the conventions of standard English capitalization, punctuation, and spelling when writing.

KNOWLEDGE OF LANGUAGE

3. Apply knowledge of language to understand how language functions in different contexts, to make effective choices for meaning or style, and to comprehend more fully when reading or listening.

VOCABULARY ACQUISITION AND USE

4. Determine or clarify the meaning of unknown and multiple-meaning words and phrases by using context clues, analyzing meaningful word parts, and consulting general and specialized reference materials, as appropriate.

5. Demonstrate understanding of figurative language, word relationships, and nuances in word meanings.

6. Acquire and use accurately a range of general academic and domain-specific words and phrases sufficient for reading, writing, speaking, and listening at the college- and career-readiness level; demonstrate independence in gathering vocabulary knowledge when encountering an unknown term important to comprehension or expression.

Language Standards, Grade 6 Students

Common Core State Standards	What It Means to You
CONVENTIONS OF STANDARD ENGLISH	
1. Demonstrate command of the conventions of standard English grammar and usage when writing or speaking.	You will correctly understand and use the conventions of English grammar and usage, including
a. Ensure that pronouns are in the proper case (subjective, objective, possessive).	making sure pronouns are in the proper case
b. Use intensive pronouns (e.g., *myself, ourselves*).	using intensive pronouns
c. Recognize and correct inappropriate shifts in pronoun number and person.	correcting shifts in pronoun number and person

Common Core State Standards	What It Means to You
d. Recognize and correct vague pronouns (i.e., ones with unclear or ambiguous antecedents).	correcting unclear connections between pronouns and antecedents
e. Recognize variations from standard English in their own and others' writing and speaking, and identify and use strategies to improve expression in conventional language.	identifying your own and others' errors in speaking and writing and using strategies to improve expression
2. Demonstrate command of the conventions of standard English capitalization, punctuation, and spelling when writing.	You will correctly use the conventions of English capitalization, punctuation, and spelling, including
a. Use punctuation (commas, parentheses, dashes) to set off nonrestrictive/parenthetical elements.	punctuation to set off information that is not essential to the meaning of the sentence
b. Spell correctly.	spelling

KNOWLEDGE OF LANGUAGE

3. Use knowledge of language and its conventions when writing, speaking, reading, or listening.	You will apply your knowledge of language in different contexts by
a. Vary sentence patterns for meaning, reader/listener interest, and style.	using various sentence patterns
b. Maintain consistency in style and tone.	keeping a consistent style and tone

VOCABULARY ACQUISITION AND USE

4. Determine or clarify the meaning of unknown and multiple-meaning words and phrases based on grade 6 reading and content, choosing flexibly from a range of strategies.	You will understand the meaning of grade-level appropriate words and phrases by
a. Use context (e.g., the overall meaning of a sentence or paragraph; a word's position or function in a sentence) as a clue to the meaning of a word or phrase.	using context clues
b. Use common, grade-appropriate Greek or Latin affixes and roots as clues to the meaning of a word (e.g., *audience, auditory, audible*).	using Greek or Latin roots

Common Core State Standards	What It Means to You
c. Consult reference materials (e.g., dictionaries, glossaries, thesauruses), both print and digital, to find the pronunciation of a word or determine or clarify its precise meaning or its part of speech.	using reference materials
d. Verify the preliminary determination of the meaning of a word or phrase (e.g., by checking the inferred meaning in context or in a dictionary).	inferring and verifying the meanings of words in context
5. Demonstrate understanding of figurative language, word relationships, and nuances in word meanings.	You will understand figurative language, word relationships, and slight differences in word meanings by
a. Interpret figures of speech (e.g., personification) in context.	interpreting figures of speech in context
b. Use the relationship between particular words (e.g., cause/effect, part/whole, item/category) to better understand each of the words.	analyzing relationships between words
c. Distinguish among the connotations (associations) of words with similar denotations (definitions) (e.g., *stingy, scrimping, economical, unwasteful, thrifty*).	distinguishing among words with similar definitions
6. Acquire and use accurately grade-appropriate general academic and domain-specific words and phrases; gather vocabulary knowledge when considering a word or phrase important to comprehension or expression.	You will learn and use grade-appropriate vocabulary.

© Corbis

Facing Fear

"Do one thing every day that scares you."

—Eleanor Roosevelt

1

PLAN

STREAM TO START

Motivate students to read the collection texts, and spark their curiosity about the collection by playing the video and watching it in class. After students view the video, ask them to think about two things they hope to learn about experiencing fear and how fear affects people. Call on volunteers to share their responses.

PERFORMANCE TASK PREVIEW

Point out to students that they will complete two performance tasks at the end of the collection. The performance tasks will require them to further analyze the selections in the collection and to synthesize ideas about these analyses. Students will present their findings in a variety of products.

ACADEMIC VOCABULARY

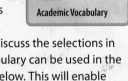

> *View It!*
> Professional Development Podcast:
> **Academic Vocabulary**

Students can acquire facility with the academic vocabulary words through frequent, repeated exposure as they analyze and discuss the selections in the collection. Academic vocabulary can be used in the instructional contexts shown below. This will enable students to incorporate the academic vocabulary words into their working vocabulary.

- Collaborative Discussion at the end of each selection
- Analyzing the Text questions for each selection
- Selection-level Performance Task
- Vocabulary instruction (for Critical Vocabulary and/or for Vocabulary Strategy)
- Language Conventions
- End-of-collection Performance Task for all selections in the collection

ASK STUDENTS to review the Academic Vocabulary word list for this collection. You may wish to pronounce each word aloud so students hear the correct pronunciation. Then, discuss the definitions and the related forms for each word. Remind students that they will encounter these five academic vocabulary words throughout the collection.

Facing Fear

In this collection, you will explore how people experience fear and how fear affects the brain and the body.

 Stream to Start   hmhfyi.com   Channel One News®

COLLECTION
PERFORMANCE TASK Preview

After reading this collection, you will have the opportunity to complete two performance tasks:

- In one, you will present a response to one of the selections from the collection.
- In the second, you will write an informative essay about a fear using information found in selections from the collection and your own research.

ACADEMIC VOCABULARY

Study the words and their definitions in the chart below. You will use these words as you discuss and write about the texts in this collection.

Word	Definition	Related Forms
evident (ĕv´ĭ-dənt) *adj.*	easily seen or understood; obvious	evidence, evidently
factor (făk´tər) *n.*	someone or something that has an affect on an event, a process, or a situation	factorable
indicate (ĭn´dĭ-kāt´) *tr.v.*	to point out; also, to serve as a sign or symbol of something	indication, indicator, indicative
similar (sĭm´ə-lər) *adj.*	alike in appearance or nature, though not identical; having features that are the same	similarly, similarity
specific (spĭ-sĭf´ĭk) *adj.*	concerned with a particular thing; also, precise or exact	specifically, specifics, specification

2

📓 myNotebook

As students read, analyze, and discuss the texts in this collection, encourage them to create a *my*WordList folder in *my*Notebook to build their own personal word lists.

- **Annotate** Students can highlight vocabulary terms and other unfamiliar words and save each highlighted term to *my*Notebook.
- **Organize** Within *my*Notebook, students can drag each word into the *my*WordList folder.
- **Elaborate** Ask students to add details to the entry for each word, such as a definition, other forms of the word, and a sample sentence.

English Language Support

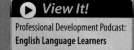 **View It!**
Professional Development Podcast:
English Language Learners

ENGAGE WITH THE COLLECTION TOPIC

Draw students' attention to the title of the collection, Facing Fear. Explain that *facing* is a multiple-meaning word. Here, it means "confronting with courage." Tell students that this collection focuses on what fear is and how people react to and overcome their fears.

ACCESS PRIOR KNOWLEDGE Ask students why it is important for people to understand how fear affects them. Discuss why understanding fear can help a person overcome fearful situations.

TAKING NOTES

Use this strategy to help students learn how to take notes as they read or discuss a text.

- **First**, before reading, provide students with a graphic organizer they can use for notetaking, such as a story map, timeline, character chart, or argument frame. Explain the purposes of each section of the organizer.
- **Then**, display a passage from a text, and ask students to take notes in the graphic organizer, reminding them to write down important and memorable ideas and details in their appropriate locations.
- **Next**, have students gather into small groups to present and explain each point listed on their graphic organizer, along

with reasons for having included each one. Tell groups that their task is to come to agreement about which notes are accurate and significant and most likely to be useful.

- **Finally**, distribute a single, blank copy of the graphic organizer to each group; have the groups complete it together, according to the conclusions they reached in the discussion. Have representatives from each group present their graphic organizer to the class for discussion.

 Collection 1 Digital Resources for English Language Support

LANGUAGE WORKSHOP
Designated English Learners

Use Teacher Resources > Language Workshop to support English learners in composing personal narratives, adding detail by expanding noun phrases, and sharing ideas by asking and answering questions.

Text in FOCUS **VIDEOS**

These videos will help students learn how to visualize a story and how to preview a text. Have students use **Text in Focus Practice** to apply those skills.

COLLECTION 1 DIGITAL OVERVIEW

| my SmartPlanner | eBook | myNotebook | my WriteSmart | fyi hmhfyi.com |

Collection 1 Lessons	Media	Teach and Practice
Student Edition | eBook	▶ Video Links HISTORY A&E Channel One News	**Close Reading and Evidence Tracking**
ANCHOR TEXT Short Story by Graham Salisbury "The Ravine"	◀ Audio "The Ravine"	**Close Read Screencasts** • Modeled Discussion (lines 1–7) • Close Read Application PDF (lines 297–308) **Text in Focus** • Visualizing (line 291) **Strategies for Annotation** • Analyze Language • Describe Stories: Characters and Setting • Using Context Clues
CLOSE READER Short Story by René Saldaña, Jr. "The Jumping Tree"	◀ Audio "The Jumping Tree"	
Short Story by Margaret Peterson Haddix "Fine?"	◀ Audio "Fine?"	**Strategies for Annotation** • Describe Stories: Plot and Suspense • Greek Roots
Poem by Maya Angelou "Life Doesn't Frighten Me"	◀ Audio "Life Doesn't Frighten Me"	**Strategies for Annotation** • Analyze Structure
ANCHOR TEXT Online Article by kidshealth.org "Fears and Phobias"	▶ Video HISTORY® Fear ◀ Audio "Fears and Phobias"	**Close Read Screencasts** • Modeled Discussion (lines 107–114) • Close Read Application PDF (lines 147–162) **Text in Focus** • Previewing the Text (line 1) **Strategies for Annotation** • Cite Evidence • Prefixes That Mean "Not"
CLOSE READER Magazine Article by Dana Hudepohl "Face Your Fears: Choking Under Pressure Is Every Athlete's Worst Nightmare"	◀ Audio "Face Your Fears: Choking Under Pressure Is Every Athlete's Worst Nightmare"	
Informational Text by Glenn Murphy "In the Spotlight" from *Stuff That Scares Your Pants Off!*	◀ Audio "In the Spotlight"	**Strategies for Annotation** • Determine Central Idea and Details
CLOSE READER Magazine Article by Jason Koebler "Face Your Fears and Scare the Phobia Out of Your Brain"	◀ Audio "Face Your Fears and Scare the Phobia Out of Your Brain"	
Online Science Exhibit by The California Science Center "Wired for Fear"	▶ Video *Wired for Fear*	
Collection 1 Performance Tasks: **A** Present a Response to Literature **B** Write an Informative Essay	fyi hmhfyi.com	**Interactive Lessons** **A** Giving a Presentation **B** Writing Informative Texts **B** Using Textual Evidence
	For Systematic Coverage of Writing and Speaking & Listening Standards	**Interactive Lessons** Writing as a Process Participating in Collaborative Discussions

For foundational
skills and reading
intervention support: READ180

Assess		Extend	Reteach
Performance Task	✅ *Assess It Online!*	**Teacher eBook**	**Teacher eBook**
Writing Activity: Informative Essay	Selection Test	**Describe Plot: Conflict**	**Describe Stories: Character Development > Level Up Tutorials >** Character Traits > Character Motivation > Making Inferences About Characters
Writing Activity: Narrative	Selection Test	**Explain Point of View > Interactive Whiteboard Lesson >** Point of View	**Describe Stories: Plot > Level Up Tutorials** > Plot Stages > Plot: Sequence of Events > Conflict
Speaking Activity: Response to Literature	Selection Test	**Analyze Structure: Rhyme Scheme > Interactive Whiteboard Lesson >** Sound Devices in Poetry	**Analyze Structure: Lyric Poetry**
Writing Activity: Summary	Selection Test	**Write a Summary > Interactive Whiteboard Lesson >** Write a Summary	**Cite Evidence > Level Up Tutorial >** Reading for Details
Writing Activity: Letter	Selection Test	**Analyze Style > Interactive Whiteboard Lesson >** Word Choice and Tone	**Determine Central Idea and Details > Level Up Tutorial >** Main Idea and Supporting Details
Media Activity: Podcast	Selection Test	**Integrate Information**	**Interpret Information: Visual and Sound Elements**
A Present a Response to Literature **B** Write an Informative Essay	Collection Test		

Lesson Assessments Writing as a Process Participating in Collaborative Discussions	**Standards Support and Enrichment**	For more instruction and practice in reading literary and informational texts, language, spelling, and speaking and listening, see Teacher Resources > Standards Support and Enrichment.
	For Designated English Language Instruction	To provide scaffolded support specific to the needs of English Learners during Designated English Language instruction, use the selection- and standards-aligned lessons found in Teacher Resources > Language Workshop.

Collection 1 Lessons	Key Learning Objective	Performance Task	Vocabulary Strategy
ANCHOR TEXT **Short Story by Graham Salisbury** **"The Ravine," p. 3A** Lexile 680L	**The student will be able to . . .** describe characters and setting and make inferences in the context of a short story.	Writing Activity: Informative Essay	Context Clues
Short Story by Margaret Peterson Haddix **"Fine?" p. 17A** Lexile 770L	**The student will be able to . . .** describe plot elements and analyze point of view in a short story.	Writing Activity: Narrative	Greek Roots
Poem by Maya Angelou **"Life Doesn't Frighten Me," p. 37A**	**The student will be able to . . .** describe the structure of a lyric poem and identify repetition and rhyme scheme.	Speaking Activity: Response to Literature	
ANCHOR TEXT **Online Article by kidshealth.org** **"Fears and Phobias," p. 41A** Lexile 1080L	**The student will be able to . . .** cite textual evidence to analyze text features and structure.	Writing Activity: Summary	Prefixes That Mean "Not"
Informational Text by Glenn Murphy **from *Stuff That Scares Your Pants Off!*** **"In the Spotlight," p. 51A** Lexile 1110L	**The student will be able to . . .** determine central ideas and supporting details in informational text.	Writing Activity: Letter	Suffixes That Form Nouns
Online Science Exhibit by The California Science Center **"Wired for Fear," p. 59A**	**The student will be able to . . .** analyze the purpose of a video and understand the visual and sound elements used in it.	Media Activity: Podcast	

Collection 1 Performance Tasks:

A Present a Response to Literature
B Write an Informative Essay

Language Conventions	English Language Support	Differentiated Instruction	CLOSE READER Selection
Recognize Variations from Standard English	• Improve Reading Fluency • Exchange Ideas • Standard English Variations	**For Standard English Learners:** Analyze Language **When Students Struggle:** Character Development **To Challenge Students:** Describe Characters **For Students with Disabilities:** Comprehension Strategies	Short Story by René Saldaña, Jr. "The Jumping Tree," p. 16b **Lexile 810L**
Commas and Dashes	• Read Closely • Word Study • Understand Cohesion • Understand Text Structure • Understand Character • Understand Language Choices	**When Students Struggle:** Order Events **For Standard English Learners:** Comparative Forms of Adjectives **To Challenge Students:** Describe Stories: Plot	
	• Read Closely		
Subjective and Objective Pronouns	• Evaluate Language Choices • Read Closely • Exchange Information • Improve Reading Fluency • Determine Word Meanings • Use Subjective and Objective Pronouns	**For Students with Disabilities:** Physical Aids **When Students Struggle:** Compare and Contrast	Magazine Article by Dana Hudepohl "Face Your Fears: Choking Under Pressure Is Every Athlete's Worst Nightmare," p. 50b **Lexile 870L**
Possessive Pronouns	• Read Closely • Adapt Language Choices • Learn More About Affixes • Understand Cohesion • Examine Language Choices	**When Students Struggle:** Main Ideas and Details **To Challenge Students:** Make Connections	Magazine Article by Jason Koebler "Face Your Fears and Scare the Phobia Out of Your Brain," p. 58b **Lexile 1420L**
	• Use Technical Words • Take Notes • Link Ideas	**For Standard English Learners:** Pronunciation	
A Adverbs **B** Compound Sentences	**A** Plan a Presentation Provide Text Evidence Use Adverbials Modify to Add Details **B** Write Informative Texts Link Ideas Understand Text Structure Use Language Resources	**A** **For Standard English Learners:** Adapt Speech **For Students with Disabilities:** Use Visual Cues **When Students Struggle:** Practice Speaking Techniques **To Challenge Students:** Create an Advertisement **B** **For Standard English Learners:** Conjugate Verbs **When Students Struggle:** Add Relevant Evidence **For Students with Disabilities:** Evaluate the Essay **To Challenge Students:** Conduct an Interview	

ANCHOR TEXT — The Ravine

Short Story by Graham Salisbury

Why This Text?

Students regularly read realistic fiction in school and on their own. This lesson explores the specific ways author Graham Salisbury develops characters and setting in "The Ravine."

Key Learning Objective: The student will be able to describe characters and setting and make inferences in the context of a short story.

For practice and application:

Close Reader selection
from "The Jumping Tree"
Short Story by René Saldaña Jr.

RL 1 Cite textual evidence; make inferences.
RL 2 Determine a theme or central idea; provide a summary.
RL 3 Describe story elements.
RL 4 Determine the meaning of words and phrases.
RL 5 Analyze structure.
W 2 Write informative/explanatory texts.
W 9a Draw evidence from literary texts.
SL 1 Engage effectively in a range of collaborative discussions.
L 1e Recognize variations from standard English.
L 3a Vary sentence patterns.
L 4a Use context as a clue to the meaning of a word or phrase.
L 4c Consult reference materials.
L 4d Verify preliminary determination of the meaning of a word.

▲ Text Complexity Rubric

Quantitative Measures	**The Ravine** Lexile: 680L
Qualitative Measures	**Levels of Meaning/Purpose** single level of complex meaning
	Structure somewhat complex story concepts
	Language Conventionality and Clarity figurative, less accessible language
	Knowledge Demands increased amount of cultural and literary knowledge useful
Reader/Task Considerations	• Teacher determined • Vary by individual reader and type of text • See the Text X-Ray for suggested Reader/Task Considerations.

TEXT X-RAY

English Language Support
Before teaching, use the Text X-Ray for an overview of the text's complexity. The Text X-Ray and the supports and scaffolds in the Teacher's Edition will help you guide students of different skill levels.

Meaning Making

Language Development

Effective Expression

Content Knowledge

Foundational Skills

Text Complexity: Qualitative Measures

Levels of Meaning/Purpose

single level of complex meaning

Help students make and support inferences.

- Teacher's Edition side notes, pp. 3, 5, 8, 10, 12, 13
- English Language Support, pp. 3, 8
- Strategies for Annotation, p. 13
- Make Inferences, p. 13

▶ *Use It!* **Interactive Whiteboard Lessons:** Making Inferences

ZOOM IN ON **MAKING INFERENCES** Tell students an author sometimes leaves things out of a story and lets readers figure them out on their own. Readers do this by making **inferences**, or logical guesses, based on text details and personal knowledge and experience.

- Read aloud lines 13–30 as students follow. Discuss what Vinny's friend is doing to Vinny. *(teasing him)*
- Then have small groups reread the lines and make an inference about why Joe-Boy teases Vinny. Remind them to use details from the text and their own experiences. *(Joe-Boy is teasing Vinny because he knows that Vinny is nervous.)*
- Let volunteers share inferences and explain what details or experiences they used in making those inferences.

Structure

somewhat complex story concepts

Help students understand the terms and factors associated with character and setting in a story.

- Teacher's Edition side notes, pp. 3, 4, 5, 6, 7, 8, 9, 11, 13
- English Language Support, p. 9
- When Students Struggle, p. 7
- Close Read Screencasts, p. 3
- Strategies for Annotation, p. 10, 13
- Describe Stories: Character and Setting, p. 13
- Performance Task, p. 14

To reteach character development, see

- Describe Stories: Character Development, p. 16a

▶ *Use It!* **Level Up Tutorials:** Character Traits; Character Motivation; Making Inferences About Characters

ZOOM IN ON **UNDERSTANDING CHARACTER** Explain that characters have **traits**, or features, and **motivations**, or reasons for acting. Analyzing what a character does and why can help readers understand an author's message.

- Read aloud lines 121–132 while students follow the text.
- Have students list two things they think the text will tell them about Vinny's character.
- Let students read the text to confirm their ideas about Vinny's character.
- After they finish reading, have small groups discuss what they learned about Vinny.

Language Conventionality and Clarity

figurative, less accessible language

Teach unfamiliar vocabulary in context.

- Teacher's Edition Critical Vocabulary notes, pp. 4, 10, 11, 15
- English Language Support, p. 11
- Applying Academic Vocabulary, p. 5
- Strategies for Annotation, p. 15
- Vocabulary Strategy: Using Context Clues, p. 15

Help students analyze language, sentence structure, and the use of dialect in a narrative.

- Teacher's Edition side notes, p. 4, 6, 7, 9, 12, 16
- English Language Support, p. 8, 16
- Strategies for Annotation, p. 6
- Language Conventions: Recognize Variations from Standard English, p. 16

ZOOM IN ON **ANALYZING REPETITION** Explain that writers often repeat words to produce certain effects. Have pairs read lines 38–53 aloud, alternating after every 10 or 11 lines.

- Have listeners note repeated words and phrases. *(too soon, Two weeks and one day, fourteen, louder)*
- Ask the pairs to discuss how the **repetition** affects their ideas about the main character and what he worries about. *(It shows that Vinny is thinking about how the boy died too young and that it is too soon for anyone to be swimming in the same place. The repetition of louder makes the waterfall seem dangerous.)*

Knowledge Demands

increased amount of cultural and literary knowledge useful

Support English Learners in understanding the cultural references in the text.

- Teacher's Edition Background note, p. 3
- Content Area Connection, p. 12

 Visualizing

ZOOM IN ON **BUILDING KNOWLEDGE OF SETTING** Note that the **setting,** or place, of this text is a Hawaiian island. The descriptions of the setting help set the **mood,** or atmosphere, of the selection.

- Model how to think about setting by reading aloud lines 1–7.
- Point out words that describe the setting, and ask volunteers to define them. *(ravine, jungle, tangled trees, muddy trail, cool breeze, Hawaiian hillside pastures)*
- Discuss with the whole class their impressions of the setting. Ask, *Do you think it is warm? How does the description of the jungle make you feel? Is Vinny happy to be on the trail?*

Suggested Reader/Task Considerations

You might consider the following before assigning this selection to students.

- Do students have the skills to make inferences to understand connections between parts of the text?
- Are students mature enough to understand the concerns of the main character?

ZOOM IN ON **SUPPORTING COMPREHENSION**

- Review making **inferences:** When you make an inference, you figure out something that the author has not explained or described in the text. Have pairs read lines 110–121 and discuss what they can infer about the main character's relationship with his mother.
- Before students read, ask them to consider what it means to be a friend. Have small groups discuss whether a friend makes fun of a person's fears and concerns. As students read, ask them to connect the ideas raised in their discussions with those expressed in "The Ravine."

Graham Salisbury Have students read the information about the author. Explain that Salisbury's work focuses on the need to make choices in life and how young people struggle with this need wherever they may grow up. Making choices can be confusing and even frightening; Salisbury feels that as a writer he has a responsibility to explore these issues with readers through the authentic experiences and characters he creates.

SETTING A PURPOSE Direct students to use the Setting a Purpose prompt to focus their reading. Remind them to write down questions as they read.

Describe Stories: Character and Setting (LINES 1–12)   RL 3

Explain to students that the **characters,** the people or animals the story is about, and the **setting,** or time and place of a story, are important story elements that an author usually identifies early in a story. The author quickly establishes who the main character or characters are and what the problem might be.

 CITE TEXT EVIDENCE Have students read lines 1–12 and identify the story characters and setting, including who is the main character. *(The characters are Vinny, Joe-Boy, Mo, and Starlene; the setting is a jungle ravine. Vinny is the main character.)*

Make Inferences (LINES 8–12)   RL 1

Explain that readers often have to figure out something that an author has not explained. Tell students that in these cases, readers may need to make an **inference,** or a logical guess based on facts and one's own knowledge and experience, to understand a story clearly.

B **ASK STUDENTS** to reread lines 8–12 and state an inference they can make about any of the characters or the setting. *(Possible responses: Vinny is the main character; the characters will talk about the dead boy; the ravine is a little scary and/or dangerous.)*

English Language Support

To help students understand how to make an inference, read lines 8–12 aloud and express an inference. *(The author writes about a boy drowning and then wonders if it really happened. This suggests that the characters will talk about the dead boy.)*

Graham Salisbury (b. 1944) *was born in Pennsylvania but grew up in Hawaii. Growing up with a distant mother and without a father, who was killed in World War II, Salisbury lacked guidance. His characters explore choices similar to those he faced—making and keeping friends and learning honesty and courage. Their struggles, like Salisbury's, also take place in a Hawaiian setting. Among his many writing awards are the Boston Globe/Horn Book award and a School Library Journal Best Book of the Year award.*

The Ravine

Short Story by Graham Salisbury

SETTING A PURPOSE As you read, pay attention to how a tragic event affects Vinny. Write down any questions you have while reading.

 myNotebook

As you read, save new words to *myWordList.*

When Vinny and three others dropped down into the ravine,[1] they entered a jungle thick with tangled trees and rumors of what might have happened to the dead boy's body.

The muddy trail was slick and, in places where it had fallen away, flat-out dangerous. The cool breeze that swept the Hawaiian hillside pastures above died early in the descent.

There were four of them—Vinny; his best friend, Joe-Boy; Mo, who was afraid of nothing; and Joe-Boy's *haole*[2] girlfriend, Starlene—all fifteen. It was a Tuesday in July, two weeks and a day after the boy had drowned. If, in fact, that's what had happened to him.

 Close Read

B

---

[1] **ravine** (rə-vēn´): a deep, narrow valley made by running water.
[2] **haole** (hou´lē): in Hawaii, a white person or non-native Hawaiian.

The Ravine   **3**

Close Read Screencasts   Close Read

Modeled Discussions

Have students click the *Close Read* icon in their eBook to access a screencast in which readers discuss and annotate lines 1–7, a key passage that introduces the setting and a central issue of the story.

As a class, view and discuss the video. Then have students pair up to do an independent close read of an additional passage—Vinny's moment of decision about whether or not to jump (lines 297–308).

Analyze Language RL 4, L 1e

(LINES 26–29)

Explain to students that **dialect** is a form of language spoken in a specific place by a particular group of people. Tell them that a dialect varies from standard English in different ways and that they need to pay attention as they read to make sure they understand its meaning and use.

C **ASK STUDENTS** to reread lines 26–29, point out the variations from standard English, and then restate the boys' dialogue in standard English. Ask them how this use of dialect helps them better understand the characters.

Describe Stories: RL 1, RL 3
Character (LINES 38–53)

Explain to students that characters in a story have **traits,** or personal qualities, and **motivations,** or reasons why they do things, just as real people do. These elements, as well as story events, contribute to a character's **development** throughout a story.

D **ASK STUDENTS** to reread lines 38–53 and tell what they learn about Vinny's feelings in these paragraphs. *(Vinny feels more concerned about the missing boy than his friends do; this makes him a little afraid or anxious about what will happen on the hike.)*

CRITICAL VOCABULARY

gnarly: The word *gnarly* is a descriptive, sensory word that helps readers imagine what the trees in the ravine look and feel like.

ASK STUDENTS to discuss what they think a gnarly tree would look and feel like and how that description adds to their ideas about the setting and atmosphere of the story. *(The tree would feel rough and bumpy; it would look oddly shaped and maybe a little scary or uninviting. This description adds darkness and danger to the feel of the jungle and to the story.)*

Vinny slipped, and dropped his towel in the mud. He picked it up and tried to brush it off, but instead smeared the mud spot around until the towel resembled something someone's dog had slept on. "Tst," he said.

Joe-Boy, hiking down just behind him, laughed. "Hey, Vinny, just think, that kid walked where you walking."

"Shuddup," Vinny said.

20 "You prob'ly stepping right where his foot was."

Vinny moved to the edge of the trail, where the ravine fell through a twisted jungle of **gnarly** trees and underbrush to the stream far below. He could see Starlene and Mo farther ahead, their heads bobbing as they walked, both almost down to the pond where the boy had died.

C "Hey," Joe-Boy went on, "maybe you going be the one to find his body."

"You don't cut it out, Joe-Boy, I going . . . I going . . . "

"What, cry?"

30 Vinny scowled. Sometimes Joe-Boy was a big fat babooze.

They slid down the trail. Mud oozed between Vinny's toes. He grabbed at roots and branches to keep from falling. Mo and Starlene were out of sight now, the trail ahead having cut back.

Joe-Boy said, "You going jump in the water and go down and your hand going touch his face, stuck under the rocks. *Ha ha ha . . . a ha ha ha!*"

D Vinny winced. He didn't want to be here. It was too soon, way too soon. Two weeks and one day.

40 He saw a footprint in the mud and stepped around it.

The dead boy had jumped and had never come back up. Four search and rescue divers hunted for two days straight and never found him. Not a trace. Gave Vinny the creeps. It didn't make sense. The pond wasn't that big.

He wondered why it didn't seem to bother anyone else. Maybe it did and they just didn't want to say.

Butchie was the kid's name. Only fourteen.

Fourteen.

Two weeks and one day ago he was walking down this 50 trail. Now nobody could find him.

The jungle crushed in, reaching over the trail, and Vinny brushed leafy branches aside. The roar of the waterfall got louder, louder.

gnarly
(när´lē) *adj.*
Something that is *gnarly* has many knots and bumpy areas on its surface.

FOR STANDARD ENGLISH LEARNERS

Analyze Language Display lines 17–20 of the story and follow these steps:

- Highlight in yellow: *where you walking, Shuddup,* and *prob'ly.*
- Rewrite the words and phrases in standard English and read them aloud.
- Discuss the differences between the two versions.

ASK STUDENTS to read the dialogue aloud—first, as it is in the story, then in standard English. Have partners repeat with other story dialect as needed.

Vinny, just think, that kid walked where you walking."

"Shuddup," Vinny said.

Starlene said it was the goddess that took him, the one that lives in the stone down by the road. She did that every now and then, Starlene said, took somebody when she got lonely. Took him and kept him. Vinny had heard that legend before, but he'd never believed in it.

Now he didn't know what he believed.

60   The body had to be stuck down there. But still, four divers and they couldn't find it?

Vinny decided he'd better believe in the legend. If he didn't, the goddess might get mad and send him bad luck. Or maybe take *him*, too.

Stopstopstop! Don't think like that.

"Come on," Joe-Boy said, nudging Vinny from behind. "Hurry it up."

Just then Starlene whooped, her voice bouncing around the walls of the ravine.

70   "Let's *go*," Joe-Boy said. "They there already."

Moments later, Vinny jumped up onto a large boulder at the edge of the pond. Starlene was swimming out in the brown water. It wasn't murky brown, but clean and clear to a depth of maybe three or four feet. Because of the waterfall you had to yell if you wanted to say something. The whole place smelled of mud and ginger and iron.

Starlene swam across to the waterfall on the far side of the pond and ducked under it, then climbed out and edged along the rock wall behind it, moving slowly, like a spider. Above,
80   sun-sparkling stream water spilled over the lip of a one-hundred-foot drop.

Mo and Joe-Boy threw their towels onto the rocks and dove into the pond. Vinny watched, his muddy towel hooked around his neck. Reluctantly, he let it fall, then dove in after them.

The cold mountain water tasted tangy. Was it because the boy's body was down there decomposing?[3] He spit it out.

He followed Joe-Boy and Mo to the waterfall and ducked under it. They climbed up onto the rock ledge, just as Starlene
90   had done, then spidered their way over to where you could climb to a small ledge about fifteen feet up. They took their time because the hand and footholds were slimy with moss.

---

[3] **decomposing** (dē´kəm-pōz´ĭng): starting to decay and fall apart.

APPLYING ACADEMIC VOCABULARY

factor	indicate

THINK-PAIR-SHARE Have students turn to a partner to discuss the following questions. Guide students to include the academic vocabulary words *factor* and *indicate* in their responses. Ask volunteers to share their responses with the class.

- What **factors** affect the characters in the story?
- What do these ideas **indicate** about each character's traits and motivation? Remember to consider setting in your discussion.

CLOSE READ

Describe Stories: Character and Setting (LINES 54–87)   RL 1, RL 3

Character Explain to students that authors often reveal character traits through a character's reactions to other characters and their ideas.

E **ASK STUDENTS** to reread lines 54–65 and tell what they think Vinny's thoughts about the goddess reveal about him. *(Possible responses: Vinny is uneasy; his fear of what may or may not be in the pond is making him question his senses and his beliefs. He is upset that his fears rather than his reason seem to be in control.)*

Setting Explain to students that the setting of a story is often a factor that affects a character's development.

F **CITE TEXT EVIDENCE** Have students reread lines 71–87 and cite words and phrases that indicate how the setting is making Vinny uneasy and afraid. *(line 75: whole place smelled; lines 80–81: one-hundred-foot drop; line 84: Reluctantly; line 87: body, decomposing)*

Make Inferences   RL 1
(LINES 54–81)

Explain that readers learn much about a character's personality from his or her actions and ideas. Tell them that often readers can make inferences about a character's traits by combining details from the story with their own knowledge and experience.

G **ASK STUDENTS** to review references to Starlene in lines 54–81 and then describe her personality based on what they find. *(Possible responses: Starlene is imaginative, curious, energetic, friendly, brave, and probably a leader in many situations.)*

Analyze Language

RL 4,
L 3a

(LINES 93–102)

Explain to students that authors vary the length, structure, and pattern of sentences in their writing to create reader interest or emphasis or to develop meaning. Authors will also use **repetition,** or repeated words or phrases, to create emphasis and drama.

H CITE TEXT EVIDENCE Have students review lines 93–102 and point out specific instances of sentence variations and repetition that create interest and drama. *(Line 95: short phrases, repeated word* then; *lines 97–98: repeated words* the one; *lines 101–102: repeated words* That was; *short, one-sentence paragraphs)*

Describe Stories:

RL 1,
RL 3

Character (LINES 110–117)

Explain to students that **character development** is how a character changes or becomes better known to the reader over the course of a story.

I ASK STUDENTS to reread lines 110–117, identify another conflict that is affecting Vinny, and describe what this tells readers about Vinny's personality. *(Vinny's mother told him not to go to the ravine, but his father said Vinny should go back so he wouldn't be scared anymore; Vinny respects his parents but is confused by their comments.)*

Starlene jumped first. Her shriek echoed off the rocky cliff, then died in the dense green jungle.

Mo jumped, then Joe-Boy, then Vinny.

The fifteen-foot ledge was not the problem.

It was the one above it, the one you had to work up to, the big one, where you had to take a deadly zigzag trail that climbed up and away from the waterfall, then cut back and forth to a foot-wide ledge something more like fifty feet up.

That was the problem.

That was where the boy had jumped from.

Joe-Boy and Starlene swam out to the middle of the pond. Mo swam back under the waterfall and climbed once again to the fifteen-foot ledge.

Vinny started to swim out toward Joe-Boy but stopped when he saw Starlene put her arms around him. She kissed him. They sank under for a long time, then came back up, still kissing.

Vinny turned away and swam back over to the other side of the pond, where he'd first gotten in. His mother would kill him if she ever heard about where he'd come. After the boy drowned, or was taken by the goddess, or whatever happened to him, she said never to come to this pond again. Ever. It was off-limits. Permanently.

But not his dad. He said, "You fall off a horse, you get back on, right? Or else you going be scared of it all your life."

©Getty Images

6 Collection 1

Strategies for Annotation ✏ 🖻 *Annotate it!*

Analyze Language

RL 4, L 3a

Share these strategies for guided or independent analysis:

- Highlight in yellow repeated words or phrases.
- Underline short, dramatic sentences that create emphasis or drama.
- Reread your underlined and highlighted text, noting any overlaps.
- On a note, record any insights about the author's writing techniques.

It was the one above it, the one you had to work up to, the big one, where you had to take a deadly zigzag trail that climbed up and away from the waterfall, then cut back and forth to a foot-wide ledge something more like fifty feet up.

<u>That was</u> the problem.

Repeated short text adds tension.

<u>That was</u> where the boy had jumped from.

His mother scoffed and waved him off. "Don't listen to him, Vinny, listen to me. Don't go there. That pond is haunted." Which had made his dad laugh.

But Vinny promised he'd stay away.

But then Starlene and Joe-Boy said, "Come with us anyway. You let your mommy run your life, or what?" And Vinny said, "But what if I get caught?" And Joe-Boy said, "So?"

Vinny mashed his lips. He was so weak. Couldn't even say no. But if he'd said, "I can't go, my mother won't like it," they would have laughed him right off the island. No, he had to go. No choice.

So he'd come along, and so far it was fine. He'd even gone in the water. Everyone was happy. All he had to do now was wait it out and go home and hope his mother never heard about it.

When he looked up, Starlene was gone.

He glanced around the pond until he spotted her starting up the zigzag trail to the fifty-foot ledge. She was moving slowly, hanging on to roots and branches on the upside of the cliff. He couldn't believe she was going there. He wanted to yell, *Hey, Starlene, that's where he* died!

But she already knew that.

Mo jumped from the lower ledge, yelling, "Banzaiiii!" An explosion of coffee-colored water erupted when he hit.

Joe-Boy swam over to where Starlene had gotten out. He waved to Vinny, grinning like a fool, then followed Starlene up the zigzag trail.

Now Starlene was twenty-five, thirty feet up. Vinny watched her for a while, then lost sight of her when she slipped behind a wall of jungle that blocked his view. A few minutes later she popped back out, now almost at the top, where the trail ended, where there was nothing but mud and a few plants to grab on to if you slipped, plants that would rip right out of the ground, plants that wouldn't stop you if you fell, nothing but your screams between you and the rocks below.

Vinny's stomach tingled just watching her. He couldn't imagine what it must feel like to be up there, especially if you were afraid of heights, like he was. *She has no fear*, Vinny thought, *no fear at all. Pleasepleaseplease, Starlene. I don't want to see you die.*

Starlene crept forward, making her way to the end of the trail, where the small ledge was.

CLOSE READ

Analyze Language
RL 4,
L 3a

(LINES 147–152)

Explain to students that authors use **repetition,** or repeated words or phrases, to create emphasis and drama in their writing. Tell students that repeated words can also create a rhythm in language that propels the reader forward through the text.

Ⓙ CITE TEXT EVIDENCE Have students review lines 147–152, point out specific instances of repetition, and explain the effect this repetition has for the reader. *(Repeated words include* where, plants that; *author uses them in short, rhythmic phrases to create a rush toward the end of the paragraph, as if the reader is falling into the ravine as the language describes.)*

Describe Stories:
RL 1,
RL 3

Character (LINES 153–157)

Explain to students that authors develop the traits of their main characters throughout a story, adding to and refining the characters' personalities by revealing more and more details about them.

Ⓚ CITE TEXT EVIDENCE Have students reread lines 153–157 and identify new information they have learned about Vinny. *(Vinny is afraid of heights, and he is afraid that Starlene or another of his friends might die jumping into the pond, just as the dead boy did.)*

WHEN STUDENTS STRUGGLE . . .

To guide students' comprehension of character development throughout a story, have individuals or partners complete a character web for Vinny like the one shown. Have them refer back to the beginning of the story as needed to create as complete a description of Vinny as possible.

LEVEL UP TUTORIALS For additional support, assign the following *Level Up* tutorial: **Character Traits.**

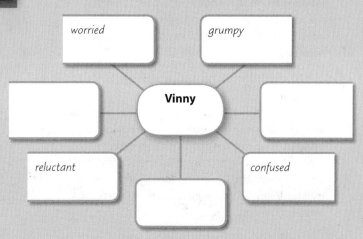

Make Inferences   RL 1
(LINES 162–165)

Tell students that authors sometimes leave things out of a story that readers need to figure out or think about on their own.

Ⓛ ASK STUDENTS why Vinny might want to hug Starlene. *(Starlene and Vinny are friends, and Vinny is afraid she might die when she jumps off the high ledge.)*

English Language Support

Read Closely Point out the words in italic type in line 165. Explain that the slanted type is italic and using it is a way to call attention to certain words. Have students work in small groups to look through the selection to find italic type. Ask them to discuss why italic type is used. *(to voice Vinny's thoughts, to tell what other characters are feeling)* Have volunteers share what their groups concluded about the italic type.

Describe Stories: RL 1, RL 3
Character (LINES 184–197)

Explain to students that authors develop characters in a story by showing their actions and words and by describing their reactions to events and to other characters' actions.

Ⓜ ASK STUDENTS to explain Vinny's idea that "It was asking for it" as a reaction to Starlene's jump. *(Vinny is more concerned about what happened to the dead boy than the others; he thinks Starlene is not taking the death or the dangerous jump seriously enough and that she will get into some kind of trouble because of that.)*

Ⓝ CITE TEXT EVIDENCE Have students reread lines 189–197 and then describe Joe-Boy's personality, using both his actions and Vinny's reaction to them. *(Joe-Boy likes to tease Vinny; he is confident and exuberant and sometimes too careless of others' feelings. Vinny thinks Joe-Boy is being reckless and careless right now.)*

160 　Joe-Boy popped out of the jungle behind her. He stopped, waiting for her to jump before going on.

　Vinny held his breath.

　Starlene, in her cutoff jeans and soaked T-shirt, stood perfectly still, her arms at her sides. Vinny suddenly felt like hugging her. Why, he couldn't tell. *Starlene, please.*　Ⓛ

　She reached behind her and took a wide leaf from a plant, then eased down and scooped up a finger of mud. She made a brown cross on her forehead, then wiped her muddy fingers on her jeans.

170 　She waited.

　Was she thinking about the dead boy?

　She stuck the stem end of the leaf in her mouth, leaving the rest of it to hang out. When she jumped, the leaf would flap up and cover her nose and keep water from rushing into it. An old island trick.

　She jumped.

　Down, down.

　Almost in slow motion, it seemed at first, then faster and faster. She fell feetfirst, arms flapping to keep balance so she

180 wouldn't land on her back, or stomach, which would probably almost kill her.

　Just before she hit, she crossed her arms over her chest and vanished within a small explosion of rusty water.

　Vinny stood, not breathing at all, praying.

　Ten seconds. Twenty, thirty . . .

　She came back up, laughing.

　She shouldn't make fun that way, Vinny thought. It was　Ⓜ dangerous, disrespectful. It was asking for it.

　Vinny looked up when he heard Joe-Boy shout, "Hey,

190 Vinny, watch how a man does it! Look!"

　Joe-Boy scooped up some mud and drew a stroke of lightning across his chest. When he jumped, he threw himself out, face and body parallel to the pond, his arms and legs spread out. *He's crazy,* Vinny thought, *absolutely insane.* At the last second Joe-Boy folded into a ball and hit. *Ca-roomp!* He came up whooping and yelling, "*Wooo!* So *good!* Come on, Vinny, it's hot!"

　Vinny faked a laugh. He waved, shouting, "Naah, the water's too cold!"　Ⓝ

English Language Support

Improve Reading Fluency Have students work with a partner to choral read the text and dialogue starting on page 7, line 129. First, model by reading ten lines of the text with a student and then stopping and providing feedback about the student's pronunciation and expression. Next, have student partners proceed with the reading until line 199, stopping every ten lines to review pronunciation and expression.

200   Now Mo was heading up the zigzag trail—Mo, who
hardly ever said a word and would do anything anyone ever
challenged him to do. *Come on, Mo, not you, too.*

     Vinny knew then that he would have to jump.

     Jump, or never live it down.

     Mo jumped in the same way Joe-Boy had, man-style,
splayed out in a suicide fall. He came up grinning.

     Starlene and Joe-Boy turned toward Vinny.

     Vinny got up and hiked around the edge of the pond,
walking in the muddy shallows, looking at a school of small
210 brown-backed fish near a ginger patch.

     Maybe they'd forget about him.

     Starlene torpedoed over, swimming underwater. Her body
glittered in the small amount of sunlight that penetrated the
trees around the rim of the ravine. When she came up, she
broke the surface smoothly, gracefully, like a swan. Her blond
hair sleeked back like river grass.

     She smiled a sweet smile. "Joe-Boy says you're afraid to
jump. I didn't believe him. He's wrong, right?"

     Vinny said quickly, "Of course he's wrong. I just don't
220 want to, that's all. The water's cold."

     "Naah, it's nice."

     Vinny looked away. On the other side of the pond Joe-Boy
and Mo were on the cliff behind the waterfall.

     "Joe-Boy says your mom told you not to come here. Is
that true?"

     Vinny nodded. "Yeah. Stupid, but she thinks it's haunted."

     "She's right."

     "What?"

     "That boy didn't die, Vinny. The stone goddess took him.
230 He's in a good place right now. He's her prince."

     Vinny scowled. He couldn't tell if Starlene was teasing him
or if she really believed that. He said, "Yeah, prob'ly."

     "Are you going to jump, or is Joe-Boy right?"

     "Joe-Boy's an idiot. Sure I'm going to jump."

     Starlene grinned, staring at Vinny a little too long. "He is
an idiot, isn't he? But I love him."

     "Yeah, well . . . "

     "Go to it, big boy. I'll be watching."

     Starlene sank down and swam out into the pond.
240 *Ca-ripes.*

The Ravine   **9**

TO CHALLENGE STUDENTS . . .

Describe Characters Starlene is a minor character in the story who
nevertheless has a strong role in helping Vinny understand his feelings.
Explain that an author will often develop a particular side of a minor
character to add depth to another character's development.

ASK STUDENTS to write a profile of Starlene based on Salisbury's
descriptions and her interactions with others in the story. Have them include
how her actions and words affect Vinny's feelings and actions throughout
the story.

CLOSE READ

Analyze Language   RL 4
(LINES 212–216)

Explain to students that an author uses sensory
details that appeal to readers' senses of sight, touch,
smell, taste, and hearing to help readers get a clear
picture of a story and its characters. Tell them that a
simile is a kind of descriptive language that compares
two unlike things using the words *like* or *as*.

Ⓞ CITE TEXT EVIDENCE Have students tell what
sensory language, including similes, the author
uses in lines 212–216 and how this helps them
picture Starlene and the pond more clearly. *(Possible
answers: torpedoed; glittered; small amount of sunlight;
penetrated the trees; blond; similes "like a swan," "like
river grass." This description shows how calm and
confident Starlene is; it also makes the pond seem less
dangerous.)*

Describe Stories: RL 1, RL 2, RL 3
Character and Setting
(LINES 217–240)

Explain to students that authors use dialogue to
create authentic characters and to show a character's
traits and development in a story.

Ⓟ CITE TEXT EVIDENCE Have students reread
Starlene and Vinny's conversation (lines 217–240) and
then **summarize,** or retell in their own words, what
factors Vinny has been worrying about. *(Vinny is afraid
to jump; he is worried about his mom telling him not to
come to the ravine and about the boy who died there.
And he is worried about what Joe-Boy will think of him.
Starlene asks Vinny about all these things, which helps
readers recall them more easily.)*

English Language Support

To help students describe what Vinny has been
experiencing, have them work in pairs to reread lines
217–240 and brainstorm words that describe Vinny.
(caring, worried, afraid, nervous, scared) Have students
use their words to write three sentences about why
Vinny is worried.

Make Inferences
RL 1

(LINES 267–271)

Explain to students that sometimes readers need to use what the author writes as well as their own knowledge and experience to understand a character more deeply.

Q **ASK STUDENTS** to explain why Vinny has an urge to fly as he looks down into the ravine. *(Vinny wants to be able to stop worrying and being afraid. Being a glider, bird, or leaf would allow him to fly away and leave the worry behind him; there would be nothing to fear.)*

CRITICAL VOCABULARY

rivulet: The author uses the word *rivulets* to help explain why the trail is wet and muddy.

ASK STUDENTS to discuss how the word *rivulets* helps them picture the trail and the cliff more clearly. *(The use of the word* rivulets *shows how even some small streams of water can make the trail dangerous.)*

cascade: The author uses the word *cascading* to describe the power of the waterfall.

ASK STUDENTS to discuss how the word *cascading* works with other words in the paragraph to describe the waterfall. *(The word* cascading *tells about what Vinny sees; the word* roaring *tells what he hears; the words* its mist dampened the air he breathed *tell what he can feel on his body from the powerful waterfall.)*

Vinny ripped a hank[4] of white ginger from the ginger patch and smelled it, and prayed he'd still be alive after the sun went down.

He took his time climbing the zigzag trail. When he got to the part where the jungle hid him from view, he stopped and smelled the ginger again. So sweet and alive it made Vinny wish for all he was worth that he was climbing out of the ravine right now, heading home.

But of course, there was no way he could do that.

250 Not before jumping.

He tossed the ginger onto the muddy trail and continued on. He slipped once or twice, maybe three times. He didn't keep track. He was too numb now, too caught up in the insane thing he was about to do. He'd never been this far up the trail before. Once he'd tried to go all the way, but couldn't. It made him dizzy.

When he stepped out and the jungle opened into a huge bowl where he could look down, way, way down, he could see their three heads in the water, heads with arms moving slowly 260 to keep them afloat, and a few bright rays of sunlight pouring down onto them, and when he saw this, his stomach fluttered and rose. Something sour came up and he spit it out.

It made him wobble to look down. He closed his eyes. His whole body trembled. The trail was no wider than the length of his foot. And it was wet and muddy from little **rivulets** of water that bled from the side of the cliff.

The next few steps were the hardest he'd ever taken in his life. He tried not to look down, but he couldn't help it. His gaze was drawn there. He struggled to push back an 270 urge to fly, just jump off and fly. He could almost see himself spiraling down like a glider, or a bird, or a leaf.

His hands shook as if he were freezing. He wondered, *Had the dead boy felt this way?* Or had he felt brave, like Starlene or Joe-Boy, or Mo, who seemed to feel nothing.

Somebody from below shouted, but Vinny couldn't make it out over the waterfall, roaring down just feet beyond the ledge where he would soon be standing, **cascading** past so close its mist dampened the air he breathed.

The dead boy had just come to the ravine to have fun, 280 Vinny thought. Just a regular kid like himself, come to swim

rivulet
(rĭv′yə-lĭt) *n.* A *rivulet* is a small brook or stream.

cascade
(kăs-kād′) *v.* Something that can *cascade* will fall, pour, or rush in stages, like a waterfall over steep rocks.

---

[4] **hank** (hăngk): a coiled or looped bundle of something, such as rope or yarn.

Strategies for Annotation   ✏️ 📄 Annotate it!

Describe Stories: Character and Setting
RL 1, RL 3

Share these strategies for guided or independent analysis:
- Highlight in yellow a character's thoughts or feelings.
- Highlight in green a character's actions.
- Highlight in blue a character's spoken words.
- Review your highlights. On a note, record what all of them together seem to indicate about the character.

Vinny thought he heard a voice, small and distant. Yes. Something inside him, a tiny voice pleading, *Don't do it. Walk away. Just turn and go and walk back down.*

"... I can't," Vinny whispered.

You can, you can, you can. Walk back down.

Vinny waited.

And waited.

> ## "The next few steps were the hardest he'd ever taken in his life."

and be with his friends, then go home and eat macaroni and cheese and watch TV, maybe play with his dog or wander around after dark.

But he'd done none of that.

Where was he?

Inch by inch Vinny made it to the ledge. He stood, swaying slightly, the tips of his toes one small movement from the **precipice**.

Far below, Joe-Boy waved his arm back and forth. It was dreamy to see—back and forth, back and forth. He looked so small down there.

For a moment Vinny's mind went blank, as if he were in some trance, some dream where he could so easily lean out and fall, and think or feel nothing.

A breeze picked up and moved the trees on the ridge-line, but not a breath of it reached the fifty-foot ledge.

Vinny thought he heard a voice, small and distant. Yes. Something inside him, a tiny voice pleading, *Don't do it. Walk away. Just turn and go and walk back down.*

" . . . I can't," Vinny whispered.

You can, you can, you can. Walk back down.

Vinny waited.

And waited.

Joe-Boy yelled, then Starlene, both of them waving.

Then something very strange happened.

Vinny felt at peace. Completely and totally calm and at peace. He had not made up his mind about jumping. But something else inside him had.

Thoughts and feelings swarmed, stinging him: *Jump! Jump! Jump! Jump!*

But deep inside, where the peace was, where his mind wasn't, he would not jump. He would walk back down.

precipice
(prĕs´ə-pĭs) *n.*
A *precipice* is an overhanging or extremely steep area of rock.

FOR STUDENTS WITH DISABILITIES

Students may struggle with the idea that the text on page 11, lines 292–312 describes what Vinny is seeing, feeling, and thinking as he stands on the ledge. Guide students to read the definition of *precipice* on the page. Draw a simple picture of a precipice on the board and confirm that students understand that Vinny is standing on the edge of the precipice and thinking about jumping into the water. Have students reread lines 292–312 and ask them what Vinny decided.

TEACH

CLOSE READ

Describe Stories: Character (LINES 279–312)

RL 1,
RL 3

Explain to students that one way authors develop characters is by describing thoughts and feelings the character has.

R ASK STUDENTS to reread lines 279–283 and then tell what these lines help explain about Vinny and his fears. *(Vinny realizes that he has been thinking about how the dead boy was just like him and now that boy has disappeared; he is afraid that he might make a similar mistake.)*

S CITE TEXT EVIDENCE Have students review lines 297–312. Ask whether they think Vinny will jump or walk back down and why. *(Possible answer: Vinny will walk back down because he feels peaceful; he trusts himself.)*

CRITICAL VOCABULARY

precipice: The author uses the word *precipice* to describe the ledge where Vinny is standing.

ASK STUDENTS why they think the author chose to use the word *precipice* here rather than a word such as *edge* or *cliff*. *(The word* precipice *sounds more dangerous; it helps readers understand how the ledge overhangs the water and makes clear how Vinny feels as he stands there, looking down over the edge.)*

Text in Focus English Language Support

Visualizing (LINE 291)

Have students view the **Text in Focus** video on this page of their eBook to learn how to use descriptive details to visualize the story's characters, setting, and events. Then have students use **Text in Focus Practice** to apply what they have learned.

CLOSE READ

Make Inferences

RL 1

(LINES 313–318)

Remind students that sometimes readers need to use both what the author has written and their own knowledge and experience to figure out something an author wants them to know.

T **CITE TEXT EVIDENCE** Have students explain how they know after reading lines 317–318 that Vinny will walk back down the trail and not jump. *(The others jumped with a leaf in their mouth, so when Vinny spits the leaf out of his mouth, the reader knows he will not jump.)*

COLLABORATIVE DISCUSSION Have small groups list Vinny's feelings and behavior throughout the story. Then have them discuss how Vinny's feelings and actions were influenced by the boy's death. Remind students to cite evidence from the text to support their ideas.

ASK STUDENTS to share any questions they generated in the course of reading and discussing the selection.

English Language Support

Exchange Ideas Before students begin their discussion, provide the following tips.

- Use *who, what, where,* and *when* to start questions about Vinny's feeling and actions.
- Paraphrase the key ideas in another student's comments to help clarify ideas.
- Take time to tell other people in the group that they have brought up an interesting idea. Then ask a question about their idea.

No! No, no, no!

Vinny eased down and fingered up some mud and made a cross on his chest, big and bold. He grabbed a leaf, stuck it in his mouth. *Be calm, be calm. Don't look down.*

After a long pause he spit the leaf out and rubbed the cross to a blur.

320 They walked out of the ravine in silence, Starlene, Joe-Boy, and Mo far ahead of him. They hadn't said a word since he'd come down off the trail. He knew what they were thinking. He knew, he knew, he knew.

At the same time the peace was still there. He had no idea what it was. But he prayed it wouldn't leave him now, prayed it wouldn't go away, would never go away, because in there, in that place where the peace was, it didn't matter what they thought.

Vinny emerged from the ravine into a brilliance that surprised him. Joe-Boy, Starlene, and Mo were now almost 330 down to the road.

Vinny breathed deeply, and looked up and out over the island. He saw, from there, a land that rolled away like honey, easing down a descent of rich Kikuyu grass pasture-land, flowing from there over vast highlands of brown and green, then, finally, falling massively to the coast and flat blue sea.

He'd never seen anything like it.

Had it always been here? This view of the island?

He stared and stared, then sat, taking it in.

He'd never seen anything so beautiful in all his life.

COLLABORATIVE DISCUSSION With a small group, discuss how Vinny's feelings and behavior are influenced by the boy's tragic death. Refer to events in the story to support your ideas.

CONTENT-AREA CONNECTION

Geography and Geology Remind students that "The Ravine" is set in Hawaii where the author grew up. The state of Hawaii is in the Pacific Ocean and it is made up of several islands. These islands are volcanic, or formed by volcanoes erupting over millions of years. Volcanoes continue to erupt frequently on the island of Hawaii that is also known as the Big Island. A new volcanic island is starting to form under the ocean about 20 miles from the Big Island.

Activity After reading the story, have students work in pairs to research how ravines are formed in Hawaii. Encourage students to make posters that include photographs of Hawaiian ravines and a paragraph about how they are formed. You might collaborate with geography or science teachers to have students present their findings in both classes.

Describe Stories: Character and Setting

Like real people, characters have personalities, drive, and life-changing events. To describe characters in terms of how they appear in stories, you can use these terms:

- **Character traits** are the qualities shown by a character, such as physical traits (tall, brown eyes) or expressions of personality (kind, anxious).
- **Character motivation** is the reason or reasons a character acts, feels, or thinks in a certain way.
- **Character development** is how a character changes throughout a story.

Think about your impressions of the characters in "The Ravine." What traits and motivations does Vinny exhibit throughout the story?

In a story like "The Ravine," the setting is a key factor in the events of the story and how the characters react to it and each other. The **setting** is the time and place in which the action occurs. The time can be a particular time of day, season, year, or historical period. The place can be an outside location, a room, a building, or a country.

Setting can affect characters by influencing their values, beliefs, and emotions or by affecting the way they live and interact with other characters. What impact does the setting have on Vinny?

Make Inferences

Readers often make inferences to figure out something an author has not explained. An **inference** is a logical guess that is based on facts and one's own knowledge and experience. To support your inference, you may need to **cite evidence,** or provide examples and quotations from the story. For example, you can make an inference about Vinny and Joe-Boy's friendship.

Evidence from the Story	My Own Knowledge	Inference
• Joe-Boy is Vinny's "best friend." • Joe-Boy teases Vinny about finding the body.	Sometimes friends tease each other in a friendly way, but this teasing does not seem kind.	They may be friends, but Joe-Boy is not especially nice to Vinny.

TEACH

CLOSE READ

Describe Stories: Character and Setting

Help students understand the terms and the factors that are part of both character and setting in a story. Then focus on characters and have volunteers describe at least one example of each character term (trait, motivation, development) from the story.

Next, review the information about how setting can influence the characters in a story. Prompt students to provide examples of the influence of setting on the characters in "The Ravine."

Make Inferences

Help students understand that making inferences is a way to figure out things that are not directly explained in a story. Ask volunteers to provide examples of inferences they make. Or you can provide one yourself, such as how when you see someone laughing, you can infer that he or she is happy; no one needs to tell you.

Then review the steps shown in the chart that explain the factors involved in making an inference. Walk through the steps with students to make the inference about Joe-Boy and Vinny's friendship. Then use the chart to make additional inferences in other sections of the story together.

Strategies for Annotation   📝 🗂 *Annotate it!*

Describe Stories: Character and Setting

Share these strategies for guided or independent analysis:

- Highlight in yellow factors about the setting, such as time and place, including details of the place.
- Highlight in green a character's thoughts and actions in response to elements of the setting.
- Review your highlights. On a note, record what effects the setting has had on the character.

Vinny winced. He didn't want to be here. It was too soon, way too soon. Two weeks and one day. He saw a footprint in the mud and stepped around it.

The dead boy had jumped and had never come back up. . . . Gave Vinny the creeps. It didn't make sense. The pond wasn't that big.

PRACTICE & APPLY

Analyzing the Text

RL 1,
RL 3,
RL 5

Possible answers:

1. *Vinny knows the boy was fourteen, was named Butchie, and disappeared two weeks ago; they think he jumped into the pond and drowned, but no one has found his body. Vinny thinks it is creepy that the boy hasn't been found, and he doesn't know whether to believe Starlene's claim that the goddess took Butchie.*

2. *It smells of "mud and ginger and iron"; there is "a one-hundred-foot drop" above the pond; climbing is hard and dangerous because the hand and footholds are "slimy with moss"; the high ledge is just a foot wide. The setting is important because the story's plot and conflict center on the real potential for danger in the jungle ravine.*

3. *Vinny is confused by his parents' messages about being in a dangerous place like the ravine. Vinny lacks confidence, because he calls himself "weak" and knows he lets others tell him what to do. Vinny also feels guilty for breaking his promise; he cares about keeping his word.*

4. *Before the characters jump, they prepare by smearing mud on their bodies. It is likely that they have watched others make jumps like these and seen others in their school or community perform these same rituals; they feel these rituals will protect them.*

5. *Near the beginning of the story, Vinny sees himself as "weak" and worries about how his friends see him. At the end, he has found "peace" within himself, and says he knows what his friends are thinking, but he is calm and accepting of his decision. He is the same only in that he still thinks about his friends' opinion of him. The difference is that he finds peace with making his own decision.*

6. *The author ends the story with Vinny noticing the intense beauty of the view in front of him, as if for the first time. The descriptions add to the story's power, because they show how Vinny's perspective has moved from being mostly inside himself to what is outside of him. It shows how he has grown by making his own choice.*

English Language Support

Guide students to work in small groups to answer the questions on this page. Each group should answer one question. When all the groups are finished, they can take turns presenting their answers to the class. Encourage students to provide their classmates with useful feedback.

 eBook *Annotate It!*

Analyzing the Text

RL 1, RL 3, RL 5,
W 2a-f, W 9a

Cite Text Evidence   Support your responses with evidence from the text.

1. **Summarize** Review lines 38–65. In your own words, describe what Vinny knows about the dead boy. Explain his thoughts and feelings about this past event.

2. **Draw Conclusions** Review lines 71–100. What are some examples of language the author uses to describe the setting? Why is the setting important to the story?

3. **Cite Evidence** Reread lines 110–132 and think about what the author wants us to understand about Vinny. What words would you use to describe Vinny's character traits?

4. **Make Inferences** Before jumping, the characters perform certain rituals. Reread lines 163–206 to review how they prepare to jump. What inferences can you make about the characters' feelings and their reasons for these rituals?

5. **Analyze** Consider Vinny's feelings and actions throughout the story. How is Vinny different by the end of the story? How is he the same?

6. **Critique** Review the story's ending in lines 319–339 and examine the descriptions the author provides. Do you think the ending makes the story more powerful? Why or why not?

PERFORMANCE TASK

Writing Activity: Informative Essay Write a two- or three-paragraph essay to compare and contrast the character traits of Vinny and Joe-Boy.

- Introduce your topic by briefly describing the characters and their relationship to each other.

- Next, tell about how their character traits are different. Use examples from the text to support your ideas.

- Then indicate the character traits that the boys share or that are similar. Include evidence from the text.

Assign this performance task.

PERFORMANCE TASK

W 2a-f,
W 9a

Writing Activity: Informative Essay Have students work independently. Direct them to

- create a chart of each character's words, thoughts, feelings, and actions
- use the chart to list character traits for each boy
- group similar traits and different traits in separate paragraphs

Remind students to create an introductory paragraph that briefly describes the boys' friendship and states students' compare-and-contrast approach.

Critical Vocabulary

gnarly   rivulet   cascade   precipice

Practice and Apply With a partner, discuss the following questions. Then work together to write a sentence for each vocabulary word.

1. Which vocabulary word goes with *twisted*? Why?

2. Which vocabulary word goes with *edge*? Why?

3. Which vocabulary word goes with *trickle*? Why?

4. Which vocabulary word goes with *pouring*? Why?

Vocabulary Strategy: Using Context Clues

When you encounter an unfamiliar word in your reading, one way to figure out the meaning is to use context clues. **Context clues** are hints about the meaning of an unknown word that may be found in the words, phrases, sentences, and paragraphs that surround that unknown word. Look at this example:

> **And it was wet and muddy from little rivulets of water that bled from the side of the cliff.**

To figure out the meaning of *rivulets*, look for clues in the surrounding words and ideas in the sentence. The sentence says that the rivulets of water "bled" from the cliff. This helps you imagine water flowing from the cliff in the same way that blood flows from a cut or scrape on your arm; the blood looks like a running stream. Combining this image with the word "little," you can imagine that rivulets might be little streams. Then use a dictionary to confirm your guess: A *rivulet* is "a small brook or stream."

Practice and Apply Reread "The Ravine" and find the following words. Look at the surrounding words and sentences for clues to each word's meaning. Fill out a chart like the one shown.

Word	Context Clues	My Guessed Definition	Dictionary Definition
winced (lines 35–39)			
scoffed (lines 116–120)			
parallel (lines 192–194)			

Critical Vocabulary

Answers:

1. *The word **gnarly** goes with* twisted *because both words can describe something that is bent or bumpy. Sentence: The gnarly branch was a great scratching post for my cat.*

2. *The word **precipice** goes with* edge *because both words describe a place where the ground drops away. Sentence: We could see a rock climber hanging from the precipice high above us.*

3. *The word **rivulet** goes with* trickle *because both words describe small streams of something. Sentence: I watched the rivulets of chocolate sauce drip off my ice cream.*

4. *The word **cascading** goes with* pouring *because both words describe something flowing fast and powerfully. Sentence: The water was cascading down the slide and into the pool.*

Vocabulary Strategy: Using Context Clues

Word	Context Clues	My Guessed Definition	Dictionary Definition
winced	*Joe-Boy is being morbid and teasing.*	*showing that you are uncomfortable*	*to flinch, or startle, as in pain or distress*
scoffed	*his mother disagrees and "waves him off"*	*made a face to show she did not agree*	*showed or expressed scorn*
parallel	*he jumped, "his arms and legs spread out"*	*his face and body are facing the pond*	*relating to two planes that do not intersect*

 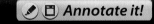

Using Context Clues

Have students locate the sentences containing *winced*, *scoffed*, and *parallel* in the selection. Tell them to use their eBook annotation tools to do the following:

- Highlight each word.
- Reread the surrounding words and sentences, looking for clues to the word's meaning.
- Underline any clues you find, such as examples, synonyms, or antonyms.
- Review your annotations and try to infer the word's meaning.

> Joe-Boy said, "You going jump in the water and go down and your hand going touch his face, stuck under the rocks. . . . "
>
> Vinny winced. He <u>didn't want to be here</u>. It was <u>too soon, way too soon</u>. Two weeks and one day.

winced: "shook" or "flinched"?

Language Conventions: Recognize Variations from Standard English

L 1e

Tell students that variations from standard English, such as dialect, can be effective ways to create authentic characters in a story. Explain that it is important when writing to understand when it is appropriate to use variations such as dialect and when these variations might be inappropriate or confusing.

Answers:

1. S'up *for* What's up; goin' *for* going.
   Rewritten sentence: "What's up, Denise? How is it going?" asked Claire.

2. dunno *for* don't know.
   Rewritten sentence: "I don't know," he mumbled.

3. *omitting space between* never ever.
   Rewritten sentence: I will never ever go back to that sad old place again.

4. Gimme *for* Give me; ya *for* you.
   Rewritten sentence: "Give me a break!" scoffed Tina. "I saw you there with Jill, you liar!"

5. hangin' *for* hanging; lookin' *for* looking; lookin' for no trouble *for* looking for any trouble; know what I'm sayin' *for* do you know what I'm saying.
   Rewritten sentence: I was just hanging out with some friends at the mall. We weren't looking for any trouble. Do you know what I'm saying?

Language Conventions: Recognize Variations from Standard English

L 1e

Writers often use words in dialogue that vary from Standard English to bring their characters to life. Writers may also use dialect to convey information about a community in which a character lives. **Dialect** is a form of language that is spoken in a particular region by the people who live there. In "The Ravine," the author uses the following sentences to give his characters an informal and conversational voice.

> "Shuddup," Vinny said.
> "You prob'ly stepping right where his foot was."
> "Hey," Joe-Boy went on, "maybe you going be the one to find his body."
> *Stopstopstop! Don't think like that.*

Notice the informal spelling of *Shut up* and *probably* in the first two sentences. These variations indicate informal speech patterns that many people use every day. The phrase "maybe you going be the one" is an example of incorrect grammar that can be a part of dialect. In the last sentence, the words *Stopstopstop* are run together to indicate the urgency of Vinny's thoughts. A character's way of speaking can help you better understand that character.

Practice and Apply Read the sentences and identify the variations from standard English. Then rewrite each sentence to show that you understand what is being said.

1. "S'up, Denise? How's it goin'?" asked Claire.

2. Jake did not want to answer. He shrugged his shoulders. "I dunno," he mumbled.

3. I refuse. I quit. I will neverever go back to that sad old place again.

4. "Gimme a break!" scoffed Tina. "I saw ya there with Jill, ya liar!"

5. I was just hangin' out with some friends at the mall. We weren't lookin' for no trouble. Know what I'm sayin'?

English Language Support

Standard English Variations Read aloud each Practice and Apply item with students following along in their books. Point out variations from standard English. Discuss why the dialect in the story is appropriate. (*The language is realistic and reflects how kids often talk to each other.*)

- Ask volunteers to write each item on the board and underline the variations from standard English. Point out how the apostrophe takes the place of letters in some of the words.
- Pair students, and ask them to write each item on a sheet of paper and underline the variations from standard English. Then ask them to work with a partner to rewrite each sentence.
- Ask students to work independently to rewrite the sentences and share them with a group. Have students point out what similarities they notice about the dialect in these sentences. (*Possible answers: not pronouncing the ng in -ing, combining two words either by running them together—neverever—or by taking parts of both words—dunno.*)

Describe Plot: Conflict

RL 3

TEACH

Review that a good story plot centers on a **conflict,** which is a problem or struggle between opposing forces that triggers the action and events of the story. Explain these points to students:

- An **external conflict** involves a character who struggles against an outside force, such as nature, a physical obstacle, or another character.
- An **internal conflict** is one that occurs within a character, such as a character struggling with fear or sadness.

Explain that a story may include both external and internal conflicts. Tell students, however, that a reader can usually determine which conflict is most central to the plot of a story by deciding which conflict most consistently affects the plot's events and the main character's development as the story progresses.

PRACTICE AND APPLY

Display and review examples of each type of conflict from "The Ravine" with students. Possible examples include:

- Lines 1–30
- Lines 38–53
- Lines 110–128
- Lines 153–188
- Lines 229–250
- Lines 267–303

For each example, have students discuss the conflict as internal, external, or both and explain how the conflict connects to the plot and moves it forward.

INDEPENDENT READING

Invite students to explore the use of internal and external conflicts in the short story "Fine?" (another selection in Collection 1) or in a short story or novel they may be reading on their own. Have them identify examples of conflict and explain the effects of each one on the story's plot and characters, as appropriate.

Describe Stories: Character Development

RL 3

RETEACH

Review the terms *character, character traits, motivation,* and *character development.* Provide examples from "The Ravine" by reading aloud or having students read aloud passages from the selection. Ask students to identify an instance of each term in the relevant passage. Use these passages:

- Lines 1–12: character
- Lines 191–197: character traits
- Lines 122–132: character motivation
- Lines 306–312: character development

Remind students that an author develops particular characters throughout a story, using characters' actions, traits, thoughts, feelings, and interactions with others to show readers how a particular character changes. Have partners review the story together to find examples of character development and share examples with the rest of the class.

 LEVEL UP TUTORIALS Assign one or more of the following *Level Up* tutorials: **Character Traits; Character Motivation; Making Inferences About Characters.**

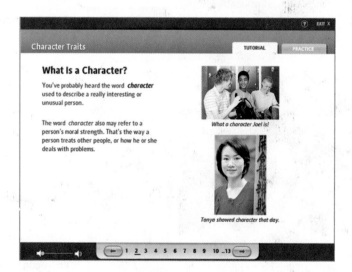

INDEPENDENT READING

Individual students can apply these skills to another selection in Collection 1 or to a short story or novel they may be reading on their own. After their analysis, have them share their ideas about character development with other students in the class.

from **The Jumping Tree**

Short Story by René Saldaña, Jr.

Why This Text

Students may be more familiar with fiction written from a third-person point of view than they are with first-person narratives. The narrator of "The Jumping Tree" is the story's main character, and readers perceive story events from his perspective. With the help of the close-reading questions, students will make inferences about the narrator and what motivates him based on his description of the events. This close reading will lead students to develop a deeper understanding of the elements of a first-person fictional story.

Background Have students read the background and information about the author. Introduce the selection by pointing out that René Saldaña, Jr. was inspired to write by a love of storytelling, and that this love of storytelling is evident in his writing. Point out that Saldaña is known for his issue-oriented stories about life as he experienced it growing up Latino in South Texas and Georgia.

SETTING A PURPOSE Ask students to pay attention to how the narrator's feelings and actions advance the plot. Do his actions make sense based on their prior knowledge?

Standards Support

- cite textual evidence to support inferences
- describe how a story's plot unfolds in a series of episodes
- describe how the characters respond or change as the plot moves toward a resolution
- analyze how an author develops the point of view of the narrator in text

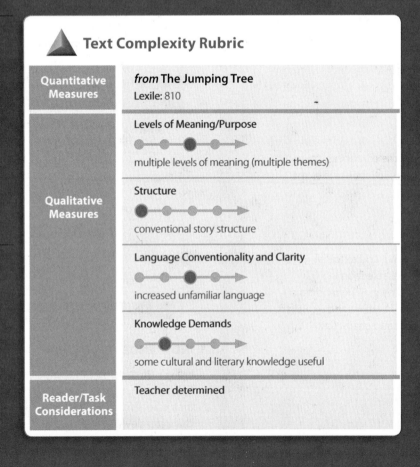

Text Complexity Rubric

Quantitative Measures	*from* **The Jumping Tree** Lexile: 810
Qualitative Measures	**Levels of Meaning/Purpose** multiple levels of meaning (multiple themes)
	Structure conventional story structure
	Language Conventionality and Clarity increased unfamiliar language
	Knowledge Demands some cultural and literary knowledge useful
Reader/Task Considerations	Teacher determined

Strategies for CLOSE READING

Analyze Character

Students should read this story carefully all the way through. Close-reading questions at the bottom of the page will help them focus on a narrator's motivations and interactions. As they read, students should jot down comments or questions about the text in the margins.

WHEN STUDENTS STRUGGLE . . .

To help students analyze the characters in "The Jumping Tree," have them work in small groups to fill out a chart like the one shown below.

CITE TEXT EVIDENCE For practice in analyzing and understanding a character's traits and motivations, ask students to cite text evidence for each point in the chart.

	INFERENCE	EVIDENCE
How does the narrator feel about himself in relation to others?	nervous about cousin's visit	"I didn't know exactly how to entertain him."
	need to impress other kids	"I hadn't done much to get the older kids' respect this summer."
	self-conscious of his age	"I didn't want to do things that were for kids."
What motivates the narrator to act the way he does?	He wants to belong.	"I had to prove that I could belong to this group."
	He doesn't want to lose face.	"I had to go through with this deal."
	His "manhood" is at stake.	"It was a question of manhood."

Background René Saldaña, Jr. *was inspired to become a writer by his grandfather, who was a first-rate storyteller. Saldaña was also motivated by his students when he taught middle school and high school. He told them about the beginnings of his book The Jumping Tree, and as they wrote alongside him in class, he was inspired to continue his story.*

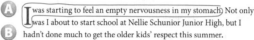

from THE JUMPING TREE

Short Story by René Saldaña, Jr.

CLOSE READ
Notes

1. **READ ▶** As you read lines 1–30, begin to collect and cite text evidence.
   - Circle the phrase that tells how the narrator feels as the story begins.
   - In the margin, explain why the narrator feels this way.
   - Underline the names of the other characters introduced in these lines.

A
B
I was starting to feel an empty nervousness in my stomach. Not only was I about to start school at Nellie Schunior Junior High, but I hadn't done much to get the older kids' respect this summer.

My cousin Jorge, who was a full two years older, was visiting from Mier across the border. This didn't happen too often because we visited my family in Mexico two or three weekends out of the month, and my tío[1] Jorge, Jorge's father, didn't own a car, so Jorge had to wait until my uncle could borrow some transportation. Jorge wouldn't start school for another two weeks, so he wanted to take a vacation in

10 the States.

Odd how just across the border, only some forty-five minutes away, people still walked to work, there was still a milkman, a water truck brought drinking water to each house, and fruit and vegetable **vendors** drove or walked up and down streets selling their wares.

[1] **tío** (tē'ō): Spanish for "uncle."

The narrator is concerned that he will not be able to compete with older kids.

vendors:
people who sell things

3

1. **READ AND CITE TEXT EVIDENCE** Point out that the narrator (the "I" in the story) is also the main character. Since the story events are presented from the narrator's point of view, it's necessary to make inferences about his actions and motivations based on text evidence and your own experience.

A **ASK STUDENTS** to infer the narrator's character traits by citing specific textual evidence in lines 1–30. Responses may include references to evidence in lines 1–3 and 29–30.

Critical Vocabulary: vendors (line 14) What do the "vendors" indicate about life across the border? *Life there may be slower paced, with goods being sold by individuals instead of big stores.*

When I'd visit my cousin, he'd always make certain I had a good time. We'd spend hours on end in his father's carpentry shop sawing blocks of wood into rough imitations of cars and planes. We'd shave planks of wood until they felt smooth on the palms of our hands or our cheeks. We'd use the shavings later on for **kindling** or confetti,
20 and we'd dig our fingers into the mountains of sawdust, sometimes as deep as our elbows.

So, when he came up to Peñitas, I wanted to make sure there was always something doing. Since he was older, I didn't want to do things that were for kids, but I didn't know exactly how to entertain him.

At the beginning of summer, Tío Nardo had hammered a few slats of wood to my granddad's mesquite tree in the middle of the backyard, called it a tree house, and we were set. It was just like in *The Brady Bunch*.[2] Only their tree house actually resembled a house, with its walls, windows, roof, and floor. We had to imagine all that. All we
30 had, really, were flat places to sit on. But it was enough for us.

One day after Jorge arrived, Ricky was over, and we came up with a jumping and gymnastics competition. Actually, Ricky came up with the idea because he was good at that stuff. He was always saying,

---

[2] **The Brady Bunch:** popular TV show of the 1960s and 1970s.

kindling:
bits of dry wood used to start a fire

2. ◀ REREAD Reread lines 15–24. What can you infer about the narrator's feelings toward his cousin? Underline text evidence that supports your inference.

He seems to get along with his cousin, and they have fun together. He also wants to impress his cousin.

3. READ ▶ As you read lines 31–70, continue to cite textual evidence.

- Underline text that reveals the narrator's thoughts and feelings about jumping.
- Circle details that describe the setting.
- In the margin, explain the narrator's thoughts as his turn to jump approaches.

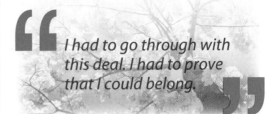

I had to go through with this deal. I had to prove that I could belong.

"Look at this," and he'd tumble, pop a cartwheel, flip backward, or walk on his hands. Once he even walked across the top of a fence like a tightrope walker. Its sharp points didn't seem to bother him.

Ricky explained the rules as we stood under the **mammoth** mesquite. "Okay, we're going to climb the tree and start from there." He pointed to the slat where I normally sat. "Then jump down to that
40 branch there and grab hold." His finger slid across the sky from the plank to a branch that stretched out below it. Easy enough. "Then whoever can do the best trick is the winner and king of the world."

"What do you mean by trick?" asked Jorge.

"You know, flips, swinging back and forth, then letting go, seeing who can land the fanciest."

Ⓒ All this time I'm thinking, *Okay, jump, grab, let go, and pray I land standing. No fancy-schmancy stuff for me. Just do the thing.*

But Jorge was the oldest of us, and the strongest; Ricky was the gymnast; and I was the youngest and the smallest, the one who had
50 something to prove to these guys. I had to go through with this deal. I had to prove that I could belong to this group, could be a man.

"*Orale pues*,"[3] said Jorge. "Let's climb up."

And so we did, hand over hand, foot after foot, until we all reached the top and we **sidled** to the edge of the jumping place. When I saw how far the branch was from this spot, then how far the ground was from that branch, I decided to do the minimum, a jump and
Ⓓ release. After all, I was only in the summer after my fifth-grade year. What could they expect?

---

[3] *orale pues* (ō-rä′lä pwäs): Spanish slang meaning "let's go, then" or "all right, then."

mammoth:
gigantic, enormous

sidle:
to move sideways

4

5

---

2. **REREAD AND CITE TEXT EVIDENCE**

Ⓑ **ASK STUDENTS** to suggest one reason for the narrator's insecurity. Students should point out the references to his age in lines 3 and 23.

3. **READ AND CITE TEXT EVIDENCE** In this section the author reveals the narrator's thoughts directly.

Ⓒ **ASK STUDENTS** why they think the author uses this technique. Cite a specific example in the text. *Students should cite the italicized text in lines 46–47.*

Critical Vocabulary: kindling (line 19) What does "kindling" suggest about life in Mier? *Students should see that there is little technology.*

Critical Vocabulary: mammoth (line 37) What things might be characterized as "mammoth"? *Students might suggest mountains, skyscrapers, and dinosaurs.*

Critical Vocabulary: sidle (line 54) How does "sidle" help you visualize the setting? *Students might say that visualizing boys standing side by side on a ledge helps you appreciate the danger they face.*

Jorge went first. Ricky and I stood back, watching. My Mexican
60 jumping bean heart was making it hard to concentrate on the task at
hand. Even at this age I knew that people could learn a lot from their
bodies' reactions to a situation: hand over open fire burns: remove
hand immediately; hunger pangs: eat; heart grasping at sides of throat
fighting to get out alongside that morning's breakfast: don't jump!

But, I am Mexican. I could not—strike that—would not back
down. I would do the deed. It was a question of manhood. *¿Macho o
mujeringa? ¡Pues macho!*[4]

Jorge screamed "*¡Aiee!*" and jumped. He swung like a trapeze
artist at the Circus Vargas.[5] I whistled. Then I was one step closer to
70 having to jump.

(E) Ricky stepped up. "We'll see you down there, *primo*,"[6] he said.
"Yeah—down there." I forced a smile.

He jumped and it was like he and the branch were one. The rough
bark of the mesquite melted into a smooth bar in his hands. He

---
[4] *¿Macho o mujeringa? ¡Pues macho!* (mä'chō ō mōō'hār-ē'ä): Spanish slang for "Manly or weak and cowardly! Manly!"
[5] **Circus Vargas:** California-based traveling circus.
[6] *primo* (prē'mō): Spanish for "cousin," literally, but also used to mean "pal" or "close friend."

(margin note, left:)
He cannot
back down,
but he will do
the minimum
and hope for
the best.

---

4. ◀ REREAD Reread lines 48–67. Why does the narrator decide to go through with the jump? Make an inference about the narrator based on his reasoning. Support your answer with explicit textual evidence.

Even though the narrator is nervous about jumping, he wants to
impress Jorge and Ricky. He is jumping to prove to himself and to
Jorge and Ricky that he "could belong to this group" of older kids.

5. READ ▶ As you read lines 71–115, continue to cite textual evidence.
• Underline details that convey the narrator's fear as he jumps.
• Circle details that suggest the narrator has a sense of humor about the events.

6

---

swung forward, let go, twisted, caught the bar again, swung toward
me, flipped, all the while holding on to the branch, released, flipped
in the air once, and stuck the landing. A perfect 10, even from the
Russian judge.

I was next.
80 "*Orale*,[7] jump!" It sounded like an echo, they were so far away. I
glanced down at them. A big mistake. My stomach was a better
jumper than I because it was already flipping and turning. But I was
at the edge of the board. I'd made a **contract** with myself, for my sake,
signed in blood.

I began to rock back and forth, back and forth, back and forth,
trying for courage.

The time had come. It was my destiny to fly, to live on the very
edge of life, a life James Bond would be jealous of. So I dug my toes
into my tennis shoes, took a deep breath, fought closing my eyes,
90 stretched out my arms and did it.

I saw myself from below somehow. My body like Superman's
flying over Metropolis. The branch growing bigger, closer. Within
reach. All I had to do was to grab hold now. Just let the momentum[8]
carry me toward the branch. The bark, rough on my palms, would be
my safe place. All I had to do was close my fingers around the branch.
Then swing and . . .

But my chubby little soon-to-be-sixth-grade fingers failed me.
I felt the branch slipping from my fingers. And so, like Superman
confronted by kryptonite, I fell.
100 As the ground came closer, I tried to remember my PE coach's
exact advice on how to fall. Had he told his little bunch of munchkins
to roll onto our backs, or to put out our arms and hands? I had only a
split second to make up my mind.

I stretched out my arms to break my fall.

What broke was my left wrist. When I rolled over and looked at
the sky, I knew I had failed.

---
[7] *orale:* Spanish slang meaning "let's do it" or "let's go."
[8] **momentum:** the characteristic of a moving body that is caused by its mass and its motion.

(margin note, right:)
contract:
agreement

7

---

4. REREAD AND CITE TEXT EVIDENCE Explain that the narrator sees reasons for and against jumping.

(D) **ASK STUDENTS** to cite evidence showing that the narrator is trying to talk himself out of making the jump. *Students should cite lines 57 and 64.*

5. READ AND CITE TEXT EVIDENCE Explain that the author includes Spanish phrases to give the characters authenticity.

(E) **ASK STUDENTS** to cite evidence showing that the characters are using slang. *Students should cite lines 71, 80, and 108–109.*

Critical Vocabulary: contract (line 83) What are some "contracts" people make with themselves? *Students might suggest eating healthy, learning a language, or practicing the piano an hour a day.*

FOR ELL STUDENTS Ask English-speaking volunteers to describe to ELL students the actions referred to in the gymnastics-related expressions. *tumble, pop a cartwheel, flip backward, flips, swinging back and forth, release, and stuck the landing.*

F Or so I thought. When I returned from the doctor's that evening, arm encased in a cast, my cousins couldn't stop talking about it. "*Y, que padre*,"⁹ they said, caressing my cast. "A cast, Rey. You know," said
110 Jorge, "that's the best. It's better than a scar. I wish I had one. How does it feel?" It was my badge of courage. And it couldn't have come at a better time. I just knew that the guys at school would look at my cast and wonder how I had busted my arm. Had I fought a gang? Had I fallen from a motorbike? Or something else just as manly? The girls, too, would be impressed. It was just the break I needed.

* *Y, que padre* (ē kä pä′drä): American Spanish for "And, how great."

6. ◀ **REREAD AND DISCUSS** Reread lines 107–115. With a small group, explain what Rey means when he says that the result of the jump "was just the break I needed."

SHORT RESPONSE

Cite Text Evidence   Review your notes on Rey's thoughts and actions throughout the story. What words would you use to describe his character traits? For example, you might describe him as brave, anxious, or foolish. **Cite text evidence** from the story in your response.

Rey is uncertain and anxious as the story begins. He wants to show his older cousin a good time, but is not sure how to do that. Impressing other people is also important to him. He wants to prove that he "could belong to this group, could be a man." He proves to himself that he can fit in with older kids by actually jumping. Jumping also proves that Rey is brave after all.

8

---

6. **REREAD AND DISCUSS USING TEXT EVIDENCE**   The word *break* is used in two ways: the narrator *breaks* his arm, and the narrator gets the *break* he needs.

F **ASK STUDENTS** to cite text evidence to show that the narrator thinks it was all worth it. *Students should cite lines 107–115.*

SHORT RESPONSE

Cite Text Evidence   Student responses will vary but should use text evidence to support their positions. Students should

- describe the kind of person Rey is
- give reasons for Rey's decision
- cite evidence to show how Rey felt at the end

TO CHALLENGE STUDENTS . . .

For more context, students can read the short story "La Bamba" by Gary Soto. The protagonist in the story is named Manuel, and has a similar personality to that of Rey, the narrator of "The Jumping Tree."

ASK STUDENTS to read "La Bamba" and then to compare and contrast the protagonist Manuel with the narrator of "The Jumping Tree."

- In what ways are the two boys tested? *Manuel performs in front of his school and is nervous about his performance and worried about what everyone will think. Rey "performs" for his cousin and his friend and desperately wants to impress them.*
- What is similar about the ways the boys emerge from the central occurrence of each story? *In each case, the boy can be thought of as failing. However, they are both wildly appreciated after the event—Manuel for entertaining everyone so well and Rey for having a cast, which was a badge of honor.*

DIG DEEPER

1. With the class, return to Question 4, Reread. Have students share their responses to the question.

   ASK STUDENTS what the narrator had to do to convince himself to make the jump in lines 48–67.

   - Have students describe what is happening to the narrator in lines 59–64 and why he takes that as a sign. What can students infer about his resolve at this point in the story?

   - Ask students about the shift in perspective that occurs in lines 65–67. Have them draw conclusions about the significance of being Mexican and what is meant by "a question of manhood." Why do you think the narrator will not allow himself to back down?

   - Ask students why they think the author chose to use Spanish slang in lines 66–67.

2. With the class, return to Question 6, Reread and Discuss. Have students share the results of their discussion.

   ASK STUDENTS to discuss whether or not making the jump was the right thing for Rey to do and whether it was believable under the circumstances.

   - Have students tell whether they think it would have made a difference to Rey if he had ended up with a worse injury, or if the other kids hadn't been so impressed.

   - Have groups support their ideas using text evidence. Groups should cite evidence in which the author shows that in Latino culture a challenge to one's machismo might seem more devastating than any kind of bodily harm.

   - Have groups analyze what other factors were involved in Rey's decision. Ask whether Rey's age was a factor in his need to prove himself and also played a part in his decision to take a physical risk. Students might present evidence showing that Rey's insecurity led him to believe that his failure to act would be perceived as weakness.

   ASK STUDENTS to return to their Short Response answer and revise it based on the class discussion.

CLOSE READING NOTES

Fine?

Short Story by Margaret Peterson Haddix

Why This Text?

As students read fiction in school and on their own, they will encounter more complex story plots. This lesson guides students to identify and analyze plot elements and explores how an author builds suspense in a realistic fiction story.

▶ **View It!**

Professional Development Podcast:

Text-Dependent Analysis

Key Learning Objective: The student will be able to describe plot elements and analyze point of view in a short story.

RL 1 Cite textual evidence; make inferences.

RL 3 Describe story elements.

RL 4 Determine the meaning of words and phrases.

RL 5 Analyze structure.

RL 6 Explain point of view.

W 3 Write narratives to develop real or imagined experiences.

SL 1 Engage effectively in a range of collaborative discussions.

L 2a Use commas and dashes to set off nonrestrictive elements.

L 4 Determine or clarify the meaning of words and phrases, choosing from a range of strategies.

L 4a Use context as a clue to the meaning of a word or phrase.

L 4b Use Greek roots as clues to the meaning of a word.

L 6 Acquire and use accurately grade-appropriate general academic and domain-specific words and phrases.

 ## Text Complexity Rubric

Quantitative Measures	**Fine?** Lexile: 770L

Levels of Meaning/Purpose

multiple levels of meaning (multiple themes)

| Qualitative Measures | |

Structure

no major shifts in chronology; occasional use of flashback

Language Conventionality and Clarity

increased unfamiliar, academic, or domain-specific words

Knowledge Demands

moderately complex theme

| Reader/Task Considerations | • Teacher determined
• Vary by individual reader and type of text
• See the Text X-Ray for suggested Reader/Task Considerations. |

English Language Support
Before teaching, use the Text X-Ray for an overview of the text's complexity. The Text X-Ray and the supports and scaffolds in the Teacher's Edition will help you guide students of different skill levels.

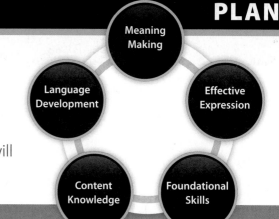

Meaning Making

Language Development

Effective Expression

Content Knowledge

Foundational Skills

Text Complexity: Qualitative Measures

Levels of Meaning/Purpose

multiple levels of meaning (multiple themes)

Help students analyze point of view.

- Teacher's Edition side notes, pp. 18, 19, 20, 22, 26, 27, 28, 33
- English Language Support, p. 22
- Explain Point of View, p. 33
- Performance Task, p. 34

Help students understand character.

- English Language Support, p. 27

To help students explain point of view, see

- Explain Point of View, p. 36a

 Use It! **Level Up Tutorial:** Third-Person Point of View

Use It! **Interactive Whiteboard Lesson:** Point of View

***ZOOM IN ON* EXPLAINING POINT OF VIEW** Before students read, explain that **point of view** is the perspective from which a writer chooses to tell the story. This selection is told in the **third-person point of view**. This means a narrator's voice, not a character's, tells the story. Explain how this differs from first-person point of view. *(The narrator is a character in the story.)* Have students read lines 1–69 and then discuss the following questions as a class:

- If this story were in the first-person point of view, what pronoun would the narrator use while telling the story? *(first-person pronouns, such as I and me)*
- How would the story be different if it were told from Bailey's point of view? *(The reader might know less about what Baily is thinking.)*

Structure

no major shifts in chronology; occasional use of flashback

Help students understand how a plot progresses through a story.

- Teacher's Edition side notes, pp. 17, 18, 19, 21, 24, 25, 28, 29, 30, 31, 32, 33
- English Language Support, pp. 23, 30, 31
- When Students Struggle, pp. 20, 29
- Strategies for Annotation, pp. 25, 33
- Describe Stories: Plot and Suspense, p. 33

Help students understand how setting interacts with plot.

- Teacher's Edition side note, p. 23

To reteach plot, see

- Describe Stories: Plot, p. 36a

Use It! **Level Up Tutorial:** Plot Stages; Plot; Sequence of Events; Conflict

***ZOOM IN ON* UNDERSTANDING PLOT** After students have read the selection, explain that writers organize events into a **plot**, or connected actions that tell what happens in a story.

- Review the elements of a plot: **exposition, rising action, climax, falling action,** and **resolution**.
- Ask pairs to locate and identify each plot element in the story. Have them use the following sentence frames:
  Lines _____ in the text show the _____ part of the plot. Two details from the text that support our ideas are _____.
- Have pairs share their responses with the class.

Language Conventionality and Clarity

increased unfamiliar, academic, or domain-specific words

Teach unfamiliar vocabulary in context.

- Teacher's Edition Critical Vocabulary notes, pp. 17, 20, 23, 27, 31, 33, 35
- English Language Support, p. 20
- Applying Academic Vocabulary, p. 18
- Vocabulary Strategy: Greek Roots, p. 35
- Strategies for Annotation, p. 35

Help students achieve greater facility in analyzing and using language.

- Teacher's Edition side notes, pp. 25, 31, 35, 36
- English Language Support, p. 17, 18, 21, 26, 35
- Language Conventions: Commas and Dashes, p. 36

ZOOM IN ON **UNDERSTANDING LANGUAGE CONVENTIONS**
Explain that language conventions include the grammar, spelling, and punctuation in a text. Display lines 1–15 and have students scan the text's punctuation. Draw attention to the ellipses in lines 9 and 15.

- Write the term *ellipsis* on the board and explain that it can indicate something missing.
- Writers also use ellipses to show pause in thought or action.
- Read both sentences and ask students to explain the meaning of the ellipses. *(line 9: the technician remembers that people who don't like enclosed spaces might have trouble; line 15: Bailey continues to think about what might happen.)*
- Encourage students to find and interpret ellipses in the selection.

Knowledge Demands

moderately complex theme

Help students clarify the setting and health context of the selection.

- Teacher's Edition Background note, p. 17
- Content-Area Connection, p. 31

ZOOM IN ON **USING CONTEXT CLUES** Before students read, review the Teacher's Edition Background note. Point out medical terms in the selection, e.g., *claustrophobic* (line 9), *technician* (line 16), and *tumor* (line 65). Introduce the following strategy:

- As students read each paragraph or section, have them record any difficult words in a notebook.
- Ask them to reread to find context clues, or words and phrases that suggest the meaning, for the difficult words. If they still cannot understand the term, have them consult a dictionary.
- Ask them to write a definition for each word in their notebooks.

Suggested Reader/Task Considerations

You might consider the following before assigning this selection to students.

- Will the plot interest students?
- Will the theme of the text make some students uncomfortable?

ZOOM IN ON **SUPPORTING COMPREHENSION**

- Give an overview of typical hospitals and the kind of care that people expect to receive there. Discuss why some people might be nervous there. Let students share impressions of hospitals in the community.
- Tell students that they will read a narrative, or story, about a girl's experience at a hospital. To avoid overwhelming students, divide the story into segments. Have students read independently, pausing after each segment to review events and to ask and answer questions.

Margaret Peterson Haddix Have students read the information about Haddix. Ask them to read the title, look at the photograph, and think about what Haddix might be writing about in this story.

Background If necessary, explain to students that *MRI*, an acronym they will read in line 1, stands for *Magnetic Resonance Imaging*, a medical test that uses a powerful magnet and radio waves to present pictures and provide information about organs and structures within the body. The person taking the test lies on a flat table that is part of the MRI scanner; the table slides into the space surrounded by the magnet. The person taking the test must lie still in the small, enclosed area. An MRI procedure usually takes about 30 to 60 minutes, but may last longer.

SETTING A PURPOSE Direct students to use the Setting a Purpose prompt to focus their reading. Remind them to write down questions as they read.

Describe Stories: Plot and Suspense (LINES 4–15)

RL 1,
RL 3,
RL 5

Tell students that the series of events in a story is called the **plot.** The plot usually centers on a **conflict,** or struggle, faced by the main character. Explain that **suspense** is a feeling of growing tension and excitement that makes the reader curious to find out what happens.

Ⓐ **CITE TEXT EVIDENCE** Have students read lines 4–15 and point out clues in the text that help them identify the conflict and sentences that create suspense. *(Clues about the MRI machine and lines 11–15 tell about the struggle Bailey faces. Lines 5–6 and 14–15 create suspense by making readers want to find out what's wrong with Bailey.)*

CRITICAL VOCABULARY

technician: By using the word *technician*, the author helps readers imagine the scene at a hospital lab.

ASK STUDENTS to explain why an MRI machine requires a technician to operate it. *(It is probably a complicated, sensitive machine, so only someone who is knowledgeable about it and trained to use it can operate it.)*

Margaret Peterson Haddix (b. 1964) *dreamed about writing novels as a child. Her interest in writing was sparked by her father's imaginative tales; however, she did not think she could support herself writing stories. She worked as a newspaper reporter after college but never gave up her dream. Eventually, Haddix quit her job and began working on her first novel. Haddix has now written more than a dozen young adult novels.*

Fine?

Short Story by Margaret Peterson Haddix

SETTING A PURPOSE As you read, pay attention to the clues that help you understand how Bailey feels and thinks about her life.

"Contrary to popular opinion," the MRI **technician** says, "this is not a torture device, it was not invented by aliens, and it does not enable us to read your thoughts."

Bailey looks doubtfully at the huge machine in front of her. She has already forgotten what MRI stands for. Does that mean there's really something wrong with her?

Ⓐ "Just joking," the man says. "But you wouldn't believe the questions I get. This won't be a problem for you at all unless . . . you're not claustrophobic, are you?"

"No," Bailey says. But she has to think about the question. Wearing a hospital gown, sitting in a wheelchair, she has a hard time remembering what and who she is. Bailey Smith, sophomore at Riverside High School, all-around ordinary kid.

But I won't be ordinary if that machine finds something awful in my brain . . . .

technician
(tĕk-nĭsh´ən) *n.* A *technician* is a person who does skilled practical work using specific equipment.

(t) ©Jeff Malet Photography/Newscom; (c) © KidStock/Blend Images/Corbis

Fine? **17**

English Language Support

Read Closely Display and read aloud lines 11–13. Explain that the text gives information about Bailey. Invite volunteers to follow these steps:

- Highlight in yellow words that tell about setting.
- Underline key words that describe Bailey.
- Highlight in green phrases that tell what Bailey might be worried about.

ASK STUDENTS to tell why Bailey is at a hospital and why she feels worried.

Wearing a hospital gown, sitting in a wheelchair, she has a hard time remembering what and who she is. Bailey Smith, sophomore at . . .

CLOSE READ

Explain Point of View
RL 6

(LINES 16–21)

Explain to students that **point of view** refers to how a writer chooses to narrate a story. When a story is told from **first-person point of view,** the narrator is a character in the story and uses pronouns such as *I, me,* and *we.* When a writer uses **third-person point of view,** the narrator is not a character, but is more like a voice that tells the story.

B **ASK STUDENTS** to reread lines 16–21 and determine whether the story is told using first-person or third-person point of view. Have students explain their reasoning. *(The story is told using third-person point of view; the narrator is not a character in the story and does not use first-person pronouns.)*

Describe Stories: Plot
RL 1,
RL 3,
RL 5

(LINES 22–31)

Explain to students that **exposition** is the first stage of a typical story plot. Tell them that this stage provides important background information and introduces the setting and characters.

C **CITE TEXT EVIDENCE** Have students reread lines 22–31 and identify specific examples of background information they learn about Bailey's mother. Ask them to tell how Bailey feels about her mother. *(Bailey's mother frequently makes comments—about bra straps, about having a date for homecoming, and about Bailey's changing tastes in music—that embarrass Bailey.)*

B "Good," the technician is saying. "Because I have to admit, some people do go a little nutso in there." He's a short man with glasses; he seems amused that some people might not enjoy his precious machine.

20 "Bailey will be fine," Bailey's mother says firmly from behind the wheelchair.

C "Mom," Bailey protests, shorthand for "Mom, you're embarrassing me," "Mom, you're bugging me," "Mom, you're driving me crazy." Bailey has said that word that way a thousand times in the past couple of years: When her mother said she shouldn't let her bra straps show. When her mother thought people went to homecoming *with dates.* When her mother asked why Bailey didn't like Hanson's music anymore. The complaint "Mom" was usually so perfect at conveying

30 Bailey's thoughts. But it sounds all wrong in this huge, hollow room.

"Well," the technician says, "time to get this over with."

Bailey lies down on a narrow pallet[1] sticking out of the machine like a tongue. The technician starts to pull a covering over her head, then stops.

"Almost forgot," he says. "Want to listen to the radio while you're in there?"

"Okay," Bailey says.

"What station?"

40 Bailey starts to say Z-98, the station everyone at school listens to, the only station Bailey ever turns on.

"Country 101?" the technician teases. "Want to hear cowboys crying in their beer?"

"No," Bailey says. She surprises herself by deciding, "Something classical."

As soon as she's in the tube, Bailey regrets her choice. All those throbbing violins, those crashing cymbals—Bailey knows next to nothing about classical music and cares about it even less. The slow, cultured voice of the announcer—

50 "And now we'll hear Mozart's finest concerto, at least in my humble opinion"—could drive anyone crazy. Or nutso, as the technician had said.

---

[1] **pallet** (păl´ĭt): a bed-like platform, sometimes covered with padding or cloth.

18 Collection 1

APPLYING ACADEMIC VOCABULARY

evident	specific

THINK-PAIR-SHARE Have students turn to a partner to discuss the following questions. Guide students to include the academic vocabulary words *evident* and *specific* in their responses. Ask volunteers to share their responses with the class.

- What thoughts and actions make Bailey's fears and anxiety **evident**?
- Which **specific** events and plot developments add suspense to the story?

"All right," the technician's voice comes over her headphones. He's in the control room, but he sounds a million miles away. "Hold very still, and we'll get started."

There's a noise like the clip-clop of horses' hooves—not real horses, but maybe a mechanical kind someone might create if he'd never heard real ones. The noise drowns out the classical music, and in losing it, Bailey realizes why she asked

60 for it in the first place: She knew she'd never have to listen to it again. If she'd chosen Z-98, some song she liked might be ruined for her forever. She could imagine hearing an Ace of Base song six months from now and thinking, *That's the song that was playing the day they found out about my brain tumor—* **D**

But if there's a tumor, will I even be alive six months from now?

Something catches in Bailey's throat and she has to swallow a cough.

70 *Silly,* she chides herself. *Nobody's said anything about a tumor.* The only real possibility the emergency room doctor mentioned, ordering all these tests, was a stroke, which was too ridiculous to think about. Old people had strokes. Bailey is only sixteen.

Maybe they'll just find out I made the whole thing up.

But she hadn't. Her arm had gone totally numb, right there **E** in algebra class. She hadn't been able to feel the pencil in her fingers. And she hadn't been able to see right, she hadn't been able to hear much—Mr. Vickers's raspy voice had seemed to

80 come at her through a tunnel. Still, she might not have said anything about it if Mr. Vickers hadn't called on her to go work a problem on the board.

"I can't . . . ," she tried to say, but she couldn't seem to make her brain think the words right, she couldn't get her mouth to move. She tried to stand up but fell down instead. Mr. Vickers had Paula Klinely take her to the nurse, the nurse called her mother, and now she's in an MRI tube listening to the clip-clop of fake horses.

The clip-clopping stops and the violins come back.

90 "You moved," the technician says over the headphones with the same tone of exaggerated patience as the classical music announcer. "We'll have to do that one again. The less you move, the quicker we'll be done."

Fine? **19**

CLOSE READ

Explain Point of View RL 6
(LINES 62–67)

Remind students that the use of third-person point of view helps reveal a character's thoughts and feelings. Explain that, at times, an author may choose to include thoughts a character is having within his or her mind. Point out that these thoughts are indicated by the use of italicized text, as in lines 62–67.

D ASK STUDENTS to reread lines 62–67 and tell how the author's inclusion of Bailey's internal thoughts helps readers understand what she is going through. *(Learning Bailey's thoughts helps readers get a better understanding of her fear that she might have something terribly wrong with her.)*

Describe Stories: Plot and Suspense (LINES 76–88) RL 1, RL 2, RL 3, RL 5

Remind students that exposition provides background information about a story's setting, characters, and conflict. Then explain that a flashback can be used to add expository information. Explain that a **flashback** is an interruption of the action to show events that took place at an earlier time.

E CITE TEXT EVIDENCE Ask students to summarize the flashback in lines 76–88 and then tell how it helps explain why Bailey is having an MRI. *(Earlier that day in math class, Bailey lost feeling in her arm, couldn't speak, and fell down.)* Then ask them to tell how the flashback adds to the story's suspense. *(The details make it clear that something serious happened to Bailey; the flashback makes readers want to find out just what is wrong with her.)*

English Language Support

Word Study Write these letter combinations on the board and review them with students.

- *mb* is pronounced /m/ in *thumb*
- *mn* is pronounced /m/ in *autumn*
- *kn* is pronounced /n/ in *knife*
- *gn* is pronounced /n/ in *sign*
- *ph* is pronounced /f/ in *photograph*
- *gh* is pronounced /f/ in *tough*

Use the selection words *million* (line 54) and *numb* (line 76) to discuss how *m* and *mb* make the same sound. Repeat with other letter combinations. Remind students that knowing these combinations will help them pronounce and spell words correctly.

ASK STUDENTS to work with a partner to scan the selection or use a dictionary or the Internet to find one example of each letter combination. Have partners write a sentence with each example and then read them aloud to each other.

Explain Point of View

RL 3,
RL 6

(LINES 94–110)

Remind students that third-person point of view helps readers understand what a character thinks or feels and what that character is like.

F **CITE TEXT EVIDENCE** Have students review lines 94–110 and explain what Bailey is imagining. Then ask them to tell what her imaginings tell readers about her. *(Bailey is imagining what people might say about her at her funeral. These thoughts show that she seems to enjoy drama; she might even be a bit vain and shallow, as evidenced by what she thinks Allison should say about her and by the line "what else the technician might be impressed by.")*

CRITICAL VOCABULARY

reminisce: The author uses the word *reminisce* to describe how Bailey imagines her best friend talking about her at Bailey's funeral.

ASK STUDENTS to explain why the author used *reminisce* instead of *say*. *(Using* reminisce *helps show Bailey's thoughts, that Allison would remember her fondly and with enjoyment to others.)*

English Language Support

Ask students to read the definition of *reminisce* and practice pronouncing the word. Then ask them to list some possible synonyms. *(remember, recall, recollect, think back)* Have students work in pairs to discuss how replacing *reminisce* with a synonym would affect readers. Encourage them to read aloud the sentence (lines 98–101) with each synonym to help them with their discussion.

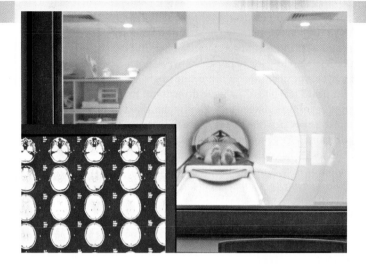

©Martin Barraud/Alamy

"I'm sorry," Bailey apologizes, though she's not sure he can hear her. If she's going to die at sixteen, she wants people to remember her as a nice person. She can imagine people giving testimonials at her funeral: *She was always so good, so kind to animals and people alike.* Her best friend, Allison, could **reminisce**, *And if she found a spider indoors, she was always very careful about carrying it outside instead of killing it.* She hopes Allison would remember to say that. Maybe this technician would even come to the funeral.

I never get close to the patients, he might say. *I view everyone as just another brain scan. But here was a kid who was always so gracious and noble. She knew she was dying, but she was always concerned about other people. She always asked about my family, my pets, my—*

Bailey can't think what else the technician might be impressed by her asking about. She decides he should break down in sobs at that point.

The clip-clopping starts again. Bailey concentrates on not moving. She's very glad the MRI can't read her thoughts.

When the MRI is finally done and the technician pulls her out of the tube, Bailey scans his face for some expression—of pity, maybe, or better yet, boredom.

"Well?" she says.

reminisce
(rĕm´ə-nĭs´) *v.*
When you *reminisce*, you remember past experiences or events.

WHEN STUDENTS STRUGGLE . . .

Have students create a sequence chart to show the order of the events in the story. Point out that the events are not described in order so far; the event in the flashback in lines 76–88 will be the first event in their chart.

Bailey has a scary episode in math class and is taken to the school nurse. ▶ ▶

 LEVEL UP TUTORIALS For additional support, assign the following *Level Up* tutorial: **Plot: Sequence of Events.**

"What?" he asks, looking down at the controls that lower her pallet.

"What did you find?" she asks, forgetting that she is
120 supposed to be acting like she cares more about his dog than her life.

"Oh, I'm not allowed to discuss results with patients," the technician says. "Your doctor will review everything and then talk to you."

He's less chatty now. Does that mean anything?

Bailey climbs back into the wheelchair—something else that's ridiculous, because isn't she perfectly capable of walking now? The technician pushes her out to the waiting room, where Bailey's mother is intently reading *Golf Digest*. To the
130 best of Bailey's knowledge, Bailey's mother has never played golf in her entire life.

"Well?" Bailey's mother asks. But she directs the question to Bailey, not the technician. "Are you all right?"

"I'm fine," Bailey insists.

Bailey's mother lays her hand on Bailey's shoulder, something she never would have done under normal circumstances. Bailey doesn't pull away.

The technician is on the phone.

"They have a room ready for you now," he reports. "An
140 aide will be by in a few minutes to take you up there."

He leaves, and Bailey and her mother are alone.

"Do you really feel okay?" Bailey's mother asks. "You haven't had another . . . episode?"

"No. I've just got a little headache," Bailey says. But it's just the edge of a headache—nothing Bailey would mention if she weren't in the hospital. "Do I really have to stay all night?"

"That's what the doctor said. They can't schedule the other tests until tomorrow. And—" Mom stops and starts over. "Look at it as a chance to play hooky. To avoid biology class."
150 She smiles brightly at Bailey, and Bailey resists the urge to retort, "I'd rather dissect[2] frogs than die." But she realizes she'd said exactly the reverse only a week ago in the school cafeteria: "I'd rather die than dissect a frog." She remembers the exact moment she spoke the words: Sunlight had been streaming in the window behind Allison, grease was congealing on the school lunch tacos, all her friends were laughing.

---

[2] **dissect** (dĭ-sĕktʹ): to cut apart or separate into pieces, especially to study more closely.

Fine? **21**

CLOSE READ

Describe Stories: Plot and Suspense (LINES 125–149)

RL 1,
RL 3,
RL 5

Plot Tell students that a plot stage called **rising action** follows the plot's exposition. Explain that in the rising action stage, events occur that make the story's conflict more complicated.

G CITE TEXT EVIDENCE Ask students to review lines 125–149 and determine what is going to happen as a result of Bailey's MRI. *(She will be staying overnight at the hospital.)* How does this rising action add to the conflict? *(It means that Bailey's situation might be more serious, since she has to stay at the hospital.)*

Suspense Explain to students that authors can build suspense by raising questions in readers' minds. Point out how, in line 125, Bailey notices that the technician is "less chatty now" and she wonders what that might mean. Then, in lines 135–137, Bailey's mother "lays her hand on Bailey's shoulder," an act that is "something she never would have done under normal circumstances."

H ASK STUDENTS to review lines 147–149, where the narrator notes that Bailey's mother "stops and starts over." What questions does this raise in the reader's mind? *(Possible response: It makes the reader wonder whether Bailey's mom has reasons to be worried that she doesn't want to share with Bailey.)*

English Language Support

Understand Cohesion Display this sentence: "'What did you find?' she asks, forgetting that she is supposed to be acting like she cares more about his dog than her life." (lines 119–121)

- Underline *you, she, his,* and *her*. Remind students that the underlined words are pronouns, or words that take the place of nouns or other pronouns. Confirm that students understand that *she* and *her* refers to Bailey in line 114 and *his* refers to the technician in line 113.

- Work with students to correct the references in this sentence: *The teachers told the students they would get a day off.* Underline *they* and ask which noun *they* refers to. *They* could refer to *teachers* or *students*. There are several ways to make this sentence clear. One way is as follows: *The teachers told the students to expect an extra vacation day.* Ask volunteers to rephrase the sentence, giving the teachers the vacation day, e.g., *The teachers told the students that teachers would get a day off.*

Explain Point of View
RL 1,
RL 6

(LINES 157–172)

Remind students that third-person point of view uses a narrator who is not a character in the story. Explain that a narrator called **third-person limited** knows the thoughts of just one character, usually the main character.

I CITE TEXT EVIDENCE Ask students to review lines 157–159 and explain why the narrator includes Bailey's thoughts. (*Her thoughts show how terrified she is.*) Then have them identify a clue the third-person limited narrator gives in lines 165–171 that suggests what Bailey thinks her mother might really be thinking. (*The lines "Mom wouldn't dare criticize Bailey's eating habits if she thought something was really wrong" indicate that Bailey hopes that her mother's remark is a good sign.*)

J CITE TEXT EVIDENCE Have students reread lines 165–172 and then explain how the third-person limited narrator adds tension by raising a question. (*In lines 165–171, the narrator shares what Mom says and tells that she laughs. But then, in line 172, when the narrator asks, "Would she?" it makes the reader wonder what Mom is really thinking.*)

English Language Support

Practice understanding how the third-person limited narrator continues to add tension on this page. Read lines 182–184 aloud, starting with "Then she . . .," having students follow along in the text. Ask students to reread the lines and explain what the narrator is communicating about how Bailey is feeling about her illness. (*Even though Bailey is trying to be brave, the fact that the narrator shares that she is thinking about how people will remember her shows that Bailey is scared that she is seriously ill and might die.*)

I *Oh, God, did I bring this on myself?* Bailey wonders. *I didn't really mean that. God, I'll dissect a billion frogs if you want me to. If you let me live.* But she knows from TV disease-160 of-the-week movies that bargaining with God never works.

"Mom, what do you think is wrong with me?" Bailey asks, and is amazed that the question comes out sounding merely conversational. She wants to whimper.

Mom keeps her smile, but it seems even less genuine now.

"I'm no doctor," she says. "But I think you blacked out because you skipped lunch to do your history report. That's all."

"I had a candy bar," Bailey says.

J "My point exactly," Mom says, and laughs, and Bailey 170 feels much better. Mom wouldn't dare criticize Bailey's eating habits if she thought something was really wrong.

Would she?

Bailey's room is in the main part of the hospital, not the pediatric wing, a fact that worries Bailey's mom.

"Are you sure?" she asks the aide who is skillfully maneuvering Bailey's wheelchair past several carts of dinner trays. "She's only sixteen. Don't they—"

"Listen, lady, I just go where they send me," the aide responds. He's a thin man with sallow skin and a dark braid 180 hanging down his back. Bailey can't decide if he would have been considered cool or a scuzz in high school. Probably a scuzz if he ended up as a hospital aide. Then she decides she shouldn't think things like that, not if she wants people to remember her as a nice person.

The aide is explaining to Mom that lots of kids have checked in lately; the pediatric wing is full. He makes it sound like a hotel everyone wants to stay at.

"But if she's not in the pediatric wing, I can't spend the night with her," Mom frets.

190 "Nope. Not according to what they tell me," the aide agrees.

K They arrive at the door of Bailey's room. At first glance Bailey thinks the mistake is even bigger than Mom feared: She's been given a bed in a nursing home. The room is crowded with people at least a decade or two older than Bailey's own grandparents. Then Bailey realizes that only one of the old people is actually in a bed. The rest are visitors.

"Coming through," the aide says, only barely missing knocking down one man's cane and another man's walker.

200 "Oh, look, Aunt Mabel's got a roommate," someone says. "Won't that be nice."

But they're all looking back and forth from Bailey to her mother, obviously confused.

"She fainted," Bailey's mother announces. "She's just in for a few tests."

It's a cue for Bailey to say, once more, "Mom!" This time she keeps her mouth shut and her head down.

The old people nod and smile. One woman says, "She looks just like my granddaughter. I'm sure she'll be fine," as if

210 the resemblance could save Bailey's life. Another woman adds, "You know those doctors. They just don't want to get sued."

As Bailey silently climbs from the chair to the bed she sees that her mother is smiling back at the old people, but the corners of her mouth are tighter than ever.

A nurse appears and whips a curtain between Bailey's bed and the old people. The aide fades away with a strange little wave, almost a salute. That one hand gesture makes Bailey want to call after him: *Wait! What happens to most of the people you wheel around? Do they die?*

220 But the nurse has begun asking questions.

"I know some of these won't apply to you," she apologizes, "but it's hospital policy . . . ."

Bailey can't help giggling at "Do you wear dentures?" and "Do you have any artificial limbs?" The nurse zips through the questions without looking up, until she reaches "Do you do recreational drugs?"

"No," Bailey says. They asked that in the emergency room, too.

"Are you sure?" The nurse squints suspiciously at Bailey.

230 "Yes," Bailey says. "I have never done drugs." She spaces the words out, trying to sound **emphatic**, but it comes out all wrong.

"My daughter," Bailey's mother interjects, "has never taken anything stronger than aspirin."

It's true, and Bailey's glad it's true, but she wants to sink through the floor with humiliation at her mother's words.

How can she care about humiliation at a time like this?

Someone comes and takes ten vials of blood from Bailey's arm. Someone else starts what he calls an IV port on the back

emphatic
(ĕm-făt´ĭk) *adj.*
If something is *emphatic*, it is expressed in a definite and forceful way.

Fine? **23**

CLOSE READ

Describe Stories: Setting (LINES 192–220)

RL 1, RL 5

Explain to students that an author provides descriptions about the story's **setting,** or where the plot's action takes place. Tell them that descriptions of settings help readers imagine the place where events happen and often provide clues to a character's actions, thoughts, or feelings.

K **CITE TEXT EVIDENCE** Have students review lines 192–220 and identify clues that tell about the hospital room that Bailey has been moved to and about her reactions to the room and her situation. *(Possible answers: room is full of old people; climbs from the chair to the bed; A nurse appears and whips a curtain between Bailey's bed and the old people. The room is unfamiliar; Bailey feels uncertain; she knows her mother is uncertain, too, as shown in lines 213–214.)*

CRITICAL VOCABULARY

emphatic: The author uses the word *emphatic* to show how Bailey is trying to sound.

ASK STUDENTS to explain how the word *emphatic* works with other words in the paragraph to describe what Bailey is trying to communicate. *(Bailey is telling the nurse that she has "never done drugs" and she "spaces the words out." However, the words "it comes out all wrong" show that being emphatic doesn't help her express herself clearly.)*

English Language Support

Understand Text Structure Discuss narrative structure with students. Tell them that narratives need to be structured so that readers understand the events. Ask students how narratives are most often organized. (sequentially or chronologically) Remind students that other types of text are structured in other ways. For example, arguments are organized logically around reasons and evidence.

- Work with students to use connecting words or phrases *(first/next/ at the beginning)* to write sentences stating the sequence of events in the selection up to this point.

- Have students work with a partner to write a sequence of events for the story using connecting words or phrases such as *for example, in the first place, as a result,* and *on the other hand*. Remind students to include sentences that show how Bailey's feelings are changing.

- Ask students to write a paragraph about what has happened in the selection so far. Encourage them to use transition words such as *consequently, specifically, however,* and *moreover* to describe the sequence of events.

Describe Stories: Plot

RL 3,
RL 5

(LINES 249–258)

Remind students that rising action includes events that develop and intensify the conflict.

L **ASK STUDENTS** to tell what event develops in lines 249–258 and how this rising action intensifies the story's conflict. *(Bailey's mother is told that visiting hours are over and she must leave. This intensifies the situation for Bailey because she now has to face her worries about being in the hospital all by herself.)*

English Language Support

Point of View To help students understand point of view, clarify that the although there is dialogue on page 24, a narrator who is not part of the story is actually providing the point of view. Point out the dialogue in line 244. Help students see how this line might change if Bailey were telling the story. *("Good," he says when I open my eyes.)*

©Helen King/Corbis

240 of Bailey's left hand. It's basically a needle taped into her vein, ready for any injection she might need. Someone else takes her blood pressure and makes Bailey push on his hands with her feet, then close her eyes and hold her arms out straight.

"Good," the man says when Bailey opens her eyes.

I did that right? So I'm okay? Bailey wants to ask. But something about lying in a hospital bed has made Bailey mute. She can barely say a word to her own mother, sitting two feet away.

"Visiting hours are over," the man tells Mom in a flat voice.

250 "But my daughter—," Mom protests, and stops, swallows hard. Bailey is stunned. Mom is never at a loss for words. "She's only sixteen, and—"

"No visitors after five. Hospital policy," the man says, but there's a hint of compassion in his voice now. "We'll take good care of her. I promise."

"Well . . ." Still Mom hesitates. She looks at Bailey. "I know the Montinis didn't really want to take Andrew overnight, they were just being nice, and with your dad away . . ."

24 Collection 1

Andrew is Bailey's younger brother, seven years old
and, everyone agrees, a pure terror. Bailey's dad is away on
a business trip. Mom couldn't even reach him on the phone
from the emergency room. Bailey can't see why Mom is telling
her what she already knows. Then Bailey understands: Mom is
asking Bailey for permission to leave.

They're going to make you leave anyway, Bailey wants
to say. *What do you want me to do?* But it's strange. For a
minute Bailey feels like she's the mother and her mother is the
daughter.

"Go on," she says magnanimously.³ "I'll be fine."

But as soon as her mother is out the door, Bailey wants to
run after her, crying, "Mom-mee! Don't go!" just like she used
to do at preschool, years and years and years ago.

Once they're alone together, Bailey's roommate, Mabel, gets
gabby.

"Ten days I've been lying in this hospital bed," she
announces, speaking to the TV as much as to Bailey. "First
they say it's my kidneys, then it's my bladder—or is that the
same thing? I forget. Then there's my spleen—"

Bailey can't imagine lying in any hospital bed for ten
days. She's already antsy, after just two hours. The sheets are
suffocating her legs. She hated that spring in junior high when
she signed up for track and Mom made her finish the whole
season. But now she longs to run and run and run, sprints and
relays and maybe even marathons.

*I've never run a marathon. What else will I never get to do
if I die now?*

Bailey is glad when Mabel distracts her by announcing
joyfully, "Oh good, dinner."

An aide slides a covered tray in front of Mabel and one in
front of Bailey.

"We didn't know what you wanted, 'cause you weren't here
last night," the aide says accusingly.

Bailey lifts the cover. Dinner is some kind of meat covered
in brown gravy, green beans blanched to a sickly gray, mashed
potatoes that could pass for glue, gummy apples with a slab
of soggy pie dough on top—food Bailey would never eat in a

---
³ **magnanimously** (măg-năn′ə-məs-lē): to do something in a courageous, kind,
unselfish way.

CLOSE READ

Describe Stories: Plot and Suspense (LINES 279–286)

RL 3,
RL 5

Remind students that a flashback interrupts a story's
action to show events that happened at an earlier time.

(M) ASK STUDENTS to review lines 279–286 and then
tell how the flashback adds to Bailey's worries. *(When
she recalls how she hated track, Bailey realizes that if
she's really sick she may never get to do many things,
such as run a marathon.)* Then ask students to explain
how the flashback also reinforces what they have
learned about Bailey's relationship with her mother.
*(Noting that Bailey hated track adds to the reader's
understanding that Bailey feels her mother doesn't
understand her.)*

Analyze Language

RL 1,
RL 4

(LINES 293–296)

Tell students that authors use descriptions to help
readers visualize a scene. Explain that **sensory details**
are words and phrases that appeal to the reader's
senses of sight, hearing, touch, smell, and taste.

(N) CITE TEXT EVIDENCE Have students review lines
293–296 and identify examples of sensory details
that describe Bailey's dinner. *(covered in brown gravy;
blanched to a sickly gray; could pass for glue; gummy;
soggy)* Ask why they think the author includes
these descriptions. *(Possible response: to show how
unappetizing it is)*

Strategies for Annotation 🖊 📱 Annotate it!

Describe Stories:
Plot and Suspense

RL 3,
RL 5

Have students use their eBook annotation tools to analyze the text. Ask
them to do the following:

- Highlight in yellow events or thoughts that are occurring in the
  present.
- Highlight in green a flashback, an event that has occurred earlier.
- Review your highlights. On a note, record why you think the
  flashback is included.

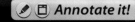

Bailey can't imagine lying in any hospital bed for ten . . .
suffocating her legs. She hated that spring in junior high when she
signed up for track and Mom made her finish the whole season.
But now she longs to run and run and run, sprints and relays and
maybe even marathons. *I've never run a marathon. What else will I
never get to do if I die now? . . .* joyfully, *"Oh good, dinner."*

Explain Point of View

RL 1,
RL 3,
RL 6

(LINES 320–332)

Remind students that when a story is told from third-person limited point of view, the narrator knows and may share one character's inner thoughts with readers.

CITE TEXT EVIDENCE Ask students to review lines 320–332, tell what Bailey's inner thoughts are, and explain why the narrator shares Bailey's thoughts with readers. *(Bailey is stunned to realize that life is still going on around her, and she thinks about what she would be doing if this were a normal day. Knowing her thoughts helps readers understand how Bailey's situation is so shocking and hard for her to understand.)*

English Language Support

Use a Variety of Verbs Display lines 315–317. Read the lines aloud while students follow along in their texts. Point out that there are several sentences that are missing verbs, or action words, and are therefore incomplete. Ask volunteers to identify the sentence fragments. *(Pancakes for breakfast. Chicken salad for lunch. Meat loaf and chocolate cake.)* Explain that in everyday speech, people don't also talk in complete sentences. The author uses the sentence fragments to show that Bailey is listing the types of things she could eat the next day.

ASK STUDENTS to work in pairs to rewrite the incomplete sentences as complete sentences. *(Possible responses: Bailey could check the box to have pancakes for breakfast. For lunch, she could choose chicken salad. At dinner, her choice would be meat loaf and chocolate cake.)*

---

million years. And yet, somehow, she finds that she can eat it, and does, every bite.

See? she wants to tell someone. *I'm healthy. So healthy I* 300 *can eat this slop and not die.*

Beside her tray is a menu for the next day. Bailey studies it as carefully as a cram sheet for some major final exam. Hospital Food 101, maybe. If she were still here for dinner tomorrow night, she'd have a choice of meat loaf or fried chicken, chocolate cake or ice cream.

But of course she won't be here tomorrow night. Because they're going to find out, first thing tomorrow, that there's nothing wrong with her.

She hopes.

310 The aide comes back for Bailey's tray.

"You didn't fill that out," she says, pointing at Bailey's menu.

"I'm just here overnight. I don't need to—," Bailey protests.

"Fill it out anyway," the aide orders.

Meekly, Bailey puts check marks in little boxes. Pancakes for breakfast. Chicken salad for lunch. Meat loaf and chocolate cake.

It doesn't matter. If she's still here tomorrow night, she knows, she won't be hungry.

320 The aide glances out Bailey's window. "Man, look at that traffic," she moans.

Bailey looks up, puzzled, and the aide has to explain: "Rush hour."

It's five forty-five. Bailey is stunned that the rest of the world is going on outside this hospital room. She is stunned to realize that she should be at marching band practice, right now, with Mr. Chaynowski ordering them to do a final run-through of "Another Opening, Another Show," before marching back to the school, packing up her clarinet, joking 330 with her friends.

It's too weird to think about. She's actually glad when Mabel flips on the local news.

Three hours later Bailey is ready to scream. She can't stand the TV. It's into sitcoms now, old-lady ones Bailey never watches. Bailey has never noticed before, but on TV everyone smiles all the time. Everyone laughs at everything.

How dare they?

Searching desperately for something to distract her, Bailey notices her backpack, cast off in the corner. She pulls out her 340 algebra book.

She is a normal sixteen-year-old. Sixteen-year-olds do homework on Tuesday nights.

Bailey missed the end of class, when Mr. Vickers assigns the homework, but he always assigns the odd problems. She takes out a pencil and paper, and imagines what Mr. Vickers will say on Thursday: *Bailey, good to have you back. Remember to make up the homework.*

Bailey will use her airiest voice: *Oh, it's already done. Here.* And he'll stare in amazement.

350 *Why, Bailey,* he'll say, admiration creeping into his voice. *You're such a* **conscientious** *student.*

Mr. Vickers is straight out of college, and a real hottie. Lots of girls have crushes on him.

Why, there you were on the verge of death, he might say. *And you still—*

Bailey doesn't want to think anymore about what Mr. Vickers might say. The numbers swim in front of her eyes.

The phone rings. Mabel answers it and grunts disappointedly, "It's for you."

360 Bailey picks up her phone.

"Oh, Bay-ley!" It's Allison.

Bailey is suddenly so happy she can't speak. She grins as widely as someone on TV.

"Bailey?" Allison asks. "Are you all right?"

"I'm fine," Bailey says. But she's not happy anymore. Allison's voice is all wrong, and so is Bailey's. She can't seem to make her words come out right.

"Well," Allison says, and stops. It strikes Bailey that Allison doesn't know what to say either. Allison—who usually 370 talks so much she could get a speeding ticket for her mouth.

"What'd you think? That I was going to be the dead person in the yearbook for our class?" Bailey jokes desperately. Their yearbook came out last week, and Allison had gone on and on about how every year the senior class had someone die, usually in a car wreck, and that person got a whole page of the yearbook dedicated to him. Last year the dead person was the head cheerleader, so there were lots of pictures. Allison and Bailey and their friends had spent an entire lunch period

conscientious

(kŏn´shē-ĕn´shəs) *adj.* If someone is *conscientious*, that person is very careful and thorough.

CLOSE READ

Explain Point of View

RL 1, RL 2, RL 6

(LINES 345–357)

Remind students that a third-person limited narrator knows one character's thoughts and feelings.

P **ASK STUDENTS** to reread lines 345–357 and summarize what the narrator shares. *(Bailey imagines a conversation with her attractive math teacher in which she impresses him with her conscientiousness.)* Ask students to tell possible reasons why the narrator shares Bailey's imaginations. *(Possible responses: She is a normal teenager who daydreams; daydreaming gives her something else to focus on other than her current situation; the scene reinforces character traits, such as being a little bit vain and shallow.)*

CRITICAL VOCABULARY

conscientious: Bailey uses the word *conscientious* to describe herself in a conversation she imagines having.

ASK STUDENTS why Bailey might have liked to hear herself described as *conscientious* by Mr. Vickers, instead of *hardworking* or *dependable*. *(Bailey is imagining how Mr. Vickers, a young teacher, would be impressed that she completed her homework in the hospital. She might have chosen the word* conscientious *because it makes her sound more admirable and sophisticated.)*

English Language Support

Understand Character Tell students that as they read, they are learning about the characters in a selection through the details that the author includes. Ask students who the main characters are in the selection. *(Bailey and her mother)* Discuss briefly what students know and think about Bailey and her mother.

- Organize students into pairs, and have them make a word web of ten words to describe Bailey. Provide additional support by starting a web on the board, with words such as *good student, hard worker, critical.*

- Have students work independently to write sentences describing what they know about each of the following: Bailey's physical appearance and age, Bailey's positive character traits, Bailey's negative character traits, and Bailey's reaction to her situation.

- Ask students to write a paragraph describing Bailey's relationship with her mother, providing quotes from the text to support their conclusions.

Describe Stories: Plot and Suspense (LINES 379–388)
RL 1,
RL 3,
RL 5

Remind students that rising action includes events that develop and intensify a story's conflict. Explain that the rising action will lead to a turning point for the main character when the story reaches its **climax,** or most exciting part.

Q CITE TEXT EVIDENCE Have students reread lines 379–388 and identify sentences that show what Bailey and Allison realize. *(The lines "It had been funny last week. It isn't now," make it clear that the girls realize how what was once a joke is possibly a reality.)* **Then ask students to predict what this rising action might lead to as the story reaches its climax. Explain to students that a prediction is a logical guess about what might happen next in a story.** *(Possible responses: Bailey will find out her test results (negative or positive); Bailey will have another fainting episode.)*

Explain Point of View
(LINES 406–419)
RL 1,
RL 6

Remind students that a third-person limited narrator shares one character's thoughts and feelings. Explain that, at times, readers need to think about why a character responds a certain way to events.

R CITE TEXT EVIDENCE Have students reread lines 406–419 and identify words and phrases that describe how Bailey responds to her mother's news. *(Possible responses: "automatically, like a robot," "the words have no meaning anymore.")* **Ask students to tell why they think Bailey responds in this way.** *(Possible responses: She feels very alone, scared, or numb; she is realizing that she has to handle this on her own.)*

FOR STANDARD ENGLISH LEARNERS

Comparative Forms of Adjectives. Tell students that when they compare two or more things In formal English, they should not use both *-er* and *more* to form a comparative adjective or *-est* and *most* to form a superlative adjective. Write lines 381–385 on the board and underline *biggest* and *better.* Discuss how the sentence uses the comparative and superlative forms correctly. Then have students practice by rewriting the comparative forms in standard English.

- Bailey thought her classmates were more funnier last week. (*more funny* or *funnier*)

- Alison was more happier than Bailey. (*more happy* or *happier*)
- It would have been most easiest for Bailey's mother to get to the hospital by car. (*easiest*)

Discuss the answers with students and encourage them to notice how other adjectives in the comparative and superlative forms are used in the selection.

---

imagining what a memorial page might say for everyone in their class.

"Imogene Rogers, world's biggest airhead, floated off into outer space . . . John Vhymes, biggest show-off, thought he had a better idea for running heaven than God does . . . Stanley Witherspoon, died two years ago but nobody noticed until now . . . "

It had been funny last week. It isn't now. Bailey hears Allison inhale sharply. Bailey tries to pretend she didn't say anything.

"So what happened after I left?" Bailey asks. "Anything good?"

"Everyone was just talking about you," Allison says. "Do you know what's wrong yet?"

Suddenly Bailey can't talk to Allison. She just can't.

"Listen, Al, some nurse is coming in in a minute to take my blood pressure. I'll call you later, okay?"

It isn't really a lie. They're always coming in to take her blood pressure.

Allison hangs up. Bailey hopes Mabel's hearing is as bad as her kidneys.

Bailey is surprised that she can fall asleep. She's even more surprised when they wake her up at 6 A.M. for an electro-cardiogram.

"But my mom—," she protests groggily.

"They don't want to test your mom's heart," the aide says. "They want to test yours."

Bailey is climbing into the wheelchair when the phone rings.

"Oh, Bailey," her mother's voice rushes at her. "They said you were already up. I was just getting ready to come down there, but something awful happened—the car won't start. I called Triple A, but it's going to be an hour before they get out here. I'm looking for someone to give me a ride or loan me a car. . . . I am so sorry. This is incredibly bad timing. Are you okay?"

It's easiest for Bailey to say automatically, like a robot, "I'm fine."

"I'll get there as soon as I can," Mom assures her.

"I know. That's fine," Bailey says. But the words have no meaning anymore.

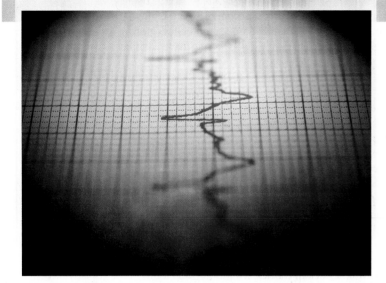

©Corbis Bridge / Alamy

420　　Down in the EKG room they put cold gel on Bailey's chest and the technician runs a probe[4] along Bailey's rib cage. Even though the technician is a woman, Bailey is embarrassed because the probe keeps running into her breasts.

"Um-hmm," the technician mutters to herself.

Bailey knows better now than to ask what the "Um-hmm" means. She can't see the TV screen the technician peers into. The technician pushes harder and harder on the probe, until it feels like an animal trying to burrow between Bailey's ribs. Bailey can't help crying out.

430　　The technician looks up, surprised, as if she'd forgotten that Bailey is an actual human being, capable of feeling pain.

"Sorry," she says, and pushes the probe down even harder.

I am just a body here, Bailey thinks. *Nobody here knows or cares that I'm nice to animals and small children, that I do my homework on time. That I'm a person.* She wants to say something to make the technician really see her, but the longer Bailey lies on the cold table in her hospital gown, the more she feels like all her personality is leaching away. She is just a body.

Is that what it's like to die?

---
[4] **probe** (prōb): a small device or instrument used to gather information.

Fine?　**29**

CLOSE READ

Describe Stories: Plot
RL 1,
RL 2,
RL 3

(LINES 430–438)

Explain to students that as a story's plot develops, the main character often undergoes changes as a result of events.

S **CITE TEXT EVIDENCE** Have students review lines 430–438. Have students point out text evidence that shows how Bailey feels during the EKG. *(Possible responses: "I am just a body here"; "Nobody knows or cares. . . . That I'm a person"; "all her personality is leaching away.")* Then ask students to summarize how Bailey has changed from the beginning of the story. *(Possible response: At first, she was scared, and she dealt with her fears by daydreaming and trying to distract herself. Now, she is starting to realize that she is alone and no one seems to care or be able to help her.)*

WHEN STUDENTS STRUGGLE...

To support students' comprehension of plot and character development, have them create a chart to show how Bailey responds to events in the story. Guide students to note how Bailey increasingly feels that she is no longer a person, but just a body.

LEVEL UP TUTORIALS For additional support, assign the following *Level Up* tutorials: **Plot Stages; Conflict.**

Event	How Bailey responds
She has an MRI.	She imagines what people might say about her at her funeral.
She talks to Allison on the phone.	She tries to joke about her situation but realizes it's not funny.
Her mom calls to say she will be late.	She responds "automatically, like a robot."
She has an EKG.	She feels pain but thinks about how she is just a body that no one cares about.

Describe Stories: Plot and Suspense (LINES 449–486)

RL 1, RL 3, RL 5

Remind students that suspense is a feeling of growing tension that builds as a story progresses. Explain that tension builds as a story reaches its climax, or most exciting moment.

T CITE TEXT EVIDENCE Ask students to review lines 449–482 and tell how the author builds the suspense that leads to the climax of Bailey's realization in line 483. *(The author builds suspense by telling how Bailey wants her mother to help her and then showing that that won't happen. Bailey reaches a turning point at the climax when she comes to realize that she is utterly alone, her future is uncertain—and that, through no choice of her own, she might actually die.)*

English Language Support

Before students complete the activity above, read aloud lines 450–457 as students follow along in the text. Explain that these lines help show what Bailey is thinking and feeling. Have volunteers read aloud lines 456–457. Ask: What emotion must Bailey be feeling when she learns her mother is stuck in traffic? *(disappointment)* Is this the only time in the selection that Bailey has felt this way? *(no)* Have students read to the end of the page independently and discuss what Bailey has realized about her situation. Then ask students to complete the activity.

---

440   Another technician in another room repeats the procedure—the cold gel, the hard probe—on Bailey's neck and shoulders, checking out the blood vessels that lead to her brain.

      This woman talks constantly—about her kids, her garden, her diet—but it's not like she's really talking to Bailey. Even when the woman asks a direct question, "Have you ever heard of a geranium growing like that?" the woman doesn't stop long enough for Bailey to answer.

      Bailey is crying, and the woman doesn't even notice.

450   Bailey thinks she'll have to dry her tears and wipe her eyes before she sees her mother. She can't wait to see her mother. She wants Mom to think about all these horrible things so Bailey doesn't have to. She wants Mom there to remember what Bailey is really like, so Bailey can remember how to act normal.

      But when Bailey gets back to her room, there's only a message. Mom's stuck in traffic.

> " **Bailey is standing on the edge of something awful, balanced between two possible futures.** "

      Mom left the number for the Montinis' car phone, but Bailey doesn't call it. She turns her head to the wall so her 460 roommate won't see, and lies in bed sobbing silently. She's not sure if she's crying about the stalled traffic or the painful probe or the shame of having made jokes about dead people in the yearbook. Or the fact that whatever made Bailey faint yesterday might also make her die. *It really could happen,* Bailey thinks. *People die of terrible diseases all the time. There's no reason that it shouldn't happen to me.*

TO CHALLENGE STUDENTS...

Describe Stories: Plot Have students work singly or in pairs to imagine that they are preparing to shoot a movie version of "Fine?" Tell them to create storyboard illustrations of moments from each plot stage of the story. Remind students that they want to make the scenes visually interesting, so they may need to experiment with "camera angles" and try out more than one illustration to create different points of view.

ASK STUDENTS to explain their choices for each storyboard's point of view and approach and its connection to the plot of the story.

For the first time Bailey realizes none of her fears have been real before. When she imagined the MRI technician speaking at her funeral, the memorial page in the yearbook, Mr. Vickers's response to her devotion to algebra, even her personality leaching away, it was just a fantasy to her. Role-playing. A game.

But Bailey is standing on the edge of something awful, balanced between two possible futures. On one side is the life she's always known: homework and marching band and jokes with Allison and groans at her mother. Health. A future just like her past. And on the other side, over the cliff into whatever her illness is, is more time in hospital beds, more technicians seeing her innards but not really seeing her, more time crying alone. And maybe—death. Bailey longs fervently for her normal life back. In her mind it positively glows, an utterly joyous existence. Ordinary never looked so good.

But it's not her choice which future she gets.

"Hello?" someone calls tentatively.

Bailey pauses to hide the evidence of her crying before she turns. But, strangely, she's not crying anymore.

A man pulls the curtain around her bed, to give some privacy from her roommate.

"I'm Dr. Rogers, your neurologist," he says. "I've looked at all your test results, and—"

Bailey's heart pounds. She can barely hear him for the surge of blood in her ears. She feels dizzier than she felt yesterday, when everyone said she fainted.

"Shouldn't my mom be here to hear this?" Bailey asks. "She's coming soon."

Dr. Rogers looks at his watch.

"No. I can't wait."

He's treating me like I'm a grown-up, Bailey marvels. But the thought has an echo: *Grown-up enough to die.*

"This is a classic case," Dr. Rogers is saying. "I'm surprised nobody caught it yesterday. They still would have wanted the tests, just to be sure. . . . What you had was a migraine headache."

A headache? Not a stroke? Not a tumor? As soon as Dr. Rogers has said the inoffensive word, all the possibilities Bailey feared instantly recede. She's a million miles away from that frightening cliff now. Of course she isn't going to die.

Fine? **31**

CLOSE READ

Analyze Language RL 4
(LINES 491–493)

Remind students that authors use sensory details to help readers imagine a scene.

U CITE TEXT EVIDENCE Have students review lines 491–493. Ask what words and phrases help them imagine how Bailey responds to what the neurologist is about to tell her. *(Possible answer: Phrases like "heart pounds," "surge of blood in her ears," and "feels dizzier" help readers understand that she is in a state of fearful excitement.)*

Describe Stories: Plot and Suspense (LINES 500-507) RL 1, RL 2, RL 3, RL 5

Explain that a plot stage called **falling action** follows the climax and eases the tension in the story.

V CITE TEXT EVIDENCE Ask students to reread lines 500–507 and summarize the falling action. *(The neurologist tells Bailey that what she experienced was a migraine headache.)* Then ask them to explain how Bailey responds. *(She is "instantly" relieved and "a million miles away from that frightening cliff now.")*

English Language Support

Direct students' attention to lines 500–507. Explain that they can summarize the falling action by identifying the most important words.

- First, have students reread the lines and create a list of what they think are the five most important words.
- Then have pairs compare and discuss their lists. Ask them to choose the most important five words from both lists.
- Next, have pairs work with other pairs to compare lists and make a final list of the most important five words.
- Finally, have students summarize the falling action independently, including the five words from the list.

CONTENT-AREA CONNECTION

Health Project lines 500–507 and read the lines aloud. To help students understand the term *migraine*, tell them that migraine headaches affect many people. Doctors may not always realize that a teenager is suffering from migraines because different people have different symptoms.

Activity After students have completed reading the story, have them work in small groups to research migraine headaches. Ask students to write a paragraph about some of the causes of migraine headaches. Students should then create a list of symptoms from their research and finally write about some of the treatments for these types of headaches. Ask students to share their research with the class.

Describe Stories: Plot and Suspense (LINES 510–528)

RL 1,
RL 3,
RL 5

Explain to students that the final plot stage is called the **resolution,** which reveals how the story's problem or conflict gets solved.

Ⓦ CITE TEXT EVIDENCE Ask students to explain why Bailey "barely listens" in lines 510–520 as the doctor explains the link between chocolate and migraines. *(She is so relieved to know she is "getting her ordinary life back" that she cannot focus on his words.)*

Ⓧ CITE TEXT EVIDENCE Have students compare lines 526–528 with how Bailey thinks about her mother at the beginning of the story. Ask them to explain how the author ties the resolution of the story to what readers learn at its beginning. *(When Bailey says, "'Mom,'" at the end, it reminds readers of how, at the beginning of the story, her biggest complaint was that her mother often said the most embarrassing things.)*

COLLABORATIVE DISCUSSION Have partners work together to briefly chart the events during Bailey's visit to the hospital. Then have them use their chart to discuss each event and tell how Bailey responds to it. Remind students to cite evidence from the text to support their ideas.

ASK STUDENTS to share any questions they generated in the course of reading and discussing the selection.

English Language Support

Support Opinions Before students begin their discussion, provide the following sentence frames to help them support their opinions and persuade others.

For clarification
I agree with _____, but can you say more about
_____.

For persuasion:
I think _____ because it says _____ in the selection.
For counterargument:
You said that _____, but I read _____ in the selection and I think it supports a different opinion.

How silly she'd been, to think she might. How silly, to think he'd tell her she was dying without her mother there.

510   Dr. Rogers is still talking, about the link between chocolate and migraines, about how common migraines are for young girls, about how it was perfectly normal for Bailey to get the symptoms of a migraine headache before her head even began to hurt. But Bailey barely listens. She's thinking about getting her ordinary life back—ordinary life with maybe a headache every now and then. Bailey doesn't care—her head barely even hurt yesterday. She doesn't expect a mere headache to change anything at all. She waits for the glow to fade from her view of her ordinary life, and it does, but not entirely. Even with
520   headaches she has a pretty good life.

Bailey's mother rushes into the room just then, apologizing right and left.

"Doctor, you must think I'm a terrible mother, not to be here at a time like this. What did you find out? Please tell me—it was just a fluke, right?"

"Mom," Bailey protests, in humiliation, with perfect emphasis.   **Ⓧ**

The complaint never sounded so wonderful before.

COLLABORATIVE DISCUSSION Being hospitalized and waiting to hear about her test results is an emotional experience for Bailey. With a partner, discuss the events that take place during her stay. How does each event help you understand more about Bailey's thoughts and feelings?

Describe Stories: Plot and Suspense

RL 3, RL 5

Stories, such as "Fine?", follow a pattern called a **plot,** which is the series of events in the story. At the center of a good plot is a conflict. A **conflict** is a problem or struggle between opposing forces that triggers the action and events. Most plots have the following stages:

- **Exposition** provides background and introduces the setting and characters. The conflict is also introduced at this stage.
- **Rising action** includes events that develop and intensify the conflict.
- The **climax** is the story's most exciting part and a turning point for the main character.
- **Falling action** eases the tension, and events unfold as a result of the climax.
- The **resolution** is the final part of the plot and reveals how the problem is solved.

To keep you involved and excited about the plot, a writer will often create suspense. **Suspense** is a feeling of growing tension and excitement that makes a reader curious about what will happen next in a story. At the start of "Fine?", you learn about the story's conflict—Bailey is in a hospital undergoing tests—and you want to find out more.

Explain Point of View

RL 6

In literature, the **narrator** is the voice that tells the story. A writer's choice of narrator is known as **point of view.**

First-Person Point of View	Third-Person Point of View
The narrator is a character in the story.	The narrator is not a character in the story but more like a voice that tells it.
The narrator uses the pronouns *I, me,* and *my* to refer to himself or herself.	The narrator uses the pronouns *he, she,* and *they* to refer to the characters.
The narrator tells about his or her thoughts and feelings, but does not know what other characters are thinking and feeling.	A narrator called **third-person omniscient** knows what ALL the characters think and feel.
	A narrator called **third-person limited** knows the thoughts and feelings of just one person, usually the main character.

Think about the following questions to help you analyze point of view:

- How does the author's choice of point of view affect the story?
- What does the choice of narrator help you learn about characters and events?

Fine? **33**

CLOSE READ

Describe Stories: Plot and Suspense

RL 3, RL 5

Help students understand the terms and how each plot stage helps a story progress. Then use the story to ask questions about each plot stage, such as *How can you tell that the resolution of the story occurs when Dr. Rogers arrives to talk to Bailey? (This scene resolves the conflict, when Bailey realizes she is not seriously ill.)*

Next, review the information about how suspense adds tension and excitement to a story. Ask students to point out events and occurrences that add suspense in "Fine?"

Explain Point of View

RL 6

Guide students to understand that determining the narrator and the point of view used in a story will help them understand characters and story events.

Point out that in a story told using first-person point of view, events are filtered through the narrator's perspective, and readers may feel that the narrator is speaking directly to them. Then discuss differences between third-person limited and third-person omniscient points of view and the effects each point of view might have.

Strategies for Annotation 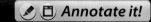 Annotate it!

Describe Stories: Plot and Suspense

RL 3, RL 5

Share these strategies for guided or independent analysis:

- Highlight in yellow expository details that give you more information about the characters.
- Highlight in green expository details that provide more information about the conflict.
- Review your highlights. On a note, record how these details add suspense.

Bailey's mother lays her hand on Bailey's shoulder, something she never would have done under normal circumstances. . . .

"They have a room ready for you now," he reports. . . .

". . . I've just got a little headache," Bailey says. . . . the edge of a headache—nothing Bailey would mention if she weren't in the hospital.

Analyzing the Text

RL 1, RL 3, RL 5, RL 6

Possible answers:

1. *The point of view is third-person limited. The narrator is not a character in the story and knows only what Bailey feels.*

2. *Internal conflicts: Bailey worries about what the MRI will find. She worries whether she'll be alive in six months. She wonders about her funeral service.*
External conflicts: Bailey's mom embarrasses her in front of the technician. Bailey is ready to scream after watching television for three hours.

3. *Bailey is trying to find ways to distract herself; the fantasy that she imagines about her math teacher highlights that Bailey is just a normal teenager, prone to flights of fancy and somewhat self-centered.*

4. *Their conversation heightens the tension as Bailey tries to make light of possibly being the "dead person in the yearbook." Something that the friends joked about could become reality, which adds to the suspense as part of the rising action.*

5. *Exposition: Bailey is in a hospital having an MRI. Her mother is also with her. The setting, major characters, and conflict are introduced.*
Rising Action: Bailey and Allison joke about death, but the call ends when they realize the joke isn't funny anymore. This heightens the suspense.
Climax: Bailey realizes her ordinary life is threatened and she must accept this. This is her turning point.
Falling Action: The tension falls. Bailey sees that she must accept and appreciate what life offers.
Resolution: Bailey has a treatable ailment. She realizes she won't die now and that she has a pretty good life.

6. *The author connects the end with the beginning by having Bailey complain about her mom. However, by the end, Bailey realizes how important life is, as she thinks, "The complaint never sounded so wonderful before."*

7. *If the author had used first-person point of view, the important lesson might have been lost in Bailey's personality or been expressed less clearly. For example, Bailey might have left out telling the yearbook anecdote because it doesn't reflect well on her.*

✎ 📋 **eBook** *Annotate It!*

Analyzing the Text

RL 1, RL 3, RL 5, RL 6, W 3a-e

Cite Text Evidence Support your responses with evidence from the text.

1. **Identify** Reread lines 1–15. Identify the point of view of the story. Explain how you can tell which point of view is being used.

2. **Infer** An **external conflict** is a character's struggle against an outside force. An **internal conflict** takes place inside a character's mind. Go back through the story and record examples of the internal and external conflicts that Bailey faces.

3. **Draw Conclusions** Review lines 333–357. What does this passage tell you about Bailey's character?

4. **Evaluate** Reread the conversation Bailey has with her friend Allison in lines 371–395. How does the scene add suspense to the plot?

5. **Analyze** The plot of "Fine?" centers on Bailey's fear of what her illness is. Go back through the story and make a list of important events. Label each event to identify what happens at each stage of the plot—exposition, rising action, climax, falling action, and resolution. Explain how each event fits its plot stage.

6. **Connect** Reread lines 22–31 and 521–527. Explain why the author repeats Bailey's complaint. What does the author want you to know about Bailey at the end of the story?

7. **Analyze** How would the story be different if Bailey was the narrator? Name a detail that Bailey might leave out and explain why.

PERFORMANCE TASK

Writing Activity: Narrative The story "Fine?" presents Bailey's thoughts and feelings about her impending diagnosis. Write a one- or two-page narrative that describes the situation from Bailey's mother's point of view.

- Think about and decide whether you will tell the story using first- or third-person point of view.
- Follow the actual story; do not change the events or plot.
- Include relevant details that Bailey shares with her mother.

Assign this performance task.

PERFORMANCE TASK

W 3a-e

Writing Activity: Narrative Have students work independently. Remind them to make language choices and include events that make Bailey's mother's perspective clear. Direct them to

- create a plot line or chart to note the events to include in the narrative
- decide whether they will use first- or third-person point of view
- write the narrative, following their plot chart

Critical Vocabulary

technician	reminisce	emphatic	conscientious

Practice and Apply Complete the sentences with words that show that you understand the meaning of each vocabulary word.

1. We are going to have a TV **technician** come to our house because . . .

2. I like to hear old Uncle Al **reminisce** because . . .

3. The jury foreperson read the verdict in an **emphatic** voice because . . .

4. I am very **conscientious** when I do my chores because . . .

Vocabulary Strategy: Greek Roots

You can often determine the meaning of an unfamiliar word by examining its root. A **root** is a word part that contains the core meaning of the word. For example, *tech* comes from a Greek root that can mean "art," "skill," or "craft." You can find this root in the word *technician* and use its meaning to figure out that *technician* refers to someone who has a specific skill.

Practice and Apply The Greek root *tech* is found in a number of English words. Choose a word from the web that best completes each sentence. Use your understanding of the root's meaning as well as context clues to figure out the meaning of each word.

1. The artist has a special _____ that she uses to create her sculptures.

2. The audience wished that the scientist would use plain English instead of _____ to explain her latest invention.

3. Raul likes to be the first to purchase the latest _____ in computers.

4. The suspected thief was released from jail because of a _____.

PRACTICE & APPLY

Critical Vocabulary

Possible answers:

1. . . . we are not getting clear reception.

2. . . . he remembers and tells great stories about his past and the things kids did before television, computers, and other forms of technology existed.

3. . . . she wanted listeners in the courtroom to understand the jury's finding.

4. . . . I want to do a good job.

Vocabulary Strategy: Greek Roots

Answers:

1. *technique*

2. *technobabble*

3. *technology*

4. *technicality*

English Language Support

Have students work in pairs to complete the Practice and Apply sections on this page. Tell them to take turns reading each item aloud before writing an answer. Encourage them to use context clues and a dictionary to help them complete the activities.

Strategies for Annotation [✎ 🗖 Annotate it!]

Greek Roots

Have students locate the sentence containing *technician* in the selection. Tell them to use their eBook annotation tools to do the following:

- Highlight in yellow the word *technician*.
- Underline the Greek root *tech*. Write a note that defines its meaning.
- Reread the surrounding words and sentences, looking for clues to the word's meaning. Highlight clues in green.
- Review the annotations and try to infer the word's meaning.

"Contrary to popular opinion," the MRI technician says, "this is not a torture device, it was not invented by aliens, and it does not enable us to read your thoughts."

Bailey looks doubtfully at the huge machine in front of her.

> someone good with machines

Language Conventions: Commas and Dashes

L 2a

Tell students that commas and dashes are used to help communicate ideas clearly. Use the examples from "Fine?" to point out that if the nonrestrictive phrase enclosed within the commas or dashes were removed, the sentences would still make sense. Explain that if the commas or dashes were not used, the sentences would be difficult to follow and would confuse readers.

Answers:

1. *The concert tickets—I just bought them yesterday—were expensive and nonrefundable.*

2. *Mr. Jackson, who moved here from Texas, was introduced to us as the new principal.*

3. *Nola's voice, never loud to begin with, dropped to an airy whisper in the library.*

4. *Sharon eyed the sunrise, deep red clouds and wispy flares of pink, through the dining room window.*

5. *Our agreed-upon rule is that the drummer—not the guitarist or the keyboardist—is responsible for making sure the entire drum kit makes it to the show.*

Assess It Online!

Online Selection Test
- Download an editable ExamView bank.
- Assign and manage this test online.

L 2a

Language Conventions: Commas and Dashes

Commas can make the meaning of sentences clearer by separating certain words, phrases, or clauses. Commas can be used to set off nonrestrictive elements. A **nonrestrictive element** is a phrase or clause that can be removed from the sentence without changing the sentence's basic meaning. Notice how commas are used in the following sentence from the story "Fine?"

> The only real possibility the emergency room doctor mentioned, ordering all these tests, was a stroke . . .

If you remove the phrase *ordering all these tests*, the basic meaning of the sentence is still clear.

Like commas, **dashes** can also be used to set off nonrestrictive elements. Dashes are used most often when the nonrestrictive element indicates a more abrupt break in thought. Notice how dashes are used in this example from the story.

> The slow, cultured voice of the announcer—"And now we'll hear Mozart's finest concerto, at least in my humble opinion"—could drive anyone crazy.

Using commas and dashes to set off nonrestrictive elements helps to communicate meaning and information clearly. Look at the examples from the story again. If the commas and dashes were not included, the sentences would be confusing and difficult to follow.

Practice and Apply Use commas or dashes as indicated to set off the nonrestrictive element in each sentence.

1. The concert tickets I just bought them yesterday were expensive and nonrefundable. (dashes)

2. Mr. Jackson who moved here from Texas was introduced to us as the new principal. (commas)

3. Nola's voice never loud to begin with dropped to an airy whisper in the library. (commas)

4. Sharon eyed the sunrise deep red clouds and wispy flares of pink through the dining room window. (commas)

5. Our agreed-upon rule is that the drummer not the guitarist or the keyboardist is responsible for making sure the entire drum kit makes it to the show. (dashes)

36 Collection 1

English Language Support

Understand Language Choices Write Bailey's observation about a woman at the hospital in lines 444–445 on the board: "This woman talks constantly—about her kids, her garden, her diet—but it's not like she's really talking to Bailey." Read aloud the material enclosed by the dashes.

- Work with students to read the sentence aloud without the material in dashes, telling students that the sentence is still correct without those words.

- Read the sentence aloud with students, pausing at the dashes. Point out that the sentence is correct without the material in dashes, but

ask students to explain why the author included the material. *(Possible answer: The information about what the woman is talking about helps the reader understand Bailey's thoughts and situation.)* Lead students in a discussion about how this writer uses nonrestrictive elements to develop the characters in the story.

- Have pairs of students find examples of nonrestrictive clauses set off by commas or dashes in the selection. Then have them discuss how these nonrestrictive elements help them understand the characters in the selection, even though they are not necessary to the sentences.

Explain Point of View

TEACH

An author can develop point of view in a story in a number of ways. Explain these devices to students:

- **Voice** refers to a unique use of language that allows readers to "hear" the narrator's human personality. An author can develop the narrator's voice to show a particular attitude or sensibility.
- **Dialogue** is written conversation between two or more characters. Dialogue reveals point of view by presenting what characters think and say. Verbs, adverbs, or adverbial phrases may be included to indicate how characters express their speech, such as "barked" or "in a hesitant way."
- **Internal monologue** refers to thoughts that a character has within his or her own mind. Internal monologue is usually indicated by italicized type.

Explain that whether a story is told from first- or third-person point of view, an author may use any of these devices to help readers gain a deeper understanding of the story's characters, events, or thematic ideas.

PRACTICE AND APPLY

Discuss the following examples from the story:

- Lines 230–237: Ask a student to read the passage aloud. Then ask students why the narrator speaks directly to readers in lines 235–237. *(Possible responses: to verify that Bailey has never done drugs; to make readers wonder why Bailey cares about being humiliated by her mother in such a serious situation)*
- Lines 16–24: Have students identify words and phrases the narrator uses to express feelings in the dialogue. *(Possible responses: "seems amused," "says firmly," "protests")*
- Lines 14–15, 157–159, and 465–466: Ask students to explain why the narrator presents Bailey's internal monologues. *(Possible responses: The internal monologues take readers inside Bailey's mind; they make her ideas more direct than if the narrator expressed them for her.)*

Invite students to review "Fine?" to find more examples of how point of view is developed through dialogue, internal monologue, and the narrator's voice. Have them explain the effect of each example.

 INTERACTIVE WHITEBOARD LESSON Use **Point of View** for additional instruction.

Describe Stories: Plot

RETEACH

Review the five stages of a story plot: exposition, rising action, climax, falling action, and resolution. Then use a graphic organizer such as the following to fill in events from "Fine?" or from "The Ravine."

Plot Stage	Examples from Story
Exposition	
Rising Action	
Climax	
Falling Action	
Resolution	

Review the story with students to fill in the organizer. As they provide examples, have students explain how the example fits within that particular plot stage.

 LEVEL UP TUTORIALS Assign the following *Level Up* tutorials: **Plot Stages; Plot: Sequence of Events; Conflict.**

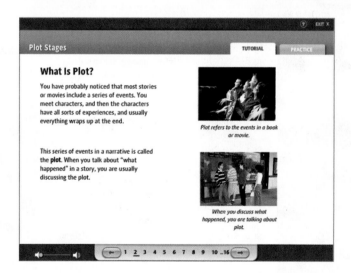

INDEPENDENT READING

Individual students can apply these skills to another selection in Collection 1 or to a short story or novel they may be reading on their own. After their analysis, have them share their ideas about plot stages with other students in the class.

Life Doesn't Frighten Me

Poem by Maya Angelou

Why This Text?

Poetry is a powerful way for people to express emotions, offering the reader insights or new ways of thinking. This lesson explores the structure of a lyric poem and how it is used to express emotions and ideas.

Key Learning Objective: The student will learn about the structure of a lyric poem and be able to identify repetition and rhyme scheme.

RL 1 Cite textual evidence.
RL 2 Determine a theme or central idea of a text.
RL 4 Determine the meaning of words and phrases.
RL 5 Analyze structure.
RL 6 Explain how an author develops the point of view of the speaker.
SL 1 Engage effectively in a range of collaborative discussions.
SL 4 Present claims and findings logically to accentuate main ideas or themes; use appropriate eye contact, adequate volume, and clear pronunciation.
SL 6 Adapt speech to a variety of contexts and tasks.

Text Complexity Rubric

Quantitative Measures	**Life Doesn't Frighten Me** N/A
Qualitative Measures	**Levels of Meaning/Purpose** single level of simple meaning **Structure** regular stanzas with some liberties taken **Language Conventionality and Clarity** some figurative language **Knowledge Demands** experience includes unfamiliar aspects
Reader/Task Considerations	• Teacher determined • Vary by individual reader and type of text • See the Text X-Ray for suggested Reader/Task Considerations.

English Language Support

Before teaching, use the Text X-Ray below for an overview of the text's complexity. The Text X-Ray and the supports and scaffolds in the Teacher's Edition will help you guide students of different skill levels.

Meaning Making

Language Development

Effective Expression

Content Knowledge

Foundational Skills

Text Complexity: Qualitative Measures

Levels of Meaning/Purpose

single level of simple meaning

Help students analyze speaker and tone in a lyric poem.

• Teacher's Edition side notes, pp. 37, 38

To reteach the elements of lyric poetry, see

• Analyze Structure: Lyric Poetry, p. 40a

 Use It! Level Up Tutorial: Elements of Poetry

ZOOM IN ON **ANALYZING SPEAKER** Tell students that the **speaker** is the voice that readers hear in the poem. Like the narrator of a story, the speaker might use a first- or third-person point of view.

• Ask students what words in the first stanza of the poem identify the speaker. *(me)* From what point of view is the poem told? *(first person)*

• Have partners read the poem aloud. Ask them to discuss who they think the speaker is. Encourage them to look for clues in specific lines. *(Possible answers: The speaker "talks" in the way a child would; she is a girl; she mentions how boys pull her hair.)*

Structure

regular stanzas with some liberties taken

Help students analyze the structure of a lyric poem.

• Teacher's Edition side notes, pp. 37, 38, 39
• English Language Support, p. 37
• Strategies for Annotation, p. 39
• Analyze Structure, p. 39

To teach rhyme scheme, see

• Analyze Structure: Rhyme Scheme, p. 40a

 Use It! Interactive Whiteboard Lesson: Use Sound Devices

ZOOM IN ON **UNDERSTANDING THE ELEMENTS OF A POEM** Introduce students to the poetic elements listed in the chart on page 39. Increase students' understanding of the organization and elements of a poem by having them work through these steps with a partner:

• Count the number of **stanzas** in the poem. *(9)*
• Identify two **couplets**. *(Possible responses: "Bad dogs barking loud/ Big ghosts in a cloud"; "Panthers in the park/Strangers in the dark")*
• Write the **rhyme** scheme of lines 28–32. *(aabbc)*
• Identify the line that is repeated. Tell what this line shows us about the speaker. *("Life doesn't frighten me at all." The repetition of this line shows the speaker's desire to be brave and overcome her fears.)*

Language Conventionality and Clarity

some figurative language

Teach unfamiliar vocabulary in context.

- Applying Academic Vocabulary, p. 38

Guide students to write about and discuss the language of poetry.

- Teacher's Edition side notes, p. 38
- English Language Support, p. 39
- Performance Task, p. 40

ZOOM IN ON **ANALYZING THE LANGUAGE OF POETRY** Tell students that poets sometimes use as few words as possible to convey meaning or create a particular sound. Point out lines in this poem that seem to be missing a word. Although some of the ideas in lines that rhyme are connected, the poet has chosen to leave out the word that connects those ideas.

- Display lines 13–21 on the board.
- Ask pairs to rewrite the lines, inserting any missing elements. *(I go boo **and** make them shoo; I make fun **of** the way they run; I just smile **and** they go wild)*
- Have volunteers read their rewritten versions and then the original verse. Discuss the effect of the additional words on the sound of the poem. *(The pace slows; the lines lose momentum and emphasis.)*

Knowledge Demands

experience includes unfamiliar aspects

Support English Learners in understanding important ideas about the poet and the poem.

- Teacher's Edition Author's note, p. 37

ZOOM IN ON **BUILDING CONTEXT** Help students understand some of the ideas referred to in the poem.

- Explain that Mother Goose (line 7) is the fictional author of nursery rhymes and tales. Point out that some are quite frightening and the characters often face danger or undergo harm.
- Tell students that the word *boo* in line 13 is often shouted by someone jumping out from a hiding place with the intent of scaring another person.
- Have students reread the poem and identify unfamiliar words. Discuss them as a class.

Suggested Reader/Task Considerations

You might consider the following before assigning this poem to students.

- Do students have prior experience with reading poetry?
- Will students be able to comprehend the poem?

ZOOM IN ON **SUPPORTING COMPREHENSION**

- Display a word web with "poetry" in the middle. Ask volunteers to name ideas and characteristics they associate with poetry. Prompt them by naming poems that they might know. Add details to the web and explain what students should look for as they read.
- Before analyzing the poem, facilitate comprehension by reading the poem aloud. Then read it a second time, pausing to ask students what ideas are brought out in each stanza.

Maya Angelou Have students read the information about the author. Explain that much of Angelou's poetry focuses on people's emotional responses to hardship and loss. Many critics believe that in order for her poems to be appreciated, they must be performed. Angelou frequently recited her poems to large crowds, and she was one of only two poets in history to have read a poem at a presidential inauguration. Her reading won a Grammy award in the category for "Best Spoken Word."

SETTING A PURPOSE Direct students to use the Setting a Purpose prompt to focus their reading. Remind them to write down questions as they read.

Analyze Language (LINES 1–12)   RL 1, RL 4, RL 6

Explain to students that a **lyric** poem is a poem that expresses the personal thoughts and feelings of a speaker. The **speaker** of a lyric poem can be the poet or an invented character who has had an experience that he or she is responding to.

Ⓐ **CITE TEXT EVIDENCE** Have a student or students reread lines 1–12 aloud. Ask them to tell who they think the speaker is and why. *(The speaker lists many things that often scare children and says that he or she is not afraid of them; the speaker is probably a child.)*

Analyze Structure (LINES 1–12)   RL 1, RL 4, RL 5

Explain that lyric poems were originally written to be sung; therefore, they often have a musical quality. Poets use sound devices such as repetition and rhyme to create this quality.

- **Repetition** is a technique in which a sound, word, phrase, or entire line is repeated.
- A **rhyme scheme** is a pattern of end rhymes in a poem. A common rhyme scheme is a **couplet,** which is a rhymed pair of lines.

Ⓑ **CITE TEXT EVIDENCE** Have a student or students reread lines 1–6, then lines 7–12 aloud. After each set of lines, ask students to identify examples of rhyme and repetition and to explain their effects in the poem. *(Rhymes such as wall/hall and loud/cloud link the examples of frightening things. Repetition: The use of "doesn't frighten me at all" emphasizes the speaker's claim of fearlessness.)*

Maya Angelou (1928–2014) *was born Marguerite Annie Johnson in St. Louis, Missouri. Though a childhood trauma led her to stop speaking for five and a half years, Angelou grew up to pursue a career as a singer and actor. She later turned to writing as her main form of expression, and in 1970, her best-selling autobiography* I Know Why the Caged Bird Sings *made her an international literary star. She is widely admired as a fearless and inspiring voice.*

Life Doesn't Frighten Me

Poem by Maya Angelou

SETTING A PURPOSE As you read, think about the images and ideas that the poem brings to your mind.

 Ⓐ
Shadows on the wall
Noises down the hall
Life doesn't frighten me at all   Ⓑ
Bad dogs barking loud
5   Big ghosts in a cloud
Life doesn't frighten me at all.

Mean old Mother Goose
Lions on the loose
They don't frighten me at all
10   Dragons breathing flame
On my counterpane[1]
That doesn't frighten me at all.

---

[1] **counterpane:** a bedspread.

(tr) ©ZUMA/Alamy Images; (c) ©Phillip Lee Harvey/First Light (Toronto)

Life Doesn't Frighten Me   **37**

English Language Support

Read Closely Display or project lines 1–12 for students. Choral read the lines with students. Have volunteers identify the repeated phrases and highlight the lines that contain a similar phrase in yellow. *(lines 3, 6, 9, and 12)* Reread each similar line and note the differences. *(Lines 3 and 6 are the same, while lines 9 and 12 have different words at the beginning.)*

ASK STUDENTS to tell why the speaker repeats these similar lines. *(to stress that nothing can scare her)*

Analyze Structure
RL 5

(LINES 13–27)

Tell students that the length of the lines of a poem contributes to the poem's rhythm and meaning. Poets decide how long each line will be and how each one will end, whether in rhyme, repeating words, or other natural breaks. Have students reread lines 13–27 aloud, either individually or as a group.

C **ASK STUDENTS** to tell how the length of the lines affects the poem's rhythm and meaning. *(The short sentences speed up the pace of the poem, giving it a more lively feeling. The longer sentences slow the pace down, shifting to a more serious feeling.)*

Analyze Language
RL 1,
RL 4

(LINES 41–44)

Explain to students that repetition can affect a poem's tone. The **tone** of a poem conveys the speaker's attitude toward his or her subject. For example, a poem can express anger, sadness, or humor. Have students reread lines 41–44 aloud.

D **CITE TEXT EVIDENCE** Ask students to identify the repetition in lines 41–44 and to explain how the repetition contributes to the poem's tone. *(The repetition gives the poem a persuasive tone, as if the speaker is trying to convince herself of her fearlessness as well as the reader. The repeating phrase "Not at all" gives more emphasis to this feeling.)*

COLLABORATIVE DISCUSSION Have partners make a list of words and phrases from the poem that help them determine its main message. Have them discuss why they think the poet wrote the poem. Then have them share their ideas with the larger group.

ASK STUDENTS to share any questions they generated in the course of reading and discussing this selection.

I go boo
Make them shoo
15 I make fun
Way they run
I won't cry
So they fly
I just smile
20 They go wild
Life doesn't frighten me at all.

Tough guys in a fight
All alone at night
Life doesn't frighten me at all.

25 Panthers in the park
Strangers in the dark
No, they don't frighten me at all.

That new classroom where
Boys all pull my hair
30 (Kissy little girls
With their hair in curls)
They don't frighten me at all.

Don't show me frogs and snakes
And listen for my scream,
35 If I'm afraid at all
It's only in my dreams.

I've got a magic charm
That I keep up my sleeve,
I can walk the ocean floor
40 And never have to breathe.

D
Life doesn't frighten me at all
Not at all
Not at all.
Life doesn't frighten me at all.

© Leslie Evans Illustration

COLLABORATIVE DISCUSSION With a partner, discuss what the poem's main message might be, based on the images, words, and phrases in it. Why do you think the poet wrote this poem?

APPLYING ACADEMIC VOCABULARY

similar	evident

THINK-PAIR-SHARE Have students turn to a partner to discuss the following questions. Guide students to include the academic vocabulary words *similar* and *evident* in their responses. Ask volunteers to share their responses with the class.

- What are some specific examples of how the speaker makes her feelings **evident** in the poem?

- Have you had any experiences that are **similar** to the speaker's experiences? Describe them.

Analyze Structure

RL 4, RL 5, RL 6

"Life Doesn't Frighten Me" is a lyric poem. **Lyric poetry** is a poetic form in which a single speaker expresses his or her thoughts and feelings. Lyric poetry can take many different forms and can address all types of topics, including complex ideas or everyday experiences.

Similar to a narrator in fiction, a **speaker** in poetry is the voice that "talks" to the reader. The speaker may be the poet or a fictional character. Even if a poem uses the pronouns *I* or *me*, it does not mean that the poet is the speaker. Clues in the title and in individual lines can help you determine the speaker and his or her situation.

To analyze the speaker in a lyric poem, ask yourself:

- Who is speaking? How do I know?
- What ideas does the speaker want to communicate? Why?

Poets use structure and poetic elements to create mood, express ideas, and reinforce meaning in their work. Most poems are meant to be heard, not just read. A poem's sounds are as carefully chosen as its words. The following elements are often present in lyric poetry as well as other forms of poetry.

> A **stanza** is a group of two or more lines that form a unit in a poem.
>
> **Repetition** is a technique in which a sound, word, phrase, or line is repeated.
>
> A **rhyme scheme** is a pattern of rhymes at the ends of lines. A rhyme scheme is noted by assigning a letter of the alphabet, beginning with *a*, to each line. Lines that rhyme are given the same letter.
>
> A **couplet** is a rhymed pair of lines.

As you read a poem, either silently or aloud, look at and listen to its different elements. Ask yourself:

- How does repetition add to the poem's meaning or emphasize its ideas?
- What patterns can I find in the poem's rhyme scheme? What rhythms do they add to the poem?
- What sounds are emphasized in the poem's rhyme scheme? Why might this be?

Life Doesn't Frighten Me **39**

CLOSE READ

Analyze Structure

RL 4, RL 5, RL 6

Explain to students that determining who the speaker is in a poem will help them better understand the poem's meaning. Help them answer the bulleted questions to analyze who the speaker is in "Life Doesn't Frighten Me." Have them identify clues in specific lines that help them know who the speaker is. Then have them discuss the ideas and feelings the speaker is trying to communicate.

Next, review the information about poetic elements. Have students give examples to explain how each element contributes to the mood and meaning of a poem. Then discuss the bulleted questions, having students provide examples from the poem to support their ideas.

English Language Support

Guide students to work in small groups to answer the questions on page 40. Each group should answer one question. When all the groups are finished, they can take turns presenting their answers to the class. Encourage students to provide their classmates with useful feedback.

Strategies for Annotation 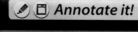 *Annotate it!*

Analyze Structure

RL 4, RL 5

Have students use their eBook annotation tools to identify the poem's rhyme scheme as follows:

- Highlight in yellow the word *wall* and any words that rhyme with it.
- Highlight in green any last words that don't rhyme with the yellow highlighted words, and any other words that rhyme with it.
- Assign the lines that are highlighted in yellow the letter *a*. Assign the lines highlighted in green the letter *b*.
- Identify any patterns in the rhyme scheme in remaining stanzas.

> Shadows on the wall
>
> Noises down the hall
>
> Life doesn't frighten me at all
>
> Bad dogs barking loud
>
> Big ghosts in a cloud
>
> Life doesn't frighten me at all.

Life Doesn't Frighten Me **39**

PRACTICE & APPLY

Analyzing the Text

RL 1, RL 2,
RL 4, RL 5,
RL 6

Possible answers:

1. *The line "Boys all pull my hair" shows that the speaker is most likely a girl in elementary school. Topics and phrases such as "Mother Goose," and "bad dogs barking loud" show that the speaker is most likely young. Repeating the line "Life doesn't frighten me" shows that she wants to be brave. Referring to "kissy little girls" shows that she does not see herself that way.*

2. *Some examples of rhyme schemes used are aabccb in the second stanza, couplets in the third stanza, and aab in the fourth and fifth stanzas. The poem uses a variety of rhyme schemes; some are very simple, while others are more sophisticated.*

3. *Shadows, noises, and dogs barking could all be real; lines 5, 7, 8, and 10–11 refer to imaginary things. All, however, are things that young children might be afraid of and help to emphasize that the speaker is young. They also point out that young children are fearful of things both real and imaginary.*

4. *The shorter line lengths and couplets make the rhythm change to a simpler, choppier, singsong effect.*

5. *The rhyme schemes and rhythms are simple; there is repetition and many lines are rhythmic and fairly short, like nursery or jump-rope rhymes; the topics and word choices are ones that a young child would choose. Together, they create a lively, realistic portrayal of a young girl trying to be brave and confident. The repetition of "Life doesn't frighten me at all" emphasizes the speaker's desire to not be frightened. At the end, the increased repetition of the phrase "Not at all" emphasizes that the child may be working very hard to be unafraid, chanting the phrase to convince herself that it is true.*

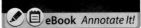

Analyzing the Text

RL 1, RL 2, RL 4,
RL 5, RL 6, SL 4,
SL 6

Cite Text Evidence   Support your responses with evidence from the text.

1. **Infer** Review lines 1–9 and lines 37–40. What conclusions can you draw about the speaker's age and personality?

2. **Analyze** Examine and identify the different rhyme schemes the poet uses. What general statement could you use to describe the poem's rhyme scheme?

3. **Draw Conclusions** Reread lines 1–21. Which scary things are clearly imaginary? Which are possibly real? What effect does this variety of things create in the poem?

4. **Evaluate** Read aloud lines 1–24. Notice the change to couplets and shorter line lengths in the third stanza. What effect does this change have on your reading?

5. **Synthesize** Explain how the structure of the poem and the repetition of the line "Life doesn't frighten me at all" help convey the meaning of the poem. Do you think the speaker of the poem is truly not afraid? Why or why not?

PERFORMANCE TASK

Speaking Activity: Response to Literature Different people can read the same poem aloud in very different ways. Prepare an oral reading of all or a part of "Life Doesn't Frighten Me."

- Every person finds his or her own meanings in a poem. Review the poem and write a statement that summarizes its meaning to you.

- Next, practice reading the poem aloud. At first, focus on the different rhythms, repetition, and sounds.
- Try giving different "personalities" to your reading until you find one that you like.
- Practice until you can read the poem smoothly. Then read it aloud to a small group.

Assign this performance task.

PERFORMANCE TASK

SL 4, SL 6

Speaking Activity: Response to Literature Have students work independently. As they practice, have them try speaking in front of a mirror or recording their reading and listening to it. Direct them to

- keep the meaning of the poem in mind as they speak
- use their voices effectively, speaking with adequate volume and clear pronunciation
- use gestures and facial expressions to emphasize rhythm and feeling

Analyze Structure: Rhyme Scheme

TEACH

Tell students that poets use the sounds of words to help them emphasize meaning, create rhythm, or express emotion. Review that one technique poets use is rhyme, and explain these points:

- **Rhyme** is the repetition of sounds at the end of words, as in the words *pig* and *dig*.
- **End rhyme,** in which rhyming words come at the ends of lines, is the most common type of poetic rhyme.
- **Internal rhyme** is rhyme that occurs within a line of poetry.

Explain that a pattern of end rhymes in a poem is called a rhyme scheme. A **rhyme scheme** is one poetic device that poets often use to give a poem a regular beat, or rhythm. This rhyme and rhythm can help a poet

- convey a particular feeling, experience, or idea
- reinforce the meaning or message of the poem

A rhyme scheme can be identified by assigning a letter to each line in a poem. Lines that rhyme are assigned the same letter. Here is an example from "Life Doesn't Frighten Me" (lines 33–36):

Don't show me frogs and snakes	*a*
And listen for my scream,	*b*
If I'm afraid at all	*c*
It's only in my dreams.	*b*

The rhyme scheme for this stanza is *abcb*. Explain that a poem may have many different rhyme schemes throughout its length, each carefully chosen by the poet to create the rhythm and expression he or she wants to convey to readers.

PRACTICE AND APPLY

Have students work with a partner to analyze the rhyme schemes in "Life Doesn't Frighten Me" stanza by stanza. As they work, ask them to note what effect each rhyme scheme has in the poem and how it makes them feel as readers.

COLLABORATIVE DISCUSSION

After partners complete their analysis, have each pair discuss their responses with the entire class.

 INTERACTIVE WHITEBOARD LESSON Use **Sound Devices in Poetry** for additional instruction.

Analyze Structure: Lyric Poetry

RETEACH

Review that a lyric poem is a kind of poem in which the speaker expresses personal feelings or emotions. Explain that most poems, other than narrative poems, are lyric poems. Remind students of these common poetic elements:

- A **stanza** is a group of two or more lines that form a unit.
- **Repetition** is a technique in which a sound, word, phrase, or line is repeated.
- A **rhyme scheme** is a pattern of rhymes at the ends of lines.
- A **couplet** is a rhymed pair of lines.
- The **speaker** of a poem is the voice that "talks" to the reader. In a lyric poem, the speaker can be the poet, but it doesn't have to be.

To understand a poem well, readers must focus on all its elements and how the poet uses them to create different effects. Readers do this by paying attention to the words and details in the poem.

For example, have students reread aloud lines 28–32 of "Life Doesn't Frighten Me." Ask students what the words "Boys all pull my hair" suggest about the speaker. *(that she is a girl)* Then have them tell what the lines "(Kissy little girls/With their hair in curls)" suggest about the speaker. *(She feels different from the other children in the class.)*

Have students identify and discuss other elements in the poem. Use these questions:

- How many stanzas does the poem have? How are the stanzas alike and how are they different?
- What are the speaker's thoughts and feelings? How similar are they to your own experiences?

INDEPENDENT READING

Individual students or partners can apply these skills to another lyric poem of their choosing. Have them identify specific poetic elements, including the speaker, and the details from the poem that helped them identify these elements.

Fears and Phobias

my **SmartPlanner**   Create lesson plans and access resources online.

Online Article by kidshealth.org

Why This Text?

Students regularly encounter informational text on a variety of topics. This lesson explores the use of text features to organize information and analyze text structure.

▶ **View It!**

Professional Development Podcast:

Informational Text

Key Learning Objective: The student will be able to cite textual evidence to analyze text features and structure.

For practice and application:

Close Reader selection

"Face Your Fears: Choking Under Pressure Is Every Athlete's Worst Nightmare"
Magazine Article by Dana Hudepohl

RI 1   Cite textual evidence; make inferences.
RI 2   Determine a central idea; provide a summary.
RI 3   Analyze text elements.
RI 4   Determine the meaning of words and phrases.
RI 5   Analyze structure.
RI 6   Determine an author's purpose.
W 2   Write informative/explanatory texts.
W 4   Produce clear and coherent writing.
SL 1   Engage effectively in a range of collaborative discussions.
L 1a   Ensure that pronouns are in the proper case.
L 4a   Use context as a clue to the meaning of a word or phrase.
L 4b   Use common Greek or Latin affixes as clues to meaning.
L 4d   Verify preliminary determination of the meaning of a word.
L 6   Acquire and use accurately grade-appropriate general academic and domain-specific words and phrases.

 Text Complexity Rubric

Quantitative Measures	**Fears and Phobias** Lexile: 1080L

Levels of Meaning/Purpose

two topics

Structure

organization of main ideas and details complex; but clearly stated and generally sequential

Qualitative Measures

Language Conventionality and Clarity

increased unfamiliar, academic, or domain-specific words

Knowledge Demands

some specialized knowledge required

Reader/Task Considerations
- Teacher determined
- Vary by individual reader and type of text
- See the Text X-Ray for suggested Reader/Task Considerations.

English Language Support Before teaching, use the Text X-Ray for an overview of the text's complexity. The Text X-Ray and the supports and scaffolds in the Teacher's Edition will help you guide students of different skill levels.

Meaning Making

Language Development

Effective Expression

Content Knowledge

Foundational Skills

Text Complexity: Qualitative Measures

Levels of Meaning/Purpose

two topics

Help students cite evidence in support of important ideas.

- Teacher's Edition side notes, pp. 41, 43, 44, 47
- English Language Support, pp. 42, 44, 46
- When Students Struggle, p. 44
- Close Read Screencasts, p. 41
- Strategies for Annotation, p. 47
- Cite Evidence, p. 47

To reteach citing evidence, see

- Cite Evidence, p. 50a

 Use It! **Level Up Tutorial:** Reading for Details

ZOOM IN ON **CITING EVIDENCE** Tell students that authors of informational text provide **evidence** in the form of **facts, examples, explanations, definitions, direct quotations,** and other **details** to help readers understand the **central idea,** or most important idea.

- Have pairs of students reread lines 107–125.
- Have them make a statement identifying a central idea. *(Phobias develop for different reasons.)*
- Ask students to provide two pieces of evidence to support this central idea. *(A phobia may be caused by a scary experience. The brain then triggers a fear reaction every time the person think about that situation. Some people's personality traits make them more sensitive to fear.)*

Structure

organization of main ideas and details complex; but clearly stated and generally sequential

Help students analyze the structure of an online article.

- Teacher's Edition side notes, pp. 41, 42, 43, 46, 47
- Analyze Structure, p. 47
- Performance Task, p. 48

 Previewing the Text

To teach how to write a summary, see

- Write a Summary, p. 50a

 Use It! **Interactive Whiteboard Lesson:** Summarizing Text

ZOOM IN ON **ANALYZING STRUCTURE** Preview the article, drawing attention to the **subheads.** Explain that each subhead indicates that a new **central idea,** or main idea, will be developed.

- Tell students that one way to focus on the most important ideas and details is to phrase the subhead as a question. The answers to that question will include key points of that section.
- Have students work with a partner to write each subhead as a question. Point out that two of the subheads are already questions. *(How does fear work? What fears do people have? What are childhood fears? What are phobias? How are phobias overcome?)*
- After students have read the article, assign each pair one of the questions to answer in two or three sentences. Have pairs share their answers with the class.

Language Conventionality and Clarity

increased unfamiliar, academic, or domain-specific words

Teach unfamiliar vocabulary in context.

- Teacher's Edition Critical Vocabulary notes, pp. 42, 43, 45, 49
- English Language Support, p. 49
- Applying Academic Vocabulary, p. 43
- Strategies for Annotation, p. 49
- Vocabulary Strategy: Prefixes that Mean "Not", p. 49

Help students to discuss and read informational text.

- Teacher's Edition side notes, pp. 42, 45, 46
- English Language Support, p. 46

Guide students to identify and use subjective and objective pronouns.

- Teacher's Edition side notes, p. 50
- English Language Support, p. 50
- Language Conventions: Subjective and Objective Pronouns, p. 50

ZOOM IN ON **USING CONTEXT CLUES** Tell students that **context clues,** or words and phrases that surround an unfamiliar word, can help them define that word. Stress that the context clue can also be in another sentence. Have pairs of students locate each of the following words, identify a context clue, and define the word:

- *hesitates,* line 1 *("split second," "after a long, slow climb": pauses or stops)*
- *vulnerable,* line 69 *("unsure": unprotected, nervous)*
- *interfere,* line 89 *("normal activities," "feel afraid to walk to school," "avoid a field trip": get in the way of)*
- *generating,* line 129 *("triggers," "false alarm": creating)*

Let students share their clues and definitions.

Knowledge Demands

some specialized knowledge required

Support English Learners in understanding the content of the text.

- Teacher's Edition Background note, p. 41

[HISTORY] For more background, students can view the video "Fear" in their eBooks.

ZOOM IN ON **BUILDING SCIENTIFIC KNOWLEDGE** Before students read, have them view the video in their eBooks. Ask them to note answers to the questions below. Discuss their responses after viewing:

- What is the function of the brain stem? *(It controls involuntary processes in the body.)*
- What is the responsibility of the limbic system? *(to process emotions)*
- What is the amygdala? *(It is a tiny portion of tissue in each hemisphere of the brain; it controls people's emotions.)*

Suggested Reader/Task Considerations

You might consider the following before assigning this article to students.

- Will students be able to maintain their attention throughout their reading of the article?
- Will any questions asked about this text be too complex for students to answer?

ZOOM IN ON **SUPPORTING COMPREHENSION**

- Preview the article with students, pointing out the subheadings that divide it into several sections. Suggest that students read one section at a time with a partner. Before moving on to the next section, have them discuss what they learned.
- Assign small groups one or more of the questions on page 48. Have them use graphic organizers to outline their answers.

TEACH

CLOSE READ

 For more context and historical background, students can view the video *Fear* in their eBooks.

Background Have students read the scientific information that helps explain the ordinary feelings of fear we experience. Explain that everyone experiences fear in varying degrees. The knowledge and insight into fear that science can bring help us understand the purposes fear has for the human body and human survival. The article identifies different types of fear and shows that understanding the fear response helps control it.

SETTING A PURPOSE Direct students to use the Setting a Purpose prompt to focus their reading.

Cite Evidence (LINES 1–5)   RI 1

Explain to students that when they make an **inference** while reading, they use facts and details from the text and their own knowledge to make a logical guess.

A   CITE TEXT EVIDENCE Have students reread lines 1–5. Ask them to make an inference about what it is like to ride a roller coaster and to identify text details and their own knowledge that support their inference. *(Riding a roller coaster is scary but fun; hang on the handrail, sweating, heart racing, bracing for the wild ride; have ridden or watched others ride.)*

Analyze Structure (LINES 6–12)   RI 1, RI 5

Explain that informational texts are often organized using **text features,** such as boldface or colored type, **headings** (titles), or **subheadings** (section titles). Each text feature indicates specific information the author wants the reader to know.

B   CITE TEXT EVIDENCE Have students describe how the subheading "What Is Fear?" and its section fit into the structure of the article. *(The section is key because it provides a common definition of fear for the reader.)*

 English Language Support

Previewing the Text (LINE 1)

Have students view the **Text in Focus** video on this page of their eBook to learn how to preview a nonfiction text. Then have students use **Text in Focus Practice** to apply what they have learned.

Background *Most people experience fear now and then; fear is an ordinary part of life. Some fears may be overcome quickly; others may continue, in varying degrees, for a lifetime. Science provides knowledge and insight into why we experience fear and why sometimes our fears seem out of control. Whether it is a fear of spiders, a fear of the dark, or a fear of flying, using science to understand the physical and emotional responses that we call fear is the first step toward conquering it.*

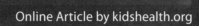

Fears and Phobias

Online Article by kidshealth.org

SETTING A PURPOSE As you read, pay attention to the details that explain the nature of fear and how fear can affect everyday life, both physically and emotionally.

A The roller coaster hesitates for a split second at the peak of its steep track after a long, slow climb. You know what's about to happen—and there's no way to avoid it now. It's time to hang onto the handrail, palms sweating, heart racing, and brace yourself for the wild ride down.

 Text in FOCUS

What Is Fear?

B Fear is one of the most basic human emotions. It is programmed into the nervous system and works like an instinct. From the time we're infants, we are equipped with the survival instincts necessary to respond with fear when we
10 sense danger or feel unsafe.

Fear helps protect us. It makes us alert to danger and prepares us to deal with it. Feeling afraid is very natural—and

 (tl) ©Corbis, (tr)©Superstock

Close Read Screencasts

Modeled Discussions

Have students click the *Close Read* icon in their eBook to access a screencast in which readers discuss and annotate a passage from lines 107–114 in the section under the heading "What Causes Phobias?" This passage provides some information about what causes phobias.

As a class, view and discuss the video. Then have students pair up to do an independent close read of an additional passage—a discussion of how people might overcome their phobias (lines 147–162).

Analyze Language RI 4

(LINES 26–29)

Remind students that **quotation marks** are punctuation that normally set off a speaker's exact words. Sometimes they are used to indicate a term that has a special meaning, such as that someone is using these words with a meaning beyond the words themselves.

C **ASK STUDENTS** to reread lines 26–29 and point out the phrases in quotation marks. *("fight or flight"; "all clear")* Have students tell what the phrases mean and why they think the phrases are emphasized this way. *(Meanings: fight danger or run away; danger is gone; the author wants readers to understand these terms clearly and remember them.)*

Analyze Structure (SIDEBAR) RI 5

Explain to students that a **sidebar** is a part of an article that contains information that is related but slightly different from the basic information the author is explaining. Tell students that this information is often set off in a box or colored space, near to other text it is somewhat related to.

D **CITE TEXT EVIDENCE** Ask students to find a sidebar in the article. *(purple box titled "FEAR OR FUN?")* Have them reread the sidebar and tell how the ideas in it differ from the rest of the article but are still related to it. *(It is about fear, but it presents the idea that scary things terrify some people, whereas others love to be scared; this isn't mentioned in the article.)*

CRITICAL VOCABULARY

activate: When we feel danger, our brain starts a reaction that causes many changes in our bodies.

ASK STUDENTS what physical responses are activated by the signal from the nervous system. *(heart beats faster, pressure increases, skin sweats)*

trigger: The article explains that a reaction to danger can be caused instantly, but sometimes that cause is not dangerous at all.

ASK STUDENTS how the fear reaction is triggered and turned off by the brain in only seconds. *(When the brain perceives no danger, it stops the reaction.)*

---

helpful—in some situations. Fear can be like a warning, a signal that cautions us to be careful.

Like all emotions, fear can be mild, medium, or intense, depending on the situation and the person. A feeling of fear can be brief or it can last longer.

How Fear Works

When we sense danger, the brain reacts instantly, sending signals that **activate** the nervous system. This causes physical
20 responses, such as a faster heartbeat, rapid breathing, and an increase in blood pressure. Blood pumps to muscle groups to prepare the body for physical action (such as running or fighting). Skin sweats to keep the body cool. Some people might notice sensations in the stomach, head, chest, legs, or hands. These physical sensations of fear can be mild or strong.

This response is known as "fight or flight" because that is exactly what the body is preparing itself to do: fight off the danger or run fast to get away. The body stays in this state of fight-flight until the brain receives an "all clear" message and
30 turns off the response.

Sometimes fear is **triggered** by something that is startling or unexpected (like a loud noise), even if it's not actually dangerous. That's because the fear reaction is activated instantly—a few seconds faster than the thinking part of the brain can process or evaluate what's happening. As soon as the brain gets enough information to realize there's no danger ("Oh, it's just a balloon bursting—whew!"), it turns off the fear reaction. All this can happen in seconds.

activate

(ăk´tə-vāt´) *v.* To *activate* something means to cause it to start working.

trigger

(trĭg´ər) *v.* To *trigger* something means to cause it to begin.

D **FEAR OR FUN?**

Some people find the rush of fear exciting. They might seek out the thrill of extreme sports and savor the scariest horror flicks. Others do not like the experience of feeling afraid or taking risks. During the scariest moments of a roller coaster ride one person might think, "I'll never get on this thing again—that is, if I make it out alive!" while another person thinks, "This is awesome! As soon as it's over, I'm getting back on!"

English Language Support

Evaluate Language Choices Display lines 21–23 of the text. Ask students to
- Highlight in yellow the parenthetical information (such as running or fighting).
- Highlight in green the words physical action.

ASK STUDENTS to discuss with a partner how the text in parentheses is related to physical action. *(examples of physical activity.)* Have students evaluate the author's language choices, using the following sentence starters:

Why does the author _____?

I think the author did this because _____.

E ## Fears People Have

Fear is the word we use to describe our emotional reaction to
40 something that seems dangerous. But the word "fear" is used
in another way, too: to name something a person often feels
afraid of.

People fear things or situations that make them feel unsafe
or unsure. For instance, someone who isn't a strong swimmer
might have a fear of deep water. In this case, the fear is helpful
because it cautions the person to stay safe. Someone could
overcome this fear by learning how to swim safely.

F A fear can be healthy if it cautions a person to stay safe
around something that could be dangerous. But sometimes a
50 fear is unnecessary and causes more caution than the situation
calls for.

Many people have a fear of public speaking. Whether it's
giving a report in class, speaking at an assembly, or reciting
lines in the school play, speaking in front of others is one of
the most common fears people have.

People tend to avoid the situations or things they fear. But
this doesn't help them overcome fear—in fact, it can be the
reverse. Avoiding something scary reinforces a fear and keeps
it strong.

60 People can overcome unnecessary fears by giving
themselves the chance to learn about and gradually get used
to the thing or situation they're afraid of. For example, people
who fly despite a fear of flying can become used to unfamiliar
sensations like takeoff or **turbulence**. They learn what to
expect and have a chance to watch what others do to relax
and enjoy the flight. Gradually (and safely) facing fear helps
someone overcome it.

Fears During Childhood

Certain fears are normal during childhood. That's because fear
can be a natural reaction to feeling unsure and vulnerable—
70 and much of what children experience is new and unfamiliar.

Young kids often have fears of the dark, being alone,
strangers, and monsters or other scary imaginary creatures.
School-aged kids might be afraid when it's stormy or at a first
sleepover. As they grow and learn, with the support of adults,
most kids are able to slowly conquer these fears and outgrow
them.

turbulence
(tûr´byə-ləns) *n.* In
flying, *turbulence*
is an interruption
in the flow of wind
that causes planes to
rise, fall, or sway in a
rough way.

Fears and Phobias **43**

APPLYING ACADEMIC VOCABULARY

similar	specific

THINK-PAIR-SHARE Have students turn to a partner to discuss the
following questions. Guide students to include the academic vocabulary
words *similar* and *specific* in their responses. Ask volunteers to share their
responses with the class.

- Which fears that people have are **similar** to each other?
- How do **specific** fears and phobias affect different people in different
ways?

Analyze Structure   RI 1, RI 5
(SUBHEADS)

Explain to students that authors often use subheads
to present important ideas and to organize
information into sections for readers. Readers can use
these subheads to find specific kinds of information
within the text.

E **CITE TEXT EVIDENCE** Have students find and
read aloud the subheads above lines 39 and 68. *(Fears
People Have; Fears During Childhood)* Ask them to tell
how the subheads are related and how they help
the reader understand the information that follows
them. *(Each one names a category of "Fears"; they tell
the reader what type of fears will be explained in that
section of the text.)*

Cite Evidence   RI 1, RI 5
(LINES 43–67)

Explain that authors often organize similar
information into a series of paragraphs.

F **CITE TEXT EVIDENCE** Ask students to list some
fears people have. *(deep water, public speaking, flying)*
Then have them describe a helpful or healthy fear
and an unnecessary fear and tell how they found the
information. *(looking under the subhead "Fears People
Have")*

CRITICAL VOCABULARY

turbulence: The author uses the word *turbulence*
to describe a specific kind of sensation that may
occur during flying. The phrase "It's just turbulence"
might be frightening to someone who doesn't fly
often.

ASK STUDENTS to discuss why an interruption in
the flow of the wind makes turbulence terrifying.
Have them consider what turbulence feels like to
a passenger. *(A plane flying into a steady wind flies
smoothly. If the plane bounces, as it does during
turbulence, it may seem like the plane is no longer
flying or that it is falling out of the sky.)*

Cite Evidence (LINES 77–106)

RI 1,
RI 3

Remind students that they need to support conclusions or statements they make about a text by citing information from the text.

G **CITE TEXT EVIDENCE** Have students reread lines 77–106 and then make a statement about that section of the text, citing evidence from the text. *(Possible answer: A person with a phobia may feel unsafe in an everyday, safe situation. Seeing a dog or riding an elevator are usually safe, but a person with a phobia about dogs or elevators would be scared; lines 86–92.)*

English Language Support

Read Closely Have students work with a partner to reread lines 77–106. Ask partners to take turns reading paragraphs aloud while the other student takes notes about the important ideas. Then have them each write a statement and use their notes to provide text evidence. Invite volunteers to share their statements and text evidence with the class.

Analyze Language

RI 1,
RI 4

(LINES 108–110)

Explain to students that **boldface type** indicates a word or phrase that the reader should note. Tell students that authors often emphasize terms whose meaning most readers would not know and/or may not know how to pronounce.

CITE TEXT EVIDENCE Have students reread lines 108–110 to identify and pronounce a boldface term they find there. *(amygdala)* Ask them to find the words that define what the term means and its function in the body. *(meaning: a tiny brain structure; function: keeps track of experiences that trigger strong emotions)*

Some kids are more sensitive to fears and may have a tough time overcoming them. When fears last beyond the expected age, it might be a sign that someone is overly fearful, worried, or anxious. People whose fears are too intense or last too long might need help and support to overcome them.

80

G **Phobias**

A phobia is an intense fear reaction to a particular thing or a situation. With a phobia, the fear is out of proportion to the potential danger. But to the person with the phobia, the danger feels real because the fear is so very strong.

Phobias cause people to worry about, dread, feel upset by, and avoid the things or situations they fear because the physical sensations of fear can be so intense. So having a phobia can interfere with normal activities. A person with a phobia of dogs might feel afraid to walk to school in case he or she sees a dog on the way. Someone with an elevator phobia might avoid a field trip if it involves going on an elevator.

90

A girl with a phobia of thunderstorms might be afraid to go to school if the weather forecast predicts a storm. She might feel terrible distress and fear when the sky turns cloudy. A guy with social phobia experiences intense fear of public speaking or interacting, and may be afraid to answer questions in class, give a report, or speak to classmates in the lunchroom.

It can be exhausting and upsetting to feel the intense fear that goes with having a phobia. It can be disappointing to miss out on opportunities because fear is holding you back. And it can be confusing and embarrassing to feel afraid of things that others seem to have no problem with.

100

Sometimes, people get teased about their fears. Even if the person doing the teasing doesn't mean to be unkind and unfair, teasing only makes the situation worse.

▶ Close Read **What Causes Phobias?**

Some phobias develop when someone has a scary experience with a particular thing or situation. A tiny brain structure called the **amygdala** (pronounced: uh-mig-duh-luh) keeps track of experiences that trigger strong emotions. Once a certain thing or situation triggers a strong fear reaction, the amygdala warns the person by triggering a fear reaction every

H 10

44 Collection 1

WHEN STUDENTS STRUGGLE . . .

Have individuals or partners use a Comparison-Contrast Chart to compare fears and phobias. Ask them to highlight similarities in one color and differences in another. Students may choose different aspects to compare than the ones shown here.

	Fears	*Phobias*
What It Is	*basic emotion, warning*	*intense fear, false alarm*
What It Is Not	*sign of weakness*	*sign of weakness*
How It Works	*brain signals "fight or flight"*	*brain signals "fight or flight"*

LEVEL UP TUTORIALS For additional support, assign the following *Level Up* tutorial: **Reading for Details.**

© Uli Wiesmeier/Corbis

time he or she encounters (or even thinks about) that thing or situation.

Someone might develop a bee phobia after being stung during a particularly scary situation. For that person, looking at a photograph of a bee, seeing a bee from a distance, or even walking near flowers where there *could* be a bee can all trigger the phobia.

120   Sometimes, though, there may be no single event that causes a particular phobia. Some people may be more sensitive to fears because of personality traits they are born with, certain genes[1] they've inherited, or situations they've experienced. People who have had strong childhood fears or anxiety may be more likely to have one or more phobias.

Having a phobia isn't a sign of weakness or **immaturity**. It's a response the brain has learned in an attempt to protect the person. It's as if the brain's alert system triggers a false alarm, generating intense fear that is out of proportion to the

immaturity
(ĭm´ə-tyŏŏr´ĭ-tē) *n.*
Immaturity is the state of not being fully developed or grown.

---

[1] **genes** (jēnz): the parts of cells that give a living thing its physical characteristics and make it grow and develop; a person's genes come from their parents and other blood relatives.

FOR STUDENTS WITH DISABILITIES

Students may struggle to hold the student book in position while reading this selection and others. A rubber mat on a desk can help prevent the book from slipping while turning the pages of the book. A page turning device may also be required to make reading easier. For students who prefer to read and listen to the eBook, a pointer or typing stick with rubber strips attached to prevent slipping can assist in manipulating keyboard navigation keys.

CLOSE READ

RI 1,
RI 4

Analyze Language
(LINES 116–119)

Explain to students that authors often repeat certain words or phrases to catch readers' attention and clarify an important set of facts. This repetition produces a rhythm in language that helps engage readers and push them forward.

Ⓘ CITE TEXT EVIDENCE   Have students review lines 116–119, find the use of repetition, and discuss how this repetition affects them. *(repetition of* bee *three times; different instances of seeing a bee indicate that a real bee isn't necessary to provoke a phobia.)*

RI 1,
RI 4

Analyze Language (LINE 123)

Explain to students that authors often need to use technical terms in an article that covers scientific topics. Note that if authors had to stop to define these terms, the flow of the text would be interrupted. Instead, authors use footnotes, which provide a definition at the bottom of the page. Explain that a superscript number links each word to its definition.

Ⓙ CITE TEXT EVIDENCE   Have students reread line 123, identify the word with a superscript number, and read its definition. *(genes)*

CRITICAL VOCABULARY

immaturity: The author uses the word *immaturity* to remind the reader not to think that a phobia might simply be something only a child would have.

ASK STUDENTS to discuss what kinds of fear reactions might be the result of immaturity. *(A child might be frightened of a clown or a shadow because these are misunderstood or new and surprising; once he or she got older, that fear would probably go away.)*

Analyze Structure

RI 1,
RI 5

(LINES 132–158)

Explain to students that authors use the overall structure of an article to present important ideas about the topic in a logical sequence.

 ASK STUDENTS to review the article's subheadings in order, including this last one. Have them explain the sequence of ideas the subheadings of each section show. (*Sections first tell what fear is and how it works. Next, readers learn about different types of fears and about phobias and what causes them. Finally, the last section presents a solution for overcoming phobias.*)

L **CITE TEXT EVIDENCE** Have students reread lines 132–158 and explain how the important ideas and details in this section connect to the rest of the article. (*This section is about facing a fear and getting used to it. Each step focuses on gradually decreasing the person's fear until the brain adjusts its response to whatever was causing the phobia. The section uses a phobia of dogs as its example, a phobia that was discussed in earlier sections as well.*)

COLLABORATIVE DISCUSSION Have students form partnerships to locate text evidence that defines the differences between fears and phobias. Students can discuss examples as further definition of the differences and explain why fears and phobias are useful, harmful, or both.

ASK STUDENTS to share any questions they generated in the course of reading and discussing the selection.

English Language Support

Exchange Information Have students work with a partner to create a compare and contrast chart of text evidence that defines the differences between fears and phobias. Remind students to list the line number beside each piece of information. Then have students use the information in their charts to help in their explanations about the usefulness and harmfulness of fears and phobias.

---

130 situation. Because the fear signal is so intense, the person is convinced the danger is greater than it actually is.

Overcoming Phobias **K**

People can learn to overcome phobias by gradually facing their fears. This is not easy at first. It takes willingness and bravery. Sometimes people need the help of a therapist[2] to guide them through the process.

Overcoming a phobia usually starts with making a long list of the person's fears in least-to-worst order. For example, with a dog phobia, the list might start with the things the person is least afraid of, such as looking at a photo of a dog. It 140 will then work all the way up to worst fears, such as standing next to someone who's petting a dog, petting a dog on a leash, and walking a dog.

Gradually, and with support, the person tries each fear situation on the list—one at a time, starting with the least fear. The person isn't forced to do anything and works on each fear until he or she feels comfortable, taking as long as needed.

A therapist could also show someone with a dog phobia how to approach, pet, and walk a dog, and help the person to try it, too. The person may expect terrible things to happen 150 when near a dog. Talking about this can help, too. When people find that what they fear doesn't actually turn out to be true, it can be a great relief.

A therapist might also teach relaxation practices such as specific ways of breathing, muscle relaxation training, or soothing self-talk. These can help people feel comfortable and bold enough to face the fears on their list.

As somebody gets used to a feared object or situation, the brain adjusts how it responds and the phobia is overcome.

Often, the hardest part of overcoming a phobia is getting 160 started. Once a person decides to go for it—and gets the right coaching and support—it can be surprising how quickly fear can melt away.

COLLABORATIVE DISCUSSION Fears and phobias are related, but they are quite different in some ways. With a partner, use evidence from the text to discuss these differences. Which response can be useful? Which one can be harmful, and why?

---

[2] **therapist** (thĕr´ə-pĭst): a person who is skilled in treating mental or physical illness.

English Language Support

Improve Reading Fluency Have students work with partners to read the text in Overcoming Phobias. First, use lines 132–135 to model for students how to read informational text. Have students follow along in their books as you read the text in measured tones. Then, have partners take turns reading aloud each paragraph in the section. Encourage students to provide feedback and support for pronouncing multisyllabic words. Remind students that when they are reading informational text aloud for an audience they should avoid reading too quickly and pace their reading so that the audience has time to understand difficult concepts and/or examples.

Cite Evidence

RI 1

To support analysis of any text that you read, you need to be able to **cite evidence,** or provide specific information from the text. Evidence can include details, facts, statistics, quotations, and examples. The chart shows different ways to cite evidence from an informational text such as "Fears and Phobias."

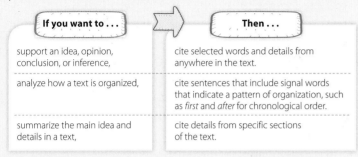

If you want to . . .	Then . . .
support an idea, opinion, conclusion, or inference,	cite selected words and details from anywhere in the text.
analyze how a text is organized,	cite sentences that include signal words that indicate a pattern of organization, such as *first* and *after* for chronological order.
summarize the main idea and details in a text,	cite details from specific sections of the text.

After reading "Fears and Phobias," imagine that you came to the conclusion that when we are afraid, our bodies respond in many ways. To support your conclusion, you could cite lines 18–25 as examples from the text.

Analyze Structure

RI 5

Text features are design elements such as boldface type and headings that highlight the organization and important information in a text. You can use text features to get an idea of the topics in a text. They can also help you locate particular topics or ideas after reading. Text features include:

- A **heading** is a kind of title that identifies the topic of the content that follows it. Headings often appear at the beginning of a chapter or article.
- A **subheading** is a kind of title that usually indicates the beginning of a new topic or section within a chapter or article. A subheading helps you identify the main idea of the text that follows.
- A **sidebar** is additional information that is usually set in a box alongside or within an article.

Analyze text features by asking yourself these questions:

- What text features does the text include?
- Which features help me preview and locate main ideas in the text?
- How does information under a particular heading fit into the whole text? What important ideas does it contain?

CLOSE READ

Cite Evidence

RI 1

Help students understand the terms and concepts that are necessary for citing evidence when making statements about and analyzing an informational text. Have students focus on both the types of evidence or specific information (details, facts, statistics, quotations, examples) as well as the purposes for citing evidence shown in the chart (supporting an idea, analyzing text, summarizing.)

Then remind students that all of these purposes and information can be used together for a variety of reasons when gathering information from an article. Have students reread lines 18–25 from "Fears and Phobias" to verify the conclusion discussed here.

Analyze Structure

RI 5

Help students understand that using text features makes it easier for them to understand important information in an article. Stress that the author uses text features to help the reader. Go over each of the features shown in the bulleted list, and review examples of each in the text.

Next, have students answer the questions that are listed at the bottom of the page. Tell them to refer to headings or details from the article itself and to discuss how the article's structure helps the reader better understand the information presented.

Strategies for Annotation 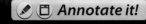 *Annotate it!*

Cite Evidence

RI 1

Share these strategies for guided or independent analysis:

- Highlight in yellow evidence supporting an idea, opinion, conclusion, or inference.
- Highlight in green text features that help organize or call attention to important details.
- Review your highlights. On a note, jot down a summary of the information presented.

How Fear Works

When we sense danger, the brain reacts instantly, sending signals that activate the nervous system. This causes physical responses, such as a faster heartbeat, rapid breathing, and an increase in blood pressure. Blood pumps to muscle groups to prepare the body for physical action.

Analyzing the Text

RI 1, RI 3, RI 5, RI 6

Possible answers:

1. *When a sense of danger is caused, the effect is that our heart beats faster, we breathe more quickly, and our blood pressure increases. When the brain learns a situation is not dangerous, it sends signals to turn off the fear reaction.*

2. *The text says that some phobias may arise from a "particularly scary situation" but that others may be related to personality traits or to genes a person has inherited.*

3. *The author says that it takes willingness and bravery to overcome a phobia. Therapy might include making a list of least-to-worst possible events and working through each one, or it might include relaxation techniques, such as breathing exercises. The author thinks that overcoming a phobia is worth the effort, because having one can be "exhausting and upsetting" and can cause people to "miss out on opportunities."*

4. *Fear is an emotion. In our body, it works like an instinct to help protect us from danger. Examples include the fear we feel at the beginning of a roller coaster ride or a fear of deep water if a person cannot swim. A phobia is an intense fear that is out of proportion to the actual danger. An example used in the text is a person with a bee phobia who might be very fearful when walking near flowers.*

5. *The sidebar explains that some people find fear exciting and others do not like the experience. It helps the reader understand that two people might view experiences such as horror movies or roller coaster rides differently; even though their physical reactions may be similar, their emotional reactions are not.*

6. *The author first presents ideas about fear, what it is, how it works, and what fears people have and when they have them. Then the author discusses phobias, what causes them, and how they can be overcome.*

Analyzing the Text

RI 1, RI 3, RI 5, RI 6, W 2, W 4

Cite Text Evidence Support your responses with evidence from the text.

1. **Cause/Effect** Events are often related by **cause and effect**: one event brings about the other. The event that happens first is the **cause**; the one that follows is the **effect**. Reread lines 18–38. Examine the text and identify examples of cause-and-effect relationships.

2. **Cite Evidence** What causes phobias? Cite evidence from the text that explains where phobias come from.

3. **Draw Conclusions** Review lines 132–162. What factors are important in helping people overcome phobias? Explain whether the author believes it is worthwhile to try to overcome phobias and why.

4. **Compare** Explain how a fear is different from a phobia. Identify examples of each that the author presents.

5. **Interpret** What additional information does the sidebar provide? How does it add to your understanding of the article?

6. **Analyze** Use the headings in "Fears and Phobias" to examine the main ideas the author presents. In your own words, describe the way the author orders the information.

PERFORMANCE TASK

Writing Activity: Summary Write a summary of "Fears and Phobias." A **summary** is a brief retelling of a text in your own words. You should cover only the main ideas and most important details. Your summary should be no more than one-third the length of the original text.

• Review the article to identify the main ideas.

• Introduce the summary by writing a topic sentence that explains the main purpose of the article.

• Tell what a fear is, what a phobia is, and how they are different. Cite evidence from the text.

• Conclude your summary by telling why the article is useful or important.

PERFORMANCE TASK

RI 2, W 2, W 4

Assign this performance task.

Writing Activity: Summary Have students work independently. Direct them to briefly retell the information in the text in their own words. Emphasize that their summary should

• be less than one-third as long as the text

• stress main ideas

• begin with a topic sentence

• differentiate between a fear and a phobia

• tell why the article was useful

Critical Vocabulary

L 4a, L 4b, L 4d, L 6

activate   trigger   turbulence   immaturity

Practice and Apply Answer each question and explain your response.

1. Which of the following is an example of **activate**? Why?
   unplugging a computer   pressing the power button on a computer

2. Which of the following is most likely to **trigger** an allergy? Why?
   getting stung by a bee   watching a movie about bees

3. Which of the following involves **turbulence**? Why?
   a canoe trip on a quiet lake   a canoe trip on a rushing, rocky river

4. Which of the following is an example of **immaturity**? Why?
   explaining why you are upset   crying when you don't get your way

Vocabulary Strategy: Prefixes That Mean "Not"

A **prefix** is a word that appears at the beginning of a base word to form a new word. Many prefixes that mean "not" come from Latin, the language of ancient Rome. One example is the vocabulary word *immaturity* (*im + maturity*). To figure out the meaning of a word that contains a prefix and a base word, follow these steps.

- Think of the meaning of each word part separately.
- Use this information as well as context clues to define the word.

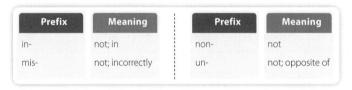

Prefix	Meaning		Prefix	Meaning
in-	not; in		non-	not
mis-	not; incorrectly		un-	not; opposite of

Practice and Apply Use the prefixes in the chart and context clues to help you determine a meaning for the boldface word in each sentence.

1. Not having Sunday hours at the library is **inconvenient** for people who work during the week.

2. The group agreed that their protest would be a **nonviolent** one.

3. Being late to the party was **unintentional;** we were stuck in traffic!

4. The careless reporter **misquoted** the mayor's remarks.

PRACTICE & APPLY

Critical Vocabulary

L 4a, L 4b, L 4d, L 6

Answers:

1. *pressing the power button on a computer; because doing this starts a process in the computer*

2. *getting stung by a bee; because it may set off an allergic reaction*

3. *a canoe trip on a rushing, rocky river; because it involves roughness and unsteadiness*

4. *crying when you don't get your way; someone who is more grown up would be able to explain something in a calm way*

Vocabulary Strategy: Prefixes That Mean "Not"

Answers:

1. *inconvenient:* not convenient

2. *nonviolent:* not violent; peaceful

3. *unintentional:* not on purpose

4. *misquoted:* incorrectly stated

English Language Support

Determine Word Meanings Give students additional practice in determining the meaning of unknown words. Write the following words on the board: *incurable, impossible, mislead, nonsense, unknown.* Have pairs of students copy the words, underline the prefixes, and write definitions. Tell them to confirm their definitions by looking up each word in a dictionary.

Strategies for Annotation   🖊 📋 *Annotate it!*

Prefixes That Mean "Not"

L 4a, L 4b, L 4d, L 6

Have students locate the words *unsafe, unsure,* and *unnecessary* in lines 43–51. Tell them to use their eBook annotation tools to do the following:

- Highlight in yellow each word that contains a prefix that means "not."
- Underline the base word of each highlighted word.
- Highlight in green any words in the sentence that help you determine the meanings of these words.
- Apply the idea of "not" to the meanings of the base words to confirm the overall meanings.

People fear things or situations that make them feel <u>unsafe</u> or <u>unsure</u>. For instance, someone who isn't a strong swimmer might have a fear of deep water. In this case, the fear is helpful because it cautions the person to stay safe.

Language Conventions: Subjective and Objective Pronouns

L 1a

Tell students that pronouns are most often misused when the speaker does not pay attention to the case of the pronoun. Review with students how a pronoun can be either in the **subjective** or **objective** case depending on if it is being used as a **subject** in a sentence or as an **object** of a verb or preposition.

Answers:

1. *him*

2. *they*

3. *me*

4. *they*

5. *I*

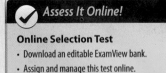

Assess It Online!

Online Selection Test
- Download an editable ExamView bank.
- Assign and manage this test online.

Language Conventions: Subjective and Objective Pronouns

L 1a

A **pronoun** is a word that takes the place of a noun or another pronoun. Personal pronouns take different forms, or cases, depending on how they are used in a sentence. A pronoun in the **subjective case** is one that is used as the subject of a sentence. A pronoun in the **objective case** is one that is used as an object of a verb or preposition. Here are some examples from "Fears and Phobias."

> Subjective Case: *It is programmed into the nervous system.*
> Objective Case: *Fear helps protect us.*

Pronouns can also be singular or plural in number. This chart shows the singular and plural forms of the subjective and objective case.

		Subjective	Objective
Singular	First person	I	me
	Second person	you	you
	Third person	she, he, it	her, him, it
Plural	First person	we	us
	Second person	you	you
	Third person	they	them

Pronouns can be misused, especially in compound subjects and objects. Use a **subject pronoun** if the pronoun is part of a compound subject. Use an **object pronoun** if the pronoun is part of a compound object.

Practice and Apply Choose the correct pronoun to complete each sentence.

1. Carlos took swimming lessons to help (him, it) overcome a fear of deep water.

2. When some people experience extreme fear, (you, they) may feel sick or dizzy.

3. I do not like small spaces. Being in an elevator makes (her, me) very anxious.

4. Danielle and Ramon explained how (he, they) use breathing exercises to help stay relaxed.

5. Leia and (I, me) are sometimes teased about our fears.

English Language Support

Use Subjective and Objective Pronouns Write the following sentences on the board. Work with students to choral read each sentence, replacing the object with all possible pronouns. Discuss why certain pronouns do not work in each sentence.

- I *(subjective pronouns: you, she, he, we, they)* took the book from *(objective pronouns: him, her, them, you)*.
- They *(subjective pronouns: you, we)* were singing in front of *(objective pronouns: me, us, you, him, her it)*.

Ask volunteers to underline the subjective pronoun in each sentence. Discuss which subjective pronouns work in each sentence, making sure that students understand that objective pronouns may also have to be changed.

- Have students work independently to write sentences using each of the subjective and objective pronouns from the chart on page 50. Have them read their sentences aloud to a partner. Then have partners use different pronouns in their sentences, reading them aloud to check their replacements.

INTERACTIVE WHITEBOARD LESSON
Write a Summary

RI 2,
W 2,
W 4

Learn the Skill ▶ How to Summarize Literary Texts ▶ **The Steps**

Steps for Summarizing

Read the following summary of the short story "Seventh Grade" by Gary Soto.

Click Steps 1–4 to see examples of each summary feature.

Original Text

Step 1

Step 2

Step 3

Step 4

The short story "Seventh Grade" by Gary Soto tells about a seventh grader named Victor who lives in Fresno, California. Victor likes a girl at school named Teresa and spends a lot of time trying to get up the courage to talk to her. Victor's friend, Michael, suggests that Victor get Teresa's attention by scowling at her because he thinks girls like this. In the end, though, Victor gets Teresa's attention by pretending to be good at speaking French in French class. The two then make plans to study together.

TEACH

Explain to students that **summarizing** is briefly retelling the important ideas of a text in one's own words. Before students begin the Performance Task, explain the steps for writing a summary:

- **Step 1:** List the title, author, and text type.
- **Step 2:** Identify the author's main ideas. Explain that a **main idea** is the most important idea about a topic. It can be an overall main idea for the whole article as well as a main idea for an individual section or paragraph.
- **Step 3:** Identify key details. Tell students that **details** are facts, examples, definitions, anecdotes, quotations, and other elements that explain and support the main ideas.

Finally, explain that a summary should be brief—no more than one-third the length of the original text.

PRACTICE AND APPLY

After completing the Practice and Apply screens of the IWB lesson, have students review "Fears and Phobias" and offer their own summaries of each section of the article. Students can then use these section summaries to write their summary of the entire article.

Cite Evidence

RI 1

RETEACH

Remind students that it is not just enough to read an informational article; they need to be able to go back and find specific information they just read in order to support their ideas, opinions, statements, and conclusions about a topic. Explain that citing evidence is also necessary when summarizing, reinforcing what they have learned, or conducting research.

Have students return to "Fears and Phobias" to find different types of evidence, such as the following:

- **facts or statistics** that support ideas
- **details** that support important ideas
- **examples** of different fears and phobias

Then have partners practice stating a conclusion and citing evidence to support it from the text.

LEVEL UP TUTORIALS Assign the following *Level Up* tutorial (section on Nonfiction): **Reading for Details**

INDEPENDENT READING

Individual students can apply these skills to a magazine article or a textbook they may be reading on their own. Have them state conclusions or give opinions about the text and then cite evidence from their reading to support their ideas.

Face Your Fears: Choking Under Pressure Is Every Athlete's Worst Nightmare

Magazine Article by Dana Hudepohl

Why This Text

Students often finish reading a magazine article without a complete understanding of the author's central (or main) ideas. Articles such as this one by Dana Hudepohl may have more than one complex central idea. Guide students to recognize that some central ideas are directly stated, while others are implied. With the help of the close-reading questions, students will cite text evidence to support analysis of ideas that are explicitly stated as well as implied. This close reading will lead students to develop a coherent understanding of the most important ideas and supporting evidence in an informational text.

Background Have students read the background information that defines the meaning of "choking" as used in athletics. Introduce the selection by sharing this definition: "Choking refers to the failure to perform well during a key moment." Point out that as a health writer, Dana Hudepohl uses information about athletes' experiences to discuss the handling of fear and stress effectively while dealing with the pressure to succeed at competitive sports.

SETTING A PURPOSE Ask students to pay close attention to the central ideas in this article and to the text evidence that supports those ideas. How soon does Hudepohl present the article's central idea?

Standards Support

- cite textual evidence
- determine the central (or main) ideas in a text
- provide a summary of a text distinct from personal opinions and judgments
- analyze the interactions among individuals, events, or ideas in a text

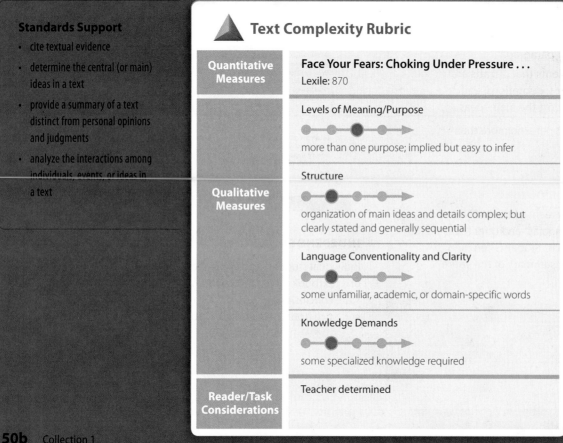

Text Complexity Rubric

Quantitative Measures

Face Your Fears: Choking Under Pressure . . .
Lexile: 870

Qualitative Measures

Levels of Meaning/Purpose
more than one purpose; implied but easy to infer

Structure
organization of main ideas and details complex; but clearly stated and generally sequential

Language Conventionality and Clarity
some unfamiliar, academic, or domain-specific words

Knowledge Demands
some specialized knowledge required

Reader/Task Considerations

Teacher determined

Strategies for CLOSE READING

Cite Evidence

Students should read this article carefully all the way through. Close-reading questions at the bottom of the page will help them focus on a thorough analysis of the central (or main) ideas and on the evidence, including details, facts, statistics, quotations, examples, and anecdotes, that support them. As they read, students should record comments or questions about the text in the side margins.

WHEN STUDENTS STRUGGLE . . .

To practice citing evidence that supports the central ideas of an informational text, students should work in small groups to fill out a two-column chart such as the one shown below.

CITE TEXT EVIDENCE For practice in providing textual evidence from an informational text, ask students to examine the evidence that supports a central (or main) idea.

Central Idea	Text Evidence
It is possible for athletes to overcome their fear and succeed.	Wilkinson faced her fears the night before the final round of diving and was able to move on and win.
	Lindquist overcame her fears by staying focused on the job at hand.
	Hickman doesn't allow fear to overcome her during a race but, like Lindquist, focuses on the job that needs to get done.

Background *In athletics, choking refers to the failure to perform well during a key moment. For example, a golfer who misses an easy putt in the closing moments of a tournament is said to have "choked." In this article from* Sports Illustrated for Women, *three competitors offer their advice on how to handle fear and stress effectively while dealing with pressure to succeed.*

Face Your Fears:
Choking Under Pressure Is Every Athlete's Worst Nightmare

Magazine Article by Dana Hudepohl

CLOSE READ
Notes

1. **READ ▶** As you read lines 1–31, begin to collect and cite text evidence.

- In the margin, briefly explain what is happening in lines 1–7.
- Circle the key to Wilkinson's victory and the reaction of the fans (lines 8–12).
- Underline details that describe Wilkinson's experience at her first international meet.

(A) As she stood on the 10-meter platform at the Sydney Olympics, Laura Wilkinson knew she had to nail her fourth dive to clinch the gold. The pressure was intense: Head-to-head against the toughest divers in the world, she had to be flawless. "In a way I felt I was putting more pressure on myself than I could handle," says Wilkinson, 23. "But I felt like I had nothing to lose. There are more important things than fear."

With that calm attitude, she aced her fourth and fifth dives and won the gold. Her upset victory (she went from fifth to first after three dives) stunned competitors and fans. The key to Wilkinson's victory? Confidence, which was something she had worked on developing in her training.

Laura Wilkinson had to move beyond her fear while diving at the Olympics.

9

---

1. **READ AND CITE TEXT EVIDENCE** Explain to students that the central idea in the first paragraph (lines 1–7) is not stated directly, but implied. Explain that in order to identify an implied central idea, students need to examine the details to determine what the writer intended.

(A) ASK STUDENTS to examine the details to infer the central idea of the first paragraph by citing specific textual evidence from lines 1–7. *Responses may include references to evidence in lines 3–7.*

FOR ELL STUDENTS Explain that *head-to-head* is an idiomatic phrase (or expression). Ask students if they know what it means. How does the idiomatic phrase help suggest the central idea of the paragraph? *Students should see that it expresses the pressure and fear Wilkinson felt, which she knew she had to move beyond in order to win.*

Wilkinson did well on her dives after facing her fears and went on to win the gold medal.

B "When you push away your nerves and refuse to think about them, they come on full force at the most important time: right during the meet," says Wilkinson. So, alone in her hotel room in Sydney, Wilkinson faced her fears the night before the final round of diving. "I let everything hit me: What would happen if I did well? What would happen if I did badly? What am I afraid of?" she recalls. "I was literally shaking just thinking about it, feeling scared and
20 nervous. When I had the courage to stand up to what I was feeling, it didn't seem so bad anymore. I was able to move on."

Wilkinson knows what it's like to get hung up in doubts and anxieties. At her first international meet, she says she was seized by a feeling of near panic. "I was afraid of embarrassing myself and [as a result] I just choked," she says. It took her several meets to get over the experience, which sports psychologists say is not unusual.

"Every player chokes at some point—it's a natural response to competitive stress," says Todd Ryska, a professor of sport psychology at the University of Texas-San Antonio. "Athletes fear it most because
30 of the stigma. No one wants to be the one everyone's talking about in the locker room."

Find Your Focus

D Choking is not a mistake out of nowhere like a shanked[1] golf shot; it's usually the result of misplaced focus. Athletes who avoid choking concentrate on the process (what do I have to do right now?), which is

---

[1] **shank:** a golf term meaning "to accidentally hit a golf ball with the wrong part of the golf club."

---

a positive mental approach. Those who choke tend to dwell on the outcome (what will happen if I don't win?) and its potentially unpleasant **consequences.**

C Letting your attention wander can also lead to trouble. Barb Lindquist, who swam for Stanford from 1987 to 1991, recalls how she
40 felt at her first big meet (the U.S. Open) as she listened to the announcer reciting the accomplishments of her competitors. "I was 16 and I was next to a swimmer that I had read about. I got really flustered by hearing her accomplishments," she says. "I didn't concentrate on my race and was all shaky afterward. I finished last."

Now 31 and a triathlete,[2] Lindquist hasn't had any problems since then. While swimming, she repeats to herself the words "long and strong." On the bike she thinks about her pedal **technique**, and while running she visualizes balloons pulling up her legs to make her feel light. "If you're thinking about each of those things along the way and
50 pushing yourself, you can't really choke," says Lindquist, who finished 2000 ranked seventh in the world.

E Once choking symptoms kick in they're difficult to stop. Libbie Hickman, 35, found this out when she was running the 5,000 meters at the '96 Olympic trials. Hickman led until the last 100 meters, when three runners passed her. "I remember thinking, I'm not doing it. I'm not going to make the team," she says. "As soon as you start focusing on the negative you're dead."

---

[2] **triathlete:** a person who participates in a three-part athletic contest, which generally includes swimming, biking, and running.

---

consequences:
results

technique:
way of accomplishing a task

She focused on negative thoughts and went from first place to finish fourth.

---

2. **◄ REREAD** Reread lines 13–21. Wilkinson says confidence was the key to her Olympic victory. In the margin, list two details that support her statement.

3. **READ ►** As you read lines 32–51, underline the negative effects of fear and stress on Barb Lindquist at her first big meet.

4. **◄ REREAD AND DISCUSS** With a small group, discuss the main ideas the writer presents under the heading "Find Your Focus." Include facts and examples in lines 32–37 and the specific experiences of Barb Lindquist in your discussion.

5. **READ ►** Read lines 52–68. In the margin, summarize Hickman's experiences at the 1996 and 2000 Olympic trials.

---

2. **REREAD AND CITE TEXT EVIDENCE**

B **ASK STUDENTS** to examine the way Wilkinson built confidence before her Olympic diving victory. *Students should note that when Wilkinson pushed away her nerves and faced her fears, she was able to gain confidence in her ability to win—and won the gold medal.*

3. **READ AND CITE TEXT EVIDENCE** Like Laura Wilkinson, Barb Lindquist also knows about the negative effects of fear and stress and a lack of focus on a sports competition.

C **ASK STUDENTS** to find and cite the details that also demonstrate the negative effects of pressure and fear on Barb Lindquist at her first big meet. *Students should cite examples from lines 32–51.*

4. **REREAD AND DISCUSS USING TEXT EVIDENCE**

D **ASK STUDENTS** to appoint a reporter for each group to discuss the main ideas in the section titled "Finding Your Focus." *Students should cite evidence from lines 32–51.*

5. **READ AND CITE TEXT EVIDENCE**

E **ASK STUDENTS** to read their margin notes to a partner and then write one response that gives an objective summary of Libbie Hickman's experiences at the Olympic trials, using a strong central idea for the summary. *Students should cite evidence from lines 52–68.*

Critical Vocabulary: consequences (line 37) Have students share examples of times when they faced consequences as a result of having done something foolish.

Critical Vocabulary: technique (line 47) Have students explain "technique" as it is used here.

She threw out her fear and finished third.

What Hickman learned from that experience helped her at the 2000 trials. "I started getting passed in the last lap, and the fear of coming in fourth again jumped in my head," she says. "But instead of letting that fear sit there, I threw it out, focused on the job that needed to be done and saw the finish line." The result: She finished third.

60

It's Just a Game

perspective:
viewpoint

 F

If you have a bad experience, keep it in **perspective**. "Not to minimize the importance of competition, but it's still only a portion of life," says Ryska. Your friends and teammates will still accept you even when you don't perform up to expectations—theirs or yours.

"You have to look forward," says Lindquist. "You only fail in a race if you haven't learned something from it."

---

6. **◀ REREAD** Reread lines 63–68. Summarize the important idea under the heading "It's Just a Game."

It's important to remember that competition is only one part of life.

SHORT RESPONSE

Cite Text Evidence What is the central idea of this article? Review your reading notes, and **cite text evidence** that supports this idea.

The central idea of this article is that it is possible to overcome fear and succeed. In the article, all three athletes are unsuccessful until they find a way to deal with their fear and overcome it. For example, when Laura Wilkinson "faced her fears" instead of ignoring them, she was able to "move on" and win. Barb Lindquist and Libbie Hickman both overcame their fear by learning to focus on the job at hand instead of the other people competing. As long as you learn from your failures, you haven't failed at all.

12

---

6. **REREAD AND CITE TEXT EVIDENCE** Ryska warns athletes not to focus their energies on bad experiences in sports.

F **ASK STUDENTS** to cite evidence that supports the most important idea in the last section titled "It's Just a Game." *Students should cite textual evidence from lines 63–68.*

Critical Vocabulary: perspective Ask how "perspective" fits into Ryska's discussion of learning from a bad experience. *Ryska, a professor of sport psychology, wants athletes to maintain a reasonable outlook after a negative competitive experience.*

SHORT RESPONSE

Cite Text Evidence Student responses will vary, but students should cite text evidence to support the central idea. Students should

- explain what the central idea of the article is
- give reasons for their point of view
- cite specific evidence from the text to support their viewpoint

---

TO CHALLENGE STUDENTS . . .

For more context about female athletes in competitive sports, students can conduct Internet research on other notable female athletes such as Mia Hamm, Lisa Leslie, or Billie Jean King.

ASK STUDENTS what they have learned about women's participation in athletics. How has their opinion of female athletes broadened from their research? *Students should recognize that female athletes often face many struggles in order to succeed. Like male athletes, they have had to learn from their failures in order to succeed.*

DIG DEEPER

With the class, return to Question 4, Reread and Discuss. Have students share the results of their discussion.

ASK STUDENTS whether they were satisfied with the outcome of their small-group discussions. Have each group share the main ideas they found in the section called "Find Your Focus." What specific evidence from the text did the groups cite to support their choice of the most important ideas in this section? What compelling evidence from the article did each group cite about the specific experiences of Barb Lindquist, who now focuses on the process (what she has to do right now) in order to win?

- Encourage students to tell whether there was any compelling textual evidence cited by group members who did not agree with the central ideas found by the group.
- Have groups tell how they used Lindquist's experiences as an example of an athlete who has found her focus.
- After students have shared the results of their group's discussion, ask whether another group shared any ideas that seemed particularly insightful.

ASK STUDENTS to return to their Short Response answer and to revise it based on the class discussion.

In the Spotlight

Informational Text by Glenn Murphy

Why This Text?

Students regularly encounter informational text on a variety of topics. This lesson explores the central ideas and details in an article about a common fear—glossophobia.

▶ **View It!**

Professional Development Podcast:

Text-Dependent Analysis

Key Learning Objective: The student will be able to determine central ideas and supporting details in informational text.

For practice and application:

Face Your Fears and Scare the Phobia Out of Your Brain
Magazine Article by Jason Koebler

Close Reader selection
"Face Your Fears and Scare the Phobias Out of Your Brain"
Magazine Article by Jason Koebler

RI 1 Cite textual evidence; make inferences.
RI 2 Determine a central idea; provide a summary.
RI 3 Analyze text elements.
RI 4 Determine the meaning of words and phrases.
RI 5 Analyze structure.
RI 6 Determine an author's purpose.
W 2 Write informative/explanatory texts.
W 4 Produce clear and coherent writing.
W 9b Draw information from informational texts to support analysis.
SL 1 Engage effectively in a range of collaborative discussions.
L 1a Ensure that pronouns are in the proper case.
L 4a Use context as a clue to the meaning of a word or phrase.
L 4b Use common Greek or Latin affixes as clues to meaning.
L 4d Verify preliminary determination of the meaning of a word.
L 6 Acquire and use accurately grade-appropriate general academic and domain-specific words and phrases.

▲ Text Complexity Rubric

Quantitative Measures	**In the Spotlight** Lexile: 1110L

Levels of Meaning/Purpose

single purpose, explicitly stated

Qualitative Measures

Structure

organization of main ideas and details complex, but mostly explicit; may exhibit disciplinary traits

Language Conventionality and Clarity

increased, unfamiliar academic, or domain-specific words

Knowledge Demands

somewhat complex concepts

Reader/Task Considerations

• Teacher determined
• Vary by individual reader and type of text
• See the Text X-Ray for suggested Reader/Task Considerations.

English Language Support
Before teaching, use the Text X-Ray for an overview of the text's complexity. The Text X-Ray and the supports and scaffolds in the Teacher's Edition will help you guide students of different skill levels.

Meaning Making

Language Development

Effective Expression

Content Knowledge

Foundational Skills

Text Complexity: Qualitative Measures

Levels of Meaning/Purpose

single purpose, explicitly stated

Help students determine main ideas in an informational text.

- Teacher's Edition side notes, pp. 51, 53, 54, 55
- English Language Support, p. 51
- When Students Struggle, p. 53
- Strategies for Annotation, p. 55
- Determine Central Ideas, p. 55

ZOOM IN ON **DETERMINING CENTRAL IDEAS** Tell students that the **central idea** of an entire text is often suggested by the details rather than stated directly. To find the central idea, readers must look at the topic of the text and the most important ideas in each paragraph or section.

- Give students time to review and take notes on the selection.
- Have partners discuss and develop a statement about the central idea.
- Ask them to share their central ideas with the class. *(Possible response: While glossophobia is a problem because it produces extreme anxiety about speaking in public, it is not life threatening, and it can be overcome.)*

Structure

organization of main ideas and details complex, but mostly explicit; may exhibit disciplinary traits

Help students use the structure of an informational text to determine central ideas and details.

- Teacher's Edition side notes, pp. 51, 52, 53, 55
- Determine Details, p. 55

To reteach how to determine central ideas and details, see

- Determine Central Idea and Details, p. 58a

 Use It! **Level Up Tutorial:** Main Idea and Supporting Details

ZOOM IN ON **USING STRUCTURE** Explain that authors present information in a way that will convey their central ideas and details most effectively. Review these patterns of organization: **compare-and-contrast, cause-effect, problem-solution order, chronological order.**

- Have students read lines 10–12. Ask what they think they will learn in the "The Reality." Then have them read lines 80–83. Ask: What will "The Lowdown" explain? *(how to overcome glossophobia)*
- Based on these answers, ask students to identify the organizational pattern the author is using. *(problem-solution order)*
- As a class, complete these sentence frames:
  Glossophobia is a problem because _____.
  Glossophobia can be overcome by _____.

Language Conventionality and Clarity

increased, unfamiliar academic, or domain-specific words

Teach unfamiliar vocabulary in context.

- Teacher's Edition Critical Vocabulary notes, pp. 52, 54, 57
- English Language Support, p. 57
- Applying Academic Vocabulary, p. 52
- Vocabulary Strategy: Suffixes That Form Nouns, p. 57

Guide students to discuss and write about informational text using conventions of standard English.

- Teacher's Edition side notes, pp. 54, 58
- English Language Support, pp. 54, 58
- Language Conventions: Possessive Pronouns, p. 58

To teach how to analyze style, see

- Analyze Style, p. 58a

▶ *Use It!* **Interactive Whiteboard Lesson:** Use Word Choice and Tone

ZOOM IN ON **ANALYZING CONNOTATIONS** Tell students that authors of informational text, like short story writers or poets, choose their words carefully both for their dictionary definitions and for their **connotations,** or ideas and feelings associated with them.

- Display the following sentences from the selection:

  Lines 5–6: "Shoved out onstage, or to the front of the class, people like this will literally lose their voice." *(pushed, propelled, thrust)*

  Lines 27–28: "Being booed and pelted with rotten vegetables if we do badly?" *(whacked, struck, hit)*

- Read each sentence and discuss connotations of the highlighted words. Ask pairs to choose words with the closest connotation and to explain their choices. *(thrust; whacked)*

Knowledge Demands

somewhat complex concepts

Provide English Learners with background on the text.

- Teacher's Edition Author's note, p. 51

ZOOM IN ON **BUILDING KNOWLEDGE OF KEY TERMS** Tell students that the suffix *–phobia* means "fear."

- Explain that word parts are often combined with *–phobia* to describe a type of fear. Glosso is the Greek word for "tongue." Therefore, *glossophobia* is "fear of speaking."
- List other common phobias that include these words in their names: *hydro-* (water); *pyro-* (fire); *claustro-* (enclosed place).
- Have students write and define each new word they create.

Suggested Reader/Task Considerations

You might consider the following before assigning this informational text to students.

- Will students be able to set a purpose that will help them focus on important ideas?
- Do students have adequate experience with imagery and figurative language to allow them to understand the text?

ZOOM IN ON **SUPPORTING COMPREHENSION**

- Survey the class to see who dreads speaking in front of others or knows someone who does. Explain that this text offers some strategies to help overcome such fears.
- Display the following quotation: "They just stand there gaping like helpless goldfish pulled out of the water . . ." This simile compares frightened speakers to goldfish. Ask what idea is brought out through the comparison. *(The speakers are literally gasping for breath or suffocating from fear of being in the "spotlight.")*

TEACH

CLOSE READ

Glenn Murphy Have students read the information about Glenn Murphy and the title, subtitle, and byline for this selection. Discuss what they think an "Explainer team" might do and why Murphy might have been a part of it. Then ask them what they think this selection might be like—funny, serious, informative, entertaining, and so on.

SETTING A PURPOSE Direct students to use the Setting a Purpose prompt to focus their reading. Remind them to write down questions as they read.

Determine Central Idea   RI 1, RI 2
(LINES 1–12)

Explain to students that a **central**, or **main**, **idea** is the most important idea an author wants the reader to know. A central or main idea can apply to a whole text, to a section of the text, or to a paragraph.

(A) **CITE TEXT EVIDENCE** Have students reread lines 1–12 and then state the main idea of the paragraph. *(People who are afraid of speaking in public have a fear called "glossophobia.")*

Analyze Structure (LINES 1–12)   RI 1, RI 5

Explain that **supporting details** are words, phrases, or sentences that tell more about an important idea or topic.

(B) **CITE TEXT EVIDENCE** Ask students to name details in lines 1–12 that tell about glossophobia. *(People who have it are afraid of speaking in public; they lose their voice on stage; they want to run away or cry; it can be scarier than actual physical danger.)*

English Language Support

Read Closely Display lines 1–10 of the text. Read the lines aloud and highlight the words as shown in this sample.

- Reread the highlighted phrases aloud with students. Help them describe in their own words the images that the words create in their minds.
- Have pairs of students work together to list other phrases from lines 1–10 that they can picture in their minds. Invite them to highlight these in the displayed text.

Glenn Murphy *is an expert in explaining science concepts for kids, teenagers, and adults. After receiving his Masters in Science Communication from London's Imperial College of Science, Technology and Medicine, Murphy managed the Explainer team at the Science Museum in London, England. This experience led to his first book,* Why Is Snot Green? *With the sequel,* How Loud Can You Burp?, *and several more books, Murphy continues to explain science topics with humor and energy.*

In the Spotlight

from Stuff That Scares Your Pants Off!

Informational Text by Glenn Murphy

SETTING A PURPOSE As you read, focus on the science facts that explain why some people are afraid of speaking in public and how this fear may be overcome.

THE FEAR   Some of us are fine with the idea of standing in front of huge crowds of people. But others would happily bungee off a 200-foot bridge, or dive into a shoal of circling sharks, rather than experience the sheer terror of facing an audience. Shoved out onstage, or to the front of a class, people like this will quite literally lose their voice. The mouth may open, but the words won't come out. They just stand there gaping like helpless goldfish pulled out of water, their weak limbs quaking with fear, feeling like they want to
10 run, hide, or cry. If that sounds like you, then you are one of the world's many, many sufferers of glossophobia—the fear of speaking (or trying to speak) in public.

(t) © Glenn Murphy, (c) ©Superstock

- Ask pairs of students to list all the words and phrases from lines 1–10 that create images in their minds. Have them discuss why using this kind of language helps the author convey meaning to readers.

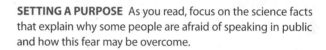

facing an audience. Shoved out onstage, or to the front of a class, people like this will quite literally lose their voice. The mouth may open, but the words won't come out.

Determine Details

RI 1,
RI 2,
RI 3

(LINES 34–47)

Explain to students that there are many things that authors use as supporting details. Tell students that **examples,** such as stories or experiences, are one type of detail that authors often use to help explain an idea.

C **CITE TEXT EVIDENCE** Have students identify examples used as supporting details in lines 34–47. *(Staring is a signal of fighting; we don't usually stare at people when we talk to them; we shift our eyes, so that eye contact doesn't signal that we want to fight.)*

CRITICAL VOCABULARY

ambush: The author uses the word *ambushed* to describe something that might happen to people.

ASK STUDENTS how early humans might have been ambushed and how that might connect to some people's fear of speaking in public. *(People could be ambushed or attacked by large animals or other humans; when speaking in public, people feel that same sense of danger because of being surrounded by an audience.)*

aggression: The author says that staring is a sign of aggression in primates.

ASK STUDENTS why people who are speaking in public might feel aggression from the audience. *(The audience is watching; this can feel like staring and aggression and trigger the older fear of being attacked.)*

confidence: The author says that a person needs confidence to be onstage.

ASK STUDENTS how having confidence is important when speaking or performing. *(Having confidence can help you believe that the audience is interested in what you have to say and won't want to harm you.)*

The Reality

Glossophobia is amazingly common—there are usually at least four or five kids in every grade who have it, and it's very common in adults too because you generally don't "grow out" of glossophobia. It takes help or practice to get over it. This is because it's basically a type of social phobia—a fear of being watched, judged, or sized up by other people (especially strangers, and especially large numbers of them).

20   So where does it come from, and what use is it? I mean, if fear of the dark, heights, and dangerous animals helped keep our ancestors from being **ambushed,** what good is a fear of speaking to people? Wouldn't being able to speak to big groups have helped those early humans to communicate? The ones who were best at it, you'd think, could become chiefs, kings, and emperors. If speaking is that useful, what is this fear trying to protect us from? Being booed and pelted with rotten vegetables if we do badly?

30   Well, the answer is—nothing, really. There's no real danger involved in speaking to people. But the action of standing there and being watched can trigger a much older and more useful fear—the fear of being surrounded, threatened, and attacked by other people.

Throughout the animal world, and especially in primates (the group that includes humans, gorillas, and chimpanzees), staring at someone is a signal of fighting or **aggression.** Even when we chat with people we trust and like, we don't stare them down while we talk. Instead, we shift the focus of our eyes around the other person's face—from their eyes to their 40 mouth and nose and back again—and we glance away every so often during the conversation. (If you don't believe me, try it with a friend. Sit close to each other and just stare while you talk, without looking away, for one minute. You'll probably find you both start to feel really uncomfortable very quickly!) All of this helps to break up the eye contact, and reassures each person that the other is still friendly. Without it, a long burst of eye contact feels like the buildup to a fight.

Now multiply that one staring pair of eyes by thirty, and you have some idea of why standing up to speak in front of 50 a class can feel so unnerving. Multiply it by 500 or 1,000, and you see why it takes a lot of **confidence** to be onstage in a packed theater. Even though the audience is (probably)

ambush
(ăm´bŏŏsh) *v.* Some animals *ambush* their prey by hiding and then attacking as the prey comes near them.

aggression
(ə-grĕsh´ən) *n.* Angry, violent behavior or action is called *aggression.*

confidence
(kŏn´fĭ-dəns) *n.* A person who has *confidence* believes in his or her abilities or ideas.

APPLYING ACADEMIC VOCABULARY

evident	factor

THINK-PAIR-SHARE Have students turn to a partner to discuss the following questions. Guide students to include the academic vocabulary words *evident* and *factor* in their responses. Ask volunteers to share their responses with the class.

- What things make it **evident** that someone has glossophobia?
- Are there **factors** that contribute to glossophobia? What are they?

friendly, the sensation is like being surrounded by an angry tribe, and all your brain wants to do is get you out of there. So that's what it prepares you to do. The "fight-or-flight" system kicks in, making your heart rate increase, your breathing tight and rapid, your muscles tense, and your guts feel queasy[1] (as blood is directed away from them). The whole time you're trying to speak or perform, your brain is saying, "OK—any minute now we make a run for it, right? Get ready ... readyyy ... readyyyyyyyyyyy ... "

For some people, this feels quite thrilling. But for glossophobics, it's absolutely terrifying.

But if you think about it, there really is nothing to be afraid of this time. Unlike the fear of water, heights, and the dark, there's no real danger present at all. Even if you speak or perform really badly, it's not like the audience is going to kill you—the worst response you'll get is silence, booing, or rotten fruit and veggies. None of these are pleasant, but none of them can actually harm you either.

Happily, this also makes glossophobia a perfect example of a fear you can beat with simple practice. Since there's no real danger, it's much easier to work up from speaking to one, to two, to ten, to thirty people. Believe it or not, you can go from stage-phobic to star performer in no time!

The Chances

The odds of being killed by a classroom or theater full of people just because you're speaking to or performing for them? Zero. Unless you're really, really bad ...

No, really—it's zero. Just kidding.

The Lowdown

The fear of being "in the spotlight" is extremely common and, to those who suffer from it, extremely powerful. But it's also extremely easy to work through, given a bit of effort. Since there's no real danger involved, it's just a matter of convincing your brain that you don't need the "fight-or-flight" system to kick in when you're speaking or performing before people. How do you do that? Practice!

---

[1] **queasy** (kwē´zē): nauseated; sick to your stomach.

In the Spotlight **53**

TEACH

CLOSE READ

Determine Central Idea and Details (LINES 48–75)

RI 1,
RI 2,
RI 3

Explain to students that authors will often take several paragraphs to develop a central idea and its supporting details.

D **CITE TEXT EVIDENCE** Have students reread lines 48–75 and then describe its central idea and some details that support this idea. *(Central idea: Glossophobia is terrifying for those who have it, but people can overcome it through practice. Details: Glossophobia makes you feel surrounded by "an angry tribe"; the "fight-or-flight" system makes a person want to run away, but there is no real danger, so you can practice and get over it.)*

Analyze Language
(SUBHEADS)

RI 4

Explain that authors often use subheads to help organize the information in their writing. Tell students that subheads can help readers understand the flow of ideas in a text. Explain the meaning of *lowdown* (slang for "the whole truth") to students.

E **ASK STUDENTS** to explain how the subhead "The Lowdown" is related to, or follows from, the other subheads in the selection. *(The first subhead is "The Reality"; that section describes what glossophobia is. The next subhead, "The Chances," is humorous and keeps the text lighthearted. "The Lowdown" section gives readers "the whole truth"—that glossophobia can be overcome with practice.*

WHEN STUDENTS STRUGGLE ...

Have partners record main ideas and details as they read. Have them begin with lines 13–19 and continue throughout the selection as you guide them. (See the **Interactive Graphic Organizers for Reading** for a chart.)

LEVEL UP TUTORIALS For additional support, assign the following *Level Up* tutorial: **Main Idea and Supporting Details.**

Main Idea: Glossophobia is a type of social phobia.
Detail 1: It's a fear of being watched.
Detail 2: It is common.
Detail 3: You generally don't grow out of it.

TEACH

CLOSE READ

Determine Central Idea and Details (LINES 87–112)

RI 1,
RI 2,
RI 3

Remind students that a central idea can be stated in one paragraph and then developed through a few or several following paragraphs.

Ⓕ CITE TEXT EVIDENCE Have students reread lines 87–112 and state the central idea and some details that support it. (Central idea: There are a lot of ways to build confidence when speaking to an audience. Details: join a speaking group; join an acting or a debating club; try a different kind of performance.)

CRITICAL VOCABULARY

distract: The author believes you can distract a speaker from thinking about the audience as they speak.

ASK STUDENTS to explain helpful and not-so-helpful ways to distract someone when they are going to speak before an audience. (Helpful: Make sure they focus on their ideas and not the people; have them look above the audience rather than at it. Not-so-helpful: Waving or making other gestures; staring at them intently; moving about too much in your seat as you listen.)

COLLABORATIVE DISCUSSION Have partners discuss what they have learned about glossophobia and record their ideas. Suggest that they organize their ideas based on central, or main, ideas and supporting details as much as possible.

ASK STUDENTS to share any questions they generated in the course of reading and discussing the selection.

English Language Support

Adapt Language Choices Before students begin their work recording their ideas, tell them that it is important to think about their audience in the discussion. Remind them to adjust their language choices to

- explain their ideas
- provide feedback on what their partner says
- support their main ideas with details

There are lots of ways of working through your fears and building your confidence before audiences. The most direct (and powerful) way is to join a school, church, or community speaking group, where you can be coached on how to give speeches. At first, you may practice alone or with one or two people. Then, as you get more confident, you can work up to larger and larger groups, until before you know it you're speaking to whole school assemblies, church congregations, or community groups! The best thing is that in many cases you get to talk about whatever you want, whether it's "Ten Ways to Make a Better World" or "My Love of Dinosaurs."

Ⓕ If that doesn't sound like any kind of fun, then you can get experience with speaking in front of audiences without speaking directly to them. In acting or debating clubs, you can practice talking to small groups of people while being watched by an audience, but without having to look straight at them. Plus the act of concentrating on your lines or on the argument will help **distract** you from the many watching eyes. When you get really good at it, you might even forget the audience is there!

And if you really can't imagine speaking in front of crowds at all, then you can work up to it (or at the very least gain a lot more confidence) by trying other types of performance instead. Ever wanted to dance? How about play guitar, or sing? Learning a performing art of any kind will help you get over your fears of an audience if you eventually take it to the stage.

So if you're one of the world's many perform-o-phobes, don't worry—the "treatment" for it may turn out to be the most fun you've ever had. The prescription looks like this: take a handful of guitar, acting, or dance lessons, rock a roomful of people with your mad new skills, and call me in the morning!

distract
(dĭ-străkt´) v. To distract is to pull attention away from something or someone.

COLLABORATIVE DISCUSSION With a partner, discuss the facts and ideas that explain glossophobia and why it is a fear that people must work at overcoming.

TO CHALLENGE STUDENTS . . .

Make Connections Is it possible to overcome most phobias or not? Have small groups of students discuss different phobias they have read about in this collection; remind them to review "Fears and Phobias" if needed. Then have partners or small groups work together to choose another phobia, such as a fear of flying or a fear of heights, and propose a plan for helping someone overcome it. Tell them to write specific steps in their plan of action and to explain why their plan should work.

Determine Central Idea

RI 2, RI 3

In informational text, the **central idea,** or **main idea,** is the most important idea that an author of a text wants you to know about the topic. You can look for the central idea of the entire text and you can look for the central idea in each paragraph.

The **topic sentence** of a paragraph states the paragraph's central idea. In informational text, the topic sentence is often the first sentence in a paragraph. However, it may appear anywhere in the paragraph. Sometimes the central idea is not directly stated but implied, or suggested by details. To identify an **implied** central idea, you need to examine the details to determine what the writer intends.

To find the central idea, follow these steps:
- Identify the specific topic of each paragraph or section.
- Examine all the details the author includes.

Ask what idea or message the details convey about the topic.

Stated Central Idea	Implied Central Idea
Lines 87–97: Central idea at the beginning of a paragraph Lines 13–19: Central idea at the end of a paragraph	Lines 48–61: Implied central idea People who have glossophobia when speaking in public experience increased heart rate, rapid breathing, and queasiness.

Determine Details

RI 2, RI 3

Supporting details are words, phrases, or sentences that tell more about the central idea. Facts, opinions, examples, statistics, and anecdotes are all supporting details that writers may use depending on the type of writing.

- A **fact** is a statement that can be proved.
- An **opinion** is a statement that expresses a person's beliefs, feelings, or thoughts. An opinion cannot be proved.
- An **example** is a specific instance that helps to explain an idea, such as a personal story or experience.
- A **statistic** is a fact that is expressed in numbers.
- An **anecdote** is a short account of an interesting incident.

Reread lines 87–97. Ask yourself these questions:
- What is the central idea of this paragraph?
- What details, such as facts and examples, support the main idea?

In the Spotlight **55**

CLOSE READ

Determine Central Idea

RI 2, RI 3

Help students understand the terms *central* or *main idea, topic sentence, stated central idea,* and *implied central idea.* Have volunteers define or explain each term.

Review the bulleted list of steps to follow when finding central ideas. Then have partners return to the selection to look up the examples listed in the chart. Have students read each example aloud, and ask volunteers to explain each one.

Determine Details

RI 2, RI 3

Help students understand the term *supporting details* and then discuss each type of detail listed in the lesson. Ask students to give examples of each type of detail.

Next, have students reread lines 87–97 and answer the questions at the bottom of the page.

English Language Support

Guide students to work in small groups to answer the questions on page 56. Each group should answer one question. When all the groups are finished, they can take turns presenting their answers to the class. Encourage students to provide their classmates with useful feedback.

Strategies for Annotation

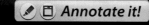 **Annotate it!**

Determine Central Idea and Details

RI 2, RI 3

Share these strategies for guided or independent analysis:
- Highlight in yellow a central or main idea.
- Highlight in green the details that support that idea.
- Review your highlights. On a note, jot down a summary of the information presented, including whether the central idea is stated or implied.

There are lots of ways of working through your fears and building your confidence before audiences. The most direct (and powerful) way is to join a school, church, or community speaking group, where you can be coached on how to give speeches. At first, you may practice alone or with one or two people. Then, as you get more confident, you can work up to larger and larger groups, until before you know it you're

Analyzing the Text

RI 1, RI 2,
RI 3, RI 4,
RI 5, RI 6

Possible answers:

1. *Words: circling sharks, sheer terror, gaping like a helpless goldfish, quaking with fear. This description quickly creates a vivid image of what it is like to experience glossophobia; it makes the intensity of the phobia clear.*

2. *The central idea of these lines is that glossophobia comes from our basic instinct to protect ourselves from other people who might hurt us. This idea is important because it shows that this phobia is understandable and might be controllable.*

3. *The experiment helps the reader experience a mild version of the fear that people with glossophobia feel more intensely; it makes a fear that seems a little far fetched in daily life feel more real and concrete.*

4. *Examples include joining a speaking group, joining an acting or debate club, or trying other types of performance such as dancing, playing an instrument, or singing. Some facts: There's no real danger in speaking in front of people; you don't need the fight-or-flight response to kick in when you're speaking; a speaking group is a place where you can get coached in giving speeches. Some opinions: It's extremely easy to work through; the best thing is that . . . you get to talk about whatever you want.*

5. *The central idea is that glossophobia is a serious fear that can be overcome by understanding how it works and practicing ways to make sure that the fight-or-flight response is not triggered so easily or intensely. "The Fear" gives a vivid image of glossophobia; "The Reality" explains how the phobia works in our bodies and that the key is that there is no real danger in speaking in front of an audience; "The Chances" and "The Lowdown" describe ways to overcome the phobia gradually and with practice.*

6. *Examples of humor include: your brain saying "OK—any minute now . . ."; not like the audience is going to kill you; "The Chances" section. The article is written as if the author is speaking directly to the reader. This style works well here because it gives a lighthearted approach to a topic that might be frightening to many readers. (See the Extend lesson, "Analyze Style" for related instruction.)*

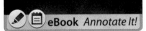
eBook *Annotate It!*

Analyzing the Text

RI 1, RI 2, RI 3,
RI 4, RI 5, RI 6,
W 2a-f, W 9b

Cite Text Evidence Support your responses with evidence from the text.

1. **Interpret** Reread lines 1–12. What words and phrases does the author use to create a vivid image of glossophobia? Explain why this description is important.

2. **Infer** What is the central idea of lines 20–33 in "In the Spotlight"? Explain why this is an important idea in the article.

3. **Draw Conclusions** Reread lines 34–47. Explain why the experiment the author proposes is valuable to the reader.

4. **Analyze** The author states that glossophobia is ". . . extremely easy to work through, given a bit of effort" (lines 80–82). What examples support this idea? List one fact and one opinion about this idea.

5. **Summarize** What is the central idea of "In the Spotlight"? Explain how each section of the article supports this central idea.

6. **Evaluate** The author uses an informal, humorous writing style. What examples in the text show this style? Tell why the author probably used this style here and how well you think it works.

PERFORMANCE TASK

Writing Activity: Letter Imagine that you are an advice columnist. Answer a letter from a reader who would like advice on how to cure glossophobia.

- Review "In the Spotlight." Identify the main ideas about curing glossophobia.

- Decide which suggestions you will advise the reader to use. Cite explicit evidence from "In the Spotlight" to support your suggestions.
- Create an alias, or a fake name, for the reader you are responding to.
- Read your letter aloud to a partner to see if it is clear and helpful.

Assign this performance task.

PERFORMANCE TASK

W 2a-f, W 9b

Writing Activity: Letter Have students work independently to write their letter, and then have them work with a partner to review and revise if necessary. Emphasize that they should

- think about the person they are writing to (Is it a child, an adult, a teen-ager? How severe is his or her phobia?)
- review "In the Spotlight" and include specific suggestions from it
- create aliases for both the reader and themselves as the columnist
- review the letter with a partner

Critical Vocabulary

ambush   aggression   confidence   distract

Practice and Apply Answer each question and explain your response.

1. Which situation is an example of an **ambush**?
   a. a person who is hiding suddenly jumps out
   b. a dog runs out from a yard to greet someone walking by

2. Which situation shows **aggression**?
   a. a friend gives you a pat on the back
   b. a dog growls at someone walking by

3. Which group shows **confidence**?
   a. a debate team that is eager to begin a contest
   b. a marching band that decides not to be in a parade

4. Which of these would be a way to **distract** someone?
   a. waiting quietly while the person talks to someone else
   b. waving at a person who is giving a speech

Vocabulary Strategy: Suffixes That Form Nouns

A **suffix** is a word part that appears at the end of a root or base word to form a new word. Some Latin suffixes, such as -ance, -ence, and -ant, can be added to verbs to form nouns. If you can recognize the verb that a suffix is attached to, you can often figure out the meaning of the noun formed from it.

Suffix	Meaning
-ance, -ence	the act of, the condition of, the state of
-ant	one that performs or causes an action

For example, -ence is added to confide to make confidence. One meaning of confide is "to tell in secret." Confidence means "trust or the act of confiding."

Practice and Apply Identify the verb in each underlined word. Use context clues to define the noun. Use a dictionary to confirm your definitions.

1. The <u>performance</u> was sold out in only one hour.

2. We celebrated my uncle's <u>emergence</u> as a great writer.

3. Mrs. Lowenstein is the attorney for the <u>defendant</u> in the trial.

4. She won her case because an <u>informant</u> testified at the trial.

Critical Vocabulary

Answers:

1. ***a.;*** *being hidden is an important aspect of an ambush*

2. ***b.;*** *the dog is scary and threatening, which is part of aggression*

3. ***a.;*** *the team's eagerness shows they are sure of themselves*

4. ***b.;*** *waving could take their attention away from their speaking*

Vocabulary Strategy: Suffixes That Form Nouns

Answers:

1. ***perform:*** *the act of performing, a public presentation*

2. ***emerge:*** *coming forth*

3. ***defend:*** *the person being defended*

4. ***inform:*** *a person who provides information to another person*

English Language Support

Learn More About Affixes Point out to students that some root or base words can be combined with several different suffixes. For example, the word *emerge*, as in *emergence*, can also be part of the word *emergent*, with the suffix *-ent*. Help students understand that the suffix *-ent* is a variation of *-ant*, and has the same meaning. Have pairs of students examine the word *confidence* to find out what word is formed if the suffix *-ant* replaces the suffix *-ence*. Have students use a dictionary to determine the meaning of *confidant*.

PRACTICE & APPLY

Language Conventions: Possessive Pronouns

L 1a

Review with students that a **possessive pronoun** shows ownership, as in *I possess that book; it is mine.* Remind students that pronouns must agree with the noun they refer to in number (singular, plural), in gender, and in person (first, second, third). Have students practice using the pronouns orally in their own sentences before completing the Practice and Apply exercises.

Answers:

1. *their*

2. *her*

3. *ours*

4. *my*

5. *its*

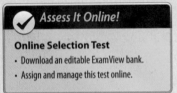

Assess It Online!

Online Selection Test
- Download an editable ExamView bank.
- Assign and manage this test online.

Language Conventions: Possessive Pronouns

L 1a

Pronouns are words that take the place of nouns or other pronouns. Personal pronouns change form to show how they function in a sentence. A **possessive pronoun** shows ownership. Here are some examples from "In the Spotlight":

> Instead, we shift the focus of <u>our</u> eyes around the other person's face—from <u>their</u> eyes to <u>their</u> mouth and nose and back again . . .

In this sentence, both *our* and *their* are examples of possessive pronouns. Both are used to indicate ownership: *our* refers to the subjective pronoun *we*, and *their* refers to the "other person."

The chart shows possessive pronouns in either singular (one person) or plural (more than one person) form.

		Use Before Nouns	Use in Place of Nouns
Singular			
	First person	my	mine
	Second person	your	yours
	Third person	her, his, its	hers, his, its
Plural			
	First person	our	ours
	Second person	your	yours
	Third person	their	theirs

Practice and Apply Complete the sentences with the correct possessive pronoun. Remember that pronouns must agree with the noun they refer to in number, gender, and person.

1. The team felt confident; they felt _____ chances of winning were high.

2. Jenna was worried; _____ fear of heights made riding the roller coaster scary for her.

3. Kevin and I worked together on that project. That project is _____.

4. I speak next week. I need to practice _____ speech.

5. The dog pressed _____ face against the window.

English Language Support

Understand Cohesion Review with students that possessive pronouns show ownership. Tell students that possessive pronouns are useful in writing clearly and concisely.

- Work with students to read the chart in the student edition. Point to or hold items around the classroom and say sentences aloud using each term in the chart, such as "This book is your book." Ask students to echo each sentence.
- Before students complete the Practice and Apply items, model the activity. Say, "This pen is mine." Write the sentence on the board and underline *mine*. Tell students that the sentence could be written "This pen is my pen." Show students that the word *mine* can replace the phrase *my pen*. Help students create more sentences based on the chart on page 58. Read each sentence aloud and underline the possessive pronoun.
- After students have completed the Practice and Apply items, ask them to write sentences about giving a speech using the possessive pronouns in the student edition chart.

Analyze Style

RI 4

TEACH

Explain to students that a piece of writing usually has a particular style. A **style** is a manner of writing; it involves *how* something is said rather than *what* is said. Each writer has a style, which is his or her unique way of communicating ideas.

Tell students that several literary elements contribute to a writer's style. Discuss these elements with them:

- **word choice**—the way words and phrases are used to express ideas
- **sentence structure**—the types, patterns, and lengths of sentences used, including fragments (pieces of sentences)
- **imagery**—words and phrases that appeal to a reader's five senses
- **tone**—the writer's attitude toward the subject, such as serious, playful, mocking, sympathetic

With students, examine the following passages in "In the Spotlight" to identify different elements of the author's style.

- **Lines 1–12:** *imagery* describing how it feels to be glossophobic
- **Lines 13–28:** varied *sentence structure* that moves the reader forward, creates drama (statements, questions)
- **Lines 48–61:** *word choices* that create a funny, playful *tone*

English Language Support

Examine Language Choices Remind students that the author's word choices not only express ideas, but produce different effects on the reader. Word choices also signal tone. Discuss the term *perform-o-phobe* (line 113). Discuss the meaning of the term. *(someone who has a phobia of performing)* Tell students that this is not actually a word. Explain that the author uses this made-up word because he is trying to make a serious topic more playful.

PRACTICE AND APPLY

Have students work in small groups to identify additional examples of Glenn Murphy's style in "In the Spotlight." Then, depending on whether students have completed the Analyzing the Text questions, have them write or revise their responses to question 6 as they feel necessary.

 INTERACTIVE WHITEBOARD LESSON Use **Word Choice and Tone** for additional instruction.

Determine Central Idea and Details

RI 2

RETEACH

Review the terms *central* or *main idea, supporting details, stated main idea,* and *implied main idea.* Then give an example of a main idea: "Glossophobia is a common phobia among children and adults." Ask students to name some types of supporting details that an author might include to support this idea. *(facts, examples, statistics)* Have a few students take turns stating main ideas and naming types of details that might support that idea, including opinions and anecdotes as well as facts, examples, and statistics. Next, review how to figure out an implied main idea:

- Look at the title, subheadings, and details.
- Decide what all the information says about the topic.

 LEVEL UP TUTORIALS Assign the following *Level Up* tutorial: **Main Idea and Supporting Details**

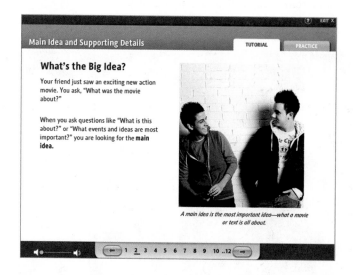

INDEPENDENT READING

Individual students can apply these skills to a current magazine article or nonfiction book they may be reading on their own. Have them state main ideas and supporting details, including whether each main idea is stated or implied in the text.

Face Your Fears and Scare the Phobia Out of Your Brain

Magazine Article by Jason Koebler

Why This Text

Students often finish reading a magazine article without a thorough understanding of the author's central (or main) ideas. Articles such as this one by Jason Koebler may have more than one complex central idea. Guide students to recognize that some central ideas are directly stated, while others need to be inferred by analyzing textual evidence. With the help of the close-reading questions, students will determine the central ideas by examining the textual evidence (details, facts, statistics, quotations, examples, and anecdotes). This close reading will lead students to develop a coherent understanding of the most important ideas in an informational text.

Background Have students read the background information that suggests the definition of *phobia* as used in psychology. Introduce the selection by sharing this definition: "A phobia is a marked and persistent fear and avoidance of a particular object or situation." Point out that as a science reporter, Jason Koebler uses scientific information about people's phobias to discuss a new form of therapy.

SETTING A PURPOSE Ask students to pay close attention to the central ideas in this article and to the interactions among individuals, ideas, and events in the text. How soon does Koebler present the article's central idea?

Standards Support

- cite textual evidence to support what the text says explicitly
- cite textual evidence to support inferences drawn from the text
- determine central (or main) ideas in a text
- analyze central ideas to provide an objective summary of a text

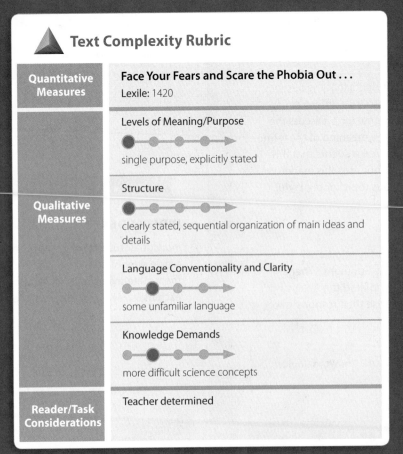

Text Complexity Rubric

Quantitative Measures

Face Your Fears and Scare the Phobia Out . . .
Lexile: 1420

Qualitative Measures

Levels of Meaning/Purpose

single purpose, explicitly stated

Structure

clearly stated, sequential organization of main ideas and details

Language Conventionality and Clarity

some unfamiliar language

Knowledge Demands

more difficult science concepts

Reader/Task Considerations

Teacher determined

Strategies for CLOSE READING

Determine Central Idea

Students should read this article carefully all the way through. Close-reading questions at the bottom of the page will help them focus on a thorough analysis of the central ideas and the details that support them. As they read, students should record comments or questions about the text in the side margins.

WHEN STUDENTS STRUGGLE . . .

To help students determine the central idea of a text, have them work in small groups to fill out a chart such as the one shown below as they analyze the article.

CITE TEXT EVIDENCE For practice analyzing the central idea of a text, ask students to examine the details and evidence that support the central idea.

> **Central Idea:** *Exposure therapy helps eliminate fears and phobias from the brain.*
>
> **Detail 1:** *Parts of the brain that produce fear became inactive after people were exposed to the thing they feared.*
>
> **Detail 2:** *Exposure therapy changes the way the brain reacts to fear.*
>
> **Detail 3:** *Parts of the brain that react to fear remained inactive for at least six months.*
>
> **Detail 4:** *After six months, when people were exposed to the thing they feared, they were no longer afraid.*

Background *It is wise to be afraid of things that can hurt you. But when a fear is excessive and not based on reality, it becomes a phobia. In his article for U.S. News & World Report, science journalist* **Jason Koebler** *examines how a new form of therapy may be the first step to completely eliminating fears and phobias from our brains in the near future.*

Face Your Fears and Scare the Phobia Out of Your Brain

Magazine Article by Jason Koebler

1. **READ ▷** As you read lines 1–22, begin to collect and cite text evidence.

   - In the margin, restate the main idea in lines 1–4.
   - Underline text that explains why a person may choose to undergo "exposure therapy."
   - In the margin, list the steps that participants follow (lines 18–22).

CLOSE READ Notes

Ⓐ It turns out facing your fears really does work—researchers at Northwestern University have found that just one positive **exposure** to spiders had lasting effects in people with arachnophobia[1] six months later.

Ⓑ   The parts of the brain responsible for producing fear remained relatively inactive six months after patients underwent a single two-hour "exposure therapy" session in which they were able to touch a live tarantula. The brain changes were seen immediately after therapy
10 and remained essentially the same six months later, according to Katherina Hauner, lead author and therapist of the study, which appears in Monday's Proceedings of the National Academy of Sciences.

[1] **arachnophobia:** a fear of spiders.

Facing fears can actually help people overcome them.

exposure: *state of being left unprotected*

13

---

1. **READ AND CITE TEXT EVIDENCE** Explain that the central idea in this first paragraph is stated directly.

   Ⓐ **ASK STUDENTS** to read their margin notes to a partner and then write one response that best states the central (or main) idea of the first paragraph, citing textual evidence to support it. *Responses will include references to evidence in lines 1–4.*

   Critical Vocabulary: exposure (line 3) Have students explain *exposure* as it is used here. Why is the word used to describe this type of therapy? *This therapy exposes people to the object or situation that they fear.*

   FOR ELL STUDENTS Explain that *It turns out (that)* (line 1) is an idiomatic phase (or expression). Ask students what it means. *It means "to be found to be something."*

   ASK STUDENTS to look for other idiomatic phrases (or expressions) and cite them in the margin.

*Touch a live
tarantula
1. with a
paintbrush
2. with a
gloved hand
3. with a bare
hand*

"These people had been clinically afraid of spiders since childhood . . . they'd have to leave the house if they thought there was a spider inside," she says. According to the NIH, about 8 percent of people have a "specific phobia," considered to be a "marked and persistent fear and avoidance of a specific object or situation."

Over the course of two hours, participants touched a live tarantula with a paintbrush, a gloved hand, and eventually their bare hand. "It's 20 this idea that you slowly approach the thing you're afraid of. They learned that the spider was predictable and controllable, and by that time, they feel like it's not a spider anymore."

(D) The study sheds light on the brain responses to fear and the changes that happen when a fear is overcome. Immediately after therapy, activity in the participants' amygdalas, the part of the brain believed to be responsible for fear responses, remained relatively **dormant** and stayed that way six months later when participants were exposed to spiders.

*dormant:
inactive*

---

2. ◀ **REREAD AND DISCUSS** Reread lines 1–22. With a small group, discuss whether the evidence convinces you that exposure therapy works. Cite facts and examples from the text to support your opinions.

3. **READ** ▶ As you read lines 23–35, continue to cite textual evidence.

• Underline what happens in the brain during exposure therapy.
• Circle the fears that exposure therapy treats best and underline the fears it does not treat.

14

(C) Hauner says the study proves that exposure therapy works and 30 can potentially be used to develop new treatment methods for people with extreme phobias. She says a similar method can be used on people with fears of confined spaces, heights, flying, blood, and more.

"It has to be an **innocuous** object or situation—it's not a phobia if you're scared of sharks and don't want to go in shark-infested water," she says. "That's called being safe."

*innocuous:
not causing
harm or
offense*

---

4. ◀ **REREAD** Reread lines 23–35. Summarize the study in lines 23–28 in your own words.

Exposure therapy changes the way the brain reacts to fear, and that change lasts for at least six months.

---

5. **READ** ▶ As you read lines 36–42, underline text that explains future uses of exposure therapy.

15

---

2. **REREAD AND DISCUSS USING TEXT EVIDENCE**

(B) **ASK STUDENTS** to appoint a reporter for each group to cite specific textual evidence, including scientific facts and examples, to support their opinions about the effectiveness of exposure therapy. *Students should cite evidence from lines 1–22.*

3. **READ AND CITE TEXT EVIDENCE**

(C) **ASK STUDENTS** to locate and cite specific examples of the fears that exposure therapy treats successfully as well as the fears it doesn't treat. *Students should cite specific textual examples from lines 29–35.*

Critical Vocabulary: dormant (line 27) Ask how *dormant* fits into Koebler's discussion of the brain's responses to fear and the changes that occur when a fear is overcome. *Right after exposure therapy, the part of the brain responsible for fear responses remained inactive for at least six months.*

4. **REREAD AND CITE TEXT EVIDENCE**

(D) **ASK STUDENTS** to cite textual evidence (scientific facts and examples) that supports the main idea in a brief summary of the study. *Students should cite specific evidence from lines 23–28.*

5. **READ AND CITE TEXT EVIDENCE**

(E) **ASK STUDENTS** to cite textual evidence, based on the inferences and conclusions that therapists have drawn from the study, to explain possible future uses of exposure therapy. *Students should cite evidence from lines 36–42.*

Critical Vocabulary: innocuous (line 33) Have students explain **innocuous** as it is used here. Encourage them to cite innocuous objects or situations. *Students should be able to explain harmless objects or situations that can cause phobias, such as fear of thunder or of Friday the 13th, that are innocuous in reality.*

CLOSE READ
Notes

E **F**

In the near future, therapists might be able to inhibit the part of the brain responsible for fear or stimulate the region of the brain responsible for blocking fear in order to begin new therapies.

stimulate:
excite

40   "There's already techniques we use to **stimulate** regions of the brain to treat depression and OCD,"[2] she says. "It's not too far off in the future that we can use these techniques to treat other types of disorders."

   [2] **OCD:** OCD, or obsessive-compulsive disorder, is an anxiety disorder characterized by intrusive thoughts and repetitive behaviors.

---

6. ◀ **REREAD**   Reread lines 36–42. What is the main idea of this section?

In the future, exposure therapy might be used to treat different problems.

SHORT RESPONSE

Cite Text Evidence   Which information from the text most convinces you of the effectiveness of exposure therapy? **Cite text evidence** with specific facts and examples from the text.

The Northwestern University study provided the most convincing evidence about the effectiveness of exposure therapy. During the study, participants overcame a fear of spiders by learning that they are "predictable" and "controllable." This proves that exposure therapy works for people with specific phobias. The study also indicates that exposure therapy is effective in the long term. Participants were not afraid of spiders six months after the study.

16

---

6. **REREAD AND CITE TEXT EVIDENCE**

F **ASK STUDENTS** to cite textual evidence to support the central idea. *Support for the central idea is that exposure therapy might help therapists to find new ways to treat phobias or other types of psychological problems.*

Critical Vocabulary: stimulate (line 39) Have students share their definitions of *stimulate*. Ask how *stimulate* fits into the scientific discussion. *Koebler wants to share the study's findings that stimulating areas of the brain can treat certain disorders.*

SHORT RESPONSE

Cite Text Evidence   Students should

- explain whether or not they were convinced of the effectiveness of exposure therapy
- give reasons for their point of view
- cite specific evidence from the text to support their viewpoint

---

TO CHALLENGE STUDENTS . . .

For more context about fears and phobia, students can view the video titled "Fear" in their eBooks.

ASK STUDENTS to compare the aspects of fear that the scientists in the video are researching with the aspects of fear the scientists in the article are researching. *Students should note that the scientists in the video are concerned with discovering why human beings are afraid while the scientists in the article are researching how people can overcome their fears. Ask students to cite evidence to support their explanation.*

DIG DEEPER

With the class, return to Question 2, Reread and Discuss. Have students share the results of their discussion.

ASK STUDENTS whether they were satisfied with the outcome of their small-group discussions. Have each group share what the majority opinion was of the group. What persuasive evidence from the text did the group cite to support this opinion?

- Encourage students to tell whether there was any convincing evidence cited by group members holding the minority opinion about the effectiveness of exposure therapy. If so, why didn't it sway the group's opinion?
- Have groups explain whether or not they found sufficient persuasive evidence to support their point of view. Did everyone agree as to what made the evidence sufficient? How did the group resolve any differences of opinion?
- After groups have shared the results of their group discussion, ask whether another group shared any findings that persuaded them to change their opinion.

ASK STUDENTS to return to their Short Response answer to revise it, adding essential facts and examples, or deleting unnecessary details, based on the class discussion.

*my*SmartPlanner Create lesson plans and access resources online.

MEDIA **Wired for Fear**

Online Science Exhibit by The California Science Center

Why This Text?

Students encounter many different kinds of information online, particularly in videos. This lesson explores an online science exhibit with an animated video that tells how the brain deals with fear.

Key Learning Objective: The student will be able to analyze the purpose of a video and understand the visual and sound elements used in it.

RI 1 Cite textual evidence; make inferences.
RI 2 Determine a central idea; provide a summary.
RI 3 Analyze text elements.
RI 4 Determine the meaning of words and phrases, including technical meanings.
RI 5 Analyze structure.
RI 6 Determine an author's point of view or purpose.
RI 7 Integrate information presented in different media or formats.
SL 1 Engage effectively in a range of collaborative discussions.
SL 2 Interpret information presented in diverse media and formats; explain how it contributes to a topic.
SL 4 Present claims and findings to accentuate main ideas.
SL 5 Include multimedia components and visual displays in presentations.
L 4a Use context as a clue to a word's meaning.
L 4c Consult reference materials to determine meaning.
L 4d Verify preliminary determination of the meaning of a word.

 Text Complexity Rubric

Quantitative Measures	**Wired for Fear** Lexile: N/A
Qualitative Measures	**Levels of Meaning/Purpose** more than one purpose; implied, but easy to infer
	Structure sophisticated graphics, essential to understanding the text; may also provide information not otherwise conveyed in the text
	Language Conventionality and Clarity increased unfamiliar language
	Knowledge Demands complex concepts
Reader/Task Considerations	• Teacher determined • Vary by individual reader and type of text • See the Text X-Ray for suggested Reader/Task Considerations.

English Language Support Before teaching, use the Text X-Ray below for an overview of the text's complexity. The Text X-Ray and the supports and scaffolds in the Teacher's Edition will help you guide students of different skill levels.

Meaning Making

Language Development

Effective Expression

Content Knowledge

Foundational Skills

Text Complexity: Qualitative Measures

Levels of Meaning/Purpose

more than one purpose; implied, easy to infer

Help students determine the purpose and meaning of an online science exhibit.

- Teacher's Edition side notes, pp. 60, 61

To teach how to integrate information, see

- Integrate Information, p. 62a

 Use It! **Interactive Whiteboard Lesson:** Main/Central Idea and Details

ZOOM IN ON DETERMINING MEANING AND PURPOSE Organize students into mixed-ability pairs or small groups. Have them watch the video once and then play it again, pausing at logical points. During each pause, students should ask and answer questions they have about the part they just watched. Encourage them to replay the portions of the video until their questions have all been answered. Then ask groups to complete these sentence frames.

- The **main idea** of the video is that _____. *(the brain has an effective, complex system in place for dealing with the threat of danger)*
- The **purpose** of the video is to _____. *(inform viewers of the way the brain works when faced with danger)*

Structure

sophisticated graphics, essential to understanding the text; may also provide information not otherwise conveyed in the text

Help students interpret information from the visual and sound elements of an online exhibit.

- Teacher's Edition side notes, p. 60
- Interpret Information, p. 61

To reteach how to interpret information, see

- Interpret Information, p. 62a

 Use It! **Level Up Tutorial:** Analyzing Visuals

ZOOM IN ON INTERPRETING INFORMATION Point out that the video includes **subtitles,** or lines of text that show what the narrator is saying.

- Ask students why they think the creator of the video included this text element in addition to the narration. *(Because the information includes vocabulary and complicated ideas unfamiliar to the viewer, it is helpful to both hear and see it.)*
- Play the video once with the sound; then play it again without the sound. Ask students how the lack of sound affects their viewing of the film. *(Possible responses: Students may say that the film doesn't hold their attention as well without the sound; the music and other sound effects help to emphasize important ideas; hearing the narrator explain what is happening makes the explanation clearer.)*

Language Conventionality and Clarity

increased unfamiliar language

Teach unfamiliar vocabulary in context.

- Applying Academic Vocabulary, p. 60

Help students determine the meaning of technical words.

- Teacher's Edition side notes, p. 59
- English Language Support, p. 59

Guide students to discuss and write about the information in the text.

- English Language Support, p. 61
- Performance Task, p. 62

ZOOM IN ON **USING TRANSITIONS** Write these transitional words and phrases on the board: *first, then, next, finally, before, after; also, because, as a result of; but, however, in contrast.* Review with students how these words and phrases help to show relationships between ideas.

- Have pairs of students write three sentences that include transitions from the board about the functions/relationships of these parts of the body during the fear response: the sensory organs and the thalamus; the amygdala and the brain stem; the hypothalamus and hormones.
- Encourage them to watch the video several times to check the accuracy of their statements.
- Have pairs take turns sharing their sentences with the class.

Knowledge Demands

complex concepts

Support English Learners in understanding necessary background information.

- Teacher's Edition Background note, p. 59

ZOOM IN ON **BUILDING SCIENTIFIC BACKGROUND** Give students an overview of each part of the video:

- The first part (00:00–1:08) introduces the potentially dangerous situation and how the awareness of danger reaches the amygdala, or fear control center.
- The second part (1:09–2:22) explains which parts of the brain are involved in sending out the initial response to a possible threat.
- The third section (2:23–3:03) tells what happens when the danger is confirmed or found to be a false alarm.
- The final part of the video (3:04–4:05) explains how the brain creates a memory from this situation that will help the person react to similar situations in the future.

Suggested Reader/Task Considerations

You might consider the following before assigning this video to students.

- Will students be able to remember the information they learn from the video and connect the ideas?
- Will students understand the technical terms in the video?

ZOOM IN ON **SUPPORTING COMPREHENSION**

- Have small groups of students create their own graphic representations of the way in which the brain and body react to the fear stimulus. Have groups present their charts to the class.
- Discuss the various components of the video such as the introductory sequence, the use of the model, the subtitles, and the sound elements including the music and narration. Have students think about one part of the video that they thought was effective and one part that they did not find interesting. Let them to share their ideas with a partner.

Background Have students read the background information. Explain that scientists, by using increasingly advanced technologies, are now able to understand that signs of danger activate different pathways in the brain. The scientist who helped make this online exhibit has created experiments that show fear signals traveling through two different pathways in the brain. Each of these pathways is essential in helping people successfully react to danger.

SETTING A PURPOSE Direct students to read the Setting a Purpose section to help them focus their attention as they explore the online exhibit. Remind them to generate questions as they view and read the information.

Analyze Technical Meaning   RI 4

Explain to students that this online exhibit contains several words and terms about the brain. Some of these words, such as *amygdala*, they have read earlier in the selections "Fears and Phobias" and "In the Spotlight"; others may not be familiar to them. Tell students that they can approach these difficult-sounding words as they would any word that they do not know while they are reading.

A CITE TEXT EVIDENCE Discuss ways that students approach unknown words while they are viewing or studying information. *(context clues, rereading or replaying, look up in a dictionary)* As needed, remind students of these choices, explaining that they should not continue reading or watching if they are not able to come up with at least a basic meaning of the word, such as "a part of the brain that sends signals to the body."

English Language Support

Have students work with a partner to view "Wired for Fear." Instruct them to turn off the sound and read the subtitles of the video and take notes on the words that they find difficult. Remind them that they can stop the video to give themselves time to copy a word. Then have them use the strategies above to write definitions for the words on their list. Finally, have them view the video with the sound turned on, stopping the video as necessary to review their definitions.

Background *The study and science of fear involves the work of many scientists over many years. These scientists have explored exactly how the body deals with fear as a nervous impulse. They have conducted research and used computer-generated brain imaging to study activity in the brain. Their work has revealed different brain structures, paths, and cells that help to explain fear and how the whole body responds to the fear alarm.*

MEDIA ANALYSIS

Wired for Fear

Online Science Exhibit by The California Science Center

SETTING A PURPOSE "Fear is a full-body experience." This is how the website Goosebumps! The Science of Fear introduces its topic "Fear and the Brain." This website includes a collection of videos, articles, and images that covers several aspects of how the body, especially the brain, processes sensory information (what we see, hear, feel, smell, touch) and alerts us to what might be harmful to us.

The section of the website titled "Wired for Fear" provides information on the specific areas and cells of the brain that activate our responses to scary situations. This web page includes a video that you can access to watch an animated version of how the brain processes fear reactions. As you watch the video, note how these pathways connect to the brain's threat center and show why fear can be a good thing. Write down any questions you have during viewing.

(tl) ©Sebastian Kaulitzki/Alamy Images; (tr) ©Fotolia

English Language Support

Use Technical Words Before watching the video, display concrete examples of sound and visual elements students will encounter in the online exhibit:

- an animated sequence
- a photography still
- an example of narration

Explain the terms *animated, still, narration,* and any other terms that describe the examples as you discuss them together.

CLOSE READ

AS YOU VIEW Tell students that they will be viewing an online science exhibit, including an animated video. Explain that video creators use a variety of visual and sound elements to convey information in their videos. Then have students read the AS YOU VIEW section to help them focus on the elements used in the video to convey information.

Interpret Information
RI 1, RI 4,
RI 6, SL 2

Explain that video creators use different **visual elements,** things you see, and **sound elements,** things you hear, to convey information. Tell students that visual elements can include **stills** (motionless photos) or **animation** (illustrations made to move or appear alive). Sound elements can include music and **narration** (words spoken by a narrator).

Point out that many videos include printed text as well, including a feature called subtitles. **Subtitles** are printed words that appear on the screen and show what a narrator or character is saying.

B CITE EVIDENCE As students watch the video, have them list the different visual and sound elements it uses. *(stills, animation, diagrams, music, narration, subtitles)*

Next, explain to students that a video creator has a **purpose,** or intent, for making the video. A purpose for a video can be to inform, entertain, persuade, or express thoughts or feelings, just as with a story or article.

C ASK STUDENTS to decide the basic purpose of the video as they watch it. *(to inform)*

COLLABORATIVE DISCUSSION As students discuss the content of the video in small groups, they might work together to make a diagram showing the brain pathways that are activated in response to fear. Students can use this diagram to discuss the new ideas and information they learned from the video.

ASK STUDENTS to share any questions they generated in the course of viewing and discussing the online exhibit and animated video.

MEDIA

Format: Online science exhibit
Running Time: 4:05

B AS YOU VIEW As you view the animated video, consider how the information is presented. Notice how the video introduces and explains new terms and ideas using text, sound, and visuals.

Consider how the use of these three elements helps you understand the scientific terms and ideas presented. As needed, pause the video to make notes about what impresses you or about ideas you might want to talk about later. Replay or rewind so that you can clarify anything you do not **C** understand.

COLLABORATIVE DISCUSSION With a small group, discuss how the brain pathways of our body's fear response work. What new ideas or information did you learn about fear and the brain from the video? Cite specific terms and segments from the video and tell what you learned from them.

©Vogt Productions/California Science Center Foundation

APPLYING ACADEMIC VOCABULARY

factor	indicate

THINK-PAIR-SHARE Have students turn to a partner to discuss the following questions. Guide students to include the academic vocabulary words *factor* and *indicate* in their responses. Ask volunteers to share their responses with the class.

- Which **factors** trigger the freeze response?
- How does the human body **indicate** that the brain has received signals that danger is present?

Interpret Information

Like other media, the video "Wired for Fear" was created for a specific purpose. The **purpose,** or intent, of any video or form of media is usually to inform, entertain, persuade, or express the feelings or thoughts of the creator. In meeting the purpose, the creator uses words as well as visual and sound elements to convey information.

Visual elements that can be used in animated videos include:

 Stills — images that are motionless, such as illustrations or photographs. In "Wired for Fear," a still of an illustration of the brain is used to point out where the amygdala is located.

 Animation — the process of creating images that appear to move and seem alive. Animation can be created through drawings, computer graphics, or photographs. For example, the hiking scenes in "Wired for Fear" are an animation cycle of drawings.

Visual elements can help viewers understand **technical terms,** which are the words and phrases used in a particular profession or field of study. For example, by showing the amygdala as a kind of master computer that processes information, the animated model in "Wired for Fear" helps viewers better understand the amygdala and what it does. Using light to highlight brain pathways is another way that the video's visuals help to explain the content in a memorable way.

Sound elements include what you hear in a video:

 Music — sounds created by singing, playing instruments, or using computer-generated tones. Music is often included in videos to create a mood.

 Narration — the words as well as the expression and quality of voice used by the narrator. In "Wired for Fear," the narrator uses emphasis and expression to connect the words to the visuals being shown.

To interpret visual and sound elements in a video, ask questions such as the following:

- Does the video use stills or animation? What purpose do they serve? How do they aid my understanding of the topic?
- How does the music match the video's topic or content? How does the music create or add to a mood?
- What does the narration add to the video?

TEACH

CLOSE READ

Interpret Information

Guide students through the instruction, helping them identify parts and elements of "Wired for Fear" that correspond to each element or term discussed in the instruction. As students identify elements, ask them to explain how each one conveys information to the viewer. Clarify technical terms as needed, and review the video together when necessary to remind students of its content and approach.

Review technical terms from the exhibit, such as *amygdala, adrenaline, hippocampus,* and so on. Have students explain the terms in their own words to show their understanding of the content. Explain that the scientists who regularly work with these terms have a much more detailed knowledge of the terms' meanings; however, for the purposes of introduction to the topic, it is enough for students to understand the terms in a more basic way.

Remind students to use the bulleted questions to review and discuss the video. Tell them to write notes to remind themselves of their ideas and any questions they have for further investigation of the information found in this online exhibit.

English Language Support

Taking Notes Remind students that one way to understand a text is to take notes about the content. Model by reading the first paragraph on page 61 and writing some notes from the text, for example, "purpose is to inform, entertain, persuade, or express feelings." Then combine the notes into one summary sentence.

- Read aloud the second paragraph on the page about visual elements. Clarify terms and content. Then work as a group to write a sentence about the paragraph. Encourage the group to use the words *and*, *but*, or *so* in their sentence.

- Have pairs of students take turns reading aloud the sections that describe visual and sound elements. As one student reads, the other should take notes. Review compound and complex sentences. Then encourage students to create compound and complex sentences to make connections between the ideas.

- Ask students to work independently to read the page and take notes. Review compound, complex, and compound-complex sentences before having students write a summary using each type of sentence.

Analyzing the Media

RI 1, RI 2,
RI 3, RI 4,
RI 5, RI 6,
RI 7

Possible answers:

1. *The hiker is about to stumble upon something in his path; he is not sure if it is a snake or not. The video shows how the hiker's body responds to (1) identify possible danger, (2) process the sensory information it receives, and (3) decide if the danger is real or not.*

2. *We might freeze or change facial expression; heart rate, blood pressure, and sweating increase. The brain stem, facial muscles and nerves, the hypothalamus, and the hormones released by the hypothalamus all play a part in activating these responses.*

3. *The title helps you understand that the brain works in a way that is similar to wiring for lights and electricity. The lights help focus your attention on the area being discussed; the lighted railroad tracks use a familiar example of forward motion to help explain the motion of information along the pathways.*

4. *The female voice is calm and easy to listen to. The music shifts to match the mood of each scene. Both music and narration help underline important ideas about how the amygdala works.*

5. *The video is an effective way to learn about the topic. Although the visual effects are not overly sophisticated, they help frame the important ideas in a way that helps viewers grasp them. The sound elements are appropriate; they emphasize ideas, but they are not too obvious.*

Analyzing the Media

RI 1, RI 2, RI 3,
RI 4, RI 5, RI 6,
RI 7, W 6, SL 2,
SL 5

Cite Text Evidence   Support your responses with evidence from the media.

1. **Summarize** What situation does the hiker face in "Wired for Fear"? Describe how the video explains what the hiker experiences.

2. **Cause/Effect** Review the sequence that uses the animated model. What are some ways our bodies respond when the amygdala senses danger? What parts of the brain activate these responses?

3. **Infer** Explain the title "Wired for Fear." Why does the video use flashing lights and graphics that show movement in the animated model of how the brain processes potential danger?

4. **Integrate** Describe the music and narration used in the video. In what ways do they support the purpose of the video?

5. **Critique** Think about the purpose of this video. Consider the techniques that are used to support the information presented. Do you think "Wired for Fear" is an effective informational video? Why or why not?

PERFORMANCE TASK

Media Activity: Podcast Create an audio recording for a podcast movie review of the video "Wired for Fear." You can work alone or with a partner.

- Focus on a few elements of the video that particularly impressed you. Include both positive and negative impressions that you think are relevant. Write notes about these impressions.

- Explain how each element you have chosen clarifies the topic, using examples from the video. Present ideas for additional information that could be included in this type of video. Write notes about these elements and examples.

- Use your notes to create an outline or draft of your podcast review.

- Create the recording of your review alone or with a partner, using a conversational approach. Share your review with a larger group.

FOR STANDARD ENGLISH LEARNERS

Some students may have difficulty with the **pronunciation** of both letters in certain final consonant clusters, including *st* as in *podcast*, and others such as *ft*, *nd*, *sk*, *sp*, *pt*, and *ct*. After students have written their outline or draft of the podcast review, suggest that they underline words with final consonant clusters. Then have them practice their review with a partner before sharing with a larger group, paying particular attention to the pronunciation of the underlined words.

Assign this performance task.

PERFORMANCE TASK

W 6, SL 2,
SL 5

Media Activity: Podcast Have student partners or peer groups critique each other's podcasts before they present them to the whole class.

- Students should give ideas for how their partners might improve their recordings.
- Students can review the suggestions and decide which ones to incorporate into their podcasts.
- Students can record their podcasts again for posting on the Web.

Integrate Information

RI 7

TEACH

Remind students that both the video "Wired for Fear" and the excerpt from "In the Spotlight" they read earlier tell about the fear response. Tell students that they can integrate the ideas in these two selections. Explain that to **integrate** or **synthesize** means to take individual pieces of information and combine them in order to have a better understanding of a topic. Then explain these steps to synthesize, or integrate, information:

- **Find the central idea.** The **central idea,** or main idea, is the most important idea in a text or a video. It can be a central idea for a whole article or video; it can also be a central idea for a section or a paragraph of the whole selection.
- **Identify supporting details.** After you determine a central idea, think about and list the important details that give information about it.
- **Make connections.** Think about the relationships among all the ideas in the text and video. In what ways are they connected? How are they similar? How are they different? How does one idea relate to or expand your understanding of the other?
- **Integrate ideas.** Take individual pieces of information and combine them in order to gain a better understanding of a topic.

PRACTICE AND APPLY

Work with students to organize their ideas about the video and the excerpt in a chart like the one below. Then have them use the information in the chart to write a paragraph that integrates some central ideas and details about the topic from both sources.

Source	Central Idea(s)	Details

English Language Support

Link Ideas Review connecting words with students. Write phrases such as *for example, in the first place, as a result,* and *on the other hand* on the board. Challenge pairs of students to use the information in their charts and these phrases to write sentences that integrate the central ideas and details from both sources.

Interpret Information: Visual and Sound Elements

SL 2

RETEACH

Remind students that the creators of videos use different visual and sound elements to convey information. Review the following elements and their purposes with students:

- **Stills** are motionless images such as illustrations and photographs. They can help viewers figure out what things look like.
- **Animation** is the process of creating images that appear to move and seem to be alive. Animations can show how something moves or works.
- **Music** includes sounds created by singing, instruments, or computer-generated tones. It can help create a mood.
- **Narration** includes the words used by a narrator. It can provide information that helps explain the topic and the visuals being shown. As a voice, narration can provide emphasis and expression.
- **Subtitles** are the narration shown in printed words on the screen; these are meant to help hearing-impaired people understand the narration. Subtitles can also be used to describe music or other sound effects that are important to understanding mood or the actions taking place in the video.

English Language Support

Use Technical Words Have students work in pairs to read each word and its explanation aloud. Ask them to use a dictionary to look up any unfamiliar words. Then have them write simple complete sentences using each term. *(Possible answers: The stills help viewers see things. Animations make things look as if they are moving. We listen to music every day. The narration explains what the video is showing. Subtitles are printed words that tell what is happening.)*

PRACTICE AND APPLY

Have students watch another informational video. As they watch, have them list the different kinds of visual and sound elements in it. Ask students to tell how each element contributed to the video and conveyed information.

FACING FEAR

The FYI site provides links to online articles from a variety of magazines and newspapers. Help students choose a few articles to read to further their exploration of the topic Facing Fear.

NOVELWISE

Students can unlock the power of novels with this unique resource. Help students read through longer works with these tips:

- Find a Book
- Before You Read
- As You Read
- After You Read

Each book includes introductory material, worksheets, graphic organizers, and discussion guides.

ADDITIONAL TEXTS BY COLLECTION

Suggest students read the following:

- "The Raven" by Edgar Allen Poe
- "Psalm 23" from the King James Bible

Read aloud the poems, and then ask students to identify their themes. *(fear of death or separation, reassurance in the face of fear)*

NONFICTION CONNECTIONS

Suggest that students increase their reading of informational texts. The nonfiction connections include

- speeches
- diaries
- true-life accounts
- newspaper articles
- political cartoons

Creating an Independent Reading Program

BUILD A CLASSROOM LIBRARY

A classroom library full of books and other media offers students a rich and accessible reading environment.

- Designate a bookcase as the classroom library.
- Organize books into broad categories such as fiction, fantasy, biography, and informational text.
- Ask your school or local librarian to recommend other trade books you could include in your classroom library.
- Create a checkout system. You may want to put an index card in a pocket at the back of each book or use a cell phone to take a photo of each student with the book he or she wants to check out. (Delete the photo when the student returns the book.)

- Use a box or crate for returns. Students should place their returned books in the box.
- Assign volunteers to take turns with library upkeep.

CREATE LIBRARY RULES

Work with students to create a list of library rules, such as these:

- Check out one book at a time.
- Return a book before you check out a new one.
- Sign the checkout card and place it in the Checkout Box.
- Use a shared digital spreadsheet to create an online catalog and to track books.

PERFORMANCE TASK A

Interactive Lessons
To help you complete this task, use *Giving a Presentation.*

Present a Response to Literature

People in the literary works in this collection have to face a fear. Look back at these texts and share your response to one of them. Explain your understanding of the text's meaning and convince others that your interpretation is valid.

A successful response to literature

- includes a clear thesis statement
- provides background information
- provides a variety of evidence to support the thesis
- ends by restating the thesis
- uses effective verbal and nonverbal elements

W 2a–b Write informative texts.
W 9a Draw evidence from literary texts to support analysis.
SL 4 Present claims and findings.
SL 6 Adapt speech to a variety of contexts and tasks.

PLAN

Choose a Topic Which literary work from the collection interests you most? Re-read it, studying it closely for details. Choose a text with at least one literary element that is important to your understanding of the work as a whole.

Develop a Thesis Draft a thesis statement, or controlling idea, that sums up the main point you will make in your response. The thesis statement should clearly identify your purpose and explain one literary element of the text, such as character, conflict, or theme.

Gather Evidence Use the annotation tools in your eBook to find evidence from the text to support your thesis. Save your evidence to *my*Notebook, in a folder titled *Collection 1 Performance Task.* Try to include various kinds of support, such as direct quotations, paraphrased lines, details, and examples.

ACADEMIC VOCABULARY

As you plan, write, and review your draft, try to use the academic vocabulary words.

evident
factor
indicate
similar
specific

myNotebook

"Fine?"

"Go on," she says magnanimously. "I'll be fine."

But as soon as her mother is out the door, Bailey wants to run after her, crying "Mom-mee! Don't go!"

This passage shows how Bailey is trying to be brave and grown-up but is still very frightened.

English Language Support

Plan a Presentation Make sure students understand that their responses should focus on their own interpretations of the text. Explain that the drafts of their thesis statements may simply state a general or basic idea that they want to prove; they may revise their thesis to more specifically answer the question *How?* or *Why?* after they gather evidence. Have pairs discuss their literary-response plans using the sentence frames and questions below.

- The text I have chosen for my response is _____.

PERFORMANCE TASK A

PRESENT A RESPONSE TO LITERATURE

W 2a–b,
W 9a,
SL 4, SL 6, L 1, L 3b

Introduce students to the Performance Task by reading the introductory paragraph with them and reviewing the criteria for what makes a good response to literature. Remind students that their responses should examine how literary elements in the text affect the overall meaning.

PLAN

CHOOSE A TOPIC

To help students narrow their topic selection, have them list their three favorite texts from the collection. Then have them refer to their reading notes to identify the literary elements that they think had the strongest impact on each text. Encourage students to select the topic that they are most interested in analyzing and interpreting further.

English Language Support

Provide Text Evidence Draw students' attention to the excerpt from "Fine?" and help them identify the dialogue and the description of Bailey's fear and her efforts to overcome it. Explain that this example shows how a quotation can support interpretations about a character.

- One literary element I will explain in my response is _____.
- My thesis, or the main point I want to make is _____.
- To support my thesis, I will look for evidence that shows _____.

What would you want to learn if you were listening to a presentation on this topic?

Students can use their conversations to help them select evidence to support their theses.

English Language Support

Adjust Language Choices Tell students that using clear, precise language helps them convey their ideas and convince their audience. Have small groups brainstorm words that relate to the literary elements in their theses. For example, students examining character might list *traits, attitude, behavior, thoughts, feelings,* and *appearance.* Students can use their word lists, along with the evidence they have gathered, to write main-idea statements to support their theses.

PRODUCE

DRAFT YOUR RESPONSE

Encourage students to use an outline or graphic organizer to plan their drafts. Remind them that each paragraph should relate clearly to the thesis statement.

LANGUAGE CONVENTIONS

Point out that adverbs indicate manner and are usually formed by adding the suffix *-ly* to an adjective. Clarify that a phrase or clause may also function as an adverbial. As students create their drafts, encourage them to add adverbs to help readers understand when, where, how, or why an event occurred.

English Language Support

Use Adverbials Explain that an **adverbial** is a word or group of words that answers the question *When? Where? How?* or *Why?* in a sentence. Share the following examples of adverbials with students. Have them take turns with partners using the examples in sentences.

Adverbials

To provide details about...	Example
time	later, yesterday, after school
manner	quickly, carefully
place	outside, on the table
cause	because they felt nervous, to relax

Consider Purpose and Audience How can you explain your interpretation of the text? What evidence will convey your ideas to your audience? Keeping your purpose and audience in mind will help you maintain the right tone and include the right information.

Interactive Lessons
To help you plan your purpose and audience, complete the following lesson:
· Knowing Your Audience

PRODUCE

myWriteSmart

Draft Your Response Write out your response to the literary work you have selected. As you draft your response, keep the following in mind:

- The introduction should state the title and author of the work, clearly explain the thesis, and provide any necessary background information.
- In the body, discuss your main ideas. Each idea should include evidence that supports the thesis. Explain what each piece of evidence shows.
- Restate the thesis in the conclusion and give an overall impression or insight into the work.

Write your rough draft in *my*WriteSmart. Focus on getting your ideas down, rather than perfecting your choice of language.

Interactive Lessons
To help you organize your response, complete the following lessons:
· The Content of Your Presentation
· Style in Presentation

Language Conventions: Modify to Add Details

Adverbs are words that modify, or describe, verbs, adjectives, or other adverbs. They provide details about time, place, manner, and cause. Read the following passage from "The Ravine."

" Vinny watched, his muddy towel hooked around his neck. Reluctantly, he let it fall, then dove in after them. "

Notice how the adverb "reluctantly" tells more about how Vinny lets the towel fall. Look for places where you can add details about the time, manner, place, or cause of an event.

REVISE

myWriteSmart

Practice Your Response Read your response to literature aloud. Practice using verbal and nonverbal elements to engage the audience. You can write cues on the text of your presentation about the verbal and nonverbal elements you plan to use in presenting your ideas.

- Show enthusiasm through your voice so your audience will feel enthusiasm for your response.

Have your partner or a group of peers review your draft in *my*WriteSmart. Ask them to note any evidence that does not support the thesis.

English Language Support

Modify to Add Details Have students exchange drafts with a partner. Ask students to write three *When?, Where?, How?,* or *Why?* questions about their partner's draft. Encourage students to use adverbials to answer the questions. **ALL PROFICIENCIES**

- Grab your audience's attention by using the pitch of your voice for emphasis.
- Speak more slowly than you do in conversation, to help listeners understand you. Pause to let important points sink in.
- Look audience members in the eye. Use gestures and facial expressions to show your feelings and add emphasis.

Interactive Lessons
To practice verbal and nonverbal elements, complete the following lesson:
- Delivering Your Presentation

Evaluate Your Response Have your partner or group of peers review your planned response. Use the following chart to revise your draft.

Questions	Tips	Revision Techniques
Did I include the author and title of the literary work in my introduction?	**Highlight** the author and title.	**Add** a sentence or phrase naming the author and title.
Does my introduction have a clear thesis?	**Underline** the thesis. **Highlight** the literary element and your main point about it.	**Add** a sentence that clearly states the thesis.
Are the main ideas clear? Does each main idea support the thesis?	**Highlight** each main idea.	**Revise** the body of your response so that the main ideas are clear.
Is each main idea supported by evidence?	**Underline** each supporting detail, example, or quotation.	**Add** details, examples, or quotations to support ideas. **Explain** the significance of each piece of evidence.
Did I use adverbs to provide details about time, place, manner, or cause?	**Underline** all adverbs that provide details.	**Add** adverbs to provide details about time, place, manner, or cause.
Does my conclusion restate the thesis?	**Highlight** the restatement.	**Add** a restatement of the thesis.

PRESENT

Share Your Response Finalize your response and choose a way to share it with your audience. Consider these options:

- Present your response as a speech to the class.
- Record your response as a webcast.

PERFORMANCE TASK A

FOR STANDARD ENGLISH LEARNERS

Adapt Speech Remind students of the differences between formal speech and informal conversation. As they practice their responses, encourage students to pay special attention to words that end with consonant clusters. Speaking slowly and clearly can help them focus on pronouncing the final consonant in each word.

REVISE

EVALUATE YOUR RESPONSE

As students use the chart to evaluate their responses, remind them to examine both the relevance and sufficiency of evidence for each main idea. Use a student sample to model revision techniques for adding and explaining evidence.

PRESENT

SHARE YOUR RESPONSE

Remind students to use volume, expression, and pacing to emphasize their points. Let speakers respond to audience questions and comments either after their class speeches or through post-speech online discussions.

FOR STUDENTS WITH DISABILITIES

Use Visual Cues Encourage students to use highlighting to create visual cues that will alert them when to pause or stress certain words and phrases. Students may also read their responses from a projector screen as they record a video of their presentation.

WHEN STUDENTS STRUGGLE...

Practice Speaking Techniques Let students view a recording of a model presentation before they present their own responses. Pause the recording intermittently to point out examples of strong speaking techniques, such as maintaining eye contact or using voice modulation and inflection. Encourage students to focus on one technique at a time as they practice their responses with a partner.

USE THE SCORING RUBRIC

Assign three students to score each presentation, with each student focusing on one of the three rubric categories. Ask students to write a brief explanation of the reasons for their score.

REFLECT ON THE PROCESS

In addition to reflecting on the effectiveness of their presentations, ask students to reflect on their planning, producing, and revising. They should consider not only what they learned but also what they might do differently in future assignments. Have students discuss their answers to the following questions in small groups:

- How did writing the response affect your interpretation of the text?
- What were the most important revisions that you made to strengthen your draft?
- What was the most challenging aspect of the process? What strategies did you use to address the challenge?

PERFORMANCE TASK A RUBRIC
RESPONSE TO LITERATURE

	Ideas and Evidence	Organization	Language
4	• The introduction clearly states the thesis. • The response includes insightful interpretation of the text. • All background information appropriate for the audience is included. • Relevant evidence supports the thesis. • The conclusion effectively summarizes the thesis.	• The ideas and evidence are organized logically throughout the speech. • Verbal and nonverbal elements effectively emphasize main points and hold the audience's attention.	• The response reflects a formal style. • Standard English is used appropriately throughout the response. • Sentence beginnings, lengths, and structures vary and have a rhythmic flow. • Grammar and usage are correct.
3	• The introduction states a thesis. • The response includes interpretation of the text. • Some background information is included, but some details are left out. • Most evidence supports the thesis. • The conclusion restates the thesis.	• The organization of ideas and evidence is logical in most places. • Verbal and nonverbal elements emphasize some main points and sometimes hold the audience's attention.	• The style becomes informal in a few places. • Standard English is used appropriately, with few problems. • Sentence beginnings, lengths, and structures vary somewhat. • Some grammatical and usage errors are present.
2	• The introduction identifies a thesis, but it is not clearly stated. • The response includes little interpretation of the text. • Several background details are included, but important information is omitted. • The evidence is not always clear or relevant. • The conclusion includes an incomplete summary of the thesis.	• The organization of ideas and evidence is confusing in some places, and does not follow a pattern. • Verbal and nonverbal elements are sparse or misplace emphasis.	• The style becomes informal in many places. • The use of standard English is inconsistent. • Sentence structures rarely vary, and some fragments are present. • Grammar and usage are incorrect in many places, but the speaker's ideas are still clear.
1	• The introduction is confusing and does not state a thesis. • The response includes no interpretation of the text. • Background information is missing. • The thesis is not supported by evidence. • The conclusion is missing.	• A logical organization is not used; ideas and evidence are presented randomly. • Verbal and nonverbal elements are not used to emphasize main points, or their inappropriate use detracts from the response.	• The style is inappropriate. • The use of standard English is minimal. • Repetitive sentence structure and fragments make the response hard to follow. • Many grammatical and usage errors change the meaning of ideas.

TO CHALLENGE STUDENTS...

Create an Advertisement Challenge students to use their literary responses to create an advertisement that encourages viewers to read their literary text. Students should select the strongest evidence from their responses to support their opinions. Encourage students to incorporate visual or multimedia elements and to include persuasive techniques.

Interactive Lessons
To help you complete this task, use
• *Writing Informative Texts*
• *Using Textual Evidence*

Write an Informative Essay

In "Fears and Phobias" and other lessons in this collection, you learned about fear. Now use the texts you have read and your own research to write an informative essay about a fear.

A successful informative essay

- provides an introduction that catches the reader's attention and clearly states the topic
- logically organizes main ideas and supporting evidence
- includes evidence such as facts, definitions, examples, and quotations
- uses appropriate transitions to connect ideas
- provides a conclusion that supports the topic

Mentor Text Notice how this introduction from "In the Spotlight" catches the reader's attention and also states the topic.

> " Some of us are fine with the idea of standing in front of huge crowds of people. But others would happily bungee off a 200-foot bridge . . . rather than experience the sheer terror of facing an audience. . . . If that sounds like you, then you are one of the world's many, many sufferers of glossophobia—the fear of speaking (or trying to speak) in public. "

PLAN

Determine Your Topic Review the selections in the collection. Choose the fear that you want to learn more about.

Gather Information Jot down important facts, examples, and definitions, including

- what causes this type of fear
- what happens to our bodies in response to this fear
- what methods can be used to overcome this fear

Do Research Use print and digital sources to find additional definitions, information, and quotations from experts.

- Search for little-known facts. Make sure facts are credible.
- Cite real-life examples of people living with this fear.

W 2a–f Write informative texts.

W 4 Produce clear and coherent writing.

W 5 Strengthen writing as needed.

W 8 Gather relevant and credible information from multiple print and digital sources while avoiding plagiarism and providing basic bibliographic information.

fyi
hmhfyi.com

Visit hmhfyi.com to explore your topic and enhance your research.

myNotebook
Use the annotation tools in your eBook to find evidence to support your ideas. Save each piece of evidence to your notebook.

ACADEMIC VOCABULARY
As you write about fear, be sure to use the academic vocabulary words.

evident
factor
indicate
similar
specific

WRITE AN INFORMATIVE ESSAY

W 2a–f, W 4, W 5, W 8

Introduce students to the Performance Task by reading the introductory paragraph with them and reviewing the criteria for what makes a good informative essay. Remind students that a good informative essay includes evidence that supports the main points the writer makes. Students may complete this Performance Task in connection with their study of the brain and the nervous system. Coordinate with science teachers as appropriate.

PLAN

DETERMINE YOUR TOPIC

To help students select a topic, have them work in small groups to list the different types of fears that they read about in the collection. For each type, have group members take turns stating one thing they learned about the fear and one question they have about the fear.

English Language Support

Write Informative Texts Have pairs use the Mentor Text excerpt to discuss the following questions:

- What is the relationship between the first two sentences? What signal word helps you identify this relationship? Why would the author use this text relationship in the introduction?

- What part of the text informs readers of the topic? What do you learn about the topic from this part of the text?

Encourage students to refer back to the Mentor Text and their discussion notes as they plan and write introductions for their informative essays.

PERFORMANCE TASK B

PLAN

DO RESEARCH

Point out that Internet search engines can help students find websites that may contain the kinds of information they are looking for. Suggest that students be as specific as possible when typing in key words for their web searches.

PRODUCE

WRITE YOUR ESSAY

Make sure students use their outlines as a guide for their first draft, and point out that each main idea should be supported by the details and evidence they included in their outlines. Explain that some examples and evidence might be better presented as visuals, which students should prepare now as well.

FOR STANDARD ENGLISH LEARNERS

Conjugate Verbs Explain that students should use formal English in their essays. Remind them to use the correct form of the verb *to be* that agrees with the subject. Ask students to identify the example of formal language in the following sentence pairs:

- His stomach be fluttering like a butterfly./His stomach was fluttering like a butterfly.
- They was taught relaxation techniques to use when they felt anxious./They were taught relaxation techniques to use when they felt anxious.

English Language Support

Link Ideas Have students choose transitions to complete the sentences below. Then have pairs discuss the relationship between each set of ideas.

- Claustrophobia is the fear of being in small spaces. ____, many people who have claustrophobia do not like riding in elevators. (*For example/However*)
- The brain activates the body's "fight or flight" response when it senses danger. ____, the heart rate and blood pressure increase. (*As a result/Therefore*)

Consider Your Purpose and Audience Think about who will read you essay and what you want them to know.

Organize Your Ideas Create an outline to organize your ideas in a logical sequence. Make sure each idea follows from the previous idea and leads into the next idea.

Interactive Lessons
For help in planning your essay, use
- Using Textual Evidence: Writing an Outline

> **I.** Use Roman numerals for main topics.
>   A. Indent and use capital letters for subtopics.
>   1. Indent and use numbers for supporting facts and details.
>   2. Indent and use numbers for supporting facts and details.

PRODUCE

myWriteSmart

Write Your Essay Review your notes and your outline as you begin your draft.

- Begin your introduction with an unusual comment, fact, quote, or personal anecdote.
- Develop your main ideas with supporting facts, details, examples, and quotations from experts.
- Use transitions such as *in addition to* and *also* to connect ideas.
- Include website links and visuals, such as charts, graphs, or photos, to add depth to your essay.
- In your conclusion, restate your main idea and summarize supporting details and facts.

Write your rough draft in *my*WriteSmart. Focus on getting your ideas down, rather than perfecting your choice of language.

Interactive Lessons
For help in writing your draft, use
- Writing Informative Texts: Organizing Ideas

Language Conventions: Connect Ideas

The use of a lot of simple sentences in your writing can make it hard to understand how details are connected. Two other sentence structures can help you clarify ideas. A **compound sentence** consists of two or more independent clauses joined together. A **complex sentence** consists of one independent clause and one or more dependent clauses.

In the following paragraph from "Fears and Phobias," a dependent clause is added to the first sentence and an independent clause is added to the second sentence.

> " Like all emotions, fear can be mild, medium, or intense, depending on the situation and the person. A feeling of fear can be brief or it can last longer. "

Look for places where you can use compound and complex sentences to make your ideas clearer and your writing smoother.

English Language Support

Understand Text Structure Tell students that categorizing the information they gather according to "big ideas" can help them determine an organizational structure for their essays. Have students write two or three big-idea questions about their topic, such as *What Is It? What Causes It?* and *How Can People Overcome It?* Have them use different colors to highlight facts and details in their source notes that help answer each question. Students can then use their answers to write central ideas in their outlines.

Review Your Draft Have your partner or a group of peers review your draft. Use the following chart to revise your draft.

Have your partner or a group of peers review your draft in *my*WriteSmart. Ask your reviewers to note any details that do not support your ideas.

Questions	Tips	Revision Techniques
Does my introduction grab readers' attention?	**Highlight** the introduction.	**Add** an interesting fact, example, or quotation that illustrates the topic.
Does my introduction clearly state the topic?	**Underline** the topic sentence.	**Add** a sentence that clearly states the topic.
Are my main ideas organized in a clear and logical way?	**Highlight** each main idea. **Underline** transitions.	**Reorder** ideas so that each one flows easily to the next. **Add** appropriate transitions to connect ideas and clarify the organization.
Do I support each main idea with evidence?	**Underline** each supporting fact, definition, example, or quotation.	**Add** facts, details, examples, or quotations to support ideas.
Do I use compound and complex sentences to make relationships between ideas clear?	**Underline** each compound and complex sentence.	**Combine** some simple sentences to form compound and complex sentences.
Does my conclusion support the topic?	**Highlight** the conclusion.	**Add** a statement that summarizes the main ideas.

PRESENT

Create a Finished Copy Finalize your essay and choose a way to share it with your audience. Consider these options:

- Present your essay as a speech to the class.
- Record your essay as a news report and share it on a school website.

PERFORMANCE TASK B

PRODUCE

LANGUAGE CONVENTIONS

Explain that in a compound sentence, independent clauses may be joined with a comma and a coordinating conjunction (such as *and, but,* or *so*). Complex sentences use connecting words such as *when, even though,* or *because* to form a dependent clause. A comma separates a dependent clause that comes before the independent clause. Model the following examples:

- He is afraid of heights. He avoids tall buildings. *(simple)*
- He is afraid of heights, so he avoids tall buildings. *(compound)*
- He avoids tall buildings because he is a afraid of heights. *(complex)*
- Because he is a afraid of heights, he avoids tall buildings. *(complex)*

REVISE

REVIEW YOUR DRAFT

Have students answer each question in the chart to determine how they can improve their drafts. Invite volunteers to model their revision techniques.

PRESENT

CREATE A FINISHED COPY

Students can present their essays as news reports or as blogs on school or personal websites. Encourage others to read the essays and to write comments about them. The authors can then respond to the comments.

WHEN STUDENTS STRUGGLE . . .

Add Relevant Evidence Have students ask peer reviewers to evaluate their supporting evidence by answering the following questions:

- Which pieces of evidence are unclear? Why?
- What questions do you have about my main points?

Students should use the reviewer's feedback to add relevant facts, details, examples, or quotations that further develop their main points.

English Language Support

Use Language Resources Explain that writers often clarify and connect ideas by referring back to a noun with a synonym. Have students identify the pair of synonyms in the following:

- People may experience different physical responses to fear, such as sweaty palms or sensations in the stomach. These reactions may range from mild to strong. *(responses, reactions)*

Encourage students to find opportunities to link ideas with synonyms in their essays. Suggest that they consult a dictionary or thesaurus to clarify meaning.

PERFORMANCE TASK B

USE THE SCORING RUBRIC

Have partners exchange final drafts of their informative essays. Then ask them to score their partner's essay using the rubric. Each student should write a paragraph explaining the reasons for the score given in each category.

REFLECT ON THE PROCESS

Tell students that taking the time to reflect on their writing process in this task will help them apply what they learned and improve their writing in future assignments. Ask students to think about how well their essays engaged and informed readers. Then, have them answer the following questions:

- What were the best sources of information on your topic?
- What are the strongest pieces of evidence in your essay?
- What were the most surprising or interesting facts that you learned about your topic?

PERFORMANCE TASK B RUBRIC
INFORMATIVE ESSAY

	Ideas and Evidence	Organization	Language
4	• The introduction is appealing, is informative, and catches the reader's attention; the topic is clearly identified. • The topic is well developed with clear main ideas supported by facts, details, definitions, examples, and quotations from reliable sources. • The conclusion effectively summarizes the information presented.	• The organization is effective and logical throughout the essay. • Transitions logically connect related ideas.	• A consistent, formal writing style is used throughout. • Language is strong and precise. • A variety of simple, compound, and complex sentences is used to show how ideas are related. • Spelling, capitalization, and punctuation are correct. • Grammar, usage, and mechanics are correct.
3	• The introduction could be more appealing and engaging; the topic is clearly identified. • One or two important points could use more support, but most main ideas are well supported by facts, details, definitions, examples, and quotations from reliable sources. • The conclusion summarizes the information presented.	• The organization of main ideas and details is confusing in a few places. • A few more transitions are needed to connect related ideas.	• The writing style is inconsistent in a few places. • Language is too vague or general in some places. • Sentences vary somewhat in structure. • Some spelling, capitalization, and punctuation mistakes occur. • Some grammar and usage errors are present.
2	• The introduction is only partly informative; the topic is unclear. • Most important points could use more support from relevant facts, details, definitions, examples, and quotations from reliable sources. • The conclusion is unclear or only partially summarizes the information presented.	• The organization of main ideas and details is logical in some places, but it often doesn't follow a pattern. • More transitions are needed throughout to connect related ideas.	• The writing style becomes informal in many places. • Language is too general or vague in many places. • Compound and complex sentences are hardly used. • Spelling, capitalization, and punctuation are often incorrect but do not make reading difficult. • Grammar and usage are often incorrect, but the writer's ideas are still clear.
1	• The introduction is missing or confusing. • Supporting facts, details, definitions, examples, or quotations are unreliable or missing. • The conclusion is missing.	• The organization is not logical; main ideas and details are presented randomly. • No transitions are used, making the essay difficult to understand.	• The style is inappropriate for the essay. • Language is too general to convey the information. • The use of too many simple sentences makes the essay monotonous and choppy and the relationships between ideas unclear. • Spelling, capitalization, and punctuation are incorrect and distracting throughout. • Many grammatical and usage errors change the meaning of the writer's ideas.

FOR STUDENTS WITH DISABILITIES

Evaluate the Essay Provide students with a copy of a student essay to score over an extended period. Explain that by scoring an essay, they will better understand how their own work is assessed. Have students cite examples from the essay that support their reasons for the score given in each category.

TO CHALLENGE STUDENTS . . .

Conduct an Interview Challenge students to interview someone who has personally experienced a fear or helped someone overcome a fear. Students may incorporate quotations from the interview in their essays or include interview transcripts or recordings as a special feature.

©Doug Norman/Alamy

Animal Intelligence

❝Each species, however inconspicuous and humble, . . . is a masterpiece.❞

—Edward O. Wilson

71

STREAM TO START

Motivate students to read the collection texts, and spark their curiosity by playing the video for the class. Have students use information gained by watching the video to identify two things they hope to learn from reading about animals, their intelligence, and other qualities. Ask volunteers to share their responses.

PERFORMANCE TASK PREVIEW

Point out to students that they will complete two performance tasks at the end of the collection. The performance tasks will require them to further analyze the selections in the collections and to synthesize ideas about these analyses. Students will present their findings in a variety of products.

ACADEMIC VOCABULARY

> ▶ **View It!**
> Professional Development Podcast:
> **Academic Vocabulary**

Students can acquire facility with the academic vocabulary words through frequent, repeated exposure as they analyze and discuss the selections in the collection. Academic vocabulary can be used in the instructional contexts shown below. This will enable students to incorporate the academic vocabulary words into their working vocabulary.

- Collaborative Discussion at the end of each selection
- Analyzing the Text questions for each selection
- Selection-level Performance Tasks
- Vocabulary instruction (for Critical Vocabulary and/or for Vocabulary Strategy)
- Language Conventions
- End-of-collection Performance Task for all selections in the collection

ASK STUDENTS to review the Academic Vocabulary word list for this collection. You may wish to pronounce each word aloud so students can hear the correct pronunciation. Then, discuss the definitions and the related forms for each word. Remind students that they will encounter these five academic vocabulary words throughout the collection.

COLLECTION 2

Animal Intelligence

In this collection, you will explore various perspectives on the intelligence of animals.

Stream to Start   hmhfyi.com   Channel One News®

COLLECTION

PERFORMANCE TASK Preview

After reading this collection, you will have the opportunity to complete two performance tasks:

- In one, you will write a literary analysis in which you analyze an animal as the narrator or main character of a story.
- In the second, you will give an informative presentation in which you explore how animals show intelligence.

ACADEMIC VOCABULARY

Study the words and their definitions in the chart below. You will use these words as you discuss and write about the texts in this collection.

Word	Definition	Related Forms
benefit (bĕn´ə-fĭt) *n.*	something that provides help or improves something else	beneficial
distinct (dĭ-stĭngkt´) *adj.*	easy to tell apart from others; not alike	distinctly, distinctness, distinctive, distinction
environment (ĕn-vī´rən-mənt) *n.*	surroundings; the conditions that surround someone or something	environmental, environmentalism
illustrate (ĭl´ə-strāt´) *v.*	to show, or clarify, by examples or comparing	illustratable, illustrator, illustration, illustrative, illustrational, illustratively
respond (rĭ-spŏnd´) *v.*	to make a reply; answer	responder, response

72

▤ myNotebook

As students read, analyze, and discuss the texts in this collection, encourage them to create a *my*WordList folder in *my*Notebook to build their own personal word lists.

- **Annotate** Students can highlight vocabulary terms and other unfamiliar words and save each highlighted term to *my*Notebook.
- **Organize** Within *my*Notebook, students can drag each word into the *my*WordList folder.
- **Elaborate** Ask students to add details to the entry for each word, such as a definition, other forms of the word, and a sample sentence.

English Language Support

ENGAGE WITH THE COLLECTION TOPIC

Draw students' attention to the title of the collection, Animal Intelligence. Explain that intelligence refers to "the ability to think and reason, as well as acquire knowledge." Tell students that this collection explores animals' mental abilities along with other unique qualities that make them such an important part of our world.

ACCESS PRIOR KNOWLEDGE Read the quotation on page 71 aloud, clarifying the definitions of unfamiliar words for students. Then have students discuss the meaning of the quotation. What examples from the animal world support the idea the quote expresses?

THINK-WRITE-PAIR-SHARE

Use this strategy to encourage collaborative discussion about the texts in this collection.

- *First*, display a question about an aspect of a text that students have read or are in the process of reading.
- *Then*, tell students to examine the text and consider possible responses to the question. Have them each write answers to the question.
- *Next*, pair students and ask them to share their thoughts with their partners. Remind pairs to ask each other clarifying questions as they discuss their responses.

When students finish, have them revise their written responses to reflect any changes to their ideas that may have arisen during discussion.

- *Finally*, have students share their revised answers with the entire class.

▶ Collection 2 Digital Resources for English Language Support

LANGUAGE WORKSHOP
Designated English Learners

Use the Teacher Resources > Language Workshop to support English learners in describing characters, improving cohesion by using language resources, and collaborating to produce informational texts.

● Text in FOCUS VIDEOS

These videos will help students learn how to analyze point of view and how to monitor comprehension. Have students use **Text in Focus Practice** to apply those skills.

my SmartPlanner | eBook | myNotebook | *my* WriteSmart | fyi hmhfyi.com

Collection 2 Lessons	Media	Teach and Practice	
Student Edition | eBook	▶ Video Links HISTORY A&E Channel One News	**Close Reading and Evidence Tracking**	
ANCHOR TEXT Short Story by P. G. Wodehouse "The Mixer"	▶ Video **HISTORY®** *Modern Marvels: Dogs* ◀ Audio "The Mixer"	**Close Read Screencasts** • Modeled Discussion 1 (lines 23–32) • Modeled Discussion 2 (lines 269–276) • Close Read Application PDF (lines 529–535)	**Text in Focus** • Analyzing Point of View (line 175) **Strategies for Annotation** • Explain Point of View • Describe Characters' Responses • Greek Suffix *-ize*
CLOSE READER Short Story by Maureen Crane Wartski "The Pod"	◀ Audio "The Pod"		
Speech by George Graham Vest "Tribute to the Dog"	◀ Audio "Tribute to the Dog"		**Strategies for Annotation** • Trace and Evaluate an Argument • Use a Print or Digital Dictionary
Poem by Nancy Wood "Animal Wisdom" Poem by Mary TallMountain "The Last Wolf"	◀ Audio "Animal Wisdom" ◀ Audio "The Last Wolf"		**Strategies for Annotation** • Determine Meanings of Words and Phrases
ANCHOR TEXT Science Writing by Dorothy Hinshaw Patent from *How Smart Are Animals?*	◀ Audio from *How Smart Are Animals?*	**Close Read Screencasts** • Modeled Discussion 1 (lines 21–32) • Modeled Discussion 2 (lines 121–132) • Close Read Application PDF (lines 147–156)	**Text in Focus** • Monitoring Comprehension (line 110) **Strategies for Annotation** • Summarize Text • Verify Word Meaning
CLOSE READER Informational Text by DeShawn Jones "Can Animals Feel and Think?"	▶ Video **HISTORY®** ◀ Audio "Can Animals Feel and Think?"		
Informational Text by Peter Christie from *Animal Snoops: The Wondrous World of Wildlife Spies*	◀ Audio from *Animal Snoops: The Wondrous World of Wildlife Spies*		**Strategies for Annotation** • Integrate Information • Analyze Text: Anecdote • Synonyms
CLOSE READER Science Writing by Mary Kay Carson "Bats!"	◀ Audio "Bats!"		
Collection 2 Performance Tasks: **A** Write a Literary Analysis **B** Give an Informative Presentation	fyi hmhfyi.com	**Interactive Lessons** **A** Writing Informative Texts **A** Using Textual Evidence	**B** Writing Informative Texts **B** Conducting Research **B** Giving a Presentation

For Systematic Coverage of Writing and Speaking & Listening Standards	**Interactive Lessons** Writing an Argument Analyzing and Evaluating Presentations	

Assess		Extend	Reteach
Performance Task	**Assess It Online!**	**Teacher eBook**	**Teacher eBook**
Writing Activity: Informative Essay	Selection Test	**Analyze Language: Irony**	**Explain Narrator and Point of View > Level Up Tutorials** > Point of View > First-Person Point of View > Third-Person Point of View > Narrator and Speaker
Speaking Activity: Discussion	Selection Test	**Persuasive Techniques**	**Trace Elements of an Argument > Level Up Tutorials** > Elements of an Argument > Analyzing Arguments > Evidence > Persuasive Techniques
Writing Activity: Informative Essay	Selection Test	**Analyze Structure: Poetry**	**Determine Meanings: Imagery > Interactive Whiteboard Lesson** > Figurative Language and Imagery
Writing Activity: Informative Essay	Selection Test	**Draw Conclusions**	**Summarize Text > Level Up Tutorial >** Summarizing
Media Activity: Informative Presentation	Selection Test	**Take Notes**	**Analyze Text:** Anecdote
A Write a Literary Analysis **B** Give an Informative Presentation	Collection Test		

Lesson Assessments

Writing an Argument
Analyzing and Evaluating Presentations

Standards Support and Enrichment

For more instruction and practice in reading literary and informational texts, language, spelling, and speaking and listening, see Teacher Resources > Standards Support and Enrichment.

For Designated English Language Instruction

To provide scaffolded support specific to the needs of English Learners during Designated English Language instruction, use the selection- and standards-aligned lessons found in Teacher Resources > Language Workshop.

Collection 2 Lessons	Key Learning Objective	Performance Task	Vocabulary Strategy
ANCHOR TEXT **Short Story by P. G. Wodehouse** **"The Mixer," p. 73A** Lexile 770L	**The student will be able to . . .** describe how characters respond and change and analyze point of view in a short story.	Writing Activity: Informative Essay	Greek Suffix -ize
Speech by George Graham Vest **"Tribute to the Dog," p. 93A** Lexile 1170L	**The student will be able to . . .** trace and evaluate an argument and identify persuasive techniques in a speech.	Speaking Activity: Discussion	Use a Print or Digital Dictionary
Poem by Nancy Wood **"Animal Wisdom," p. 99A** **Poem by Mary TallMountain** **"The Last Wolf," p. 99A**	**The student will be able to . . .** understand how personification and imagery emphasize themes and ideas in poetry and learn how to paraphrase these ideas.	Writing Activity: Informative Essay	
ANCHOR TEXT **Science Writing** **by Dorothy Hinshaw Patent** **from *How Smart Are Animals?* p. 105A** Lexile 1130L	**The student will be able to . . .** summarize central ideas and important details and determine author's purpose.	Writing Activity: Informative Essay	Verify Word Meaning
Informational Text by Peter Christie **from *Animal Snoops:*** ***The Wondrous World*** ***of Wildlife Spies,* p. 117A** Lexile 1020L	**The student will be able to . . .** analyze how anecdotes and text features contribute to the structure of a text.	Media Activity: Informative Presentation	Synonyms

Collection 2 Performance Tasks:

A Write a Literary Analysis
B Give an Informative Presentation

Language Conventions	English Language Support	Differentiated Instruction	CLOSE READER Selection
Intensive Pronouns	• Understand Cohesion • Use Verbs and Verb Phrases • Read Closely • Improve Reading Fluency • Word Study	**When Students Struggle:** Describe Characters' Responses **For Students with Disabilities:** Comprehension Strategies **To Challenge Students:** Analyze Characters **For Standard English Learners:** Indefinite Articles	Short Story by Maureen Crane Wartski "The Pod," p. 92b **Lexile 810L**
Relative Pronouns *who* and *whom*	• Understand Text Structure • Understand Cohesion • Analyze Language		
	• Culturally Responsive Instruction • Read Closely • Analyze Language • Exchange Ideas and Information • Connect Ideas	**When Students Struggle:** Paraphrase Text	
Pronoun Number	• Understand Text Structure • Understand Cohesion • Improve Reading Fluency	**When Students Struggle:** Analyze Text **For Standard English Learners:** Pronunciation	Informational Text by DeShawn Jones "Can Animals Feel and Think?" p. 116b **Lexile 1010L**
Capitalization	• Analyze Language • Read Closely • Exchange Ideas and Information • Write Brief Texts	**When Students Struggle:** Analyze Text **To Challenge Students:** Compare and Contrast **For Students with Disabilities:** Listening Strategies	Science Writing by Mary Kay Carson "Bats!," p. 128b **Lexile 990L**
A Condense Ideas **B** Nouns and Noun Phrases	**A** Write a Literary Analysis Justify Opinions Understand Text Structure Condense Ideas **B** Provide Text Evidence Plan an Informative Presentation Link Ideas	**A** **To Challenge Students:** Strengthen a Conclusion **For Standard English Learners:** Use Prepositions **When Students Struggle:** Connect Ideas **For Students with Disabilities:** Evaluate the Analysis **B** **For Standard English Learners:** Adapt Speech **When Students Struggle:** Use Quotations **For Students with Disabilities:** Give a Small Group Presentation **To Challenge Students:** Share Resources	

ANCHOR TEXT The Mixer

Short Story by P. G. Wodehouse

Why This Text?

As students encounter increasingly challenging texts, they must be able to analyze more diverse and difficult story elements. This lesson focuses on character development and the effects of narrator and point of view in a humorous, classic short story by P.G. Wodehouse.

▶ **View It!**

Professional Development Podcast:

Text-Dependent Analysis

Key Learning Objective: The student will be able to describe how characters respond and change, and analyze point of view in a short story.

For practice and application:

The Pod

Close Reader selection
"The Pod"
Short Story by Maureen Crane Wartski

RL 1 Cite textual evidence; make inferences.
RL 3 Describe story elements.
RL 4 Determine meaning of words and phrases.
RL 5 Analyze structure.
RL 6 Explain point of view.
RL 10 Read and comprehend literature.
W 2 Write informative/explanatory texts.
SL 1 Engage effectively in a range of collaborative discussions.
L 1b Use intensive pronouns.
L 4 Determine or clarify the meaning of words and phrases, choosing from a range of strategies.
L 4a Use context as a clue to the meaning of a word or phrase.
L 4b Use Greek affixes as clues to the meaning of a word.
L 6 Acquire and use accurately grade-appropriate general academic and domain-specific words and phrases.

▲ **Text Complexity Rubric**

Quantitative Measures	**The Mixer** Lexile: 770L
	Levels of Meaning/Purpose ●—●—●—●—→ single level of complex meaning
Qualitative Measures	**Structure** ●—●—●—●—→ somewhat complex story concepts
	Language Conventionality and Clarity ●—●—●—●—→ contextual ambiguous language
	Knowledge Demands ●—●—●—●—→ experience includes unfamiliar aspects
Reader/Task Considerations	• Teacher determined • Vary by individual reader and type of text • See the Text X-Ray for suggested Reader/Task Considerations.

TEXT X-RAY

English Language Support
Before teaching, use the Text X-Ray below for an overview of the text's complexity. The Text X-Ray and the supports and scaffolds in the Teacher's Edition will help you guide students of different skill levels.

Meaning Making · Language Development · Effective Expression · Content Knowledge · Foundational Skills

Levels of Meaning/Purpose

single level of complex meaning

Help students analyze characters' responses to events.

- Teacher's Edition side notes, pp. 73, 74, 76, 78, 79, 80, 81, 82, 84, 86, 88, 89
- English Language Support, p. 79
- When Students Struggle, pp. 80, 86
- Close Read Screencasts, p. 73
- Strategies for Annotation, pp. 84, 89
- Describe Characters' Responses, p. 89

▶ *Use It!* **Level Up Tutorials:** Methods of Characterization, Character Motivation

***ZOOM IN ON* ANALYZING CHARACTERS' RESPONSES** Tell students a character is a person or animal who takes part in a story. An author can develop a character through the way other characters in the text react to him or her.

- Read aloud lines 87–90. Have students describe the different ways the narrator and Mother react to the man.
- Ask students to explain Mother's reaction. *(She sensed something threatening or untrustworthy about the man.)*
- Point out that analyzing Mother's response helps readers learn more about the man and increases their interest in finding out why he wants a dog.

Structure

somewhat complex story concepts

Help students analyze the role of the narrator in a short story.

- Teacher's Edition side notes, pp. 73, 74, 75, 76, 78, 81, 82, 83, 87, 89
- English Language Support, p. 87
- Strategies for Annotation, p. 77
- Explain Point of View, p. 89

Guide students to recognize irony created by the point of view.

- Teacher's Edition side notes, pp. 77, 85
- English Language Support, pp. 77

To reteach explain point of view, see

- Explain Narrator and Point of View, p. 92a

Text in FOCUS Analyzing Point of View

▶ *Use It!* **Level Up Tutorials:** Point of View; First-Person Point of View; Third-Person Point of View; Narrator and Speaker; Irony

***ZOOM IN ON* ANALYZING THE NARRATOR** Tell students that the **narrator** is the voice that tells the story. Explain that it is from the narrator's **point of view** that the reader learns what happens in a story.

- Display the first paragraph on page 75. Read it aloud.
- Ask students to describe what they might expect in a story being told by a dog. *(Possible answers: humor, dog may not always know what humans are thinking.)*
- Explain that **irony** is the difference between what is expected and what actually happens. Work with students to explain the irony in the portrayal of events by the narrator, a dog. *(While the narrator thinks he is helping, in fact, he has been creating an uproar with his barking and running around.)*
- Encourage students to look for places in the story where the narrator's point of view creates irony.

Language Conventionality and Clarity

contextual ambiguous language

Teach unfamiliar vocabulary in context.

Teacher's Edition Critical Vocabulary notes, pp. 74, 75, 78, 82, 85, 91

- English Language Support, p. 79
- Applying Academic Vocabulary, p. 75
- Strategies for Annotation, p. 91
- Vocabulary Strategy: Greek Suffix *–ize*, p. 91

Help students to use language to express ideas and information in writing and discussion.

- Teacher's Edition side notes, pp. 88, 92
- English Language Support, pp. 74, 78, 82, 83, 85, 88, 92
- Language Conventions: Intensive Pronouns, p. 92

ZOOM IN ON **USING CONTEXT** Before reading, review the strategy of using context clues to define the colloquial or slang expressions.

- Display lines 396–400. Underline the phrase "lifted the roof off." Point out that this expression has an overall meaning different from the individual words.
- Have students look for words and phrases in the passage that help them to define this expression. Guide them to use "But I didn't bark" to define "lifted the roof off" as "bark loudly."
- Remind students to use this strategy when they encounter unknown expressions in their reading.

Knowledge Demands

experience includes unfamiliar aspects

Support English Learners in understanding the cultural references in the text as well as information about the subject.

- Teacher's Edition Author's note, p. 73
- Content-Area Connection, p. 76

 For more historical background, students can view the video "Modern Marvels: Dogs" in their eBooks.

ZOOM IN ON **BUILDING BACKGROUND KNOWLEDGE** Explain that some of the narrator's behavior is meant to reflect the attributes, or positive traits, associated with dogs.

- Ask students what qualities come to their minds when they think of dogs. Encourage them to draw on their prior knowledge to answer and list their responses on the board. *(Possible answers: loyal, loving, courageous)*
- As students read, have them identify ways in which the narrator demonstrates these qualities.

Suggested Reader/Task Considerations

You might consider the following before assigning this story to students.

- Do students have the necessary skills to comprehend this story?
- Will the story engage students and keep their attention?

ZOOM IN ON **SUPPORTING COMPREHENSION**

- Before students read, ask them to describe typical dog behaviors, such as barking, running in circles, jumping, and tail-wagging. Explain that the narrator of this story is a dog. Tell students that the humor of the story comes from the discrepancy between the dog's reasons for his actions and the humans' interpretations of them. Encourage students to note these differences as they read.
- To capture students' attention, read the first 47 lines aloud and answer any questions. Then have students read through line 86 independently. Continue to alternate reading aloud with students' silent reading, clarifying important ideas during each transition.

CLOSE READ

For more context and historical background, students can view the video *Modern Marvels: Dogs* in their eBooks.

P.G. Wodehouse Have students read the information about the author. Explain that Wodehouse remains one of Britain's most popular humorists. A number of British television shows have been based on his writings, such as *Jeeves and Wooster* and *Blandings.* Explain that Wodehouse often incorporated British slang and colloquialisms in his writing. Point out that "mixer" refers to one's ability to get along with others in a social setting, but that "mixer" is also British slang for "a troublemaker."

SETTING A PURPOSE Direct students to use the Setting a Purpose prompt to focus their reading. Remind them to write down questions as they read.

Describe Characters' Responses (LINES 1–10)   RL 1, RL 3

Explain to students that a **character** is a person, animal, or imaginary creature that takes part in a story's series of events, called the **plot.** Tell them that good readers pay attention to how characters respond to events.

Ⓐ **CITE TEXT EVIDENCE** Have students read lines 1–10 and identify the main character. Ask them to tell whether they think the character has a positive or negative outlook on life using evidence from the story. *(The main character, a dog, seems to have a positive outlook, since he says that he looks forward to learning new things.)*

Explain Point of View   RL 1, RL 6
(LINES 1–10)

Tell students that a story's **narrator** is the voice that tells the story. Explain that in a story told using **first-person point of view,** the narrator is a character in the story and uses first-person pronouns such as *I, me,* and *my.*

Ⓑ **CITE TEXT EVIDENCE** Have students reread lines 1–3 and tell how they know the story is told using first-person point of view. *(The narrator uses the first-person pronouns I and my.)*

VIDEO

P. G. Wodehouse (1881–1975) *was born in England. Although Wodehouse always wanted to be a writer, as a young man he was forced to work at a London bank to make a living. This career did not last long. After only two years, Wodehouse left the bank and began writing full time. In 1904, Wodehouse left England for New York. There, Wodehouse began writing plays and musicals in addition to novels and short stories. Wodehouse later added many movie screenplays to his long list of writing accomplishments.*

The Mixer

Short Story by P. G. Wodehouse

SETTING A PURPOSE As you read, pay attention to how a dog's actions affect his master's plans. Write down any questions you have while reading.

 myNotebook

As you read, save new words to *my*WordList.

Looking back, I always consider that my career as a dog proper really started when I was bought for the sum of half a crown[1] by the Shy Man. That event marked the end of my puppyhood. The knowledge that I was worth actual cash to somebody filled me with a sense of new responsibilities. It sobered me. Besides, it was only after that half-crown changed hands that I went out into the great world; and, however interesting life may be in an East End public-house,[2] it is only when you go out into the world that you really broaden your mind and begin to see things.

Ⓑ

Ⓐ

10

---

[1] **half a crown:** another name for a *half-crown,* a British coin that is no longer in use; was worth two shillings and sixpence, or about 30 pennies (pence).
[2] **public-house:** a place, such as a bar, that is allowed to sell alcoholic beverages.

(t) ©Getty Images; (c) ©keith taylor/Alamy Images; (cr) ©age fotostock

The Mixer   73

Close Read Screencasts   Close Read

Modeled Discussions

Have students click the *Close Read* icon in their eBook to access a screencast in which readers discuss and annotate the following key passages:

- Blackie's analysis of his behavior and heritage (lines 23–32)
- how Blackie decides on a course of action (lines 269–276)

As a class, view and discuss the video. Then have students pair up to do an independent close read of an additional passage—Blackie's take on how Fred and the Shy Man interact (lines 529–535).

Explain Point of View

RL 1,
RL 6

(LINES 21–25)

Tell students that when a story is told using first-person point of view, the author, writing as the narrator, decides how much or how little the narrator will share with the audience about himself, other characters, or story events.

C CITE TEXT EVIDENCE Have students reread lines 21–25 and identify a personal trait that the narrator discusses. Ask them to explain whether they think the narrator knows himself well. *(He says his "restlessness" is a "marked trait." He seems to know himself well, because he identifies patterns in his behavior; he has always been "anxious to get on to the next thing.")*

Describe Characters' Responses (LINES 41–47)

RL 3

Remind students that paying attention to how characters respond to events will help them better understand characters and story events.

D ASK STUDENTS to reread lines 41–47 and summarize how the narrator responds to strangers compared to his mother. *(The narrator seems to respond calmly to strangers, while his mother barks at every stranger.)*

CRITICAL VOCABULARY

surfeit: The narrator is telling how his grandfather died from paste.

ASK STUDENTS to tell how the word *surfeit* adds humor here, since the narrator is relating that his grandfather died from eating too much paste. *(The word surfeit adds humor because paste is not a food, but a dog might think it was something good to eat.)*

Within its limitations, my life had been singularly full and vivid. I was born, as I say, in a public-house in the East End, and however lacking a public-house may be in refinement and the true culture, it certainly provides plenty of excitement. Before I was six weeks old, I had upset three policemen by getting between their legs when they came round to the sidedoor, thinking they had heard suspicious noises; and I can still recall the interesting sensation of being chased seventeen times round the yard with a broom-handle
20 after a well-planned and completely successful raid on the larder. These and other happenings of a like nature soothed for the moment but could not cure the restlessness which has always been so marked a trait in my character. I have always been restless, unable to settle down in one place and anxious to get on to the next thing. This may be due to a gipsy³ strain in my ancestry—one of my uncles traveled with a circus—or it may be the Artistic Temperament,⁴ acquired from a grandfather who, before dying of a **surfeit** of paste in the property-room of the Bristol Coliseum, which he was
30 visiting in the course of a professional tour, had an established reputation on the music-hall stage as one of Professor Pond's Performing Poodles.

I owe the fullness and variety of my life to this restlessness of mine, for I have repeatedly left comfortable homes in order to follow some perfect stranger who looked as if he were on his way to somewhere interesting. Sometimes I think I must have cat blood in me.

The Shy Man came into our yard one afternoon in April, while I was sleeping with Mother in the sun on an old sweater
40 which we had borrowed from Fred, one of the barmen. I heard Mother growl, but I didn't take any notice. Mother is what they call a good watch-dog, and she growls at everybody except Master. At first when she used to do it, I would get up and bark my head off, but not now. Life's too short to bark at everybody who comes into our yard. It is behind the public-house, and they keep empty bottles and things there, so people are always coming and going.

surfeit
(sûr´fĭt) *n.* A *surfeit* is an excessive amount of something, such as food or drink.

³ **gipsy** (jĭp´sē): also *gypsy* or *Gypsy*; a member of a race of people who travel from place to place, rather than living in one place.
⁴ **Artistic Temperament:** a manner of thinking or acting said to be common among artists (painters, musicians, writers, actors); often used to explain traits such as sensitivity, odd or unusual behavior, or nervousness.

APPLYING ACADEMIC VOCABULARY

distinct	illustrate	respond

THINK-PAIR-SHARE Have students turn to a partner to discuss the questions below. Encourage students to include the academic vocabulary words *distinct*, *illustrate*, and *respond* in their responses. Let volunteers share their responses with the class.

- How does the narrator's **distinct** point of view and the way he **responds** to events affect your understanding of the story?
- What examples in the text **illustrate** your answer to this question?

Besides, I was tired. I had had a very busy morning, helping the men bring in a lot of cases of beer and running into the saloon to talk to Fred and generally looking after things. So I was just dozing off again when I heard a voice say, "Well, he's ugly enough." Then I knew that they were talking about me.

I have never disguised it from myself, and nobody has ever disguised it from me, that I am not a handsome dog. Even Mother never thought me beautiful. She was no Gladys Cooper herself, but she never hesitated to **criticize** my appearance. In fact, I have yet to meet anyone who did. The first thing strangers say about me is "What an ugly dog!"

I don't know what I am. I have a bull-dog kind of a face, but the rest of me is terrier. I have a long tail which sticks straight up in the air. My hair is wiry. My eyes are brown. I am jet black with a white chest. I once overheard Fred saying that I was a Gorgonzola cheese-hound,[5] and I have generally found Fred reliable in his statements.

When I found that I was under discussion, I opened my eyes. Master was standing there, looking down at me, and by his side the man who had just said I was ugly enough. The man was a thin man, about the age of a barman and smaller than a policeman. He had patched brown shoes and black trousers.

"But he's got a sweet nature," said Master.

This was true, luckily for me. Mother always said, "A dog without influence or private means, if he is to make his way in the world, must have either good looks or **amiability**." But, according to her, I overdid it. "A dog," she used to say, "can have a good heart without chumming with every Tom, Dick, and Harry he meets. Your behavior is sometimes quite undog-like." Mother prided herself on being a one-man dog. She kept herself to herself, and wouldn't kiss anybody except Master—not even Fred.

Now, I'm a mixer. I can't help it. It's my nature. I like men. I like the taste of their boots, the smell of their legs, and the sound of their voices. It may be weak of me, but a man has only to speak to me, and a sort of thrill goes right down my spine and sets my tail wagging.

criticize
(krĭt´ĭ-sīz´) v. To criticize is to tell someone what you think is wrong with them.

amiable
(ā´mē-ə-bəl) n. To be amiable is to be good-natured and friendly.

[5] **Gorgonzola cheese-hound:** Gorgonzola is a bumpy, crumbly cheese with many swirls of blue mold in it; based on this phrase, the dog probably has a bumpy, sort of wrinkly face or body.

The Mixer   75

CLOSE READ

Explain Point of View

RL 1,
RL 6

(LINES 76–86)

Remind students that readers learn about a first-person narrator by what he or she shares with readers.

(E) CITE TEXT EVIDENCE Explain that a "mixer" refers to someone who is outgoing and "mixes" well with others. Have students reread lines 76–86 and tell how they know the narrator's description of himself as a "mixer" seems accurate. (*He compares himself to his mother, explaining that while she was "a one-man dog," the smells and sounds of ALL men give him a "thrill."*)

CRITICAL VOCABULARY

criticize: The narrator says that he is used to having everyone *criticize* his appearance.

ASK STUDENTS to tell why the narrator might not be bothered when others *criticize* him by saying "'What an ugly dog!'" (*Possible response: He knows that he is "not a handsome dog," so criticism from others about what he looks like doesn't upset him.*)

amiable: The narrator uses the word *amiability* to describe one of two qualities the average dog must possess.

ASK STUDENTS to discuss what the narrator means when he relates his mother's words that a dog "'must have either good looks or amiability.'" (*Possible response: He means that people are drawn to a dog that is attractive to look at. If a dog is not good-looking, the dog needs to have a pleasant nature in order to get attention from people.*)

English Language Support

Understand Cohesion Display this sentence (lines 15–21): "Before I was six weeks old, I had upset three policemen by getting between their legs when they came round to the sidedoor, thinking they had heard suspicious noises; and I can still recall the interesting sensation of being chased seventeen times round the yard with a broom-handle after a well-planned and completely successful raid on the larder."

• Circle the words *Before, when,* and *after.* Explain to students that the circled words are **transitions,** or words that connect ideas.

Transitions can show cause and effect, compare ideas or show a sequence of events.

• Point out the word *after* and work with students to explain how it signals when events occur.

• Have pairs examine and explain how the circled words connect the events the sentence describes.

• Have students work together to identify and analyze other sentences on page 74 that use transitional words and phrases to connect events.

Explain Point of View

RL 1,
RL 6

(LINES 87–105)

Remind students that in first-person point of view, readers learn about other characters from the narrator's perspective.

F **CITE TEXT EVIDENCE** Have students reread lines 87–95 and summarize what the Shy Man is like. *(According to the narrator, the man seems "silent" and "brooding.")* Then have students point out clues that indicate that there might be more to what is going on than the narrator understands. *(The man doesn't respond to the narrator's friendly nature; Mother growls at the man.)*

G **ASK STUDENTS** to reread lines 96–105. Point out that the narrator seems rather innocent about what is going on. Have students explain why Master is praising the dog so highly. *(He wants to sell the dog for a good price.)* Explain that readers need to pay attention to how the narrator's innocent nature may cause him to misinterpret events.

Describe Characters'

RL 1,
RL 3

Responses (LINES 116–130)

Remind students that readers learn about the characters by paying attention to how characters respond to plot events.

H **ASK STUDENTS** to reread lines 116–130 and tell what they learn about the narrator as he responds to leaving home and to his new owner's actions. *(The dog is excited that he is "off to see life," which illustrates that he looks forward to new experiences. He is not upset when he gets kicked; he just stops barking. This could show that he is a quick learner, not easily bothered, or eager to please.)* Point out to students that the dog's "voice" also gives clues to his personality. Ask students what words they would use to describe his personality. *(excitable, friendly, optimistic, somewhat innocent)*

I wagged it now. The man looked at me rather distantly. He didn't pat me. I suspected—what I afterwards found to be the case—that he was shy, so I jumped up at him to put him at his ease. Mother growled again. I felt that she did not approve.

"Why, he's took quite a fancy to you already," said Master.

The man didn't say a word. He seemed to be brooding on something. He was one of those silent men. He reminded me of Joe, the old dog down the street at the grocer's shop, who lies at the door all day, blinking and not speaking to anybody.

Master began to talk about me. It surprised me, the way he praised me. I hadn't a suspicion he admired me so much. From what he said you would have thought I had won prizes and ribbons at the Crystal Palace. But the man didn't seem to be impressed. He kept on saying nothing.

When Master had finished telling him what a wonderful dog I was till I blushed, the man spoke.

"Less of it," he said. "Half a crown is my bid, and if he was an angel from on high you couldn't get another ha' penny out of me. What about it?"

A thrill went down my spine and out at my tail, for of course I saw now what was happening. The man wanted to buy me and take me away. I looked at Master hopefully.

"He's more like a son to me than a dog," said Master, sort of wistful.

"It's his face that makes you feel that way," said the man, unsympathetically. "If you had a son that's just how he would look. Half a crown is my offer, and I'm in a hurry."

"All right," said Master, with a sigh, "though it's giving him away, a valuable dog like that. Where's your half-crown?"

The man got a bit of rope and tied it round my neck.

I could hear Mother barking advice and telling me to be a credit to the family, but I was too excited to listen.

"Good-bye, Mother," I said. "Good-bye, Master. Good-bye, Fred. Good-bye, everybody. I'm off to see life. The Shy Man has bought me for half a crown. Wow!"

I kept running round in circles and shouting, till the man gave me a kick and told me to stop it.

So I did.

I don't know where we went, but it was a long way. I had never been off our street before in my life and didn't know the whole world was half as big as that. We walked on and on, and the man jerking at my rope whenever I wanted to stop and

CONTENT-AREA CONNECTION

Science Note that when the narrator describes himself as shouting or talking, human characters perceive him as barking. Scientists who study canine communication (and many dog owners) believe that different barks communicate different messages. Dogs may bark one way when a stranger approaches and another way when their humans return home.

Activity Invite small groups to prepare reports about the ways dogs communicate with each other and with humans. Suggest that they narrow their focus to concentrate either on vocal or non-vocal forms of expression. Remind them to use reliable sources.

look at anything. He wouldn't even let me pass the time of the day with dogs we met.

When we had gone about a hundred miles and were just going to turn in at a dark doorway, a policeman suddenly stopped the man. I could feel by the way the man pulled at my rope and tried to hurry on that he didn't want to speak to the policeman. The more I saw of the man, the more I saw how shy he was.

> ## "He's more like a son to me than a dog," said Master, sort of wistful."

"Hi!" said the policeman, and we had to stop.

"I've got a message for you, old pal," said the policeman. "It's from the Board of Health. They told me to tell you you needed a change of air. See?"

"All right!" said the man.

"And take it as soon as you like. Else you'll find you'll get it given you. See?"

I looked at the man with a good deal of respect. He was evidently someone very important, if they worried so about his health.

"I'm going down to the country tonight," said the man.

The policeman seemed pleased.

"That's a bit of luck for the country," he said. "Don't go changing your mind."

And we walked on, and went in at the dark doorway, and climbed about a million stairs, and went into a room that smelt of rats. The man sat down and swore a little, and I sat and looked at him.

Presently I couldn't keep it in any longer.

"Do we live here?" I said. "Is it true we're going to the country? Wasn't that policeman a good sort? Don't you like policemen? I knew lots of policemen at the public-house. Are

CLOSE READ

Explain Point of View   RL 6

(LINES 138–150)

Tell students that point of view can be used to create **irony** and humor. Explain that irony is a contrast between what is expected and what actually exists or happens.

ASK STUDENTS to reread lines 137–150. Have them summarize what message the policeman is trying to get across to the Shy Man. *(He wants the Shy Man to get out of town.)* Then ask them to explain why the narrator's interpretation of this message is ironic. *(It is ironic because the narrator thinks the Shy Man is a well-respected, "important" man, and that is not at all what the policeman thinks.)* Ask students to explain what this tells them about how much they can trust the narrator's observations. *(His misinterpretations show that his observations should not be trusted.)*

English Language Support

To help students recognize irony, read lines 137–150 aloud.

- Ask students what Blackie thinks the policeman means. *(He thinks the policeman is really concerned about the Shy Man's health.)*
- Have students explain what the policeman really means. *(The policeman is telling the Shy Man to leave the area.)*
- Guide students to use the dialogue, as well as the policeman's obvious familiarity with the man, to make inferences about the Shy Man's occupation.

Strategies for Annotation   ✎ 🖥 *Annotate it!*

Explain Point of View   RL 6

Share these strategies for guided or independent analysis:

- Highlight in yellow sarcastic statements the policeman makes.
- Highlight in green what the narrator thinks the policeman's remarks mean.
- On a note, record an insight about the narrator's nature and whether his observations can be trusted.

"I've got a message for you, old pal," said the policeman. "It's from the Board of Health. They told me to tell you you needed a change of air. See?"

"All right!" said the man.

"And take it as soon as you like. Else you'll find you'll get it given you. See?"

I looked at the man with a good deal of respect. He was evidently someone very important, if they worried so about his health.

Describe Characters' Responses (LINES 163–175)

RL 1,
RL 3

Explain that noticing how characters respond to plot events will help them understand the characters.

J **CITE TEXT EVIDENCE** Ask students to explain how the dog responds to his new surroundings. *(He is excited and "talks" a lot to his new owner.)* Ask why it doesn't bother the dog when the man "wallops" him. *(Possible response: He knows the man is his "boss.")*

Explain Point of View

RL 1,
RL 6

(LINES 173–175)

Explain that sometimes readers' understanding of what is happening in a story is limited by a first-person narrator. An **unreliable narrator** is one who shares limited or mistaken knowledge with readers.

K **CITE TEXT EVIDENCE** Ask students to reread lines 173–175. Ask them how they know the narrator of the story is unreliable. *(The dog is mistaken by calling his new owner "the shyest man I had ever met." He thinks the man hits him because "it hurt him to be spoken to.")*

CRITICAL VOCABULARY

wallop: The author uses the word *walloped* to tell how the Shy Man hits the dog with a stick.

ASK STUDENTS to tell why the author might have chosen the word *walloped* instead of words such as *hit* or *struck*. *(Possible responses: It is more descriptive; readers can see and hear the action.)*

Analyzing Point of View (line 175)

Have students view the **Text in Focus** video in their eBook to analyze how the dog's point of view shapes his understanding of people and events. Have students use **Text in Focus Practice** to apply what they have learned.

---

160 there any other dogs here? What is there for dinner? What's in that cupboard? When are you going to take me out for another run? May I go out and see if I can find a cat?"

"Stop that yelping," he said.

"When we go to the country, where shall we live? Are you going to be a caretaker at a house? Fred's father is a caretaker at a big house in Kent. I've heard Fred talk about it. You didn't meet Fred when you came to the public-house, did you? You would like Fred. I like Fred. Mother likes Fred. We all like Fred."

170 I was going on to tell him a lot more about Fred, who had always been one of my warmest friends, when he suddenly got hold of a stick and **walloped** me with it.

"You keep quiet when you're told," he said.

He really was the shyest man I had ever met. It seemed to hurt him to be spoken to. However, he was the boss, and I had to humor him, so I didn't say any more.

We went down to the country that night, just as the man had told the policeman we would. I was all worked up, for I had heard so much about the country from Fred that I had always wanted to go there. Fred used to go off on a motor-

180 bicycle sometimes to spend the night with his father in Kent, and once he brought back a squirrel with him, which I thought was for me to eat, but Mother said no. "The first thing a dog has to learn," Mother used often to say, "is that the whole world wasn't created for him to eat."

It was quite dark when we got to the country, but the man seemed to know where to go. He pulled at my rope, and we began to walk along a road with no people in it at all. We walked on and on, but it was all so new to me that I forgot how tired I was. I could feel my mind broadening with every

190 step I took.

Every now and then we would pass a very big house which looked as if it was empty, but I knew that there was a caretaker inside, because of Fred's father. These big houses belong to very rich people, but they don't want to live in them till the summer so they put in caretakers, and the caretakers have a dog to keep off burglars. I wondered if that was what I had been brought here for.

"Are you going to be a caretaker?" I asked the man.

"Shut up," he said.

wallop
(wŏl´əp) v. To *wallop* is to hit or strike with a hard blow.

English Language Support

Use Verbs and Verb Phrases Write on the board: "We went down to the country that night, just as the man had told the policeman we would." Underline "had told" and explain that the past perfect tense describes an action that occurred before another past event.

- Help students understand how the past perfect tense shows which event happened first. *(talking to the policeman first)*
- Have partners identify other past perfect verbs in lines 176–184 and explain the sequence of the events.

200 So I shut up.

After we had been walking a long time, we came to a cottage. A man came out. My man seemed to know him, for he called him Bill. I was quite surprised to see the man was not at all shy with Bill. They seemed very friendly.

"Is that him?" said Bill, looking at me.

"Bought him this afternoon," said the man.

"Well," said Bill, "he's ugly enough. He looks fierce. If you want a dog, he's the sort of dog you want. But what do you want one for? It seems to me it's a lot of trouble to take, when

210 there's no need of any trouble at all. Why not do what I've always wanted to do? What's wrong with just fixing the dog, same as it's always done, and walking in and helping yourself?"

"I'll tell you what's wrong" said the man. "To start with, you can't get at the dog to fix him except by day, when they let him out. At night he's shut up inside the house. And suppose you do fix him during the day, what happens then? Either the bloke[6] gets another before night, or else he sits up all night with a gun. It isn't like as if these blokes was ordinary blokes. They're down here to look after the house. That's their job,

220 and they don't take any chances."

It was the longest speech I had ever heard the man make, and it seemed to impress Bill. He was quite humble.

"I didn't think of that," he said. "We'd best start in to train this tyke at once."

Mother often used to say, when I went on about wanting to go out into the world and see life, "You'll be sorry when you do. The world isn't all bones and liver." And I hadn't been living with the man and Bill in their cottage long before I found out how right she was.

230 It was the man's shyness that made all the trouble. It seemed as if he hated to be taken notice of.

It started on my very first night at the cottage. I had fallen asleep in the kitchen, tired out after all the excitement of the day and the long walks I had had, when something woke me with a start. It was somebody scratching at the window, trying to get in.

Well, I ask you, I ask any dog, what would you have done in my place? Ever since I was old enough to listen, Mother had

---

[6] **bloke** (blōk): a British term for a man or a fellow.

The Mixer   79

TEACH

CLOSE READ

Explain Point of View
RL 1,
RL 6

(LINES 211–224)

Remind students that they know the dog is an unreliable narrator who has limited knowledge of what is happening in the story. Explain that readers need to pay close attention to interpret information that the narrator tells about.

(L) **ASK STUDENTS** to interpret what the man and his friend are talking about in lines 211–224. Have them make inferences about how they might be planning to "train" the narrator. (*Possible responses: Bill is wondering why they can't just "fix" a watchdog at a home they want to rob. The Shy Man explains that that method is too difficult, and that caretakers don't take any chances. The details aren't clear, but it sounds like they are going to train the narrator to do something that will help them rob a house with a caretaker in it.*)

English Language Support

Explain that **inferences** are logical guesses based on details in the text and our own prior knowledge.

• Model how to make an inference: *Based on lines 215–220, I can tell that Bill and the Shy Man are worried about the caretakers of the houses and their dogs. I already know that the Shy Man had been in trouble with police. This helps me infer that they are planning to rob one of the houses.*

• Provide this sentence frame to guide students to make an inference: When the men say they want to "train" the narrator, I can infer that they plan to _____ . *(use him to help them commit their crime)*

English Language Support

Read Closely Project lines 211–224 on the board. Tell students that **paraphrasing,** or restating sentences, in their own words, can help them understand important ideas about plot and character.

• Work with students to define unknown words and expressions in the second sentence. Then guide them to restate what the Shy Man is saying. (*The only time to get close to the dog to harm him is during the day when he's outside.*)

• Have pairs define unfamiliar words and phrases in the passage and explain the Shy Man's conflict in their own words.

• Ask students to restate in standard English the dialogue in lines 213–220. Have them share their passages with a partner.

The Mixer   **79**

Describe Characters' Responses (LINES 240–251)

RL 1,
RL 3

Remind students that paying attention to how characters respond to plot events will help readers understand them more deeply.

Ⓜ CITE TEXT EVIDENCE Have students reread lines 240–251 and explain why the narrator barks. *(Someone is climbing in the window; his mother taught him to bark when this happens. As he notes, "It is the ABC of a dog's education.")*

told me over and over again what I must do in a case like this.
240 It is the ABC of a dog's education. "If you are in a room and you hear anyone trying to get in," Mother used to say, "bark. It may be some one who has business there, or it may not. Bark first, and inquire afterwards. Dogs were made to be heard and not seen."

I lifted my head and yelled. I have a good, deep voice, due to a hound strain in my pedigree,[7] and at the public-house, when there was a full moon, I have often had people leaning out of the windows and saying things all down the street. I took a deep breath and let it go.

250 "Man!" I shouted. "Bill! Man! Come quick! Here's a burglar getting in!"

---

[7] **pedigree** (pĕd´ĭ-grē´): an animal's list of ancestors, or family members; a family tree.

©Derek James Seaward/Corbis

WHEN STUDENTS STRUGGLE . . .

Guide students' comprehension of how characters respond and change throughout a story by having students, alone or in pairs, create a chart that shows how the dog responds. As the story progresses, have them add events and responses to the chart.

LEVEL UP TUTORIALS For additional support, assign the following *Level Up* tutorial: **Character Motivation.**

Then somebody struck a light, and it was the man himself. He had come in through the window.

He picked up a stick, and he walloped me. I couldn't understand it. I couldn't see where I had done the wrong thing. But he was the boss, so there was nothing to be said.

If you'll believe me, that same thing happened every night. Every single night! And sometimes twice or three times before morning. And every time I would bark my loudest, and
260 the man would strike a light and wallop me. The thing was baffling. I couldn't possibly have mistaken what Mother had said to me. She said it too often for that. Bark! Bark! Bark! It was the main plank of her whole system of education. And yet, here I was, getting walloped every night for doing it.

I thought it out till my head ached, and finally I got it right. I began to see that Mother's outlook was narrow. No doubt, living with a man like Master at the public-house, a man without a trace of shyness in his composition, barking was all right. But circumstances alter cases. I belonged to
270 a man who was a mass of nerves, who got the jumps if you spoke to him. What I had to do was to forget the training I had had from Mother, sound as it no doubt was as a general thing, and to adapt myself to the needs of the particular man who had happened to buy me. I had tried Mother's way, and all it had brought me was walloping, so now I would think for myself.

So next night, when I heard the window go, I lay there without a word, though it went against all my better feelings. I didn't even growl. Someone came in and moved about in the
280 dark, with a lantern, but, though I smelt that it was the man, I didn't ask him a single question. And presently the man lit a light and came over to me and gave me a pat, which was a thing he had never done before.

"Good dog!" he said. "Now you can have this."

And he let me lick out the saucepan in which the dinner had been cooked.

After that, we got on fine. Whenever I heard anyone at the window I just kept curled up and took no notice, and every time I got a bone or something good. It was easy, once you had
290 got the hang of things.

It was about a week after that the man took me out one morning, and we walked a long way till we turned in at some big gates and went along a very smooth road till we came to a

CLOSE READ

Describe Characters' Responses (LINES 254–256, 271–290)
RL 1, RL 3

Tell students that when characters change as a result of events, it often signals a key moment in the plot.

N CITE TEXT EVIDENCE Ask students why the narrator responds the way he does when the man wallops him. (*He stops barking, because, as he has noted before, the man is "the boss."*)

O CITE TEXT EVIDENCE Have students reread lines 271–290. Ask them to tell how the narrator's response to the man entering through the window changes, and why. (*The dog decides not to bark when the man comes in, even "though it went against all my better feelings." He decides to ignore his training because "all it had brought me was walloping."*)

Explain Point of View
RL 1, RL 6
(LINES 287–290)

Remind students that readers need to pay close attention to interpret information from an unreliable narrator.

P ASK STUDENTS to make an inference about why the man is training the dog to behave this way. (*Possible response: He is training the dog in order to help him rob a house. If the dog is in the house, he will not bark when he sees the Shy Man enter through a window.*)

What happens?	How does the dog respond?	Why?
The man enters through the window.	He barks and barks until he gets walloped.	He learned it from his mother.
The dog thinks about the situation.	He doesn't bark when the man enters.	He doesn't want to get walloped. He gets a reward.

Explain Point of View
(LINES 300–316)

RL 1,
RL 6

Tell students that when they make an inference about the limited information they get from a first-person narrator, they should follow up to find out whether it is correct.

Q **CITE TEXT EVIDENCE** Ask students to reread lines 300–316 and tell whether events match their inferences about why the man was training the dog. *(Possible response: Yes; the Shy Man is selling the dog to a caretaker so that he later can rob the house.)*

Describe Characters' Responses (LINES 317–327)

RL 1,
RL 3

Remind students that characters often change in response to story events.

R **CITE TEXT EVIDENCE** Have students reread lines 317–327 and describe how the narrator's feelings change. Ask whether the reasons the narrator gives for this change make sense to them. *(Possible responses: He becomes "very depressed" because he misses the Shy Man. I think his explanation that "dogs are dogs, and they are built like that" is sad in this case, but it makes sense, because dogs are loyal, faithful animals.)*

CRITICAL VOCABULARY

mope: The author uses the word *moped* to help show how the narrator behaves after he is sold to a new owner.

ASK STUDENTS to discuss how the word *moped* helps them picture the dog and how he behaves. *(Possible response: The word* moped *helps me see him lying down, head on his paws, with a sad, dejected look on his face.)*

---

great house, standing all by itself in the middle of a whole lot of country. There was a big lawn in front of it, and all round there were fields and trees, and at the back a great wood.

The man rang a bell, and the door opened, and an old man came out.

"Well?" he said, not very cordially.

300   "I thought you might want to buy a good watch-dog," said the man.

"Well, that's queer, your saying that," said the caretaker. "It's a coincidence. That's exactly what I do want to buy. I was just thinking of going along and trying to get one. My old dog picked up something this morning that he oughtn't to have, and he's dead, poor feller."

"Poor feller," said the man. "Found an old bone with phosphorus on it, I guess."

"What do you want for this one?"

310   "Five shillings."[8]

"Is he a good watch-dog?"

"He's a grand watch-dog."

"He looks fierce enough."

"Ah!"

So the caretaker gave the man his five shillings, and the man went off and left me.

At first the newness of everything and the unaccustomed smells and getting to know the caretaker, who was a nice old man, prevented my missing the man, but as the day

320   went on and I began to realize that he had gone and would never come back, I got very depressed. I pattered all over the house, whining. It was a most interesting house, bigger than I thought a house could possibly be, but it couldn't cheer me up. You may think it strange that I should pine for the man, after all the wallopings he had given me, and it is odd, when you come to think of it. But dogs are dogs, and they are built like that. By the time it was evening I was thoroughly miserable. I found a shoe and an old clothes-brush in one of the rooms, but could eat nothing. I just sat and **moped**.

330   It's a funny thing, but it seems as if it always happened that just when you are feeling most miserable, something nice

mope
(mōp) *intr.v.* To *mope* is to be gloomy, miserable, and not interested in anything.

---

[8] **five shillings:** a shilling is a coin of the United Kingdom that is no longer in use; it was worth 12 pennies (pence).

English Language Support

Improve Reading Fluency Emphasize the importance of paying attention to punctuation when reading aloud. Commas signal where to pause and show which groups of words should be read together.

- Display lines 317–329 and highlight the commas. Then model how to read it, using an appropriate pace and expression.

- Ask partners to take turns reading the paragraph aloud to each other. Have them give helpful feedback on the pace and expression with which their partner reads.

happens. As I sat there, there came from outside the sound of a motor-bicycle, and somebody shouted.

It was dear old Fred, my old pal Fred, the best old boy that ever stepped. I recognized his voice in a second, and I was scratching at the door before the old man had time to get up out of his chair.

Well, well, well! That was a pleasant surprise! I ran five times round the lawn without stopping, and then I came back and jumped up at him.

"What are you doing down here, Fred?" I said. "Is this caretaker your father? Have you seen the rabbits in the wood? How long are you going to stop? How's Mother? I like the country. Have you come all the way from the public-house? I'm living here now. Your father gave five shillings for me. That's twice as much as I was worth when I saw you last."

"Why, it's young Blackie!" That was what they called me at the saloon. "What are you doing here? Where did you get this dog, Father?"

"A man sold him to me this morning. Poor old Bob got poisoned. This one ought to be just as good a watch-dog. He barks loud enough."

"He should be. His mother is the best watch-dog in London. This cheese-hound used to belong to the boss. Funny him getting down here."

We went into the house and had supper. And after supper we sat and talked. Fred was only down for the night, he said, because the boss wanted him back next day.

"And I'd sooner have my job than yours, Dad," he said. "Of all the lonely places! I wonder you aren't scared of burglars."

"I've got my shot-gun, and there's the dog. I might be scared if it wasn't for him, but he kind of gives me confidence. Old Bob was the same. Dogs are a comfort in the country."

"Get many tramps here?"

"I've only seen one in two months, and that's the feller who sold me the dog here."

As they were talking about the man, I asked Fred if he knew him. They might have met at the public-house, when the man was buying me from the boss.

"You would like him," I said. "I wish you could have met."
They both looked at me.

"What's he growling at?" asked Fred. "Think he heard something?"

The Mixer **83**

y

TEACH

CLOSE READ

Explain Point of View
RL 1, RL 6

(LINES 341–346, 367–373)

Remind students that the narrator of this story sometimes "talks" to other characters. Explain that this device is useful in a number of ways.

(S) ASK STUDENTS to reread lines 341–346 and then explain how it reinforces what readers know about the narrator's personality. *(Possible response: It reminds readers how excitable and friendly the dog is.)* Ask them to explain how it also adds to the story's humor. *(Possible response: The dog's "speech" is entertaining because it seems a lot like what a friendly dog might actually say, and how he might say it, asking lots of questions about many different topics, all at one time.)*

(T) CITE TEXT EVIDENCE Have students reread lines 367–373. Ask them whether they think Fred understands what Blackie is saying and how they know this. *(When Fred asks "'What's he growling at?" it is clear he doesn't understand what Blackie is saying.)*

English Language Support

Culturally Responsive Instruction Initiate a class discussion to help students think more deeply about the role dogs play in peoples' lives.

ASK STUDENTS how Fred's father feels about the narrator staying in his house. Why does he feel this way? Have students discuss whether Fred's father should feel this way, knowing what they do about the narrator's "training." Then have pairs interview each other about the ways in which dogs perform important functions in society. Encourage students to draw on their prior experiences to identify roles that dogs might fulfill, such as guards, searchers, or rescuers. Then ask volunteers to share their ideas with the class.

FOR STUDENTS WITH DISABILITIES

Students may struggle with a story of this length.

- Organize the text into manageable segments.
- Have students read each segment with a partner or listen to the audio recording in their eBooks as they follow along.
- Have them annotate confusing or difficult parts with sticky notes.

The Mixer **83**

Describe Characters' Responses (LINES 403–408)

RL 1,
RL 3

Explain to students that as they read, they can ask themselves questions about how a character responds to an event to learn more about the character.

Ⓤ CITE TEXT EVIDENCE Ask students why Blackie doesn't bark when the Shy Man enters the house and what this tells them about Blackie. *(He is very excited to see the man again, but he "remembered in time how shy he was," and stays quiet. Blackie is mistaken about the man's personality and his intentions, but Blackie is a very obedient dog.)*

The old man laughed.

"He wasn't growling. He was talking in his sleep. You're nervous, Fred. It comes from living in the city."

"Well, I am. I like this place in the daytime, but it gives me the pip[9] at night. It's so quiet. How you can stand it here all the time, I can't understand. Two nights of it would have me
380 seeing things."

His father laughed.

"If you feel like that, Fred, you had better take the gun to bed with you. I shall be quite happy without it."

"I will," said Fred. "I'll take six if you've got them."

And after that they went upstairs. I had a basket in the hall, which had belonged to Bob, the dog who had got poisoned. It was a comfortable basket, but I was so excited at having met Fred again that I couldn't sleep. Besides, there was a smell of mice somewhere, and I had to move around, trying
390 to place it.

I was just sniffing at a place in the wall when I heard a scratching noise. At first I thought it was the mice working in a different place, but, when I listened, I found that the sound came from the window. Somebody was doing something to it from outside.

If it had been Mother, she would have lifted the roof off right there, and so should I, if it hadn't been for what the man had taught me. I didn't think it possible that this could be the man come back, for he had gone away and said nothing
400 about ever seeing me again. But I didn't bark. I stopped where I was and listened. And presently the window came open, and somebody began to climb in.

Ⓤ I gave a good sniff, and I knew it was the man.

I was so delighted that for a moment I nearly forgot myself and shouted with joy, but I remembered in time how shy he was, and stopped myself. But I ran to him and jumped up quite quietly, and he told me to lie down. I was disappointed that he didn't seem more pleased to see me. I lay down.

It was very dark, but he had brought a lantern with him,
410 and I could see him moving about the room, picking things up and putting them in a bag which he had brought with him.

---

[9] **pip:** a slang term for a minor illness; here, probably an upset stomach from being nervous or worried.

Describe Characters' Responses

RL 1,
RL 3

Share these strategies for guided or independent analysis:

- Highlight in yellow the main character's thoughts or feelings.
- Highlight in green the main character's actions.
- Review your highlights. On a note, record what they tell you about the character.

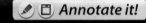

I gave a good sniff, and I knew it was the man.

I was so delighted that for a moment I nearly forgot myself and shouted with joy, but I remembered in time how shy he was, and stopped myself. But I ran to him and jumped up quite quietly, and he told me to lie down. I was disappointed that he didn't seem more pleased to see me. I lay down.

Every now and then he would stop and listen, and then he would start moving round again. He was very quick about it, but very quiet. It was plain that he didn't want Fred or his father to come down and find him.

I kept thinking about this peculiarity of his while I watched him. I suppose, being chummy myself, I find it hard to understand that everybody else in the world isn't chummy too. Of course, my experience at the public-house
420 had taught me that men are just as different from each other as dogs. If I chewed Master's shoe, for instance, he used to kick me, but if I chewed Fred's, Fred would tickle me under the ear. And, similarly, some men are shy and some men are mixers. I quite appreciated that, but I couldn't help feeling that the man carried shyness to a point where it became **morbid**. And he didn't give himself a chance to cure himself of it. That was the point. Imagine a man hating to meet people so much that he never visited their houses till the middle of the night, when they were in bed and asleep. It was silly. Shyness had always
430 been something so outside my nature that I suppose I have never really been able to look at it sympathetically. I have always held the view that you can get over it if you make an effort. The trouble with the man was that he wouldn't make an effort. He went out of his way to avoid meeting people.

I was fond of the man. He was the sort of person you never get to know very well, but we had been together for quite a while, and I wouldn't have been a dog if I hadn't got attached to him.

morbid
(môr´bĭd) *adj.* A *morbid* quality or feeling is one that is unhealthy or unwholesome, like an illness or disease.

The Mixer **85**

CLOSE READ

Explain Point of View
RL 1, RL 6

(LINES 427–434)

Remind students that a first-person narrator may have a limited understanding of events, and that irony is a contrast between what is expected and what really exists.

V **CITE TEXT EVIDENCE** Ask students to reread lines 427–434 and then tell how Blackie is mistaken about the Shy Man and what the man is doing. Have them tell why this is ironic. *(Blackie thinks the man is so shy that he avoids visiting the house during the day. This is ironic because the man is not shy, but is a burglar and has come to rob the house.)*

CRITICAL VOCABULARY

morbid: The author uses the word *morbid* to help show what Blackie thinks about the Shy Man's behavior.

ASK STUDENTS to discuss how the word *morbid* helps them understand how very mistaken Blackie is about the man. *(Possible response: Using* morbid *shows that Blackie thinks the man's shyness is a really serious problem for the man and that Blackie doesn't understand the man's personality at all.)*

English Language Support

Word Study Write the following on the board: *stop + ed = stopped* (line 400); *put + ing = putting* (line 411); *chum + y = chummy* (line 417).

Explain that when we when add a suffix that begins with *y* or a vowel to a one-syllable word with a short vowel sound and final consonant, we double that consonant (except for the letter *x*). However, when we add a suffix that begins with a consonant to such words, we do not double the final consonant.

ASK STUDENTS to add the indicated suffix to each word below. Have them rewrite the new word with the correct spelling. *(dogged; swimmer; dropping; sadder; sadly; crablike; gripped; grimly; slippery; fitness; mixer; crabby)*

dog + ed = ___   **sad + er** = ___   **grip + ed** = ___   **fit + ness** = ___

swim + er = ___   **sad + ly** = ___   **grim + ly** = ___   **mix + er** = ___

drop + ing = ___   **crab + like** = ___   **slip + ery** = ___   **crab + y** = ___

Describe Characters' Responses (LINES 439–451)

RL 1,
RL 3

Remind students to ask themselves why a character chooses to act in a particular way.

 CITE TEXT EVIDENCE Ask students to reread lines 439–451. Ask them to explain the reasons Blackie decides to go get Fred. *(He thinks that the men "would get along splendidly," and that it would give the Shy Man "the confidence which he needed.")* Then ask them to explain what this tells them about Blackie. *(Possible response: It shows that Blackie is a kind-hearted dog that wants to be helpful to his master.)*

As I sat and watched him creep about the room, it suddenly came to me that here was a chance of doing him a real good turn in spite of himself. Fred was upstairs, and Fred, as I knew by experience, was the easiest man to get along with in the world. Nobody could be shy with Fred. I felt that if only I could bring him and the man together, they would get along splendidly, and it would teach the man not to be silly and avoid people. It would help to give him the confidence which he needed. I had seen him with Bill, and I knew that he could be perfectly natural and easy when he liked.

It was true that the man might object at first, but after a while he would see that I had acted simply for his good, and would be grateful.

The difficulty was, how to get Fred down without scaring the man. I knew that if I shouted he wouldn't wait, but would be out of the window and away before Fred could get there. What I had to do was to go to Fred's room, explain the whole situation quietly to him, and ask him to come down and make himself pleasant.

The man was far too busy to pay any attention to me. He was kneeling in a corner with his back to me, putting something in his bag. I seized the opportunity to steal softly from the room.

Fred's door was shut, and I could hear him snoring. I scratched gently, and then harder, till I heard the snores stop. He got out of bed and opened the door.

"Don't make a noise," I whispered. "Come on downstairs. I want you to meet a friend of mine."

At first he was quite peevish.[10]

"What's the idea," he said, "coming and spoiling a man's beauty-sleep? Get out."

He actually started to go back into the room.

"No, honestly, Fred," I said, "I'm not fooling you. There *is* a man downstairs. He got in through the window. I want you to meet him. He's very shy, and I think it will do him good to have a chat with you."

"What are you whining about?" Fred began, and then he broke off suddenly and listened. We could both hear the man's footsteps as he moved about.

---

[10] **peevish** (pē´vĭsh): discontented or ill-tempered; cranky.

WHEN STUDENTS STRUGGLE . . .

Help students continue the chart they began on page 80.

- Together, identify the event that happens on page 86. Have pairs explain what Blackie does and why.
- Review students' charts. Then have pairs read page 87 and record the next event, as well as Blackie's response and motivation.
- Point out that although readers know the real reason behind Blackie's actions, the characters in the story interpret them differently. Lead a whole-class discussion on how this lack of understanding leads to humor.

LEVEL UP TUTORIALS For additional support, assign the following *Level Up* tutorial: **Character Motivation.**

Fred jumped back into the room. He came out, carrying
something. He didn't say any more but started to go
480 downstairs, very quiet, and I went after him.

There was the man, still putting things in his bag. I was
just going to introduce Fred, when Fred gave a great yell.

I could have bitten him.

"What did you want to do that for, you chump?"[11] I said.
"I told you he was shy. Now you've scared him."

He certainly had. The man was out of the window
quicker than you would have believed possible. He just flew
out. I called after him that it was only Fred and me, but at
that moment a gun went off with a tremendous bang, so he
490 couldn't have heard me.

I was pretty sick about it. The whole thing had gone
wrong. Fred seemed to have lost his head entirely. Naturally
the man had been frightened with him carrying on in that
way. I jumped out of the window to see if I could find the man
and explain, but he was gone. Fred jumped out after me, and
nearly squashed me.

It was pitch dark out there. I couldn't see a thing. But
I knew the man could not have gone far, or I should have
heard him. I started to sniff round on the chance of picking
500 up his trail. It wasn't long before I struck it.

Fred's father had come down now, and they were
running about. The old man had a light. I followed the trail,
and it ended at a large cedar tree, not far from the house.
I stood underneath it and looked up, but of course I could not
see anything.

"Are you up there?" I shouted. "There's nothing to be
scared at. It was only Fred. He's an old pal of mine. He works
at the place where you bought me. His gun went off by
accident. He won't hurt you."

510 There wasn't a sound. I began to think I must have made
a mistake.

"He's got away," I heard Fred say to his father, and just as
he said it I caught a faint sound of someone moving in the
branches above me.

"No he hasn't!" I shouted. "He's up this tree."

"I believe the dog's found him, Dad!"

"Yes, he's up here. Come along and meet him."

---

[11] **chump:** a stupid or silly person.

What happens?	How does Blackie respond?	Why?
The Shy Man comes in the window of the big house.	Blackie runs to get Fred.	Blackie wants Fred and the Shy Man to become friends.

CLOSE READ

Explain Point of View   RL 6
(LINES 481–496)

Explain to students that point of view can be used
to create humor, for example, when a first-person
narrator has only a limited understanding of what is
going on.

Ⓧ **ASK STUDENTS** to reread lines 481–496 and
then imagine the action in the scene. Ask them to tell
why the scene is entertaining, given what they know
about Blackie's understanding of the events. *(Picturing
the scene is entertaining because Blackie is barking and
barking, trying to "explain" things, while the Shy Man
leaps out the window and Fred shoots and jumps out
the window after him.)*

English Language Support

Understand Text Structure Draw a simple plot
diagram on the board and label the climax at the peak.
Tell students that this is the point of greatest excitement
in the story. After the climax, it becomes clear how the
story will end.

ASK STUDENTS to work with a partner to identify the
climax of the story. Have pairs predict what they think
will happen next. *(Blackie finds the Shy Man for Fred
and his father; the Shy Man will likely be arrested.)*

Describe Characters' Responses (LINES 536–547)

RL 1,
RL 3

Remind students that they should pay attention to how characters respond or change as a story's plot progresses.

Ⓨ CITE TEXT EVIDENCE Have students reread lines 536–547 and tell whether they think Blackie has changed as a result of his experiences. *(Possible response: Blackie has not changed very much; he says he "couldn't understand it," and says that "Men are so odd." He remains true to his happy-go-lucky character, saying that he "stopped worrying about it.")*

COLLABORATIVE DISCUSSION Have partners create a graphic organizer, such as a flow chart, that outlines the Shy Man's plan, and note what caused the plan to fail. Remind students to cite evidence from the text to support their ideas.

ASK STUDENTS to share any questions they generated in the course of reading and discussing the selection.

English Language Support

Exchange Ideas Provide students with a flow chart and explain its purpose.

- Have students respond to the Collaborative Discussion question, rereading key passages and noting important ideas in their flow charts.
- Form small, mixed-ability groups to discuss the details members included in their flow charts. Explain that they must agree on which ideas are most relevant.
- Distribute one blank flow chart to each group to complete by writing the ideas that the group has chosen. Let groups take turns sharing their charts.

Fred came to the foot of the tree.

"You up there," he said, "come along down."

520 Not a sound from the tree.

"It's all right," I explained, "he *is* up there, but he's very shy. Ask him again."

"All right," said Fred, "stay there if you want to. But I'm going to shoot off this gun into the branches just for fun."

And then the man started to come down. As soon as he touched the ground I jumped up at him.

"This is fine!" I said. "Here's my friend Fred. You'll like him."

But it wasn't any good. They didn't get along together at 530 all. They hardly spoke. The man went into the house, and Fred went after him, carrying his gun. And when they got into the house it was just the same. The man sat in one chair, and Fred sat in another, and after a long time some men came in a motor-car, and the man went away with them. He didn't say good-bye to me.

When he had gone, Fred and his father made a great fuss of me. I couldn't understand it. Men are so odd. The man wasn't a bit pleased that I had brought him and Fred together, but Fred seemed as if he couldn't do enough for me having 540 introduced him to the man. However, Fred's father produced some cold ham—my favorite dish—and gave me quite a lot of it, so I stopped worrying over the thing. As Mother used to say, "Don't bother your head about what doesn't concern you. The only thing a dog need concern himself with is the bill of fare.[12] Eat your bun, and don't make yourself busy about other people's affairs." Mother's was in some ways a narrow outlook, but she had a great fund of sterling common sense.

COLLABORATIVE DISCUSSION What was the Shy Man's plan? How does the plan go wrong and why? With a partner, discuss these questions and whether the plan made sense.

---

[12] **bill of fare:** a list of items that are available, as on a menu.

TO CHALLENGE STUDENTS . . .

Analyze Characters Point out to students that while Blackie has not changed a great deal by the end of the story, he is quite philosophical in his approach to life. For example, in lines 545–546, he reflects on his mother's advice that a dog should focus on what's in front of him and to not "'make yourself busy about other people's affairs.'"

ASK STUDENTS in small groups or as partners to review the story to find other life lessons Blackie shares, and discuss which they think are the most useful.

Describe Characters' Responses

RL 3

Every good story has strong characters and an interesting plot. A **character** is a person, animal, or even an imaginary creature who takes part in a story. A **plot,** as you already know, is the series of events in a story.

When you read a story, it is interesting to see how characters respond to events or change as the plot moves toward its resolution. Authors illustrate characters' responses through their actions, thoughts, feelings, and interactions with other characters. When Blackie, the main character in "The Mixer," is sold to the Shy Man, he is thrilled, saying that he's "off to see life.'" Blackie's response to this event tells you that he enjoys new experiences.

Look for more examples of characters' responses to the plot as you analyze "The Mixer." Ask yourself: How does the character respond when something happens to him or her? What does that tell me about the character?

Explain Point of View

RL 6

A story's **narrator** is the voice that tells the story. Point of view is the perspective from which the story is told. A **first-person** point of view means a character from the story is the narrator. When a story is told in first-person point of view, the narrator

- may be a major or minor character
- tells the story using first-person words like *I, me,* and *my*
- tells about his or her thoughts and feelings
- does not know what other characters are thinking or feeling

Sometimes point of view can be used to create irony and humor. **Irony** is a contrast between what is expected and what actually exists or happens. For example, it is ironic that Blackie calls his new owner "the Shy Man," because the man turns out not to be shy at all.

In "The Mixer," look for ways the narrator and point of view shape the way the story is told and how the narration creates irony. Ask yourself:

- Does the narrator understand everything that is happening?
- How is my understanding of the story limited by what the narrator knows or decides to tell?
- What events in the story are surprising?

The Mixer   **89**

CLOSE READ

Describe Characters' Responses

RL 1, RL 3

Help students understand the terms. Point out that in most stories, the main character undergoes a change in response to events and in order to resolve the story's conflict. Ask students to tell why a main character might change as a story's plot progresses. *(Possible responses: in order to grow; to meet a goal or face a challenge; to keep a story interesting)*

Ask students to give examples of how Blackie responded to events or changed in "The Mixer."

Explain Point of View

RL 1, RL 6

Guide students to understand how a first-person point of view narrator helps shape a story. Point out that in a story that uses first-person point of view, it can feel like the narrator is speaking directly to readers, which makes it feel personal, but that the narrator cannot know exactly what other characters are thinking.

Next, discuss that when irony is used, readers often realize something that the characters do not. Prompt students to give examples of how they know something that Blackie does not.

Strategies for Annotation   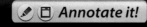 *Annotate it!*

Describe Characters' Responses

RL 3

Share these strategies for guided or independent analysis:

- Highlight in yellow events that take place.
- Highlight in green how the main character responds to the event.
- On a note, record what the character's response tells you about him.

It was quite dark when we got to the country, but the man seemed to know where to go. He pulled at my rope, and we began to walk along a road with no people in it at all. We walked on and on, but it was all so new to me that I forgot how tired I was. I could feel my mind broadening with every step I took.

The Mixer   **89**

PRACTICE & APPLY

Analyzing the Text

RL 1, RL 3, RL 5, RL 6, RL 10

Possible answers:

1. *Words such as* I, me, *and* my *show that the story is told in first-person point of view. The narrator is a dog who began his days "in an East End public-house," but was sold to someone he calls "the Shy Man."*

2. *He can be overly friendly; he loves humans and loves getting attention from them. Unlike his mother, who is loyal to one master, he is not a one-person dog.*

3. *After being walloped several times for barking, Blackie figures out that he should forget what he learned from his mother and keep quiet. This shows that Blackie can adapt to new situations.*

4. *It helps the reader understand that the Shy Man will likely try to break into the house, and imagine that the plan may go wrong, since Blackie is so excited to see Fred.*

5. *Blackie loves men and is happy when he is sold to the Shy Man. He is loyal to his owner even when the man mistreats him. When the Shy Man finally gives him a reward for not barking, he thinks his mother has given him the wrong advice. Blackie is so devoted to the Shy Man that he doesn't realize the man is committing a burglary and thinks his unexpected arrival is a chance for the Shy Man to meet his other friends from the saloon.*

6. *He describes the man as not giving "himself a chance to cure himself of [shyness]"; he says the man "wouldn't make an effort. He went out of his way to avoid meeting people." This is ironic because Blackie's view is the opposite of the truth; the Shy Man is not shy; he avoids meeting people because, as a thief, he does not want to be seen.*

7. *Blackie's role as the narrator creates the humor of the story; knowing his "thoughts" makes the story funny. The reader still knows what the Shy Man is doing, even though Blackie doesn't. Blackie also shows the reader what it is like to be a dog.*

FOR STANDARD ENGLISH LEARNERS

Review the rules about using indefinite articles before nouns and encourage students to check for correct usage when proofreading their essays. Provide these sentences for practice:

- The Shy Man has a attitude from the beginning of the story that is suspicious. To Blackie, he seems like a honest man. But, in fact, he is a thief. (*an attitude; an honest man; a thief*)

 eBook *Annotate It!*

Analyzing the Text

RL 1, RL 3, RL 5, RL 6, RL 10, W 2a-f

Cite Text Evidence Support your responses with evidence from the text.

1. **Identify** Reread lines 1–10. Identify clues that help you explain the story's point of view. What is the point of view and who is the narrator?

2. **Infer** Reread lines 72–86. Describe the dog's character. How is his personality the same as or different from any other dog's personality?

3. **Interpret** Review the events in lines 232–286. How does Blackie respond to his training? Explain what this tells you about his character.

4. **Draw Conclusions** Review lines 334–355, when Fred appears at the country house. Explain why this event helps you understand the attempted burglary.

5. **Analyze** How is Blackie affected by events in the story?

6. **Analyze** Review lines 416–438. Tell what Blackie says that illustrates how he views the Shy Man. What is ironic about Blackie's view?

7. **Analyze** What effect does Blackie's role as the narrator have on the story?

PERFORMANCE TASK

Writing Activity: Informative Essay In "The Mixer," Blackie is mistaken about why the Shy Man seems so quiet. Write a one-page essay that explains the Shy Man's motivation for not speaking.

- Review the story. Make notes about events and situations that help you understand the man's character.
- Describe the man's character, using evidence from the text.

- Tell how the man responds to Blackie and to other characters in the story.
- Give concrete examples that illustrate why the man does not speak.
- Use appropriate transitions such as *furthermore, one reason,* and *in addition* to clarify relationships among your ideas.
- Provide a concluding statement that supports your explanation.

Assign this performance task.

PERFORMANCE TASK

W 2a-f

Writing Activity: Informative Essay Have students work independently. Direct them to

- create a chart to list events and evidence about the Shy Man's character and motivation
- use the chart to explain what each event tells them about his character

Remind them to take notes on evidence from the text that they will include in their essays.

Critical Vocabulary

L 4, L 4b, L 6

surfeit criticize amiable wallop mope morbid

Practice and Apply Answer each question.

1. Have you ever consumed a **surfeit** of sweets? How did you feel afterwards?

2. When did you ever **criticize** someone? Why?

3. Have you ever been impressed by an **amiable** person? Why?

4. Have you ever wanted to **wallop** something? What was the result?

5. Do you ever **mope** about a situation? Tell when and why.

6. Have you ever felt that someone was being **morbid**? Tell how that person acted.

Vocabulary Strategy: Greek Suffix *-ize*

The Greek suffix *-ize* often creates a verb when it is added to a noun. For example, the vocabulary word *criticize* means "to find fault with"—in other words, to act as a critic. In this case, the suffix *-ize* means "to become or be like." If you can recognize the noun that the suffix *-ize* is attached to, you can often figure out the meaning of the verb that is formed. The chart shows some meanings of the suffix *-ize*.

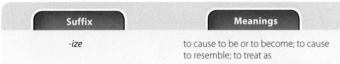

Suffix	Meanings
-ize	to cause to be or to become; to cause to resemble; to treat as

Practice and Apply Complete each sentence with one of the following words. Then identify the noun in each word and its meaning. Use the information in the chart to write a definition for each boldface word.

dramatize idolize authorize equalize jeopardize

1. The store walls were plastered with posters of singers that teens _____ .

2. Poor judgment and rash behavior could _____ our secret mission.

3. This note will _____ you to spend lunchtime in the library.

4. I am writing a play to _____ my grandmother's life story.

5. You need to sit on the other end of the seesaw to _____ the weight.

Critical Vocabulary

L 4, L 4b, L 6

Possible answers:

1. *I had too much candy at a movie once, and my stomach was upset the rest of the day.*

2. *I criticized my brother when he slammed the door too hard.*

3. *I am always impressed by my grandma's amiability. She is always friendly and happy, no matter what.*

4. *I wanted to wallop my bike yesterday. When I got home, I wanted to ride it, but it had a flat tire.*

5. *When I found out I couldn't visit a friend, I moped all afternoon.*

6. *Once, my cousin was being morbid when she wouldn't stop talking about how it was possible to have a broken toe and not know about it.*

Vocabulary Strategy: Greek Suffix *-ize*

Answers:

1. *idolize: idol; treat as an idol*

2. *jeopardize: jeopardy, danger; put in jeopardy or danger*

3. *authorize: author; the creator of a book, story, or other written work; give permission for*

4. *dramatize: drama, a play; treat as a drama*

5. *equalize: equal; a person or thing that is the same as another in some way; cause to be equal*

Strategies for Annotation   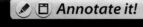 Annotate it!

Greek Suffix *–ize*

L 4a, L 4b

Have students locate the sentence containing *criticize* in the selection. Tell them to use their eBook annotation tools to do the following:

- Highlight the word in yellow.
- Underline the suffix *-ize*.
- On a note, write the base word and its meaning.
- Highlight in green any context clues you find in the surrounding text.
- Try to infer the word's meaning. Combine the meanings of *-ize* ("to act as") and of *critic* to think about what *criticize* might mean.

. . . I am not a handsome dog. Even Mother never thought me beautiful. She was no Gladys Cooper herself, but she never hesitated to criticize my appearance. In fact, I have yet to meet anyone who did. The first thing strangers say about me is "What an ugly dog!"

Criticize: act as a critic

Language Conventions: Intensive Pronouns

L 1b

Clarify for students that intensive pronouns are used primarily to emphasize who is doing, has done, or will do something. Using the example sentences, point out that if the intensive pronoun is removed, the sentence still makes sense. Adding the intensive pronoun emphasizes who is performing the action.

Answers:

1. *themselves*

2. *myself*

3. *herself*

4. *yourself*

5. *himself*

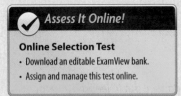

Assess It Online!

Online Selection Test
- Download an editable ExamView bank.
- Assign and manage this test online.

Language Conventions: Intensive Pronouns

L 1b

Intensive pronouns are formed by adding *-self* or *-selves* to certain personal pronouns and are used to intensify, or emphasize, the nouns or pronouns to which they refer. Like other pronouns, they also change their form to express person, number, and gender.

	First Person	Second Person	Third Person
Singular	myself	yourself	himself, herself, itself
Plural	ourselves	yourselves	themselves

Here is an example of an intensive pronoun from "The Mixer."

Then somebody struck a light, and it was the man <u>himself</u>.

The intensive pronoun *himself* emphasizes Blackie's surprise at seeing his new owner breaking into his own home. Here are some more examples:

The dog <u>itself</u> hid the bone.
He took the car home <u>himself</u>.
You ate the whole cake <u>yourself</u>!
The scouts will clean the room <u>themselves</u>.

Keep in mind that standard English does not include forms such as *hisself* and *theirselves*, even though *his* and *their* are common possessive pronouns. The correct forms in these cases are *himself* and *themselves*.

Practice and Apply Complete each sentence with the correct intensive pronoun.

1. The students _____ made all the refreshments.

2. I _____ had the best audition.

3. Judith _____ is to blame.

4. You _____ have to take responsibility for this.

5. Rico will finish the diorama _____ .

English Language Support

Understand Cohesion Remind students that intensive pronouns can refer to a noun or to another pronoun. They directly follow the noun or pronoun that they intensify and must agree in number and gender with their referent.

- Display the Practice and Apply sentences and list the following choices for each blank: 1. *theirselves, themselves*; 2. *myself, myselve*; 3. *herself, itself*; 4. *yourselve, yourself*; 5. *myself, himself*. Have students work in pairs to choose the correct pronoun.

- Have students complete the Practice and Apply activity with a partner. Discuss their answers and then ask them to write an original sentence containing an intensive pronoun. Have pairs share their sentences with the class.

- Have students choose two sentences from the story and rewrite them to include intensive pronouns. Have volunteers read both versions to the class.

Analyze Language: Irony

RL 4

TEACH

Remind students that **irony** is a contrast between what appears to be true and what is really true. It is often used as a source of humor in fiction texts. Explain different types of irony to students:

- **Situational irony** is a contrast between what a reader or character expects and what actually exists or happens.
- **Dramatic irony** refers to when the reader or viewer knows something that a character does not know.
- **Verbal irony** exists when someone knowingly exaggerates or says one thing and means another.

PRACTICE AND APPLY

Discuss examples of different types of irony found in "The Mixer." Possible examples include:

- Situational irony: Blackie's training by the Shy Man (lines 252–264); his disappointment that Fred and the Shy Man do not get along (lines 529–538)
- Dramatic irony: the sale of Blackie to the caretaker (lines 300–316)
- Verbal irony: the Master's statement to the Shy Man (lines 114–115); the policeman's statements to the Shy Man (lines 138–140)

Invite students to find other examples of different types of irony in "The Mixer," or from other texts or movies with which they are familiar. Have them describe each example and explain its effect.

English Language Support

Read Closely Adapt the Collection Opener strategy, Think-Write-Pair-Share, to help students locate examples of irony.

- **First,** assist students in looking through the text for additional examples of irony. Have them each write an example and explain its effect.
- **Next,** have pairs share their responses. Remind students to ask each other clarifying questions. Then have students revise their responses to reflect any changes resulting from the discussions.
- **Finally,** have students share their answers with the class.

Explain Narrator and Point of View

RL 6

RETEACH

Review the terms *narrator, first-person point of view,* and *third-person point of view.* Remind students that sometimes a narrator is unreliable, like Blackie in "The Mixer." Explain that an **unreliable narrator** may be untrustworthy because he has bad intentions or simply because he is naïve (lacking in wisdom, experience, or judgment). Ask students why Blackie in "The Mixer" is an unreliable narrator.

Remind students how to identify point of view.

- **Look at the pronouns** in the story. A first-person narrator uses pronouns like *I, me,* or *my.* A third-person narrator uses pronouns like *he, her,* or *their.*
- **Identify the narrator.** Is the narrator a voice that is a character in the story or not? How can you tell? Is the narrator unreliable? How do you know?
- **Analyze the effects.** Point out that a first-person narrator does not know what others are thinking. A third-person narrator may know the thoughts of all or some of the characters. An unreliable narrator cannot be trusted to understand or share everything that is going on.

 LEVEL UP TUTORIALS Assign one or more of the following *Level Up* tutorials: **Point of View; First-Person Point of View; Third-Person Point of View; Narrator and Speaker.**

INDEPENDENT READING

Individual students can apply these skills to another selection in Collection 1 or 2, or to a short story or novel they may be reading on their own. After their analysis, have them share their ideas about narrator and point of view with other students in the class.

The Pod

Short Story by Maureen Crane Wartski

Why This Text

Students often read a short story without understanding how the elements of a story interact. The characters may respond to the events of the plot and change as the plot moves forward. With the help of the close-reading questions, students will recognize how the characters respond or change as the plot moves toward a resolution of the conflict. This close reading will also guide students to understand how the author develops the narrator's point of view.

Background Have students read the background and the information about the author. Tell students that Maureen Crane Wartski is a naturalized American citizen who was born in Japan. The author of many novels for children and young adults, she is also an expert watercolorist, blending storytelling and art in her young-adult novels and in the quilts she makes.

SETTING A PURPOSE Ask students to pay close attention to how the plot unfolds in a series of episodes and how a main character responds or changes as the plot moves toward a resolution. How soon into the story can students begin to identify the conflict?

Standards Support

- cite textual evidence
- describe how a story's plot unfolds in a series of episodes (or events)
- describe how a character responds or changes as the plot moves toward a resolution
- explain how an author develops the point of view of the narrator

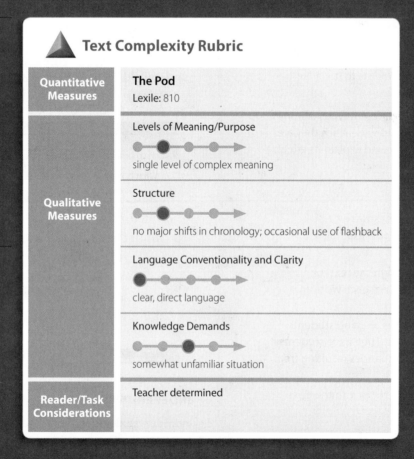

Text Complexity Rubric

Quantitative Measures

The Pod
Lexile: 810

Qualitative Measures

Levels of Meaning/Purpose
single level of complex meaning

Structure
no major shifts in chronology; occasional use of flashback

Language Conventionality and Clarity
clear, direct language

Knowledge Demands
somewhat unfamiliar situation

Reader/Task Considerations
Teacher determined

Strategies for CLOSE READING

Describe Characters' Responses

Students should read this short story carefully all the way through. Close-reading questions at the bottom of the page will help them analyze how a main character responds or changes as the plot moves toward a resolution. As they read, students should record comments or questions about the text in the side margins.

WHEN STUDENTS STRUGGLE . . .

To help students understand the way a character responds or changes as the plot moves toward a resolution, have them work in small groups to fill out a story map such as the one shown below as they analyze the story.

CITE TEXT EVIDENCE The power of a story such as this one comes from a main character's response to events in the plot. For practice in tracking how the character changes as the action moves forward, have students complete the story map.

> *Setting:* Jesse's house; a road by the ocean

> *Major Characters:* Jesse and his cousin Pete
>
> *Minor Characters:* Jesse's mother, the dolphin, the dolphin's pod

> *Plot/Problem:* Jesse is annoyed at his cousin Pete for his boring lectures about "fish" (marine mammals), but then Jesse is faced with having to rescue a dolphin.

> *Event 1:* Jesse leaves the house to escape Pete's dull lecture and his family's pity.

> *Event 2:* Jesse finds a wounded, stranded dolphin and tries to rescue it.

> *Event 3:* Jesse tries to call Pete for help. He wishes he had paid more attention.

> *Outcome:* As he remembers Pete's lecture, Jesse saves the dolphin and returns him to his pod. Jesse realizes he needs to return to his own family.

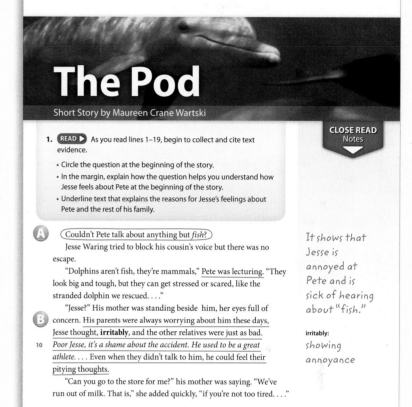

Background **Maureen Crane Wartski** *was born in Ashiya, Japan, in 1940. Her European and Asian heritage and her deep connection with nature have strongly influenced her writing. In addition, Wartski is an accomplished artist. Like her writing, her watercolors often portray the natural world. Here she writes about dolphins, which, like whales, travel together in groups called "pods."*

The Pod
Short Story by Maureen Crane Wartski

CLOSE READ
Notes

1. **READD ▶** As you read lines 1–19, begin to collect and cite text evidence.
   - Circle the question at the beginning of the story.
   - In the margin, explain how the question helps you understand how Jesse feels about Pete at the beginning of the story.
   - Underline text that explains the reasons for Jesse's feelings about Pete and the rest of his family.

Ⓐ ⟨Couldn't Pete talk about anything but *fish*?⟩

Jesse Waring tried to block his cousin's voice but there was no escape.

"Dolphins aren't fish, they're mammals," Pete was lecturing. "They look big and tough, but they can get stressed or scared, like the stranded dolphin we rescued. . . ."

"Jesse?" His mother was standing beside him, her eyes full of concern. His parents were always worrying about him these days, Jesse thought, **irritably**, and the other relatives were just as bad.

10 *Poor Jesse, it's a shame about the accident. He used to be a great athlete. . . . Even when they didn't talk to him, he could feel their pitying thoughts.*

"Can you go to the store for me?" his mother was saying. "We've run out of milk. That is," she added quickly, "if you're not too tired. . . ."

It shows that Jesse is annoyed at Pete and is sick of hearing about "fish."

Ⓑ

irritably: *showing annoyance*

19

---

1. **READ AND CITE TEXT EVIDENCE**   Explain to students that Wartski begins the story by describing the main characters, Jesse and his cousin Pete, and by establishing the conflict of the plot.

Ⓐ **ASK STUDENTS** to determine how Jesse feels about Pete and the rest of his family since his accident by examining Jesse's thoughts, words, and actions and by citing specific textual evidence in lines 1–19. *Responses may include specific references to evidence in lines 1–3, 8–12, and 16–19.*

Critical Vocabulary: irritably (line 9) Have students share their definitions of *irritably*. Why does Wartski° use the word to describe Jesse's response to his family's concern about him? *Students should point out that Jesse is annoyed by his parents' (and his other relatives') worried looks and attitude toward him since his accident.*

He no longer enjoys the family reunions.

He is no longer star of the soccer team and cannot get an athletic scholarship.

He feels that his future is smashed and that he is a cripple.

"... And I want to make sure to visit the Cape Cod Stranding Network." Pete was droning on. "They have a hotline, and they do great work...."

Yada, yada, yada. "Sure Mom," Jess said. *Anything to get away from Pete's lectures and all those pitying eyes.*

20   He snatched up car keys from the table in the entryway, grabbing his windbreaker as he limped out the door. Once outside, he wished he'd brought his parka—the wind had an icy sting—but he wasn't going back into the house.

C   He'd always enjoyed the annual Waring family reunion, when cousins, uncles and aunts from all over the country got together and rented a house on New England's Cape Cod, but this March was different. It was the first time the clan had gathered since the accident.

D   Jesse didn't want to think about how a man driving a pickup had jumped a red light, slamming into his car and fracturing his legs.

30   Until then Jesse had been the star of the school soccer team, certain of an athletic scholarship.

"Not anymore," he muttered, then frowned as he realized he'd passed the store. Well, OK, there was a convenience store about 30 miles away, and the drive would give him some needed alone time.

At first, the silence was great.

But as Jesse drove on the road that wound beside the ocean, he kept thinking how his future had been smashed along with his legs. Pep talks that people gave him made it worse. He was a cripple, and

---

2.   ◀ REREAD   Reread lines 7–14. How does Jesse respond to the accident? Explain what this tells you about his character. Support your answer with explicit textual evidence.

Jesse responds with anger and frustration. He seems annoyed by his mother and Pete and resents what he sees as their pity.

---

3.   READ ▶   As you read lines 20–40, continue to cite textual evidence.
   • Underline the text that shows what Jesse was like before the accident.
   • Note in the margin how this event has changed him.

20

---

he knew it. These days Jesse always felt as if there was a tight, hard
40   knot in his chest.

On **impulse**, he turned the wheel, pulling into an empty parking lot that faced the water. He got out and limped down some stairs. Except for screeching seagulls and a few scattered rocks, the beach was deserted.

Suddenly, Jesse tensed. *That rock ... did it move?* He took a step closer and saw that it was no rock.

The dolphin wasn't very big, not even four feet long. When Jesse hobbled over, the big fish ... *mammal,* according to Pete ... rolled an eye at him. How long had it been there? It was breathing, but its sides
50   were heaving painfully.

E F   Fragments of Pete's endless **monologue** came back to him. His cousin had said that a dolphin's rib structure wasn't built to protect it on land. The body weight of this creature was slowly compressing its vital organs, and if it didn't get back into the water soon, it could die. It was going to low tide and the waves seemed far away. The best thing to do was to call Pete, who would know what to do. Jesse reached for his cell phone.

It wasn't there. He'd left it in the pocket of his parka! He could drive home and get Pete, but that would mean leaving the dolphin.

impulse:
a sudden urge

monologue:
a long speech

He realizes that Pete's knowledge might be important.

---

4.   ◀ REREAD   As you reread lines 28–35, compare Jesse's life before and after the accident. Why do you think he misses the convenience store? Support your answer with explicit textual evidence.

Jesse was a soccer star before the accident and always liked seeing family. Now he feels that his old life is over. He is so distracted that he drives past the store.

---

5.   READ ▶   As you read lines 41–61, continue to cite textual evidence.
   • Underline the text that tells what Jesse thinks about immediately after he sees the stranded dolphin.
   • Circle the text that shows how Jesse's feelings toward Pete have changed, and restate the change in the margin.

21

---

2.   REREAD AND CITE TEXT EVIDENCE

B   ASK STUDENTS to cite explicit textual evidence that shows how Jesse's response to his accident reveals his character and shows how he has changed since the crash. *Students should cite specific evidence from lines 8–12.*

3.   READ AND CITE TEXT EVIDENCE

C   ASK STUDENTS to read their margin notes to a partner and then write one response that best states how Jesse has changed since his accident, citing specific textual evidence. *Students should cite examples in lines 24–27, 30–31, and 36–40.*

FOR ELL STUDENTS Review the meaning of the phrasal verb **pull into** (line 41), pointing out that in the context of the story, it means "to put the car in a parking space." Point out the differences in the meaning of the verb with and without the preposition.

4.   REREAD AND CITE TEXT EVIDENCE

D   ASK STUDENTS to evaluate the significance of the event in which Jesse drives past the convenience store. What does it show about Jesse's state of mind since the accident? *Students should cite evidence from lines 28–31 and 32–34.*

5.   READ AND CITE TEXT EVIDENCE

E   ASK STUDENTS to read their margin notes to a partner and then write one response that shows why Jesse's feelings toward Pete have changed, citing specific textual evidence. *Students should cite examples in lines 51–56 and 58–59.*

Critical Vocabulary: impulse (line 41) Have students give examples of instances when someone has followed an impulse. *Students should cite times when they have seen someone act rashly.*

Critical Vocabulary: monologue (line 51) Ask students to share definitions of *monologue* and to use it in a sentence.

60 Would it be alive when he got back? He knew nothing about this creature except that it was helpless.

G The dolphin's eyes rolled again, and Jesse felt a sudden jolt of **empathy**.

It looked as scared as he had felt when they'd wheeled him into the emergency room that afternoon.

H "Hey, Bud, . . ." Jesse knelt down beside the dolphin. "OK, I just can't leave you here to die. But how do I get you back into the water?"

Even if he managed to drag this creature that weighed — what? maybe 75 pounds? back into the water, the coarse sand might damage 70 its skin. Jesse looked helplessly toward the gray ocean and was surprised to see dark shapes **arcing** out of the waves. A *pod*[1]—Pete's word—was out there.

"I think your family's waiting for you, Bud." Carefully, Jesse reached out and patted the dolphin. Was it his imagination that his touch made the dolphin calmer?

I Jesse didn't want to waste time thinking about that. He was trying to remember what Pete had said about how, when he'd helped rescue a stranded dolphin, he had put the creature on a sort of blanket sling and carried that **contraption** down to the water. Well, he didn't 80 have a blanket handy, so his windbreaker would have to do.

Carefully, Jesse scooped a hollow in the soft sand under the dolphin's head, then eased part of the windbreaker under it. He was streaming with sweat by the time he managed to maneuver as much of the dolphin as possible onto its makeshift "blanket," then began to drag the dolphin toward the water.

[1] **pod:** a school (or family) of dolphins or other sea mammals.

empathy:
identifying with someone else's feelings or situation

arcing:
making a curved path

contraption:
a device

---

6. **◀ REREAD AND DISCUSS** *Irony* is a contrast between what is expected and what actually happens. With a small group, discuss how Jesse's feelings about Pete's lectures may be changing. What makes this change surprising?

7. **READ ▶** As you read lines 62–75, continue to cite textual evidence.

- Underline the text that demonstrates how Jesse continues to benefit from Pete's lecture as he cares for the dolphin.
- Circle the text that shows that Jesse is comparing himself to the dolphin.

22

Twice, his legs buckled under him, tumbling him backward onto the sand, but he kept going until water was lapping around his ankles.

"Almost there, Bud," Jesse gritted.

As Jesse waded knee-deep into the water, the dolphin made some 90 kind of noise and then began to swim.

"Woo hoo!" Jesse yelled, then yelped in **dismay**. The dolphin was swimming back toward the shore.

What was wrong with the crazy creature? Pete's voice began to drone in Jesse's mind again, recounting his own dolphin rescue; "*The dolphin was **disoriented**. It kept heading for the shore. We had to guide it back into the deep water. . . .*"

Jesse waded deeper, past the breakers. Icy waves broke against him as he tried to head off the young dolphin. When he'd finally managed that, it wouldn't turn. He wished he had paid more attention to Pete's 100 lecture, but wishing never helped.

J Waves sent freezing spumes into his face. "Bud, you've got to save yourself." Jesse gritted through chattering teeth. "Nobody's going to do it for you. If you give up, you're finished. . . ."

Suddenly, as if it had at last understood, the young dolphin turned toward deeper water and began to swim toward the pod. Waiting dolphins arced nearer as if in welcome, and watching them, Jess thought of his own family. They'd be worried because he'd been gone so long.

My pod, he thought.

dismay:
feeling alarmed

disoriented:
confused

It is ironic because in the past he has thought Pete's lectures were boring.

---

8. **◀ REREAD** Reread lines 66–75. What does Jesse do to care for the dolphin? How do his actions show that Jesse is changing as the story moves forward? Support your answer with explicit textual evidence.

Jesse does not want to leave the stranded dolphin alone, and he tries to make it feel calmer. He tries to figure out how to get the animal back into the water. Jesse's empathy for the dolphin helps him lose his anger and take responsibility for the dolphin and himself.

9. **READ ▶** As you read lines 76–117, continue to cite textual evidence.

- Underline the actions Jesse takes to get the dolphin back into the water.
- In the margin, tell why it is ironic that Jesse remembers Pete's words.

23

---

6. **REREAD AND DISCUSS USING TEXT EVIDENCE**

F **ASK STUDENTS** to appoint a reporter for each group to cite specific textual evidence that shows irony in the text and how Jesse's point of view toward Pete and his lectures may be changing. *Students should cite specific evidence from lines 51–57 and 58–59.*

7. **READ AND CITE TEXT EVIDENCE**

G **ASK STUDENTS** to cite specific textual evidence to show that Jesse is beginning to relate to the wounded, frightened dolphin and its situation. *Students should cite evidence from lines 62–65 and 73–75.*

Critical Vocabulary: empathy (line 63), **arcing** (line 71), and **contraption** (line 79) Have students share their definitions of the words and use each in a sentence. How does the use of *empathy* lead you to realize that Jesse is beginning to relate to the dolphin?

8. **REREAD AND CITE TEXT EVIDENCE**

H **ASK STUDENTS** to cite textual evidence that shows how Jesse's actions toward the dolphin indicate a change in his character as the plot moves toward a resolution. *Jesse's response to the dolphin's distress suggests that his feelings toward his family, and himself, have changed. Students should cite evidence in lines 66–67, 68–72, and 73–75.*

9. **READ AND CITE TEXT EVIDENCE**

I **ASK STUDENTS** to read their margin notes to a partner, and then create one response that best represents the ironic situation posed by Jesse's attempt to remember Pete's words. *Students should cite textual evidence in lines 76–85, 93–100, and 101–105.*

Critical Vocabulary: dismay (line 91) and **disoriented** (line 95) Ask students to define *dismay* and *disoriented*. Point out that *dis-* is often used as a prefix, meaning "not" or "away from," as in *disoriented*. Have them cite other words with *dis-*.

110 He was freezing as he limped back to his car, but he was grinning, and he was happier than he'd been in a long while.

He was going to drive to the nearest store and call Pete, who would probably contact the Cape Cod Stranding Network hotline that he'd been talking about. The CCSN would make sure that Bud didn't strand again.

"But that's not going to happen anyway," Jesse said aloud.

He had a feeling the young dolphin was finally on the right track.

10. **◄ REREAD** As you reread lines 101–117, explain why what Jesse says to the dolphin could really be applied to himself. To whom might Jesse be referring when he says that the young dolphin is "on the right track"?

Like the dolphin, Jesse has to save himself and change his attitude. He can't give up. When he says that the dolphin is "on the right track," he is probably also referring to himself.

SHORT RESPONSE

Cite Text Evidence Explain how events in the story change Jesse's feelings about his cousin Pete. How does this response to Pete show that Jesse himself has changed as he struggled to rescue the stranded dolphin? **Cite text evidence** to support your response.

At the beginning of the story, Jesse is tired of listening to Pete's lectures about sea mammals, which Jesse calls "fish." However, when Jesse encounters the stranded dolphin, he tries to call Pete for advice, something he would not have done before. He tries to remember what Pete has said about rescuing dolphins. As he remembers Pete's lecture, he realizes that he will have to make a makeshift blanket to carry the dolphin to the ocean, and he will have to take the dolphin into deep water. By remembering Pete's words, Jesse saves the dolphin—and himself—in the process.

24

10. **REREAD AND CITE TEXT EVIDENCE**

Ⓙ ASK STUDENTS to cite specific textual evidence and line numbers to support the idea that Jesse's identification with the dolphin is complete. By ending the story with Jesse's perception that "the young dolphin was finally on the right track," students should infer that Jesse could be referring to himself. *Students should cite evidence from lines 101–103, 104–109, and 110–117.*

SHORT RESPONSE

Cite Text Evidence Student responses will vary, but students should cite evidence from the text to support their ideas. Students should

- explain how Jesse's response to Pete changes as the plot moves toward the resolution of the conflict
- give reasons for their point of view
- cite specific evidence from the text to track how the narrator's point of view toward Jesse changes.

TO CHALLENGE STUDENTS . . .

For more content about dolphins, students can conduct research online or in the library on these fascinating creatures.

ASK STUDENTS to discover more information about the intelligence of dolphins by writing a research report. Some research topics about dolphins might include

- how dolphins communicate
- fascinating facts about dolphins, whales, and porpoises
- swimming with dolphins

With the class, discuss these elements of a research report after students have chosen a topic.

PLAN YOUR RESEARCH

- Write questions about your topic.
- Research your topic and take notes.
- Organize your notes.
- Write an outline based on your notes.

WRITE YOUR REPORT

- Keep your purpose and audience in mind.
- Write a first draft.
- Revise your report, and proofread it.
- Check that your bibliography is correct.

PUBLISH AND SHARE

- Make a final copy of your report.
- Publish and share it.

ASK STUDENTS what they hope to discover about dolphins as they research their report. How is the information they find similar to, yet different from, the facts in "The Pod"?

DIG DEEPER

With the class, return to Question 6, Reread and Discuss. Have students share the results of their discussion.

ASK STUDENTS whether they were pleased with the outcome of the small-group discussions. Have each group share the details of its discussion about irony in "The Pod." How did each group define the term *irony* in the context of the story? What made the situation in the story ironic? *Students should recognize that the situation in which Jesse finds himself with the stranded dolphin is ironic because what is expected to happen does not actually happen, in a surprising twist of the plot. Jesse had not cared about what his cousin Pete had to say about dolphins or their rescue before, and now he is faced with having to save one that is stranded. Jesse's feelings toward his cousin Pete are also ironic because he begins to realize that he should have paid attention to Pete's lectures about "fish" (really, marine mammals) as he tries hard to remember Pete's words about how to rescue a dolphin.*

Encourage groups to share any other ideas they may have had about irony in the story. For example, is there a discrepancy between what seems to be and what is? What textual evidence did group members cite to support the idea that the narrator's point of view toward Jesse changed too abruptly?

- Guide each group to tell how it decided on the ironic details of the story. Were there any group members who did not agree with the decision of the group? If so, how did the group resolve any conflicts or differences of opinion?

- After groups have shared the results of their discussion, ask whether another group had shared any ideas they wish they had thought of.

ASK STUDENTS to return to their Short Response answer and to revise it based on the class discussion about the conflict between Jesse and Pete and the change in Jesse's feelings toward his cousin by the end of the story. Remind students to cite textual evidence to support any revisions to their response.

CLOSE READING NOTES

Tribute to the Dog

Speech by George Graham Vest

Why This Text?

Students frequently encounter persuasive arguments in texts, in media, and in conversations. This lesson investigates a speech in which a lawyer presents an argument in praise of man's one true friend, that trusty animal: the dog.

▶ **View It!**

Professional Development Podcast:

Teaching Argument

Key Learning Objective: The student will be able to trace and evaluate an argument and identify persuasive techniques in a speech.

RI 1   Cite textual evidence.

RI 2   Determine central idea; provide a summary.

RI 4   Determine the meaning of words and phrases.

RI 5   Analyze structure.

RI 8   Trace and evaluate the argument and specific claims in a text.

SL 1   Engage effectively in a range of collaborative discussions.

SL 1a Come to discussions prepared and draw on preparation to probe and reflect on ideas.

SL 4   Present claims and findings logically; use appropriate eye contact, volume, and pronunciation.

L 1a   Use relative pronouns correctly.

L 4   Determine or clarify the meaning of words and phrases, choosing from a range of strategies.

L 4a   Use context as a clue to the meaning of a word or phrase.

L 4c   Consult reference materials.

L 6   Acquire and use grade-appropriate words and phrases.

▲ Text Complexity Rubric

Quantitative Measures

Tribute to the Dog

Lexile: 1170L

Qualitative Measures

Levels of Meaning/Purpose

single purpose, explicitly stated

Structure

organization of main ideas and details complex, but clearly stated and generally sequential

Language Conventionality and Clarity

more complex sentence structure

Knowledge Demands

everyday knowledge required

Reader/Task Considerations

- Teacher determined
- Vary by individual reader and type of text
- See the Text X-Ray for suggested Reader/Task Considerations.

English Language Support Before teaching, use the Text X-Ray for an overview of the text's complexity. The Text X-Ray and the supports and scaffolds in the Teacher's Edition will help you guide students of different skill levels.

Meaning Making

Language Development

Effective Expression

Content Knowledge

Foundational Skills

Text Complexity: Qualitative Measures

Levels of Meaning/Purpose

single purpose, explicitly stated

Help students analyze the appeals in an argument.

- Teacher's Edition side notes, pp. 94, 95
- Analyze the Meaning of Words and Phrases, p. 95

To further students' understanding of appeals, see

- Persuasive Techniques, p. 98a

▶ **Use It!** Level Up Tutorials: Analyzing Arguments; Persuasive Techniques

ZOOM IN ON ANALYZING PERSUASIVE TECHNIQUES Explain the terms **emotional appeal** and **logical appeal**. An **emotional appeal** is a message that creates strong feelings such as fear or pity. A **logical appeal** relies on reasoning and facts. Then have students work with a partner to identify the statements below as an emotional appeal or a logical one. Ask them to explain their responses.

- A survey shows that 97% of the students using this study method improved their test grades. Sign up now! *(logical)*
- This new study method will send you to the head of the class in no time. Sign up now! *(emotional)*
- If you do not use this mouthwash, you will find yourself alone, friendless, abandoned. Buy it today! *(emotional)*
- This mouthwash is proven to kill the bacteria that cause tooth decay and bad breath. Buy it today! *(logical)*

Structure

organization of main ideas and details complex; but clearly stated and generally sequential

Help students trace and evaluate an argument.

- Teacher's Edition side notes, pp. 93, 94, 95
- English Language Support, p. 93
- Strategies for Annotation, p. 95
- Trace and Evaluate an Argument, p. 95

To reteach trace and evaluate an argument, see

- Trace Elements of an Argument, p. 98a

▶ **Use It!** Level Up Tutorials: Elements of an Argument; Analyzing Arguments; Evidence; Persuasive Techniques

ZOOM IN ON TRACING AND EVALUATING AN ARGUMENT Use the sentence frames below to help students identify the elements of the **argument**. Have them complete the frames in small groups after reading the text.

- The counterargument in the first paragraph appears in____. *(the first sentence)*

  To support this counterargument, the speaker says _____. *(accept any examples given in the first paragraph)*

- The speaker's claim, found in the second paragraph, states that ____. *(a dog is the truest friend a man can have)*

  To support his claim, the speaker says _____ and _____. *(accept any examples or elaborative details)*

Language Conventionality and Clarity

more complex sentence structure

Teach unfamiliar vocabulary in context.

- Teacher's Edition Critical Vocabulary notes, pp. 93, 94, 97
- Applying Academic Vocabulary, p. 94
- Strategies for Annotation, p. 97
- Vocabulary Strategy: Using a Dictionary, p. 97

Guide students to acquire facility in using spoken and written language.

- Teacher's Edition side notes, pp. 94, 98
- English Language Support, pp. 96, 98
- Performance Task, p. 96
- Language Conventions: Relative Pronouns *who* and *whom*, p. 98

ZOOM IN ON **INTERPRETING FIGURATIVE LANGUAGE** Display and highlight the following sentence as shown.

"When riches take wings, and reputation falls to pieces, he is as constant in his love as the sun in its journey through the heavens."

Explain that to make points effectively, the speaker chooses words and phrases that create vivid pictures in listeners' minds.

- Assign a different highlighted phrase to small groups and have them discuss its meaning.
- Have each group share its finding with the class.
- As a whole class, paraphrase the sentence and then compare it to the original to determine the impact of figurative language on persuasiveness.

Knowledge Demands

everyday knowledge required

Support English Learners in understanding the context of the argument.

- Teacher's Edition Background note, p. 93

ZOOM IN ON **BUILDING CONTEXT** Help students understand the case that led to this closing argument.

- Tell students that the case was tried in Missouri where the law still allows a farmer to kill a dog that is maiming or attacking livestock.
- Explain that Leonidas Hornsby had lost many sheep to dogs. He threatened to kill the next dog that entered his property. When Old Drum, a neighbor's dog, wandered into his yard, Hornsby told his nephew to scare it off with a few shots. The next day Old Drum's owner found his dog dead. The owner sued, and after four trials and an appeal, Hornsby had to pay damages.

Suggested Reader/Task Considerations

You might consider the following before assigning this argument to students.

- Do students have an adequate familiarity with the structure and purpose of arguments to understand this text?
- Will reading this text benefit students' critical thinking skills, memory, and attention?

ZOOM IN ON **SUPPORTING COMPREHENSION**

- Define the purpose of an argument: to persuade listeners to take a certain action or accept a certain position. List the elements of a well-crafted argument: claim, reasons, evidence, counterargument. Help students define these terms before reading the text.
- Explain that in order to evaluate, or judge the effectiveness, of an argument, students must pay careful attention to its reasons, evidence, and counterarguments. Distribute sticky notes and have pairs label the parts of the arguments.

Background Have students read the background. Tell students that not only did the speech become a favorite of dog lovers, but that the town where the speech was given, Warrensburg, Missouri, erected a statue to honor the dog, Old Drum, and George Graham Vest.

SETTING A PURPOSE Direct students to use the Setting a Purpose prompt to focus their reading. Remind them to write down questions as they read.

Trace and Evaluate an Argument (LINES 1–12)

RI 1,
RI 5,
RI 8

Explain that a **speech** is a talk or public address in which a speaker presents an argument. Tell students that an **argument** expresses a **claim,** or position on a problem, and supports it with **reasons** and evidence. Point out that reasons are statements that explain an action or belief and that **evidence** can include facts, statistics, and other information.

Ⓐ **ASK STUDENTS** to review lines 1–12. Ask them to use the text, title, and background information to predict what argument the speaker will make. *(The speaker may be leading up to an argument that a person's dog will never desert him or her.)*

Explain that a **counterargument** is an argument made to address opposing viewpoints.

Ⓑ **CITE TEXT EVIDENCE** Have students reread lines 4–8 and identify two examples of evidence the speaker includes in his counterargument. *(The speaker notes that a person may lose the "faith" of "those who are nearest and dearest to" him, and that money can be lost "perhaps when he needs it most.")*

CRITICAL VOCABULARY

malice: The word *malice* is used to discuss false friends.

ASK STUDENTS to reread lines 9–12. Have them tell why the author might have chosen the phrase "to throw the stone of malice." *(Because* malice *can mean "a desire to harm others," the phrase "to throw the stone of malice" gives readers a mental picture of how false friends might hurt a person.)*

Background *As a young lawyer,* **George Graham Vest** *(1830–1904) represented a man seeking payment for his dog, which had been shot by a sheep farmer. In this closing speech of the trial, Vest ignores the evidence given at trial; instead, he gives a moving tribute to dogs in general. Some said it was a perfect piece of oratory; others exclaimed that the jury was moved to tears. Vest's client won the case. Eight years later, Vest was elected to the U.S. Senate. His speech is now regarded as a classic tribute to "man's best friend."*

TRIBUTE TO THE DOG

Speech by George Graham Vest

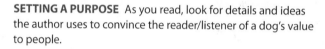

SETTING A PURPOSE As you read, look for details and ideas the author uses to convince the reader/listener of a dog's value to people.

Ⓐ Ⓖentlemen of the Jury: The best friend a man has in the world may turn against him and become his enemy. His son or daughter that he has reared[1] with loving care may prove ungrateful. Those who are nearest and dearest to us, those whom we trust with our happiness and our good name may become traitors to their faith. The money that a man has, he may lose. It flies away from him, perhaps when he needs it most. A man's reputation may be sacrificed in a moment of ill-considered action. The people who are prone to fall on
10 their knees to do us honor when success is with us, may be the first to throw the stone of **malice** when failure settles its cloud upon our heads.

Ⓑ

malice
(măl´ĭs) *n. Malice* is a desire to harm others or to see someone suffer.

[1] **reared:** raised; guided to grow into an adult.

English Language Support

Understand Text Structure Clarify the definition of *counterargument:* an answer to objections that opponents might raise. A counterargument usually follows the claim. Here, Vest presents the counterargument first.

- Discuss the counterargument presented in the first paragraph. Ask students to identify the objection that it responds to and what it suggests that the speaker will claim. *(objection: why do people need dogs if they have each other; claim: dogs make better friends than people do)*

TEACH

CLOSE READ

Trace and Evaluate an Argument (LINES 13–25)

RI 1,
RI 5,
RI 8

C **CITE TEXT EVIDENCE** Have students reread lines 13–25 and point out the speaker's claim, reasons, and evidence. *(Claim in first sentence: A man's dog is his only true friend. Reasons and evidence: A dog stays loyal through all hardships and will guard and protect its master when all others desert him.)*

Explain that to **evaluate** a speaker's argument is to decide whether it is effective, logical, and convincing.

D **ASK STUDENTS** to evaluate lines 13–25 and explain whether the argument is effective or not. *(The argument is effective; it logically points out ways that a dog is a person's only true friend.)*

Analyze Meanings of Words and Phrases (LINES 26–34)

RI 1,
RI 4

Explain that **persuasive techniques** are methods a speaker uses to convince others. One type, an **emotional appeal,** is a message that creates strong feelings in the audience, such as fear, pity, or vanity.

E **CITE TEXT EVIDENCE** Ask students to reread lines 26–34 and point out words and phrases that create strong feelings. *(friendless and homeless; faithful dog asks no higher privilege; faithful and true even in death.)*

CRITICAL VOCABULARY

treacherous, prosperity, embrace: The author chooses the words *embrace, treacherous,* and *prosperity* in order to be precise and convincing.

ASK STUDENTS to think of synonyms for *embrace, treacherous,* and *prosperity,* and tell why the chosen words are more exact. *(Possible responses: Embrace is more precise than hug; treacherous is more vivid than disloyal; prosperity is more exact than success.)*

COLLABORATIVE DISCUSSION Have groups list specific reasons the speaker provides for his argument.

ASK STUDENTS to share any questions they generated in the course of reading and discussing the selection.

C The one absolutely unselfish friend that man can have in this selfish world, the one that never deserts him, the one that never proves ungrateful or **treacherous** is his dog. A man's dog stands by him in **prosperity** and in poverty, in health and in sickness. He will sleep on the cold ground, where the wintry winds blow and the snow drives fiercely, if only he may be near his master's side. He will kiss the hand that has
20 no food to offer. He will lick the wounds and sores that come in encounters with the roughness of the world. He guards the
D sleep of his pauper[2] master as if he were a prince. When all other friends desert, he remains. When riches take wings,[3] and reputation falls to pieces, he is as constant in his love as the sun in its journey through the heavens.

E If fortune drives the master forth, an outcast in the world, friendless and homeless, the faithful dog asks no higher privilege than that of accompanying him, to guard him against danger, to fight against his enemies. And when the last
30 scene of all comes, and death takes his master in its **embrace** and his body is laid away in the cold ground, no matter if all other friends pursue their way,[4] there by the graveside will the noble dog be found, his head between his paws, his eyes sad, but open in alert watchfulness, faithful and true even in death.

treacherous
(trĕch´ər-əs) *adj.* A *treacherous* person is untrustworthy and likely to betray others.

prosperity
(prŏ-spĕr´ĭ-tē) *n.* *Prosperity* means having success, particularly having enough money.

embrace
(ĕm-brās´) *n.* An *embrace* is a hug or encirclement, showing acceptance.

COLLABORATIVE DISCUSSION The author of this speech argues that a dog is more faithful to its owner than the owner's friends and family. With a small group, identify text evidence and other details that support this argument.

---

[2] **pauper** (pô´pər): someone who is extremely poor.
[3] **take wings:** disappear; vanish.
[4] **pursue their way:** continue with their lives; move on.

APPLYING ACADEMIC VOCABULARY

benefit	respond

THINK-PAIR-SHARE Have students turn to a partner to discuss the questions below. Guide students to include the academic vocabulary words *benefit* and *respond* in their responses. Ask volunteers to share their responses with the class.

• How does the speaker's evidence **benefit** his argument?

• How might an audience **respond** to the speaker's emotional appeals? Explain.

Trace and Evaluate an Argument

RI 5, RI 8

"Tribute to the Dog" is a **persuasive speech,** which is a talk or public address that has a clear argument. An **argument** expresses a position and supports it with reasons and evidence. To analyze how an argument is constructed, you can **trace,** or follow the reasoning of, an argument as follows:

- Identify the **claim,** which is the speaker's position on the issue or problem.
- Look for **support,** which consists of reasons and evidence to prove the claim. **Reasons** are statements made to explain an action or belief. **Evidence** includes specific facts, statistics, and examples.
- Notice whether the author includes a **counterargument,** an argument made to address opposing viewpoints.

To find these elements, identify and analyze particular sentences or paragraphs that contribute to the development of the speaker's argument. After you trace an argument, you can **evaluate,** or judge, its effectiveness or whether or not the evidence is logical and convincing. Ask yourself:

- Has the speaker included enough reasons and evidence to support the claim?
- Do the ideas make sense? Do they flow in a logical way?
- Has the speaker thought about opposing ideas and provided counterarguments?

Analyze the Meanings of Words and Phrases

RI 4

"Tribute to the Dog" was written to persuade listeners to agree with the speaker's opinion. To convince an audience, a speaker can use a variety of **persuasive techniques,** which are methods used to influence others. One effective persuasive technique is the **emotional appeal,** which is a message that uses language or images that create strong feelings in the listener.

Identifying emotional appeals helps the audience understand how a speaker is trying to persuade them. In "Tribute to the Dog," when the speaker says that a dog "will kiss the hand that has no food," he is making an emotional appeal to the audience's feelings about their pets. Look for more examples of emotional appeals as you analyze "Tribute to the Dog."

Tribute to the Dog **95**

CLOSE READ

Trace and Evaluate an Argument

RI 5, RI 8

Help students understand the terms and make distinctions to clarify their meaning; for example, ask them how *reasons* are similar to but different from *evidence*. (*Reasons and evidence are ways a speaker supports his or her claim. Reasons are statements that explain a position; evidence includes specific facts, statistics, and examples that support the claim.*)

Next, discuss the information about how to evaluate an argument. Have students use the questions to explore how they might evaluate the speaker's ideas in "Tribute to the Dog." Have them cite examples from the text in their responses.

Analyze the Meanings of Words and Phrases

RI 4

Guide students to understand how emotional appeals can be very persuasive. Point out that advertising often uses persuasive techniques that appeal to our fears, pity, or vanity, such as a shampoo ad that promises "the shiny, lustrous locks you long for." Ask volunteers to suggest more examples.

Then have students identify emotional appeals the speaker uses in "Tribute to the Dog" that touch on strong feelings people have for their pets. (*Possible examples: "The one absolutely unselfish friend that man can have in this selfish world," "he is as constant in his love as the sun in its journey through the heavens."*)

Strategies for Annotation 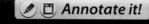 Annotate it!

Trace and Evaluate an Argument

RI 5, RI 8

Share these strategies for guided or independent analysis:

- Highlight in yellow the speaker's claim.
- Highlight in green key phrases that show evidence for the speaker's claim.
- On a note, record the types of evidence the speaker uses.
- Review your highlights. On a note, record whether you think the claim and evidence are effective.

The one absolutely unselfish friend that man can have in this selfish world . . . the one that never proves ungrateful or treacherous is his dog. A man's dog stands by him in prosperity and in poverty, in health and in sickness. He will sleep on the cold ground . . . if only he may be near his master's side.

Analyzing the Text

RI 1, RI 2, RI 4, RI 5, RI 8

Possible answers:

1. *Vest claims that a dog is the one friend that will always be loyal and never desert his master.*

2. *The counterargument is that a man can lose his family, friends, reputation, and supporters in hard times. The counterargument is forceful and dramatic; it creates a strong, black-and-white contrast that will draw the readers' feelings to the opposite claim, in the next paragraph, that a man's dog will never desert him.*

3. *A dog always stands by its master, regardless of his master's circumstances; a dog will always care for and protect his master; a dog is always loyal. The reasons and evidence the author presents are clear, strong, and logical, and they back up the claim in a moving way.*

4. *The author describes a scene of loneliness and dying, focusing on appealing to the readers' fear of living and dying alone. He uses phrases such as "an outcast in the world, friendless and homeless" and "by the graveside the noble dog be found" to represent his appeal.*

5. *The author's reasons and evidence support his claim that a dog is man's only true friend. The order of ideas could be improved; by presenting his counterarguments first, it takes a long time to arrive at his claim.*

English Language Support

Exchange Information and Ideas Form five small groups to answer the questions on this page. Assign one of the questions to each group. When all the groups finish, have them take turns presenting their answers to the class. Encourage class members to provide useful feedback.

eBook *Annotate It!*

Analyzing the Text

RI 1, RI 2, RI 4, RI 5, RI 8, SL 1a, SL 4

Cite Text Evidence   Support your responses with evidence from the text.

1. **Identify** What claim does Vest make in his speech?

2. **Infer** Reread lines 1–12. Identify the counterargument Vest presents. Why might he have chosen to begin the speech with a counterargument?

3. **Summarize** Reread lines 13–25. Summarize the reasons and evidence Vest uses to support his claim. Explain whether he successfully supports his claim.

4. **Analyze** Review lines 26–34. What is Vest's final appeal to his audience? What emotion does he appeal to? What words and phrases does Vest use to represent this appeal?

5. **Evaluate** Review Vest's claim and how he supports it. Do his ideas make sense to you? Do you find his argument persuasive? Why or why not?

PERFORMANCE TASK

Speaking Activity: Discussion In a small-group panel discussion, tell why you agree or disagree with the speech "Tribute to the Dog," providing your own claim with support for your opinion.

- Prepare for the discussion by reviewing the speech and listing evidence from the text to support your opinion.

- When it's your turn to speak, present your claims and support in a logical way. Be sure to make eye contact with members of the panel, speak at an appropriate volume, and pronounce words clearly.

- Appoint a group leader to begin the discussion.

- Make sure each person on the panel has a chance to speak.

Assign this performance task.

PERFORMANCE TASK

SL 1, SL 1a, SL 4

Speaking Activity: Discussion Have students prepare for the discussion by

- composing a claim that clearly states their position
- listing examples and evidence from the text that supports their claim
- ordering their points in a logical way

During the discussion, remind them to speak clearly and to listen attentively to other speakers.

Critical Vocabulary

L 4, L 4c, L 6

malice   **treacherous**   **prosperity**   **embrace**

Practice and Apply   Answer each question.

1. If someone shows **malice,** is he or she acting kind or cruel? Explain.

2. If someone was **treacherous,** would you share a secret with that person? Explain.

3. If a country has **prosperity,** how do its citizens feel? Why?

4. Which would you rather have in your **embrace**—a dog or a porcupine? Explain.

Vocabulary Strategy:
Using a Print or Digital Dictionary

When you come across an unfamiliar word in a text, you can use strategies, such as context clues, to help you determine the meaning. If those strategies do not work, you should use a print or digital dictionary to find the correct definition. Here is an example of a dictionary entry.

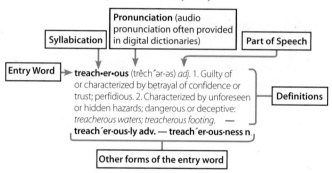

Practice and Apply   Use a print or digital dictionary to explore words found in "Tribute to the Dog."

1. Reread lines 9–12. Look up *prone*. How many meanings are shown? Which meaning is used in the sentence?

2. Reread lines 22–23. Look up *desert*. How many entries for *desert* are shown? Which entry and meaning is used in the speech?

3. Reread lines 23–25. Look up *constant*. What is the meaning of *constant* in the sentence? What other form of *constant* do you find?

PRACTICE & APPLY

Critical Vocabulary

L 4, L 4c, L 6

Possible answers:

1. *Cruel, because that person would have hurt someone in some way.*

2. *I would not, because the person is likely to tell my secret to others.*

3. *They are probably happy, because their country is successful; many of them are probably successful as well.*

4. *I would rather have a dog in my embrace, because a dog is soft and friendly and easier to put my arms around. A porcupine is prickly and a wild animal. Touching a porcupine could be dangerous.*

Vocabulary Strategy: Using a Print or Digital Dictionary

Possible answers:

1. *Two meanings are shown; "having a tendency; inclined" is the meaning used in the speech.*

2. *Three entries are shown; the third entry, with the meaning "to leave empty or alone; abandon," is used in the speech.*

3. *The meaning in the sentence is "steadfast in purpose, loyalty, or affection; faithful"; the other form found is constantly.*

Strategies for Annotation 🖉 🗎 *Annotate it!*

Using a Print or Digital Dictionary

L 4a, L 4c

Have students locate the sentence containing *constant* (lines 23–25). Tell them to use their eBook annotation tools to do the following:

- Highlight the word.
- Look in nearby sentences for clues to the word's meaning.
- Underline any clues you find, such as synonyms or antonyms.
- Compare your annotations with the meanings you found in the dictionary, and decide the word's meaning as it is used in the sentence.

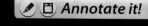

other friends desert, he remains. When riches take wings, and reputation falls to pieces, he is as constant in his love as the sun in its journey through the heavens.

constant = same?

Language Conventions: Relative Pronouns *who* and *whom*

L 1a

Tell students that to decide whether to use the relative pronouns *who* or *whom*, they need to identify the words they modify in sentences. Discuss the two basic rules: *Who* is used with subjects, and *whom* is used with objects. Provide additional example sentences as needed.

Answers:

1. *who*

2. *whom*

3. *whom*

4. *who*

5. *whom*

6. *who*

7. *who*

8. *whom*

 Assess It Online!

Online Selection Test
- Download an editable ExamView bank.
- Assign and manage this test online.

Language Conventions: Relative Pronouns *who* and *whom*

L 1a

The relative pronouns *who* and *whom* relate, or connect, adjective clauses to the words they modify in sentences. Deciding when to use *who* or *whom* can be confusing. Here are two simple rules:

- The relative pronoun *who* is used with subjects.
- The relative pronoun *whom* is used with objects.

Take a look at how *who* and *whom* are used in these sentences.

Those who are nearest and dearest to us may betray us.
People with whom we trust our happiness may become traitors.

The relative pronoun *who* is used in the first sentence because it relates the adjective clause to the subject, *those (people)*. In the second sentence, the relative pronoun *whom* is used because it is the object of the preposition *with*.

Practice and Apply Complete each sentence with the correct relative pronoun *who* or *whom*.

1. My brother, _____ lives in Florida, owns a potbellied pig.

2. My uncle, for _____ I have the highest regard, needs my help.

3. The owner hired the woman _____ he interviewed last week.

4. I have a friend _____ walks dogs for a living.

5. My sister, with _____ I share a room, is not an especially tidy person.

6. Tanya knows a doctor _____ specializes in caring for injured birds.

7. Darius is the one _____ will buy food for our pets.

8. The person to _____ I spoke was Dr Nash, the vet.

English Language Support

Understand Cohesion Explain that relative pronouns function as either a subject or an object in the subordinate clause. The subjects tells whom or what the clause is about; the object receives the action of the verb or follows a preposition. Remind students to use *who* when the pronoun functions as a subject and *whom* when it functions as a object.

- Write sentences 1 and 5 on the board with the correct relative pronoun. Point out that in sentence 1, *who* is the subject of the clause "who lives in Florida." In sentence 5, *whom* is the object of the preposition *with*. Explain the pronoun function in sentences

2–4 and elicit responses, then have students complete sentences 7 and 8 on their own.

- Have pairs complete the Practice and Apply sentences. Ask volunteers to share their answers and explain the function of the pronoun in the subordinate clauses. (*1, 4, 6, 7: pronoun is the subject of the clause; 2, 5, 8: the pronoun is the object of the preposition; 3: pronoun is the direct object of interviewed*)

Persuasive Techniques

TEACH

Writers of persuasive texts can use a variety of techniques to convince readers to agree with their positions. Remind students that an **emotional appeal** is a message that creates strong feelings in readers or listeners. Explain and discuss with students these additional persuasive techniques:

- A **logical appeal** is a way of writing or speaking that relies on logic and facts. It appeals to people's reasoning or intellect rather than their emotions. Example: *Numerous studies and research show that students who miss breakfast perform more poorly in school. It's clear that we must make sure that every child has a healthy breakfast.*

- **Loaded language** consists of words with strongly positive or negative connotations, intended to influence a reader's or listener's attitude. Example: *Our country's flag, the symbol of liberty, should be present in every classroom to remind students of our hard-won freedoms.*

PRACTICE AND APPLY

Display lines 13–25 from "Tribute to the Dog." With students, discuss examples of the persuasive techniques the author uses. Invite them to review each sentence and identify whether it includes an emotional appeal, a logical appeal, loaded language, or a combination of these techniques.

Invite students to explore other sources that employ persuasive techniques, such as editorials, letters to the editor, and electronic or print advertising. Have them identify examples of emotional appeals, logical appeals, and loaded language, and evaluate their effectiveness.

English Language Support

Analyze Language Tell students that a word has a dictionary definition, or **denotation,** but it may also have a **connotation,** or certain feelings or ideas associated with it. Point out the word *liberty* in the "loaded language" example under **TEACH**. Explain that it means freedom, but it also evokes feelings of patriotism and pride.

- Write these words from lines 13–25 on the board: *unselfish, prince, constant.*
- Help students recognize the connotations of each word. (*unselfish: noble, self-sacrificing; prince: very special, royal; constant: dependable, always there for someone*)
- Ask students how the use of these words makes them feel about dogs.

Trace Elements of an Argument

RETEACH

Review the terms *argument, claim, support, reasons,* and *evidence.* Then give an example of a claim that might be used in an argument in a middle-school newspaper editorial, such as "Required physical education classes no longer have a place in middle schools."

Remind students how to identify point of view.

- Invite students to present reasons and evidence that a writer might use to support the claim. (*Possible responses: Students have many opportunities to get exercise on their own; class time is better spent on academic subjects.*)
- Then suggest an opposing claim, such as "Because regular physical exercise is essential to a healthy mind, physical education in school is more important than ever." Ask students to tell how the writer might counter this claim. (*Possible response: Fitness begins at home.*)

 LEVEL UP TUTORIALS Assign one or more of the following *Level Up* tutorials: **Elements of an Argument; Analyzing Arguments; Evidence; Persuasive Techniques.**

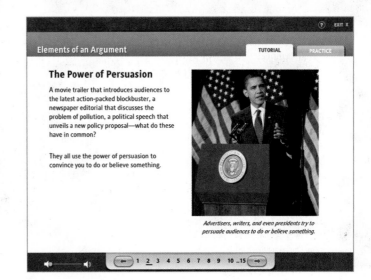

INDEPENDENT READING

Students can apply the skills to a current editorial from a print or online newspaper or magazine. Have them work independently to identify the claim, support, and any counterarguments. Have them evaluate whether the editorial is effective.

Animal Wisdom

The Last Wolf

Poem by Nancy Wood

Poem by Mary TallMountain

Why This Text?

In reading poetry, students experience carefully chosen language that has been arranged to create certain impressions and insights. This lesson focuses on how each poet uses personification and imagery to express specific emotions and ideas with poetic language.

> ▶ **View It!**
>
> Professional Development Podcast:
>
> **Text-Dependent Analysis**

Key Learning Objective: The student will understand how personification and imagery emphasize themes and ideas in poetry and will learn how to paraphrase these ideas.

RL 1 Cite text evidence to support analysis and inferences.

RL 2 Determine theme; provide a summary.

RL 4 Determine the meaning of words and phrases.

RL 10 Read and comprehend literature.

W 2 Write explanatory texts.

W 4 Produce clear and coherent writing.

W 9a Draw evidence from literary texts to support analysis and reflection when applying grade 6 Reading standards to literature.

SL 1 Engage effectively in a range of collaborative discussions.

L 5a Interpret figures of speech (e.g., personification) in context.

 Text Complexity Rubric

	Animal Wisdom Lexile: Not applicable	**The Last Wolf** Lexile: Not applicable
Quantitative Measures		
Qualitative Measures	**Levels of Meaning/Purpose** single level of complex meaning	**Levels of Meaning/Purpose** single level of complex meaning
	Structure no obvious voice or sense of speaker, or omniscient speaker	**Structure** free verse, no particular patterns
	Language Conventionality and Clarity some figurative language	**Language Conventionality and Clarity** some figurative language
	Knowledge Demands some cultural and literary knowledge useful	**Knowledge Demands** simple, single theme
Reader/Task Considerations	• Teacher determined • Vary by individual reader and type of text • See the Text X-Ray for suggested Reader/Task Considerations.	

English Language Support

Before teaching, use the Text X-Ray for an overview of the text's complexity. The Text X-Ray and the supports and scaffolds in the Teacher's Edition will help you guide students of different skill levels.

Meaning Making

Language Development

Effective Expression

Content Knowledge

Foundational Skills

Text Complexity: Qualitative Measures

▲ Levels of Meaning/Purpose

Help students use strategies to understand a poem's language and meaning.

- Teacher's Edition side notes, pp. 100, 101, 102, 103
- English Language Support, p. 101
- When Students Struggle, p. 102
- Strategies for Annotation, pp. 101, 103
- Determine Meanings of Words and Phrases, p. 103

To reteach how to determine the meaning of imagery and figurative language, see

- Determine Meanings: Imagery, p. 104a

▶ ***Use It!*** **Interactive Whiteboard Lessons:** Figurative Language and Imagery

ZOOM IN ON **ANALYZING POETRY** Tell students that they will read two poems about nature. Explain that both poems contain words used in different ways to create **images** that appeal to the senses. Students will need to read each poem more than once in order to fully understand the meaning that the poet intended. Write the following steps on the board and have students implement them as they read "Animal Wisdom:"

1. Read the poem aloud without pausing.

2. Try to answer the question: What is this poem about?

3. Read the poem a second time, noticing specific details that help answer your questions.

4. Paraphrase, or write in your own words, lines that are difficult to understand. Then write what you think the poem means.

5. With a partner, review your paraphrases. Then find details in the poem that support your interpretation.

▲ Structure

Help students understand the structure of a poem.

- English Language Support, p. 99

To teach the structure of a poem, see

- Analyze Structure: Poetry, p. 104a

▶ ***Use It!*** **Interactive Whiteboard Lessons:** Form in Poetry

ZOOM IN ON **EXAMINING THE STRUCTURE OF A POEM** Explain that students will read two poems written in free verse.

- Write a verse from a nursery rhyme, such as "Humpty Dumpty," on the board. Point out the general uniformity of line lengths. Then read it aloud, emphasizing its regular rhyme and meter.
- Display lines 1–8 of "The Last Wolf." Ask students what they notice about the length of these lines. *(They differ.)* Then read the lines aloud. Ask students how the sound differs from that of the nursery rhyme. Explain that free verse has no regular rhythm or rhyme.

▲ Language Conventionality and Clarity

Teach unfamiliar vocabulary in context.

- Applying Academic Vocabulary, p. 100

Guide students to discuss and write about the language of poetry.

- Teacher's Edition side notes, p. 102
- English Language Support, pp. 99, 103, 104
- Performance Task, p. 104

ZOOM IN ON **USING CONTEXT** Write these lines from "The Last Wolf" on the board: "the last wolf hurried toward me/ through the ruined city/ and I heard his baying echoes/ down the steep smashed warrens."

- Tell students that they can use the words surrounding an unfamiliar word to help define it.
- Highlight *baying*. Ask volunteers to identify words that hint at what it might mean. *(wolf, heard, echoes)*
- Have students work with a partner to define *baying*. Ask them to share their definitions. *(howling, barking)*

▲ Knowledge Demands

Support English Learners in understanding the context of "The Last Wolf."

- Teacher's Edition Background note, p. 99

ZOOM IN ON **BUILDING CONTEXT** Promote understanding of context in "The Last Wolf."

- Explain that "The Last Wolf" is set in a ruined, apparently abandoned city. Although it is not clear what has caused this destruction, by the end of the poem it is clear that the humans who created the city are responsible.
- Point out that the title "The Last Wolf" gives readers a clue about the poet's message. Have students use the background information and their knowledge of the setting to speculate on the title's meaning. Encourage them to find images and details in the text to support or disprove their ideas.

▲ Suggested Reader/Task Considerations

You might consider the following before assigning these poems to students.

- Do students have the necessary visualization skills to read these poems?
- Can students make connections between ideas in these poems and learning that has occurred in other classes?

ZOOM IN ON **SUPPORTING COMPREHENSION**

- After the initial reading of each poem, ask pairs of students to reread each stanza and draw images that the words suggest. Have partners share their sketches and discuss differences and similarities in their portrayals.
- Read the Background note on page 99 aloud to the class. Elicit prior knowledge of Native American groups, including information gained from other classes. Discuss why these societies valued nature and how they showed it respect.

Background Have students read the background and the information about the poets. Explain that they are going to read two poems that reflect on people's beliefs about people, animals, and nature through the imagined thoughts and ideas of animals. The first poem focuses on the connections among animals, people, and nature. The second poem conveys a perception about people's effects on the environment.

SETTING A PURPOSE Direct students to use the Setting a Purpose prompt to focus their reading. Remind them to write down questions as they read.

English Language Support

Culturally Responsive Instruction Before reading, encourage a class discussion to elicit students' knowledge of poetry.

ASK STUDENTS if they know any poems in any other languages. Encourage volunteers to recite lines or stanzas from these poems and explain what they are about. As a class, discuss why poems are often easier to remember than passages from a story. Then form small groups to discuss characteristics of poetry with which students are already familiar. Use their ideas as a springboard for introducing background knowledge needed in order to read "Animal Wisdom" and "The Last Wolf," including form (free verse) and the importance of punctuation and line breaks.

Background *People and animals are in constant interaction with each other. It is not surprising, then, that animals have long been a favorite focus of poets and storytellers. In particular, Native American literature and culture express a strong reverence for animals and the land, air, and water they share with us. Many Native American poems are prayers, thanking animals for food, clothing, and shelter, as well as the intelligence they seem to possess about the natural world.*

Animal Wisdom   The Last Wolf

Poem by Nancy Wood   Poem by Mary TallMountain

Nancy Wood (b. 1936) *is a poet, novelist, and photographer who lives on the edge of the natural wilderness that inspires her. Her artistic work focuses on the people of the Southwest, including the Native American people of the Taos Pueblo near her home in Santa Fe, New Mexico. Wood has produced more than 25 photography books. She has also published numerous books of poetry and fiction for adults and children.*

Mary TallMountain (1918–1994) *was born in a small village along the Yukon River in Alaska. After her Athabaskan mother became seriously ill, TallMountain was adopted and taken away from her village. Living far from her family and home, TallMountain felt like an outsider. Many of her poems and stories reflect her struggles to reconnect with nature and her lost home far to the north. Her writing is highly praised as part of the renaissance of Native American literature during the last few decades of the 20th century.*

SETTING A PURPOSE As you read, look for details and ideas that illustrate each poet's understanding of wild animals, their intelligence, and the environment.

(tbg) ©John E Marriott/Corbis; (tl) ©Getty images; (cr) Photograph by Myron Wood, ©Pikes Peak Library District; (br) ©Lance Woodruff/Lance Woodruff

---

English Language Support

Read Closely Prepare students to read the poems. Display lines 1–11 of "Animal Wisdom." Explain that poets, like prose writers, use transitional words and phrases to connect the ideas. These words may show a sequence of events, compare ideas, or indicate a cause-and-effect relationship.

- Help students find and highlight transition words and phrases. *(At first, until, as)* Ask them what these words tell about the way the ideas are linked. *(in sequence)*

- Have students work with a partner to identify the type of organization used in these lines. Then ask them to list events in the order in which they occur.

- Have pairs identify the transition words and phrases as well as the organizational pattern that they indicate. Then ask them to explain why the poet chose to order her ideas in this way. *(This organization emphasizes that animals were here before humans and provided the "wisdom" that went into shaping the world.)*

Determine Meaning of Words and Phrases

RL 1,
RL 4,
L 5a

(LINES 1–17)

Explain that **figurative language** is a way of using words to express ideas that are not literally true. One type, called **personification,** is language that gives human qualities to an animal, object, or idea.

A CITE TEXT EVIDENCE Have students reread lines 1–11 to find and explain examples of personification. *(In lines 3–4, Turtle speaks; in lines 9–11, Bear speaks; the poet gives animals the human ability to speak ideas and thoughts.)*

Explain that another type of figurative language is **imagery,** the use of words and phrases that appeal to the senses.

B CITE TEXT EVIDENCE Have students close their eyes as you reread lines 12–17 aloud. Ask them to identify words and phrases that appealed to their senses and why. *(fiery heat; soared; penetrating vision; laughter)*

Tell students that one way to better understand a poem is to paraphrase it. Explain that to **paraphrase,** you restate or express the poet's ideas in your own words, without changing or adding to the poem's meaning.

C ASK STUDENTS to reread lines 1–5 and then paraphrase their meaning. *(Possible response: The animals did not take the time to discover the world around them and enjoy life until Turtle pointed it out to them.)*

Animal Wisdom
by Nancy Wood

A
At first, the wild creatures were too busy
to explore their natural curiosity until
Turtle crawled up on land. He said:
What's missing is the ability
5   to find contentment in a slow-paced life.

C

As the oceans receded, fish sprouted whiskers.
Certain animals grew four legs and were able
to roam from shore to shore. Bear stood
upright and looked around. He said:
10 What's missing is devotion
to place, to give meaning to passing time.

B
Mountains grew from fiery heat, while
above them soared birds, the greatest
of which was Eagle, to whom penetrating
15 vision was given. He said: What's missing
is laughter so that arguments
can be resolved without rancor.[1]

After darkness and light settled their differences
20 and the creatures paired up,
people appeared in all the corners of
the world. They said: What's missing
is perception.[2] They began to notice
the beauty hidden
D
25 in an ordinary stone,
the short lives of snowflakes,
the perfection of bird wings, and

---
[1] **rancor** (răng´kər): long-lasting resentment or anger.
[2] **perception** (pər-sĕp´shən): the ability to understand something, usually through the senses; also insight, intuition.

APPLYING ACADEMIC VOCABULARY

benefit	environment

THINK-PAIR-SHARE After reading both poems, have pairs discuss the questions below. Encourage students to use the academic vocabulary words *benefit* and *environment* in their responses. Then ask volunteers to share their responses with the class.

- In "Animal Wisdom," how do people **benefit** from observations that the animals make?
- How does the use of the **environment** differ in the two poems? How is it similar?

the way a butterfly speaks
through its fragility.[3] When they realized

30 they had something in common with animals,
people began saying the same things.
They defended the Earth together,
though it was the animals who insisted

D on keeping their own names.

---

[3] **fragility** (frə-jĭl′ĭ-tē): easily broken, damaged, or destroyed; frail.

©DLILLC/Corbis

CLOSE READ

Determine Meaning of Words and Phrases

RL 1, RL 4

(LINES 23–34)

Remind students that imagery is the use of words and phrases that appeal to the senses. Point out that imagery helps readers to create a picture in their minds.

D **ASK STUDENTS** to close their eyes as you reread lines 23–34 aloud, beginning with "They began to notice . . ." Have them describe the effect of the imagery and other language in these lines. (*Possible response: The reader feels a sense of connectedness and peace with the coming together of nature, animals, and people, along with an idea that the animals continue to have wisdom beyond what people have learned.*)

English Language Support

Analyze Language Write *personification* on the board and circle *person.* Guide students to use the word part to recall that **personification** is a type of figurative language that gives human qualities to an animal, object, or idea.

- Have small groups identify personification in lines 18–29. (*"After darkness and light settled their differences"* (lines 18–19), *"the short lives of snowflakes"* (line 26), *"the way a butterfly speaks through its fragility"* (lines 28–29).)
- Ask them to explain what this personification emphasizes. (*that nature is alive; that there is a deliberation and method in every aspect of nature*)

Strategies for Annotation   ✐ 🖺 *Annotate it!*

Determine Meaning of Words and Phrases

RL 1, RL 4

Share these strategies for guided or independent analysis:

- Highlight in yellow examples of imagery.
- Tell which sense(s) the imagery appeals to.
- Use a note to explain the effect of each example.

As the oceans receded, fish sprouted whiskers.

Certain animals grew four legs and were able

to roam from shore to shore. Bear stood

upright and looked around. He said:

Determine Meaning of Words and Phrases

RL 1,
RL 4,
L 5a

(LINES 1–19)

Remind students that to paraphrase, they restate the meaning of a piece of writing in their own words.

E **ASK STUDENTS** to paraphrase lines 1–8. *(Possible response: The only living wolf ran to me through the destroyed city. I heard his bark echo through the wrecked buildings and the highrises that were still standing.)*

Next, explain that imagery can create mood and give additional meaning to writing. Point out that imagery shows, rather than tells, the reader what is happening; it helps a reader picture the scene in his or her mind.

F **ASK STUDENTS** to reread lines 1–4 and to describe what meaning and mood these lines create for them. *(Possible answer: These lines make me see the last wolf running through destroyed buildings; the mood is sad, depressed, and lonely.)*

G **CITE TEXT EVIDENCE** Ask students to identify imagery in lines 9–14. *(Possible answers: flickering red and green; wild loping gait; clutter and rubble)*

Remind students that personification is language that gives human qualities to an animal, object, or idea.

H **CITE TEXT EVIDENCE** Ask students to reread lines 15–26. Have them tell whether or not the poet uses personification in this poem and why they think so. *(Possible answers: Yes; in lines 15–18, the poem talks about the wolf's voice and shows him going from room to room; the poet makes us feel that the wolf has human emotions; the wolf does things that a real wolf would not do.)*

COLLABORATIVE DISCUSSION Have partners work together to discuss their ideas and to cite evidence from the poems to support them. Then have them share their ideas with the larger group.

ASK STUDENTS to share any questions they generated in the course of reading and discussing this selection.

The Last Wolf
by Mary TallMountain

the last wolf hurried toward me
through the ruined city
and I heard his baying echoes
down the steep smashed warrens[1]
5   of Montgomery Street and past
the few ruby-crowned highrises
left standing
their lighted elevators useless

passing the flickering red and green
10 of traffic signals
baying his way eastward
in the mystery of his wild loping gait
closer the sounds in the deadly night
through clutter and rubble of quiet blocks
15 I heard his voice ascending[2] the hill
and at last his low whine as he came
floor by empty floor to the room
where I sat
in my narrow bed looking west, waiting
20 I heard him snuffle[3] at the door and
I watched
he trotted across the floor
he laid his long gray muzzle
on the spare white spread
25 and his eyes burned yellow
his small dotted eyebrows quivered

Yes, I said.
I know what they have done.

COLLABORATIVE DISCUSSION The authors of these poems have a deep appreciation for wildlife. In what ways do the different animals they write about demonstrate their intelligence?

---

[1] **warrens** (wôr'ənz): overcrowded living areas.
[2] **ascending** (ə-sĕnd'ĭng): rising up.
[3] **snuffle** (snŭf'əl): sniff.

WHEN STUDENTS STRUGGLE...

To help students learn to paraphrase, help them understand the difference between paraphrasing and summarizing. Tell them that when you paraphrase, you restate the text in your own words without shortening it or leaving anything out. When you summarize, you just tell the main idea of the text in your own words.

ASK STUDENTS to reread the poem. Then have partners take turns paraphrasing stanzas. Have them discuss any ideas they don't understand.

 LEVEL UP TUTORIALS For additional support, assign the following *Level Up* tutorial: **Paraphrasing.**

Determine Meanings of Words and Phrases

RL 1, RL 4

Imagery is the use of words and phrases in a way that allows readers to picture, or imagine, how something looks, feels, sounds, smells, or tastes. Effective imagery helps create a picture, or image, in the mind of the reader. To find imagery in a piece of writing, ask yourself, "What details help me picture what the author is describing?" In "The Last Wolf," the author uses imagery to describe a wolf entering the city:

> and I heard his baying echoes
> down the steep smashed warrens
> of Montgomery Street and past
> the few ruby-crowned highrises
> left standing

The sensory details in these lines help the reader imagine how the wolf sounds and what he sees as he runs. The phrase, "the few ruby-crowned highrises" illustrates the use of **figurative language,** or language that is not literally true, as part of the poem's imagery.

Figurative language is often used to create imagery. **Personification** is a type of figurative language in which an object or an animal is given human qualities. In "Animal Wisdom," a turtle talks the way a person would.

> Turtle crawled up on land. He said:
> What's missing is the ability
> to find contentment in a slow-paced life.

As you analyze "Animal Wisdom" and "The Last Wolf," look for more examples of imagery and personification in their language.

One way to clarify the meanings of words and phrases in a poem is to paraphrase them. **Paraphrasing** is restating text in your own words. An effective paraphrase is written in simpler language and is about the same length as the original text. The chart shows a paraphrase of a stanza from "The Last Wolf."

Original Text	Paraphrase
he laid his long gray muzzle on the spare white spread and his eyes burned yellow his small dotted eyebrows quivered	The wolf laid his head on the bed and stared with intense emotion at the person there.

Be sure to avoid using exact wording from the original text when you paraphrase. If you use exact words, you would need to enclose the words with quotation marks, but generally, quotes are not part of paraphrasing.

CLOSE READ

Determine Meaning of Words and Phrases

RL 1, RL 4, L 5a

Use the examples to help students understand imagery and personification. Guide them to find additional examples of imagery and personification in each poem. Then have partners reread each poem and discuss the impact of imagery and personification in each one.

Next, review how to paraphrase. Point out how the paraphrased text says the same thing as the lines of the poem, just using different words. Have volunteers discuss the meaning of other sets of lines in the poem and have them take turns paraphrasing each one.

English Language Support

Exchange Ideas and Information Form five small groups to answer the questions on page 104. Assign one question to each group. When the groups finish, let them take turns presenting their answers to the class. Encourage the class to provide useful feedback.

Strategies for Annotation   🖊 📖 *Annotate it!*

Determine Meaning of Words and Phrases

RL 1, RL 4

Have students use their eBook annotation tools to identify personification in "Animal Wisdom." Ask them to do the following:

- Highlight in yellow the object, animal, or idea that is personified.
- Highlight in blue the human quality that the object, animal, or idea is being given.
- On a note, jot down the effects each example of personification has on the reader.

As the oceans receded, fish sprouted whiskers.

Certain animals grew four legs and were able

to roam from shore to shore. Bear stood

upright and looked around. He said:

What's missing is devotion

to place, to give meaning to passing time.

PRACTICE & APPLY

Analyzing the Text
RL 1, RL 2,
RL 4, RL 10

Possible answers:

1. *A bear is being personified; the poet has Bear think and speak as a human would.*

2. *The phrase "fiery heat" suggests that the mountains were formed by volcanoes; "above them soared birds" creates an image of birds gliding high in the sky above the mountains.*

3. *Paraphrase of lines 28–34: When people realized that they shared the world with animals, they began saying what the animals had been saying before. Then both animals and people worked to take care of the earth.*
   The animals want to keep their own names because they want to remain distinct from people, perhaps to emphasize their own importance and unique wisdom.

4. *Imagery: flickering red and green; baying; wild loping gait; clutter and rubble; quiet blocks; voice ascending; low whine; narrow bed. The imagery appeals to sight, hearing, and perhaps touch as readers imagine being the person in the bed.*

5. *The author admires the wolf and also feels sorry for it; she feels the wolf understands and expresses the sadness that she feels herself. She feels that people have destroyed the environment by building cities that fall to ruin and forgetting about the other animals that need the resources of the world in order to survive.*

English Language Support

Connect Ideas Before students begin their essays, remind them to use transition words and phrases to link ideas and to help readers understand the differences and similarities between the poets' attitudes. Explain that **transition words and phrases** help continue an idea in a piece of writing.

- Use these words and phrases to show how things are alike: *in the same way, similarly, likewise, too.*
- Use these words and phrases to show how things are different: *in contrast to, unlike, on the other hand, yet, however, on the contrary.*

eBook *Annotate It!*

Analyzing the Text
RL 1, RL 2, RL 4,
RL 10, W 2a-f,
W 4, W 9a

> *Cite Text Evidence*   Support your responses with evidence from the text.

1. **Identify** Reread lines 6–11 of "Animal Wisdom," noticing the use of personification. What is being personified?

2. **Analyze** Examine lines 12–17 of "Animal Wisdom." Find two examples of imagery and describe the image that each suggests.

3. **Interpret** Paraphase lines 28–34 of "Animal Wisdom." Why do you think the animals "insisted/on keeping their own names"?

4. **Identify** Reread lines 9–19 of "The Last Wolf." Identify the imagery the author uses here, and explain which senses it appeals to.

5. **Analyze** What opinion does author TallMountain have of the wolf and of people and their effect on the environment?

PERFORMANCE TASK

Writing Activity: Informative Essay Write a one-page essay in which you compare and contrast how the writer of each poem feels about wildlife.

- In what ways are both writers' attitudes about animals alike?
- In what ways is the imagery in these poems the same? In what ways is it distinct, or different?
- Compare and contrast the way each author presents the idea of animal intelligence and how this wisdom can benefit people.

- Support your ideas with the imagery each author uses.
- Use appropriate transitions to clarify the relationships among your ideas.
- Provide a concluding statement.
- Share your essay by reading it aloud in a small group.

Assign this performance task.

PERFORMANCE TASK
W 2a–f, W 4,
W 9a

Writing Activity: Informative Essay Have students work independently. Direct them to

- create Venn diagrams or simple charts to compare and contrast the writers' attitudes, use of imagery, and ideas about animal intelligence
- create an introductory paragraph that captures readers' attention
- present each set of ideas in a separate paragraph
- include imagery and other evidence from the poems that supports their ideas

Analyze Structure: Poetry

RL 5

TEACH

Explain to students that the **form** of a written work is its structure or organization. One of the elements of a poem's form is the arrangement of its words and lines on the page. A poem's form is closely tied to its meaning; this makes the form of a poem important to the message of the poem. Explain these elements of a poem's form:

- A **line** is just what it says it is: the text that appears on one line. The line is the core unit of a poem; it can be a single word, part of a sentence, an entire sentence, or even more than one sentence.
- A **line break** is the place where a poet chooses to end a line. Explain that line breaks do not always signal the end of a sentence or thought. A line break can occur in the middle of a sentence or phrase to create a meaningful pause or emphasis.
- A **stanza** is a group of two or more lines that form a unit in a poem. Stanzas in a poem may or may not have the same number of lines. Usually, each stanza expresses a separate idea or feeling.

Explain to students that poets use all of these elements of form to build the poem's meaning. The form, combined with the words and phrases used in the poem, creates the message the poet wants to convey to the reader.

PRACTICE AND APPLY

Display "Animal Wisdom" or "The Last Wolf" for students. Work with them to analyze the poem's form. Have them:

- tell how many lines and stanzas the poem has
- describe how each thought begins and ends
- explain the effects that are created by the poem's line breaks
- compare and contrast each stanza and explain how each one fits into the overall structure of the poem

Then ask students to read the poem aloud a few times, taking turns reading each stanza. Guide them to express the meaning of the poem, using the line breaks and other elements of form to guide them.

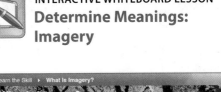

INTERACTIVE WHITEBOARD LESSON   RL 4

Determine Meanings: Imagery

Learn the Skill ▸ What Is Imagery?

What Is Imagery?

Find Out

Imagery refers to the vivid language and details writers use to create word pictures. Imagery draws on **sensory language**, words that appeal to the senses of sight, hearing, smell, taste, and touch.

RETEACH

Review that **imagery** consists of words and phrases that appeal to a reader's five senses. Remind students that sensory details describe how things look, feel, smell, sound, and taste; this use of imagery helps readers imagine what the author or poet is describing.

Use the Interactive Whiteboard Lesson "Figurative Language and Imagery" to help students learn to identify sensory details and imagery. Focus on these steps:

- **Step 1: Identify sensory language.** Look for words and phrases that appeal to your senses of sight, hearing, smell, taste, and touch. What does the writer want you to see or hear? Can you imagine the taste or touch of something in the writing?
- **Step 2: Analyze the meaning.** Think about what you felt and imagined as you read the text. What mood or emotion was created? Which words and phrases helped create that mood?

COLLABORATIVE DISCUSSION

Have students work in small groups to apply the steps to "Animal Wisdom" and "The Last Wolf." Have groups compare their results.

ANCHOR TEXT | How Smart Are Animals?

Science Writing by Dorothy Hinshaw Patent

Why This Text?

Students frequently encounter scientific information in nonfiction texts, both online and in books. This lesson explores animal intelligence through the lens of science and experiments, asking this central question: What is intelligence?

 **View It!**
Professional Development Podcast:
Text Complexity

For practice and application:

Can Animals Feel and Think?

Close Reader selection
"Can Animals Feel and Think?"
Informational Text by DeShawn Jones

Key Learning Objective: The student will be able to summarize central ideas and important details and determine author's purpose.

RI 1 Cite textual evidence; make inferences.
RI 2 Determine a central idea; provide a summary.
RI 3 Analyze text elements.
RI 5 Analyze structure.
RI 6 Determine an author's purpose.
RI 10 Read and comprehend literary nonfiction.
W 2 Write informative/explanatory texts.
W 9 Draw evidence from informational texts to support analysis.
SL 1 Engage effectively in a range of collaborative discussions.
L 1c Recognize and correct inappropriate shifts in pronoun number and person.
L 4a Use context as a clue to meaning.
L 4c Consult reference materials.
L 4d Verify preliminary determination of meaning.
L 6 Acquire and use accurately grade-appropriate words and phrases.

▲ Text Complexity Rubric

Quantitative Measures	**How Smart Are Animals?** Lexile: 1130L

Levels of Meaning/Purpose

more than one purpose implied; easily identified from context

Qualitative Measures

Structure

organization of main ideas and details complex, but clearly stated and generally sequential

Language Conventionality and Clarity

increased unfamiliar, academic, or domain-specific words

Knowledge Demands

complex science concepts

Reader/Task Considerations

- Teacher determined
- Vary by individual reader and type of text
- See the Text X-Ray for suggested Reader/Task Considerations.

English Language Support

Before teaching, use the Text X-Ray for an overview of the text's complexity. The Text X-Ray and the supports and scaffolds in the Teacher's Edition will help you guide students of different skill levels.

Meaning Making

Language Development

Effective Expression

Content Knowledge

Foundational Skills

Text Complexity: Qualitative Measures

Levels of Meaning/Purpose

more than one purpose implied; easily identified from context

Help students determine author's purpose and improve comprehension.

- Teacher's Edition side notes, pp. 105, 107, 108, 109, 112, 113
- English Language Support, p. 105
- Close Read Screencasts, p. 105
- Determine Author's Purpose, p. 113

Help students draw conclusions.

- Teacher's Edition side notes, pp. 106, 108, 110

To teach students to draw conclusions, see

- Draw Conclusions, p. 116a

 Text in FOCUS Monitoring Comprehension

 Use It! **Interactive Whiteboard Lessons:** Author's Purpose and Perspective

ZOOM IN ON DETERMINING AUTHOR'S PURPOSE After students finish reading, review the kinds of details that the author includes in her text. *(facts, examples, factual anecdotes, definitions)* Suggest that these details indicate that the author's purpose is **to provide information**.

- Have small groups skim the text to find instances of each type of detail. Ask volunteers to share their details.
- Then have groups discuss whether the author accomplishes her purpose and explain why or why not. Let groups share their opinions, reasons, and evidence with the class.

Structure

organization of main ideas and details complex, but clearly stated and generally sequential

Help students summarize text.

- Teacher's Edition side notes, pp. 106, 107, 109, 110, 111, 113
- English Language Support, p. 106
- When Students Struggle, p. 108
- Strategies for Annotation, p. 113
- Summarize Text, p. 113

To reteach summarize text, see

- Summarize Text, p. 116a

 Use It! **Level Up Tutorial:** Summarizing

ZOOM IN ON SUMMARIZING TEXT Before students read the text, remind them that a **summary** includes only the main idea and the most important details.

- Ask students to reread lines 133–139.
- Have them work with a partner to complete the following summary:

  Determining animals' intelligence is a problem because _____. *(It can't be measured in the same way that we measure human intelligence, and it is very different from human intelligence.)*
- Have pairs join small groups to compare their summaries.

Language Conventionality and Clarity

increased unfamiliar, academic, or domain-specific words

Teach unfamiliar vocabulary in context.

- Teacher's Edition Critical Vocabulary notes, pp. 106, 107, 108, 110, 111, 115
- Applying Academic Vocabulary, p. 107
- Strategies for Annotation, p. 115
- Vocabulary Strategy: Verify Word Meaning, p. 115

Help students increase their facility with spoken and written language.

- Teacher's Edition side notes, pp. 112, 116
- English Language Support, pp. 110, 111, 112, 116
- Performance Task, p. 114
- Language Conventions: Pronoun Number, p.116

ZOOM IN ON **PRETEACHING VOCABULARY** Before students read the selection, write the Critical Vocabulary terms on the board and identify the sentence from the text in which they appear. Discuss the meaning of each word, considering both its definition and the way it is used in the sentence. Then have students write original sentences that include each word. Review sentences for accuracy.

Knowledge Demands

complex science concepts

Support English Learners in understanding the scientific concepts in the text.

- Teacher's Edition Background note, p. 105
- Student Edition footnotes, pp. 107, 109, 110

ZOOM IN ON **BUILDING SCIENTIFIC UNDERSTANDING** Explain that in this text students may encounter unfamiliar scientific terms or ideas. Practice these strategies with them to support understanding.

- Show how footnotes in the text explain technical or specialized terms. Have students turn to page 108. Read aloud the last sentence on the page: "Clever Hans . . . of animals." Point out the superscript number after *behavioral scientists* and the corresponding footnote at the bottom of page 109. Ask a volunteer to read the definition aloud.
- Explain that authors often include a word or phrase after an unusual term in order to explain it in familiar language. Read the sentence on page 109, lines 126–131, as students follow along. Point out the information in parentheses that explains the type of test and each factor of the test.

Suggested Reader/Task Considerations

You might consider the following before assigning this informational text to students.

- Will students be able to comprehend the concepts presented in this text?
- Will students be interested in the content of this text?

ZOOM IN ON **SUPPORTING COMPREHENSION**

- Assign five mixed-ability groups one of the sections designated by subheadings. Have them annotate their sections and identify the most important ideas. Have groups share their findings.
- To stimulate interest, pose this question: Do animals possess intelligence? Let students draw upon prior knowledge and experience to respond. Record responses on the board and elicit examples to support opinions. Then discuss why the question might be important.

Dorothy Hinshaw Patent Have students read and discuss the information about the author. Explain that Dorothy Hinshaw Patent began her work as a zoologist. Later, she used that knowledge to begin writing for young readers, explaining complex scientific topics using language that is easy to understand. Tell students that she has also written books on complex topics such as insect communication, bacteria, habitats, and animal intelligence.

SETTING A PURPOSE Have students use the Setting a Purpose prompt to focus their reading. Ask them to write down questions as they read.

Determine Author's Purpose (LINES 1–10)

RI 1, RI 6

Explain that an **author's purpose** is the writer's main reason for writing a text. Discuss the possible purposes an author might have, such as to inform, entertain, express thoughts or feelings, or persuade.

Ⓐ **CITE TEXT EVIDENCE** Have students tell what they think the author's purpose is for this selection and why they think this. *(to inform readers about intelligence in animals; the title and first section head ask how smart animals are; the byline says it is science writing)*

Ⓑ **ASK STUDENTS** to reread lines 1–10 and tell how they think this text/story relates to the topic. *(It tells about Villa, a dog who helps a girl in a storm; Villa might be considered a smart animal.)* Ask why the author may have decided to begin this scientific article with this story. *(The author is using this example to catch readers' interest and get them involved in the topic.)*

English Language Support

Clarify that authors have different reasons for writing.

- Help students to identify the primary purpose of the texts they have read in this collection. *("The Mixer," to entertain; the poems, to express thoughts and feelings, "Tribute," to persuade)*

- Preview this text with students. Point out that it is organized into sections, each with its own heading. Read the headings aloud. Discuss what they indicate about the author's purpose. *(She wants to share knowledge, or inform.)*

- As students read, have them identify the kinds of details that help accomplish this purpose.

Dorothy Hinshaw Patent (b. 1940) *was born in Minnesota. As a child, Patent loved animals and being outdoors, spending much of her time exploring the woods near her home. Her love of animals led her to study animals when she went to college. After college, Patent worked as a scientist for several years. Then she decided to start writing nature books for children so she could share her love of the natural world with others. Patent has now published over 100 books for children and young adults.*

from How Smart Are Animals?

Science Writing by Dorothy Hinshaw Patent

SETTING A PURPOSE As you read, focus on the distinct characteristics that indicate intelligence and how scientists try to discover these traits in animals.

How Smart Is Smart?

The blizzard came on suddenly, with no warning. Eleven-year-old Andrea Anderson was outside near her home when the storm struck. The sixty- to eighty-mile-an-hour winds drove her into a snowdrift, and the snow quickly covered her up to her waist. Unable to get out, she screamed desperately for help. Through the swirling wind, Villa, a year-old Newfoundland dog[1] belonging to Andrea's neighbors, heard her cries. Villa had always been content to stay inside her dog run, but now she leapt over the five-foot fence and rushed to Andrea's side.

10 First she licked the girl, then began circling around her,

©Dorothy Hinshaw Patent

---

[1] **Newfoundland dog** (nōō´fən-lənd): a large strong dog bred in Newfoundland, Canada, and having a thick, usually black coat.

How Smart Are Animals? **105**

Close Read Screencasts ▶ Close Read

Modeled Discussions

Have students click the *Close Read* icon in their eBooks to access two screencasts in which readers discuss and annotate the following key passages:

- a discussion of two ways to interpret Villa's behavior (lines 21–32)
- the talents and factors that scientists believe are part of intelligence (lines 121–132)

As a class, view and discuss at least one of these videos. Then have students pair up to do an independent close read of an additional passage that discusses the difficulties involved in studying animal thought (lines 147–156).

Summarize Text

RI 1,
RI 2

(LINES 16–32)

Explain that to **summarize** means to briefly restate the central ideas and important details of a text in your own words. Remind students that a **central idea** is the most important point in a paragraph, section, or entire work and that **details** are the support for a central idea.

C **CITE TEXT EVIDENCE** Ask students to reread lines 16–32 and tell what details support the idea that Villa's actions did not show intelligence. (*Villa didn't understand danger; she acted on instinct, not on her own thinking.*)

D **ASK STUDENTS** to summarize the section "How Smart Is Smart?" (*Possible answer: Scientists thought that animal behavior like Villa's was instinct, not intelligence, but since the 1960s, different experiments have shown that some animals' behavior is intelligent.*)

Draw Conclusions

RI 1,
RI 2

(LINES 40–42)

Explain to students that a **conclusion** is a belief based on evidence, experience, and reasoning. A good, or valid, conclusion follows logically from the facts or statements on which it is based.

E **CITE TEXT EVIDENCE** Present students with this conclusion: *A trained animal may not be showing intelligence.* Ask them to reread lines 40–42 and tell what this conclusion is based on. (*An animal trained to perform a trick doesn't necessarily **know** what it is doing.*)

CRITICAL VOCABULARY

evolve: The word evolve connects dogs and wolves; wolves and dogs share many characteristics because they gradually changed and developed together over a long period of time.

ASK STUDENTS to discuss why the author points out that dogs evolved from wolves. (*The author is making a connection between the protective instinct of wolves in the wild and Villa; this is an example of Villa's behavior being instinct rather than intelligence, since dogs and wolves are related to each other.*)

---

packing down the snow with her paws. Next, Villa stood still as a statue in front of the girl with her paws on the packed snow. The dog waited until Andrea grabbed her, then strained forward, pulling the girl from the drift. As the storm raged around them, Villa led the way back to Andrea's home.

Villa won the Ken-L Ration Dog Hero of the Year award in 1983 for her bravery, loyalty, and intelligence. Her feat was truly impressive—understanding that Andrea needed help and performing the tasks necessary to save her. We can all admire Villa and envy Andrea for having such a loyal friend. But did Villa's heroic behavior exhibit intelligence? Some scientists would say that, while Villa certainly is a wonderful animal, her behavior was unthinking, perhaps an instinctive holdover from the protective environment of the wolf pack, where the adult animals defend the pups against danger. After all, dogs **evolved** from wolves, which are highly social animals. They would say that Villa just acted, without really understanding the concept of danger or thinking about what she was doing. Up until the 1960s, this view of animals prevailed among scientists studying animal behavior. But nowadays, a variety of experiments and experiences with different creatures are showing that some animals have impressive mental abilities.

20

C

30

evolve
(ĭ-vŏlv´) v. When animals and plants *evolve*, they gradually change and develop into different forms.

D

Do Animals Think?

If dogs might think, what about bees, rats, birds, cats, monkeys, and apes? How well do animals learn? How much of their experiences can they remember? Can they apply what they may have learned to new challenges in their lives? Are animals aware of the world around them? How might it be possible to learn about and evaluate the intelligence of different animals?

It is easy to confuse trainability with thinking. But just because an animal can learn to perform a trick doesn't mean that it knows what it is doing. In the IQ Zoo in Hotsprings, Arkansas, for example, animals perform some amazing tasks. A cat turns on the lights and then plays the piano, while a duck strums on the guitar with its bill. Parrots ride tiny bicycles and slide around on roller skates. At John F. Kennedy Airport in New York, beagles work for the Food and Drug Administration, sniffing at luggage and signaling when they

40

E

APPLYING ACADEMIC VOCABULARY

distinct	illustrate

THINK-PAIR-SHARE Have students turn to a partner to discuss the questions below. Guide students to include the academic vocabulary words *distinct* and *illustrate*. Ask volunteers to share their responses with the class.

- Which **distinct** behaviors show animals' intelligence and which do not?
- What examples does the author use to **illustrate** these distinctions?

perceive drugs or illegal foods in the baggage. Dolphins and
50 killer whales at marine parks perform some spectacular feats,
and their behavior is often linked into a story line so that it
appears they are acting roles, as humans would in a movie or
play. These animals may seem to be behaving in an intelligent
fashion, but they are just repeating behavior patterns they
have been trained to perform for food rewards. The drug-
sniffing beagle has no concept of drug illegality, and the duck
doesn't understand or appreciate music. They aren't thinking
and then deciding what to do.

Studying the intelligence of animals is very tricky. During
60 the nineteenth and early twentieth centuries, people readily
attributed human emotions and mental abilities to animals.
Even learned scientists had great faith in animal minds—
"An animal can think in a human way and can express
human ideas in human language," said the respected Swiss
psychiatrist[2] Gustav Wolff in the early 1900s.

Wolff's statement was inspired by Clever Hans, a horse
that appeared to show remarkable intelligence. A retired
schoolteacher trained Hans as he would a child, with
blackboards, flash cards, number boards, and letter cards.
70 After four years of training, Hans was ready to perform in
public. When asked to solve a numerical problem, Hans would
paw the answer with his hoof. He shook his head "yes" and
"no," moved it "up" and "down," and turned it "right" or "left."
Hans would show his "knowledge" of colors by picking up a
rag of the appropriate shade with his teeth. Many scientists
of the time came to watch Hans and tried to figure out how
he performed his amazing feats; they went away impressed.
Hans appeared to understand human language and to have
mastered arithmetic.
80 Then Oskar Pfungst, a German experimental
psychologist,[3] uncovered Hans's secret by using what is now a
standard scientific method—the double blind experiment.[4]

attribute
(ə-trĭb´yo͞ot) *tr.v.* If you
attribute something
to a person, thing, or
event, you believe
that they cause it or
have it.

---

[2] **psychiatrist** (sī-kī´ə-trĭst): a doctor who deals with mental illness.
[3] **experimental psychologist** (sī-kŏl´ə-jĭst): a person trained to do research and
testing that deals with the processes of the human mind and human behavior.
[4] **double blind experiment:** an experiment in which neither the research subjects
nor the scientists know the correct responses; both sides of the experiment are
kept "in the dark" about the phenomena in question until the study ends.

How Smart Are Animals? **107**

Summarize Text RI 1, RI 2
(LINES 49–58)

Remind students that a summary is a brief retelling of
a central idea and important details that support it.

(F) CITE TEXT EVIDENCE Have students reread
lines 49–58, decide what the central idea is, and then
summarize it, including details from the text. *(Possible
response: The repeated behavior of trained animals
doesn't show that the animal is intelligent. They are
deciding what to do; they are doing things for a reward.)*

Determine Author's RI 6
Purpose (LINES 59–79)

Explain that authors often want to inform their
readers in an entertaining and engaging way.

(G) ASK STUDENTS to review the story told in
lines 59–79 and then decide why the author told
it. *(Possible response: The author wanted to use an
engaging, real-life example of people's belief in animal
intelligence to illustrate that the intelligence of animals
is tricky to study and understand.)*

CRITICAL VOCABULARY

attribute: In this article, the word *attribute*
describes how people tend to believe that an
animal's behavior shows intelligence when the
behavior may be due to some other factor.

ASK STUDENTS to discuss why humans might
attribute intelligence to an animal. *(People see
animals do things that are similar to what humans do
and think animals are intelligent in the same way.)*

English Language Support

Understand Text Structure Call attention to the headings in the
selection and explain that they signal a new section in the text. Explain
that each section develops a point related to the topic of animal
intelligence. To identify this point, have students examine the main idea
of each paragraph in the section.

- Read aloud the second paragraph under "Do Animals Think?"
Work with students to identify the sentence that expresses the
paragraph's main idea. ("It is easy to confuse trainability with
thinking.")

- Have pairs read the second paragraph and outline the main idea
and supporting details.

- Ask students to write a summary of the main idea and important
details in the second paragraph. Have them predict what they will
learn in the rest of this section.

Determine Author's Purpose (LINES 85–97)

RI 1,
RI 6

Explain that authors will often recreate a scene to help readers feel that they are experiencing what actually took place.

 CITE TEXT EVIDENCE Have students review lines 85–97 and point out specific words and phrases that recreate the scene. Have them explain why the author uses this language. (*lean . . . forward; then relax; sign of relief, then stopped pawing; moved his head from side to side or up and down; nodded his head; began to tap his hoof; straightened his head; stood at attention. In line 94, the author says, ". . . Pfungst was able to prove his point." The author uses the language in this scene to help readers better understand how Hans used people's movements and how Pfungst proved his point.*)

Draw Conclusions

RI 1,
RI 2

(LINES 102–105)

Explain to students that authors will sometimes make a reference to a related idea without really explaining it. They are expecting readers to draw a conclusion on their own.

 ASK STUDENTS to reread lines 102–105 and discuss what the author means by this phrase: "Clever Hans taught psychology some important lessons." (*Psychologists thought Hans understood human language, but actually Hans did what people wanted by watching their movements. Psychologists learned that people communicate through their actions as well as their language.*)

CRITICAL VOCABULARY

phenomenon: The word *phenomenon* describes the fact that Clever Hans the horse seemed to be able to understand language and do mathematics.

ASK STUDENTS to discuss why no one understood how Hans could do such remarkable and unusual feats. (*People wanted to believe he was a phenomenon, or something completely unique, when he actually wasn't.*)

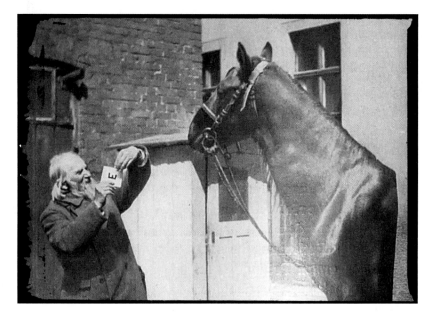

When the horse was asked a question, no one in his presence knew the answer. Under these conditions, Clever Hans was no longer so "smart"; he couldn't come up with the correct responses. By observing the horse and the audience when the answer was known, Pfungst discovered that Hans was very sensitive to the smallest movements of the people watching. They would lean ever so slightly forward until he had pawed 90 the correct number of times, then relax. He watched for that sign of relief, then stopped pawing. His trainer unknowingly moved his head from side to side or up and down just enough for Hans to take a cue as to what to do. At the end of his investigation, Pfungst was able to prove his point. He stood in front of Hans without asking any question. He nodded his head slightly, and the horse began to tap his hoof. When Pfungst straightened his head, Hans stood at attention.

Ever since the embarrassment of Clever Hans, psychologists have been extremely wary of falling into the 100 same trap. They are ready to call upon the "Clever Hans **phenomenon**" whenever an animal seems to be exhibiting intelligent behavior. Clever Hans taught psychology some important lessons, but the incident may also have made

phenomenon
(fĭ-nŏm´ə-nŏn´) *n.*
A *phenomenon*
is an unusual or
remarkable fact or
event.

©Karl Krall, Denkende Tiere, S. 38

WHEN STUDENTS STRUGGLE . . .

To help students understand the five parts of the Structure of Intellect test, use a chart like the one shown. Have them fill in each of the five main factors and then add other words below that mean roughly the same thing as the official term. Ask students to come up with more than one definition or to cite examples of the type of thinking discussed.

LEVEL UP TUTORIALS For additional support, assign the following *Level Up* tutorial: **Reading for Details.**

behavioral scientists[5] too cautious about the mental abilities of animals.

Animals that are easy to train may also be very intelligent. Some of the most trainable creatures, such as dolphins, are also the most likely candidates for genuine animal thinking. But finding ways to get at animals' real mental capacity can be very difficult.

110

What Is Intelligence?

We humans recognize a "smart" person when we meet one; we know who is a "brain" and who is not. In school, we take IQ tests, which are supposed to give a numerical measure of our "intelligence." But these days, the whole concept of intelligence is being reevaluated. The older, standard IQ tests measure only a limited range of mental abilities, concentrating on mathematics and language skills. Creativity, which most people would agree is a critical element in the meaningful application of intelligence, has not traditionally been evaluated

120 by such tests, and other important mental skills have also been ignored. But things are changing. Many scientists believe that dozens of different talents are a part of intelligence. In fact, more than a hundred factors of intelligence have been written about in scientific literature. Psychologists are now developing tests that measure intelligence more accurately and more broadly. The SOI (Structure of Intellect) test, for example, evaluates five main factors of intelligence: cognition (comprehension), memory, evaluation (judgment, planning, reasoning, and critical decision making), convergent

130 production (solving problems where answers are known), and divergent production (solving problems creatively). Each of these is broken down further into many subcategories.

But what about animals? We can't hand them a pencil and paper and give them a test, and we can't ask them what they're thinking. We must find other ways of measuring their "smarts." And that's not the only problem. Since the lives of animals are so different from ours, we can't apply human standards to them. We must develop different ideas of what animal intelligence might be.

---

[5] **behavioral scientists:** researchers who study human and animal behavior and mental processes.

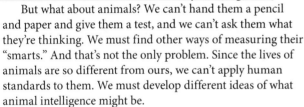

Structure of Intellect Test				
cognition	memory	evaluation	convergent production	divergent production
thinking	remembering	judging deciding	finding the right answer	solving problems creatively

CLOSE READ

Determine Author's Purpose (LINES 121–132)   RI 6

Explain that thinking about an author's purpose for including a particular section in a piece of writing can help them understand the whole piece of writing better.

J ASK STUDENTS to review lines 121–132 and explain why the author included this information. *(The information illustrates how broad and complicated the concept of human intelligence is and how complex it is to try and measure it. This helps readers begin to understand how much more difficult animal intelligence might be to study.)*

Summarize Text   RI 1, RI 2
(LINES 126–132)

Explain to students that when authors discuss complex topics they often break the overall idea into parts, or details. Readers can summarize these details to help understand the central idea.

K CITE TEXT EVIDENCE Have students reread lines 126–132 and identify the parts of the Structure of Intellect test. *(cognition, memory, evaluation, convergent production, divergent production)* Then have them summarize the central idea that these details support. *(Psychologists are thinking about intelligence in a broader and more accurate way; the SOI test is an example of this more complex thinking.)*

Text in FOCUS English Language Support

Monitoring Comprehension (line 110)

Have students view the **Text in Focus** video on this page of their eBook to learn how to monitor their comprehension of this complex text. Then have students use **Text in Focus Practice** to apply what they have learned.

Draw Conclusions

RI 1,
RI 2

(LINES 140–148)

Explain to students that they can draw conclusions from text to help them think about what might come next.

(L) **CITE TEXT EVIDENCE** Ask students to draw a conclusion based on lines 140–148. *(Possible response: Animal intelligence is different from intelligence in humans, so scientists need to create new ways to test for intelligence in animals.)* Then have students explain how this paragraph logically leads into the next section of text. *(The next section is about studying animal thought, which is a logical follow-up to finding new ways to study animal intelligence.)*

Summarize Text

RI 1,
RI 2

(LINES 153–164)

Tell students that summarizing a section of text can help them better understand what they have read and help them remember central ideas more easily.

(M) **CITE TEXT EVIDENCE** Have students reread lines 153–164, point out the main idea, and summarize the section. *(The main idea is that different abilities of animals affect experiments. Rhesus monkeys seemed to do better than cebus monkeys in tests using colored objects. But cebus monkeys have different color vision; once gray objects were used instead of colored objects, cebus monkeys actually did better than the rhesus monkeys.)*

CRITICAL VOCABULARY

inconsistency: The author uses the word *inconsistency* to describe one of the difficulties (pitfalls) of studying the behavior of animals.

ASK STUDENTS to discuss how inconsistency affects scientific tests of animal intelligence. *(Possible responses: Animals, like people, do not always respond to the same situation in the same way; people cannot tell if an animal sometimes just doesn't want to do a specific test.)*

---

140 The concept of intelligence was thought up by humans, and our thinking about it is tied up with our own human system of values. The things that are important to animals can be different from those that matter to humans. When studying animals, we must test them in situations that have meaning for their lives, not ours, and not just look to see how much they resemble us.

Studying Animal Thought

Many pitfalls await the scientist trying to interpret animals' behavior and make inferences about their intelligence. One is **inconsistency**. An animal might breeze through what we
150 consider a difficult learning task and then fail when presented with what seems obvious to us. When an animal can't perform well, we don't know if it really cannot solve the problems put to it or if it just doesn't want to. Sometimes the difficulty lies in the perceptive abilities of the animals. The animal may have the mental ability and the desire to solve the problem but is unable to make the discriminations[6] being asked of it. For example, a researcher using colored objects to compare learning in a cebus monkey and in a rhesus monkey first found that the rhesus scored much better than the cebus.
160 But rhesus monkeys have color vision that is essentially the same as ours, while the cebus's is significantly different. When the design of the experiment was changed and gray objects were substituted for the colored ones, the cebus monkeys actually did a little better than the rhesus.

Scientists studying animals in nature can run into difficulties in interpreting their results if they don't pay very close attention to what they see and hear. C. G. Beer of Rutgers University in New Jersey spent long hours studying laughing gull behavior. Early on, he interpreted what he called
170 the "long call" as a signal that was the same for each bird and that was made on all occasions. But when he recorded a variety of long calls and played them back to the gulls, he noticed that the birds didn't always respond in the same way. There were differences in the calls that were hard for a human researcher to hear. Beer then realized that the long call was actually so individualized that it helped distinguish one bird from another! The more carefully he listened to the calls and

inconsistency
(ĭn´kən-sĭs´tən-sē) *n.*
If something shows *inconsistency*, it does not always behave or respond the same way every time.

---

[6] **discriminations** (dĭ-skrĭm´ə-na´shəns): fine distinctions; small differences.

English Language Support

Improve Reading Fluency Discuss the characteristics of scientific texts, including the use of specific vocabulary, lengthy sentences, and formal style.

- Display lines 192–206. Read each sentence aloud, repeating any words that may be unfamiliar to students. Then read the entire passage, modeling the appropriate pace and expression.
- Have students take turns reading sentences aloud in sequence. Continue alternating until all students have read. Then, as a class, read the entire passage aloud.

watched the gulls' reactions to them, the more **complexity** and variety he found in both the calls and the responses. From this
180 work Beer concluded: "We may often misunderstand what animals are doing in social interaction because we fail to draw our distinctions where the animals draw theirs."

Measuring Animal Intelligence

Keeping all these concerns in mind, we can list some factors of intelligence that might be measurable or observable in animals—speed of learning, complexity of learned tasks, ability to retrieve information from long-term memory, rule learning, decision-making and problem-solving capacity, counting **aptitude**, understanding of spatial relations, and ability to learn by watching what others do. More advanced
190 signs of intelligence are tool manufacture and use, symbolic communication, and ability to form mental concepts.

With such a list of capabilities that might be involved with intelligence, it seems that scientists should be able to analyze and compare the intelligence of animals. But it's one thing to decide to test intelligence and another to design experiments that will measure it. You may read somewhere that rats, for example, are smarter than pigeons. But finding ways to compare the accomplishments of different species is virtually impossible. Animals are just too varied in their physical
200 makeup and in their life styles. Scientists have found that different kinds of animals learn better under different sorts of conditions, so the same experiment usually can't be used meaningfully on a rat and a pigeon. In addition, some animals have evolved special mental skills to deal with their particular environments. They might appear especially intelligent on one measure of brain power and very dull on another.

Dealing with wild animals presents new problems. Laboratory pigeons and rats have been bred for many generations in captivity. They are used to cages and to
210 humans, and large numbers are easy to acquire. Wild animals may not perform well in the laboratory because they are afraid or because the setting is so strange to them. And because wild animals are often hard to come by, the experimenter must usually work with only a small number of individuals. Variations of "intelligence" from one individual to the next can significantly affect the results. Primates—apes and monkeys—are among the most intelligent animals, and apes

complexity
(kəm-plĕkʹsĭ-tē) *n.* *Complexity* is the state of having many different parts that are connected in a tangled or layered way.

aptitude
(ăpʹtĭ-tōōdʹ) *n.* An *aptitude* for something is an ability to easily and quickly learn how to do it.

How Smart Are Animals? **111**

CLOSE READ

Summarize Text
RI 1,
RI 2

(LINES 183–216)

Explain that when summarizing a large section of text, it is necessary to isolate the central ideas of each paragraph.

N CITE TEXT EVIDENCE Have students identify the sentences that contain central ideas in lines 183–216 and restate those ideas in their own words. *(Lines 183–185: There are some factors of animal intelligence that we can observe or measure. Lines 197–199: It is very difficult to compare intelligence across different kinds of animals. Line 207: Wild animals present new problems for researchers.)*

> #### CRITICAL VOCABULARY
>
> **complexity**: The author uses the word *complexity* to describe the gulls' calls and responses; it can also apply to many other parts of the selection.
>
> **ASK STUDENTS** to discuss why there is such complexity in understanding how animals learn. *(Humans may interpret animal communication or behavior one way without understanding it completely.)*
>
> **aptitude**: The word *aptitude* is a synonym for the words *skill* and *talent*. Aptitude includes the capacity to *learn* skills, as in a "talent for counting."
>
> **ASK STUDENTS** to discuss how one element of intelligence is having the aptitude to absorb knowledge and turn it into a skill. *(Students should note how both animals and humans **learn** by processing information and then using that information to perform a task.)*

English Language Support

Understand Cohesion Explain that **transitions,** words such as *and, but, or, however,* and *unlike,* can show how ideas are related. Display lines 154–164. Highlight both instances of the word *but.* Explain that *but* often signals a **contrast,** or difference.

- Have students reread lines 160–161. Then help them complete this sentence frame to show the relationship between the two types of monkeys: Cebus monkeys and rhesus monkeys have _____. *(different types of color vision)*

- Have pairs explain the differences expressed in lines 154–156 and 160–161 and then share their explanations in small groups. *(Intelligence and willingness are different and separate from sensory abilities. The animal may understand the task but not be able to taste, feel, smell, see, or hear subtle distinctions.)*

- List words that also signal a contrast: *although, however, in contrast.* Have partners use these words to restate the ideas in lines 154–156 and 160–161.

Determine Author's Purpose (LINES 220–227)

RI 1,
RI 6

Explain to students that this selection is one part of a longer book by this author. Point out that an author will often wrap up a particular section of a book by making a statement or conclusion that moves the reader forward to the next part of the book.

CITE TEXT EVIDENCE Have students reread lines 220–227 and identify the author's purpose. Ask them why they think this. (*The author wants to persuade readers that determining animal intelligence is worth the effort despite the difficulty. The last sentence seems to show that the rest of the book will discuss more studies of animal intelligence and what scientists have learned from them.*)

COLLABORATIVE DISCUSSION Have small groups define the concept of "highly trainable" animals and what that would mean when working with different animals. Ask students to review the article to find ways scientists have tried to measure intelligence in animals. Remind students to cite evidence from the text to define the differences between an intelligent animal and one that can perform a trick.

ASK STUDENTS to share any questions they generated in the course of reading and discussing the selection.

English Language Support

Exchange Information and Ideas Tell students that in order to conduct an effective discussion they must be prepared.

- Display a Venn diagram with the phrase *highly trainable* in one circle and *intelligent* in the other.
- Have small groups find details from the text that help define and explain each concept. Have students record their findings in a Venn diagram like the one on the board.
- Have students refer to their diagrams in their discussions.

seem closer to our idea of "smart" than monkeys. But a bright monkey may score as well on a test as an ape, while a dull one may be outclassed by a rat. For these reasons, behavioral scientists have realized that trying to compare the intelligence of different animals is a very challenging problem.

220

That doesn't mean, however, that trying to find out how animal minds function is not worth the effort. We can learn a great deal through studying how various kinds of animals solve problems and how they use their mental abilities to survive in their natural environments.

COLLABORATIVE DISCUSSION Can we know for certain whether an animal is showing intelligence, or whether it is simply highly trainable? What are some challenges scientists face in trying to determine animal intelligence? Discuss these questions with a small group. Be sure to cite evidence from the text.

FOR STANDARD ENGLISH LEARNERS

Pronunciation Some students may struggle with the pronunciation of words commonly used in organized peer discussions. For example, they may pronounce the initial /th/ sound in such words as *that, than, their, those*, etc., as /d/. Display this sentence (lines 223–224): "That doesn't mean, however, that trying to find out how animal minds function is not worth the effort." Read the sentence aloud several times, emphasizing initial /th/ sounds. Have students echo your reading.

Summarize Text

RI 2

One way to check your understanding of what you are reading is to summarize it. When you **summarize,** you briefly restate in your own words the central ideas and important details of a text. A **central idea** is the most important point in a paragraph, section, or an entire work. **Details** are the support for the central idea.

This chart shows how to summarize the section "Measuring Animal Intelligence" in *How Smart Are Animals?* The central idea and a sample detail from each paragraph is recorded.

Central Idea	Detail
There are many ways intelligence in animals could be measured. *(lines 183–191)*	Tests might include creating and using tools.
It is difficult to design useful tests and to compare different species. *(lines 192–206)*	An experiment used on a rat might not be useful for testing a pigeon.
Using wild animals in a lab is problematic. *(lines 207–222)*	They might not perform well in a strange setting.

Summary The section "Measuring Animal Intelligence" focuses on how animal intelligence might be tested. While there are many ways animal intelligence could be measured, testing is also problematic. Designing useful tests, comparing different species, and using wild animals are some of the challenges scientists face.

Generally, a summary is no more then one-third the length of the original text and includes just the facts—not your personal opinions. Try summarizing other sections of the selection as you analyze *How Smart Are Animals?*

Determine Author's Purpose

RI 6

A writer's main reason for writing a text is called the **author's purpose.** The purpose may be to inform, entertain, persuade, or express thoughts and feelings. Most writers do not state their reason for writing. Their purpose is suggested through the information they present. A text can also have more than one purpose. To determine an author's purpose for writing, ask yourself these questions:

- Why is the writer telling me this?
- What does the writer want me to think about this topic?

CLOSE READ

Summarize Text

RI 2

Help students review and restate the definitions of the terms *central idea* and *details.* Then have them relate the terms to the idea of summarizing in their own words.

Go through the chart and isolate the lines offered that show central ideas and key details. Have students explain why these lines are part of a good summary.

Next, go through the summary that is shown. Have students link the restatements in the summary to the original ideas. Discuss why a summary is always shorter than the original text. *(It lists only central ideas and important details.)* Then help students summarize other sections of the text.

Determine Author's Purpose

RI 6

Remind students that authors make decisions about how to present information and about what effects they want to have on their readers. Point out that an author wants readers to keep on reading, and this requires writers to engage their audience in different ways, while still serving the overall purpose of the writing.

Have students discuss the different purposes for writing and how they align with readers' reasons for reading. Then review the bulleted points that will help students to determine author's purpose.

Strategies for Annotation   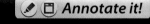 Annotate it!

Summarize Text

RI 2

Share these strategies for guided or independent analysis:

- Highlight in yellow central ideas that could be combined or shortened for a summary.
- Highlight in green key details that may be included in a summary.
- Review your highlights. On a note, record shortened and combined versions in your own words that might go into your summary.

Keeping all these concerns in mind, we can list some factors of intelligence that might be measurable or observable in animals—speed of learning, complexity of learned tasks, ability to retrieve information from long-term memory, rule learning, decision-making and problem-solving capacity, counting aptitude, understanding of spatial relations, and. . . .

PRACTICE & APPLY

Analyzing the Text
RI 1, RI 2,
RI 3, RI 5,
RI 6

Possible answers:

1. The author's main purpose is to inform or explain. Lines 20–25 discuss whether Villa was thinking or just acting on instinct, and lines 30–32 talk about experiments and experiences, so the author will probably discuss evidence about whether and how animals think.

2. The author wants to use a dramatic account to pique the reader's interest in the topic. Also, the anecdote illustrates that animals may be able to think.

3. The story about Clever Hans is included to show that even scientists can mistake animal trainability for intelligence. It is an effective example because it shows in detail how difficult it is for humans to determine an animal's intelligence.

4. Main ideas include that there are many pitfalls to interpreting animal behavior and intelligence, and that studying animals in nature can also have its drawbacks. Possible summary: The section points out that interpreting animal behavior can be tricky because scientists cannot know everything about animal perceptions and desire to complete a task. It also discusses how, even when animals are studied in the wild, scientists can misunderstand or not notice behaviors.

5. The author does not directly answer the question. Instead, she shows how difficult it is to answer the question. The author does this by sharing examples and studies that illustrate the challenges scientists face, such as a flawed experiment that attempted to measure intelligence in rhesus and cebus monkeys.

Analyzing the Text
RI 1, RI 2, RI 3,
RI 5, RI 6, RI 10,
W 2, W 9

Cite Text Evidence   Support your responses with evidence from the text.

1. **Infer** Reread lines 1–32 of *How Smart Are Animals?* What is the author's main purpose for writing? Explain how you know this.

2. **Infer** The author introduces the topic with an **anecdote,** a short account of an event. Explain the author's purpose for including this event.

3. **Evaluate** Review lines 33–110. Why does the author include the information about Clever Hans? Tell whether or not this example is effective and why.

4. **Summarize** Review lines 147–182. What main ideas and details does the author present? Write a summary of the section.

5. **Analyze** Review the main ideas the author discusses in each section of the excerpt. Tell whether or not the author answers the question "How smart are animals?" and explain why.

PERFORMANCE TASK

Writing Activity: Informative Essay Write a one-page essay to explain the author's purpose in writing *How Smart Are Animals?*

- Review the selection. Note clues that help you determine the author's purpose in writing it.

- Summarize important ideas from the text. Cite relevant textual evidence to support your analysis, such as facts, definitions, details, and examples that help show the author's purpose.

PERFORMANCE TASK
W 2,
W 9

Assign this performance task.

Writing Activity: Informative Essay Have students work independently. Suggest that they

- begin with a statement of the author's purpose
- continue with text clues that show this purpose
- create a list of important ideas and details from the text that support their statement about the author's purpose
- use their list to craft a summary that explains this purpose

Remind students to conclude with a simple statement that restates the author's purpose.

Critical Vocabulary

L 4a, L 4c,
L 4d, L 6

evolve	attribute	phenomenon
inconsistency	complexity	aptitude

Practice and Apply Answer each question.

1. Which Vocabulary word goes with *complicated*? Why?

2. Which Vocabulary word goes with *irregular*? Why?

3. Which Vocabulary word goes with *change*? Why?

4. Which Vocabulary word goes with *event*? Why?

5. Which Vocabulary word goes with *assign*? Why?

6. Which Vocabulary word goes with *talent*? Why?

Vocabulary Strategy: Verify Word Meaning

When you encounter an unfamiliar word in text, there are several ways you can **verify**, or check, its meaning. One way is to look for context clues in words, sentences, or paragraphs that surround the unfamiliar word. When you can't figure out the meaning of a word using context clues, you can look it up in a dictionary. Try to figure out the meaning of *aptitude* in this text.

> **Lin is so intelligent. She has an aptitude for solving difficult problems.**

If you are unfamiliar with the meaning of the word *aptitude,* you can tell from the surrounding text that it has something to do with intelligence, even though the text doesn't state the word's exact meaning. When you consult a dictionary, you will find that *aptitude* means "an inherent ability, as for learning; a talent."

Practice and Apply Complete the chart for the words listed. First, record context clues that give clues about each word's meaning. Consult a dictionary to verify the word's meaning and then write the definition.

Word	Context Clues	Dictionary Definition
feat (lines 16–19)		
wary (lines 98–100)		
virtually (lines 196–199)		

Critical Vocabulary

L 4a, L 4c, L 4d

Answers:

1. *complexity; both words mean that something has many layers or factors involved in it.*

2. *inconsistency; both words mean that something does not happen the same way every time.*

3. *evolve; both words mean that something is becoming different or not staying the same.*

4. *phenomenon; both words mean something that happens.*

5. *attribute; both words mean to give something a particular quality or trait.*

6. *aptitude; both words mean a skill or ability.*

Vocabulary Strategy: Verify Word Meaning

Word	Context Clues	Dictionary Definition
feat	*won; award; impressive*	*an act of great courage, skill, or imagination*
wary	*embarrassment; falling into the same trap*	*on guard; cautious*
virtually	*difficult to compare; impossible*	*practically; nearly*

Strategies for Annotation  *Annotate it!*

Verify Word Meaning

L 4a, L 4c, L 4d

Have students locate the sentences containing *feat, wary,* and *virtually* in the selection. Tell them to use their eBook annotation tools to do the following:

- Highlight each word. Reread the surrounding words and sentences, looking for clues to the word's meaning.
- Underline any clues, such as examples, synonyms, or antonyms.
- Try to infer the word's meaning and write it down on a note.
- Check your preliminary meaning in a dictionary.

Villa won the Ken-L Ration Dog Hero of the Year award in 1983 for her bravery, loyalty, and intelligence. Her feat was truly impressive—understanding that Andrea needed help and performing the tasks necessary to save her.

PRACTICE & APPLY

Language Conventions: Pronoun Number

L 1c

Tell students that we use pronouns to avoid repeating the same proper nouns over and over again. Note that to avoid confusion, proper pronouns that agree in number with the nouns they are replacing must be used.

Help students identify antecedents by testing all nouns in a sentence as possible antecedents. This will help them hear which pronoun or noun antecedent works best in the sentence.

Answers:

1. *them* should be *him*

2. *their* should be *its*; also accept *his* or *her*

3. *her* should be *their*; *it* should be *them*

4. *them* should be *her*; *him* should be *them*

5. *you* should be *they*

 Assess It Online!

Online Selection Test
- Download an editable ExamView bank.
- Assign and manage this test online.

Language Conventions: Pronoun Number

L 1c

A **pronoun** is a word used in the place of one or more nouns or pronouns. An **antecedent** is the noun or pronoun to which a pronoun refers. A pronoun must agree with its antecedent in number. In other words, if an antecedent is singular, you should use a singular pronoun. If an antecedent is plural, you should use a plural pronoun. Read this passage from *How Smart Are Animals?*

> But what about animals? We can't hand them a pencil and paper and give them a test, and we can't ask them what they're thinking. We must find other ways of measuring their "smarts."

The antecedent, *animals*, is plural, so the pronouns *them* and *their* are also plural.

It is important to recognize and correct shifts in pronoun number. Read this sentence:

> Marcus gave his dog some treats. His dog gobbled it up.

The pronoun *it* is singular, and does not match its plural antecedent, *treats*. This shift in number makes the sentence confusing. The correct pronoun to use is *them*.

Here's another example of a shift in pronoun number:

> A scientist has to be careful when designing an experiment so that their results will be valid.

The pronoun *their* is plural, and does not match its antecedent, *scientist*, which is singular. The correct pronoun to use is *his* or *her*.

Practice and Apply Correct the shift in pronoun number in each sentence. Some sentences have more then one mistake.

1. At the aquatic park, my uncle trains dolphins to retrieve objects. The dolphins learn quickly and bring the objects back to them.

2. The puppy ran around the park, howling, looking for their owner.

3. Mother blue jays are fiercely protective of her young and will chase away any predators that might threaten it.

4. Barry and Mitch groomed the horse, Princess, after they fed them. Princess whinnied softly as if to say goodnight to him.

5. Zoo visitors are enthusiastic when you see the big cats.

116   Collection 2

English Language Support

Understand Cohesion Display this chart and review it with the class:

Singular	Plural
I/me/my/mine	we/us/our/ours
you/yours	you/yours
he/him/his	they/them/their/theirs
she/her/hers	
it/its	

- Display each Practice and Apply sentence, and circle the antecedent with which the pronoun agrees. Then help students choose the correct pronoun from the chart.
- Have students work in pairs to identify the errors in the sentences. Have each partner take turns choosing pronouns from the chart that will correct the mistake(s).
- Have students write their own sentences in which personal pronouns disagree with the antecedents. Have them exchange papers with partners and correct the errors.

116 Collection 2

Draw Conclusions

RI 1,
RI 2

TEACH

Explain to students that a **conclusion** is a statement of belief based on evidence, experience, and reasoning. Tell them that a **valid,** or well-supported, conclusion is one that logically follows from the statements or facts upon which it is based. Together, discuss these different types of facts and statements that an author might present in a text:

- **Evidence** is a specific piece of information, such as a fact, a quotation, an example, a statistic, an anecdote, a personal experience of the author, or another person connected to the text, among other things.
- **Experience** refers to anything the reader previously knows or has encountered before.
- **Reasoning** is the use of logic and careful thinking.

Explain that as readers think about the ideas presented in informational texts such as *How Smart Are Animals?* they are constantly drawing conclusions using the facts and statements that the author presents. (Point out that drawing conclusions is not limited to informational text; readers follow the same process to arrive at conclusions when reading fiction, poetry, drama, or any other kind of text.)

PRACTICE AND APPLY

Display the following sections from *How Smart Are Animals?* for students. Have them work in groups to draw conclusions based on the prompts shown.

- **Lines 1–15:** Why does Villa help Andrea?
- **Lines 111–132:** What defines intelligence?
- **Lines 157–182:** Why do scientists need to be careful when they study animals?
- **Lines 183–227:** What would prove animal intelligence?

Have students identify the evidence from the text and/or their own experience that they used in drawing conclusions. Have members of the groups share their reasoning as they came to a conclusion.

Summarize Text

RI 2

RETEACH

Review the terms *central idea, details,* and *summarize.* Provide examples of central ideas and details from *How Smart Are Animals?* by reading aloud or having students read aloud sentences, words, or phrases from the selection.

Next, model summarizing text by using the first passage below, presenting a written summary to students. Break the summary down into its central idea and the details that support it. Then have partners summarize the other two passages.

- **Lines 16–28:** theories on Villa's behavior
- **Lines 59–65:** belief that animals are like humans
- **Lines 66–97:** the story of Clever Hans

Have partners share their summaries with the rest of the class. Students should discuss differences and similarities and how well each summary conveys the meaning of the text.

 LEVEL UP TUTORIALS Assign the following *Level Up* tutorial: **Summarizing**

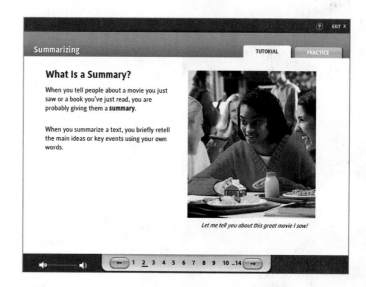

INDEPENDENT READING

Individual students can apply their summarizing skills to another selection in Collection 2, or to a magazine article or textbook passage they may be reading on their own. After their analysis, have them share summaries of what they have read with other students in the class.

Can Animals Feel and Think?

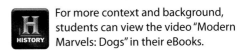

For more context and background, students can view the video "Modern Marvels: Dogs" in their eBooks.

Informational Text by DeShawn Jones

Why This Text

Students may finish reading an informational text without a full understanding of the author's central ideas. Informational texts such as this one by DeShawn Jones may have more than one complex central idea. Remind students that they must identify the central idea when they summarize text. With the help of the close-reading questions, students will determine the central ideas by examining the supporting details. This close reading will lead students to understand the most important ideas and supporting details in an informational text.

Background Have students read the background information about some of the early philosophers and scientists, such as René Descartes, who thought about or studied animal behavior. Introduce the selection by telling students that since the turn of the twenty-first century, many aspects of animal communication, animal emotions, and animal thought processes that experts thought they had understood are being reexamined, and startling new conclusions are being reached.

SETTING A PURPOSE Ask students to pay attention to the central ideas in this informational text and to the author's point of view and purpose for having written this article. How soon into the text can students begin to identify the central idea?

Standards Support

- cite textual evidence
- determine a central idea of a text and how it is conveyed through particular details
- provide a summary of a text distinct from personal opinions or judgments
- determine an author's point of view and purpose

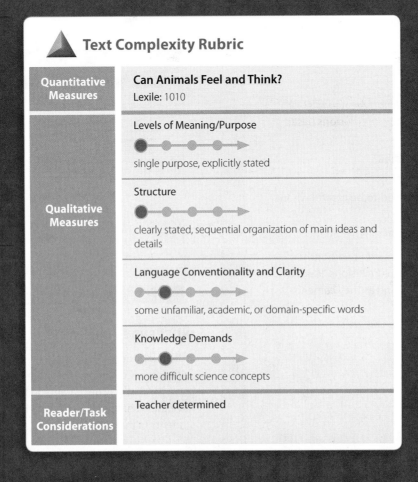

Text Complexity Rubric

Quantitative Measures

Can Animals Feel and Think?
Lexile: 1010

Qualitative Measures

Levels of Meaning/Purpose
single purpose, explicitly stated

Structure
clearly stated, sequential organization of main ideas and details

Language Conventionality and Clarity
some unfamiliar, academic, or domain-specific words

Knowledge Demands
more difficult science concepts

Reader/Task Considerations
Teacher determined

Strategies for CLOSE READING

Summarize Text

Students should read this article carefully all the way through. Close-reading questions at the bottom of the page will help students focus on a central idea and on the details that support it in order to summarize text. As they read, students should record comments or questions about the text in the side margins.

WHEN STUDENTS STRUGGLE . . .

To help students summarize the entire text by focusing on one central idea and its supporting details, have students work in a small group to fill out a chart such as the one shown below as they analyze the informational text.

CITE TEXT EVIDENCE For practice in summarizing, have students first record the central idea and supporting details in the text as a whole or in parts of the text.

Central Idea	Supporting Details
Many scientists now believe that animals, like humans, can feel and think.	Many mammals, such as dogs and elephants, seem to feel emotions such as fear, joy, and grief.
	Some animals, such as pigs and birds, are able to learn or solve problems.
	Animal and human brains have a cerebral cortex, which is responsible for feeling pain, fear, and grief.
	Regardless of brain size, some animals seem to be able to think.
	Animals are more like humans than once thought.

Summary: *Scientists now believe that animals, such as mammals and birds, can feel emotions and actually think. Like humans, animals have a cerebral cortex that is responsible for feeling pain, fear, and grief. Also, having a large brain is not necessary for thinking, as evidenced by Betty the crow. Scientists now think that animals are more like humans than once thought.*

Background *For most of history, people have believed that animals are totally unlike human beings. A great scholar from the 1600s, René Descartes (dā kärt'), described animals as "machines"—incapable of thinking. In the early 1900s, the scientist Ivan Pavlov performed experiments that led many to believe that animals always acted predictably. In recent years, however, scientists have studied animal emotions and thought processes.*

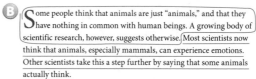

Can Animals Feel and Think?

Informational Text by DeShawn Jones

CLOSE READ
Notes

1. **READ ▶** As you read lines 1–13, begin to collect and cite text evidence.
   - Circle the central idea in the first paragraph, and underline the details that support the idea.
   - Circle the central idea in the second paragraph, and underline the supporting details.
   - In the margin, paraphrase each of the two central ideas.

A B Some people think that animals are just "animals," and that they have nothing in common with human beings. A growing body of scientific research, however, suggests otherwise. Most scientists now think that animals, especially mammals, can experience emotions. Other scientists take this a step further by saying that some animals actually think.

Think about what most dogs do when you scold them. They lower their heads and slink off to some secluded spot. Only when they sense that you are no longer angry do they come back out. On the other
10 hand, when you return home after a day at school, your dog probably leaps around you, tail wagging furiously. But, do these reactions really indicate that dogs and other mammals feel emotions? They certainly seem to.

Many scientists now believe that animals can feel and think.

Dogs and other mammals seem to feel emotions.

25

---

1. **READ AND CITE TEXT EVIDENCE** Explain that the central idea is the most important idea in the text as a whole or in a paragraph or section of text. Tell students that when you summarize text, you briefly restate in your own words the central idea and the details that support it.

A **ASK STUDENTS** to determine the central idea in each of the first two paragraphs (lines 1–13) and the specific details that convey each central idea. *Responses may include references to the central ideas in lines 1–3 and 11–13 and the supporting details in lines 3–11.*

FOR ELL STUDENTS Explain that "on the other hand" (lines 9–10) is an idiomatic phrase (or expression) that points to a contrast of two things or ideas.

ASK STUDENTS to look for other words and phrases that show comparison, such as *like* or *as*, or contrast, such as *however, while,* and *but,* and cite them in the margin.

C There are plenty of examples that seem to indicate that animals feel emotions such as fear, anger, joy, and grief. If the antelope did not feel fear, it would stand still or continue grazing instead of sprinting away at the sight of a cheetah. Mammals such as dolphins, chimpanzees, and rats show the feeling of joy in their love of playful activity. Elephants show signs of long-lasting grief when a member of

20 the herd dies. Other mammals such as sea lions, bears, and moose also seem to become upset by a death in their group.

Whether or not animals can actually think is a more difficult question. Do animals, for example, have the **capacity** to learn, solve problems, or guess what other animals are thinking? Research suggests that some animals can do this and more.

Chimpanzees in large captive colonies often cooperate with certain other chimpanzees in the colony. They have then been observed to suddenly switch **alliances** and seemingly double-cross each other. This behavior suggests that chimpanzees can, like

30 humans, change their minds or feel **resentment**.

Pigs offer an interesting example of problem solving. A scientist from Bristol University discovered that stronger pigs looking for food would follow the lead of a weaker but smarter pig. The smarter pig would find the food. Then, the smarter pig would trick the stronger pig by distracting it. While the stronger pig wasn't looking, the smarter pig would dive in and gobble up the food.

capacity:
ability

alliances:
loyalties

resentment:
anger

---

2. **◀ REREAD** Write a summary of lines 1–13.

Although some people believe that animals are unlike humans, most scientists now think that some animals can feel emotions and actually think. The reactions of dogs when you scold them, for example, seem to confirm that some animals experience emotions.

---

3. **READ ▶** As you read lines 14–36, continue to cite textual evidence.

• Circle a sentence in lines 14–21 that informs the reader of the author's point of view.

• Underline at least one fact or example in each paragraph that supports the author's point of view.

26

The Cerebral Cortex in Different Species

Bird   Frog

Monkey   Cat   Rabbit

Human   Chimpanzee

The part of the brain colored pink in these diagrams is the cerebral cortex. The cerebral cortex is the part of the brain that gives the capacity to feel pain, fear, and grief.

D

His purpose is to show that animal brains and human brains both have a cerebral cortex.

E Perhaps the most amazing example of an animal thinking involves not a mammal, but a bird. Betty the crow makes her home in a laboratory in Oxford, England. She devised an **ingenious** solution

40 for getting a treat in the form of food that scientists had inserted in a long tube. When she first tried to get the treat, she stuck her beak into the tube but found that the tube was too deep for her beak to reach the treat. Undaunted, she picked up a piece of wire that the scientists had placed beforehand in her cage. She bent the wire into a hook and used the hook to lift the treat from the tube. She did this not once, but repeatedly. What really amazed the scientists observing Betty was that she had never seen a piece of wire before. But this bird figured out the challenge, decided to use the wire, and then shape it into the perfect tool for getting the treat.

ingenious:
clever

---

4. **READ ▶** As you read lines 37–53, continue to cite textual evidence.

• Circle the central idea in lines 37–49 and lines 50–53, and underline at least one detail that supports each central idea.

• In the margin, explain the author's purpose for including the diagram, chart, and captions.

27

---

2. **REREAD AND CITE TEXT EVIDENCE**

B **ASK STUDENTS** to include each of the two central ideas and supporting details they cited from the first two paragraphs in their summary of lines 1–13. *Responses may include references to lines 1–6 and 7–13.*

3. **READ AND CITE TEXT EVIDENCE**

C **ASK STUDENTS** to find the author's point of view about the topic and the evidence (details, facts, and examples) he uses to support it. *Students should cite textual evidence from lines 14–36, including references to specific evidence from lines 14–21.*

Critical Vocabulary: capacity (line 23) Have students explain *capacity* as Jones uses it here.

Critical Vocabulary: alliances (line 28) and **resentment** (line 30) Ask students to cite situations in which someone might make alliances with a group but then feel resentment.

4. **READ AND CITE TEXT EVIDENCE** Explain that the author's purpose is the reason the author writes something. In an informational text, the purpose may be to explain information or even to persuade the reader to agree with the author's point of view.

D **ASK STUDENTS** to read their margin notes to a partner and then explain the author's purpose for including the diagram, labels, and caption, as well as the chart on the next page. *By presenting graphic and textual evidence about animals' brains, Jones is illustrating his point of view about the capacity of some animals to feel and think.*

Critical Vocabulary: ingenious (line 39) Have students explain *ingenious* as Jones uses it here. Why does he use the word to describe Betty the crow? *Jones wants to show that the bird has the ability to problem-solve and even to make a tool, suggesting the capacity of the bird to think.*

The chart and caption demonstrate that brain size does not indicate an animal's intelligence.

Brain Weights of Different Species	
Species	Brain Weight
Elephant	6,000 grams
Adult Human	1,350 grams
Monkey	97 grams
Dog	72 grams
Cat	30 grams
Owl	2.2 grams

Some insects, despite having a brain the size of a pinhead, can seemingly behave as intelligently as bigger animals. Larger animals need larger brains to interpret more sensory information and to control their greater number of muscles.

50 What these examples seem to show is that animals are more like us than we may have once thought. It seems clear that animals can feel a range of emotions. It seems just as clear that some animals show an uncanny ability to do what appears to be "thinking."

5. **◀ REREAD AND DISCUSS** Reread lines 37–53. With a small group, discuss whether the facts and examples the author cites provide sufficient support for his point of view. Be sure to consider the information presented in the diagram, chart, and captions.

SHORT RESPONSE

Cite Text Evidence Write a summary of the article. Review your reading notes, and **cite text evidence** in your summary.

Scientists now think that animals, such as mammals and birds, can feel emotions and actually think. Dogs and elephants appear to show emotions, and chimpanzees and pigs can act in clever, thoughtful ways. A crow shaped a wire into a tool that could help her get food. So, having a large brain is not necessary for thinking. Animals certainly seem capable of thinking and feeling.

28

5. **REREAD AND DISCUSS USING TEXT EVIDENCE** Jones offers graphic and textual evidence to support his point of view.

Ⓔ ASK STUDENTS to appoint a reporter for each group, then cite specific graphic and textual evidence to explain their position as to whether Jones's evidence is sufficient to support his point of view. *Students should cite specific evidence from the diagram and chart, as well as from lines 37–53.*

SHORT RESPONSE

Cite Text Evidence Student responses will vary, but students should use the central idea and supporting details from the text, as well as specific textual evidence, in their summaries. Students should:

- briefly state the central idea of the text as a whole and the details that support it.
- provide a summary distinct from personal opinions or judgments.
- cite specific evidence from the text to support the points made in the summary.

TO CHALLENGE STUDENTS . . .

For more context about animals' abilities and emotions, have students research interesting facts about crows. They can also find videos of Betty the crow online, as well as other videos showing crows using their intelligence in other ways, such as using passing traffic to break nuts.

ASK STUDENTS to share the information they discovered about crows, and how it compares with what they may have previously thought about these birds. *Students may present information about crows being social birds that sometimes live in roosts of hundreds of thousands of individuals. Crows are considered to be among the smartest and most adaptable birds; they can recognize guns and supposedly read traffic lights. They communicate with each other, and there are many tales of their being able to count.*

DIG DEEPER

With the class, return to Question 5, Reread and Discuss. Have students share the results of their discussion.

ASK STUDENTS whether they were pleased with the outcome of their small-group discussions. Have each group share what the majority opinion was regarding the sufficiency of the author's evidence to support his point of view. What convincing evidence did the groups cite from the text to support this opinion?

- Encourage students to tell whether there was any compelling evidence cited by group members holding the opposite opinion. If so, why didn't it sway the group?
- Have groups explain how they decided whether or not they had found sufficient evidence to support their opinion. Did everyone in the group agree as to what made the evidence sufficient? How did the group resolve any conflicts or differences of opinion?

After students have shared the results of their group's discussion, ask whether another group shared any findings they wish they had considered.

ASK STUDENTS to return to their summary of the article in their Short Response answer and to revise it based on the class discussion.

Animal Snoops: The Wondrous World of Wildlife Spies

Informational Text by Peter Christie

Why This Text?

Students will encounter an increasing variety of nonfiction texts as they progress through middle and high school. This lesson focuses on elements of nonfiction and the author's use of anecdotes as an effective way to provide information.

▶ **View It!**

Professional Development Podcast:

Informational Text

Key Learning Objective: The student will be able to analyze how anecdotes and text features contribute to the structure of a text.

For practice and application:

Bats!

Science Writing by Mary Kay Carson

Close Reader selection
"Bats!"
Science Writing by Mary Kay Carson

RI 1 Cite textual evidence; make inferences.

RI 2 Determine central idea; provide a summary.

RI 3 Analyze text.

RI 4 Determine the meaning of words and phrases.

RI 5 Analyze structure.

RI 6 Determine author's purpose and explain how it is conveyed in the text.

RI 7 Integrate information.

W 2 Write informative/explanatory texts.

W 7 Conduct short research projects.

SL 1 Engage effectively in a range of collaborative discussions.

SL 5 Include multimedia components and visual displays in presentations.

L 2 Demonstrate command of capitalization.

L 4c Consult reference materials.

L 5 Demonstrate understanding of nuances in word meanings.

L 6 Acquire and use grade-appropriate words and phrases.

▲ Text Complexity Rubric

Quantitative Measures	**Animal Snoops: The Wondrous World of Wildlife Spies** Lexile: 1020L
Qualitative Measures	**Levels of Meaning/Purpose**  single topic
	Structure  implicit description text structure
	Language Conventionality and Clarity  some unfamiliar, academic, or domain-specific words
	Knowledge Demands  more difficult science concepts
Reader/Task Considerations	• Teacher determined • Vary by individual reader and type of text • See the Text X-Ray for suggested Reader/Task Considerations.

English Language Support Before teaching, use the Text X-Ray for an overview of the text's complexity. The Text X-Ray and the supports and scaffolds in the Teacher's Edition will help you guide students in different proficiencies and skill levels.

Meaning Making

Language Development

Effective Expression

Content Knowledge

Foundational Skills

Text Complexity: Qualitative Measures

Levels of Meaning/Purpose

single topic

Help students analyze anecdotes and other aspects of the text.

- Teacher's Edition side notes, pp. 117, 118, 119, 120, 121, 122, 123, 124, 125
- When Students Struggle, p. 121
- Strategies for Annotation, p. 125
- Analyze Text: Anecdote, p. 125

To reteach anecdote, see

- Analyze Text: Anecdote, p. 128h

 Use It! Interactive Whiteboard Lesson: Reading Informational Text

***ZOOM IN ON* ANALYZING ANECDOTES** Before students read, write the term *anecdote* on the board and help them define (*a brief narrative, or story, that often illustrates an important idea*). Tell students that the author uses anecdotes to help readers remember and visualize the information he conveys.

- Read aloud the anecdote in lines 128–140. Ask students to identify these elements: **setting** (*the East African savannah*); **character** (*the dik-dik*); **plot** (conflict: *threat the wild dog poses to the dik-dik*; climax: *the dik-dik's escape, thanks to the go-away bird*).
- Ask students what information the author conveys through this anecdote. (*Eavesdropping can sometimes save animals' lives.*)
- Remind students to look for other important ideas conveyed by anecdotes as they read the text.

Structure

implicit description text structure

Help students integrate information from different sources.

- Teacher's Edition side notes, pp. 117, 118, 119, 120, 121, 125
- Strategies for Annotation, p. 120
- Integrate Information, p. 125

 Use It! Level Up Tutorial: Synthesizing Information

***ZOOM IN ON* INTEGRATING INFORMATION** Review with students the definition of *integrate* on page 125. After students have read the text, ask them how the photograph and caption helped them better understand the topic.

- Have students work with a partner to reread the selection and identify other places where they would insert a photograph or other visual aid.
- Have pairs describe the images they would choose and explain how each would reinforce or add information to the main idea of that part of the text.

Language Conventionality and Clarity

some unfamiliar, academic, or domain-specific words

Teach unfamiliar vocabulary in context.

- Teacher's Edition Critical Vocabulary notes, pp. 117, 118, 119, 123, 127
- Applying Academic Vocabulary, p. 118
- Strategies for Annotation, p. 127
- Vocabulary Strategy: Synonyms, p. 127

Help students increase their facility with the language of informational text.

- Teacher's Edition side notes, pp. 123, 124, 128
- English Language Support, pp. 117, 122, 123, 124, 128
- Language Conventions: Capitalization, p. 128

***ZOOM IN ON* DEFINING COMPOUND WORDS** Tell students that this selection includes several **compound words,** two or more words joined together to form a new word. Explain that the meanings of these individual words can help readers define the compound word.

- List these words on the board: *wildlife* (line 31); *fireflies* (line 81); *nighttime* (line 89); *treetop* (line 151).
- Model how to define *wildlife* from the meanings of *wild* and *life*. *(creatures that live in the wild or wilderness)*
- Have pairs define the other three words and share their meanings. Encourage students to use this strategy when they encounter other compound words.

Knowledge Demands

more difficult science concepts

Support English learners in understanding the scientific concepts in the text.

- Teacher's Edition Author's note, p. 117
- Content-Area Connection, p. 119
- Performance Task, p. 126
- Student Edition footnotes, pp. 118, 119, 120, 121, 122, 123

***ZOOM IN ON* BUILDING SCIENTIFIC UNDERSTANDING** Explain that students may unfamiliar scientific terms or ideas in the text.

- Before students read, review the pronunciation of the names of different animals, such as langurs and macaques on page 123.
- Suggest that students note the names of unfamiliar animals and use the Internet and/or print references to find out more about them.
- Encourage students to use the footnotes to help them define unfamiliar terms. Ask a volunteer to read a footnote to the class.

Suggested Reader/Task Considerations

You might consider the following before assigning this informational text to students.

- Will students be able to visualize what is being described in the text?
- Will students be engaged by the text and motivated to read it?

***ZOOM IN ON* SUPPORTING COMPREHENSION**

- Have students use their eBook tools to highlight descriptive words and phrases as they read. At the end of each section, ask volunteers to explain the mental images evoked by the words and phrases they have identified.
- Before students begin, read the first four paragraphs aloud to introduce the author's style and to create interest in the topic. Then have students read with a partner. After they finish each passage, ask them what they have learned and what they predict the next passage will be about.

TEACH

CLOSE READ

Peter Christie Have students read the information about the author. Tell students that Christie studied both science and writing in college. Note that writers are often advised to "write what they know." Christie uses what he knows about science to inform readers, in an entertaining and easy-to-understand way, about scientific topics.

SETTING A PURPOSE Direct students to use the Setting a Purpose question to focus their reading. Remind students to write down questions that arise as they read.

Analyze Text: Anecdote RI 1, RI 3
(LINES 1–13)

Explain that an **anecdote** is a short account of an event. Tell students that authors often use anecdotes to make a point or to provide information in an entertaining and/or memorable way.

Ⓐ **CITE TEXT EVIDENCE** Have students identify what kind of evidence is given in lines 1–13, tell what idea it introduces, and explain how it fits into the text's structure. *(This anecdote is a good introduction because the descriptive language, the crime, and the memorable parrot catch readers' attention.)*

Integrate Information RI 5, RI 7
(HEADING)

Point out to students that the author uses headings within this text. A heading is just one type of **text feature,** or an element that helps organize or call attention to important information.

Ⓑ **ASK STUDENTS** to explain what or how the heading adds to the text. *(The heading introduces the parrot anecdote in a funny way with its repetition of words that begin with b. It helps readers get ready for a good story.)*

CRITICAL VOCABULARY

eavesdrop: Christie explains how the parrot behaved while thieves took things from the home. Instead of using *listening,* he uses *eavesdropping.*

ASK STUDENTS why it would be important to be quiet while eavesdropping on a conversation. *(Eavesdropping means to listen to something secretly. If you make noise, the people you are listening to might discover you.)*

Peter Christie (b. 1962) *loved exploring nature in the fields and streams of his native Canada as a child. As a freelance science author and editor, he enjoys writing for young people because they are naturally curious. Young people also love a good story, and for Christie, the best science writing is about telling a story. In his explorations of animal behavior and intelligence, Christie continues to find many stories to tell.*

from
ANIMAL SNOOPS:
The Wondrous World of Wildlife Spies

Informational Text by Peter Christie

SETTING A PURPOSE As you read, pay attention to the distinct ways animals snoop and spy on other animals in their environment and the reasons why they do this.

Presenting: The Bird-Brained Burglar Bust   Ⓑ

The house in Memphis, Tennessee, sat empty: the coast was clear for a robbery. Quickly and secretively, the three young burglars checked the windows and doors and found a way in. They piled up computers, DVD players, and other electronic equipment.

Ⓐ   The thieves talked as they worked, paying no attention to the parrot, nearly motionless in its cage. Only when the crooks were ready to make their getaway did the bird finally pipe up. "JJ," it said plainly. "JJ, JJ."

10   Marshmallow—a six-year-old green parrot—had been quietly **eavesdropping**. And the private-eye parrot had learned a thing or two, including the nickname of one of the robbers: J.J.

eavesdrop
(ēvz´drŏp´) *intr.v.* To *eavesdrop* is to listen secretly to others' private conversations.

Animal Snoops: The Wondrous World of Wildlife Spies   **117**

English Language Support

Analyze Language Explain that the author often uses informal language. Display lines 1–13.

- Help students identify and define idiomatic or slang expressions. *(the coast was clear, make their getaway, pipe up)*
- Have pairs use context clues to define the informal expressions. *("coast was clear": no one was around; "make their getaway": escape without being detected; "pipe up": speak)*

Analyze Text: Anecdote

RI 1, RI 3

(LINES 19–25)

Explain that authors use anecdotes to connect and support ideas in their writing in the same way they might use facts or examples.

C **CITE TEXT EVIDENCE** Have students reread lines 19–25. Ask them to tell what idea the author has introduced by using the anecdote about Marshmallow. (*The author has connected the anecdote with the central idea that animals are good at watching and listening to other animals (lines 23–25).*)

Analyze Structure

RI 1, RI 5

(LINES 29–34)

Point out that the author is presenting ideas about the nature of animal communication.

D **CITE TEXT EVIDENCE** Have students reread lines 29–34 and cite details that describe the nature of animal communication. Ask what effect the reference to social media has for the reader. (*Animal communication is often loud, bright, and easy to understand; it is like social media, where many people can see or read what you've written. The reference to social media makes the idea very understandable because most readers will have used social media.*)

CRITICAL VOCABULARY

foil: This word shows the effect of the bird's actions.

ASK STUDENTS how the bird's actions foil the thieves. (*The bird foils the thieves by saying the thief's name and making them think it will tell the police.*)

predator: Christie is telling why animals spy on each other. One reason is to learn about predators.

stake: The author explains that animals have something to gain or lose by eavesdropping.

ASK STUDENTS why an animal may want "early warning" about a predator and what might be at stake. (*If a predator wants to eat an animal, it would be good to know that soon because the animal's life might be at stake.*)

The burglars fled but soon realized that the parrot knew too much. "They were afraid the bird would stool[1] on them," said Billy Reilly, a local police officer. When the thieves returned to the crime scene to nab the bird, police captured them.

20 **C** The Memphis crooks hadn't counted on Marshmallow's talents as an eavesdropper. Why would they? Few people imagine that animals can be highly skilled spies and snoops. Yet nature is filled with them.

More and more, scientists are discovering that creatures—from bugs to baboons—are experts at watching, listening, and prying into the lives of other animals. While Marshmallow's eavesdropping helped to **foil** human criminals, wild spies work for their own benefit. Spying can be the best or fastest way to find food or a mate, or get early warning of a **predator**.

30 **D** Until recently, researchers preferred to think of communication between animals as similar to two people talking privately. But wildlife sounds and signals are often loud or bright enough that it is easy for others to listen in. It's like having conversations on social media that every one of your friends—and maybe some of your enemies—can read.

Animal messages are often detected by audiences that were not meant to get wind of[2] them. Hungry gopher snakes, for example, use foot-drumming signals between kangaroo rats to locate a snaky snack. Female chickadees listen in on singing contests of territorial[3] males when choosing a mate.

40 Biologists call it eavesdropping. It sounds sneaky, but it works well. And some animals are doubly sneaky, changing their behavior when they expect to be overheard. The animal communication network is far more complicated than researchers used to believe.

The **stakes** in wild spy games are high. Eavesdropping can determine whether animals mate, find a home, or enjoy a sneaky life instead of meeting sudden death. It can reveal

foil
(foil) *tr.v.* If you *foil* someone, you stop that person from being successful at something.

predator
(prĕd´ə-tər) *n.* A *predator* is an animal that survives by eating other animals.

stake
(stāk) *n.* A *stake* is something that can be gained or lost in a situation, such as money, food, or life.

---

[1] **stool**: a slang term meaning to tell on someone else, especially to spy on someone or to inform the police; to be a stool pigeon.
[2] **get wind of**: to learn of or find out about.
[3] **territorial** (tĕr´ĭ-tôr´ē-əl): displaying the behavior of defending an area, or territory, from other animals.

118 Collection 2

APPLYING ACADEMIC VOCABULARY

environment	benefit

THINK-PAIR-SHARE Have students work with a partner to discuss the following questions. Encourage them to use the academic vocabulary words *environment* and *benefit* in their responses. Then ask volunteers to share their responses with the class.

- What role does the **environment** of the animals mentioned in the text play in their spying?
- How does spying or eavesdropping **benefit** each animal?

whom they should trust and even affect the evolution of songs and signals.

50   Naturally clever secret agents learn things from snooping that help them survive and pass their genes to the next generation. It's one more tool that crafty creatures use to understand the world around them.

Ⓔ ## The Hungry Spy: Spying and Prying Predators

The path home was one the eastern chipmunk had traveled a hundred times before: under the ferns to the narrow tunnel into his burrow. The small animal ran briskly through the quiet Pennsylvania forest.

Suddenly, a flash and a sting. The startled chipmunk jumped. Dried leaves scattered. A sharp pain seared his
60   haunches.[4] Scrambling away, he glimpsed the motionless length of a timber rattlesnake.

The ambush had succeeded. The deadly serpent had lain coiled and still for many hours, waiting. Even now, after striking, the snake was in no hurry. She would track down the chipmunk's lifeless body after her venom had done its work.

Patience is among the most practiced skills of a rattlesnake. Snooping is another. Before choosing an ambush site, timber rattlesnakes study the habits of their prey. Using their highly sensitive, flickering tongues, the snakes use scent
70   clues to reveal the routines of rodents and other tasty animals.

Ⓖ

Their tongues are so remarkable that they also pry into the hunting habits of other rattlesnakes. Scenting the difference between a recently fed rattlesnake and a hungry one, they use the clues to hide where another snake has dined and the hunting is likely to be successful.

For many animals, snooping and spying can mean the difference between a full stomach and starvation. Some creatures, like the rattlesnake, spy on the habits of their prey. Others **intercept** private communication—and think of the
80   signals as a call to supper.

Photinus fireflies, for instance, broadcast their mating messages with a light show. These plant-eating beetles flash

intercept
(ĭn′tər-sĕpt′) *v.* To *intercept* is to stop or interrupt something.

---

[4] **haunches** (hônch′əz): the hips, buttocks, and upper thighs of an animal.

CONTENT-AREA CONNECTION

Science Display the quotation on page 71 that introduces this collection: "Each species, however inconspicuous and humble . . . is a masterpiece." Help students connect the ideas they have discussed with this observation.

Activity Have students work in pairs to choose one animal in this selection that best exemplifies the idea expressed in the quotation. Have them consult print and digital resources to learn more about how this animal communicates. Ask pairs to create posters showing the major aspects of the animal's communication system. Encourage them to integrate illustrations or diagrams. Have pairs present their posters to the class.

TEACH

CLOSE READ

Integrate Information
RI 5, RI 7

(HEADINGS)

Direct students' attention to the heading. Note that this is the second boldface red heading the author has included in the selection.

Ⓔ **ASK STUDENTS** to explain what this heading tells them about the next section of the text and how it connects to the first section. (*This heading tells readers that the focus of this section will be on how predators use communication. The first section was more general and explained that animal communication is complicated; the second section gives more specific examples about predator communication.*)

Analyze Text: Anecdote
RI 1, RI 3

(LINES 54–70)

Remind students that authors often use anecdotes to illustrate important ideas.

Ⓕ **CITE TEXT EVIDENCE** Have students reread lines 54–70, identify the central idea, and explain how the idea is illustrated in the text. (*The central idea is how one predator finds and ambushes its prey; the anecdote in lines 54–65 shows this.*) Then ask students to share words or phrases that make the anecdote interesting or memorable and to tell why. (*Memorable language might be "path home," "under the ferns," "narrow tunnel," or "a flash and a sting"; the language places the chipmunk in a place that is familiar to it and then suddenly describes the quick attack of the snake.*)

Ⓖ **CITE TEXT EVIDENCE** Have students explain how the snake found its prey and point out the information in the text. (*The snake used its tongue to find scent clues that told it where the rodent often traveled.*)

> **CRITICAL VOCABULARY**

intercept: The author is making a distinction between animals that spy on other animals and animals that intercept signals that other animals are making or sending.

ASK STUDENTS to describe how an animal might intercept another animal's communication.

CLOSE READ

Analyze Text: Anecdote
RI 1,
RI 3

(LINES 90–96)

Point out to students that the author often introduces an anecdote by describing the animal's location.

H **CITE TEXT EVIDENCE** Have students cite sensory words in lines 90–96 that help them imagine the setting, and tell how this language elaborates on ideas in the text. (*still-frigid, tuneless chorus, Waug, waug, waug, ice has barely loosed its grip, marsh-bottom muck; Picturing the setting helps connect the anecdote to the idea of intercepted signals more easily.*)

Integrate Information
RI 5,
RI 7

(PHOTO, CAPTION, LINES 85–89)

Explain that photographs and captions are other types of text features. Photographs provide visual information. Captions can provide new information or reinforce information in the text. Captions are often paired with visual features such as photos.

I **ASK STUDENTS** to reread lines 85–89, explain why the photograph and caption fit into the section "The Hungry Spy: Spying and Prying Predators," and tell how these elements help them better understand the text. (*The photograph shows a firefly that becomes a meal because a different kind of firefly—a predator—looks for the flashes of the smaller firefly and eats it. Together, the photo and the caption help the reader better understand how the signal of one animal can be intercepted and used by a predator to find its prey.*)

luminescent[5] abdomens to wow potential mates on warm North American summer nights.

A bigger relative is named *Photuris*. They also blink biological tail lights during courtship, but are not always looking for a mate. These fireflies are predators that eat their smaller *Photinus* cousins. They spy on their blinking prey and follow the flashing beacon to a nighttime meal.

90 In the still-frigid early spring of northern Europe, a male moor frog begins his tuneless chorus: *Waug, waug, waug.*

H Not minding that the ice has barely loosed its grip on the pond edge, the frog has emerged from wintering beneath marsh-bottom muck. He's all set to attract female moor frogs the moment they wake from chilly months of sleep.

Waug, waug, waug… **WHAM!**

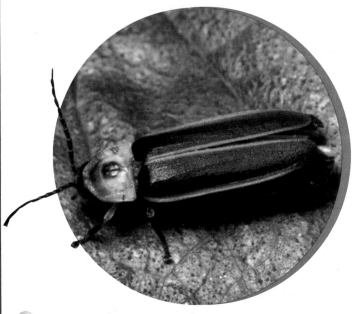

I A flashing *Photinus* firefly looks good to his mate—but he looks delicious to his *Photuris* cousin!

©Scott Camazine/Alamy Images

---
[5] **luminescent** (lo͞o′mə-nĕs′ənt): brightly lit up.

120 Collection 2

Strategies for Annotation 🖊 📋 Annotate it!

Integrate Information
RI 5,
RI 7

Have students use their eBook annotation tools to analyze the text. Ask students to do the following:

- Highlight in yellow each photograph and/or caption.
- Find text that corresponds to the photograph and caption. Underline that text.
- Write a note that sums up the additional information the photograph and caption provide.

A flashing **Photinus** firefly looks good to his mate—but he looks delicious to his **Photuris** cousin!

looking for a mate. These fireflies are <u>predators that eat their smaller *Photinus* cousins.</u> They spy on their blinking prey and follow the flashing beacon to a nighttime meal.

With a lightning strike, the long, lance-like bill of a white stork jabs through the marsh grass and snatches up the singing frog. In an instant, the tireless music-maker becomes the dinner of a spy.

White storks are master eavesdroppers. They rely on the songs of moor frogs to guide them when they're hunting. The birds are so skillful that they can stealthily follow frog sounds to within two or three strides of an unsuspecting singer.

Some spies can intercept signals sent by plants. Bright flowers invite bees and other animals to come for a meal of pollen or nectar (and to pollinate the plants at the same time). Scientists believe that the most symmetrical flowers—where each half mirrors the other like two sides of a face—help bees and birds recognize them as healthy, with top-quality pollen and nectar.

But crab spiders are deadly spies: they love to eat honeybees and know all about this flower-bee communication system. These sneaky spiders build their bee-trapping webs next to good-looking, symmetrical blooms that bees are more likely to visit.

Deep Secrets Overheard

Tick, tick, creak.

In the eerie, deep-water gloom off the coast of Norway, an enormous sperm whale makes mysterious noises before it abruptly rakes its toothy mouth through a school of swimming squid.

Scientists believe the whale is using echolocation[6]—in the same way bats use echoes of their ultrasonic[7] chirps to "see" in the dark. The whale's ticks and creaks help it zero in on prey.

But the sounds may also help distant sperm whales to find a good meal. The whales' echolocation sounds travel far, farther than the length of Manhattan Island. Sly sperm whales may eavesdrop to learn where another whale is hunting successfully, and drop by for lunch.

---

[6] **echolocation** (ĕk´ō-lō-kā´shən): a system used by some animals to locate objects around them; the animals produce high-pitched sounds and "listen" for the sounds to come back.

[7] **ultrasonic** (ŭl´trə-sŏn´ĭk): not able to be heard by humans; above the range of sound waves that humans can hear.

Animal Snoops: The Wondrous World of Wildlife Spies **121**

CLOSE READ

Analyze Text: Anecdote   RI 3

(LINES 105–115)

Direct students' attention to lines 105–115.

J ASK STUDENTS to tell how the information in these paragraphs is similar to or different from earlier information about other animal spies. *(A crab spider figures out where its prey is and then waits there, just like the timber rattlesnake does. The crab spider does not use its sense of smell, though. It recognizes which flowers bees like and builds a web near them to catch bees as they fly to the flowers.)*

Integrate Information   RI 4, RI 7

(HEADING, LINES 116–127)

Point out the boldface, red heading that introduces a new section.

K ASK STUDENTS to reread the heading and the three paragraphs that follow it. Have them explain how the heading introduces or gives a hint about the text. *(The word "Deep" hints at the fact that the text talks about ocean-dwelling animals. "Overheard" and "Tick, tick, creak" hint at the idea that whales listen in on the sounds of other whales to find food.)*

WHEN STUDENTS STRUGGLE...

For each anecdote, have students fill out a chart to keep track of how various animals communicate or use spying to survive. Have individuals fill in the chart after they reread lines 90–100. Have partners compare their charts and go back to the text if their details don't match.

 LEVEL UP TUTORIALS For additional support, assign the following *Level Up* tutorial: **Reading for Details.**

Animal	How and Why It Communicates	How and Why It Spies
moor frog	sings to attract mate	
white stork		listens to moor frog's song to hunt and eat

Analyze Text: Anecdote   RI 3

(LINES 128–134)

Explain that when authors describe a setting, it is important that they include details to which readers can easily relate. Readers need to be able to picture what the author is describing.

L ASK STUDENTS to explain why the author mentions a Labrador dog in the anecdote. *(The author mentions a Labrador dog because it is reasonably familiar to readers and will help them understand the size of a dik-dik more clearly. This, in turn, helps readers understand why the dik-dik relies on a bird sitting in a tree to alert it to danger.)*

English Language Support

Analyze Language Write the following on the board: "The insistent cry had an electric effect on the dik-dik." (line 135)

- Ask students what the word *electric* means in this context. Elicit from students synonyms that could replace the word. *(instant, shocking, sudden)*

- Repeat the sentence using each word that volunteers suggest. Ask students to explain how each synonym changes the impact of the sentence.

Live and Let Die: Spying and Prying to Stay Alive

The tiny antelope jerked his head up to listen.

He was a Gunther's dik-dik, a miniature antelope no larger
130 than a Labrador dog. The tall grasses of the East African
savannah[8] surrounded him like a curtain: he was well hidden
from leopards and hyenas, but predators were also concealed
from him. Through the chattering of birds and insects, the
dik-dik recognized a familiar sound: *Gwaa, gwaa, gwaa.*

The insistent cry had an electric effect on the dik-dik.
He leaped and bolted through the grass. The fleeing animal
glimpsed the source of the sound—on a nearby tree sat a
white-bellied go-away bird, sentinel of the savannah. Beyond
it, barely visible above the grass, were the large black ears of a
140 hunting wild dog.

Go-away birds are known for their noisy alarm call; the
gwaa is thought by some to sound like a person shouting
"g'away." These social birds feed together in chattering groups.
A loud, urgent *gwaa* cry is a signal to other go-away birds that
an eagle, wild dog, or other predator has been spotted nearby.

Many of these dangerous hunters also eat dik-diks.
The wary antelopes use every trick in the book to avoid
becoming a meal—including eavesdropping on go-away bird
communication. Unable to see far on the grassy savannah,
150 dik-diks rely on the birds, which spot approaching predators
from treetop lookouts.

For many animals, spying is a life-and-death business.
Creatures that catch warning signals meant for others may
stay one step ahead of enemies. Iguanas on the Galápagos
Islands, for instance, keep their ears open even though they
never utter a sound themselves.

Galápagos marine iguanas feed on algae in the sea. When
they're basking on rocks along the shore, young iguanas are
a prime target for hungry Galápagos hawks. Another favorite
160 hawk meal is the Galápagos mockingbird, but these birds
have something to say about it: a distinctive chirp warns
other mockingbirds a hawk is approaching. Marine iguanas

---

[8] **savannah** (sə-văn´ə): a flat grassland environment, located in or near the tropics.

English Language Support

Reading Closely Display page 123 and highlight the dashes used in lines 171, 175, 184, and 195. Explain that dashes draw attention to the words that follow; the phrases or clauses set off by a dash often add information about another word in the sentence.

- Read each sentence that contains a dash aloud. Ask students to explain what they learn from the expression set off by the dash.

- Have pairs suggest two other sentences on this page in which a dash could emphasize and set off words or phrases add more explanation. Let partners take turns writing sentences on the board.

- Ask students to rewrite each sentence without a dash. Then have partners explain the punctuation they used and the effect of the change on the sentence.

eavesdrop on mockingbird conversations. They can tell the alarm from other songs and calls and will dash for cover when they hear it.

Some animal snoops are born recognizing the warning signals of different creatures; others, such as bonnet macaques, have to learn. These monkeys of southern India often pal around with langur monkeys. Langurs are good lookouts, and
170 macaques will quickly scramble up a tree when they overhear a langur warning cry—as long as the macaques have learned the correct langur language.

Scientists say bonnet macaques at one animal reserve[9] respond to recorded Nilgiri langur alarm shrieks but are slower to flee after a similar cry by Hanuman langurs—which would rarely be seen there. Farther north, only Hanuman langurs are common and bonnet macaques there have learned the opposite langur language. They jump at the sound of Hanuman warnings but are less bothered by Nilgiri cries.

180 Eavesdropping on the alarm signals of other animals is useful, but spying on predators directly also has advantages. Geometrid moths, for instance, are slow, night-flying moths that can be easily overtaken by hunting bats. To make up for their sluggish speed, the moths have espionage skills—they can track bat radar.

Many moths are stone deaf, but geometrid moths have ears that tune into the ultrasonic frequency bats use when navigating by echolocation. Not only can they hear a bat approaching, geometrid moths can also tell how close it is.
190 If a bat is nearer than two bus lengths away, a moth will begin evasive zigzag flying. Closer than one bus length and the moth folds its wings and **plummets** to the ground, where the bat won't follow.

plummet
(plŭm´ ĭt) v. If you _plummet_, you fall straight down, suddenly and steeply.

Pop and Stop

The seagrass is alive with the sound of music.

Singing fish—male Gulf toadfish—are performing their bizarre courtship serenade in the azure waters off the coast of Florida: _Grunt, grunt, trrrrrrt._ It's a song only a female

---

[9] **animal reserve:** an area of land that is protected to preserve wild animals that are often rare or endangered.

Animal Snoops: The Wondrous World of Wildlife Spies   **123**

CLOSE READ

Analyze Language
RI 1, RI 4
(LINES 166–172)

Explain to students that the author, Peter Christie, is known for making complex scientific topics interesting to read about and understandable for his nonscientific readers. To accomplish this, he uses somewhat informal language that is familiar to most readers.

CITE TEXT EVIDENCE Ask students to identify an example of informal language in this paragraph. Then have them tell what effect the language has on the text. (_The phrase "pal around" is informal; it helps readers understand that the two types of monkeys share a friendly relationship._)

Analyze Text: Anecdote
RI 1, RI 3, RI 4
(LINES 194–197)

Remind students that the author has used a number of anecdotes to present information about how animals communicate.

CITE TEXT EVIDENCE Have students reread lines 194–197, identify clues that tell them this is the beginning of an anecdote, and explain how the anecdote will add to the ideas in the text. (_It tells about a specific animal; it describes a setting, like a story does; it includes sound words, which earlier anecdotes have included. It will add more information about animals' signals to each other._)

CRITICAL VOCABULARY

plummet: Christie describes how a moth escapes from a predator.

ASK STUDENTS to distinguish between falling to escape an enemy and plummeting to escape an enemy. (_Falling implies a slower or less purposeful descent. Plummeting implies a fast, straight, downward descent that might more successfully leave a predator behind._)

Analyze Text

RI 1,
RI 3

(LINES 200–206)

○ **ASK STUDENTS** to reread lines 200–206 and then explain how this example of animal spying is similar to or different from another example in the selection. *(Possible response: This example is similar to that of the male moor frog, whose mating song attracts not only females of the species but also potential predators. This example is different in that the singing toadfish also intercepts a signal from its predator, the bottlenose dolphin, and will stop singing as soon as it knows a dolphin is near.)*

COLLABORATIVE DISCUSSION Have partners or small groups review the selection, section by section, and list the different types of communication and spying described in the selection. Ask students to draw conclusions about whether the communication habits described are evidence of animal intelligence. Remind students to cite evidence from the text to support their ideas.

ASK STUDENTS to share any questions they generated in the course of reading and discussing the selection.

English Language Support

Exchange Ideas and Information To help students prepare for their Collaborative Discussion activity, provide these sentence stems and explain their purposes:

- *to state the conclusion*: The way in which animals communicate (is/is not)_____.
- *to state the reason for this conclusion*: I think this because _____.
- *to present supporting evidence*: One example that supports my conclusion is _____. Another example that supports my conclusion is _____.

toadfish could like… unless an appreciative bottlenose dolphin is also in the audience.

200   Dolphins love to eat toadfish, and they eavesdrop on the singing fish to find their dinner. But the dolphins aren't the only spies in the sea: the toadfish spy on the dolphins, too. Dolphins make a low-frequency "pop" sound when they use sonar to reveal toadfish hidden under dense seagrass. The fish listen for popping from hunting dolphins, and stop singing when the sound gets near.

COLLABORATIVE DISCUSSION With a partner or a small group, discuss facts and examples in the text that illustrate animals' abilities to snoop on other animals. Discuss whether or not these examples prove that animals have intelligence.

FOR STUDENTS WITH DISABILITIES

Some students may struggle to hear the post-reading discussion. Use these strategies to facilitate their participation and comprehension:

- Arrange chairs in a circle so that all students face each other when they speak.
- Remind students that only one person should speak at a time.
- Write key ideas that come up in the discussion on the board.
- Consider holding an online text discussion.

Analyze Text: Anecdote

RI 3

Peter Christie begins *Animal Snoops* with an anecdote about a parrot that helped police officers catch some burglars. An **anecdote** is a short account of an event that is usually intended to entertain or make a point. Authors often use an anecdote to introduce or give an example of an important idea in a way that is easy to understand and remember. Think about how the anecdote in *Animal Snoops* introduces animals' observation of other animals and the issue of animal intelligence. Look for more anecdotes as you analyze *Animal Snoops*.

Integrate Information

RI 5, RI 7

Authors of nonfiction texts often include features that draw the readers' attention or provide information in visual ways. For example, a text may contain larger or darker type that highlights certain ideas. These are **text features,** or elements such as boldface type, headings, and subheadings, that help organize and call attention to important information. Text features help readers better understand a text and its topic. Text features also include:

Photographs	Captions
visual records of real people and objects in real settings. Photographs help readers understand exactly what something looks like.	brief explanations of what is in a photograph. Captions can indicate how the photographs relate to the text.

Good readers integrate the information in text features, such as photos and captions, with the information in the text. To **integrate,** or synthesize, information means to take individual pieces of information and combine them in order to develop a coherent understanding of a topic. Think about the new or important ideas you learned as you read this text. How does the author use photographs and captions to help clarify those ideas?

Look for more examples of text features, including photographs and captions, as you analyze *Animal Snoops*. Be sure to synthesize the information in the text and in each text feature to gain a better understanding of what you read.

CLOSE READ

Analyze Text: Anecdote

RI 3

Tell students that both writers and speakers—including teachers—use anecdotes. Help students understand that even though Peter Christie's anecdotes are made up, they do describe events that could happen. His descriptive language and storytelling style make the anecdotes both interesting to read and easy to remember.

Have students share details that they remember from *Animal Snoops*. Discuss what elements they remember most readily and how the visual images and sound effects that Christie includes in his anecdotes play a part in helping them recall information.

Integrate Information

RI 5, RI 7

Review text features with students and discuss what their purpose is. Explain that text features such as headings and subheadings are organizers; they tell readers what's coming up. Boldface words have meaning that is important to the overall topic. Photographs and captions add interest and provide more information.

Briefly review *Animal Snoops* with students and talk about the role that specific text features play in the selection.

Strategies for Annotation
Annotate it!

Analyze Text: Anecdote

RI 3

Share these strategies for guided or independent analysis:

- Within each anecdote, highlight in yellow the name of the predator, the hunting animal.
- Highlight in blue the name of the prey, the hunted animal.
- Underline words or phrases that tell how the predator spies to catch its meal or how the prey spies to avoid being eaten.
- Use a note to emphasize facts that are especially interesting to you.

Suddenly, a flash and a sting. The startled chipmunk jumped. Dried leaves scattered. A sharp pain seared his haunches. Scrambling away, he glimpsed the motionless length of a timber rattlesnake.

The ambush had succeeded. The deadly serpent had lain coiled and still for many hours, waiting. Even now, after...

PRACTICE & APPLY

Analyzing the Text
RI 1, RI 2,
RI 3, RI 4,
RI 5, RI 7

Possible answers:

1. *The anecdote introduces the ideas that animals listen to and watch other animals and humans and that they also communicate in different ways.*

2. *Animals are like spies and snoops because they are experts at finding out about other animals. Like human spies and snoops who listen to what other people say and do and report about them, animals listen to or watch other animals and either take action or give warnings about what they see, hear, or smell.*

3. *The statement means that if the animals are not successful at detecting enemies or finding prey, it could mean that they get killed by predators, do not find a mate, cannot find food to eat, or will not find a home.*

4. *Spying helps animals stay alive in two ways. One way is that spying helps them find food to eat. For example, some fireflies follow the lights of other, smaller fireflies and then catch and eat them. Storks follow the sound of frogs' mating songs to find the frogs and eat them. Spying also lets animals know where their enemies are so they can stay safe from them. For example, the dik-dik antelope listens for warning signals from white-bellied go-away birds, which mean danger is near. Iguanas avoid getting eaten by hawks by listening for the alarm calls of mockingbirds.*

5. *A rattlesnake gathers information using its tongue to detect scents. A sperm whale gathers information using its own sounds. Both animals gather information to find prey.*

6. *The photo shows what a Photinus firefly looks like. The caption reinforces the idea that the firefly's flashing light looks good to both a mate and a predator.*

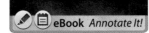

Analyzing the Text
RI 1, RI 2, RI 3,
RI 4, RI 5, RI 7,
W 2, W 6, W 7,
SL 5

Cite Text Evidence   Support your responses with evidence from the text.

1. **Analyze** The author uses an anecdote to introduce the topic. What important ideas are illustrated in the anecdote?

2. **Infer** The author refers to the animals in the text as spies and snoops. What does he mean by this?

3. **Interpret** In line 45, the author says "The stakes in wild spy games are high." What does this statement mean?

4. **Summarize** Review lines 128–193. What is the central idea of this section? Explain how the author elaborates on this idea.

5. **Compare** A rattlesnake and a sperm whale find their prey in different ways. Review lines 54–75 and lines 116–127. How does each animal gather information? How does each use that information?

6. **Synthesize** What important idea does the photograph and caption of the firefly (below line 96) help you understand?

PERFORMANCE TASK

Media Activity: Informative Presentation Do research to find out more about an animal mentioned in *Animal Snoops.*

- Choose one animal from the text.
- Do research to find more information about the animal, including its environment and its behavior.

- Use both print and digital sources for your research.
- Synthesize the information from the text with your research to present a slideshow presentation that describes the animal and how it lives. Include photographs with captions in your presentation.

PERFORMANCE TASK
W 2, W 6,
W 7, SL 5

Assign this performance task.

Media Activity: Informative Presentation Have students work independently. Provide this guidance:

- Remind students to view and evaluate digital resources.
- Have students use a KWL chart to organize their ideas, recording what they know (K), questions (what they want to know—W), and what they learn (L).

- Ask students to use text features such as headings, photographs, and captions.

Critical Vocabulary

L 4c, L 5, L 6

| eavesdrop | foil | predator | stake | intercept | plummet |

Practice and Apply Describe what is alike and different about the two words in each pair.

1. *eavesdrop* and *listen*

2. *foil* and *intercept*

3. *stake* and *reward*

4. *predator* and *enemy*

5. *plummet* and *fall*

Vocabulary Strategy: Synonyms

A **synonym** is a word that has the same meaning or similar meaning as another word. However, the words are not all interchangeable. For example, the word *big* has many synonyms, such as *large, bulky, huge*, and *enormous*. You can have a big appetite, but you would not have a bulky appetite. You can use a **thesaurus,** or a book of synonyms, to find the precise word to describe *appetite*. Thesauruses are available in print and digital versions.

Look at how *eavesdrop* and its synonyms—*overhear* and *snoop*—are used in these sentences.

> The parrot decided to eavesdrop when it heard the burglars talking.

> The parrot happened to overhear the burglars.

> The neighbors decided to snoop in the backyard to see if the burglars dropped any valuables.

Does the sentence completed with *eavesdrop* mean exactly the same as the sentences completed with *overhear* and *snoop*? How are the meanings of the three sentences different?

Practice and Apply Read each sentence. Think about the meaning of the underlined word in each one. Then look up the word in a print or digital thesaurus. Choose a synonym that gives the sentence a more precise meaning. Discuss your choices with a partner.

1. Gopher snakes <u>notice</u> foot-drumming signals between kangaroo rats.

2. Some birds give out <u>noisy</u> warning signals when a predator is nearby.

3. Hunting bats can easily overtake the <u>slow,</u> night-flying geometrid moth.

PRACTICE & APPLY

Critical Vocabulary

L 4c, L 5, L 6

Possible answers:

1. *eavesdrop/listen; both are about using your ears to hear things; eavesdropping is about listening secretly.*

2. *foil/intercept; both tell about ways to affect someone else's progress; foil means to stop someone from being successful, while intercept simply means to interrupt, but not necessarily to cause what is happening to stop.*

3. *stake/reward; both tell about something of value to someone; stakes can be won or lost, and imply a risky activity of some kind; a reward is something that is earned and is usually associated with something positive.*

4. *predator/enemy; both tell about someone or something probably causing harm; a predator hunts another animal (prey) and eats it; an enemy may do different kinds of harm in different ways.*

5. *plummet/fall; both involve being in the air or upright and then ending up on the ground or not upright; plummet means falling fast and steeply; fall means simply moving downward, with no particular speed involved.*

Vocabulary Strategy: Synonyms

Possible answers:

1. *detect, perceive*

2. *blaring, piercing, shrill*

3. *sluggish, plodding, pokey, dawdling*

Strategies for Annotation 🖊 📋 *Annotate it!*

Synonyms

L 5

Share this strategy for guided or independent analysis:

- Explore the author's use of synonyms for "to listen."
- Highlight in pink each occurrence of a word or phrase that means the same or almost the same as "to listen" or "someone who listens."
- On a note, write more synonyms for "to listen" that you know.
- Review the synonyms and try using each of them in a sentence.

> More and more, scientists are discovering that creatures— from bugs to baboons—are experts at watching, listening, and prying into the lives of other animals. While Marshmallow's eavesdropping helped to **foil** human criminals, wild spies work for their own benefit. Spying can be the best or fa
>
> hear, attend

Language Conventions: Capitalization

L2

Remind students that many proper nouns name specific places, such as *America, Florida,* and *France.* Proper adjectives are formed from proper nouns. Some proper adjectives are formed by adding an ending to the noun: *American, Floridian.* Other proper adjectives have a slightly different form than the noun from which they are formed, like *French.* Guide students to form phrases with proper adjectives based on your state, region, city, and so on (for example, *Midwestern city,* or *Californian*). Write the phrases and talk about the capitalization of the proper adjectives.

Answers:

1. *Italian; My sister and I love Italian cooking.*

2. *British; Jamaica was formerly a British colony.*

3. *Pacific Northwest; The Pacific Northwest region of the United States has many national forests.*

4. *English; We visited the English countryside.*

5. *Austrian; We enjoyed strolling through the quaint Austrian village.*

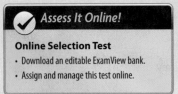

✓ Assess It Online!

Online Selection Test
- Download an editable ExamView bank.
- Assign and manage this test online.

Language Conventions: Capitalization

L2

In your writing, you will need to apply the rules of capitalization to proper adjectives. **Proper adjectives** are formed from **proper nouns**, which name specific people, places, and things. Proper adjectives are always capitalized and often end in the letters *n, an, ian, ese,* and *ish.* Many proper adjectives describe cultural references or locations.

In the following sentence from *Animal Snoops,* note how the proper adjective is capitalized.

> The tall grasses of the East African savannah surrounded him like a curtain: he was well hidden from leopards and hyenas, but predators were also concealed from him.

The chart shows two types of proper adjectives that require capitalization.

Type	Example
cultural references	*The Chinese dumplings were delicious. Erin is taking African dance lessons.*
location	*We live close to the Canadian border. During our trip, we visited many Midwestern cities.*

Practice and Apply Identify the proper adjectives that should be capitalized in each sentence. Then write the sentences correctly.

1. My sister and I love italian cooking.

2. Jamaica is formerly a british colony.

3. The pacific northwest region of the United States has many national forests.

4. We visited the english countryside.

5. We enjoyed strolling through the quaint austrian village.

English Language Support

Write Sentences Work with students to review the capitalization rules for proper adjectives.

- Assist students in identifying the proper adjective in each Practice and Apply sentence. Have them rewrite each sentence correctly.

- Direct pairs of students to lines 90, 116, and 168 in the text. Ask them to write each sentence using a proper adjective. Remind them that the proper adjective will appear before the noun it modifies, not after it. *(in the still-frigid early northern European spring; off the Norwegian coast; these southern Indian monkeys)*

- After students complete the Practice and Apply, ask them to rewrite the sentences using proper nouns. Have pairs compare their sentences and discuss how the change affects the flow and sound of the sentence. *(the cooking of Italy; a colony of Britain; the Pacific Northwest of the United States; the countryside of England; the quaint village in Austria)*

Taking Notes

TEACH

Explain to students that taking notes as they read will help them understand the text and remember information more fully. Point out that taking notes is especially useful when reading informational text. Explain these points:

- Taking notes can help you sort through information in a text and find the most important ideas.
- Use clues in the headings and subheadings to find big or important ideas.
- Write down only the most important details that support each big idea.
- Use as few words as possible to record ideas and details. Do not write ideas and details word-for-word from the text.
- Notes about a section of text should be much shorter than the actual text.

One way to take notes is to **categorize** information, or put ideas into groups. Point out to students that much of *Animal Snoops* concentrates on predators and prey. Have students record notes in a two-column list, with columns labeled "Predator" and "Prey."

PRACTICE AND APPLY

Review lines 54–65 of *Animal Snoops* with students. Create a two-column chart as shown and model entering "timber rattlesnake" in the Predator column and "chipmunk" in the Prey column.

Predator	Prey
timber rattlesnake	chipmunk

Assign individual students a section of *Animal Snoops*. Have them reread the section and take notes as described. Ask students assigned to the same section to meet and compare notes. Have a spokesperson from each group talk about differences in the individual notes as well as how the notes helped them remember the information.

Students may use this note-taking procedure when they read any informational text, whether for pleasure or for school assignments.

Analyze Text: Anecdote

RETEACH

Review the term *anecdote* and and revisit the first one in *Animal Snoops* (lines 1–18). Discuss these points:

- What animal is listening or spying? *(a parrot)*
- What is the result of the spying? *(The police catch thieves.)*
- What makes this anecdote a good beginning? *(It connects to the title,* Animal Snoops, *and to the topic of animal communication; the language is dramatic, like an action movie, which makes it engaging for the reader.)*
- How does the anecdote provide and connect to other information about the topic? *(It gives a concrete example of animal snooping and leads to a discussion of how animals listen to and watch other animals and humans.)*

Remind students that asking and answering these questions will help them remember the information in the text more easily.

Have partners review another anecdote in *Animal Snoops* and address the same set of questions. Have partners share information about their anecdote with the class. Remind them to explain how their anecdote is connected to a particular section of the text and why the author chose to include it there.

INDEPENDENT READING

Students can apply the skill to another piece of informational text written in a narrative or storytelling style. Students should remember that each anecdote, in addition to being engaging, provides information on the author's topic. After reading an anecdote, readers should pause and think about why the author included it. They can ask themselves questions such as these:

- Why did the author include this?
- What information does the anecdote provide?
- What makes the anecdote interesting or easy to remember?

English Language Support

Read Closely Have students use the Think-Write-Pair-Share strategy to analyze an anecdote they have read.

- *First,* direct students' attention to the three questions listed above.
- *Then,* have students write answers.
- *Next,* have them share answers with a partner.
- *Finally,* have students adjust and share their answers with the entire class.

Bats!

Science Writing by Mary Kay Carson

Background Have students read the background information about bats, the author Mary Kay Carson, and Bat Conservation International (BCI). Introduce the selection by reminding students that in cultures worldwide, people may tell scary stories or anecdotes about bats, such as that bats are the souls of sleeping people or that bats in a building means something evil will happen. Encourage students to share their own stories. Then, tell students that this article will give them real facts about what it turns out are pretty amazing creatures.

SETTING A PURPOSE Ask students to pay attention to the information given in the text and the information presented in photographs, illustrations, and charts. Tell them to note how visual elements add to their understanding of the text.

Standards Support

- cite textual evidence
- analyze how a key idea is introduced, illustrated, and elaborated in a text
- integrate information presented in different formats

Text Complexity Rubric

Quantitative Measures

Bats!
Lexile: 990

Qualitative Measures

Levels of Meaning/Purpose

single purpose, explicitly stated

Structure

some sophisticated graphics, occasionally essential to understanding the text

Language Conventionality and Clarity

some unfamiliar, academic, or domain-specific words

Knowledge Demands

some specialized knowledge required

Reader/Task Considerations

Teacher determined

Strategies for CLOSE READING

Integrate Information

Students should read this science essay carefully all the way through. Close-reading questions at the bottom of the page will help them to collect and cite text evidence to better understand the text. As they read, students should jot down comments or questions about the text in the margins.

WHEN STUDENTS STRUGGLE . . .

To help students integrate information in "Bats!," have them work in small groups to fill out a chart like the one shown below.

CITE TEXT EVIDENCE For practice in integrating information, ask students to tell what text evidence supports the facts given by the author.

Text Feature	Information It Provides
Selection Text (pages 29–34)	The text explains what makes bats such unique creatures.
A Bat's Body (page 30)	The illustrations and labels help convey what happens when bats fly and what happens if these parts are injured.
Echolocation: Seeing with Sound (page 33)	The graphic and text explains and clarifies the process of echolocation.
Batty Myths (page 34)	This feature gives examples of popular misconceptions about bats.

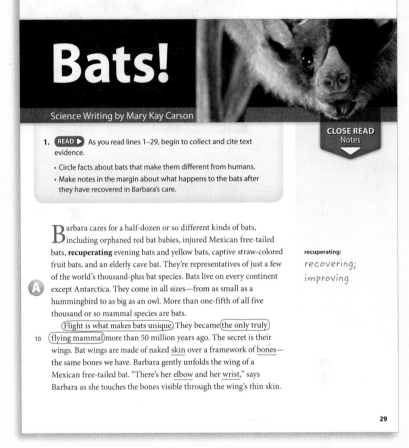

Bats!

Science Writing by Mary Kay Carson

CLOSE READ
Notes

1. **READ ▶** As you read lines 1–29, begin to collect and cite text evidence.

   • Circle facts about bats that make them different from humans.
   • Make notes in the margin about what happens to the bats after they have recovered in Barbara's care.

Barbara cares for a half-dozen or so different kinds of bats, including orphaned red bat babies, injured Mexican free-tailed bats, **recuperating** evening bats and yellow bats, captive straw-colored fruit bats, and an elderly cave bat. They're representatives of just a few of the world's thousand-plus bat species. Bats live on every continent except Antarctica. They come in all sizes—from as small as a hummingbird to as big as an owl. More than one-fifth of all five thousand or so mammal species are bats.

Flight is what makes bats unique. They became the only truly flying mammal more than 50 million years ago. The secret is their wings. Bat wings are made of naked skin over a framework of bones— the same bones we have. Barbara gently unfolds the wing of a Mexican free-tailed bat. "There's her elbow and her wrist," says Barbara as she touches the bones visible through the wing's thin skin.

recuperating:
recovering;
improving

29

---

1. **READ AND CITE TEXT EVIDENCE** The author tells readers that bats come in all sizes.

   Ⓐ ASK STUDENTS to find the examples cited by the author to prove that bats come in all sizes. *Bats can be as small as a hummingbird or as big as an owl.*

   Critical Vocabulary: recuperating (line 3) Have students share their definitions of *recuperating*. Ask why a recuperating bat might need the kind of help Barbara offers them. *Because the bats are recovering from some sort of injury, Barbara can help them get well faster and also determine when they are well enough to be set free.*

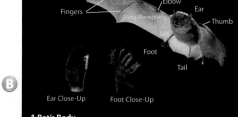

Arm
Elbow
Fingers
Ear
Wing Membrane
Thumb
Foot
Tail
Ear Close-Up
Foot Close-Up

A Bat's Body

A bat's body is adapted to its airborne lifestyle. Its flexible wings are made up of arm and hand bones covered in a thin hairless membrane of skin. The feet lock into a clamped position when the bat's asleep so it can hang from its roost while resting. And a bat's large ears help it hear the echoed sounds it bounces off prey and obstacles in flight.

maneuver:

to change movement or direction

Barbara releases the bats that are able to fly and feed themselves. The bats that can't fly or find food travel with Barbara as bat ambassadors.

"And her thumb," she continues, pointing to the small nub[1] halfway down the top of the wing. Bats are master fliers. Their flapping wings propel them forward with speed and **maneuver** them around trees,
20 after insects, and into crevices.[2]

When a bat can't fly, it's in trouble. Many of Barbara's bat patients have broken or hurt wings. "The wing injuries can often be treated," says Barbara. She sometimes does bat surgery, putting pins in the broken bones. "Finger injuries will heal well, but the upper arm is much harder," says Barbara. Only bats that can fly and catch insects on their own are released back into the wild. Outside the bat barn is a big flight cage where recuperating bats exercise and can catch bugs. When—and if—they can feed themselves, Barbara releases them back into the wild. Those that can't make it on their own become bat ambassadors, traveling with Barbara to events that teach people the truth about bats.
30 Bats are unique among mammals in other ways besides flight. In general, the bigger the mammal, the longer it lives. An elephant might live seventy years, a dog fifteen years, or a hamster only two years.

---

[1] **nub:** bump, bony protrusion.
[2] **crevices:** small gaps.

Bats break this rule. Even small bats can live forty or more years. For their size, bats are the longest-lived mammals on earth. Bats also reproduce slowly for their size. A mouse might have dozens of babies per year. Most kinds of bats give birth only once a year to a single pup. "One lost bat baby is a lost generation," says Barbara.

While the bat babies get milk, most adults in the bat barn eat live mealworms. "They're live beetle **larvae**," says Barbara. "I order eighty
40 thousand mealworms a month." Most North American bats are insect-eaters. They have mouths full of sharp teeth to quickly crunch up insects as they fly. Each of the 1,100 different kinds of bats is especially adapted to the particular food it eats. Fruit-eating bats have big eyes and powerful noses to see and smell the ripe tropical fruit available year round. Nectar-eating bats also live in warm places with year-round flowers. They have long noses and tongues to reach deep into flowers and slurp up nectar. There are bats that snag fish with their strong-clawed feet, bats that catch birds in midair, and even bats that ambush mice on the ground! The infamous vampire bats of
50 Central and South America drink the blood of mammals and birds.

Most bats do their eating at night. They are nocturnal animals. So how do bats manage to fly around and find their food in the dark? Many fruit-eating bats have extra-big eyes, just like other nocturnal creatures. The African straw-colored fruit bats that Barbara cares for have dog-like faces—the reason these kinds of bats are often called flying foxes. "They depend on their eyesight and sense of smell to find fruit," explains Barbara.

larvae:

young, wingless, often wormlike form of an insect

---

2. ◀ **REREAD** Reread lines 9–18. Underline the parts of a bat's body that humans also have. Study the image of the bat. How does showing body parts similar to a human's help you better understand a bat's body? Support your answer with explicit textual evidence.

A bat's body is like a human's because they both have common parts: arms, fingers, and ears. But humans do not have wings or large ears that help them find food.

3. **READ** ▶ As you read lines 30–85, continue to cite textual evidence.

• Underline text that explains how bats get food, including their use of sound.
• Make brief notes about echolocation in the margin.

Critical Vocabulary: maneuver (line 17) The text says that *maneuvering* is something that helps bats get around trees, find insects, and get into small places. Have students share examples of when they had to maneuver in order to do something or get someplace. Then, ask students to share their definitions of *maneuver*.

FOR ELL STUDENTS Clarify the meaning of *ambassadors* in this context. Explain that in politics, an ambassador is the representative of a country's government in another country. In this text, the bats that can't fly "represent" all the other bats in Barbara's events and lectures.

2. **REREAD AND CITE TEXT EVIDENCE**

B **ASK STUDENTS** to explain how the information in the graphic helps them understand the information in lines 13–24. *Seeing the bat's fingers, arm, elbow, and other parts helps me to understand how it flies and what happens when these parts are injured.*

3. **READ AND CITE TEXT EVIDENCE**

C **ASK STUDENTS** to cite text evidence in lines 39–50 that shows how different bats have adapted to eat different foods. *North American bats have sharp teeth to crunch insects as they fly; fruit-eating bats have big eyes and powerful noses to see and smell fruit; nectar-eating bats have long noses and tongues to reach deep into flowers; some bats snag fish with their strong-clawed feet.*

Critical Vocabulary: larvae (line 39) Barbara orders eighty thousand beetle larvae a month for the bats to eat. Ask students what, based on this fact, they think the larvae will look like. Then, ask students to share their definitions of *larvae*.

Insect-eating bats are different. "Hearing is most important for them," says Barbara. "They can also smell and see, but echolocation is the biggest part of finding their food." These bats get around and hunt in the dark by "seeing" with sound.

Echolocation lets bats "see" things by bouncing sounds off what is in front of them. This is how they catch food.

E Echolocation means locating something with echoes. Like sonar, it's a way to get information about something by bouncing sounds off it. Echolocating bats make loud calls and then listen for the echoes. The reflected sounds carry information about distance, speed, density, and size. A bat's brain turns the information into a kind of picture that helps the night-flying bat avoid trees, zero in on prey, and speed through caves. An echolocating bat "sees" its surroundings—caves, telephone poles, other bats, birds, and its prey—with sound. Bat echolocation is so precise that a bat can find a moth, tell how big it is, and know in which direction and at what speed it's moving, all in complete darkness. And it gathers all this information quickly enough to catch the moth while flying through a forest.

"It's why echolocators have such large ears," explains Barbara. Their big, sensitive ears collect the echoes like tiny satellite dishes. The strange faces of many bats are also echolocation tools. Those wrinkly lips and ears, leaf-shaped snouts called noseleafs, and bumpy foreheads focus the calls and echoes. Some bats even shout their calls through their megaphone-like nose. Bats are the loudest flying animals around! Their short calls or shouts are as loud as a smoke detector. Luckily for us, those echolocation calls are ultrasonic—too high pitched for humans to hear. So what is all the plainly heard chatter about inside Barbara's bat barn? "They're communicating," explains Barbara. Besides using ultrasonic calls to echolocate, bats use **audible** chirps, trills, buzzes, clicks, and purrs to talk to one another.

audible:
clear, loud

---

4. ◀ **REREAD AND DISCUSS** Reread lines 51–61. In a small group, discuss the following question: If bats can see quite well, why is echolocation important to them?

5. **READ** ▶ As you read lines 86–107 and the list of "Batty Myths" on page 34, continue to cite evidence.

- Underline ways that bats communicate with one another.
- Circle two ways that bats are important to their ecosystems.
- Underline three "batty" myths that you find surprising.

32

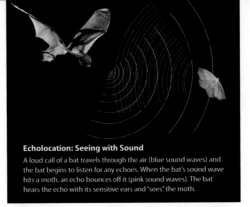

Echolocation: Seeing with Sound
A loud call of a bat travels through the air (blue sound waves) and the bat begins to listen for any echoes. When the bat's sound wave hits a moth, an echo bounces off it (pink sound waves). The bat hears the echo with its sensitive ears and "sees" the moth.

F What do bats talk about? The normal stuff—food, friends, mates, territory, and complaints. The most talkative bats seem to be those that live in big colonies. Think of the mother bat coming home to Bracken Bat Cave after a night of hunting bugs. How does she find her pup among the millions of bats? One way she zeros in on her baby is by calling to it, and then the pup calls back to her. Barbara and other scientists have identified more than twenty different calls in Mexican free-tailed bats. Many were first discovered from studying the recorded conversations among the colony of fifty or so free-tailed bats in Barbara's barn. "They may even use a sort of grammar," says Barbara. "They put all of these little clicks and buzzes and trills together in certain ways to make certain meanings."

The fact that bats communicate with a complex language adds to what scientists are learning about these marvelous and misunderstood mammals. Though many people once scorned them as flying **vermin**, we now know that bats are intelligent, social, long-lived creatures more closely related to monkeys than mice. And no matter where they live or what they eat, each bat species plays an important role in its ecosystem. Bats are important controllers of insects. Fruit bats pollinate plants and spread seeds that grow forests. Cave-dwelling bats and the guano[3] they make support hundreds of unique cave species of insects, fungi,[4] and bacteria found nowhere else.

vermin:
pests

[3] **guano:** the waste that bats produce.
[4] **fungi:** mushrooms.

33

---

4. **REREAD AND DISCUSS USING TEXT EVIDENCE**

D **ASK STUDENTS** to assign a reporter for each group to present specific text evidence to support what they have learned about bats. Building on their text evidence, have students discuss how bats differ from other mammals, why flying is so important to bats, and what the eating habits of bats are.

5. **READ AND CITE TEXT EVIDENCE**

E **ASK STUDENTS** Ask students to find and cite information both in the text and in the illustration caption on p. 33 that explains how bats hear and the importance of echolocation. *Students should cite information in lines 62–73 as well as information from the illustration and the caption.*

Critical Vocabulary: audible (line 85) The text gives examples of things that are audible, such as chirps, trills, buzzes, clicks, and purrs. Based on this, what do you think the word *audible* means?

Critical Vocabulary: vermin (line 100) Have students share their definitions of *vermin*. Ask them why the appearance of vermin at a family picnic would be a disaster. *The presence of vermin would disgust people and ruin the picnic.*

CLOSE READ
Notes

BATTY MYTHS

People still believe all kinds of crazy things about bats. Here are six of the most commonly misunderstood bat facts.

Bats Are Not Blind. All bats have eyes and can see quite well.

Most Bats Do Not Have Rabies. Like any wild animal, bats should not be touched, especially one found on the ground, which is more likely to be sick. However, getting rabies from a bat is very rare.

Bats Do Not Get Tangled In People's Hair. Bats are too good at flying for that— plus they generally avoid humans.

Bats Do Not Suck Blood. Not even the three species of vampire bats that live in Central and South America suck blood. They lap it up with their tiny tongues. No vampire bats live in the United States, except in zoos.

Bats Are Not Flying Mice. DNA evidence shows that bats are not closely related to rodents. Some scientists believe they are more like **primitive** primates.

Bats Are Not Pests In Need Of Extermination. Bats can be safely removed from an attic or home without harming them. Bats are important pest controllers, often eating their own weight in pest insects every night.

primitive:
simple, not advanced

6. ◀ **REREAD** Reread lines 86–97. Why might bats in big colonies be the most talkative?

Bats in big colonies might be most talkative because they have to communicate with many other bats.

SHORT RESPONSE

Cite Text Evidence   Explain how the information in the photos helps you understand the ways insect-eating bats communicate and find food. Be sure to **cite text evidence** in your response.

The picture of the bat and the moth shows the bat using echolocation, which lets the bat "see" its food. Both pictures show the bat's ears, which let it hear the echo of whatever is in front of it. The bat then knows how big something is and how quickly it's moving. The echolocation calls that bats use to find prey are ultrasonic, but they use other sounds to communicate with each other. They use sounds like buzzes and clicks to make a complex language.

34

TO CHALLENGE STUDENTS . . .

For more context about bats and organizations devoted to their protection, students can research the Ann W. Richards Congress Avenue Bridge in Austin, Texas, and the work done by Bat Conservation International (BTI) to both educate people about bats and protect bats and their habitats.

ASK STUDENTS what they have learned about the bats that spend their summers in Austin, Texas, at the Ann W. Richards Congress Avenue Bridge. Why do the bats go there? *They migrate from Mexico and stay under the bridge because it is safe and protected.* What kinds of bats are attracted to the area? *For the most part, the area is populated by Mexican free-tailed bats.* Why does the presence of bats attract tourists? *Tourists are attracted to the area because of the huge number of bats there in the summer—about 1.5 million (more than the population of Austin).* What contributions has Bat Conservation International (BTI) made to protect bats in the area? *BTI has educated the population about bats, telling residents that they have nothing to fear as long as they don't try to handle the bats. As a result, residents have grown to appreciate the bats and their contribution to the city.* What other work does BTI do? *BTI works worldwide to protect bats from persecution by humans, habitat loss, and environmental pollution.*

6. **REREAD AND CITE TEXT EVIDENCE**

(F) **ASK STUDENTS** to provide reasons to support their ideas on why bats in large colonies would be more talkative. *Students should mention that bats in large colonies have more bats to communicate with and may learn many different calls.*

Critical Vocabulary: primitive (line 13 in the list of Batty Myths) Have students share their definitions of *primitive*. What does the phrase *primitive primate* mean? *an early form of primate, a primate in an early stage of development*

SHORT RESPONSE

Cite Text Evidence   Students' responses will vary but should include evidence from photos and illustrations that support their answers. Students should:

• explain how bats communicate.
• explain how bats find food.

DIG DEEPER

With the class, return to Question 4, Reread. Have students share the results of their discussion.

ASK STUDENTS what additional information they have learned about bats, in particular how they hear and what they contribute to ecosystems. Remind students to cite text and visual evidence that supports what they have learned.

- Have students explain echolocation and why it is a unique ability. *Echolocation allows bats to get information about something by bouncing sounds off of it. As they use echolocation, bats make loud sounds and then listen for the echoes. The reflected sound of the echoes carries information about distance, speed, density, and size. This information enables the bat to "see" its surroundings.*

- Encourage students to use information gleaned from the chart and illustration on page 33. *The illustration in the chart shows how a bat tracks the sound made by a moth. The sound waves made by the moth travel and send a message (an echo) back to the bats. This echo allows bats, with their highly sensitive ears, to "see" the moth.*

- Have groups summarize their findings on bats and discuss why or why not bats are good for ecosystems. *Flight is what makes bats unique because they are the only mammal that can fly. When a bat can't fly, it's in trouble because without flying it has no way to get food. Bats feed mostly on insects, but different kinds of bats have developed different methods for catching and eating their food. Bats are nocturnal animals, which means that they are active only at night. But, because of echolocation they can "see" and hunt at night. Their heightened sense of smell also helps bats hunt at night. Bats make all kinds of sounds and appear to be able to communicate with each other in a complex language, especially when they are gathered together in large colonies. Bats are important controllers of insects and wherever they are they play an important role in their ecosystem. Most of the myths about bats—for example, that they are blind or get tangled in people's hair—are not true.*

ASK STUDENTS to return their Short Responses and revise them based on their discussion.

CLOSE READING NOTES

ANIMAL INTELLIGENCE

The FYI site provides links to online articles from a variety of magazines and newspapers. Help students choose a few articles to read to further their exploration of the topic Animal Intelligence.

NOVELWISE

Students can unlock the power of novels with this unique resource. Help students read through longer works with these tips:

- Find a Book
- Before You Read
- As You Read
- After You Read

Each book includes introductory material, worksheets, graphic organizers, and discussion guides.

ADDITIONAL TEXTS BY COLLECTION

Suggest students read the following:

- "There Was an Old Man with a Beard" by Edward Lear

Read aloud the limerick and then ask students to analyze the structure. Ask them how the form of the limerick helps convey its meaning.

NONFICTION CONNECTIONS

Suggest that students increase their reading of informational texts. The nonfiction connections include:

- speeches
- diaries
- true-life accounts
- newspaper articles
- political cartoons

Creating an Independent Reading Program

STUDENTS CHOOSE THEIR OWN BOOKS

Students who choose their own books will read more actively.

- Discuss with students how they already choose books. Record their responses on a chart, poster, or word cloud.
- Ask students if they prefer certain types of books over others. Do they have favorite topics or authors? What would make them consider different genres, topics, or authors?
- Encourage students to choose books in pairs or trios, so they can talk about their reading with others, or have designated days where students can "shop" for the books they want to read.
- Explain that it's okay to abandon a book that doesn't fit. Model scenarios where this might be the case.

STRATEGIES FOR SELECTING A BOOK

Help students select books of suitable difficulty, content, and interest.

- Have students preview a book by skimming its table of contents, the amount of text on a page, and its illustrations.
- Ask students to read the first two pages. How many words did they not know? (More than five means the book is too difficult; three is about right.) Can the students summarize what they've read? Can they start to make predictions? (If so, the book is on level.)
- Ask students to read to page 5. Is the book making them think or stop and clarify? (If so, how much? They should have to think and clarify some. If they don't, the book is too easy. If they can't make any sense of it, the book is too hard.)
- If the book they've chosen meets these criteria and interests them, students may continue reading.

PERFORMANCE TASK A

Interactive Lessons

To help you complete this task, use
• *Writing Informative Texts*
• *Using Textual Evidence*

Write a Literary Analysis

In "The Mixer" you read a story from a dog's perspective. In other selections in this collection, you learned about various aspects of animal intelligence and behavior. Draw from the ideas and examples in these selections to help you write an analysis of the dog as the main character and narrator in "The Mixer."

A successful literary analysis

- provides a clear thesis statement, or controlling idea
- clearly organizes ideas and concepts
- presents examples and quotations to support ideas
- provides a conclusion that leaves the reader with an insight or memorable impression

W 2a–f Write explanatory texts.
W 4 Produce clear and coherent writing.
W 5 Develop and strengthen writing as needed.
W 9a Draw evidence from literary or informational texts to support analysis, reflection, and research.
W 10 Write routinely over extended time frames.

PLAN

Develop a Thesis Draft a thesis statement, or controlling idea, which sums up the main point you will make in your analysis. The thesis statement should clearly identify the point you want to make about the dog in "The Mixer."

Analyze the Text Review "The Mixer." Jot down information about the dog's personality and character traits and how these influence how he narrates the story. Consider the following questions as you analyze the text.

- What character traits are revealed through the dog's thoughts and actions?
- How does the dog view the other characters in the story?
- Explain the struggle or conflict that the dog faces. Tell how the dog responds to the conflict.
- What do the dog's actions tell you about him?
- Identify whether the dog changes or grows as a result of the story's events. How is the dog different at the end of the story?

ACADEMIC VOCABULARY

As you plan and present your analysis, be sure to use the academic vocabulary words.

benefit
respond
environment
distinct
illustrate

WRITE A LITERARY ANALYSIS

W 2a–f, W 4, W 5, W 9a, W 10

Introduce students to the Performance Task by reading the introductory paragraph with them and reviewing the criteria for what makes a good literary analysis. Remind students that in a literary analysis, a writer uses story details to support a thesis, or a main point he or she wants to make about a story.

PLAN

ANALYZE THE TEXT

Explain to students that, when analyzing a character in a story, a reader often has to make inferences based on evidence from the story. Remind students that when they make inferences, they should use details from a story plus what they know from experience to figure out something a writer doesn't say directly.

English Language Support

Write a Literary Analysis Make sure students understand that their analysis of the dog's character in "The Mixer" should relate to ideas about animal intelligence included in other collection texts. To help them develop a thesis, have small groups share opinions about animal intelligence, drawing on evidence from collection texts to support their ideas. Then have students use a two-column chart to connect these opinions to the character of the dog.

Animal Intelligence	Blackie
Animals can't understand humans.	Blackie suffers as a result of misunderstanding humans.

Finally, have students use their discussion notes to write thesis statements for their analyses. Explain that although they may later revise these statements, a "working thesis" will help focus their analyses and information gathering.

PERFORMANCE TASK A

PLAN

GATHER EVIDENCE

Suggest that students prepare an outline to help them organize evidence into separate paragraphs for each main idea. The information should be presented in a sequence that is coherent and logical.

PRODUCE

WRITE YOUR ANALYSIS

Remind students that the introduction should identify the text's title and author. It should briefly describe the story in a way that engages readers and leads naturally to the thesis statement.

English Language Support

Justify Opinions Using the Student Model that accompanies *Interactive Lessons*: Writing Informative Texts, have students highlight quotations from Longfellow. Then have pairs discuss the following:

- What methods did the author use to introduce quotations in this text?
- Which quotations do you think are most effective? Why?

Encourage students to refer to the annotated text and discussion notes as they add quotes to their analysis.

TO CHALLENGE STUDENTS . . .

Strengthen a Conclusion Challenge students to strengthen their conclusions by using one of the following techniques:

- Relate the subject of the essay to a larger idea outside of the text.
- Include a quotation that sums up the main idea or offers a new insight.
- Raise a question for the audience.

Gather Evidence Use the annotation tools in your eBook to find evidence from the text to support your thesis. Save your evidence to *my*Notebook, in a folder titled *Collection 2 Performance Task*. Include different kinds of support, such as direct quotations.

Interactive Lessons
For help in integrating information and evidence, use
- Using Textual Evidence: Synthesizing Information

⊟ myNotebook

🗏 "The Mixer"

"I have always been restless, unable to settle down in one place and anxious to get on to the next thing."

In this sentence, the dog reveals aspects of his personality.

Consider Your Purpose and Audience Think about who will read your analysis, and what you want them to know.

PRODUCE

✓ myWriteSmart

Draft the text for your analysis in *my*WriteSmart. Focus on listing and developing your ideas, rather than perfecting your choice of language.

Write Your Analysis Review your notes as you begin your draft.

- Write a thesis statement that includes the main point you want to make about the dog's character.
- Focus on the events of the story. Include evidence, such as examples and quotations, to support your ideas.
- Describe the dog's response to conflict and its impact on him.
- Use transitions, such as *next* or *yet* to organize your ideas.
- Write a conclusion that summarizes your interpretation and focuses on the most important ideas you want to convey.

Interactive Lessons
For help in organizing your analysis, use
- Writing Informative Texts: Introductions and Conclusions

Language Conventions: Condense Ideas

When you write a rough draft, you should just focus on getting your ideas down. Afterwards, you can work on choosing more precise words. In this rough draft, notice how the writer repeats ideas and uses the same structure for every sentence.

> ❝ 'The Mixer' is a strange tale about a dog. It is funny. The dog narrates the story. You get to see humans through the dog's eyes. You learn a lot about how dogs behave. You also learn about how humans behave. Dogs misunderstand a lot about human behavior. The dog just wants to please. He often suffers. He doesn't understand what humans expect. ❞

English Language Support

Understand Text Structure Review the following examples of organizational structures:

- *Order of Importance:* Organize reasons and evidence from most important to least important, or vice versa.
- *Chronological Order:* Introduce main points in the order in which they occur.

Have pairs review the information they have gathered, discuss the connections between ideas, and use their conversations to help choose a logical organizational structure.

In this draft, the writer combines sentences and adds prepositional phrases and more precise modifiers to create detailed sentences.

> ❝ 'The Mixer' is an unusually funny tale because a dog narrates the story. Through the dog's eyes, you learn that dogs misunderstand a lot when it comes to human behavior. Although the dog just wants to please, he often suffers as a result of not understanding humans' expectations. ❞

REVISE

my WriteSmart

Review Your Draft Have your partner or a group of peers review your draft. Use the following chart to revise your draft.

Have your partner or a group of peers review your draft in *my*WriteSmart. Have them note if any ideas do not follow a logical sequence.

Questions	Tips	Revision Techniques
Does my introduction include a clear thesis statement?	**Underline** the thesis statement. Highlight the main points about the dog.	**Add** a sentence that clearly states the thesis.
Are my main ideas presented logically?	**Highlight** each main idea. **Underline** transitions.	**Reorder** ideas so that each one flows easily into the next. **Add** appropriate transitions.
Is each main idea supported by evidence from the story?	**Underline** each supporting detail, example, or quotation.	**Add** details, examples, or quotations to support ideas. **Explain** each piece of evidence.
Do I use prepositional phrases and precise modifiers to add more detail?	**Highlight** each prepositional phrase. **Underline** each modifier.	**Add** prepositional phrases and modifiers to make sentences more descriptive.
Do I restate the thesis in the conclusion?	**Highlight** the conclusion.	**Add** a restatement of the thesis.

PRESENT

Create a Finished Copy Finalize your analysis and choose a way to share it with your audience. You might share your analysis with a magazine or website that focuses on animals.

PERFORMANCE TASK A

PRODUCE

LANGUAGE CONVENTIONS

Tell students to look for places in their drafts where consecutive sentences begin with the same subject. Suggest that students try to combine the sentences by using compound verbs or by using a subordinate clause to show the relationship between ideas.

REVISE

REVIEW YOUR DRAFT

As students evaluate supporting evidence, remind them to make sure that each detail, example, or quotation clearly relates to the main idea.

PRESENT

CREATE A FINISHED COPY

Students may want to share their analyses with the class. Allow discussion time for students to compare and contrast their ideas.

FOR STANDARD ENGLISH LEARNERS

Use Prepositions Explain that in formal English, the prepositions *in* and *on* describe location. For example, *in* describes a specific point or enclosed space, while *on* refers to the surface of something. Review the following:

- The dog was *in* the kitchen when he heard someone.
- The man patted the dog *on* the head.

WHEN STUDENTS STRUGGLE...

Connect Ideas Have pairs read aloud their drafts, and let partners summarize their understanding of the main ideas. Have students take notes on these summaries and identify areas where the partners' understanding differed from their intended meaning. Encourage them to suggest and discuss revisions to help clarify connections between ideas.

English Language Support

Condense Ideas A *relative pronoun* such as *who* or *that* introduces a clause. Show how to condense these sentences with relative pronouns.

This is a story about a dog. The dog misunderstands human behavior. *(This is a story about a dog that misunderstands human behavior.)*

Blackie's mother has given him advice. He realizes this advice is wrong. *(Blackie's mother gives him advice that he realizes is wrong.)*

PERFORMANCE TASK A

USE THE SCORING RUBRIC

Have students work in pairs and score each other's analysis using the rubric. Then ask each student to write a brief paragraph explaining his or her reasons for the score.

REFLECT ON THE PROCESS

Ask students to reflect on the entire writing process, not only the final product. Encourage them to consider what they learned from completing this performance task, as well as what they might improve in future assignments. Have students write short responses to the following questions:

- What process did you use to develop your thesis statement?
- How did you decide which evidence to include?
- What did you learn about character and point of view by writing your analysis?

PERFORMANCE TASK A RUBRIC
LITERARY ANALYSIS

	Ideas and Evidence	Organization	Language
4	• The introduction is engaging, tells the title and author of the work, and presents a clear thesis statement. • Important points are supported by specific, relevant details. • The conclusion effectively summarizes the analysis and gives an original idea or insight about the work.	• The organization of important points and supporting details is effective and logical throughout the analysis. • Transitions logically connect related ideas.	• The analysis reflects an appropriately formal style. • Language is precise and presents ideas in an original way. • Sentences vary in structure and have a rhythmic flow. • Spelling, capitalization, and punctuation are correct. • Grammar, usage, and mechanics are correct.
3	• The introduction tells the title and author of the work but could be more engaging; the introduction includes a thesis statement. • One or two important points need more support. • The conclusion summarizes most of the analysis but does not give an original idea or insight to think about.	• The organization of important points and supporting details is confusing in a few places. • A few more transitions are needed to connect related ideas.	• The writing style is inconsistent in a few places. • Most language is precise. • Sentences vary somewhat in pattern and structure. • Some spelling, capitalization, and punctuation mistakes occur. • Some grammar and usage errors are present.
2	• The introduction tells the title and author of the work, but the thesis statement is vague. • Most important points could use more supporting details; details are often too general. • The conclusion is incomplete or unclear and does not present a new idea or insight.	• The organization of most important points is logical, but many supporting details are misplaced. • More transitions are needed throughout to connect related ideas.	• The writing style becomes informal in many places. • Language is repetitive or too general in many places. • Sentence structures hardly vary; some fragments or run-on sentences occur. • Spelling, capitalization, and punctuation are often incorrect but do not make reading difficult. • Grammar and usage are often incorrect, but the writer's ideas are still clear.
1	• The introduction does not include the title and author of the work or the thesis statement. • Supporting details are irrelevant or missing. • The conclusion is missing.	• The organization is not logical; important ideas are presented randomly. • No transitions are used, making the analysis difficult to understand.	• The style is inappropriate for the analysis. • Language is inaccurate, repetitive, and too general. • Sentence structure is repetitive and monotonous; fragments and run-on sentences make the analysis hard to follow. • Spelling, capitalization, and punctuation are incorrect and distracting throughout. • Many grammatical and usage errors change the meaning of the writer's ideas.

FOR STUDENTS WITH DISABILITIES

Evaluate the Analysis Before students score their analyses with a partner, let them review the scoring rubric and identify one or two areas for improvement. Have each student ask a peer to read the analysis and make suggestions for editing in those areas. Tell students to ask peers to clarify or explain the suggestions before they incorporate any changes.

Interactive Lessons

To help you complete this task, use
• *Writing Informative Texts*
• *Conducting Research*
• *Giving a Presentation*

Give an Informative Presentation

In the excerpt from "How Smart Are Animals?" you learned about animal behavior and intelligence. Now draw from the ideas in this text and others in this collection as well as your own research, to help you give a presentation on how animals exhibit intelligence.

A successful informative presentation

- includes a clear thesis statement
- presents ideas in a logical sequence
- includes evidence such as facts, definitions, concrete details, and graphics to support ideas
- uses effective verbal and nonverbal elements
- ends with a conclusion that restates the thesis

Mentor Text Notice how this example from "Animal Snoops" offers support for the idea that animals are intelligent.

> " The thieves talked as they worked, paying no attention to the parrot, nearly motionless in its cage. Only when the crooks were ready to make their getaway did the bird finally pipe up. 'JJ,' it said plainly. 'JJ, JJ.'
>
> Marshmallow—a six-year-old green parrot—had been quietly eavesdropping. . . . "

W 8 Gather relevant information.
SL 4 Present claims, findings, and evidence.
SL 5 Include visual displays.
SL 6 Adapt speech to a variety of contexts and tasks.

Visit hmhfyi.com to explore your topic and enhance your research.

myNotebook

Use the annotation tools in your eBook to find evidence to support your ideas. Save each detail to your notebook.

PLAN

Gather Information Review the excerpts from "How Smart Are Animals?" and "Animal Snoops: The Wondrous World of Wildlife Spies." Jot down facts, definitions, quotations, and examples that support the following ideas:

- Distinguish different ways that animals show intelligence.
- Identify how scientists measure animal intelligence.
- Consider how an animal's environment can affect intelligence.

Do Research Find sources online using appropriate keywords. Also use your school library to research books and magazines for visuals, such as graphs and charts, that illustrate your ideas.

ACADEMIC VOCABULARY

As you write about animal intelligence, be sure to use the academic vocabulary words.

benefit
respond
environment
distinct
illustrate

Collection Performance Task B **133**

GIVE AN INFORMATIVE PRESENTATION

W 8, SL 4, SL 5, SL 6

Introduce students to the Performance Task by reading the introductory paragraph with them and reviewing the criteria for what makes a good informative presentation. Remind students that a good informative presentation provides evidence to support the main ideas the speaker wants the audience to understand.

PLAN

GATHER INFORMATION

As students review the collection texts for evidence supporting their ideas about animal intelligence, encourage them also to note evidence that might support opposing viewpoints. Then students can identify evidence to refute these views as they conduct research.

English Language Support

Provide Text Evidence Review the different types of evidence and encourage students to look for each type as they gather information on their topic.

fact: basic piece of information that can be proven, such as when an event took place
definition: explanation of the meaning of a word or term
quotation: another person's statement about a topic, usually someone regarded as an expert in the field

example: specific sample or type that is representative of something

After students review the collection texts for information about animal intelligence, have small groups answer and discuss these questions: *What main point do you want to make about animal intelligence? What key ideas relate to your main point? What evidence in the texts supports your ideas? What other evidence will you look for as you conduct research?* Tell students that their conversations will help guide research and planning.

PERFORMANCE TASK B

PLAN

DO RESEARCH

Remind students doing research on the Internet to look for details about the author, the sponsoring organization, and the date the website was published. All of these details can help students determine whether the website is a credible one.

PRODUCE

DRAFT YOUR PRESENTATION

Remind students to use their hierarchy charts as a guide for their first draft. The introduction should clearly state the thesis and preview what will follow. Explain that beginning each paragraph with one of their main ideas will help students present their information logically.

FOR STANDARD ENGLISH LEARNERS

Adapt Speech Remind students of the differences between formal speech and informal conversation. As they practice their presentations, encourage students to pay special attention to words containing the digraph *th* in initial, medial, and final positions. Speaking slowly and clearly can help them focus on following the rules of standard English to pronounce the the digraphs.

WHEN STUDENTS STRUGGLE...

Use Quotations Provide the following sentence frames to help students add direct quotations to their presentations:

- [Source name] argues, "[quote]."
- According to [source name], "[quote]."
- "[Quote]," says [source name].

Organize Your Ideas A hierarchy chart can help you present your ideas logically.

Consider Your Purpose and Audience Think about who will listen to your presentation, and what you want them to know.

PRODUCE

Interactive Lessons
For help with research, use
- Conducting Research: Using the Library for Research

Write your rough draft in *my*WriteSmart. Focus on getting your ideas down rather than perfecting your choice of language.

Draft Your Presentation Review your notes and the information in your hierarchy chart as you begin your draft.

- Write a thesis statement. The thesis states your topic and your main idea about the topic.
- Develop your ideas with facts, definitions, details, quotations, and visuals.
- Use transitions to help you sequence ideas logically and also to show how they are related.
- Restate your thesis in your conclusion.

Interactive Lessons
For help in writing your draft, use
- Writing Informative Texts: Elaboration

Interactive Lessons
For help in practicing your presentation, use
- Giving a Presentation: Delivering Your Presentation

Practice Your Presentation Practice your speech aloud with a group of friends or in front of a mirror.

- Speak loudly and slowly.
- Use your voice to add meaning to your ideas. To stress an important idea, change the **modulation**, or pitch, of your voice.
- Match your gestures and facial expressions to ideas that you want to emphasize. For example, raising your voice while pointing to a chart or diagram will signal to your audience that you are making an important point.
- Make eye contact by glancing at your friends or at different objects in the room.

English Language Support

Plan an Informative Presentation Discuss the differences between an essay and a presentation. In a presentation, students can use visuals as well as verbal and nonverbal techniques to illustrate key points. Before students practice their presentations, suggest the following strategies:

- Decide when to pause or use gestures to introduce visuals or to emphasize ideas. Add cues such as highlighting to help you remember.
- Circle any word that you're unsure how to pronounce. Consult a dictionary to confirm the pronunciation.

Language Conventions: Nouns and Noun Phrases

A **noun phrase** consists of a noun and all the words that modify the noun. Read this excerpt from "How Smart Are Animals?"

> " Some scientists would say that, while Villa certainly is a wonderful animal, her behavior was unthinking, perhaps an instinctive holdover from the protective environment of the wolf pack . . . "

Notice how the noun phrases clarify what scientists believe about Villa's behavior. Look for places where you can add noun phrases to help explain details and examples.

REVISE

Evaluate Your Presentation Have your partner or a group of peers review the draft of your presentation. Use the following chart to revise it.

myWriteSmart

Have your partner or a group of peers review your draft in *my*WriteSmart and note any main ideas that are not supported.

Questions	Tips	Revision Techniques
Does my introduction include a clear thesis statement?	**Underline** the thesis statement. **Highlight** the topic and your main point about the topic.	**Add** a sentence that clearly states the thesis.
Are my main ideas presented logically?	**Highlight** each main idea. **Underline** transitions.	**Reorder** ideas so that each one flows easily to the next. **Add** appropriate transitions.
Is each main idea supported by evidence?	**Underline** each supporting detail, example, or quotation.	**Add** facts, details, examples, quotations, and visuals to support ideas. **Explain** the importance of the evidence.
Do I use noun phrases to provide details?	**Highlight** all noun phrases that provide details.	**Add** noun phrases that provide details and explain key ideas.
Do I restate the thesis in my conclusion?	**Underline** the conclusion.	**Add** a restatement of the thesis.

PRESENT

Give Your Presentation Finalize your presentation and choose a way to share it with your audience. You might convert your presentation into a multimedia presentation.

Collection Performance Task B **135**

PRODUCE

LANGUAGE CONVENTIONS

Encourage students to look for places where they can add an adjective to a noun to provide more details.

REVISE

EVALUATE YOUR PRESENTATION

Encourage students to make suggestions that will ensure that the ideas are presented coherently.

PRESENT

GIVE YOUR PRESENTATION

Students may share their presentations in class or on a school website.

English Language Support

Use Language Resources Students can connect ideas using words that are related but are different parts of speech. *(frequent, frequency)* Share this example:

People have *approached* the measurement of animal intelligence in different ways. Some of these *approaches* are less reliable than others.

English Language Support

Link Ideas Share the list of connecting words and phrases. Encourage students to use them when linking ideas and evidence. Make sure students understand the type of relationship that each transition shows.

Transitions	Relationship
first, next, before, after, later	time order
so, because, as a result, since	cause and effect
similarly, in contrast, however, instead	comparison or contrast

FOR STUDENTS WITH DISABILITIES

Give a Small Group Presentation If individuals are not comfortable with addressing the whole class, allow them to share their presentation with a small group. To help them avoid feeling nervous or distracted while they're speaking, help them select an object located behind the audience to focus on. Encourage students to try making direct eye contact with audience members at the beginning or end of the presentation or when they pause to show a visual.

PERFORMANCE TASK B

USE THE SCORING RUBRIC

Have partners score each other's presentation by comparing it with each point on the rubric. Following the presentations, encourage pairs to discuss their assessments. Students should use language from the rubric to explain the reasons for the score they gave.

REFLECT ON THE PROCESS

Explain that taking the time to reflect on the planning and delivery of their presentations will help students prepare for future assignments. Ask students to evaluate how well their presentations engaged and informed the audience. Then have them answer the following questions:

- How did you determine if your sources were reliable?
- What strategies did you use to find and select evidence for your presentation?
- How did you decide what visuals to include?
- What nonverbal elements of your presentation do you think were most effective?

PERFORMANCE TASK B RUBRIC
INFORMATIVE PRESENTATION

	Ideas and Evidence	Organization	Language
4	• The introduction clearly states the thesis. • The topic is well developed with clear main ideas supported by facts, details, definitions, and examples from reliable sources. • The conclusion effectively summarizes the thesis.	• The organization of main ideas and details is effective and logical throughout the presentation. • Verbal and nonverbal elements effectively emphasize main points and hold the audience's attention.	• The presentation reflects a formal style. • Language is strong and precise. • Sentences vary in pattern and structure. • Grammar, usage, and mechanics are correct.
3	• The introduction states a thesis. • One or two important points could use more support, but most main ideas are well supported by facts, details, definitions, and examples from reliable sources. • The conclusion restates the thesis.	• The organization of main ideas and details is confusing in a few places. • Verbal and nonverbal elements effectively emphasize some main points and sometimes hold the audience's attention.	• The style is inconsistent in a few places. • Language is too vague or general in some places. • Sentences vary somewhat in pattern and structure. • Some grammar and usage errors are present.
2	• The introduction identifies a thesis, but it is not clearly stated. • Most important points could use more support from relevant facts, details, definitions, and examples from reliable sources. • The conclusion is unclear or only partially summarizes the thesis.	• The organization of main ideas and details is logical in some places, but it often doesn't follow a pattern. • Verbal and nonverbal elements are sparse or misplace emphasis.	• The style becomes informal in many places. • Language is too general or vague in many places. • Sentence pattern and structure hardly vary; some fragments occur. • Grammar and usage are often incorrect, but the ideas are still clear.
1	• The introduction is confusing and does not state a thesis. • Supporting facts, details, definitions, or examples are unreliable or missing. • The conclusion is missing.	• The organization is not logical; main ideas and details are presented randomly. • Verbal and nonverbal elements are not used to emphasize main points, or their inappropriate use detracts from the presentation.	• The style is inappropriate. • Language is too general to convey the information. • Sentence structure is repetitive and monotonous; fragments make the presentation hard to follow. • Many grammatical and usage errors change the meaning of ideas.

TO CHALLENGE STUDENTS . . .

Share Resources Challenge students to compile and curate a list of links to online resources on animal behavior and intelligence. Students may post these links on a section of the school website.

©13/Corbis

Dealing with Disaster

"Through every kind of disaster and setback and catastrophe. We are survivors."

—Robert Fulghum

137

STREAM TO START

Motivate students to read the collection texts, and spark their curiosity about the collection by playing the video. After students view the video, ask them to suggest common responses to catastrophic events. Call on volunteers to share their responses.

PERFORMANCE TASK PREVIEW

Point out to students that they will complete two performance tasks at the end of the collection. The performance tasks will require them to further analyze the selections in the collection and to synthesize ideas about these analyses. They will present their findings in a variety of products.

ACADEMIC VOCABULARY

> ▶ **View It!**
> Professional Development Podcast:
> **Academic Vocabulary**

Students can acquire facility with the academic vocabulary words through frequent, repeated exposure as they analyze and discuss the selections in the collection. Academic vocabulary can be used in the following instructional contexts. This will enable students to incorporate the academic vocabulary words into their working vocabulary.

- Collaborative Discussion at the end of each selection
- Analyzing the Text questions for each selection
- Selection-level Performance Task
- Vocabulary instruction (for Critical Vocabulary and/or for Vocabulary Strategy)
- Language Conventions
- End-of-collection Performance Task for all selections in the collection

ASK STUDENTS to review the Academic Vocabulary word list for this collection. You may wish to pronounce each word aloud so students hear the correct pronunciation. Then, discuss the definitions and the related forms for each word. Remind students that they will encounter these five academic vocabulary words throughout the collection.

COLLECTION 3

Dealing with Disaster

In this collection, you will discover how people react in the face of disaster.

Stream to Start

hmhfyi.com

Channel One News®

COLLECTION

PERFORMANCE TASK Preview

After reading this collection, you will have the opportunity to complete two performance tasks:

- In one, you will create a multimedia presentation with a partner or small group.
- In the second, you will write a narrative about what happens after a ship hits an iceberg.

ACADEMIC VOCABULARY

Study the words and their definitions in the chart below. You will use these words as you discuss and write about the texts in this collection.

Word	Definition	Related Forms
circumstance (sûr´kəm-stăns´) n.	a condition or fact that affects an event	circumstantial, circumstantially
constraint (kən-strānt´) n.	something or someone that limits or restricts another's actions	constrain
impact (ĭm´păkt´) n.	something striking against another; also, the effect or impression of one thing on another	impaction
injure (ĭn´jər) tr.v.	to hurt or cause damage	injurer, injurious, injury, injuriously, injuriousness
significant (sĭg-nĭf´ĭ-kənt) adj.	meaningful; important	significantly, significance

myNotebook

As students read, analyze, and discuss the texts in this collection, encourage them to create a *my*WordList folder in *my*Notebook to build their own personal word lists.

- **Annotate** Students can highlight vocabulary terms and other unfamiliar words and save each highlighted term to *my*Notebook.
- **Organize** Within *my*Notebook, students can drag each word into the *my*WordList folder.
- **Elaborate** Ask students to add details to the entry for each word, such as a definition, other forms of the word, and a sample sentence.

English Language Support

View It!

Professional Development Podcast:
English Language Learners

ENGAGE WITH THE COLLECTION TOPIC

Draw students' attention to the title of the collection, Dealing with Disaster. Explain that *disaster* means "a sudden event that causes great damage or loss of life." Tell students that this collection focuses on people who cope with different types of disasters.

ACCESS PRIOR KNOWLEDGE Have students name disasters with which they are familiar. Ask volunteers to suggest the needs that people might have when a disaster strikes. Encourage them to consider the importance of communication in responding to disasters.

LEARNING CIRCLES

Use this strategy to deepen students' understanding of the the texts in this collection and to encourage collaboration.

- *First*, organize the class into small groups of three or four.
- *Then*, have members of each group select their individual roles. For example, one student can note unfamiliar vocabulary, another can identify and consider interesting language, and another can prepare questions about the text and take notes.
- *Next*, read aloud or present an audio recording of the text to the class, reminding students to perform the tasks associated with their selected roles.

- *Finally*, explain that each group member is expected to share what he or she noted about the text, to respond to others by asking clarifying questions, and to build on the comments of the member who is sharing.

Collection 3 Digital Resources for English Language Support

LANGUAGE WORKSHOP
Designated English Learners

Use the Teacher Resources > Language Workshop to support English learners in explaining cause-effect text relationships, connecting ideas by using transitional words, and sharing ideas by providing useful feedback.

VIDEOS

These videos will help students learn how to build background and identify a sequence of events. Have them use **Text in Focus Practice** to apply those skills.

Collection 3 Lessons	**Media**	**Teach and Practice**
Student Edition | **eBook**	▶ **Video Links** HISTORY A&E Channel One News	**Close Reading and Evidence Tracking**
ANCHOR TEXT — **Informational Text by Brenda Z. Guiberson** "Mammoth Shakes and Monster Waves: Destruction in 12 Countries"	▶ **Video HISTORY®** *The Science of Tsunamis* ◀ **Audio** "Mammoth Shakes and Monster Waves: Destruction in 12 Countries"	**Close Read Screencasts** • Modeled Discussion 1 (lines 39–49) • Modeled Discussion 2 (lines 150–159) • Close Read Application PDF (lines 340–351)	**Text in Focus** • Build Background **Strategies for Annotation** • Analyze Structure: Cause and Effect • Determine Meaning: Technical Language • Greek Affixes
CLOSE READER — **Book Review by David Holahan** "Moby-Duck"	◀ **Audio** "Moby-Duck"	
Poem by Rita Williams-Garcia *from* "After the Hurricane" **Poem by Natasha D. Trethewey** "Watcher, After Katrina, 2005"	◀ **Audio** *from* "After the Hurricane" ◀ **Audio** "Watcher, After Katrina, 2005"	**Strategies for Annotation** • Analyze Structure • Determine Meanings of Words and Phrases
Short Story by James Berry "The Banana Tree"	◀ **Audio** "The Banana Tree"	**Strategies for Annotation** • Determine Meaning: Dialect • Determine Meaning: Figurative Language • Use Context Clues
CLOSE READER — **Short Story by Ray Bradbury** "There Will Come Soft Rains"	◀ **Audio** "There Will Come Soft Rains"	
ANCHOR TEXT — **History Writing by Walter Lord** *from A Night to Remember*	◀ **Audio** *from A Night to Remember*	**Close Read Screencasts** • Modeled Discussion (lines 42–49) • Close Read Application PDF (lines 155–163)	**Text in Focus** • Identifying Sequence (line 39) **Strategies for Annotation** • Analyze Text: Narrative Nonfiction • Analyze the Meanings of Words and Phrases • Specialized Vocabulary
CLOSE READER — **Newspaper Article by Guy Trebay** "On the Titanic, Defined by What They Wore" **Diagram** "The Discovery of the Titanic"	◀ **Audio** "On the Titanic, Defined by What They Wore" ▶ **Video HISTORY®**	
Documentary by James Cameron *from Titanic at 100: Mystery Solved*	▶ **Video HISTORY®** *from Titanic at 100: Mystery Solved*	
Collection 3 Performance Tasks: **A** Create a Multimedia Presentation **B** Write Narrative Nonfiction	**fyi** hmhfyi.com	**Interactive Lessons** **A** Conducting Research **A** Using Media in a Presentation	**B** Writing Narratives **B** Writing as a Process

For Systematic Coverage of Writing and Speaking & Listening Standards

Interactive Lessons

Conducting Research
Evaluating Sources

Assess		Extend	Reteach
Performance Task	✅ *Assess It Online!*	**Teacher eBook**	**Teacher eBook**
Speaking Activity: Discussion	Selection Test	**Discussion Etiquette**	**Analyze Structure: Cause and Effect > Level Up Tutorial >** Cause-and-Effect Organization
Writing Activity: Poem	Selection Test	**Analyze Structure: Meter**	**Compare Poetic Forms > Interactive Whiteboard Lesson >** Form in Poetry **Level Up Tutorial >** Elements of Poetry
Writing Activity: Narrative	Selection Test	**Draw Conclusions**	**Determine Meaning: Figurative Language > Level Up Tutorial >** Figurative Language
Writing Activity: Research	Selection Test	**Formulate Research Questions**	**Analyze Meaning: Style > Level Up Tutorials >** Author's Style > Tone > Imagery
Media Activity: Multimedia Presentation	Selection Test	**Cite Evidence in a Presentation > Interactive Whiteboard Lesson >** Cite Textual Evidence	**Elements of a Documentary**
A Create a Multimedia Presentation **B** Write Narrative Nonfiction	Collection Test		

Lesson Assessments Conducting Research Evaluating Sources	**Standards Support and Enrichment**	For more instruction and practice in reading literary and informational texts, language, spelling, and speaking and listening, see Teacher Resources > Standards Support and Enrichment.
	For Designated English Language Instruction	To provide scaffolded support specific to the needs of English Learners during Designated English Language instruction, use the selection- and standards-aligned lessons found in Teacher Resources > Language Workshop.

Collection 3 Lessons	Key Learning Objective	Performance Task	Vocabulary Strategy
ANCHOR TEXT **Informational Text by Brenda Z. Guiberson** **"Mammoth Shakes and Monster Waves: Destruction in 12 Countries," p. 139A** **Lexile 1140L**	**The student will be able to . . .** identify and analyze cause-and-effect organization and determine meanings of technical language in an informational text.	Speaking Activity: Discussion	Greek Affixes
Poem by Rita Williams-Garcia *from* **"After the Hurricane," p. 157A** **Poem by Natasha D. Trethewey** **"Watcher, After Katrina, 2005," p. 157A**	**The student will be able to . . .** analyze and compare poetic form and learn how poets use form, alliteration, and tone to express feelings and ideas.	Writing Activity: Poem	
Short Story by James Berry **"The Banana Tree," p. 171A** **Lexile 820L**	**The student will be able to . . .** identify and analyze how dialect and imagery, including figurative language, bring a story to life.	Writing Activity: Narrative	Context Clues
ANCHOR TEXT **EXEMPLAR** **History Writing by Walter Lord** *from A Night to Remember*, **p. 185A** **Lexile 1070L**	**The student will be able to . . .** analyze elements of narrative nonfiction, including how authors establish style and tone in their writing.	Writing Activity: Research	Specialized Vocabulary
Documentary by James Cameron *from Titanic at 100: Mystery Solved*, **p. 197A**	**The student will be able to . . .** understand the features and analyze the purpose of a documentary, as well as integrate its information with other sources.	Media Activity: Multimedia Presentation	

Collection 3 Performance Tasks:

A Create a Multimedia Presentation

B Write Narrative Nonfiction

Language Conventions	English Language Support	Differentiated Instruction	CLOSE READER Selection
Shifts in Pronoun Person	• Analyze Cause/Effect Relationships • Word Study • Determine Meaning • Learning Circles • Improve Reading Fluency • Draw Conclusions	**When Students Struggle:** • Cause-and-Effect Organization • Integrate Information **To Challenge Students:** Make Comparisons **For Students with Disabilities:** Discussion Roles	Book Review by David Holahan "Moby-Duck," p. 156b **Lexile 1340L**
	• Read Closely • Learning Circles • Understand Language Choices • Culturally Responsive Instruction • Cite Evidence • Write Literary Texts	**For Standard English Learners:** Grammar **When Students Struggle:** Analyze Structure **To Challenge Students:** Interpret Symbolism	
Capitalization	• Analyze Language • Determine Meaning: Dialect • Using Participles and Gerunds • Determine Meaning: Figurative Language • Provide Textual Evidence • Write with Correct Capitalization	**For Standard English Learners:** • Pronunciation • Verb Tenses **When Students Struggle:** Dialect **To Challenge Students:** Analyze Characters	Short Story by Ray Bradbury "There Will Come Soft Rains," p. 184b **Lexile 920L**
Consistency in Style and Tone	• Use Context Clues • Analyze Meaning: Style • Analyze Text • Evaluate Language Choices	**When Students Struggle:** Point of View **To Challenge Students:** Analyze a Diagram **For Students with Disabilities:** Making Research Manageable	Newspaper Article by Guy Trebay *"On the Titanic, Defined by What They Wore,"* p. 196b **Lexile 1450L** Diagram "The Discovery of the Titanic," p. 196b
	• View Closely • Interpret Diverse Media	**To Challenge Students:** Analyze Style	
B Sequence of Tenses	**A** Plan a Multimedia Presentation Express Opinions Adapt Language Choices **B** Write Narrative Nonfiction Adapt Language Choices Understand Text Structure	**A** **For Standard English Learners:** Use Stress Patterns **When Students Struggle:** Integrate Multimedia Elements **For Students with Disabilities:** Extend the Completion Time **To Challenge Students:** Plan an Awareness Campaign **B** **When Students Struggle:** Brainstorm Imagery Ideas **For Standard English Learners:** Adapt Speech **For Students with Disabilities:** Pre-record the Presentation **To Challenge Students:** Create a Multimedia Presentation	

ANCHOR TEXT

Mammoth Shakes and Monster Waves: Destruction in 12 Countries

Informational Text by Brenda Z. Guiberson

Why This Text?

Students frequently read informational texts that are structured in a variety of ways. This lesson guides students to explore how one author uses cause-and-effect organization in an informational text.

 ▶ **View It!**
Professional Development Podcast:
Text Complexity

Key Learning Objective: The student will be able to identify and analyze cause-and-effect organization and determine meanings of technical language in an informational text.

For practice and application:

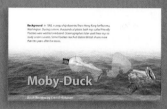
Moby-Duck

Close Reader selection
"Moby-Duck"
Book Review by David Holahan

RI 1 Cite text evidence.
RI 2 Determine central idea; provide a summary.
RI 4 Determine the meaning of words and phrases.
RI 5 Analyze structure.
RI 7 Integrate information.
SL 1a Come to discussions prepared.
SL 1b Follow rules for discussions.
SL 1c Pose and respond to questions.
SL 1d Review key ideas and demonstrate understanding.
SL 5 Include multimedia components and visual displays in presentations.
L 1c Recognize and correct inappropriate shifts in pronoun person.
L 4a Use context as a clue to the meaning of a word or phrase.
L 4b Determine or clarify meaning using common Greek affixes.
L 6 Acquire and use grade-appropriate words and phrases.

 ### Text Complexity Rubric

	Mammoth Shakes and Monster Waves: Destruction in 12 Countries
Quantitative Measures	Lexile: 1140L

Levels of Meaning/Purpose

more than one purpose; implied but easy to infer

Structure

implicit text structure

Qualitative Measures

Language Conventionality and Clarity

more complex descriptions

Knowledge Demands

some specialized knowledge required

Reader/Task Considerations
- Teacher determined
- Vary by individual reader and type of text
- See the Text X-Ray for suggested Reader/Task Considerations.

Making

Language Development

Effective Expression

Content Knowledge

Foundational Skills

Text Complexity: Qualitative Measures

Levels of Meaning/Purpose

more than one purpose; implied but easy to infer

Help students determine meaning of words and phrases.

- Teacher's Edition side notes, pp. 139, 140, 144, 149, 152, 153
- English Language Support, pp. 139, 144
- Close Read Screencasts, p. 139
- Strategies for Annotation, p. 149
- Determine Meanings of Words and Phrases, p. 153

Guide students to apply the Learning Circles strategy to comprehend the text.

- English Language Support, p. 148

Help students synthesize information.

- Teacher's Edition side note, p. 152
- English Language Support, p. 152
- When Students Struggle, p. 147

ZOOM IN ON DETERMINING MEANINGS OF WORDS AND PHRASES Tell students that informational texts often contain **technical language**, or terms that are specific to a particular field of study or topic. Model for students how to determine meanings of unfamiliar words and phrases by using context clues, footnotes, and reference materials.

- As students read, have them use a chart to list the technical words and phrases that they encounter, along with the words' definitions.
- After students have finished the text, have them join small groups to compare their charts and explain how they determined the meanings of the words and phrases they listed.

Structure

implicit text structure

Help students analyze text structure.

- Teacher's Edition side notes, pp. 140, 141, 143, 144, 145, 146, 147, 148, 149, 150, 151, 153
- English Language Support, pp. 140, 141, 148
- When Students Struggle, p. 143
- Strategies for Annotation, pp. 146, 153
- Performance Task, p. 154
- Analyze Structure: Cause and Effect, p. 153

To reteach how to identify cause and effect, see

- Analyze Structure: Cause and Effect, p. 156a

▶ *Use It!* *Level Up* Tutorial: Plot and Cause-and-Effect Organization

ZOOM IN ON RECOGNIZING CAUSE-AND-EFFECT ORGANIZATION Tell students that a **cause-and-effect** pattern of organization is one method that writers use to connect events. Two events are related by cause and effect when one event brings about, or causes, the other. One cause can produce multiple effects.

- Have small groups work together to fill in a cause-and-effect graphic organizer as they read the first section of the article (lines 1–29).
- Then have groups share their work with the class.
- Have students work in pairs to repeat this exercise as they read each remaining section of the article.

Language Conventionality and Clarity

more complex descriptions

Teach unfamiliar academic vocabulary in context.

- Teacher's Edition Critical Vocabulary notes, pp. 140, 144, 145, 146, 149, 150, 155
- Applying Academic Vocabulary, p. 141
- Strategies for Annotation, p. 155
- Vocabulary Strategy: Greek Affixes, p. 155

Help students understand the language of the text.

- Teacher's Edition side notes, pp. 142, 156
- English Language Support, pp. 142, 150, 156
- Language Conventions: Shifts in Pronoun Person, p. 156

ZOOM IN ON **AVOIDING SHIFTS IN PRONOUN PERSON** Remind students that a **pronoun** is used in place of a noun. Explain that the noun that the pronoun refers to is called the **antecedent**. The pronoun must agree with its antecedent. For example, a first-person pronoun cannot refer to a third-person noun. Display the following sentence:

> When Sara saw the enormous ocean wave, _____ (they/we/she/you) ran from the beach.

- Guide students to identify the antecedent in the sentence (*Sara*).
- Then have pairs read the sentence aloud with each answer choice.
- Ask them to decide which pronoun agrees with its third-person antecedent.

Knowledge Demands

some specialized knowledge required

Help students integrate information about the topic from text, visuals, and multimedia.

- Teacher's Edition Background note, p. 139
- Teacher's Edition side note, p. 142
- English Language Support, p. 148

 Building Background

 For more historical background, students can view the video "The Science of Tsunamis" in their eBooks.

ZOOM IN ON **INTEGRATING INFORMATION FROM TEXT, VISUALS, AND MULTIMEDIA** Share with students the information in the Background note on Teacher's Edition page 139. Remind students that when they encounter unfamiliar terms or concepts in the article, they can use a variety of resources to clarify information.

- Before students begin to read, model how to use a footnote to pronounce and define a term.
- Remind students that the charts and photographs can help clarify information.
- Have students view the History video to provide context and historical background.

Suggested Reader/Task Considerations

You might consider the following before assigning this informational text to students:

- Do students have the necessary attention to read and comprehend an informational article of this length?
- Do students have the necessary visualization skills to imagine what is being described in the text?

ZOOM IN ON **SUPPORTING COMPREHENSION**

- Use the article's subheadings to divide the reading into manageable segments. Have students read in mixed-ability groups, and provide opportunities for students to ask questions and discuss the text after completing each section.
- Tell students that the author uses vivid and precise language to help readers picture complicated events. As you read aloud the first paragraph, encourage them to focus on descriptive details to create mental images of the earthquake. Ask volunteers to share their images.

CLOSE READ

For more context and historical background, students can view the video "The Science of Tsunamis" in their eBooks.

Brenda Z. Guiberson Have students read the information about the author.

Background Explain that many tectonic plates make up Earth's surface, and they fit together like a giant jigsaw puzzle. They move very slowly, over long periods of time. Occasionally, plates get snagged on one another. Tension builds as the plates continue to move. When the plates break free, the energy released results in an earthquake.

SETTING A PURPOSE Direct students to use the Setting a Purpose prompt to focus their reading. Remind them to write down questions as they read.

Determine Meaning: Technical Language (LINES 1–8)   RI 1, RI 4

Tell students that **technical language** refers to terms suited to a particular topic or field of study. Explain that sometimes readers can use clues in the text to help them determine the meaning of technical language. Good readers will also use a dictionary or glossary to help them determine or confirm a term's meaning.

Ⓐ CITE TEXT EVIDENCE Have students review lines 1–8 and use text clues that help them identify the meaning of *plate*, as it is used here. (*The phrase "a big chunk of earth" helps explain that, in this context, plate refers to huge slabs of earth.*)

Ⓑ ASK STUDENTS to find the term *Richter scale* in line 8 and to tell how the footnote helps explain what it is. (*The footnote tells what the scale is and whom it was named for.*) Tell students that if there is no footnote or glossary entry, they should check a dictionary.

English Language Support

Point out the word *scale* in line 8 and explain that it has several meanings. Write the following definitions on the board: (1) a series of musical tones; (2) a system of classifying according to relative size, strength, amount, etc.; (3) a thin, small, overlapping plate that forms part of the covering of a fish.

ASK STUDENTS to choose the correct meaning of *scale* based on the context of the line and the information in the footnote. (*definition 2*)

Brenda Z. Guiberson *wanted to be a jungle explorer when she was a child. Much of her childhood was spent swimming, watching birds and salmon, and searching for arrowheads near her home along the Columbia River in the state of Washington. After volunteering at her child's school, Guiberson became interested in writing nature books for children. She says that she writes for the child in herself, the one who loves adventure, surprises, and learning new things—a jungle explorer in words.*

MAMMOTH SHAKES AND MONSTER WAVES,
Destruction in 12 Countries

Informational Text by Brenda Z. Guiberson

SETTING A PURPOSE As you read, pay attention to how earthquakes affect people, animals, the land, and the ocean, and think about how people explain and deal with the impact of these damaging events.

myNotebook

As you read, mark up the text. Save your work to *myNotebook*.
- Highlight details
- Add notes and questions
- Add new words to *myWordList*

Head for the Hills! It's Earth Against Earth

Ⓐ For centuries, a big chunk of earth under the Indian Ocean known as the India plate has been scraping against another chunk of earth, the Burma plate. At eight o'clock in the morning on December 26, 2004, this scraping reached a breaking point near the island of Sumatra in Indonesia. A 750-mile section of earth snapped and popped up as a new 40-foot-high cliff. This created one of the biggest earthquakes ever, 9.2 to 9.3 on the Richter scale.[1] At a hospital, oxygen tanks tumbled and beds lurched. At a mosque, the dome
10 crashed to the floor. On the street, athletes running a race fell   Ⓑ

---

[1] **Richter scale** (rĭk´tər): a scale ranging from 1 to 10 that expresses the amount of energy released by an earthquake; named after Charles Richter, an American seismologist.

(cl) ©Corbis; (c) © Getty Images; (cr) ©Corbis

Close Read Screencasts   Close Read

Modeled Discussions

Have students click the *Close Read* icon in their eBook to access two screencasts in which readers discuss and annotate the following key passages:
- how the tsunami waves were created (lines 39–49)
- the rescue of a trapped survivor (lines 150–159)

As a class, view and discuss at least one of these videos. Then have students pair up to do an independent close read of an additional passage on the shortcomings of the Pacific Ocean warning system (lines 340–351).

Analyze Structure: Cause and Effect (LINES 13–18; 19–24)

RI 1,
RI 5

Tell students that authors can organize their writing using **cause-and-effect organization.** Explain that two events are related when one event brings about, or causes, the other. The event that happens first is the **cause;** the one that follows is the **effect.** One cause can have one or many effects.

C **CITE TEXT EVIDENCE** Have students reread lines 13–18, identify a cause, and summarize its effects. *(cause: the earthquake; effects: islands rise and sink, villages fill with water and fish, planet vibrates half an inch)*

D **ASK STUDENTS** to reread lines 19–24 and explain why the author includes this text. *(The author tells about one man's experience, which describes other immediate effects of the earthquake.)*

Determine Meaning: Technical Language

RI 1,
RI 4

(LINES 32–38)

Remind students that technical language refers to terms suited to a particular topic or field of study.

E **CITE TEXT EVIDENCE** Have students review lines 32–33, give the meaning of the term *epicenter*, and tell how they know this. *(Footnote gives meaning; context clues, such as "near" and "earthquake," help to clarify.)* Then have them review lines 34–38 and repeat the process for *tsunami*. *(Footnote gives meaning; context clues, such as "swallowed up," and the distance the wave travels show how huge it is.)*

CRITICAL VOCABULARY

rupture: The author uses the word *ruptured* to show how the ocean floor burst and broke.

ASK STUDENTS to tell how *ruptured* helps them to understand or imagine the event better than words such as *cracked* or *broke*. *(Possible response: The word* ruptured, *along with the other words in the text, helps readers picture the huge event. You can almost see the sea floor splitting apart.)*

---

to the ground and a hotel crumbled. Houses on stilts swayed and collapsed. A man tried to grab a fence that jumped back and forth, up and down, and side to side. The quake, the longest ever recorded, lasted 10 minutes. Some islands rose up, and others sank, leaving "fish now swimming around in once idyllic, palm-fringed villages," wrote Madhusree Mukerjee. The shaking was so severe that it caused the entire planet to vibrate one half inch. And that was just the beginning.

20 Maslahuddin Daud, a fisherman, said, "I had barely started fishing when the earthquake struck. The earth shook violently, coconut trees crashed noisily against each other, and people fell down in prayer. . . . I lingered at the beach to talk with an older fisherman. We watched the water drain from the beach, exposing thousands of fish." He saw a huge wave filling the horizon. Someone yelled, "*Air laut naik*"—"The sea is coming"—but tourists stayed on the beach, and locals collected flopping fish stranded by the receding water. Few seemed to understand that destruction was rolling their way at the speed of a jetliner.

The Sea Is Coming?

30 All along the shorelines of a dozen countries, villagers, tourists, royalty, and soldiers were in the path of monster waves able to cross the entire ocean. People near the epicenter[2] of the earthquake were swallowed up in less than 30 minutes. The tsunami[3] didn't reach others for an hour, two hours, even six hours or more. Without a warning system, hundreds of thousands of people were caught unawares, many so far away from the source of the wave that they never even knew there had been an earthquake.

Yet earth against earth was the cause of all their problems. 40 When the sea floor **ruptured**, trillions of tons of water were

Close Read

rupture
(rŭp´chər) *v.* To *rupture* means to break open or burst.

---

[2] **epicenter** (ĕp´ĭ-sĕn´tər): the point of the earth's surface directly above the focus of an earthquake.
[3] **tsunami** (tsōō-nä´mē): a huge ocean wave caused by an underwater earthquake or volcanic eruption.

English Language Support

Analyze Cause/Effect Relationships Tell students that writers may use a cause-and-effect pattern of organization to show relationships between events. In this pattern, one event (the cause) brings about another event (the effect). Have students reread lines 19–24.

• Work with students to list the events described in these lines. *(earthquake struck, the earth shook, trees crashed, people prayed, water drained from beach)* Guide them to see that the earthquake caused the events that followed.

F instantly pushed up 40 feet by the rising land. Then the water came back down, and the collapse created a series of waves. These were not wind-whipped waves moving along at a few miles per hour. They were tsunami waves, racing out at 500 miles per hour. In deep water, the waves caused hardly a blip, but whenever one reached a coastline, the bottom slowed in the shallow water while the top kept coming, higher and higher, until massive walls of water, some over 100 feet high, smashed into land with the strength of many hurricanes.

50   The waves just kept coming, salty and polluted, with the second more powerful than the first, then the third and fourth, all so cluttered with debris that they became moving piles of concrete and cars, boats and coconuts, wood and tin, nails and glass, survivors and corpses. A shopkeeper said the noise was "like a thousand drums." As wave after wave smashed through villages, children were pulled from the arms of parents, clothing was ripped from bodies, and people and their possessions were flipped over, cut, and punched. Some were swept two miles inland, while others were caught in the
60 backwash[4] and carried out to sea. When the water started to drain, survivors shimmied down from coconut trees or other high places feeling dazed and confused. Weak voices called out to them from vast piles of debris. It was a changed world, soggy and broken; nothing looked familiar, nothing at all.

This was the scene in many countries around the Indian Ocean. The waves swamped the Aceh Province of Indonesia, surged through Sri Lanka, Thailand, Myanmar (Burma), Bangladesh, Malaysia, and India, flooded the Maldives and Seychelles, and eventually reached Africa. In Aceh,
70 169,000 died quickly, but death was also reported 16 hours and 5,300 miles away in South Africa. The tsunami left 225,000 dead, 500,000 injured, and millions without homes or jobs. One-third of the dead were children, and 9,000 were tourists. Plain luck helped some to survive. Only a few received a warning.

---

[4] **backwash** (băk´wôsh´): a backward flow of water.

APPLYING ACADEMIC VOCABULARY

impact	constraint

THINK-PAIR-SHARE Ask pairs to answer and discuss the questions below. Guide students to include the vocabulary words *impact* and *constraint* in their responses. Let volunteers share their responses with the class.

- What is the **impact** of the natural disasters on people and animals?
- What **constraints** did rescue and medical workers have to deal with following the natural disasters described in the article?

TEACH

CLOSE READ

For more context and historical background, students can view the video "The Science of Tsunamis" in their eBooks.

Analyze Structure: Cause and Effect (LINES 39–49)   RI 2, RI 5

Explain to students that one way to identify and understand cause-and-effect organization is to look for signal words, such as *cause, because, effect, led to,* and *since,* that show how events are related.

F **ASK STUDENTS** to reread lines 39–49. Have them point out a signal word *(the word* cause *in line 39)* and then summarize how "earth against earth" caused tsunami waves to form. *(Possible response: When the huge plates scraped against each other, all the ocean waters were pushed up, and giant waves were created when the water came back down. The giant, powerful waves kept moving toward land.)* Then ask students how this paragraph fits into the text's overall structure and develops the ideas of the text. *(This paragraph develops the idea of how the earthquake and the tsunami were connected and how people who did not feel the earthquake would soon see its effects in the tsunami. This paragraph fits into the text's overall structure by connecting information in the first section with information in the second section.)*

English Language Support

Have students work with a partner to summarize lines 39–49. Provide the following sentence frames to guide students' responses.

The earth plates _____.

This caused the water to _____.

When the water came down, _____.

The waves_____.

Integrate Information RI 7

(LINES 65–75, DIAGRAM)

Explain to students that a **diagram** is an illustration that can show the relationship between the parts of a whole. Tell them that readers **integrate** ideas when they put together, or **synthesize,** individual pieces of information to better understand a subject.

G **ASK STUDENTS** to review lines 65–75 and the diagram that appears at the end of the section titled "The Sea Is Coming?" Ask them how the diagram and its caption, along with the text in lines 65–75, help them better understand the event. *(Possible response: I read in lines 65–75 how many countries were affected by the tsunami, but the diagram helps me understand how gigantic it was and how far the waves traveled.)*

Analyze Language RI 1, RI 4

(LINES 79–85)

Explain that a **simile** is a type of figurative language that compares two unlike things using the word *like* or *as.* Point out the simile in lines 79–80, "like some great monster was slurping it up with a straw." Explain how the simile helps readers imagine something so unusual.

H **CITE TEXT EVIDENCE** Ask students to review lines 80–85, identify another simile, and explain what the simile helps them imagine. *(The simile "longboats were bobbing up and down like toys in a bathtub" helps readers picture that the tsunami was so powerful, it made sturdy objects, like boats, seem like toys.)*

G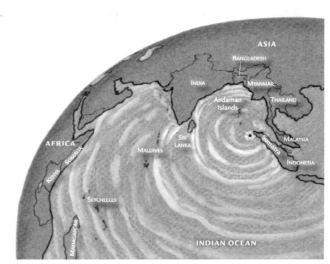

Racing at 500 miles per hour, the first wave took 20 minutes to reach Sumatra, 2 hours to Sri Lanka, 3½ hours to the Maldives, and 7½ hours to reach Africa. Traveling across the ocean at just two feet high, the waves piled up in shallow water to form great surges that reached 20 feet, 40 feet, and even much higher.

Text in FOCUS
Trumpeting Elephants, Skittering Crabs, and the Power of Story

On a beach in Thailand, 10-year-old Tilly Smith was enjoying Christmas vacation and building sand castles with her sister. She noticed hundreds of tiny crabs scuttling out of the water. Then she saw the sea retreat far back into the ocean, like some great monster was slurping it up with a straw. No one seemed to notice, so she started to play again but then stood up in alarm as the sea turned white, churning with bubbles. A great wave was building up on the horizon as far as she could see. Fishermen's longboats were bobbing up and down like toys in a bathtub. Tilly remembered a geography lesson two weeks earlier at her school in England. These were the warning signs she had just learned. A tsunami was coming! Her mother wasn't convinced, but Tilly persuaded her father to get the hotel staff to evacuate guests while she alerted those

80

142 Collection 3

English Language Support

Word Study Review these sounds represented by the letter *c.*

- *c* stands for the /k/ sound in *can* and *core*
- *c* stands for the /s/ sound in *voice* and *pace*

Tell students that when *c* is followed by the vowel *e, i,* or *y,* it often (but not always) makes the /s/ sound.

Use the word *ocean* to point out an exception. Explain that in *ocean, c* makes the /sh/ sound, even though it is followed by *e.*

ASK STUDENTS to sort the following words according to the sound represented by the letter *c.* Before students begin, pronounce each word and clarify the meaning of any unfamiliar words.

vacation	notice	coming
evacuate	racing	scrambled
coast	cattle	decide

(/k/ sound—vacation, coming, evacuate, scrambled, coast, cattle; /s/ sound—racing, notice, decide)

90 on the beach. With this warning, they became some of the few
survivors in the area.

On another beach, an eight-year-old named Amber Mason
was riding on an elephant called Ning Nong. The elephant
started to trumpet loudly and paw the ground with feet able
to sense low vibrations. The mahout[5] riding with her tried to
calm the animal, but the elephant charged up a hill. While
the girl, elephant, and mahout made it safely to high ground,
others on the beach couldn't outrun the tsunami waves that
soon followed.

100 Before the waves hit Sri Lanka, all the animals in a
national park started to behave strangely. Monkeys chattered
with terror, snakes went rigid, cattle bolted, and flamingos
took flight. All of them scrambled to the highest places
they could reach, and the keepers, who had never seen such
behavior, decided to follow.

Near the Similan Islands off the western coast of Thailand,
local divers saw dolphins jump madly around them and then
torpedo far out to sea. "Quick, follow them," they urged the
captain. They knew stories of animals that help and thought
110 these dolphins could sense something unusual that the divers
could not detect. Because, along with several other boats, they
followed the dolphins to deep water, they were spared the
smashing blow of the tsunami.

Closer to shore, Wimon, a fisherman, was eating
watermelon when the strangeness began. The water turned
murky with rocks bubbling at the top. He looked up to see
the beach stretching out five times its normal width. Had
there ever been such a low tide? Suddenly he was thrown off
his bench and felt weightless. His boat bobbed up and down
120 in a strange wave that surged past to flood his village to the
tops of the coconut trees. He worried about his wife and
two daughters, who couldn't swim. Then he saw the second
wave, spitting, rising even higher than the first. Should he
head straight into it? He watched other fishermen try, and
their boats split apart. He decided to go sideways, was lifted
20 feet, 30 feet, until he was surrounded by a hazy mist and
felt weightless again. He fell with a slam but survived. Of the
24 longboats in the area, his was the only one still intact.

---

[5] **mahout** (mə-hout´): a keeper and driver of an elephant.

CLOSE READ

Analyze Structure: Cause and Effect (LINES 92–113)

RI 1,
RI 5

Remind students that authors can use cause-and-effect relationships to organize ideas and information.

I **CITE TEXT EVIDENCE** Have students examine the cause-and-effect relationships in lines 92–113. Ask them to tell how the author organizes information that shows how some of the effects caused by the tsunami were alike. *(The author puts together information about how different animals, like elephants, creatures in a national park, and dolphins, all seemed to sense that danger was coming.)*

Remind students that signal words such as *because* and *as a result* can help readers determine how causes and effects are related.

J **ASK STUDENTS** to reread lines 111–113, identify a signal word, and explain how this text fits into the overall structure of the text. *(The signal word* because *helps point out that some divers survived the tsunami because they decided to follow dolphins out to deeper water. This cause-and-effect information fits into this section of text by explaining why some people survived the tsunami.)*

Text in FOCUS English Language Support

Building Background

Have students view the **Text in Focus** video in their eBook to build background that will help them better comprehend the article. Then have them use **Text in Focus Practice** to apply what they have learned.

WHEN STUDENTS STRUGGLE . . .

Explain that one cause can produce many effects. Reread lines 83–105 with students and help them identify the cause of the events described in the passage. Record the cause in a cause-and-effect graphic organizer. Then have pairs work together to identify the effects and add them to the graphic organizer.

 LEVEL UP TUTORIALS For additional support, assign the following *Level Up* tutorial: **Cause-and-Effect Organization.**
Interactive Graphic Organizer: Cause-and-Effect Chart

Determine Meaning: Technical Language
RI 1, RI 4

(LINES 129–142)

Remind students that technical language refers to terms suited to a particular topic or field of study, and that footnotes and context clues can help them determine the meaning of these terms.

(K) CITE TEXT EVIDENCE Ask students to review lines 129–142, tell the meaning of *aboriginal*, and explain how they know this. *(Footnote gives the meaning; context clues, such as "ancient tribes" and "ancient stories," clarify that* aboriginal *refers to people who have lived in an area for a long time.)*

Analyze Structure
RI 1, RI 5

(LINES 150–159)

Explain to students that, in order to show how a situation develops over time, an author may present a sequence of events. Signal words and phrases, such as *first*, *later on*, and *finally*, help make the order of events clear to readers.

(L) CITE TEXT EVIDENCE Have students review lines 150–159 and point out words and phrases that make the sequence of events clear. *(After; After two days; On the third day; Finally on the fifth day)* Then ask them to summarize the situation and tell why the author might have included it. *(A deliveryman was trapped for five days. Possible response: to show how difficult survival and rescue were after the tsunami)*

> ### CRITICAL VOCABULARY
>
> **gauge:** The author uses the word *gauge* to describe how ancient tribes observe nature and make judgments about the world around them.
>
> **ASK STUDENTS** to tell how gauging natural factors has helped ancient tribes survive. *(Possible response: By gauging changes in the depth of the sea and being alert to how creatures behave, they were more aware that something unusual was about to take place.)*

The ancient tribes on the remote Andaman and Nicobar
130 Islands have lived close to nature for centuries. They are said to detect changes by the smell of the wind and **gauge** the depth of the sea with the sounds of their oars. Every minute they pay close attention to the cries of birds and the behavior of animals. These natural clues warned them that something big was about to occur, and the stories of the forefathers told them what to do. "When the earth shakes, the sea will rise up onto the land. . . . Run to the hills or get into a boat and go far out to sea."

Some members of aboriginal[6] groups survived the tsunami
140 because they read the signs of nature; heeded ancient stories; packed up their children, baskets, nets, arrows, and embers; and headed for the hills. Most people, however, lost their homes and precious possessions. Almost all wild animals, including tigers, elephants, water buffalo, monkeys, and birds, survived in good shape. Endangered orangutans and other creatures that live in the rain forests of Sumatra were not affected by the tsunami until it was all over. The trees are an easy source of timber, and forest creatures are losing vast acres of habitat as people rebuild.

gauge
(gāj) *tr.v.* To *gauge* something is to measure it or judge it, as in to make an estimate.

Swamped and Scared

150 People caught in the tsunami suffered many injuries. After the waves receded, some were caught under deep piles of debris. A trapped deliveryman named Romi called and called for help but received no response. After two days, rain fell, and he was able to collect water for drinking. Mosquitoes feasted on him at night. On the third day, more people were trudging through the murky water to look for survivors. Four men tried to rescue Romi, but they failed. Finally on the fifth day, 25 men worked four hours and were finally able to haul him through miles of debris. All around, tens of thousands of corpses
160 needed to be buried quickly. Elephants and bulldozers were brought in to help with the wreckage.

As survivors returned to their villages, they often found that nothing remained—no familiar landmarks, no driveway, car, or motorbike. The house was gone and everything in it, including toothbrush, comb, lipstick, and frying pan. Power

---

[6] **aboriginal** (ăb´ə-rĭj´ə-nəl): having lived in an area from the beginning; earliest known.

was out, and phones were dead. According to one survivor, "Many people were literally left with nothing—not even coins in their pockets or clothes on their backs." They suffered from breathing problems after swallowing mud, sand, and toxic
170 water. Before starting to rebuild, many spent days, and then weeks, looking for lost relatives.

On the first day, those nearest the earthquake were **traumatized** by 37 more tremors. During the next days, there were more earthquakes: 18 on Monday, 5 on Tuesday, 7 on Wednesday, 7 on Thursday, 9 on Friday. Each time the ground trembled, people who still had shelter scampered outside, "joining the others who feared that the walls and ceiling would fall in on them," wrote Barry Bearak.

The tsunami left a huge problem of contaminated water.
180 In Sri Lanka, for instance, 40,000 wells were destroyed and the freshwater aquifer[7] became toxic. In the Maldives, 16 coral reef atolls[8] lost their freshwater and may be uninhabitable until decades of monsoons can refresh the supply. Other countries had similar problems as the salty waves mixed with freshwater and sewers. Thousands of banana, rice, and mango plantations were destroyed by thick layers of salty sludge. For drinking, Spain and Australia delivered gigantic water purifying machines. Military ships from the United States and Singapore made freshwater from the sea, and several
190 companies sent water purifiers, including one that could turn raw sewage into drinking water in seconds. Some purifiers were lightweight and could be flown in by helicopter to areas that lost all road and bridge access.

As people sought help for severe injuries, supplies were scarce. At one hospital only 5 of 956 health workers were available. Barry Bearak wrote, "Little in the way of supplies was kept in the emergency room—no IVs, no painkillers, few bandages. As in many poor nations, new patients were examined and then their families were sent to buy drugs,
200 syringes, and other items needed for treatment." When health workers ran out of anesthetic, ice cubes were used to deaden the pain. When they ran out of suture threads, wounds were wrapped in plastic snipped from seat covers or left open. The

traumatize
(trô′mə-tīz′, trou′-) *tr.v.*
To *traumatize* means to upset or shock someone, causing emotional and mental pain.

---

[7] **aquifer** (ăk′wə-fər): an underground layer of earth, sand, or gravel that holds and can release water.
[8] **atolls** (ăt′ôlz′): ringlike coral islands and reefs that nearly or entirely enclose a body of water.

CLOSE READ

Analyze Structure: Cause and Effect (LINES 179–193)

RI 1, RI 5

Explain to students that one cause can have multiple effects, and that some of those events then lead to more cause-and-effect relationships.

Ⓜ CITE TEXT EVIDENCE Have students reread lines 179–186 and identify effects the tsunami had on water supplies. *(Possible responses: Freshwater supplies became contaminated; saltwater mixed with sewer systems; crops and plantations were ruined.)*

Ⓝ ASK STUDENTS to summarize information from lines 187–193 about what had to happen as a result of the problems with water. Then have them tell why the author used this cause-and-effect structure to present this information. *(Possible responses: Solutions had to be found; many countries supplied systems for purifying water. This structure helps readers see how the effects of the quake and the tsunami developed and increased the danger for everyone involved.)*

CRITICAL VOCABULARY

traumatize: The author says that those close to the earthquake were traumatized by the many tremors that followed.

ASK STUDENTS to tell why the "next days" continued to be traumatizing. *(Possible response: There were many more earthquakes over the next several days, and people were in a state of fear and distress from the constant danger.)*

English Language Support

Determine Meaning Tell students that they can learn the meaning of an unfamiliar word in several ways. Read aloud lines 139–142 and explain that the word *aboriginal* comes from Latin, meaning "from the beginning."

- Read the footnote aloud. Then guide students to identify context clues that can help explain the meaning of *aboriginal*. ("read the signs of nature," "ancient stories")

- Ask pairs to look up synonyms for *aboriginal*. Explain that synonyms, or words that mean nearly the same thing, can help them understand and remember the word's meaning. *(Possible responses: native, ancient, original)*

- Ask students to write original sentences that contain *aboriginal*. Let volunteers share their sentences with the class.

Analyze Structure: Cause and Effect (LINES 220–228)

RI 1,
RI 5

Tell students that a cause-and-effect pattern of organization can help authors present complicated information and help readers understand it.

⊙ **CITE TEXT EVIDENCE** Ask students to review lines 220–228 and cite examples of cause-and-effect relationships that the author uses to present information. (*Possible responses: Foreigners had not been allowed in Aceh Province earlier, but now their help was welcome. Relief workers were afraid to go into war zones, so peace talks were held among different groups to work together as a community.*) Ask students what these relationships explain. (*Lines 220–221: They explain how war zones made relief efforts more complicated.*)

> #### CRITICAL VOCABULARY
>
> **antibiotic**: The author uses the word *antibiotics* as part of a list of supplies from relief workers.
>
> **ASK STUDENTS** to discuss why antibiotics would be needed in regions that were affected by the tsunami. (*Many people had infections; water and hospital supplies were contaminated by bacteria.*)

ones who had wounds cleaned but not stitched were actually lucky. After three days, those with stitches often developed fatal infections when contaminated water was trapped inside their injury.

Relief workers from around the world eventually arrived with vaccines, **antibiotics**, food, blankets, tents, field hospitals, 210 building supplies, and mosquito nets. In general, health care was well planned and prevented the outbreak of diseases, but the number of dead and wounded could be overwhelming. Sometimes tourists were treated before villagers. Villagers were treated before Burmese immigrant workers. Friends and family were treated before strangers. In India, people called Dalits, "untouchables," traditionally judged to be "less than human," were denied aid, even fresh drinking water. Social problems that exist before a disaster get magnified or changed afterward.

antibiotic
(ăn′tĭ-bī-ŏt′ĭk) *n.* An *antibiotic* is a drug used in medicine to kill bacteria and to cure infections.

Rebuilding

220 Parts of India, Sri Lanka, and Indonesia were war zones before the tsunami, and these situations complicated relief efforts. In Indonesia, for instance, no foreigners had been allowed into Aceh Province for years because of the fighting. After so many died, however, foreign help was welcomed. Later, peace talks were held to aid the relief efforts because workers were afraid to go into war zones. Groups felt it was time for Muslims, Hindus, Christians, and Buddhists to work together as members of a world community.

In many areas it was both the custom and law that women 230 could enter the water only if fully clothed and wearing a head scarf. Therefore, most of them had never learned to swim, and the waves killed three times more women than men. Before the tsunami, women in Aceh Province had a hard time finding spouses because large numbers of men had died fighting in the long guerrilla⁹ war. After the tsunami, thousands of men were left without wives and children, and there were many new marriages.

In some areas, unscrupulous people saw a chance to increase their wealth during the chaos. A powerful

---

⁹ **guerrilla** (gə-rĭl′ə): irregular military; a guerrilla war is one fought by small, irregular bands of soliders that try to undermine the enemy.

Strategies for Annotation 🖊 📋 Annotate it!

Analyze Structure: Cause and Effect

RI 5,
RI 7

Share these strategies for guided or independent analysis:

- Highlight in yellow an event, or cause, that could lead to other events.
- Highlight in green effects that have already occurred as a result of this event.
- Review your highlights. On a note, integrate causes and effects and then explain what you have learned.

[women] could enter the water only if fully clothed and wearing a head scarf. Therefore, most of them had never learned to swim, and the waves killed three times more women . . . thousands of men were left without wives and children, and there were many new marriages.

240 corporation, the Far East Company, for instance, tried to take land from villagers in Laem Pom, Thailand, who had lived on a beautiful beach for many years. With all documents gone, it was hard to prove ownership of the land. A local woman named Dang decided to fight when the company posted a bodyguard to keep them out. Not only did the survivors want to rebuild, but they were desperate to search through the debris for bodies. Dang told her story to Parliament, but nothing changed. Finally she asked her neighbors to bring whatever documents they had; as a group, they would
250 challenge the bodyguard. "He might be able to stop one of us, or even a few or us, but he can't stop all of us," she said. Twenty-seven families gathered together and were able to walk past the bodyguard. They set up a camp on a concrete slab.

An official offered Dang a bribe of five furnished houses plus a scooter and telephone if she would leave. Dang refused and eventually received donations of 30,000 baht (about $830); 10,000 bricks; 5,000 tiles; and help from Thai students. Erich Krauss wrote, "It reminded her that there were still good people in this world—people whose hearts were large enough
260 to care about the people of Laem Pom."

A man named Wichien missed the tsunami because he was inland diving for river sand used to make ceramics. His wife, Nang, tried to escape on a truck but got caught in a traffic jam. She had worked since the age of six and once learned how to harvest coconuts, so she was able to shimmy

©Getty Images

CLOSE READ

Analyze Structure: Cause and Effect (LINES 238–260)

RI 1,
RI 5,
RI 7

Remind students that when they look for cause-and-effect relationships, they need to integrate pieces of information to help them understand a larger idea.

P **CITE TEXT EVIDENCE** Ask students to reread lines 238–253 and tell the cause-and-effect relationships the author describes. *(A company tried to take land from villagers; a woman decided to fight; she and 27 other families set up camp on the land.)* Then have them reread lines 254–260 and summarize how the situation turned out. *(The villagers were able to reclaim and rebuild their community.)*

Q **ASK STUDENTS** to review lines 258–260. Have them integrate the information in these lines with what they have read in lines 238–253 and explain why the author included these cause-and-effect relationships. *(Possible response: The author wants readers to know that when terrible things happen, other bad things might also happen, but that good things can come out in the end.)*

WHEN STUDENTS STRUGGLE . . .

Have individuals or partners complete a graphic organizer, similar to the one shown, to integrate information.

Have students write summary sentences to tell what the author explains in lines 238–253 and in lines 254–260. Guide them to put together these two ideas to create a larger one.

| A company tried to take land away from villagers. | + | Donations helped the villagers reclaim their land. | = | After a disaster, people may do both bad and good things. |

LEVEL UP TUTORIALS For additional support, assign the following *Level Up* tutorial: **Synthesizing Information.**

Analyze Structure: Cause and Effect (LINES 271–287)

RI 5

Remind students that authors use cause-and-effect organization to show the relationship between events.

Ⓡ **ASK STUDENTS** to review lines 271–287. Ask them to tell how the events in these lines are related to the earlier examples the author provides about relief and rebuilding efforts. *(Possible response: Like the examples of what happened in Aceh Province and to villagers in Laem Pom, the events in these lines show how religion and politics got in the way of providing relief to tsunami survivors.)*

English Language Support

Have pairs review earlier examples of obstacles that got in the way of relief and rebuilding efforts. One partner can reread and report on the example in lines 220–228; the other can reread and report on lines 238–260. Pairs can then discuss how those examples are similar to the events in lines 271–287. Encourage students to express their ideas using a variety of verbs *(show how, suggest that, indicate that).*

---

up a tree. She managed to hold on at the top even as ants swarmed over her body. As she called out to Buddha, she could hear what sounded like "a thousand children calling out for their parents and a thousand parents calling out for their

270 children."

After spending several days in a hospital, she and her husband discovered that part of their house remained standing but needed much repair. Some materials were provided by a group who also brought Bibles and instructions to read certain sections. "Our God will help you," they said, and then sent a van to take them to church. This was confusing to Nang because, according to Erich Krauss, "She was a Buddhist. She loved going to the temple to pray with the monks. When the wave had taken her under, she had

280 called out to the great Buddha."

The church group never really provided the help Nang wanted, so she took a job cleaning the house of a local official. She then discovered "rice cookers, gas stoves, dishes, bowls" stored in a room instead of being distributed to villagers who needed them. When Nang asked for a rice cooker, "the leader's assistant would say she would get something tomorrow but the tomorrow they talked about never came," said Erich Krauss.

Wonderful assistance was donated to the tsunami survivors but many of them also had to deal with theft,

290 deception, and disappointment. Relief workers had the best success when they found out what the local people needed, included them in the planning, and then made sure necessary materials were delivered. For example, when villagers wanted to rebuild using traditional methods, engineers gave them a demonstration showing that a similar but stronger house design would hold up better in the next earthquake. Models were made of both types of houses and put on a "shake table" to imitate an earthquake. When the traditional house crumbled and the reinforced house did not, all agreed the new

300 design would be better. Then they worked together to include features that fit the lifestyle of the village.

Tree Zones

Many people noticed that some shorelines were damaged much more than others, even though they were close together. A study in October 2005 by seven nations that included

---

English Language Support

Learning Circles Use the strategy introduced on page 138a to deepen students' understanding and to encourage collaboration.

- First, organize the class into small groups of three or four. Divide the text into the nine sections introduced by headings. Assign one or two sections to each group.
- Then, have members of each group select their individual roles. For example, one student can note unfamiliar vocabulary, another can identify and consider interesting language, and a third can prepare questions about the text and take notes.
- Next, read aloud or present an audio recording of the text to the class, reminding students to perform the duties associated with their selected roles. Explain that each of them is expected to share his or her notes about the text with the group.
- Finally, have students discuss their findings. Encourage them to respond by asking clarifying questions and to build on the comments of the group member who is sharing.

ecologists, botanists, geographers, a forester, and a tsunami wave engineer found that "areas with trees suffered less destruction than areas without trees." They calculated that 30 trees per 100 square meters could reduce the maximum flow of the waves by more than 90 percent. "Just like the degradation of wetlands in Louisiana almost certainly increased Hurricane Katrina's destructive powers," they concluded, "the degradation of mangroves in India magnified the tsunami's destruction." They found similar results in areas where coral reefs had been destroyed to make shrimp farms. Houses with landscaping also experienced much less scouring and water damage.

After the study of beach damage, local communities decided to replant mangrove forests and clean out debris from coral reefs. These inexpensive actions will provide benefits not just for the villagers but also for sea creatures that use forest roots and coral for food, shelter, and nurseries.

In some areas, people have not been allowed to rebuild their homes along shorelines and must move inland. In crowded countries with little available land, this has not been easy. Fishermen suffered the most damage from the tsunami, and they prefer to live by the sea to watch their boats and nets. After the tsunami, some were sent to live in places so far from the sea that the transportation costs were more than their earnings as fishermen.

Warnings

The 2004 tsunami revealed that the Indian Ocean was in desperate need of a tsunami warning system, and 25 seismic stations[10] relaying information to 26 information centers were installed. Signs were also put up to identify evacuation routes. Still, the system is not yet perfect. Another earthquake and tsunami struck Indonesia on July 17, 2006, but warnings were not passed along in time, and another 600 people died. Some suggest that the loudspeakers used by mosques to call Muslims to prayer would be effective for broadcasting tsunami warnings.

---

degradation
(dĕg´rə-dā´shən) *n.* Damage done to something in nature, by weather or water for example, is called *degradation.*

[10] **seismic stations** (sīz´mĭk stā´shənz): places that have sensors to detect ground motion, a clock, and a recorder for collecting data; must have several stations connected to a network to provide enough data to detect and locate earthquakes.

TEACH

CLOSE READ

Analyze Structure: Cause and Effect (LINES 302–321)
RI 1, RI 5

(S) CITE TEXT EVIDENCE Ask students to name a cause and an effect in lines 302–316. *(Cause: People noticed some shorelines were more damaged than others. Effect: A study found that trees and reefs reduced damage.)* Ask how this relationship fits into the text structure. *(It shows how people used information about the damage to contribute to the rebuilding process.)*

> **CRITICAL VOCABULARY**
>
> **degradation**: The author uses the word *degradation* to describe the Louisiana wetlands before Hurricane Katrina.
>
> **ASK STUDENTS** why the author chose the word *degradation* here rather than a word such as *destruction*. *(The word* degradation *is more exact because it refers to damage from weather.)*

Determine Meaning: Technical Language
RI 1, RI 4

(LINES 330–333)

(T) CITE TEXT EVIDENCE Have students explain seismic stations and tell how they know this. *(Context: "warning system"; "relaying information to 26 . . . centers"; Footnote: details about equipment and what happens there.)*

Strategies for Annotation 🖊 🖥 *Annotate it!*

Determine Meaning: Technical Language
RI 4

Share these strategies for guided or independent analysis:

- Highlight in yellow a technical term in the text.
- Highlight in green context clues for the term.
- Highlight in blue details in any footnotes that tell more about the term.
- Review your highlights. On a note, write your explanation of the term.

desperate need of a tsunami warning system, and 25 seismic stations relaying information to 26 information centers . . .

seismic stations . . . places that have sensors to detect ground motion, a clock, and a recorder for collecting data; stations connected to a network . . . to detect and locate earthquakes.

seismic station: a place with equipment that watches for earthquakes

Analyze Structure: Cause and Effect (LINES 352–363)

RI 1,
RI 5

Explain to students that sometimes authors present cause-and-effect relationships as possible solutions to a problem by suggesting that, if one thing takes place, something else will happen as a result.

U ASK STUDENTS to reread lines 352–363 and summarize a possible way to help scientists predict earthquakes. (*Possible response: By studying movement patterns of foraminifera, it might be possible to get an advance warning of earthquakes.*)

Remind students that signal words and phrases can help readers identify relationships between events.

V CITE TEXT EVIDENCE Have students reread lines 361–363, find a signal word, and explain how these lines fit into the overall structure of the text. (*because; They illustrate one way nature may give early warnings about earthquakes and elaborate on the "Warnings" section.*)

CRITICAL VOCABULARY

magnitude: The author uses the word *magnitude* to refer to an earthquake's measurement on the Richter scale.

ASK STUDENTS to discuss how the word *magnitude* connects with other words in the paragraph to tell about an earthquake's power. (*Words and phrases, such as "underwater earthquakes," "big tsunami waves," and "mega events," connect with* magnitude *to describe large, powerful natural occurrences.*)

---

340 The 2004 event also revealed that the Pacific Ocean warning system, in use since the 1960s, had only three of its six seafloor pressure sensors in working order. Money for upkeep had been scarce, even though tsunamis are common in the Pacific Ocean. In 1946 a tsunami started by an Alaska quake killed 159 people in Hilo, Hawaii, 3,000 miles away. Another Alaska quake in 1964 was a 9.2 magnitude, the biggest ever recorded in North America. It killed 115 people in Alaska, and the tsunami that followed killed another 16 people in Oregon and California. After the 2004 tsunami scare, the
350 United States provided more funds to expand and update the warning system.

Nature may provide advance warning signs of earthquakes if we learn to read them. In underwater studies along fault lines, for instance, interesting changes have been found in the populations of single-celled microorganisms called foraminifera. These tiny creatures, with shells the size of a grain of sand, are very particular about their environment. When the elevation of land changes, the organisms relocate. In underwater earthquake areas, they seem to move about 5
360 to 10 years before the great shaking caused by uplifting plates. Scientists hope to learn more about this because it is possible that the foraminifera can provide warnings for disasters of huge proportions.

The "Orphan Tsunami"

It takes an underwater earthquake of **magnitude** 9.0 or above to generate big tsunami waves. Several events like this have already occurred on the West Coast of the United States, but few people have heard about them. The evidence has only recently been found, and much of it was not in places where scientists usually look. These mega events sometimes occurred
370 when people with a written language were not around to record them.

The last event was over 300 years ago and has been called an "orphan tsunami" because some witnesses had no idea where it came from. The Samurai in Japan kept records of crop production for hundreds of years. On January 27, 1700, they recorded huge waves along 600 miles of coastline that caused flooded fields, ruined houses, fires, and shipwrecks. Since the Samurai were thousands of miles from the quake,

magnitude
(măg´nĭ-tōōd´) *n.*
Magnitude is a measure of the amount of energy released by an earthquake.

150 Collection 3

English Language Support

Improve Reading Fluency Select a paragraph or a passage from the text for repetitive oral reading. Work with individuals, or pair students who have low fluency rates with more fluent peers. Have the student read the passage aloud several times as you give guided feedback. With each reading, focus on a different element of fluency. Check for expression and volume, phrasing, smoothness, and pace.

they did not feel the shaking. To them, the big waves were a
380 mysterious "high tide." Legends in Japan refer to this flooding
event also.

Where did this orphan tsunami come from? Thousands of
miles across the ocean, Native American myths in the Pacific
Northwest provide a possible answer. Tribes from California
and on up the coast to Vancouver Island have many stories that
refer to a day when the earth shook and the ocean crashed,
leaving villages wiped out and canoes stranded high in trees.
Often the event is described as a battle between a great whale
and a thunderbird. Makah elder Helma Ward said, "The tide
390 came in and never left. There was a whale in the river and
the people couldn't figure out how it got there." To pinpoint
the date, scientists have found evidence of a magnitude-9
earthquake off the Washington coast that warped the seafloor
on January 26, 1700. At the same time, a whole forest died just
before the growing season began, and soil samples reveal great
saltwater flooding in many coast areas.

> **There was a whale in the river and the people couldn't figure out how it got there.**

The epicenter of this earthquake was just off the coast of
Washington and Oregon, where the Juan de Fuca plate pushes
under the North American plate in the same manner as the
400 Burma and India plates. The next big earthquake here will
threaten 10 million people along 500 miles of coastline that
includes large cities like Seattle, Portland, San Francisco, and
Vancouver, B.C. A warning system has been added off the
West Coast and evacuation routes established. Scientists now
monitor 24 hours a day and must live within five minutes of
their work because some coastal areas could be swallowed up in
15 minutes, and every minute of advance warning will count.

The blend of myth and evidence found in the earth has
brought scientists and Native Americans to share a new way

CLOSE READ

Analyze Structure: Cause and Effect (LINES 374–396) RI 5

Remind students that authors use cause-and-effect relationships to show how events are connected.

W **ASK STUDENTS** to reread lines 374–396 and explain how events in January of 1700 might have been connected to each other. *(An underwater earthquake that might have taken place could have been responsible for tsunamis on the northwest coast of North America and as far away as Japan.)*

TO CHALLENGE STUDENTS...

Make Comparisons In lines 397–407, the author discusses how an earthquake where the Juan de Fuca plate and North American plates meet might affect that region.

ASK STUDENTS to discuss how this region and those affected by the 2004 tsunami are alike and different. Have partners or small groups discuss questions like these:

- How are the human and animal populations in the regions alike and different?
- In what ways might relief efforts and challenges be similar? How might they be different?
- If an earthquake or tsunami struck in the Pacific Northwest, would responses by officials be similar or different from those you read about in Thailand? How?

Determine Meaning: Technical Language

RI 1,
RI 4

(LINES 423–435)

Point out that the author says in lines 408–410 that a field of study called geomythology tries to connect cultural myths with actual natural events that occurred long ago.

Ⓧ CITE TEXT EVIDENCE Ask students to review lines 423–435 and summarize an example the author provides of geomythology. *(Possible response: A myth from India tells of a group of temples that was destroyed by angry gods in the seventh century. The 2004 tsunami revealed structures in the place where the temples were supposedly located.)*

COLLABORATIVE DISCUSSION Before partners begin their discussion, have students work independently to draw their own conclusions about connections between myths and real-life events. Point out to partners that there is no one correct response. In their discussions, remind students to cite evidence from the text to support their ideas.

ASK STUDENTS to share any questions they generated in the course of reading and discussing the selection.

English Language Support

Draw Conclusions Before students begin their discussion, provide the following sentence stems:

According to the "Seven Pagodas" myth,

_____ .

The 2004 tsunami uncovered _____ .

Other myths _____ .

Archeologists might find myths useful because

_____ .

---

410 of looking at the past called geomythology. Ancient stories tell us that events happened before and will happen again. Science studies the danger, while stories enrich the record and provide clues about frequency. Native Americans have developed a new interest too. Ron Brainard, chairman of the Coos Tribal Council in Coos Bay, Oregon, asked his mother to tell the stories again because before they didn't listen.

Now You See It, Now You Don't

In the disaster of 2004, coral beds rose up to become land, and several islands sank. These events were recorded by eyewitnesses, cameras, satellites, and other measuring
420 devices. Sinking islands are more than myths. Six islands visited by early European explorers are now gone, some just under the waves.

In 1798, John Goldingham, a British astronomer and traveler to India, wrote down the details of a myth about the "Seven Pagodas," a group of temples from the seventh century that was swallowed up by the sea. The city was reported to be so beautiful that the gods sent a flood to engulf six of its seven temples.

That was the myth. Then came the 2004 tsunami, with
430 ferocious waves that shifted great volumes of beach sand. This scouring revealed handmade blocks and carvings of a lion, the head of an elephant, and a horse in flight, all at the mythical location of the Seven Pagodas. Did the tsunami uncover an ancient mythical place? Archaeologists have dated the carvings to the seventh century and are busy studying.

Myths from the South Pacific also tell of deities that "fish up" islands from the water and sometimes throw them back. Ancient tales around the world are providing clues about other prehistoric seismic events. When it's earth against earth,
440 nature keeps a record, and human survivors will always have a story to tell.

COLLABORATIVE DISCUSSION The last section of "Mammoth Shakes and Monster Waves" describes possible connections between myths and real-life events. With a partner, use evidence from the text to discuss whether you think legends can explain actual events in our earth's history.

Analyze Structure: Cause and Effect

Writers often use patterns of organization to help explain particular ideas. One commonly used pattern is **cause-and-effect** organization, which shows the relationship between an event and its **cause** (an event or action that makes another event happen) or **effect** (the outcome of an event or action). For example, the author of "Mammoth Shakes and Monster Waves" explains that a huge underwater earthquake took place on December 26, 2004. The text then gives details about what happened after this event. The earthquake was the cause that resulted in multiple effects.

To analyze cause-and-effect relationships:

- Look for words and phrases, such as *because, cause, effect, led to,* and *since,* that help you identify specific relationships between events.
- Determine how the ideas or events are related. A single cause can have one or multiple effects. More than one cause can lead to one effect.

Often, a visual such as a diagram can also help you understand the relationship between events. A diagram is an illustration that shows how something works or the relationship between the parts of a whole. When you examine a diagram in a text, you integrate its information with that of the text. To **integrate,** or **synthesize,** means to take individual pieces of information and combine them in order to gain a better understanding of a subject.

Determine Meanings of Words and Phrases

RI 4

Technical language refers to a group of terms suited to a particular field of study or topic. The terms *epicenter, Richter scale,* and *seismic stations* in "Mammoth Shakes and Monster Waves" are all technical terms related to earthquakes. Often technical words are defined in the text or in footnotes. For example, the term *Richter scale* in line 8 is defined in a footnote. However, the word *plate* in line 3 is not. *Plate* in this instance does not mean "a dish." In this selection, it has a specific meaning related to earthquakes. As you analyze the selection, refer to a dictionary to help you determine how words are used in the text.

CLOSE READ

Analyze Structure: Cause and Effect

RI 5, RI 7

Help students understand the terms, and how an author might use cause-and-effect organization to present and explain ideas in an informational text. Review each section of "Mammoth Shakes and Monster Waves" and discuss how each one focuses on particular causes, effects, or cause-and-effect relationships.

Next, help students see that when they integrate, or synthesize, visual and written information, they gain deeper understanding of a topic and a text. Discuss how diagrams help readers integrate information, and ask students to provide examples.

Determine Meanings of Words and Phrases

RI 4

Guide students to understand that identifying and determining the meaning of technical language will help them better understand what they read. Invite volunteers to provide examples of technical language they have learned, or provide an example yourself.

Point out to students that if a technical language term is not clearly explained in the text through a footnote or context clues, they should always use a print or online dictionary to confirm its meaning.

Strategies for Annotation ✎ ▣ *Annotate it!*

Analyze Structure: Cause and Effect

RI 5, RI 7

Share these strategies for guided or independent analysis:

- Highlight in yellow an anticipated event, or cause, that could lead to other events.
- Highlight in green effects that have already occurred as a result of this possibility.
- Review your highlights. On a note, integrate what you have learned about from these pieces of information.

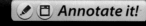

Burma and India plates. The next big earthquake here will threaten 10 million people along 500 miles of coastline that . . . Vancouver, B.C. A warning system has been added off the West Coast and evacuation routes established. Scientists now monitor 24 hours a day and must live within five minutes of . . .

PRACTICE & APPLY

Analyzing the Text

RI 1, RI 2, RI 4, RI 5, RI 7, RI 10

Possible answers:

1. *Two chunks of earth under the Indian Ocean had been scraping against each other for a long time. On December 26, 2004, the scraping caused a huge chunk of earth to reach a breaking point, causing an earthquake.*

2. *By combining the information in the diagram, caption, and the text, you understand that the Maldives and Seychelles are islands, and the impact of the tsunami would cause these islands to be under water because of the height and speed of the waves.*

3. Aboriginal *is used to describe native or original members of a region. The word helps explain that these people had a vast, long-term knowledge of the region that helped them understand the impact the tsunami would have; they knew to pay attention to the animals' reactions, to the changes in the water's depth, and to their own stories that told of similar significant circumstances long ago.*

4. *The tsunami set off a chain of cause-and-effect relationships. For example, the destruction caused by the tsunami killed many people and left many others lost or stranded, which caused others to search for them. The water left behind was contaminated, which made people sick. Many injured people needed medical help, but supplies weren't available or took a long time to come. As a result, many could not be helped, or suffered even more because of water contamination.*

5. *More seismic stations and more information centers were installed. It was also suggested that loudspeakers used by mosques to call Muslims to prayer be used to broadcast warnings. Scientists also think that nature can provide warning signs. Certain microorganisms relocate when the elevation of the land changes.*

FOR STUDENTS WITH DISABILITIES

Make sure that students who have physical disabilities are given roles in the discussion that allow them to participate actively. For example, a student who has difficulty speaking may prefer to participate as a note taker or may need more time to express his or her ideas. Hearing-impaired students will benefit if the group follows turn-taking rules and if each speaker uses clear diction and a moderate pace.

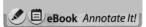
eBook Annotate It!

Analyzing the Text

RI 1, RI 4, RI 5, RI 7, RI 10, SL 1a-d, SL 5

Cite Text Evidence   Support your responses with evidence from the text.

1. **Summarize** Reread lines 1–18. Explain how the earthquake starts.

2. **Synthesize** Review lines 30–75 and examine the diagram that follows this text. What information do you learn from the diagram and the caption that helps you understand what the author means by "flooded the Maldives and Seychelles"?

3. **Analyze** Review lines 129–142. Then reread the footnote for *aboriginal*. What does the footnote explain that helps you understand the people's response to the tsunami?

4. **Cause/Effect** Review lines 150–219. What cause-and-effect relationships can you identify in this section? Explain how the ideas and events are related.

5. **Interpret** Reread lines 330–363. What kinds of warning systems have proved useful as a result of lessons learned from this tsunami?

PERFORMANCE TASK

Speaking Activity: Discussion With a small group, discuss the cause of the tsunami and its effects. Use details from "Mammoth Shakes and Monster Waves" in your discussion.

-   Each member of the group should review the text and take notes on causes and effects.
-   Appoint a member of the group to lead the discussion. The group leader should make sure that each group member has a chance to contribute his or her ideas to the discussion.
-   Appoint a note taker to record the causes and effects that the group agrees on.
-   Together, make a chart that shows these cause-and-effect relationships. Show how one event led to another and had multiple effects.
-   Share your chart with the rest of the class.

Assign this performance task.

PERFORMANCE TASK

SL 1a-d, SL 5

Speaking Activity: Discussion Have students work independently. Direct them to

-   prepare for the discussion by creating a chart to list causes and effects
-   take turns contributing ideas during the discussion

Have groups integrate their ideas in one chart that shows the cause-and-effect relationships they discussed.

Critical Vocabulary

rupture	gauge	traumatize
antibiotic	degradation	magnitude

Practice and Apply   For each vocabulary word, choose the sentence that best fits its meaning.

1. rupture   After a freezing evening, my car's engine would not start.
       After I drove over broken glass, my car got a flat tire.

2. gauge   We figured out that the storm left eight inches of snow.
       We were amazed by the beauty of the snowstorm.

3. traumatize   Joan prefers cats to dogs because she thinks dogs are noisy.
       Joan fears dogs because she was bitten by one.

4. antibiotic   The doctor gave me medicine for an ear infection.
       The doctor told me to get plenty of rest.

5. degradation   The soil improved after compost was worked into it.
       The soil lacked nutrients after the drought.

6. magnitude   The earthquake was measured to be quite small.
       The earthquake occurred at 5:50 in the evening.

Vocabulary Strategy: Greek Affixes

An **affix** is a word part that can be added to the beginning or the end of a base word to form a new word. Many affixes come from ancient Greek. Knowing the meaning of Greek affixes can help you recognize and understand related words as well as build your vocabulary.

The Greek prefix *anti-* means "opposite" or "against." The word *antibiotics* refers to medicines that work against infections. Other words that share the Greek affix *anti-* include *antidote, antifreeze, antisocial,* and *anticrime.*

Practice and Apply   Use a chart like the one shown to explore the meaning of more words with Greek affixes. List other words that share each affix. Be sure to use a dictionary to confirm the meanings of the other words.

Greek Affix	Meaning	Example	Other Words
auto-	"self, same"	*autograph*	
geo-	"Earth"	*geography*	
-phone	"sound, voice"	*telephone*	
-ism	"an action or characteristic"	*criticism*	

PRACTICE & APPLY

Critical Vocabulary

Answers:

1. *After I drove over broken glass, my car got a flat tire.*

2. *We figured out that the storm left eight inches of snow.*

3. *Joan fears dogs because she was bitten by one.*

4. *The doctor gave me medicine for an ear infection.*

5. *The soil lacked nutrients after the drought.*

6. *The earthquake was measured to be quite small.*

Vocabulary Strategy: Greek Affixes

Greek Affix	Meaning	Example	Related Words
auto-	"self, same"	*autograph*	*automatic, autobiography, autopilot*
geo-	"Earth"	*geography*	*geology, geopolitics, geocentric*
-phone	"sound, voice"	*telephone*	*microphone, headphone, speakerphone*
-ism	"an action or characteristic"	*criticism*	*heroism, terrorism, optimism*

Strategies for Annotation   ✐ 🗐 *Annotate it!*

Greek Affixes

Have students locate the sentence containing *geomythology* in the selection. Ask them to use their eBook annotation tools to do the following:

- Highlight in yellow the word *geomythology.*
- Underline the Greek affix they know, *geo-.* Notice the base word, *mythology,* and think about its meaning.
- Highlight in green any context clues that might help you understand the word's meaning.
- Review your annotations and try to infer the word's meaning.

The blend of myth and evidence found in the earth ha[s] brought scientists and Native Americans to share a ne[w] 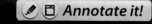 of looking at the past called geomythology. Ancient stories tell us that events happened before and will happen again. Science studies the danger, while stories enrich the record and provide clues about frequency. . . .

> geomythology = stories based on real geological events?

Language Conventions: Shifts in Pronoun Person

L 1c

Tell students that readers can get confused when a pronoun does not agree in number with its antecedent, because it is hard to tell who is speaking or being spoken to. In addition to examining examples of shifts in pronoun person, present additional examples of sentences in which the pronouns agree in number with their antecedents, and have students tell why they agree.

Answers:

1. *they* should be *she*

2. *They* should be *We*

3. *its* should be *their*

4. *Our* should be *Your*

5. *you* should be *they*

 Assess It Online!

Online Selection Test
- Download an editable ExamView bank.
- Assign and manage this test online.

L 1c

Language Conventions: Shifts in Pronoun Person

A **pronoun** is a word that is used in place of a noun or another pronoun. The word that the pronoun refers to is its **antecedent.** Pronouns should always agree in number with their antecedents. Read this sentence from "Mammoth Shakes and Monster Waves":

> As survivors returned to their villages, they often found that nothing remained—no familiar landmarks, no driveway, car, or motorbike.

The pronouns *their* and *they* both agree with their third-person antecedent, *survivors*.

It is important to recognize and correct shifts in pronoun person. Read this sentence:

> When people are terrified and anxious, we often don't make thoughtful decisions.

The antecedent *people* is third person, but the pronoun *we* does not match because it is first person. This shift in person makes the sentence awkward and confusing. The correct pronoun to use is *they*.

Here's another example of a shift in pronoun person:

> I heard wood splintering and glass breaking. Your heart started to beat like a drum.

The antecedent *I* is first person, but the pronoun *Your* is second person. The correct pronoun to use is *My*.

Practice and Apply Correct the shift in pronoun person in each sentence.

1. Megan was determined in her efforts to collect supplies to help the flood victims. By the end of the week, they had a truckload of goods to ship out.

2. Exhausted, we watched the sun set over the horizon. They were so tired, but still amazed at how beautiful it was.

3. I was inspired by the story about the people who helped transport its elderly neighbors from the storm site.

4. The captain shouted, "All of you need to move these vehicles. Our cars cannot block the street!"

5. Zoo visitors are enthusiastic when you see the big cats.

English Language Support

Use Pronouns Point out that the word *antecedent* comes from the Latin *ante* ("before") and *cedere* ("to go"). Explain that an **antecedent** is a word or a group of words to which a pronoun refers.

- Read each Practice and Apply sentence aloud as students follow the text. Ask volunteers to identify the pronoun and its antecedent. Then work with students to correct the shift in pronoun person.

- Let pairs work together to correct the Practice and Apply sentences. Then have the pairs join small groups to compare and check their work.

- List five pronouns on the board. Have students write sentences in which each pronoun refers back to an antecedent. Ask volunteers to read their sentences to the class.

Discussion Etiquette

SL 1a,
SL 1b,
SL 1c,
SL 1d

TEACH

Understanding and acquiring speaking and listening skills is essential for collaborative discussions. Explain these points about discussion etiquette to students:

- To collaborate effectively, members of a discussion group must prepare ideas and notes ahead of time.
- As needed, groups should choose and assign roles, such as a member to lead the discussion and a member who will take notes.
- Members should engage in active speaking and listening. An active speaker stays on topic, addresses others, uses eye contact, and speaks clearly. An active listener stays focused on the topic and on the speakers, maintaining eye contact.
- Members collaborate by asking speakers follow-up questions, restating ideas to show comprehension, or asking questions for clarification.
- Members treat each other with consideration and respect. They may disagree, but in a constructive way. Listeners should not interrupt a speaker, although a group leader might need to make sure a speaker stays on topic. A group leader should also be sure that every member is given opportunities to contribute ideas.

PRACTICE AND APPLY

Provide an opportunity for students to engage in collaborative discussion groups. Give groups a topic to discuss about "Mammoth Shakes and Monster Waves," such as the challenges and successes of relief efforts after the tsunami, or global efforts to predict and prepare for earthquakes and tsunamis.

Have group members prepare for the discussion by reviewing the text and noting ideas to contribute. When groups meet, have them select one member to lead the discussion, and review etiquette guidelines before they begin. Afterwards, review with the whole class how the discussions worked or how they could be improved next time.

 INTERACTIVE LESSON For further practice on discussion etiquette, have students complete the *Interactive Speaking and Listening Lesson* on **Participating in Collaborative Discussions.**

Analyze Structure: Cause and Effect

RI 5

RETEACH

Remind students that authors of informational text organize ideas and information in ways to help readers understand the ideas they present. Explain that cause-and-effect organization shows how events are related. Review these points with students:

- A **cause** is an event that makes something else happen, and an **effect** is what happens as a result.
- A single cause can have many effects.
- Signal words such as *when, because, so,* and *as a result* can help readers notice cause-and-effect relationships.

Ask students to identify causes and effects in the following passages from "Mammoth Shakes and Monster Waves":

- Lines 65–75 (area around the Indian Ocean)
- Lines 200–207 (medical issues)

Then choose one or two sections and have students explain why the author included it and how it fits into the text's structure.

 LEVEL UP TUTORIALS Assign the following *Level Up* tutorial: **Cause-and-Effect Organization**

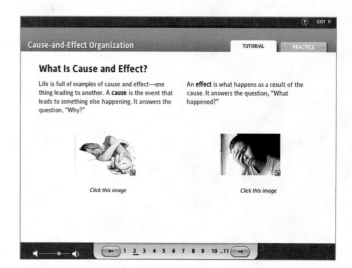

INDEPENDENT READING

Students can apply these skills to another selection, such as "Animal Snoops" in Collection 2, or to an informational text they may be reading on their own. Have students tell about the cause-and-effect relationships and structure they learned about.

Moby-Duck

Book Review by David Holahan

Background Have students read the background and information about the lost cargo of bath toys. The problem of ocean pollution has gained the attention of the media and public in recent years. Most of the articles produced and consumed today—from food containers to cell phones to cars—are made with plastic or plastic components. A great deal of this plastic does not end up in landfills. Rather, it finds its way into rivers, which lead almost invariably to the ocean.

SETTING A PURPOSE Ask students to pay attention to how cause-and-effect relationships underlie much of the book review. How does the reviewer use them to organize his writing?

Standards Support

- cite textual evidence
- determine a central idea of a text
- determine the meaning of words
- analyze how particular elements of a text fit into its structure
- determine an author's point of view
- integrate information presented in different formats

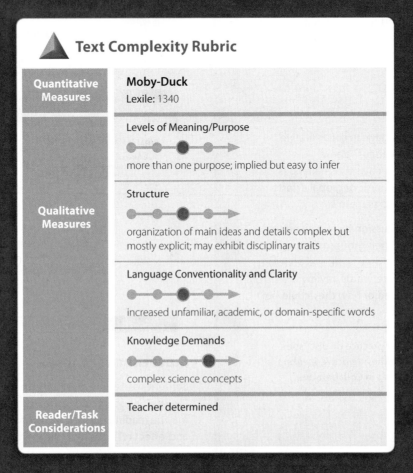

Text Complexity Rubric

Quantitative Measures	**Moby-Duck** Lexile: 1340
Qualitative Measures	**Levels of Meaning/Purpose** more than one purpose; implied but easy to infer
	Structure organization of main ideas and details complex but mostly explicit; may exhibit disciplinary traits
	Language Conventionality and Clarity increased unfamiliar, academic, or domain-specific words
	Knowledge Demands complex science concepts
Reader/Task Considerations	Teacher determined

Strategies for CLOSE READING

Analyze Structure

Students should read this book review carefully all the way through. Close-reading questions at the bottom of the page will help them focus on a thorough analysis of the cause-and-effect relationships. As they read, students should jot down comments or questions about the text in the margins.

WHEN STUDENTS STRUGGLE . . .

To help students analyze the structure of Holahan's review, have them work in small groups to fill out a chart like the one shown below.

CITE TEXT EVIDENCE For practice in analyzing the structure of a book review, ask students to cite text evidence for some of the cause-and-effect relationships.

Cause	Effect(s)
28,800 plastic ducks spill into the north Pacific.	". . . the author's quest more than a decade later to track their journey . . ." (lines 12–13)
Donovan Hohn decides to write a book about the lost plastic ducks.	"He would . . . help to clean up beaches in Alaska . . ." (lines 23–24) "The author also trolled for plastic on the high seas . . ." (lines 27–28)
Ocean currents in the north Pacific are circular.	"Two thousand of the Floatees . . . are stuck in . . . the North Pacific Gyre." (caption, p. 39) ". . . where our floating industrial waste stream often is aggregated." (lines 34–35)
Plastic things are meant to be thrown away.	". . . barely five percent of all plastic we use is recycled." (lines 59–60) ". . . that's what makes them so . . . profitable" (lines 61–62)

Background *In 1992, a cargo ship departed from Hong Kong for Tacoma, Washington. During a storm, thousands of plastic bath toys called Friendly Floatees were washed overboard. Oceanographers later used these toys to study ocean currents. Some Floatees reached distant British shores more than ten years after the storm.*

Moby-Duck

Book Review by David Holahan

CLOSE READ Notes

1. **READ ▶** As you read lines 1–31, begin to collect and cite evidence.
   • Underline what will happen to readers who read *Moby-Duck*.
   • In the margin, explain what the book's subtitle lets you know.
   • In the margin, summarize lines 19–31.

Donovan Hohn's narrative about his monomaniacal[1] quest for the elusive yellow duck(s) bobbing somewhere upon the **intractable** oceans is more than a little Melvillian.[2] The plastic (not rubber) duckies that were cast so carelessly upon the waters are a symbol of our collective, all-consuming sin. <u>Readers of this book will never again smile benignly at cloying little bath toys.</u>

The plot of *Moby-Duck* (which has an epically long subtitle: "The True Story of 28,800 Bath Toys Lost at Sea and of the Beachcombers, Oceanographers, Environmentalists, and Fools, Including the Author, Who Went In Search of Them") revolves around the 1992 spill of 28,800 bathtub accessories from a massive container ship in the north Pacific, and the author's quest more than a decade later to track their

---
[1] **monomaniacal:** obsessed with one idea or subject.
[2] **Melvillian:** similar to the writings of author Herman Melville, specifically to the novel *Moby Dick*, the tale of a crew in search of a great white whale.

intractable:
uncontrollable

The book is about the author's quest to learn more about thousands of bath toys lost at sea.

37

1. **READ AND CITE TEXT EVIDENCE** Explain to students that the book's title, *Moby-Duck*, is a play on words referring to the great nineteenth-century whaling novel, *Moby Dick*.

A **ASK STUDENTS** why Holahan might open his review by telling readers that the book will change their view about plastic bath toys. *Students should recognize that the reviewer thinks the book is a success. Before reading the book, a person might see "cloying little bath toys." But after reading it, the person will see "a symbol of our collective, all-consuming sin." Reading the book, then, will cause people to learn important lessons about seemingly mundane items.*

Critical Vocabulary: intractable (line 2) Have students share their definitions of *intractable*. What makes the oceans intractable? *They are huge. They are deep and cover the planet. The currents and waves are strong and never stop.*

journey from China to purportedly pristine places like Hawaii and Alaska, and possibly through Northwest Passage to Maine. Will the author find one of these indestructible icons of domestic bliss on the bounding main, or along some secluded spit of sand, as other beachcombers have? Or will his odyssey end in failure, like that of the doomed Pequod?[3]

B 20   A former school teacher, Hohn got the idea for the book from a student's essay about the spill and toyed with the idea of writing about it from the safety of his home in New York City. His wife was expecting, after all. But he soon was consumed by the watery tale and the search for answers. So off he went, again and again. He would comb and help to clean up beaches in Alaska, which—despite being America's "Last Frontier"—is awash in startling amounts of debris: fishing gear, bottles, cans and the rest of the relentless plastic flotsam of our ever expanding civilization. The author also trolled for plastic on the high seas, shoved off with scientists studying oceanic currents, and booked a cruise on a container ship like the one that **disgorged**
30   all those duckies (beavers, frogs, and turtles spilled, too, but these, clearly, are less **charismatic** commercial litter).

[3] **Pequod:** Captain Ahab's ship in Melville's novel *Moby Dick*.

Hohn was going to write about the spill from home, but got actively involved in tracking plastic flotsam around the world.

disgorged:
poured out

charismatic:
appealing; charming

2. ◀ REREAD   Reread lines 19–31. Look up and define the words *debris* and *flotsam*. Use these words to explain where Hohn's search led him and what he found.

"Debris" means scattered remains or rubble. "Flotsam" means wreckage that floats after a ship has sunk. Hohn's search led him to beaches in Alaska, where he cleaned up vast amounts of debris, including bottles and cans. He also looked for flotsam in the high seas, studied oceanic currents, and rode on a container ship.

3. READ ▶   As you read lines 32–41, continue to cite text evidence.

• Underline what people once believed about the ocean.
• Study the map showing where ocean currents carried the shipwrecked toys.
• Underline information about the Great Pacific Garbage Patch in the text and in the caption.

38

C This map shows where the Floatees traveled between the time they went overboard in 1992 and 2007. Two thousand of the Floatees, along with the Great Pacific Garbage Patch, are stuck in the circular currents of the North Pacific Gyre.

D   Cleaning up a remote beach where grizzly bears forage is hardly the answer to plastic pollution, it turns out. The shoreline will be well littered again in no time. And where does that leave the oceans, where our floating industrial waste stream often is aggregated by the currents into places with names like the Great Pacific Garbage Patch? The oceans were once thought to be too vast for us to properly befoul—even Rachel Carson[4] thought as much for a time. The Great Pacific Garbage Patch is roughly the size of Texas and growing, and
40   plastic has become as common as plankton in many places. Birds and fish mistake the smaller portions for food.

[4] **Rachel Carson:** American conservationist, scientist, ecologist, and marine biologist; often credited with being the founder of the environmental movement.

4. ◀ REREAD AND DISCUSS   Review lines 32–41 and the map. With a small group, integrate information from the text and the map to explain the many effects of a single cause: the spill of 28,800 bathtub toys.

5. READ ▶   As you read lines 42–54, continue to cite text evidence. Underline the descriptive words and phrases Holahan uses to describe Hohn's writing.

39

---

2. **REREAD AND CITE TEXT EVIDENCE**

B **ASK STUDENTS** what caused Hohn to search for the toy ducks. *He read a student essay about the toy duck spill and was consumed by the story. He wanted to get answers.*

3. **READ AND CITE TEXT EVIDENCE**

C **ASK STUDENTS** to discuss the effects of ocean currents on plastic trash. *The map shows that the currents move plastic trash all over the world. But some of the currents are circular, so they aggregate the trash in giant "garbage patches."*

Critical Vocabulary: disgorged (line 29) Have students give the meaning of the base word *gorged*. *ate greedily* So what does *disgorged* mean? *threw out*

Critical Vocabulary: charismatic (line 31) Have students suggest synonyms of the adjective *charismatic*. *appealing, alluring, charming, magnetic*

4. **REREAD AND DISCUSS USING TEXT EVIDENCE**

D **ASK STUDENTS** in each group to describe three chains of events: one that leads to the author on an Alaskan beach, one that leads to 2,000 Floatees in the Great Pacific Garbage Patch, and one that leads to birds and fish eating plastic. *Students may want to draw a flowchart to show these cause-and-effect chains. They should note the following chains: 1) Toys spill ⟶ student essay ⟶ Hohn consumed by story ⟶ Hohn travels to Alaska; 2) Toys spill ⟶ currents move toys ⟶ 2,000 toys stuck in North Pacific Gyre; 3) toys spill ⟶ currents move toys and other plastic trash ⟶ birds and fish eat small pieces of plastic.*

5. **READ AND CITE TEXT EVIDENCE**

E **ASK STUDENTS** to summarize what Holahan says about Hohn's writing. *Students should explain that Holahan thinks Hohn is an accomplished writer whose style suits his subject.*

E
F
Hohn, who is now the features editor at *GQ* [magazine], writes with precision and passion about what he sees and learns on his various travels and about his discussions with scientists, mariners, do-gooders, and beachcombers. His writing is lively and literate, filled with vivid descriptions, telling context, and lightly seasoned with quotes from Melville and others. He knows a symbol when one bobs into his **ken**, and what to do with it: "Here, then, is one of the 50 meanings of the duck. It represents this vision of childhood—the hygienic childhood, the safe childhood, the brightly colored childhood in which everything, even bathtub articles, have been designed to please the childish mind, much as the golden fruit in that most famous origin myth of paradise 'was pleasant to the eyes' of childish Eve."

ken:
knowledge;
awareness

---

6. **◀ REREAD** Reread lines 42–54. Is this a positive or negative review of Hohn's book? Cite evidence from the text to support your answer.

This is a positive review of Hohn's book. Holahan praises Hohn by saying he writes with "precision and passion." He compliments his writing by calling it "lively and literate" and says that Hohn uses "vivid descriptions." Holahan also provides a quotation from the book to give an example of Hohn's effective use of symbols.

---

7. **READ ▶** As you read lines 55–78, continue to cite text evidence.

• Circle environmental "cons" and underline real solutions to reducing the amount of trash in the ocean.

• Explain in the margin what the technique of "greenwashing" means. Be sure to read the footnote that defines the term.

40

❝❝So what is the answer to oceans beset by a rising tide of indestructible trash?❞❞

H
G
The author also knows a clever con when he sees one. He concludes that "Keep America Beautiful" approaches, which are largely spawned and bankrolled by the very corporations that are producing all the plastic detritus, are not the answer. There is no way to keep much of anything beautiful when barely five percent of all 60 plastic we use is recycled. The whole point of plastic things is that they are made to be thrown away; that's what makes them so darn consumer-friendly and profitable. What companies are doing with their "Let's Not Litter" PR is to "greenwash"[5] their own sizeable and systemic culpability, according to Hohn.

So what is the answer to oceans beset by a rising tide of indestructible trash? One is people like boat captain Charlie Moore, a self-made scientist and activist, who works to raise public awareness of the problem and lobbies for more enlightened regulations and corporate practices. Others Hohn encounters are volunteering their 70 time and money to clean up our collective mess.

[5] **greenwashing:** a practice in which a company deceptively promotes the idea that its product is good for the environment when that is not the case.

Greenwashing is a technique companies use to appear concerned about the environment when they may actually be doing the environment harm.

41

---

6. **REREAD AND CITE TEXT EVIDENCE**

F **ASK STUDENTS** to cite phrases with positive connotations that tell them that the reviewer admires Hohn's work. *Students should cite phrases that are complimentary of Hohn's writing ability.*

7. **READ AND CITE TEXT EVIDENCE** Holahan introduces the term "greenwash" to describe corporations' attempts to appear environmentally friendly. The term is an adaptation of the verb *whitewash*—to cover up one's crimes or sins.

G **ASK STUDENTS** what might cause a company to pursue a *greenwashing* campaign. *Students should note that the companies "are producing all the plastic detritus." They need customers to keep buying their products, so they want customers to have favorable ideas about the companies and their products.*

Critical Vocabulary: ken (line 48) Have students share their definitions of *ken*, and ask them to use the noun in sentences.

FOR ELL STUDENTS Point out the phrase *a clever con* in line 55. Tell students that the term means "a swindle" or "a trick." The word *con* is an abbreviation for *confidence,* and the kind of swindle it describes involves first winning the victim's confidence.

CLOSE READ
Notes

But the author wonders if such solutions, nibbling around the edges, are enough: "I'd like to share Moore's faith in the arc of progress . . . but I had a hard time imagining the bright future he saw, in which we Americans would trade conspicuous consumption for cradle-to-cradle manufacturing practices, disposable plastics for zero-waste policies and closed ecological loops. I had a hard time because such a future seemed to me **inimical** to the American gospel of perpetual economic growth."

inimical:
unfriendly;
hostile

8. **◄ REREAD** Reread lines 55–78. Summarize why certain actions are "cons," according to Hohn.

Certain companies that make plastic products will fund campaigns about keeping the environment clean but do not change their practices. Hohn calls these actions "cons" because they are deceptive.

SHORT RESPONSE

Cite Text Evidence At the beginning of this review, Holahan says that "Readers of this book will never again smile" at "little bath toys." Do you agree or disagree with this statement, now that you know about the life of the Floatees? Support your response by **citing text evidence**.

Sample response: I agree with Holahan's statement about the Floatees. Before reading this review, I never imagined that these little yellow ducks could be a part of a "floating industrial waste stream." But now that I have learned about the spill described in the book and how far the ducks spread from the map, I will view the "little bath toys" differently from now on. They symbolize a huge environmental problem that impacts people all over the world.

42

---

8. **REREAD AND CITE TEXT EVIDENCE**

Ⓗ **ASK STUDENTS** to discuss the results of the cons mentioned by the reviewer. *The cons can lead to consumers being fooled: buying and throwing away plastic products while they believe that recycling "keeps America beautiful." Consumers will think favorably of companies with a "let's not litter" message, even though those very companies are to blame for plastic trash.*

Critical Vocabulary: inimical (line 77) Have students suggest synonyms of *inimical* that could be used in this context. *opposed, adverse, unfavorable*

SHORT RESPONSE

Cite Text Evidence Students should:

- tell whether they agree or disagree with the statement.
- explain how they viewed bath toys before reading the essay.
- give examples of the effect of the essay on their opinions.

TO CHALLENGE STUDENTS . . .

To deepen their knowledge of the problem of ocean plastics, students can research the causes and effects online.

ASK STUDENTS to research where most of the plastic trash in oceans comes from. Students can pursue this topic by investigating the paths that plastic takes to reach oceans, or by examining what kinds of plastic objects are found in oceans. *Students should realize that most plastic trash is consumer waste that washes into gutters, streams, and rivers that flow into the ocean. Coastal towns and cities are the main source of this kind of plastic. Fishing boats are another major source. The global fishing fleet is enormous—and responsible for a staggering amount of flotsam such as abandoned nets. The shipping industry, from container ships to cruise liners, is the last major source. Anything that washes off these boats—bags, Styrofoam, nylon ropes, plastic ducks—becomes ocean trash.*

Have students research some of the consequences of plastic trash in the oceans. This topic relates mainly to marine animals and ocean ecosystems. *Students should note that ocean plastic gradually breaks down into smaller and smaller pieces. The tiniest pieces are taken up by microorganisms, thus entering the food chain. Larger pieces are eaten directly by fish, seabirds, and turtles. And the largest pieces—nets, lines, and ropes—pose deadly hazards to some of the ocean's most charismatic animals, such as dolphins, seals, otters, and whales.*

DIG DEEPER

1. With the class, return to Question 1, Read. Have students share their explanations of the book's subtitle.

   ASK STUDENTS to discuss how Holahan uses the subtitle as a device to help frame his review.

   - Have students reread lines 7–31 and cite text evidence of the groups mentioned in the subtitle. Students should realize that Holahan gives an overview of the book by telling how the author, at various points in his quest, joins each of the groups that are searching for the plastic ducks. *Holahan writes that the author wonders whether he will find a duck on "some secluded spit of sand, as other beachcombers have" (lines 16–17). He writes that the author will later "comb and help to clean up beaches in Alaska" (line 24), thus joining the ranks of beachcombers and environmentalists. And finally Holahan notes that the author sails with "scientists studying oceanic currents" (line 28)— that is, oceanographers.*

2. With the class, return to Question 4, Reread and Discuss. Have students share the main points of their discussion.

   ASK STUDENTS why cleaning up the plastic on beaches is not a solution to plastic pollution.

   - Students should understand that cleaning up beaches only addresses a result of the problem, not the cause. *The sources of plastic pollution aren't changed by cleaning up beaches. Plastic trash will still get into the ocean, and ocean currents will still move it onto beaches. Until people stop letting trash get into the oceans, the beaches will be littered with plastic.*

   ASK STUDENTS to return to their Short Response answer and revise it based on the class discussion.

CLOSE READING NOTES

from After the Hurricane

Watcher
After Katrina, 2005

Poem by Rita Williams-Garcia

Poem by Natasha D. Trethewey

Why These Texts?

Poetry provides students with opportunities to experience feelings and ideas in striking and unusual ways. This lesson focuses on how each poet uses the elements of poetry to explore the aftermath of Hurricane Katrina.

▶ **View It!**

Professional Development Podcast:

Text Complexity

Key Learning Objective: The student will analyze and compare poetic form and learn how poets use form, alliteration, and tone to express ideas.

RL 1 Cite text evidence.
RL 2 Determine theme or central idea; provide a summary.
RL 4 Determine the meaning of words and phrases.
RL 5 Analyze structure.
RL 6 Explain how an author develops point of view.
RL 9 Compare and contrast texts in different forms.
W 3d Use precise words and phrases, relevant descriptive details, and sensory language.
SL 1 Engage effectively in a range of collaborative discussions.

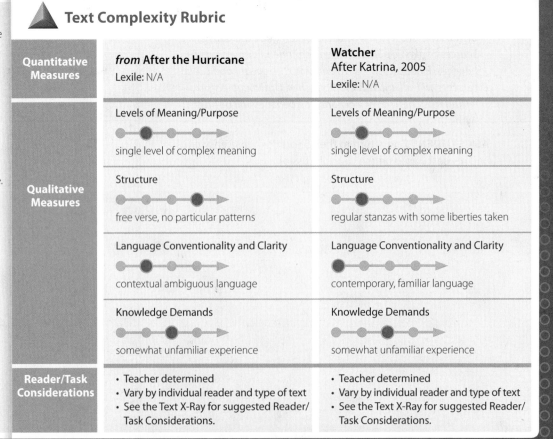

▲ **Text Complexity Rubric**

	from After the Hurricane	Watcher After Katrina, 2005
Quantitative Measures	Lexile: N/A	Lexile: N/A
Qualitative Measures	Levels of Meaning/Purpose — single level of complex meaning	Levels of Meaning/Purpose — single level of complex meaning
	Structure — free verse, no particular patterns	Structure — regular stanzas with some liberties taken
	Language Conventionality and Clarity — contextual ambiguous language	Language Conventionality and Clarity — contemporary, familiar language
	Knowledge Demands — somewhat unfamiliar experience	Knowledge Demands — somewhat unfamiliar experience
Reader/Task Considerations	• Teacher determined • Vary by individual reader and type of text • See the Text X-Ray for suggested Reader/Task Considerations.	• Teacher determined • Vary by individual reader and type of text • See the Text X-Ray for suggested Reader/Task Considerations.

English Language Support Before teaching, use the Text X-Ray for an overview of the text's complexity. The Text X-Ray and the supports and scaffolds in the Teacher's Edition will help you guide students of different skill levels.

Meaning Making
Language Development
Effective Expression
Content Knowledge
Foundational Skills

Text Complexity: Qualitative Measures

▲ Levels of Meaning/Purpose

Help students analyze how poetic techniques convey point of view and tone.

- Teacher's Edition side notes, pp. 158, 159, 162, 164, 166
- English Language Support, pp. 157, 159, 164

Guide students to apply the Learning Circles strategy to comprehend the text.

- English Language Support, p. 157

Help students analyze the speaker's feelings.

- English Language Support, p. 163

 Use It! *Level Up* Tutorial: Rhythm

ZOOM IN ON **ANALYZING THE TEXT** Explain that poets use many techniques, or tools, to convey the speaker's **point of view,** or how he or she chooses to narrate the poem, and to create a **tone,** or attitude, that affects a reader's emotions. Ask students to think about how the poet uses repeated lines and images, as they listen to you read the first two stanzas of "After the Hurricane." Then have pairs reread the stanzas closely and use the following sentence frames to discuss it:

- A word that describes the speaker's tone is _____.
- The repeated lines in lines 1–24 show _____.
- The images in lines 14–15 make me think of _____.

Have pairs share and discuss their responses with the class.

▲ Structure

Help students analyze poetic form.

- Teacher's Edition side notes, pp. 158, 160, 161, 163, 165, 166, 167, 168, 169
- English Language Support, p. 169
- When Students Struggle, pp. 161, 166
- Strategies for Annotation, pp. 165, 168
- Analyze Structure, pp. 165, 168
- Compare and Contrast Poetic Forms, p. 169

To teach students to analyze structure, see

- Analyze Structure: Meter, p. 170a

To reteach how to analyze poetic form, see

- Compare Poetic Forms, p. 170a

▶ **Use It!** Interactive Whiteboard Lesson: Form in Poetry
Level Up Tutorial: Elements of Poetry

ZOOM IN ON **COMPARING AND CONTRASTING POETIC FORMS** Tell students that a poem's **form** is the way its words and lines are arranged on the page. Explain that **free-verse** poems do not follow fixed rules, but poems in a **traditional** form follow rules about the number of lines in a **stanza,** or group of lines, rhythm and rhyme patterns, and line lengths.

- After students have read both poems, ask partners to compare and contrast the form of the poems.
- Then, as a class, discuss the ways in which the form of each poem fits the meaning and tone that the speakers convey.

▲ Language Conventionality and Clarity

Teach how to evaluate and analyze how poets use language to produce different effects.

- Teacher's Edition side notes, pp. 159, 166, 167, 169
- English Language Support, pp. 158, 162, 170
- Applying Academic Vocabulary, p. 159
- Strategies for Annotation, p. 169
- Determine Meanings of Words and Phrases, p. 169

ZOOM IN ON **ANALYZING LANGUAGE CHOICES** Explain that poets carefully choose words and phrases to convey meaning, produce emotional responses, and establish a **tone**, or the speaker's attitude, toward the subject.

- Ask each group to prepare a three-column chart with the following heads atop the columns: Alliteration (the repeating of consonant sounds at the beginning of words), Imagery, Rhythm.
- Have the groups read the poems aloud, pausing after each stanza to record examples of the categories on their charts.
- Discuss ways in which the words and phrases the groups identified help express the tone of each poem.

▲ Knowledge Demands

Help students understand the historical context of the poems.

- Teacher's Edition Background note, p. 157

ZOOM IN ON **BUILDING HISTORICAL KNOWLEDGE** Help students understand references to the aftermath of Hurricane Katrina in the poem "After the Hurricane." Explain the following.

- The first stanza describes terrible conditions that people endured as they sheltered in the Superdome.
- The reference to "actors drowning" in line 23 reflects the fact that in real life hundreds of people drowned in New Orleans after the hurricane.

▲ Suggested Reader/Task Considerations

You might consider the following before assigning these poems to students:

- Will students be engaged with the subject matter of the poems?
- Will the poems maintain students' interest throughout the lesson?

ZOOM IN ON **SUPPORTING COMPREHENSION**

- Tell students that the speakers in both poems share first-hand experiences of one of the most devastating disasters ever to hit the United States.
- Break up the reading of "After the Hurricane" by pausing after every one or two stanzas to discuss what the speaker is describing and to help students relate the speaker's experiences to the experiences of other people in New Orleans at the time.

TEACH

CLOSE READ

Background Have students read the background and information about the authors. Explain that the loss and devastation caused by Hurricane Katrina was enormous. Thousands of residents of the city of New Orleans evacuated, leaving homes, jobs, and businesses behind, and in many cases separating their families. Thousands of others had no transportation or were too poor to travel. Tell students that the two poems they will read capture the struggles and emotions of different people who did not evacuate, and were then trapped in a city without power, water, or food.

SETTING A PURPOSE Direct students to use the Setting a Purpose prompt to focus their reading. Remind them to write down questions as they read.

English Language Support

Learning Circles Use the strategy introduced on page 138a to deepen students' understanding and to encourage collaboration.

- First, organize the class into small groups of three or four. Assign each group one of the three sections of the poem divided by asterisks (* * *).
- Then, have group members select individual roles. For example, one student can note unfamiliar vocabulary, another can identify and consider interesting language, and a third can prepare questions about the text and take notes.
- Next, read aloud or present an audio recording of the text, reminding students to perform the duties associated with their selected roles. Explain that each of them will share his or her notes about the text with the group.
- Finally, have students discuss their findings. Encourage them to ask clarifying questions and to build on the comments of other group members.

English Language Support

Read Closely Display lines 1–11 for students and read them aloud. Explain that poets use punctuation to signal the kind of pause they want the reader to experience. For example, if there is no punctuation at the end of a line, the poet wants the reader to barely pause; if there is a period, the poet wants the reader to come to a full stop. The way the poet uses punctuation affects the meaning of the poem.

Background On August 29, 2005, Hurricane Katrina ripped through the Gulf coast. It was one of the strongest storms to hit the United States in the last 100 years. With winds of more than 125 miles per hour, Katrina caused massive damage all along the coast. But no city was affected more than New Orleans. Almost 80 percent of the city was underwater; thousands of people were left homeless. Almost 2,000 people lost their lives, and hundreds more were missing. Years after the hurricane, parts of the city have still not been rebuilt.

from After the Hurricane
Poem by Rita Williams-Garcia

Watcher
After Katrina, 2005
Poem by Natasha D. Trethewey

Rita Williams-Garcia (b. 1957) *was writing stories and trying to get them published by the time she was twelve years old. Today, her writing draws on her experiences growing up in New York City and, more significantly, the issues faced by urban black teenagers in the modern world. For Williams-Garcia, writing for young people is her passion and her mission. She believes that teens hunger for stories that reflect their circumstances, and she hopes her writing strengthens their understanding of themselves and others.*

Natasha D. Trethewey (b. 1966) *has deep ties to the Gulf coast. She was born in Gulfport, Mississippi, and returned to the Gulf coast often as a child, spending her summers there with her mother's family and in New Orleans with her father. Her father, also a poet, encouraged her to write poems on long car trips to keep her from getting bored. Trethewey was named poet laureate of the United States in 2012. Her collection of poems* Native Guard *won the Pulitzer Prize in poetry in 2007.*

SETTING A PURPOSE As you read each poem, pay attention to the events that take place and how each speaker reacts to them.

ASK STUDENTS to read lines 1–11 aloud, pausing as needed. Have them describe how the punctuation affects meaning. (*Short phrases separated by commas emphasize the conditions after the hurricane; one long, run-on sentence emphasizes the speaker's disbelief that this is real life and not a movie.*)

CLOSE READ

Analyze Structure
RL 1,
RL 5

(LINES 1–15)

Explain to students that in poetry, **form** is the way in which the words and lines are arranged on the page. Tell students that some forms of poetry have rules to follow, and some do not. Explain that **free verse** is poetry that has no rules; it has no regular patterns in line length, rhyme, or rhythm.

A CITE TEXT EVIDENCE Ask students to reread lines 1–15. Have them analyze the lines of the poem and tell how they know what kind of poem it is. *(The lines of the poem are different lengths, and there are no set patterns of rhyme or rhythm. Therefore, the poem is free verse.)* Then ask students how these lines contribute to the development of ideas in the poem. *(These lines describe the setting and events after the hurricane; they also develop the personality of the speaker.)*

Explain Point of View
RL 1,
RL 6

(LINES 16–24)

Remind students that the speaker in a poem is the voice that "talks" to the reader. The speaker may be the poet or a fictional character. Clues in the title and in the lines of the poem can help the reader determine who the speaker is.

B CITE TEXT EVIDENCE Have students reread lines 16–24. Have them identify details in the poem that help them understand who the speaker is. *(The phrase "King, Jasper, and I'd rent/ after band practice" suggests that the speaker is a young person who plays in a band.)*

After the Hurricane
Poem by Rita Williams-Garcia

A

If toilets flushed,
if babies slept,
if faucets ran,
old bodies didn't die in the sun,
5   if none of it were real,
if we weren't in it,
this could be a disaster movie with
helicopters whipping up sky overhead,
Special Effects brought in to create Lake George
10   and not the great Mississippi
          meeting Lake Pontchartrain.
Out-of-work waiters would pose as policemen,
locals as extras paid in box lunches.
For set design, dump raw sewage, trash everywhere,
15   news trucks, patrol cars, army tanks, Humvees.

B

If none of it were real,
if we weren't in it,
this could be a big-budget disaster flick
King, Jasper, and I'd rent
20   after band practice
like we did last Tuesday watching *Titanic* on Grandmama's
sofa.
That Jasper could *laaaugh* at all the actors drowning
while the band played—*glub, glub, glub*—to the death.

25   But this ain't that. We're waist high in it.
Camera crews bark, "Big Mike! Get this, over here!"
"Roll tape."
"Got that?"
"Good God!"
30   "Shut it down."

©Alexander Widding/Corbis

English Language Support

Understand Language Choices Write line 25 on the board: "But this ain't that. We're waist high in it." Point out to students that the author has the speaker use nonstandard English to create a certain effect and to help readers understand the speaker's personality.

- Work with individual students to restate the line using standard English.
- Have pairs find examples of nonstandard English in lines 31–40. Ask them to rewrite the lines in standard English.

- Have students identify and restate examples of nonstandard English in lines 31–40. Then form small groups to discuss the effect the author creates by using nonstandard English. Suggest that students compare the original and corrected versions of the lines and comment on which version seems more authentic and more powerful.

This ain't hardly no picture.
We're not on location.
We're herded. Domed in,
feels like for good

35 unless you caught a bus like Ma
or Jasper's family (save Jasper).
I still want to smash a camera,
break a lens, make them stop shooting.
But King says, "No, Freddie. Gotta show it.

40 Who'd believe it without film?"

Still no running water, no food, no power, no help.
The world is here but no one's coming.
The Guard[1] is here with rifles pointed.
The Red Cross got their tables set up.

45 Weathermen, anchors,[2] reporters, meteorologists,
a fleet of black Homeland SUVs.
The world is here
but where is the water? The food? The power?
The way to Ma or Jasper's people.

50 They just herd us, split us, film us, guard us.
No one said feed us. No one brought water.
The world is here but no one's coming.
Helicopters overhead beat up on our skies.

* * *

Miracle One.

55 King noses around the news guys,
runs back to Jasper and me.
"There's water trucks held up on the highway.
Gallons, girl! Water by the gallons.
Fresh drinking water.

60 Clean shower water.
See that, Freddie. The water company loves us.
Somebody thought to send us water."
Even with our trumpets drowned, King's chest swells.
He booms, "Brass Crew, are you with me?

65 Let's get outta here, bring back some water."

---

[1] **The Guard:** the National Guard of the United States, units of reserve soldiers that are controlled by each state of the United States. The National Guard responds to both the federal (national) and state governments for a variety of emergency needs, both in this country and abroad.

[2] **anchors** (ăng´kərs): people who organize and read the news on media newscasts (television, radio, online); they work with a team of reporters, camera operators, and so on to report the news.

APPLYING ACADEMIC VOCABULARY

impact	circumstance	significant

THINK-PAIR-SHARE Have students turn to a partner to discuss the following questions. Encourage them to include the vocabulary words *impact, circumstance,* and *significant* in their responses. Ask volunteers to share their responses with the class.

- What is the **impact** of the situation on the speaker?
- Why is the speaker's attitude about her **circumstances significant?**

TEACH

CLOSE READ

Determine Meaning: Tone (LINES 31–40)

RL 1,
RL 4

Explain to students that the **tone** of a poem expresses the poet's attitude and how he or she feels toward a subject. The words and phrases that a poet uses can help the reader understand the speaker's personality or elicit a certain response from the reader. (Explain that the speaker is taking shelter in the Superdome in New Orleans; this is what the poet means by using the phrase "Domed in.")

C CITE TEXT EVIDENCE Ask students to reread lines 31–40. Have students tell how the speaker feels and identify words and phrases that the poet uses to help readers understand this. (*The speaker is angry; the lines "I still want to smash a camera, / break a lens, make them stop shooting" show this.*)

English Language Support

Read aloud lines 31–34 and lines 35–38, pausing after each to have students identify the most powerful words and phrases. Discuss what these words and phrases indicate about how the speaker feels.

- Lines 31–34 (Words and phrases: *"ain't hardly no picture," "herded," "domed in"*; speaker's feelings: *angry, frustrated*)
- Lines 35–38 (Words and phrases: *"smash," "break," "make them stop shooting"*; speaker's feelings: *angry*)

FOR STANDARD ENGLISH LEARNERS

Grammar Write these sentence pairs on the board:

- This ain't hardly no picture. / This is not a movie.
- We not on location. / We're not on location.

Read the sentences aloud and ask students to identify the standard English *(those on the right)* and the nonstandard sentences *(on the left)*. Then ask pairs to identify other examples of nonstandard English on this page. Discuss why nonstandard English seems appropriate in this poem.

CLOSE READ

RL 1,
RL 4,
RL 5

Analyze Structure:
Repetition (LINES 66–76)

Explain that poets choose words for a poem for both meaning and sound. The sound of a word or line can help emphasize the meaning, create rhythm, or affect a reader's emotions. **Repetition** is the use of a sound, word, phrase, or line more than once. Repetition helps create emphasis, rhythm, and meaning within the structure of the poem, and it can make lines more memorable.

D **CITE TEXT EVIDENCE** Ask students to identify examples of repetition in lines 66–76 and explain their effects on the development of ideas in the poem. *(Possible response: The use of "how can I leave" and "be happy to leave" emphasize the speaker's mixed feelings about getting out of a terrible place and leaving her family behind.)*

How can I leave TK and Grandmama?
How can I leave, and be happy to leave?
Watch me. Just watch me
high step on outta here
70 for the water I say I'll bring back.
Honest to God, I heard "Brass Crew" and was gone.
I heard *Elbows up,*
natural breath!
That was enough.
75 How can I leave, and be happy to leave?
Easy. As needing to breathe new air.

King's got a First Trumpet stride. Jasper walks.
I lick the salt off my bare arms,
turn to look back at the people
80 held up by canes, hugging strollers, collapsible
black and newly colored people,
women with shirts for head wraps.
Salt dries my tongue.
I turn my eyes from them and walk.
85 I don't have to tell myself
it's not a school project for Ms. LeBlanc,
"The Colored Peoples of Freddie's Diorama."[3]

---

[3] **diorama** (dī′ə-răm′ə): a three-dimensional scene in which models of people, animals, or other objects are arranged in natural poses against a painted background.

Green pasted just so, around the huts just so.
The despair just right.
90 It's not my social studies diorama
depicting "Over There," across the Atlantic,
the Pacific. Bodies of water.
Way, way over there.
The refugees of the mudslides,
95 refugees of the tsunami,
refugees of Rwanda.
No. It is US. In state. In country.
Drowned but not separated by
bodies of water or by spoken language.
100 The despair is just right, no translation needed.
We are not the refugees in my social studies diorama.
We are 11th graders,
a broken brass line,
old homeowners, grandmamas, head chefs, street
105 performers, a saxophonist mourning the loss of his Selmer
horn of 43 years and wife of 38 years. We are aunties,
dry cleaners, cops' daughters, deacons, cement mixers,
auto mechanics, trombonists without trombones, quartets
scattered, communion servers, stranded freshmen, old
110 nuns, X-ray technicians, bread bakers, curators,[4] diabetics,
shrimpers,[5] dishwashers, seamstresses, brides-to-be, new
daddies, taxi drivers, principals, Cub Scouts crying, car
dealers, other dealers, hairstylists, too many babies, too
many of us to count.
115 Still wearing what we had on when it hit.
When we fled,
or were wheeled, piggybacked, airlifted, carried off.
Citizens herded.
We are Ms. LeBlanc, social studies teacher, a rag wrapped
120 around her head,
And Principal Canelle. He missed that last bus.

* * *

___

[4] **curators** (kyŏŏ-rāˊtərs): people who manage and oversee; most often describes those who manage a museum and its collection of art.

[5] **shrimpers** (shrĭmpˊərs): people who catch shrimp—small edible sea animals with a semi-hard outer shell.

After the Hurricane **161**

Analyze Structure
RL 1, RL 5

(LINES 88–121)

Explain to students that free verse poetry does not have a regular pattern of rhyme or rhythm. Explain that **rhythm** is the musical quality, or "beat," heard in a poem. The rhythm in a free verse poem often sounds like everyday speech, or conversation. Poets often develop this rhythm using repetition or by including lines of various lengths.

E CITE TEXT EVIDENCE Ask students to reread lines 88–121. Ask them to explain how the poet creates rhythm and the sound of everyday speech in the poem. Have them identify words and phrases in the poem that support their answer. (*The poet creates rhythm by repeating words and phrases, such as "just so," "over there," and "refugees"; she uses short phrases that emphasize place, such as "No. It is US. In state. In country." She uses long lines and lists descriptions of people in lines 104–114.*)

WHEN STUDENTS STRUGGLE . . .

Guide students in understanding the rhythm of the poem. Reread lines 88–96 aloud, paying little attention to the punctuation. Ask students to tell whether they had a hard time understanding the meaning of the lines.

Next, discuss how some lines of the poem end with a period, some with a comma, and some with no punctuation. Then reread the poem aloud, using the punctuation to pause for meaning and understanding as the poet intended. Point out how the different line breaks and punctuation affect the rhythm.

ASK STUDENTS to tell how paying attention to the punctuation in the poem creates rhythm and meaning. Have students reread the lines aloud.

LEVEL UP TUTORIALS For additional support, assign the following *Level Up* tutorial: **Rhythm.**

Explain Point of View

RL 1,
RL 6

(LINES 122–125; 136–154)

Review with students that, like a story has a narrator, a poem often has a speaker. The speaker is the voice that "talks" to the reader. The words and details in the poem tell the reader many things about the speaker.

F **CITE TEXT EVIDENCE** Ask students to name the speaker of the poem and tell where they found this detail. *(The speaker's name is Fredericka; she says her name in line 128.)*

G **ASK STUDENTS** to reread lines 122–125 and tell what the speaker and her friends have done. Have students tell what she means by the phrase "Minor Miracle." *(They have left the shelter of the Superdome; the speaker thinks it is amazing, a miracle, that they have been able to walk past the National Guard.)*

H **ASK STUDENTS** to reread lines 136–154. Have them describe what these lines in the poem tell the reader about the speaker. *(The questions and answers are thoughts that the speaker has while she and her friends march out of the shelter. It shows that, although she has doubts, she is determined and thinks that leaving the shelter is the right thing to do.)*

English Language Support

Help students understand that the speaker is recalling the thoughts she would have when she marched in holiday parades with her band. Point out the verb phrase *would ask* in line 136. Explain that the helping verb *would* combined with the present-tense verb (*ask*) signals a habitual or repetitive action in the past.

Minor Miracle.
We walk past the Guard.
You'd think they'd see us
125 marching on outta here.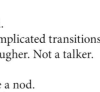
You'd think they'd stop us. Keep us domed.
But we're on the march, a broken brass line.
King, Jasper, and me, Fredericka.

King needs to lead; I need to leave.
130 Been following his lead since
band camp. Junior band. Senior band.
Box formations, flying diamonds, complicated transitions.
Jasper sticks close. A horn player, a laugher. Not a talker.
See anything to laugh about?
135 Jasper sticks close. Stays quiet. Maybe a nod.

Keeping step I would ask myself,
Aren't you ashamed? No.
Of band pride? No.
You band geek. So.
140 Aren't you ashamed? No.
You want to parade? So.
Raise your trumpet? So.
Aren't you ashamed? No.
To praise Saint Louis?
145 "Oh, when the saints go marching in?"
Aren't you ashamed? No.
Of strutting krewe⁶
On Mardi Gras? The Fourth of July?
These very streets
150 Purple and gold, bop
Stars and Stripes, bop
Aren't you ashamed?
To shake and boogie?
Aren't you ashamed?

---

⁶ **krewe** (kroō): any of several groups of people who organize and participate in the annual Mardi Gras carnival in New Orleans.

TO CHALLENGE STUDENTS . . .

Interpret Symbolism Have students work in small groups to discuss how unpredictable and devastating hurricanes such as Katrina can be for everyone involved. Then ask students to consider a larger idea that the poem represents about coping with an unpredictable event. What broader life lessons does the poem address through the speaker and her friends? Remind students to use examples from the poem to support their ideas.

155 To enjoy your march,
while Grandmama suffers
and no milk for TK?
Tell the truth. Aren't you ashamed?
No. I'm not ashamed.
160 I step high, elbows up.
Band pride.

King asks, "Freddie, what you thinking?"
I say, "I'm not thinking, King."
But I'm dried out on the inside.
165 Hungry talks LOUD, you know.
"Let's try the Beauxmart. The Food Circle. Something."

King knows better. He doesn't say.
Still, we go and find (no surprise)
the Beauxmart's been hit. Stripped. Smashed.
170 Forget about Food Circle and every corner grocery.
Nothing left but rotten milk,
glass shards.[7] Loose shopping carts.
Jasper sighs. Grabs a cart.

Stomach won't shut up.
175 Talking. Knotting. Cramping. I whine,
"Let's go to Doolie's."
Again, King knows better. Still, we go,
almost passed right by. Didn't see it until
Jasper points. King sighs.
180 Check out the D in Doolie's, blown clear off.
The outside boarded up, chained up, locked.
Black and red spray-painted:
LOOTERS WILL BE SHOT.

---

[7] **shards** (shärds): small pieces of something that has been broken.

CLOSE READ

Analyze Structure

RL 1, RL 5

(LINES 155–166)

Review with students that the rhythm of a free verse poem sounds like everyday speech. Explain that the arrangement of the lines of a poem contributes to that rhythm. Poets decide how long each line will be and how they will end—for example, in rhyme, repeating words, or other natural breaks.

CITE TEXT EVIDENCE Ask students to reread lines 155–166 aloud. Have them cite specific lines to explain how the length and endings of the lines contribute to the rhythm of the poem. (*The short sentences give the poem a fast pace. The lines ending in questions and answers make it sound like a conversation.*)

English Language Support

Culturally Responsive Instruction Begin a class discussion about how the speaker deals with her inner conflict. Reread lines 136–161. Ask volunteers why the speaker feels guilty about leaving the Superdome. (*She has left TK and Grandmama behind.*)

ASK STUDENTS to explain how the speaker's identity as a band member influences her response to the situation. Have small groups discuss why the speaker imagines herself proudly marching in a parade. Encourage students to consider ways that community or social organizations can help people cope with disaster.

Explain Point of View

RL 1, RL 6

(LINES 184–200)

Review with students that poets develop the point of view by showing the speaker's feelings and ideas.

 CITE TEXT EVIDENCE Have students reread lines 184–200 and tell how the speaker feels. Ask them how her attitude has changed since the beginning, and ask them to identify words and details the poet uses to help them understand this. *(Possible response: Earlier in the poem, the speaker feels determined to make things better. Now she is dismayed about the devastation and how it has affected the city and its people. The words and phrases "I can't believe it," "believe," "No bop step, high step," and "Just walk" help me understand these feelings.)*

Determine Meaning: Tone

RL 1, RL 4

(LINES 201–208)

Remind students that the **tone** of a poem expresses the poet's attitude and feelings toward a subject.

K **ASK STUDENTS** to reread and analyze the tone of lines 201–208. Have them explain the poet's feelings, using words and phrases from the text to support their ideas. *(Possible response: The poet's tone is sad, angry, disappointed, and resentful. Word choices such as "the Big Empty," "good for nothing," "heavy stink," and "full of ghosts" describe how the poet feels these people have been abandoned and forgotten.)*

I can't believe it.

185 Doolie who buys block tickets to home games
Doolie who sponsors our team bus
Band instruments, uniforms (all underwater),
Chicken bucket championships. The band eats half-price.
My eyes say, *Freddie, believe the spray paint*:

190 *Big Sean Doolie will shoot the looters.*
Yeah. Big Sean Doolie.
Believe.

King (First Trumpet) was right,
he doesn't make me (Second) like I'm second.

195 A simple, "Come on, Brass. Let's get this water."
I follow King. Jasper pushes the cart.
First, Second, Third. No bop step,
high step, no feather head shake,
no shimmy[8] front, boogie back.

200 Just walk.

"Hear that?"
Another helicopter overhead.
Another chopper stirring up the Big Empty.
Wide blades good for nothing but whirling up

205 heavy heat, heavy stink on empty streets
full of ghosts and mosquitoes.
Swat all you want. Look around.
Nothing here but us in Big Empty.

---

[8] **shimmy** (shĭm´ē): to do the shimmy, a dance involving rapid shaking of the body.

CONTENT-AREA CONNECTION

SCIENCE Tell students that the scientific name for a hurricane (or a typhoon) is *tropical cyclone*. These huge storms form over warm ocean waters and can produce winds of more than 100 miles per hour. They produce storm surges and heavy rains that can flood coastal areas. Landslides, flash floods, and debris carried by high winds present additional hazards. When a hurricane begins, it is assigned a name to distinguish it from other tropical storms that may be forming at the same time. The World Meteorological Organization assigns names based on an alphabetical list that repeats every seven years for Atlantic hurricanes. The names of extremely destructive storms—such as Katrina—are retired from the list and replaced by another name that begins with the same letter.

Activity Have small groups research how hurricanes form, where they form, and how scientists predict, study, and track the storms. If possible, collaborate with a science teacher to help students narrow the focus of their research. Students can then present their reports in both classes.

Analyze Structure

RL 5

A poem's **form** is the way its words and lines are arranged on a page. Some forms are also defined by poetic devices, such as rhyme and rhythm. A poem's form is closely linked to its meaning, which makes the poem's form important to its message.

Free verse is a form of poetry with no regular patterns of rhyme, rhythm, or line length. When poets write free verse, they can create rhythms that they think will best communicate their ideas.

"After the Hurricane" is written in free verse, which the poet can use to portray the sounds and rhythms of everyday speech. In lines 16–24, the poet uses both short and long line lengths to create rhythms that make the words sound like a person telling you a story. Line length can also be used to call attention to certain words and ideas.

To analyze free verse, ask questions such as the following:

- What ideas is the poet expressing? How does the use of free verse support those ideas?
- What rhythms are created by the line lengths in the poem? How do these poetic devices add to my understanding of the poem?

Notice where the poet ends each line as you analyze "After the Hurricane."

Analyzing the Text

RL 1, RL 2, RL 4, RL 5, RL 6

Cite Text Evidence   Support your responses with evidence from the text.

1. **Summarize** Reread lines 1–30. How does the speaker describe what happens after the hurricane? What does the speaker compare the scene to?

2. **Analyze** Review lines 101–121 and examine how the poet arranges the words and lines. Describe the variations in line lengths. What circumstances is the poet trying to explain, and how does the form support those ideas?

3. **Compare** Review lines 129–161, in which the speaker tells about the friends' roles in the band. Compare these ideas with those in lines 184–200. How has the hurricane affected the friends' roles and changed the speaker's feelings? Explain which words show this.

TEACH

CLOSE READ

Analyze Structure

RL 5

Review with students that when analyzing free verse, they should pay attention to line breaks, how the lines are grouped, and the effects these choices have on the sound and feel of the poem. Have students discuss the bulleted questions as they analyze the poem. Help students look at each stanza and discuss ways the line breaks emphasize specific ideas and emotions in the poem.

Analyzing the Text

Possible answers: RL 1, RL 2, RL 4, RL 5, RL 6

1. *The speaker describes how unreal the world feels, how nothing works and how strange it feels. She compares the scene to the set of a disaster movie, how all these things seem unreal, except that they are all too real.*

2. *The lines start off short, then become longer and denser, and then get shorter again. The poet shows that many people were affected by the hurricane, for many reasons. Long lines show the huge number and diversity of lives that have been uprooted.*

3. *First, the speaker shows "pride" as a "band geek," in King's role as leader, and in the sophisticated steps they execute. Later, however, she is discouraged by how people who once supported each other have become enemies after the hurricane. At the end, words like* simple, *the repeated* no *to dance moves, and "Just walk" show how disappointed she is.*

Strategies for Annotation   *Annotate it!*

Analyze Structure

RL 5

Have students use their eBook annotation tools to analyze the form of "After the Hurricane." Ask them to do the following:

- Count the number of lines in each group.
- Highlight repeating words.
- On a note, jot down any patterns in line length or rhythm they find.

King needs to lead; I need to leave. / Been following his lead since

band camp. Junior band. Senior band.

Box formations, flying diamonds, complicated transitions.

Jasper sticks close. A horn player, a laugher. Not a talker.

See anything to laugh about?

Jasper sticks close. Stays quiet. Maybe a nod.

The word *band* repeats. Affects rhythm.

Analyze Structure

RL 5

(LINES 1–12)

Remind students that in poetry, **form** is the way in which the words and lines are arranged on the page. Explain that a poem is made up of lines and stanzas. A **line** is the core unit of a poem. A **stanza** is a group of two or more lines. The place where a line ends is called a **line break.**

A **ASK STUDENTS** to reread lines 1–12. Work with them to analyze the poem's form. Have them count the lines and stanzas and tell how each thought begins and ends.

Review that poems come in many different forms. Some poems, such as free verse, do not follow any fixed rules for number of lines, line length, or pattern of rhythm and rhyme. Others, called **traditional** poems, follow fixed rules.

B **ASK STUDENTS** to analyze the poem's lines, stanzas, and patterns of rhythm and rhyme. Have students tell what kind of poem it is. *(There are three lines in each stanza. Each stanza includes a shorter line and two longer lines. The beat repeats regularly throughout the poem. Therefore, the poem is traditional.)*

Determine Meanings of Words and Phrases

RL 1, RL 4

(LINES 1–12)

Explain to students that **alliteration** is the repetition of consonant sounds at the beginning of words. Poets often use alliteration to give a poem rhythm or to direct attention to certain words.

C **CITE TEXT EVIDENCE** Have students reread lines 1–12 and find two instances of alliteration. Ask how these phrases affect their response to the poem. *(Line 3: "sat on the stoop"; Line 9: "signs of a storm." Possible response: The rhythm helps readers to notice details of the scene and understand the watcher's situation.)*

Watcher
After Katrina, 2005
by Natasha D. Trethewey

A At first, there was nothing to do but watch.
For days, before the trucks arrived, before the work
of cleanup, my brother sat on the stoop[1] and watched.

B He watched the ambulances speed by, the police cars;
5 watched for the looters who'd come each day
to siphon[2] gas from the car, take away the generator,

the air conditioner, whatever there was to be had.
He watched his phone for a signal, watched the sky
for signs of a storm, for rain so he could wash. **C**

10 At the church, handing out diapers and water,
he watched the people line up, watched their faces
as they watched his. And when at last there was work,

[1] **stoop** (sto͞op): a small porch or staircase that leads up to the door of a house or other building.

[2] **siphon** (sī´fən): to move a liquid up and out of a container, over a barrier, and into a new container, using an inverted, U-shaped tube.

WHEN STUDENTS STRUGGLE...

Display the poem for students. Have students use a chart such as the following to guide them as they analyze the form of the poem.

ASK STUDENTS what kind of poem this is. *(traditional)*

Lines in Each Stanza	three, except for the last line, which is by itself
Stanzas	eight
Other Elements	rhythm

 LEVEL UP TUTORIALS For additional support, assign the following *Level Up* tutorial: **Elements of Poetry.**

he got a job, on the beach, as a *watcher*.
Behind safety goggles, he watched the sand for bones,
15   searched for debris that clogged the great machines.

Riding the prow of the cleaners, or walking ahead,
he watched for carcasses³—chickens mostly, maybe
some cats or dogs. No one said *remains*.⁴ No one

had to. It was a kind of faith, that watching:
20   my brother trained his eyes to bear
the sharp erasure⁵ of sand and glass, prayed

there'd be nothing more to see.

COLLABORATIVE DISCUSSION With a partner, use evidence from
the poems to discuss what happened during Hurricane Katrina
and how people who experienced it were affected.

---

³ **carcasses:** (kär´kəs-əz): dead bodies; usually referring to dead animals that
have been killed for food.

⁴ **remains** (rĭ-mānz´): all that is left after other parts have been taken away, used
up, or destroyed; here, refers to dead bodies of people.

⁵ **erasure** (ĭ-rā´shər): an act or instance of erasing—removing by rubbing, wiping,
or scraping; the state of being erased.

CLOSE READ

Analyze Structure
(LINES 13–22)

RL 1,
RL 5

Explain to students that the form of a poem affects
its pace, feeling, rhythm, and tone. For example, line
lengths can speed up or slow down the pace of a
poem and help create rhythm. Line breaks can affect
the poem's tone and how ideas are emphasized.

D CITE TEXT EVIDENCE Ask students what ideas
the poet stresses in lines 13–15 and how she does
this. *(These lines explain the job of a watcher. The poet
emphasizes this by beginning line 13 with the phrase "he
got a job" and describing what a watcher does.)*

E ASK STUDENTS to examine the poem's form in
lines 16–22 and explain the effects that are created by
the poem's line lengths, breaks, and stanzas. *(Possible
response: The line lengths and breaks give the poem a
conversational rhythm and somber tone. The last stanza
only has one line, which gives emphasis to the hope that
there will be no more death and destruction.)*

COLLABORATIVE DISCUSSION To prepare for the
discussion, have students make a short list of ideas they
want to discuss with their partner. Explain that they
might want to sort their ideas into categories, such
as things that happened before, during, and after the
hurricane. Remind students to cite evidence from the
poem to support their ideas.

ASK STUDENTS to share any questions they generated
in the course of reading and discussing this selection.

English Language Support

Cite Evidence Before students begin their discussion,
provide the following sentence stems:
After the hurricane, some people _____.
Other people _____.
There was not enough _____.
The hurricane _____.

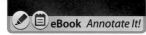

Analyze Structure   RL 5

Review the information about the elements of a poem's form and how they affect its rhythm and meaning. Work with students to identify examples of how these elements affect rhythm and meaning in "Watcher." Then have partners reread the poem and discuss how the stanzas in the poem express and help build the poem's meaning.

Analyzing the Text   RL 1, RL 2, RL 4, RL 5

Possible answers:

1. *The first line is shorter than the others, which are about the same length. The shorter line emphasizes the theme of the poem, which is watching the unfortunate incidents that occur after the storm.*

2. *The third line in the second stanza ends with a comma, so the reader knows that a thought will continue in the next stanza. The fourth and fifth stanzas work this way, and the sixth and seventh stanzas do, too. The author may have used this structure to give rhythm to the list of many unfortunate incidents that the brother sees.*

Analyze Structure   RL 5

Many poems are written in traditional form. Poems in **traditional form** follow fixed rules, such as a certain number of lines, a rhyme scheme, and a definite structure.

A **line** of poetry is simply that: the text that appears on one line. The line is the core unit of a poem and can be a complete sentence, part of a sentence, or even a single word. Poets use **line breaks,** or the places where lines of poetry end, to add emphasis to certain words and phrases.

A **stanza** is a group of two or more lines that form a unit in a poem. A stanza is like a paragraph in prose. Depending on the form, the stanzas of a poem

- may or may not have the same number of lines
- will, most often, express a separate idea or emotion

In a traditional form, the stanzas are often a determined length.

When you analyze traditional forms of poetry, think about questions like the following:

- What specific idea does each stanza express?
- Why might the poet have chosen to use this form to structure the poem?
- Taken together, how do the stanzas help build the poem's meaning?

In the poem "Watcher," notice the number of lines in each stanza and how the ideas in the stanzas are connected through the use of the poem's form.

Analyzing the Text   RL 1, RL 2, RL 4, RL 5

Cite Text Evidence   Support your responses with evidence from the text.

1. **Interpret** Reread lines 1–3 of "Watcher." What do you notice about the length of each line? How does the shortest line contribute to the poem's meaning?

2. **Draw Conclusions** Reread lines 4–9 of "Watcher." What clues tell you that these stanzas work together as a complete idea? Do other stanzas in the poem work the same way? Why do you think the author chose to structure the poem this way?

Strategies for Annotation

Analyze Structure   RL 5

Have students use their eBook annotation tools to analyze the form of "Watcher." Ask them to do the following:

- Highlight in yellow words that are emphasized in each line.
- Highlight in green repeated words.
- On a note, jot down how the emphasis on these words affects the rhythm and meaning of the poem.

Riding the prow of the cleaners, or walking ahead,

he watched for carcasses—chickens mostly, maybe

some cats or dogs. No one said *remains*. No one

repeating the phrase "No one" is key to meaning.

Determine Meanings of Words and Phrases

RL 4

One of many poetic elements poets use is called alliteration. **Alliteration** is the repetition of consonant sounds at the beginning of words. This line from "After the Hurricane" includes two examples of alliteration:

> **Out-of-work waiters would pose as policemen,**

The repeated *w* and *p* sounds add a bouncing rhythm to the line. The rhythm creates an almost lighthearted feeling for this part of the poem, where the poet shows how the speaker's situation could be a movie, except that it is actually happening.

By adding rhythm and repetition, alliteration can also affect meaning and tone. **Tone** refers to the poet's attitude and how he or she feels about a topic. The repeated *w* sound in lines 45–49 in "After the Hurricane" points out important words, such as *Weathermen, world, where, water,* and *way.* It helps create a tone that shows that the topic makes the poet feel a certain way about the incidents taking place in the aftermath of the storm.

Look for more examples of alliteration and its effect on tone as you analyze the two poems.

Compare and Contrast Poetic Forms

RL 9

To compare and contrast poetic forms, especially free verse and traditional forms, examine the following:

- the structure of the stanzas, including number of lines and line length
- emphasis created by line breaks
- the use of rhythm
- rhyme scheme or lack of rhyme
- imagery
- the use of alliteration

Notice how "After the Hurricane" and "Watcher" convey meaning through the use of their different forms.

TEACH

CLOSE READ

Determine Meanings of Words and Phrases

RL 4

Review the examples of alliteration in "After the Hurricane." Discuss how they contribute to the rhythm, meaning, and tone of the poem.

Ask students to identify additional examples of alliteration and discuss its effect on the poem's tone.

Compare and Contrast Poetic Forms

RL 9

Work with students to compare and contrast the two poems. Use a Comparison-Contrast chart to record how the poetic elements are alike and different. Students can use the chart to discuss how the different forms help each poet convey meaning.

English Language Support

Have small mixed-ability groups complete a three-column Interactive Comparison-Contrast Chart. Ask students to add the poem titles at the top of columns 2 and 3, and then to list the following elements in column 1: *stanza length, line breaks, rhythm, imagery, alliteration.* Next, have the groups record their analyses of these elements for each poem. Before discussing how the forms help convey meaning, let groups complete this sentence frame for each poem: This poem conveys ideas about _____.

Strategies for Annotation 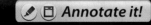 *Annotate it!*

Determine Meanings of Words and Phrases

RL 4

Have students use their eBook annotation tools to analyze the text. Ask them to do the following:

- Highlight the alliterative words.
- On a note, record whether each example contributes to rhythm, meaning, or tone.
- Review your annotations and summarize how the use of alliteration contributes to rhythm, meaning, and tone.

Minor Miracle. / We walk past the Guard.

You'd think they'd see us / marching on outta here.

You'd think they'd stop us. Keep us domed.

But we're on the march, a broken brass line.

King, Jasper, and me, Fredericka.

> "think they'd" contributes to the rhythm.

Analyzing the Texts

RL 1, RL 4,
RL 5, RL 6,
RL 9

Possible answers:

1. *Words beginning with* h *include* hear, helicopter, heavy, heat, here. *The* h *sound brings to mind the word* hurricane *from the title. The* h *sounds add to the weary, tired tone, like a heavy sigh.*

2. *The* w *sound is heard most often in "Watcher," and, like in "After the Hurricane," it creates a tone of feeling tired and worn out.*

3. *The tone in "Watcher" is formal. The speaker is relating what her brother sees in the aftermath of the storm. The tone of "After the Hurricane" is more informal because the speaker is a teenager and relates incidents in the aftermath of the storm in a more casual and sometimes playful manner.*

4. *"After the Hurricane" is structured using free verse, while "Watcher" is more formal, composed of three-line stanzas and ending with a single line. The general rhythm in each poem is somewhat similar, using patterns that sound like natural speech.*

5. *The form of "After the Hurricane" matches the personality of its speaker, a teenaged girl. The speaker sometimes speaks playfully about a very serious situation. The gender and age of the speaker in "Watcher" is unclear, but the speaker is quieter and more serious. The poem's form supports this by using tight, regular stanzas with ideas that continue from the end of one stanza to the beginning of the next.*

English Language Support

Divide the class into small groups to answer the questions. Have each group answer one question. When all the groups are finished, let them take turns presenting their answers to the class. Encourage classmates to provide useful feedback.

English Language Support

Write Literary Texts Have students work independently to choose a topic, message, and audience for their poems. Then ask partners to help each other brainstorm words that convey the imagery they want to include in their poems. Monitor students' work and intervene as needed.

 eBook *Annotate It!*

Analyzing the Texts

RL 1, RL 4, RL 5,
RL 6, RL 9, W 3d

Cite Text Evidence Support your responses with evidence from the text.

1. **Interpret** Read aloud lines 201–208 of "After the Hurricane." What examples of alliteration do you hear? How does this sound connect with the topic and title, and what tone or feeling does this alliteration evoke?

2. **Identify** Read aloud "Watcher" and identify the alliterative sound you hear most often. Which words are emphasized with this sound? How does it relate to the tone and meaning of the poem?

3. **Compare** How is the tone in "Watcher" similar to or different from the tone in "After the Hurricane"? Tell why.

4. **Compare** Review how "After the Hurricane" and "Watcher" are structured. How are their structures and general use of rhythm alike? How are they different?

5. **Analyze** A poem's form can affect its meaning. How does each poem's form support the personality of the speaker that you hear in the poem's words and rhythms?

PERFORMANCE TASK

Writing Activity: Poem Write a poem about a disaster you have read about recently. Your poem can be written in free verse or in a structured form with stanzas.

- First, choose the event you will write about. Make sure you have enough information about what it was like.
- Decide on the main idea or message you want to convey. Do you want to create a vivid picture of the event or share a strong emotion?

- Think about your likely audience. Will they be familiar with the event?
- Decide who will be the speaker in your poem.
- Use imagery to bring the event to life.
- As you write your poem, be sure you choose a form that will best convey your ideas.

Assign this performance task.

PERFORMANCE TASK

W 3d

Writing Activity: Poem Have students work independently. Tell them to

- choose only words that are necessary and that enhance meaning
- use words describing what the speaker hears, says, sees, smells, and feels
- choose the best way to present the message students want to convey

Have students share their poems with the class.

Analyze Structure: Meter

TEACH

Review with students that **rhythm** is the musical quality, or "beat," heard in a poem, created by the pattern of stressed and unstressed syllables in a line of poetry. Rhythm helps a poet emphasize words or ideas, or suggest a mood or action. In many poems, the rhythm varies from line to line or stanza to stanza, depending on the effect the poet intends to create.

Next, explain to students that **meter** is a regular pattern of stressed and unstressed syllables in a poem. Point out that many poems have rhythm, but not all poems with rhythm have a regular meter. Tell students that in order to have meter, a poem must faithfully follow an established pattern of stressed and unstressed syllables throughout the entire poem, or at least through most of it.

Then, explain to students that each unit of meter is known as a foot and that a **foot** of meter is made up of one stressed syllable and one or two unstressed syllables. Tell students that different types of meter are identified by the number and type of feet found in each line of poetry. Provide definitions of the different types of feet in English poetry:

- An **iamb** is made up of two syllables: unstressed, stressed.
- A **trochee** is made up of two syllables: stressed, unstressed.
- A **spondee** is made up of two syllables: stressed, stressed.
- An **anapest** is made up of three syllables: unstressed, unstressed, stressed.
- A **dactyl** is made up of three syllables: stressed, unstressed, unstressed.

If possible, explore an example of one or two of these types of feet with students.

PRACTICE AND APPLY

Have students work together to explore patterns of stressed and unstressed syllables in familiar nursery rhymes, such as "Humpty Dumpty," "Little Miss Muffet," and "Jack and Jill." Then have students analyze "Watcher" or another poem of their choosing for rhythm and meter, reminding them that not all poems that have rhythm have a regular meter.

INTERACTIVE WHITEBOARD LESSON
Compare Poetic Forms

Learn the Skill ▸ What Role Does Form Play in Poetry?

What Role Does Form Play in Poetry?

Find Out

In poetry, form is the way words and lines are arranged on the page. Form may also involve patterns of rhythm and rhyme. Poets choose forms that are well-suited to the thoughts they wish to express.

RETEACH

Use the whiteboard lesson to review form, the role it plays in poetry, and these steps for comparing form:

- **Step 1: Examine Line Length and Stanzas** Compare the number of lines per stanza and how the stanzas are organized. Note the emphasis created by the line breaks.
- **Step 2: Look for a Rhyme Scheme** Remind students to look for rhyme patterns; rhythm created by rhyming words, repetition, or alliteration; or regular patterns of stressed and unstressed syllables.
- **Step 3: Analyze the Effects of Form** Compare the effects each form has on the meaning of the poem. Have students analyze how specific lines and stanzas develop meaning within the overall form or structure of a poem.

Next, work with students to analyze a traditional poem and a free verse poem using the whiteboard lesson. Help them recognize which elements are important to each form and how poets use these elements to express their ideas in a compelling way.

LEVEL UP TUTORIALS Assign the following *Level Up* tutorial: **Elements of Poetry**

INDEPENDENT READING

Have students work in groups to apply the steps to "The Last Hurricane" and "Watcher," to poems from Collection 2, or to other poems they are reading. Have groups compare their results.

The Banana Tree

Short Story by James Berry

Why This Text?

Students often encounter stories from diverse cultures and literary traditions. These stories enable them to appreciate differences and similarities among many people. This lesson explores how one writer uses literary techniques to show the relationship between a boy and his father.

Key Learning Objective: The student will be able to identify and analyze how dialect and imagery, including figurative language, enrich a story.

For practice and application:

There Will Come Soft Rains
Short Story by Ray Bradbury

Close Reader selection:
"There Will Come Soft Rains,"
Short Story by Ray Bradbury

RL 1 Cite textual evidence.
RL 2 Determine a theme or central idea; provide a summary.
RL 4 Determine the meaning of words and phrases.
RL 5 Analyze structure.
RL 10 Read and comprehend literature.
W 3d Write narratives: Use precise words, relevant details, and sensory language.
SL 1 Engage effectively in a range of collaborative discussions.
L 2 Demonstrate command of the conventions of standard English capitalization.
L 4 Determine or clarify meaning of multiple-meaning words.
L 4a Use context as a clue to meaning.
L 5a Interpret figures of speech.
L 6 Acquire and use grade-appropriate academic vocabulary and domain-specific words and phrases.

Text Complexity Rubric

Quantitative Measures	**The Banana Tree** Lexile: 820L
Qualitative Measures	**Levels of Meaning/Purpose** multiple levels of meaning (multiple themes)
	Structure no major shifts in chronology; occasional use of flashback
	Language Conventionality and Clarity figurative, less accessible language
	Knowledge Demands somewhat unfamiliar situation
Reader/Task Considerations	• Teacher determined • Vary by individual reader and type of text • See the Text X-Ray for suggested Reader/Task Considerations.

English Language Support

Before teaching, use the Text X-Ray for an overview of the text's complexity. The Text X-Ray and the supports and scaffolds in the Teacher's Edition will help you guide students of different skill levels.

Meaning Making

Language Development

Effective Expression

Content Knowledge

Foundational Skills

Text Complexity: Qualitative Measures

Levels of Meaning/Purpose

multiple levels of meaning (multiple themes)

Help students determine meanings of figurative and descriptive language.

- Teacher's Edition side notes, pp. 171, 174, 175, 176, 177, 178, 179, 180, 181
- English Language Support, pp. 171, 178
- Strategies for Annotation, pp. 176, 181
- Determine Meanings: Figurative Language, p. 181

To reteach how to determine meanings in figurative language, see

- Determine Meaning: Figurative Language, p. 184a

▶ **Use It!** *Level Up* Tutorial: Figurative Language

Interactive Graphic Organizer: Conclusions Chart

ZOOM IN ON **DETERMINING MEANINGS OF FIGURATIVE LANGUAGE** Give the definitions of **simile, metaphor,** and **personification** and elicit examples from volunteers. Explain that writers use these types of **figurative language** to make comparisons that help readers form pictures in their minds. Ask students to look for figurative language as they read the story; then have them answer and discuss these questions:

- What is a good example of personification in the story?
- What two things are being compared in this example?
- Did the figurative language help you form images in your mind?

Next, let students work in pairs or small groups to find and analyze examples of similes and metaphors in the story, using these questions as a model.

Structure

no major shifts in chronology, occasional use of flashback

Help students understand dialect.

- Teacher's Edition side notes, pp. 172, 173, 175, 177, 179, 181
- English Language Support, p. 172
- When Students Struggle, p. 175
- Strategies for Annotation, p. 173
- Determine Meanings: Dialect, p. 181

ZOOM IN ON **DETERMINING MEANINGS: DIALECT** Explain that **dialect** is a different form of a language spoken in a particular region. Writers may include dialect in the **dialogue,** or conversation between two or more characters. Students will encounter words that are spelled according to the way people say them in the characters' Jamaican dialect. To help students understand the dialect, suggest that they read the dialogue aloud or listen to the eBook audio while following the text.

After they read the story, have pairs locate passages of dialect and take turns reading them aloud. To extend the activity,

- create a class "glossary" that lists the standard English versions of the words
- discuss what the dialect adds to the emotional tone of the story

Language Conventionality and Clarity

figurative, less accessible language

Teach vocabulary in context.

- Teacher's Edition Critical Vocabulary notes, pp. 173, 174, 176, 177, 183
- Applying Academic Vocabulary, p. 172
- Vocabulary Strategy: Use Context Clues, p. 183
- Strategies for Annotation, p. 183

Help students understand the language and conventions used in the text.

- English Language Support, p. 177, 184
- Language Conventions: Capitalization, p. 184

ZOOM IN ON **PREVIEWING CRITICAL VOCABULARY** Introduce the vocabulary for the selection.

- List the Critical Vocabulary terms on the board.
- As a class, identify familiar affixes and roots and record them next to the words.
- Use each word in a sentence. Then guide students to define the words based on the context.
- Have pairs write sentences for each word and share them with the class.

Knowledge Demands

somewhat unfamiliar situation

Help students understand the cultural and geographical context of the story.

- Teacher's Edition Author note, p. 171
- Content-Area Connection, p. 174

ZOOM IN ON **BUILDING CULTURAL KNOWLEDGE** Before reading, discuss the extreme poverty found in Jamaica's agricultural communities. Frequent hurricanes hit the island, causing floods and damaging crops and buildings. Rural road conditions are poor. Many houses are built with flimsy scrap materials, and most lack electricity and running water. Preview the photograph on page 178 to help students understand the setting of the story.

- Have students jot down questions about the setting as they read.
- After reading, let students share their questions. Help them find answers by revisiting the text or by consulting reference sources.

Suggested Reader/Task Considerations

You might consider the following before assigning this story to students:

- Do students have the necessary inferencing, visualizing, and questioning skills to comprehend the story?
- Do students have adequate experience regarding the dialect used in the story to understand it?

ZOOM IN ON **SUPPORTING COMPREHENSION**

- The author's vivid descriptions provide ample opportunities for visualizing. To enhance inferencing and questioning skills, have small groups speculate about daily life of the people in Canerise Village.
- Explain that while English is the official language of Jamaica, the people speak in a dialect that reflects the island's heritage. It mixes elements of English, African, Spanish, and French, along with Irish, British, and American idioms. Preview the dialect by reading examples aloud and paraphrasing them.

James Berry Have students read the information about the author. Explain that James Berry moved to the United States during World War II looking for opportunity. Though he returned to Jamaica four years later, he stayed there for only two years, then moved to England, again seeking opportunity. Berry, reflecting on his experiences, has explained that the movements of people bring change, development, and enlightenment. He endeavors to do the same with his poetry and stories.

SETTING A PURPOSE Direct students to use the Setting a Purpose question to focus their reading. Remind students to write down questions as they read.

Determine Meaning: Figurative Language

RL 1,
RL 4,
L 5a

(LINES 5–12)

Explain to students that **figurative language** is language that uses words and phrases in an imaginative way to express ideas that are not literally true. Tell students that one type of figurative language is called **personification,** in which an animal, object, or event is described as behaving in a human way.

(A) **CITE TEXT EVIDENCE** Have students reread lines 5–12 and identify two examples of personification. *(Lines 5–6: "...the hurricane meant to show it was merciless..."; line 12: "...trees crouched.")* Ask students how this language helps readers understand the setting. *(It helps show the danger and power of the hurricane; it creates a sense of fear and possible injury.)*

James Berry (b. 1924) *was raised in a tiny seaside village in Jamaica. At seventeen, he left home for the United States. Unhappy there, he returned to Jamaica four years later. Although Berry moved to England in 1948, much of his writing focuses on his early Caribbean home. He chooses to use the local language of his childhood in his writing because he wants to express the experience of living in his home village. Berry has won many literary awards for his poetry and stories.*

THE BANANA TREE

Short Story by James Berry

SETTING A PURPOSE As you read, pay attention to the clues that help you understand the relationship between the boy and his father. Write down any questions you have while reading.

In the hours the hurricane stayed, its presence made everybody older. It made Mr. Bass see that not only people and animals and certain valuables were of most importance to be saved.

(A) From its very buildup the hurricane meant to show it was merciless, unstoppable, and, with its might, changed landscapes.

All day the Jamaican sun didn't come out. Then, ten minutes before, there was a swift shower of rain that raced by and was gone like some urgent messenger-rush of wind. And again everything went back to that quiet, that unnatural quiet. It was as if trees crouched quietly in fear. As if, too, birds knew they should shut up. A thick and low black cloud had covered the sky and shadowed everywhere, and made it seem like

(t) ©Sal Idriss; (c) ©Getty Images

English Language Support

Analyze Language Students may have difficulty following the long, imaginative descriptions that appear throughout the story. Before reading, discuss the story's setting and let volunteers speculate about the problems a hurricane might bring to such a place.

• Divide the story into short segments. Have pairs pause after each segment to ask and answer questions about the hurricane's effects on the village.

• Ask students to take notes about the hurricane's effects as they read. Then have them share and discuss their notes with a partner.

• After reading, ask small groups to cite the most striking images of the hurricane's effects and to describe what happened in their own words.

CLOSE READ

Determine Meaning:
Dialect (LINES 47–48)

RL 4

Explain to students that **dialect** is a form of language that is spoken in a particular region by people who live there. Tell students that authors often use dialect to create characters who sound authentic. In **dialogue,** or written conversation between two or more characters, dialect connects the characters to the particular setting of the story and to each other.

(B) **ASK STUDENTS** to reread lines 47–48 and explain what Mr. Jetro Bass is saying and to whom. (*Mr. Bass is telling his children that the storm is bad, but it will be over soon.*) Ask students what this tells them about Mr. Bass. (*Possible response: He cares about his children and wants them to feel safe.*)

English Language Support

Hearing dialect spoken aloud may help students better make connections with standard English words. Ask students to use context clues to explain what is being said in the dialogue in lines 51–61. If students have difficulty, read aloud the dialect or have them listen to the audio in their eBooks as they read along with the text.

ASK STUDENTS to provide the standard English versions of these words:

- chil'run (*children*)
- das' (*that's*)
- bwoy (*boy*)
- somet'ing (*something*)
- nothin' (*nothing*)

---

night was coming on. And the cloud deepened. Its deepening spread more and more over the full stretch of the sea.

The doom-laden afternoon had the atmosphere of Judgment Day[1] for everybody in all the districts about. Everybody knew the hour of disaster was near. Warnings
20 printed in bold lettering had been put up at post offices, police stations, and school-yard entrances and in clear view on shop walls in village squares.

Carrying children and belongings, people hurried in files and in scattered groups, headed for the big, strong, and safe community buildings. In Canerise Village, we headed for the schoolroom. Loaded with bags and cases, with bundles and lidded baskets, individuals carrying or leading an animal, parents shrieking for children to stay at their heels, we arrived there. And looking around, anyone would think the whole of
30 Canerise was here in this vast superbarn of a noisy chattering schoolroom.

With violent gusts and squalls the storm broke. Great rushes, huge bulky rushes, of wind struck the building in heavy, repeated thuds, shaking it over and over and carrying on.

Families were huddled together on the floor. People sang, sitting on benches, desks, anywhere there was room. Some people knelt in loud prayer. Among the refugees' noises a goat bleated, a hen fluttered or cackled, a dog whined.
40 Mr. Jetro Bass was sitting on a soap box. His broad back leaned on the blackboard against the wall. Mrs. Imogene Bass, largely pregnant, looked a midget beside him. Their children were sitting on the floor. The eldest boy, Gustus, sat farthest from his father. Altogether, the children's heads made seven different levels of height around the parents. Mr. Bass forced a reassuring smile. His toothbrush mustache[2] moved about a little as he said, "The storm's bad, chil'run. Really bad. But it'll blow off. It'll spen' itself out. It'll kill itself." **(B)**

Except for Gustus's, all the faces of the children turned up
50 with subdued fear and looked at their father as he spoke.

---

[1] **Judgment Day:** a religious term for the end of the world.
[2] **toothbrush mustache** (mŭs´tăsh´): a small, rectangular unshaven area of hair on a man's upper lip.

APPLYING ACADEMIC VOCABULARY

significant	impact	injure

THINK-PAIR-SHARE Ask pairs to answer and discuss the questions below. Encourage them to use the academic vocabulary words *significant, impact,* and *injure* in their discussions. Let volunteers share their responses with the class.

- Is the size of the Bass family **significant** to Gustus's relationship with his father?
- What **impact** did the storm have on the family?
- Did the storm physically or emotionally **injure** the family?

"Das true wha' Pappy say," Mrs. Bass said. "The good Lord won' gi' we more than we can bear."

Mr. Bass looked at Gustus. He stretched fully through the sitting children and put a lumpy, blistery hand—though a huge hand—on the boy's head, almost covering it. The boy's clear brown eyes looked straight and unblinkingly into his father's face. "Wha's the matter, bwoy?" his dad asked.

He shook his head. "Nothin', Pappy."

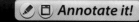

"Wha' mek you say nothin'? I sure somet'ing bodder
60 you, Gustus. You not a bwoy who frighten easy. Is not the hurricane wha' bodder you? Tell Pappy."

"Is nothin'."

"You're a big bwoy now. Gustus—you nearly thirteen. You strong. You very useful fo' you age. You good as mi right han'. I depen' on you. But this afternoon—earlier—in the rush, when we so well push to move befo' storm broke, you couldn' rememba a t'ing! Not one t'ing! Why so? Wha' on you mind? You harborin' t'ings from me, Gustus?"

Gustus opened his mouth to speak but closed it again.
70 He knew his father was proud of how well he had grown. To strengthen him, he had always given him "last milk"[3] straight from the cow in the mornings. He was thankful. But to him his strength was only proven in the number of innings he could pitch for his cricket team. The boy's lips trembled. What's the good of tellin' when Pappy don' like cricket. He only get vex[4] an' say it's an evil game for idle hands! He twisted his head and looked away. "I'm harborin' nothin', Pappy."

"Gustus . . ."

80 At that moment a man called, "Mr. Bass!" He came up quickly. "Got a hymnbook, Mr. Bass? We want you to lead us singing."

The people were sitting with bowed heads, humming a song. As the **repressed** singing grew louder and louder, it sounded mournful in the room. Mr. Bass shuffled, looking around as if he wished to back out of the suggestion. But his rich voice and singing leadership were too famous. Mrs. Bass

repress

(rĭ-prĕs´) v. If you *repress* something, you hold it back or try to stop it from happening.

---

[3] **last milk:** the last milk taken from milking a cow; this milk is usually the richest in nutrients and taste.

[4] **vex:** dialect for *vexed*, meaning "annoyed."

The Banana Tree **173**

CLOSE READ

Determine Meaning: Dialect (LINES 57–78)

RL 1, RL 4

Explain to students that writers will often use dialect in other parts of a story in addition to dialogue.

C **CITE TEXT EVIDENCE** Ask students to find the text in which Mr. Bass asks Gustus what is bothering him. *(lines 57–61)* Have students restate what happens in these lines in their own words.

D **ASK STUDENTS** to reread lines 62–79, point out the lines of dialect, and take turns restating events in their own words. *(Dialect: lines 62–68, lines 75–78; Gustus's father is saying that he noticed Gustus wasn't helpful as they rushed to the shelter. Gustus is thinking about how to explain his feelings to his father.)*

E **ASK STUDENTS** to reread lines 75–78 and tell why the author presents some of Gustus's thoughts in dialect here. *(The dialect brings the reader directly into Gustus's mind, making readers feel closer to how Gustus feels about his father.)*

CRITICAL VOCABULARY

repress: The word *repressed* describes the singing.

ASK STUDENTS why the singing was repressed and why it is growing louder. *(The people who were singing were trying not to be heard, maybe in order to not alarm others or because they were upset. It is growing louder as more people join in.)*

Strategies for Annotation ✏️ 🖥️ Annotate it!

Determine Meaning: Dialect

RL 4

Have students reread lines 57–61. Ask them to use their eBook annotation tools to:

- Highlight informally spelled words.
- Underline parts of the sentence where words have been omitted or used informally.
- Review the highlights. On a note, record formal versions of the dialogue.

[. . .] "Wha's the matter, bwoy?" his dad asked.

What is the matter, boy?

He shook his head. "Nothin', Pappy."

"Wha' mek you say nothin'? I sure somet'ing bodder you, Gustus. You not a bwoy who frighten easy. Is not the hurricane wha' bodder you? Tell Pappy."

**Determine Meaning:
Figurative Language**

RL 1,
RL 4,
L 5a

(LINES 98–102)

Remind students that personification is language that gives an object, animal, or event human qualities.

F **CITE TEXT EVIDENCE** Have students reread lines 98–102 to identify examples of personification and explain how they know this. *(Lines 101–102; the author gives the wind human qualities by saying it mocks, screams, whistles, and smashes things.)*

G **ASK STUDENTS** to explain what effect the personification in lines 101–102 has for the reader. *(By making the wind seem human, the author creates a relationship between the people who are singing and the wind that is mocking them and their need for safety.)*

CRITICAL VOCABULARY

mocked: The author writes that the wind mocked someone or something.

ASK STUDENTS who or what the wind is mocking. Can the wind actually mock anyone? *(The wind is mocking the people who are singing and seeking safety. The wind cannot really mock anything because the wind does not have emotions such as scorn or contempt.)*

---

already had the hymnbook in her hand, and she pushed it at her husband. He took it and began turning the leaves as he
90 moved toward the center of the room.

Immediately Mr. Bass was surrounded. He started with a resounding chant over the heads of everybody. "Abide wid me; fast fall the eventide . . . " He joined the singing but broke off to recite the next line. "The darkness deepen; Lord, wid me, abide . . . " Again, before the last long-drawn note faded from the deeply stirred voices, Mr. Bass intoned musically, "When odder helpers fail, and comfo'ts flee . . . "

In this manner he fired inspiration into the singing of hymn after hymn. The congregation swelled their throats,
100 and their mixed voices filled the room, pleading to heaven from the depths of their hearts. But the wind outside **mocked** viciously. It screamed. It whistled. It smashed everywhere up.

Mrs. Bass had tightly closed her eyes, singing and swaying in the center of the children who nestled around her. But Gustus was by himself. He had his elbows on his knees and his hands blocking his ears. He had his own worries.

mock
(mŏk) *v.* To *mock* someone is to treat them with scorn or contempt.

© Shutterstock

174 Collection 3

CONTENT-AREA CONNECTION

Geography Tell students that Jamaica is an island of rolling hills and beaches in the Caribbean Sea, 600 miles south of Florida. Jamaica's first inhabitants, the Tainos, called the island Xaymaca, which means "land of wood and water." Christopher Columbus reached the island in 1494 and claimed it for Spain. The Spanish enslaved the Tainos, and by 1600, they had all died off, mostly due to diseases brought by the settlers. In 1655 the British invaded the island and claimed it for England. Later, English settlers developed sugar plantations on the coastal plains and brought thousands of enslaved Africans to work there. After many slave uprisings, slavery was finally abolished in 1838. Many freed people, called Maroons, moved inland and formed small rural settlements, such as the village described in "The Banana Tree."

Activity After students read the story, have small groups research the geography and culture of Jamaica. Students might also compare the Maroons' struggle for freedom with the civil rights movement in the United States. Have students present their findings to the class.

What's the good of Pappy asking all those questions when he treat him so bad? He's the only one in the family without a pair of shoes! Because he's a big boy, he don't need anyt'ing an' must do all the work. He can't stay at school in the evenings an' play cricket[5] because there's work to do at home. He can't have no outings with the other children because he has no shoes. An' now when he was to sell his bunch of bananas an' buy shoes so he can go out with his cricket team, the hurricane is going to blow it down.

It was true: the root of the banana was his "navel string."[6] After his birth the umbilical cord[7] was dressed with castor oil and sprinkled with nutmeg and buried, with the banana tree planted over it for him. When he was nine days old, the nana midwife[8] had taken him out into the open for the first time. She had held the infant proudly and walked the twenty-five yards that separated the house from the kitchen, and at the back showed him his tree. "'Memba when you grow up," her toothless mouth had said, "it's you nable strings feedin' you tree, the same way it feed you from you mudder."

Refuse from the kitchen made the plant flourish out of all proportion. But the rich soil around it was loose. Each time the tree gave a shoot, the bunch would be too heavy for the soil to support; so it crashed to the ground, crushing the tender fruit. This time, determined that his banana must reach the market, Gustus had supported his tree with eight props. And as he watched it night and morning, it had become very close to him. Often he had seriously thought of moving his bed to its root.

Muffled cries, and the sound of blowing noses, now mixed with the singing. Delayed impact of the disaster was happening. Sobbing was everywhere. Quickly the atmosphere became sodden with the wave of weeping outbursts.

---

[5] **cricket** (krĭk´ĭt): an English sport similar to baseball.

[6] **navel string:** a term for the umbilical cord.

[7] **umbilical cord** (ŭm-bĭl´ĭ-kəl kôrd): the cord through which an unborn baby (fetus) receives nourishment from its mother; a person's navel is the place where the cord was attached.

[8] **nana midwife:** a woman who helps other women give birth and cares for newborn children.

The Banana Tree **175**

TEACH

CLOSE READ

Determine Meaning: Dialect (LINES 107–115)   RL 1, RL 4

Explain that authors often use dialect to show a character's internal thoughts.

H CITE TEXT EVIDENCE Have students reread lines 107–115 and cite differences between the author's use of dialect here and in earlier dialogue. *(Gustus's internal thoughts are longer and more expressive than his spoken words. Fewer words are shortened and sentences are longer than the spoken dialect.)*

I ASK STUDENTS why Gustus's internal thoughts are more expressive than his conversations with his father. *(The author wants to show that Gustus is not telling his father everything that he is thinking about.)*

Determine Meaning: Figurative Language   RL 1, RL 4, L 5a
(LINES 116–125)

Remind students that figurative language is language that expresses ideas that are not literally true.

J CITE TEXT EVIDENCE Have students identify an example of figurative language in lines 116–125. Ask them to explain its meaning in the story. *(Lines 123–125; this idea from the midwife explains that Gustus is responsible for the tree and feels a close connection to it.)*

WHEN STUDENTS STRUGGLE . . .

To improve students' understanding, ask them to list words in dialect along with standard terms as they read. Using the sample, model how to prepare a chart while reading the paragraph that begins in line 116.

Words in Dialect	Respelling / Restatement
Memba	Remember
nable	navel
mudder	mother

TEACH

CLOSE READ

Determine Meaning: Figurative Language

RL 1,
RL 4,
L 5a

(LINES 154–163)

Emphasize to students that the author uses figurative language, including personification, to describe the wind in this passage. Tell students that another example of figurative language is a simile. Explain that a **simile** is an expression that compares two unlike things using the words *like* or *as*.

(K) CITE TEXT EVIDENCE Have students reread lines 154–163 and identify examples of figurative language. Ask students what affect this language has on the story. (*Examples: "wind sneered"; "shirt was fluttering . . . like a boat sail"; "belligerent wind"; wind was "merciless"; wind "bellowed . . . and drummed . . . slapped." The language makes the wind into another character, a character Gustus must struggle against.*)

> #### CRITICAL VOCABULARY
>
> **grimace**: Gustus grimaced in the wind.
>
> **ASK STUDENTS** why Gustus grimaced. What emotion made him grimace? Have students ever grimaced? Why? (*Gustus grimaces because his struggle is so difficult. Students' reasons for grimacing will vary but should relate to difficult experiences and/or emotions.*)

Mrs. Bass's pregnant belly heaved. Her younger children were upset and cried, "Mammy, Mammy, Mammy . . ."

Realizing that his family, too, was overwhelmed by the surrounding calamity, Mr. Bass bustled over to them. Because their respect for him bordered on fear, his presence quieted all immediately. He looked around. "Where's Gustus! Imogene . . . where's Gustus!"

"He was 'ere, Pappy," she replied, drying her eyes. "I dohn know when he get up."

Briskly Mr. Bass began combing the schoolroom to find his boy. He asked; no one had seen Gustus. He called. There was no answer. He tottered, lifting his heavy boots over heads, fighting his way to the jalousie.[9] He opened it, and his eyes gleamed up and down the road but saw nothing of the boy. In despair Mr. Bass gave one last thunderous shout: "Gustus!" Only the wind sneered.

By this time Gustus was halfway on the mile journey to their house. The lone figure in the raging wind and shin-deep road flood was tugging, snapping, and pitching branches out of his path. His shirt was fluttering from his back like a boat sail. And a leaf was fastened to his cheek. But the belligerent wind was merciless. It bellowed into his ears and drummed a deafening commotion. As he **grimaced** and covered his ears, he was forcefully slapped against a coconut tree trunk that lay across the road.

When his eyes opened, his round face was turned up to a festered[10] sky. Above the tormented trees a zinc sheet writhed, twisted, and somersaulted in the tempestuous flurry. Leaves of all shapes and sizes were whirling and diving like attackers around the zinc sheet. As Gustus turned to get up, a bullet drop of rain struck his temple. He shook his head, held grimly to the tree trunk, and struggled to his feet.

Where the road was clear, he edged along the bank. Once, when the wind staggered him, he recovered with his legs wide apart. Angrily he stretched out his hands with clenched fists and shouted, "I almos' hol' you that time. . . . Come solid like that again, an' we fight like man an' man!"

grimace
(grĭm´ĭs) *v.* If you *grimace*, you twist your face in an unattractive way because you are unhappy, disgusted, or in pain.

---

[9] **jalousie** (jăl´ə-sē): a window blind or shutter with adjustable thin slats.
[10] **festered** (fĕs´tərd): infected and irritated; diseased.

176 Collection 3

Strategies for Annotation ✐ 🗐 Annotate it!

Determine Meaning: Figurative Language

RL 4,
L 5a

Have students reread lines 164–170. Ask them to use their eBook annotation tools to do the following:

- Highlight examples of personification in yellow.
- Highlight examples of similes in blue.
- Highlight other figurative language in green.
- Review your annotations. On a note, describe how these examples affect how you see Gustus's situation.

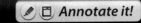

festered sky. Above the tormented trees a zinc sheet writhed,

twisted, and somersaulted in the tempestuous flurry. Leaves

of all shapes and sizes were whirling and diving like attackers

around the zinc sheet. As G_____ to get up, a bullet

drop of rain struck his temp___ ___his head, held grimly

Gustus is in danger.

When Gustus approached the river he had to cross, it was flooded and blocked beyond recognition. Pressing his chest against the gritty road bank, the boy closed his weary eyes on the brink of the spating river. The wrecked footbridge had become the harboring fort for all the debris, branches, and monstrous tree trunks which the river swept along its course. The river was still swelling. More accumulation arrived each moment, ramming and pressing the bridge. Under pressure it was cracking and shifting minutely toward a turbulent forty-foot fall.

Gustus had seen it! A feeling of dismay paralyzed him, reminding him of his foolish **venture**. He scraped his cheek on the bank looking back. But how can he go back? He has no strength to go back. His house is nearer than the school. An' Pappy will only strap him for nothin' . . . for nothin' . . . no shoes, nothin', when the hurricane is gone.

With trembling fingers he tied up the remnants of his shirt. He made a bold step, and the wind half lifted him, ducking him in the muddy flood. He sank to his neck. Floating leaves, sticks, coconut husks, dead ratbats, and all manner of feathered creatures and refuse surrounded him. Forest vines under the water entangled him. But he struggled desperately until he clung to the laden bridge and climbed up among leafless branches.

His legs were bruised and **bore** deep scratches, but steadily he moved up on the slimy pile. He felt like a man at sea, in the heart of a storm, going up the mast of a ship. He rested his feet on a smooth log that stuck to the water-splashed heap like a black torso. As he strained up for another grip, the torso came to life and leaped from under his feet. Swiftly sliding down, he grimly clutched some brambles.

The urgency of getting across became more frightening, and he gritted his teeth and dug his toes into the debris, climbing with maddened determination. But a hard gust of wind slammed the wreck, pinning him like a motionless lizard. For a minute the boy was stuck there, panting, swelling his naked ribs.

He stirred again and reached the top. He was sliding over a breadfruit limb when a flutter startled him. As he looked and saw the clean-head crow and glassy-eyed owl close together,

venture
(věn′chər) *n.*
A *venture* is a dangerous, daring, or poorly planned task or activity.

bore
(bôr) *v.* (past tense of *bear*) If you say a person *bore* something, you mean they carried it or had it on them; it is visible in some way.

The Banana Tree **177**

English Language Support

Use Participles and Gerunds Have students reread the paragraph beginning with line 175 and use their eBook annotation tools to underline the words ending in *-ing*. Explain that a **participle** is an *-ing* form of a verb used as an adjective; a **gerund** is an *-ing* form used as a noun.

- Have students list the *-ing* words in the paragraph on the board and name the verb from which each word was formed. Then ask partners to identify which *-ing* words are used as verbs, participles or gerunds.

CLOSE READ

Determine Meaning: Imagery (LINES 176–185)
RL 1, RL 4

Explain to students that **imagery** consists of words and phrases that appeal to a reader's five senses. Tell students that authors use imagery to help readers imagine what characters are experiencing.

L CITE TEXT EVIDENCE Ask students to find examples of imagery in lines 176–185 and tell how this language affects them. *("Pressing"; "gritty"; "wrecked"; "harboring"; "swept along"; "swelling"; "ramming"; "cracking"; "turbulent." The language allows the reader to see, hear, and feel the violence of the flooded river and to picture Gustus on the riverbank.)*

Determine Meaning: Dialect (LINES 186–192)
RL 1, RL 4

Remind students that authors use dialect to help them create authentic characters.

M CITE TEXT EVIDENCE Have students reread lines 186–192 and point out where the language changes to dialect. *(line 190)* Ask students why the author changes to dialect here. *(The change to dialect pulls the reader closer to Gustus's experience by showing his direct thoughts. It also emphasizes Gustus's difficult feelings about his father in personal language.)*

CRITICAL VOCABULARY

venture: The author describes Gustus's experience as a venture.

ASK STUDENTS what other words the author might have used to show the same or similar idea. What makes *venture* the best choice? *(Gustus's mission to save his tree is dangerous, daring, and poorly planned. The word* adventure *might have been used, but its positive connotation makes* venture *a better choice.)*

bore: Gustus's legs bore deep scratches.

ASK STUDENTS why the author might have chosen the word *bore* instead of the word *had*. *(Bore is a more powerful word than* had. *It has the added connotation of carrying something, and these scratches are like a burden that Gustus bears.)*

CLOSE READ

Determine Meaning: Figurative Language

RL 1,
RL 4,
L 5a

(LINES 220–229)

Remind students that figurative language is used to express ideas that are not literally true. Authors use it for comparison, emphasis, and emotional effect. Explain that a **metaphor** is a comparison of two things that are basically not alike but have some qualities in common. Tell students that a metaphor does not include the words *like* or *as*, which is how it is different from a simile.

N **CITE TEXT EVIDENCE** Have students identify examples of figurative language, including simile, metaphor, and personification, in lines 220–229. *(examples: "whose white heart was a needly splinter, murdered by the wind"; "terrorized trees"; "writhing in turmoil"; "collapsed like an open umbrella")* Ask students to tell what each example describes in their own words.

English Language Support

To help students recognize figurative language, clarify for them the meanings of unfamiliar words and phrases, such as *needly splinter, writhing,* and *turmoil.*

ASK STUDENTS TO explain what has happened to the tree. *(It has been split open and knocked down by the wind.)* Then ask what is meant by the "white heart" of the tree stump. *(It is the central core of the tree, which is a lighter color than the outside of the tree.)*

© Shutterstock

there was a powerful jolt. Gustus flung himself into the air and fell in the expanding water on the other side. When he surfaced, the river had dumped the entire wreckage into the gurgling gully. For once the wind helped. It blew him to land.

220 Gustus was in a daze when he reached his house. Mud and rotten leaves covered his head and face, and blood caked around a gash on his chin. He bent down, shielding himself behind a tree stump whose white heart was a needly splinter, murdered by the wind.

He could hardly recognize his yard. The terrorized trees that stood were writhing in turmoil. Their thatched house had collapsed like an open umbrella that was given a heavy blow. He looked the other way and whispered, "Is still there! That's a miracle. . . . That's a miracle."

230 Dodging the wind, he staggered from tree to tree until he got to his own tormented banana tree. Gustus hugged the tree. "My nable string!" he cried. "My nable string! I know you would stan' up to it, I know you would."

FOR STANDARD ENGLISH LEARNERS

Pronunciation Some students may have difficulty pronouncing both letters in certain final consonant clusters, such as *ft, nd, ld, sk, sp, pt,* and *ct.* Explain that the dialect in this story reflects the way Gustus leaves off final consonants when he says words that end in these clusters.

- Point out *stan'* in line 233 and ask students to spell the complete word. *(stand)* Read the sentence aloud in standard English, emphasizing *stand,* and have students repeat it after you: "I knew you would stand up to it, I knew you would."

- Then have pairs look for two more words on page 179 in which the final consonant has been replaced with an apostrophe. *(hol', line 245; groun', line 247)* Write them on the board.

- Work with students to rephrase in standard English the sentences in which the words appear. Practice saying them aloud.

The bones of the tree's stalky leaves were broken, and the wind lifted them and harassed them. And over Gustus's head the heavy fruit swayed and swayed. The props held the tree, but they were squeaking and slipping. And around the plant the roots stretched and trembled, gradually surfacing under loose earth.

240   With the rags of his wet shirt flying off his back, Gustus was down busily on his knees, bracing, pushing, tightening the props. One by one he was adjusting them until a heavy rush of wind knocked him to the ground. A prop fell on him, but he scrambled to his feet and looked up at the thirteen-hand bunch of bananas. "My good tree," he bawled, "hol' you fruit. . . . Keep it to you heart like a mudder savin' her baby! Don't let the wicked wind t'row you to the groun' . . . even if it t'row me to the groun'. I will not leave you."

But several attempts to replace the prop were futile. The
250   force of the wind against his weight was too much for him. He thought of a rope to lash the tree to anything, but it was difficult to make his way into the kitchen, which, separate from the house, was still standing. The invisible hand of the wind tugged, pushed, and forcefully restrained him. He got down and crawled on his belly into the earth-floor kitchen. As he showed himself with the rope, the wind tossed him, like washing on the line, against his tree.

The boy was hurt! He looked crucified against the tree. The spike of the wind was slightly withdrawn. He fell, folded
260   on the ground. He lay there unconscious. And the wind had no mercy for him. It shoved him, poked him, and molested his clothes like muddy newspaper against the tree.

As darkness began to move in rapidly, the wind grew more vicious and surged a mighty gust that struck the resisting kitchen. It was heaved to the ground in a rubbled pile. The brave wooden hut had been shielding the banana tree but in its death fall missed it by inches. The wind charged again, and the soft tree gurgled—the fruit was torn from it and plunged to the ground.

270   The wind was less fierce when Mr. Bass and a searching party arrived with lanterns. Because the bridge was washed away, the hazardous roundabout journey had badly impeded them.

Talks about safety were mockery to the anxious father. Relentlessly he searched. In the darkness his great voice

TO CHALLENGE STUDENTS . . .

Analyze Characters Remind students that this story is told primarily from Gustus's perspective and not his father's. Ask students to imagine what Mr. Bass might be going through as he leaves the shelter and looks for Gustus. Would his trek through the storm have been as difficult as Gustus's? How might that have affected him? Have students discuss the traits that Mr. Bass seems to have and how his approach to parenting might be developing as he searches for his son. Students should support their analysis with details from the text.

CLOSE READ

Determine Meaning: Dialect (LINES 245–248)   RL 4

Emphasize to students the emotional content in this dialogue between Gustus and his tree.

Q   ASK STUDENTS to reread lines 245–248. Have them tell why the tree is so important to Gustus. *(Gustus is desperate for his tree to survive so that his life can change. All of his hopes are caught up in the tree and its fruit.)* Ask them to tell whether the dialect helps or interferes with their understanding of Gustus's emotion, and why. *(Possible responses: I enjoy the dialect because it helps me imagine how difficult and important this situation is for Gustus. I don't like the dialect because it slows me down, or is hard to understand.)*

Determine Meaning: Figurative Language   RL 1, RL 4, L 5a
(LINES 258–262)

Remind students that the author has used a variety of figurative language in this story.

P   CITE TEXT EVIDENCE Ask students how the author continues to portray the wind as a separate character. *(The author uses personification to give the wind human traits: the wind had no mercy; shoved him, poked him, molested his clothes. All these make the wind seem as if it is acting personally against Gustus.)*

Q   ASK STUDENTS to reread line 259 and tell what two things are being compared and how they are alike and different. *(The line compares the wind to a spike without using the words like or as; this is a metaphor. These two things are different because a spike is very solid, but the wind is not. They are alike because in this moment the wind was sharp and forceful, like a weapon or spike.)*

Determine Meaning: Imagery (LINES 276–280)

RL 1,
RL 4

Remind students that imagery is the use of words that describe sensory details and appeal to a reader's senses of sight, hearing, taste, smell, or touch.

Ⓡ CITE TEXT EVIDENCE Have students find examples of imagery in lines 276–280 and explain how they help readers picture the scene. *(Examples: echoed, wrenching, ripping; the words help readers picture Mr. Bass's frantic actions.)*

Determine Meaning: Figurative Language

RL 1,
RL 4,
L 5a

(LINES 281–284)

Remind students that the author has used figurative language in a variety of ways throughout the story.

Ⓢ CITE TEXT EVIDENCE Have students reread lines 281–284 and identify the simile. *("shivering and twitching like a propped-up man...")* Ask them how this vivid (and somewhat gruesome) description gives insight into Mr. Bass's emotions. *(Mr. Bass was in fear that his son might be dead. He was probably preparing himself or expecting to find a gory scene.)*

COLLABORATIVE DISCUSSION Have partners discuss what both Gustus and his father are like and why they have been having difficulties. As they discuss this father-son relationship and how it might change, have them cite text evidence to support their ideas.

ASK STUDENTS to share any questions they generated in the course of reading and discussing this selection.

English Language Support

Provide Textual Evidence Provide the following sentence stems and encourage students to complete them during their discussion.

- Gustus feels that his father _____.
- He feels this way because _____.
- Gustus's father is _____ because _____.
- Their relationship might change because _____.

echoed everywhere, calling for his boy. He was wrenching and ripping through the house wreckage when suddenly he vaguely remembered how the boy had been fussing with the banana tree. Desperate, the man struggled from the ruins,
280 flagging the lantern he carried.

The flickering light above his head showed Mr. Bass the forlorn and pitiful banana tree. There it stood, shivering and twitching like a propped-up man with lacerated throat and dismembered head. Half of the damaged fruit rested on Gustus. The father hesitated. But when he saw a feeble wink of the boy's eyelids, he flung himself to the ground. His bristly chin rubbed the child's face while his unsteady hand ran all over his body. "Mi bwoy!" he murmured. "Mi hurricane bwoy! The Good Lord save you. . . . Why you do this? Why
290 you do this?"

"I did want buy mi shoes, Pappy. I . . . I can't go anywhere ' cause I have no shoes. . . . I didn' go to school outing at the factory. I didn' go to Government House. I didn' go to Ol' Fort in town."

Mr. Bass sank into the dirt and stripped himself of his heavy boots. He was about to lace them to the boy's feet when the onlooking men prevented him. He tied the boots together and threw them over his shoulder.

Gustus's broken arm was strapped to his side as they
300 carried him away. Mr. Bass stroked his head and asked how he felt. Only then grief swelled inside him and he wept.

COLLABORATIVE DISCUSSION Think about what happens at the end of "The Banana Tree." With a partner, discuss how the storm may change the relationship between Gustus and his father. Use text evidence to support your ideas.

Determine Meanings: Figurative Language

RL 4

Great stories help readers feel as if they can see and hear the characters and action. **Imagery,** or rich sensory details, is one device authors use to help readers imagine a scene. Here is an example from "The Banana Tree":

> Floating leaves, sticks, cocnut husks, dead ratbats, and all manner of feathered creatures and refuse surrounded him. Forest vines under the water entangled him.

The details that appeal to your senses of sight and touch help you recognize that the author is using imagery.

Figurative language is language that uses words and expressions to express ideas that are different from their literal meanings. One type of figurative language, **personification** is when an animal, object, or phenomenon is described as behaving in a human way. The phrase "Only the wind sneered" is an example of personification from "The Banana Tree."

Identifying imagery and figurative language helps you determine the intended meaning of words and phrases and better understand what you read. To identify imagery, figurative language, and personification, ask:

- Do descriptions use rich sensory details? How is this imagery useful?
- Does the author use figurative language, such as personification, to make comparisons? How does it add to the story?

Look for additional imagery, figurative language, and personification as you analyze "The Banana Tree."

Determine Meanings: Dialect

RL 4

Dialect is a form of language that is spoken in a particular region by the people who live there. Writers use dialect to make dialogue sound authentic. In "The Banana Tree," the characters speak a Jamaican dialect in which English words are mixed with African words, pronunciations, and expressions:

> "Wha' mek you say nothin'? I sure somet'ing bodder you, Gustus. You not a bwoy who frighten easy."

One way to understand dialect is to read the text aloud to help you hear the sounds and rhythms of the language. Look for more examples of personification and dialect as you analyze "The Banana Tree."

The Banana Tree **181**

Determine Meanings: Figurative Language

RL 4

Discuss the literary terms with students. Ask them to discuss the example shown and to explain the meaning of other examples in the text. Have volunteers identify examples of imagery and figurative language in the story that they found to be particularly effective at creating an image in their minds. Discuss why these passages were so effective, using the bulleted questions as needed to prompt students' discussion.

Determine Meanings: Dialect

RL 4

Discuss the definition of the term *dialect*, using the example shown. Talk with students about clues in the text and other knowledge of language they used to determine the meaning of the dialect in the story. Have them explain the effects of dialect on the story, such as creating an informal tone and developing authentic characters. Then point out that the United States has many, many dialects. Have volunteers share examples from their own travels or other experiences. Finally, have students share (classroom-appropriate) examples of teenage or popular dialect that they know or use themselves.

Strategies for Annotation ✏ 🗐 *Annotate it!*

Determine Meanings: Figurative Language

RL 4, L 5a

Share these strategies for guided or independent analysis:

- Underline effective examples of imagery in the story.
- Highlight in yellow examples of personification.
- Highlight in blue examples of simile or metaphor.
- Review the annotations. On a note, explain the meaning of each one and the effect it has on the text.

from the house, was still standing. The invisible hand of the wind tugged, pushed, and forcefully restrained him. He got down and crawled on his belly into the earth-floor kitchen. As he showed himself with the rope, the wind tossed him, like washing on the line, against his tree.

PRACTICE & APPLY

Analyzing the Text

RL 1, RL 2,
RL 4, RL 5,
RL 10

Possible answers:

1. *"Violent gusts and squalls," "heavy, repeated thuds," "huddled together on the floor," animals "bleated," "fluttered or cackled," "whined." By including details that help readers see and hear the approaching hurricane and how people and animals have gathered in a small place to seek shelter from it, the author sets the stage for the conflict and makes readers want to find out what will happen.*

2. *The author wants readers to get a sense of Gustus's own voice and learn what is important to him.*

3. *He is tied to the banana tree emotionally because it was planted especially for him at his birth. It also will bear fruit that he can sell to buy the shoes he wants.*

4. *He is telling the wind how angry he is. He is also saying that he is not afraid, perhaps to chase his fear away.*

5. *Gustus was very determined to take care of his beloved tree and to take control of his life by buying himself the shoes he needs to do the things he wants.*

6. *Some examples of personification are "tormented banana tree," "I know you would stan' up to it, I know you would," "bones of the tree's stalky leaves," "the wind . . . harassed them." Personification in this story helps readers to understand the storm (and nature as a whole) as another character in the story—an angry, harsh, and destructive character.*

7. *The imagery helps readers see, hear, and feel the setting, characters, and events in vivid ways. The characters are in a desperate struggle with nature—a very powerful opponent. The strong imagery brings readers closer to the struggles of Gustus and Mr. Bass.*

FOR STANDARD ENGLISH LEARNERS

Verb Tenses Remind students that the summary of an experience should be written in the past tense. Review the rules for past-tense forms of regular verbs. Then provide the following sentences for students to complete.

- It (rain, rained) for five days without stopping.
- Soon the river (overflow, overflowed) its banks.
- Rescuers (row, rowed) a boat to our house to help us get out.

Have partners exchange their sentences and review them for errors in tense.

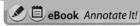

Analyzing the Text

RL 1, RL 2, RL 4,
RL 5, RL 10,
W 3d

Cite Text Evidence   Support your responses with evidence from the text.

1. **Infer** Review lines 32–39. What sensory details does the author use in these paragraphs? Explain why the author would use strong imagery near the beginning of the story.

2. **Draw Conclusions** Reread lines 69–78. Toward the end of the paragraph, the writing shifts to dialect. Why is the author's choice to write Gustus's thoughts in dialect significant?

3. **Summarize** Review lines 107–134. Explain why the banana tree is so important to Gustus.

4. **Interpret** Read lines 171–175 aloud. In your own words, tell what Gustus is saying to the wind.

5. **Draw Conclusions** Think about the danger and injuries Gustus faced because he would not let the hurricane constrain him. What conclusion can you draw about Gustus's character?

6. **Interpret** Reread lines 230–235. What are two examples of personification the author uses? What impact does the personification have on the story?

7. **Evaluate** How does the strong imagery in the story add to your understanding of the ideas the author wants to share?

PERFORMANCE TASK

Writing Activity: Narrative Write a description of a bad storm that you have experienced.

- First, write a summary of the event.
- Next, fill in sensory details. What did you see, feel, and hear?
- As you record your details, use specific nouns, verbs, and adjectives to create a clear picture of what you experienced.

- Use personification to make animals, buildings, or things in nature behave like humans.
- Review your writing to add or clarify details of the event.

Assign this performance task.

PERFORMANCE TASK

W 3d

Writing Activity: Narrative Have students work independently to

- summarize ideas before writing the narrative
- choose vivid, sensory words to convey details
- read their draft aloud to a partner, asking for feedback

Students can present narratives to the class and discuss each storm.

Critical Vocabulary

L 4, L 4a, L 6

repress	mock	grimace	venture	bore

Practice and Apply Complete each sentence.

1. Jorge wished he could **repress** the loud noises because . . .

2. Hank didn't like it when Gail began to **mock** his singing because . . .

3. I had to **grimace** when I saw the menu choices because . . .

4. Mom said to think twice about taking a **venture** to the pond because . . .

5. The piano **bore** evidence of heavy use because . . .

Vocabulary Strategy: Use Context Clues

Context clues are the words or phrases surrounding a word that provide hints about a word's meaning. Context clues can help you determine the correct meaning of **multiple-meaning words,** which are words that have more than one meaning.

In "The Banana Tree," Gustus's "legs were bruised and *bore* deep scratches." The word *bore* can have several meanings, including

- "to make a hole or drill into"
- "to make weary by being dull and tedious"
- "the past tense of *bear*," (as in "have as a visible characteristic")

The context clues help you figure out that in the example, *bore* means "the past tense of *bear*" as in "have as a visible characteristic."

Knowing whether a multiple-meaning word is being used as a noun, verb, modifier, or another part of a sentence can also help you determine its meaning. You can tell that *bore* is being used as a verb in the example.

Practice and Apply Choose the correct meaning of each boldface word.

1. Drake's mother asked him to keep a close **watch** on his younger brother.
    a. the act of looking or observing attentively
    b. a small timepiece

2. Lena was surprised to see daffodils blooming so early in the **spring.**
    a. to leap or jump suddenly
    b. the season between winter and summer

3. Ms. Hamilton wondered why Nate wasn't **present.**
    a. gift
    b. in attendance

The Banana Tree **183**

Critical Vocabulary

L 4,
L 4a,
L 6

Possible answers:

1. *. . . he needed some quiet time to finish his work.*

2. *. . . he thought he had a pretty good voice!*

3. *. . . the choices were all horrible.*

4. *. . . she had heard there might be a thunderstorm.*

5. *. . . it was used for all our community events.*

Vocabulary Strategy: Use Context Clues

Answers:

1. **a.** *the act of looking or observing attentively*

2. **b.** *the season between winter and summer*

3. **b.** *in attendance*

Strategies for Annotation   📝 🔲 *Annotate it!*

Use Context Clues

L 4,
L 4a,
L 6

Have students locate the words *files, rich, treat, wave,* and *blow* (lines 23, 87, 108, 138, 227). Ask them to use their eBook annotation tools to do the following:

- Write at least two meanings for each word.
- Highlight each word in yellow.
- Underline words or phrases that have clues to each word's meaning.
- Record the meaning of the word as used in context. Decide if it matches a meaning you wrote down earlier and write why or why not.

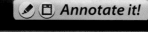

Carrying children and belongings, people hurried in files and in scattered groups, headed for the big, strong, and safe community buildings. . . .

The Banana Tree **183**

PRACTICE & APPLY

Language Conventions: Capitalization

Tell students that the examples in the chart show just a few examples of common and proper nouns. Invite volunteers to come up with additional examples for each category and write each example for the rest of the class.

Answers:

1. *The Red Cross will arrive on Wednesday.*

2. *In 2005, the city of New Orleans was devastated by Hurricane Katrina.*

3. *Reporters gathered in the city square to hear what Mayor Reynolds had to say.*

4. *Many nurses and physicians, including Doctor Webb, helped hurricane victims in the emergency room at Mercy Hospital.*

5. *Mr. and Mrs. Carter spent several weeks at the Pleasant Valley Shelter.*

 Assess It Online!

Online Selection Test
- Download an editable ExamView bank.
- Assign and manage this test online.

Language Conventions: Capitalization

A **common noun** is a general name for a person, place, thing, or idea. Common nouns are not capitalized. A **proper noun** is one that names a specific or particular person, place, thing, or idea. Each word in a proper noun begins with a capital letter. Examples include the names of people, titles, countries, and religions. In the following example, notice how proper nouns are capitalized:

> As the hurricane headed toward Jamaica, Gustus went with his parents, Mr. Jetro Bass and Mrs. Imogene Bass, to the strong and safe community buildings of Canerise Village.

The chart gives some additional examples.

Common Nouns	Proper Nouns
sheriff	Sheriff Ryan
museum	Heritage Museum
tropical storm	Tropical Storm Irene

Practice and Apply Correct each sentence so that all proper nouns are capitalized.

1. The red cross will arrive on Wednesday.

2. In 2005, the city of New orleans was devastated by hurricane Katrina.

3. Reporters gathered in the city square to hear what mayor Reynolds had to say.

4. Many nurses and physicians, including doctor Webb, helped hurricane victims in the emergency room at Mercy hospital.

5. Mr. and mrs. Carter spent several weeks at the Pleasant Valley shelter.

English Language Support

Write with Correct Capitalization Review the definitions of common and proper nouns. Display a two-column chart with the headings Common Nouns and Proper Nouns. Ask volunteers to list examples under each category.

- Read the Practice and Apply sentences aloud. Work with students to identify the proper nouns in each sentence that should be capitalized.

- Have partners identify the proper nouns and rewrite each sentence using correct capitalization. Then have two pairs exchange and review each other's work.

- Write a list of ten common and proper nouns on the board, but do not capitalize the proper nouns. Ask students to write sentences containing the nouns with correct capitalization. Have them share their work with a partner and explain their capitalization decisions.

Draw Conclusions

TEACH

Tell students that to **draw conclusions** means to combine evidence from a story, your own experience or knowledge, and logical reasoning to make broader statements about a story or elements within it.

- Have volunteers share conclusions in their own lives. For example, students might combine the fact of clear skies with their knowledge to conclude that they don't need an umbrella.
- Point out that in the example above, the students combine **evidence,** or a specific piece of information that supports a claim (the clear skies), with what they know (rain rarely falls from a clear sky) to draw a conclusion (the umbrella was unnecessary).
- Emphasize that when drawing conclusions based on a text, the reader combines evidence from the text with his or her own previous experience or knowledge.

Have students reread lines 80–90 of "The Banana Tree." Discuss how, based on these lines, a reader can draw conclusions about Mr. Bass's standing in the community. Model the use of a Conclusions Chart as you work with students to draw a conclusion about Mr. Bass.

PRACTICE AND APPLY

Have pairs of students work together to draw conclusions about Gustus's **character traits,** or the qualities shown by a character, in "The Banana Tree." Have them use a Conclusions Chart as they work.

- Have partners review the story section by section.
- Ask them to record events, actions, and dialogue that show Gustus's personality.
- Tell them to record their own experiences and knowledge that help them draw some conclusions.
- Have them explain their reasoning for each conclusion.

Have students share their completed charts with another pair of students and discuss the conclusions they have drawn about Gustus's character traits.

 INTERACTIVE GRAPHIC ORGANIZERS Have students download and complete a **Conclusions Chart** as they practice.

Determine Meaning: Figurative Language

RETEACH

Review these terms with students:

- **Literal language** consists of words and phrases that are used according to their dictionary definition.
- **Figurative language** consists of words and phrases that are used in an imaginative way to express ideas *beyond* the literal meanings of the words.

Review that **personification** is the giving of human qualities to an animal, object, phenomena, idea, or anything that is not specifically human. It is a type of figurative language.

Have students discuss these examples from "The Banana Tree":

- **Lines 5–7:** The words *meant to show it was merciless* give the wind a motive that wind does not literally have.
- **Lines 159–163:** The wind is called *belligerent,* and it *bellowed* and *drummed*. These words are human traits.

Have students suggest ways that the wind and the river in the story might be personified. Have them picture each as a person and describe how that person acts. Have students focus on word choices that give human qualities to these natural elements.

 LEVEL UP TUTORIALS Assign the following *Level Up* tutorial: **Figurative Language**

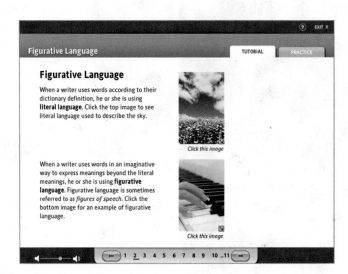

INDEPENDENT READING

Have partners work together to find examples of personification in "The Banana Tree" or in other selections in Collections 1 or 2.

There Will Come Soft Rains

Short Story by Ray Bradbury

Why This Text

Students may have difficulty accepting the idea of a story where the main character is a house with human attributes. In "There Will Come Soft Rains," Ray Bradbury uses a "dying" house to represent his vision of the future—a post-apocalyptic world devoid of humans, one in which a house and its appliances are the last things to go. With the help of the close-reading questions, students will understand how personification can be used to make abstract ideas seem clear.

Background Have students read the information about Ray Bradbury in the background. Point out that "There Will Come Soft Rains," although set in the future, is deeply rooted in the 1950s, when the world was still reeling from the devastating effects of World War II and the dropping of the atom bomb. It was a time when the war-weary American public rushed to embrace the American Dream and all the technology that went with it, including a wide range of "modern" appliances. Many of Bradbury's stories, including this one, focus on the threat of war and an out-of-control technology.

SETTING A PURPOSE Ask students to pay attention to the way the author uses personification and other figurative language to deliver a strong message about world peace.

Standards Support

- cite textual evidence
- draw inferences about events based on clues in the text
- analyze how a theme is conveyed through particular details
- determine the meaning of words and phrases, including figurative language

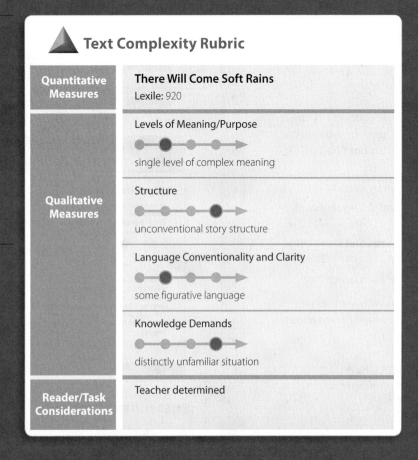

Text Complexity Rubric

Quantitative Measures	**There Will Come Soft Rains** Lexile: 920
Qualitative Measures	Levels of Meaning/Purpose single level of complex meaning
	Structure unconventional story structure
	Language Conventionality and Clarity some figurative language
	Knowledge Demands distinctly unfamiliar situation
Reader/Task Considerations	Teacher determined

Strategies for CLOSE READING

Determine Meanings: Figurative Language

Students should read this story carefully all the way through. Close-reading questions at the bottom of the page will help them understand how the author uses figurative language, including personification, to create meaning. As they read, students should jot down comments or questions about the text in the margins.

WHEN STUDENTS STRUGGLE . . .

To help students understand how personification is used in "There Will Come Soft Rains," have them work in small groups to fill out a chart like the one shown below.

CITE TEXT EVIDENCE For practice in recognizing how the author uses personification, have them find examples in the text and add them to the chart.

Examples of Personification	Effect
". . . the fire in ten billion angry sparks moved with flaming ease from room to room and then up the stairs." (lines 152–153)	The personification of the fire makes it seem cruel and unfeeling; it doesn't care what it destroys.
". . . blind robot faces peered down with faucet mouths gushing green chemical." (lines 166–167)	The robot is dying a slow and painful death; "faucet mouths" allows you to visualize the force of the chemicals it spews.
". . . the stove could be seen making breakfasts at a psychopathic rate . . ." (lines 203–204)	The stove is seen as animate—going crazy as it dies.
"Deep freeze, armchair, film tapes, circuits, beds, and all like skeletons thrown in a cluttered mound deep under . . ." (lines 208–210)	The dying of the house replicates the dying of the people who lived there. The contents of the house are its "bones," which are buried underground.

Background Ray Bradbury (1920–2012) was born in a small town named Waukegan, Illinois. He was hired to write short stories for a radio show at the age of 14 and joined the Los Angeles Science Fiction Society at the age of 16. In 1953, he published his most famous book, Fahrenheit 451, which warned of the dangers of book censorship. In all, Ray Bradbury wrote 27 novels and over 600 short stories.

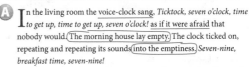

There Will Come Soft Rains

Short Story by Ray Bradbury

CLOSE READ
Notes

1. **READD** ▶ As you read lines 1–15, begin to collect and cite evidence.
   - Underline examples of personification in the text.
   - In the margin, define "voice-clock," using clues from the text.
   - Circle two phrases that help you infer that no people are in the house.

(A) In the living room the voice-clock sang, *Ticktock, seven o'clock, time to get up, time to get up, seven o'clock!* as if it were afraid that nobody would. The morning house lay empty. The clock ticked on, repeating and repeating its sounds into the emptiness. *Seven-nine, breakfast time, seven-nine!*

In the kitchen the breakfast stove gave a hissing sigh and ejected from its warm interior eight pieces of perfectly browned toast, eight eggs sunny side up, sixteen slices of bacon, and two coffees.

"Today is August 4, 2026," said a second voice from the kitchen
10 ceiling, "in the city of Allendale, California." It repeated the date
(B) three times for memory's sake. "Today is Mr. Featherstone's birthday. Today is the anniversary of Tilita's marriage. Insurance is payable, as are the water, gas, and light bills."

Somewhere in the walls, relays clicked, memory tapes glided under electric eyes.

A voice-clock is a clock that talks.

43

---

1. **READ AND CITE TEXT EVIDENCE**

(A) **ASK STUDENTS** to make an inference about the various types of appliances mentioned. What is their function? *They tell the inhabitants of the house what to do; they give factual information; they keep repeating things over and over.*

Eight-one, tick-tock, eight-one o'clock, off to school, off to work,
run, run, eight-one! But no doors slammed, no carpets took the soft
tread of rubber heels. It was raining outside. The weather box on the
20 front door sang quietly: "Rain, rain, go away; rubbers, raincoats for
today . . . " And the rain tapped on the empty house, echoing.

Outside, the garage chimed and lifted its door to reveal the
waiting car. After a long wait the door swung down again.

At eight-thirty the eggs were shriveled and the toast was like
stone. An aluminum wedge scraped them into the sink, where hot
water whirled them down a metal throat which digested and flushed
them away to the distant sea. The dirty dishes were dropped into a
hot washer and emerged twinkling dry.

Nine-fifteen, sang the clock, *time to clean.*

30 Out of **warrens** in the wall, tiny robot mice darted. The rooms
were acrawl with the small cleaning animals, all rubber and metal.
They thudded against chairs, whirling their moustached runners,
kneading the rug nap, sucking gently at hidden dust. Then, like
mysterious invaders, they popped into their burrows. Their pink
electric eyes faded. The house was clean.

Ten o'clock. The sun came out from behind the rain. The house
stood alone in a city of rubble and ashes. This was the one house left
standing. At night the ruined city gave off a radioactive glow which
could be seen for miles.

The metal
throat is a
drain in a sink.

warrens:
small, crowded
spaces

C

D

Ten-fifteen. The garden sprinklers whirled up in golden founts,
40 filling the soft morning air with scatterings of brightness. The water
pelted windowpanes, running down the charred west side where the
house had been burned evenly free of its white paint. The entire west
face of the house was black, save for five places. Here the silhouette in
paint of a man mowing a lawn. Here, as in a photograph, a woman
bent to pick flowers. Still farther over, their images burned on wood
in one titanic instant, a small boy, hands flung into the air; higher up,
the image of a thrown ball, and opposite him a girl, hands raised to
catch a ball which never came down.

The five spots of paint—the man, the woman, the children, the
50 ball—remained. The rest was a thin charcoaled layer.

The gentle sprinkler rain filled the garden with falling light.
Until this day, how well the house had kept its peace. How
carefully it had inquired, "Who goes there? What's the password?"
and, getting no answer from lonely foxes and whining cats, it had shut
up its windows and drawn shades in an old-maidenly preoccupation
with self-protection which bordered on a mechanical **paranoia.**

It quivered at each sound, the house did. If a sparrow brushed a
window, the shade snapped up. The bird, startled, flew off! No, not
even a bird must touch the house!

The boy and
the girl were
playing catch
with a ball.

F

E

paranoia:
a psychotic
disorder
characterized
by delusions of
persecution

---

2. ◀ **REREAD** Reread lines 1–15. What kind of "personality" does the
house have? Support your answer with explicit textual evidence.

The house seems like a living thing. It is cheerful and efficient. The
clock speaks in rhyme, and the stove cooks a perfect breakfast for
four.

3. **READ** ▶ As you read lines 16–38, continue to cite text evidence.

• Underline examples of personification in the text.
• In the margin, explain what the author is referring to when he says "a
metal throat."
• Circle what makes the city visible for miles.

4. ◀ **REREAD** Reread lines 35–38. What conclusion can you draw from
the text about what happened to the rest of the houses in the town?

The rest of the houses were probably destroyed by a nuclear
weapon—the city "gave off a radioactive glow." The author also
refers to the city as "ruined," which would mean something bad had
happened.

5. **READ** ▶ As you read lines 39–59, continue to cite text evidence.

• Underline examples of personification in the text.
• In the margin, explain what the boy and girl were doing when the
nuclear event occurred.
• Circle the sentence that lets you know something bad is about to
happen to the house.

---

2. **REREAD AND CITE TEXT EVIDENCE** Have students think
about what the house's cheerful, efficient personality suggests
about the lives of its inhabitants.

B **ASK STUDENTS** to make an inference about the people
from what we know about the house. *The sing-songy repetition of*
the date (lines 11–12) suggests that the human inhabitants are
childlike, and need to be told what to do.

3. **READ AND CITE TEXT EVIDENCE** The narrator describes
breakfast being "whirled down" a metal throat.

C **ASK STUDENTS** why the author used the words *metal*
throat to describe a sink drain? What effect does it create? *It*
makes it seem like the breakfast is being "gobbled up" by the sink.

Critical Vocabulary: warrens (line 29) Have students explain
the meaning of *warrens.* Which word in this paragraph is a
synonym of *warrens*? *The word* burrows *(line 33) means the same*
thing.

4. **REREAD AND CITE TEXT EVIDENCE** Explain that lines 35–38
tell you that there is only one house left standing, that the rest of
the houses have been destroyed.

D **ASK STUDENTS** what they can conclude about the people
in the town. *They are all dead.*

5. **READ AND CITE TEXT EVIDENCE** In lines 54–56, the house
shuts up its windows and draws its shades in an "old maidenly
preoccupation with self-protection."

E **ASK STUDENTS** to explain what the house is reacting to.
What causes it to shut down? *There is no response when the house*
asks for the password, so it shuts down automatically.

Critical Vocabulary: paranoia (line 56) Have students explain
the meaning of *paranoia.* What does this term tell you about the
house? *The house is suspicious of everything.*

The attendants are the machines in the house; the gods are the people who lived there.

It was looking for its owners, the people who once lived there.

60   The house was an altar with ten thousand attendants, big, small, servicing, attending, in choirs. But the gods had gone away, and the ritual of the religion continued senselessly, uselessly.

Twelve noon.

A dog whined, shivering, on the front porch.

The front door recognized the dog voice and opened. The dog, once huge and fleshy, but now gone to bone and covered with sores, moved in and through the house, tracking mud. Behind it whirred angry mice, angry at having to pick up mud; angry at inconvenience.

70   For not a leaf fragment blew under the door but what the wall panels flipped open and the copper scrap rats flashed swiftly out. The offending dust, hair, or paper, seized in miniature steel jaws, was raced back to the burrows. There, down tubes which fed into the cellar, it was dropped into the sighing vent of an incinerator which sat like evil Baal[1] in a dark corner.

The dog ran upstairs, hysterically yelping to each door, at last realizing, as the house realized, that only silence was here.

G   It sniffed the air and scratched the kitchen door. Behind the door, the stove was making pancakes which filled the house with a rich baked odor and the scent of maple syrup.

80   The dog frothed at the mouth, lying at the door, sniffing, its eyes turned to fire. It ran wildly in circles, biting at its tail, spun in a frenzy, and died. It lay in the parlor for an hour.

Two o'clock, sang a voice.

H   Delicately sensing decay at last, the regiments of mice hummed out as softly as blown gray leaves in an electrical wind.

[1] **Baal:** In the Bible, the god of Canaan, whom the Israelites came to recognize as a false god.

6.   **◄ REREAD AND DISCUSS**   Reread lines 39–50. In a small group, discuss what conclusions you can draw about the nuclear event, based on the silhouettes, or outlines, on the side of the house.

7.   **READ ►**   As you read lines 60–96, continue to cite text evidence.

• Underline examples of personification in the text.
• In the margin, explain who the attendants and gods are.
• In the margin, explain why the dog yelps at each door.

46

Two-fifteen.

The dog was gone.

In the cellar, the incinerator glowed suddenly and a whirl of sparks leaped up the chimney.

90   *Two thirty-five.*

Bridge[2] tables sprouted from patio walls. Playing cards fluttered onto pads in a shower of pips.[3] Martinis manifested on an oaken bench with egg-salad sandwiches. Music played.

But the tables were silent and the cards untouched.

At four o'clock the tables folded like great butterflies back through the paneled walls.

[2] **bridge:** a card game.
[3] **pips:** symbols on the front of a playing card that denote the suit.

8.   **◄ REREAD**   Reread lines 65–89. What inferences can you make about what killed the dog? What happens to the dog's body after it dies? Cite textual evidence to support your inference.

The dog died of radiation poisoning or starvation. It "sniffed the air and scratched the kitchen door" where "the stove was making pancakes which filled the house with a rich baked odor." The dog then "frothed at the mouth" and died. The mice clean up the dog's body, "sensing decay at last," and then they put his body in the incinerator, which "glowed suddenly" while "sparks leaped up the chimney."

47

6.   **REREAD AND DISCUSS USING TEXT EVIDENCE**   Discuss the "five spots of paint" left on the side of the house.

F   **ASK STUDENTS**   how these "spots" were created. What details in the text tell you? *The house had been charred on the west side except for places where people had been, where the paint shows through.*

7.   **READ AND CITE TEXT EVIDENCE**   In this section of text, the dog realizes that there is no one home.

G   **ASK STUDENTS**   to make an inference about why the dog thought the people were still at home. What details in the text tell you? *The dog smelled the pancakes that the stove was automatically making* (lines 77–79).

FOR ELL STUDENTS   Some students may be familiar with the adjective *sore,* as in "a sore loser," rather than the noun. Explain that in this context, *sore* means "a painful spot."

8.   **REREAD AND CITE TEXT EVIDENCE**

H   **ASK STUDENTS**   what they can infer about the way life is valued in this future based on the treatment of the dog. *Students should infer that life is not highly valued. The dog's remains are swept away in a very mechanical fashion and then everyday life proceeds as usual.*

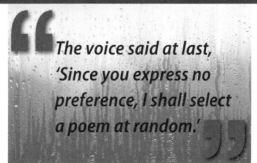

> " The voice said at last, 'Since you express no preference, I shall select a poem at random.' "

Four-thirty.
The nursery walls glowed. Animals took shape: yellow giraffes, blue lions, pink antelopes, lilac panthers cavorting in crystal substance. The walls were glass. They looked out upon color and fantasy. Hidden films clocked through well-oiled sprockets, and the walls lived. The nursery floor was woven to resemble a crisp cereal meadow. Over this ran aluminum roaches and iron crickets, and in the hot, still air butterflies of delicate red tissue wavered among the sharp aromas of animal spoors! There was the sound like a great matted yellow hive of bees within a dark bellows, the lazy bumble of a purring lion. And there was the patter of okapi[4] feet and the murmur of a fresh jungle rain, like other hoofs, falling upon the summer-starched grass. Now the walls dissolved into distances of parched weed, mile on mile, and warm endless sky. The animals drew away into thorn brakes[5] and water holes.

It was the children's hour.
Five o'clock. The bath filled with clear hot water.
Six, seven, eight o'clock. The dinner dishes manipulated like magic tricks, and in the study a *click.* In the metal stand opposite the hearth

---

[4] **okapi:** an animal, similar to a giraffe, with zebra striping.
[5] **thorn brakes:** clumps of thorns; thickets.

---

9. (READ ▶) As you read lines 97–140, continue to cite text evidence.

• Underline examples of personification in the text.
• In the margin, explain why "not one will know of the war" (line 132).
• Circle evidence that helps you infer that the animals are not real.

48

---

where a fire now blazed up warmly, a cigar popped out, half an inch of soft gray ash on it, smoking, waiting.
Nine o'clock. The beds warmed their hidden circuits, for nights were cool here.

120   *Nine-five.* A voice spoke from the study ceiling:
"Mrs. McClellan, which poem would you like this evening?"
The house was silent.
The voice said at last, "Since you express no preference, I shall select a poem at random." Quiet music rose to back the voice. "Sara Teasdale. As I recall, your favorite. . . ."

(J)   *There will come soft rains and the smell of the ground,*
And swallows circling with their shimmering sound;

And frogs in the pools singing at night,
And wild plum trees in **tremulous** *white;*

130   *Robins will wear their feathery fire,*
Whistling their whims on a low fence-wire;

(I)   *And not one will know of the war, not one*
Will care at last when it is done.

Not one would mind, neither bird nor tree,
If mankind perished utterly;

And Spring herself, when she woke at dawn
Would scarcely know that we were gone."

The fire burned on the stone hearth, and the cigar fell away into a mound of quiet ash on its tray. The empty chairs faced each other
140   between the silent walls, and the music played.
(K)   At ten o'clock the house began to die.
The wind blew. A falling tree bough crashed through the kitchen window. Cleaning solvent, bottled, shattered over the stove. The room was ablaze in an instant!

tremulous:

quivering;
shaking

The animals
and plants will
not realize
that there
were once
people, before
a war.

---

10. (◀ REREAD AND DISCUSS) Reread lines 126–137. The title of this poem is "There Will Come Soft Rains." In a small group, discuss why Bradbury might have borrowed this title for his story.

11. (READ ▶) As you read lines 141–189, continue to cite evidence.

• Underline examples of personification in the text.
• In the margin, explain what the "twenty snakes" are.
• Circle the names of parts of the body.

49

---

9. (READ AND CITE TEXT EVIDENCE)   Have students revisit lines 132–137 from Teasdale's poem.

(I) ASK STUDENTS   to explain what these lines of poetry have to do with the rest of the story. Why does the author include them here? *They address the present situation. The author is saying that no one will remember our world or care that it is gone.*

FOR ELL STUDENTS Explain that a sprocket is a toothed wheel that helps a mechanism or another wheel move. Ask for a volunteer to give you examples of machines that may have this kind of wheel.

10. (REREAD AND DISCUSS USING TEXT EVIDENCE)

(J) ASK STUDENTS   to reread lines 126–129 to hear the words "There will come soft rains" in context. Have them discuss what the title says about Bradbury's vision of the world after it destroys itself. What will it look like? *Bradbury sees it as a paradise with no memory of anything having existed before.*

11. (READ AND CITE TEXT EVIDENCE)   Have students note that *personification* in this section refers to death and dying.

(K) ASK STUDENTS how the author uses personification to make the death of the house more vivid. *He "humanizes" it by using words that refer to parts of the body.*

Critical Vocabulary: tremulous (line 129) Have students explain the meaning of *tremulous*. How does this word help you visualize the plum trees? *The trees are hopeful as new brides.*

"Fire!" screamed a voice. The house lights flashed, water pumps shot water from the ceilings. But the solvent spread on the linoleum, licking, eating, under the kitchen door, while the voices took it up in chorus: "Fire, fire, fire!"

The house tried to save itself. Doors sprang tightly shut, but the windows were broken by the heat and the wind blew and sucked upon the fire.

150

The house gave ground as the fire in ten billion angry sparks moved with flaming ease from room to room and then up the stairs. While scurrying water rats squeaked from the walls, pistoled their water, and ran for more. And the wall sprays let down showers of mechanical rain.

But too late. Somewhere, sighing, a pump shrugged to a stop. The quenching rain ceased. The reserve water supply which had filled baths and washed dishes for many quiet days was gone.

160

The fire crackled up the stairs. It fed upon Picassos and Matisses in the upper halls, like delicacies, baking off the oily flesh, tenderly crisping the canvases into black shavings.

Now the fire lay in beds, stood in windows, changed the colors of drapes!

And then, reinforcements.

From attic trapdoors, blind robot faces peered down with faucet mouths gushing green chemical.

The fire backed off, as even an elephant must at the sight of a dead snake. Now there were twenty snakes whipping over the floor, killing the fire with a clear cold venom of green froth.

170

But the fire was clever. It had sent flame outside the house, up through the attic to the pumps there. An explosion! The attic brain which directed the pumps was shattered into bronze shrapnel on the beams.

The fire rushed back into every closet and felt of the clothes hung there.

The house shuddered, oak bone on bone, its bared skeleton cringing from the heat, its wire, its nerves revealed as if a surgeon had

The twenty snakes are a green chemical meant to put out the fire.

torn the skin off to let the red veins and capillaries quiver in the scalded air. Help, help! Fire! Run, run! Heat snapped mirrors like the first brittle winter ice. And the voices wailed, Fire, fire, run, run, like a tragic nursery rhyme, a dozen voices, high, low, like children dying in a forest, alone, alone. And the voices fading as the wires popped their sheathings like hot chestnuts. One, two, three, four, five voices died.

180

In the nursery the jungle burned. Blue lions roared, purple giraffes bounded off. The panthers ran in circles, changing color, and ten million animals, running before the fire, vanished off toward a distant steaming river. . . .

190

Ten more voices died. In the last instant under the fire avalanche, other choruses, **oblivious,** could be heard announcing the time, playing music, cutting the lawn by remote-control mower, or setting an umbrella frantically out and in, the slamming and opening front door, a thousand things happening, like a clock shop when each clock strikes the hour insanely before or after the other, a scene of maniac confusion, yet unity; singing, screaming, a few last cleaning mice darting bravely out to carry the horrid ashes away! And one voice, with **sublime** disregard for the situation, read poetry aloud in the fiery study, until all the film spools burned, until all the wires withered and the circuits cracked.

200

The fire burst the house and let it slam flat down, puffing out skirts of spark and smoke.

In the kitchen, an instant before the rain of fire and timber, the stove could be seen making breakfasts at a psychopathic rate, ten dozen eggs, six loaves of toast, twenty dozen bacon strips, which, eaten by fire, started the stove working again, hysterically hissing!

oblivious:
unknowing

sublime:
excellent

The stove makes breakfast.

---

12. ◀ REREAD AND DISCUSS Reread lines 149–185. In a small group, discuss the ways in which the "personalities" of the fire and the house create an impression of war.

13. READ ▶ As you read lines 190–216, continue to cite text evidence.
- Underline examples of personification.
- In the margin, describe two actions that happen at both the beginning and the end of the story.

12. REREAD AND DISCUSS USING TEXT EVIDENCE

Ⓛ **ASK STUDENTS** to cite examples of personification used to describe the cruelty of the fire. *Students may cite "angry sparks"; "crackled up the stairs"; "fed upon" paintings like they were "delicacies . . . tenderly crisping the canvases into black shavings."*

13. READ AND CITE TEXT EVIDENCE

Ⓜ **ASK STUDENTS** to discuss the behavior of the mechanical appliances. What does it say about machines? *They are unthinking and unfeeling; they do what they're programmed to do.*

Critical Vocabulary: oblivious (line 191) Why does the author describe the machines as oblivious? *The machines don't care about anything.*

Critical Vocabulary: sublime (line 198) What does "sublime disregard" say about the voice of the poetry reader? *It is too "refined" to notice that everything around it is on fire.*

There Will Come Soft Rains **184g**

The crash. The attic smashing into kitchen and parlor. The parlor into cellar, cellar into subcellar. Deep freeze, armchair, film tapes, circuits, beds, and all like skeletons thrown in a cluttered mound deep
210 under.

Smoke and silence. A great quantity of smoke.

Dawn showed faintly in the east. Among the ruins, <u>one wall stood alone.</u> Within the wall, a last voice said, over and over again and again, even as the sun rose to shine upon the heaped rubble and steam:

"Today is August 5, 2026, today is August 5, 2026, today is . . ."

The voice-clock announces the date.

14. ◀ REREAD AND DISCUSS Reread lines 212–216. In a small group, discuss your responses to the ending. What is ironic, or unexpected, about the way the story ends?

SHORT RESPONSE

Cite Text Evidence What overall effect does the author's personification of the house have on the reader as the house burns down? **Cite text evidence** to support your ideas.

When the writer says "The house tried to save itself," it almost feels like the house literally made the choice to defend itself. The house falling apart makes the reader empathize—it's like a person is dying. The author compares parts of the house to a human body, as when he refers to the "attic brain" being "shattered" or when he says "its nerves revealed as if a surgeon had torn the skin off" when referring to the wiring.

52

---

14. (REREAD AND DISCUSS USING TEXT EVIDENCE) Have students discuss the end of the world as depicted in lines 207–215.

 ASK STUDENTS to cite evidence showing that technology outlives humans. *They may note that the date has moved ahead another day (it is now August 5), but the people have not.*

SHORT RESPONSE

Cite Text Evidence Students' responses should include text evidence that supports their positions. They should:

- cite examples of personification and other figures of speech.
- draw conclusions about the story's theme.
- examine the effect of word choice on meaning.
- make inferences about events and characters.

TO CHALLENGE STUDENTS . . .

To help students deepen their understanding of Bradbury's writing, tell them that he has often speculated in writing on the impact of future technology on the world.

ASK STUDENTS to find out more about Bradbury's views of technology. Have them research the following questions:

- What does Bradbury think of the Internet, the automobile, virtual reality, and other inventions?
- Which elements of some of his stories and other writings actually predicted some aspect of the future?
- Which elements were way off the mark?

After students have completed their research, have them present their findings about Bradbury's views and writings to the class.

DIG DEEPER

1. With the class, return to Question 3, Read. Have students share their responses.

ASK STUDENTS to think about the role of the machines in the story.

- Students can make inferences about how this technology would affect people's daily lives. What does it say about the importance of the individual in this society? What does it say about free will?

- Students can list the machines' directives and messages and write a description of each. What does this suggest about who's in charge? Why might they want people to listen to these messages all day long?

- Have students consider a society completely run by machines. Is that in our future? What can we do to prevent Bradbury's dark vision from becoming a reality? Is there a connection between war and the use of technology?

2. With the class, return to Question 5, Read. Have students share their responses.

- Have students make inferences how people's lives were affected by the war. What does the house's "preoccupation with self-protection" suggest about people's state of mind? Why was it so important to be barricaded from the outside world? What inferences can they make from the necessity of a password?

- Have students think about how the climate of paranoia affected people's relationships with each other.

3. With the class, return to Question 9, Read. Have students share their responses.

- Have students analyze Teasdale's poem. What common threads can they find?

- Have students find similarities between the poem and the story. Have them analyze their common threads. How do the authors attempt to convey their messages?

ASK STUDENTS to return to their Short Response answer and revise it based on the class discussion.

CLOSE READING NOTES

ANCHOR TEXT EXEMPLAR
A Night to Remember

History Writing by Walter Lord

Why This Text?

Students regularly read narrative nonfiction in school and on their own. This lesson examines the realistic style and tone of a work long considered a turning point in the genre of history writing—author Walter Lord's objective yet emotional account of the sinking of the *Titanic*.

Key Learning Objective: The student will be able to analyze elements of narrative nonfiction, including how authors establish style and tone in their writing.

For practice and application:

Close Reader selections
"On the *Titanic*, Defined by What They Wore"
Newspaper Article by Guy Trebay
"The Discovery of the *Titanic*"
Diagram

RI 1 Cite text evidence; make inferences.
RI 3 Analyze text elements.
RI 4 Determine the meaning of words and phrases.
RI 5 Analyze structure.
RI 10 Read and comprehend literary nonfiction.
W 7   Conduct short research projects.
W 8   Gather relevant information from multiple sources.
SL 1 Engage effectively in a range of collaborative discussions.
L 3b Maintain consistency in style and tone.
L 4a Use context as a clue to meaning.
L 4c Consult reference materials.
L 4d Verify preliminary determination of meaning.
L 6   Use grade-appropriate academic and domain-specific words and phrases.

▲ Text Complexity Rubric

Quantitative Measures	**A Night to Remember** Lexile: 1070L

Levels of Meaning/Purpose

more than one purpose; implied, easily identified from context

Qualitative Measures

Structure

no major shifts in chronology; occasional use of flashback

Language Conventionality and Clarity

some figurative language

Knowledge Demands

some specialized knowledge required

Reader/Task Considerations

- Teacher determined
- Vary by individual reader and type of text
- See the Text X-Ray for suggested Reader/Task Considerations.

English Language Support Before teaching, use the Text X-Ray for an overview of the text's complexity. The Text X-Ray and the supports and scaffolds in the Teacher's Edition will help you guide students of different proficiencies and skill levels.

Meaning Making

Language Development

Effective Expression

Content Knowledge

Foundational Skills

Text Complexity: Qualitative Measures

Levels of Meaning/Purpose

more than one purpose; implied, easily identified from context

Help students analyze style and tone.

- Teacher's Edition side notes, pp. 185, 186, 187, 189, 190, 191, 192, 193
- English Language Support, p. 187
- Strategies for Annotation, p. 193
- Analyze the Meanings of Words and Phrases, p. 193

To reteach analyzing style, see

- Analyze Meaning: Style, p. 196a

 Use It! Level Up Tutorials: Author's Style; Tone; Imagery

ZOOM IN ON **ANALYZING THE MEANINGS OF WORDS AND PHRASES** Tell students that an author's **style** is the way he or she expresses ideas. It includes the **tone**, or attitude toward the subject, along with literary elements such as **word choice**, **sentence structure**, **imagery**, and **point of view**.

- Ask students to describe the type of style they would expect to find in a history text. Then read the first paragraph of *A Night to Remember*.
- Have students discuss how the style and tone of this paragraph is similar to or different from a typical historical text.
- After students read the selection, ask small groups to list adjectives that describe the author's style and tone.

Structure

no major shifts in chronology; occasional use of flashback

Help students analyze narrative nonfiction.

- Teacher's Edition side notes, pp. 185, 188, 189, 190, 192, 193, 194
- English Language Support, p. 188
- When Students Struggle, p. 191
- Close Read Screencasts, p. 185
- Strategies for Annotation, p. 189
- Analyze Text: Narrative Nonfiction, p. 193

 Identifying Sequence

ZOOM IN ON **ANALYZING NARRATIVE NONFICTION** Tell students that the word *narrative* means "story." Explain that **narrative nonfiction** presents real-life events in a way that reads like a fictional story. In *A Night to Remember*, the author uses a variety of literary elements and story-telling techniques to describe the sinking of the *Titanic*. List the following elements of narrative nonfiction on the board: *vivid imagery, factual details, eyewitness accounts,* and *suspense*. Define and discuss the elements with the class; then, as students read the selection, ask them to note examples of each one in the text.

Language Conventionality and Clarity

some figurative language

Teach unfamiliar academic vocabulary in context.
- Teacher's Edition Critical Vocabulary notes, pp. 186, 187, 188, 195
- Vocabulary Strategy: Specialized Vocabulary, p. 195
- Strategies for Annotation, p. 195

Help students interpret idioms.
- English Language Support, p. 187

Guide students to create a consistent style and tone in their writing.
- English Language Support, p. 196
- Language Conventions: Consistency in Style and Tone, p. 196

ZOOM IN ON **USING SPECIALIZED VOCABULARY** Point out that nonfiction often employs **specialized vocabulary**, or terms related to a particular subject, activity, or job. Explain that while students can often derive the meaning of a specialized term from context clues, they should also consult a dictionary to confirm the definition. Tell students to check all of the definitions listed for the word and to select the one that best relates to the subject of the text. As students read *A Night to Remember*, have them use a three-column chart like the one on page 195 to note and define the specialized vocabulary they encounter.

Knowledge Demands

some specialized knowledge required

Provide information about the author of the selection.
- Teacher's Edition Author note, p. 185

Help students formulate research questions.
- Teacher's Edition side notes, pp. 186, 191

To teach formulating research questions, see
- Formulate Research Questions, p. 196a

 Use It! **Interactive Whiteboard Lesson:** Doing Research on the Web

ZOOM IN ON **FORMULATING RESEARCH QUESTIONS** Tell students that as they read *A Night to Remember*, questions may arise about certain events, actions, people, or details.

- Have students jot down their questions as they read.
- After reading, have small groups share their questions and sort them into two categories: simple questions that have easy, short answers, and questions that require longer, more complex answers.
- Explain that answering complex questions will likely require collecting information from different sources.

Suggested Reader/Task Considerations

You might consider the following before assigning this informational text to students:
- Will students find the topic of this narrative nonfiction engaging?
- Do students have prior experience with the genre that will help them manage the content?

ZOOM IN ON **SUPPORTING COMPREHENSION**

- Many students will be familiar with the tragic tale of the Titanic. Elicit from volunteers information they already know about the event. Explain that this selection helps us understand what it was like to be aboard the sinking ship.
- Ask students to share other examples of narrative nonfiction they have encountered. Discuss the author's purpose in writing this kind of nonfiction. Guide students to understand that the author presents factual information in a way that will engage and entertain the reader.

Walter Lord Have students read the information about the author. Explain that Lord's work created a new way to present history that made it come alive. He had worked as an advertising executive and knew how to make history appeal to a reader through a combination of small details and emotions. He was praised for allowing readers to form their own impression of the events of that night. He has said about the *Titanic* that he was trying to show how wealth or rank has little to do with someone being brave or good or bad.

SETTING A PURPOSE Direct students to use the Setting a Purpose prompt to focus their reading. Remind them to write down questions as they read.

Analyze Text: Narrative Nonfiction (LINES 1–3)
RI 1, RI 3

Explain to students that narrative nonfiction like *A Night to Remember* tells about real-life people and events in a way that seems like fiction. Tell them that because the story being told is real, the details in the text must match the actual details of the event.

A **CITE TEXT EVIDENCE** Have students reread lines 1–3 and identify details that would have to match what really happened that night. (*White Star Liner* Titanic, *Frederick Fleet, weather and moon conditions*)

Analyze Meaning: Style (LINES 4–6)
RI 1, RI 4

Explain that an author's **style** is his or her unique way of communicating ideas. Tell students that an author's **word choices,** such as using powerful verbs, precise nouns, and vivid adjectives or adverbs, are one way an author affects readers' experiences and creates a personal writing style.

B **CITE TEXT EVIDENCE** Have students reread lines 4–6 to identify powerful verbs, nouns, adjectives, or adverbs. Ask them to describe the effect these words have. (*Possible responses: "Blazed with stars" and "polished plate glass" create a vivid picture of a quiet, beautiful night at sea.*)

Walter Lord (1917–2002) *studied law at college, but he never practiced as a lawyer. After receiving his degree, he worked in a business information service in New York City. It was there that he got interested in writing. Lord's approach to writing changed the way many people read history. By mixing research and interviews, Lord connected readers to the immediacy of historical events. In particular, his account of the sinking of the* Titanic *is widely respected as an accurate, heartfelt account of a tragic disaster on the high seas.*

from A Night to Remember
History Writing by Walter Lord

SETTING A PURPOSE As you read, pay attention to the details that engage you in the circumstances of this historical event.

High in the crow's-nest of the new White Star Liner *Titanic*, Lookout Frederick Fleet peered into a dazzling night. It was calm, clear and bitterly cold. There was no moon, but the cloudless sky blazed with stars. The Atlantic was like polished plate glass; people later said they had never seen it so smooth.

This was the fifth night of the *Titanic*'s maiden voyage to New York, and it was already clear that she was not only the largest but also the most glamorous ship in the world.

10 Even the passengers' dogs were glamorous. John Jacob Astor had along his airedale Kitty. Henry Sleeper Harper, of the publishing family, had his prize Pekingese Sun Yatsen. Robert W. Daniel, the Philadelphia banker, was bringing back a champion French bulldog just purchased in Britain. Clarence Moore of Washington also had been dog-shopping,

(t) ©AP Images; (c) ©Frazer Hudson/Corbis

Close Read Screencasts Close Read

Modeled Discussions

Have students click the *Close Read* icon in their eBook to access a screencast in which readers discuss and annotate lines 42–49, a key passage that describes the viewpoint of the watchmen in the crow's-nest of the *Titanic* as they first encounter the iceberg.

As a class, view and discuss the video. Then have students pair up to do an independent close read of an additional passage—another description of the ship's encounter with the iceberg (lines 155–163).

Analyze Meaning: Style (LINES 23–36)   RI 4

Explain to students that analyzing the length, type, and punctuation of the sentences in a text can help them better understand what the author wants to tell them and the author's style.

C ASK STUDENTS to reread lines 23–26 and discuss the structure of the sentences. Students should note how the sentences and punctuation chosen have an effect on the reader and help the reader experience the action described. (*The author uses shorts bursts of information linked by ellipses that show the passage of time. In this way, he represents a long night of watching with little talking.*)

Formulate Research Questions (LINES 29–31)

Explain to students that while they read and analyze text, they might think of questions they would like answered by further research. They should write these down for discussion later.

D ASK STUDENTS to reread lines 29–31 and pose a question they might want answered. (*Students may wonder why the* Titanic *was "racing" through an area with icebergs everywhere; they may also want to check the time and date for accuracy.*)

CRITICAL VOCABULARY

knot: The word *knot* is a nautical term that students may not know. Explain that $22\frac{1}{2}$ knots is equal to about 24 miles per hour, which may not seem fast. However, because of the *Titanic's* size, this speed is actually prodigious; stopping or turning a big ship traveling that fast is very difficult.

ASK STUDENTS to discuss why the author used a nautical term to discuss the ship's speed. Have students point out other ship-related vocabulary. (*The author wants to add authenticity to the account, so he uses terms that are used on an ocean liner, such as* rigging, knot, port, stem, forecastle deck, bow, starboard, *and* crow's-nest bell.)

---

but the 50 pairs of English foxhounds he bought for the Loudoun Hunt weren't making the trip.

That was all another world to Frederick Fleet. He was one of six lookouts carried by the *Titanic*, and the lookouts didn't

20   worry about passenger problems. They were the "eyes of the ship," and on this particular night Fleet had been warned to watch especially for icebergs.

C So far, so good. On duty at 10 o'clock . . . a few words about the ice problem with Lookout Reginald Lee, who shared the same watch . . . a few more words about the cold . . . but mostly just silence, as the two men stared into the darkness.

Now the watch was almost over, and still there was nothing unusual. Just the night, the stars, the biting cold, the wind that whistled through the rigging[1] as the *Titanic* raced

D
30   across the calm, black sea at 22½ **knots**. It was almost 11:40 P.M. on Sunday, the 14th of April, 1912.

Suddenly Fleet saw something directly ahead, even darker than the darkness. At first it was small (about the size, he thought, of two tables put together), but every second it grew larger and closer. Quickly Fleet banged the crow's-nest bell three times, the warning of danger ahead. At the same time he lifted the phone and rang the bridge.

"What did you see?" asked a calm voice at the other end.

"Iceberg right ahead," replied Fleet.

40   "Thank you," acknowledged the voice with curiously detached courtesy. Nothing more was said.

For the next 37 seconds Fleet and Lee stood quietly side by side, watching the ice draw nearer. Now they were almost on top of it, and still the ship didn't turn. The berg towered wet and glistening far above the forecastle deck, and both men braced themselves for a crash. Then, miraculously, the bow began to swing to port.[2] At the last second the stem[3] shot into the clear, and the ice glided swiftly by along the starboard side. It looked to Fleet like a very close shave.

knot
(nŏt) *n.* a *knot* is a unit of speed used by ships. One knot is equal to one nautical mile, or about 1.85 kilometers per hour.

---

[1] **rigging** (rĭg´ĭng): the system of ropes, wires, pulleys, and hardware needed on the ship to hoist cargo, open hatches, or raise signal flags.
[2] **port**: the left-hand side of a ship facing forward.
[3] **stem**: the curved upright beam to which the hull timbers are joined to form the front of the ship.

186   Collection 3

Text in FOCUS   English Language Support

Identifying Sequence (LINE 39)

Have students view the **Zoom In** video on this page of their eBook to learn how to identify the sequence of events that led to the ship's sinking. Then have students use **Zoom In Practice** to apply what they have learned.

50 At this moment Quartermaster George Thomas Rowe was standing watch on the after bridge. For him too, it had been an uneventful night—just the sea, the stars, the biting cold. As he paced the deck, he noticed what he and his mates called "Whiskers 'round the Light"—tiny splinters of ice in the air, fine as dust, that gave off myriads of bright colors whenever caught in the glow of the deck lights.

Then suddenly he felt a curious motion break the steady rhythm of the engines. It was a little like coming alongside a dock wall rather heavily. He glanced forward—and stared
60 again. A windjammer, sails set, seemed to be passing along the starboard[4] side. Then he realized it was an iceberg, towering perhaps 100 feet above the water. The next instant it was gone, drifting astern[5] into the dark.

Meanwhile, down below in the First Class dining saloon on D Deck, four other members of the *Titanic*'s crew were sitting around one of the tables. The last diner had long since departed, and now the big white Jacobean room was empty except for this single group. They were dining-saloon stewards, **indulging** in the time-honored pastime of all
70 stewards off duty—they were gossiping about their passengers.

Then, as they sat there talking, a faint grinding jar seemed to come from somewhere deep inside the ship. It was not much, but enough to break the conversation and rattle the silver that was set for breakfast next morning.

Steward James Johnson felt he knew just what it was. He recognized the kind of **shudder** a ship gives when she drops a propeller blade, and he knew this sort of mishap meant a trip back to the Harland & Wolff shipyard at Belfast— with plenty of free time to enjoy the hospitality of the port.
80 Somebody near him agreed and sang out cheerfully, "Another Belfast trip!"

In the galley just to the stern, Chief Night Baker Walter Belford was making rolls for the following day. (The honor of baking fancy pastry was reserved for the day shift.) When the

indulge
(ĭn-dŭlj´) *v.* If you *indulge* in something, you allow yourself to do or have something you want.

shudder
(shŭd´ər) *n.* A *shudder* is a strong shiver or tremor.

---

[4] **starboard:** the right-hand side of a ship facing forward.
[5] **astern:** behind a ship.

A Night to Remember **187**

CLOSE READ

Analyze Meaning: Style (LINES 53–56)

RI 4

Explain to students that authors use strong **imagery,** or words and details that appeal to the five senses, to heighten the effects of their writing. In nonfiction, this device allows readers to gain a sense of what people in a scene actually experienced.

Ⓔ **ASK STUDENTS** to reread lines 53–56. Have them tell what "Whiskers 'round the Light" means and why the author included this detail. (*Possible response: It means tiny pieces of ice in the air, glowing in the lights. The tiny pieces of ice looked like whiskers. Lord includes it to reveal how cold and icy it was.*)

CRITICAL VOCABULARY

indulge: The word *indulging* refers to the stewards and their pastime of gossiping.

ASK STUDENTS to discuss how indulging in gossip is treating yourself. Ask whether others on the ship might be treating, or indulging, themselves in other ways. (*The stewards aren't supposed to gossip but are allowing themselves to do it. Some passengers are indulging in the luxury of the ship.*)

shudder: The word *shudder* describes something the steward felt and thought he recognized from other experiences.

ASK STUDENTS to demonstrate what a shudder is and discuss what it feels like, particularly in a large object like a huge ship. (*Students should shiver or shake and note how it would feel like an earthquake, an avalanche, or a heavy weight falling on the ground near where you were standing.*)

English Language Support

Use Context Clues Tell students an idiom is a common phrase that expresses a meaning different from the meaning of its actual words. Use a whiteboard to project lines 47–49 and highlight the expressions "shot into the clear" and "close shave."

- Help students interpret the meaning of each expression. Then have partners restate the sentences to explain the event in their own words.

- Guide students to use context clues to determine the meaning of each expression. Once students arrive at the correct interpretation, have them write a description of the events.

- Ask pairs to determine the meaning of each expression from context. Let volunteers share their definitions and correct as necessary. Then have students write their own sentences using each expression.

Analyze Text

RI 1,
RI 3

(LINES 88–106)

Remind students that authors of narrative nonfiction use details described by real-life people to retell real-life events. Explain to students that eyewitnesses tell their personal stories; these stories become a powerful group narrative of the events.

Ⓕ CITE TEXT EVIDENCE Have students tell how the author illustrates the moment when the *Titanic* hits the iceberg in lines 88–106. Ask what effect this text has for the reader. (*The author uses eyewitness accounts. Some are personal, like Frolicher's connection to a Zurich lake ferry; others give the reader different ways to imagine the sensation of the ship hitting the iceberg.*)

English Language Support

Display the phrase *eyewitness account*. Explain that an eyewitness is someone who was actually there to see an event. An account is a story told about a real event. Tell students that the quotations in lines 93, 98, and 99–100 are taken directly from other books or newspaper articles in which people who survived the *Titanic* disaster told their own stories.

CRITICAL VOCABULARY

jar: The author uses the word *jar* to describe the sensation passengers felt as the ship bumped up against the iceberg and scraped along its side.

ASK STUDENTS to note the words in the definition that have similar meaning, such as *jolt, shock,* and *scraping.* Have students discuss other ways the author describes the sensation here and on the previous page. Remind students to be aware of similar descriptions throughout the rest of the text.

ominous: This word describes the jolt Mrs. Stephenson felt in the San Francisco earthquake.

ASK STUDENTS to discuss why the jolt would give the passengers an ominous warning of what lies ahead. (*The odd motion of the ship indicates that it has been damaged and may not be able to stay afloat as a result.*)

jolt came, it impressed Belford more strongly than Steward Johnson—perhaps because a pan of new rolls clattered off the top of the oven and scattered about the floor.

The passengers in their cabins felt the **jar** too, and tried to connect it with something familiar. Marguerite Frolicher, a
90 young Swiss girl accompanying her father on a business trip, woke up with a start. Half-asleep, she could think only of the little white lake ferries at Zurich making a sloppy landing. Softly she said to herself, "Isn't it funny . . . we're landing!"

Major Arthur Godfrey Peuchen, starting to undress for the night, thought it was like a heavy wave striking the ship. Mrs. J. Stuart White was sitting on the edge of her bed, just reaching to turn out the light, when the ship seemed to roll over "a thousand marbles." To Lady Cosmo Duff Gordon, waking up from the jolt, it seemed "as though somebody had
100 drawn a giant finger along the side of the ship." Mrs. John Jacob Astor thought it was some mishap in the kitchen.

It seemed stronger to some than to others. Mrs. Albert Caldwell pictured a large dog that had a baby kitten in its mouth and was shaking it. Mrs. Walter B. Stephenson recalled the first **ominous** jolt when she was in the San Francisco earthquake—then decided this wasn't that bad. Mrs. E. D.

jar
(jär) *n.* A *jar* can be a jolt or shock, as well as a harsh, scraping sound.

ominous
(ŏm′ə-nəs) *adj.* Something that is *ominous* is frightening or threatening.

©Underwood & Underwood/Corbis

TO CHALLENGE STUDENTS...

Analyze a Diagram Have students use online sources to locate a diagram of the deck plans for the *Titanic* and any photos they can find. Ask students to locate the places specifically identified in this selection.

ASK STUDENTS to use the diagram to trace the movements of the passengers as well as the points of contact with the iceberg and the areas of the ship that were affected.

Appleton felt hardly any shock at all, but she noticed an unpleasant ripping sound . . . like someone tearing a long, long strip of calico.

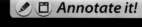

110   The jar meant more to J. Bruce Ismay, Managing Director of the White Star Line, who in a festive mood was going along for the ride on the *Titanic*'s first trip. Ismay woke up with a start in his de-luxe suite on B Deck—he felt sure the ship had struck something, but he didn't know what.

    Some of the passengers already knew the answer. Mr. and Mrs. George A. Harder, a young honeymoon couple down in cabin E-50, were still awake when they heard a dull thump. Then they felt the ship quiver, and there was "a sort of rumbling, scraping noise" along the ship's side. Mr. Harder

120 hopped out of bed and ran to the porthole. As he looked through the glass, he saw a wall of ice glide by.

    The same thing happened to James B. McGough, a Gimbels buyer from Philadelphia, except his experience was somewhat more disturbing. His porthole was open, and as the berg brushed by, chunks of ice fell into the cabin.

    Like Mr. McGough, most of the *Titanic*'s passengers were in bed when the jar came. On this quiet, cold Sunday night a snug bunk seemed about the best place to be. But a few shipboard die-hards were still up. As usual, most were in the

130 First Class smoking room on A Deck.

    And as usual, it was a very mixed group. Around one table sat Archie Butt, President Taft's military aide; Clarence Moore, the traveling Master of Hounds; Harry Widener, son of the Philadelphia streetcar magnate; and William Carter, another Main Liner. They were winding up a small dinner given by Widener's father in honor of Captain Edward J. Smith, the ship's commander. The Captain had left early, the ladies had been packed off to bed, and now the men were enjoying a final cigar before turning in too. The conversation

140 wandered from politics to Clarence Moore's adventures in West Virginia, the time he helped interview the old feuding mountaineer Anse Hatfield.

    Buried in a nearby leather armchair, Spencer V. Silver-thorne, a young buyer for Nugent's department store in St. Louis, browsed through a new best seller, *The Virginian*. Not far off, Lucien P. Smith (still another Philadelphian)

TEACH

CLOSE READ

Analyze Meaning: Style (LINES 107–109; LINES 120–121)

RI 1, RI 4

Explain that authors often use comparisons to help readers understand difficult concepts or experiences.

G **CITE TEXT EVIDENCE** Ask students to describe the comparison being made in lines 107–109. *(Mrs. Appleton compares an unpleasant ripping sound she heard to someone tearing calico cloth. What she heard is the ripping of the side of the ship, but she doesn't know that yet.)* Ask students why the author would include this. *(It appeals to readers' sense of hearing; other details of hitting the iceberg have been mostly about feeling and sight.)*

H **CITE TEXT EVIDENCE** Ask students to point out the description of the ice in lines 120–121. *(The iceberg is described as a wall.)* Have students explain what they think this would look like. *(The ice would be so large that it would fill the porthole view like a wall.)*

Analyze Text (LINES 131–142)

RI 1, RI 3

Explain that the authors of nonfiction use authentic details to support their accounts of events.

I **CITE TEXT EVIDENCE** Have students explain how the details in lines 131–142 elaborate on people and ideas in the text. *(Students should cite passengers' names and the details about their lives that help readers imagine the real people affected by this event.)*

Strategies for Annotation   ✎ ▤ *Annotate it!*

Analyze Text: Narrative Nonfiction

RI 1, RI 3

Share these strategies for guided or independent analysis:

- Highlight in yellow the actual details of the events.
- Highlight in green real-life people.
- Highlight in blue opinions that survivors had.
- Review your highlights. On a note, analyze how the details, real-life people, and real opinions elaborate on the event of the *Titanic* hitting the iceberg.

The same thing happened to James B. McGough, a Gimbels buyer from Philadelphia, except his experience was somewhat more disturbing. His porthole was open, and as the berg brushed by, chunks of ice fell into the cabin. . . .

. . . Sunday night a snug bunk seemed about the best place to be. But a few shipboard die-hards were still up.

Analyze Text

RI 1,
RI 3

(LINES 149–165; 178–186)

Remind students that narrative nonfiction tells about real-life people and events, but in a way that is often structured like a fictional story. Explain that certain details or events may be revisited for emphasis or suspense, just as a story's plot unfolds in stages.

J **ASK STUDENTS** why the author has decided to retell even more passengers' reactions to the ship hitting the iceberg. *(The author wants to show the variety of reactions that different passengers had to this moment.)* Ask students how this style is different from a newspaper article. *(Possible response: A newspaper article would probably report events in chronological order and not describe the same moment several times.)*

K **CITE TEXT EVIDENCE** Ask students to cite details in lines 178–186 that show how this scene relates to an earlier scene in the text. *(The details "once Fleet phoned the warning"; "hard-a-starboard"; "those 37 seconds of breathless waiting" connect this scene to the scene in lines 42–49 where lookouts Fleet and Lee spot the iceberg, phone in the warning, and wait—for 37 seconds.)*

Analyze Meaning: Style

RI 1,
RI 4

(LINES 157–165)

Remind students that **style** is an author's unique way of communicating ideas. Tell students that authors use sentence structure, punctuation, and details to create certain effects and meaning for the reader.

L **CITE TEXT EVIDENCE** Ask students to explain how the punctuation (dash and ellipses) and event details in lines 157–165 create meaning for the reader. *(The dash is like the jolt of the collision; ellipses let readers feel that they are running from room to room. The details of watching chunks of ice break off and the iceberg sliding into the darkness bring the scene to life.)*

---

struggled gamely through the linguistic[6] problems of a bridge game with three Frenchmen.

150   At another table the ship's young set was enjoying a somewhat noisier game of bridge. Normally the young set preferred the livelier Café Parisien, just below on B Deck, and at first tonight was no exception. But it grew so cold that around 11:30 the girls went off to bed, and the men strolled up to the smoking room.

Somebody produced a deck of cards, and as they sat playing and laughing, suddenly there came that grinding jar. Not much of a shock, but enough to give a man a start— Mr. Silverthorne still sits up with a jolt when he tells it. In an instant the smoking-room steward and Mr. Silverthorne
160   were on their feet . . . through the aft door . . . past the Palm Court . . . and out onto the deck. They were just in time to see the iceberg scraping along the starboard side, a little higher than the Boat Deck. As it slid by, they watched chunks of ice breaking and tumbling off into the water. In another moment it faded into the darkness astern.

Others in the smoking room were pouring out now. As Hugh Woolner reached the deck, he heard a man call out, "We hit an iceberg—there it is!"

Woolner squinted into the night. About 150 yards astern
170   he made out a mountain of ice standing black against the starlit sky. Then it vanished into the dark.

The excitement, too, soon disappeared. The *Titanic* seemed as solid as ever, and it was too bitterly cold to stay outside any longer. Slowly the group filed back, Woolner picked up his hand, and the bridge game went on. The last man inside thought, as he slammed the deck door, that the engines were stopping.

He was right. Up on the bridge First Officer William M. Murdoch had just pulled the engine-room telegraph handle
180   all the way to "Stop." Murdoch was in charge of the bridge this watch, and it was his problem, once Fleet phoned the warning. A tense minute had passed since then—orders to Quartermaster Hitchens to turn the wheel hard-a-starboard[7] . . . a yank on the engine-room telegraph for "Full Speed Astern" . . . a hard push on the button closing the watertight doors . . . and finally those 37 seconds of breathless waiting.

---

[6] **linguistic** (lĭng-gwĭs´tĭk): of or relating to language.
[7] **hard-a-starboard:** hard to the right.

Now the waiting was over, and it was all so clearly too late. As the grinding noise died away, Captain Smith rushed onto the bridge from his cabin next to the wheel-house.[8] There were
190 a few quick words:

"Mr. Murdoch, what was that?"

"An iceberg, sir. I hard-a-starboarded and reversed the engines, and I was going to hard-a-port[9] around it, but she was too close. I couldn't do any more."

"Close the emergency doors."

"The doors are already closed."

They were closed, all right. Down in boiler room No. 6, Fireman Fred Barrett had been talking to Assistant Second Engineer James Hesketh when the warning bell sounded and
200 the light flashed red above the watertight door leading to the stern. A quick shout of warning—an ear-splitting crash—and the whole starboard side of the ship seemed to give way. The sea cascaded in, swirling about the pipes and valves, and the two men leaped through the door as it slammed down behind them.

Barrett found things almost as bad where he was now, in boiler room No. 5. The gash ran into No. 5 about two feet beyond the closed compartment door, and a fat jet of sea water was spouting through the hole. Nearby, Trimmer George
210 Cavell was digging himself out of an avalanche of coal that had poured out of a bunker with the impact. Another stoker mournfully studied an overturned bowl of soup that had been warming on a piece of machinery.

It was dry in the other boiler rooms further aft, but the scene was pretty much the same—men picking themselves up, calling back and forth, asking what had happened. It was hard to figure out. Until now the *Titanic* had been a picnic. Being a new ship on her maiden voyage, everything was clean. She was, as Fireman George Kemish still recalls, "a good job . . . not
220 what we were accustomed to in old ships, slogging our guts out and nearly roasted by the heat."

All the firemen had to do was keep the furnaces full. No need to work the fires with slice bars, pricker bars, and rakes. So on this Sunday night the men were taking it easy—sitting

---

[8] **wheel-house** (hwēl´hous´): an enclosed area, usually on the bridge, from which the ship is controlled.
[9] **hard-a-port:** hard to the left.

CLOSE READ

Formulate Research Questions (LINES 191–201)

Explain to students that it may be difficult to understand all of the action on the *Titanic* without learning more about how an ocean liner behaves at top speed in the open ocean.

M **ASK STUDENTS** to reread lines 191–201 and discuss questions that arise from the text that they might want to research and answer later. *(Possible responses: Why did they steer the ship the way Murdoch described? What are the emergency doors and the warning bell?)*

Analyze Meaning: Tone (LINES 196–213)

RI 1, RI 4

Explain to students that an author's **tone** is his or her attitude toward the subject. Tell students that tone is often described using adjectives such as *funny*, *serious*, or *ominous*.

N **CITE TEXT EVIDENCE** Ask students to describe the author's tone in lines 196–213. Have them cite details to support their ideas. *(Possible responses: The tone is tense, gripping, objective, engaged. Details: Warning bells are sounding; lights are flashing; men are shouting; the sea is pouring in; some men are racing for their lives; others are studying their supper. Some students may see Lord's tone as a bit removed; he makes little jokes, such as "They were closed, all right" and describes a man mourning his soup. The tone is not entirely straightforward.)*

WHEN STUDENTS STRUGGLE . . .

To help students follow shifts in the narrative point of view, have partners create a chart to track people and the events in different locations. Use the sample to model how to record the action in lines 178–213. Have students create new charts for other sections of text as they continue reading.

	Bridge	Boiler Rooms
People	Captain Smith	Fireman Barrett
	First Officer Murdoch	Engineer Hesketh
Events	pulled handle to "Stop"	warning bell

TEACH

CLOSE READ

Analyze Text

RI 1,
RI 3

(LINES 227–233)

Explain to students that this selection is an excerpt from the book *A Night to Remember*. Tell students that the book goes on to describe the evacuation and eventual sinking of the *Titanic* and that this excerpt is the first chapter of the book.

O **ASK STUDENTS** to reread lines 227–233, thinking about the fact that this selection is the first chapter of a book. Have them tell how this paragraph elaborates on key events in the text. *(Possible responses: It pulls together the events so far; it describes the confusion on the ship about what has happened; it describes how hard it was for people to believe that anything dangerous or life threatening could happen to the* Titanic.*)*

Analyze Meaning:

RI 1,
RI 4

Tone (LINES 234–255)

Remind students that an author's tone is his or her attitude toward the subject and that tone is usually described using adjectives such as *humorous*, *suspenseful*, or *angry*.

P **CITE TEXT EVIDENCE** Ask students to describe the author's tone in lines 234–255. Is it similar to or different from the rest of the selection? Have them cite details to support their ideas. *(Possible responses: The tone is objective, authentic, reliable. It is similar to earlier sections. Details: events are recorded in time order; there are facts about the* Californian *and its crew; there is nothing overly dramatic about the language.)*

COLLABORATIVE DISCUSSION Before meeting with their partners, have students look back through *A Night to Remember* to list the parts they liked most and why. Remind them to include details from the text and reasons for their choices. Partners can then discuss their lists together, referring back to the text to discuss specific parts.

ASK STUDENTS to share any questions they generated in the course of reading and discussing the selection.

around on buckets and the trimmers' iron wheel-barrows, shooting the breeze, waiting for the 12-to-4 watch to come on.

Then came that thud . . . the grinding, tearing sound . . . the telegraphs ringing wildly . . . the watertight doors crashing down. Most of the men couldn't imagine what it was—the
230 story spread that the *Titanic* had gone aground just off the Banks of Newfoundland. Many of them still thought so, even after a trimmer came running down from above shouting, "Blimey! We've struck an iceberg!"

About ten miles away Third Officer Charles Victor Groves stood on the bridge of the Leyland Liner *Californian*, bound from London to Boston. A plodding 6000-tonner, she had room for 47 passengers, but none were being carried just now. On this Sunday night she had been stopped since 10:30 P.M., completely blocked by drifting ice.
240 At about 11:10 Groves noticed the lights of another ship, racing up from the east on the starboard side. As the newcomer rapidly overhauled the motionless *Californian*, a blaze of deck lights showed she was a large passenger liner. Around 11:30 he knocked on the Venetian door of the chart room and told Captain Stanley Lord about it. Lord suggested contacting the new arrival by Morse lamp, and Groves prepared to do this.

Then, at about 11:40, he saw the big ship suddenly stop and put out most of her lights. This didn't surprise Groves very
250 much. He had spent some time in the Far East trade, where they usually put deck lights out at midnight to encourage the passengers to turn in. It never occurred to him that perhaps the lights were still on . . . that they only seemed to go out because she was no longer broadside but had veered sharply to port.

COLLABORATIVE DISCUSSION With a partner, review *A Night to Remember* and point out sections or passages that you especially enjoyed or found fascinating. Identify specific details and reasons why you found them engaging, useful, or memorable.

Analyze Text: Narrative Nonfiction

RI 3

Narrative nonfiction reads much like a fictional story, except that the characters, setting, and events are real rather than imaginary.

Using a real person's experiences and actual details of the events on the *Titanic* gives readers a full, clear picture of what the experience was like. As you analyze *A Night to Remember,* use these questions to identify elements of narrative nonfiction:

- What real-life details of setting and events are included? Why?
- Who are the real-life people, or characters, in the text?
- How is this text different from a newspaper article or a fictional story about the event?

Analyze the Meanings of Words and Phrases

RI 4

Style refers to a writer's unique way of communicating ideas. Many literary elements, including word choice, sentence structure, imagery, point of view, voice, and tone contribute to a writer's style.

Tone is the writer's attitude toward his or her subject. Adjectives are often used to describe the tone of a text, such as *serious, humorous, sarcastic,* and *respectful.*

The style and tone an author uses help readers understand ideas and makes the writing memorable. In *A Night to Remember*, the author describes the *Titanic* as "the most glamorous ship in the world," adding that "Even the passengers' dogs were glamorous." He supports that idea by describing a list of wealthy passengers—and their dogs. The careful details, precise choice of words, and slightly humorous tone help make up the author's style.

To analyze style and tone, think about these elements:

- **Word choice:** Does the author use powerful verbs, precise nouns, and vivid adjectives or adverbs? How does the author's word choice affect the tone of the text?
- **Sentence structure:** Are most sentences long or short? Does the author use a variety of sentence types?
- **Literary devices:** Does the author use strong imagery and sensory details, or devices such as repetition or exaggeration?

Look for more examples of Walter Lord's style and tone.

CLOSE READ

Analyze Text: Narrative Nonfiction

RI 3

Help students understand the differences between narrative nonfiction and a newspaper article or a fictional story. Point out the differences between characters, settings, and events that are made up in fiction and the real-life elements in narrative nonfiction. Discuss how narrative nonfiction can recreate a real-life experience for readers using real-life details and eyewitness accounts. Have students find examples of these elements in the selection.

Analyze the Meanings of Words and Phrases

RI 4

Help students understand that an author's use of words and phrases produces a style that communicates his or her ideas in a unique way. Ask volunteers to offer examples of different styles they have encountered in other articles and books.

Then, discuss the details of style and tone listed from *A Night to Remember*, going over elements of word choice, sentence structure, and literary devices that create style and tone.

Strategies for Annotation   ✎ ▣ *Annotate it!*

Analyze the Meanings of Words and Phrases

RI 1,
RI 4

Share these strategies for guided or independent analysis:

- Highlight important word choices in yellow.
- Highlight elements of sentence structure in green.
- Highlight details about point of view in blue.
- Review your highlights. On a note, record what tone this scene suggests to you.

Then came that thud . . . the grinding, tearing sound . . . the telegraphs ringing wildly . . . the watertight doors crashing down. . . . the story spread that the *Titanic* had gone aground just off the Banks of Newfoundland. Many of them still thought so, even after a trimmer came . . . shouting, "Blimey! We've struck an iceberg!"

Analyzing the Text

RI 1, RI 3, RI 4, RI 5, RI 10

Possible answers:

1. *Words: "eyes of the ship"; "Fleet had been warned to watch especially for icebergs"; "ice problem." A likely prediction is that the ship will hit an iceberg.*

2. *The tone is serious, almost ominous. Words and phrases, such as "stood quietly," "braced themselves," "miraculously," and "close shave," add to the seriousness of the tone.*

3. *The author presents sounds and sensations from the point of view of different passengers and crew members. The reader gets a rich, full idea of the moment and understands that it was a different experience for every person aboard the ship.*

4. *The real-life accounts the author chooses are personal, sometimes humorous, and full of sensory details. He includes quotations, personal memories, and a variety of imaginative descriptions from the passengers. These elements make the text personal and authentic to the reader.*

5. *The events on the Titanic are becoming chaotic. Water is rushing in, but many people are still not aware of the danger. On the Californian, an officer was experiencing a quiet night on the ship and was not surprised when the lights went out on the large ship that had passed earlier. The calmness on the Californian contrasts sharply with the Titanic. The last lines create suspense and foreshadow the tragic events to come.*

6. *The crises are dramatic and lend themselves to storytelling. The atmosphere of the Titanic and the style of its wealthy passengers contribute elements similar to stories about royalty. The personal accounts add drama and the opportunity for readers to care about specific people.*

English Language Support

Divide the class into small groups to answer the questions. Have each group answer one question. When all the groups are finished, let them take turns presenting their answers to the class. Encourage classmates to provide useful feedback.

FOR STUDENTS WITH DISABILITIES

Work with students with learning disabilities to divide the research process into specific, numbered stages (for example, 1. research websites; 2. research texts, 3. collect and sort notes, etc.). Provide students with a checklist to fill in as each task is completed. Give students a due date to complete each task and monitor individual progress.

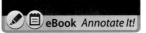

Analyzing the Text

RI 1, RI 3, RI 4, RI 5, RI 10, W 7

Cite Text Evidence   Support your responses with evidence from the text.

1. **Predict** Sometimes writers use **foreshadowing,** a hint that a future event will take place in the text. Reread lines 18-26. What words, phrases, and sentences does the author use to hint at a future event? What might you predict will happen?

2. **Interpret** Reread lines 42–49. Describe the tone of this passage. Which words help convey the tone?

3. **Identify Patterns** Reread lines 71–87. How does the author describe the ship striking the iceberg? Explain the significance of the author's choice to present ideas this way.

4. **Analyze** Reread lines 88–109. What elements contribute to the author's style in these lines? Describe the impact these elements have on the text.

5. **Compare** Review lines 234–255. How do the events on the *Californian* compare with the events happening on the *Titanic*? How does this section contribute to the development of the events?

6. **Evaluate** The author could have written the facts about the sinking as a piece of informational text. Instead, he wrote narrative nonfiction and included the words and experiences of people on the ship. Is Lord's telling of the events effective? Explain why.

PERFORMANCE TASK

Writing Activity: Research Conduct research to find out what happened to the *Titanic* after it struck the iceberg. Look for information that will help you form a full picture of the events.

- Use research sources—websites, encyclopedias, nonfiction books, and documentaries.
- Look for firsthand accounts from survivors.
- Take notes and record the sources of your information.

Assign this performance task.

PERFORMANCE TASK

W 7

Writing Activity: Research Have students work independently to

- use a wide variety of research sources and different types of accounts
- organize their research into notes and sources

Explain that resources from the time period, such as newspapers, or current resources, such as interviews or recollections by survivors, might be available.

Critical Vocabulary

L 4a, L 4c, L 4d, L 6

knot	indulge	shudder	jar	ominous

Practice and Apply Answer each question.

1. Who would be more likely to be discussing a **knot**? Why?
   the captain of an ocean liner   a racecar driver

2. If you like chocolate, which of these might you **indulge** in? Why?
   a glass of lemonade   a hot fudge sundae   a pizza

3. Which of the following might make you **shudder**? Why?
   sweeping the floor   remembering a bad dream   buying a gift

4. Which of these would you describe as a **jar**? Why?
   closing a window   bumping into someone   taking a deep breath

5. Which of these might be an **ominous** sound? Why?
   a door creaking open   a doorbell ringing   music

Vocabulary Strategy: Specialized Vocabulary

The term **specialized vocabulary** refers to words and terms that are used in a particular occupation, activity, or field of study. Some specialized vocabulary, such as *starboard*, is used primarily by people when discussing sailing. Other terms, such as *knot*, may be familiar but have a special meaning in that field. Sometimes readers may be able to use context to determine the meaning of specialized vocabulary. In most cases, however, it is best to use a dictionary to find out or confirm a word's meaning.

Practice and Apply Use a chart like the one here to explore the meaning of specialized vocabulary about ships and sailing. Use a dictionary as well as context to determine the precise meaning of each word.

Term	Guessed Meaning	Dictionary Meaning
crow's nest (line 1)		
bridge (line 37)		
bow (line 46)		
windjammer (line 60)		

PRACTICE & APPLY

Critical Vocabulary

L 4a, L 4c, L 4d, L6

Possible answers:

1. *the captain of an ocean liner, because the speed of a ship is measured in knots*

2. *a hot fudge sundae, because I would be treating myself to chocolate*

3. *remembering a bad dream, because that would be upsetting and might make me shake*

4. *bumping into someone, because that would feel like a jolt or a push*

5. *a door creaking open, because someone might be sneaking up on me*

Vocabulary Strategy: Specialized Vocabulary

Term	Guessed Meaning	Dictionary Meaning
crow's-nest	*a room at the top of a ship, used to watch for danger ahead*	*a small platform at the top of a ship, with a railing and windscreen, used to watch for danger ahead*
bridge	*the captain's room*	*a crosswise platform or enclosed area above the main deck from which the ship is controlled*
bow	*the front half of a ship*	*the front end of a ship or boat, or either of the sides of this front end*
windjammer	*a small sailing ship*	*a large sailing ship*

Strategies for Annotation ✏️ 🖥 *Annotate it!*

Specialized Vocabulary

L 4a, L 4c, L 4d, L 6

Have students locate the words *broadside*, *porthole*, and *trimmer* in the selection. Tell them to use their eBook annotation tools to do the following:

- Highlight each word.
- Underline any context clues you find in the surrounding text.
- Review the annotations. On a note, write a guess about the word's meaning. Then look it up in a dictionary.

. . . Nearby, Trimmer George Cavell was digging himself out of an avalanche of coal that had poured out of a bunker with the impact. Another stoker mournfully studied an overturned b[
trimmer: someone who moved coal?

PRACTICE & APPLY

Language Conventions: Consistency in Style and Tone

L 3b

Tell students that an abrupt change in style and tone can cause the reader's attention to drift or even confuse the reader. Review the example from *A Night to Remember* and discuss the elements of consistent style and tone. Then read through the Practice and Apply activity with students. Have students work independently to revise the paragraphs and then share revisions among the whole group.

Possible answers:

"Just because I've never been fishing on a lake before doesn't mean I don't know what I'm doing," Jenn told Morgan. She reached in the bait bucket and fearlessly threaded an earthworm on the hook of her fishing pole. "See?" she smirked. "I can handle this!"

Morgan grinned. "Be careful you don't rock the canoe," he replied.

Jenn's eyes suddenly got a wicked glint. "Check this out!" she chortled. She stood up and marched vigorously in place. The canoe rocked dangerously from side to side.

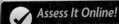

Assess It Online!

Online Selection Test
- Download an editable ExamView bank.
- Assign and manage this test online.

Language Conventions: Consistency in Style and Tone

L 3b

Good readers notice a change in style or tone. If a writer's style or tone changes abruptly, it can be jarring and cause the reader to lose focus or misunderstand ideas.

As a writer, you should work to maintain a consistent style and tone. Take a look at this excerpt from *A Night to Remember*:

> Meanwhile, down below in the First Class dining saloon on D Deck, four other members of the *Titanic*'s crew were sitting around one of the tables. The last diner had long since departed, and now the big white Jacobean room was empty except for this single group. They were dining-saloon stewards, indulging in the time-honored pastime of all stewards off duty—they were gossiping about their passengers.

Walter Lord uses a consistent style and tone in his writing. His sentences flow smoothly, and he uses precise word choices to describe people and their surroundings clearly and vividly. He creates a lightly humorous tone by using the formal-sounding phrase "indulging in the time-honored pastime" to describe the everyday activity of gossiping.

Practice and Apply Edit the paragraphs to make them more consistent in style and tone.

"Just because I've never been fishing on a lake before doesn't mean I don't know what I'm doing," Jenn told Morgan. She reached in the bait bucket and fearlessly threaded an earthworm on the hook of her fishing pole. "See?" she smirked. "I can handle this!"

Morgan grinned. He said to be careful that she didn't rock the canoe.

Jenn laughed. "Check this out!" she chortled. Jenn stood up. She marched. She marched like she was in a parade. The canoe rocked from side to side. Talk about dangerous. Wasn't that a crazy thing to do?

English Language Support

Evaluate Language Choices Review some of the elements that help to create a consistent style and tone: smooth transitions, formal versus informal language, precise word choices, and clear descriptions.

- Read the Practice and Apply paragraphs aloud as student follow in their texts. Guide students to notice the changes in style and tone after the first paragraph. Explain that instead of continuing the dialogue, Morgan's comment is reported indirectly. Point out the contrast between the long, complex sentences in the first paragraph and the short, choppy sentences that follow. Then work with students to revise the paragraphs for a more consistent style and tone.

- Choral read the Practice and Apply paragraphs and conduct a class discussion to identify problem areas. Then ask pairs to rewrite the second and third paragraphs to make them consistent with the style and tone of the first paragraph.

Formulate Research Questions

W 5

TEACH

Explain to students that the first step in conducting research on the Internet is to write questions to guide that research. Share these guidelines:

1. **Choose a topic** Decide what topic you will research, such as the construction of the *Titanic*.

2. **Brainstorm questions** Quickly brainstorm and write down as many questions about the topic as you can. Work with a partner or small group to improve the number of questions. Aim for at least ten to twenty questions.

3. **Analyze and sort the questions** Explain that some questions are better research questions than others.

   - "Closed" questions will have short answers, such as simple facts or yes and no answers.

   - "Open" questions require a long answer and often begin with the words *how* or *why*.

Explain that open questions make the best research questions because they aren't easy to answer. Open questions require searching through several sources, finding different kinds of information, and integrating, or putting all the information together. Open questions and their answers provide the opportunity to learn the most interesting and surprising information about a topic.

PRACTICE AND APPLY

Display a two-column chart with the heads "Closed" and "Open." Ask students to refer to questions they wrote down while reading *A Night to Remember* and to formulate new ones. Have volunteers share questions and tell where each question should be recorded in the chart. Discuss each question as a group and decide if it is being recorded in the correct column.

Next, have small groups or partners work together to formulate questions. Assign a topic or have students choose their own. Ask students to create charts of their questions to share and discuss with the class. Have students keep their charts to help them with Performance Tasks and other activities as needed.

 INTERACTIVE WHITEBOARD LESSON Use **Doing Research on the Web** to provide instruction in online research.

Analyze Meaning: Style

RI 4

RETEACH

Review that **style** is an author's unique way of writing; it is *how* something is written rather than *what* is written. Remind students that the following literary elements are part of style:

- **word choice:** the author's use of powerful, vivid, and precise words to express ideas

- **sentence structure:** the author's use of a variety of sentence types for different effects

- **imagery:** words and phrases that appeal to the five senses

- **tone:** the author's attitude toward the subject

Read aloud these passages from *A Night to Remember*. Ask students to identify elements of style and explain the meaning each element conveys in the text.

- **Lines 32–41:** imagery; word choices
- **Lines 94–101:** sentence structure; imagery; tone
- **Lines 169–171:** word choice; imagery

 LEVEL UP TUTORIALS Assign one or more of these *Level Up* tutorials: **Author's Style**; **Tone**; **Imagery**

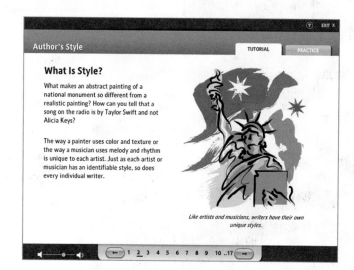

INDEPENDENT READING

Individual students can apply these skills to another selection in Collection 3 or to their independent reading. After their analysis, have them discuss the styles of other writers with a partner or small group.

On the Titanic, Defined by What They Wore

Newspaper Article by Guy Trebay

Why This Text

Students do not always take the time to analyze the meanings of words and phrases as they are used in a text. Newspaper articles like this one by Guy Trebay include key ideas and word choices that must be analyzed to be understood. With the help of the close-reading questions, students will analyze Trebay's key ideas and word choices. This close reading will help students understand the content of the article.

Background Have students read the background information. Introduce the selection by telling students that the *Titanic* was a brand new ship that was built with new technology, such as electric watertight doors. Many people believed the ship could not sink. Maybe that explains why there were not enough lifeboats on board and so many people died. Tell students that Guy Trebay is an award-winning style writer for the *New York Times*.

SETTING A PURPOSE Ask students to look up words they do not know. Does analyzing the meanings of words and phrases help them understand what they are reading?

Standards Support

- cite textual evidence
- analyze how a key idea is introduced
- determine the meaning of words and phrases as they are used in a text
- integrate information presented in different formats

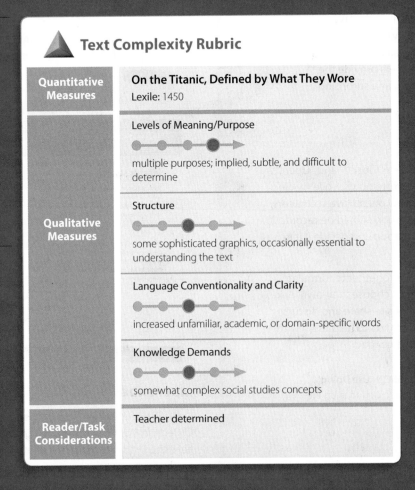

Text Complexity Rubric

Quantitative Measures

On the Titanic, Defined by What They Wore
Lexile: 1450

Qualitative Measures

Levels of Meaning/Purpose

multiple purposes; implied, subtle, and difficult to determine

Structure

some sophisticated graphics, occasionally essential to understanding the text

Language Conventionality and Clarity

increased unfamiliar, academic, or domain-specific words

Knowledge Demands

somewhat complex social studies concepts

Reader/Task Considerations

Teacher determined

Strategies for CLOSE READING

Analyze Meanings of Words and Phrases

Students should read this newspaper article carefully all the way through. Close-reading questions at the bottom of the page will help them focus on a thorough analysis of the text. As they read, students should jot down comments or questions about the article in the side margins.

WHEN STUDENTS STRUGGLE . . .

To help students analyze the meanings of words and phrases, have them work in a small group to fill out a chart, such as the one shown below, as they analyze the text.

CITE TEXT EVIDENCE For practice in analyzing words and phrases as they are used in a text, ask students to cite sentences that contain powerful verbs, vivid adjectives, or precise nouns; define the specific word; and explain Trebay's use of the word in the text.

sentence with specific word: "Tatters and scraps, they emerged from the deep coated with mire and miraculously although tenuously intact." (lines 1–2)	definition: tenuously, adverb: without much substance or strength	Trebay's use of the word: Trebay lets readers know that the clothes that were recovered from the Titanic were barely intact and could easily fall apart or be destroyed.
sentence with specific word:	definition:	Trebay's use of the word:

Background On April 10th, 1912, the RMS Titanic left Southampton, England, for New York City on its first and only voyage. The Titanic had been called "unsinkable" and was the most luxurious passenger liner of its day. On April 15th, the ship collided with an iceberg and sank. Over 1,500 people died in the freezing waters. The wreckage was discovered in 1985, but the ship remains on the ocean floor to this day. The Titanic has been immortalized through film, books, television series, songs, exhibits—and in this recent newspaper article.

On the **Titanic,** Defined by **What They Wore**

Newspaper Article by Guy Trebay

CLOSE READ
Notes

1. **READ ▶** As you read lines 1–34, begin to cite text evidence.
   - In the margin, explain what you think the article's title means.
   - In the margin, paraphrase what the second sentence says.
   - Underline items recovered from the *Titanic*.

Tatters and scraps, they emerged from the deep coated with mire and miraculously although tenuously intact. Treated with the reverence due relics of perhaps the greatest maritime tragedy and with all the care modern conservation science could summon, they were restored, put on display and then offered this week in an exceptional **(A)** single-lot auction of the more than 5,000 objects (with a current estimated worth of $190 million) that salvagers of the Titanic found scattered across the North Atlantic seabed.

A surprising amount of ephemera[1] defied logic to survive the
10 sinking of the unsinkable ocean liner that went to the bottom 100 years ago on April 15.

Most astonishing of all the recovered items, it would seem, were the articles of clothing either carried or worn by passengers before the 882-foot-long liner sank in icy water. The ship broke apart and shot to

---
[1] **ephemera:** things that are useful for only a short time.

Passengers on the Titanic wore distinctive clothing.

More than 5,000 restored objects salvaged from the Titanic, valued at $190 million, were put up for auction.

53

---

1. **READ AND CITE TEXT EVIDENCE** Discuss the meaning of the word *salvagers* (line 7).

A **ASK STUDENTS** to read aloud their paraphrase of the second sentence to a partner. Have them work with their partner to improve their paraphrase and include text evidence. *Students should cite evidence of the auction (line 6) and should cite the "5,000 objects . . . that salvagers of the Titanic found . . ." (lines 6–7).* Have them underline examples of some of the 5,000 objects up for auction.

the bottom; its contents fell more slowly, fluttering to the depths like grim leaf fall.

And there, in the lightless saline netherworld, a vest, a trilby hat, a pair of laced boots, a belted valise and an alligator bag (along with a huge range of artifacts) lay scattered across a broad apron of

20 remnants.

The wreck was discovered in 1985 and the objects were brought to the surface over the course of seven **expeditions.** Perhaps more than the teacups or perfume flacons, the garments eerily conjure lives lost that clear April night, so much so that when the Academy Award-winning designer Deborah L. Scott prepared to create costumes for James Cameron's blockbuster 1997 film "Titanic," she covered her office walls with photographs of the Titanic's passengers to absorb the sartorial[2] elements that enliven character.

The removable celluloid collars with laundry marks inside, the

30 man's vest with a single vertical buttonhole for a watch chain and fob, the homespun finery packed away by village girls as a trousseau[3] for an imaginary future: these sorts of detail were employed by Ms. Scott to summon the beings who once inhabited garments that in some cases, though it is hard to imagine, survived their owners.

Consider, for instance, Marion Meanwell's handbag.

Using public records, newspaper accounts at the time and the recollections of survivors, historians like Richard Davenport-Hines, author of "Voyagers of the Titanic: Passengers, Sailors, Shipbuilders,

expedition:

a journey taken by a group of people

[2] **sartorial:** related to clothing.
[3] **trousseau:** a bride's personal possessions.

---

2. ◀ REREAD Reread lines 21–34. Where did Deborah L. Scott find inspiration for her costume designs for the 1997 movie?

She used pictures of Titanic passengers to get the feeling of the kinds of clothing they typically wore.

---

3. READ ▶ As you read lines 35–80, continue to cite text evidence.

• In the margin, paraphrase the quote at the top of the next page.
• Underline information that helps you understand Mrs. Meanwell's story.
• In the margin, explain why it was so important to have credentials.

54

> **As was true of many ocean voyagers of the time, Mrs. Meanwell was on a passage intended to be a momentous alteration of a settled life.**

Like many people who travelled across the ocean, Mrs. Meanwell was seeking a new and different future.

Aristocrats, and the Worlds They Came From," have pieced together

40 fragmentary biographies of victims like Mrs. Meanwell (nee Ogden), a British milliner[4] traveling aboard the Titanic on a third-class ticket.

As was true of many ocean voyagers of the time, Mrs. Meanwell was on a passage intended to be a momentous alteration of a settled life. First chartered to sail on the liner Majestic, Mrs. Meanwell rebooked on the Titanic after that vessel was removed from regular service. Tucked into her handbag were a number of documents, among them a letter from the London landlords Wheeler Sons & Co.

This **innocuous** note, stating blandly that "we have always found Meanwell a good tenant and prompt in payment of her rent," carried

50 an extra freight of meaning for an immigrant hoping to build a new life.

"If you were coming over without **credentials** or with no prospect of work," Mr. Davenport-Hines said, it was not uncommon for examiners at Ellis Island to refuse entry to new arrivals and to send them home as "vagrants or tramps."

Then as now, an alligator bag was a luxury item, a satchel of substance carried by a woman whose own social authority it advertised. Mrs. Meanwell was parted from her alligator bag on the night the Titanic sank and, while she perished, her purse did not.

[4] **milliner:** hatmaker.

innocuous:

plain, innocent

credentials:

evidence of authority

Without credentials, a person could be denied entry to the United States.

55

---

2. REREAD AND CITE TEXT EVIDENCE

Ⓑ **ASK STUDENTS** to cite text evidence to support their answer. *Students should cite text from lines 24–27, "when . . . Scott prepared to create costumes for . . . 'Titanic' she covered her office walls with photographs of the Titanic's passengers . . ."*

3. READ AND CITE TEXT EVIDENCE

Ⓒ **ASK STUDENTS** to cite textual evidence that helps them understand Marion Meanwell's story. *Students should underline evidence about Meanwell's background, (lines 41 and 65), her plans (lines 42–44 and 65–67), and evidence of the credentials she carried in her handbag (lines 48–49).*

Critical Vocabulary: expedition (line 22) Have students define *expedition* as Trebay uses it here. *Students should explain that these expeditions are journeys to the sunken* Titanic.

Critical Vocabulary: innocuous (line 48) Ask students to compare their definitions. Why does Trebay describe the note as innocuous? *Students should recognize that Trebay is drawing attention to the contrast between how plain the note might seem to us today and how important it was to Meanwell, as well as what a meaningful clue it was to Meanwell's story.*

Critical Vocabulary: credentials (line 52) Have students share their definitions. Did Mrs. Meanwell have credentials? What did she have? *She had a letter from her landlord, her marriage license, and her parents' wedding license.*

60　"Inside it was her marriage license, as well as her parents' wedding license," said David Galusha, a conservator for Premier Exhibition, the Atlanta-based company that sold the Titanic relics, along with the video archives of its salvage expeditions and the intellectual rights to create objects using the R.M.S. Titanic "brand."

"She had sold everything, was a widow and was moving to the United States to be with her daughter, who had two children, to assist with them," Mr. Galusha said of Mrs. Meanwell.

That the bag survived was owed in part to the fact that the objects scattered from the wreck spent the last century, "two miles down, in 70　an environment with no light, and hardly any oxygen," the conservator said. There was something else. "The thickness of the alligator skin, the quality, is no comparison to what you would find today," Mr. Galusha said. "There was a general attitude at the time of making things durable, things that would stand the test of time."

That they did so is an unexpectedly moving aspect of a tale so often rehearsed that its human dimensions are sometimes overlooked. "Titanic" may be, as some claim, one of the most universally recognized names in the English language. Yet the lives at the heart of the story are easily forgotten, transformed into facile metaphors and 80　symbols of gender and class.

---

4. ◀ **REREAD**　Reread lines 42–80. Why does the author include the narrative history about Mrs. Meanwell? Cite text evidence in your response.

The story of Mrs. Meanwell represents one of the "lives at the heart" of the history of the Titanic. The details of her life are remembered thanks to the study of "a number of documents" recovered from her alligator handbag.

5. **READ** ▶　As you read lines 81–114, continue to cite text evidence.

• Underline the role that clothing played after the *Titanic* sank.
• In the margin, explain what the names of first-class passengers reveal about the gap between social classes.
• In the margin, paraphrase what Cohen says about the *Titanic* as a stage.

56

> **The Titanic was this stage where people were performing certain versions of themselves, for all kinds of audiences.**

E　There is the tragic noblesse of the first-class passengers, people named Straus and Widener and Guggenheim; the hopeless scrabbling of the businessmen and boys traveling in second class, some kept at gunpoint from entering lifeboats that went off half-filled; and the wretched doom of those nameless victims at the bottom of the social scale.

"They were all judged finally on their clothes and the quality of their clothes," Mr. Davenport-Hines said, adding that among the aspects of the story most laden with pathos is the contemporary 90　depiction of bodies frozen into life jackets and hauled from the North Atlantic and sorted by class, largely according to what else they had on.

Clothes, said Lisa Cohen, a biographer whose book "All We Know" delineates the lives of three early modernist women—Mercedes de Acosta, Madge Garland, Esther Murphy—in part by using the "soft history" of fashion to demonstrate that our surfaces **elucidate** "our depths," as the author said.

The identity masquerade that artists like Cindy Sherman explore to theatrical effect was on prominent view aboard the floating theater 100　of an ocean passage, Ms. Cohen said. The Titanic was in that sense a stage prop moving across what was by all accounts a flat and unthreatening ocean and also across the proscenium[5] of a new century.

F　"The Titanic was this stage where people were performing certain versions of themselves, for all kinds of audiences," Ms. Cohen said. "It was a transitional space in a transitional period, a time of self-invention right before the war."

---

[5] **proscenium:** the part of the stage in front of the curtain.

First-class passengers are remembered by name, as individuals, but the lower classes are nameless.

elucidate:
explain

The Titanic was the stage, and the passengers were performers.

57

---

4. **REREAD AND CITE TEXT EVIDENCE**

D **ASK STUDENTS** to cite text evidence to support their explanation of why the author chose to include the narrative history about Mrs. Meanwell. *Answers will vary. Students may cite that her story represents one of the "lives at the heart" of the history of the Titanic (line 78), or that "a number of documents" in her handbag revealed details of her life (line 46).*

5. **READ AND CITE TEXT EVIDENCE**

E **ASK STUDENTS** to cite text evidence to support their explanation of what the names of first-class passengers reveal about the gap between social classes. *Students should cite evidence from lines 81–86.*

FOR ELL STUDENTS Don't let students confuse *conservator* and *conservative*. Explain that a conservator is a person responsible for items in an exhibit or museum, while *conservative* usually describes traditional views, and the opposition to severe change.

Critical Vocabulary: elucidate (line 97) Ask students to compare their definitions of *elucidate*. Then have them define the related word *lucid*. Discuss connotations of the word *elucidate* and why Trebay chose this word.

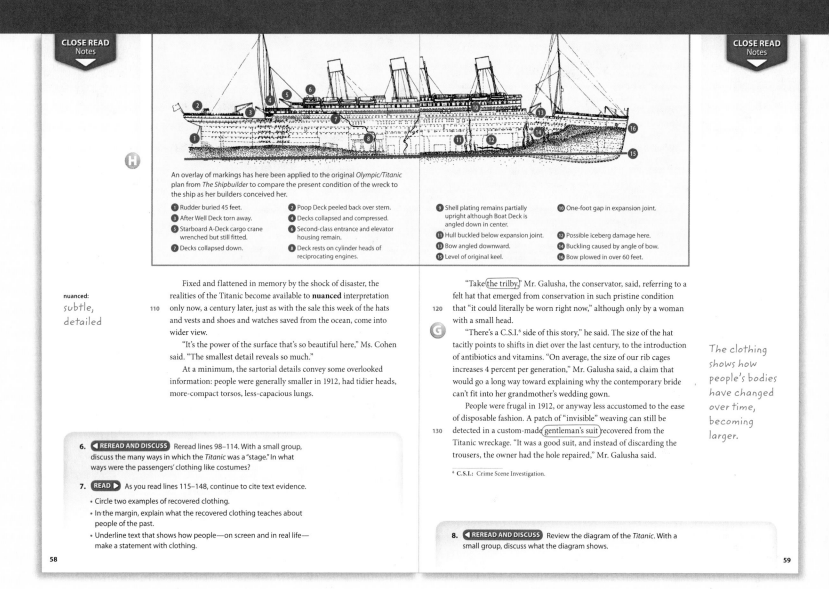

An overlay of markings has here been applied to the original *Olympic/Titanic* plan from *The Shipbuilder* to compare the present condition of the wreck to the ship as her builders conceived her.

❶ Rudder buried 45 feet.
❷ Poop Deck peeled back over stern.
❸ After Well Deck torn away.
❹ Decks collapsed and compressed.
❺ Starboard A-Deck cargo crane wrenched but still fitted.
❻ Second-class entrance and elevator housing remain.
❼ Decks collapsed down.
❽ Deck rests on cylinder heads of reciprocating engines.
❾ Shell plating remains partially upright although Boat Deck is angled down in center.
❿ One-foot gap in expansion joint.
⓫ Hull buckled below expansion joint.
⓬ Possible iceberg damage here.
⓭ Bow angled downward.
⓮ Buckling caused by angle of bow.
⓯ Level of original keel.
⓰ Bow plowed in over 60 feet.

nuanced:
subtle, detailed

Fixed and flattened in memory by the shock of disaster, the realities of the Titanic become available to **nuanced** interpretation
110 only now, a century later, just as with the sale this week of the hats and vests and shoes and watches saved from the ocean, come into wider view.

"It's the power of the surface that's so beautiful here," Ms. Cohen said. "The smallest detail reveals so much."

At a minimum, the sartorial details convey some overlooked information: people were generally smaller in 1912, had tidier heads, more-compact torsos, less-capacious lungs.

> **6.** ◀ **REREAD AND DISCUSS** Reread lines 98–114. With a small group, discuss the many ways in which the *Titanic* was a "stage." In what ways were the passengers' clothing like costumes?
>
> **7.** **READ** ▶ As you read lines 115–148, continue to cite text evidence.
> • Circle two examples of recovered clothing.
> • In the margin, explain what the recovered clothing teaches about people of the past.
> • Underline text that shows how people—on screen and in real life—make a statement with clothing.

58

"Take the trilby," Mr. Galusha, the conservator, said, referring to a felt hat that emerged from conservation in such pristine condition
120 that "it could literally be worn right now," although only by a woman with a small head.

"There's a C.S.I.[6] side of this story," he said. The size of the hat tacitly points to shifts in diet over the last century, to the introduction of antibiotics and vitamins. "On average, the size of our rib cages increases 4 percent per generation," Mr. Galusha said, a claim that would go a long way toward explaining why the contemporary bride can't fit into her grandmother's wedding gown.

People were frugal in 1912, or anyway less accustomed to the ease of disposable fashion. A patch of "invisible" weaving can still be
130 detected in a custom-made gentleman's suit recovered from the Titanic wreckage. "It was a good suit, and instead of discarding the trousers, the owner had the hole repaired," Mr. Galusha said.

[6] **C.S.I.:** Crime Scene Investigation.

The clothing shows how people's bodies have changed over time, becoming larger.

> **8.** ◀ **REREAD AND DISCUSS** Review the diagram of the *Titanic*. With a small group, discuss what the diagram shows.

59

---

6. **REREAD AND DISCUSS USING TEXT EVIDENCE**

F **ASK STUDENTS** to cite specific text evidence in their discussion, with line numbers and references to support their conclusions. *Students should cite line 104 and note that clothes were part of people's attempts at "performing certain versions of themselves . . ."*

7. **READ AND CITE TEXT EVIDENCE**

G **ASK STUDENTS** to cite text evidence to support their explanation of what the recovered clothing teaches about people of the past. *Students should cite lines 122–127 as evidence that people's bodies have changed over time, becoming larger.*

Critical Vocabulary: nuanced (line 109) Ask volunteers to read their definitions of *nuanced*. Ask students to explain the meaning of *nuanced* as it is used here.

8. **REREAD AND DISCUSS USING TEXT EVIDENCE**

H **ASK STUDENTS** to appoint a reporter for each group to explain what happened to the ship at the numbered locations on the diagram. Students should describe the damage to such parts of the ship as the various decks, the hull, the rudder, and the bow.

FOR ELL STUDENTS Explain the word *frugal*. Tell students that frugal people are careful about spending money on things they don't really need. Encourage students to give you an example of what a frugal person might do.

Critical Vocabulary: amalgam (line 145) Ask students to explain the meaning of *amalgam* as it is used here. In what way are clothes an amalgam? *They are a mixture of various fabrics, colors, and styles.*

196f Collection 3

Though they largely passed into legend, those who lost their lives in the epoch-making shipwreck were never "characters," said Deborah Nadoolman Landis, the curator of "Hollywood Costume," an exhibition exploring the role costume design plays in cinema history that will open in October at the Victoria and Albert Museum in London. "A character is a pretend person, and real people lost their lives," in the wreck of the Titanic, said Ms. Landis, an Academy
140   Award-nominated designer. <u>On-screen, their clothes served a crucial function, as flashcard symbols of social identity.</u> "One of the ways you make people real in movies is through clothes."

People are to a surprising extent what they imagine themselves to be every time they get dressed, Ms. Landis said. "<u>Our clothing is an **amalgam** of what we are</u>: the shoes, the vest, the trousers, the suit jacket purchased at different times," she said. "<u>Clothes hold us together</u> in so many ways. They're the closest thing to our bodies, our pulse."

amalgam:
mixture

SHORT RESPONSE

Cite Text Evidence   What information in the article and the diagram helps you understand how the trip was different for first-class passengers and steerage passengers of the *Titanic*? Be sure to **cite text evidence** from the diagram in your response.

The diagram shows that there were separate entrances for the different classes (for example, the second-class entrance is shown in the diagram). These entrances went to different deck levels, which were separate for the different classes. People were identified by the clothing they wore or the items they brought with them, but they were also identified by where they were situated on the ship. They were not only separated by the quality of the clothes they wore— they were physically separated from one another by location.

60

SHORT RESPONSE

Cite Text Evidence   Student responses will vary, but they should cite evidence from the article to support their comparison. Students should:

- compare the experience of first-class and steerage passengers on the *Titanic*.
- cite evidence from the text.
- cite evidence from the diagram.

TO CHALLENGE STUDENTS . . .

For more context and historical background, students can view the video "Titanic at 100: Mystery Solved" in their eBooks.

ASK STUDENTS to use the newspaper article by Trebay as well as the audio and video evidence to write a paragraph describing the sinking of the *Titanic*. *Students should write paragraphs that include descriptive details of the events as they are described in the article and the video.*

DIG DEEPER

With the class, return to Question 8, Reread and Discuss. Have students share the results of their discussion.

ASK STUDENTS whether they were satisfied with the outcome of their small-group discussions. Have each group share their review of the diagram. What text evidence can they identify that supports their review?

- Encourage students to tell whether there was any disagreement about what the diagram shows. Did examining the diagram closely and discussing evidence help to resolve the disagreement?
- Have groups explore the text for further evidence that supports what they found in the diagram.
- After students have shared the results of their group's discussion, ask whether another group found evidence they would like to include in their findings.

ASK STUDENTS to return to their Short Response answer and revise it based on the class discussion.

MEDIA *Titanic* **at 100: Mystery Solved**

Documentary by James Cameron

Why This Text?

Students regularly encounter documentaries in various venues. This lesson showcases various features of a documentary while bringing students along on an expedition to discover how and why the *Titanic* sank.

> ▶ **View It!**
> Professional Development Podcast:
> **Text-Dependent Analysis**

Key Learning Objective: The student will be able to understand the features and analyze the purpose of a documentary, as well as integrate its information with other sources.

RI 1 Cite evidence.
RI 2 Determine central idea; provide a summary.
RI 7 Integrate information presented in different media.
W 4 Produce clear and coherent writing.
W 7 Conduct short research projects.
SL 1 Engage effectively in a range of collaborative discussions.
SL 2 Interpret information presented in diverse media.
SL 5 Include multimedia components and visual displays in presentations.

 ### Text Complexity Rubric

Quantitative Measures	***Titanic* at 100: Mystery Solved** Lexile: N/A

Qualitative Measures

Levels of Meaning/Purpose

single level of complex meaning

Structure

organization of main ideas and details is highly complex; not explicit, must be inferred by the reader

Language Conventionality and Clarity

increased unfamiliar, academic, or domain-specific words

Knowledge Demands

somewhat complex concepts

Reader/Task Considerations

- Teacher determined
- Vary by individual reader and type of text
- See the Text X-Ray for suggested Reader/Task Considerations.

English Language Support Before teaching, use the Text X-Ray for an overview of the text's complexity. The Text X-Ray and the supports and scaffolds in the Teacher's Edition will help you guide students of different skill levels.

Meaning
Making

Language
Development

Effective
Expression

Content
Knowledge

Foundational
Skills

Text Complexity: Qualitative Measures

Levels of Meaning/Purpose

single level of complex meaning

Help students interpret diverse media.
- Teacher's Edition side notes, pp. 197, 198, 199
- English Language Support, pp. 199, 200
- Interpret Diverse Media, p. 199

To reteach interpreting media, see
- Elements of a Documentary, p. 200a

ZOOM IN ON **INTERPRETING DIVERSE MEDIA** Explain that a **documentary** is a film, video, or audio program that presents factual information about a topic. Have students view the film clip three times. During each viewing, have them pay particular attention to just one of the following elements and note how it is used:

- voice-over narration
- interviews
- animation

Then have students discuss how each element helps integrate, or pull together, the many pieces of information that are presented, and how it helps make the information clear to viewers.

Structure

organization of main ideas and details is highly complex; not explicit, must be inferred by the reader

Help students integrate information.
- Teacher's Edition side notes, pp. 197, 199
- English Language Support, p. 200
- Performance Task, p. 200
- Integrate Information, p. 199

▶ *Use It!* **Level Up Tutorial:** Synthesizing Information

To teach citing text evidence, see
- Citing Evidence in a Presentation, p. 200a

▶ *Use It!* **Interactive Whiteboard Lesson:** Citing Textual Evidence

ZOOM IN ON **INTEGRATING INFORMATION** Tell students that when they assemble facts and details from more than one source or form, they are **integrating information**. After students view the film clip, have small groups discuss what it added to their understanding of the *Titanic*.

Language Conventionality and Clarity

increased unfamiliar, academic, or domain-specific words

Teach unfamiliar academic vocabulary in context.

- English Language Support, p. 197
- Applying Academic Vocabulary, p. 198

ZOOM IN ON **DETERMINING WORD MEANING** Tell students that with a video, they can use the visual context to help determine the meanings of unfamiliar words. Model how to pause the clip and look for visual clues to the meaning of the terms *bow* and *stern*.

- Before students view the video, instruct them to jot down any unfamiliar terms that they encounter.
- During their second viewing, have students pause at these terms to examine the visual context. Ask volunteers to identify any visual elements that helped them determine meaning.

Knowledge Demands

somewhat complex concepts

Help students understand the historical background of the documentary.

- Teacher's Edition Background note, p. 197

ZOOM IN ON **BUILDING HISTORICAL BACKGROUND** Have students read and discuss the Background note on page 197.

- Invite students to share any prior knowledge of the expedition.
- Review what students already know about the sinking of the *Titanic*.
- After they view the clip, discuss and list new information they learned.

Suggested Reader/Task Considerations

You might consider the following before assigning this documentary to students:

- Do students have an interest in the genre?
- Do students have prior experience with the genre that will help them manage the content?

ZOOM IN ON **SUPPORTING COMPREHENSION**

- Explain that advances in technology have made the documentary genre more popular. People make documentaries to present information, to inform people about issues, and to motivate people to take action. Have small groups share ideas about documentaries that they would like to see or make.
- Have students recall and review other documentaries that they have seen. Elicit examples, such as nature films, biographies, or public-service videos. Encourage students to cite the specific features of any documentaries that they have found memorable.

Background Have students read the background information about *Titanic at 100: Mystery Solved*. Explain that for years people didn't know exactly what caused the *Titanic* to sink. The discovery of the ship in 1985 by ocean explorers offered the possibility for scientists to find new clues to help them piece together the mystery. By studying the *Titanic*'s wreckage on the ocean floor, the expedition hoped to uncover facts and details that would help them come closer to proving theories discussed for decades.

SETTING A PURPOSE Direct students to use the Setting a Purpose text to focus their attention as they watch and listen to the documentary. Remind them to generate questions as they view the film clip.

Interpret Diverse Media

RI 7, SL 2

Explain to students that a **documentary** is a fact-based film that tells about real-life people, places, and events. As a form, it often combines interviews, eyewitness accounts, and other sources to present information about a particular topic.

Ⓐ ASK STUDENTS to integrate information from the Background and Setting a Purpose sections to discuss what kinds of images the documentary may include. *(Possible responses: photos of the* Titanic *on the ocean floor; filmed interviews with experts; diagrams of the ship.)*

Integrate Information

RI 7, SL 2

Explain that to **integrate** information means to put together facts, details, and other evidence from one source or from several sources in order to develop a better understanding of a topic.

Ⓑ ASK STUDENTS to integrate the information from *A Night to Remember,* the information presented here, and their own knowledge of documentary film to discuss what kind of information each source will contribute to the topic. *(Possible responses: the film is about current events, and the excerpt is about the past; both tell about a group of people brought together by a significant event.)*

Background *On April 14, 1912, at 11:40 P.M. ship's time, the great passenger ship RMS* Titanic *struck an iceberg in the North Atlantic Ocean. Hours later, in the early morning of April 15,* Titanic *plunged through the deep, frigid waters to the bottom of the sea.* Titanic *lay on the ocean floor undiscovered, until 1985, when it was finally found by ocean explorer Bob Ballard. In 2010, a group of the world's top underwater experts from the Woods Hole Oceanographic Institute took part in an expedition to the wreckage site to find out what might have caused the catastrophe.*

MEDIA ANALYSIS

from TITANIC at 100: Mystery Solved

Documentary by James Cameron

SETTING A PURPOSE Did *Titanic* have a fatal flaw? Was *Titanic* a weak ship? The research team in the documentary clip you are about to view believes they finally know the answers to these century-old questions. Using the team's images of the remains of the ship and interviews with experts, **Ⓐ** the documentary describes the dramatic circumstances of *Titanic*'s sinking.

As you view the documentary, pay attention to how scientists and other experts use the expedition's information to understand exactly how and why *Titanic* sank. Also pay attention to similarities and differences you notice between what the documentary reveals and what you learned in reading the narrative from *A Night to Remember*. **Ⓑ**

(cbg) ©Getty Images; (inset) ©68/Corbis

English Language Support

View Closely Explain that people use specialized vocabulary—in this case, nautical terms—to talk about ships and sailing. Point out that knowing these terms will help them better understand how the *Titanic* broke apart and sank. Pause the documentary from time to time and model how to use visual cues and, where necessary, a dictionary to determine the meanings of such unfamiliar words such as *bow, stern, deckhouse, tower,* and *galley deck.*

TEACH

CLOSE READ

AS YOU VIEW Have students read this section to help them focus their viewing on how the information is presented and how it helps them understand the sinking of the *Titanic* with more depth. Remind them to pause, replay, or rewind the video to make notes, ask questions, or discuss anything they do not understand.

Interpret Diverse Media

RI 7,
SL 2

Explain that documentary filmmakers use different kinds of features to present a variety of information.

○ ASK STUDENTS to review the features listed in the As You View section and discuss what each feature is. *(Possible response: Narration is the voice of someone who is not on screen.)* Then have students integrate the information presented here with their own knowledge to discuss how each feature could be used. *(Possible responses: Interviews could present experts' opinions. Music could create suspense.)*

As students view the video, ask them to integrate the information from different features in the film, as well as from the excerpt from *A Night to Remember*, to reach a deeper understanding of the night the *Titanic* sank.

COLLABORATIVE DISCUSSION Have students work in a small group to list pieces of new evidence the expedition found. Then have them work together to describe the conclusions scientists drew from each piece of evidence. Students can then discuss whether these conclusions seem appropriate and logical.

ASK STUDENTS to share any questions they generated in the course of viewing and discussing the documentary.

MEDIA

Format: Documentary
Running Time: 5:02

AS YOU VIEW As you view the clip from the documentary, consider how the information is presented and the impact it has on your understanding of the sinking of *Titanic*. Notice how the documentary explains the scientists' ideas, using different combinations of animation, interviews, film clips, narration, and sound, including music. Consider how each of these elements helps you understand the sequence of events and how scientists now interpret those events. As needed, pause the video and write notes about what impresses you and about ideas or questions you might want to talk about later. Replay or rewind the video so that you can clarify anything you do not understand.

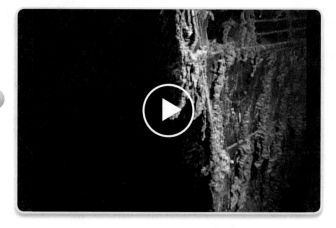

COLLABORATIVE DISCUSSION With a small group, discuss how the discovery of new evidence has changed ideas about why the RMS *Titanic* sank. What techniques does the film clip use to convey these new ideas and evidence? Cite specific segments from the documentary to support your conclusions about what you learned.

APPLYING ACADEMIC VOCABULARY

constraint	significant

THINK-PAIR-SHARE Have partners answer and discuss the questions below. Encourage them to use the vocabulary words *constraint* and *significant* in their responses. Ask volunteers to share their responses with the class.

- What **constraints** did scientists experience when exploring the *Titanic*?
- How did **significant** improvements in imaging and other equipment help scientists to learn more about the *Titanic's* sinking?

Interpret Diverse Media

A **documentary** is a nonfiction film that tells about important people, historic places, or major events. The purpose of a documentary may be to inform, to explain, or to persuade. Filmmakers gather information about a topic and present the material in an engaging way by using features such as these:

Feature of a Documentary	How the Feature Might Be Used
Voice-over narration: the voice of an unseen speaker	• tells viewer what is most important • summarizes key scenes or events
Interviews: question-and-answer conversations	• provide information from experts • present another side to the story
Animation: the process of displaying images so they appear to move	• heightens interest • provides visual support for complex ideas • summarizes key ideas visually
Footage: recorded material such as reenactments, film clips, or news reports	• brings the topic to life • provides details of a historical time • reveals insights
Primary sources: material such as photos, diaries, or recordings from an event	• show real-life experiences • provide details of a historical time • provide reliable evidence

To interpret the information presented in *Titanic at 100: Mystery Solved*, examine the film's features and learn what new evidence they contribute to the topic of why *Titanic* sank. As you review the documentary ask yourself:

- How is each feature used?
- What new information is presented?

Integrate Information

To **integrate** information means to take individual pieces of information and synthesize, or combine, them in order to develop a coherent, or clearer, understanding of a topic. Think about new or important information presented in *Titanic at 100*. Then think about important information presented in *A Night to Remember*. To integrate information from both sources, ask yourself:

- What specific information does each source contribute?
- What features do the sources share? What features are unique to each source?

Titanic at 100: Mystery Solved **199**

TO CHALLENGE STUDENTS...

Analyze Style How does Walter Lord's style in *A Night to Remember* compare to that of James Cameron's style in *Titanic at 100: Mystery Solved*? Have students discuss how Lord's and Cameron's approaches to the *Titanic* are the same and different. Remind them to discuss style in terms of word choice, sentence structure, imagery, and tone. Have them present their ideas to others when they are finished.

CLOSE READ

Interpret Diverse Media

Help students understand the different kinds of features used by documentary filmmakers to convey information. Discuss which features were included in the clip from *Titanic at 100: Mystery Solved*.

Next, have students name the feature that they found was the most powerful in conveying information in the documentary. *(Possible answer: The animation was the strongest feature in the documentary. It showed how the* Titanic *sank and broke apart.)*

English Language Support

Review the features of a documentary by locating and replaying specific examples in *Titanic at 100*. Guide students to identify and repeat the name of each feature. If possible, have small groups view and locate these features in other documentaries.

Integrate Information

Remind students that they watched a documentary and read a historical narrative about the sinking of the *Titanic*. Help students understand that you can connect the ideas between both of these sources. Point out that when you put together the information from more than one source, you **integrate,** or synthesize, it.

Discuss with students the kinds of information *A Night to Remember* added to their understanding of what happened to the *Titanic*. *(Possible answer: It gave firsthand information about what was happening on the ship and how the people on board reacted to the initial problem.)*

Analyze Media

RI 2,
RI 7

Possible answers:

1. *The central idea is that the Titanic sank because of stresses that no structure could withstand, rather than previous ideas that it was a weak ship or had fatal flaws. This is based on new findings about where debris from the ship landed on the ocean floor, the position of important pieces of that debris, and the discovery of a large section of the ship that was previously thought to have been destroyed.*

2. *Primary sources include reports from experts and 2-D and 3-D photos of the ship's wreckage on the ocean floor. The filmmaker uses these materials as evidence for what happened as the ship sank.*

3. *The filmmaker uses voiceover narration while showing scenes of the Titanic's wreckage and how the ship broke apart. The narrator describes events that happened after the Titanic hit the iceberg and summarizes key discoveries and important points in the documentary.*

4. *The filmmaker uses a reenactment that is supported by real photos and expert analysis to describe and show what happened; uses interviews with experts to provide insights and further information; and uses animation to show how the wreckage broke apart.*

5. *The evidence is convincing because of new information gathered from photos and from interviews. Experts can learn a lot from the location and position of the debris and from examining the actual wreckage itself.*

6. *The description and dialogue in A Night to Remember present eyewitness accounts and tell events as they happen, so the reader feels the drama, tension, and fear, and learns details of the actual experience. The documentary presents events visually and with audio, such as screams and crash sounds, bringing the event to life. The new information in the documentary helps the viewer understand how the ship sank.*

English Language Support

Organize the class into six small groups and assign one question to each group. When all the groups have finished, let them take turns presenting their answers to the class. Encourage the class to provide each group with useful feedback.

Analyze Media

RI 7, W 4,
SL 2, SL 5

Cite Text Evidence   Support your responses with evidence from the media.

1. **Infer** What is the **central idea,** or most important idea about a topic, that the filmmaker wants to convey in *Titanic at 100: Mystery Solved*? Explain how this idea is supported in the documentary.

2. **Interpret** What primary sources are included in the film clip? Explain how and why the filmmaker uses these materials.

3. **Analyze** When does the filmmaker use voiceover narration? What information do you learn from the narration that images alone don't convey?

4. **Analyze** Which features does the filmmaker use to help you understand the actual events that took place during the sinking of *Titanic* and how the passengers and crew reacted to these events?

5. **Evaluate** Do you find the new evidence about *Titanic* convincing? Why or why not?

6. **Integrate** Using information from *A Night to Remember* and from *Titanic at 100: Mystery Solved*, explain how effectively the two sources present events and bring them to life. What techniques unique to each source, print and media, help you understand the issues surrounding *Titanic*'s voyage?

PERFORMANCE TASK

Media Activity: Multimedia Presentation: Create a multimedia presentation or poster that describes how the excerpt from *A Night to Remember* and the film clip from *Titanic at 100: Mystery Solved* work together to give you a clearer understanding of what happened the night *Titanic* sank.

-   Integrate information from the text with information from the documentary.

-   Create an outline or detailed description of your presentation. Cite evidence for each piece of information. Include quotations.

-   Gather visuals, such as graphics, photos, and illustrations that clarify your ideas.

-   Decide how to organize and present your work. Share your poster display or computer presentation with the class.

Assign this performance task.

PERFORMANCE TASK

RI 7, W 4,
SL 2, SL 5

Media Activity: Multimedia Presentation Have students work in pairs to

-   decide what elements and information they want to include
-   organize the big ideas into an outline
-   create different slides that include text and visuals that support those ideas
-   design the slides and add special effects, if appropriate

Cite Evidence in a Presentation

RI 1

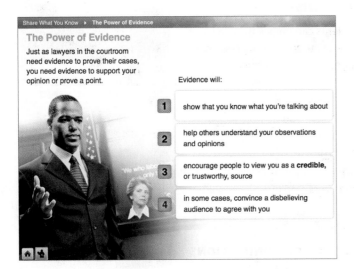

The Power of Evidence

Just as lawyers in the courtroom need evidence to prove their cases, you need evidence to support your opinion or prove a point.

Evidence will:

1. show that you know what you're talking about
2. help others understand your observations and opinions
3. encourage people to view you as a **credible**, or trustworthy, source
4. in some cases, convince a disbelieving audience to agree with you

TEACH

Before students work on the Performance Task, use the whiteboard lesson to review what evidence is and why it is important. Discuss these steps for citing textual evidence:

- **Step 1: Mark Up Details in the Text** Explain that if students cannot mark up the text, they can take notes from it. Remind them to record the title or URL of the source and a page reference, if applicable.
- **Step 2: Find Directly Stated Evidence** When you find evidence you want to use, paraphrase or summarize it in your own words. If you want to cite some text exactly as it appears in the work, put quotation marks around it.
- **Step 3: Make Logical Inferences** Combine details in the text with your own knowledge to make an inference, or a logical guess.

After finishing the whiteboard lesson, explain to students that when making a presentation, they will need to cite evidence to support each main idea. Also explain that evidence for a presentation might include photos and diagrams, information in charts or graphs, and film clips.

PRACTICE AND APPLY

Have students reread *A Night to Remember* and watch *Titanic at 100* again. Ask them to cite evidence to support their ideas about why the *Titanic* sank. Students can use the evidence in their presentations.

Elements of a Documentary

RI 7, SL 2

RETEACH

Remind students that documentary filmmakers use different features to convey and integrate information. Review the following features and the ways they might be used by filmmakers:

- **Voice-over narration** is the voice of an unseen speaker. The narration tells viewers what is most important and summarizes key scenes or events.
- **Interviews** are question-and-answer conversations. They provide information from experts or the experiences of people related to an event.
- **Animation** is the process of displaying images so they appear to move. Animation heightens interest, provides visual support for complex ideas, and summarizes key ideas visually, making them easier to understand.
- **Footage** is recorded material, such as reenactments, film clips, or news reports.
- **Primary sources** are materials such as photos, diaries, or recordings from an event. They show real-life experiences, provide details of a historical time, and provide reliable evidence.

Display *Titanic at 100* for students. Go through the documentary together. Ask students to look for one film feature at a time. Pause when students identify one and discuss it together, deciding what its intended effect was and whether the feature is successful or not. Discuss how to integrate the information from each feature with other features in the film and then restate it together. Continue until students feel comfortable with most or all of the film features.

PRACTICE AND APPLY

Have students watch another documentary, approaching it as a close viewing opportunity, as with *Titanic at 100*. Ask students to work on their own to list the different kinds of features in the documentary and what the intent of each feature was. Have students compare lists and then tell how each feature contributed to the documentary and helped them integrate and understand information.

DEALING WITH DISASTER

The FYI site provides links to online articles from a variety of magazines and newspapers. Help students choose a few articles to read to further their exploration of the topic Dealing with Disaster.

NOVELWISE

Students can unlock the power of novels with this unique resource. Help students read through longer works with these tips:

- Find a Book
- Before You Read
- As You Read
- After You Read

Each book includes introductory material, worksheets, graphic organizers, and discussion guides.

ADDITIONAL TEXTS BY COLLECTION

Suggest students read:

- "The Story of an Eyewitness" by Jack London
- *from* Snow-bound: A Winter Idyll by John Greenleaf Whittier
- *from* The Diary of Samuel Pepys, "The Great London Fire, 1666"

Have students pick two works and compare points of view.

NONFICTION CONNECTIONS

Suggest that students increase their reading of informational texts. The nonfiction connections include

- speeches
- diaries
- true-life accounts
- newspaper articles
- political cartoons

Creating an Independent Reading Program

DAILY SCHEDULED TIME

Daily scheduled time for independent reading allows students to finish the books they select, and helps them develop good independent reading habits.

- Schedule a time when students can read quietly, such as before the bell rings or at the end of class. Try to keep the same time each day.
- Ask students to pick a reasonable length of time to read. Appoint a student to monitor the time.

EXPECTATIONS FOR READING

Clear expectations will help students develop good lifelong reading habits.

- Work with students to create rules for silent reading time. Post the rules where they can be seen.
- Work with parents and families to establish a homework reading policy. Encourage parents to read with their students. Give them a progress report they can fill out to track reading.
- Hold reading contests throughout the school year. Start with easily accomplished tasks, like reading for the most days in a row. As the year goes on, make the contests more challenging, such as reading 5 news articles in a week or reading books of over 75 pages.

PERFORMANCE TASK A

Interactive Lessons

To help you complete this task, use
• *Conducting Research*
• *Using Media in a Presentation*

Create a Multimedia Presentation

Would you know what to do in the event of a natural disaster, such as the tsunami you read about in this collection? With a partner, create a multimedia presentation on how to prepare for a tsunami or other natural disaster, using "Mammoth Shakes and Monster Waves," other selections from this collection, and your own research.

W 8 Gather relevant information.
SL 4 Present claims, findings, and evidence.
SL 5 Include multimedia components and visual displays.
SL 6 Adapt speech to a variety of contexts and tasks.

A successful multimedia presentation

- has a clear and consistent focus
- presents ideas clearly and logically
- includes graphics, text, music, and/or sound that effectively supports key points
- is organized in a way that is interesting and appropriate to purpose and audience
- conveys the presenter's knowledge of the topic

PLAN

Gather Information Use the annotation tools in your eBook to gather information about the survivors from "Mammoth Shakes and Monster Waves" and other texts. What can you learn about preparedness from their actions? Save each piece of information to *my*Notebook, in a folder titled *Collection 3 Performance Task*.

hmhfyi.com

Visit hmhfyi.com to explore your topic and enhance your research.

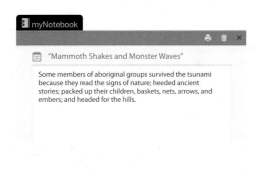

myNotebook

"Mammoth Shakes and Monster Waves"

Some members of aboriginal groups survived the tsunami because they read the signs of nature; heeded ancient stories; packed up their children, baskets, nets, arrows, and embers; and headed for the hills.

ACADEMIC VOCABULARY

As you plan and deliver your presentation, be sure to use the academic vocabulary words.

circumstance
constraint
impact
injure
significant

CREATE A MULTIMEDIA PRESENTATION

W 8, SL 4, SL 5, SL 6

Introduce students to the Performance Task by reading the introductory paragraph with them and reviewing the criteria for what makes a good multimedia presentation. Point out to students that the purpose for their presentation will be to inform others. Students may complete this Performance Task in connection with their study of Earth science. Coordinate with science teachers as appropriate.

PLAN

DO RESEARCH

Explain to students that because they are making a multimedia presentation, they will be looking for more than text sources as they do research. Point out that students should look for graphics, music, sounds, and video that will convey relevant information to viewers at the same time as it engages them.

English Language Support

Plan a Multimedia Presentation Remind students that their presentations should focus on how to prepare for a specific type of natural disaster. As students review the collection texts for information about disaster preparedness, encourage them to note facts, details, and examples related to the event that they have chosen. Ask pairs to answer and discuss the following questions:

- What type of disaster is the topic of your presentation?
- What information from the collection texts relates to your topic?

- What information will you look for as you do further research?
- What types of media will support your key ideas?
- How will multimedia elements help engage and inform your audience?

Students can use their conversations to help them focus their research and plan their presentations.

English Language Support

Express Opinions Point out that students' presentations will offer recommendations on how to prepare for hypothetical, not actual, situations. As students discuss their ideas, model how to use helping verbs, such as *can, could, should, would,* and *might,* to express opinions about possibilities or expectations of their disaster. Share the following examples:

• If you think a hurricane *might* strike in your area, you *should* cover your windows.

• An earthquake *can* happen at any moment, but many people don't know how they *would* protect themselves in a shaking building.

• Having a first aid kit *could* help save someone's life.

Encourage students to include these helping verbs in their presentations.

PRODUCE

DRAFT AND DESIGN YOUR PRESENTATION

Explain to students that the text and multimedia components need to work together to present information to viewers. Remind students that all multimedia should support the points they want to make in their presentations. Suggest that students choose only the best examples to include, so as to avoid overwhelming their audience.

WHEN STUDENTS STRUGGLE ...

Integrate Multimedia Elements Make sure students understand that each multimedia component in a presentation should help emphasize the main idea. Have small groups discuss ways to integrate multimedia effectively into their presentations. For example, they might animate a disaster-preparedness checklist or incorporate a video showing the effects of a disaster or illustrating a survival skill.

Do Research Review at least two print and digital sources to find out what you can do to prepare for a tsunami or other natural disaster.

Interactive Lessons
For help with conducting research, use
• Conducting Research: Types of Sources

• Consider these research questions: What are the warning signs? What can you do before, during, and after the disaster?

• Find facts, details, and examples to support your points.

• Identify multimedia components—such as graphics, maps, videos, or sound—that emphasize your points.

• Use credible sources. Use keywords to find books in the library. Use an Internet search engine to find other sources.

Organize Your Ideas Create an outline that identifies each topic and subtopic in your presentation. Then map out your ideas in a graphic organizer, such as a storyboard, to help you present them clearly and logically.

Consider Your Purpose and Audience Who will watch and listen to your presentation? What do you want your audience to know?

PRODUCE

my WriteSmart

Produce a rough draft of your presentation using the authoring software of your choice. Then upload your draft to *my*WriteSmart for a peer and teacher review.

Draft and Design Your Presentation Think about how you want your presentation to look. Choose type styles and graphics that are appropriate for your purpose.

• Draft main ideas as headlines followed by bullets that list supporting evidence and information.

• Choose multimedia components that emphasize your most significant points. Make sure you have a clear purpose for each one.

• Check that all text and visuals are large and clear enough so that everyone in the audience can see them.

Interactive Lessons
For help in drafting your presentation, use
• Using Media in a Presentation: Using Presentation Software

English Language Support

Adapt Language Choices Students' headings and bulleted lists should contain the key words and details that they will explain during the presentation. Ask students to share their headings and bulleted lists with a partner. Have them ask each other these questions to adjust word choices.

• Which words are most important to my main points?

• What words could make my points clearer?

• Does each bullet item relate to its heading?

REVISE

Evaluate Your Presentation Use the rubric on the following page to evaluate your presentation. Work with your partner to determine whether your presentation has the intended impact. Consider the following:

- Check that your ideas are clearly and logically presented.
- Verify that your text includes specific and accurate information.
- Examine your visuals to make sure they are relevant and support key points.

Practice Your Presentation Take turns practicing your presentation with your partner. You may want to make a recording of your presentation and watch it together.

- Begin your presentation with a statement that captures the attention of your audience. Then state your thesis, or controlling idea.
- Don't just read your main and supporting ideas. Explain each point.
- Use your voice effectively. Speak loudly enough to be heard, varying your pitch and tone. Avoid using slang words.
- Maintain eye contact. Look directly at individuals in your audience.
- Use gestures and facial expressions to emphasize ideas and express emotion.

PRESENT

Deliver Your Presentation Finalize your multimedia presentation and share it with your audience. Consider the following options:

- Use your presentation to present a news report about emergency preparedness.
- Make a video recording of your presentation and share it on your class or school website.
- Organize a group discussion to share your ideas about emergency preparedness where you live.

myWriteSmart

Have a group of peers review your draft in *my*WriteSmart, along with your multimedia elements. Ask your reviewers to note any ideas or visuals that are unclear or not in a logical sequence.

Interactive Lessons
For help with practicing your presentation, use
· *Using Media in a Presentation:* Building and Practicing Your Presentation

FOR STUDENTS WITH DISABILITIES

Extend the Completion Time Help students divide their work into manageable segments they can complete over an extended time period. For example, students may prepare and practice the introduction, main body, and conclusion of their presentations at different times. If students create videos of their presentations, suggest they record different sections separately and then combine the sections later. You might also consider modifying students' schedules to let them complete the task during the times of the day that they work more productively, such as early in the day or directly after an activity period.

REVISE

EVALUATE YOUR PRESENTATION

Suggest that partners work together to critique each other's multimedia presentations. Point out that students should not only evaluate the evidence but the presentation as well. Partners may want to figure out ways that they can work together to make their presentations more effective.

PRESENT

DELIVER YOUR PRESENTATION

Students can

- present a news report using information from their presentations. Remind students that news reports answer these questions: *who, what, when, where, why,* and *how*
- work together with partners to make videos of their presentations. Students can upload their videos to the class or school website
- organize a group discussion about emergency preparations in their community. Tell students to share information from their presentations

FOR STANDARD ENGLISH LEARNERS

Use Stress Patterns As students rehearse their presentations, remind them to use formal English. For example, model how to pronounce the following with stress on the second syllable, not the first: *today, decide, refuse, repeat, resist.*

Have partners practice with similar words from their own presentations.

USE THE SCORING RUBRIC

Assign three students to score each presentation, with each student focusing on just one of the three rubric categories. Ask students to write a brief explanation of the reasons for the score they've given.

REFLECT ON THE PROCESS

Tell students that taking the time to reflect on their planning and presentation processes for this task will help them apply what they've learned and improve their skills. Ask students to think about how well their presentations informed their audience. Then have them briefly respond to the following questions:

- What were your best sources of information on your topic?
- What multimedia elements in your presentation were most effective?
- Was your delivery of the presentation engaging?

PERFORMANCE TASK A RUBRIC
MULTIMEDIA PRESENTATION

	Ideas and Evidence	Organization	Language
4	• The introduction clearly identifies the topic and its purpose and engages the audience. • Important points and steps are supported with relevant facts and details. • The conclusion effectively summarizes the topic and restates the purpose.	• The organization is effective; points and steps are arranged logically. • Text, visuals, and sound are combined in a coherent manner. • Transitions effectively link the steps and inform the reader.	• Oral and written language has a formal style. • Language is precise; unfamiliar terms are explained. • Spelling, capitalization, and punctuation are correct. • Grammar and usage are correct.
3	• The introduction clearly identifies the topic and its purpose but could be more engaging. • Most important points and steps are supported with relevant facts and details. • The conclusion partially summarizes the information and generally restates the purpose.	• The organization is generally effective, but one or two points or steps are out of sequence. • Text, visuals, and sound are mostly combined in a coherent manner. • A few more transitions are needed to link the steps and clarify the information.	• Oral and written language style is inconsistent in a few places. • Most language and terms are precise and clear. • Some spelling, capitalization, and punctuation mistakes occur. • Some grammar and usage errors occur.
2	• The introduction is only partly informative; the topic and purpose are unclear. • Most important points need more support from relevant facts and details. • The conclusion summarizes some of the information but does not restate the purpose.	• The organization has gaps in logic and a confusing sequence. • Text, visuals, and sound are combined in a disorganized way. • More transitions are needed throughout to link important points.	• The language becomes informal in many places. • Some language is precise; some unfamiliar terms are undefined. • Spelling, capitalization, and punctuation are often incorrect, but the ideas are still clear. • Several grammar and usage errors occur.
1	• There is no introduction. • Supporting facts and details are unreliable or missing. • The conclusion is missing.	• The organization is not logical; the sequence of points and steps is disjointed. • Visuals and sound are missing. • No transitions are used, making the presentation difficult to understand.	• The style is inappropriate for the presentation. • Language is too general; unfamiliar terms are not defined. • Spelling, capitalization, and punctuation are incorrect and distracting throughout. • Grammar and usage errors interfere with meaning.

TO CHALLENGE STUDENTS . . .

Plan an Awareness Campaign Challenge students to use data from their presentations to develop plans for a campaign to make the public more aware of disaster preparedness. Encourage students to consider the different communication strategies for sharing information with a wide audience. Students should develop a theme for the campaign and plan informational videos, pamphlets, posters, etc.

Interactive Lessons

To help you complete this task, use
• *Writing Narratives*
• *Writing as a Process*

Write Narrative Nonfiction

In *A Night to Remember*, Walter Lord uses real people's experiences along with facts to give a moment-by-moment account of the events that happened the night the *Titanic* hit an iceberg. Using the same style and tone as Lord, you will write a narrative nonfiction account of the events that happened after the ship hit the iceberg.

W 3a–e Write narratives.
W 4 Produce clear and coherent writing.
W 5 Develop and strengthen writing.
W 6 Use technology to produce and publish writing.

A successful nonfiction narrative

- establishes a situation that introduces real people, places, and events
- organizes an event sequence that unfolds naturally and logically
- uses elements, such as setting, conflict, and dialogue; pacing; and descriptive details to develop people, places, and events
- uses precise words and sensory language to convey events and maintains a consistent style and tone
- provides a conclusion that follows from and reflects on the events

Visit hmhfyi.com to explore your topic and enhance your research.

Mentor Text In this excerpt, notice how the author uses sensory details and precise verbs to convey tension.

 myNotebook

Use the notebook in your eBook to record examples of narrative techniques in the selections that show pacing or descriptive details.

" The berg towered wet and glistening far above the forecastle deck, and both men braced themselves for a crash. "

PLAN

Gather Facts Use print and online sources to research firsthand accounts of events that happened after the *Titanic* hit the iceberg. Then reread the firsthand accounts in *A Night to Remember*. Think about how your research compares to the facts in *A Night to Remember*. Decide which firsthand accounts you will use in your narrative.

ACADEMIC VOCABULARY

As you plan, write, and review your narrative, be sure to use the academic vocabulary words.

circumstance
constraint
impact
injure
significant

WRITE NARRATIVE NONFICTION

W 3a-e, W 4, W 5, W 6

Introduce students to the Performance Task by reading the introductory paragraph with them and reviewing the criteria for what makes a good narrative nonfiction account. Point out that writers of good narrative nonfiction use many of the same literary elements that are found in good stories.

English Language Support

Adapt Language Choices Read aloud the Mentor Text excerpt as students follow along in their texts. Discuss how the verb *towered* in the excerpt creates a more precise meaning than the synonym *stood*. Point out that *towered* helps the reader imagine the feeling that something gigantic is looming above them. Encourage students to analyze other examples of words that help create precise meaning in *A Night to Remember*.

PLAN

ESTABLISH THE SITUATION

Remind students that it is important to map out the sequence of events they will tell about in their narrative nonfiction account. This will help students produce clear and coherent writing. Explain that briefly describing the people, places, and events in their narratives will also help students create vivid scenes and imagery when they begin to write.

English Language Support

Write Narrative Nonfiction Students may require different levels of support as they search for firsthand accounts in print and online sources.

- Monitor students closely as they work in small groups to identify useful and reliable print and online sources.
- Have students share and compare print and online sources with partners. Have them work together to evaluate the usefulness and reliability of the sources.

- Have students create and test a list of keywords to use for online searches. Ask them to rate and display their list of suggested keywords and recommended websites for the class.

PERFORMANCE TASK B

WHEN STUDENTS STRUGGLE...

Brainstorm Imagery Ideas Have students review the information they have gathered and make a list of the mental images they want to convey to readers. Then have pairs work together to jot down words and phrases that describe the sights, sounds, scents, tastes, or feelings that best communicate those images.

PRODUCE

WRITE YOUR NARRATIVE

Remind students to refer to their flow charts as they write their drafts. In particular, point out that students need to pay close attention to make sure that the events and details they use are from real life—that they were actually things that happened and were connected to the *Titanic*. Ask students to keep sensory details in mind as they transform their thoughts into words.

Establish the Situation Narrative nonfiction tells a true story about events that really happened. Identify the events and details of the *Titanic* that you think will have the greatest impact. Then consider how you will develop your narrative.

- Decide who the narrator will be. A narrator can be an observer or a person in the narrative.
- Keep in mind that *A Night to Remember* features strong imagery as well as descriptions of emotions and small details. The author's tone is tense. Consider how you will apply a similar style and tone in your narrative.

Organize Your Information In narrative nonfiction, the story is told in chronological order, or the order in which the events took place. A graphic organizer, such as a flow chart, can help you to describe events in a logical way.

Consider Your Purpose and Audience Focus on the important details and circumstances that you want your audience to understand.

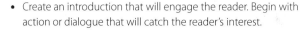
PRODUCE

Write Your Narrative Review your notes and the information in your flow chart as you begin your draft.

- Create an introduction that will engage the reader. Begin with action or dialogue that will catch the reader's interest.
- Use your chart to describe the sequence of events. Include descriptive details to make your story come alive.
- Use short sentences for fast-paced action. Use longer sentences to put more emphasis on a major event.
- Choose precise words and phrases that involve the senses and capture the action.
- Bring your narrative to a conclusion by telling how the events ended and giving the reader a new insight.

WriteSmart

Write your rough draft in *my*WriteSmart. Focus on getting your ideas down, rather than on perfecting your choice of language.

Interactive Lessons
For help in writing your draft, use
- *Writing Narratives: Narrative Techniques*

English Language Support

Understand Text Structure Distribute or display the Student Model that accompanies *Interactive Lessons: Writing Narratives*. Ask students to explain how the writer uses imagery and descriptive details in the first paragraph to engage interest. Point out that the story is organized sequentially, using connecting words such as *then* and *when*. Then discuss the writer's use of short and long sentences to control the pacing of the story. Review the following examples from the Student Model:

- Shorter sentences to show fast-paced action: *Sirak stood up. He walked over to Pravat... Sirak looked down at his clothes. His own clothes and jeans were black. "Come join us," he told Pravat and smiled.*
- Longer sentences to emphasize major ideas or events: *He was little when his family had left their home to move to Miami, but he hadn't forgotten the ugly cawing noise of those disgusting, big black birds.*
- Post an annotated copy of the model that students can refer to as they write.

Language Conventions: Verbs and Verb Phrases

A **verb** expresses an action, a condition, or state of being. Helping verbs such as *is*, *could*, *has*, and *might*, can be combined with verbs to form **verb phrases**. The **tense** of a verb is actually a form of the verb that shows the time of the action. The tenses of verbs and verb phrases allow you to describe present, past, and future events. Read the following passage.

> " Marguerite Frolicher, a young Swiss girl accompanying her father on a business trip, woke up with a start. Half-asleep, she could only think of the little white lake ferries at Zurich making a sloppy landing. "

The author uses different tenses of verbs and verb phrases to describe actions that happened in the past as well as actions that are still ongoing.

REVISE

Evaluate Your Nonfiction Narrative Have your partner or group of peers review your draft. Use this chart to revise it.

Questions	Tips	Revision Techniques
Do I use narrative elements such as setting, conflict, and dialogue?	**Underline** details that show when and where the experience happened.	**Add** details about setting and conflict. Include dialogue for some of the survivors.
Do I use a clear and consistent point of view?	**Highlight** pronouns such as *I, my, you, he,* and *she.*	**Change** pronouns that cause a shift in the point of view.
Do I tell events in chronological order?	**Underline** words that show time order.	**Connect** events with words and phrases that show time order.
Do I use sensory language to develop the events?	**Underline** words and phrases that appeal to the senses.	**Add** words and phrases that describe sights, sounds, and feelings.
Do I use verbs and verb phrases to tell when events occurred?	**Highlight** verbs and verb phrases.	**Add** verbs and verb phrases that describe when the action takes place.
Does my conclusion tell how the situation ended?	**Underline** the conclusion.	**Add** a sentence that tells how the situation ended.

myWriteSmart

Have a partner or a group of peers review your draft in *my*WriteSmart. Ask your reviewers to note any events that seem out of sequence or language that is unclear or confusing.

Interactive Lessons
For help in revising your draft, use
• *Writing as a Process: Revising and Editing*

PRESENT

Create a Finished Copy Finalize your narrative. You might present it as an author's reading to the class.

FOR STANDARD ENGLISH LEARNERS

Adapt Speech Remind students of the differences between formal speech and informal conversation. As they practice their narrative presentations, encourage students to pay special attention to words ending in final *g*. Suggest that speaking slowly and clearly can help them focus on their pronunciation.

PERFORMANCE TASK B

REVISE

LANGUAGE CONVENTIONS

Have students check their drafts against their graphic organizer to make sure they have used verb tenses that accurately reflect the sequence of events. Tell students to look for places in their draft where they can add verbs and verb phrases to clarify when actions and events take place.

REVISE

EVALUATE YOUR NONFICTION NARRATIVE

Explain to students that, like good stories, narrative nonfiction is more engaging when it includes sensory details and vivid action words. Suggest that students use a thesaurus to replace vague words with more interesting ones that precisely describe events, feelings, and thoughts. Explain that this is a good way to develop and strengthen their writing.

PRESENT

CREATE A FINISHED COPY

Students can

• present their narratives to the class. Remind students that they should read with expression

• post their narratives as a blog on a personal or school website. Suggest that others write comments after they read the narrative

• dramatize their narratives in a one-person show. Students may want to create visuals and props to support their dramas as they perform them

FOR STUDENTS WITH DISABILITIES

Prerecord the Presentation Give students the option of pre-recording their narrative presentations. Students can work with a partner to make a video or audio recording, Allow them to work at their own pace, editing and revising their recordings to achieve a smooth presentation.

PERFORMANCE TASK B

USE THE SCORING RUBRIC

Have students score their own narratives using the three rubric categories. Then have pairs exchange narratives and use the language of the rubric to discuss how the writing can be improved in each category.

REFLECT ON THE PROCESS

Ask students to reflect on the experience of writing their narratives. Prompt them to think about the details of planning, producing, and revising that went into their finished product. Have students consider what they learned. Then ask small groups to discuss these questions:

- How did you clarify the sequence of events?
- Did you maintain a consistent point of view and tone throughout?
- How did you use sensory language and vivid details?
- Did your conclusion offer a new insight on the event?

PERFORMANCE TASK B RUBRIC
NARRATIVE NONFICTION

	Ideas and Evidence	Organization	Language
4	• The introduction identifies the experience and setting and creates a strong impression. • Background information helps to explain events. • Dialogue, description, and reflection re-create the experience. • The conclusion reflects on the significance of the experience and leaves readers with a new insight on the event.	• The organization is smooth, effective, and logical; events are organized chronologically. • Pacing is clear and effective. • Transitions logically connect events in sequence.	• Point of view, style, and tone are consistent and effective. • Sensory language and vivid details creatively reveal people, places, and events. • Sentences are varied and have a rhythmic flow. • Tense in verbs and verb phrases is used correctly and clarifies the sequence of events. • Spelling, grammar, usage, and mechanics are correct.
3	• The introduction identifies the experience and setting but could be more compelling. • More background is needed to explain one or two events. • Dialogue and description generally re-create the experience. • The conclusion reflects on the experience.	• The organization is generally logical; the sequence of events is confusing in a few places. • Pacing is somewhat clear. • More transitions would make the sequence of events clearer.	• Point of view, style, and tone are inconsistent in a few places. • Some sensory language is used to reveal some people, places, and events. • Sentences are somewhat varied. • Some errors in the use of tense in verbs and verb phrases occur. • Some spelling, grammar, usage, or mechanics errors occur.
2	• The introduction briefly mentions the experience and only hints at the setting. • More background is needed throughout. • Dialogue and description are limited or missing entirely. • The conclusion only hints at the significance of the experience.	• The organization is confusing; missing or extraneous events are distracting. • Pacing is choppy and ineffective. • Few transitions are used throughout.	• Point of view, style, and tone are inconsistent. • Sensory language and details are mostly lacking. • Sentences hardly vary; some fragments or run-on sentences are present. • The use of tense in verbs and verb phrases to help establish sequence of events is mostly lacking. • Multiple spelling, grammar, usage, or mechanics errors occur, but ideas are clear.
1	• The introduction does not present an identifiable experience. • Necessary background is missing. • Dialogue and description are unrelated or missing. • There is no conclusion.	• There is no evident organization or sequence of events. • There is no evident pacing of events. • Transitions are not used, making the narrative difficult to understand.	• Point of view, style, and tone are never established. • Sensory language is not used. • Sentences do not vary; several fragments and run-on sentences are present. • Incorrect use of tense in verbs and verb phrases makes the sequence of events difficult to understand. • Significant spelling, grammar, usage, or mechanics errors create confusion and misunderstanding of ideas.

TO CHALLENGE STUDENTS...

Create a Multimedia Presentation Challenge students to present their narrative as a multimedia presentation. Encourage them to include elements such as photographs, voice-over narration, animation, and clips from reenactments and news reports.

© Fred de Noyelle/Godong/Corbis

Making Your Voice Heard

❝When people don't express themselves,
they die one piece at a time.**❞**

—Laurie Halse Anderson

STREAM TO START

Motivate students to read the collection texts, and spark their curiosity by playing the video for the class. After students view the video, ask them to identify two things they hope to learn from reading about how people express their ideas. Ask volunteers to share their responses.

PERFORMANCE TASK PREVIEW

Point out to students that they will complete a performance task at the end of the collection. The performance task will require them to further analyze the selections in the collection and to synthesize ideas about their analysis. Students will present their findings in a speech.

ACADEMIC VOCABULARY

> ▶ **View It!**
> Professional Development Podcast:
> **Academic Vocabulary**

Students can acquire facility with the academic vocabulary words through frequent, repeated exposure as they analyze and discuss the selections in the collection. Academic vocabulary can be used in the instructional contexts shown below. This will enable students to incorporate the academic vocabulary words into their working vocabulary.

- Collaborative Discussion at the end of each selection
- Analyzing the Text questions for each selection
- Selection-level Performance Task
- Vocabulary instruction (for Critical Vocabulary and/or for Vocabulary Strategy)
- Language Conventions
- End-of-collection Performance Task for all selections in the collection

ASK STUDENTS to review the Academic Vocabulary word list for this collection. You may wish to pronounce each word aloud so students hear the correct pronunciation. Then, discuss the definitions and the related forms for each word. Remind students that they will encounter these five academic vocabulary words throughout the collection.

Making Your Voice Heard

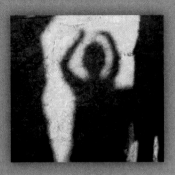

In this collection, you will explore the many ways people express their ideas—and themselves.

Stream to Start   hmhfyi.com   Channel One News®

COLLECTION
PERFORMANCE TASK Preview

At the end of this collection, you will write a speech in which you present an argument either in favor of or against owning exotic animals, using selections from the collection to provide ideas, information, and support. Your challenge will be to justify your opinion with appropriate facts and examples and to convince others to share your opinion.

ACADEMIC VOCABULARY

Study the words and their definitions in the chart below. You will use these words as you discuss and write about the texts in this collection.

Word	Definition	Related Forms
appropriate (ə-prō´prē-ĭt) *adj.*	suitable or acceptable for a particular situation, person, place, or condition	appropriately, appropriateness
authority (ə-thôr´ĭ-tē) *n.*	an accepted source, such as a person or text, of expert information or advice	authoritative
consequence (kŏn´sĭ-kwĕns´) *n.*	something that logically or naturally follows from an action or condition	consequent, consequently, consequential
justify (jŭs´tə-fī´) *v.*	to demonstrate or prove to be just, right, reasonable, or valid	justifiably, justifiable, justification
legal (lē´gəl) *adj.*	permitted by law; of, related to, or concerned with law	legally, legalism, legality, legalize

---

☰ myNotebook

As students read, analyze, and discuss the texts in this collection, encourage them to create a *my*WordList folder in *my*Notebook to build their own personal word lists.

- **Annotate** Students can highlight vocabulary terms and other unfamiliar words and save each highlighted term to *my*Notebook.
- **Organize** Within *my*Notebook, students can drag each word into the *my*WordList folder.
- **Elaborate** Ask students to add details to the entry for each word, such as a definition, other forms of the word, and a sample sentence.

English Language Support

ENGAGE WITH THE COLLECTION TOPIC

Draw students' attention to the title of the collection, Making Your Voice Heard. Explain that *to express yourself* means "to tell others what you think or how you feel about something." *Making your voice heard* refers to your speaking voice and writer's voice and to your ideas. People express themselves in different ways to communicate their ideas to others.

ACCESS PRIOR KNOWLEDGE Read the quotation on page 209 aloud, clarifying the definitions of unfamiliar words for students. Then have students discuss the meaning of the quotation. What "pieces" of a person "die" when they don't express themselves?

DISCUSSION WEB

Use the strategy to help students learn how to support an argument.

- *First,* write a focusing question on the board: *Should people be allowed to keep wild animals as pets?* Introduce "Wild Animals Aren't Pets" and "Let People Own Exotic Animals," explaining that they concern a debatable topic, one that people hold differing opinions about. Have students read the texts.
- *Then,* after students have finished reading, point out that more than one answer to the focus question is possible. Each answer may be supported by reasons and evidence.

Lead students in a discussion of possible answers to the focus question, guiding them to identify information needed to construct a sound argument for each answer.
- *Next,* provide students with graphic organizers they can use to identify reasons and evidence and to structure arguments to support each contrasting opinion.
- *Finally,* have students select one opinion and, using their organizers, write a brief argument in its support.

Collection 4 Digital Resources for English Language Support

LANGUAGE WORKSHOP
Designated English Learners

Use the Teacher Resources > Language Workshop to support English learners in justifying opinions, using verbs to express inferences, and participating in discussions.

 VIDEOS

This video will help students learn how to compare arguments. Have students use **Text In Focus Practice** to apply the skills.

COLLECTION 4 DIGITAL OVERVIEW

my SmartPlanner | eBook | myNotebook | *my* WriteSmart | fyi hmhfyi.com

Collection 4 Lessons	Media	Teach and Practice
Student Edition | eBook	▶ **Video Links** HISTORY A&E Channel One News®	**Close Reading and Evidence Tracking**
Short Story by Sabine R. Ulibarrí **"My Wonder Horse"**	▶ **Audio** "My Wonder Horse"	**Strategies for Annotation** • Determine Theme • Interpret Figures of Speech in Context
ANCHOR TEXT Editorial by USA TODAY **"Wild Animals Aren't Pets"** Commentary by Zuzana Kukol **"Let People Own Exotic Animals"**	◀ **Audio** "Wild Animals Aren't Pets" ◀ **Audio** "Let People Own Exotic Animals"	**Close Read Screencasts** "Wild Animals Aren't Pets" • Modeled Discussion (lines 9–16) • Close Read Application PDF (lines 42–48) "Let People Own Exotic Animals" • Modeled Discussion (lines 4–9) • Close Read Application PDF (lines 16–21)	**Text in Focus** • Comparing Arguments (line 1) **Strategies for Annotation** • Trace and Evaluate an Argument • Analyze the Meaning of Words and Phrases • Part-to-Whole Analogies
CLOSE READER Informational Text **"Views on Zoos"**	◀ **Audio** "Views on Zoos"	
EXEMPLAR Short Story by Sandra Cisneros **"Eleven"**	◀ **Audio** "Eleven"	**Strategies for Annotation** • Analyze Word Choice and Tone • Denotations and Connotations
CLOSE READER Short Story by Avi **"What Do Fish Have to Do with Anything?"**	◀ **Audio** "What Do Fish Have to Do with Anything?"	
Poem by Pat Mora **"A Voice"** Poem by Langston Hughes **"Words Like Freedom"**	◀ **Audio** "A Voice" ◀ **Audio** "Words Like Freedom"	**Strategies for Annotation** • Determine the Meaning of Figurative Language
Collection 4 Performance Task: Present an Argument in a Speech	fyi **hmhfyi.com**	**Interactive Lessons** Writing an Argument Using Textual Evidence Giving a Presentation

For Systematic Coverage of Writing and Speaking & Listening Standards	**Interactive Lessons** Using Textual Evidence Using Media in a Presentation

For foundational skills and reading intervention support:

Assess		Extend	Reteach
Performance Task	✅ *Assess It Online!*	**Teacher eBook**	**Teacher eBook**
Writing Activity: Informative Essay	Selection Test	**Explain Point of View and Narrator > Interactive Whiteboard Lesson >** Point of View	**Determine Theme: > Level Up Tutorial >** Theme
Writing Activity: Argument	Selection Test	**Paraphrase**	**Compare and Contrast: Arguments > Level Up Tutorials >** Elements of an Argument > Analyzing Arguments
Speaking Activity: Collaborative Discussion	Selection Test		**Characterization > Interactive Whiteboard Lesson >** Character Development **Analyze Style > Level Up Tutorial >** Author's Style
Writing Activity: Poem	Selection Test	**Determine Theme > Interactive Whiteboard Lesson >** Theme/Central Idea	**Determine Meaning: Figurative Language > Level Up Tutorial >** Figurative Language
Present an Argument in a Speech	Collection Test		

Lesson Assessments Using Textual Evidence Using Media in a Presentation	**Standards Support and Enrichment**	For more instruction and practice in reading literary and informational texts, language, spelling, and speaking and listening, see Teacher Resources > Standards Support and Enrichment.
	For Designated English Language Instruction	To provide scaffolded support specific to the needs of English Learners during Designated English Language instruction, use the selection- and standards-aligned lessons found in Teacher Resources > Language Workshop.

Collection 4 Lessons	Key Learning Objective	Performance Task	Vocabulary Strategy
Short Story by Sabine R. Ulibarrí **"My Wonder Horse," p. 211A** **Lexile 610L**	**The student will be able to . . .** interpret themes and identify internal and external conflict in the context of a short story.	Writing Activity: Informative Essay	Interpret Figures of Speech in Context
ANCHOR TEXT **Editorial by USA TODAY** **"Wild Animals Aren't Pets," p. 223A** **Lexile 1170L** **Commentary by Zuzana Kukol** **"Let People Own Exotic Animals," p. 223A** **Lexile 1180L**	**The student will be able to . . .** trace and evaluate an argument, analyze persuasive techniques, and compare and contrast two arguments on the same topic.	Writing Activity: Argument	Part-to-Whole Analogies
EXEMPLAR **Short Story by Sandra Cisneros** **"Eleven," p. 233A** **Lexile 1090L**	**The student will be able to . . .** analyze an author's style and tone and describe characterization in a short story.	Speaking Activity: Collaborative Discussion	Denotations and Connotations
Poem by Pat Mora **"A Voice," p. 241A** **Poem by Langston Hughes** **"Words Like Freedom," p. 241A**	**The student will be able to . . .** identify figurative language and analyze tone in poetry.	Writing Activity: Poem	

Collection 4 Performance Task:

Present an Argument in a Speech

Language Conventions	English Language Support	Differentiated Instruction	CLOSE READER Selection
Improving Expression	• Analyze Language • Summarize Conflict • Word Study • Support Opinions • Adapt Language Choices	**When Students Struggle:** Internal and External Conflict **To Challenge Students:** Analyze Setting **For Standard English Learners:** • Irregular Reflexive Pronouns • Subject-Verb Agreement	
Spell Words Correctly	• Trace and Evaluate an Argument • Analyze Language • Express Opinions • Discussion Web • Write and Spell Words Correctly • Paraphrase	**When Students Struggle:** Persuasive Language **For Students with Disabilities:** Spell Correctly	Informational Text "Views on Zoos," p. 232b
Punctuating Dialogue	• Evaluate Language Choices • Express Inferences and Conclusions • Write Dialogue • Write and Spell Words Correctly • Paraphrase	**When Students Struggle:** Make Inferences **To Challenge Students:** Analyze Point of View **For Standard English Learners:** Pronunciation	Short Story by Avi "What Do Fish Have to Do with Anything?" p. 240b **Lexile 430L**
	• Improve Reading Fluency • Evaluate Language • Analyze Language Choices • Analyze Tone	**When Students Struggle:** Analyze Tone **To Challenge Students:** Analyze Perspective **For Students with Disabilities:** Compare Metaphors and Similies	
Adverbial Phrases	Plan to Present an Argument Use Academic Words Adapt Language Choices Express Opinions	**For Standard English Learners:** Adapt Speech **When Students Struggle:** Organize Information **For Students with Disabilities:** Practice on Camera **To Challenge Students:** Create a Public Service Video	

My Wonder Horse

Short Story by Sabine R. Ulibarrí

Why This Text?

Students regularly encounter complex works of fiction that present a variety of challenges. This lesson explores the themes and conflicts in a coming-of-age story in which a boy struggles to come to terms with life and its challenges.

► View It!

Professional Development Podcast:

Text-Dependent Analysis

Key Learning Objective: The student will be able to interpret themes and identify internal and external conflict in the context of a short story.

RL 1 Cite text evidence; make inferences.
RL 2 Determine a theme or central idea.
RL 3 Describe story elements.
RL 4 Determine the meaning of words and phrases.
RL 5 Analyze structure.
RL 6 Explain point of view.
W 2 Write informative/explanatory texts.
W 6 Use technology to produce and publish writing.
W 7 Conduct short research projects.
SL 1 Engage effectively in a range of collaborative discussions.
L 1e Recognize variations from standard English and identify and use strategies to improve expression.
L 4a Use context as a clue to meaning.
L 4d Verify preliminary determination of meaning.
L 5a Interpret figures of speech.
L 6 Acquire and use grade-appropriate general academic vocabulary.

▲ Text Complexity Rubric

Quantitative Measures	**My Wonder Horse** Lexile: 610L
Qualitative Measures	**Levels of Meaning/Purpose**  multiple levels of meaning (multiple themes)
	Structure 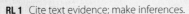 complex, unfamiliar story concepts
	Language Conventionality and Clarity  figurative, less accessible language
	Knowledge Demands somewhat unfamiliar experience
Reader/Task Considerations	• Teacher determined • Vary by individual reader and type of text • See the Text X-Ray for suggested Reader/Task Considerations.

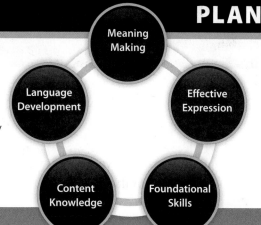

TEXT X-RAY **English Language Support** Before teaching, use the Text X-Ray for an overview of the text's complexity. The Text X-Ray and the supports and scaffolds in the Teacher's Edition will help you guide students of different skill levels.

Text Complexity: Qualitative Measures

Levels of Meaning/Purpose

multiple levels of meaning (multiple themes)

Help students determine theme.

- Teacher's Edition side notes, pp. 211, 213, 218, 219, 220
- English Language Support, p. 211
- Strategies for Annotation, p. 219
- Determine Theme, p. 219

To teach students to examine point of view and narrator, see

- Explain Point of View and Narrator, p. 222a

To reteach how to determine theme, see

Determine Theme, p. 222a

 Use It! **Interactive Whiteboard Lesson:** Point of view
Level Up Tutorial: Theme

ZOOM IN ON DETERMINING THEME Explain that a **theme** is the message of a story. Readers can determine a theme by paying attention to symbols the author uses and lessons the characters learn. A **symbol** is a person, place, or thing that stands for something else, such as an idea.

- Read aloud lines 68–71 and point out the phrase "a white horse occupied my dreams."
- Ask students what the narrator's dreams are like. *(He is dreaming of adventures involving the white horse.)* What is he feeling? *(anticipation)*
- Point out that dreams often stand for wishes in stories.

Structure

complex, unfamiliar story concepts

Help students describe the conflict in a short story.

- Teacher's Edition side notes, pp. 212, 213, 215, 216, 219, 220
- English Language Support, p. 212, 216
- Strategies for Annotation, p. 221
- When Students Struggle, p. 215
- Describe Stories: Conflict, p. 219

ZOOM IN ON DESCRIBING STORIES: CONFLICT
Explain that stories are built around a central internal or external **conflict**, or struggle.

- Give an example of an external conflict, such as a character having a disagreement with another character, and an internal conflict, such as a character having difficulty deciding between two options.
- Ask pairs of students to list examples of external and internal conflicts. Encourage them to think about books they have read to find examples.

Language Conventionality and Clarity

figurative, less accessible language

Teach unfamiliar academic vocabulary in context.
- Teacher's Edition Critical Vocabulary notes, pp. 212, 213, 214, 215, 216, 218
- English Language Support, p. 216
- Applying Academic Vocabulary, p. 213
- Vocabulary Strategy: Interpret Figures of Speech in Context, p. 221
- Strategies for Annotation, p. 221

Guide students to recognize figurative language.
- Teacher's Edition side notes, p. 214
- English Language Support, pp. 211, 212, 214

Help students adjust language for use in different situations.
- Teacher's Edition side note, p. 222
- English Language Support, pp. 216, 218, 222

ZOOM IN ON **INTERPRETING FIGURES OF SPEECH** Review the strategy of questioning to determine the meanings of figures of speech.
- Display lines 50–52. Underline the sentences "He is a statue. He is an engraving." Point out that *he* refers to the horse and an *engraving* is a picture. What does the description tell the reader about how the narrator sees the horse? (*The horse is proud, impressive, and beautiful.*)
- Remind students to use questions to help them understand figures of speech.

Knowledge Demands

somewhat unfamiliar experience

Support English learners in understanding information about the author and subject.
- Teacher's Edition Background note, p. 211
- Image of horse, p. 217

ZOOM IN ON **BUILDING BACKGROUND KNOWLEDGE** Explain that the Wonder Horse is the leader of a herd of wild horses and that the other horses are mares, or female horses.
- Explain what *lasso* (line 32) means. (*A rope with a loop used to capture horses and cows by throwing it around the animal's neck.*)
- Ask students how wild horses might be different from tame horses. List their responses on the board. (*Possible answers: not trained, not fed regularly, not used to being fenced in, don't have horseshoes*)

Suggested Reader/Task Considerations

You might consider the following before assigning this short story to students.
- Are students able to make inferences in order to understand figurative language?
- Have students encountered enough of the vocabulary used to understand the story?

ZOOM IN ON **SUPPORTING COMPREHENSION**
- Explain that personification means to give human traits to an animal, thing, or idea. Ask students how a horse might be given human traits. (*walking tall, shaking head in anger, waiting impatiently*)
- Have students record confusing words and phrases as they read. Then have students pause frequently and discuss problematic language with a partner.

Sabine R. Ulibarrí Have students read the information about the author. Then, explain that "My Wonder Horse" could be classified as a coming-of-age story. Explain that in a coming-of-age story, the main character is a young person who goes on adventures and often faces internal struggles as he or she learns important lessons—sometimes harsh ones—about life and becoming an adult.

Setting a Purpose Direct students to use the Setting a Purpose prompt to focus their reading. Remind students to write down questions as they read.

Determine Theme (LINES 1–12)   RL 1, RL 2

Explain that a theme is a message about life that the writer shares with the reader. Tell them that a theme is usually not stated directly, so readers must figure it out on their own. Explain that one way to determine a theme is to notice important symbols, which are people, places, or things that stand for something else.

Ⓐ CITE TEXT EVIDENCE Have students reread the title and lines 1–12. Ask them to cite the ideas the white horse stands for. Then, have them tell how these ideas might be an important part of the theme in the story. (Possible response: The story says the white horse stands for "fantasy, liberty, and excitement," and "dreams." Because the narrator is telling about his youth, one theme may be a message about the strength and importance of a young person's dreams.)

English Language Support

To help students understand the theme, define and discuss *fantasy, liberty,* and *dreams.* With the group, discuss what the white horse stands for in the narrator's mind.

Sabine R. Ulibarrí (1919–2003) *was born in Tierra Amarilla, a small town in northern New Mexico. Much of his work focuses on preserving the history of this region. Although Ulibarrí is considered one of the most famous Mexican American writers, he did not actually begin to write until he was in his forties. Before that, he was a teacher. Like "My Wonder Horse," most of Ulibarrí's work was originally written in Spanish. This version of "My Wonder Horse" was translated by Thelma Campbell Nason.*

My Wonder Horse

Short Story by Sabine R. Ulibarrí

SETTING A PURPOSE As you read, pay attention to why the narrator is fascinated by the Wonder Horse. Write down any questions you have while reading.

🔲 myNotebook

As you read, mark up the text. Save your work to *my*Notebook.
- Highlight details
- Add notes and questions
- Add new words to *my*WordList

Ⓐ He was white. White as memories lost. He was free. Free as happiness is. He was fantasy, liberty, and excitement. He filled and dominated the mountain valleys and surrounding plains. He was a white horse that flooded my youth with dreams and poetry.

Around the campfires of the country and in the sunny patios of the town, the ranch hands talked about him with enthusiasm and admiration. But gradually their eyes would become hazy and blurred with dreaming. The lively talk
10 would die down. All thoughts fixed on the vision evoked by the horse. Myth of the animal kingdom. Poem of the world of men.

White and mysterious, he paraded his harem through the summer forests with lordly rejoicing. Winter sent him to the plains and sheltered hillsides for the protection of his

(c) ©Getty Images

English Language Support

Analyze Language Explain to students that one tool writers use in fiction is figurative language, or language that does not mean exactly what the words say. Figurative language often compares one thing to another to help the reader understand what the writer wants to say. Explain that when one thing is compared to another thing using the word *like* or *as,* it is called a simile.

- Read aloud the sentence, "He was free. Free as happiness is" in lines 1–2. Ask students to describe what "being free" means. (*being able to do what you want to do or go where you want to go*) How does being free make them feel? (*happy, excited*) Point out the word *as.* Ask students what *free* is being compared to. (*happiness*) Discuss that by saying that the horse is free and then comparing freedom to happiness, the writer is also saying that the horse is like happiness.

Describe Stories: Conflict (LINES 19–34)

RL 1,
RL 3

Explain to students that every story centers on a **conflict**—a problem or struggle that the main character faces. Tell them that an **internal conflict** is a struggle that takes place within a character. An **external conflict** involves a struggle with a force outside the main character, such as nature, a physical obstacle, or another character.

B CITE TEXT EVIDENCE Ask students to reread lines 19–34 and identify the external conflict that the narrator tells about. *(He wants to capture the white horse.)* Ask them to tell how they know this will be a challenge. *(Many have tried, but no one has ever captured the Wonder Horse.)*

English Language Support

Summarize Conflict Explain to students that *conflict* means "a problem or struggle." In stories, the main character faces one or more conflicts. Review the idea of external and internal conflict. Read lines 19–34 aloud with students following along in their books, defining terms as necessary. Then have pairs of students write brief summaries of the conflict described in these lines using complete sentences and the key words *conflict* and *character*. *(Possible response: The main character's conflict is that he wants to catch the white horse, and it is going to be hard because no one has ever done it before.)*

CRITICAL VOCABULARY

lethargy: The author uses the word *lethargy* to describe the feelings that the narrator experiences in the late afternoon.

ASK STUDENTS to point out words in the surrounding text that are related to *lethargy*. *(Possible responses: "slowly," "Listless and drowsy," "dozing")* Then, ask them to tell why *lethargy* is a good choice to explain how one might feel in the late afternoon. *(Possible response: It is a time of day when people often feel sleepy or lack energy.)*

---

females. He spent the summer like an Oriental potentate[1] in his woodland gardens. The winter he passed like an illustrious warrior celebrating a well-earned victory.

20 He was a legend. The stories told of the Wonder Horse were endless. Some true, others fabricated. So many traps, so many snares, so many searching parties, and all in vain. The horse always escaped, always mocked his pursuers, always rose above the control of man. Many a valiant cowboy swore to put his halter and his brand on the animal. But always he had to confess later that the mystic[2] horse was more of a man than he.

I was fifteen years old. Although I had never seen the Wonder Horse, he filled my imagination and fired my ambition. I used to listen open-mouthed as my father and the ranch hands talked about the phantom horse who turned into 30 mist and air and nothingness when he was trapped. I joined in the universal obsession—like the hope of winning the lottery—of putting my lasso on him some day, of capturing him and showing him off on Sunday afternoons when the girls of the town strolled through the streets.

It was high summer. The forests were fresh, green, and gay. The cattle moved slowly, fat and sleek in the August sun and shadow. Listless and drowsy in the **lethargy** of late afternoon, I was dozing on my horse. It was time to round up the herd and go back to the good bread of the cowboy camp. Already 40 my comrades would be sitting around the campfire, playing the guitar, telling stories of past or present, or surrendering to the languor of the late afternoon. The sun was setting behind me in a riot of streaks and colors. Deep, harmonious silence.

I sit drowsily still, forgetting the cattle in the glade. Suddenly the forest falls silent, a deafening quiet. The afternoon comes to a standstill. The breeze stops blowing, but it vibrates. The sun flares hotly. The planet, life, and time itself have stopped in an inexplicable way. For a moment, I don't understand what is happening.

50 Then my eyes focus. There he is! The Wonder Horse! At the end of the glade, on high ground surrounded by summer green. He is a statue. He is an engraving. Line and form and white stain on a green background. Pride, prestige, and art

lethargy
(lĕth´ər-jē) *n.* In a state of *lethargy*, a person experiences drowsiness, inactivity, and a lack of energy.

---

[1] **Oriental potentate** (pōt´n-tāt´): Asian king.
[2] **mystic** (mĭs´tĭk): inspiring a sense of mystery and wonder.

English Language Support

Analyze Language Choices Point out that the author chooses words carefully to produce different effects on the reader. Display this sentence: "Suddenly the forest falls silent, a deafening quiet." Highlight the terms *suddenly* and *deafening quiet*.

- Point out the word *suddenly* and work with students to explain how it signals a change in the scene.
- Have pairs of students examine and explain the shades of meaning in the phrase *deafening quiet*.

incarnate in animal flesh. A picture of burning beauty and virile[3] freedom. An ideal, pure and invincible, rising from the eternal dreams of humanity. Even today my being thrills when I remember him.

A sharp neigh. A far-reaching challenge that soars on high, ripping the virginal fabric of the rosy clouds. Ears at the point. Eyes flashing. Tail waving active defiance. Hoofs glossy and destructive. Arrogant ruler of the countryside.

The moment is never-ending, a momentary eternity. It no longer exists, but it will always live. . . . There must have been mares. I did not see them. The cattle went on their indifferent way. My horse followed them, and I came slowly back from the land of dreams to the world of toil. But life could no longer be what it was before.

That night under the stars I didn't sleep. I dreamed. How much I dreamed awake and how much I dreamed asleep, I do not know. I only know that a white horse occupied my dreams and filled them with vibrant sound, and light, and turmoil.

Summer passed and winter came. Green grass gave place to white snow. The herds descended from the mountains to the valleys and the hollows. And in the town they kept saying that the Wonder Horse was roaming through this or that secluded area. I inquired everywhere for his whereabouts. Every day he became for me more of an ideal, more of an idol, more of a mystery.

It was Sunday. The sun had barely risen above the snowy mountains. My breath was a white cloud. My horse was trembling with cold and fear like me. I left without going to mass. Without any breakfast. Without the usual bread and sardines in my saddlebags. I had slept badly but had kept the **vigil** well. I was going in search of the white light that galloped through my dreams.

On leaving the town for the open country, the roads disappear. There are no tracks, human or animal. Only a silence, deep, white, and sparkling. My horse breaks trail with his chest and leaves an unending wake, an open rift, in the white sea. My trained, concentrated gaze covers the landscape

vigil
(vĭj´əl) *n.* A *vigil* is an act or a time of watching, often during normal sleeping hours.

---

[3] **virile** (vîr´əl): having or showing male spirit, strength, vigor, or power.

My Wonder Horse **213**

CLOSE READ

Determine Theme
RL 1, RL 2, RL 4
(LINES 50–61)

Remind students that an author can use a symbol to help develop a theme in a story.

C **CITE TEXT EVIDENCE** Ask students to reread lines 50–61 and identify words that tell what the Wonder Horse stands for in the narrator's mind. *(Possible responses: "Pride, prestige," "virile freedom," "challenge," "defiance")* Ask why these ideas might be important to a young person. *(Possible responses: Pride, prestige, and freedom are ideas that tell what a young person might want to attain; challenge and defiance speak of things that a young person wants to have or to express, but that may be beyond reach.)* What theme is the author developing with this language? *(Possible response: The dreams we have when we are young are important to us all our lives.)*

Describe Stories: Conflict (LINES 79–85)
RL 1, RL 3

Explain that sometimes a character faces a conflict that is both internal and external.

D **CITE TEXT EVIDENCE** Ask students to reread lines 79–85 and tell how the narrator shows that his quest is an internal conflict as well as an external one. *(Describing that he was "going in search of the white light that galloped through my dreams" shows that the quest is also internal; his search is something he does during the day, in the external world, and he also dreams about it at night.)*

CRITICAL VOCABULARY

vigil: The word *vigil* describes the narrator's efforts to watch for the horse.

ASK STUDENTS to tell why the author might have chosen the word *vigil* to describe the narrator's efforts. *(Possible response: A vigil can describe a period of time, rather than a simple watch; because it often refers to watching at night, vigil also describes how the narrator sees the horse in his dreams.)*

APPLYING ACADEMIC VOCABULARY

appropriate	consequence	justify

Think-Pair-Share Have students turn to a partner to discuss the questions below. Encourage students to include the academic vocabulary words *appropriate, consequence,* and *justify* in their responses. Let volunteers share their responses with the class.

- How are the words the author chose **appropriate** for describing the white horse?
- Do you think the narrator understands what the **consequences** of his plan will be?
- How does the narrator **justify** leaving without going to mass or eating breakfast?

Analyze Language

RL 1,
RL 3,
RL 4,
L 5a

(LINES 95–100)

Tell students that in **figurative language,** words are used in an imaginative way to express ideas that are not literally true. Explain that authors might use figurative language to emphasize an idea or help readers picture a scene or image.

(E) CITE TEXT EVIDENCE Ask students to reread lines 95–100 and identify examples of figurative language. *("Together, we turned to stone," "A glove hurled into my face.")* Have students explain what images and ideas each figure of speech illustrates. Then, ask them to tell what story elements each example elaborates on for the reader. *(The first helps readers picture how still and connected the narrator and the horse are. The second helps emphasize the challenge that the horse presents for the narrator. Both elaborate on the internal and external conflict.)*

English Language Support

Explain that a challenge is an invitation to a competition or a test of ability. Throwing a glove was once a common way to challenge someone, or invite them to compete. Have a pair demonstrate this by having one member throw a prop glove on the ground and complete the saying, "I challenge you to a game of _____." Demonstrate "turning to stone" and have the group act out being very still. Then have pairs of students practice writing and saying sentences that use the phrase *still as stone.*

CRITICAL VOCABULARY

mandate: The author uses the word *mandate* to explain what the narrator believes the white horse is trying to communicate to him.

ASK STUDENTS to reread line 100. Ask them to tell why the author might have described the horse's scream as both "a challenge and a mandate." *(Possible response: A challenge involves two beings in a contest to show which is superior; a mandate is more like a command, so it shows that the narrator sees the horse as an authority.)*

©Corbis

from horizon to horizon, searching for the noble silhouette of the talismanic[4] horse.

It must have been midday. I don't know. Time had lost its meaning. I found him! On a slope stained with sunlight. We saw one another at the same time. Together, we turned to stone. Motionless, absorbed, and panting, I gazed at his beauty, his pride, his nobility. As still as sculptured marble, he allowed himself to be admired.

100   A sudden, violent scream breaks the silence. A glove hurled into my face.[5] A challenge and a **mandate.** Then something surprising happens. The horse that in summer takes his stand between any threat and his herd, swinging

mandate
(măn´dāt´) *n.* A *mandate* is an authoritative command or instruction.

---

[4] **talismanic** (tăl´ĭs-măn´ĭk): possessing or believed to possess magical power.

[5] **A glove hurled into my face:** a defiant challenge. Historically, one man challenged another to a duel by throwing down a glove, or gauntlet.

English Language Support

Analyze Language Say aloud, "A challenge and a mandate." Ask volunteers to define *mandate. (an order or command)* Ask students to describe the effect of the word *mandate. (official, formal, important)*

ASK STUDENTS to work in small groups to look up *mandate* in the dictionary and find four synonyms, e.g., *instruction, order, ruling, decree.* Have them replace *mandate* with each synonym. Help students discuss or write how the sentence changes with the word substitutions.

back and forth from left to right, now plunges into the snow.
Stronger than they, he is breaking trail for his mares. They
follow him. His flight is slow in order to conserve his strength.

I follow. Slowly. Quivering. Thinking about his
intelligence. Admiring his courage. Understanding his
courtesy. The afternoon advances. My horse is taking it easy.

One by one the mares become weary. One by one, they
110 drop out of the trail. Alone! He and I. My inner ferment[6]
bubbles to my lips. I speak to him. He listens and is quiet.

He still opens the way, and I follow in the path he leaves
me. Behind us a long, deep trench crosses the white plain.
My horse, which has eaten grain and good hay, is still strong.
Under-nourished as the Wonder Horse is, his strength is
waning. But he keeps on because that is the way he is. He does
not know how to surrender.

I now see black stains over his body. Sweat and the wet
snow have revealed the black skin beneath the white hair.
120 Snorting breath, turned to steam, tears the air. White spume
above white snow. Sweat, spume,[7] and steam. Uneasiness.

I felt like an executioner. But there was no turning back.
The distance between us was growing relentlessly shorter.
God and Nature watched indifferently.

I feel sure of myself at last. I untie the rope. I open the
lasso and pull the reins tight. Every nerve, every muscle
is tense. My heart is in my mouth. Spurs pressed against
trembling flanks. The horse leaps. I whirl the rope and throw
the obedient lasso.

130 A frenzy of fury and rage. Whirlpools of light and fans
of transparent snow. A rope that whistles and burns the
saddletree. Smoking, fighting gloves. Eyes burning in their
sockets. Mouth parched. Fevered forehead. The whole earth
shakes and shudders. The long, white trench ends in a wide,
white pool.

Deep, gasping quiet. The Wonder Horse is mine! Both still
trembling, we look at one another squarely for a long time.
Intelligent and realistic, he stops struggling and even takes a
hesitant step toward me. I speak to him. As I talk, I approach
140 him. At first, he flinches and **recoils**. Then he waits for me.
The two horses greet one another in their own way. Finally,

recoil
(rĭ-koil´) *v.* To *recoil*
from something is
to shrink back, as if
in fear.

---

[6] **ferment** (fûr´mĕnt´): agitation or excitement.
[7] **spume** (spyōōm): foam or froth.

CLOSE READ

Describe Stories: Conflict (LINES 112–124)

RL 1,
RL 3,
RL 5

Remind students that an external conflict is a struggle
the main character has with an outside force, such
as another character or nature, and that an internal
struggle is one that takes place within a main
character.

F CITE TEXT EVIDENCE Ask students to reread
lines 112–124 and explain how the narrator's external
conflict, his desire to capture the Wonder Horse,
causes an internal conflict to develop in the story.
*(Possible response: As the narrator gets closer to his goal,
he says he "felt like an executioner" because he knows
the white horse is "under-nourished" and tiring from
breaking the trail through the snow.)*

CRITICAL VOCABULARY

recoil: The author uses the word *recoils* to describe
how the white horse reacts when the narrator
draws near.

ASK STUDENTS to tell why the white horse recoils.
Then, ask how the word helps them picture the
scene. *(Possible responses: The horse recoils because
he is afraid or unsure of what the narrator might do,
or because the horse has very little experience around
humans; the word* recoils *helps readers picture how
the horse draws back suddenly when the narrator
comes closer and speaks to him.)*

WHEN STUDENTS STRUGGLE . . .

To guide students' comprehension of internal and external conflict, use a
chart like the one shown and have individuals complete the column on
external conflict. Have them refer back to the beginning of the story as
needed to find text evidence.

Then, guide students to complete the right column of the chart to explore
the internal conflict that develops in lines 112–124.

Guide students to clarify the connection between the external conflict and
the internal conflict. *(If the narrator had not had such a strong desire to capture
the white horse, he would not feel the inner turmoil he feels now as he gets closer
to his goal.)*

External Conflict	Internal Conflict
The narrator wants to capture the white horse.	
Text Evidence	**Text Evidence**
"I joined in the universal obsession . . . of putting my lasso on him some day, of capturing him and showing him off" (lines 30–33)	

CLOSE READ

Describe Stories: Conflict (LINES 144–161)

RL 1, RL 3, RL 5

Tell students that characters may respond in surprising ways when they resolve, or settle, a conflict.

G **CITE TEXT EVIDENCE** Have students reread lines 144–161 and describe how the narrator's response to leading the Wonder Horse through the town causes a surprising shift in the story. *(He feels "triumphant" and "exultant," but when the horse slips and falls, he feels the creature's "humiliation." He begins to feel the pain of the horse and not just his own pride.)*

H **ASK STUDENTS** to examine lines 158–161 and tell whether they think the narrator feels that resolving this external conflict of capturing the horse has been worth it. *(Possible response: He may not feel it has been worth it because he feels the animal's humiliation so deeply and must realize that it was all his own doing.)*

English Language Support

Have students think about the main character's mixed feelings about catching the horse. Read lines 144–161 aloud as students follow along. Review what the horse symbolizes, or stands for, in lines 1–5. Encourage students to think about how the resolution of the external conflict creates an internal conflict for the main character. Finally, discuss whether the character thinks that catching the horse was a good thing.

CRITICAL VOCABULARY

indignity: The narrator uses the word *indignity* to describe what has happened to the white horse.

ASK STUDENTS to tell why this event would be such an indignity for the white horse. *(Possible responses: The white horse is legendary for escaping capture, and now he has been captured by a very young man and taken through town for everyone to see; the horse has slipped and fallen in front of townspeople, and that is deeply embarrassing.)*

I succeed in stroking his mane. I tell him many things, and he seems to understand.

Ahead of me, along the trail already made, I drove him toward the town. Triumphant. Exultant. Childish laughter gathered in my throat. With my newfound manliness, I controlled it. I wanted to sing, but I fought down the desire. I wanted to shout, but I kept quiet. It was the ultimate[8] in happiness. It was the pride of the male adolescent. I felt myself 150 a conqueror.

G Occasionally the Wonder Horse made a try for his liberty, snatching me abruptly from my thoughts. For a few moments, the struggle was renewed. Then we went on.

It was necessary to go through the town. There was no other way. The sun was setting. Icy streets and people on the porches. The Wonder Horse full of terror and panic for the first time. He ran, and my well-shod horse stopped him. He slipped and fell on his side. I suffered for him. The **indignity**. The humiliation. Majesty degraded. I begged him not to 160 struggle, to let himself be led. How it hurt me that other people should see him like that!

Finally we reached home.

"What shall I do with you, Mago?[9] If I put you into the stable or the corral, you are sure to hurt yourself. Besides, it would be an insult. You aren't a slave. You aren't a servant. You aren't even an animal."

I decided to turn him loose in the fenced pasture. There, little by little, Mago would become accustomed to my friendship and my company. No animal had ever escaped 170 from that pasture.

My father saw me coming and waited for me without a word. A smile played over his face, and a spark danced in his eyes. He watched me take the rope from Mago, and the two of us thoughtfully observed him move away. My father clasped my hand a little more firmly than usual and said, "That was a man's job." That was all. Nothing more was needed. We understood one another very well. I was playing the role of a real man, but the childish laughter and shouting that bubbled up inside me almost destroyed the impression 180 I wanted to create.

indignity
(ĭn-dĭgʹnĭ-tē) *n.* An *indignity* is something that offends, insults, or injures one's pride or dignity.

H

---

[8] **ultimate** (ulʹtə-mĭt): the greatest extreme; maximum.
[9] **Mago** (mäʹgô): Spanish: magician, wizard.

English Language Support

Word Study Write the word *indignity* on the board. Underscore *in-* and *-ity*. Ask volunteers to name the word parts. *(prefix and suffix)* Ask students to define *in-*. *("not")* Then focus students' attention on *-ity*. Tell students that the suffix *-ity* means "state or quality." Ask volunteers to define *dignity*. *("the state of deserving respect")* In groups, brainstorm other words with the suffix *-ity*, such as *captivity, inability*, and *nobility*.

ASK STUDENTS to work in pairs to use each word in a sentence that discusses the horse or boy in the story.

©Makarova Viktoria/Shutterstock

TO CHALLENGE STUDENTS...

Analyze Setting Have partners work together to analyze the setting choices the author makes and their impact. Point out to them that the author presents scenes from high summer and deep winter.

ASK STUDENTS to examine the image of the horse and discuss how it captures setting and plot elements. Then, have them discuss the following:

- What feelings and qualities do you associate with deep winter? With high summer?
- What is the importance of the narrator's first seeing the Wonder Horse in summer, as well as his capture of the horse in winter? How might the story be different if the seasons had been reversed for each event?

Determine Theme

RL 2

(LINES 207–213)

Tell students that readers can determine a story's theme by thinking about the lessons the main character learns. Remind them that a story can have more than one theme.

ASK STUDENTS to review lines 207–213 and suggest possible themes suggested by the lessons the narrator learns from the Wonder Horse. Point out that because a theme is a complete idea it should be expressed in a complete sentence, such as "Sometimes events are both happy and sad." *(Possible responses: Things that are free cannot ever be captured; Growing up means realizing that some things are beyond possession; We learn important lessons from things that cannot stay with us.)*

CRITICAL VOCABULARY

indomitable: The narrator uses the word *indomitable* to describe the white horse's spirit.

ASK STUDENTS to tell why they think the narrator says he was "rejoicing" to learn about the white horse's indomitable spirit. *(Possible responses: He is filled with joy because the white horse has taught him that some things cannot ever be captured and will always remain free.)*

COLLABORATIVE DISCUSSION Have students think about the question and form their own response before discussing the question with a partner. Point out that there is no one correct answer to the question. Remind students to cite evidence from the text to support their ideas.

ASK STUDENTS to share any questions they generated in the course of reading and discussing the selection.

That night I slept little, and when I slept, I did not know that I was asleep. For dreaming is the same when one really dreams, asleep or awake. I was up at dawn. I had to go to see my Wonder Horse. As soon as it was light, I went out into the cold to look for him.

The pasture was large. It contained a grove of trees and a small gully. The Wonder Horse was not visible anywhere, but I was not worried. I walked slowly, my head full of the events of yesterday and my plans for the futures. Suddenly

190 I realized that I had walked a long way. I quicken my steps. I look apprehensively around me. I begin to be afraid. Without knowing it, I begin to run. Faster and faster.

He is not there. The Wonder Horse has escaped. I search every corner where he could be hidden. I follow his tracks. I see that during the night he walked incessantly, sniffing, searching for a way out. He did not find one. He made one for himself.

I followed the track that led straight to the fence. And I saw that the trail did not stop but continued on the other side. It was a barbed-wire fence. There was white hair on the wire.

200 There was blood on the barbs. There were red stains on the snow and little red drops in the hoofprints on the other side of the fence.

I stopped there. I did not go any farther. The rays of the morning sun on my face. Eyes clouded and yet filled with light. Childish tears on the cheeks of a man. A cry stifled in my throat. Slow, silent sobs.

Standing there, I forgot myself and the world and time. I cannot explain it, but my sorrow was mixed with pleasure. I was weeping with happiness. No matter how much it hurt me,

210 I was rejoicing over the flight and the freedom of the Wonder Horse, the dimensions of his **indomitable** spirit. Now he would always be fantasy, freedom, and excitement. The Wonder Horse was transcendent. He had enriched my life forever.

My father found me there. He came close without a word and laid his arm across my shoulders. We stood looking at the white trench with its flecks of red that led into the rising sun.

indomitable
(ĭn-dŏmʹ ĭ-tə-bəl)
adj. Something or someone that is *indomitable* is unable to be tamed or defeated.

COLLABORATIVE DISCUSSION Think about what the narrator learns about the Wonder Horse. Does he have to capture the Wonder Horse to learn these things? Why or why not? With a partner, discuss your response. Point out text evidence that supports your ideas.

English Language Support

Support Opinions Explain that supporting opinions with details from the text will help students be more convincing. Have them use the following sentence frames to prepare for their Collaborative Discussion.

- I think the narrator did not have to capture the horse to learn what he did because _____.
- I disagree because _____.
- This quotation from the text backs up my opinion: _____.

Determine Theme

RL 2

A **theme** is a story's message about life or human nature. The theme is different from the **topic,** which is simply the subject the author is writing about. A topic can be stated in a few words. However, it usually takes at least one full sentence to express the theme of a text. In addition, a text may have more than one theme.

A story's theme is not stated directly. Instead, readers need to figure it out using particular details in the text. To determine a story's theme, notice the following:

- the title of the story, which can suggest an important idea or symbol
- the main conflict faced by the main character and the lessons the character learns
- important statements that the narrator or main character make
- the setting, which can affect the characters and influence action
- **symbols,** which can be a person, place, or thing that stands for something beyond itself

As you analyze "My Wonder Horse," think about the important messages about life the author wants to share with readers. Use these ideas to determine the theme of the story.

Describe Stories: Conflict

RL 3, RL 5

Every story centers on a conflict. A **conflict** is the problem or struggle that the main character faces.

- An **internal conflict** is a struggle that takes place within a character. An internal conflict is expressed through the character's thoughts and actions. The struggle often involves a decision the character must make.
- An **external conflict** is a struggle with a force outside of the character, such as another character, society, or nature.

To determine the conflicts in a story, ask yourself:

- What problems or struggles does the main character face?
- Is each struggle external or internal?

"My Wonder Horse" contains both external and internal conflicts. As you analyze "My Wonder Horse," notice the conflicts the main character faces.

CLOSE READ

Determine Theme

RL 2

Help students understand the difference between a topic and a theme by providing examples from familiar stories, such as the following: *The topic of "Goldilocks and the Three Bears" is "a fairy tale about a girl and a family of bears." The story's theme comes from lessons Goldilocks learns, such as "Don't go in someone's house without permission!"*

Next, discuss the elements readers can use to figure out story themes. Provide examples of symbols that students might be familiar with, such as our country's flag as a symbol of freedom, a heart as a symbol of love, and a dove as a symbol of peace.

Describe Stories: Conflict

RL 1, RL 3, RL 5

Help students understand that conflict is an important part of every story. Clarify the difference between internal and external conflict by having students suggest examples of each and discussing each one together. Discuss how a story can include more than one conflict, as well as both internal and external conflicts. Then, guide students to answer the bulleted questions to identify internal and external conflicts the narrator faces in "My Wonder Horse."

Strategies for Annotation ✐ 🖉 Annotate it!

Determine Theme

RL 2

Share these strategies for guided or independent analysis:

- Highlight in yellow phrases that tell about the narrator's response to stories about the white horse.
- Underline details that tell why the narrator wants to capture the white horse.
- Review your annotations and think about lessons you can take from them. On a note, record statements about these lessons, or themes.

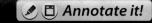

... wants to impress others ...

I was fifteen years old. Although I had never seen the W___ Horse, he filled my imagination and fired my ambition. I used to listen open-mouthed . . . I joined in the universal obsession . . . of putting my lasso on him some day, of capturing him and showing him off on Sunday afternoons when the girls of the town strolled through the streets.

PRACTICE & APPLY

Analyzing the Text

RL 1, RL 2,
RL 3, RL 4,
RL 5

Possible answers:

1. *He is admired by many; he has a harem; he escapes all kinds of traps; he will not be caught or tamed by man. The men admire the horse's independence, freedom, cleverness, masculinity, and superiority.*

2. *He is fifteen and, like others, he is obsessed with capturing the horse. It is a challenge that will make him feel like an adult and look grown up in the eyes of others.*

3. *Words and phrases that stand out include "a statue," "an engraving," "pride, prestige, and art incarnate in animal flesh," "virile freedom," and "an ideal." The narrator is in awe of the horse and views him as a prize.*

4. *The horse is the symbol. The narrator becomes more mature as he realizes that the horse cannot be captured.*

5. *The narrator wants to capture the horse. Having seen the horse in the summer, the narrator becomes obsessed with the horse for months.*

6. *The narrator has caught the horse but the horse is still struggling to get away.*

7. *It takes a long time to grow up; You cannot capture or imprison freedom; The road to adulthood is full of difficult choices; Sometimes we learn important lessons from painful experiences.*

FOR STANDARD ENGLISH LEARNERS

Review the rules about irregular reflexive pronouns. Encourage students to check for correct usage when they proofread their essays. Provide these sentences for practice:

- The horse hurt hisself when he jumped the fence. He didn't want his mares to be left by theirselves for too long. So he made hisself jump over the high fence.
(himself, themselves, himself)

Analyzing the Text

RL 1, RL 2, RL 3,
RL 4, RL 5, W 2,
W 7

> **Cite Text Evidence**   Support your responses with evidence from the text.

1. **Identify** Reread lines 6–25. What does the Wonder Horse do that makes him legendary? Tell what qualities and characteristics of the horse the men admire.

2. **Infer** Reread lines 26–34. What does the narrator tell about himself? Explain how this information helps you understand why he wants to capture the Wonder Horse.

3. **Analyze** Reread lines 50–57. Tell which words and phrases stand out in the description of the horse. What do these words suggest about the narrator's view of the horse?

4. **Interpret** What symbol is present in the story? What meaning does it have for the narrator?

5. **Cause/Effect** Reread lines 62–78. What is the internal conflict? How has this conflict developed and intensified?

6. **Analyze** Review lines 154–180. Describe an external conflict in the story.

7. **Connect** Think about conflicts in the story, and what the narrator learns from the Wonder Horse, its capture, and its escape. What are some important messages or themes the author shares?

PERFORMANCE TASK

Writing Activity: Informative Essay
Find out more about wild mustangs or other wild animals of the West. Then write a one- or two-page informative essay.

- Use online and print resources to find information about your topic.

- Take notes about the animals' population, location, habits, and any threats to their existence.

- Share your essay with the class.

Assign this performance task.

PERFORMANCE TASK

W 2, W 6,
W 7

Writing Activity: Informative Essay Have students work independently. Direct them to

- think of keywords they can use to conduct research online
- take notes on information to include in their essays, and keep track of their sources
- create an outline to organize their essay

Remind them to include an introduction and a conclusion for their essays.

Critical Vocabulary

L 4a, L 4d, L 5a, L 6

lethargy	vigil	mandate
recoil	indignity	indomitable

Practice and Apply Answer each question and explain your answer.

1. Would you be more likely to experience **lethargy** after a good night's sleep or if you had very little sleep? Explain.

2. Would a bird enthusiast be more likely to hold an owl-watching **vigil** at night or during the day?

3. If a leader gives a clear **mandate,** are people more or less likely to listen to that person? Explain.

4. Would you be more likely to **recoil** from a snake or from an apple? Explain.

5. Which do you see as the greater **indignity**—tripping and falling in public or giving the wrong answer to a question in class?

6. If the opposing team is **indomitable,** is your team likely to win or lose?

Vocabulary Strategy: Interpret Figures of Speech in Context

Writers often use **figures of speech,** or language that communicates meanings beyond the literal meaning of words to help them express ideas in imaginative ways. Here are three common figures of speech.

A **simile** is a comparison between two unlike things that uses the words *like* or *as*.	A **metaphor** is a comparison of two unlike things that does *not* use the words *like* or *as*.	**Personification** is giving human qualities to an animal, thing, or idea.

In "My Wonder Horse," there is "Only a silence, deep, white, and sparkling." This example of personification helps you see silence in a new and interesting way. The silence is compared to the snow and is personified as sparkling. The brightness of the snow helps you understand what *sparkling* means.

Practice and Apply Write a definition for each boldface word. Then use a dictionary to confirm your answers.

1. The **avaricious** sponge soaked up all the water on the counter.

2. Except for one sturdy bench, the stage props were as **flimsy** as a house made of paper.

Critical Vocabulary

L 4a, L 4d, L 5a, L 6

Possible answers:

1. *I would feel lethargy after getting very little sleep because I would be very tired.*

2. *The vigil would be at night because owls are usually out at night, not during the day.*

3. *People are more likely to listen because if he or she has a mandate, that person has the authority to give a command.*

4. *I would recoil from a snake because it might be dangerous and I would be afraid.*

5. *I think giving the wrong answer in class is a greater indignity; it hurts my pride more to give the wrong answer than to trip accidentally.*

6. *Our team is more likely to lose; the other team appears to be undefeatable.*

FOR STANDARD ENGLISH LEARNERS

As students answer the questions, remind them of the rules for subject-verb agreement. The subject and verb have to agree in number, so when they are writing their answers, the verb should be plural, as in a possible answer to item 3, "People are more likely to listen . . ." When students are referring to a single person or thing, the verb should be singular, as in item 6, "Our team is . . ."

Vocabulary Strategy: Interpret Figures of Speech in Context

1. *greedy*

2. *not well built*

Strategies for Annotation   📝 📖 *Annotate it!*

Interpret Figures of Speech in Context

RL 4, L 5a

Have students review lines 58–61 and focus on the word *arrogant*. Tell them to use their eBook annotation tools to do the following:

- Underline the word *arrogant*.
- Highlight in yellow the metaphor "Arrogant ruler of the countryside."
- Highlight in green clues that tell more about the horse's behavior.
- Review your annotations and try to infer the word's meaning. Use a dictionary to check the meaning.

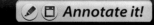

A sharp neigh. A far-reaching challenge that soars on high, ripping the virginal fabric of the rosy clouds. Ears at the point. Eyes flashing. Tail waving active defiance. Hoofs glossy and destructive. Arrogant ruler of the countryside.

"angry" or "proud" . . . ?

Language Conventions: Improving Expression

L 1e

Tell students that writers choose whether to use formal language, informal language, or a mix of both, depending on their reasons for writing and the audience they are writing for. Explain to students that when they write it is important to use language that is appropriate for their audience and to be consistent to avoid confusing readers.

Verbally illustrate the concepts for students by providing an example, such as when they might need help completing a task. Ask them how they might ask someone their own age (*"Give me a hand?" "A little help here?"*) as opposed to asking an adult (*"Would you help me, please?"*).

Possible revision:

"Hey," Karla heard her say. "Where are you going?"

"I'm on my way to lunch," said Karla as she turned around.

"How have your classes been today?" asked Ms. Hansen.

"Been better," sighed Karla. "Today is not one of my best days."

 **Assess It Online!**

Online Selection Test
• Download an editable ExamView bank.
• Assign and manage this test online.

Language Conventions: Improving Expression

L 1e

The author of "My Wonder Horse" chose **formal language,** or Standard English to describe the horse, the setting, and the narrator's thoughts. The author of "The Ravine" (Collection 1) included **informal language,** such as *shuddup,* to mimic how teenagers actually sound. Another author might use **slang,** or made-up words and ordinary words with new meanings, to create situations and characters that are authentic to a particular place and time.

Sometimes writers use a blend of informal and formal language to express certain ideas, or mix formal language with slang to create or highlight a contrast. Sometimes, however, a writer's methods of expression cause problems for the reader. Here are two strategies you should use to improve expression in writing:

• **Consider your audience.** Is your audience a group of students your own age, younger children, or professional adults? With students your own age, you can use more informal language, but slang might confuse younger students. You show respect for an older or professional audience by using a formal tone.

• **Use a consistent method of expression.** Knowing your audience will help you choose your tone. Your method of expression should be consistent. When a writer starts to stray from one method of expression to another, readers may be confused and wonder to whom the writer is speaking.

Practice and Apply Edit and revise the dialogue to match the tone of the first paragraph.

As Karla passed the principal's office, she thought about how she admired that Ms. Hansen was quiet, but kind and direct. Karla's thoughts were interrupted when she heard Ms. Hansen's door open behind her.

"Hey," Karla heard Ms. Hansen say. "Where ya headed?"

"To get some grub," said Karla as she turned around.

"Whatcha been doing today?" asked Ms. Hansen.

"Been better," sighed Karla. "Epic fail."

English Language Support

Adapt Language Choices Discuss formal and informal language with students, reviewing the definitions in their books as necessary. Remind them that writers usually use a consistent type of language in their writing because it can be confusing to the reader to change the language. However, point out that writers may change language to make readers pay attention to important ideas. Encourage students to think about how language is used as they read other selections.

• Read the first paragraph of the Practice and Apply aloud. Ask students whether it has a formal or informal tone. *(formal)* Then read the first sentence of the dialogue aloud and ask the same question. *(informal)* To scaffold the rest of the activity, restate "Where ya headed?" in formal language and have students repeat it. *(Where are you going?)*

• Have students complete the Practice and Apply activity with a partner. Discuss their answers, then ask them to add an original sentence to the dialogue written in formal language. Have pairs share their sentences with another pair and explain what makes the language formal.

INTERACTIVE WHITEBOARD LESSON
Explain Point of View and Narrator

RL 6

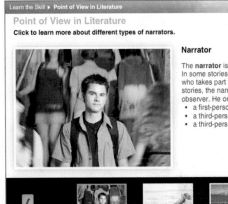

Learn the Skill ▶ Point of View in Literature

Point of View in Literature
Click to learn more about different types of narrators.

Narrator

The **narrator** is the voice that tells a story. In some stories, the narrator is a character who takes part in the action. In other stories, the narrator is an outside observer. He or she can be:
- a first-person narrator
- a third-person limited narrator
- a third-person omniscient narrator

Narrator   First-Person Narrator   Third-Person Limited Narrator

TEACH

As you use the whiteboard lesson, discuss what a story's point of view is and why it matters. Help students understand these points:

- **Point of view** is the vantage point from which the story is told. It is determined by the author's choice of narrator.
- The **narrator** is the "voice" that tells a story.
- Most stories use **first-person point of view,** in which the story is told by a character in the story, or **third-person point of view,** in which the story is told by someone *not* in the story.

Once students understand these points, discuss how to identify point of view in a story.

- **Step 1: Look at the Pronouns** Remind students that pronouns are words that stand in for nouns. Help them identify them in the sample.
- **Step 2: Identify the Narrator** Discuss who the narrator is in the sample story.
- **Step 3: Analyze the Effects** Talk about what information readers do and do not learn from different types of narrators and points of view.

COLLABORATIVE DISCUSSION

After completing the Practice and Apply section of the whiteboard lesson, have partners review "My Wonder Horse" to identify the point of view the author uses and to analyze its effects. Have partners discuss their findings with other pairs of students.

Determine Theme

RL 2

RETEACH

Review with students that a **theme** is a lesson about life or human nature. Explain that most often, a story's themes are not stated directly in the text, but that readers must figure them out on their own. Remind students that elements such as the following can help readers identify a story's themes:

- important conflicts the main character faces and how they are resolved
- what key symbols in the story stand for, and what a character learns from them
- story elements, such as its title and settings, that influence what happens in the story

Have partners review "My Wonder Horse" together. Ask them to write complete sentences that express important messages readers can learn from the story. Then, discuss students' responses together.

 LEVEL UP TUTORIALS Assign the following *Level Up* tutorial: **Theme**

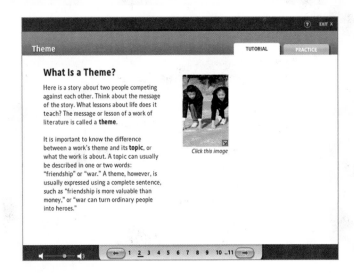

Theme   TUTORIAL   PRACTICE

What Is a Theme?

Here is a story about two people competing against each other. Think about the message of the story. What lessons about life does it teach? The message or lesson of a work of literature is called a **theme**.

It is important to know the difference between a work's theme and its **topic**, or what the work is about. A topic can usually be described in one or two words: "friendship" or "war." A theme, however, is usually expressed using a complete sentence, such as "friendship is more valuable than money," or "war can turn ordinary people into heroes."

Click this image

1 2 3 4 5 6 7 8 9 10 ..11

INDEPENDENT READING

Have students apply these skills to another selection they have read, such as "The Ravine" (Collection 1) or "The Banana Tree" (Collection 3). Students can also apply them to a short story or novel they may be reading on their own. Invite students to share their ideas about theme with the class.

ANCHOR TEXT
Wild Animals Aren't Pets

ANCHOR TEXT
Let People Own Exotic Animals

Editorial by USA TODAY

Commentary by Zuzana Kukol

Why These Texts?

Students regularly encounter arguments online and in print that present opposing viewpoints on a single topic. This lesson reviews the arguments made in an editorial and a responding commentary on the issue of personal ownership of exotic animals.

▶ **View It!**
Professional Development Podcast:
Teaching Argument

For Practice and Application:

Close Reader selection
"Views on Zoos"
Informational Text

Key Learning Objective: The student will be able to trace and evaluate an argument, analyze persuasive language, and compare and contrast two arguments on the same topic.

RI 1	Cite text evidence.	
RI 2	Determine central idea; provide a summary.	
RI 3	Analyze text elements.	
RI 4	Determine the meaning of words and phrases.	
RI 5	Analyze structure.	
RI 6	Determine author's point of view.	
RI 8	Trace and evaluate an argument.	
RI 9	Compare and contrast arguments.	
W 1	Write arguments.	
W 7	Conduct short research projects.	
SL 1	Engage effectively in discussions.	
L 2b	Spell correctly.	
L 4a	Use context as clue to meaning.	
L 5b	Use analogies to understand meaning.	
L 6	Acquire and use grade-appropriate general academic vocabulary.	

▲ Text Complexity Rubric

	Wild Animals Aren't Pets	**Let People Own Exotic Animals**
Quantitative Measures	Lexile: 1170L	Lexile: 1180L
Qualitative Measures	**Levels of Meaning/Purpose** more than one purpose; implied, easily identified from context	**Levels of Meaning/Purpose** single purpose, explicitly stated
	Structure clearly stated, sequential organization of main ideas and details	**Structure** clearly stated, sequential organization of main ideas and details
	Language Conventionality and Clarity some unfamiliar language	**Language Conventionality and Clarity** clear, direct language
	Knowledge Demands everyday knowledge required	**Knowledge Demands** everyday knowledge required
Reader/Task Considerations	• Teacher determined • Vary by individual reader and type of text • See the Text X-Ray for suggested Reader/Task Considerations.	

English Language Support

Before teaching, use the Text X-Ray for an overview of the text's complexity. The Text X-Ray and the supports and scaffolds in the Teacher's Edition will help you guide students of different skill levels.

Meaning Making

Language Development

Effective Expression

Content Knowledge

Foundational Skills

Text Complexity: Qualitative Measures

 Levels of Meaning/Purpose

Help students to trace and evaluate an argument.

- Teacher's Edition side notes, pp. 223, 224, 226, 227
- English Language Support, pp. 223, 224, 225, 230
- When Students Struggle, p. 228
- Close Read Screencasts, pp. 223, 227
- Strategies for Annotation, p. 226
- Trace and Evaluate an Argument, p. 226
- Performance Task: Argument, p. 230

To reteach paraphrasing, see

- Paraphrase, p. 232a
- English Language Support, p. 232a

▶ *Use It! Level Up* **Tutorials:** Elements of an Argument; Analyzing Arguments

ZOOM IN ON **TRACING AND EVALUATING AN ARGUMENT** Explain that an **argument** has a **claim** and reasons or **evidence** that support it. The first step is to identify the claim and evidence. Then readers can evaluate the evidence to see how well it supports the claim. Tell students that they will read how two writers present different claims and evidence on the same topic. They will need to evaluate both arguments. After students have read the editorial, have them use these sentence frames to discuss the argument with a partner.

- Another way of stating the claim in the title is _____.
- The authors think there should be stronger laws to _____.

▲ **Structure**

Help students compare and contrast arguments.

- Teacher's Edition side notes, pp. 228, 230
- English Language Support, p. 228
- Compare and Contrast Arguments, p. 230

To reteach Compare and Contrast Arguments, see

- Compare and Contrast: Arguments, p. 232a

 Comparing Arguments

ZOOM IN ON **COMPARING AND CONTRASTING ARGUMENTS** Remind students that there are two **arguments** on the same topic in their text. Some arguments will try to convince using **logic**, and others with **emotion**.

- Have students work with a partner to identify how each statement below is trying to convince the reader.
1. Wild animals need our help. When you keep one as a pet, you help save the planet! (*emotion*)
2. Over half of all chimpanzees adopted as pets are given up before they reach adulthood. (*logic*)

▲ Language Conventionality and Clarity

Teach unfamiliar academic vocabulary in context.

- Teacher's Edition Critical Vocabulary notes, pp. 224, 225, 227
- Applying Academic Vocabulary, p. 225
- English Language Support, p. 232
- Language Conventions: Spell Words Correctly, p. 232

Teach analyzing words and phrases for loaded language.

- Teacher Edition side notes, pp. 227, 228, 229
- English Language Support, p. 228
- Strategies for Annotation, p. 229

Help students understand Part-to-Whole Analogies:

- Vocabulary Strategy: Part-to-Whole Analogies, p. 231
- Strategies for Annotation, p. 231

ZOOM IN ON **ANALYZING LOADED LANGUAGE** To help students understand the term *loaded language*, draw a balance on the board with *For* and *Against* on each side. Explain that a *loaded* word or phrase has a weight on one side or the other that tilts the balance of the reader's feelings. Work with students to assign the following phrases from the arguments to each side of the balance, clarifying meanings as needed:

- *freedom to have pets, animals to love, people were horrified, animals were innocent victims* (for, for, against, against)

▲ Knowledge Demands

Help students to understand the background of the topic.

- Teacher's Edition Background note, p. 223

ZOOM IN ON **BUILDING BACKGROUND KNOWLEDGE** Familiarize students with the following information:

- Write *editorial* on the board. Explain that an editorial is one kind of opinion article published in newspapers. An editorial shows the opinion of the people in charge of the newspaper.
- Explain that *commentary* is also opinion writing, but is usually written by a reader of the paper who wants to express her or his opinion to other readers.

▲ Suggested Reader/Task Considerations

You might consider the following before assigning these arguments to students:

- Do students know how to connect the ideas and details they will encounter in the text?
- Will students be able to formulate questions about the ideas in the text and to think about those ideas from different perspectives?

ZOOM IN ON **SUPPORTING COMPREHENSION**

- Tell students that they will be reading two texts on the same topic. Remind them to refer back to the editorial if they are not sure what the writer of the commentary is discussing.
- Tell students that these texts express strong opinions that readers need to question. Have them write questions that challenge statements in the texts, for example, *Is this true?* or *Why/Why not?*

TEACH

CLOSE READ

Background Have students read the background information and briefly discuss their own knowledge, experience, or opinions about the issues.

Unsigned Editorials "Wild Animals Aren't Pets" is an editorial that appeared in the newspaper *USA TODAY*. On the opinion and editorial pages of many newspapers, editorials are unsigned, meaning that they do not name the author. Unsigned editorials are usually written by a member of the newspaper's editorial board. Commentary, such as "Let People Own Exotic Animals," is always signed so that readers know that the editorial reflects a particular person's point of view.

SETTING A PURPOSE Direct students to use the Setting a Purpose prompt to focus their reading.

 Text in FOCUS English Language Support

Comparing Arguments

(Setting a Purpose)

Have students view the **Text in Focus** video on this page of their eBook to learn how to compare the features of each writers' argument. Then have students use **Text in Focus Practice** to apply what they have learned.

Trace and Evaluate an Argument (LINES 1–8)

RI 1, RI 8

Tell students that an **argument** expresses a position on a problem. Explain that an argument is made up of a **claim,** the writer's position on the topic, and **support,** which includes reasons and evidence, such as facts and statistics, that support the claim.

A CITE TEXT EVIDENCE Have students review the title of the editorial and lines 1–8 and explain how they know what the writer's claim is. (*The title states the writer's claim, the opinion that wild animals aren't pets; the phrase "potentially tragic" helps point out the writer's position.*)

Background *Wild animals are animals that live in nature. They can be as rare as a snow leopard or as common as a tree squirrel. Although many states have laws that prohibit owning a wild animal, thousands of people in the United States keep animals such as wolves, pythons, crocodiles, and bears as pets. Some people want to make it illegal to have these kinds of pets. They argue that these animals pose a safety and health risk to people and the environment. Others claim that with proper care, wild animals can safely live in captivity.*

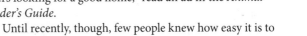

WILD ANIMALS AREN'T PETS

LET PEOPLE OWN EXOTIC ANIMALS

Editorial by USA TODAY

Commentary by Zuzana Kukol

SETTING A PURPOSE As you read, focus on the facts and examples used to justify the points in the editorial by *USA TODAY* and the commentary by Zuzana Kukol, president and co-founder of Responsible Exotic Animal Ownership. Think about which points are convincing to you and which are not.

 Text in FOCUS

Wild Animals Aren't Pets
Editorial by USA TODAY

In many states, anyone with a few hundred dollars and a yen[1] for the unusual can own a python, a black bear or a big cat as a "pet." For $8,000 a baby white tiger can be yours. Sometimes, wild animals are even offered free: "Siberian tigers looking for a good home," read an ad in the *Animal Finder's Guide*.

Until recently, though, few people knew how easy it is to own a wild animal as a pet. Or how potentially tragic.

A

(bg), (b) ©Siede Preis/Getty Images; (c) ©Bhushan Patil Photography/Getty Images

[1] **yen** (yĕn): a strong desire or inclination.

Close Read Screencasts

 Close Read

Modeled Discussions

Have students click the *Close Read* icon in their eBook to access a screencast in which readers discuss and annotate lines 9–16, a key passage that includes the central claim of an argument.

As a class, view and discuss the video. Then, have students pair up to do an independent close read of an additional passage—support for the author's argument (lines 42–48).

Trace and Evaluate an Argument (LINES 9–23, LINES 24–25)

RI 1, RI 8

Tell students that when they read an argument, they should **trace** it, or follow its reasoning, by identifying the writer's claim and support. Remind them that support includes reasons and evidence that back up a claim.

B CITE TEXT EVIDENCE Have students review lines 9–16 and identify reasons that back up the claim that wild animals aren't pets. *(Lines 14–16: "...public safety, common sense and compassion for animals all dictate the same conclusion: Wild animals are not pets.")*

C CITE TEXT EVIDENCE Have students trace the argument by identifying and explaining an example used as support. *(Lines 17–23: The Zanesville, Ohio, incident where many animals had to be shot supports the claim by showing how these wild animals are a threat to public safety; it also shows the horror of having to kill the animals to protect people.)*

CRITICAL VOCABULARY

exotic: The author uses the word *exotic* to describe animals from other parts of the world.

dictate: The word *dictate* is used here to explain a situation that requires a logical conclusion.
ASK STUDENTS to discuss the distinction between exotic animals and wild animals. Are all wild animals exotic, or not? Have students discuss how the terms are used in the editorial. Then, ask them to discuss what reasons might dictate that exotic animals should only be kept in zoos and not by private individuals.

Next, tell students that support for an argument often includes **counterarguments,** which are statements that address opposing viewpoints. Explain that a strong argument anticipates opposing viewpoints and presents counterarguments that will disprove them.

D ASK STUDENTS to review lines 24–25 and **paraphrase** the sentences, meaning retell them in their own words. *(Possible response: The author's counterargument is that statistics about deaths caused by "exotic" animals are irrelevant.)*

After Terry Thompson set his exotic animals free in Zanesville, Ohio, a sign on an expressway warned motorists that the animals were on the loose in the area.

But just as a 2007 raid on property owned by football star
10 Michael Vick laid bare the little known and cruel world of dogfighting, a story that unfolded in a small Ohio city recently opened the public's eyes to the little known, distressing world of "**exotic**" pets. We're not suggesting that people who own these animals are cruel. Many surely love them. But public safety, common sense and compassion for animals all **dictate** the same conclusion: Wild animals are not pets.

If that weren't already obvious, it became more so when collector Terry Thompson opened the cages on his Zanesville farm, springing dozens of lions, tigers, bears and other wild
20 creatures before killing himself. With animals running loose and darkness closing in, authorities arrived with no good choices to protect the public. They shot all but a handful of the animals as the nation watched, transfixed[2] and horrified.

Owners of "exotic" animals claim they rarely maim or kill. But is the death rate really the point?

exotic
(ĭg-zŏt´ĭk) *adj.*
Something that is *exotic* is from another part of the world.

dictate
(dĭk´tāt´) *v.* To *dictate* something is to require it to be done or decided.

---

[2] **transfixed** (trăns-fĭkst´): motionless, as with terror, amazement, or other strong emotion.

224 Collection 4

ENGLISH LANGUAGE SUPPORT

Evaluate Language Project lines 14–16. Highlight the sentence "But public safety . . ." and read it aloud. Explain to students that this sentence contains the main claim of the argument and reasons that support it.

- Work with students to identify the claim. *(Wild animals are not pets.)* Have groups discuss what the claim means.
- Have pairs work together to understand the reasons that support the claim—safety, common sense, and compassion for animals—by restating them in their own words. *(Sample answers: keeping people safe, things people should know, caring for animals)*

In 2009, a 2-year-old Florida girl was strangled by a 12-foot-long Burmese python, a family pet that had gotten out of its aquarium. That same year, a Connecticut woman was mauled and disfigured by a neighbor's pet chimp. Last year, a

30 caretaker was mauled to death by a bear owned by a Cleveland collector. In Zanesville, it was the animals themselves, including 18 rare Bengal tigers, who became innocent victims.

Trade in these beautiful creatures thrives in the USA, where thousands are bred and sold through classified ads or at auctions centered in Indiana, Missouri and Tennessee. There's too little to stop it.

A 2003 federal law, which forbids the interstate transport of certain big cats, has stopped much of the trade on the Internet, according to the Humane Society of the U.S. But

40 monkeys, baboons and other primates were left out, and measures to plug that hole have twice stalled in Congress.

Only collectors who exhibit animals need a federal license. Those, such as Thompson, who keep the animals as "pets" are left alone, unless states intervene.[3] And many do not. Eight—Alabama, Idaho, Ohio, Nevada, North Carolina, South Carolina, West Virginia and Wisconsin—have no rules, and in 13 others the laws are lax,[4] according to Born Free USA, which has lobbied for years for stronger laws.

After the Cleveland bear-mauling, then-Ohio Gov. Ted

50 Strickland issued an emergency order to ban possession of wild animals. While it exempted[5] current owners, Thompson might have been forced to give up his **menagerie** because he had been cited for animal cruelty. We'll never know. Strickland's successor, John Kasich, let the order expire.

menagerie
(mə-năjʹə-rē) *n.*
A *menagerie* is a collection of live wild animals, often kept for showing to the public.

---

[3] **intervene** (ĭnʹtər-vēnʹ): to come between so as to block or change an action.

[4] **lax** (lăks): not rigorous, strict, or firm.

[5] **exempted** (ĭg-zĕmptʹəd): freed or excused from following a law or duty which others must obey.

Wild Animals Aren't Pets **225**

APPLYING ACADEMIC VOCABULARY

authority	legal

THINK-PAIR-SHARE Have students turn to a partner to discuss the questions below. Encourage students to include the academic vocabulary words *authority* and *legal* in their responses. Call on volunteers to share their responses with the class.

- Is the author of the editorial an **authority** on the topic of owning wild animals?
- Have efforts to use the **legal** system to control the trade in exotic animals worked?

CLOSE READ

Trace and Evaluate an Argument (LINES 42–48)

RI 1, RI 8

Trace an Argument Remind students that when they trace an argument they follow its reasoning by identifying the author's claim and its support.

(E) **ASK STUDENTS** to reread lines 42–48 and tell the author's opinion of how states regulate exotic animals. (*The author feels that state governments are not doing enough.*) Ask what support the editorial offers for this opinion. (*The author provides facts about states that have few or no laws regulating ownership.*)

English Language Support

To help students understand the connection between the reference to Thompson in line 43 and the list of states in lines 45–47, project the first two paragraphs on page 224. Highlight "a small Ohio town" and reread lines 17–20 aloud. Ask students what city and state Terry Thompson lived in. (*Zanesville, Ohio*) Point out that Ohio is one of the states in line 45 that has no rules about keeping wild animals as pets.

Evaluate an Argument Explain to students that when they **evaluate** an argument, they examine it and decide whether the evidence and claim connect logically and if ideas make sense.

(F) **CITE TEXT EVIDENCE** Remind students of the author's claim that "wild animals aren't pets." Then, have students reread lines 42–48 and evaluate whether the evidence supports the author's claim. (*Possible response: The evidence does not logically support the author's claim; it suggests another claim, government should do more to regulate ownership.*)

CRITICAL VOCABULARY

menagerie: The word *menagerie* is used to describe the wild animals kept by a mentally unstable owner. Note that *menagerie* often refers to animals that are exhibited by their owner.

ASK STUDENTS to review lines 42–48. Ask students to tell whether the animal owner was also an exhibitor of his menagerie. (*No; the author uses Thompson as an example of someone who just kept the animals as pets.*)

PRACTICE & APPLY

Trace and Evaluate an Argument

RI 8

Help students understand the terms and types of reasons and evidence an author might use to support a claim. Ask volunteers to identify types of support in the editorial.

Clarify for students the difference between tracing an argument (identifying claims and support) and evaluating it (determining whether it is logical and effective). Review how to evaluate an argument and prompt students to apply the steps to "Wild Animals Aren't Pets."

Analyzing the Text

RI 1, RI 2, RI 5, RI 8

Possible answers

1. The claim "Wild animals aren't pets" is in the title.

2. A man set dozens of wild animals free; authorities killed most of the animals to protect the public. The editorial uses this to show why wild animals are not pets.

3. Exotic pet owners claim these animals rarely kill or maim. The editorial says it isn't the number of killings that matters; what matters is that they kill innocent victims, and their owners cannot always control them.

4. One federal law stopped trade on the Internet, but it did not cover baboons and other primates. Federal laws do not license keeping wild animals, and few states have strong laws to regulate this.

5. The author makes some convincing points, but the editorial is hard to follow. Reasons and evidence in the final three paragraphs are about legal issues that are not stated clearly enough to support the claim.

eBook *Annotate It!*

Trace and Evaluate an Argument

RI 8

The editorial you have just read is an **argument,** which is a carefully stated claim supported by reasons and evidence. An argument is made up of two parts. The **claim** is the writer's position on a problem or issue. The **support** is the reasons and evidence that help prove the claim. **Reasons** are statements made to explain a belief. **Evidence** is a specific reference, such as a fact, statistic, quotation, or opinion that is used to support a claim. Support in an argument is usually for or against an issue; it is used to justify a viewpoint.

To **trace,** or follow the reasoning, of an argument:

- Identify the claim, or the writer's position on the issue.
- Look for reasons and specific types of evidence (facts, statistics, quotations, or opinions) that support the claim.
- Identify **counterarguments,** which are statements that address opposing viewpoints.

To **evaluate** an argument, or decide whether it makes sense and is convincing:

- Determine whether the evidence supports the claim in a logical way.
- Make sure ideas are presented in a way that makes sense and is clear.
- Determine whether the counterarguments are adequately addressed.

As you analyze the editorial, look at how the author constructs and supports the argument.

Analyzing the Text

RI 1, RI 2, RI 5, RI 8

Cite Text Evidence   Support your responses with evidence from the text.

1. **Identify** What is the claim of the editorial? Where is it found?

2. **Summarize** Reread lines 17–23. What specific evidence is used in this paragraph to support the editorial's claim?

3. **Interpret** Reread lines 24–32. What counterargument does the author address?

4. **Summarize** Reread lines 37–48. What legal issues make it possible for people to own exotic pets?

5. **Evaluate** Do you think the writer's argument is convincing? Cite reasons and evidence from the text that you feel were the weakest or the strongest.

226   Collection 4

Strategies for Annotation   *Annotate it!*

Trace and Evaluate an Argument   RI 8

Share these strategies for guided or independent analysis:

- On a note, record the author's claim.
- Use a different color to highlight each piece of evidence presented to support the claim.
- Review your highlights. On another note, record whether you think the evidence supports the claim in a logical way.

In 2009, a 2-year-old Florida girl was strangled by a 12-foot-long Burmese python, a family pet that had gotten out of its aquarium. That same year, a Connecticut woman was mauled and disfigured by a neighbor's pet chimp. Last year, a caretaker was mauled to death by a bear owned by a Cleveland collector.

TEACH

CLOSE READ

Trace and Evaluate an Argument (LINES 4–15)

RI 1, RI 8

Remind students that an **argument** expresses a position on an issue, and that an argument is made up of a **claim,** the writer's position on the topic, and **support,** which may include reasons and evidence.

A **CITE TEXT EVIDENCE** Have students read lines 4–15 and identify the author's claim. *("Responsible private ownership of exotic animals should be legal if animal welfare is taken care of.")* Then, ask them to **paraphrase,** or tell in their own words, reasons the author presents to support her claim. *(Possible response: The author's reasons include that most exotic animals born in captivity are cared for in well-regulated settings. They are also valuable in case a particular animal faces extinction.)*

Analyze Language

RI 4

(LINES 10–12)

Tell students that authors often try to persuade readers of something. To do this, they use different **persuasive techniques,** which are methods of influencing others to agree with certain opinions or to take action. Using loaded language is one persuasive technique; **loaded language** consists of words with strong positive or negative connotations. A word's **connotations** are the ideas or feelings that we attach to the word, as opposed to its dictionary meaning.

B **ASK STUDENTS** to review lines 10–12 and tell what connotations the phrase "federally inspected facilities" has and why. *(It has strong positive connotations in this context; it suggests that federal agencies have looked at and approved of the places in which the animals are kept, so the places are trustworthy.)*

CRITICAL VOCABULARY

regulate: The word *regulate* refers to controlling or directing something so that it follows a set of rules or laws.

ASK STUDENTS to discuss what they think the author means when she states that "we cannot regulate insanity." *(Possible response: There is no way anyone can control when, how, or if people become insane or unstable.)*

Let People Own Exotic Animals
by Zuzana Kukol

The recent tragedy in Zanesville, Ohio brought back the question of whether private ownership of wild and exotic animals should be legal.

The simple answer is yes. Responsible private ownership of exotic animals should be legal if animal welfare is taken care of. Terry Thompson didn't represent the typical responsible owner. He had a criminal record and animal abuse charges. What Thompson did was selfish and insane; we cannot **regulate** insanity.

A

10 **B** People keep exotic animals for commercial[1] reasons and as pets. Most exotic animals—such as big cats, bears or apes—are in commercial, federally inspected facilities. These animals are born in captivity, and not "stolen" from the wild. Captive breeding eliminates the pressure on wild populations, and also serves as a backup in case the animals go extinct.[2]

regulate
(rĕgʹyə-lāt´) *v.* If you *regulate* something, you control or direct it according to a rule, principle, or law.

(t), (bbg) ©Siede Preis/Getty Images, (b) ©Sue Ogrocki/AP Images

---

[1] **commercial** (kə-mûrʹshəl): of or relating to commerce or trade.
[2] **extinct** (ĭk-stĭngktʹ): no longer existing or living.

Close Read Screencasts

 Close Read

Modeled Discussions

Have students click the *Close Read* icon in their eBook to access a screencast in which readers discuss and annotate lines 4–9, a key passage that introduces the author's claim and presents reasons to support it.

As a class, view and discuss the video. Then, have students pair up to do an independent close read of evidence presented in lines 16–21.

Compare and Contrast: Arguments (LINES 16–21)

RI 1,
RI 4

Tell students that readers can **compare and contrast** two arguments by examining whether the claim is backed up by logical, convincing support and looking at the language used.

(C) CITE TEXT EVIDENCE Ask students to compare the evidence in lines 16–21 with that presented in lines 26–32 in "Wild Animals Aren't Pets." Ask them how the two sets of evidence are alike and different. (*Possible response: The two texts discuss similar evidence about people killed by captive exotic animals. However, the language in "Wild Animals Aren't Pets," such as "strangled" and "mauled and disfigured," is much more emotional. Lines 16–21 here use more positive language, such as "dangers from exotic animals are low," and "only 3.25 people per year are killed."*)

English Language Support

Remind students that to *compare* means to show how two things are similar; *contrast* means to show differences. Work with them to reread lines 16–21 and 26–32, answering any questions before identifying the evidence that is the same and different.

Analyze Language

RI 1,
RI 4

(LINES 22–25)

Remind students that authors may use loaded language as a persuasive technique.

(D) ASK STUDENTS to find an example of loaded language in lines 22–25 and explain why the author uses it. (*The repeated word* freedom *is loaded language because the author wants readers to relate the ownership of exotic animals to their own freedom.*)

COLLABORATIVE DISCUSSION Before partners meet, have students decide which editorial most closely matches their own views. Point out to students that there is no one "correct" view. Remind them to cite supporting evidence.

ASK STUDENTS to share any questions they generated in the course of reading and discussing the selections.

Dangers from exotic animals are low. On average in the United States, only 3.25 people per year are killed by captive big cats, snakes, elephants and bears. Most of these fatalities are owners, family members, friends and trainers voluntarily
20 on the property where the animals were kept. Meanwhile, traffic accidents kill about 125 people per day.

If we have the freedom to choose what car to buy, where to live, or what domestic animal to have, why shouldn't we have the same freedom to choose what species of wild or exotic animal to own and to love?

Would the Ohio situation be any different if the animals were owned by a government and their caretaker released them? Is this really about private ownership, or is it about certain people's personal issues with exotics in captivity?
30 If society overreacts and bans exotics because of actions of a few deranged[3] individuals, then we need to ban kids, as that is the only way to totally stop child abuse, and we need to ban humans, because that is the only way to stop murder. Silly, isn't it?

COLLABORATIVE DISCUSSION With a partner, discuss whether the editorial or the commentary most closely matches your point of view. Point out specific passages or ideas in each text with which you strongly agree or disagree.

---

[3] **deranged** (dĭ-rānjd´): mentally unbalanced; insane.

English Language Support

ANALYZE LANGUAGE Read lines 22–25 aloud, emphasizing the word *freedom*. Then read the same lines again without the word. For example: "If we can choose what car to buy . . . why shouldn't we be able to choose what species of wild or exotic animal to own and to love?"

- List *be able to choose, have the freedom to choose,* and *can choose* on the board. Call on volunteers to read each phrase aloud and assign a connotation to each phrase: positive, negative, or neutral. (*neutral, positive, neutral*)

Analyze the Meaning of Words and Phrases

RI 4

When a writer makes an argument for or against an issue, he or she will often use persuasive techniques to convince readers to see things their way. **Persuasive techniques** are methods used to influence others to adopt a certain opinion or belief or to act a certain way.

Persuasive techniques can make a strong argument even more powerful. They can also be used to disguise flaws in weak arguments. One persuasive technique that writers use is loaded language. **Loaded language** consists of words and phrases with strongly positive or negative connotations. (**Connotations** are meanings that are associated with a word *beyond* its dictionary meaning.)

To help you analyze loaded language:

- Look for words in the text that have strong impact. Think about how these words make you feel.
- Ask yourself if the argument is strong without the use of these words.

As you analyze "Let People Own Exotic Animals," look for examples of loaded language.

Analyzing the Text

RI 1, RI 2, RI 3, RI 4

Cite Text Evidence   Support your responses with evidence from the text.

1. **Identify** What is the claim of the commentary? Where is it found?

2. **Summarize** Reread lines 10–15. According to the writer, where are most exotic animals kept and what is the benefit of breeding them?

3. **Analyze** Reread lines 16–21. What specific evidence does the writer use to support the argument that people should be allowed to own exotic animals? Explain how the evidence is or is not directly related to the claim.

4. **Interpret** Review lines 30–33. What examples of loaded language do you find? What are the positive or negative associations of these words?

CLOSE READ

Analyze the Meaning of Words and Phrases

RI 1, RI 4

Guide students to understand that writers use loaded language as a persuasive technique to influence others. Point out *simple* in line 4 and *deranged* in line 31. Invite volunteers to explain the positive connotations of *simple* and the negative connotations of *deranged*. (*Something that is simple is easy or obvious. Someone who is deranged is highly dangerous.*) Then, have students explain whether the sentences are as persuasive if the words *simple* and *deranged* are removed. (*Possible response: Both sentences would be less persuasive.*)

Analyzing the Text

RI 1, RI 2, RI 3, RI 4, RI 8

Possible answers:

1. *Lines 4–6: "Responsible private ownership of exotic animals should be legal if animal welfare is taken care of."*

2. *Most exotic animals are in facilities inspected by the government. Benefits: captive breeding helps support wild populations; may prevent extinction.*

3. *Statistics show that very few people involved with exotic pets are killed each year; many more are killed in traffic accidents. The first statistic is directly about wild animals, but the second is not.*

4. *Words: overreacts, bans, deranged, child abuse, murder. These words have negative connotations and are used to show that arguments against exotic pets are not logical.*

Strategies for Annotation

Analyze the Meaning of Words and Phrases

RI 4

Share these strategies for guided or independent analysis:

- Highlight in yellow words that are examples of loaded language.
- Underline the full sentences in which the words appear.
- Review your highlights. On a note, tell whether the argument would be as strong without the loaded language.

The simple answer is yes. Responsible private ownership of exotic animals should be legal if animal welfare is taken care of. Terry Thompson didn't represent the typical responsible owner.

PRACTICE & APPLY

Compare and Contrast: Arguments
RI 1, RI 8, RI 9

Guide students to understand the steps to take to compare and contrast two arguments. Ask students to compare the types of evidence each author provides and determine how well the evidence supports their arguments. Have students point out examples of loaded language.

Analyzing the Text
RI 1, RI 2, RI 4, RI 6, RI 8, RI 9

Possible answers:

1. *The claim of the editorial is that people should not own wild animals as pets. The claim of the commentary is that responsible people should be allowed to allowed to own wild animals as pets. Both writers present adequate evidence in the form of facts, information, and statistics that support their claims.*

2. *Editorial: Words such as "potentially tragic," "cruel world," "no good choices," "innocent victims," and "beautiful creatures" try to convince readers that the writer has the interests of wild animals at heart and make the content seem reasoned. Commentary: The words "selfish and insane," "we cannot regulate insanity," and "why shouldn't we have the same freedom" show an impatient attitude and make the content seem less logical and more emotional.*

3. *The counterargument the author includes is that Terry Thompson is not the typical exotic pet owner because he already had been charged with animal abuse .*

4. *Both editorials use strong evidence and persuasive language to support their claims; students may find the first text more authoritative; it shows that accidents can happen, so better laws are needed.*

English Language Support

Express Opinions Write these statements on the board:

Laws about owning exotic pets should be tougher. Better laws would probably end problems.

Laws about owning exotic pets must be tougher. Better laws would definitely end problems.

- Have pairs read the statements aloud and describe the effect of each set. *(suggestion; a strong opinion.)*

COMPARE TEXTS

Compare and Contrast: Arguments
RI 8, RI 9

When you **compare and contrast** two arguments on the same issue, you analyze how each argument is presented. First, you trace and evaluate each argument: identify its claim, follow its support and reasoning, and decide whether it is convincing. Then you determine how each author's viewpoint or attitude toward the issue differs.

To compare and contrast persuasive writing texts:

- Look at the evidence each writer provide as support—facts, examples, statistics. Does the evidence support the claim in a logical way?
- Determine if the writers are trying to be persuasive by appealing to your emotions, to your logic, or to both. Look for words with strong positive or negative connotations.

Analyzing the Text
RI 1, RI 2, RI 4, RI 6, RI 8, RI 9, W 1a-b, W 7

Cite Text Evidence   Support your responses with evidence from the texts.

1. **Compare** Compare each writer's claim and the kinds of evidence that support it. Does each author include enough evidence to support the claim?

2. **Evaluate** Examine each text and identify examples of loaded language. For each text, tell whether the author's word choices are effective and why.

3. **Identify** Reread lines 4–9 of "Let People Own Exotic Animals." What counterargument does the author address?

4. **Critique** Which argument do you think is more authoritative? Why?

PERFORMANCE TASK

Writing Activity: Argument Write an argument telling whether or not you would own a particular exotic animal and why.

- First, conduct research on owning a specific exotic animal. Take notes on the care, safety, and feeding of this animal.

- Next, decide whether you would or would not own this animal as a pet.
- Then draft your essay, starting with a clearly stated claim.
- Use your research notes to provide evidence that supports your claim.

Assign this performance task.

PERFORMANCE TASK
W 1a-b, W 7

Writing Activity: Argument Have students work independently. Direct them to

- choose the exotic animal they will write about
- keep track of their research sources so they can cite information from them
- draft an essay about whether they would or would not own this type of animal
- state their claim near the beginning of the essay
- organize ideas and evidence in a logical way

Critical Vocabulary

L 4a, L 5b, L6

exotic	dictate	menagerie	regulate

Practice and Apply Answer each question, choosing one or more responses.

1. Which of the following could be described as **exotic**?
   a food from another country   a backpack   a rare type of orchid

2. Which of the following is something our government can **dictate**?
   how birthdays could be celebrated   taxes people have to pay

3. Which of these might you find in a **menagerie**?
   monkeys   a stuffed lion   stars

4. Which of the following are things we could **regulate**?
   laughter   dreams   how fast people should drive

Vocabulary Strategy: Part-to-Whole Analogies

An **analogy** presents a relationship between pairs of words. Sometimes writers use analogies to explain unfamiliar ideas. A typical analogy begins with a pair of items that are related in some way. One of the most common analogies is part to whole. Here is an example, displayed first as a sentence and then with special symbols:

> *Baseball card* is to *collection* as *tiger* is to *menagerie*.
>
> **baseball card : collection :: tiger : menagerie**

Both versions express a part-to-whole relationship: *baseball card* and *tiger* are parts; *collection* and *menagerie* are wholes. In the second version, the single colon stands for "is to" and the double colon stands for "as." Examining the full analogy helps you understand how the word pairs are related.

Practice and Apply Complete each part-to-whole analogy by choosing the letter of the best answer.

1. petal : _____ :: child : family
   a. flower
   b. stem

2. chapter : book :: _____ : army
   a. uniform
   b. soldier

3. Ohio : _____ :: lettuce : salad
   a. United States
   b. Zanesville

4. elbow : arm :: people : _____
   a. business
   b. population

Compare Texts **231**

Critical Vocabulary

L 4a, L 5b, L 6

Possible answers:

1. *a food from another country; a rare type of orchid*

2. *taxes people have to pay*

3. *monkeys*

4. *how fast people should drive*

Vocabulary Strategy: Part-to-Whole Analogies

1. *a*   3. *a*

2. *b*   4. *b*

English Language Support

Discussion Web Help students collaborate to complete the performance task on page 230.

- First, write a focusing question frame on the board: *Should people be allowed to keep_____ as pets?* Then, have students research the animal they chose.

- Then, after students research, point out that the focus question may have more than one answer. Have pairs of students work together to create a written outline of a sound argument for each focus question answer.

- Next, provide students with web diagrams. Have them discuss and identify reasons and evidence to support each contrasting opinion.

- Finally, have students use their organizers and appropriate technology to write their arguments, including counterarguments.

Strategies for Annotation   🖊 📋 *Annotate it!*

Part-to-Whole Analogies   L 5b

Have students use part-to-whole analogies to clarify word meaning. Tell them to use their eBook annotation tools to do the following:

- Underline the phrase *animal welfare*.
- Highlight in yellow words that tell what *animal welfare* is a part of.
- Find another part-to-whole analogy nearby. Highlight it in green.
- Review the analogies and try to clarify meaning. If animal abuse is not part of responsible ownership, and animal welfare is, then *animal welfare* must be about caring for animals one owns.

> The simple answer is yes. Responsible private ownership of exotic animals should be legal if animal welfare is taken care of. Terry Thompson didn't represent the typical responsible owner. He had a criminal record and animal abuse charges. 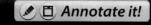 Thompson did was selfish and insane; we cannot reg
>
> welfare: "care"?

PRACTICE & APPLY

Language Conventions: Spell Words Correctly

L 2b

Explain to students that it is important to proofread their writing to check for words that are often misspelled because they are close in spelling. Most spell-check programs will not catch these types of errors because *loose* and *lose* are not misspellings; they are spelling errors in context only, and spell-check programs do not understand the context.

Point out to students that another reason they should proofread their writing is that when a reader gets distracted or confused by a misspelled word, it takes away from the writer's point and lessens the impact of what he or she is trying to say.

Answers:

1. *accept*

2. *further*

3. *advise*

4. *bear*

5. *brake*

6. *effect*

7. *passed*

8. *than*

FOR STUDENTS WITH DISABILITIES

For students with visual impairments, read the answer choices aloud letter by letter so that students can compare spellings when choosing between commonly confused words. Students using screen reader software can have their screen readers spell out words they are unsure about that sound similar and might be confused.

Language Conventions: Spell Words Correctly

L 2b

The main reason for writing is to communicate ideas with others. That's why it is extremely important for writers to use and spell words correctly.

Many common words, such as *loose* and *lose,* are spelled differently and sound slightly different, but they are close enough to be easily confused or misused. Look at this example from "Wild Animals Aren't Pets":

> **With animals running loose and darkness closing in, authorities arrived with no good choices to protect the public.**

The word *loose* is commonly misspelled as *lose,* which is a different word with a different meaning. If the writer had misspelled *loose* as *lose,* readers would have been confused and distracted. The following words are often confused:

advice/advise
lie/lay
passed/past
than/then
two/too/to
their/there/they're

Practice and Apply Choose the word from each commonly confused pair that correctly completes each sentence.

1. Gena would not (accept/except) Mindy's offer of a ride to school.

2. Do not discuss this any (farther/further) with the police until you have seen a lawyer.

3. The lawyer will (advice/advise) you of your rights.

4. The rusty fire escape did not look like it could (bare/bear) the weight of a small child.

5. Russell slammed his foot on the (brake/break) to avoid hitting the duck crossing the road in front of him.

6. The judge's ruling today will have a significant (affect/effect) on similar cases waiting to be heard.

7. Malia (passed/past) the library on her way to the store.

8. We would rather see a movie (than/then) go to the park.

English Language Support

Write and Spell Words Correctly Before students complete the Practice and Apply items, model thinking through the first item by saying: *I'm going to read the sentence aloud to hear how it sounds with each answer choice. When I say* accept *and* except *aloud it helps me hear the difference between the words.*

- Ask students to write each Practice and Apply sentence on the board. Call on volunteers to read each sentence aloud. Correct the pronunciation of the answer choices as needed and then ask students to identify the correct answers.

- Have student pairs complete the items and then ask them to write new sentences for each word in the word pairs. Then have partners check each other's sentences to see if the words were used correctly.

- Once students have completed the Practice and Apply sentences, tell them to go back and rework each sentence so that it correctly uses the other answer choice. Call on volunteers to read their examples to the class.

Paraphrase

RI 2

TEACH

Discuss with students that learning to paraphrase ideas will help them better understand and retain what they have read. Explain these points to students:

- When you **paraphrase** an author's idea, you restate the idea in your own words.
- A paraphrase does not change the author's original meaning. By paraphrasing, you restate an author's idea in a way that will help you remember it or explain it to others.

Explain that paraphrasing is different from summarizing. When you summarize, you retell the main points and important details; a summary is usually shorter than the original text. When you paraphrase, you use your own words to restate an important idea; a paraphrase may be about the same length as the original text.

PRACTICE AND APPLY

Display lines 30–33 from "Let People Own Exotic Animals." Guide students to paraphrase the author's main idea.

- Discuss the idea the author is trying to explain. Work with students to paraphrase it, such as *Just because a few owners of exotic animals are irresponsible doesn't mean no one should be allowed to own them. It would make as much sense as saying we could end child abuse by outlawing people from having children.*
- Point out how the paraphrase does not include every detail the author includes, but that it restates an important idea and an example that illustrates it.

Present other examples from the two texts and have partners or individual students paraphrase them. Use passages such as these:

- "Wild Animals Aren't Pets": lines 1–8; lines 26–32; lines 37–41
- "Let People Own Exotic Animals": lines 10–15; lines 16–21; lines 22–29

Have students share their work with the class or a larger group.

English Language Support

Paraphrase Review that paraphrasing can help students check that they understand the text. Model what to do when having difficulty paraphrasing a sentence using lines 30–33 from "Let People Own Exotic Animals." Say: *I know this sentence says something important, but when I try to paraphrase it, I run into words I don't understand. I think I need to find these words in a dictionary. Then I can be sure that I'm not changing the author's original meaning when I paraphrase.*

Compare and Contrast: Arguments

RI 8, RI 9

RETEACH

Review with students how to trace and evaluate an argument. Then, remind them that when they compare and contrast two arguments, they

- determine how the claims or positions differ
- compare and contrast how each uses evidence
- analyze the effects of each author's word choices

Have students compare evidence in lines 33–36 of "Wild Animals Aren't Pets" with evidence in lines 10–15 of "Let People Own Exotic Animals." As needed, point out that

- both authors cite evidence that thousands of exotic animals are bred and sold in this country
- the first author uses the evidence to show that there is not enough regulation of the practice
- the second author uses the evidence to point out that breeding exotic animals helps sustain wild populations and may help prevent extinction

Have partners compare and contrast the two arguments and then share their ideas with the class.

 LEVEL UP TUTORIALS Assign one or more of the following *Level Up* tutorials: **Elements of an Argument; Analyzing Arguments**

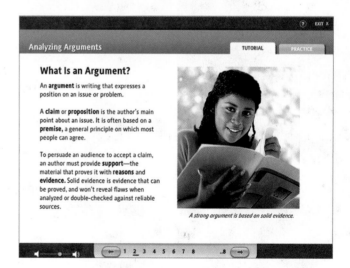

INDEPENDENT READING

Individual students can apply these skills to two editorials or letters to the editor that present opposing views on a single topic. After their analysis, have them share their ideas on comparing and contrasting arguments with other students in the class.

Views on Zoos

Why This Text

It might be difficult for students to evaluate arguments with different points of view, or to identify the reasons and evidence a writer uses to support a case. In "Views on Zoos," students will compare and contrast different viewpoints on the same subject, taking into account supporting evidence and the writer's use of persuasive techniques. With the help of the close-reading questions, students will determine the validity of each writer's claim based on a set of objective criteria.

Background Have students read the background information about zoos. Point out that in "Views on Zoos," they will read various arguments for and against zoos. Point out, however, that there are many kinds of zoos, and not all of them are featured in the article. There are urban and suburban zoos, sprawling open-air zoos, safari parks, game reserves, and petting zoos. There are even zoos dedicated to exhibiting one animal species alone. At the Jurong Bird Park in Singapore, there are more than 1,000 flamingoes living in a sprawling African-wetlands habitat, where they are treated to a daily simulated thunderstorm!

SETTING A PURPOSE Ask students to pay attention to the way the writers use loaded language and other persuasive techniques to strengthen their arguments.

Standards Support

- cite textual evidence
- determine an author's point of view in a text
- trace and evaluate the argument and specific claims in a text
- compare and contrast

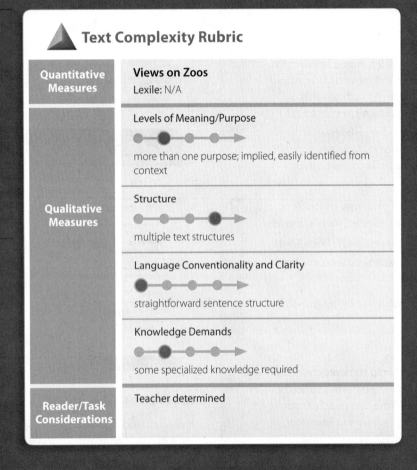

Text Complexity Rubric

Quantitative Measures

Views on Zoos
Lexile: N/A

Qualitative Measures

Levels of Meaning/Purpose

more than one purpose; implied, easily identified from context

Structure

multiple text structures

Language Conventionality and Clarity

straightforward sentence structure

Knowledge Demands

some specialized knowledge required

Reader/Task Considerations

Teacher determined

Strategies for CLOSE READING

Compare and Contrast: Arguments

Students should read the texts carefully all the way through. Close-reading questions at the bottom of the page will help them understand how a writer uses persuasive techniques to make an argument. As they read, students should jot down comments or questions about the text in the margins.

WHEN STUDENTS STRUGGLE . . .

To help students analyze and compare arguments, have them work in small groups to fill out a chart like the one shown below.

CITE TEXT EVIDENCE For practice in identifying evidence supporting an argument, have students cite evidence from the texts for and against the existence of zoos.

Evidence for Zoos	Evidence Against Zoos
"Animals that are constantly . . . life on this planet." (Functions of a Zoo, lines 3–14)	"I couldn't help noticing . . . they seemed defeated." (Sonia's Blog, lines 21–23)
"I loved seeing the animals." (Sonia's Blog, line 32)	"I felt bad . . . they couldn't be themselves." (Sonia's Blog, lines 33–34)
"Zoo conditions for animals have improved vastly." (Innocent and Imprisoned, line 8)	"The zoo inmates are all innocent." (Innocent and Imprisoned, line 7)
"Zoos also provide their customers an education." (Innocent and Imprisoned, line 29)	"Information gained from . . . in unnatural situations." (Innocent and Imprisoned, lines 27–28)

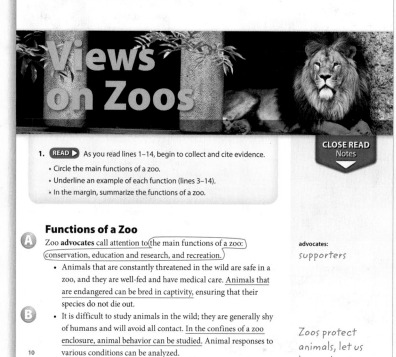

Background *The oldest known zoo existed in Hierakonpolis, Egypt, more than 5,500 years ago. It had hippos, elephants, baboons, and wildcats. In ancient times, a zoo was meant to display a leader's power and wealth. The purpose of today's zoos is different. For example, when the popular and vast Bronx Zoo opened in 1899, its purpose was to preserve native animals and promote zoology. Today, some people question whether zoos should exist at all.*

Views on Zoos

CLOSE READ
Notes

1. **READ ▶** As you read lines 1–14, begin to collect and cite evidence.
- Circle the main functions of a zoo.
- Underline an example of each function (lines 3–14).
- In the margin, summarize the functions of a zoo.

Functions of a Zoo

(A) Zoo **advocates** call attention to (the main functions of a zoo: conservation, education and research, and recreation.)
- Animals that are constantly threatened in the wild are safe in a zoo, and they are well-fed and have medical care. Animals that are endangered can be bred in captivity, ensuring that their species do not die out.

(B) - It is difficult to study animals in the wild; they are generally shy of humans and will avoid all contact. In the confines of a zoo enclosure, animal behavior can be studied. Animal responses to various conditions can be analyzed.
- Human beings have a natural curiosity about animals. Millions of people who otherwise could observe only a few animals in their lives can visit a zoo and marvel at the diversity of life on this planet.

10

advocates:
supporters

Zoos protect animals, let us learn about them, and provide a place to have fun.

63

---

1. **READ AND CITE TEXT EVIDENCE** Have students think about the three main functions of a zoo.

(A) **ASK STUDENTS** to tell which function is primarily devoted to helping animals. *Students should cite protection of animals.* Which is primarily devoted to helping humans? *Students should cite providing a place to have fun.*

Critical Vocabulary: advocates (line 1) Have students share their definitions. What does a human rights advocate do? *A human rights advocate works to support human rights.*

Sonia's Blog

Who I Am, What I Do—Every Day

Saturday, June 18

The zoo! I visited the zoo with mom today. It's the same zoo she visited with her Mom. Mom said she remembers that the first thing you would see was a cage with two Siberian[1] tigers in it. But now the tigers have a new home, a huge area about the size of three football fields. They need it—they are huge themselves. One of the tigers weighs more than 600 pounds! They are my absolute favorite animals there. Go on the web and find some images of them, you'll understand.

10　We couldn't see everything in just one day, and luckily Mom and I both like the same animals. That means no snakes or insects! I always say I like all animals, so I'm a bit embarrassed to admit that I prefer the furry, cuddly ones (but when a tiger looks you in the eye, you know it isn't very cuddly).

There were elephants (cuddly?) and giraffes! Hippos! Monkeys of all kinds! I started wondering where they all came

[1] **Siberian:** from a region in northern Russia.

The entry is about going to the zoo.

from, and how they liked it here. I talked to some zookeepers. I

20　guess it's obvious, but they all love animals, too. They take good care of them, and know each one's personality. But I couldn't help noticing a sad look in some of the animals' eyes. And they seemed defeated.

I can go jogging all around the pond and across the park, and then go with Mom to our friends way across town just to visit, that's what I can do. And then come home, and go to school the next day. Some of the animals had a faraway look that seemed to say how far they wanted to go, too. One of the

30　keepers told me that a Siberian tiger (I know, I can't stop talking about those giant cats) can travel over 600 miles. Well, that's a long way away from the zoo.

So, I had a mixed experience. I loved seeing the animals, but I felt bad for some of them because they couldn't be themselves. I know, that's just me thinking I know what an animal would feel. But here's what I think: If you put me in a big apartment with everything I might need, it would be great. For a day or two. And then I would want to go and do the things I do every day and be myself. That's what this blog is all

40　about.

What do you think about zoos? As usual, I want your comments.

---

2. ◀ REREAD Reread lines 3–14 of "Functions of a Zoo". Restate the reasons zoo advocates cite in support of the existence of zoos.

Animals in zoos are better cared for than in the wild, and their species can be protected. People can study the animals and their behavior. Visitors can learn more about the animals on the planet.

3. READ ▶ As you read lines 1–41 of "Sonia's Blog," continue to cite evidence.

- In the margin, state the topic of Sonia's blog entry.
- Circle some positive statements Sonia makes about the zoo.
- Underline some critical statements Sonia makes about the zoo.

4. ◀ REREAD Reread lines 1–10 of "Sonia's Blog". Explain how the zoo has changed over the years. Cite text evidence in your response.

Sonia's mother remembered "a cage with two Siberian tigers in it." However, when Sonia visits the zoo, the tigers have "a new home" that is the size of "three football fields."

64

65

---

2. **REREAD AND CITE TEXT EVIDENCE** Have students think about the three functions of zoos listed here.

B **ASK STUDENTS** to paraphrase the information in the second bulleted point (lines 7–10). *Students may say that animals in captivity are easier to study than animals in the wild.*

3. **READ AND CITE TEXT EVIDENCE** The blogger has positive and negative things to say about her trip to the zoo.

C **ASK STUDENTS** to think about the phrase "they seemed defeated" (line 23). What does this comment refer to? *It refers to the animals' expressions.* What effect do these words have on the reader? *They make you feel sorry for the animals.* Does this comment support or criticize zoos? *It criticizes zoos.*

4. **REREAD AND CITE TEXT EVIDENCE**

D **ASK STUDENTS** to read the blogger's comments comparing her mother's zoo experience with her own (lines 3–9). Have them make a general statement about how people's thinking about zoos has changed. *There is more humane treatment of animals now, as well as an attempt to reproduce the animals' natural habitat.*

FOR ELL STUDENTS ELL students may not have a good understanding of the measure of a mile. Explain to them that 600 miles is equivalent to 965 kilometers.

Association of Zoos and Aquariums

accredits:

guarantees that something conforms to certain rules and standards

The Association of Zoos and Aquariums (AZA) is an organization that **accredits** zoos, mostly in North America. This means that the AZA carefully makes sure that animals in zoos have suitable living environments, live together in their natural social groups, and are well taken care of, helping the animals to follow their natural behavior.

Most well-known zoos are members of the AZA, but of the animal exhibits in the United States, fewer than 10% are accredited. Worldwide, there are more than 10,000 zoos.

Most animal exhibits in the U.S. and around the world are not accredited.

AZA Statistics on Accredited Zoos	
Accredited Zoos and Aquariums	221
Animals	752,000
Species	6,000
Threatened or Endangered Species	1,000
Annual Visitors	175 million
Annual Student Learners	12 million
Jobs Supported	142,000
Annual Contribution to U.S. Economy	$16 billion

5. **READ** As you read lines 1–9 of "Association of Zoos and Aquariums" and study the chart, continue to cite text evidence.

- Underline text that explains what the association is and the duties it carries out.
- In the margin, summarize lines 7–9.
- In the chart, circle the number of species housed in accredited zoos.

6. **REREAD** Reread lines 1–9 and study the chart. What evidence could you cite that supports the existence of zoos?

The AZA ensures that animals are comfortable in zoos. The chart illustrates that zoos preserve endangered species and serve to educate millions of students.

66

G # Innocent and Imprisoned

Robert McGuinness   **July 22**

H The elephant behind the fence is bobbing her head repeatedly, a sign of "zoochosis"—distress resulting from being in a zoo. In the wild, elephants roam about 30 miles each day in large groups. But not here, and one wonders what crime she could have committed to be behind bars. That's not the way it works, though. Violent and unpredictable animals are not the kind that are exhibited in zoos. The zoo inmates are all innocent.

Of course, zoo conditions for animals have improved **vastly.** Cramped cages and incorrect diets have been replaced with open spaces and well-researched care. But it is impossible to recreate the living environment of a dolphin or a polar bear. A forty-year-long study showed that polar bears—along with lions, tigers, and cheetahs—exhibit great evidence of stress in captivity.

So why are these animals locked up? One answer to the question is conservation, but only a tiny number of zoos breed animals for conservation, and they release very few animals. During the twentieth century, there were 145 attempts to reintroduce populations into the wild, and only 16 of them were successful. The only way to **guarantee** a species' survival is to preserve them in the wild. Anyway, fewer than 15% of the animals on display are endangered. Many of the others are in zoos because of their "**charisma.**" These are animals that paying customers want to see.

There's another reason for keeping animals under lock and key: research. In some cases, this may be helpful to the animal populations as a whole, but to me it seems unscientific. Information gained from studying animals in unnatural situations is only reliable about animals in unnatural situations.

10

20

vastly:
greatly

guarantee:
ensure

charisma:
charm

7. **READ** As you read lines 1–45 of "Innocent and Imprisoned," cite text evidence.

- Underline evidence in lines 14–23 that opposes the existence of zoos.
- Circle the counterargument in lines 24–28. Underline evidence that addresses this counterargument.
- In the margin, restate the claim of the editorial in your own words.

67

---

5. **READ AND CITE TEXT EVIDENCE** Have students look at lines 7–9, stating that "fewer than 10% [of all zoos] are accredited."

E **ASK STUDENTS** to cite two pieces of evidence that can be used to support this statement. *Students should cite line 9, "Worldwide, there are more than 10,000 zoos," as well as Accredited Zoos and Aquariums shown in the chart (221 are accredited).*

6. **REREAD AND CITE TEXT EVIDENCE**

F **ASK STUDENTS** what evidence they can cite that supports the idea that zoos should be better regulated. *Students may cite the fact that fewer than 10% of all zoos are accredited—which means most of them are not (lines 8–9).*

Critical Vocabulary: accredits (line 2 of "Association of Zoos and Aquariums") Have students explain the meaning of *accredits*. What inference can be made about the zoos the AZA accredits? *They have passed AZA inspections and/or demonstrated compliance with certain regulations.*

7. **READ AND CITE TEXT EVIDENCE**

G **ASK STUDENTS** to consider the words in the title, "innocent" and "imprisoned." What inferences can you make about the writer's argument based on the title? *The writer will probably say that zoo animals are "innocent" and shouldn't be locked up.*

Critical Vocabulary: vastly (line 8) What else can students think of that has improved *vastly* over the years? *Students may suggest computers and cell phone technology.*

Critical Vocabulary: guarantee (line 19) What does it mean when a you get a lifetime *guarantee* on a piece of merchandise? *The company will fix or replace the item if it malfunctions.*

Critical Vocabulary: charisma (line 22) Ask students to name zoo animals they think have the greatest *charisma*. *Students may name seals, chimpanzees, or dolphins.*

There is no zoo that serves animals, so we should take care of animals in the wild.

30   Zoos also provide their customers an education. In most cases, however, the information given about an animal is very brief and presented on a small sign that few people bother to read. People tend to talk to their friends as they watch the exotic animals, rather than learn about their particular traits and characteristics. Visitors may watch in surprise as lions choose the freezing outdoors over heated shelters, but never learn that these animals once roamed freely throughout Europe.

   The final main reason for having zoos is entertainment. This is obviously unfair to the animals that are imprisoned to entertain
40 us. There are numerous television shows and movies that show us animals in their natural environments, behaving in ways that are natural to them.

   A zoo that really suited animals would be a failure. It would be huge, and many of the animals would remain out of sight. The money spent supporting zoos would be better used trying to save animals in their natural surroundings, where they belong.

---

8. ◀ **REREAD AND DISCUSS** Reread lines 1–45. With a small group, discuss whether you find the writer's argument convincing. Cite reasons and evidence from the text that you find are the strongest or the weakest.

SHORT RESPONSE

Cite Text Evidence   What is your position on the existence of zoos? Write an argument in favor of or against zoos. **Cite text evidence** to support your claim and address any counterarguments.

Sample response: I am in favor of the existence of zoos. Zoos serve an important educational function for both students like Sonia and researchers. Zoos also protect endangered species. The AZA ensures that animals are safe and comfortable. Even people who think zoos should be abolished, like McGuinness, have to admit that "conditions for animals have improved vastly."

68

TO CHALLENGE STUDENTS . . .

To increase students' familiarity with different kinds of zoos, have them conduct research on zoos in their area and beyond.

ASK STUDENTS to choose a zoo to research.

- Have them use a chart similar to the one on page 66 to list facts and figures about their zoo.
- Have groups compare and contrast their zoo with the rest of the nation's zoos on a number of criteria, including how many of each kind of animal there are.
- Groups can establish their own criteria for rating zoos, such as the animals' diets, medical treatment, exercise, interaction with their peers, and how well their zoo environments replicate the conditions of home.
- Have students give their zoo a "rating."

ASK STUDENTS to conduct research on zoos around the world. Have them include information such as:

- the number of animals.
- the variety of animals.
- the number of visitors.
- the treatment of old or sick animals.

After groups have completed their research, they can work together to rate the zoos based on predetermined criteria.

---

8. **REREAD AND DISCUSS USING TEXT EVIDENCE**

Ⓗ **ASK STUDENTS** to assign a reporter for each group to share the strong and the weak evidence. *Strong evidence: "zoochosis" (line 2); stress in captivity (line 13); only 16 of 145 attempts at reintroducing populations were successful (lines 17–19). Weak evidence: research is unscientific (lines 25–26); few people bother to read (line 31); a suitable zoo would be a failure (line 42).*

SHORT RESPONSE

Cite Text Evidence   Students should:

- make an argument for or against zoos.
- cite supporting text evidence for the argument.
- address counterarguments using reason and logic.
- use persuasive techniques such as loaded language.
- choose words that have positive or negative connotations.

DIG DEEPER

1. With the class, return to Question 3, Read. Have students share their responses.

   ASK STUDENTS to review lines 35–39 of "Sonia's Blog" and analyze the analogy the writer uses comparing herself to the animals in the zoo. Have them discuss the following points:

   - How is the "big apartment" like a zoo?
   - How would the writer feel about living in the big apartment at first?
   - How would she feel about it in the long term?
   - How does she imagine the animals feel about living in a zoo?
   - Students can use their answers to draw conclusions about the writer's overall feeling about zoos.

2. With the class, return to Question 8, Reread and Discuss. Have students share their responses.

   ASK STUDENTS to discuss this writer's point of view about zoos.

   - Have students think about the word *zoochosis*. What specific connotations does this word carry? Does the use of this term help or hinder the effectiveness of the writer's argument?
   - Have students discuss how effectively the McGuinness article addresses the bulleted claims in "Functions of a Zoo" (lines 1–14). Does McGuinness provide counterarguments for each of the claims made?
   - Do students agree with McGuinness? Are there flaws in his logic? Does he provide enough evidence to support his conclusions?

   ASK STUDENTS to return to their Short Response answer and revise it based on the class discussion.

CLOSE READING NOTES

EXEMPLAR **Eleven**

Short Story by Sandra Cisneros

Why This Text?

Realistic fiction regularly engages young people with characters they can recognize and relate to on many levels. This lesson explores how a character named Rachel responds and changes to story events and the techniques the author uses to create a believable story and memorable characters.

Key Learning Objective: The student will be able to analyze an author's style, tone, and characterization in a short story.

For Practice and Application:

Close Reader selection
"What Do Fish Have to Do with Anything?"
Short Story by Avi

RL 1 Cite textual evidence; make inferences.

RL 3 Describe how a story's characters respond or change as the plot moves toward a resolution.

RL 4 Determine the meaning of words and phrases.

SL 1a Come to discussions prepared.

SL 1b Follow rules for discussions.

SL 1c Pose and respond to questions with elaboration and detail.

SL 1d Review key ideas expressed and demonstrate understanding of multiple perspectives.

L 2 Demonstrate command of standard English punctuation.

L 4c Consult reference materials.

L 5c Distinguish among connotations of words with similar denotations.

L 6 Acquire and use grade-appropriate academic words.

▲ Text Complexity Rubric

Quantitative Measures	**Eleven** Lexile: 1090L
Qualitative Measures	**Levels of Meaning/Purpose** single level of complex meaning
	Structure one consistent point of view
	Language Conventionality and Clarity less straightforward sentence structure
	Knowledge Demands common, everyday experience
Reader/Task Considerations	• Teacher determined • Vary by individual reader and type of text • See the Text X-Ray for suggested Reader/Task Considerations.

English Language Support

Before teaching, use the Text X-Ray for an overview of the text's complexity. The Text X-Ray and the supports and scaffolds in the Teacher's Edition will help you guide students of different skill levels.

Meaning Making
Language Development
Effective Expression
Content Knowledge
Foundational Skills

Text Complexity: Qualitative Measures

Levels of Meaning/Purpose

single level of complex meaning

Help students understand characterization.

- Teacher's Edition side notes, pp. 233, 234, 235, 237
- English Language Support, pp. 234
- Describe Characters' Responses, p. 237

To reteach characterization, see

- Characterization, page 240a

ZOOM IN ON UNDERSTANDING CHARACTERIZATION Explain that authors can describe characters by showing how the characters think.

- Read aloud lines 17–20.
- Highlight the words "the way you grow old . . . inside a tree trunk." Circle the word *grow*. Draw a cross-section of a tree showing layers.
- Ask students to describe what Rachel means. (*As people grow older, new layers grow over old ones*.)
- Guide students to understand how Rachel sees getting older: As you age, your younger self is still part of you.

Structure

one consistent point of view

Help students analyze style and tone.

- Teacher's Edition side notes, pp. 233, 235, 236, 237
- English Language Support, p. 233
- Strategies for Annotation, p. 237
- When Students Struggle, p. 236
- Analyze Word Choice and Tone, p. 237

Help students analyze dialogue.

- Teacher's Edition side note, p. 234

To reteach analyze style, see

- Analyze Style, p. 240a

▶ *Use It!* **Level Up Tutorials:** Author's Style

ZOOM IN ON ANALYZING STYLE AND TONE Tell students that **style** is about *how* something is said, not *what* is said. For example, different people might wear the same hat in different ways. The hat is the same, but *how* it is worn changes, and the difference affects how the person looks.

- Explain that changing words and sentence structures in a story can produce a different effect for the reader.
- Give the following examples: *I hate that being eleven still feels like being ten./It feels great to finally turn eleven*
- Ask students what is different about the two sentences. (*one is grumpy, one is happy*) Point out that both are about the same thing, turning eleven.

Language Conventionality and Clarity

less straightforward sentence structure

Teach unfamiliar academic vocabulary in context.
- Teacher's Edition Critical Vocabulary notes, pp. 234, 235
- Critical Vocabulary, p. 239

Help students understand connotations.
- Vocabulary Strategy: Denotations and Connotations, p. 239
- English Language Support, p. 239
- Strategies for Annotation, p. 239

Teach punctuating dialogue.
- Language Conventions: Punctuating Dialogue, p. 240
- English Language Support, p. 240

ZOOM IN ON **UNDERSTANDING CONNOTATION AND DENOTATION** To help students understand **connotation** and **denotation**, label a Venn diagram with *Positive Feeling*, *Neutral Feeling*, and *Negative Feeling*. Write *soaring* on the left, *tall* in the center, and *looming* on the right.

- Say, *I see a tall building*. Ask volunteers to replace the word *tall* with *soaring* or *looming*. Help students identify which word gives the sentence a positive or negative feeling.
- Repeat with the word *wet* and the sentence: *The ground was wet*. Have students list words for wet with different connotations. (*slimy, soggy, dewy, shiny*) Have small groups sort the words in a Venn diagram and write sentences using them.

Knowledge Demands

common, everyday experience

Help students to understand the background of the author.
- Teacher's Edition Author note, p. 233

ZOOM IN ON **BUILDING BACKGROUND KNOWLEDGE** Remind students that author Sandra Cisneros was shy when she was a child. Point out that the character Rachel is shy too.

- Read aloud lines 41–48.
- Ask students to describe how shyness affects Rachel in this passage. (*She finds it hard to speak up for herself.*)
- Have students identify and present to the class other examples of how Rachel's shyness makes the story's events hard for her.

Suggested Reader/Task Considerations

You might consider the following before assigning the selection:
- Will the text engage the interest of the students?
- Do students believe that they will be able to read and understand the text?

ZOOM IN ON **SUPPORTING COMPREHENSION**

- To capture students' interest, alternate reading to students with students reading silently, answering questions and clarifying ideas during each transition.
- Explain that the numbers in the first sentence are all ages. Have students restate the numbers as ages. (*eleven years old, ten years old, etc.*)

CLOSE READ

Sandra Cisneros Have students read the information about the author. Tell them that despite having six brothers Cisneros was shy and introverted as a child. Her family moved often, and it was difficult for her to make friends. She became a quiet observer of life and expressed herself through writing. Cisneros often writes about Mexican and Mexican American women, bringing to life their strength and ability to rise above poverty.

SETTING A PURPOSE Direct students to use the Setting a Purpose prompt to focus their reading. Remind them to write down questions as they read.

Describe Characters'   RL 1, RL 3
Responses (LINES 1–16)

Explain that one way readers learn about characters in a story is through the characters' words, thoughts, and actions.

A   **CITE TEXT EVIDENCE** Ask students how Rachel feels about birthdays and to explain how they know this. *(Rachel thinks birthdays are not as good as people say they are. She says "you don't feel eleven at all"; "you're still ten . . . underneath the year that makes you eleven.")*

B   **ASK STUDENTS** to explain what Rachel means in lines 2–6 and lines 10–16 about feeling older. *(Possible response: Rachel believes that your younger self is still part of you as you grow older. She knows that there will be times when you will feel and behave more like the younger you—and it's okay to do that.)*

Analyze Word Choice   RL 4

(LINES 10–11)

Explain to students that a writer's **word choice,** the language used to express an idea, has a direct impact on readers' understanding of characters.

C   **ASK STUDENTS** to reread lines 10–11 and describe the language. *(Possible responses: informal; like an eleven-year-old talking to you)* Have students tell why the author might choose this kind of language. *(It helps the reader understand Rachel; it tells readers that Rachel is telling the story in her own words and from her point of view.)*

Sandra Cisneros (b. 1954) *is one of seven children born to her Mexican father and Mexican American mother. When Cisneros was eleven, her family moved to a poor neighborhood in Chicago. Cisneros's first novel,* The House on Mango Street, *published in 1984, paints a picture of this neighborhood and the people who lived in it. It took Cisneros eight years to write the book. Cisneros has won many awards for her poems, short stories, and novels. She now lives in San Antonio, Texas.*

Eleven

Short Story by Sandra Cisneros

SETTING A PURPOSE As you read, pay attention to how the narrator feels and the clues that help you understand why she feels the way she does.

A   What they don't understand about birthdays and what they never tell you is that when you're eleven, you're also ten, and nine, and eight, and seven, and six, and five, and four, and three, and two, and one. And when you wake up on your eleventh birthday you expect to feel eleven, but you don't. You open your eyes and everything's just like yesterday, only it's today. And you don't feel eleven at all. You feel like you're still ten. And you are—underneath the year that makes you eleven. **B**

10   Like some days you might say something stupid, and **C** that's the part of you that's still ten. Or maybe some days you might need to sit on your mama's lap because you're scared, and that's the part of you that's five. And maybe one day when you're all grown up maybe you will need to cry like if you're **B**

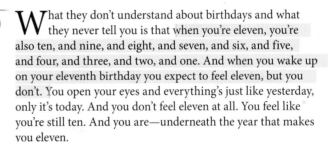

(t) ©Eric Gay/AP Images; (c) ©Neil Webb/Corbis

Eleven   **233**

English Language Support

Evaluate Language Choices Display lines 10–16. Explain that the narrator's informal language helps show the reader who she is, but this kind of language does not always follow English grammar rules. Underline "Like some days you might say" in line 10, "like if you're three" in lines 14–15, and "Maybe she's feeling three" in line 16.

- Have students rewrite each phrase in formal English. *(Some days you might say; as if you were three; she may be feeling like she's three years old.)*

Analyze Dialogue
RL 1,
RL 3,
RL 4

(LINES 32–48)

Remind students that **dialogue** is written conversation between two or more characters. Dialogue brings characters to life and advances the **plot,** or series of events in a story.

D **CITE TEXT EVIDENCE** Have students reread lines 32–48 and analyze the purpose of this part of the story, citing lines of dialogue that contribute to the development of the plot. (*The dialogue between Mrs. Price and the students brings the character of Mrs. Price to life and sets up the conflict between her and Rachel.*)

Describe Characters' Responses
RL 1,
RL 3

(LINES 49–51)

Remind students that characters in a story have **traits,** or personal qualities, that are revealed as the plot unfolds and characters respond to one another.

E **CITE TEXT EVIDENCE** Have students reread lines 49–51, and then identify some character traits of Mrs. Price and Rachel and the specific words and phrases that help to reveal these traits. (*Mrs. Price is impatient and dismissive of Rachel when she says, "'Of course it's yours'"; Rachel is timid toward an authority figure even though she knows Mrs. Price is not being fair: "Because she's older and the teacher, she's right and I'm not."*)

CRITICAL VOCABULARY

rattle: Rachel compares her eleven years of life to pennies rattling around in a tin box. **ASK STUDENTS** why the author might have chosen this comparison. (*It emphasizes how immature Rachel feels; she feels a little hollow or empty inside.*) Note that *rattling* is a sensory word that conjures up a distinct sound; demonstrate the sound.

raggedy: Rachel describes the red sweater as "all raggedy and old," as well as ugly. **ASK STUDENTS** how the word *raggedy* contributes to their understanding of how Rachel feels about the sweater. (*The word* raggedy *has a negative feeling, as if the person who owns it doesn't take care of it or can't have a better one. It helps you visualize the sweater and understand why Rachel loathes it.*)

---

three, and that's okay. That's what I tell Mama when she's sad and needs to cry. Maybe she's feeling three.

Because the way you grow old is kind of like an onion or like the rings inside a tree trunk or like my little wooden dolls that fit one inside the other, each year inside the next one.

20 That's how being eleven years old is.

You don't feel eleven. Not right away. It takes a few days, weeks even, sometimes even months before you say Eleven when they ask you. And you don't feel smart eleven, not until you're almost twelve. That's the way it is.

Only today I wish I didn't have only eleven years **rattling** inside me like pennies in a tin Band-Aid box. Today I wish I was one hundred and two instead of eleven because if I was one hundred and two I'd have known what to say when Mrs. Price put the red sweater on my desk. I would've known

30 how to tell her it wasn't mine instead of just sitting there with that look on my face and nothing coming out of my mouth.

"Whose is this?" Mrs. Price says, and she holds the red sweater up in the air for all the class to see. "Whose? It's been sitting in the coatroom for a month."

"Not mine," says everybody. "Not me."

"It has to belong to somebody," Mrs. Price keeps saying, but nobody can remember. It's an ugly sweater with red plastic buttons and a collar and sleeves all stretched out like you could use it for a jump rope. It's maybe a thousand years old

40 and even if it belonged to me I wouldn't say so.

Maybe because I'm skinny, maybe because she doesn't like me, that stupid Sylvia Saldívar says, "I think it belongs to Rachel." An ugly sweater like that, all **raggedy** and old, but Mrs. Price believes her. Mrs. Price takes the sweater and puts it right on my desk, but when I open my mouth nothing comes out.

"That's not, I don't, you're not . . . Not mine," I finally say in a little voice that was maybe me when I was four.

"Of course it's yours," Mrs. Price says. "I remember you

50 wearing it once." Because she's older and the teacher, she's right and I'm not.

Not mine, not mine, not mine, but Mrs. Price is already turning to page thirty-two, and math problem number four. I don't know why but all of a sudden I'm feeling sick inside, like the part of me that's three wants to come out of my eyes, only I squeeze them shut tight and bite down on my teeth real

rattle
(răt´l) *v.* If you hear something *rattle*, it is making a short, fast knocking sound as it moves.

raggedy
(răg´ĭ-dē) *adj.* Something that is *raggedy* is worn out, torn, or frayed.

English Language Support

Express Inferences and Conclusions Display and read aloud lines 60–65. Underline the last three lines.

- Work with students to perform the actions in each sentence, using a piece of paper to represent the sweater. Prompt students with questions such as *How do you think Rachel feels about the sweater? If you were doing the same thing with, say, a shirt, what feelings would you have about it?*

hard and try to remember today I am eleven, eleven. Mama is making a cake for me for tonight, and when Papa comes home everybody will sing Happy birthday, happy birthday to you.

60 But when the sick feeling goes away and I open my eyes, the red sweater's still sitting there like a big red mountain. I move the red sweater to the corner of my desk with my ruler. I move my pencil and books and eraser as far from it as possible. I even move my chair a little to the right. Not mine, not mine, not mine.

In my head I'm thinking how long till lunchtime, how long till I can take the red sweater and throw it over the schoolyard fence, or leave it hanging on a parking meter, or bunch it up into a little ball and toss it in the **alley**. Except when math

70 period ends Mrs. Price says loud and in front of everybody, "Now, Rachel, that's enough," because she sees I've shoved the red sweater to the tippy-tip corner of my desk and it's hanging all over the edge like a waterfall, but I don't care.

"Rachel," Mrs. Price says. She says it like she's getting mad. "You put that sweater on right now and no more nonsense."

"But it's not—"

"Now!" Mrs. Price says.

alley
(ăl´ē) *n.* An *alley* is a narrow street or passage behind or between city buildings.

« You put that sweater
on right now and
no more nonsense. »

This is when I wish I wasn't eleven, because all the years inside of me—ten, nine, eight, seven, six, five, four, three,
80 two, and one—are pushing at the back of my eyes when I put one arm through one sleeve of the sweater that smells like cottage cheese, and then the other arm through the other and stand there with my arms apart like if the sweater hurts me and it does, all itchy and full of germs that aren't even mine.

That's when everything I've been holding in since this morning, since when Mrs. Price put the sweater on my desk, finally lets go, and all of a sudden I'm crying in front of everybody. I wish I was **invisible** but I'm not. I'm eleven and

invisible
(ĭn-vĭz´ə-bəl) *adj.* If something is *invisible*, you cannot see it.

Eleven **235**

TO CHALLENGE STUDENTS...

Analyze Point of View Tell students to discuss how the characters and events of "Eleven" would be different if told from a point of view other than Rachel's. What if Mrs. Price or one of Rachel's classmates were telling the story? How would it be different if an omniscient narrator (someone not involved in the story but who has knowledge of the characters and events) were telling the story? Have students take turns retelling the story from one of these different points of view.

ASK STUDENTS to share their ideas with the class.

CLOSE READ

Describe Characters' Responses (LINES 66–77)

RL 1, RL 3

Explain that additional character traits are revealed as characters respond to new story developments.

F **CITE TEXT EVIDENCE** Have students reread lines 66–77 and cite text that shows the tension between Mrs. Price and Rachel. *(Lines 71–77 show Mrs. Price and Rachel growing more upset with each other.)* Have students explain what this scene tells readers about each character. *(Rachel's attempt to move the sweater away from herself makes Mrs. Price annoyed, and it shows how stubborn Rachel is. Soon Mrs. Price is angry, too.)*

Analyze Word Choice and Tone (LINES 78–84)

RL 4

Point out that this paragraph contains vivid **sensory details,** words that appeal to the reader's senses. Explain to students that **tone,** or the writer's attitude toward the subject, is often shown through details.

G **ASK STUDENTS** to reread lines 78–84. Ask what these details add to readers' understanding of Rachel and how they affect the tone of the paragraph. *(Possible response: The sensory details help readers see, feel, and smell the sweater as Rachel does; they clearly show Rachel's misery and disgust. The scene is a bit dramatic for the situation to show how upset Rachel is at having to put on the sweater and at not being able to speak up for herself.)*

CRITICAL VOCABULARY

alley: Rachel wants to throw the red sweater over a fence, hang it on a parking meter, or toss it into an alley. **ASK STUDENTS** to think about these three choices and tell how tossing something into an alley is similar to the other two actions. *(Rachel wants to get rid of the sweater. An alley can be a hidden, neglected place. If you toss something into one, you probably hope it will never be found.)*

invisible: When Rachel bursts into tears in class, she wishes she were invisible. **ASK STUDENTS** to explain why Rachel wants to be invisible. *(She doesn't want anyone to see her crying, as if she were three years old.)* Ask students if they have ever wanted to be invisible.

Eleven **235**

Analyze Word Choice and Tone (LINES 97–109)

RL 1,
RL 4

Remind students that word choice is one way authors set the tone in a story.

H **CITE TEXT EVIDENCE** Have students reread lines 97–106, describe the tone, and cite text that creates it. *(The tone is angry and a little sad. The words "stupid Phyllis Lopez," "even dumber than Sylvia," and "pretends like everything's okay" show Rachel's anger at her classmates and Mrs. Price. When Rachel thinks "only it's too late," we know she is sad because her birthday has been spoiled.)*

I **ASK STUDENTS** to reread lines 107–109 and tell where they have read them before. *(lines 1–4; lines 78–80, when Rachel puts on the sweater)* Ask why Cisneros repeats these words at these places in the story. *(Possible responses: The words emphasize Rachel's idea that birthdays do not mean immediate knowledge or maturity; growing up is a long process and sometimes people step back to a younger age. The repetition of these words ties the story together.)*

COLLABORATIVE DISCUSSION Have partners discuss Mrs. Price and Rachel's classmates and how their actions make Rachel feel. Ask how Rachel's feelings might be different if these characters had acted differently. Encourage students to describe what Mrs. Price and the other students could have done to make Rachel feel safe and more welcome in the classroom. Remind students to cite evidence for their ideas.

ASK STUDENTS to share any questions they generated in the course of reading and discussing the selection.

WHEN STUDENTS STRUGGLE . . .

To guide students' comprehension of the story's ending, have them reread lines 97–106. Why isn't Rachel happy, excited, or joyful at the end? Have students discuss the related phrases "only Mrs. Price pretends like everything's okay" and "only it's too late" and the inferences readers need to make to understand how Rachel feels. Have students use an Inference Chart like the one shown to record their ideas.

LEVEL UP TUTORIALS Assign the following *Level Up* tutorial: **Make Inferences About Characters**

---

it's my birthday today and I'm crying like I'm three in front
90   of everybody. I put my head down on the desk and bury my
face in my stupid clown-sweater arms. My face all hot and spit
coming out of my mouth because I can't stop the little animal
noises from coming out of me, until there aren't any more
tears left in my eyes, and it's just my body shaking like when
you have the hiccups, and my whole head hurts like when you
drink milk too fast.

But the worst part is right before the bell rings for lunch.
That stupid Phyllis Lopez, who is even dumber than Sylvia
Saldívar, says she remembers the red sweater is hers! I take it
100 off right away and give it to her, only Mrs. Price pretends like
everything's okay.

Today I'm eleven. There's a cake Mama's making
for tonight, and when Papa comes home from work we'll
eat it. There'll be candles and presents and everybody will
sing Happy birthday, happy birthday to you, Rachel, only it's
too late.

I'm eleven today. I'm eleven, ten, nine, eight, seven, six,
five, four, three, two, and one, but I wish I was one hundred
and two. I wish I was anything but eleven, because I want
110 today to be far away already, far away like a runaway balloon,
like a tiny o in the sky, so tiny-tiny you have to close your eyes
to see it.

COLLABORATIVE DISCUSSION With a partner, discuss how the story events and other characters affect the narrator's feelings. Cite specific passages to support your ideas.

Evidence	Your Knowledge	Inference
Mrs. Price pretends everything's okay.	When people pretend something is okay, it usually isn't.	Rachel thinks Mrs. Price should admit she was wrong.
Rachel says it's too late for a happy birthday.	Rachel doesn't mean the time of day.	The sweater incident has upset Rachel and ruined her birthday.

Analyze Word Choice and Tone RL 4

A piece of writing usually has a particular style. A **style** is a manner of writing; it involves *how* something is said rather than *what* is said. Style is shown through elements such as

- **word choice**—the way words and phrases are used to express ideas
- **sentence structure**—the types, patterns, and lengths of sentences used, including fragments (pieces of sentences)
- **dialogue**—realistic conversation between characters
- **tone**—the writer's attitude toward the subject, such as *serious, playful, mocking,* and *sympathetic*

The author's choice to tell "Eleven" from Rachel's point of view affects the style of the writing. For example, reread the first paragraph. Note that the writer uses a combination of long and short sentences and conversational words as if Rachel were talking directly to you. When Rachel describes how she feels about turning eleven, the tone might be described as *annoyed* or *grumpy.* These style elements draw us into Rachel's world and help us see the story from her perspective.

As you analyze "Eleven," find other examples of these techniques that reveal the writer's style and the tone of the story.

Describe Characters' Responses RL 3

The way a writer develops characters is known as **characterization.** Writers develop their story characters through the characters' words, thoughts, and actions. They also use other methods, such as describing how a character looks, telling how other characters react to him or her, and by commenting directly on the character through the use of a narrator.

By noticing and analyzing these methods of characterization, readers can better understand what motivates the characters and makes them behave the way they do. As you analyze Rachel's character, ask yourself:

- What does she look like?
- What does she think about turning eleven?
- How does Mrs. Price treat her?
- How does Rachel respond to the conflict in the story?

As you analyze "Eleven," look for more examples of the author's characterization of Rachel as well as other characters in the story.

Eleven **237**

CLOSE READ

Analyze Word Choice and Tone RL 4

Help students review the elements of style present in "Eleven." As they reread the first paragraph, have students think about how the elements work together to contribute to the tone and style of the story. As students continue to analyze the story, have them focus on how the author uses the techniques of word choice, sentence structure, dialogue, and tone to create a compelling character and story.

Describe Characters' Responses RL 1, RL 3

Help students understand that characterization in a story is ongoing. Writers don't describe their characters fully when they are introduced. Readers don't know or understand a character completely until we see how he or she responds to story events and interacts with other characters. Explain that readers must also make inferences about what a character's responses and interactions reveal about him or her.

After discussing how the author establishes Rachel's point of view, ask students to return to the story and discuss why Mrs. Price is dismissive of Rachel, or why Rachel's classmates don't support her. Remind students to support their ideas with text evidence. *(Possible responses: Perhaps Rachel acts like a know-it-all [calls her classmates "stupid," "dumb"], or she is self-conscious and doesn't make friends easily [she is skinny, thinks Sylvia doesn't like her].)*

Strategies for Annotation ✎ 🖥 *Annotate it!*

Analyze Word Choice and Tone RL 4

Have students use their eBook annotation tools to analyze the text:

- Highlight in yellow words that have an impact on meaning and tone.
- Underline examples of different types and lengths of sentences, including fragments.
- On a note, jot down how you would describe the tone of the passage.

Not mine, not mine, not mine, but Mrs. Price is already turning to page thirty-two, and math problem number four. I don't know why but all of a sudden I'm feeling sick inside, like the part of me that's three wants to come out of my eyes, only I squeeze them shut tight and bite down on my teeth real hard and try to remember today I am eleven, eleven.

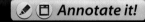 tone is "upset," "angry"

PRACTICE & APPLY

Analyzing the Text

RL 1,
RL 3,
RL 4

Possible answers:

1. *Although you are a year older, you are still the same person you were before; you don't immediately change and mature; you still have the younger you inside. The author uses these words because it sounds like something an adolescent would say, sort of annoyed or exasperated but vivid and clear.*

2. *Other similes: "like the rings inside a tree trunk," "like my little wooden dolls that fit one inside the other"; all three similes refer to the fact that as you grow older, you add another layer (or ring, or doll) to the person who already exists. The younger you does not disappear.*

3. *Rachel's inability to speak up for herself makes her feel small and powerless, and this makes her miserable. When Rachel says, "Because she's [Mrs. Price] older and the teacher, she's right and I'm not," you can tell she feels that turning eleven hasn't made her old enough or strong enough to contradict an authority figure such as Mrs. Price.*

4. *Rachel starts pushing the sweater away, so it is falling off her desk. Mrs. Price is annoyed by this, and then demands that Rachel put on the sweater. The injustice of not being heard or believed and being ordered to put on something that does not belong to her is more than Rachel can bear. She can't be invisible, so she bursts into uncontrollable crying.*

5. *Rachel's unkind remarks about Phyllis and Sylvia show that she is angry and defensive. She is focusing her anger about the sweater incident on them. Although this is immature, her comments might be justified because Phyllis should have spoken up sooner, and Sylvia, as well as other classmates, may have known the sweater was not Rachel's but did not back her up with Mrs. Price.*

6. *The tone at the end of the story is sad. Despite knowing she will be celebrating her birthday with her family, Rachel wants to disappear, to be "far away like a runaway balloon."*

7. *The author uses a casual, conversational style. The author uses many long sentences and repeats words to replicate the narrator's thought patterns.*

FOR STANDARD ENGLISH LEARNERS

Pronunciation As they prepare for discussion, remind students of the rules for pronouncing the /sh/ and /ch/ digraph in standard English. Have students practice saying words such as *teacher, Rachel, share,* and *shame.*

 **eBook** *Annotate It!*

Analyzing the Text

RL 1, RL 3, RL 4,
SL 1a, SL 1b,
SL 1c, SL 1d

Cite Text Evidence Support your responses with evidence from the text.

1. **Draw Conclusions** In "Eleven," Rachel says that when you're eleven, you're also ten, nine, eight, seven, six, five, four, three, two, and one. What does Rachel mean by this and why do you think the author chose these words to convey that meaning?

2. **Interpret** Reread lines 17–20. When Rachel says that growing old is "like an onion," she is using a **simile,** a comparison that uses the word *like* or *as.* What other similes does she use in lines 17–20, and what meaning do all the similes convey?

3. **Synthesize** Explain how Rachel's inability to speak up to Mrs. Price contributes to how she feels about turning eleven.

4. **Analyze** What are the consequences of Rachel's being unable to speak up to Mrs. Price? Explain why Rachel has such a negative reaction to wearing the sweater.

5. **Evaluate** Reread lines 97–101. What do Rachel's words about Phyllis and Sylvia reveal about her character? Are Rachel's comments justified? Why or why not?

6. **Analyze** How would you describe the tone at the end of the story? What techniques does the author use to convey this tone?

7. **Analyze** How would you describe the author's style? Describe some of the aspects that convey the author's style.

PERFORMANCE TASK

Speaking Activity: Collaborative Discussion In a small group, discuss the role of Mrs. Price as a minor character in "Eleven." Together, explain why Mrs. Price's actions are an important part of the story.

- Appoint one member of the group to take notes.
- List words that describe Mrs. Price.
- Describe Rachel's reactions to Mrs. Price as an authority figure.

- Discuss how the first-person point of view with Rachel as narrator affects how Mrs. Price is described and how the reader sees her.
- When the discussion is finished, review the key ideas expressed. Then share the group's ideas with the rest of the class. Be sure to point out examples in the story that support the group's ideas.

Assign this
performance task.

PERFORMANCE TASK

SL 1a–d

Speaking Activity: Collaborative Discussion Ask students to create an inference chart to help them describe Mrs. Price. Direct each group to

- follow the rules for successful discussions
- pose and respond to questions thoughtfully
- review discussion notes before sharing them with the class

Critical Vocabulary

rattle   raggedy   alley   invisible

Practice and Apply Use what you know about the Vocabulary words to answer the questions.

1. Which Vocabulary word goes with *narrow*? Why?

2. Which Vocabulary word goes with *noisy*? Why?

3. Which Vocabulary word goes with *shredded*? Why?

4. Which Vocabulary word goes with *hidden*? Why?

Vocabulary Strategy:
Denotations and Connotations

A word's **denotation** is its dictionary meaning. A word's **connotation** includes the feelings and ideas associated with it. For example, the dictionary definition of the word *frigid* is "extremely cold." The word *wintry* also means "cold," but the two words can have different connotations.

Writers use connotations of words to communicate positive or negative feelings. *Frigid* has the negative connotation of meaning the weather is so cold that you do not want to be outside in it. In contrast, *wintry* has a more positive connotation and may bring to mind crisp air or cheery snow flurries. Each word creates a different tone in the writing and elicits different feelings in the reader.

In "Eleven," Rachel describes the sweater as *raggedy,* which means "tattered, worn out." From this, you can tell that Rachel is angry partly because the sweater is in bad shape. Thinking about a word's connotation will help you to understand the writer's purpose in using that word.

Practice and Apply Read the words in each group below. (The first word in each group is from "Eleven.") Look up any words you do not know in a dictionary. Then arrange each group of words in order from positive to negative connotation. Discuss your responses with a partner or small group.

1. *skinny, thin, gaunt, narrow, scrawny*

2. *raggedy, torn, ripped, frayed, shredded, tattered*

3. *hanging, dangling, drooping, falling, swinging*

4. *rattling, shaking, quivering, wobbling, jerking, jiggling*

5. *shoved, pushed, guided, propelled, crammed, forced*

6. *squeezed, jammed, crushed, stuffed, condensed, smashed, compressed*

PRACTICE & APPLY

Critical Vocabulary

Answers:

1. **alley**; *an alley is usually narrow and cramped, hard to pass through.*

2. **rattling**; *if something is rattling, it is making a knocking noise.*

3. **raggedy**; *if something is raggedy, it is torn and shredded.*

4. **invisible**; *something that is hidden is invisible; it cannot be seen.*

Vocabulary Strategy:
Denotations and Connotations

There is no correct order for each group of words; however, students should be able to justify the order of the words based on the positive and negative feelings they feel each word carries with it.

Possible answers:

1. *thin, narrow, skinny, scrawny, gaunt*

2. *frayed, torn, ripped, raggedy, tattered, shredded*

3. *swinging, dangling, hanging, drooping, falling*

4. *jiggling, quivering, wobbling, rattling, shaking, jerking*

5. *guided, propelled, pushed, shoved, crammed, forced*

6. *condensed, compressed, squeezed, stuffed, jammed, crushed, smashed*

Strategies for Annotation   📝 🖥 *Annotate it!*

Denotations and Connotations

Have students locate the sentences containing *skinny, hanging, shoved,* and *squeeze* in the selection. Tell students to use their eBook annotation tools to do the following:

- Highlight each word.
- Reread the surrounding words and sentences, looking for clues to the word's meaning and connotation.
- Underline any clues you find.
- Review your annotations. On a note, write down the positive or negative connotations the word has in the story.

I don't know why but all of a sudden I'm feeling sick inside, like the part of me that's three wants to come out of my eyes, only I squeeze them shut tight and bite down on my teeth real hard and try to remember today I am eleven, eleven.

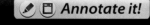

negative; keep shut, hide away

Language Conventions: Punctuating Dialogue

L2

Tell students that another type of written dialogue includes a divided quotation that is all one sentence. In these cases, the first letter of the second part of the quotation is not capitalized. Display and discuss this example with students:

"I think," said Sylvia, "it belongs to Rachel."

However, when a divided quotation is two separate sentences, you must capitalize the first word of the second part. Display and discuss this example with students:

"Of course it's yours," declared Mrs. Price. "You wore it last week, as I recall."

Answers:

Corrections needed are shown in yellow, highlighted text.

1. *"Birthdays are not what you expect them to be," said Rachel.*

2. *Mrs. Price glared at me and said, "It is not appropriate to burst into tears in the middle of class."*

3. *"You think I'm skinny, don't you?" asked Rachel.*

4. *"I don't," replied Sylvia.*

5. *"The sweater is mine," admitted Phyllis. "I left it in the coatroom and forgot all about it."*

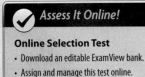
Assess It Online!

Online Selection Test
- Download an editable ExamView bank.
- Assign and manage this test online.

Language Conventions: Punctuating Dialogue

L2

Dialogue is written conversation between two or more characters. In fiction, dialogue is usually set off with quotation marks. Keep the following rules in mind when you write dialogue:

- Put quotation marks before and after a speaker's exact words.
- Place punctuation marks, such as commas, question marks, and periods, inside the quotation mark.
- If a speaker tag, such as *she said,* comes before the quotation, set a comma after the speaker tag.
- If a speaker tag follows the exact words of the quotation, set a comma after the quotation but before the closing quotation mark.

Note how the following dialogue from "Eleven" follows the rules for punctuating dialogue:

> **"Whose is this?" Mrs. Price says, and she holds the red sweater up in the air for all the class to see. "Whose? It's been sitting in the coatroom for a month."**
>
> **"Not mine," says everybody. "Not me."**
>
> **"It has to belong to somebody," Mrs. Price keeps saying, but nobody can remember.**

Practice and Apply Rewrite the incorrectly punctuated sentences, adding or correcting the punctuation as needed.

1. "Birthdays are not what you expect them to be" said Rachel.

2. Mrs. Price glared at me and said It is not appropriate to burst into tears in the middle of class.

3. "You think I'm skinny, don't you"? asked Rachel.

4. I don't," replied Sylvia.

5. "The sweater is mine, admitted Phyllis. I left it in the coatroom and forgot all about it."

English Language Support

Write Dialogue Remind students that dialogue has different punctuation rules than narration does. To punctuate dialogue correctly, writers need to pay careful attention to which words are actually said aloud by the characters.

- Display the Practice and Apply sentences. Highlight the places where punctuation needs to be added or removed and list the following choices for each place: (1) *be,"* or *be."* (2) *said, "It . . . class."* or *said "it . . . class.* (3) *you."* or *you?"* (4) *"I don't,"* or *I don't,* (5) *mine." . . ."I* or *"mine," . . .I.*

- Have students complete the Practice and Apply activity with a partner. Discuss their answers and have them make any corrections they think are needed. Ask them to work together to write a sentence of dialogue that has correct punctuation and share it with the class.

- Have students write two original sentences of dialogue between Rachel and Mrs. Price about the sweater, using correct punctuation. Call on volunteers to present their sentences to the class.

INTERACTIVE WHITEBOARD LESSON

Characterization

RL 3

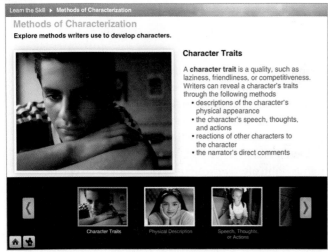

RETEACH

Before groups discuss Mrs. Price for the Performance Task, use the Interactive Whiteboard Lesson to review **characterization,** or how writers develop characters. Use these sections:

- Methods of Characterization
- Describing Characters

Tell students that authors may not employ all of these methods of characterization for each character. Explain that students can use these steps to analyze any character:

- **Step 1: Find Key Details** A close reading of the first exchange between Mrs. Price and the class may reveal important details. For example, the owner of the red sweater does not speak up.
- **Step 2: Create a Character Map** Write down important details, organized by type of detail.
- **Step 3: Infer Character Traits** Can you infer anything about Mrs. Price from the owner's reluctance to claim the sweater? What about from Mrs. Price's words to Rachel, "Of course it's yours"?

Remind students that **motivation** is the reason why a character acts, feels, or thinks a certain way. Ask students what might motivate Mrs. Price's actions. Then, complete the Practice & Apply sections of the Interactive Whiteboard Lesson.

COLLABORATIVE DISCUSSION

Have students discuss what details they should look for when analyzing characters. Then, have them apply these insights to the Performance Task for "Eleven."

Analyze Style

RL 4

RETEACH

Review the elements of style with students:

- **Word choice:** the way words and phrases, including figurative language, are used to express ideas
- **Sentence structure:** the types, patterns, and lengths of sentences used, including fragments (pieces of sentences)
- **Dialogue:** realistic conversation between characters
- **Tone:** the writer's attitude toward the subject

With students, examine the following passages in "Eleven" to identify different elements of the author's style.

- **Lines 17–20:** word choices that incorporate figurative language to make comparisons that clarify meaning
- **Lines 21–24:** varied sentence structure that mimics conversation
- **Lines 71–77:** realistic dialogue that brings the characters to life, creates drama, and advances the plot

Ask students to find other examples in "Eleven" that contribute to author Sandra Cisneros's style.

LEVEL UP TUTORIALS Assign the following *Level Up* tutorial: **Author's Style**

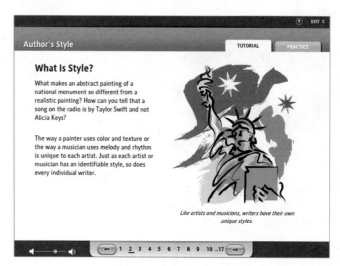

INDEPENDENT READING

Individual students can apply these skills to another selection in Collection 4 or to a short story or novel they may be reading on their own. After their analysis, have them share their ideas about the elements of style with other students in the class.

What Do Fish Have to Do with Anything?

Short Story by Avi

Why This Text

Students may have difficulty understanding why the characters in a story behave the way they do. In this story, the complex relationships between a boy, his mother, and a homeless man become clear only with an analysis of each character's motivations. Students will study the characters' reactions and determine why they behave in the ways they do as the plot moves forward. With the help of the close-reading questions, students will better understand each character's motivations and why they react to each other as they do.

Background Have students read the background information about the author. Point out that because of his lifelong dysgraphia (inability to distinguish letters), Avi often fails to see spelling errors in his work. Although he cites the discovery of the computer spellchecker as "one of the happiest moments of his life," he knows it's far from perfect, and must work doubly hard to get things right, often rewriting his work "fifty or sixty times" before he's satisfied. As students read this story, have them note that despite its apparent simplicity it represents many hours of hard work.

SETTING A PURPOSE Ask students to pay attention to the way the author uses word choice, sentence structure, dialogue, and tone to reveal character.

Standards Support

- cite textual evidence
- describe how characters respond or change as the plot moves toward a resolution
- analyze the impact of specific word choice on meaning and tone

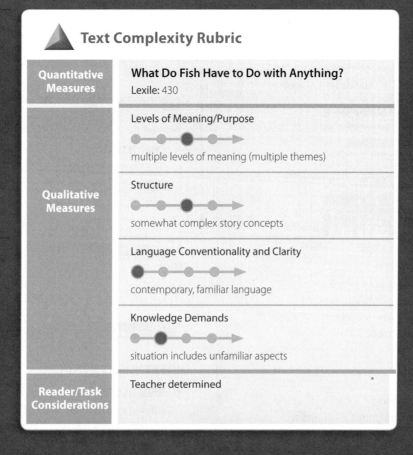

Text Complexity Rubric

Quantitative Measures

What Do Fish Have to Do with Anything?
Lexile: 430

Qualitative Measures

Levels of Meaning/Purpose

multiple levels of meaning (multiple themes)

Structure

somewhat complex story concepts

Language Conventionality and Clarity

contemporary, familiar language

Knowledge Demands

situation includes unfamiliar aspects

Reader/Task Considerations

Teacher determined

Describe Characters' Reactions

Students should read this story carefully all the way through. Close-reading questions at the bottom of the page will help them analyze the way characters respond or change as the plot moves toward a resolution. As they read, students should jot down comments or questions about the text in the margins.

WHEN STUDENTS STRUGGLE . . .

To help students identify examples of how character is revealed in "What Do Fish Have to Do with Anything?," have them work in small groups to fill out a chart like the one below.

CITE TEXT EVIDENCE For practice in recognizing a character's motivations, have students explain what each character's actions or reactions reveal about the character.

Action or Reaction	What It Reveals
Mrs. Markham carefully cuts a half-inch piece of cake (line 39) and explains that it is a portion. (lines 45–46)	Mrs. Markham needs everything to be in order in her world.
Mrs. Markham tells Willie to do his homework rather than answering his question about her being unhappy. (lines 85–86)	Mrs. Markham doesn't want to deal with the fact that she is unhappy.
Willie gives the homeless man money. (lines 127–128)	Willie is compassionate and he wants to find out why his mother is nervous about the man.
The homeless man says he believes Willie about the cave fish. (lines 270–277)	Although he doesn't trust much, the man has judged that Willie is straightforward.

Background *Avi says he became a writer out of sheer stubbornness. In elementary school and high school, he failed many subjects, not knowing that he suffered from a serious learning disability. Still, he was determined to prove that he could write if he set his mind to it. First, Avi wrote for adults with little success. He didn't discover his true audience until he became a father and took an interest in writing for children and young adults. He has written over 70 books and received the Newbury Medal and the Newbury Honor award for his work.*

What Do Fish Have to Do with Anything?

Short Story by Avi

CLOSE READ
Notes

1. **READ ▶** As you read lines 1–23, begin to collect and cite text evidence.

• Underline details that describe Willie's behavior.
• In the margin, explain why Willie feels lonely.
• Circle details that describe the man Willie sees (lines 17–23).

Every day at three o'clock Mrs. Markham waited for her son, Willie, to come out of school. <u>They walked home together.</u> If asked why she did it, Mrs. Markham would say, "Parents need to watch their children."

As they left the schoolyard, Mrs. Markham inevitably asked, "How was school?"

<u>Willie would begin to talk, then stop.</u> He was never sure his mother was listening. She seemed **preoccupied** with her own thoughts. She had been like that ever since his dad had abandoned

10 them six months ago. No one knew where he'd gone. Willie had the feeling that his mother was lost too. It made him feel lonely.

One Monday afternoon, as they approached the apartment building where they lived, she suddenly tugged at him. "Don't look that way," she said.

Willie feels lonely because his mother has been distracted since his father left.

preoccupied:
absorbed in thought

69

1. **READ AND CITE TEXT EVIDENCE** In lines 17–23, the author describes the man sitting on the milk crate.

Ⓐ **ASK STUDENTS** about the man's appearance. What can you infer about him from details in the text? *He is probably homeless ("His matted, streaky gray hair hung like a ragged curtain over his dirty face."); he is begging for money ("One hand was palm up.").*

Critical Vocabulary: preoccupied (line 8) Have students explain the meaning of *preoccupied*. How does Willie's mother's preoccupation affect Willie? *It makes him think she doesn't care about him.*

"Where?"

"At that man over there."

B Willie stole a look over his shoulder. A man, whom Willie had
A never seen before, was sitting on a red plastic milk crate near the curb.
His matted, streaky gray hair hung like a ragged curtain over his
20 dirty face. His shoes were torn. Rough hands lay upon his knees. One
hand was palm up. No one seemed to pay him any mind. Willie was
certain he had never seen a man so utterly alone. It was as if he were
some spat-out piece of chewing gum on the pavement.

"What's the matter with him?" Willie asked his mother in a
hushed voice.

Keeping her eyes straight ahead, Mrs. Markham said, "He's sick."
She pulled Willie around. "Don't stare. It's rude."

"What kind of sick?"

As Mrs. Markham searched for an answer, she began to walk
30 faster. "He's unhappy," she said.

"What's he doing?"

"Come on, Willie, you know perfectly well. He's begging."

"Do you think anyone gave him anything?"

"I don't know. Now, come on, don't look."

"Why don't you give him anything?"

"We have nothing to spare."

---

2. ◀ **REREAD** Reread lines 1–23. What does Willie's action in line 17
reveal about his character? Support your answer with text evidence.

*Willie is a curious boy who wants to learn about things he doesn't
know about. He also may be a little disobedient since he disregards
his mother's request not to look "that way" at the man.*

3. **READ** ▶ As you read lines 24–61, continue to cite text evidence.

• Underline the questions that Willie asks his mother in lines 24–36.
• In the margin, restate in your own words the most significant thing
Mrs. Markham says in lines 49–52.
• Circle what Mrs. Markham does that reminds Willie of the homeless
man.

70

When they got home, Mrs. Markham removed a white cardboard
box from the refrigerator. It contained pound cake. Using her thumb
as a measure, she carefully cut a half-inch piece of cake and gave it to
D 40 Willie on a clean plate. The plate lay on a plastic mat decorated with
images of roses with diamondlike dewdrops. She also gave him a glass
of milk and a folded napkin. She moved slowly.

Willie said, "Can I have a bigger piece of cake?"

Mrs. Markham picked up the cake box and ran a **manicured** pink
fingernail along the nutrition information panel. "A half-inch piece is
a portion, and a portion contains the following health requirements.
Do you want to hear them?"

"No."

C "It's on the box, so you can believe what it says. Scientists study
50 people, then write these things. If you're smart enough you could
become a scientist. Like this." Mrs. Markham tapped the box. "It pays
well."

Willie ate his cake and drank the milk. When he was done he
took care to wipe the crumbs off his face as well as to blot his milk
mustache with the napkin. His mother liked him to be neat.

His mother said, "Now go on and do your homework. Carefully.
You're in sixth grade. It's important."

Willie gathered up his books that lay on the empty third chair. At
the kitchen entrance he paused and looked back at his mother. She
60 was staring sadly at the cake box, but he didn't think she was seeing it.
Her unhappiness made him think of the man on the street.

manicured:
*trimmed and
polished*

*You can trust
what you read
if it comes
from a source
of authority.*

---

4. ◀ **REREAD** Reread lines 37–52. What can you infer about Mrs.
Markham based on her dialogue and the description of her
behavior?

*Mrs. Markham accepts things at face value. She doesn't look beneath
the surface of what she reads and does not ask deep questions.*

5. **READ** ▶ As you read lines 62–88, continue to cite text evidence.

• Underline each occurrence of the word *unhappiness*.
• Circle answers that Mrs. Markham gives that do not really address
Willie's questions.
• In the margin, explain the salesman's quotation in line 81.

71

---

2. **REREAD AND CITE TEXT EVIDENCE** Point out how the
author's word choice expresses ideas. Have students look at the
word *stole* in the sentence "Willie stole a look over his shoulder"
(line 17).

B **ASK STUDENTS** to think about the word's connotation. Is it
positive or negative? *It is negative.* Why does the author say that
Willie "stole" a look? *Willie is doing something forbidden.*

3. **READ AND CITE TEXT EVIDENCE** Explain that the dialogue in
lines 49–52 reveals Mrs. Markham's character.

C **ASK STUDENTS** to think about the line "It's on the box, so
you can believe what it says." What do these words tell you about
Mrs. Markham? *She is rigid and authoritarian; she believes in rules.*

4. **REREAD AND CITE TEXT EVIDENCE** Have students note the
way Mrs. Markham measures and cuts the cake (lines 38–40).

D **ASK STUDENTS** to analyze her behavior. What does it tell
you about her? *She doesn't trust her instincts.* In line 40, Mrs.
Markham puts the cake on a "clean plate." Why is that detail
important? *The author is emphasizing Mrs. Markham's insistence on
being "proper."*

5. **READ AND CITE TEXT EVIDENCE**

E **ASK STUDENTS** what they know about Mrs. Markham that
might explain her behavior. *She wants to ward off further
discussion of "unhappiness"; she wants Willie to do well in school; she
wants him to be successful.*

Critical Vocabulary: manicured (line 44) Have students
explain the meaning of *manicured*. Ask them what Mrs.
Markham's "manicured" nails say about her. *She cares about
appearances.*

"What *kind* of unhappiness do you think he has?" he suddenly asked.

"Who's that?"

"That man."

Mrs. Markham looked puzzled.

"The begging man. The one on the street."

"Oh, could be anything," his mother said, **vaguely**. "A person can be unhappy for many reasons." She turned to stare out the window, as
70 if an answer might be there.

"Is unhappiness a sickness you can cure?"

E "I wish you wouldn't ask such questions."

"Why?"

F After a moment she said, "Questions that have no answers shouldn't be asked."

"Can I go out?"

"Homework first."

Willie turned to go again.

"Money," Mrs. Markham suddenly said. "Money will cure a lot of
80 unhappiness. That's why that man was begging. A salesman once said to me, 'Maybe you can't buy happiness, but you can rent a lot of it.' You should remember that."

"How much money do we have?"

"Not enough."

"Is that why you're unhappy?"

"Willie, do your homework."

Willie started to ask another question, but decided he would not get an answer. He left the kitchen.

vaguely:

with
uncertainty

The salesman
suggests that
money can at
least make
people
somewhat
happy.

6. **◀ REREAD AND DISCUSS** Reread lines 62–88. In a small group, discuss the reasons why Mrs. Markham avoids responding to Willie's questions about unhappiness.

7. **READ ▶** As you read lines 89–134, continue to cite text evidence.
   • Underline instances of Willie looking at the homeless man.
   • In the margin, describe the way the dog and Willie are similar.
   • Circle the text in which Willie disobeys his mother (lines 120–134).

72

The apartment had three rooms. The walls were painted mint
90 green. Willie walked down the hallway to his room, which was at the front of the building. By climbing up on the windowsill and pressing against the glass he could see the sidewalk five stories below. The man was still there.

It was almost five when he went to tell his mother he had finished his school assignments. He found her in her dim bedroom, sleeping. Since she had begun working the night shift at a convenience store —two weeks now—she took naps in the late afternoon.

For a while Willie stood on the **threshold**, hoping his mother would wake up. When she didn't, he went to the front room and
100 looked down on the street again. The begging man had not moved.

Willie returned to his mother's room.

"I'm going out," he announced—softly.

Willie waited a decent interval for his mother to waken. When she did not, he made sure his keys were in his pocket. Then he left the apartment.

By standing just outside the building door, he could keep his eyes on the man. It appeared as if he had still not moved. Willie wondered how anyone could go without moving for so long in the chill October air. Was staying still part of the man's sickness?
110 During the twenty minutes that Willie watched, no one who passed looked in the beggar's direction. Willie wondered if they even saw the man. Certainly no one put any money into his open hand.

G A lady leading a dog by a leash went by. The dog strained in the direction of the man sitting on the crate. His tail wagged. The lady pulled the dog away. "Heel!" she commanded.

The dog—tail between his legs—scampered to the lady's side. Even so, the dog twisted around to look back at the beggar.

Willie grinned. The dog had done exactly what Willie had done when his mother told him not to stare.
120 Pressing deep into his pocket, Willie found a nickel. It was warm
H and slippery. He wondered how much happiness you could rent for a nickel.

Squeezing the nickel between his fingers, Willie walked slowly toward the man. When he came before him, he stopped, suddenly nervous. The man, who appeared to be looking at the ground, did not move his eyes. He smelled bad.

threshold:

piece of wood
or stone
beneath a
door; doorway

Both Willie
and the dog
did the
opposite of
what they
were told and
acknowledged
the homeless
man.

73

6. **REREAD AND DISCUSS USING TEXT EVIDENCE** In lines 74–75, Mrs. Markham tells Willie, "Questions that have no answers shouldn't be asked."

F **ASK STUDENTS** to discuss Willie's response to this comment. What does he say? *"Can I go out?"* Why might he say that? What might be on his mind? *He might be planning to go out and see the homeless man.*

7. **READ AND CITE TEXT EVIDENCE** In lines 113–115, the lady pulls the dog away from the homeless man and gives the command "Heel!"

G **ASK STUDENTS** why Willie identifies with the dog. *They are both being pulled away reluctantly from the homeless man.* How is the lady like his mother? *They are both severe and controlling.*

Critical Vocabulary: vaguely (line 68) Have students share definitions. How do you feel when someone gives a "vague" answer? *Students may say they feel impatient or frustrated.*

Critical Vocabulary: threshold (line 98) Have students share definitions of *threshold*. Explain that the word is used in expressions such as "the threshold of adulthood." What does this expression mean? *It means "the start of adulthood."*

FOR ELL STUDENTS Clarify the meaning of *decent*. Explain that, as it is used in the text, it means "fairly good."

"Here." Willie stretched forward and dropped the coin into the man's open right hand.

"God bless you," the man said hoarsely as he folded his fingers
130 over the coin. His eyes, like high beams on a car, flashed up at Willie, then dropped.

Willie waited for a moment, then went back up to his room. From his window he looked down on the street. He thought he saw the coin in the man's hand, but was not sure.

After supper Mrs. Markham readied herself to go to work, then kissed Willie good night. As she did every night, she said, "If you have regular problems, call Mrs. Murphy downstairs. What's her number?"

"274-8676," Willie said.

"Extra bad problems, call Grandma."
140 "369-6754."

"Super special problems, you can call me."

"962-6743."

"Emergency, the police."

"911."

"Lay out your morning clothing."

"I will."

"Don't let anyone in the door."

"I won't."

"No television past nine."
150 "I know."

"But you can read late."

Willie has all
of these phone
numbers
because his
mother wants
him to be
prepared in
case of an
emergency.

---

8. **◀ REREAD** Reread lines 120–134. Why does Willie give money to the homeless man, especially since his mother told him to stay away?

Willie wants to find out what made his mother nervous. Willie also feels compassion for the homeless man after seeing so many people ignore him.

9. **READ ▶** As you read lines 135–164, continue to cite text evidence.

- In the margin, explain why Willie has all these phone numbers.
- Underline what Willie learns about the fish that live in caves.
- Circle the teacher's responses to Willie's questions.

74

"You're the one who's going to be late," Willie reminded her.

"I'm leaving," Mrs. Markham said.

After she went, Willie stood for a long while in the hallway. The empty apartment felt like a cave that lay deep below the earth. That day in school Willie's teacher had told the class about a kind of fish that lived in caves. These fish could not see. They had no eyes. The teacher had said it was living in the dark cave that made them like that.

160 Willie had raised his hand and asked, "If they want to get out of the cave, can they?"

"I suppose."

"Would their eyes come back?"

"Good question," she said, but did not give an answer.

Before he went to bed, Willie took another look out the window. In the pool of light cast by the street lamp, Willie saw the man.

On Tuesday morning when Willie went to school, the man was gone. But when he came home from school with his mother, he was there again.

170 "*Please* don't look at him," his mother whispered with some urgency.

During his snack, Willie said, "Why shouldn't I look?"

"What are you talking about?"

"That man. On the street. Begging."

"I told you. He's sick. It's better to act as if you never saw him. When people are that way they don't wish to be looked at."

---

10. **◀ REREAD** Reread lines 154–164. What does the dialogue between Willie and his teacher reveal about Willie's character?

Willie is inquisitive and intelligent. The inability of Willie's teacher to answer his question shows that Willie often asks complicated questions that are difficult to answer.

11. **READ ▶** As you read lines 165–217, continue to cite text evidence.

- Underline details that show Willie's father was unhappy.
- In the margin, make an inference about why Willie's mother wishes Willie would not ask about her being unhappy.
- Circle the moment in the conversation when Willie mentions the sightless fish.

75

---

8. **REREAD AND CITE TEXT EVIDENCE**

H ASK STUDENTS to cite text evidence suggesting one reason why Willie gives the man money. *In line 121 Willie wonders "how much happiness you could rent for a nickel," suggesting that he wants to make the man happy, if only temporarily.*

9. **READ AND CITE TEXT EVIDENCE** Have students review the teacher's response in line 164: "'Good question,' she said, but did not give an answer."

I ASK STUDENTS to think about another person in the story that has been unwilling to give Willie an answer. *Mrs. Markham*

10. **REREAD AND CITE TEXT EVIDENCE**

J ASK STUDENTS to think about Willie's questions about the fish. What does he want to know? *He wants to know if they can get out of the cave and if their eyes would come back (lines 160–16 3).* Cite text evidence suggesting that Willie feels like he's living in a cave. *Willie's "empty apartment felt like a cave" (line 155).*

11. **READ AND CITE TEXT EVIDENCE** Mrs. Markham says she doesn't want to talk about her unhappiness because it "hurts" (line 200). Willie thinks there's something she's not telling him.

K ASK STUDENTS what Willie wants to know. *He wants to know if his mother is ashamed.* What is Mrs. Markham's response? *She doesn't answer the question; she gets irritated.*

"Why not?"

Mrs. Markham pondered for a while. "People are ashamed of being unhappy."

180 Willie looked thoughtfully at his mother. "Are you sure he's unhappy?"

"You don't have to ask if people are unhappy. They tell you all the time."

"How?"

"The way they look."

"Is that part of the sickness?"

"Oh, Willie, I don't know. It's just the way they are."

contemplate:

think about

Willie **contemplated** the half-inch slice of cake his mother had just given him. A year ago his parents seemed to be perfectly happy.

190 For Willie, the world seemed easy, full of light. Then his father lost his job. He tried to get another but could not. For long hours he sat in dark rooms. Sometimes he drank. His parents began to argue a lot. One day, his father was gone.

For two weeks his mother kept to the dark. And wept.

Ⓚ

Willie's mother doesn't want to talk about her unhappiness because it is a painful subject for her and possibly for Willie.

Willie looked at his mother. "You're unhappy," he said. "Are *you* ashamed?"

Mrs. Markham sighed and closed her eyes. "I wish you wouldn't ask that."

"Why?"

200 "It hurts me."

"But are you ashamed?" Willie persisted. He felt it was urgent that he know. So that he could do something.

She only shook her head.

Willie said, "Do you think Dad might come back?"

She hesitated before saying, "Yes, I think so."

Willie wondered if that was what she really thought.

"Do you think Dad is unhappy?" Willie asked.

"Where do you get such questions?"

"They're in my mind."

210 "There's much in the mind that need not be paid attention to."

Ⓛ

"Fish who live in caves have no eyes."

"What are you talking about?"

"My teacher said it's all that darkness. The fish forget how to see. So they lose their eyes."

76

"I doubt she said that."

"She did."

Ⓜ

"Willie, you have too much imagination."

After his mother went to work, Willie gazed down onto the street. The man was there. Willie thought of going down, but he knew he

220 was not supposed to leave the building when his mother worked at night. He decided to speak to the man the next day.

That afternoon—Wednesday—Willie stood before the man. "I don't have any money," Willie said. "Can I still talk to you?"

Ⓝ

The man lifted his face. It was a dirty face with very tired eyes. He needed a shave.

"My mother," Willie began, "said you were unhappy. Is that true?"

"Could be," the man said.

"What are you unhappy about?"

The man's eyes narrowed as he studied Willie **intently.** He said,

230 "How come you want to know?"

Willie shrugged.

"I think you should go home, kid."

"I am home." Willie gestured toward the apartment. "I live right here. Fifth floor. Where do you live?"

"Around."

"*Are* you unhappy?" Willie persisted.

The man ran a tongue over his lips. His Adam's apple bobbed. "A man has the right to remain silent," he said, and closed his eyes.

intently:

with close attention

---

12. **◀ REREAD** Reread lines 195–217. Why does Willie bring up the sightless fish during their conversation?

Willie might be connecting his mother's refusal to address her unhappiness and answer his questions with the fish who have lost their eyes. Both the fish and Mrs. Markham are failing to acknowledge certain details about their circumstances.

13. **READ ▶** As you read lines 218–264, continue to cite text evidence.

- Underline text that describes the man's appearance and behavior.
- Circle what the homeless man says to Willie in lines 237–247.
- In the margin, explain why Willie wants to find the cure for unhappiness.

77

Critical Vocabulary: contemplate (line 188) Have students share definitions. What is the difference between *contemplating* and *thinking*? *Students may say that contemplating is a deeper level of thought.*

FOR ELL STUDENTS Explain that the verb *pondered* is similar in sound to the verb *wondered*, which means "thought about something, considered something."

12. **REREAD AND CITE TEXT EVIDENCE**

Ⓛ **ASK STUDENTS** to reread the lines surrounding Willie's statement, "Fish who live in caves have no eyes" (line 211). What has his mother said about his questions? *She wonders where he gets such questions, and then says that there's a lot in the mind that needs no attention.* What does her statement have to do with fish in caves? *Willie is implying that she is living in a kind of cave.*

13. **READ AND CITE TEXT EVIDENCE**

Ⓜ **ASK STUDENTS** what the dialogue in lines 218–264 reveals about Willie's character. *He is curious about the world, and he is also sincere. He believes he can find out how to help his mother.*

Critical Vocabulary: intently (line 229) After they share definitions, have pairs of students look at each other *intently.*

Willie remained standing on the pavement for a while before
240 retreating back to his apartment. Once inside he looked down from
the window. The man was still there. For a moment Willie was
certain the man was looking at the apartment building and the floor
where Willie lived.

The next day, Thursday—after dropping a nickel in the man's
palm—Willie said, "I've never seen anyone look so unhappy as you
do. So I figure you must know a lot about it."

The man took a deep breath. "Well, yeah, maybe."

Willie said, "And I need to find a cure for it."

"A *what*?"

250 "A cure for unhappiness."

The man pursed his cracked lips and blew a silent whistle. Then
he said, "Why?"

"My mother is unhappy."

"Why's that?"

"My dad went away."

"How come?"

"I think because he was unhappy. Now my mother's unhappy
too—all the time. So if I found a cure for unhappiness, it would be a
good thing, wouldn't it?"

260 "I suppose. Hey, you don't have anything to eat on you, do you?"

Willie shook his head, then said, "Would you like some cake?"

"What kind?"

"I don't know. Cake."

Willie wants to find the cure for unhappiness because his dad was unhappy when he left and his mom is unhappy now.

14. ◀ REREAD Reread lines 218–264. What does the homeless man's
dialogue and behavior suggest about his character?

The description of the homeless man conveys that his life is a painful
struggle. His dialogue suggests that he may be embarrassed or
ashamed of his situation.

15. READ ▶ As you read lines 265–297, continue to cite text evidence.

- Underline the reasons why the homeless man believes Willie.
- Circle Willie's "grown-up name."
- In the margin, note differences between Willie's discussion with the
  man in lines 270–283 and his conversation with his mother in lines
  211–217.

78

"Depends on the cake."

On Friday Willie said to the man, "I found out what kind of cake
it is."

"Yeah?"

"Pound cake. But I don't know why it's called that."

"Long as it's cake it probably don't matter."

270 Neither spoke. Then Willie said, "In school my teacher said there
are fish who live in caves and the caves are so dark the fish don't have
eyes. What do you think? Do you believe that?"

"Sure."

"You do? How come?"

"Because you said so."

"You mean, just because someone *said* it you believe it?"

"Not someone. You."

Willie was puzzled. "But, well, maybe it *isn't* true."

The man grunted. "Hey, do you believe it?"

280 Willie nodded.

"Well, you're not just anyone. You got eyes. You see. You ain't no
fish."

"Oh." Willie was pleased.

"What's your name?" the man asked.

"Willie."

"That's a boy's name. What's your grown-up name?"

"William."

"And that means another thing."

"What?"

290 "I'll take some of that cake."

Willie started. "You will?" he asked, surprised.

"Just said it, didn't I?"

Willie suddenly felt excited. It was as if the man had given him a
gift. Willie wasn't sure what it was except that it was important and he
was glad to have it. For a moment he just gazed at the man. He saw
the lines on the man's face, the way his lips curved, the small scar on
the side of his chin, the shape of his eyes, which he now saw were blue.

The man trusts what Willie says and gives direct answers to his questions. Willie's mother does not trust Willie and says he asks too many questions.

16. ◀ REREAD AND DISCUSS Reread lines 270–283. In a small group,
discuss why the homeless man says Willie's "got eyes." Cite evidence
from the text to support your interpretation.

79

14. REREAD AND CITE TEXT EVIDENCE

Ⓝ **ASK STUDENTS** what details in the text reveal things about
the homeless man's character. *Students may point out details such*
as the man's dirty face and tired eyes (line 224) and his cracked lips
(line 251). He is clearly in bad shape and is not trying to do anything
about it. His initial words—"Could be", "How come you want to
know?" (lines 227 and 230)—reveal that he feels he has no reason to
trust people.

15. READ AND CITE TEXT EVIDENCE Have students think about
what the homeless man says to Willie in lines 275 and 281.

Ⓞ **ASK STUDENTS** to explain the effect these words have on
Willie. *He feels like he's being taken seriously.* What else does the
man say that makes Willie feel like he is being taken seriously? *The*
homeless man asks for Willie's "grown-up name" (line 286).

16. REREAD AND DISCUSS USING TEXT EVIDENCE

Ⓟ **ASK STUDENTS** to review lines 281–282. Cite the words
that Willie has been longing to hear. *Students may suggest "You're*
not just anyone." Why is this important to Willie? *Willie needs to feel*
special, unique, and respected.

FOR ELL STUDENTS Explain that the contraction *ain't* is
a colloquialism. Challenge a volunteer to guess what the
contraction stands for.

Q "I'll get the cake," Willie cried and ran back to the apartment. He
300 snatched the box from the refrigerator as well as a knife, then hurried
back down to the street. "I'll cut you a piece," he said, and he opened
the box.

"Hey, that don't look like a pound of cake," the man said.

Willie, alarmed, looked up.

"But like I told you, it don't matter."

Willie held his thumb against the cake to make sure the portion
was the right size. With a poke of the knife he made a small mark for
the proper width.

Just as he was about to cut, the man said, "Hold it!"

Willie looked up. "What?"

310 "What were you doing there with your thumb?"

"I was measuring the size. The right portion. A person is
supposed to get only one portion."

"Where'd you learn that?"

"It says so on the box. You can see for yourself." He held out the
box.

The man studied the box then handed it back to Willie. "That's
just lies," he said.

"How do you know?"

"William, how can a box say how much a person needs?"

320 "But it does. The scientists say so. They measured, so they know.
Then they put it there."

"Lies," the man repeated.

Willie began to feel that this man knew many things. "Well, then,
how much should I cut?" he asked.

The man said, ⟨"You have to look at me, then at the cake, and then
you're going to have to decide for yourself."⟩

"Oh." Willie looked at the cake. The piece was about three inches
wide. Willie looked up at the man. After a moment he cut the cake
into two pieces, each an inch and a half wide. He gave one piece to the
330 man and kept the other in the box.

*Willie
measures a
piece of cake
the same way
his mother
does.*

---

17. **READ ▶** As you read lines 298–349, continue to cite text evidence.

- In the margin, explain why Willie measures the cake the way he does.
- Circle the man's advice to Willie on the amount of cake to cut.
- Underline the man's "cure for unhappiness." In the margin, explain
  what he means.

"God bless you," the man said as he took the piece and laid it in
his left hand. He began to break off pieces with his right hand and put
them in his mouth one by one. Each piece was chewed thoughtfully.
Willie watched him eat.

When the man was done, he licked the crumbs on his fingers.

"Now I'll give you something," the man said.

"What?" Willie said, surprised.

"The cure for unhappiness."

"You know it?" Willie asked, eyes wide.

340 The man nodded.

"What is it?"

"It's this: <u>What a person needs is always more than they say.</u>"

R "Who's *they?*" Willie asked.

The man pointed to the cake box. "The people on the box," he
said.

In his mind Willie repeated what he had been told, then he gave
the man the second piece of cake.

The man took it, saying, "Good man," and he ate it.

Willie grinned.

*The homeless
man means
that a strict
measurement
cannot
determine
what each
individual
needs.*

---

18. **◀ REREAD** Reread lines 305–349. Why does Willie give the man all
of the cake? In what ways does his decision indicate that he has
changed as a person?

*Willie gives him the cake because he understands that other
people may need more than we may be led to believe. This decision
indicates that Willie has learned to think for himself and
recognized that every individual has his or her own needs.*

---

17. **READ AND CITE TEXT EVIDENCE**

Q **ASK STUDENTS** to summarize the two contrasting views on
the amount of cake to cut. *Willie wants to measure it out carefully
the way his mother does, on the advice of the "experts"; the man tells
Willie he has to decide for himself no matter what the experts say.*

18. **REREAD AND CITE TEXT EVIDENCE** In line 344, the man
responds to Willie's question with the words "The people on the
box."

R **ASK STUDENTS** what the man means by this. Who are "the
people on the box"? *They are the experts his mother says know
everything about how much cake a person needs.*

350　The next day was Saturday. Willie did not go to school. All morning he kept looking down from his window for the man, but it was raining and he did not appear. Willie wondered where he was, but could not imagine it.

Willie's mother woke about noon. Willie sat with her while she ate her breakfast. "I found the cure for unhappiness," he announced.

"Did you?" his mother said. She was reading a memo from the convenience store's owner.

"It's 'What a person needs is always more than they say.'"

His mother put her papers down. "That's nonsense. Where did
360　you hear that?"

"That man."

"What man?"

"On the street. The one who was begging. You said he was unhappy. So I asked him."

"Willie, I told you I didn't want you to even look at that man."

"He's a nice man. . . ."

"How do you know?"

"I've talked to him."

"When? How much?"

370　Willie shrank down. "I did, that's all."

"Willie, I forbid you to talk to him. Do you understand me? Do you? Answer me!" She was shrill.

"Yes," Willie said, but he'd already decided he would talk to the man one more time. He needed to explain why he could not talk to him anymore.

Willie is going to explain why he is not allowed to talk to him.

19. **READ ▶** As you read lines 350–375, continue to cite text evidence.

- Underline Willie's mother's reaction to the cure for unhappiness.
- Circle the text that tells you Willie's mother is angry with him.
- In the margin, restate the reason why Willie is going to speak to the man again.

20. **◀ REREAD** Reread lines 365–375. Why is Willie's mother so upset with him? What is Willie's reaction to her anger?

Willie's mother is upset because he disobeyed her and because she is afraid for his safety. Willie listens to her but decides he is going to see the man one more time in spite of his mother's feelings.

82

> ## What a person needs is always more than they say.

On Sunday, however, the man was not there. Nor was he there on Monday.

"That man is gone," Willie said to his mother as they walked home from school.

380　"I saw. I'm not blind."

"Where do you think he went?"

"I couldn't care less. But you might as well know, I arranged for him to be gone."

Willie stopped short. "What do you mean?"

"I called the police. We don't need a nuisance like that around here. Pestering kids."

"He wasn't pestering me."

"Of course he was."

"How do you know?"

390　"Willie, I have eyes. I can see."

Willie glared at his mother. "No, you can't. You're a fish. You live in a cave."

Willie wants to be called William because he is maturing and being called by a "grown-up name" reflects that.

21. **READ ▶** As you read lines 376–400, continue to cite text evidence.

- Underline details in lines 376–386 that explain what has happened to the homeless man.
- Circle the dialogue that refers to the sightless fish.
- In the margin, explain why Willie insists on being called William.

83

19. **READ AND CITE TEXT EVIDENCE** In line 369, Mrs. Markham asks, "When? How much?" when Willie tells her he has talked to the man.

S **ASK STUDENTS** about this remark. Why does she ask "How much?" What is she concerned about? *She wants to know how many times they have spoken; she is concerned that a homeless man has gotten too friendly with her son.*

20. **REREAD AND CITE TEXT EVIDENCE** In line 370, the author describes Willie's reaction to his mother's anger. Have students think about what Willie does and says. Have them think about the author's choice of words.

T **ASK STUDENTS** how Willie's attitude is affected by his mother's harsh words. What does he do? *He "shrank down."* What does he say? *"I did, that's all."* What is happening to Willie? *Students may say that he is withdrawing or that he no longer wants to explain himself.*

21. **READ AND CITE TEXT EVIDENCE** Have students review the last paragraphs of the story (lines 391–400), in which Willie asserts himself, calling his mother "a fish."

U **ASK STUDENTS** What else does Willie say to his mother that shows the influence of the homeless man? *Students may cite the following: "My name isn't Willie. It's William," and "What a person needs is always more than they say!" (lines 395–397).*

CLOSE READ
Notes

"Fish?" retorted Mrs. Markham. "What do fish have to do with anything? Willie, don't talk nonsense."

"My name isn't Willie. It's William. And I know how to keep from being unhappy. I do!" He was yelling now. "What a person needs is always more than they say! *Always!*"

He turned on his heel and walked back toward the school. At the corner he glanced back. His mother was following. He kept going. She
400 kept following.

22. **◀ REREAD** Reread lines 376–400. What does the sightless fish represent to Willie? Why does he call his mother a fish? Cite explicit textual evidence in your answer.

The fish represent a willingness to be "blind" to real life. He calls his mother a fish because she refuses to listen to Willie, does not respect the homeless man as an individual, and will not confront her own unhappiness.

SHORT ANSWER

Cite Text Evidence How does Willie grow and change as the story progresses? Review the notes you took as you read and **cite text evidence** in your response.

At first Willie is a curious but timid boy. His questions to his mother about the homeless man and about her own unhappiness are not answered. Eventually, his curiosity gets the best of him and he finally speaks to the man. The conversation changes Willie's outlook on life. The homeless man speaks to him as an adult and gives him the "cure for unhappiness" which is "What a person needs is always more than they say." The encounter teaches Willie the importance of thinking for himself. The final scene in which he calls his mother a "fish" and insists on being called "William" reveals that Willie has matured and learned to think for himself and to respect individuals.

84

22. **REREAD AND CITE TEXT EVIDENCE**

Ⓥ ASK STUDENTS why Willie was angry at his mother. *She had sent the police to remove the homeless man and thought that she knew better than Willie.* What did Willie think of her actions? *He thought she couldn't see what was really happening.*

SHORT RESPONSE

Cite Text Evidence Students should:

- explain how the author develops characters and how they respond and change during the course of the story.
- interpret characters through their words and actions.
- analyze characters' motivations.
- examine the techniques the author uses to create realistic characters and dialogue.

TO CHALLENGE STUDENTS . . .

Tell students that Avi, the author of this story, is skilled at creating realistic dialogue for his characters. Giving each character his or her own voice enables readers to go beyond the literal meanings of the words and into the characters' minds. Explain that sometimes the meaning of dialogue lies more in what is not said than what is said. Some writers find it helpful to "act out" the dialogue first, to get a sense of what the character might really say in a particular situation.

ASK STUDENTS to work with a partner or small group to write new dialogue for this story. Have them invent exchanges between Willie, Mrs. Markham, and/or the homeless man in any combination. (They may even want to invent a conversation involving all three characters!) They can create a new scene, or add dialogue to a scene that exists. After they have written their dialogue, have them read it aloud to the class.

DIG DEEPER

With the class, return to Question 17, Read. Have students share their responses.

ASK STUDENTS to think about the way the author uses the simple act of cutting a cake to reveal character.

- Have students describe the cake-cutting methods used by Mrs. Markham and the homeless man.
- Have students make an inference about Mrs. Markham's insistence on measuring each slice. What might explain her inflexibility?
- Have students draw conclusions about the life of the homeless man based on his ideas about cake cutting.
- Have students contrast the way Willie cuts the cake at the beginning and at the end of the story. How does the homeless man's idea about giving people more than they ask for help Willie to become his own person?
- Students may include text evidence that shows how the homeless man's ideas challenged Willie's beliefs about himself, his mother, homeless people, blind adherence to authority, and virtually everything he'd been taught previously.

ASK STUDENTS to return to their Short Response answer and revise it based on the class discussion.

A Voice

Words Like Freedom

Why These Texts?

The function of poetry is to rouse emotion, and immigration and freedom are two topics that evoke strong emotions. This lesson focuses on the different ways in which poets stir emotion and express personal thoughts.

Key Learning Objective: The student will learn how to identify figurative language and analyze tone in poetry.

RL 1 Cite textual evidence to support analysis and inferences.

RL 2 Determine a theme or central idea.

RL 3 Describe how characters respond or change.

RL 4 Determine the meaning of words and phrases.

RL 6 Explain how an author develops the point of view of the speaker.

RL 9 Compare and contrast texts.

W 3d Write narratives; use precise words and phrases.

SL 1 Engage effectively in a range of collaborative discussions.

▲ Text Complexity Rubric

	A Voice Lexile: N/A	Words Like Freedom Lexile: N/A
Quantitative Measures		
Qualitative Measures	Levels of Meaning/Purpose single level of complex meaning	Levels of Meaning/Purpose single level of complex meaning
	Structure regular stanzas with some liberties taken	Structure regular stanzas with some liberties taken
	Language Conventionality and Clarity some figurative language	Language Conventionality and Clarity clear, direct language
	Knowledge Demands some cultural and literary knowledge useful	Knowledge Demands cultural and literary knowledge essential to understanding
Reader/Task Considerations	• Teacher determined • Vary by individual reader and type of text • See the Text X-Ray for suggested Reader/Task Considerations	

English Language Support Before teaching, use the Text X-Ray for an overview of the text's complexity. The Text X-Ray and the supports and scaffolds in the Teacher's Edition will help you guide students of different skill levels.

Meaning Making

Language Development

Effective Expression

Content Knowledge

Foundational Skills

Text Complexity: Qualitative Measures

▲ Levels of Meaning/Purpose

Help students learn how to analyze a poem's tone.

- Teacher's Edition side notes, pp. 242, 243, 244, 245
- English Language Support, p. 245
- When Students Struggle, p. 243
- Analyze Tone, p. 245

To reteach tone, see

 Use It! **Level Up Tutorial:** Tone

ZOOM IN ON ANALYZING A POEM'S TONE Remind students that a poem's tone is a feeling that comes from the poet or speaker, not from the reader.

- Give students the following examples and have them identify the tone: *The birds were chirping, the sun was shining.* (happy) *The memory brought tears to her eyes.* (sad)
- Divide the class into groups by tone: *joyous, thoughtful, offended,* and *sarcastic.* Have each group write two sentences in their assigned tone and share them with the class.

▲ Structure

Help students understand how to identify the speaker in a poem.

- Teacher's Edition Side Notes, pp. 242, 243

▶ **Use It!** **Level Up Tutorial:** Narrator and Speaker

To help students structure and write a poem, see

- Performance Task, p. 246

▶ **Use It!** **Interactive Whiteboard Lessons:** Form in Poetry

ZOOM IN ON IDENTIFYING THE SPEAKER OF A POEM Explain to students that a speaker in a poem is similar to a narrator in a story.

- Display lines 5–8 of "Words Like Freedom." Circle the pronouns *me* and *I.* Ask students who these pronouns identify. *(the speaker)* Circle the pronoun *you.* Ask students who the poet is speaking to. *(the reader)*
- Display lines 1–4 of the poem and have pairs find the pronoun that identifies the speaker. *(my)*

Language Conventionality and Clarity

Guide students to discuss and write about figurative language.

- Teacher's Edition side notes, pp. 242, 243, 245
- English Language Support, p. 242
- Strategies for Annotation, p. 245
- Determine the Meaning of Figurative Language, p. 245

To reteach figurative language, see

- Determine Meaning: Figurative Language, p. 246a

 Use It! **Level Up Tutorial:** Figurative Language

ZOOM IN ON **UNDERSTANDING FIGURATIVE LANGUAGE** Review the definitions of **similes** and **metaphors.** Tell students that poets often use these figures of speech to bring out a certain feeling or image.

- Display lines 22–24 of "A Voice." Highlight the words *spunky* and *peacock.* Point out the definition of *spunky* and have students look up the definition of *peacock.* Ask students who the speaker is describing as "spunky as a peacock." *(the speaker's mother)* Have volunteers describe the feeling or image they get from this phrase.
- Have pairs work together to write sentences describing the speaker's mother in their own words.

▲ Knowledge Demands

Support English learners in understanding the context of the two poems.

- Teacher's Edition Background note, p. 241
- English Language Support, p. 241
- Content-Area Connection, p. 244

ZOOM IN ON **BUILDING CONTEXT** Promote understanding of context in "A Voice." Explain that it is about three generations of the same immigrant family.

- Display the words "your father" in line 8. Ask students what the family relationship is between the speaker and the subject's father. *(He is her grandfather.)*
- Have students work in small groups to draw a simple family tree of the people referred to in the poem.

Suggested Reader/Task Considerations

You might consider the following before assigning these poems to students.

- Will students see the relationships between the details provided in the poems?
- Do students have enough background about the topics of the poems?

ZOOM IN ON **SUPPORTING COMPREHENSION**

- Help students unpack lines 7–8 of "Words Like Freedom." Have partners discuss what kind of experiences "what I know" refers to.
- Display lines 25–29 of "A Voice." Explain that "going to the state capitol" refers to the citizenship ceremony. Explain why hoarseness would prevent someone from taking part in it.

TEACH
CLOSE READ

Background Have students read the background and information about the authors. Tell students that they are going to read two poems that reflect the writers' thoughts and feelings about two important topics: immigration and freedom.

Explain that in the early 1900s not all Mexican immigrants to the United States stayed in the country. Some immigrants returned home to Mexico when conditions improved or when they earned enough money to live more comfortably. This close proximity to their homeland allows today's Mexican Americans to have more interaction with first-generation immigrants, reinforcing cultural values and traditions and, in some cases, slowing certain changes, such as learning a new language.

Next, explain to students that during the Harlem Renaissance the new, growing African American middle class also begin advocating for racial equality. New York City became the epicenter of this movement. Three of the largest civil rights groups established their headquarters there, helping to establish a sense of community for African Americans around the country.

SETTING A PURPOSE Direct students to use the Setting a Purpose prompt to focus their reading. Remind them to write down questions as they read.

Background *In the early 1900s, more than one million Mexicans immigrated to the United States. Many came to find jobs but found discrimination as well. During the same time period, the need for workers in Northern factories of the United States caused a mass migration of African Americans from the South. Many African Americans settled in Harlem, a neighborhood of New York City. There, writers, along with artists and musicians, worked to establish a proud cultural identity. This movement was called the Harlem Renaissance.*

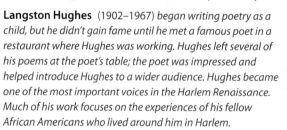 

A VOICE — Words Like FREEDOM

Poem by Pat Mora   Poem by Langston Hughes

Pat Mora (b. 1942) *was born in El Paso, Texas, to a Mexican American family that spoke both English and Spanish. Mora grew up speaking both languages, and today writes in English and in Spanish. When not writing, Mora spends much of her time encouraging children of all languages to read books. In 1996, she founded a holiday called "El día de los niños/El día de los libros." In English that means "Children's Day/Book Day."*

Langston Hughes (1902–1967) *began writing poetry as a child, but he didn't gain fame until he met a famous poet in a restaurant where Hughes was working. Hughes left several of his poems at the poet's table; the poet was impressed and helped introduce Hughes to a wider audience. Hughes became one of the most important voices in the Harlem Renaissance. Much of his work focuses on the experiences of his fellow African Americans who lived around him in Harlem.*

SETTING A PURPOSE As you read, focus on the challenges and feelings each poet expresses about being an American, paying close attention to how each poet's background affects his or her perspective.

(cr) © Cheron Bayna/Pat Mora; (br) ©Historical/Corbis

Poems **241**

Determine the Meaning of Figurative Language

RL 1,
RL 4,
L.6.5a

(LINES 7–10)

Explain that **figurative language** is a way of expressing ideas that are not literally true. Tell students that a **simile** is a comparison between two unlike things using *like* or *as*, and that a **metaphor** is a comparison of two mostly unlike things with some qualities in common that does not contain *like* or *as*.

(A) CITE TEXT EVIDENCE Ask students to reread lines 7–10 and identify the type of figurative language in line 8. *(metaphor)* Have students tell what two things are being compared and what the speaker means. *(The speaker compares the father to a judge without a courtroom, meaning that he makes all the decisions.)*

Analyze Tone (LINES 12–19)

RL 1,
RL 4,
RL 6

Explain to students that the **tone** of a poem expresses the poet's attitude toward a subject, or how he or she feels about it.

(B) CITE TEXT EVIDENCE Ask students to reread lines 12–19 and tell how the poem's subject feels, how the speaker feels, and how they know this. *(The person feels proud to speak English. The speaker is proud of this person's strength; the phrase "You liked" emphasizes this pride and shows that the speaker shares it.)* Then, ask students whether they think these feelings also describe the tone of the poem and why. *(Yes, because the poet presents them with certainty and admiration and not with humor or irony.)*

Explain Speaker (LINES 20–24)

RL 1,
RL 6

Explain to students that poems have a speaker, like stories have a narrator. Tell them that a poet uses pronouns and other clues to identify the speaker.

(C) CITE TEXT EVIDENCE Ask students to review lines 6–21 to identify clues that tell who the speaker is and is not. *(The speaker uses the pronouns* you *and* your; *when the speaker uses the pronoun* me, *so the poem is not about the speaker; it is about someone else. The person the poem tells about is from the speaker's family.)*

A VOICE
by Pat Mora

Even the lights on the stage unrelenting[1]
as the desert sun couldn't hide the other
students, their eyes also unrelenting,
students who spoke English every night

5   as they ate their meat, potatoes, gravy.
Not you. In your house that smelled like
rose powder, you spoke Spanish formal
as your father, the judge without a courtroom

in the country he floated to in the dark
10 on a flatbed truck. He walked slow
as a hot river down the narrow hall
of your house. You never dared to race past him,

to say, "Please move," in the language
you learned effortlessly, as you learned to run,
15 the language forbidden at home, though your mother
said you learned it to fight with the neighbors.

You liked winning with words. You liked
writing speeches about patriotism and democracy.
You liked all the faces looking at you, all those eyes.
20 "How did I do it?" you ask me now. "How did I do it

when my parents didn't understand?"
The family story says your voice is the voice
of an aunt in Mexico, spunky[2] as a peacock.
Family stories sing of what lives in the blood.

---

[1] **unrelenting** (ŭn´rĭ-lĕn´tĭng): steady and persistent; continuing on without stopping.
[2] **spunky** (spŭng´kē): spirited, plucky; having energy and courage.

English Language Support

Analyze Language Choices Read lines 10–16 aloud starting with "He walked slow," modeling the appropriate pace and expression.

- Have students take turns reading lines aloud. Then read the lines aloud together as a class.
- Ask students if "slow as a hot river" is a metaphor or a simile. *(simile)* Which word is most important to the meaning of *walked—hot, river,* or *slow? (slow)* Have students restate the sentence without figurative language. *(He walked slowly.)*

25 You told me only once about the time you went
to the state capitol, your family proud as if
you'd been named governor. But when you looked
around, the only Mexican in the auditorium,
you wanted to hide from those strange faces.

30 Their eyes were pinpricks,[3] and you faked
hoarseness. You, who are never at a loss
for words, felt your breath stick in your throat

like an ice-cube. "I can't," you whispered.
"I can't." Yet you did. Not that day but years later.

35 You taught the four of us to speak up.
This is America, Mom. The undo-able is done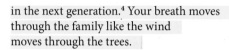

in the next generation.[4] Your breath moves
through the family like the wind
moves through the trees.

---

[3] **pinpricks** (pĭn′prĭks′): small wounds or punctures made by or as if by a pin.
[4] **generation** (jĕn′ə-rā′shən): all the people who are at the same stage of descent
from a common ancestor; grandparents, parents, and children represent three
different generations.

Poems **243**

CLOSE READ

Determine the Meaning of Figurative Language
RL 1,
RL 4,
L 5a

(LINES 25–33)

Review with students that poets use simile and metaphor to emphasize feelings or meaning.

D CITE TEXT EVIDENCE Ask students to reread lines 25–33, tell how the person in the poem feels, and identify how they know this. Remind students to explain the figurative language in these lines. *(The person is nervous, scared, anxious, intimidated. The metaphor "Their eyes were pinpricks" emphasizes being scared and judged by the audience. The simile "felt your breath stick in your throat / like an ice-cube" shows the feeling of being stopped very quickly by something, in this case suddenly not being able to speak. All these show nervousness and anxiety.)*

Analyze Tone (LINES 25–39)
RL 4,
L 5a

Remind students that tone is the poet's (writer's) attitude toward the subject. Explain to students that the feelings readers experience when reading a poem are often different from the tone of a poem.

E ASK STUDENTS how lines 25–33 make them feel. *(Possible response: nervous or sad for the person who is supposed to speak)* Then, have students describe the tone of these lines and lines 34–39 by first identifying the subject of the poem and then telling the poet's attitude toward this subject. *(The subject of the poem is the speaker's/poet's mother, as identified in line 36; the tone is proud, understanding, caring.)*

Explain Speaker (LINES 35–39)
RL 1,
RL 6

Remind students that they should identify the speaker in a poem as completely as possible.

F CITE TEXT EVIDENCE Ask students to identify who the speaker is, whose story the poem tells, and how they know this. *(The speaker is an adult child, and the poem is about this adult child's mother. Line 36 clearly states this relationship; note that readers may have already inferred this or something like it from reading the rest of the poem.)*

WHEN STUDENTS STRUGGLE...

Students may confuse tone with their own feelings as they read. Ask students to create a chart to help them distinguish the two.

Tone: How Poet Feels	How Reader Feels
Lines	Lines
Feelings	Feelings

LEVEL UP TUTORIALS For additional support, assign the following *Level Up* tutorial: **Tone**

TEACH

CLOSE READ

Analyze Tone

(LINES 1–8)

Tell students that the speaker of "Words Like Freedom" has different reactions to two words that mean almost the same thing: *freedom* and *liberty*.

G **CITE TEXT EVIDENCE** Have students reread lines 1–8 and tell how the poet's/speaker's tone changes from the first to the second stanza, and how they know this. *(The first stanza uses the words "sweet," "wonderful," "sings." The second stanza uses the word "cry.")* Ask what this tells them about the poet's feelings toward freedom and liberty. *(Possible response: In the first stanza, the speaker has a joyful tone, celebrating the meaning of freedom. In the second stanza, his tone changes to sadness. I think he is remembering all the people who have died fighting for liberty, and the costs of liberty seem very high to him. He may also be thinking about how people must fight for liberty again and again; it is a battle that never seems completely won.)*

COLLABORATIVE DISCUSSION Before partners have their discussion, have individual students list their own ideas about freedom and equality as expressed in the poem. Have partners discuss their lists and ideas together, and remind them to cite evidence from the poem as support. Then, have partners share their ideas with the larger group.

ASK STUDENTS to share any questions they generated in the course of reading and discussing this selection.

CONTENT-AREA CONNECTION

Cultural History Tell students that the Harlem Renaissance occurred between World War I and World War II. Langston Hughes published his first book of poems in 1926. African American poets, writers, musicians, and artists gathered in Harlem to create art and fight for greater civil rights.

Activity After reading the poem, have students work independently to research the Harlem Renaissance. Have students report on particular art forms or artists who were part of the movement. Students can present reports to the class or share information in another form.

WORDS LIKE FREEDOM

by Langston Hughes

There are words like *Freedom*
Sweet and wonderful to say.
On my heartstrings freedom sings
All day everyday.

5   There are words like *Liberty*
That almost make me cry.
If you had known what I know
You would know why.

COLLABORATIVE DISCUSSION With a partner, discuss how "A Voice" and "Words Like Freedom" explore ideas such as freedom and equality. Use evidence from the texts in your discussion.

©Shutterstock

TO CHALLENGE STUDENTS . . .

Author's Perspective Have students work in small groups to discuss how the poem might have been different if Hughes had written about freedom and liberty before the Civil War.

ASK STUDENTS to share their ideas about how they think freedom and liberty would be described differently, and how the poet's tone might also be different.

Determine the Meaning
of Figurative Language

RL 4

Poets often use figurative language to express ideas. A **simile** is a comparison of two things that uses the words *like* or *as*. A **metaphor** is a comparison of two things that does not use *like* or *as*. Similes and metaphors help readers see ideas in an imaginative way. The poem "A Voice" opens with a simile:

> Even the lights on the stage unrelenting as the
> desert sun couldn't hide the other students, . . .

The simile emphasizes how unforgiving and severe the stage lights seem. This comparison helps readers understand how the speaker's mother felt.

To determine the meaning of a simile or metaphor, ask yourself:

- What two ideas is the poet comparing?
- What feelings and attitudes does the simile or metaphor help explain?

As you analyze "A Voice," look for other examples of figurative language.

Analyze Tone

RL 4, RL 6

Tone is another way a writer expresses ideas. A writer's **tone** is his or her attitude toward a subject. Tone is often described with a single adjective, such as *angry, playful,* or *mocking.* Writers establish tone through thoughts, actions, images, and word choices.

An **inference** is a logical guess. Readers can identify and put together clues, such as the poet's choice of words and images, to make inferences about a poem's tone.

In "A Voice," the simile "In your house that smelled like rose powder, you spoke Spanish formal . . ." provides a clue about the home of the speaker's mother. From this, readers can infer that the **speaker,** or the voice that "talks" to the reader, has a deep understanding of what her mother's home life was like. The speaker's tone can be described as *understanding.*

Use the following clues to make inferences about tone in the poems:

- Identify the topic.
- Pay attention to images and descriptions. Are they serious, silly, or frightening?
- Decide how the speaker feels about the subject. Does he or she feel happy, sad, or angry?

CLOSE READ

Determine the Meaning
of Figurative Language

RL 4, L 5a, L 5a

Review the information about figurative language and discuss the example. Have students reread "A Voice" to find additional examples of simile and metaphor. Discuss the impact each one has on meaning and emotion.

Analyze Tone

RL 1, RL 4, RL 6

Explain to students that poets do not directly explain their attitude toward a subject. Readers need to make logical guesses, or **inferences,** about the tone the poet has toward his or her subject matter. Tell students that they make inferences by paying close attention to the details in the poem and then using those details and their own experiences to figure out what the poet doesn't directly say.

Have students analyze the tone of each poem. Ask students to identify words and details that help them understand each poet's attitude toward the subject matter.

English Language Support

To give students practice analyzing tone, remind them that in "A Voice," the poet is speaking to her mother. Read lines 30–34 aloud. Ask students to read the last two sentences in line 34 to each other and discuss how they show the poet's feelings toward her mother.

Strategies for Annotation 🖉 📄 *Annotate it!*

Determine the Meaning
of Figurative Language

RL 4

Share these strategies for guided or independent analysis:

- Highlight in yellow examples of simile.
- Highlight in blue examples of metaphor.
- On a note, jot down the meaning and effect of each example.

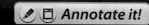

The family story says your voice is the voice of an aunt in Mexico, spunky as a peacock. Family stories sing of what lives in the blood.

actions show
blood/family
connection

Analyzing the Text

RL 1, RL 2,
RL 3, RL 4,
RL 6, RL 9

Possible answers:

1. The simile is "He walked slow as a hot river down the narrow hall of your house." The words "You never dared to race past him" help the reader infer that the speaker's mother has a sense of fear and respect for her father.

2. As an adult, the mother does not seem to understand how she could have been so brave when she was young. The simile "spunky as a peacock" connects her to an aunt in Mexico who shared these qualities.

3. The metaphor is "your father, judge without a courtroom." The metaphor explains that the father makes the decisions in the household.

4. The speaker learns from the mother to have courage and speak up for herself. The poet expresses this by saying that this message continues to be heard from one generation to the next.

5. The poet's tone is sympathetic. The poet understands that the speaker's mother wasn't always as brave as she wished to be, but the poet shows the mother as strong and imparts her wisdom and experiences to her children.

6. Using words such as "sweet" and "wonderful" with "cry" and "If you had known what I know" shows that the poet feels that the road to freedom and liberty has been long and harsh but worth the sacrifices; the tone could be described as bittersweet.

7. The metaphors both compare ideas to singing and song—the song of family history and strength that "lives in the blood" in "A Voice," and the conflicting emotions and memories that freedom's song evokes in "Words Like Freedom."

FOR STUDENTS WITH DISABILITIES

Students with disabilities may have difficulty interpreting and comparing metaphors and similes. Instruct them to work with a partner to draw the things being compared. For example, for "judge without a courtroom" in lines 5–8, tell them to draw a picture of a judge sitting in court and a picture of a father sitting at a table at home. When the two pictures are next to each other, what does the judge picture communicate about the father picture? Prompt them to consider how a father might be similar to a judge and note their ideas.

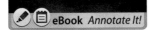

Analyzing the Text

RL 1, RL 2, RL 3,
RL 4, RL 6, RL 9,
W 3d

Cite Text Evidence Support your responses with evidence from the text.

1. **Infer** Review lines 6–14 of "A Voice," in which the speaker describes her grandfather. What is the simile in these lines? What inference can you make about the relationship between the speaker's mother and her father?

2. **Interpret** Reread lines 17–23 of "A Voice." How does the speaker's mother feel about herself as a young girl? Explain how the simile in lines 22–23 shows the connection the mother has to her family.

3. **Interpret** Reread lines 5–8 of "A Voice." Identify the metaphor in these lines. What does the metaphor tell you about the father?

4. **Connect** Reread lines 34–35 of "A Voice." What lesson does the speaker say she learned from her mother, and how does the poet express this lesson now?

5. **Interpret** Reread lines 37–39 of "A Voice." Describe the poet's tone. How does her tone help her convey the ideas she expresses?

6. **Analyze** Think about the speaker's attitude in "Words Like Freedom." How would you describe the poet's tone?

7. **Compare** Compare line 24 of "A Voice" with lines 3–4 of "Words Like Freedom." How are these metaphors similar in the experiences and ideas they address?

PERFORMANCE TASK

Writing Activity: Poem In "A Voice" and "Words Like Freedom," the poets express their opinions and make their voices heard. Write a poem in which you express your views about a freedom you enjoy, or about the freedom to have an opinion at all.

- Choose your topic. Be sure it is clear and specific.
- Choose a few adjectives that clearly tell how you feel about your topic. These words are the tone you want to create in your poem.

- Include at least one simile and one metaphor in your poem.
- Create comparisons that help express your ideas. Try a number of different ones until you find those that express your feelings in a vivid way.
- Review your word choices. Make sure they express your opinions precisely.
- Keep in mind the tone you chose as you review your work. Make adjustments as needed.

Assign this performance task.

PERFORMANCE TASK

W 3d

Writing Activity: Poem Have students work independently. Tell them to

- decide on the main idea or message they want to convey
- decide who will be the speaker in their poem
- choose their words carefully, using only words that are necessary and that enhance meaning
- use words and comparisons that describe what they hear, say, see, smell, and feel

INTERACTIVE WHITEBOARD LESSON
Determine Theme

RL 2

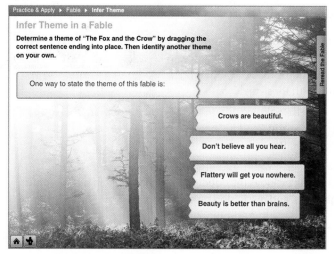

Practice & Apply ▶ Fable ▶ Infer Theme

Infer Theme in a Fable

Determine a theme of "The Fox and the Crow" by dragging the correct sentence ending into place. Then identify another theme on your own.

One way to state the theme of this fable is:

Crows are beautiful.

Don't believe all you hear.

Flattery will get you nowhere.

Beauty is better than brains.

TEACH

Use the Interactive Whiteboard Lesson to teach students how to understand and identify theme. Use the Share What You Know section to discuss lessons that people learn from life. Next, use the Learn the Skill section to discuss

- how literature can teach life lessons
- the difference between a topic and a theme: a **theme** is a message about life or human nature that tells about a topic
- the clues that reveal theme in literature

Then, focus on the steps for how to identify theme:

- **Step 1: Track the Clues** Have students examine clues in the title, subject, images, and language.
- **Step 2: Infer Theme** Explain that a theme is almost always implied rather than directly stated. Readers can identify the theme by paying attention to the words and details in a text and by asking themselves, "What big message about life is the writer trying to tell me?"

Continue with the Tips for Analyzing Theme and the Practice & Apply sections in the lesson, focusing especially on the practice exercise for a poem.

COLLABORATIVE DISCUSSION

Have students work with a partner to apply the steps to the poems "A Voice" and "Words Like Freedom." After their analysis, have them share their ideas about theme with other pairs of students in the class.

Determine Meaning: Figurative Language

RL 4

RETEACH

Review that **figurative language** is language used to express ideas that are not literally true. Explain that poets often use figurative language to compare, emphasize ideas, or create emotion. Then, discuss two types of figurative language:

- A **simile** is a comparison between two unlike things using the words *like* or *as*.
- A **metaphor** is a comparison of two mostly unlike things that have some qualities in common; it does not include the words *like* or *as*.

Give simple examples of each, prompting students with relevant questions. For example:

Life is a rollercoaster that everyone must ride.

- What two things are being compared in this figure of speech? *(life and a rollercoaster)*
- Does it include the words *like* or *as*? *(no)*
- What type of figurative language is this? *(metaphor)*

Have students try their hand at creating their own figures of speech, using familiar experiences such as movies, sports, music, and school. Discuss each example as a group.

LEVEL UP TUTORIALS Assign the following *Level Up* tutorial: **Figurative Language**

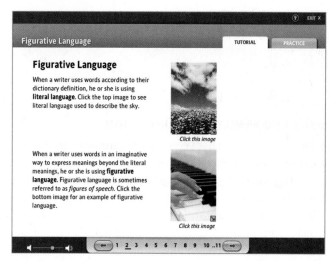

INDEPENDENT READING

Have small groups apply the skill to poetry in other collections or to poetry they are reading on their own. Ask them to explain what each figure of speech means and what effect each one has on the poem.

MAKING YOUR VOICE HEARD

The FYI site provides links to online articles from a variety of magazines and newspapers. Help students choose a few articles to read to further their exploration of the topic Making Your Voice Heard.

NOVELWISE

Students can unlock the power of novels with this unique resource. Help students read through longer works with these tips:

- Find a Book
- Before You Read
- As You Read
- After You Read

Each book includes introductory material, worksheets, graphic organizers, and discussion guides.

ADDITIONAL TEXTS BY COLLECTION

Suggest students read the following:

- "Barbara Frietchie" by John Greenleaf Whittier

Read the poem aloud to students.
Then have them analyze how the poet uses dialogue to portray the characters. Ask for volunteers to act out the exchange between Barbara Frietchie and Stonewall Jackson.

NONFICTION CONNECTIONS

Suggest that students increase their reading of informational texts. The nonfiction connections include

- speeches
- diaries
- true-life accounts
- newspaper articles
- political cartoons

Creating an Independent Reading Program

PARENT AND FAMILY COMMUNICATION

Regular communication between teachers, students, and families builds support for independent reading.

- Send home short progress notes at regular intervals. Ask students to draft notes about what they read and learned and what they liked about the book.
- Include a parent form with the student note so that the parents can record any questions or comments they may have, as well as the number of minutes or hours their student reads. Request they sign, date, and return the note.
- Encourage students to read a few pages from their book to family members, or encourage family members to read the book aloud with their student.

RECORDING BOOKS AND TEXTS READ

Using a system for recording materials read will help students remember and analyze their choices.

- Prepare a reading log or digital spreadsheet for students to use. Have them keep the logs in their reading folders or on their digital device. If you are partnering with school or municipal librarians, give them a copy of the log.
- In addition to recording the title and author of the books read, ask students to record when they started and finished the book, whether it was easy or difficult, and what they liked or disliked.
- Remind students to log their progress whenever they finish reading a book.
- Go over the log with students during their individual reading conferences.

PERFORMANCE TASK

PERFORMANCE TASK

Present an Argument in a Speech

A good argument can convince people to change their minds about a topic. Now you will draft an argument and deliver it in a speech that justifies your views on whether people should own exotic animals. Use evidence from "Wild Animals Aren't Pets" and "Let People Own Exotic Animals" to support your position.

W 1a–e Write arguments.
W 5 Develop and strengthen writing.
W 6 Use technology to produce and publish writing.
W 8 Gather relevant information from print and digital sources.
W 10 Write routinely.
SL 4 Present claims and findings.

A successful argument

- contains an engaging introduction that establishes the claim
- supports the claim with clear reasons and relevant evidence
- establishes and maintains a formal style
- uses language that effectively conveys ideas and adds interest
- includes a conclusion that follows from the argument presented and leaves a lasting impression

Mentor Text Notice how this excerpt from "Wild Animals Aren't Pets" grabs the reader's attention and establishes the claim.

> " In many states, anyone with a few hundred dollars and a yen for the unusual can own a python, black bear or a big cat as a 'pet.' For $8,000 a baby white tiger can be yours. . . . Until recently, though, few people knew how easy it is to own a wild animal as a pet. Or how potentially tragic. "

myNotebook

Use the annotation tools in your eBook to find evidence that supports your claim. Save each piece of evidence to your notebook.

PLAN

Choose Your Position Think about both sides of this argument: Should people own exotic animals? Then take the position you can argue most effectively.

Gather Information Review the evidence that supports each claim in "Wild Animals Aren't Pets" and "Let People Own Exotic Animals."

- Make a list of reasons you have taken the position you chose. Note evidence, such as facts, that will support your reasons.
- Think about counterclaims that might keep your audience from agreeing with you.

ACADEMIC VOCABULARY

As you plan and present your speech, be sure to use the academic vocabulary words.

appropriate
authority
consequence
justify
legal

PRESENT AN ARGUMENT IN A SPEECH

W 1a-e, W 5, W 6, W 8, W 10, SL 4

Introduce students to the Performance Task by reading the introductory paragraph with them. Explain to students that an argument in a speech is a carefully stated claim that is supported by reasons and evidence. Then, review the criteria for what makes a successful argument in a speech.

PLAN

GATHER INFORMATION

As students gather information, help them plan how to respond to any counterclaims that their audience might make. Guide them to prepare counterarguments to respond to these claims as needed.

Point out to students that their claim, or any counterclaims they anticipate, may be best supported by different types of evidence. For example, students may want to present their claim with facts and statistics, while a counterclaim may best be answered by anecdotes or examples. Remind students to gather several types of reasons and evidence as they work.

English Language Support

Plan to Present an Argument Point out that understanding both sides of an argument can help students support their own position. Have student pairs work together to list reasons and evidence from the collection texts that support arguments for and against owning exotic animals. Then have students use the sentence frames and questions to discuss their presentation plans with a partner.

- I think the risks of owning a wild animal are/aren't worth the benefits because _____.

- I agree with your point that _____; however, I still think that _____ because _____.
- I will look for quotations that show _____.
- I will also try to find evidence that shows _____.

What other types of evidence do you think I should look for as I do further research? Students can use their conversations to help them focus their research and develop their arguments.

PERFORMANCE TASK

FOR STANDARD ENGLISH LEARNERS

Adapt Speech Remind students of the differences between formal speech and informal conversation. As they practice their responses, encourage students to pay special attention to words ending with final *r*. Advise students that speaking slowly and clearly can help them focus on pronouncing the ending.

English Language Support

Use Academic Words Remind students to use academic language in their arguments. Provide the following sentence starters as examples.

This example clearly demonstrates _____.
The report provides evidence that _____.

PRODUCE

DRAFT YOUR ARGUMENT

Remind students that the purpose of an argument is to convince others that your claim is valid. Advise students to read aloud or listen to their arguments in their heads as they write to make sure that their points are logical and persuasive.

Explain to students that, at this stage, the goal is to make sure their most important ideas, reasons, and evidence are presented in the speech. Once students have a first draft, they can return to areas that need revising to polish their logic and their language. Guide students through the points shown to help them check the structure and logic of their draft and add, delete, or rearrange sections as needed.

WHEN STUDENTS STRUGGLE . . .

Organize Information If students have trouble organizing the information they have gathered, suggest that they work with partners to discuss their reasons and evidence. Partners can help each other evaluate the credibility and accuracy of each piece of evidence. Then have pairs work together to complete the graphic organizers showing the main claim, the reasons for the claim, and the evidence that supports each reason.

Organize Your Ideas A graphic organizer can help you present your ideas logically. Place your claim in the top box, your reasons in the next row of boxes, and your evidence in the last row.

Interactive Lessons
For help in organizing your reasons and evidence, use
• Writing Arguments: Support Reasons and Evidence

Consider Your Purpose and Audience Ask yourself: Who will listen to this speech? Which ideas will be most convincing to them? What language will you use to convey your position?

PRODUCE

my WriteSmart

Draft Your Argument As you draft your argument, keep the following in mind:

- Introduce the topic to your audience. Grab your listeners' attention with an interesting quote or surprising fact.
- State your position clearly. Use your notes and graphic organizer to create a logical sequence of your reasons and evidence. Include facts, and details that support your claim.
- Address counterclaims and tell why your position is more valid.
- Maintain a formal writing style, and use transition words and phrases such as *because, therefore,* and *for that reason* to clarify relationships between ideas.
- In your conclusion, restate your claim. Remind your audience why you believe your position is the right one.

Write your rough draft in *my*WriteSmart. Focus on getting your ideas down, rather than perfecting your choice of language.

Interactive Lessons
For help in drafting your argument, use
• Using Textual Evidence: Summarizing, Paraphrasing, and Quoting

Language Conventions: Modify to Add Details

Adverbs modify, or describe, verbs, adjectives, and other adverbs. They answer the questions *where, when, how,* and *to what extent?* In this excerpt from "Wild Animals Aren't Pets," notice how the adverb *recently* tells when the story unfolded.

> " . . . a story that unfolded in a small Ohio city recently opened the public's eyes to the little known, distressing world of 'exotic' pets. "

English Language Support

Adapt Language Choices Tell students they will need to use both verbal and nonverbal elements to persuade their audience to agree with their claims.

- Have students identify words, phrases, and sentences that they want to emphasize. Then have each student practice reading the words and sentences aloud to a partner. Encourage them to use volume, expression, and gestures to add emphasis.

Evaluate Your Speech

Evaluate Your Speech Have your partner or group of peers review the draft of your speech. Use the following chart to revise it.

Questions	Tips	Revision Techniques
Does my introduction grab the audience's attention?	**Underline** the introduction.	**Add** an interesting fact, example, or quotation.
Does my introduction present a clear claim?	**Highlight** the claim.	**Add** a claim, or replace the claim with a clearer one.
Is my claim supported with several reasons?	**Underline** the reasons that support the claim.	**Add** reasons that support the claim.
Is each reason supported by at least one piece of evidence?	**Highlight** the evidence that supports each reason.	**Add** evidence to support each reason. **Explain** each piece of evidence.
Do I use adverbs to provide details about when, where, or how events occurred?	**Highlight** adverbs.	**Add** adverbs to accurately describe how events occurred.
Do I restate my claim in the conclusion?	**Underline** the conclusion.	**Add** a restatement of the claim.

Practice Your Speech Deliver your argument as a speech to a group of peers. You can also practice in front of a mirror.

- Use your voice effectively. Speak loudly, varying your pitch and tone. Be sure to pause to emphasize important points.
- Maintain eye contact. Look directly at individuals in your audience.
- Use gestures and facial expressions that show your audience you are confident about your position.

Deliver Your Speech Finalize your speech and share it with your audience. You might present your speech as a webcast.

✔ myWriteSmart

Have your partner or a group of peers review your draft in *my*WriteSmart. Ask your reviewers to note any reasons that do not support the claim or lack sufficient evidence.

Interactive Lessons
For help in delivering your speech, use
- Giving a Presentation: Delivering Your Presentation

Collection Performance Task **249**

PERFORMANCE TASK

PRODUCE

LANGUAGE CONVENTIONS

Point out that in the excerpt on p. 248 the adverb *recently* modifies the verb *opened* to provide a detail about the time of the event. Tell students that another way they can add details to their sentences is to use adverb phrases such as *until recently, for years,* and *on the property*. Work with students to brainstorm other adverb phrases they might add to their drafts.

REVISE

PRACTICE AND EVALUATE YOUR SPEECH

Advise students to practice in front of a mirror or with a partner who can give feedback about the content and delivery. Point out that an excellent argument will sometimes be dismissed if it isn't presented well.

PRESENT

DELIVER YOUR SPEECH

Students can present their speeches as webcasts on a class or school website. Have students view at least two or three of their classmates' webcasts and demonstrate active listening by posting questions and comments in an online discussion board.

FOR STUDENTS WITH DISABILITIES

Practice on Camera Have students record a video of themselves practicing their speech. Remind them to look at the camera and use their voice effectively by varying their pitch and tone. Then have them view the video with a peer to help them identify ways that they may revise their arguments and improve their delivery.

English Language Support

Express Opinions Provide students with a list of basic or familiar modal expressions that they can use to convey attitudes or opinions or to temper statements. For example:

can, could (to express ability)
has to, must (to express obligation)
maybe, probably (to express possibility)

Encourage students to use these expressions in their speeches and in their online webcast discussions.

PERFORMANCE TASK

USE THE SCORING RUBRIC

Have students use the rubric to score their own speeches. Then have partners evaluate each other's score. Students should use the language of the rubric to provide feedback in each category.

REFLECT ON THE PROCESS

Tell students that taking the time to reflect on the planning and presentation processes in this task will help them apply what they learned and improve their skills. Ask students to think about how well their arguments persuaded the audience. Then have them answer the following questions:

- How well did your introduction grab the audience's attention?
- Which of your reasons was most convincing?
- What evidence did you use to address opposing claims?

PERFORMANCE TASK RUBRIC
ARGUMENT IN A SPEECH

	Ideas and Evidence	Organization	Language
4	• The introduction grabs the audience's attention; the claim clearly states the speaker's position on an issue. • Logical reasons and relevant evidence support the speaker's claim. • Opposing claims are anticipated and effectively addressed. • The concluding section effectively summarizes the claim.	• The reasons and evidence are organized logically throughout the speech. • Transitions effectively connect reasons and evidence to the speaker's claim.	• The speech reflects a formal style. • Sentence beginnings, lengths, and structures vary and have a rhythmic flow. • Grammar, usage, and mechanics are correct.
3	• The introduction could do more to grab the audience's attention; the speaker's claim states a position on an issue. • Most reasons and evidence support the speaker's claim. • Opposing claims are anticipated, but the responses need to be developed more. • The concluding section restates the claim.	• The organization of reasons and evidence is logical in most places. • A few more transitions are needed to connect reasons and evidence to the speaker's claim.	• The style becomes informal in a few places. • Sentence beginnings, lengths, and structures vary somewhat. • Some grammatical, usage, and mechanics errors are present.
2	• The introduction does not grab listeners' attention; the speaker's claim identifies an issue, but the position is not clearly stated. • The reasons and evidence are not always logical or relevant. • Opposing claims are anticipated but not addressed logically. • The concluding section includes an incomplete summary of the claim.	• The organization of reasons and evidence is confusing in some places, and it often does not follow a pattern. • Few transitions are used, but the speech is not difficult to understand.	• The style becomes informal in many places. • Sentence structures rarely vary, and some fragments are present. • Grammar, usage, and mechanics are incorrect in many places, but the speaker's ideas are still clear.
1	• The introduction is confusing and does not state a claim. • Supporting reasons and evidence are missing. • Opposing claims are neither anticipated nor addressed. • The concluding section is missing.	• A logical organization is not used; reasons and evidence are presented randomly. • Transitions are not used, making the speech difficult to understand.	• The style is inappropriate for the speech. • Repetitive sentence structure and fragments make the speech hard to follow. • Many grammatical and usage errors change the meaning of ideas.

TO CHALLENGE STUDENTS . . .

Create a Public Service Video Challenge students to adapt their arguments for a web video that takes a stand for or against a proposal to allow ownership of exotic pets in their community. Students should try to convince their audience of the merits of their arguments, and they should encourage a call to action.

© Images.com/Corbis

Decisions That Matter

"We must never forget that it is through our actions,
words, and thoughts that we have a choice."

—Sogyal Rinpoche

251

PLAN

STREAM TO START

Motivate students to read the collection texts, and spark their curiosity about the collection by playing the video for the class. After students view the video, ask them to list two things they hope to learn from reading about the way people approach decision-making situations. Call on volunteers to share their responses.

PERFORMANCE TASK PREVIEW

Point out to students that they will complete two performance tasks at the end of the collection. The performance tasks will require them to further analyze the selections in the collection and to synthesize ideas about these analyses. Students will present their findings in a variety of products.

ACADEMIC VOCABULARY

View It!

Professional Development Podcast:

Academic Vocabulary

Students can acquire facility with the academic vocabulary words through frequent, repeated exposure as they analyze and discuss the selections in the collection. Academic vocabulary can be used in the instructional contexts shown below.

- Collaborative Discussion at the end of each selection
- Analyzing the Text questions for each selection
- Selection-level Performance Task
- Vocabulary instruction (for Critical Vocabulary and/or for Vocabulary Strategy)
- Language Conventions
- End-of-collection Performance Task for all selections in the collection

ASK STUDENTS to review the Academic Vocabulary word list for this collection. You may wish to pronounce each word aloud so students hear the correct pronunciation. Then, discuss the definitions and the related forms for each word. Remind students that they will encounter these five academic vocabulary words throughout the collection.

COLLECTION 5

Decisions That Matter

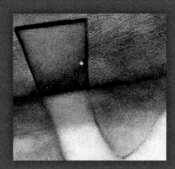

In this collection, you will explore how and why people make certain choices in their lives.

Stream to Start   hmhfyi.com   Channel One News®

COLLECTION

PERFORMANCE TASK Preview

After reading this collection, you will have the opportunity to complete two performance tasks:

- In one, you will write a personal narrative about a key decision you had to make.

- In the second, you will write an argument in which you give your views on how people's decisions shape their lives.

ACADEMIC VOCABULARY

Study the words and their definitions in the chart below. You will use these words as you discuss and write about the texts in this collection.

Word	Definition	Related Forms
achieve (ə-chēv´) *v.*	to perform or carry out with success; accomplish	achievement, achievable
individual (ĭn´də-vĭj´ōō-əl) *n.*	a single human being apart from a society or community	individuality, individualism, individually
instance (ĭn´stəns) *n.*	an example that is cited to prove or disprove a claim or illustrate a point	instances
outcome (out´kŭm´) *n.*	a natural result or consequence	outcomes
principle (prĭn´sə-pəl) *n.*	a rule or standard, especially of good behavior	principled, principles

252

---

myNotebook

As students read, analyze, and discuss the texts in this collection, encourage them to create a *my*WordList folder in *my*Notebook to build their own personal word lists.

- **Annotate** Students can highlight vocabulary terms and other unfamiliar words and save each highlighted term to *my*Notebook.
- **Organize** Within *my*Notebook, students can drag each word into the *my*WordList folder.
- **Elaborate** Ask students to add details to the entry for each word, such as a definition, other forms of the word, and a sample sentence.

English Language Support

▶ View It!
Professional Development Podcast:
English Language Learners

ENGAGE WITH THE COLLECTION TOPIC

Draw attention to the title of the collection: Decisions That Matter. Tell students that the selections in this collection explore the difficulties in making important decisions by looking at critical choices that people, both famous and ordinary, have had to make.

ACCESS PRIOR KNOWLEDGE Ask students to think about important decisions that they have had to make. Let volunteers share anecdotes, and then suggest that examining the way in which others approach this process could help them with their own decision making.

SOCRATIC SEMINAR

Use this strategy to deepen students' understanding of the texts in this collection and to encourage discussion.

- *First,* have students annotate a text as they read, noting interesting ideas, questions, and difficult or tricky passages. Students can use *my*Notebook in the eBook to record their annotations.

- *Then,* introduce the discussion by explaining that students should not only answer questions, but should respond to what's said, building on each other's ideas. Explain that they are free to take sides in the discussion, to persuade each other, and to pose additional follow-up questions. Remind them to support their ideas with textual evidence.

- *Next,* begin a discussion by posing open-ended questions related to the text, such as: "How does [*an aspect of the text*] relate to your own experience? What does your own experience tell you about [*a character's experience*]?"

- *Finally,* when discussion has ended, have students write short evaluations of their own participation, along with personal goals for future seminars.

 Collection 5 Digital Resources for English Language Support

LANGUAGE WORKSHOP
Designated English Learners

Use Teacher Resources > Language Workshop to support English learners in evaluating how a writer uses language, applying an understanding of links among reasons, and exchanging information and ideas by building on peers' responses.

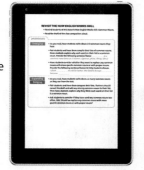

Text in FOCUS **VIDEOS**

These videos will help students learn how to analyze language and examine syntax. Have students use **Text in Focus Practice** to apply those skills.

Collection 5 Lessons	Media	Teach and Practice
Student Edition | eBook	**Video Links** HISTORY A&E Channel One News	**Close Reading and Evidence Tracking**

ANCHOR TEXT — Memoir by Colin Powell from *It Worked for Me: In Life and Leadership* Biography by Warren Brown from *Colin Powell: Military Leader*	▶ **Audio** from *It Worked for Me: In Life and Leadership* ▶ **Audio** from *Colin Powell: Military Leader*	**Close Read Screencasts** from *It Worked for Me: In Life and Leadership* • Modeled Discussion (lines 23–29) • Close Read Application PDF (lines 156–165) from *Colin Powell: Military Leader* • Modeled Discussion (lines 52–61) • Close Read Application PDF (lines 189–197)	**Text in Focus** • Analyzing Language (line 92) **Strategies for Annotation** • Analyze Text: Memoir • Analyze Text: Biography • Analogies
CLOSE READER — Autobiography by Wilma Mankiller from *Every Day Is a New Day* Essay by Susan Abbey "Community Hero: Chief Wilma Mankiller"	▶ **Audio** from *Every Day Is a New Day* ▶ **Audio** "Community Hero: Chief Wilma Mankiller"		
Short Story by R. V. Cassill "The First Day of School"	▶ **Audio** "The First Day of School"		**Strategies for Annotation** • Determine Meanings: Mood • Determine Meanings of Words and Phrases
EXEMPLAR Poem by Robert Frost "The Road Not Taken"	▶ **Audio** "The Road Not Taken"		**Strategies for Annotation** • Analyze Structure
ANCHOR TEXT — Poem by Henry Wadsworth Longfellow "Paul Revere's Ride"	▶ **Video** HISTORY® *Paul Revere* ▶ **Audio** "Paul Revere's Ride"	**Close Read Screencasts** • Modeled Discussion (lines 31–41) • Close Read Application PDF (lines 111–118)	**Text in Focus** • Examining Syntax (line 106) **Strategies for Annotation** • Analyze Structure
CLOSE READER — Poem by Joyce Sidman "The Light—Ah! The Light"	▶ **Audio** "The Light—Ah! The Light"		
News Article by Jodi Wilgoren and Edward Wong "On Doomed Flight, Passengers Vowed to Perish Fighting" TV Newscast by CBS News "Memorial Is Unveiled for Heroes of Flight 93"	▶ **Audio** "On Doomed Flight, Passengers Vowed to Perish Fighting" ▶ **Video** *Memorial Is Unveiled for Heroes of Flight 93*		**Strategies for Annotation** • Analyze Structure
Collection 5 Performance Tasks: **A** Write a Personal Narrative **B** Write an Argument	fyi hmhfyi.com	**Interactive Lessons** **A** Writing Narratives **A** Writing as a Process	**B** Writing Arguments **B** Using Textual Evidence

For Systematic Coverage of Writing and Speaking & Listening Standards

Interactive Lessons

Writing a Narrative
Producing and Publishing with Technology

For foundational
skills and reading
intervention support: READ180

Assess		Extend	Reteach
Performance Task	✅ *Assess It Online!*	**Teacher eBook**	**Teacher eBook**
Speaking Activity: Informative Presentation	Selection Test	**Analyze Tone > Interactive Whiteboard Lesson >** Word Choice and Tone	**Compare and Contrast: Memoir and Biography > Level Up Tutorials >** Author's Purpose > Biographies and Autobiographies
Writing Activity: Informative Essay	Selection Test	**Analyze Structure: Foreshadowing**	**Determine Meaning: Mood > Level Up Tutorial >** Setting and Mood
Speaking Activity: Collaborative Discussion	Selection Test	**Determine Meaning: Imagery > Interactive Whiteboard Lesson >** Figurative Language and Imagery	**Determine Theme > Level Up Tutorials >** Theme > Symbol
Writing Activity: Analysis	Selection Test	**Compare and Contrast: Two Versions of a Poem**	**Analyze Structure: Narrative Poetry > Level Up Tutorial >** Narrative Poetry
Media Activity: Commentary	Selection Test	**Evaluate Sources > Interactive Lessons >** Evaluating Sources	**Integrate Information > Interactive Graphic Organizer >** Main Idea or Main Idea and Details Chart
A Write a Personal Narrative **B** Write an Argument	Collection Test		

Lesson Assessments Writing a Narrative Producing and Publishing with Technology	**Standards Support and Enrichment**	For more instruction and practice in reading literary and informational texts, language, spelling, and speaking and listening, see Teacher Resources > Standards Support and Enrichment.
	For Designated English Language Instruction	To provide scaffolded support specific to the needs of English Learners during Designated English Language instruction, use the selection- and standards-aligned lessons found in Teacher Resources > Language Workshop.

Collection 5 Lessons	Key Learning Objective	Performance Task	Vocabulary Strategy
ANCHOR TEXT **Memoir by Colin Powell** from *It Worked for Me: In Life and Leadership*, p. 253A **Lexile 1010L** **Biography by Warren Brown** from *Colin Powell: Military Leader*, p. 253A **Lexile 1220L**	**The student will be able to . . .** identify elements of a memoir and a biography, analyze primary and secondary sources, and compare and contrast two genres on the same subject.	Speaking Activity: Informative Presentation	Analogies
Short Story by R. V. Cassill "The First Day of School," p. 271A **Lexile 780L**	**The student will be able to . . .** determine and analyze mood and describe flashback in a short story.	Writing Activity: Essay	Using a Thesaurus
EXEMPLAR **Poem by Robert Frost** "The Road Not Taken," p. 281A	**The student will be able to . . .** analyze the structure of a poem and describe how poets use symbols and structure to convey a theme.	Speaking Activity: Collaborative Discussion	
ANCHOR TEXT **EXEMPLAR** **Poem by Henry Wadsworth Longfellow** "Paul Revere's Ride," p. 285A	**The student will be able to . . .** analyze the elements of narrative poetry, including the characters, setting, and plot.	Writing Activity: Analysis	
News Article by Jodi Wilgoren and Edward Wong **Lexile 1350L** "On Doomed Flight, Passengers Vowed to Perish Fighting," p. 293A **TV Newscast by CBS News** "Memorial Is Unveiled for Heroes of Flight 93," p. 293A	**The student will be able to . . .** analyze the elements of a news report, as well as integrate information in different media.	Media Activity: Commentary	

Collection 5 Performance Tasks:

A Write a Personal Narrative

B Write an Argument

Language Conventions	English Language Support	Differentiated Instruction	CLOSE READER Selection
Correct Vague Pronouns	• Analyze Language • Use Noun Phrases • Read Closely • Understand Text Structure • Culturally Responsive Instruction • Provide Textual Evidence	**When Students Struggle:** • Message • Compare and Contrast **To Challenge Students:** • Analyze Language • Analyze Text **For Standard English Learners**: Analyze Language	Autobiography by Wilma Mankiller from *Every Day Is a New Day*, p. 270a **Lexile 1340L** Essay by Susan Abbey "Community Hero: Chief Wilma Mankiller," p. 270a **Lexile 1170L**
Varying Sentence Patterns	• Read Closely • Analyze Language • Listen Actively • Use Precise Language • Connect Ideas	**When Students Struggle:** Determine Meanings: Mood **For Standard English Learners:** Pronoun Referents	
	• Improve Reading Fluency • Determine Theme • Exchange Information and Ideas		
	• Read Closely • Word Study • Analyze Language • Exchange Information and Ideas • Interact and Collaborate	**For Students with Disabilities:** Accessible Whiteboard Formats **When Students Struggle:** Sequence of Events	Poem by Joyce Sidman "The Light—Ah! The Light," p. 292b
	• Analyze Language • Read Closely • Manipulate Language • Use Verbs and Verb Phrases • Interact and Collaborate • View Multimedia	**When Students Struggle:** Analyze Text **For Students with Disabilities:** Support for Students Challenged by Visual Cues	
A Comparative and Superlative Adjectives **B** Compound and Complex Sentences	**A** Plan a Personal Narrative Use Noun Phrases Understand Text Structure Add Comparative and Superlative Adjectives **B** Plan to Present an Argument Use Academic Words Justify an Argument with Evidence Connecting Ideas	**A When Students Struggle:** Add Descriptive Details **For Standard English Learners:** Formal and Informal Language **For Students with Disabilities:** Present an Interview **To Challenge Students:** Dramatize the Narrative **B When Students Struggle:** Clarify Reasons **For Standard English Learners:** Use Linking Verbs **For Students with Disabilities:** Debate on a Discussion Board **To Challenge Students:** Create a Public Service Ad	

COMPARE TEXTS

from It Worked for Me: In Life and Leadership

from Colin Powell: Military Leader

Memoir by Colin Powell

Biography by Warren Brown

Why These Texts?

Students read biographical texts in school and on their own. In this lesson, students will learn about Colin Powell through both a memoir and a biography, discovering how each genre reveals different aspects of one person's life.

View It!

Professional Development Podcast:
Informational Text

Key Learning Objective: The student will be able to identify elements of a memoir and of a biography, analyze sources, and compare and contrast two genres on the same subject.

For practice and application:

Close Reader selections
from Every Day Is a New Day
Autobiography by Wilma Mankiller

"Community Hero: Chief Wilma Mankiller"
Essay by Susan Abbey

RI 1	Cite text evidence.
RI 2	Determine a theme or central idea; provide a summary.
RI 3	Analyze text elements.
RI 4	Determine the meaning of words and phrases.
RI 5	Analyze structure.
RI 6	Determine author's point of view.
RI 7	Integrate information.
RI 9	Compare and contrast a memoir and a biography.
W 9b	Draw evidence from texts.
SL 1	Engage effectively in a range of collaborative discussions.
SL 4	Present claims and findings.
SL 6	Adapt speech to a variety of contexts and tasks.
L 1d	Recognize and correct vague pronouns.
L 4a	Use context as a clue to meaning.
L 5b	Use relationship between particular words to better understand each one.
L 6	Acquire and use grade-appropriate general academic vocabulary.

 **Text Complexity Rubric**

	from It Worked for Me: In Life and Leadership	*from* Colin Powell: Military Leader
Quantitative Measures	Lexile: 1010L	Lexile: 1220L
Qualitative Measures	**Levels of Meaning/Purpose** more than one purpose; implied, easily identified from context	**Levels of Meaning/Purpose** single purpose, explicitly stated
	Structure implicit text structure	**Structure** explicit text structure
	Language Conventionality and Clarity mainly conversational language	**Language Conventionality and Clarity** some unfamiliar, academic, or domain-specific words
	Knowledge Demands everyday knowledge required	**Knowledge Demands** everyday knowledge required
Reader/Task Considerations	• Teacher determined • Vary by individual reader and type of text • See the Text X-Ray for suggested Reader/Task Considerations.	

English Language Support Before teaching, use the Text X-Ray for an overview of the text's complexity. The Text X-Ray and the supports and scaffolds in the Teacher's Edition will help you guide students of different skill levels.

Meaning Making

Language Development

Effective Expression

Content Knowledge

Foundational Skills

Text Complexity: Qualitative Measures

▲ Levels of Meaning/Purpose

Help students compare and contrast elements of memoirs and biographies.

- Teacher's Edition side notes, pp. 254, 255, 256, 257, 258, 259, 260, 262, 263, 264, 265, 267
- English Language Support, pp. 256, 258, 265
- When Students Struggle, pp. 258, 263
- Close Read Screencasts, pp. 253, 260
- Strategies for Annotation, p. 259
- Analyze Text: Memoir, p. 259
- Compare and Contrast: Memoir and Biography, p. 267

To reteach how to compare and contrast memoir and autobiography, see

- Compare and Contrast: Memoir and Biography, p. 270a

 Use It! Level Up Tutorials: Author's Purpose; Biographies and Autobiographies

ZOOM IN ON DETERMINING AUTHOR'S PURPOSE Explain that an **author's purpose** is his or her reason for writing. Organize students into small groups. Have one-half of the groups answer the first set of questions below to determine Powell's purpose in the excerpt from his memoir; let the others use the second set of questions to examine his biographer's purpose.

- What kinds of incidents does Powell tell about in his memoir? What main idea does he bring out through each of these incidents and his conclusion? What is his purpose in communicating this idea? *(He describes work experiences to show how he has achieved important goals through hard work. His purpose is to persuade others to develop their potential through hard work.)*

- How is the biography organized? What kinds of details does the author include? What does this information reveal about his purpose in writing? *(The text is organized mostly in chronological order, following Powell's life from birth to his enlistment in the army. The author wants to inform readers about different aspects of Powell's life.)*

▲ Structure

Help students analyze the structure of a memoir and a biography.

- Teacher's Edition side notes, pp. 253, 261, 263, 264, 266, 267
- English Language Support, pp. 253, 254, 260, 261
- Strategies for Annotation, p. 266
- Analyze Text: Biography, p. 266
- Analyze Text: Sources, p. 267

 Use It! Interactive Whiteboard Lesson: Primary and Secondary Sources

ZOOM IN ON ANALYZING SOURCES Explain that a memoir is a **primary source**, or firsthand account, although the writer may use other primary sources in composing it; a biography is a **secondary source** that usually incorporates both primary and secondary sources. As students read the biography excerpt, have them note the primary sources it includes. *(direct quotations from Colin Powell)* Next, have them find a passage based on secondary sources. *(Possible response: the section on Harlem's history)*

▲ Language Conventionality and Clarity

Teach unfamiliar vocabulary in context.

- Teacher's Edition Critical Vocabulary notes, pp. 255, 257, 261, 262, 269
- Applying Academic Vocabulary, pp. 255, 264
- Strategies for Annotation, p. 269
- Vocabulary Strategy: Analogies, p. 269

To teach how to analyze tone, see

- Analyze Tone, p. 270a

Help students understand how to correct vague pronouns.

- English Language Support, p. 270
- Language Conventions: Correct Vague Pronouns, p. 270

 Use It! **Interactive Whiteboard Lesson:** Word Choice and Tone

ZOOM IN ON **COMPARING TONE** Explain that authors convey an attitude toward a subject through their choice of words. From the memoir, display lines 15–22; from the biography, display lines 113–119.

- Read aloud the passage from the memoir. Point out that Powell's words don't show an opinion or judgment about his parents' work lives. Help students see that his matter-of-fact tone shows an attitude of acceptance: hard work was just what people did.
- Have pairs read the second passage and list words and phrases that suggest the author's attitude toward Powell's parents. *("certainly led by example"; "never returning"; "too"; "long hours")* Have them describe the author's tone in this part of the biography. *(admiring)*

▲ Knowledge Demands

Support English learners in understanding the background of Colin Powell.

- Teacher's Edition Background note, p. 253

ZOOM IN ON **CLARIFYING REFERENCES** Explain these references in the memoir:

- The "Selma March" in lines 76–77 refers to a 1965 civil rights protest in Alabama. Thousands walked fifty miles from Selma to Montgomery to protest segregation and discrimination.
- The acronym *AWOL* (line 140) stands for "Absent Without Official Leave." Soldiers who leave base without permission are considered AWOL.

Suggested Reader/Task Considerations

You might consider the following before assigning these selections to students.

- Will students be able to remember ideas from the first selection in order to make connections to the second?
- Will students need support to compare the two selections?

ZOOM IN ON **SUPPORTING COMPREHENSION**

- After reading, have small groups review the texts and cite important ideas about Colin Powell's character. Let groups share and discuss their ideas with the class.
- Using the questions on page 267 as a guide, provide sentence starters that will help students organize their comparisons of the texts.

TEACH

CLOSE READ

Background Have students read the background information about Colin Powell. Explain that in retirement Powell has been deeply involved in efforts to help children succeed and achieve. He and his wife, Alma, founded America's Promise Alliance, an organization that is dedicated to promote and support the well-being of children from all socioeconomic backgrounds.

SETTING A PURPOSE Direct students to use the Setting a Purpose prompt to focus their reading. Remind them to write down questions as they read.

Analyze Text: Memoir

RI 1,
RI 3

(LINES 1–8)

Tell students that a **memoir** is a form of autobiographical writing in which a writer shares his or her personal experiences and observations. Explain that the elements of a memoir include the use of **first-person point of view,** which means that it is told from the writer's own perspective, using pronouns such as *I, my,* and *we.* Other elements of a memoir include descriptions of people and events important to the writer and personal thoughts and feelings.

Ⓐ CITE TEXT EVIDENCE Have students review lines 1–8, identify elements that tell them that this selection is a memoir, and explain what key idea is introduced here. *(The author uses the pronouns* I *and* me, *which show first-person point of view; he describes getting a job and the man who gave it to him, Mr. Sickser—an event and a person that were both important to him. Powell's key idea here is that work is important to him.)*

English Language Support

Explain the differences between a memoir and an autobiography: an **autobiography** usually tells the entire story of a person's life; a **memoir** focuses on selected experiences. Write *memoir* on the board and point out that it contains the same root word as "memory." Ask students what the term *memoir* suggests about the kinds of events and details authors include. *(Authors include only the most memorable events and experiences.)*

Background *Few American journeys are as varied or as respected as the journey of retired Army General Colin Powell. From his beginnings as a hard-working student, to his rescue of fellow soldiers from a burning helicopter in Vietnam, to his service in five different presidential administrations, Powell has lived his life leading by example. Many books have been written about Powell, among them one by author Warren Brown. Powell retired from public service in 2004 but continues to be vocal on political topics.*

from It Worked for Me: In LIFE and LEADERSHIP

Memoir by Colin Powell

from Colin Powell: MILITARY LEADER

Biography by Warren Brown

(tl) ©Andrew Holbrooke/Corbis; (c) ©Lawrence Manning/Corbis

SETTING A PURPOSE As you read each text, pay attention to the examples that are used to portray Colin Powell's life. Write down any questions you have while reading.

 myNotebook

As you read, mark up the text. Save your work to *my*Notebook.
- Highlight details
- Add notes and questions
- Add new words to *my*WordList

from It Worked for Me: In Life and Leadership
by Colin Powell

Back when I was a teenager in the Bronx, summer was a time for both fun and work. Starting at about age fourteen, I worked summers and Christmas holidays at a toy and baby furniture store in the Bronx. The owner, Jay Sickser, a Russian Jewish immigrant, hired me off the street as I walked past his store. "You want to make a few bucks unloading a truck in back?" he asked me. I said yes. The job took a couple of hours, and he paid me fifty cents an hour.

Ⓐ

Compare Anchor Texts **253**

Close Read Screencasts

 Close Read

Modeled Discussions

Have students click the *Close Read* icon in their eBook to access a screencast in which readers discuss and annotate lines 23–29, a key passage that includes elements of a memoir.

As a class, view and discuss the video. Then, have students pair up to do an independent close read of an additional passage in which the author shares his ideas about the nature of work (lines 156–165).

Analyze Text:

Memoir (LINES 11–29; 39–44)

RI 1,
RI 3

Explain to students that the author of a memoir may choose to tell about people or events that had a strong impact on his or her life.

Ⓑ CITE TEXT EVIDENCE Ask students what elements of memoir they find in lines 11–29. Then, have them explain how these descriptions illustrate key ideas about what is important to Powell. *(Possible responses: Powell describes people and events that had strong influences on him; his descriptions of Jay Sickser and his family show that friendship and close relationships are important to Powell; his descriptions of his Jamaican background show that his heritage is important to him and that it shapes who he is; telling about the jobs he did for Sickser shows that he was dependable and a hard worker.)*

Tell students that authors of memoirs often use a conversational, informal style of writing.

Ⓒ CITE TEXT EVIDENCE Have students review lines 39–44 and tell how the language helps to elaborate on what Powell is like as a person. *(Possible response: Powell's informal language, such as "the problem was" and "But, hey, why not? It paid better," portray him as an ordinary person with everyday concerns; he is connected to his readers in an ordinary way.)*

"You're a good worker," he told me when I'd finished. "Come back tomorrow."

10   That was the beginning of a close friendship with Jay and his family that continued through college and for the next fifty years, long after Jay had died. I worked part-time at the store a few hours a day during the summer and long hours during the Christmas season. I worked hard, a habit I got from my Jamaican immigrant parents. Every morning they left early for the garment district in Manhattan, and they came home late at night. All my relatives were hard workers. They came out of that common immigrant experience of arriving with nothing, expecting that the new life ahead of them would 20   not be easy. Jamaicans had a joke: "That lazy brute, him only have two jobs."

After I'd worked at Sickser's for a couple of years, Jay grew concerned that I was getting too close to the store and the family. One day he took me aside. "Collie," he told me with a serious look, "I want you should get an education and do well. You're too good to just be a schlepper.[1] The store will go to the family. You don't have a future here." I never thought I did, but I always treasured him for caring enough about me to say so.

30   When I was eighteen I became eligible to get a union card, which meant I could get a full-time summer job with better pay (I continued to work at Sickser's during the Christmas season). I joined the International Brotherhood of Teamsters' Local 812, the Soft Drink Workers Union. Every morning I went downtown to the union hall to stand in line to get a day's work as a helper on a soft-drink truck. It was hard work, and I became an expert at tossing wooden twenty-four-bottle Coca-Cola cases by grabbing a corner bottle without breaking it.

After a few weeks, the foreman noticed my work and asked 40   if I'd like to try driving a Coke truck. Since I was a teamster, I had a chauffeur's license and was authorized to drive a truck. The problem was that I had never driven a truck in my life. But, hey, why not? It paid better.

The next morning, I got behind the wheel of an ancient, stick shift, circa 1940 truck with a supervisor riding shotgun.[2]

---

[1] **schlepper** (shlĕp´ər): someone who carries things that are clumsy or difficult to move.

[2] **riding shotgun:** sitting in the front passenger seat of a vehicle, next to the driver; term comes from the early 1900s and refers to armed guards, often carrying shotguns, who would protect the cargo and the driver of a vehicle.

English Language Support

Expand Sentences Tell students that a memoir is often organized chronologically, or in the order in which the events occurred. Display lines 23–43. Have volunteers highlight the words and phrases that signal the sequence of events. Then discuss the events to which these words refer. Point out phrases such as "One day" (line 25) and "Every morning" (line 34) and explain to students that writers often expand sentences with adverb phrases to provide details about time. These kinds of details help readers know when things are happening in a text.

- Have small groups collaborate to write new sentences with the phrases "one day" and "every morning." Discuss how these phrases help the reader understand when something is happening.

- Have students write a summary of the events that Powell describes. Encourage them to use adverbs, adverb phrases, or prepositional phrases in their sentences to provide details. Have them exchange their work with a partner to review their summaries and the way they expanded sentences.

We carried three hundred cases, half on open racks on one side of the truck and half on the other. I asked the supervisor where we were going. "Wall Street," he said, and my heart skipped a beat as I imagined navigating the narrow streets and 50 alleys of the oldest, most **claustrophobic**, and most mazelike part of New York City. I took off with all the energy and blind optimism of youth and managed to get through the day and somehow safely delivered the three hundred cases . . . in spite of my often overenthusiastic driving. My supervisor was white-knuckled with worry that I would deliver 150 cases onto the street as the old truck leaned **precariously** at corners I was taking much too fast. Though I delivered every case, my driving skills did not impress the supervisor, and my truck-driving career was over (they still kept me on as a helper). 60 Nevertheless, I proudly took home a $20 salary that day to show my father.

The next summer, I wanted something better than standing in a crowd every morning hoping for a day's work. My opportunity came when the hiring boss announced one morning that the Pepsi plant in Long Island City was looking for porters to clean the floors, full-time for the summer. I raised my hand. I was the only one who did.

The porters at the Pepsi plant were all black. The workers on the bottling machines were all white. I didn't care. I just 70 wanted work for the summer, and I worked hard, mopping up syrup and soda that had spilled from overturned pallets.

At summer's end, the boss told me he was pleased with my work and asked if I wanted to come back. "Yes," I answered, "but not as a porter." He agreed, and next summer I worked on the bottling machine and as a pallet stacker, a more **prestigious** and higher-paying job. It wasn't exactly the Selma March, but I integrated a bottling machine crew.

Very often my best didn't turn out that well. I was neither an athlete nor a standout student. I played baseball, football, 80 stickball, and all the other Bronx sports, and I did my best, but I wasn't good at any. In school I was hardworking and dedicated, but never produced superior grades or matched the academic successes of my many high-achieving cousins. Yet my parents didn't pester me or put too much pressure on me. Their attitude was "Do your best—we'll accept your best, but nothing less."

claustrophobic
(klô´strə-fō´bĭk) adj.
A claustrophobic place feels uncomfortably closed or crowded.

precarious
(prĭ-kâr´ē-əs) adj.
If something is done in a precarious manner, it is done in a dangerously unstable or insecure way.

prestigious
(prĕ-stē´jəs) adj.
If something is prestigious, it has a greater level of people's respect or honor than others like it.

CLOSE READ

Analyze Text:
Memoir (LINES 62–77)

RI 2,
RI 3

Explain to students that thinking about the events the author of a memoir shares helps readers learn about the author.

D **ASK STUDENTS** to reread lines 62–77 and summarize the events Powell shares. *(He tells about how after working hard as a porter his boss asked him to come back the next summer. Powell shares how he got a better position and "integrated a bottling machine crew.")* Then, have students analyze why Powell shares this story and how it elaborates on what he is like as a person. *(Possible response: He wants to share how he overcame boundaries as a young man, including racial ones; it shows that he was a hard worker and could advance by proving what he was capable of doing.)*

> **CRITICAL VOCABULARY**

claustrophobic: Powell uses the word *claustrophobic* to describe how a place felt.

precariously: The word *precariously* is used to tell about how Powell drove an old truck.

ASK STUDENTS to review lines 49–59 and tell what might have happened when Powell was driving an old truck precariously in a claustrophobic area. *(Driving unsafely through crowded, narrow streets and alleys might have led to accidents.)*

prestigious: The word *prestigious* is used to describe Powell's new job.

ASK STUDENTS to review lines 72–77 and tell what was prestigious about Powell's new position and why he was proud of it. *(It paid more; it was a higher-ranking job than porter; he was the first black person to join the crew.)*

APPLYING ACADEMIC VOCABULARY

achieve	principle

THINK-PAIR-SHARE Have students review the questions below and then discuss them with a partner. Encourage pairs to include the academic vocabulary words *achieve* and *principle* in their discussions. Ask volunteers to share their responses with the class.

- What did Powell hope to **achieve** during his military career?
- What **principles** did he try to follow as a military leader?

Analyze Text:
Memoir (LINES 93–111)

RI 1,
RI 2,
RI 3

Tell students that in a memoir an author often shares personal thoughts and feelings. Explain that thinking about why the author shares this information will help them better understand the text.

E **ASK STUDENTS** to review lines 93–111 and summarize Powell's approach to jobs and his military career. (*Possible response: He says he always worked hard, even when he didn't like what he was doing.*) Then, ask them to explain how these thoughts illustrate what Powell cares about most. (*Possible response: Powell wants to show young readers that his approach worked and that they can do the same. He cares about the value of working hard and doing your best.*)

English Language Support

Make sure students understand the point of the comedian's story in lines 93–106.

- Explain that the ditch digging represents work that people consider neither important nor challenging.
- Help students summarize what happens to the first ditch digger (*He gets a better job because he works hard and does his best.*)
- Then ask, "What happened to the second digger?" (*He stayed exactly where he was because he did only the minimum amount of work.*)
- Help students paraphrase the moral of the story. (*If you work hard at whatever job you have, no matter how humble, you will get closer to achieving your goals.*)

English Language Support

Analyzing Language (LINE 92)

Have students view the **Text in Focus** video on this page of their eBook to analyze a saying Colin Powell references in his memoir. Then have students use **Text in Focus Practice** to apply what they have learned.

These experiences established a pattern for all the years and careers that came afterward. Always do your best, no matter how difficult the job, or how much you dislike it, your
90 bosses, the work environment, or your fellow workers. As the old expression goes, if you take the king's coin, you give the king his due.

I remember an old story told by the comedian Brother Dave Gardner about two ditch diggers. One guy just loves digging. He digs all day long and says nothing much. The other guy digs a little, leans on his shovel a lot, and mouths off constantly, "One of these days, I'm gonna own this company."

Time passes and guy number one gets a front-end trench machine and just digs away, hundreds of feet a day, always
100 loving it. The other guy does the minimum, but never stops mouthing off,[3] "One of these days, I'm gonna own this company." No, guy number one doesn't end up owning the company, but he does become a foreman working out of an air-conditioned van. He often waves to his old friend leaning on his shovel still insisting, "One of these days, I'm gonna own this company." Ain't gonna happen.

In my military career I often got jobs I wasn't crazy about, or I was put in situations that stretched me beyond my rank and experience. Whether the going was rough or smooth, I
110 always tried to do my best and to be loyal to my superior and the mission given to me.

---

[3] **mouthing off:** a slang term meaning to express opinions or complaints in a loud, rude manner.

TO CHALLENGE STUDENTS . . .

Analyze Language Have students discuss the expression Powell uses in lines 91–92: "if you take the king's coin, you give the king his due." Ask students to discuss or research when this expression probably originated and how it connects to modern life.

ASK STUDENTS to discuss situations in their own lives in which this expression applies to them and their actions. Have them share their ideas with the class.

On my second tour in Vietnam, I was assigned as an infantry battalion executive officer, second in command, in the 23rd Infantry Division (Americal). I was very pleased with the assignment. As it happened, I had just graduated with honors from the Command and General Staff College at Fort Leavenworth, Kansas. Shortly after I arrived in Vietnam, a photo of the top five graduates appeared in *Army Times*. The division commanding general saw it, and I was pulled up to
120 the division staff to serve as the operations officer, responsible for coordinating the combat operations of a twenty-thousand-man division. I was only a major and it was a lieutenant colonel's position. I would have preferred to stay with my battalion, but wasn't given that choice. It turned out to be very demanding and a stretch for me, but it marked a turning point in my career. Someone was watching.

Years later, as a brigadier general in an infantry division, I thought I was doing my best to train soldiers and serve my commander. He disagreed and rated me below standards. The
130 report is still in my file. It could have ended my career, but more senior leaders saw other qualities and capabilities[4] in me and moved me up into more challenging positions, where I did well.

Doing your best for your boss doesn't mean you will always like or approve of what he wants you to do; there will be times when you will have very different **priorities** from his. In the military, your superiors may have very different ideas than you do about what should be your most important mission. In some of my units my superiors put an intense
140 focus on reenlistment rates, AWOL rate, and saving bonds participation. Most of us down below would have preferred to keep our primary focus on training. Sure, those management priorities were important in principle, but they often seemed in practice to be distractions from our real work. I never tried to fight my superiors' priorities. Instead I worked hard to accomplish the tasks they set as quickly and decisively as I could. The sooner I could satisfy my superiors, the sooner they would stop bugging me about them, and the quicker I could move on to my own priorities. Always give the king his due
150 first.

priority
(prī-ôrʹĭ-tē) *n.*
A *priority* is the thing that is most important to a person in a particular situation or relationship.

---

[4] **capabilities** (kāʹpə-bĭlʹĭ-tēz): the things one is able to do or the talents one is able to develop.

CLOSE READ

Analyze Text:
Memoir (LINES 112–126; 134–150)

RI 1,
RI 3

Remind students that the author of a memoir shares experiences and observations about events in his or her life.

F CITE TEXT EVIDENCE Ask students what key idea of the memoir is illustrated in lines 112–126 and what details support this. *(Powell tells about a new position he is given when a general sees that Powell has graduated in the top five of his class from the Command and General Staff College. Powell uses this event to show how important it is to do your best all the time, no matter what the job, class, or event you are involved in.)*

G CITE TEXT EVIDENCE Have students review lines 134–150 and tell what key idea of Powell's these events illustrate. *(They illustrate the idea that one should always do the required things first and then move on to other issues. In lines 149–150, and previously in lines 90–92, Powell talks about always giving "the king his due first"; this is the idea or expression he is elaborating on. Powell is showing readers that this is a lesson he has learned and that it has served him well throughout his career.)*

CRITICAL VOCABULARY

priority: Powell uses the word *priorities* to tell about what was important to him and what was important to his superiors.

ASK STUDENTS to review lines 139–144. Ask them to tell why the priorities of Powell's superiors were different from those of lower-ranking officers, including Powell. *(Possible response: Their priorities were different because they were interested in different things. Tracking certain factors was most important to superiors, but training was more important to the lower-ranked officers.)*

FOR STANDARD ENGLISH LEARNERS

Analyze Language Display lines 98–106 of the memoir and follow these steps:

- Highlight the following: *I'm gonna own this company. Ain't gonna happen.*
- Rewrite the words and phrases in standard English and read them aloud. Discuss the differences between the two versions.

Have students explain why Powell chooses to include these expressions in his memoir. Guide them to understand that he is building understanding of a character by showing how he actually spoke.

CLOSE READ

Analyze Text:
Memoir (LINES 159–165)

RI 3

Remind students that in a memoir the author reflects on his or her life and shares important observations. Explain that readers can evaluate whether the author relates ideas in an effective way.

H ASK STUDENTS to review lines 159–165 and ask why he says he likes to "emphasize, especially to youngsters, that 99 percent of work can be seen as noble." *(Possible responses: He believes his messages about life are valuable for young people; he wants to share his belief that it doesn't matter what you do, as long as you do it well.)*

Ask students to reflect on the selection and explain whether they think Powell communicates his ideas effectively. *(Possible response: Yes; he shares specific examples and memorable events, and explains his ideas clearly in a natural, conversational way.)*

English Language Support

Have pairs find examples that support their opinions of Powell's communication skills. Provide these sentence frames for their discussions:

- Powell conveys ideas in a way that _____

- For example, he _____

English Language Support

Use Noun Phrases Display the first sentence on page 258 and underline the following: *the nation's most senior national security jobs.* Identify the underlined words as a noun phrase. Explain that it contains a noun (*jobs*) and all of its modifiers, or words that help define it. Point out that a noun phrase can contain as few as two words or, as in Powell's example, expand to many. Ask volunteers to find other noun phrases on the page. *(my government service, my life's experience, many different forums, etc.)*

By the end of my career in government, I had been appointed to the nation's most senior national security jobs, National Security Advisor, Chairman of the Joint Chiefs of Staff, and Secretary of State. I went about each job with the same attitude I'd had at Sickser's. . . .

In the years that have followed my government service, I have traveled around the country and shared my life's experience with many people in many different forums. At these events, I always emphasize, especially to youngsters, that
160 99 percent of work can be seen as noble.[5] There are few truly degrading[6] jobs. Every job is a learning experience, and we can develop and grow in every one.

If you take the pay, earn it. Always do your very best. Even when no one else is looking, you always are. Don't disappoint yourself.

H

---

[5] **noble** (nō′bəl): having or showing qualities of honor.
[6] **degrading** (dĭ-grā′dĭng): lowering or reducing in rank, dignity, respect, quality, or value.

WHEN STUDENTS STRUGGLE . . .

To guide students in determining whether Powell has communicated his ideas in an effective way, have partners work together to reflect on the selection and complete a chart like the one shown. Have students share their responses with the class.

Lines	Event or Example	Messages
11–22	Powell tells about family attitudes toward work.	Work hard. Don't expect life to be easy.

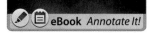
Analyze Text: Memoir   RI 3

The text *It Worked for Me* is a **memoir,** a form of autobiographical writing in which a writer shares his or her personal experiences and observations of significant events. Memoirs are often written by people who have taken part in or observed important historical events. Elements of a memoir include the following:

- **first-person point of view,** meaning that it is told from the writer's own perspective. First-person pronouns, such as *I, me, my, our,* and *we,* are used throughout the text.
- descriptions of people and events that have influenced the writer
- personal thoughts and feelings

A memoir reflects how the writer remembers his or her own life and often only focuses on a specific aspect or period in the writer's life. A memoir is often written in an informal style. In *It Worked for Me*, Colin Powell recalls how he got a job driving a truck when he had never driven one before. He says, "But, hey, why not? It paid better."

As you analyze *It Worked for Me* and other memoirs, ask questions such as these:

- What does the author want to share? Why?
- Does the author communicate his or her ideas in an effective way?

Analyzing the Text   RI 1, RI 2, RI 3, RI 4, RI 5, RI 6, RI 10

Cite Text Evidence   Support your responses with evidence from the text.

1. **Summarize** Review lines 62–77. What specific incident in his life is Powell writing about? Why might this incident be important for Powell to include in his memoir?

2. **Interpret** Review lines 87–92. What do you think is the meaning of the expression "If you take the king's coin, you give the king his due"? Why do you think Powell shares this message?

3. **Evaluate** One important element of a memoir is the inclusion of people and events that influenced the writer. Review the selection. Which person or event do you think was most influential in his life? Why do you think so?

It Worked for Me   **259**

PRACTICE & APPLY
CLOSE READ

Analyze Text: Memoir   RI 3

Discuss the elements of a memoir, and clarify that a memoir is different from an autobiography. Unlike an autobiography, which tells the full story of a person's life, a memoir usually focuses on a certain time in the author's life, or a particular aspect of it. Ask volunteers to identify what aspect of life Powell focuses on in this excerpt from his memoir. *(He focuses on how he approached his jobs and military career with an ethic of working hard and doing his best.)*

Discuss the questions readers use to analyze a memoir, and prompt students to answer them as they relate to *It Worked for Me.*

Analyzing the Text   RI 1, RI 2, RI 3, RI 4, RI 5, RI 6, RI 10

Possible answers:

1. *Powell is writing about when he got a job as a porter. He noticed that the workers who had better-paying jobs were all white. He impressed his boss by working hard and got a better-paying job. He may have included this incident to show that he was not afraid to work hard.*

2. *I think it means that if you take somebody's money for pay, you need to do that job well. I think Powell includes it because he wants readers, especially those who are young, to take his advice.*

3. *I think his parents, with their immigrant experience, were the most influential. They shaped Powell's attitudes toward life and work and set high but reasonable expectations for him.*

Strategies for Annotation   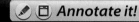 *Annotate it!*

Analyze Text: Memoir   RI 3

Share these strategies for guided or independent analysis:

- Highlight in yellow pronouns that show first-person point of view.
- Highlight in blue key phrases about people and events that influenced the author.
- Underline phrases that show the author's personal thoughts and feelings.
- Review your annotations. On a note, list key ideas that the memoir discusses.

I worked hard, a habit I got from my Jamaican immigrant parents. Every morning they left early for . . . Manhattan, and they came home late at night. All my relatives were hard workers. They came out of that common immigrant experience of arriving with nothing, . . .

> hardworking parents

Analyze Text: Biography (LINES 1–29)

RI 1,
RI 3

Tell students that a **biography** is a true account of a person's life written by another person. Explain that biographies include descriptions of events, people, and experiences that shape the subject's life.

(A) ASK STUDENTS to review lines 1–23 and identify what events the author describes. *(how the area known as Harlem developed and changed)* Ask why the author describes these events here. *(Possible responses: It is a good beginning to a biography to give details about where the subject was born; it tells readers that Powell was born in a place with a rich and changeable history.)*

(B) CITE TEXT EVIDENCE Have students reread lines 24–29 and tell how these lines elaborate on the information in lines 1–23. *(These lines explain when Colin's parents moved to Harlem; the phrases "the community was at its most prosperous" and "in the hope of finding their fortune" help explain why Luther and Maud may both have chosen Harlem as a good place to live and find work.)*

English Language Support

Read Closely Help students compare the points of view used in the memoir (first person) and in the biography. Read lines 24–35 aloud.

- Have students identify the personal pronouns used in this paragraph to tell about Colin Powell's parents. *(their, they)*
- Ask them what these pronouns indicate about the point of view used to tell the story of someone's life. *(third person)*

---

from Colin Powell: Military Leader
by Warren Brown

Colin Luther Powell was born on April 5, 1937, in New York City's Harlem district. Formerly an area of open farmland and country estates, Harlem became a residential neighborhood in the late 19th century, when a mixture of wealthy and working-class whites moved there to escape Manhattan's congested[1] downtown area. To keep pace with the growing demand for housing, real estate developers constructed magnificent town houses and apartment buildings in this uptown section. By 1900, Harlem had
10 emerged as one of the most desirable places to live in the city.

These developers overestimated the demand for housing, however, and by the early 1900s many apartments in Harlem were empty because not enough people could afford to live in such a high-rent district. Desperate to fill the vacant apartments, Harlem landlords drastically lowered their rents. The sudden availability of quality housing attracted large numbers of blacks seeking to escape the racial violence and poor living conditions in
20 the city's congested West Side ghetto, and they moved to Harlem in droves. By the beginning of World War I, 50,000 blacks resided in Harlem and formed a vibrant community with a middle-class standard of living.

Colin's parents, Luther Theopolis Powell and the former Maud Ariel McKoy, arrived in Harlem during the early 1920s, when the community was at its most prosperous.[2] Both parents were from the island of Jamaica and had left their Caribbean homeland in the hope of finding their fortune in the United States. Like so many
30 other immigrants drawn by the booming American economy during the 1920s, they settled in New York City, the thriving metropolis at the mouth of the Hudson River; with its bustling port and enormous wealth, the

---

[1] **congested** (kən-jĕst'əd): overcrowded.
[2] **prosperous** (prŏs'pər-əs): successful; well-to-do.

260 Collection 5

(tl) © Lawrence Manning/Corbis

Close Read Screencasts

Modeled Discussions

Have students click the *Close Read* icon in their eBook to access a screencast in which readers discuss and annotate lines 52–61, a key passage that includes descriptions of important historic events.

As a class, view and discuss the video. Then, have students pair up to do an independent close read of an important event in Powell's life presented in lines 189–197.

city seemed to offer limitless opportunity to anyone who sought a better life.

Neither Luther Powell nor Maud McKoy had finished high school, and so they had little choice but to join the large pool of working-class immigrants that served as the backbone of the city's labor force. Luther, a husky young man with a pleasant, round face, found work as a shipping clerk in a garment factory. At a picnic one day in the Bronx, New York City's only mainland borough, he met Maud McKoy. Shortly afterward, the pair married and made their home in Harlem.

Meanwhile, Harlem had begun to take on a special **allure**. As it became one of the few areas in the country where blacks could enjoy an unusually high quality of life, its writers, musicians, and actors celebrated their racial heritage and promoted their own culture. This awakening of black artistic and intellectual achievement came to be known as the Harlem Renaissance.

Yet underneath the surface of this growing, closely knit community lay the symptoms of decline. By 1930, 200,000 of New York City's 327,000 blacks lived in Harlem, and they were all crowded together in an area that had housed only a quarter of that number 15 years earlier. When the Great Depression began to ravage[3] the nation in the 1930s, Harlem was especially hard hit. Long lines of unemployed people in search of food and clothing stretched in front of the local churches and charity organizations. Families evicted from their apartments because they could not pay the rent crowded into the homes of relatives or lived on the street. What had previously been one of New York City's most beautiful areas began to deteriorate[4] rapidly.

It was into this black community, in desperate decline but still treasuring proud memories, that Colin Powell was born. He lived in Harlem until he was three years old; then his parents decided it was time to relocate. In 1940, Luther and Maud Powell packed their belongings; and with Colin and his sister, Marylin, who was five and a half years older than him, in tow, they followed the city's ever expanding elevated railway line northeast, across the Harlem River to the Bronx.

The Powells settled in Hunts Point, a working-class neighborhood in the southeastern section of the borough.

allure
(ə-lŏor´) *n.* An *allure* is a power of attraction, an ability to interest or entice others.

---

[3] **ravage** (răv´ĭj): destroy in a severe, drastic way.
[4] **deteriorate** (dĭ-tîr´ē-ə-rāt´): to fall apart; to break down in quality or value.

Colin Powell: Military Leader **261**

CLOSE READ

Analyze Text: Biography (LINES 64–71)

RI 3, RI 5

Explain to students that events in a biography are usually presented in **chronological order,** the order in which they occurred. Point out that dates and words and phrases such as *In 1832, after that,* and *weeks later* help readers follow the **sequence,** or order of events.

C **ASK STUDENTS** how lines 64–71 elaborate on Powell's connection to Harlem. *(These lines explain that Powell was born and lived in Harlem until he was three when, in 1940, his family moved to the Bronx.)* Have students point out words and phrases that signal the sequence of events and explain how these events fit into the overall structure of the text. *(Possible responses: "until," "then," "In 1940"; these lines continue the sequence-of-events structure that has been established so far.)*

CRITICAL VOCABULARY

allure: The word *allure* is used to describe Harlem during the 1920s.

ASK STUDENTS to review lines 44–50 and tell why Harlem might have seemed so alluring to African Americans. *(It was an area that attracted many black writers, musicians, and actors; it was a beautiful neighborhood; it was a place where black culture and achievement were celebrated.)*

English Language Support

Understand Text Structure Explain that the overall structure of this biography is chronological, but the author also presents some cause-and-effect relationships.

- Read aloud lines 51–63 and help students summarize what these details describe. *(the deterioration of Harlem)* Then have them read lines 64–71. Guide them to see the relationship between events in the two paragraphs. *(The deterioration of Harlem causes the Powells to move to the Bronx.)*

- Tell students that to help readers understand a subject more fully, biographers describe the historical context into which the person was born. Have pairs reread lines 12–63 and summarize the history of Harlem using cause-and-effect statements.

- Point out that lines 12–71 present information about the history of Harlem along with facts about Powell's parents. Have pairs discuss how events in Harlem affect the lives of Powell's parents and why the biographer chose to include this information.

Analyze Text: Biography (LINES 81–105)

RI 1,
RI 3

Remind students that a biography includes descriptions of events, people, and experiences that influenced the subject's life.

(D) CITE TEXT EVIDENCE Ask students why the author includes lines 81–105 and what details support their ideas. *(These lines illustrate more about what shaped Powell's character. Details: Growing up in a neighborhood where "children mingled unselfconsciously" with many ethnicities, Powell didn't feel different. Powell's parents, coming from Jamaica, never felt inferior and didn't allow their children to feel that way either; they wanted their children to succeed and share their "respect for formal education.")*

CRITICAL VOCABULARY

perseverance: The author uses *perseverance* to tell about a habit a focused person can develop.

ASK STUDENTS to review lines 106–112 and explain why a family member who didn't persevere might disappoint his or her entire family. *(If you were lazy, didn't try hard, or gave up easily, everyone in your family would be disappointed because your laziness would reflect poorly on them, too.)*

English Language Support

Culturally Responsive Instruction Facilitate a class discussion clarifying ideas in lines 81–105.

- Ask students why Powell felt that living in a diverse neighborhood was an advantage. *(He never thought about the color of his skin.)* How did his parents' attitude affect the way he thought of himself? *(They did not feel inferior, and neither did he.)*

- Have small groups discuss the influence of cultural backgrounds on the way people identify themselves and their place in society. Encourage students to support their opinions with evidence and to build on each other's comments.

- Provide the following stems to facilitate conversation: *I agree with _____ , I heard you say _____ , I disagree because _____ .*

The family made its home in a walk-up apartment building on Kelly Street. In time, the area would reach the extreme levels of urban decay and devastation that have come to characterize Harlem. But in the 1940s, residents called the borough "the beautiful Bronx," and Harlemites who moved into Hunts Point's blue-collar neighborhood felt that they had moved up in the world.

80

Although the local population was mainly Jewish, Hunts Point contained a mixture of New York City's various immigrant groups. Jews mixed freely with blacks, Irish, Italians, Poles, and Puerto Ricans, and their children mingled unselfconsciously in play. As a result, young Colin never paid much attention to the color of his skin. "I grew up in a neighborhood where everybody was a minority," he recalled. "I never thought there was something wrong with me because I was black."

90

The fact that his parents came from Jamaica also contributed to Colin's lack of self-consciousness about his race. Even though blacks in Jamaica were British subjects, they rarely experienced the sort of racial oppression that many black Americans, particularly those in the southern states, endured. When Powell's parents arrived in the United States, they did not view themselves as second-class citizens, and they never allowed their children to think that way either.

Instead, Luther and Maud Powell instilled[5] in their son and daughter a strong faith in the Anglican church and a

100

healthy respect for formal education. They wanted Colin and Marylin to do well in life and insisted that getting ahead in America depended on learning as much as possible. As a result, the Powell children often received lectures from their parents to "strive for a good education. Make something of your life."

Luther and Maud Powell also told their children that only hard work and **perseverance** could lead to success. Colin recalled later, "There was something of a tradition of hard work being the way to succeed, and there was simply an

110

expectation that existed in the family—you were supposed to do better. And it was a bloody disappointment to the family if you didn't."

perseverance
(pŭr´sə-vîr´əns) *n.* To have *perseverance* is to stay focused on a plan, a belief, or a purpose.

---

[5] **instilled** (ĭn-stĭld´): introduced slowly and with consistent, constant effort.

TO CHALLENGE STUDENTS . . .

Analyze Text Have students reread lines 90–97 and discuss the contrasts the author illustrates between blacks in Jamaica and black Americans. Have them research as needed and discuss the importance of these details:

- line 92, regarding blacks in Jamaica
- lines 93–94, regarding racial oppression, especially in the southern United States
- line 96, the phrase "second-class citizens"

ASK STUDENTS to summarize the differences between Jamaican blacks and blacks in America that the author feels were important in Powell's life.

Colin's parents certainly led by example. Each morning, Luther Powell left home at an early hour to catch the elevated train to his job in New York City's Garment District, and he remained there all day, never returning home from work until at least 7:00 or 8:00 in the evening. Maud Powell found a job as a seamstress, and she too spent many long hours doing her work. "It wasn't a matter of spending a great deal of time with my parents discussing things," Colin remembered. "We didn't sit down at night . . . and review the work of the day. It was just the way they lived their lives."

 I never thought there was something wrong with me because I was black.

Even though both his parents worked, young Colin never went unsupervised during the day. Maud's mother, who was known to everyone as Miss Alice, and other relatives stayed with him and his sister to enforce discipline. In addition, nearby families made a habit of watching one another's children. Marylin recalled years later that "when you walked down the street, you had all these eyes watching you."

In spite of this upbringing, Colin showed few signs during his childhood of responding to his parents' desire that he apply himself in school. Early on in elementary school, when he was about eight years old, he attempted to play hooky. The young truant estimated the time wrong, however, and arrived home too early. A family friend caught him, and a family discussion ensued. In the days that followed, an adult was always present to take Colin by the hand and lead him to the classroom door.

Colin, however, did not change his ways. As a fifth grader at Public School 39, he was such a lackluster[6] student that he landed in the slow class. At both Intermediate School 52 and Morris High School, he continued to apply himself indifferently.[7] In his own words, he "horsed around a lot" and managed to keep his grades only barely above passing. His unspectacular marks kept him from realizing an ambition to

---

[6] **lackluster** (lăk´lŭs´tər): lacking brightness and energy; dull.
[7] **indifferently** (ĭn-dĭf´ər-ənt-lē): without interest or feeling, either for or against.

Colin Powell: Military Leader **263**

Analyze Text: Biography (LINES 113–122)

RI 1, RI 3

Explain to students that biographies include quotations, which are a person's exact words. Quotations may come from the subject of the biography or from others who know the subject.

E **CITE TEXT EVIDENCE** Have students tell how lines 113–122 explain more about Powell's parents and why. *(The biographer describes how Powell's parents had long commutes and workdays. The quotation "It was just the way they lived their lives" helps readers understand that these long days were the example that Colin remembers, not long conversations.)*

Compare and Contrast: Biography and Memoir

RI 1, RI 9

(LINES 139–144)

Explain to students that when they compare and contrast a memoir and a biography they examine the way each writer presents the subject and evaluate similarities and differences.

F **CITE TEXT EVIDENCE** Have students compare descriptions of Powell as a student in this text and in *It Worked for Me*. *(The descriptions are fairly different; here, in lines 139–144, Powell is described as "lackluster" and indifferent. In lines 78–86 of his memoir, Powell says that while he didn't get outstanding grades, he was "hardworking" and "dedicated." Students should note that Powell is describing himself only as a teenager, while the biography includes information about him in fifth grade as well as in high school.)*

WHEN STUDENTS STRUGGLE . . .

To guide students in comparing and contrasting a biography and a memoir, have them create a chart like the one shown to compare aspects of Powell's life.

Powell's Life	Biography	Memoir
As a student:	Lines 139–144: "lackluster" "landed in the slow class" in fifth grade "applied himself indifferently" grades "barely above passing"	Lines 78–86: not "a standout" "hardworking and dedicated" "never produced superior grades"

 LEVEL UP TUTORIALS For additional support, assign the following *Level Up* tutorials: **Author's Purpose; Biographies and Autobiographies.**

Primary and Secondary Sources

RI 3

(LINES 148–158; 164–176)

Tell students that biographers use a variety of resources and materials to research their subject. Explain that **primary sources** are materials created by people who witnessed or took part in an event and that **secondary sources** are those made by people who were not directly involved with or may not even have been present at the event.

G **ASK STUDENTS** to reread lines 148–158 and suggest primary and secondary sources the biographer might have used. *(Possible primary sources: letters, eyewitness accounts from schoolmates such as Gene Norman [line 157] or immediate family members, autobiographical accounts from Powell; possible secondary sources: other biographical accounts, perhaps "friends of friends" who weren't present but remember general events.)*

H **ASK STUDENTS** to reread lines 164–176 and evaluate the biographer and his choice of information. *(Possible responses: The details of college costs, dates and times of when Powell enters college, and his riding the bus to get there show that the author has done an extensive amount of research into Powell's life. The information creates a clear picture of Powell as an individual.)*

Analyze Text: Biography (LINES 164–176)

RI 1, RI 3

Remind students that biographies include descriptions of experiences that shaped the subject's life.

I **CITE TEXT EVIDENCE** Have students explain how lines 164–176 tell readers more about Powell's traits and attitudes. *(Lines 164–167 describe his respect for his parents, his "ingrained sense of obedience" to them. His acceptance to college "[d]espite his low grades" shows that his overall activities probably showed his potential. Enrolling in CCNY because it cost less shows that one of his priorities is saving money.)*

attend the Bronx High School of Science, one of the nation's finest schools.

By this time, Colin had developed into a tall, strong teenager with a natural flair for leadership. At Morris High
150 School, he was elected class representative, served as treasurer of the Service League, whose members helped out around the school, and lettered in track. Neighborhood youths learned not to push him around. He moved freely among Hunts Point's various racial groups and even managed to learn some Yiddish while working after school at Sickser's, a store that sold baby furniture. In his free time, Colin and his best friend, Gene Norman, raced bicycles along the sweeping curve of Kelly Street or played games of stickball.

When Colin graduated from Morris High School in early
160 1954, he said that he wanted to become an engineer; but in reality, he had very little idea of what he wanted to do with his life. His parents, insisting that he lift himself out of Hunts Point's "$40-a-week, lower blue-collar environment," made it clear that they expected him to go to college. Colin had no particular urge to get a higher education, but he had a deeply ingrained sense of obedience to his mother and father. If they expected him to attend college, he would go.

Colin applied to New York University and to the City College of New York. Despite his low grades, both institutions
170 accepted him. Tuition costs helped Colin narrow down his choice. New York University charged students $750 per year to attend. The City College of New York, situated on 138th Street in upper Manhattan, enrolled any graduate from a New York City high school for only a token $10 fee. Accordingly, on a cold winter day in February 1954, Colin took a bus to Manhattan and began his life as a City College student.

Colin enrolled in City College's engineering program, and he did moderately well at first, ending his initial semester with a B average. But during the summer of 1954,
180 he took a mechanical drawing course, and it proved to be the most miserable summer of his life. When, on a boiling hot afternoon, his instructor asked him to imagine a cone intersecting a plane in space, Colin decided that he had had enough of engineering and dropped out of the program.

Colin decided to change his major to geology, not because of any strong interest in the subject but because he thought it

264 Collection 5

APPLYING ACADEMIC VOCABULARY

individual	instance

THINK-PAIR-SHARE Have partners read and discuss the questions below. Ask students to include the academic vocabulary words *individual* and *instance* in their discussions. Let volunteers share their responses with the class.

- How would you describe the type of **individual** that Colin Powell is?
- What **instances** from his life show these character traits?

would be easy. He did not push himself very hard and saw his average creep down to a C.

Nevertheless, Colin was about to display his first real enthusiasm for a school-related activity. During his first spring at City College, he had noticed uniformed members of the Army Reserve Officers' Training Corps walking around the campus. The ROTC offered students military training that could lead to a commission[8] as an officer in the U.S. Army. Colin decided that he liked the serious look of the members of the Pershing Rifles, the ROTC drill team, who wore small whipped cords on their uniform shoulders.

Colin already possessed a mild interest in the military. In high school, he had closely followed the unfolding of the Korean War. His interest aroused, Colin signed up for the ROTC for the fall semester of 1954 and pledged himself to the Pershing Rifles.

At that point, Colin had no intention of making the army a career. He wanted only to find a way to escape from New York City for a while and, in his own words, "have some excitement." Besides, joining the ROTC would help him find work. He expected to serve no more than two years in the army after graduating from college "and then come home and get a real job." But as it turned out, he had stumbled onto his life's calling.

COLLABORATIVE DISCUSSION With a partner, discuss which parts of Colin Powell's life you found most interesting. Point out examples in both texts that support your ideas, and tell what they indicate about Powell as an individual.

---

[8] **commission** (kə-mĭsh´ən): the act of granting an individual certain powers or authority to carry out a particular duty; also, an official document from a government granting a particular rank in the armed forces.

CLOSE READ

Compare and Contrast: Biography and Memoir

RI 1, RI 9

(LINES 199–210)

Explain that one way to compare and contrast texts is to examine the author's purpose in each one. Remind students that the two texts they have just read are excerpts from longer books.

J **CITE TEXT EVIDENCE** Have students identify the author's purpose for writing this section of the biography. *(Possible response: After reading lines 199–210, I think the biographer's purpose was to show how Powell's early years and family background helped shape him as a leader and to show how he became involved in the military. The title* Colin Powell: Military Leader *supports this.)* Then, ask students to compare these purposes with Powell's possible purposes for writing his memoir* It Worked for Me. *(Possible response: The authors have different purposes. Powell wants to show how working hard and doing one's job well is a good approach to life and a career. His title* It Worked for Me *supports this idea.)*

COLLABORATIVE DISCUSSION Before partners meet, have students independently review the memoir and the biography and take notes on the parts they found most interesting. Remind students to cite evidence from the text to support their ideas.

ASK STUDENTS to share any questions they generated in the course of reading and discussing the selection.

English Language Support

Read Closely Display lines 203-210 and highlight the phrases in quotation marks.

- Read the paragraph aloud, and then help students explain why the highlighted phrases appear in quotation marks.
- Have pairs identify the important idea emphasized by Colin Powell's own words. *(His military career happened almost by accident; he intended to spend only a short time in the army.)*

English Language Support

Exchange Information and Ideas Have students use a Think-Pair-Share strategy to prepare for discussion.

- First, have students skim both selections, selecting passages that they find interesting.
- Next, have them share these parts with a partner and identify those that they both marked. Ask them to explain why they find these ideas interesting and what details support their views.
- Encourage them to take turns volunteering these ideas in group discussions.

Analyze Text: Biography RI 1, RI 3, RI 5

Discuss the elements of a biography and how they work together to present a full, accurate picture of the subject's life. Ask students what text structure the author of *Colin Powell: Military Leader* uses for this biography and how they know this. *(sequence of events, or chronological order; information is presented in time order from when Powell was born to when he enters college and joins the ROTC)*

Analyzing the Text RI 1, RI 3, RI 5, RI 6

Possible answers:

1. *The writer is not the subject of the text. The text is written from the third-person point of view.*

2. *The author gives a brief history of Hunts Point and who lived there while Powell was growing up. It helps readers learn how the integrated, working-class surroundings and values shaped Powell.*

3. *The events take place from the early 1920s to 1954. Timelines should include his parents' arrival in Harlem, Powell's birth, the move to Hunts Point, Powell's high school graduation, college choice, and the ROTC.*

4. *His purposes were to help readers learn about, make connections with, and be inspired by Colin Powell; to show readers that Powell's road to becoming a military leader was not a straight, clear path, and that his family and surroundings shaped him enormously.*

---

eBook *Annotate It!*

Analyze Text: Biography RI 3, RI 5

The text you have just read is from a biography of Colin Powell. A **biography** is a true account of a person's life, written by another person. Elements of a biography include the following:

- **third-person point of view,** meaning that it is told by an outside narrator who is not connected to or involved in the events
- descriptions of events, people, and experiences that have shaped the subject's life
- **quotations,** or exact words, from the subject as well as from people who know or knew the subject

A writer of a biography researches many sources in order to present accurate information on an individual. The events in a biography are often presented in **chronological order,** or the order in which they occurred. Dates and words and phrases such as *by 1900, during the early 1920s, meanwhile, when Colin graduated, later,* and *during* may be used to point out the **sequence,** or order of events. For example, *Colin Powell: Military Leader* begins with "Colin Powell was born on April 5, 1937 . . ."

As you analyze the text from *Colin Powell: Military Leader* or other biographies, ask yourself questions such as the following:

- What is the author's purpose for writing the biography?
- Does the author's research include quotations from the subject or from people who knew the subject? What do the quotations tell me?
- Does the biography seem accurate? How can I tell?

Analyzing the Text RI 1, RI 3, RI 5, RI 6

Cite Text Evidence   Support your responses with evidence from the text.

1. **Infer** Review lines 24–35. How can you tell that the text is from a biography?

2. **Interpret** Review lines 72–89. What information does the author provide about Hunts Point? What do you think is the author's reason for including this information?

3. **Analyze** Review the text to determine over what period of time the events in *Colin Powell: Military Leader* take place. Then make a timeline that shows when the most important events occur.

4. **Synthesize** What purposes do you think the author had for writing *Colin Powell: Military Leader*?

266 Collection 5

Strategies for Annotation *Annotate it!*

Analyze Text: Biography RI 5

Share these strategies for guided or independent analysis:

- Highlight in yellow dates, words, and phrases that signal sequence.
- Underline the event that tells what happened at that time.
- On a note, tell what the overall structure of the text is.

Colin already possessed a mild interest in the military. In high school, he had closely followed the unfolding of the Korean War. His interest aroused, Colin signed up for the ROTC for the fall semester of 1954 and pledged himself to the Pershing Rifles.

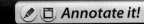

sequence of events

Analyze Texts: Sources

RI 3

Research sources can be grouped based on how closely those who created them are or were to the events being described. **Primary sources** are materials created by people who witnessed or took part in a particular event. **Secondary sources** are records of events that were created some time after the events occurred. Unlike primary sources, secondary sources are made by people who were not directly involved in an event or present when it occurred. This chart shows examples of primary and secondary sources:

Primary Sources	Secondary Sources
letters	encyclopedias
diaries	textbooks
autobiographies	biographies
eyewitness accounts	news articles

A person writing his or her memoir likely uses a number of primary sources while writing. The memoir itself is also a primary source. Someone writing a biography might use some primary sources, but the majority of the research will come from secondary sources. A biography is considered a secondary source.

Compare and Contrast: Memoir and Biography

RI 9

When you compare and contrast a memoir and a biography, you analyze the way each writer presents the subject and the events and influences in the subject's life.

Here are some questions you can ask to compare and contrast a memoir and a biography:

- What is each author's purpose for writing? Do the authors share the same purpose, or are their purposes different?
- How are the authors' presentations of events alike and different?
- How is the impression you get of the person alike and different in each text? Does the author of the memoir sound very different from the person written about in the biography? Does one text seem more accurate or reliable?

Use these questions to help you analyze *It Worked for Me* and *Colin Powell: Military Leader* and to understand a more complete picture of the subject.

TEACH

CLOSE READ

Analyze Texts: Sources

RI 3

First, explain the difference between primary and secondary sources. Review the examples in the chart, and invite students to name other primary and secondary sources. *(Other primary sources: school records; personal scrapbooks; official documents such as birth certificates. Other secondary sources: online resources that include second-hand accounts; documentary films)*

Next, discuss sources that might be used in a memoir and those that might be used in a biography. Have students suggest primary sources an author might use to write a memoir *(diaries and records, letters or e-mails, direct recollections from family members or friends)* and secondary sources the author of a biography might use *(encyclopedias, newspapers, articles, other biographies)*.

Compare and Contrast: Memoir and Biography

RI 9

Discuss the questions readers can ask to compare and contrast a memoir and a biography. Guide students to use the questions to compare and contrast the two selections. For example, have students compare and contrast lines 11–22 in Powell's memoir with lines 90–105 in Brown's biography and tell how the information is similar and different. *(Possible response: Both tell how Powell's parents valued hard work and instilled this in their children. The biography, however, also discusses race and the Powells' belief in higher education.)*

English Language Support

Condense Ideas As students compare and contrast the biography and memoir, have them write short, simple sentences that summarize the purpose, presentation, details, and tone of each text.

- Ask pairs to list their sentences in a chart with two columns, one for each text. Then have them find sentences in the two columns that express related ideas.
- Write the following example on the board: *Powell describes his early jobs. Brown tells about Powell's high school career.* Model

ways to condense these ideas into single sentences: *Both texts discuss Powell's teenage years. Powell focuses on work, but Brown emphasizes education.*

- Have pairs write sentences that condense ideas from both columns into precise, single sentences that compare and contrast the texts. Let volunteers share sentences with the class.

PRACTICE & APPLY

Analyzing the Texts
RI 3, RI 6,
RI 7, RI 9

Possible answers:

1. *Powell's purpose for writing is to share his experiences and pass along lessons and advice. The biographer's purpose for writing is to present information about Powell's background, his early years, his life as a student, and how these shaped him as a leader.*

2. *Powell remembers with fondness his job at Sickser's and how close he became to the owner. The biography only mentions that Powell worked at Sickser's. Powell remembers his job as an important event that shaped his life. Brown only mentions it briefly because he is covering many things that happened to Powell during his high school years.*

3. *Both texts describe Powell as an unremarkable student, but in his memoir, Powell says he was "hardworking and dedicated." The biography describes him as an indifferent student, and even quotes Powell saying that he "horsed around a lot." I think the biography might be a bit more reliable here; Powell is sharing a message of doing one's best in his memoir, so that is more important to him than total accuracy.*

4. *Primary sources might have included writings and accounts from Colin Powell and his sister and historical records such as grade reports and official documents. Secondary sources might have included reference works, historical accounts, and other biographical materials and information.*

5. *While the biography may have more accurate details about Powell and his life, I think Powell's memoir is most accurate in portraying him as a full human being because it helps readers see him as someone who wants to share his experiences and inspire others.*

English Language Support

Provide Textual Evidence Before students draft their informative presentations, explain that quotations, or words taken directly from a text, can help speakers convince an audience to agree with their views or interpretations. Help students find examples of how the idea of always doing his best influenced Powell. Have pairs review the selections and find a direct quotation that supports this idea. Discuss and record their quotations. Then work with students to express their own opinion about "doing their best" using a modal expression such as *can* or *has to*.

Analyzing the Texts
RI 3, RI 6, RI 7,
RI 9, W 9b, SL 4,
SL 6

Cite Text Evidence   Support your responses with evidence from the texts.

1. **Infer** What is Powell's purpose for writing his memoir? Explain how it is similar to or different from Warren Brown's purpose for writing the biography.

2. **Compare** Review lines 1–15 in *It Worked for Me* and lines 148–158 in *Colin Powell: Military Leader*. How does the portrayal of Powell's after-school job differ in each text? Explain why each author treated this event differently.

3. **Compare** Compare lines 78–86 of Powell's memoir with lines 139–147 in the biography. How are the two descriptions of Powell alike and different? Tell whether you think one is more accurate than the other and if so, why.

4. **Draw Conclusions** Review *Colin Powell: Military Leader*. What primary and secondary sources do you think the author might have used?

5. **Evaluate** Review each text. Which one do you think paints a more accurate portrayal of Colin Powell? Why?

PERFORMANCE TASK

Speaking Activity: Informative Presentation Colin Powell's advice to readers is "Always do your very best." Present a speech that explains how this principle helped shape Powell's life and career.

- As you write your speech, include information from the texts that indicates how experiences, people, and events influenced Powell.
- Be sure to present your ideas in a logical order. Include details that support each idea.

- Practice delivering your speech in a formal way, using appropriate eye contact, correct volume, and clear pronunciation.
- Check that you have not used any vague pronouns that might confuse listeners.
- When you present your speech, remember Powell's principle and do your very best!

Assign this performance task.

PERFORMANCE TASK
W 9b,
SL 4,
SL 6

Speaking Activity: Informative Presentation Direct students to

- organize their speeches in a logical way and use sequence words and phrases that help connect their ideas
- include quotations from the texts that support ideas

Have students practice giving their speech and asking for feedback.

Critical Vocabulary

L 4a, L 5b, L 6

claustrophobic	precarious	prestigious
priority	allure	perseverance

Practice and Apply Answer each question. Explain your response.

1. If you feel a room is **claustrophobic,** would you enjoy being in it? Why?

2. If a stack of dishes is balanced in a **precarious** way, will you add more to the pile or rearrange them in shorter stacks? Why?

3. Which is more **prestigious** to a marathon runner, competing in a race with friends or being invited to run in an event in another country? Why?

4. If your **priority** is to go to college and start your own company, would you work to excel in school or do just enough work to get by? Why?

5. Which job has more **allure** to a student who wants to be a journalist— delivering newspapers or writing for the school newspaper? Why?

6. If a worker wants to show her boss that she has **perseverance,** would she volunteer to complete a difficult task or take a vacation? Why?

Vocabulary Strategy: Analogies

An **analogy** presents a relationship between pairs of words. Sometimes writers use analogies to explain unfamiliar ideas. A typical analogy begins with a pair of items that are related in some way. One common word relationship is item-to-category. Here is an example, displayed first as a sentence and then using special symbols:

> *Claustrophic* is to *fear* as *newspaper* is to *periodicals.*

> **claustrophobic : fear :: newspaper : periodicals**

An **item-to-category analogy** relates an individual item (claustrophobic; newspaper) to its category (fear; periodicals). In the second version of each analogy, the single colon stands for "is to" and the double colon stands for "as." Examining each full analogy helps you understand how the word pairs are related.

Practice and Apply Complete each analogy by choosing the best answer.

1. horse : animal :: _____ : plant
   a. tomato   **b.** leaf

2. kitchen : room :: _____ : record
   a. property   **b.** diary

3. fingerprint : _____ :: oil : painting
   a. smudge   **b.** identification

4. jewels : sparkling :: _____ : prestigious
   a. awards   **b.** socks

PRACTICE & APPLY

Critical Vocabulary

L 4a, L 5b, L 6

Possible answers:

1. *No, because it feels crowded.*

2. *rearrange them in stacks because they are probably about to fall over*

3. *being invited to run in an event in another country because there is more formality and recognition involved in being asked by strangers to run in an organized event*

4. *work to excel in school because then I will get to college, which is important to me*

5. *writing for the school newspaper because the student is attracted to writing if he or she wants to be a journalist*

6. *volunteer to complete a difficult task because she will need to work steadily to complete the difficult task*

Vocabulary Strategy: Analogies

1. **a.** *tomato*

2. **b.** *diary*

3. **b.** *identification*

4. **a.** *awards*

Strategies for Annotation ✐ 🗐 *Annotate it!*

Analogies   L 5b

Have students use item-to-category analogies and their eBook annotation tools to clarify the meaning of a word in the text, *commission*.

- Reread lines 193–194 and highlight in yellow the phrases *military training* and *commission as an officer.*

- Underline other related words and phrases in the sentence.

- Think about how *military* and *training* are connected, and then consider how *commission* might be connected to *officer.*

- On a note, tell what you think *commission* means; check a dictionary.

the campus. The ROTC offered students military training that could lead to a commission as an officer in the U.S. Army.

Language Conventions: Correct Vague Pronouns

L 1d

Use the examples to identify and discuss vague pronouns. Explain to students that it is important to proofread their writing to check for vague pronouns because they can be confusing or distracting for readers. Remind students that the point of writing is to communicate ideas, and vague pronouns can make it difficult for readers to understand what a writer means to say.

Answers:

1. *James missed the concert because he was tired and he wanted to stay at home.*

2. *There are more soldiers than leaders in the military.*

3. *Second sentence: The remarks made Kelly/Ms. Patterson sound like she was complaining.*

4. *Gloria got in trouble with Mr. Goodson because she was late for school and she forgot her homework.*

5. *Second sentence: Martina/Jana thought Martina's/Jana's voice sounded strange.*

6. *According to the government report, more families are applying for help.*

Language Conventions: Correct Vague Pronouns

L 1d

Pronouns are words used in place of a noun or another pronoun, such as *he, she,* or *it.* The word that the pronoun refers to is its **antecedent.** Sometimes errors in writing occur when pronouns do not clearly refer to an antecedent. Here's an example:

> In the new movie about aliens, they have some great computer-generated imagery.

The pronoun *they* is vague because the antecedent is unclear; does it refer to the aliens or to the people who made the movie? To get rid of the vague pronoun, the sentence could be rewritten like this:

> The new movie about aliens has some great computer-generated imagery.

Sometimes a vague pronoun tries to refer to a general idea rather than a specific event. For example, *It Worked for Me* begins with a recollection of an event that led to Colin Powell's first job (lines 1–10). Line 11 begins "That was the beginning of a close friendship . . ." The pronoun *That* is vague because it does not refer directly to any particular event.

Sometimes a pronoun is vague when it could refer to more than one antecedent, like this: *When Julian and his father played chess, he often won.* The vague pronoun *he* makes it hard to tell who won. The word *he* needs to be replaced with the name of the person who won: *When Julian and his father played chess, Julian often won.*

Always review your writing to check for and correct vague pronouns.

Practice and Apply Rewrite the sentences to correct the vague pronoun.

1. James was tired and wanted to stay at home. That was the reason he missed the concert.

2. In the military, you have more soldiers than leaders.

3. Kelly frowned at Ms. Patterson's remarks. They made her sound like she was complaining.

4. Gloria was late for school, and she forgot her homework. This got her in trouble with Mr. Goodson.

5. Martina gathered her courage, took a deep breath, and called Jana. She thought her voice sounded strange.

6. According to the government report, they say that more families are applying for help.

English Language Support

Understand Cohesion Tell students that if they cannot clearly identify an antecedent, they should rewrite the sentence to clarify the noun to which the pronoun refers. Explain that sometimes they need to repeat the noun to make the meaning clear.

- Write this sentence on the board: *The boys found their seats and watched both movies. They didn't like them.* Have students highlight the pronouns in the sentence. Then guide them to draw an arrow back to the noun each pronoun replaces. Explain that the pronoun *them* could refer to either the *movies* or the *seats*. Work

with students to rewrite the second sentence in a way that makes the meaning clear: *They didn't like the movies* or *They didn't like the seats.*

- Help students identify the pronouns in the Practice and Apply sentences that lack clear antecedents. Have pairs rewrite sentences to clarify the vague pronouns.

- Have partners exchange drafts of their informative presentations. Ask them to look for examples of vague pronouns and suggest ways to eliminate the confusion.

INTERACTIVE WHITEBOARD LESSON
Analyze Tone

RI 1,
RI 4,
RL 4

Learn the Skill › How to Analyze Tone › Step 1

Analyze the Details

To analyze tone, notice the details the writer includes. Read this text from Chris Crutcher's *King of the Mild Frontier*.

Highlight details in the autobiography that show how sensitive the young Crutcher was.

Until about the age of twelve, the best use I found for my temper was to keep me from being a bawl-baby. One of the few things I could do better than almost all my peers was cry. I cried when *anybody* hit me. I cried when I was down to my last—second—cookie; when it was my brother John's turn to ride with my dad or my granddad in the gas truck; when my mother gave the second half of my Popsicle to someone else (that fell into the second-cookie category); when the New York Yankees lost a World Series game; anytime I had to share. . . .

Answer

TEACH

Use the Interactive Whiteboard Lesson to teach the skill. Begin with the Share What You Know section to explain what tone is in a work of literature. Continue with the Learn the Skill section, discussing how authors communicate tone and how tone can be described with words such as *angry, sad*, and *humorous*. Then, use the steps to analyze tone.

- **Step 1: Analyze the Details** Guide students to recognize which details in a text help them understand the tone and meaning the author intends for the reader.
- **Step 2: Examine Word Choice** Tell students that the words and phrases an author chooses to use can also affect the tone of a text and what it means to the reader. Discuss the examples and have students suggest others for discussion.
- **Step 3: Analyze the Effects** Explain to students that combining the effects of the details and the words an author chooses to use will help them understand the author's tone and intended meaning.

Continue through the lesson to explore the tips for analyzing tone and to complete the Practice & Apply sections with students.

COLLABORATIVE DISCUSSION

Have small groups review *It Worked for Me* and *Colin Powell: Military Leader* to examine the tone each author uses and to analyze the effects in each text. Tell groups to list evidence from the texts that supports their ideas and then share their ideas with the class.

Compare and Contrast: Memoir and Biography

RI 9

RETEACH

Review questions students can ask to compare and contrast a memoir and a biography: *What is each author's purpose? How are the presentations of events alike and different? What impression of the subject do you get from each author?*

Explain that comparing the impression they get of the subject from each text can be useful in determining whether the text presents a full, accurate picture of the subject. Then:

- Have students give examples from *It Worked for Me* that tell them what Colin Powell was like as a young man.
- Repeat with *Colin Powell: Military Leader*.
- Discuss how their impressions of Colin Powell from each text are alike and different.

Point out that an author's purpose may influence how the subject is presented. Have students discuss each author's purpose and examine how the purpose relates to the impression they get.

LEVEL UP TUTORIALS Assign one or more of the following *Level Up* tutorials: **Author's Purpose; Biographies and Autobiographies**

Biographies and Autobiographies

TUTORIAL   PRACTICE

What Is an Autobiography?

When your friends ask what you did over the weekend and you answer, "Well, I . . . ," you are describing a little bit of your life story. You are telling a tale from your own life.

We all share stories from our lives.

People write autobiographies to share their lives with others. An **autobiography** is a story of a person's life, told by that person. Autobiographies are written in the first-person point of view. The writer (or subject) uses the words *I, me, my*, and *we* to talk about himself or herself.

An autobiography is a story of a person's life, as told by that person.

1 **2** 3 4 5 6 7 8 9 10 ..16

INDEPENDENT READING

Individual students can apply these skills to a memoir and a biography on the same subject, in full or excerpted text. After their analysis, have them share their ideas on comparing and contrasting memoirs and biographies with the class.

Community Hero: Chief Wilma Mankiller

Biography by Susannah Abbey

from Every Day Is a New Day

Autobiography by Wilma Mankiller

Why These Texts

Readers of an autobiography and a biography about the same subject may be surprised at how different the two works are. The authors not only have different points of view but also write with different purposes, and so will focus on different aspects of the subject's life. With the help of the close-reading questions, students will analyze how the biography and autobiography portray the life of Wilma Mankiller. This close reading will lead students to compare and contrast the two works.

Background Have students read the background information about Wilma Mankiller. Introduce the selection by reminding students that as the United States pushed its frontier westward during the nineteenth century, Native Americans were displaced. The U.S. government signed hundreds of treaties with conquered tribes, relocating them to reservations. The Cherokee people were forced from their homeland in the southeast to the territory of Oklahoma.

SETTING A PURPOSE Ask students to pay attention to how the two works present elements of Mankiller's personal story. How are the presentations alike and different?

Standards Support

- cite textual evidence
- determine a central idea and summarize it
- analyze how an individual is introduced, illustrated, and elaborated
- determine an author's point of view
- compare and contrast an autobiography and a biography

Text Complexity Rubric

	Community Hero: Chief Wilma Mankiller	*from* Every Day Is a New Day
Quantitative Measures	Lexile: 1170	Lexile: 1340
Qualitative Measures	Levels of Meaning/Purpose — single purpose, explicitly stated	Levels of Meaning/Purpose — more than one purpose; implied but easy to infer
	Structure — clearly stated, sequential organization of main ideas and details	Structure — clearly stated, sequential organization of main ideas and details
	Language Conventionality and Clarity — contemporary, familiar language	Language Conventionality and Clarity — some unfamiliar language
	Knowledge Demands — simple social studies concepts	Knowledge Demands — some specialized knowledge required
Reader/Task Considerations	Teacher determined	Teacher determined

Strategies for CLOSE READING

Compare and Contrast: Biography and Autobiography

Students should read both works carefully all the way through. Close-reading questions at the bottom of the page will help them focus on a thorough analysis of how Mankiller is presented. As they read, students should jot down comments or questions about the text in the margins.

WHEN STUDENTS STRUGGLE . . .

To help students compare and contrast the biography and autobiography, have them work in small groups to fill out a chart like the one shown below.

CITE TEXT EVIDENCE For practice in comparing and contrasting the biography and autobiography, ask students to cite text evidence for each cell of the chart.

Biography	Autobiography
Author's Purpose	*Author's Purpose*
To explain how a girl from a poor family in Oklahoma became a Cherokee leader	To explain why her years in the San Francisco Bay Area were important to her
Presentation of an Event	*Presentation of an Event*
She got involved with the San Francisco Indian Center.	She joined the occupation of Alcatraz Island in 1969.
Here she became politicized and reinforced her identity as a Cherokee.	That morning . . . "my heart and mind made a quantum leap forward." (lines 7–8)
Impression of Mankiller	*Impression of Mankiller*
"She was, in truth, a natural leader." (line 49)	"I learned that sovereignty was more than a legal concept. . . It means freedom and responsibility." (lines 65–68)
She "continues to be a political, cultural, and spiritual leader. . . ." (line 74)	

Background Wilma Mankiller *(1945–2010) was born in Oklahoma, the sixth of 11 children. She grew up in a home without electricity, indoor plumbing, or a telephone. In the 1950s, the Mankiller family was relocated by the Bureau of Indian Affairs and moved to San Francisco. Mankiller was the first woman to be elected principal chief of the Cherokee Nation. As chief, she worked to improve the nation's health care, government, and education system. She continued to be an active presence in the Cherokee Nation after she left office and was particularly dedicated to working for women's rights.*

Community Hero: Chief Wilma Mankiller | *from* Every Day Is a New Day

By Susannah Abbey | By Wilma Mankiller

CLOSE READ Notes

1. **READ ▶** As you read lines 1–31 of "Community Hero," begin to collect and cite text evidence.

   • Underline facts about Wilma Mankiller's childhood.
   • Circle the role the San Francisco Indian Center played in Mankiller's life.

Community Hero: Chief Wilma Mankiller
Biography by Susannah Abbey

Wilma Mankiller <u>came from a large family that spent many years on the family farm in Oklahoma.</u> They were, of course, <u>poor, but not desperately so.</u> "As far back as I can remember there were <u>always books around our house,</u>" she recalls in her autobiography, *Mankiller: A Chief and Her People.* "<u>This love of reading</u> came from the traditional Cherokee passion for telling and listening to stories. But it also came from my parents, particularly my father . . . A love for books and reading was one of the best gifts he ever gave his children."

87

---

1. **READ AND CITE TEXT EVIDENCE** Tell students that biographies often begin with the subject's childhood. Here the biographer looks for clues about Mankiller's future in her early years as a member of a large, poor farming family in Oklahoma.

   Ⓐ ASK STUDENTS to discuss how they can distinguish facts from opinions in these lines. *Students should understand that facts are events or situations that occurred, so they can be supported by the historical record. For example, Mankiller returned to the Bay Area after spending a year at a family ranch and then got involved with the San Francisco Indian Center. An opinion is someone's view or appraisal of something. For example, Mankiller recalls that the Center was "a safe place to go, even if we only wanted to hang out." Point out that the distinction may be subtle. Have students explain why "This was not a happy time for her" (lines 16–17) is a fact. It describes an emotional state that Mankiller experienced; it can be verified by talking to her and to people who knew her then.*

1. The family was forced to relocate to San Francisco.

2. She left her family to live on her grand-mother's ranch.

3. She was inspired by people and events at the Center.

10   Unfortunately, a poor local economy made the Mankiller family an easy target for the Bureau of Indian Affairs relocation program of the 1950s. Government agents were entrusted with the job of moving rural Cherokees to cities, effectively dispersing them and allowing others to buy their traditional, oil-rich lands. In 1959 the family moved to San Francisco, where Wilma's father could get a job and where Wilma began her junior high school years. This was not a happy time for her. She missed the farm and she hated the school where white kids teased her about being Native American and about her name.

20   Mankiller decided to leave her parents and go to live with her **(A)** maternal grandmother, Pearl Sitton, on a family ranch inland from San Francisco. **(B)** The year she spent there restored her confidence and after returning to the Bay Area, she got increasingly involved with the world of the San Francisco Indian Center.

"There was something at the Center for everyone. It was a safe place to go, even if we only wanted to hang out." The Center provided entertainment, social and cultural activities for youth, as well as a place for adults to hold powwows and discuss matters of importance with other BIA relocatees. Here, Mankiller became politicized, at the
30 same time reinforcing her identity as a Cherokee and her attachments to the Cherokee people, their history and traditions.

2. **REREAD** Reread lines 10–31. In the margin, list three important events in Mankiller's life. Why does the author include information about Mankiller's childhood? Support your answer with explicit textual evidence.

The author gives information on Mankiller's childhood to help us understand her beginnings as a community leader. For example, the time spent with her grandmother gave her confidence to lead.

3. **READ** As you read lines 32–79, continue to cite textual evidence.

• Circle Mankiller's first political involvement.
• In the margin, explain why the Native American Youth Center was important to Mankiller's development as a leader. Circle an example to support your answer.
• Underline problems Mankiller encountered during her campaign.

88

> ## "Mankiller says she learned on the job. . . . But she was, in truth, a natural leader."

When a group of Native Americans occupied Alcatraz Island in November 1969, in protest of U.S. Government policies, which had, for hundreds of years, deprived them of their lands, Mankiller participated in her first major political action.

"It changed me forever," she wrote. "It was on Alcatraz . . . where at long last some Native Americans, including me, truly began to regain our balance."

In the years that followed the "occupation," Mankiller became
40 more active in developing the cultural resources of the Native American community. She helped build a school and an Indian Adult **(C)** Education Center. She directed the Native American Youth Center in East Oakland, coordinating field trips to tribal functions, hosting music concerts, and giving kids a place to do their homework or just connect with each other. The youth center also gave her the opportunity to pull together Native American adults from around Oakland as volunteers, thus strengthening their ties. Mankiller says she learned on the job, joking "my enthusiasm seemed to make up for my lack of skills." But she was, in truth, a natural leader.

50   She returned to Oklahoma in the 1970s where she worked at the Urban Indian Resource Center and volunteered in the community. In 1981 she founded and then became director of the Cherokee Community Development Department, where she orchestrated a community-based **renovation** of the water system and was instrumental in lifting an entire town, Bell, Oklahoma, out of squalor and despair. In 1983, she ran for Deputy Chief of the Cherokee Nation.

Her early organizing experiences and community work prepared her for leadership.

renovation:
upgrade;
restoration

89

---

2. **REREAD AND CITE TEXT EVIDENCE**

(B) ASK STUDENTS why certain childhood events were important. Have them cite text evidence to support their reasoning. *Students should recognize that some events were important because they had lasting effects on Mankiller, helping her become a leader of the Cherokee people. Students could mention, for example, that getting involved with the San Francisco Indian Center was important because it led to her becoming politicized, while reinforcing her identity as a Cherokee (lines 29–31).*

3. **READ AND CITE TEXT EVIDENCE**

(C) ASK STUDENTS to paraphrase Mankiller's responsibilities at the Native American Youth Center. *She was the director. She coordinated field trips. She hosted music concerts. She gave kids a place to do their homework and connect with each other. She recruited Native American adults as volunteers.* Have students explain how these duties helped Mankiller become a leader.

Critical Vocabulary: renovation (line 54) Have students share their definitions of *renovation*. If the water system was in need of renovation, what can we say about its condition? *The water system was old or had fallen into disrepair; it wasn't being maintained in good condition.*

FOR ELL STUDENTS Clarify that the noun *squalor* means "a filthy and wretched condition."

The campaign was not an easy one. <u>There had never been a woman leader of a Native American tribe.</u> She had many ideas to 60 present and debate, but <u>encountered discouraging opposition from men who refused to talk about anything but the fact that she was a woman. Her campaign days were troubled by death threats, and her tires were slashed.</u> She sought the advice of friends for ways to approach the constant insults, finally settling on a philosophy summed up by the epithet, "Don't ever argue with a fool, because someone walking by and observing you can't tell which one is the fool." In the end, Mankiller had her day: she was elected as first woman Deputy Chief, and over time her wise, strong leadership **vindicated** her supporters and proved her detractors wrong.

70   In 1985, when Chief Ross Swimmer left for Washington, D.C., Mankiller was **obligated** to step into his position, becoming the first woman to serve as Principal Chief of the Cherokee Nation. Although poor health forced her to retire from that position in 1995, Wilma Mankiller continues to be a political, cultural, and spiritual leader in her community and throughout the United States. In 1990 Oklahoma State University honored her with the Henry G. Bennett Distinguished Service Award, and in 1998, President Clinton awarded her the Presidential Medal of Freedom, the nation's highest civilian honor.

vindicate:
justify

obligate:
require

4. ◀ **REREAD AND DISCUSS** Reread lines 58–69. In a small group, discuss the possible reasons that men may have opposed having a woman as Chief. What experiences qualified Mankiller for the job? Be sure to cite evidence from the text in your discussion.

90

---

5. **READ** ▶ As you read lines 1–41 from "Every Day Is a New Day," begin to collect and cite text evidence.
- In the margin, make an inference about how Mankiller feels about her surroundings, and underline descriptive language that supports your inference.
- In the margin, summarize the indigenous people's historical connection to Alcatraz.

from Every Day Is a New Day
Autobiography by Wilma Mankiller

Though I have lived most of my life on my grandfather's Cherokee land allotment in rural Adair County, Oklahoma, I learned a great deal about **indigenous** people, governance, and land during the twenty years I spent in the San Francisco Bay Area. Soon after my Native American brothers and sisters joined the occupation of Alcatraz Island in late 1969, I made plans to visit the island. The morning I made the short journey to Alcatraz, my heart and mind made a quantum leap forward.

10   <u>Lady dawn descended on the nearly empty streets of Fisherman's Wharf, bearing the gift of a brand-new day. Fishing boats rocked in their slips, awaiting the day's journey, as shop owners sleepily prepared for the onslaught of tourists.</u> An occasional foghorn or the barking of a stray dog was the only sound other than the steady lap of the ocean against the docks. Alcatraz Island, several miles across San Francisco Bay, was barely visible as I boarded a boat for the former military and federal prison, which had recently been taken over by indigenous people and declared "Indian Land." <u>Mist and fog gave the island a dreamlike quality that seemed fitting for a place where the American dream was rejected and an Indigenous dream declared.</u>

20   The young students who occupied Alcatraz Island claimed that federal surplus lands such as Alcatraz should be returned to tribal peoples on legal and moral ground, and that treaties, land rights, and tribal **sovereignty** should be respected and honored. This was not the first relationship between indigenous people and Alcatraz. Long before Europeans arrived, Ohlones and other indigenous people of

indigenous:
original

Mankiller's surroundings are important to her. Her poetic descriptions of natural details show how much the area means to her.

sovereignty:
self-rule; independence

91

---

4. **REREAD AND DISCUSS USING TEXT EVIDENCE**

D **ASK STUDENTS** to infer why the men were against Mankiller's campaign for Deputy Chief. Have students from each group share their reasoning. *The men wouldn't talk about the issues; they just focused on the fact that Mankiller was a woman. Her friends advised Mankiller, "Don't ever argue with a fool." And there hadn't been any women leaders of Native American tribes before. All of these reasons make it seem like the men were just prejudiced against women.*

Critical Vocabulary: vindicate (line 69) Have students share their definitions of *vindicate*, and ask volunteers to use the verb in sentences.

Critical Vocabulary: obligate (line 71) Have students suggest synonyms of *obligate* that would work in this context. *bind, force, oblige*

5. **READ AND CITE TEXT EVIDENCE**

E **ASK STUDENTS** how Mankiller alerts the reader that indigenous peoples have historical connections with Alcatraz. She writes that the 1969 occupation of the island was "not the first relationship" indigenous people had with Alcatraz (lines 23–24). What were the earlier relationships? *The Ohlone and other coastal peoples used to rest on the island. The Modocs were imprisoned on the island after losing their homeland.*

Critical Vocabulary: indigenous (line 3) Have students share their definitions of *indigenous*. What distinguishes indigenous people from everyone else? *The ancestors of indigenous people originated here in the Americas; the ancestors of everyone else originated on other continents.*

Critical Vocabulary: sovereignty (line 23) Have students share their definitions of *sovereignty*, and ask volunteers to use the noun in sentences.

Alcatraz Island

At first, native peoples visited Alcatraz. For a while, it was a prison for tribal peoples. One hundred years later, American Indians occupied the island.

the coast rested and got their bearings on Alcatraz Island, called the Island of the Pelicans (Isla de los Alcatraces) after the seabirds that gathered there. In the late nineteenth century, Modocs and other tribal people were imprisoned at Alcatraz for fighting the United
30 States Army in a desperate attempt to retain their ancestral homelands. When the Spanish first settled in the mid-1700s on the land that is today California, there were more than 275,000 indigenous people living there. That changed very quickly. By 1900, fewer than 16,000 indigenous people remained. It is a miracle that even that many survived. Indigenous people of California endured widespread violence, starvation, disease, genocide, rape, and slavery. As late as 1870, a few communities in California were still paying bounties for Indian scalps or severed heads. One hundred years later, the descendants of some of the indigenous people who survived the
40 conquerors, miners, and settlers joined others at Alcatraz to find their bearings just as their ancestors had done so long ago.

6. **◀ REREAD AND DISCUSS** Reread lines 20–41. In a small group, explain why Alcatraz Island holds such importance for Mankiller.

7. **READ ▶** As you read lines 42–87, continue to cite textual evidence.
   • Underline sentences that explain what Alcatraz symbolized for younger American Indians.
   • Circle two pieces of information that Mankiller learns about sovereignty.

I visited Alcatraz several times during the nineteen-month occupation of the island. At any given time, the Alcatraz community was composed of an **eclectic** group of indigenous people, activists, civil rights veterans, students, and people who just wanted to be at a "happening." Richard Oakes, a visionary young Mohawk who emerged as an early spokesman for the Alcatraz occupiers, said, "There are many old prophecies that speak of the younger people rising up and finding a way for the People to live." (In their own
50 languages, many tribes call themselves by words that mean "the People.") Alcatraz was a catalyst for many young people who would spend their lives forging a new path for the People.
   The Alcatraz experience was certainly a **watershed** for me. The leaders articulated principles and ideas I had thought about but could not name or articulate. During the Alcatraz occupation and that period of activism, anything seemed possible. Inspired by Alcatraz, I began a four-year association with the Pit River Tribe, which was involved in a legal and political struggle to regain their ancestral lands near Mount Shasta. Mostly I worked as a volunteer at the tribe's
60 legal offices in San Francisco, but I frequently visited Pit River lands, where I learned about the history of indigenous people in California from traditional leaders. Occasionally one of the leaders would bring out an old cardboard box filled with tribal documents supporting their land claims. They treated the precious documents almost as sacred objects. At Pit River, I learned that sovereignty was more than a legal concept. It represents the ability of the People to articulate their own vision of the future, control their destiny, and watch over their lands. It means freedom and responsibility.
   Another place that had a great impact on me was the Oakland
70 Intertribal Friendship House, which served as an oasis for a diverse group of indigenous people living in a busy urban area far from their home communities. We gathered there for dinners, meetings, and to listen to a wonderful array of speakers, including Tom Porter, a Mohawk leader who spoke about his people's fight to remain separate

eclectic:
assorted; diverse

watershed:
turning point

6. **REREAD AND DISCUSS USING TEXT EVIDENCE**

F ASK STUDENTS to describe the connection Mankiller feels to the island. *Students should note that Mankiller feels connected to Alcatraz because the island is itself connected to the history of indigenous peoples, a history that is painful but vitally important to her.*

7. **READ AND CITE TEXT EVIDENCE**

G ASK STUDENTS to describe what Alcatraz meant to the occupiers. How did young Native Americans' experience on Alcatraz change them? *For some, Alcatraz was the fulfillment of an old prophecy that young people would rise up and find a way for indigenous people to live. For others, Alcatraz was a catalyst, something that made them spend the rest of their lives searching for a better path. And for Mankiller, it was a watershed, a moment when she realized important principles and decided to become an activist.*

Critical Vocabulary: eclectic (line 44) Have students share their definitions of *eclectic*. Why does Mankiller describe the group of Alcatraz occupiers as eclectic? *The group was eclectic because it was made up of different kinds of people.*

Critical Vocabulary: watershed (line 53) Have students share their definitions of *watershed*. What makes Alcatraz a watershed for Mankiller? *The Alcatraz experience was a watershed because it marked a turning point in her life.*

FOR ELL STUDENTS Clarify that in this context a catalyst is an event that causes a change or an action; in chemistry it means a substance that causes a change or an action.

and independent. He explained that the Mohawk's 1795 treaty with the United States provided that they had the "perpetual right to live on their reservations in independent sovereignty, never to be disturbed." He spoke movingly about the important role women play among his people. He said that traditional Iroquois women selected the chiefs and could **depose** them if they did not perform their duties properly. The speech had a powerful, lasting impact on me.

80

My experiences at Alcatraz and Pit River led me to cofound, with Joe Carillo, California Indians for a Fair Settlement, which encouraged California tribal people to reject a proposed settlement of all land claims for only pennies per acre. All this work helped me to understand more fully the historical context in which tribal people live our contemporary lives.

In 1976 I was further **galvanized** by a treaty conference at the Standing Rock Sioux Reservation in Wakpala, South Dakota, that

90

readied delegates for the 1977 United Nations Conference on

depose:
*overthrow;
remove*

galvanize:
excite; inspire

---

8. ◀ REREAD Reread lines 53–87. Summarize what Mankiller learns from her work at Alcatraz, with the Pit River Tribe, and in Oakland. What did her experiences teach her? Support your answer with explicit textual evidence.

Mankiller's work with various tribal leaders at these places taught her to "articulate principles and ideas" she had never been able to voice. She learned that sovereignty meant "freedom and responsibility." Her experiences at Alcatraz and Pit River inspired her to cofound an organization that united tribal people throughout California.

---

9. READ ▶ As you read lines 88–116, continue to cite textual evidence.

• Underline the relationship between political and spiritual organizations in the present and in the past.

• Circle what Mankiller thought of her experiences with the tribes.

94

> **"All peoples have the right to self-determination."**

Indigenous Rights in Geneva. I had been working as a volunteer to help indigenous people prepare for the Geneva conference by documenting the fact that from the time of initial contact with Europeans, tribal communities were treated as separate nations, and numerous agreements between the emerging United States and tribal nations were signed.

Ⓙ At Wakpala, tribal sovereignty was framed as an issue of international significance. The concept of self-determination in international law as defined by UN General Assembly Resolution 1514

100

resonates with indigenous people: "All peoples have the right to self-determination. By virtue of that right they freely determine their political status and freely pursue their economic, social, and cultural development."

Ⓘ During this time, I also came to understand that among some tribal people, including the Cherokee, there was a historical period when there was little separation between political and spiritual organizations. Cherokee spiritual leaders were involved in conducting the council meetings that provided some of the political structure whereby major decisions were made by the entire settlement. Council

110

meetings were often held after or during ceremonies, which helped prepare the people to deal with major issues affecting the community. However, in contemporary times, there is a formal separation between the political organization and spiritual practitioners.

95

---

8. **REREAD AND CITE TEXT EVIDENCE**

Ⓗ **ASK STUDENTS** to find and cite examples of lessons that Mankiller learned at the three locations. *Students should note that she learned to articulate principles and ideas (line 54), a fuller concept of sovereignty (lines 65–68), and the importance of women's role in indigenous society (lines 78–81).*

9. **READ AND CITE TEXT EVIDENCE**

Ⓘ **ASK STUDENTS** to find and paraphrase what Mankiller learned about political and spiritual organizations. *She learned that historically there wasn't much separation between the two kinds of organizations (lines 104–109).*

Critical Vocabulary: depose (line 80) Have students share their definitions of *depose*, and ask volunteers to use the verb in sentences.

Critical Vocabulary: galvanize (line 88) Have students suggest synonyms of the verb *galvanize* that would work in this context. *energize, motivate, spur*

FOR ELL STUDENTS Some students may be familiar with the expression *to be framed* as meaning "to be set up." Explain that the meaning of the phrase *was framed* in this context is "was planned."

CLOSE READ
Notes

The Alcatraz, Pit River, California Indian for a Fair Settlement, and the treaty Conference experiences were great preparation for my future role as principal chief of the Cherokee Nation.

10. ◀ REREAD AND DISCUSS Reread lines 97–103. Work with a small group to paraphrase the concept of self-determination as stated by UN General Assembly Resolution 1514. Why did this resolution mean so much to Mankiller? Cite explicit text evidence in your discussion.

SHORT RESPONSE

Cite Text Evidence In what ways is Wilma Mankiller's autobiographical account of her life different from Susannah Abbey's biography? Compare and contrast the information presented in each text. Review your reading notes for both texts, and be sure to **cite text evidence** in your response.

Mankiller focuses on her time at Alcatraz and on specific experiences that influenced the development of her thoughts and actions. Mankiller spends less time on her early life, while Abbey provides more background on Mankiller's childhood—such as her time in junior high school, which was "not a happy time for her." Mankiller does not discuss her leadership abilities, but provides details about how her experiences shaped and inspired her, especially through her association with people like Richard Oakes, Tom Porter, and Joe Carillo. Abbey writes that Mankiller is "a natural leader" with "wise, strong leadership." Mankiller writes about the history of indigenous people, while Abbey writes only about Mankiller. Mankiller expresses her feelings about her life, while Abbey uses quotes from Mankiller's autobiography and includes her own opinions of Mankiller's character.

96

TO CHALLENGE STUDENTS . . .

For deeper understanding, students can research the political and social context of the 1969 occupation of Alcatraz Island.

ASK STUDENTS what events led up to the occupation. *Students should understand that the 1960s were years of social unrest and civic protest in the United States. Ever greater numbers of U.S. troops were being sent to fight in Vietnam—a war that many Americans came to question. By the end of the decade, protests against the war were being staged on college campuses across the country. At the same time, Cesar Chavez was organizing Mexican and Chicano farm workers in California. The aim was to form a union that could increase the wages and improve living conditions for a group that had been marginalized for centuries. The 1960s were also crucial years in the civil rights movement, led by African Americans such as Martin Luther King Jr. and Malcolm X. Their efforts would eventually change the social and legal foundations of the country.*

At the time, living standards of Native Americans were among the worst in the country. Politically and economically oppressed, isolated on reservations, indigenous peoples lived in poverty. Observing the various movements of social protest in the 1960s, young Native Americans decided to take their own stand—the occupation of Alcatraz Island.

10. (REREAD AND DISCUSS USING TEXT EVIDENCE)

🔵 **ASK STUDENTS** in each group to choose a volunteer to read the group's paraphrase of Resolution 1514. Have students find and discuss earlier instances in which Mankiller examines the issue of sovereignty. *The people who occupied Alcatraz Island fought for tribal sovereignty (lines 20–24), tribal elders at the Pit River taught Mankiller the full meaning of sovereignty (lines 65–68), and Tom Porter spoke movingly about the Mohawks' long struggle for sovereignty (lines 73–78). Resolution 1514 resonated with Mankiller because it was something she'd been thinking about most of her life.*

SHORT RESPONSE

Cite Text Evidence Students should:

- describe parts of Mankiller's life presented by each text.
- describe qualities of Mankiller emphasized by each text.
- give examples of differences between the texts.

DIG DEEPER

1. With the class, return to Question 4, Reread and Discuss. Have students share the results of their discussion.

ASK STUDENTS to share the main conclusions of their group discussions.

- What kind of evidence did the groups cite for the men's opposition to Mankiller's candidacy? *Students should note that the men didn't seem to oppose Mankiller on substantive issues or differences of opinion about tribal policy. And some of the opposition was extreme, even illegal. The author records that Mankiller received death threats and had her tires slashed (lines 63–64).*

- Have groups discuss and evaluate the inferences they drew about the men's opposition. *Students will probably support their inferences that the men were prejudiced against women—especially in important roles—from the details that the author presents. The men's constant insults and refusal to engage Mankiller seriously are convincing evidence.*

- Ask students to summarize their group's conclusions about Mankiller's qualifications for the job. How did her life experiences give her skills she would need to be Deputy Chief? *Students should talk about her involvement with the San Francisco Indian Center, her participation in the Alcatraz occupation, her work at the Native American Youth Center, and her experience directing the Cherokee Community Development Department.*

2. With the class, return to Question 6, Reread and Discuss. Have students share the results of their discussion.

ASK STUDENTS to compare Alcatraz Island with its occupiers.

- What similarities did Mankiller see in the island and the young Native Americans who occupied it? *The occupiers, writes Mankiller, were the descendants of the small group of indigenous people who survived the violence and disease of European conquest. The island, declared "Indian Land" by the occupiers, was a tiny piece of California, which once belonged to their ancestors. Both were remnants of what were once greater wholes.*

ASK STUDENTS to return to their Short Response answer and revise it based on the class discussion.

CLOSE READING NOTES

The First Day of School

Short Story by R. V. Cassill

Why This Text?

Students encounter increasingly subtle and nuanced fictional texts as they read for pleasure or for school. This lesson explores the creation of suspense and tension in a story about what at first appears to be an ordinary morning of the first day of school.

▶ **View It!**

Professional Development Podcast:
Text Complexity

Key Learning Objective: The student will be able to determine and analyze mood and describe flashback in a short story.

RL 1 Cite text evidence.

RL 3 Describe story elements.

RL 4 Determine the meaning of words and phrases.

RL 5 Analyze structure.

W 2 Write explanatory texts.

W 2a Introduce a topic; organize ideas.

W 2b Develop a topic.

W 2e Establish and maintain a formal style.

W 2f Provide a concluding statement.

W 9a Draw evidence from literary texts to support analysis and reflection when applying grade 6 Reading standards to literature.

W 10 Write routinely.

SL 1 Engage effectively in a range of collaborative discussions.

L 3a Vary sentence patterns for meaning, interest, and style.

L 4a Use context as a clue to meaning.

L 4c Consult reference materials.

L 6 Acquire and use grade-appropriate general academic words; gather vocabulary knowledge.

▲ Text Complexity Rubric

Quantitative Measures	**The First Day of School** Lexile: 780L

Qualitative Measures

Levels of Meaning/Purpose

multiple levels of meaning (multiple themes)

Structure

no major shifts in chronology; occasional use of flashback

Language Conventionality and Clarity

some figurative language

Knowledge Demands

experience includes unfamiliar aspects

Reader/Task Considerations

• Teacher determined
• Vary by individual reader and type of text
• See the Text X-Ray for suggested Reader/Task Considerations.

English Language Support Before teaching, use the Text X-Ray for an overview of the text's complexity. The Text X-Ray and the supports and scaffolds in the Teacher's Edition will help you guide students of different skill levels.

Meaning Making

Language Development

Effective Expression

Content Knowledge

Foundational Skills

Text Complexity: Qualitative Measures

Levels of Meaning/Purpose

multiple levels of meaning (multiple themes)

Help students determine mood in a short story.

- Teacher's Edition side notes, pp. 271, 272, 273, 274, 275, 277
- English Language Support, pp. 271, 275
- When Students Struggle, p. 274
- Strategies for Annotation, pp. 272, 277
- Determine Meanings of Words and Phrases, p. 277

To reteach how to determine mood, see

- Determine Meaning: Mood, p. 280a

▶ **Use It!** Level Up Tutorials: Setting and Mood

ZOOM IN ON **DETERMINING MOOD** Tell students that the **mood**, or overall atmosphere, of a story influences the reader's feelings about characters and events. Display lines 84–98.

- Guide students to highlight words and phrases that show John's feelings about the information he discovers and the experience he will undergo. *("stealthily," "whispering of information," "meant to keep from him," "bitterly," "That was why you had to be," "things were worse than everybody had hoped")*
- Help students see that the ideas he expresses and the way he expresses them show his anger and bitterness.
- Ask volunteers to explain how his feelings establish the mood in this part of the story. *(They create a sense of foreboding, and anxiety.)*

Structure

no major shifts in chronology; occasional use of flashback

Help students analyze the structure of a story, including flashback.

- Teacher's Edition side notes, pp. 274, 276, 277
- English Language Support, p. 271
- Describe Stories: Flashback, p. 277

To teach how to analyze foreshadowing, see

- Analyze Structure: Foreshadowing, p. 280a

 Use It! Level Up Tutorials: Plot: Sequence of Events; Suspense and Foreshadowing

ZOOM IN ON **IDENTIFYING FLASHBACKS** Display or distribute the paragraph below and have students underline the words that signal the beginning and end of the flashback.

Mrs. Zepp waved from the gate. Turning back to the house, she caught a glimpse of the bright yellow chrysanthemum at the edge of the flower bed. <u>Suddenly, it was ten years ago</u>, and she was walking Hetty to the first day of kindergarten. Hetty, in a sunshine-colored dress, clasped her hand tightly, skipping with excitement, then slowing down to ask yet again, "Will you be there when school gets out?" Smiling, she had reassured Hetty that indeed she would. <u>Just then the creak of the gate pulled her back to the present</u>.

Language Conventionality and Clarity

some figurative language

Teach unfamiliar vocabulary in context.

- Teacher's Edition Critical Vocabulary notes, pp. 272, 273, 274, 276, 279
- Applying Academic Vocabulary, p. 273
- English Language Support, p. 279
- Vocabulary Strategy: Using a Thesaurus, p. 279

Support students' analysis of the selection.

- Teacher's Edition side notes, pp. 273, 276, 280
- English Language Support, pp. 276, 280
- Performance Task, p. 278
- Language Conventions: Varying Sentence Patterns, p. 280

ZOOM IN ON **UNPACKING SENTENCES** Discuss the variety of sentence types that appear on page 272. Model how to interpret complex sentences by displaying one from lines 34–38: "The heavy traffic in town . . . kept him awake after that."

- Explain that there is one independent clause in this sentence. Work with students to highlight its subjects *("traffic," "wail," "murmur")* and verb(s) *("kept")*.
- Then ask pairs to identify the subordinate clause. *("as somebody raced in on the U.S. highway holding the horn button down")*

Knowledge Demands

experience includes unfamiliar aspects

Support English learners in understanding the historical context of the story.

- Teacher's Edition Background note, p. 271
- Content-Area Connection, p. 276

ZOOM IN ON **BUILDING HISTORICAL CONTEXT** Read and discuss the Background notes in the Student and Teacher's Editions, page 271. Then present these additional facts related to the time period and the early days of integration:

- After a federal district court dismissed Oliver Brown's suit against the Topeka, Kansas, school, he then appealed to the Supreme Court, which decided unanimously that racial segregation of schools was "inherently unequal." In 1958, in the wake of tremendous opposition to desegregation, a Court ruling in another case required all states to integrate their schools.

Suggested Reader/Task Considerations

You might consider the following before assigning this story to students.

- Will students be interested and motivated to read this story?
- Do students have the ability to visualize important aspects of setting in the story?

ZOOM IN ON **SUPPORTING COMPREHENSION**

- To keep students engaged, help them recognize instances of foreshadowing. After reading the first pages of the story, discuss how details in lines 22–23, 34, and 38–40 develop feelings of dread and anxiety and make readers wonder what will happen on this first day of school.
- Discuss how the setting is introduced gradually. Have pairs identify details in lines 30–41, 56–69, and 101–121 that build the context and help them to visualize it.

TEACH

CLOSE READ

Background Have students read the background and information about the author. Tell students that the 1954 Supreme Court ruling is known as *Brown v. Board of Education*. In spite of the ruling, many school districts in the South resisted. In 1957 in Little Rock, Arkansas, a mob of white people and hundreds of armed guardsmen prevented the nine chosen black students from entering Central High School for weeks on end. Finally, President Eisenhower had to authorize federal troops to escort the students safely into the school. A detail of those troops remained at the school for the entire year to ensure the students' safety.

SETTING A PURPOSE Direct students to use the Setting a Purpose question to focus their reading. Remind students to write down questions as they read.

Determine Meanings: RL 1, RL 4

Mood (LINES 1–4)

Explain to students that writers create a **mood,** or feeling, in a story. In addition to the action and what the characters say, the mood helps readers understand whether a story is happy, sad, or scary, for example. Writers create mood by carefully choosing the words they use to describe the setting and characters.

A CITE TEXT EVIDENCE Ask students to tell what mood Cassill creates in lines 1–4 and to cite specific words or phrases to support their idea. (*The mood is somber or melancholy; phrases such as "souvenirs of the summer days," "rich with blue reflections," or "shadowy greens" create this mood.*)

English Language Support

Read Closely Explain that the author expects readers to make inferences in order to understand important ideas about character and plot.

- Read lines 1–8 aloud. Use a Think Aloud strategy to model how to infer from John's actions and his mother's response that he is not eager about going to school.
- Tell students that they should pay attention to details that reveal the reason for John's feelings as they read.

Background *In 1954, the United States Supreme Court ruled that segregation in public schools (the practice of having "separate but equal" schools for whites and blacks) was unconstitutional. This decision meant that schools had to begin integrating students at all levels. Schoolchildren, particularly in the southern United States, prepared to face the anger, hatred, and often violence of those who opposed this policy. In 1958, in the midst of this difficult time,* **R. V. Cassill** (1919–2002) *wrote this story.*

The First Day of School

Short Story by R. V. Cassill

SETTING A PURPOSE As you read, pay close attention to the interactions of the Hawkins family and the clues that indicate what is significant about this first day of school.

Thirteen bubbles floated in the milk. Their pearl transparent hemispheres[1] gleamed like souvenirs of the summer days just past, rich with blue reflections of the sky and of shadowy greens. John Hawkins jabbed the bubble closest to him with his spoon, and it disappeared without a ripple. On the white surface there was no mark of where it had been.

"Stop tooling[2] that oatmeal and eat it," his mother said. She glanced meaningfully at the clock on the varnished
10 cupboard. She nodded a heavy, emphatic affirmation[3] that now the clock was boss. Summer was over, when the gracious

---

[1] **hemispheres** (hĕm´ĭ-sfîrz´): half of a sphere, which is a three-dimensional circular, or ball, shape.
[2] **tooling** (tōō´lĭng): working with something, as with a tool such as a spoon.
[3] **affirmation** (ăf´ər-mā´shən): positive, strong support of the truth of something.

(cl) ©Corbis; (cr) ©Stephanie Rabemiafar/Corbis

The First Day of School **271**

English Language Support

Analyze Language Display lines 8–29, and highlight the dialogue.

- Help students name the speakers of the dialogue. Then have pairs assume the roles of John and his mother and read the dialogue aloud.
- Ask students to explain what the dialogue reveals about John's attitude and about his mother's personality. Have them share ideas in small groups. (*John appears anxious, worried that something might happen. His mother seems calm and reassuring.*)

CLOSE READ

Make Inferences
RL 1

(LINES 14–29)

Point out that sometimes readers must **make inferences,** or logical guesses based on stated information as well as their own knowledge and experience, to understand a story.

B **ASK STUDENTS** what they can infer about Audrey, about John and his mother's relationship, and about what is happening. *(Possible responses: Audrey is John's sister or maybe a visitor; John and his mother respect each other, but the mother is in charge, based on "Of course she'll go"; John and Audrey will go somewhere together.)*

Determine Meanings: Mood
RL 1, RL 4

(LINES 30–43)

C **CITE TEXT EVIDENCE** What mood does Audrey's presence create? Have students cite words that create that mood. *(Audrey is "fresh and cool"; she has "slept all right." She speaks "softly." The mood is calm and peaceful.)*

> **CRITICAL VOCABULARY**
>
> **resentment**: John feels resentment when he sees that Audrey looks well rested.
>
> **ASK STUDENTS** what John might have done that shows resentment. *(John might have frowned or set down his spoon loudly in irritation.)*

---

oncoming of morning light and the stir of early breezes promised that time was a luxury.

"Audrey's not even down yet," he said.

"Audrey'll be down."

"You think she's taking longer to dress because she wants to look nice today?"

"She likes to look *neat.*"

B 20 "What I was thinking," he said slowly, "was that maybe she didn't feel like going today. Didn't feel *exactly* like it."

"Of course she'll go."

"I meant she might not want to go until tomorrow, maybe. Until we see what happens."

"Nothing's going to happen," his mother said.

"I know there isn't. But what if it did?" Again John swirled the tip of his spoon in the milk. It was like writing on a surface that would keep no mark.

"Eat and be quiet. Audrey's coming, so let's stop this here kind of talk."

C 30 He heard the tap of heels on the stairs, and his sister came down into the kitchen. She looked fresh and cool in her white dress. Her lids looked heavy. She must have slept all right—and for this John felt both envy and a faint **resentment.** He had not really slept since midnight. The heavy traffic in town, the long wail of horns as somebody raced in on the U.S. highway holding the horn button down, and the restless murmur, like the sound of a celebration down in the courthouse square, had kept him awake after that. Each time 40 a car had passed their house his breath had gone tight and sluggish. It was better to stay awake and ready, he had told himself, than to be caught asleep.

"Daddy gone?" Audrey asked softly as she took her place across the table from her brother.

"He's been gone an hour," their mother answered. "*You know what time he has to be at the mine.*"

"She means, did he go to work today?" John said. His voice had risen impatiently. He met his mother's stout[4] gaze in a staring contest, trying to make her admit by at least some flicker of expression that today was different from any other 50 day. "I thought he might be down at Reverend Specker's," John

resentment
(rĭ-zĕnt´mənt) *n.* If you feel *resentment,* you feel anger or irritation.

---
[4] **stout** (stout): bold, brave, determined.

Strategies for Annotation ✎ 🗐 Annotate it!

Determine Meanings: Mood
RL 4

Have students use their eBook annotation tools to analyze the text. Share these strategies for guided or independent analysis:

- Highlight in yellow words or phrases that create mood.
- If the mood changes from one scene to the next, use a different color of highlighting.
- In a note, tell what mood the highlighted text creates.

> "She means, did he go to work today?" John said. His voice had risen impatiently. He met his mother's stout gaze in a staring contest, trying to make her admit by at least some flick[ ] expression that today was different from any other day
>
> mood is tense, suspenseful

said. "Cal's father and Vonnie's and some of the others are going to be there to wait and see."

Maybe his mother smiled then. If so, the smile was so faint that he could not be sure. "You know your father isn't much of a hand for waiting," she said. "Eat. It's a quarter past eight."

As he spooned the warm oatmeal into his mouth he heard the rain crow calling again from the trees beyond the railroad embankment. He had heard it since the first light came before dawn, and he had thought, Maybe the bird knows it's going to rain, after all. He hoped it would. *They won't come out in the rain,* he had thought. Not so many of them, at least. He could wear a raincoat. A raincoat might help him feel more protected on the walk to school. It would be a sort of disguise, at least.

But since dawn the sun had lain across the green Kentucky trees and the roofs of town like a clean, hard fire. The sky was as clear as fresh-washed window glass. The rain crow was wrong about the weather. And still, John thought, its **lamenting**, repeated call must mean something.

His mother and Audrey were talking about the groceries she was to bring when she came home from school at lunch time. A five-pound bag of sugar, a fresh pineapple, a pound of butter . . .

"Listen!" John said. Downtown the sound of a siren had begun. A volley of automobile horns broke around it as if they meant to drown it out. "*Listen* to them."

"It's only the National Guard, I expect," his mother said calmly. "They came in early this morning before light. And it may be some foolish kids honking at them, the way they would. Audrey, if Henry doesn't have a good-looking roast, why then let it go, and I'll walk out to Weaver's this afternoon and get one there. I wanted to have something a little bit special for our dinner tonight."

So . . . John thought . . . she wasn't asleep last night either. Someone had come **stealthily** to the house to bring his parents word about the National Guard. That meant they knew about the others who had come into town, too. Maybe all through the night there had been a swift passage of messengers through the neighborhood and a whispering of information that his mother meant to keep from him. Your folks told you, he reflected bitterly, that nothing is better than knowing. Knowing whatever there is in this world to be known. That

lament
(lə-mĕnt´) *v.* If you *lament*, you are wailing or crying as a way of expressing grief.

stealthily
(stĕl´thə-lē) *adv.* To do something *stealthily* means doing it quietly and secretly so no one notices.

APPLYING ACADEMIC VOCABULARY

achieve	outcome	principle

THINK-PAIR-SHARE Have pairs answer and discuss the questions below. Encourage them to include the academic vocabulary words *achieve, outcome,* and *principle* in their responses. Let volunteers share their responses with the class.

- What does John hope to **achieve** by insisting that Audrey stay home?
- Do such details as honking horns and crowds of people affect your expectation about the **outcome** of the morning's events?
- What **principles** guide the actions of John and Audrey's parents?

TEACH

CLOSE READ

Language Conventions: Varying Sentence Patterns
L 3a
(LINES 53–55)

Explain to students that good writers create dialogue that sounds realistic. They know that people don't always speak in complete sentences.

D **ASK STUDENTS** to notice the variety of sentence patterns in lines 53–55. Have them explain the effect of the mother's speech. (*The short sentence "Eat" seems natural and realistic; it's a normal way for parents to give reminders to children.*)

Determine Meanings: Mood (LINES 56–69)
RL 1, RL 4

Direct students' attention to John's internal thoughts as he listens to the "rain crow" and thinks about its meaning.

E **CITE TEXT EVIDENCE** Ask students to describe how John's thoughts about rain affect the mood in lines 56–69. Have students cite words or phrases that create the mood they describe. (*Even though the sun is out, John's wish for rain creates an anxious, somber mood; his thought that "Not so many of them" would come out in the rain and that he could use a raincoat as "a sort of disguise" intensify this mood.*)

CRITICAL VOCABULARY

lament: The crow's call seems to contradict the clear weather, and John thinks it means something.

ASK STUDENTS what weather would fit with a lamenting bird's cry. Ask what else John might be connecting to the bird's cry. (*Possible responses: A rainy day would fit better with a lamenting bird's cry. John may think that the crow's cry has to do with where he has to go and what might happen there.*)

stealthily: John knows his mother received new information from someone during the night.

ASK STUDENTS to describe how someone would enter a house stealthily. (*quietly, perhaps tiptoeing, knocking only lightly on the door, and whispering*)

Determine Meanings: RL 1,
RL 4
Mood (LINES 101–113)

 CITE TEXT EVIDENCE Have students tell what the mood is in lines 101–113 and what words and phrases create it. *(The words and phrases "sheltering caress," "Carefully," and "hug" create a warm, affectionate mood, though the undercurrent of tension is still there.)*

> **CRITICAL VOCABULARY**
>
> **linger**: The mother gives her daughter a lingering touch.
>
> **ASK STUDENTS** to explain how a parent who gives a child a "lingering touch" probably feels. *(The parent loves the child or perhaps is trying to comfort the child.)*

Describe Stories: RL 1,
RL 3,
RL 5
Flashback (LINES 122–142)

Explain to students that in these two paragraphs, the author presents a **flashback,** or an interruption in the current action of the story, to tell about something that took place earlier.

CITE TEXT EVIDENCE Ask students to reread lines 122–142 and identify how the flashback begins and ends, citing words and phrases that support this. *("He remembered something else from the time he was little" introduces the flashback. "Again he heard the siren and the hooting . . ." calls the character [and readers] back into the current action.)*

ASK STUDENTS to tell how this flashback develops John's character and fits into the overall structure of the story. *(Readers find out that John is self-aware and caring; his anger is caused by worry and tension. This flashback takes readers out of the present action to show something about John; it moves the story forward by helping readers understand John's actions.)*

was why you had to be one of the half dozen kids out of some nine hundred colored of school age who were going today to start classes at Joseph P. Gilmore High instead of Webster. Knowing and learning the truth were worth so much they said—and then left it to the hooting rain crow to tell you that things were worse than everybody had hoped.

100   Something had gone wrong, bad enough wrong so the National Guard had to be called out.

"It's eight twenty-five," his mother said. "Did you get that snap sewed on right, Audrey?" As her experienced fingers examined the shoulder of Audrey's dress they **lingered** a moment in an involuntary, sheltering caress. "It's all arranged," she told her children, "how you'll walk down to the Baptist Church and meet the others there. You know there'll be Reverend Chader, Reverend Smith, and Mr. Hall to go with you. It may be that the white ministers will go with you, or they may be waiting at school. We don't know. But now you
110   be sure, don't you go farther than the Baptist Church alone." Carefully she lifted her hand clear of Audrey's shoulder. John thought, Why doesn't she hug her if that's what she wants to do?

> **linger**
> (lĭng′gər) *v.* To *linger* means to leave slowly and reluctantly, not wanting to go.

> ❝ **Something had gone wrong,
> bad enough wrong so the
> National Guard had to be called out.** ❞

He pushed away from the table and went out on the front porch. The dazzling sunlight lay shadowless on the street that swept down toward the Baptist Church at the edge of the colored section. The street seemed awfully long this morning, the way it had looked when he was little. A chicken was clucking contentedly behind their neighbor's house, feeling
120   the warmth, settling itself into the sun-warmed dust. Lucky chicken.

He blinked at the sun's glare on the concrete steps leading down from the porch. He remembered something else from the time he was little. Once he had kicked Audrey's doll buggy down these same steps. He had done it out of meanness—for some silly reason he had been mad at her. But as soon as the buggy had started to bump down, he had understood how terrible it was not to be able to run after it and stop it. It had

WHEN STUDENTS STRUGGLE . . .

To guide students' analysis and comprehension of the story's mood, have students work in pairs to fill out a chart like the one shown for each of the six scenes (beginning roughly at lines 1, 30, 70, 114, 148, and 179) in the story. Remind students that authors create mood through the words they use to describe characters' actions and thoughts, as well as the setting. Students should ask themselves how the words make them feel in each scene.

 LEVEL UP TUTORIAL For additional support, assign the following *Level Up* tutorial: **Setting and Mood.**

gathered speed at each step and when it hit the sidewalk it had
spilled over. Audrey's doll had smashed into sharp little pieces
on the sidewalk below. His mother had come out of the house
to find him crying harder than Audrey. "Now you know that
when something gets out of your hands it is in the Devil's
hands," his mother had explained to him. Did she expect him
to forget—now—that that was always the way things went to
smash when they got out of hand? Again he heard the siren
and the hooting, mocking horns from the center of town.
Didn't his mother think *they* could get out of hand?

He closed his eyes and seemed to see something like a doll
buggy bump down long steps like those at Joseph P. Gilmore
High, and it seemed to him that it was not a doll that was
riding down to be smashed.

He made up his mind then. He would go today, because
he had said he would. Therefore he had to. But he wouldn't
go unless Audrey stayed home. That was going to be his
condition. His bargaining looked perfect. He would trade
them one for one.

His mother and Audrey came together onto the porch. His
mother said, "My stars, I forgot to give you the money for the
groceries." She let the screen door bang as she went swiftly
back into the house.

As soon as they were alone, he took Audrey's bare arm
in his hand and pinched hard. "You gotta stay home," he
whispered. "Don't you know there's thousands of people down
there? Didn't you hear them coming in all night long? You
slept, didn't you? All right. You can hear them now. Tell her
you're sick. She won't expect you to go if you're sick. I'll knock
you down, I'll smash you if you don't tell her that." He bared
his teeth and twisted his nails into the skin of her arm. "Hear
them horns," he hissed.

He forced her halfway to her knees with the strength of
his fear and rage. They swayed there, locked for a minute. Her
knee dropped to the porch floor. She lowered her eyes. He
thought he had won.

But she was saying something and in spite of himself he
listened to her almost whispered refusal. "Don't you know
anything? Don't you know it's harder for them than us? Don't
you know Daddy didn't go to the mine this morning? They
laid him off on account of us. They told him not to come if
we went to school."

The First Day of School **275**

Action / Setting	Words That Suggest Mood	Explanation of Mood
Lines 1–29: *John and his* *mother in kitchen*	*rich, reflections* *jabbed* *gracious . . . morning light*	*seems peaceful* *"jabbed" creates tension*

CLOSE READ

Determine Meanings: Mood (LINES 143–164)

RL 1,
RL 4

Point out to students that the mood shifts in these
paragraphs.

 CITE TEXT EVIDENCE Ask students to identify
the mood shift and to tell what words or phrases
create the mood. *(In lines 143–147, the mood is one of
certainty. John "made up his mind"; "He would go . . .
because he had said he would . . . he had to." In lines
148–151, the mood is slightly suspended as everyday
details take over. But then, in lines 152–164, John
"pinched hard," threatens to "knock you down" and
"smash you." He has "bared teeth" and "fear and rage."
All of this leads to a fearful and threatening mood.)*

Make Inferences

RL 1

(LINES 165–170)

Point out to students that, up until now, Audrey has
been a calm, quiet presence in the story. That changes
in this paragraph.

J **CITE TEXT EVIDENCE** Ask students to make
inferences about Audrey and about the situation
she and John seem to be in. Tell them to support
their inferences with text evidence. *(Audrey reveals
information that John doesn't have. Readers may infer
that she has overheard her parents talking or perhaps
that she simply better understands what was said than
John does. Readers may also infer that Audrey has not
shared information with him out of a desire to protect
him or shield him from unpleasantness.)*

English Language Support

Make sure students understand what
lines 165–170 reveal.

- What has happened to Daddy as a result of his
  children's impending actions? *(He has lost his job.)*
- What does this reveal about Daddy's character?
  (He will stand up for what is right.)
- Why has Audrey decided to share this
  information with John? *(to give him courage; to
  show how important it is that they do their part)*

Describe Stories: RL 1,
Character (LINES 171–205)   RL 3

Explain to students that line 171 marks a turning point for John and Audrey in the story.

Ⓚ ASK STUDENTS to describe the roles that John and Audrey have played up until now. Then, have them analyze the changes that occur in lines 171–205 and tell what they reveal about the characters. (*Before this point, John seemed the dominant, decision-making sibling; Audrey remained quiet. After she accuses John of being a coward, Audrey appears serene, poised, and in charge.*)

> #### CRITICAL VOCABULARY
>
> **serene**: Audrey stands up after John lets go of her, just as their mother re-enters the scene.
>
> **poise**: Audrey continues to show that she is calm and collected.
>
> **ASK STUDENTS** to explain how Audrey shows her serenity. (*She gives no hint that she and John have just been arguing.*) Ask, "How does the word *poise* apply to Audrey?" (*Audrey first appears "fresh and cool," and speaks "softly." She remains calm, polite, and determined to face whatever happens at school.*)

COLLABORATIVE DISCUSSION Have each group make a four-column chart and list each character's actions and reactions to the events of the day. Then discuss how John and Audrey were probably greeted when they arrived at school. Have students describe how people could make them feel safe and welcome when they arrived at school.

ASK STUDENTS to share any questions they generated in the course of reading and discussing the selection.

English Language Support

Listen Actively Remind students that active listening involves paying attention to important points and asking questions. During the Collaborative Discussion, have students note two new or interesting ideas. After the discussion, ask them to share the ideas they noted and explain why each is important.

Uncertainly he relaxed his grip. "How do you know all that?"

"I listen," she said. Her eyes lit with a sudden spark that seemed to come from their absolute brown depths. "But I don't let on all I know the way you do. I'm not a . . ." Her last word sunk so low that he could not exactly hear it. But if his ear missed it, his understanding caught it. He knew she had said "coward."

180   He let her get up then. She was standing beside him, **serene** and prim when their mother came out on the porch again.

"Here, child," their mother said to Audrey, counting the dollar bills into her hand. "There's six, and I guess it will be all right if you have some left if you and Brother get yourselves a cone to lick on the way home."

John was not looking at his sister then. He was already turning to face the shadowless street, but he heard the unmistakable **poised** amusement of her voice when she said, "Ma, don't you know we're a little too old for that?"

190   "Yes, you are," their mother said. "Seems I had forgotten that."

They were too old to take each other's hand, either, as they went down the steps of their home and into the street. As they turned to the right, facing the sun, they heard the chattering of a tank's tread on the pavement by the school. A voice too distant to be understood bawled a military command. There were horns again and a crescendo[5] of boos.

Behind them they heard their mother call something. It was lost in the general racket.

200   "What?" John called back to her. "What?"

She had followed them out as far as the sidewalk, but not past the gate. As they hesitated to listen, she put her hands to either side of her mouth and called to them the words she had so often used when she let them go away from home.

"Behave yourselves," she said.

serene
(sə-rēn´) *adj.* If you are *serene*, you are calm and unflustered.

poised
(poizd) *adj.* To be *poised* means to be calm and assured, showing balanced feeling and action.

COLLABORATIVE DISCUSSION With a small group, discuss how John, Audrey, and their parents react to and feel about the first day of school, citing text evidence to support your ideas.

---

[5] **crescendo** (krə-shĕn´dō): a slow, gradual increase in volume, intensity, or force.

CONTENT-AREA CONNECTION

Social Studies Many states endured turmoil over the federal desegregation law. Kentucky began school integration in 1956 to great opposition. The governor sent National Guard troops to protect the first African American students enrolled in an all-white high school.

Activity Have students write questions about school desegregation following the 1954 Supreme Court ruling. Form small groups to select a few questions for further research. Have groups prepare summaries of their findings. Then hold a class discussion in which students connect text details with actual circumstances.

Determine Meanings of Words and Phrases

RL 4

The **mood** of a story is the overall atmosphere or feeling that a writer creates for the reader. Mood can be described as cheerful, romantic, somber, peaceful, eerie, and so on. Writers create mood by

- carefully choosing words to describe the setting, characters, and plot
- using imagery that appeals to the five senses to help readers imagine how things look, feel, smell, taste, and sound
- showing what the characters think and how they talk

Using your understanding of these techniques can help you determine the meanings of words and phrases that contribute to the mood of a story. For example, John's mother says, "Eat and be quiet. Audrey's coming, so let's stop this here kind of talk." This dialogue helps the reader identify the mood as somber.

As you analyze "The First Day of School," identify the mood of different scenes, noting the techniques the writer uses to achieve that mood.

Describe Stories: Flashback

RL 3, RL 5

Events in a story are often presented in the order in which they occur. However, sometimes an author will use a **flashback,** which is an interruption of the current action to present events that took place at an earlier time. A flashback provides information that can help readers better understand a character's current situation and experience.

To identify and understand a flashback, ask yourself:

- What words indicate that this event takes place earlier in time?
- What sets the flashback in motion?
- How is the flashback connected to the current situation in the story?
- What have I learned about a character or event from the flashback?

Look for flashbacks as you analyze "The First Day of School."

CLOSE READ

Determine Meanings of Words and Phrases

RL 4

Remind students that writers create **mood,** or the overall atmosphere or feeling of a story, with the words they choose. Share the following examples of descriptive phrases with students, and talk about the mood that each creates. Talk about the subtle differences in the messages of the words' meanings and of their connotations.

- Ken slouched along the [cracked/smooth] pavement.
- Her presence made me think of the [sour/bitter] freshness of a lemon.

As students read and analyze "The First Day of School," remind them to think carefully about the meanings *and* the connotations of the words that Cassill uses.

Describe Stories: Flashback

RL 3, RL 5

Tell students authors include flashbacks for a reason. Students should always ask themselves what a flashback reveals about the characters involved and how it fits into the story's structure. A flashback may also

- provide vital or interesting information about a character
- reveal a character flaw or explain a facet of a character's personality
- foreshadow something that will happen later

Strategies for Annotation ✐ 🖻 *Annotate it!*

Determine Meanings of Words and Phrases

RL 4

Share these strategies for guided or independent analysis:

- Highlight in green words or phrases that reveal the mood of a passage.
- Write a note that identifies the mood these specific word choices create.

the others who had come into town, too. Maybe all through the night there had been a swift passage of messengers through the neighborhood and a whispering of information that his mother meant to keep from him. Your folks told you,

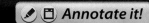

secrecy, stealth, suspense

Analyzing the Text

RL 1, RL 3,
RL 4, RL 5

Possible answers:

1. The words describing the bubbles, including pearl, gleamed, summer, rich, blue, *and* greens, *combine to suggest something beautiful and good. In contrast, the words that describe John's actions are negative, almost violent—*jabbed, disappeared, no mark of where it had been. *The mood of the paragraph changes from pleasant to threatening or ominous.*

2. John envies the chicken's total lack of awareness that something dangerous is afoot and its simple enjoyment of the sun's warmth.

3. John remembers his feeling of powerlessness when he was unable to stop the buggy. His mother's words from that event are important now, too, because John feels powerless again. But the memory pushes John to action, perhaps to feel less powerless; he decides he will go to school but only if Audrey stays home; he wants to protect her now.

4. The author recalls an earlier time when John and Audrey were young or innocent enough to hold each other's hands, yet today they are going to face "the chattering of a tank's tread," which seems especially threatening in light of the innocent childhood image just mentioned.

5. Her attitude seems to have given strength and determination to Audrey, but John's fear makes him annoyed at his mother. The mother is believable because it is normal for parents to try to protect their children from worry.

6. The mood of impending danger, menace, and suspense is still present at the end of the story, but the children's courage, their lack of hesitation, and their mother's strength combine to add a hint of hope and inspiration.

FOR STANDARD ENGLISH LEARNERS

Pronoun Referents As they write their informative essays, remind students to make sure that they use a preposition that shows the accurate relationship between ideas. Use these examples for practice:

- John is worried about what might happen to them [over, at, on] the school when they get there. *(at)*
- Their mother left the money for groceries [to, in, on] the table and then forgot it. *(on)*

Analyzing the Text

RL 1, RL 3,
RL 4, RL 5,
W 2a–b, W 2e–f,
W 9a, W 10

Cite Text Evidence Support your responses with evidence from the text.

1. **Compare** Reread lines 1–7. Compare the effect of the author's word choice in the description of the bubbles and then in the description of John's actions. What is the mood in each of these scenes? How does the mood change?

2. **Infer** Reread lines 114–121. Why does John envy the chicken?

3. **Analyze** Review lines 122–147. What is the connection between what John remembers and what is happening in the story now? Describe what you learn about John and how the flashback moves the plot of the story forward.

4. **Draw Conclusions** Reread lines 192–197. How would you describe the mood in this scene? What words does the author use that help you identify the mood?

5. **Evaluate** John's mother will not acknowledge that the day is different from any other day. How does her attitude affect her children? Do you think she is portrayed realistically? Tell why or why not.

6. **Interpret** How would you describe the mood at the end of the story? How is the mood conveyed?

PERFORMANCE TASK

Writing Activity: Informative Essay
How does John feel about his first day at this new school? Why does he resolve to go only if Audrey stays home?

- Write a one-page essay that explains John's feelings and actions about his first day at school.
- Include your ideas about why he resolves to go to school only if his sister stays home.

- Support your explanation by telling how John responds to events in his past as well as in the present.
- Cite specific examples from the text that help explain your ideas.
- Provide a concluding statement that supports your explanation of John's feelings and tells why his actions are significant.

Assign this performance task.

PERFORMANCE TASK

W 2a, W 2b,
W 2e, W 2f,
W 9a, W 10

Writing Activity: Informative Essay Have students work independently. Ask them to

- pay particular attention to what John learns in the flashback
- use a two-column chart to note events and John's reactions
- include a strong topic sentence, support for ideas, and a concluding statement that sums up the ideas

Critical Vocabulary

L 4a, L 4c, L 6

resentment	lament	stealthily
linger	serene	poised

Practice and Apply Answer these questions.

1. Why might you feel **resentment** toward a sibling who easily masters a sport you struggle to play well?

2. Would you congratulate or comfort a teammate who **laments** a game's outcome? Why?

3. If you moved **stealthily,** how would you describe your behavior?

4. Would you be more likely to **linger** at the end of a dentist appointment or at a school dance? Why?

5. Does a **serene** sky indicate stormy or sunny weather? Why?

6. If someone looked **poised** at a job interview, would that person be feeling calm or nervous? Explain.

Vocabulary Strategy: Using a Thesaurus

To express an idea clearly when you write, you need to use precise words. A thesaurus is one type of reference tool that can help. A **thesaurus** is a reference book of synonyms—words that have nearly the same meaning.

A thesaurus works like a dictionary; you simply look up the word you are interested in. You will find a list of synonyms for the word, and often a list of antonyms, or words with opposite meanings, as well. Many word-processing programs contain an electronic thesaurus tool, and there are thesauruses on the Internet as well. To use an online thesaurus:

- Look for a search box and type your word in it.
- Click on the appropriate onscreen icon (for example, a magnifying glass) and the thesaurus will display the word's definition and any number of synonyms. Antonyms may appear as well.
- You may also be able to click an icon to hear a pronunciation.

Practice and Apply Use a thesaurus to select a synonym for each of the vocabulary words on this page. Then use each synonym in a sentence that shows its meaning, as in this example for *resentment*.

Word	Synonym	Sentence
resentment	animosity	I could feel my opponent's *animosity* after I won our match.

The First Day of School **279**

PRACTICE & APPLY

Critical Vocabulary

L 4a, L 4c, L 6

Possible answers:

1. *You might feel resentment because you are jealous of the sibling's skill and are upset that you do not have that skill.*

2. *You would comfort a lamenting teammate because he or she is expressing disappointment, regret, or sadness.*

3. *You would try to make as little noise as possible; for example, you might tiptoe or whisper.*

4. *You would linger at a school dance; you linger over something because you don't want it to end.*

5. *A serene sky would be sunny; the word means "calm," "unruffled"; there would be no storm clouds or rain.*

6. *The person would be calm; the word means "composed," "in balance."*

Vocabulary Strategy: Using a Thesaurus

Possible responses:

Word	Synonym	Sentence
resentment	*bitterness*	*The bitterness of the rebuke hurt my feelings.*
serene	*peaceful*	*The peaceful cows meandered slowly across the meadow.*
lament	*wail*	*The wail of the distant train whistle made me homesick.*
poised	*composed*	*We tried to look composed and confident in spite of our nervousness.*
stealthily	*furtively*	*The thief moved furtively through the shadows.*
linger	*dawdle*	*We dawdled on the way home, not wanting such a great day to end.*

English Language Support

Use Precise Language Remind students that synonyms are words that have similar but not exactly the same meanings.

- Write these synonyms for *linger* on the board: *delay, wait, trail.* Define any that are unfamiliar to students. Then display this sentence: *He lingered on the corner hoping that Audrey would catch up.* Ask partners to identify the synonym for *linger* that best fits the meaning of the sentence. (*waited*)

- Read aloud the following twice: "John thought that if he lingered over his oatmeal long enough, it would be too late for him to go to school." Have pairs use a thesaurus to find synonyms for *linger* that would fit its meaning in the sentence. (*dawdled, dilly-dallied, hesitated*)

- Assign each pair of students a different Critical Vocabulary word. Have the students look up the thesaurus entry for the word and list the first five synonyms given. Then ask them to explain the meaning of each synonym and choose one that best relates to the term's context in the sentence.

The First Day of School **279**

Language Conventions: Varying Sentence Patterns

L 3a

Tell students that, whether they realize it or not, the texts that are most interesting to read use a variety of sentence patterns. Have students take out whatever books they are reading for pleasure and examine several paragraphs. Begin simply by asking students to choose a paragraph, count the number of words in each sentence, and share their findings. Once you've established that good writing shows sentence variety, return to the chart in the lesson. Guide students to understand the sentence structures in each example.

Possible answers:

1. *complex, changed to simple: John hadn't slept very well. The sounds of car horns and loud voices kept waking him up.*

2. *simple, changed to compound: Audrey came primly down the stairs, and the dress she had chosen looked fresh and cool.*

3. *simple, changed to compound-complex: Their mother called to them as she came onto the porch, and then she followed them down the street.*

 **Assess It Online!**

Online Selection Test
- Download an editable ExamView bank.
- Assign and manage this test online.

Language Conventions: Varying Sentence Patterns

L 3a

Authors use a variety of sentence patterns to make their writing smooth, clear, and interesting to read. A **sentence pattern** refers to how a sentence is structured. Review the sentence patterns and examples shown in the chart.

Sentence Pattern	Description and Example
Simple	one independent clause **She looked fresh and cool in her white dress.**
Compound	two or more independent clauses joined with commas and coordinating conjunctions such as *and, or, but, nor, yet, so* **He heard the tap of heels on the stairs, and his sister came down into the kitchen.**
Complex	one independent clause and one or more subordinate clauses that can be used as nouns or modifiers **He wouldn't go unless Audrey stayed home.**
Compound-Complex	two or more independent clauses and one or more subordinate clauses **As John ate his oatmeal, he heard a crow calling and he heard the sound of trucks.**

Writers pay attention to sentence patterns because the right combination of short and long sentences creates rhythm. In the opening paragraph of "The First Day of School," the author uses a combination of simple, compound, and compound-complex sentences. A rhythm of action and reflection is established, and the reader is immediately engaged.

Reread lines 30–45. Notice the contrast of long and short sections. The longer section engages you with its imagery and provides background and insight into John's character. The short segments of dialogue keep the pace of the story moving swiftly.

Practice and Apply Change the sentence pattern of each sentence or group of sentences. First, identify the original pattern used in each sentence. Then revise, using a different sentence pattern for each item.

1. John hadn't slept very well the night before because the sounds of car horns and loud voices kept waking him up.

2. Audrey came down the stairs. She acted prim. The dress she had chosen looked fresh and cool.

3. Their mother came onto the porch. She called to them. She followed them down the street.

280 Collection 5

English Language Support

Connect Ideas Review the sentence patterns in the chart. Then display lines 192–197 and read the paragraph aloud.

- Help students identify the two simple sentences in the paragraph. Then guide them to underline the subject and verb in each one. (*"A voice too distant to be understood bawled a military command." "There were horns again and a crescendo of boos."*)
- Have partners label the pattern of each sentence in the paragraph and then identify both independent and subordinate clauses. (*The*

first two sentences are complex; the second two sentences are simple. Subordinate clauses: as they went…street; As they turned…sun. Independent clauses: They were too old… hand, either; they heard… school)

- After identifying the sentence patterns in the paragraph, have students combine and rewrite sentences to create one compound sentence and one compound-complex sentence. Let students share their work with a partner.

Analyze Structure: Foreshadowing

RL 1,
RL 3,
RL 5

TEACH

Explain to students that foreshadowing occurs when a writer gives hints about something that will occur later in a story. Foreshadowing is a way to create suspense and to make readers eager to continue reading.

Tell students that authors create foreshadowing in a number of ways. They may

- give the reader direct information by mentioning an upcoming event or explaining a character's plans
- give clues about themes that will be important later
- describe (quietly and subtly) characters' reactions or observations about objects or other characters that might play an important role later
- use changes in weather or mood to hint at good or bad luck to come

Explain that these are only a few of the ways authors might use specific details to create foreshadowing.

PRACTICE AND APPLY

Remind students that readers need to be observant and thoughtful while reading in order to absorb all the clues a writer might leave for them. Explain that they can ask themselves questions such as these to recognize foreshadowing:

- Are there words or phrases about the future?
- Is there a change in the weather, setting, or mood, or a contrast among these that seems important?
- Are there objects or things about the setting that suggest a particular emotion or event?
- Do characters or the narrator see or hear something in the background that might be a hint about something to come later?

Then, display or reread with students the following passages from "The First Day of School." After each one, ask students to identify foreshadowing. Remind them to reread as if they did not know what was coming next.

- Lines 46–52 (*John is tense; mother is calm; today was different*)
- Lines 59–64 (*why wish for rain; rain crow*)
- Lines 77–78 (*why National Guard; mother still calm*)

Remind students that they should pay attention to details as they read, keeping in mind that some of those details may foreshadow events to come.

Determine Meaning: Mood

RL 4

RETEACH

Review the terms *mood* and *imagery*. Remind students that whenever authors use descriptive words to tell about a character's actions, a character's thoughts, or the setting, they are creating an overall atmosphere, or feeling, for readers.

Read aloud the first paragraph of "The First Day of School." Guide students to understand that some of the language creates a peaceful mood, but that John's jabbing motion with his spoon creates tension.

Suggest that students pause periodically as they read and ask themselves questions such as these:

- What overall feeling does this section give me?
- What words are giving me that feeling?

 LEVEL UP TUTORIALS Assign the following *Level Up* tutorial: **Setting and Mood**

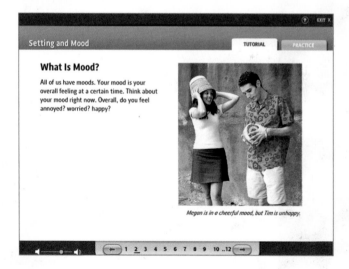

INDEPENDENT READING

Students can apply the skill of identifying mood when they read other fictional selections in Collection 5 or when reading fiction of their own choice. You might have groups of students revisit a novel that they have all read and compare their analyses of the mood in various scenes.

EXEMPLAR

The Road Not Taken

Poem by Robert Frost

Why This Text?

Poetry provides an opportunity to contemplate everyday thoughts and actions, exploring meaning and allowing the reader to see them in a different way. In this classic poem, students will discover everyday meaning through the eyes of an accomplished observer and poet, Robert Frost.

Key Learning Objective: The student will be able to analyze the structure of a poem and how poets use symbols and structure to convey a theme.

RL 1 Cite textual evidence.
RL 2 Determine theme.
RL 4 Determine the meaning of words and phrases.
RL 5 Analyze structure.
RL 10 Read and comprehend poems.
SL 1 Engage effectively in a range of collaborative discussions.
SL 1a Come to discussions prepared.
SL 1b Follow rules for discussions, set goals and deadlines, and define individual roles.
SL 1d Review key ideas and demonstrate understanding of multiple perspectives.

 Text Complexity Rubric

Quantitative Measures	**The Road Not Taken** Lexile: N/A

Levels of Meaning/Purpose

multiple levels of meaning (multiple themes)

Structure

regular stanzas, predictable rhyme scheme

Language Conventionality and Clarity

complex and varied sentence structure

Knowledge Demands

common, everyday experience

Reader/Task Considerations
- Teacher determined
- Vary by individual reader and type of text
- See the Text X-Ray for suggested Reader/Task Considerations.

Qualitative Measures

English Language Support Before teaching, use the Text X-Ray for an overview of the text's complexity. The Text X-Ray and the supports and scaffolds in the Teacher's Edition will help you guide students of different skill levels.

Meaning Making

Language Development

Effective Expression

Content Knowledge

Foundational Skills

Text Complexity: Qualitative Measures

Levels of Meaning/Purpose

multiple levels of meaning (multiple themes)

Help students determine theme in a poem.
- Teacher's Edition side notes, pp. 282, 283
- English Language Support, p. 283
- Determine Theme, p. 283

To reteach how to determine theme, see
- Determine Theme, p. 284a

 Use It! **Level Up Tutorials:** Theme; Symbol

ZOOM IN ON **DETERMINING THEME** Review the definition of **symbol** on page 283. Discuss the **symbolism** of the road, suggesting that it represents the course of one's life. Then have partners complete these sentence frames to help access the poem's **theme:**

- The speaker has a hard time choosing a road because ____. *(The view down one was limited; Both roads are "just as fair.")*
- The speaker finally chooses one road because ____. *(Fewer people have taken it.)*
- The poem's message suggests that ____. *(Possible response: Choosing the less popular course of action can greatly affect one's future— either positively or negatively.)*

Structure

regular stanzas, predictable rhyme scheme

Help students analyze the structure of a poem.
- Teacher's Edition side notes, pp. 281, 282, 283
- English Language Support, p. 281
- Strategies for Annotation, p. 283
- Analyze Structure, p. 283

 Use It! **Interactive Whiteboard Lesson:** Form in Poetry

ZOOM IN ON **ANALYZING RHYTHM** Remind students that poets create **rhythm** by stressing, or emphasizing, some syllables and not others. Explain that these stresses often call attention to ideas that the poet wants to convey.

- Read aloud the last stanza of the poem as students follow along. Have them note the stressed words or syllables that they hear most clearly.
- Read the stanza again as students check their notes. Ask volunteers to list stressed words on the board. *(Stressed syllables include "sigh," "ages," "two roads," "wood," "I," "took," "one," "that," "all.")* Discuss how the words affect the readers' understanding of the poem.

Language Conventionality and Clarity

complex and varied sentence structure

Teach unfamiliar vocabulary in context.

- Applying Academic Vocabulary, p. 282

Support students' discussion of and writing about the poem.

- Teacher's Edition side notes, p. 282
- English Language Support, p. 284
- Performance Task, p. 284

To teach how to determine meaning through imagery, see

- Determine Meaning: Imagery, p. 284a

ZOOM IN ON **DEFINING MULTIPLE MEANING WORDS** Remind students that words often have more than one meaning. Explain that poets select each word carefully, and readers must determine their intended meaning to fully understand the poem.

- Have pairs read the second stanza and look up the definitions of *fair* (line 6) and *wanted* (line 8) in a dictionary.
- Ask them to decide which meaning best fits the context of the poem.
- Let volunteers share their definitions. *(fair: pleasant or attractive; wanted: lacked)*

Knowledge Demands

common, everyday experience

Support English learners' understanding of the poet's background.

- Teacher's Edition Author note, p. 281

ZOOM IN ON **BUILDING LITERARY KNOWLEDGE** Explain that by the time Frost had finished high school, he was set on becoming a poet. Tired of being rejected by American publishers, he moved to England in 1912, and there he achieved success. In 1915 he returned to New England as a recognized poet, and from then on his reputation grew. In 1961 he read a poem at President John F. Kennedy's inauguration.

Suggested Reader/Task Considerations

You might consider the following before assigning this poem to students.

- Do students have the ability to understand the metaphorical meaning of this poem?
- Will the emphasis on analyzing the meter of the poem interfere with students' ability to appreciate reading the poem?

ZOOM IN ON **SUPPORTING COMPREHENSION**

- Conduct a Read Aloud/Think Aloud, pausing to clarify language and to help students interpret the underlying meaning of the speaker's actions and thoughts.
- Read aloud the poem and then discuss its sound and tone. Use these questions to elicit student's ideas: *Would you describe the poem as formal or conversational? Why? Would you describe the rhythm, or beat of the poem, as regular or irregular? Why? What words seem to stand out as you listen to the poem?*

Robert Frost Have students read the background and information about the author. Explain that while living in England Frost developed a great friendship with Edward Thomas, a fellow poet. The two men routinely took long walks through the countryside, with Thomas choosing a path that would allow him to show Frost a rare or special sighting. Then, before the walk was over, Thomas would often fret over what he might have shown Frost had they taken a different path. It was Thomas's behavior during these walks that Frost credited as the inspiration for "The Road Not Taken."

SETTING A PURPOSE Direct students to use the Setting a Purpose prompt to focus their reading. Remind students to write questions as they read.

Analyze Structure (LINES 1–10)   RL 1, RL 4, RL 5

Tell students that **rhyme** is the repetition of sounds at the ends of words, and that the most common type of rhyme in a poem is **end rhyme,** in which rhyming words come at the ends of lines. Explain that a pattern of end rhymes in a poem is called **rhyme scheme.**

Tell students that a rhyme scheme can be identified by assigning a letter to each line in a poem. Lines that rhyme are assigned the same letter to show the form or structure of the poem.

(A) CITE TEXT EVIDENCE Reread lines 1–10 aloud. Ask students to identify examples of rhyme and the rhyme scheme. Then, have students explain the effect of this form on the poem. *(End rhymes: wood, stood, could; both, undergrowth; fair, wear, there; same, claim. The rhyme scheme is abaab; the rhyme scheme creates rhythm and helps give the poem a serious, thought-provoking feel.)*

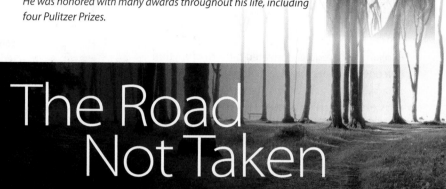

Robert Frost (1874–1963) *is considered one of the outstanding American poets of the twentieth century. Born in San Francisco, California, he moved with his family to New England when he was eleven. His first poem was published in 1894. Frost drew inspiration for much of his poetry from New England life and the countryside where he grew up and lived for most of his adult life. He was honored with many awards throughout his life, including four Pulitzer Prizes.*

The Road Not Taken

Poem by Robert Frost

SETTING A PURPOSE As you read the poem, pay attention to the thoughts and feelings the speaker has about making a choice.

> Two roads diverged[1] in a yellow wood,
> And sorry I could not travel both
> And be one traveler, long I stood
> And looked down one as far as I could
> 5 To where it bent in the undergrowth;
>
> Then took the other, as just as fair,
> And having perhaps the better claim,
> Because it was grassy and wanted wear;
> Though as for that the passing there
> 10 Had worn them really about the same,

(A)

---
[1] **diverged** (dĭ-vûrjd´): branched out; went in different directions.

English Language Support

Improve Reading Fluency Display the poem and help students identify and highlight sets of rhyming words.

- Pronounce each set of rhyming words as students repeat after you. *(wood/stood/could; both/undergrowth; fair/wear/there; claim/same; lay/day/way; black/back; sigh/I/by; hence/difference)*

- Point out which lines have end punctuation and which do not. Remind students to pause only when they see punctuation.

- Read each line aloud and have students repeat it after you. Then have pairs read the poem aloud, alternating stanzas and continuing until fluency is achieved.

> Two roads diverged in a yellow wood,
>
> And sorry I could not travel both
>
> And be one traveler, long I stood
>
> And looked down one as far as I could
>
> To where it bent in the undergrowth;

Analyze Structure
RL 4,
RL 5

(LINES 11–20)

Explain that a regular, repeated pattern of rhythm in a poem is called **meter.** Poets create meter by arranging words in a pattern of stressed and unstressed syllables. Stressed syllables are the parts of a word that are emphasized during normal speech. Unstressed syllables are those that are not emphasized. Reread lines 11–20 aloud.

B ASK STUDENTS to describe the meter, or beat, in the poem and to explain its effect. *(The meter is relatively regular, usually with four stressed syllables, or "beats" per line. Words in the poem such as both, leaves, step, and way are stressed or emphasized, which gives these words extra meaning for the reader.)*

Determine Theme
RL 2,
RL 4

(LINES 16–20)

Explain to students that a **symbol** is a person, a place, an object, or an activity that stands for something beyond itself. For example, the heart is often used as a symbol for love. Poets often use symbols as a way to add deeper meaning to the **theme,** the message they want the poem to have for the reader. Identifying and analyzing the symbols in a poem help the reader understand the poem's meaning.

C ASK STUDENTS what choosing between two roads symbolizes in lines 16–20. *(something the speaker must make a choice between in his life)* Ask students to tell what theme this symbol might suggest. *(Possible responses: not being afraid to take a chance, to try new things; following an individual path, different from most others)*

COLLABORATIVE DISCUSSION Have partners discuss their ideas and evidence about the title of the poem. As part of this discussion, ask them whether or not they think the speaker in the poem is pleased with the choice he or she made and why. Then, have students share their ideas with the larger group.

ASK STUDENTS to share any questions they generated in the course of reading and discussing this selection.

And both that morning equally lay
In leaves no step had trodden² black.
Oh, I kept the first for another day!
Yet knowing how way leads on to way,
15 I doubted if I should ever come back.

I shall be telling this with a sigh
Somewhere ages and ages hence:
Two roads diverged in a wood, and I—
I took the one less traveled by,
20 And that has made all the difference.

COLLABORATIVE DISCUSSION At the end of the poem, the speaker says that choosing the road "less traveled" has "made all the difference." However, the poem is titled "The Road Not Taken." With a partner, discuss why the poet might have titled the poem this way. Support your ideas with evidence from the poem.

(br) © Radius Images/Corbis, (bl) ©Gary Salter/Corbis

² **trodden** (trŏd´n): walked on or trampled.

APPLYING ACADEMIC VOCABULARY

individual	outcome

THINK-PAIR-SHARE Have pairs read and discuss the questions below. Ask them to include the academic vocabulary words *individual* and *outcome* in their responses. Encourage volunteers to share their answers with the class.

- What **individual** choice is the speaker of the poem considering?
- What **outcomes** might result from each choice?

Determine Theme

In a story or poem, the **theme** is the message about life or human nature that the author wants to share. Using a symbol is one way to share a theme. A **symbol** is a person, a place, an object, or an activity that stands for something beyond itself. To identify a poem's theme, keep the following clues in mind:

- The poem's title may suggest what the poem will focus on.
- A poet's use of images often helps to convey a poem's theme.
- Repeated words and phrases tell you how the **speaker,** or voice of the poem, feels.

To determine symbols and their relationship to a theme, look for:

- things, places, or people that the author emphasizes or that seem to have importance
- how the symbols are related to the theme

Look for symbols and how they add to the poet's theme as you analyze "The Road Not Taken."

Analyze Structure

RL 4, RL 5

Rhyme is the repetition of sounds at the ends of words. A pattern of rhymes developed throughout a poem is called a **rhyme scheme.** A rhyme scheme is noted by assigning a letter of the alphabet, beginning with *a*, to each line. Lines that rhyme are given the same letter. The first stanza of "The Road Not Taken" has a rhyme scheme of *abaab*.

Poems often have a regular rhythm, or meter. In poetry, **meter** is the regular pattern of stressed (ˊ) and unstressed (ˇ) syllables in a line. Take a look at the meter in these lines from "The Road Not Taken":

ˇ ˊ ˇ ˊ ˇ ˇ ˊ ˇ ˊ
And both that morning equally lay

ˇ ˊ ˇ ˊ ˇ ˇ ˊ ˇ ˊ
In leaves no step had trodden black.

If you tap your foot while you read the lines aloud, you will hear the regular meter of stressed and unstressed syllables. To analyze rhyme and meter in "The Road Not Taken" and other poems, follow these steps:

- Look for patterns to help you identify the rhyme scheme and meter.
- Consider how the rhymes and meter relate to important ideas in the poem. Do rhymes point out key words? Does the meter create a familiar rhythm?

The Road Not Taken **283**

CLOSE READ

Determine Theme

RL 2, RL 4

Review the information about theme. Then, have students reread the poem. Guide students to identify the poem's main message. Focus on how Frost describes the place where the speaker is standing, the two roads, and the speaker's thoughts and reactions. Then, have students identify symbols in the poem. Discuss the impact each one has on the theme.

English Language Support

Have students in small groups identify important symbols in the poem. Let them take turns explaining what each symbol represents and how it helps convey the poem's message. Encourage them to use these stems to express their analyses:

- One important symbol is ___.
- This symbol represents ____.
- It helps readers understand that ____.

Analyze Structure

RL 4, RL 5

Review the information about rhyme and meter. Guide students in analyzing these elements, and help them understand how they contribute to the meaning of the poem and the quiet feeling of reflection that the poem conveys.

Then, have students reread the poem aloud. Have them list words and phrases emphasized by the rhythm and describe how they relate to key ideas.

Strategies for Annotation ✏ 🖥 *Annotate it!*

Analyze Structure

RL 4, RL 5

Have students use their eBook annotation tools to identify the meter of "The Road Not Taken." Ask students to do the following:

- Highlight in yellow words or word parts that are stressed.
- Highlight in green words or word parts that are unstressed.
- On a note, identify how the meter impacts meaning.

Two roads diverged in a yellow wood,

And sorry I could not travel both

And be one traveler, long I stood

And looked down one as far as I could

To where it bent in the undergrowth;

the meter suggests the pace of walking

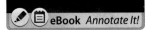
PRACTICE & APPLY

Analyzing the Text
RL 1, RL 2,
RL 4, RL 5,
RL 10

Possible answers:

1. *The yellow wood might indicate that it is autumn, when the leaves of trees turn yellow and red. As autumn leads to winter, the yellow wood might stand for nearing the end of something, such as one's youth.*

2. *The word* Road *in the title symbolizes a choice. The woods symbolize an obstacle or problem. I figured this out from the way the speaker compares both roads in the same way you would evaluate a solution.*

3. *The meter creates a rhythm similar to walking. The words equally, another day, way, and doubted are emphasized by stressed syllables and express important ideas.*

4. *A sigh can suggest regret or relief; the speaker either questions or reaffirms the decision.*

5. *There are times when you must make a choice. People are able to make decisions that shape the course of their lives. Students may say that the most important theme is that people can shape their destiny because the last line of the poem is "And that has made all the difference."*

English Language Support

Exchange Information and Ideas Adapt the collection opener strategy, Socratic Seminar, to help students prepare for and conduct their collaborative discussions.

- *First,* have students review the two texts and annotate details about each character's decision. Ask them to note what the choices reveal about Audrey and the speaker, how their decisions contribute to the theme, and how their decisions are similar or different.

- *Then,* explain that students should not only answer questions, but also respond to what is said and build on each other's ideas. They are free to take sides in the discussion, to persuade each other, and to ask additional follow-up questions. Remind them to use evidence from the text to support their ideas.

- *Next,* begin the discussion by asking how Audrey's decision is similar to or different from the one made by Frost's speaker. Encourage students to include ideas they note and to relate the characters' experiences to their own.

- *Finally,* have groups write summaries of their discussion and the conclusions they've drawn. Then let them share and evaluate their responses to the discussions, describing their own participation as well as their goals for future seminars.

Analyzing the Text
RL 1, RL 2, RL 4,
RL 5, RL 10,
SL 1a–b, SL 1d

> *Cite Text Evidence* Support your responses with evidence from the text.

1. **Infer** In line 1, the speaker describes an instance where "Two roads diverged in a yellow wood." What might "yellow wood" describe in nature, and what might the phrase be a symbol for?

2. **Interpret** Review the title of the poem and lines 1–10. What does the word "Road" symbolize in the title? What do the woods symbolize? Explain what helped you determine what the symbols mean.

3. **Analyze** Read aloud lines 11–15, tapping your foot with each stressed syllable. What physical activity does the meter remind you of? What words emphasized by stressed syllables express important ideas?

4. **Draw Conclusions** Review lines 16–20. The poet rhymes *sigh* with *I* and *less travelled by*. What conclusions can you draw about the speaker's attitude or feelings from the use of these rhyming words?

5. **Analyze** What themes do you find in the poem? Explain which theme you think is most important.

PERFORMANCE TASK

Speaking Activity: Collaborative Discussion With a small group, compare and contrast the poet's choice in "The Road Not Taken" with Audrey's choice in "The First Day of School."

- Discuss what each decision tells about the speaker in the poem and the character in the story. Think about instances in each text that support the choices they make.

- Explain how the characters' decisions contribute to the theme of each selection.

- Make sure that everyone in the group knows to be prepared for the discussion and when it will take place.

- On your own, review the texts and take notes to prepare thoughts and ideas you will bring to the discussion.

- Be sure your ideas are focused on the topic and are supported by evidence from the texts.

- During the discussion, work as a group to share your ideas and build on those of others in a collaborative way.

- Ask one person to record the group's ideas. Work together to create a summary of the discussion to share with others.

Assign this performance task.

PERFORMANCE TASK
SL 1a, SL 1b,
SL 1d

Speaking Activity: Collaborative Discussion Have students work independently to prepare for the group discussion. As students compare and contrast the choices made by the poet and the character, have them record their ideas and information on a comparison chart. Students can use the chart as a guide for their discussion. Remind students to follow the rules for discussion and define roles as needed.

INTERACTIVE WHITEBOARD LESSON
Determine Meaning: Imagery

RL 4

TEACH

Explain to students that **imagery** consists of words and phrases that appeal to a reader's five senses. Tell them that sensory details describe how things look, feel, smell, sound, and taste. This use of imagery helps readers imagine what an author or poet is describing.

As you go through the Share What You Know and Learn the Skill sections of the Interactive Whiteboard Lesson, you may want to use "The Road Not Taken" as an example. As students analyze imagery, focus on these steps:

- **Step 1: Identify Sensory Language** What does the writer want you to see or hear? Can you imagine the smell or feel of something in the poem?
- **Step 2: Analyze the Meaning** Think about what you felt and imagined as you read the text. What is the mood of the poem? Which words and phrases help create that mood?

Next, work through the Practice & Apply sections of the lesson, focusing on the section on poetry. Then, have students work as partners or in groups to apply the steps to "The Road Not Taken" or to another poem of your or their choice.

COLLABORATIVE DISCUSSION

After partners or groups have completed their analyses, have them come together and share their work. Ask students to discuss the different kinds of imagery they found and why they found them effective.

Determine Theme

RL 2,
RL 4

RETEACH

Review with students that the **theme** of a poem is the message about life or human nature that a poet communicates to the reader. The theme is often implied rather than directly stated.

Next, remind students that a **symbol** is a person, place, object, or activity that stands for something beyond itself. Review that symbols add deeper levels of meaning to a text.

Work with students to identify the theme of "The Road Not Taken." Review these steps and possible responses:

- **Examine clues in the text**. Look at the title, descriptions, and imagery. What is important in the poem? *(roads, one traveler, steps)*
- **Notice how places or objects are described**. What symbols does the poet use? How does the speaker react to these symbols? *(road, wood, leaves; speaker sees a choice)*
- **Use the clues to infer the theme**. *(In life, we must always make a choice.)*

 LEVEL UP TUTORIALS Assign these *Level Up* tutorials: **Theme; Symbol**

INDEPENDENT READING

Students can apply the skill to another poem of their choice. Have students work with a partner to use the steps for identifying a theme, including discussing symbols that are part of the poem. Have them share their analysis with other students.

*my*SmartPlanner Create lesson plans and access resources online.

ANCHOR TEXT EXEMPLAR

Paul Revere's Ride

Poem by Henry Wadsworth Longfellow

Why This Text?

Poetry provides another way to tell a story, deepening the readers' understanding of events. This lesson explores a classic narrative poem that shows the power of poetry to immortalize a person and an event decades after its occurrence.

Key Learning Objective: The student will be able to analyze the elements of narrative poetry, including the characters, setting, and plot.

For practice and application:

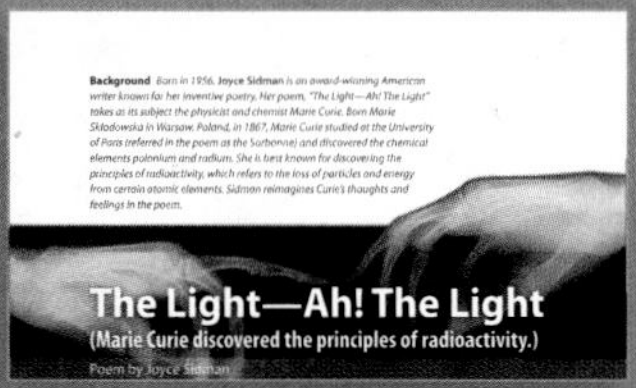

The Light—Ah! The Light
(Marie Curie discovered the principles of radioactivity.)

Close Reader selection
"The Light—Ah! The Light"
Poem by Joyce Sidman

RL 1 Cite textual evidence.
RL 2 Determine a theme.
RL 3 Describe story elements.
RL 4 Determine the meaning of words and phrases.
RL 5 Analyze structure.
RL 7 Compare and contrast reading a poem to listening to the text.
RL 9 Compare and contrast two authors' presentations of the same event.
W 2 Write explanatory texts.
W 2a Introduce a topic; organize ideas.
W 2b Develop the topic.
W 2c Use appropriate transitions.
W 2d Use precise language.
W 2e Establish and maintain a formal style.
W 2f Provide a concluding statement.
W 4 Produce clear and coherent writing.
W 9 Draw evidence from literary texts to support analysis.
W 10 Write routinely.
SL 1 Engage effectively in discussions.

Text Complexity Rubric

Quantitative Measures	**Paul Revere's Ride** Lexile: N/A
Qualitative Measures	Levels of Meaning/Purpose single level of complex meaning
	Structure regular stanzas with some liberties taken
	Language Conventionality and Clarity increased unfamiliar language
	Knowledge Demands increased amount of cultural and literary knowledge useful
Reader/Task Considerations	• Teacher determined • Vary by individual reader and type of text • See the Text X-Ray for suggested Reader/Task Considerations.

English Language Support

Before teaching, use the Text X-Ray for an overview of the text's complexity. The Text X-Ray and the supports and scaffolds in the Teacher's Edition will help you guide students of different skill levels.

Meaning Making

Language Development

Effective Expression

Content Knowledge

Foundational Skills

Text Complexity: Qualitative Measures

Levels of Meaning/Purpose

single level of complex meaning

Help students analyze the meaning of a narrative poem.

- Teacher's Edition side notes, pp. 286, 287, 288
- English Language Support, pp. 285, 287, 290
- Close Read Screencasts, p. 285

To teach how to compare two versions of a poem, see

- Compare and Contrast Two Versions of a Poem, p. 292a

 Use It! Interactive Whiteboard Lesson: Comparing Texts

ZOOM IN ON **ANALYZING NARRATIVE POETRY** Read aloud lines 73–110 as students follow along in their texts. Help students identify the suspenseful **mood**, or atmosphere, that these lines establish. To show how **imagery** and **figures of speech** help establish this mood, discuss the following questions:

- How does the metaphor in lines 79–80 show the importance of Revere's ride? *(By saying the ride "kindled the land into flame," the poet credits Revere with inspiring revolution.)*
- What figure of speech appears in lines 97–100? What words in these lines create a feeling of dread? *(Personification; Words include "black," "bare," "spectral," "aghast," and "bloody.")*

Have pairs list images that help readers visualize the sights and sounds of Revere's journey.

Structure

regular stanzas with some liberties taken

Help students analyze the structure of a narrative poem.

- Teacher's Edition side notes, pp. 285, 286, 287, 289, 290, 291
- English Language Support, p. 286
- When Students Struggle, p. 289
- Strategies for Annotation, p. 291
- Analyze Structure, p. 291
- Performance Task, p. 292

To reteach how to analyze structure, see

- Analyze Structure: Narrative Poetry, p. 292a

 Use It! Level Up Tutorial: Narrative Poetry

ZOOM IN ON **ANALYZING STRUCTURE** Explain that the action in a narrative poem, as a work of fiction, results from **characters** trying to resolve a **conflict**, or problem.

- Ask pairs to identify the major conflict and the lines that introduce it. *(The British attack the colonists [lines 6–7].)*
- Have them explain how Revere's reaction to the conflict reveals his character. *(His long journey and his willingness to confront danger show that he's determined and brave.)*
- Let pairs join small groups to discuss the conflict's resolution and the message it conveys to readers. *(The colonists rally against the British. Good overcomes tyranny.)*

Language Conventionality and Clarity

increased unfamiliar language

Teach unfamiliar vocabulary in context.

- Applying Academic Vocabulary, p. 287

Help students comprehend the language of the poem and discuss and write about its elements.

- Teacher's Edition side notes, p. 290
- English Language Support, pp. 286, 288, 290, 291, 292
- Speaking and Listening, p. 292

 Examining Syntax

ZOOM IN ON **ANALYZING POETIC LANGUAGE** Point out Longfellow's extensive use of **parallelism**, or the repetition of similar grammatical structures. Direct students' attention to line 10 ("One if by land, and two if by sea") and discuss how the parallelism helps make this line memorable.

- Ask students to reread the poem and to note other examples of parallelism.
- Have partners read their examples aloud and explain how they contribute to the poem's meaning, mood, or rhythm.

Knowledge Demands

increased amount of cultural and literary knowledge useful

Support English learners in understanding the historical context of the poem.

- Teacher's Edition Background note, p. 285

 For more historical background, students can view the video *Paul Revere* in their eBooks.

ZOOM IN ON **BUILDING HISTORICAL UNDERSTANDING** Prior to reading, have students watch the History video "Paul Revere." Review terms used in the film:

- barracks: a building or buildings that house soldiers
- militia: an army made up of citizen volunteers rather than trained soldiers
- Lead a discussion in which students share their ideas about the historical event and its presentation in the video.

Suggested Reader/Task Considerations

You might consider the following before assigning this poem to students.

- Can students set and adhere to a specific purpose for reading that will help them increase their comprehension?
- Will students know enough of the vocabulary to enable them to understand the poem?

ZOOM IN ON **SUPPORTING COMPREHENSION**

- Assign small groups one or more questions from the chart on page 291. Have them review the text to answer the questions.
- List the following words on the board: *belfry* (line 8), *muffled* (line 15), *muster* (line 27), *measured* (line 29), *encampment* (line 43), *bridle* (line 70), *fleet* (line 76), *kindled* (line 80), *gilded weathercock* (line 95). After reading the stanzas that contain these terms, pause to discuss their meanings, using context clues to help define each word.

CLOSE READ

For more context and historical background, students can view the video *Paul Revere* in their eBooks.

Background Have students read the information about the author. Tell students that Paul Revere was a silversmith in the North End section of Boston during the time when the city was struggling against the British tax policies. Revere became an activist, taking part in the Boston Tea Party and later making his famous ride to warn colonists of the approaching British. Although Revere was not the only one to ride that night, Longfellow's poem transformed him into a national folk hero.

SETTING A PURPOSE Direct students to use the Setting a Purpose prompt to focus their reading. Remind students to write questions as they read.

Analyze Structure (LINES 1–14)   RL 1, RL 5

Explain to students that **narrative poetry** is poetry that tells a story, often describing a particular event. Explain that like fiction a narrative poem contains characters, a setting, and a plot.

Ⓐ CITE TEXT EVIDENCE Ask students to reread the first two stanzas (lines 1–14). Have them explain how the beginning of this poem is similar to the beginning of a story. Ask students to support their ideas with evidence from the poem. *(line 1: The speaker of the poem is a third-person narrator; characters, lines 2 and 6: Paul Revere and a friend; setting, lines 2–3: April in '75—must infer the century, so 1775—lines 13–14: Middlesex county; plot, lines 6, 12: The British are about to attack, or "march," and Revere is preparing to warn the colonists—"Ready to ride and spread the alarm")*

English Language Support

Read Closely Display lines 1–30.

- Help volunteers identify and highlight the pronouns.
- Have pairs identify pronouns and antecedents. *(stanza 1: you / children; Who / man; stanza 2: He, his, I / Paul Revere; stanza 3: he / Paul Revere; her / the Somerset; its / hulk; stanza 4: his / Paul Revere's; he / friend; their / grenadiers)*
- Ask students to write and then share sentences that summarize the actions of each character introduced in these lines.

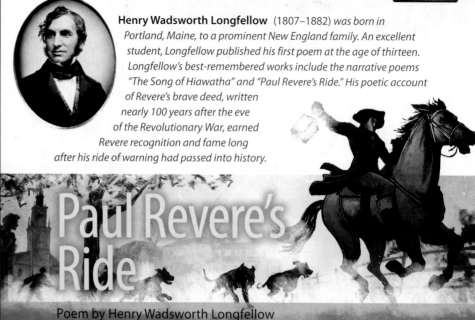

Henry Wadsworth Longfellow (1807–1882) *was born in Portland, Maine, to a prominent New England family. An excellent student, Longfellow published his first poem at the age of thirteen. Longfellow's best-remembered works include the narrative poems "The Song of Hiawatha" and "Paul Revere's Ride." His poetic account of Revere's brave deed, written nearly 100 years after the eve of the Revolutionary War, earned Revere recognition and fame long after his ride of warning had passed into history.*

Paul Revere's Ride

Poem by Henry Wadsworth Longfellow

SETTING A PURPOSE As you read, pay attention to how Longfellow honors Paul Revere in his description of the midnight ride.

> Listen, my children, and you shall hear
> Of the midnight ride of Paul Revere,
> On the eighteenth of April, in Seventy-five;
> Hardly a man is now alive
> 5 Who remembers that famous day and year.
>
> He said to his friend, "If the British march
> By land or sea from the town to-night,
> Hang a lantern aloft in the belfry arch
> Of the North Church tower as a signal light,—
> 10 One if by land, and two if by sea;
> And I on the opposite shore will be,
> Ready to ride and spread the alarm

Ⓐ

(tl) © Bettmann/CORBIS; (m) © Raul Allen Illustration

Paul Revere's Ride **285**

Close Read Screencasts ▶ Close Read

Modeled Discussions

Have students click the *Close Read* icons in their eBooks to access a screencast in which readers discuss and annotate lines 31–41, which describe Paul Revere's friend climbing up into the belfry of the Old North Church.

As a class, view and discuss this video. Then, have students work in pairs to do an independent close read of lines 111–118, in which the battle with the British begins.

Analyze Structure

RL 1, RL 5

(LINES 15–41)

Point out that Paul Revere and his friend go to different places to carry out their plan.

B **CITE TEXT EVIDENCE** Ask students to reread lines 15–41. Have students tell where Paul Revere and his friend are and how they know. *(lines 15–16: Paul Revere is in a boat rowing to the shore of Charlestown, where he sees a British warship; line 31: His friend is in the tower of the Old North Church.)* Have students explain how these 27 lines (two stanzas) fit into the overall structure of the poem. *(These lines move the narrative forward by showing the plan put into motion.)*

English Language Support

Point out "Meanwhile" (line 24) and explain that it shows a time relationship between the friend's actions and those of Paul Revere. Explain that this friend "wanders and watches" at the same time as Revere rows across the bay.

- Have students read lines 25–36 and find the word that signals a time relationship for another action in the sequence. *("Then")*
- Ask volunteers to explain the event that this word introduces. *(The friend climbs the tower.)*

Analyze Meaning:

Mood (LINES 20–30)

RL 1, RL 4

Remind students that authors choose words and phrases to show a particular feeling, or mood, that conveys meaning to the reader.

C **CITE TEXT EVIDENCE** Ask students what mood Longfellow creates in lines 20–23 and what words and phrases create this effect. *(The ship is a "phantom," blocking the moon "like a prison bar," a "black hulk." These words create a mood of tension and danger.)*

D **CITE TEXT EVIDENCE** Have students tell what words create mood in lines 24–30 and what that mood is. *("alley and street," "wanders and watches," "muster of men," "sound of arms," "tramp of feet," "measured tread"; phrases create suspense and anticipation, the approach of danger.)*

Through every Middlesex[1] village and farm,
For the country folk to be up and to arm."

15 Then he said "Good-night!" and with muffled oar
Silently rowed to the Charlestown shore,
Just as the moon rose over the bay,
Where swinging wide at her moorings[2] lay
The *Somerset*, British man-of-war;[3]
20 A phantom ship, with each mast and spar[4]
Across the moon like a prison bar,
And a huge black hulk, that was magnified   **C**
By its own reflection in the tide.

Meanwhile, his friend through alley and street
25 Wanders and watches, with eager ears,
Till in the silence around him he hears
The muster of men at the barrack door,   **D**
The sound of arms, and the tramp of feet,
And the measured tread of the grenadiers,[5]
30 Marching down to their boats on the shore.
Then he climbed the tower of the Old North Church,
By the wooden stairs, with stealthy tread,[6]
To the belfry chamber overhead,
And startled the pigeons from their perch
35 On the somber[7] rafters, that round him made
Masses and moving shapes of shade,—
By the trembling ladder, steep and tall,
To the highest window in the wall,
Where he paused to listen and look down
40 A moment on the roofs of the town
And the moonlight flowing over all.

B

[Close Read]

---

[1] **Middlesex:** a county in eastern Massachusetts—the setting of the first battle of the Revolutionary War on April 19, 1775.

[2] **moorings** (mŏŏr´ĭngs): the place where a ship is docked and secured by lines, cables, or anchors.

[3] **man-of-war:** a warship, often a large sailing ship, bearing cannons and other guns.

[4] **spar:** a pole used to support a ship's sails or rigging.

[5] **grenadiers** (grĕn´ə-dîrz´): British foot soldiers of the first regiment of the royal household.

[6] **stealthy tread** (stĕl´thē trĕd): quiet, sneaky footsteps.

[7] **somber** (sŏm´bər): gloomy, dark.

English Language Support

Word Study Explain that a vowel at the end of a syllable is usually pronounced with a long vowel sound. If a syllable ends in a consonant that follows a single vowel, that vowel sound is usually short. Use *si/lent* and *lis/ten* to illustrate this rule.

ASK STUDENTS to sort the words below according to the sounds of the vowels in their first syllable. Then have pairs compare their lists.

bel/fry *(short)*   fa/mous *(long)*   trem/bling *(short)*   mo/ment *(long)*

Beneath, in the churchyard, lay the dead,
In their night encampment on the hill,
Wrapped in silence so deep and still
45 That he could hear, like a sentinel's[8] tread,
The watchful night-wind, as it went
Creeping along from tent to tent,
And seeming to whisper, "All is well!"
A moment only he feels the spell
50 Of the place and the hour, and the secret dread
Of the lonely belfry and the dead;
For suddenly all his thoughts are bent
On a shadowy something far away,
Where the river widens to meet the bay,—
55 A line of black that bends and floats
On the rising tide like a bridge of boats.

Meanwhile, impatient to mount and ride,
Booted and spurred, with a heavy stride
On the opposite shore walked Paul Revere.
60 Now he patted his horse's side,
Now he gazed at the landscape far and near,
Then, impetuous,[9] stamped the earth,
And turned and tightened his saddle girth;[10]
But mostly he watched with eager search
65 The belfry tower of the Old North Church,
As it rose above the graves on the hill,
Lonely and spectral[11] and somber and still.
And lo! as he looks, on the belfry's height
A glimmer, and then a gleam of light!
70 He springs to the saddle, the bridle he turns,
But lingers and gazes, till full on his sight
A second lamp in the belfry burns.

A hurry of hoofs in a village street,
A shape in the moonlight, a bulk in the dark,
75 And beneath, from the pebbles, in passing, a spark
Struck out by a steed flying fearless and fleet;
That was all! And yet, through the gloom and the light,

---

[8] **sentinel** (sĕn´tə-nəl): a guard or sentry.
[9] **impetuous** (ĭm-pĕch´o͞o-əs): acting suddenly, on impulse.
[10] **saddle girth:** the strap attaching a saddle to a horse's body.
[11] **spectral** (spĕk´trəl): ghostly.

Paul Revere's Ride **287**

APPLYING ACADEMIC VOCABULARY

achieve	principle

THINK-PAIR-SHARE Have students review the following questions and then discuss them with a partner. Encourage them to include the academic vocabulary words *achieve* and *principle* in their responses. Ask volunteers to share their responses with the class.

- How did Paul Revere and his friend **achieve** their mission?
- What **principles** led Revere to take action against the British? What text examples support your view?

CLOSE READ

Analyze Structure
(LINES 42–56)

RL 1,
RL 5

Point out that here Longfellow continues his description of Revere's friend in the tower of the Old North Church.

E CITE TEXT EVIDENCE Ask students what effect lines 42–56 have on the reader and how they fit into the overall structure of the poem. *(The lines show what Revere's friend sees, hears, and feels; "lay the dead," "secret dread," and "lonely belfry" build suspense. The line "For suddenly all his thoughts are bent" turns the focus back to the British ships. These lines briefly slow the action to create tension and anticipation.)*

Describe Stories:
Plot (LINES 64–72)

RL 1,
RL 3

Explain to students that here Longfellow describes Revere waiting and watching.

F CITE TEXT EVIDENCE Ask students to tell what Revere watches in lines 64–72 and what he eventually sees. Have them use text evidence to paraphrase events in the lines. *(Revere watches the church tower [lines 64–65] and sees a light [line 69]. He mounts his horse and waits. When a second light appears [lines 70–72], he knows the British will come by sea [line 10]. Now he can spread the alarm.)*

English Language Support

Read Closely Read aloud lines 73–77. Explain that they describe how Revere's journey begins.

- Ask students what an onlooker would hear and see. *(the sound of a trotting horse; the sight of a shape moving in darkness and sparks from the horse's hooves)*
- Have them describe the mood these images create. *(These lines create a mood of furtive secrecy; Revere does not want anyone to know what he is doing for fear he might be caught.)*
- Ask, "What idea does the exclamation point emphasize?" *(that Revere's movements are nearly undetectable)*

Paul Revere's Ride **287**

Compare and Contrast: Stories and Poems

RL 1, RL 9

Have students reread lines 1–77 and then study the illustrations. Discuss what each illustration portrays in the poem, asking students to identify story elements such as characters, setting, and plot events portrayed in the illustrations.

ASK STUDENTS how these illustrations convey the idea that the "fate of a nation was riding that night" (line 78). *(Possible response: They convey a sense of urgency and danger.)*

CITE TEXT EVIDENCE Ask students to tell how these illustrations and the poem they portray compare to stories they have read in general or, more specifically, to historical stories and narratives they know. Ask students to compare and contrast how those stories do and do not seem similar to this narrative poem and how the illustrations contribute to their ideas. Have students cite evidence from the text and illustrations to support their ideas.

English Language Support

Provide these sentence frames to help students express similarities and differences between works:

- One difference between the poem and the story is _____.
- An example that shows this difference is _____.
- One similarity between the poem and the story is _____.
- An example of this similarity is _____.

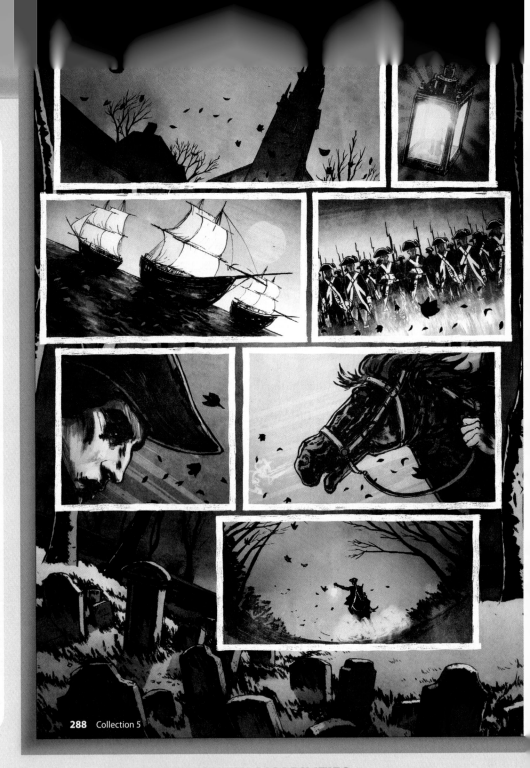

FOR STUDENTS WITH DISABILITIES

Students may have difficulty seeing text on a whiteboard or in small-print format. To increase accessibility, use the following strategies:

- Always read aloud information that is displayed.
- Avoid colored backgrounds that decrease the contrast.
- Provide text in a larger point size, such as 16 or 18.
- Use simple, uncomplicated fonts.
- Leave ample space between lines of text.

The fate of a nation was riding that night;
And the spark struck out by that steed, in his flight,
80 Kindled the land into flame with its heat.
He has left the village and mounted the steep,
And beneath him, tranquil and broad and deep,
 Is the Mystic,[12] meeting the ocean tides;
And under the alders[13] that skirt its edge,
85 Now soft on the sand, now loud on the ledge,
Is heard the tramp of his steed as he rides.

It was twelve by the village clock,
When he crossed the bridge into Medford town.
He heard the crowing of the cock,
90 And the barking of the farmer's dog,
And felt the damp of the river fog,
That rises after the sun goes down.

It was one by the village clock,
When he galloped into Lexington.
95 He saw the gilded weathercock
Swim in the moonlight as he passed,
And the meeting-house windows, black and bare,
Gaze at him with a spectral glare,
As if they already stood aghast[14]
100 At the bloody work they would look upon.

It was two by the village clock,
When he came to the bridge in Concord town.
He heard the bleating of the flock,
And the twitter of birds among the trees,
105 And felt the breath of the morning breeze
Blowing over the meadow brown.
And one was safe and asleep in his bed
Who at the bridge would be first to fall,
Who that day would be lying dead,
110 Pierced by a British musket ball.

---

[12] **Mystic:** a short river flowing into Boston Harbor.
[13] **alder** (ôl´dər): tree of the birch family.
[14] **aghast** (ə-găst´): terrified, shocked.

Paul Revere's Ride **289**

CLOSE READ

Analyze Structure
RL 1,
RL 3,
RL 5
(LINES 78–110)

Explain that rhyme contributes to a poem's rhythm, feel, and structure. Reread lines 78–86 aloud.

G **ASK STUDENTS** to explain the effect of the rhyming words. (*They emphasize ideas:* night / flight, edge / ledge, *and* rides / tides *stress the setting, the fast pace, and the distance Revere travels. These words hold the reader's attention and maintain excitement.*)

Point out that lines 78–110 describe Revere's ride. This is the **climax** of the poem, its point of greatest interest. Explain that as Longfellow describes these events he uses **foreshadowing,** a technique that hints at future events.

H **CITE TEXT EVIDENCE** Have students explain how Longfellow structures the climax of the poem, citing specific stanzas that support their ideas. (*The structure is in time order, starting with the first stanza on page 289. The next three stanzas describe successive towns on Revere's ride—Medford, Lexington, and Concord.*)

I **CITE TEXT EVIDENCE** Have students explain how lines 97–100 fit into the structure of the poem. (*They hint at the battle that will eventually take place in Lexington; they foreshadow future events.*)

 Text in FOCUS English Language Support

Examining Syntax (LINE 106)

Have students view the **Text in Focus** video on this page of their eBook to examine the poet's use of inverted syntax. Then have students use **Text in Focus Practice** to apply what they have learned.

WHEN STUDENTS STRUGGLE . . .

Students who have difficulty following the sequence of events may find it helpful to record the events on a graphic organizer such as a flow chart.

> Paul Revere and a friend plan to warn colonists about the British.

> Revere's friend watches for the British from the Old North Church. Revere rows to Charlestown to get ready to ride.

> (Students continue to list events.)

LEVEL UP TUTORIALS For additional support, assign the following *Level Up* tutorial: **Narrative Poetry.**

TEACH

CLOSE READ

Analyze Structure

**RL 3,
RL 5**

(LINES 111–130)

Explain to students that lines 111–118 are the falling action and resolution of the narrative's plot.

(J) ASK STUDENTS what Longfellow describes in lines 111–118. *(the conflict that resulted from the British attack and began the Revolutionary War)* Ask students why Longfellow begins line 111 with "You know the rest." *(The line "You know the rest" indicates that the story is ending and that the most important part is over.)*

(K) ASK STUDENTS why Longfellow includes lines 119–130. *(Possible responses: Longfellow wanted the focus to be on Revere's ride and its historical importance; he uses these lines to return to the ride and summarize its significance for the nation's people far into the future.)*

COLLABORATIVE DISCUSSION Have individuals list their ideas about Longfellow's language and intent before meeting with their partner. Have students share their ideas using their individual lists. Remind students to cite evidence from the text to support their ideas.

ASK STUDENTS to share any questions they generated in the course of reading and discussing this selection.

English Language Support

Analyze Language To prepare students for their discussion, display line 122: "A cry of defiance, and not of fear." Highlight *defiance* and *fear*.

- Discuss the definition of each highlighted word. *(defiance: "bold resistance to authority or force"; fear: "a feeling of anxiety or dread of imminent danger")* Help students understand why the poet presents them as opposites. *(Defiance carries with it a connotation of courage and fighting against injustice. Fear suggests cowering in the face of opposition.)*

- Guide students to understand Longfellow's purpose in this line. Have pairs discuss how this language appeals to American ideals, such as love of freedom, equality, and opposition to tyranny.

You know the rest. In the books you have read
How the British Regulars fired and fled,—
How the farmers gave them ball for ball,
From behind each fence and farmyard wall,
115 Chasing the redcoats down the lane,
Then crossing the fields to emerge again
Under the trees at the turn of the road,
And only pausing to fire and load.

So through the night rode Paul Revere;
120 And so through the night went his cry of alarm
To every Middlesex village and farm,—
A cry of defiance, and not of fear,
A voice in the darkness, a knock at the door,
And a word that shall echo for evermore!
125 For, borne on the night-wind of the Past,
Through all our history, to the last,
In the hour of darkness and peril and need,
The people will waken and listen to hear
The hurrying hoof-beats of that steed,
130 And the midnight message of Paul Revere.

COLLABORATIVE DISCUSSION Review the poem's final stanza. With a partner, discuss how Longfellow appeals to American ideals and virtues. Identify words and phrases from the stanza that support your ideas.

English Language Support

Read Closely Remind students that poets often use unusual word order to enhance rhythm.

- Display lines 119–121 and read them aloud. Help students identify the subjects and verbs; then discuss their positions in the sentence. Guide them to rewrite the sentence in conventional order. *(Paul Revere rode through the night, and his cry of alarm went through the night to every Middlesex village and farm.)*

- Ask students to reread the poem and choose the stanza that they think is most dramatic or powerful. Have them analyze the sentence structure and devices such as repetition in the stanza. Let them read the lines aloud and discuss their analyses in small groups.

Analyze Structure

Poetry that tells a story is called **narrative poetry.** Like a short story, a narrative poem has the following elements:

- one or more **characters** or individuals who take part in the action
- a **setting**—the time and place where the story occurs
- a **plot,** or series of events that center on a conflict faced by a main character or individual

Use the chart that follows to help you analyze narrative poetry elements.

Element	Questions to Ask and Answer
Characters or Individuals	Who takes part in the action? Who is the main character?
	What is the main character like? How would you describe his or her traits? How does he or she respond or change as the story moves on?
Setting	What information or clues tell you where and when the story takes place?
	How is the setting important to the story? What impact, if any, does it have upon the outcome?
Plot	What central conflict or struggle does the main character face?
	What important events shape the story's action?
	How is the conflict resolved?

For example, in "Paul Revere's Ride," lines 1–23 tell you about the setting:

- The action takes place on April 18, 1775.
- The description "Just as the moon rose over the bay" shows that the action takes place at night.

Sometimes narrative poetry may contain a **refrain,** the same word, phrase, or line repeated several times. Poets often use refrains to emphasize a particular word or idea or to establish a mood. A refrain can also help develop a poem's **rhythm,** or beat.

Identify the elements of narrative poetry as you analyze "Paul Revere's Ride."

CLOSE READ

Analyze Structure
RL 5

Help students understand narrative elements. Work with them to answer the questions on the chart about "Paul Revere's Ride." Small groups can work on each element and then report back to the whole group with responses and evidence from the text to support their responses.

Then, have partners reread the poem together. Have them discuss how Longfellow creates rhythm in the poem and how it helps build tension and excitement. Ask students to locate any refrains they can find in the poem. Have partners share their findings with the rest of the class and compare their ideas.

English Language Support

Exchange Information and Ideas Organize five small groups to answer the questions on page 292. Assign one question to each group. After all the groups have finished, let them take turns presenting their answers to the class. Encourage classmates to provide useful feedback.

Strategies for Annotation   ✏️ 🗐 *Annotate it!*

Analyze Structure
RL 5

Share these strategies for guided or independent analysis:

- Highlight in yellow the characters.
- Highlight in green details that describe the setting.
- Highlight in blue important events.
- On a note, write down important ideas from your annotations.

But mostly he watched with eager search / The belfry tower of the Old North Church, / As it rose above the graves on the hill,

Lonely and spectral and somber and still.
And lo! as he looks, on the belfry's height
A glimmer, and then a gleam of light!

Revere sees
the signal.

Analyzing the Text

RL 1, RL 2,
RL 3, RL 4,
RL 5

Possible Answers:

1. *Revere's friend will find out if the British are coming by land or by sea. He will hang a single lantern in the church tower if they are coming by land, or two lanterns if by sea. Once Revere sees the signal, he will ride to neighboring towns to sound the alarm.*

2. *They tell how Revere's partner hears the British soldiers moving and how he climbs to the belfry and sees British boats on the water that confirms what he heard. Sensory details include "the tramp of feet," "the measured tread," "startled the pigeons from their perch," "Masses and moving shapes of shade," "The watchful night-wind," whispering through the churchyard, and lines 55–56.*

3. *Words like "impatient," "a heavy stride," "impetuous," "watched with eager search," and "springs" all help readers see that Revere is a man of action, both careful and ready to get going on his mission. He acts impatiently because he is anxious to warn people of the attack.*

4. *It is quick and insistent; it mimics the action of Revere galloping on his horse on his mission to alert the towns.*

5. *By beginning each stanza with "It was (twelve, one, two) by the village clock," the refrain helps show the passage of time as Revere moves through the towns; it also keeps the action moving forward. Lines 97–100 and 107–110 give a glimpse of the near future—the "bloody work" of the battle to come and lives that will be lost.*

Speaking and Listening

RL 7,
SL 1

Have students listen to and analyze the audio version of "Paul Revere's Ride" in the eBook. Have them compare and contrast what they "see" and "hear" when listening to what they perceived when reading. See Extend and Reteach at the end of this selection for further instruction on comparing two versions of a poem.

English Language Support

Interact and Collaborate Have pairs select the four stanzas they want to analyze. Ask each partner to focus on two stanzas, noting the way in which they advance the plot, and write two paragraphs that develop this analysis. Partners should then combine their paragraphs and work together to write an introduction and conclusion.

✏ 📋 **eBook** *Annotate It!*

Analyzing the Text

RL 1, RL 2, RL 3, RL 4,
RL 5, RL 7, W 2a–f,
W 4, W 9a, W 10, SL 1

Cite Text Evidence Support your responses with evidence from the text.

1. **Summarize** Reread lines 6–14. What is the plan that Paul Revere discusses with his friend? What is the purpose of the plan?

2. **Analyze** Review lines 24–56. Tell what events these lines describe. What are some sensory details that help you imagine the events and settings?

3. **Analyze** Review lines 57–72. What words does the poet use to help you understand Paul Revere's character and how he behaves while he waits for a signal?

4. **Interpret** Read lines 73–86 aloud. Is the rhythm in these lines slow and leisurely, or quick and insistent? How does the rhythm contribute to the action?

5. **Identify Patterns** Review lines 87–110. How does the poet use a refrain to develop plot events? Why do you think he includes the information in lines 97–100 and 107–110? .

Speaking and Listening

Listen to an audio version of "Paul Revere's Ride." How is hearing the speech different than reading it? With a partner or small group, choose a section of the poem. Discuss how the audio version compares to reading the poem on your own.

PERFORMANCE TASK

Writing Activity: Analysis "Paul Revere's Ride" retells an event in American history. Write an essay that analyzes how the individual stanzas fit into the poem's overall structure.

- Choose three or four stanzas.
- Decide how each stanza helps develop the plot. Note the ideas you want to include.
- Take notes about details and information you will include to support your ideas.

- Plan and organize your essay. Draft the ideas you will discuss and details to support them.
- Use a formal writing style.
- Include linking and transition words to show how your ideas are related.
- Use clear, precise language.
- Be sure your introduction and conclusion help readers understand your topic.

Assign this performance task.

PERFORMANCE TASK

W 2a–f, W 4,
W 9, W 10

Writing Activity: Analysis Have students work independently.
Tell students to

- reread the poem before choosing stanzas to write about
- paraphrase each stanza and think about how each one fits into the poem's overall structure
- use a graphic organizer to organize their ideas and evidence

Compare and Contrast
Two Versions of a Poem

RL 7

TEACH

Audio Clip: in eBook

Tell students that hearing a poem read aloud helps deepen their understanding and enjoyment of the poem. Have students listen closely to the audio version of "Paul Revere's Ride," asking them to pay attention to the following:

- **Tone,** or the attitude of the speaker of the poem, such as angry, sad, serious, or humorous
- **Imagery,** or words and phrases that help you imagine how things look, feel, taste, smell, or sound
- **Mood,** or the feeling you get as you listen
- **Rhythm,** or the musical quality created by the stressed and unstressed words and syllables of the poem

Then, have students listen to the poem again, pausing when necessary to determine how the poet uses each technique to convey meaning. Have students pause after each stanza to record their ideas on a chart like the one shown.

Technique	Evidence from Poem
tone	
imagery	
mood	
rhythm	

Remind students to think about how the speaker's voice adds to the meaning of the poem. Ask students to note which stanzas in particular seem to benefit from being read aloud and to write down why they think this might be so.

COLLABORATIVE DISCUSSION

Have students hold a discussion to compare and contrast the print and audio versions of the poem. Ask students to tell which version they think better conveys the meaning of the poem and why. Do they think the poet anticipated his poem being read aloud to audiences? Why or why not? Remind students to cite examples from the poem to support their ideas.

Analyze Structure:
Narrative Poetry

RL 4,
RL 5

RETEACH

Review with students that **narrative poetry** is poetry that tells a story. Remind them that like fiction a narrative poem contains characters, a setting, and a plot. Explain that narrative poetry also contains poetic elements, such as rhyme, rhythm, and repetition.

Discuss the following elements as you guide students to identify each one in "Paul Revere's Ride":

- **Characters:** the people, animals, or imaginary creatures who take part in the action
- **Setting:** the time and place of the action
- **Plot:** the series of events in the story that center on a conflict or struggle faced by the characters

Use a story map to record the information. Then, reread the poem aloud. Discuss how the rhyme and rhythm of the poem create suspense and convey meaning.

 LEVEL UP TUTORIALS Assign the following *Level Up* tutorial: **Narrative Poetry**

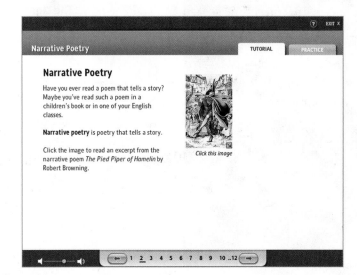

INDEPENDENT READING

Students can apply the skill to another narrative poem of their choosing. Have students work independently to identify the narrative elements. Then, have students compare their work with a partner.

The Light—Ah! The Light

Poem by Joyce Sidman

Why This Text

Students need practice analyzing the structure of narrative poetry. Narrative poetry shares many features with the short story, such as characters, setting, and plot. With the help of the close-reading questions, students will analyze the narrative structure of "The Light—Ah! The Light." This close reading will lead students to an analysis of Marie Curie's character as she is presented in the poem.

Background Have students read the background and the information about the author. Introduce the selection by telling students that Marie Curie did well in school. In 1883, however, she could not go to college in Poland because she was a woman. That did not stop her. First she attended a secret school called the Flying University. Then she moved to France and studied at the University of Paris. She discovered polonium and radium and won the Nobel Prize twice!

SETTING A PURPOSE Ask students to pay attention to details such as characters, setting, and plot. What is the first thing you learn about Marie Curie?

Standards Support

- cite textual evidence
- determine the meaning of words and phrases as they are used in a text
- analyze how a line or stanza fits into the overall structure of a text
- analyze how a line or stanza contributes to the development of the setting or plot

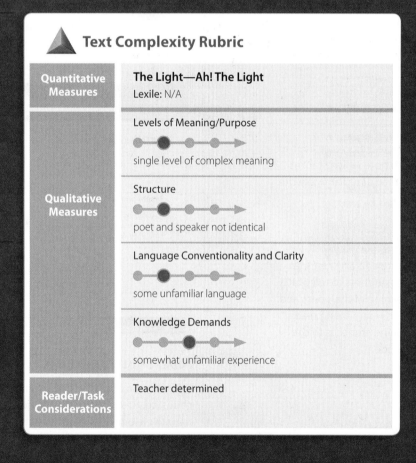

Text Complexity Rubric

Quantitative Measures

The Light—Ah! The Light
Lexile: N/A

Qualitative Measures

Levels of Meaning/Purpose
single level of complex meaning

Structure
poet and speaker not identical

Language Conventionality and Clarity
some unfamiliar language

Knowledge Demands
somewhat unfamiliar experience

Reader/Task Considerations

Teacher determined

Strategies for CLOSE READING

Analyze Structure: Narrative Poetry

Students should read the poem carefully all the way through. Close-reading questions at the bottom of the page will help them focus on a thorough analysis of the text. As they read, students should jot down comments or questions about the poem in the side margins.

WHEN STUDENTS STRUGGLE . . .

To help students determine the narrative elements of the poem, have them work in small groups to fill out a chart like the ones shown as they analyze the text.

CITE TEXT EVIDENCE For practice in analyzing narrative elements such as character, setting, and plot, ask students to cite details from the poem.

Element	Questions to Ask and Answer
Characters	**Who is the main character?** *Marie Curie* **What is the main character like?** *defiant:* "spit at the obelisk erected by the Tsar" *determined:* "Poverty, prejudice . . .I swept aside."
Setting	**What information or clues tell you where and when the story takes place?** "in Warsaw under . . . Russian rule" "Paris." **How is the setting important to the poem?** *Curie moved from Warsaw, Poland, to Paris, France, to study at "the Sorbonne."*
Plot	**What central conflict or struggle does the main character face?** "The work was brutal"; it "ravaged my skin, poisoned my blood" **How is the conflict resolved?** *Curie is satisfied by what she has accomplished in her life, despite the costs to her health.*

Background *Born in 1956, **Joyce Sidman** is an award-winning American writer known for her inventive poetry. Her poem, "The Light—Ah! The Light" takes as its subject the physicist and chemist Marie Curie. Born Marie Skłodowska in Warsaw, Poland, in 1867, Marie Curie studied at the University of Paris (referred in the poem as the Sorbonne) and discovered the chemical elements polonium and radium. She is best known for discovering the principles of radioactivity, which refers to the loss of particles and energy from certain atomic elements. Sidman reimagines Curie's thoughts and feelings in the poem.*

The Light—Ah! The Light
(Marie Curie discovered the principles of radioactivity.)

Poem by Joyce Sidman

CLOSE READ
Notes

1. **READD** ▶ As you read lines 1–34, begin to cite text evidence.
   - Underline words and phrases in lines 1–6 that reveal the setting.
   - In the margin, explain what happens in the last three stanzas.
   - Underline details that describe the effect that working with radioactive materials has on Curie.

A First of all, I am a Pole.
Manya, they called me
when I was a girl in Warsaw,
under the dark **yoke** of Russian rule.
5   We hid our Polish grammars
and spit at the obelisk erected by the Tsar.

But I was drawn to Paris
as a plant is drawn to the light.
And the Sorbonne, despite its
10 pointed little men,
shone like the sun itself.
Poverty, prejudice, the infuriating
French language—all this,
like a handful of cobwebs,
15 I swept aside.

yoke: *a wooden frame for harnessing draft animals*

Marie Curie goes to study in Paris in spite of numerous obstacles.

97

---

1. **READ AND CITE TEXT EVIDENCE**

   A **ASK STUDENTS** to cite text evidence that describes the setting, plot events, and the main character, Marie Curie. *Students should cite details about the setting from lines 1–6. They should find evidence that Curie overcame obstacles to study in Paris in lines 7–15. They should find evidence that her work to discover radium was difficult (lines 16–24). They should find evidence that the work she valued so much caused serious physical harm (lines 25–34).*

   Critical Vocabulary: yoke (line 4) Have students explain how *yoke* is used as a symbol here. How does the narrator, Curie, feel about the Russian rule? *She feels that the Poles were subjugated and were treated poorly.*

CLOSE READ
Notes

For the subject of my doctorate,
I chose uranium.
Just a lump of stone—but it shone!
The work was brutal:
20   a ton of ore to be hauled, cracked, **incinerated**
for one pure gram of radium.
I kept a bowl of it at my bedside
so I could wake at night
to its fairy glow.

25   In the end,
that glow ravaged my skin,
poisoned my blood.
I was like the shell of a burned-out tree.
Ⓑ   But what of it?
30   I, Manya,
the poor Polish girl from Warsaw,
pried open life's hidden heart
and discovered the bright burn
of its decay.

incinerate:

burn
completely

Marie Curie
does "brutal"
work as she
discovers
radium.

Marie Curie's
discoveries
cause her
severe
physical harm.

2.   ◀ **REREAD AND DISCUSS**   Reread lines 1–34. With a small group,
discuss details from the poem that convey Curie's pride in her
achievements.

SHORT RESPONSE

Cite Text Evidence   What do you learn about Marie Curie from the way she
responds to her circumstances? Review your reading notes and **cite text
evidence** in your response.

*Marie Curie is a determined, fearless woman. As a child in Warsaw
she faces frightening circumstances "under the dark yoke of Russian
rule." She leaves for Paris, where she deals with "Poverty, prejudice,
the infuriating French language" and does "brutal" work on the way
to making groundbreaking discoveries. Even when her body suffers as
a result, she feels it is worthwhile because she achieved so much.*

98

---

2.   **REREAD AND CITE TEXT EVIDENCE**

Ⓑ   **ASK STUDENTS** to cite text evidence that shows Curie's
pride in her achievements. *Students should cite evidence from lines
29–34.*

Critical Vocabulary: incinerate (line 20) Have students
determine the meaning of *incinerate* as it is used in the text.

FOR ELL STUDENTS Explain that *ore* is a rock that contains
metal. Have a volunteer explain the lines "a ton of ore to be
hauled, cracked, incinerated / for one pure gram of radium."

SHORT RESPONSE

Cite Text Evidence   Students should:

• show how Curie responds to her circumstances.
• cite textual evidence.
• draw conclusions about Curie based on the evidence.

TO CHALLENGE STUDENTS . . .

For more context and a deeper understanding of the content of
"The Light—Ah! The Light!," students can research the life and
work of Marie Curie.

ASK STUDENTS to work with a partner to write an interview
with Marie Curie. In each pair, one student will play the part of
Curie, and the other will play the part of the interviewer. Each pair
of students should identify a unique area of research, so that the
class will benefit from a broad understanding of Curie's life and
work. For example, assign each pair a period of her life, such as
"childhood in Poland," "at the Sorbonne," and "discovery of new
elements." Students should conduct their research with the goal
of writing three to five interview questions and answers that
reveal the most important details about Curie they discover.

After students have completed their research, have them
conduct their interviews in front of the class. At the end of the
interview, invite the class to ask questions of "Marie Curie" and
the interviewer, within the framework of the partners' research.
Students will answer the questions if they can, and will take one
or two useful questions that they were not able to answer as
inspiration for further research.

DIG DEEPER

With the class, return to Question 2, Reread and Discuss. Have students share the results of their discussion.

ASK STUDENTS whether they were satisfied with the outcome of their small-group discussions. Have each group share the evidence they found in the poem that showed Curie's pride in her work, then expand the conversation to include her pride in herself.

- Have volunteers read stanzas of the poem aloud.
- Have volunteers suggest evidence of Curie's pride in her heritage from the first stanza. *Students should cite line 1 as evidence that Curie is proud of being Polish. Share with students that Curie gave the name* polonium *to one of the radioactive elements she discovered, to honor her Polish heritage.*
- Ask students what Curie seems to be proud of in the second stanza. *Students might say she is proud of her courage or strength. Ask them to cite evidence to support their character analysis. Students should cite evidence such as line 15.*
- Ask students what Curie seems to be proud of in the third stanza. *Students might say she is proud of her strength or her curiosity. They should cite evidence such as line 19, "The work was brutal."*
- Ask a volunteer to reread aloud lines 30–35. Ask students if Curie sounds proud in these lines. *Students might say she is proud of her heritage, "Polish girl from Warsaw," of her strength, "pried open," and of her discovery, "discovered the bright burn."*

ASK STUDENTS to return to their Short Response on page 98, and revise their response based on the class discussion.

CLOSE READING NOTES

On Doomed Flight, Passengers Vowed to Perish Fighting

News Article by Jodi Wilgoren and Edward Wong

Memorial Is Unveiled for Heroes of Flight 93

TV Newscast by CBS News

Why These Texts?

Students regularly encounter news stories in media. This lesson explores two news stories in two different forms of media. Each one tells about the tragic and heroic events that occurred on United Flight 93 on September 11, 2001.

▶ View It!

Professional Development Podcast:
Text-Dependent Analysis

Key Learning Objective: The student will be able to analyze the elements of a news report, as well as integrate information in different media.

RI 1 Cite textual evidence.
RI 2 Determine central ideas and details.
RI 3 Analyze text elements.
RI 5 Analyze structure.
RI 7 Integrate information presented in different media.
W 8 Gather relevant information from multiple print and digital sources.
SL 1 Engage effectively in a range of collaborative discussions.
SL 2 Interpret information presented in diverse media and formats.
SL 4 Present claims and findings.
SL 5 Include multimedia components and visual displays in presentations.

 **Text Complexity Rubric**

	On Doomed Flight, Passengers Vowed to Perish Fighting	Memorial Is Unveiled for Heroes of Flight 93
Quantitative Measures	Lexile: 1350L	Lexile: N/A
Qualitative Measures	**Levels of Meaning/Purpose** single level of simple meaning (single theme)	**Levels of Meaning/Purpose** single level of simple meaning (single theme)
	Structure clearly stated, sequential organization of main ideas and details	**Structure** clearly stated, sequential organization of main ideas and details
	Language Conventionality and Clarity more complex sentence structure	**Language Conventionality and Clarity** some unfamiliar language
	Knowledge Demands distinctly unfamiliar experience	**Knowledge Demands** unfamiliar, multiple perspectives
Reader/Task Considerations	• Teacher determined • Vary by individual reader and type of text See the Text X-Ray for suggested Reader/Task Considerations.	

English Language Support

Before teaching, use the Text X-Ray for an overview of the text's complexity. The Text X-Ray and the supports and scaffolds in the Teacher's Edition will help you guide students of different skill levels.

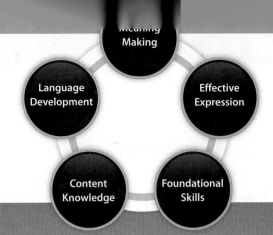

Meaning Making · Language Development · Effective Expression · Content Knowledge · Foundational Skills

Text Complexity: Qualitative Measures

▲ Levels of Meaning/Purpose

Help students interpret and integrate information from two different news reports.

- Teacher's Edition side notes, pp. 294, 295, 296, 298, 301, 302
- English Language Support, pp. 293, 300
- Interpret Information, p. 301
- Integrate Information, p. 302

To reteach how to integrate information, see

- Integrate Information, p. 302a

 Use It! Interactive Graphic Organizers: Main Idea; Main Idea and Details

***ZOOM IN ON* INTEGRATING INFORMATION** Use the following questions to help students **integrate** information from the two selections.

- What is the purpose of each report? *(The article's purpose is to inform people about events soon after they occurred. The purpose of the newscast is to revisit the event from a historical perspective and reinforce the public's view of the event.)*
- What ideas do both the article and the newscast convey about the passengers on Flight 93? *(They fought heroically to prevent terrorists from completing their plan.)*
- What new information does the newscast present? *(The intended target might have been the Capitol in Washington, D.C. A new memorial honors those lost on the flight.)*

▲ Structure

Help students analyze the structure of two different news reports.

- Teacher's Edition side notes, pp. 294, 295, 296, 297, 299
- English Language Support, pp. 293, 294, 296, 297
- When Students Struggle, p. 295
- Strategies for Annotation, pp. 297, 299
- Analyze Structure, p. 299

To reteach how to analyze structure, see

- Evaluate Sources, p. 302a

 Use It! Interactive Whiteboard Lesson: Evaluating Sources

***ZOOM IN ON* COMPARING AND CONTRASTING STRUCTURE** Pose these questions about the **structure** of the reports: What types of sources do both reports use? How do their methods of presentation differ? What effect does each have on the audience?

- Allow time for students to consider the questions and to note specific details supporting their responses.
- Have pairs combine their ideas and notes and then share their answers with the class. *(Common sources: interviews, expert testimony, witnesses. Differences: The article uses text and one graphic; the newscast uses narration with images and sounds of people and places involved in the event. Effects: The article conveys the tragic immediacy of the event; the newscast evokes feelings of national pride and patriotism.)*

▲ Language Conventionality and Clarity

Teach unfamiliar vocabulary in context.

- Applying Academic Vocabulary, pp. 294, 300

Support students' analysis of the selections through discussion and writing.

- Teacher's Edition side notes, pp. 295, 298, 300, 302
- English Language Support, p. 298

ZOOM IN ON **ANALYZING LANGUAGE** Remind students that authors choose words to create a specific effect on their audience.

- After students read lines 1–10 of the article, have small groups identify language that influences the reader's view of the events. *(die fighting, horror, harrowing, vowed, thwart, enemy)* Ask volunteers to explain the impression that these words create. *(They emphasize the passengers' bravery and the horror of the event.)*
- Have groups view the TV newscast and identify words and phrases that create the same impressions. *(ordinary people who made the extraordinary decision, storm the cockpit, chose to fight back)*

▲ Knowledge Demands

Support English learners in understanding the necessary background of both events.

- Teacher's Edition Background note, p. 293
- Content-Area Connection, p. 298
- As You View, p. 300

ZOOM IN ON **BUILDING COMPREHENSION** Make sure students understand the following words and phrases:

- *runs this into the ground* (line 36): crashes the plane
- *fallen passengers* (line 42): passengers who died
- *taken over* (line 70): seized control
- *started clicking in my mind* (lines 139–140): began to make sense

▲ Suggested Reader/Task Considerations

You might consider the following before assigning these selections to students.

- Will students need additional support to help them manage the Performance Task successfully?
- Will students be distressed by the subject of the news article?

ZOOM IN ON **SUPPORTING COMPREHENSION**

- Have mixed-ability groups brainstorm and choose a topic. Meet with each group to help them identify sources of information and develop plans for completing the task.
- Before students begin the article, tell them that it includes interviews with relatives of people who died onboard the flight. Offer those who feel uncomfortable with this content the option of reading only the following targeted passages: lines 1–19, 73–79, and 109–125.

TEACH

CLOSE READ

Background Have students read the background about the news article and the newscast. Explain that they are going to read and watch news pieces about the tragic events on United Flight 93 on September 11, 2001. Although there were no survivors of that flight, people have been able to piece together fragments of evidence that seem to indicate that the passengers decided to attack the hijackers in order to crash the plane. Though not all the facts will probably ever be known, the country counts these individuals as heroes for their actions that day.

SETTING A PURPOSE Direct students to use the Setting a Purpose question to focus their reading and viewing. Remind students to generate questions as they read and view.

Background *On September 11, 2001, four United States passenger jets were hijacked by terrorists. Two jets were flown into the World Trade Center in New York City; one jet attacked the Pentagon in Washington, D.C. The fourth hijacked jet, United Flight 93, widely believed to be headed toward the United States Capitol, was still flying as the news of the other jet crashes broke. To prevent yet another disaster, the passengers of Flight 93 banded together to end their flight, sacrificing their own lives. The passengers' valiant choice destroyed the terrorists' plans and saved the lives of countless others on that tragic day.*

MEDIA ANALYSIS

COVERING NEWS EVENTS

On Doomed Flight, Passengers Vowed to Perish Fighting
News Article by Jodi Wilgoren and Edward Wong

Memorial Is Unveiled for Heroes of Flight 93
TV Newscast by CBS News

SETTING A PURPOSE In this lesson, you'll analyze a news article that tells the story of United Flight 93. You will also view a television newscast that describes a memorial event held in 2011 that honored those who died on Flight 93. As you read and view each media selection, pay attention to how information is given and to the facts and details that reporters choose to use as they describe each event.

(t) ©Michael Henninger/ZUMA Press/Corbis; (c) Photodisc/Getty Images; (b) ©BBC Motion Gallery

Analyze Text (LINES 1–10)   RI 1, RI 3

Explain to students that news is information about events, people, and places in your community, region, the nation, and the world. Point out that journalists use the 5 *Ws* and *H* questions as an outline for writing a news story. Explain that the **5 *Ws* and *H*** questions are *who, what, when, where, why*, and *how*. Point out that by answering these questions journalists ensure that they tell the complete news story.

A **CITE TEXT EVIDENCE** Ask students to reread lines 1–10. Have students describe what key ideas and events are introduced here by citing which of the 5 *Ws* and *H* questions are answered in these lines and what the answers are. *(Possible responses: Who: passengers; What: trying to stop hijackers; Where: flying at 35,000 feet above Pennsylvania; Why: plane is maybe headed toward national landmark; How: die fighting.)*

Analyze Structure   RI 1, RI 3, RI 5

(LINES 11–32)

Explain that news articles often contain interviews of people directly or closely involved with an event.

B **CITE TEXT EVIDENCE** Ask students to tell what information lines 11–32 provide and how these lines fit into the structure of the article. *(These interviews and quotations add information about the hijackers and some of the passengers. They elaborate on what action the passengers might take and add details to the article.)*

English Language Support

Point out that not all of the information obtained through interviews appears as quotations. The authors also paraphrase information, or restate it in their own words.

- Explain that *said* and *told* often introduce information based on interviews.
- Ask pairs to find an example of paraphrasing in the passage. *(lines 11–16)*
- Discuss why the authors include both paraphrases and direct quotations.

MEDIA

On Doomed Flight, Passengers Vowed to Perish Fighting

Jodi Wilgoren and Edward Wong
New York Times, Sep. 13, 2001

A

They told the people they loved that they would die fighting.

In a series of cellular telephone calls to their wives, two passengers aboard the plane that crashed into a Pennsylvania field instead of possibly toppling a national landmark learned about the horror of the World Trade Center. From 35,000 feet, they relayed harrowing[1] details about the hijacking in progress to the police. And they vowed to try to thwart the enemy, to prevent others from dying even if they could not
10 save themselves.

B

Lyzbeth Glick, 31, of Hewitt, N.J., said her husband, Jeremy, told her that three or four 6-foot-plus passengers aboard United Airlines Flight 93 from Newark bound for San Francisco planned to take a vote about how to proceed, and joked about taking on the hijackers with the butter knives from the in-flight breakfast. In a telephone interview last night, Ms. Glick said her husband told her "three Arab-looking men with red headbands," carrying a knife and talking about a bomb, took control of the aircraft.

20 "He was a man who would not let things happen," she said of her high school sweetheart and husband of five years, the father of a 12-week-old daughter, Emerson. "He was a hero for what he did, but he was a hero for me because he told me not to be sad and to take care of our daughter and he said whatever happened he would be O.K. with any choices I make.

"He said, 'I love you, stay on the line,' but I couldn't," added Ms. Glick, 31, a teacher at Berkeley College. "I gave the phone to my dad. I don't want to know what happened."

Another passenger, Thomas E. Burnett Jr., an executive at
30 a San Francisco-area medical device company, told his wife, Deena, that one passenger had already been stabbed to death but that a group was "getting ready to do something."

[1] **harrowing** (hăr´ō ĭng): extremely distressing.

APPLYING ACADEMIC VOCABULARY

achieve	instance	outcome

THINK-PAIR-SHARE Have partners discuss the questions below. Guide students to include the academic vocabulary words *achieve*, *instance*, and *outcome* in their responses. Ask volunteers to share their responses with the class.

- What did the passengers on United Flight 93 **achieve**?
- What was the **outcome** of their actions? Cite specific **instances** to support your idea.

"I pleaded with him to please sit down and not draw attention to himself," Ms. Burnett, the mother of three young daughters, told a San Francisco television station. "And he said: 'No, no. If they're going to run this into the ground we're going to have to do something.' And he hung up and he never called back."

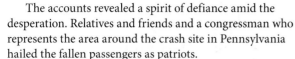

40 The accounts revealed a spirit of defiance amid the desperation. Relatives and friends and a congressman who represents the area around the crash site in Pennsylvania hailed the fallen passengers as patriots.

"Apparently they made enough of a difference that the plane did not complete its mission," said Lyzbeth Glick's uncle, Tom Crowley, of Atlanta. In an e-mail message forwarded far and wide, Mr. Crowley urged: "May we remember Jeremy and the other brave souls as heroes, soldiers and Americans on United Flight 93 who so gallantly gave their lives to save many others."

50 Like others on the doomed plane, Mr. Glick, 31, and Mr. Burnett, 38, had not originally planned to be aboard the 8 a.m. flight. Mr. Glick, who worked for an Internet company called Vividence, was heading to the West Coast on business, and Mr. Burnett, chief operating officer for Thorntec Corporation, was returning home from a visit to the company's Edison, N.J., office.

Lauren Grandcolas of San Rafael, Calif., left an early-morning message on her husband's answering machine saying she would be home earlier than expected from her
60 grandmother's funeral. Mark Bingham, 31, who ran a public relations firm, had felt too sick to fly on Monday, but was racing to make an afternoon meeting with a client in San Francisco.

The plane was airborne by 8:44 a.m., according to radar logs, and headed west, flying apparently without incident until it reached Cleveland about 50 minutes later. At 9:37, it turned south and headed back the way it came. Mr. Bingham, a 6-foot-5 former rugby player who this summer ran with the bulls in Pamplona, Spain, called his mother, Alice
70 Hoglan. "He said, 'Three guys have taken over the plane and they say they have a bomb,'" said Ms. Hoglan, a United flight attendant.

WHEN STUDENTS STRUGGLE . . .

Students may find it difficult to keep track of the people the speakers in the article are referring to when they speak. Direct students to lines 33–38. Ask students to reread this passage and discuss to whom Ms. Burnett is referring as she remembers her conversation. *(Ms. Burnett is Deena Burnett, the wife of Thomas E. Burnett Jr. He was the person who she was referring to, the passenger who said that a group was getting ready to do something.)*

Have students work in pairs to make the connections between the relatives who are speaking and the corresponding passengers who were on United Flight 93.

CLOSE READ

Analyze Meaning
RI 1, RI 4
(LINES 39–42)

Explain to students that the reporters not only include information from relatives and friends but also the responses, feelings, and ideas the relatives and friends have about the passengers' actions.

C ASK STUDENTS to reread lines 39–42 and tell why some people called the passengers patriots. *(They believe the passengers prevented the hijackers from using the plane to crash into the Capitol, an important landmark in the nation's government. Being a patriot means doing something honorable for your country, and these people believe that the passengers on the flight did that.)*

Analyze Text (LINES 64–67)
RI 1, RI 3

Point out that one of the 5 *W*s and *H* questions is *what*. Tell students that good news stories need to tell *what* happened.

D CITE TEXT EVIDENCE Have students reread lines 64–67, cite text evidence to tell what this passage is about, and tell why the reporters include it. *(line 64 tells when the flight was airborne; line 66 tells when it reached Cleveland; lines 66–67 tell that it turned around at 9:37 a.m; the path of the plane and the time when it turned around help readers understand when and why passengers became concerned.)*

English Language Support

Manipulate Language Display the sentence that begins on line 39 and clarify that *accounts* means "interviews." Then highlight *defiance* and *desperation*.

- Model how to define the words by separating their base words and affixes. Help students form sentences containing the words.

- Ask students to rewrite the sentence using *passengers* as the subject and the base forms of *defiance* and *desperation*.

Integrate Information

RI 1,
RI 7

Explain to students that **graphics** are visual elements whose purpose is to provide additional information about events. Point out that graphics may be charts, diagrams, timelines, illustrations, or other visuals.

E **CITE TEXT EVIDENCE** Ask students to describe the graphic. Have students cite the specific text it is connected to in the article and tell what information it adds to the article. *(The graphic is a map, but it includes other information, too. It shows part of the plane's route, as well as time information and the number of people on board. Together with lines 64–67 it explains the entire route of the plane from takeoff to the time it crashed in Pennsylvania.)*

English Language Support

Have partners examine the graphic and answer the following questions:

- How long was the plane in the air? *(It flew for about an hour and twenty-seven minutes.)*
- How many people were on the plane according to this graphic? *(45)*
- What does the graphic help readers to understand more clearly? *(Possible responses: the route of the flight; the dramatic change of direction; the short time in which all the events occurred)*

Make Inferences

RI 1

(LINES 73–79)

Ask students to reread lines 73–79, which report actual words that were recorded in the cockpit of the plane.

F **CITE TEXT EVIDENCE** Ask students to explain who is speaking the words heard on the transcript and to tell what details in the text tell them this. *(The man speaking was probably one of the hijackers, pretending to be the captain. The real captain did not have an Arabic accent, would not have spoken in broken English, and probably would not have said there was a bomb on board. It makes more sense that this was a hijacker trying to keep the passengers calm.)*

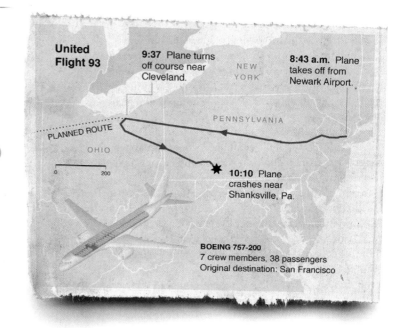

E

Map showing planned route and actual route of United Flight 93.

F

CNN reported last night that it had obtained a partial transcript[2] of cockpit chatter, and that a source who had listened to the air-traffic control tape said a man with an Arabic accent had said in broken English: "This is the captain speaking. Remain in your seat. There is a bomb on board. Stay quiet. We are meeting with their demands. We are returning to the airport."

80   Another passenger on the sparsely populated plane barricaded himself in the bathroom and dialed 911. Ms. Grandcolas tried to wake her husband, Jack, but got the answering machine. "We're having problems," she said, according to her neighbor, Dave Shapiro, who listened to the message. "But I'm comfortable," she said, and then, after a pause, added, "for now."

---

[2] **transcript:** a written or printed copy.

English Language Learners

Use Verbs and Verb Phrases Tell students that the map caption works along with the visual to inform the reader/viewer. An expanded caption that summarizes what the map is showing can be helpful to viewers. Write this text on the board: *The map shows where the plane took off and a star points to where it crashed. A dotted line represents the planned route.*

ASK STUDENTS to work with a partner to write a summary of the map contents. Ask them to pay attention to how they use verbs in their captions.

Mr. Glick, a muscular 6-foot-4 water sportsman, and
Mr. Burnett, a 6-1 former high school football player, called
their wives over and over, from about 9:30 a.m. until the crash
90   at about 10:10 a.m., chronicling[3] what was happening, urging
them to call the authorities, vowing to fight, saying goodbye.

"He sounded sad and scared, but calm at the same time,"
Ms. Glick said. "He said people weren't too panicked. They
had moved everybody to the back of the plane. The three men
were in the cockpit, but he didn't see the pilots and they made
no contact with the passengers, so my feeling is they must
have killed them."

In a radio interview with KCBS in San Francisco,
Ms. Burnett said her husband of nine years called four
100   times—first just reporting the hijacking, later asking her for
information about the World Trade Center disaster, eventually
suggesting the passengers were formulating a plan to respond.

"I could tell that he was alarmed and trying to piece
together the puzzle, trying to figure out what was going
on and what he could do about the situation," Ms. Burnett
said. "He was not giving up. His adrenaline was going. And
you could just tell that he had every intention of solving the
problem and coming on home."

Ms. Glick said that at one point, she managed to create
110   a conference call between her husband and 911 dispatchers.
"Jeremy tracked the second-by-second details and relayed
them to the police by phone," Mr. Crowley wrote in his e-mail
account of the calls. "After several minutes describing the
scene, Jeremy and several other passengers decided there was
nothing to lose by rushing the hijackers."

At the crash site near Shanksville, Pa., a local politician
and law enforcement officials said the wives' accounts
made sense.

"I would conclude there was a struggle, and a heroic
120   individual decided they were going to die anyway and,
'Let's bring the plane down here,'" said Representative
John P. Murtha, a Democrat who represents the area and
serves on the Defense Appropriations Committee.

An F.B.I. official said of Mr. Murtha's theory, "It's
reasonable what he said, but how could you know?"

---

[3] **chronicling** (krŏn´ĭ-klĭng): providing a detailed record or report.

CLOSE READ

Analyze Structure   RI 3, RI 5

(LINES 109–118)

Explain to students that details about *why* and *how*
something happened can add depth to a news story.
Discuss the question this passage seems to answer
about United Flight 93.

Ⓖ ASK STUDENTS to reread lines 109–118 and tell
what *how* and *why* questions Ms. Glick and others
believe they have answered. *(The* how *question is how
the plane probably crashed; the* why *question is why the
passengers decided to rush the hijackers.)*

English Language Support

Make sure students understand the verb *rushing* in
line 115. Explain that it means "quickly attack or try to
overcome by force."

ASK STUDENTS what the passengers understood
about the likely results of attacking the hijackers.
Have groups discuss why the passengers still
decided to take action. *(The passengers knew that
they would probably die in the attempt; however, they
also knew that they would likely die if they did nothing,
and others would die, too.)*

Strategies for Annotation   🖊 🖹 *Annotate it!*

Analyze Structure   RI 5

Share these strategies for guided or independent analysis:

- Highlight any answers to each of the 5 *W*s questions *(who, what,
  when, where, why)* in different colors.
- Underline any answers to the *H (how)* question.
- Review your annotations. On a note, write other questions or
  observations you may have based on the passage.

"I would conclude there was a struggle, and a heroic individual
decided they were going to die anyway and, 'Let's bring the plane
down here,'" said Representative John P. Murtha, a Democrat who
represents the area . . .

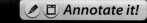

An F.B.I. official said of Mr. Murtha's theory,   Would more
information be
useful or not?

"It's reasonable what he said, but how could you know?"

Analyze Text (LINES 135–147)   RI 1, RI 3

Point out that news stories often tell about how something happened.

Ⓗ CITE TEXT EVIDENCE Ask students to reread lines 135–147 and tell how David Markmann discovered that his neighbor was on United Flight 93. Have students point out evidence in the text to support their findings. *(Markmann kept calling her but only got voice mail. Finally, he saw the list of passengers on the flight and saw her name.)* Ask students whether this description is an effective ending or not. *(Possible response: This description is effective because it focuses readers' attention back on all the passengers who died and are not coming back.)*

COLLABORATIVE DISCUSSION Have students work in small groups to discuss the information presented in the interviews with members of the passengers' families. Ask students to tell what they think happened on United Flight 93. Students can point out the evidence they used from the text to draw their conclusions. Ask students if they have any other questions about what happened. Have them share their questions with the group.

ASK STUDENTS to share any questions they generated in the course of reading and discussing the news article.

English Language Support

Read Closely Help students draw conclusions about what happened by directing them to lines 109–125. Have groups discuss what conclusion this information supports and why. Encourage them to use these sentence starters to express their conclusions and evidence:

- The details in the article indicate that _____.
- Evidence that supports this conclusion is _____.

While the women cherished their final words and their husbands' seeming heroism, other people's relatives and friends struggled to reconstruct their last conversations with their lost loved ones.

130   Between sobs, Doris Gronlund recalled how her daughter, Linda, an environmental lawyer from Long Island who was headed for a vacation in wine country with her boyfriend, Joseph DeLuca, called on Monday to relay her flight numbers, just in case anything happened.

David Markmann last saw his upstairs neighbor, Honor Elizabeth Wainio, on Sunday night, standing on her balcony in Plainfield, N.J. Ms. Wainio, 28, was a regional manager of the Discovery Channel's retail stores.

Ⓗ 140   When the Newark flight crashed, "things started clicking in my mind," Mr. Markmann said. He dialed Ms. Wainio's home number— no answer. The cell phone rang four times and went to voice mail. He called again, and again and again and again, 15 times or more, until 2 P.M. yesterday, when he saw the list of Flight 93's passengers on the United Airlines Web site.

"I wasn't getting a phone call back," he said, "so I kind of had a feeling."

COLLABORATIVE DISCUSSION If there were no survivors on Flight 93, how do we know what actually happened on the flight? With a partner, discuss the information presented by family members of the passengers. Do you think that the information provides a full account of the events? Cite evidence from the text to support your ideas.

CONTENT-AREA CONNECTION

History Discuss how the article focuses on the words, actions, and thoughts of the passengers and their families. It was published two days after the event, when not all of the facts were known. Explain that later reports had access to more information about the terrorists' plans.

Activity Have small groups find a newspaper article written several months or years after 9/11 that provides another perspective on the events related to Flight 93. Ask students to summarize the information they learn from their articles and share their summaries with the class.

Analyze Structure

RI 2, RI 3,
RI 5, RI 7

News is information on events, people, and places in your community, the nation, and the world. News reports can be found in television newscasts, online wire services, magazines, documentaries, and newspaper articles, such as the article about United Flight 93 that you just read.

In order to give a complete account of an event, newspaper articles should answer six basic questions—**who, what, when, where, why,** and **how.** Reporters often use the 5 *W*s and *H* questions as an outline for writing reports. The best news reports answer these questions and include additional information.

Newspaper articles may also use graphics. **Graphics** are visual elements whose purpose is to provide additional information about events. Graphics may be charts, maps, diagrams, timelines, or other visuals.

Look for answers to the six basic news questions and think about the purpose of the graphic as you analyze the newspaper article.

Analyzing the Media

RI 2, RI 3,
RI 5, RI 7

Cite Text Evidence   Support your responses with evidence from the text.

1. **Summarize**   Review the news story and fill out the following chart to record the story's 5 *W*s and *H*.

5 *W*s and *H* Questions	
Who is the report about?	
What happened to this person or persons?	
When did it happen?	
Where did it happen?	
Why did it happen?	
How did it happen?	

2. **Interpret**   The writer includes information about the passengers by recounting phone calls they made to family members on the ground. What is the impact of this information?

3. **Analyze and Evaluate**   What additional information does the graphic provide about United Flight 93? Explain whether this information is helpful or not, and why.

PRACTICE & APPLY

CLOSE READ

Analyze Structure

RI 3,
RI 5

Help students understand the terms. Discuss whether the news article they just read answers all of the 5 *W*s and *H* questions. Then, have them explain why answering these questions helped the journalist to write this news report. *(Answering all of these questions makes sure that the reader understands as much as possible about the topic.)*

Analyzing the Media

RI 2,
RI 3,
RI 5,
RI 7

Possible answers:

1. *Summaries should include answers to each of the six basic questions without any opinions or judgments offered about the events or the people involved, either positive or negative.*

2. *The phone calls add information about the passengers and the events on the plane that readers would not know otherwise. The information is from family members, which makes it emotionally strong, but it may also not be completely factual or objective, either in content or in the way it is presented. The personal nature of the information makes it difficult for reporters and readers to not feel something personal about the information.*

3. *The graphic provides a visual reference for the information about the flight's direction and course. It gives you a timeline that helps you understand the length of the flight. It also lists the number of passengers and crew who died on the flight. This graphic is helpful because it gives you a visual, factual context for the information being presented in the article.*

Strategies for Annotation   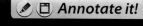 *Annotate it!*

Analyze Structure

RI 3,
RI 5

Share these strategies for guided or independent analysis:

- Highlight in yellow who this paragraph is about.
- Highlight in green where this person is.
- Highlight in blue the information that tells why the person makes the call to her husband.
- Review your highlights. On a note, explain how this text helps you understand what is happening in the news story.

Another passenger on the sparsely populated plane barricaded himself in the bathroom and dialed 911. Ms. Grandcolas tried to wake her husband, Jack, but got the answering machine. "We're having problems," she said, according to her neighbor, Dave Shapiro, who listened to the message. "But I'm comfortable," she said, and then, after a pause, added, "for now."

> tells one passenger's experience

TEACH

CLOSE READ

AS YOU VIEW Tell students that they will be watching a TV newscast from September 10, 2011, about a memorial dedication for the people who died on United Flight 93. Explain that a newscast uses different elements to communicate its story, including interviews, film clips, narration, and quotations. Have students read the As You View section to help them focus their viewing and to understand how these elements help people understand a news story.

COLLABORATIVE DISCUSSION Have students work in small groups to compare the content of the news article and newscast. Students may want to make a two-column chart to help them compare and contrast the information and insights they gathered from each news piece.

ASK STUDENTS to share any questions they generated in the course of viewing and discussing the TV interview.

English Language Support

View Multimedia Tell students that although the TV report and the article are different types of media, they share the purpose of communicating information about an event. Ask pairs to watch the video and answer these adapted 5 *Ws* and *H* questions to help them determine what facts are presented by the newscast. Have them write a brief summary of what they learn.

- What event is the report about? What is the significance of this event?
- Who was involved in this event?
- When did this event take place?
- Where did it take place?
- Why did this event occur?
- How did this event come about?

Memorial Is Unveiled for Heroes of Flight 93

Format: TV newscast
Running Time: 2:22 minutes

AS YOU VIEW As you view the newscast, consider the 5 *Ws* and *H* of news reports and how this newscast presents the answers to those questions. Notice how the newscast explains the event using a combination of interviews, film clips, narration, and quotations from different people. Consider how each of these elements helps you understand the outcome of United Flight 93, what the individuals on the plane achieved, and what the event meant to their families and to the nation.

Pause the video to write notes about ideas or questions you might want to talk about later. Note any facts or details that support your ideas. Replay or rewind the video as needed.

©BBC Motion Gallery

COLLABORATIVE DISCUSSION With a partner or small group, discuss the purpose of each news report and what you learned from it. What is the same and different about the information in each report? Tell whether you find one of the reports more compelling, and if so, why. Cite specific evidence or techniques from the reports to support your ideas.

APPLYING ACADEMIC VOCABULARY

principle	individual

THINK-PAIR-SHARE Have students turn to a partner to discuss the following questions. Guide students to include the academic vocabulary words *principle* and *individual* in their responses. Ask volunteers to share their responses with the class.

- What is a **principle** that the passengers on United Flight 93 shared?
- What did the stories told by the **individuals** who came to the memorial service reveal about the passengers on United Flight 93?

Interpret Information

The makers of news reports use different sources to provide people with information. A **source** is someone or something that provides information. News reports and newscasts use a variety of sources, including the following:

- **Experts** are people who are knowledgeable in a field or a subject area.
- **Witnesses** are people who are present at an event and can give a first-hand account of something seen, heard, or experienced.
- **Footage** is recorded material that gives information about a subject or event. Footage can include film clips, photographs, and interviews.

Interviews, which are question-and-answer conversations between two or more people, are often included in news reports. Interviews are a direct way to find out information from experts, witnesses, and others, such as family members in the newscast you just viewed, who might have information to share about an event or topic. Often, a reporter will include **quotations** from interviews, as well as other sources, as part of a news report, article, or newscast. In newscasts, like the one you just viewed, these quotations are called **sound bites.**

As you analyze the newscast "Memorial Is Unveiled for Heroes of Flight 93," consider how these elements are used and how effective each one is in conveying different types of information.

Analyzing the Media

SL 2

Cite Text Evidence Support your responses with evidence from the media.

1. **Identify and Infer** Fill out a chart like this and give one example of each type of source from the newscast.

Experts	
Witnesses	
Footage	

2. **Analyze** What do the interviews with family members help you to understand about their feelings and reactions?

3. **Interpret and Evaluate** How does the footage that shows the World Trade Center and the Pentagon affect your understanding and opinions about the events of September 11, 2001? Describe how viewing the footage of the memorial event affects your response to the actions of the passengers on United Flight 93.

FOR STUDENTS WITH DISABILITIES

Support students who may be challenged by material presented visually or orally by providing background on the event that is the topic of the newscast and watching the clip together, pausing to clarify any confusing parts. After the first viewing, have students identify questions that they have; then have them work in pairs to watch the video again to find the answers to their questions.

Interpret Information

SL 2

Help students understand the different sources that news articles and newscasts use to provide people with information, and have students identify a few of them in both the news article and the newscast.

Discuss the different information that students learned from the interviews in the article and the newscast. *(The interviews in the news article allowed readers to understand what was happening on the plane. The interviews in the newscast tell the effects of the passengers' heroic actions on the plane. The interviews tell why the passengers' actions were so important.)*

Analyzing the Media

SL 2

Possible answers:

1.

Experts	*Presidents Bush and Clinton*
Witnesses	*family members at the memorial event*
Footage	*World Trade Center on 9/11; Pentagon on 9/11; images of U.S. Capitol building; family members at the boulder memorial; names on marble wall*

2. *They want their family members to be remembered as heroes, as the first fighters at the "first battleground" of the war on terror. They also want some amount of privacy for the place where the crash happened, where the families can go to feel closer to them.*

3. *The footage reminds those who were alive at the time of their own personal reactions to the events. For those who did not view the actual attacks, this footage gives them an idea of what it was like to live through those days. Seeing the footage helps us to remember what the passengers on United Flight 93 were thinking and feeling while hearing what was happening in other places and thinking about where their plane was probably headed, shocking as it seemed at the time. It helps us to understand just how heroic their actions were.*

PRACTICE & APPLY

Integrate Information
RI 7, SL 2

Help students understand that when they integrate information they *combine separate data* in order to gain a clearer understanding of a topic. Ask students to tell what new information from the TV newscast made them better understand the events of that day. *(The TV newscast puts the events of September 11, 2001, in perspective. It states that the war on terror began that day on United Flight 93.)*

Analyzing the Media
RI 7

Possible answers:

1.

News Report	Sources Used
"On Doomed Flight . . ."	*interviews, accounts of cell-phone conversations, diagram, experts, timeline*
"Memorial Is Unveiled . . ."	*interviews, video footage, statistics (number of dead), experts, witnesses to memorial event*

2. *Time passing makes some of the facts clearer and more certain. The newscast shows that while family members still grieve, they are also moving on. It emphasizes that this event caused a momentous change in the nation and that these people are among the first heroes in the nation's battle against terrorism.*

3. *The newspaper report provides specific details about the passengers and events on the plane. The newscast, revisiting the event ten years later, honors the people described in the article and uses the memorial to emphasize the significance of their actions.*

English Language Support

Express Opinions Before students begin their commentaries, discuss the ways in which word choices can influence an audience.

- Review the use of modal verbs and verb phrases as intensifiers, and then write the following on the board: *It's important that we clean up litter around our school. Everyone _____ participate in this effort.*
- Let volunteers read the text aloud, using each of these modals in turn: *could, should, must.*
- Ask pairs to explain how the statement differs with each word and to decide which one best fits the context.

Integrate Information
RI 7, SL 2

To integrate information means to take individual pieces of information and synthesize, or combine, them in order to develop a coherent, or clearer, understanding of a topic. Think about the information you read in the news article "On Doomed Flight, Passengers Vowed to Perish Fighting." Then think about the newscast from ten years later, "Memorial Is Unveiled for Heroes of Flight 93." You can use the information from both reports to better understand what happened on September 11, 2001. To integrate information from these reports, ask yourself:

- What is the purpose of each news report? What specific information does each report contribute?
- What features do the reports share? What features are unique to each?

Analyzing the Media
RI 7, W 6, W 8, SL 1, SL 2, SL 4, SL 5

Cite Text Evidence Support your responses with evidence from the media.

1. **Interpret** Use a chart like this to list the types of sources used in each news report.

News Report	Sources Used
"On Doomed Flight..."	
"Memorial Is Unveiled..."	

2. **Integrate** Explain how the passage of ten years affects the perspective presented in the newscast in comparison with the perspective presented in the news article. How have people's views and reactions changed or remained the same over ten years?

3. **Analyze and Integrate** How do the specific details and elements presented in each news report work together to help you understand the significance of the events surrounding United Flight 93?

PERFORMANCE TASK

Media Activity: Commentary Work in a small group to create an audio recording for a commentary, or an opinion piece about a local or school news issue related to the Collection 5 topic "Decisions That Matter."

- With your group, brainstorm the local or school issue to report on.
- Conduct research and gather information about the issue.
- As a group, record opinions and have members provide comments.

Assign this performance task.

PERFORMANCE TASK
W 6, W 8, SL 1, SL 2, SL 4, SL 5

Media Activity: Commentary Tell students to briefly explain the issue and how the decision matters to the students. Explain that their opinions need to be clearly stated and supported by evidence from their research. Have groups record and review their commentary, revise as needed, and then rerecord a final version.

Evaluate Sources

RI 7,
W 8,
SL 2

TEACH

Explain to students that the object of a news story is to present news in a way that is objective, accurate, and thorough. Point out that the sources for a news story may be experts, witnesses, or footage of various kinds. Tell students that for a news story to be accurate these sources need to be trustworthy. When evaluating sources, students should ask:

- **Is the source an expert in a field or subject area?** Unnamed sources or anonymous sources should be avoided. Look for contact information, a connection to an organization, or other reliable credentials to decide if a source is credible.

- **Were the interviewed people eyewitnesses?** People who were not directly involved in a reported event are not reliable sources. For example, people who heard about a story from a friend are not reliable sources; their restatement of the information may be inaccurate or incomplete in important ways.

- **Is a published report specifically mentioned or shown?** If research, data, or reports are not specifically named or are referenced to in only vague terms, they are not credible. For example, information that follows statements such as "Research shows that . . ." is not credible.

- **Is the purpose of the information clear?** Discuss different purposes of information, such as to inform, teach, sell a product, entertain, or persuade. Decide whether the information is fact, opinion, or propaganda; this will help you decide if the information is useful or reliable for your purposes as well.

COLLABORATIVE DISCUSSION

Have partners work together to evaluate the sources in "On Doomed Flight, Passengers Vowed to Perish Fighting" and "Memorial Is Unveiled for Heroes of Flight 93." Have students make a list and tell whether they think each one is reliable and why.

 INTERACTIVE LESSON Have students complete the tutorials in this lesson: **Evaluating Sources.**

Integrate Information

RI 7

RETEACH

Remind students that when you integrate information you take individual pieces of information and combine them in order to develop a coherent understanding of a topic or event. Review the following steps with students for how to integrate information from two or more sources, such as a news article and a film, or an article and a graphic (map, diagram, chart):

- **Identify the purpose of each source.** Ask yourself why each piece of information was chosen and what effect it has on the overall source.

- **Identify specific information in each source.** List each piece of information that each source contributes to the topic. Include any graphics or other visual elements that add information.

- **Ask questions about the sources.** Think about how the sources differ from one another. What viewpoints are presented in each one?

- **Compare and contrast the sources.** Discuss how the information in each source is alike or different. What features do all the sources share? What features are only in one or two sources?

- **Integrate the information.** After comparing the sources, ask yourself: What new ideas or fuller understanding can I arrive at?

Work with students to apply these steps to "On Doomed Flight, . . . " and "Memorial Is Unveiled . . ." as a group. Decide together what each source contributes to their understanding of the flight and how their understanding is improved by reviewing both sources.

INDEPENDENT READING

Have students read two sources of information about the same event, such as an online video and a news article. Ask students to discuss the main ideas in each source. Then, have students integrate the information from both sources and discuss what greater understanding they have gained from analyzing the sources together.

 INTERACTIVE GRAPHIC ORGANIZER Students can use a **Main Idea** or **Main Idea and Details Chart** to organize and integrate information.

DECISIONS THAT MATTER

The *FYI* site provides links to online articles from a variety of magazines and newspapers. Help students choose a few articles to read to further their exploration of the topic Decisions That Matter.

NOVELWISE

Students can unlock the power of novels with this unique resource. Help students read through longer works with these tips:

- Find a Book
- Before You Read
- As You Read
- After You Read

Each book includes introductory material, worksheets, graphic organizers, and discussion guides.

ADDITIONAL TEXTS BY COLLECTION

Suggest students read the following:

- "A Psalm of Life" by Henry Wadsworth Longfellow
- "Lucinda Matlock" by Edgar Lee Masters

Read the poems aloud to students. Then have them take turns reading stanzas aloud. Ask students to identify which words and phrases stand out in the oral recitation, and why. What about each poem's structure or theme is revealed in those words and phrases?

NONFICTION CONNECTIONS

Suggest that students increase their reading of informational texts. The nonfiction connections include

- speeches
- diaries
- true-life accounts
- newspaper articles
- political cartoons

Creating an Independent Reading Program

TEACHER GUIDANCE AND FEEDBACK

As students read, carefully evaluate their progress.

- Ask students if their books seems easy, hard, or about right.
- In a private conversation, have each student read one to three pages aloud. Keep track of miscues, and ask the student a few comprehension questions.
- Make recommendations based on your assessment. If the student is struggling, suggest easier texts he or she could read to build skills. If the student isn't challenged, suggest other selections that require more effort.
- Have students set a goal for reading: for example, reading a set number of pages a day, or learning a certain number of new vocabulary words. They can track goals in their progress reports.

STUDENT-TEACHER CONFERENCING

Use one-on-one conferencing to keep track of students' progress and reactions.

- Ask students why they chose the work and how they reacted to it. Did they enjoy it and if so, why? What new information did they learn? What was easy or hard about the book? What did they do when they got to a word they didn't know?
- Listen carefully to their responses and give feedback where appropriate. Make additional recommendations to encourage further reading. If a student likes a selection, suggest works in the same series, or by the same author.
- If students are ready to begin their post-reading logs or activities, ask them whether they have questions or need clarification before they start.

COLLECTION **5**
PERFORMANCE TASK A

Interactive Lessons

To help you complete this task, use
• *Writing Narratives*
• *Writing as a Process*

PERFORMANCE TASK A

Write a Personal Narrative

W 3a–e Write narratives.
W 4 Produce clear and coherent writing.
W 5 Develop and strengthen writing as needed.
W 10 Write routinely.

In his memoir, *It Worked for Me*, Colin Powell relates experiences and feelings that lead to an important decision in his life. Like a memoir, a personal narrative also reflects experiences and feelings. However, it is much shorter than a memoir and usually deals with a single subject or event. Now you will write a personal narrative about an important decision in your life.

A successful personal narrative

- provides a captivating introduction that clearly establishes the situation

- organizes events in a sequence that unfolds naturally and logically

- uses descriptive details that offer insight on significant experiences and feelings

- uses words and phrases that create vivid images

- provides a conclusion that explains the significance of the experiences

Mentor Text In this excerpt, notice how Powell uses concrete details to relate a significant experience in his life.

> " The porters at the Pepsi plant were all black. The workers on the bottling machines were all white. I didn't care. I just wanted work for the summer and I worked hard . . .
>
> At summers end, the boss told me he was pleased with my work and asked if I wanted to come back. 'Yes,' I answered, 'but not as a porter.' He agreed, and next summer I worked on the bottling machine . . . "

≡ myNotebook

Use the annotation tools in your eBook to find examples of decisions Colin Powell made that made a significant impact on his life.

ACADEMIC VOCABULARY

As you plan and present your personal narrative, be sure to use the academic vocabulary words.

achieve

individual

instance

outcome

principle

PLAN

Establish the Situation A personal narrative is a text that describes a memorable experience or time period in a person's life. Making an important decision is often the subject of a personal narrative. Think about important decisions you have made or might have to make that will impact your future.

PERFORMANCE TASK A

WRITE A PERSONAL NARRATIVE

W 3a–e, W 4, W 5, W 10

Introduce students to the Performance Task by reading the introductory paragraph with them and reviewing the criteria for what makes a good personal narrative. Remind students that good personal narratives have many of the same characteristics that are found in good stories.

PLAN

ESTABLISH THE SITUATION

Ask that students think about the kinds of details they will need to include to make their narratives come alive for their audience. Have students ask themselves questions such as the following:

- What details will help readers understand why this decision was so important?

- What feelings do I want to share about this experience?

- How can I catch my readers' attention at the beginning of my narrative?

English Language Support

Plan a Personal Narrative Make sure students understand that their personal narratives will focus on one event. Emphasize that they should write about a decision that had a significant impact in their lives. Have students think of two decisions that they might write about. Then ask pairs to discuss these decisions using the following sentence frames and questions. Students can use their conversations to choose a topic and to plan their personal narratives.

- This decision was important in my life because _____.
- Some details about how I felt about making this decision are _____.
- This sequence of events led to this decision: First, _____. Next, _____. Then, _____. Finally, _____.
- Which of my two decisions do you think is more interesting? Why?

English Language Support

Use Noun Phrases Explain that a sensory adjective describes how something looks, sounds, feels, tastes, or smells. Help students list sensory adjectives, such as the following: *gigantic, misty, colorful, circular, deafening, howling, thunderous, rough, rigid, leathery, bitter, sweet, salty, stale, musty, floral.*

Guide students to form simple noun phrases by adding sensory adjectives to nouns.

PRODUCE

DRAFT YOUR PERSONAL NARRATIVE

Remind students that most personal narratives allow readers to see inside the mind of the writer. Tell students to let readers know what their feelings and thoughts were when facing the decisions they tell about. Point out that students should use the words *I, me,* and *my* when referring to themselves.

WHEN STUDENTS STRUGGLE . . .

Add Descriptive Details Explain that precise language captures the experience for an audience. Have partners help each other add details to their descriptions. Suggest that they consult dictionaries and thesauruses to find synonyms and antonyms to add precision and shades of meaning to their narratives.

- Consider how the decision or experience is important to you.
- Identify the feelings you have about the experience.
- Determine whether you have a story to tell.

Organize Your Ideas In a personal narrative, you are the **narrator**, or the person telling the story. A graphic organizer can help you describe the events in a logical way.

| Setting: |
| Events: |

| Details: | Feelings: |

| Conclusion: |

Interactive Lessons
For help in organizing your personal narrative, use
• Writing as a Process: Planning and Drafting
• Writing Narratives: Narrative Context

Brainstorm Details Picture your experience in your mind. Provide specific sensory details that will make the experience come alive for your readers.

Consider Your Purpose and Audience Who will read your personal narrative? What do you want your audience to understand about your experience?

PRODUCE

my WriteSmart

Draft Your Personal Narrative Review the information in your graphic organizer as you begin your draft.

- Begin with an introduction that clearly establishes your purpose and grabs the attention of your audience.
- Use the first-person point of view, and other narrative elements, such as dialogue and setting, to convey your experience and its impact on your decision.
- Refer to your graphic organizer to help you present events in a clear and logical sequence.
- Include sensory language and descriptive details.
- Conclude your narrative by explaining the impact your decision has had or will have on your life. Explain what made the experience significant for you.

Write your rough draft in *my*WriteSmart. Focus on getting your ideas down, rather than perfecting your choice of language.

Interactive Lessons
For help in drafting your personal narrative, use
• Writing Narratives: Narrative Techniques

English Language Support

Understand Text Structure Explain that most personal narratives follow a chronological pattern of organization; events unfold in the order they occurred. Point out that the events in their narratives should lead to a conclusion that shows the importance of their decisions. Ask small groups to discuss answers to the following questions: *What did this experience teach you about life? What can other people learn from your experience? How did your decision affect your life?* Students may use their conversations to help them determine a focus for their conclusions.

Review Your Draft
Have your partner or group of peers review your draft. Use the following chart to revise it.

Have your partner or a group of peers review your draft in *my*WriteSmart. Ask your reviewers to note any parts of your narrative that do not follow a logical sequence.

Questions	Tips	Revision Techniques
Does my introduction catch the audience's attention?	**Highlight** the introduction.	**Add** action, dialogue, or other details to boost the introduction.
Do I use descriptive details and sensory language?	**Underline** each example of sensory language.	**Replace** words and phrases with more vivid details and sensory language.
Do I use narrative devices, such as dialogue and setting, to bring the events to life?	**Underline** dialogue and details about setting.	**Include** dialogue to help explain events. **Add** details about time and place.
Are events arranged in a logical order?	**Highlight** each event.	**Reorder** events, if necessary.
Do I use noun phrases to describe people, places, and events?	**Underline** all noun phrases that provide details.	**Add** more noun phrases to provide details.
Does my conclusion convey the importance of the experience?	**Highlight** the conclusion.	**Add** information to explain the significance of the experience.

Language Conventions: Nouns and Noun Phrases

A **noun phrase** consists of a noun and all the words that modify the noun. You can use noun phrases to make people, places, and events more vivid for your readers. **Comparative** and **superlative** adjectives, modifiers that are used to make comparisons, can greatly expand your power to describe when used with nouns. In the following excerpt, notice how Powell makes a scene come alive by using superlative forms of adjectives to modify the noun *part*.

> " . . . my heart skipped a beat as I imagined navigating the narrow streets of the oldest, most claustrophobic, and most mazelike **part** of New York City. "

Create a Finished Copy Finalize your personal narrative and choose a way to share it. You might present your personal narrative orally to your class.

PERFORMANCE TASK A

REVISE

LANGUAGE CONVENTIONS

Explain that a comparative adjective compares two things, while a superlative adjective compares one thing to several others of the same type. For example, in the Mentor Text excerpt, Powell uses superlative adjectives to compare one neighborhood in New York City to all the others. If he were comparing the neighborhood only to his own, he might describe it as older, more claustrophobic, and more mazelike than his own. Encourage students to find places in their drafts where adding comparative or superlative adjectives can enrich meaning.

English Language Support

Add Comparative/Superlative Adjectives Tell students that the words *more* or *most* are usually added to multisyllable adjectives to form comparatives or superlatives; for shorter adjectives, the endings *-er/-ier* or *-est/-iest* are added. Have pairs identify places where they might add comparative or superlative adjectives to their drafts. Encourage them to consult dictionaries as necessary.

PRESENT

CREATE A FINISHED COPY

If students choose to present their narratives orally, remind them to read with expression. Students may also present their narratives as blog entries on the school website.

FOR STANDARD ENGLISH LEARNERS

Add Dialogue Discuss the differences between formal and informal language. Tell students that they may incorporate informal language as dialogue in their narratives. Ask students to identify the informal language in the following examples from the Mentor Text.

- "That lazy brute, him only have two jobs."
- "One of these days, I'm gonna own this company."

FOR STUDENTS WITH DISABILITIES

Present an Interview Suggest that students work in pairs to present their narratives as interviews. Have partners ask questions that prompt each other to describe their decisions and personal experiences.

PERFORMANCE TASK A

USE THE SCORING RUBRIC

Let students exchange the final drafts of their narratives with a partner. Have them use the rubric to score their partners' narratives and then write a brief paragraph using the language of the rubric to justify the scores they've given.

REFLECT ON THE PROCESS

Explain that reflecting on how they wrote their personal narratives will help students complete future writing tasks. Ask them to think about how well they achieved their purpose and reached their audience. Then have them briefly respond to the following questions:

- What sensory details helped re-create your experience?
- How well did you convey the significance of your decision to your audience?
- Did writing the personal narrative help you to better understand your experience?

PERFORMANCE TASK A RUBRIC
PERSONAL NARRATIVE

	Ideas and Evidence	Organization	Language
4	• The introduction is engaging and clearly establishes the writer's subject and situation. • Descriptive details, narrative devices, such as dialogue and setting, strong feelings, and reflection effectively re-create the experience and offer insight. • The conclusion effectively summarizes the experience and reflects on the writer's decision.	• The organization is effective; ideas are arranged logically and unfold naturally. • Details successfully clarify the relationships between the experience and decision the writer makes.	• The writing maintains a first-person point of view and reflects the personality of the writer. • Sensory language and descriptive details creatively reveal people, places, and events. • Sentence beginnings, lengths, and structures vary and have a rhythmic flow. • Spelling, capitalization, and punctuation are correct. • Grammar and usage are correct.
3	• The introduction could do more to grab the audience's attention; the writer states the subject and situation. • Most details are strong and vivid, but a few could be more relevant to the experience; some narrative elements, such as dialogue and setting, are used. • The conclusion summarizes the experience but could do more to reflect on the writer's decision.	• The organization of ideas could be clearer in a few places but is generally logical and natural. • A few more details are needed to clarify the relationships between ideas.	• The writing mostly maintains a first-person point of view but is inconsistent in some places. • Some sensory language and description is used to reveal people, places, and events. • Sentence beginnings, lengths, and structures vary somewhat. • Some spelling, capitalization and punctuation mistakes occur. • Some grammatical and usage errors are present in the narrative.
2	• The introduction does not engage the reader; the writer does not clearly state the subject and/or situation. • The details are not always strong or relevant and narrative devices, such as dialogue and setting, are not always appropriately used. • The conclusion does not adequately summarize the experience and does little to reflect on the writer's decision.	• The organization of ideas is logical in some places, but it often doesn't follow a natural or stable pattern. • Many more details are needed to clarify the relationships between ideas.	• The writer's point of view is inconsistent throughout. • Sensory language and descriptive details are mostly lacking. • Sentence structures barely vary, and some fragments or run-on sentences are present. • Several spelling and capitalization mistakes occur, and punctuation is inconsistent. • Grammar and usage are incorrect in many places.
1	• The introduction is confusing. • Narrative devices, such as dialogue and setting, and details are missing. • The conclusion is missing or does not summarize the experience and decision.	• The organization is not logical or natural; details are presented randomly. • The relationships between ideas and details are not made clear.	• The writer's point of view is inconsistent and inappropriate. • Sensory language and descriptive details are not used. • Repetitive sentence structure, fragments, and run-on sentences make the writing monotonous and hard to follow. • Spelling and capitalization are often incorrect, and punctuation is missing in several places. • Many grammatical and usage errors change the meaning of the writer's ideas.

TO CHALLENGE STUDENTS...

Dramatize the Narrative Challenge students to adapt their personal narratives to theater performances. In addition to dialogue, facial expressions, gestures, and body language, encourage students to deliver monologues, soliloquies, and asides to convey their thoughts and feelings about the experience.

Write an Argument

In "Paul Revere's Ride," Longfellow memorializes what this ride meant for the freedom of the American colonies. Draw from this poem and other texts in the collection to write an argument in which you give your views on how people's decisions, no matter how big or small, can have consequences.

A successful argument

- contains an engaging introduction that states the claim
- supports the claim with logical reasons and relevant evidence
- presents and refutes opposing claims, or viewpoints
- uses language that clarifies the relationships among claims and reasons
- concludes with a restatement of the claim

W 1a–e Write arguments.
W 4 Produce clear and coherent writing.
W 5 Develop and strengthen writing.
W 9a–b Draw evidence from literary or informational texts.
W 10 Write routinely.

PLAN

Develop a Claim Review "Paul Revere's Ride" and other texts in the collection. Use your answers to the following questions to help you develop your claim as well as reasons for your position.

- What is the outcome of the decisions each individual makes?
- How do these decisions affect the individuals and others?
- Do the decisions help these individuals achieve their goals?

Gather Evidence Use the annotation tools in your eBook to find evidence to support your claim. Save your evidence to *my*Notebook, in a folder titled *Collection 5 Performance Task*.

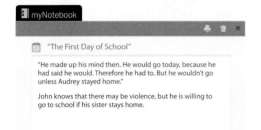

myNotebook

"The First Day of School"

"He made up his mind then. He would go today, because he had said he would. Therefore he had to. But he wouldn't go unless Audrey stayed home."

John knows that there may be violence, but he is willing to go to school if his sister stays home.

ACADEMIC VOCABULARY

As you write your argument, be sure to use the academic vocabulary words.

achieve

individual

instance

outcome

principle

PERFORMANCE TASK B

WRITE AN ARGUMENT

W 1a–e, W 4, W 5, W 9a–b, W 10

Introduce students to the Performance Task by reading the introductory paragraph with them and reviewing the criteria for what makes a good argument. Remind students that an argument needs to provide evidence to support the reasons for the writer's claim.

PLAN

GATHER EVIDENCE

Explain to students that they should anticipate readers' questions as they gather evidence to support their claims. Students should write down possible concerns and questions and prepare to answer them in their arguments. Point out that this will help them clarify their understanding and form their arguments as well as make it harder for others to disagree with the claims they express in their arguments.

English Language Support

Plan an Argument Tell students that their arguments will support a claim about the consequences of decisions. Organize the class into pairs. Have one-half of the pairs review the first two selections in the collection; assign the last three selections to the other pairs. Ask them all to identify and discuss the impact of decisions in their selections. Suggest that partners record observations and insights about each text in a chart.

Decision	Outcome	Affect on Individual	Affect on Others

After they finish, combine alternate pairs into groups of four. Have them share information and discuss the decisions made in all the collection texts. These conversations can help students develop their claims.

English Language Support

Use Academic Words Make sure students understand the differences in meaning between *affect* and *effect*. For example, in addition to analyzing the *effects* of a decision, students may also discuss factors that *affect* the decision-making process.

PRODUCE

DRAFT YOUR ARGUMENT

Explain to students that they can try several different kinds of introductions for their arguments. Suggest that students work with a partner to choose the introduction that most successfully states their claim in a way that will engage readers.

Remind students to use their evidence logically. Provide a list of transition words as needed to help students sequence their ideas in a coherent manner. Remind them that their conclusion should flow logically from the reasons and evidence they have presented in the argument.

WHEN STUDENTS STRUGGLE...

Clarify Reasons Let partners evaluate the reasoning in each other's drafts. Have them ask and answer the following questions:

- Do my reasons support my claim? Why or why not?
- Did I present my reasons in a logical order?

Encourage students to use the feedback to improve the focus of their arguments.

Organize Your Ideas A graphic organizer, such as this one, can help you to present your ideas logically.

Interactive Lessons
To help you plan your argument, complete the following lessons in Writing Arguments:
- What is a Claim?
- Reasons and Evidence

Consider Your Purpose and Audience Think about who will read your argument, and what you want them to understand. Your tone and word choice should be appealing and targeted toward them. Keep this in mind as you prepare to write.

PRODUCE

Draft Your Argument Review the information in your graphic organizer as you begin your draft.

- Begin by introducing the topic and stating your claim. Include an attention-grabbing lead, such as a quote, a story, or an interesting example. Be sure to use a formal tone.
- Write your claim and support it with reasons and evidence from the texts. Use the information in your graphic organizer to help you organize your reasons and evidence logically.
- Respond to opposing claims in your draft by explaining why your claim is more valid.
- Include transition words and phrases such as *because, therefore,* and *for that reason* that will link your claims and reasons and make your claim clearer and more coherent.
- Write a conclusion that summarizes your claim and restates the most important reasons and evidence.

my **WriteSmart**

Write your rough draft in *my*WriteSmart. Focus on getting your ideas down, rather than perfecting your choice of language.

Interactive Lessons
To help you draft your argument, complete the following lessons:
- Using Textual Evidence: Synthesizing Information
- Writing Arguments: Creating a Coherent Argument

English Language Support

Justify an Argument with Evidence Print out or display the Student Model that accompanies *Interactive Lesson:* Writing Arguments. Read the argument aloud as students follow along. Help students identify and label the details, examples, quotations, and statistics that support the writer's claim. Post an annotated copy of the model for students' reference. Explain that using different types of evidence can make an argument more convincing, and remind students that they can also support claims with examples from their own prior knowledge and experience. Have students complete hierarchy charts for their claims and ask a peer to help them assess the relevance and sufficiency of evidence.

Review Your Draft

Have your partner or group of peers review your draft. Use the following chart to revise it.

my WriteSmart

Have a partner or a group of peers review your draft in *my*WriteSmart. Ask your reviewers to note any reasons that do not support your opinion or lack sufficient evidence.

Questions	Tips	Revision Techniques
Does the introduction clearly state the claim?	**Highlight** the claim.	**Revise** the existing claim to make it clear and focused.
How well do my reasons and evidence support my claim?	**Underline** each reason. **Highlight** each piece of evidence.	**Add** more quotes or examples to support each reason. **Explain** each piece of evidence.
Are opposing claims, or viewpoints addressed?	**Highlight** any opposing claim.	**Add** transitions to set off your claim from an opposing claim.
Are compound and complex sentences used to make relationships between ideas clear?	**Underline** each compound and complex sentence.	**Combine** some simple sentences to form compound and complex sentences.
Does the conclusion include a strong restatement of the claim?	**Highlight** the conclusion.	**Add** a restatement of the claim, if necessary, to clarify.

Language Conventions: Connect Ideas

A **compound sentence** combines two independent clauses. A **complex sentence** combines an independent clause and one or more dependent clauses. Using these sentence structures will help you show how your claim and reasons and evidence are related. Notice how these sentences create coherence in this passage:

> In "Paul Revere's Ride" and "The First Day of School," two people make decisions that change the course of American history. Paul Revere embarks on a dangerous journey that leads to freedom. Because John Hawkins makes a decision along with many other black students to integrate an all-white school, he becomes a participant in the fight for civil rights. Revere's actions impact the American colonies, and Hawkins's actions impact an entire nation.

Create a Finished Copy

Choose a way to share your argument with an audience. You might present your ideas in a debate with someone who has an opposing opinion.

PERFORMANCE TASK B

REVISE

LANGUAGE CONVENTIONS

As students review their drafts, have them find places where they can make their arguments more cohesive by combining clauses to form compound and complex sentences. Remind students that an independent clause can stand on its own as a complete sentence, but a dependent clause expresses an incomplete thought.

English Language Support

Connecting Ideas Point out the word *and* in the compound sentence in the passage. Tell students that other words, such as *or, but, yet,* and *so* can connect independent clauses. Have partners identify and connect independent clauses in their drafts by creating compound sentences.

Point out the words *that* and *because* that mark the dependent clauses in the passage. Help students compile a list of additional words that they can use to create complex sentences in their drafts. *(Possible responses: after, before, even though, if, when, while)*

PRESENT

CREATE A FINISHED COPY

Students can present their ideas in a debate with classmates who have differing opinions. Remind students to take turns asking and answering questions and to listen politely to each other.

FOR STANDARD ENGLISH LEARNERS

Use Linking Verbs Remind students that they should use formal English in their arguments. For example, while students sometimes omit forms of the verb *to be* in everyday conversation, they should include linking verbs in academic language. Have students identify examples of formal English in these sentence pairs.

- She unsure about her decision. / She was unsure about her decision.
- They were risking their lives, but they decided to help anyway. / They risking their lives, but they decided to help anyway.

FOR STUDENTS WITH DISABILITIES

Debate on a Discussion Board Have students share opinions by conducting an extended online debate with classmates on a class website. As students post statements to the discussion board, remind them to support ideas and opposing views with evidence.

PERFORMANCE TASK B

USE THE SCORING RUBRIC

Have students use the rubric to score their own presentations. Then have partners exchange and evaluate each other's scores. Students should use the language of the rubric to provide feedback for each category.

REFLECT ON THE PROCESS

Encourage each student to reflect on the writing process and on the final product created for this assignment. Ask students to think about what they learned, as well as what they might improve or do differently for future assignments. Then have them write short responses to the following questions:

- How well did you engage the reader in your introduction?
- Which of your reasons was most convincing?
- What evidence did you use to address opposing claims?

PERFORMANCE TASK B RUBRIC
ARGUMENT

	Ideas and Evidence	Organization	Language
4	• The introduction skillfully pulls the reader in; the writer clearly states a claim on a topic. • Logical reasons and relevant evidence convincingly support the writer's claim. • Opposing claims are addressed and effectively refuted. • The concluding section effectively summarizes the claim and leaves a lasting impression.	• The reasons and evidence are organized logically and consistently to persuasive effect. • Transitions successfully clarify the relationships between the claim and reasons.	• The writing maintains a formal style. • Sentence beginnings, lengths, and structures vary and have a rhythmic flow. • Spelling, capitalization, and punctuation are correct. • Grammar and usage are correct.
3	• The introduction could do more to grab the audience's attention; the writer states a claim on a topic. • Most reasons and evidence support the writer's claim, but they could be more convincing. • Opposing claims are addressed, but they could be more effectively refuted. • The concluding section restates the claim and leaves a lasting impression.	• The organization of reasons and evidence is confusing in a few places. • A few more transitions are needed to connect the reasons to the claim.	• The style is informal in a few places. • Sentence beginnings, lengths, and structures vary somewhat. • Some spelling, capitalization and punctuation mistakes occur. • Some grammatical and usage errors are present in the essay.
2	• The introduction is incomplete; the writer identifies a topic, but the claim is not clearly stated. • The reasons and evidence are not always logical or relevant. • Opposing claims are anticipated but not addressed logically. • The concluding section includes an incomplete summary of the claim and does not leave a lasting impression.	• The organization of reasons and evidence is logical in some places, but it often doesn't follow a pattern. • Transitions are not adequately used to connect the reasons to the claim.	• The style becomes informal in many places. • Sentence structures barely vary, and some fragments or run-on sentences are present. • Several spelling and capitalization mistakes occur, and punctuation is inconsistent. • Grammar and usage are incorrect in many places.
1	• The introduction does not include a claim. • Supporting reasons and evidence are missing. • Opposing claims are neither anticpated nor addressed. • The concluding section is missing.	• A logical organization is not used; reasons and evidence are presented randomly. • Transitions are not used, making the essay difficult to understand.	• The style is inappropriate for the essay. • Repetitive sentence structure, fragments, and run-on sentences make the writing monotonous and hard to follow. • Spelling and capitalization are often incorrect, and punctuation is missing in most places. • Many grammatical and usage errors change the meaning of ideas.

310   Collection 5

TO CHALLENGE STUDENTS . . .

Create a Public Service Ad Challenge students to adapt their arguments for a public service ad that offers recommendations for people facing an important decision. Suggest that students present their ads as pamphlets, videos, or web pages.

©Robert Llewellyn/Corbis

What Tales Tell

"The destiny of the world is determined less by the battles that are lost and won than by the stories it loves and believes in."

—Harold Goddard

311

STREAM TO START

Motivate students to read the collection texts, and spark their curiosity about the collection by playing the video and watching it in class. After students view the video, ask them to discuss what the collection opener image and the collection quotation indicate about the values they might learn about in the collection tales. Call on volunteers to share their responses.

PERFORMANCE TASK PREVIEW

Point out to students that they will complete two performance tasks at the end of the collection. The performance tasks will require them to further analyze the selections in the collection and to synthesize ideas about these analyses. Students will present their findings in a variety of products.

ACADEMIC VOCABULARY

> **View It!**
> Professional Development Podcast:
> **Academic Vocabulary**

Students can acquire facility with the academic vocabulary words through frequent, repeated exposure as they analyze and discuss the selections in the collection. Academic vocabulary can be used in the instructional contexts listed below.

- Collaborative Discussion at the end of each selection
- Analyzing the Text questions for each selection
- Selection-level Performance Task
- Vocabulary instruction (for Critical Vocabulary and/or for Vocabulary Strategy)
- Language Conventions
- End-of-collection Performance Task for all selections in the collection

ASK STUDENTS to review the Academic Vocabulary word list for this collection. Pronounce each word aloud so students hear the correct pronunciation. Then, discuss the definitions and the related forms for each word. Remind students that they will encounter these words throughout the collection.

COLLECTION 6

What Tales Tell

In this collection, you will explore how traditional stories reveal the values of a culture.

Stream to Start   hmhfyi.com   Channel One News®

COLLECTION

PERFORMANCE TASK Preview

After reading this collection, you will have the opportunity to complete two performance tasks:

- In one, you will participate in a collaborative discussion about lessons that can be learned from stories.
- In the second, you will rewrite one of the selections in the collection as a play.

ACADEMIC VOCABULARY

Study the words and their definitions in the chart below. You will use these words as you discuss and write about the texts in this collection.

Word	Definition	Related Forms
emphasize (ĕm´fə-sīz´) v.	to give something special importance or attention	emphasis, emphatic, emphatically
occur (ə-kûr´) v.	to take place; happen	occurrence
period (pîr´ē-əd) n.	a particular length of time, often referring to a specific time in history or in a culture	periodic, periodically
relevant (rĕl´ə-vənt) adj.	important to, connected to, or significant to an issue, event, or person in some way	relevance, irrelevant, irrelevance
tradition (trə-dĭsh´ən) n.	the passing down of various elements of a culture from generation to generation; a custom	traditional, traditionally, traditionalist

312

▤ myNotebook

As students read, analyze, and discuss the texts in this collection, encourage them to create a *my*WordList folder in *my*Notebook to build their own personal word lists.

- **Annotate** Students can highlight vocabulary terms and other unfamiliar words and save each highlighted term to *my*Notebook.
- **Organize** Within *my*Notebook, students can drag each word into the *my*WordList folder.
- **Elaborate** Ask students to add details to the entry for each word, such as a definition, other forms of the word, and a sample sentence.

English Language Support

► **View It!**
Professional Development Podcast:
English Language Learners

ENGAGE WITH THE COLLECTION TOPIC

Draw students' attention to the title of the collection, What Tales Tell. Discuss that stories are told in all cultures and that often a story told by a certain country or culture will let the reader know something about what the people of that country or culture care about.

ACCESS PRIOR KNOWLEDGE Invite students to talk about stories, folktales, fables, or myths that they have read and enjoyed. Through discussion lead them toward the recognition that while the characters and situations may be fictional, stories often contain messages about life.

EXPERT GROUP JIGSAW

Use this strategy to help students compare multiple texts. By the time the activity ends, everyone in the class should be an "expert" on several texts in the collection.

- *First,* have students read each text individually, taking notes and annotating as they read. You might identify a specific aspect of each text for students to consider.
- *Then,* after students have finished reading, organize them into small "expert" groups, assigning one text to each group. Have students discuss and compare notes and observations, agreeing on the information that is most important to share with anyone who has not analyzed their text.

- *Next,* have individual "experts" change groups, gathering into "jigsaw groups." Students in these groups will share with one another the information learned in their expert groups.
- *Finally,* reconvene the original "expert groups," having members share any and all new or important information they may have learned in their "jigsaw groups."

 Collection 6 Digital Resources for English Language Support

LANGUAGE WORKSHOP
Designated English Learners

You many use the Teacher Resources > Language Workshop to support English learners in summarizing texts, condensing ideas, and sharing information in written exchanges.

 VIDEOS

These videos will help students learn how to build background and read stage directions. Have students use **Text in Focus Practice** to apply those skills.

my **SmartPlanner**	**eBook**	myNotebook	my **WriteSmart**	**fyi** hmhfyi.com

Collection 6 Lessons	Media	Teach and Practice	
**Student Edition	eBook**	▶ **Video Links** HISTORY A&E Channel One News®	**Close Reading and Evidence Tracking**	
ANCHOR TEXT **Greek Myth by Rosemary Sutcliffe** from *Black Ships Before Troy: The Story of The Iliad*	🔊 **Audio** from *Black Ships Before Troy: The Story of The Iliad*	**Close Read Screencasts** • Modeled Discussion 1 (lines 76–89) • Modeled Discussion 2 (lines 334–340) • Close Read Application PDF (lines 388–395)	**Text in Focus** • Previewing the Text (line 1) **Strategies for Annotation** • Describe Stories: Myth • Determine Theme • Cause-to-Effect Analogies
CLOSE READER **Myth by Olivia Coolidge** **"Medusa's Head"** **Poem by Agha Shahid Ali** **"Medusa"**	▶ **Video** HISTORY® 🔊 **Audio** "Medusa's Head" 🔊 **Audio** "Medusa"		
Poem by Kate Hovey **"The Apple of Discord I"**	🔊 **Audio** "The Apple of Discord I"		**Strategies for Annotation** • Determine Meanings of Words and Phrases
Chinese Folk Tale by Ai-Ling Louie *Yeh-Shen: A Cinderella Story from China*	🔊 **Audio** *Yeh-Shen: A Cinderella Story from China*		**Strategies for Annotation** • Describe Stories: Folk Tales • Describe Stories: Foreshadowing
ANCHOR TEXT **Novel by Mark Twain** **Dramatized by Joellen Bland** *The Prince and the Pauper*	🔊 **Audio** *The Prince and the Pauper*	**Close Read Screencasts** • Modeled Discussion 1 (lines 142–156) • Modeled Discussion 2 (lines 533–548) • Close Read Application PDF (lines 834–853)	**Text in Focus** • Reading Stage Directions (line 57) **Strategies for Annotation** • Describe Drama
CLOSE READER **Excerpt from Novel by Mark Twain** **Drama by Joellen Bland** **Graphic Story from Marvel Comics** *The Prince and the Pauper*	🔊 **Audio** *The Prince and the Pauper*		
Essay by Simone Payment **"The Role of Myths in Ancient Greece,"** from *Greek Mythology*	🔊 **Audio** "The Role of Myths in Ancient Greece"		**Strategies for Annotation** • Analyze Structure • Cite Evidence • Latin Roots
Collection 6 Performance Tasks: **A** Participate in a Collaborative Discussion **B** Write and Produce a Play	**fyi** hmhfyi.com	**Interactive Lessons** **A** Participating in Collaborative Discussions **A** Using Textual Evidence	**B** Writing Narratives **B** Writing as a Process **B** Giving a Presentation

	For Systematic Coverage of Writing and Speaking & Listening Standards	**Interactive Lessons** Writing Informative Texts Giving a Presentation

Assess		Extend	Reteach
Performance Task	✅ *Assess It Online!*	Teacher eBook	Teacher eBook
Writing Activity: Analysis	Selection Test	**Understand Archaic Language**	**Describe Stories: Myth > Level Up Tutorial >** Myths, Legends, and Tales
Speaking Activity: Argument	Selection Test	**Analyze Language: Symbol**	**Determine Meaning of Words and Phrases: Parody > Level Up Tutorial >** Tone
Writing Activity: Narrative	Selection Test	**Summarize Text > Interactive Whiteboard Lesson >** Summarizing Text **Interactive Lessons >** Participating in Collaborative Discussions	**Describe Stories: Foreshadowing > Level Up Tutorial >** Suspense and Foreshadowing
Speaking Activity: Dramatic Reading	Selection Test	**Describe Drama: Characterization**	**Describe Elements of Drama > Level Up Tutorial >** Elements of Drama
Speaking Activity: Discussion	Selection Test	**Generate Discussion Questions > Interactive Lessons >** Participating in Collaborative Discussions	**Analyzing Structure > Level Up Tutorials >** Main Idea and Supporting Details > Reading for Details **Interactive Graphic Organizer >** Spider Map
A Participate in a Collaborative Discussion **B** Write and Produce a Play	Collection Test		

Lesson Assessments Writing Informative Texts Giving a Presentation	**Standards Support and Enrichment**	For more instruction and practice in reading literary and informational texts, language, spelling, and speaking and listening, see Teacher Resources > Standards Support and Enrichment.	
	For Designated English Language Instruction	To provide support for English Learners during Designated English Language instruction, use the lessons found in Teacher Resources > Language Workshop.	

Collection 6 Lessons	Key Learning Objective	Performance Task	Vocabulary Strategy
ANCHOR TEXT **EXEMPLAR** **Greek Myth by Rosemary Sutcliffe** from *Black Ships Before Troy: The Story of The Iliad*, p. 313A **Lexile 1220L**	**The student will be able to . . .** describe literary elements and determine themes in a Greek myth.	Writing Activity: Analysis	Cause-to-Effect Analogies
Poem by Kate Hovey **"The Apple of Discord I," p. 331A**	**The student will be able to . . .** understand and identify the elements of a parody and learn to compare and contrast texts in different genres.	Speaking Activity: Argument	
Chinese Folk Tale by Ai-Ling Louie *Yeh-Shen: A Cinderella Story from China*, p. 335A **Lexile 1020L**	**The student will be able to . . .** describe the elements of folk tales as well as describe the use of foreshadowing.	Writing Activity: Narrative	Using a Glossary
ANCHOR TEXT **Novel by Mark Twain** **Dramatized by Joellen Bland** *The Prince and the Pauper*, p. 345A	**The student will be able to . . .** describe the elements of drama in a play.	Speaking Activity: Dramatic Reading	
Essay by Simone Payment **"The Role of Myths in Ancient Greece,"** from *Greek Mythology*, p. 363A **Lexile 970L**	**The student will be able to . . .** analyze structure and cite textual evidence.	Speaking Activity: Discussion	Latin Roots

Collection 6 Performance Tasks:

A Participate in a Collaborative Discussion

B Write and Produce a Play

Language Conventions	English Language Support	Differentiated Instruction	CLOSE READER Selection
Spell Words Correctly	• Express and Justify Opinions • Write Summaries • Understand Cohesion • Improve Reading Fluency • Modify to Add Details • Use Affixes	**When Students Struggle:** • Describe Plot • Conflict and Resolution **To Challenge Students:** Describe Character **For Students with Disabilities:** Working with Partners **For Standard English Learners:** Pronunciation	Myth by Olivia Coolidge "Medusa's Head," p. 330b **Lexile 1270L** Poem by Agha Shahid Ali "Medusa," p. 330b
	• Analyze Language • Determine Meanings • Support Opinions	**When Students Struggle:** Compare and Contrast	
Spell Words Correctly	• Understand Text Structure • Analyze Language • Write Summaries • Use Nouns and Noun Phrases • Condense Ideas • Use Affixes	**When Students Struggle:** Cause and Effect **To Challenge Students:** Analyze Point of View	
	• Read Closely • Use Context to Determine Meaning • Word Study • Use Verbs and Verb Phrases • Condense Ideas • Listen Actively	**When Students Struggle:** • Describe Plot • Determine Meaning **To Challenge Students:** Analyze Tone and Structure **For Students with Disabilities:** Preview Text **For Standard English Learners:** Pronunciation and Stress Patterns	Excerpt from Novel by Mark Twain **Lexile 920L** Drama by Joellen Bland Graphic Story from Marvel Comics *The Prince and the Pauper,* p. 362b
Parentheses	• Condense Ideas • Culturally Responsive Instruction • Express Opinions • Support Opinions • Use Linking Words • Connect Ideas	**When Students Struggle:** Determine Central Idea and Details **To Challenge Students:** Interpret Literature **For Standard English Learners:** Pronunciation	
B Use Verbs and Verb Phrases	**A** Plan a Collaborative Discussion Summarize Evidence Support Opinions Prepare to Practice and Present **B** Write and Produce a Play Use Verb Phrases Structure a Play	**A When Students Struggle:** Practice Speaking Techniques **For Standard English Learners:** Use Formal English **For Students with Disabilities:** Videotape the Discussion **To Challenge Students:** Gather Additional Evidence **B When Students Struggle:** Create a Storyboard **For Standard English Learners:** Adapt Speech **For Students with Disabilities:** Practice a Staged Reading **To Challenge Students:** Advertise the Play	

from Black Ships Before Troy: The Story of The Iliad

Greek Myth by Rosemary Sutcliff

Why This Text?

Myths have been the basis of much literature over the centuries, and students will benefit from familiarity with these classic stories. This lesson explores the character and actions of gods and goddesses in a story from classical Greek mythology.

▶ **View It!**

Professional Development Podcast:

Text Complexity

Key Learning Objective: The student will be able to describe literary elements and determine themes in a Greek myth.

For practice and application:

Background *According to Greek myth, Medusa was one of three beautiful sisters known as the Gorgons. The sisters were turned into monsters by Athena, the goddess of wisdom, who was angry at the destruction of one of her temples. Medusa was turned into a horrific creature with a gaping mouth, fragmatic eyes, and hair made of writhing snakes. Anyone who looked into Medusa's eyes was immediately turned to stone.*

Medusa's Head   Medusa

Close Reader selections

"Medusa's Head"
Myth by Olivia Coolidge

"Medusa"
Poem by Agha Shahid Ali

RL 1   Cite text evidence; make inferences.

RL 2   Determine a theme or central idea.

RL 3   Describe story elements.

RL 4   Determine the meaning of words and phrases.

RL 5   Analyze structure.

W 2   Write informative/explanatory texts.

W 2a   Introduce a topic; organize ideas.

W 2b   Develop the topic.

W 2c   Use appropriate and varied transitions.

W 2d   Use precise language and domain-specific vocabulary.

W 2e   Establish and maintain a formal style.

W 2f   Provide a concluding statement.

W 9a   Draw evidence from literary texts to support analysis.

W 10   Write routinely over extended time frames.

SL 1   Engage effectively in a range of collaborative discussions.

L 2b   Spell correctly.

L 4a   Use context as a clue to meaning.

L 5b   Use cause/effect analogies.

L 6   Acquire and use grade-appropriate general academic vocabulary.

▲ **Text Complexity Rubric**

Quantitative Measures

from **Black Ships Before Troy: The Story of THE ILIAD**
Lexile: 1220L

Levels of Meaning/Purpose

multiple levels of meaning (multiple themes)

Qualitative Measures

Structure

complex, unfamiliar story concepts

Language Conventionality and Clarity

archaic, unfamiliar language

Knowledge Demands

increased amount of cultural and literary knowledge useful

Reader/Task Considerations

• Teacher determined
• Vary by individual reader and type of text
• See the Text X-Ray for suggested Reader/Task Considerations.

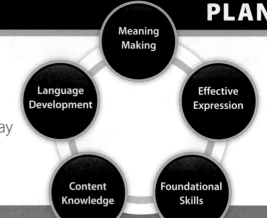

English Language Support Before teaching, use the Text X-Ray for an overview of the text's complexity. The Text X-Ray and the supports and scaffolds in the Teacher's Edition will help you guide students of different skill levels.

Text Complexity: Qualitative Measures

Levels of Meaning/Purpose

multiple levels of meaning (multiple themes)

Help students determine theme.

- Teacher's Edition side notes, pp. 316, 319, 320, 325, 326, 327
- English Language Support, pp. 314, 316, 319, 320, 325
- Close Read Screencasts, p. 313
- Strategies for Annotation, p. 327
- Determine Theme, p. 327

ZOOM IN ON **DETERMINING THEME** Review the definition of myth on page 327. Tell students that one of the purposes of **myths** in the ancient Greek culture was to teach lessons about the way people should interact with each other and with the gods and goddesses. Explain that a **theme**, or message, is often brought out through characters' actions and reactions to events and through how they resolve conflicts.

- Have students reread lines 429–437 with a partner. Ask students to state the theme of this part of the myth, using this sentence frame: Pride and anger can lead a person to _____. *(hurt others while thinking only of him or herself; refuse to fulfill his or her responsibilities)*

Structure

complex, unfamiliar story concepts

Help students describe the characteristics of a myth.

- Teacher's Edition side notes, pp. 313, 314, 315, 317, 318, 321, 322, 323, 324, 327
- English Language Support, pp. 315, 316, 317, 321, 322, 323
- When Students Struggle, pp. 319, 323
- Strategies for Annotation, pp. 317, 322
- Describe Stories: Myth, p. 327

To reteach how to describe myths, see

- Describe Stories: Myth, p. 330a

▶ *Use It!* **Level Up Tutorials:** Myths, Legends, and Tales

ZOOM IN ON **DESCRIBING MYTHS** A **myth** is a traditional story that attempts to answer questions about human nature and origins of the world. Explain that myths have their own set of elements in addition to those shared by other stories.

- A myth shows a belief in gods and goddesses. These gods and goddesses have human characteristics and often interact with humans.
- A myth has heroes with great strengths and weaknesses.
- A myth often includes a journey or a battle.
- A myth may explain nature, teach a lesson, or tell about historical events.

Organize students into groups and assign one myth characteristic to each group. Have groups take notes about their feature while reading and then share findings with the class.

Language Conventionality and Clarity

archaic, unfamiliar language

Teach unfamiliar vocabulary in context.

- Teacher's Edition Critical Vocabulary notes, pp. 315, 321, 324, 326, 329
- Applying Academic Vocabulary, p. 315
- English Language Support, p. 329
- Strategies for Annotation, p. 329
- Vocabulary Strategy: Cause-to-Effect Analogies, p. 329
- Understand Archaic Language, p. 330a

Support students' reading and analysis of the selection.

- Teacher's Edition side notes, pp. 326, 330
- English Language Support, pp. 318, 320, 324, 328, 330
- Language Conventions: Spell Words Correctly, p. 330
- Analyze Stories: Character, p. 27

▶ ***Use It!*** **Level Up Tutorial:** Using Context Clues

ZOOM IN ON **UNPACKING SENTENCES** Display this sentence from lines 370–375 on the board. Work with students to highlight the subject and the compound verbs in the independent clause. Then underline the subordinate clauses. Point out that the first and second are noun clauses that explain what Calchas told the Greeks; the third is an adverb clause that tells when Apollo's anger will "be cooled."

And Calchas watched the flight of birds and made patterns in the sand, and told them that Apollo, angry on behalf of his priest, was shooting arrows of pestilence into the camp from his silver bow; and that his anger would not be cooled until the maiden Chryseis was returned to her father.

Knowledge Demands

increased amount of cultural and literary knowledge useful

Support English Learners in understanding cultural and historical background.

- Teacher's Edition Background note, p. 313

 Building Background

ZOOM IN ON **BUILDING CULTURAL AND HISTORICAL BACKGROUND** Tell students that once Achilles stopped fighting, the war went badly for the Greeks. Finally, he allowed his best friend Patroclus to wear his armor into battle to help. But Patroclus was mistaken for Achilles and killed. Achilles flew into battle and was killed. Achilles' death is not described in the *Iliad*, but another source says that Paris shot an arrow that hit Achilles in his heel. Paris too died in the conflict.

Suggested Reader/Task Considerations

You might consider the following before assigning this selection to students.

- Do students have the attention necessary to read the entire text?
- Do students have the confidence to read a text of this length and complexity?

ZOOM IN ON **SUPPORTING COMPREHENSION**

- Break the selection into manageable parts. Have students listen to the audio recording as they read their text. After each part, have students work with a partner to summarize important ideas.
- Before reading, display the text and highlight each proper name, explaining whether it refers to a god or goddess or mortal, and if so, whether a Greek or Trojan. Have students repeat the names after you.

CLOSE READ

Background Explain to students that the ancient Greeks worshipped a number of gods and goddesses. The king of the gods, Zeus, ruled from Mount Olympus with his wife, Hera. Each deity ruled over an aspect of life. The ancient Greeks built temples and shrines to particular gods and goddesses in order to worship them and gain their favor. Some of these magnificent structures still exist and are a popular destination for tourists from around the world.

SETTING A PURPOSE Direct students to use the Setting a Purpose prompt to focus their reading. Remind students to write down questions as they read.

 Text in FOCUS English Language Support

Building Background
[THE GOLDEN APPLE]

Have students view the **Text in Focus** video on this page of their eBook to build background that will help them better comprehend these myths. Then have students use **Text in Focus Practice** to apply what they have learned.

Describe Stories:
Myth (LINES 1–8)

RL 1,
RL 3

Tell students that a **myth** is a traditional story that attempts to answer basic questions about human nature, origins of the world, mysteries of nature, or social customs. Explain that this myth involves many immortal gods and goddesses who, according to the ancient Greeks, lived atop Mount Olympus.

A **CITE TEXT EVIDENCE** Have students reread lines 1–8. Ask students what elements of Greek mythology they find in these lines and how they know a conflict begins here. (*Possible responses: Characters: Heroes, gods, and goddesses are mentioned. Events: Heroes were important because they were like gods; kings were rulers; humans might marry nonhumans, such as nymphs; gods and mortals might interact with each other. Conflict: Eris wasn't invited to the feast, and she will be angry because she is the goddess of discord.*)

Rosemary Sutcliff (1920–1992) *was a well-known British children's author and reteller of myths and legends. She spent her childhood in Malta and on other naval bases where her father was a naval officer. Sutcliff was chronically ill from a very young age and confined to a wheelchair for most of her life. Her mother, a great oral storyteller, told Rosemary many legends and myths of their native Britain. Sutcliff wrote her first novel in 1950 and never stopped; she was still writing on the morning of her death.*

from BLACK SHIPS BEFORE TROY
The Story of THE ILIAD

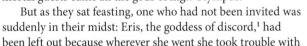

Greek Myth by Rosemary Sutcliff

SETTING A PURPOSE As you read, pay attention to how the quarrels of the gods and goddesses are relevant to the lives of the humans and the problems that occur because of their quarrels. Write down any questions you have while reading.

myNotebook

As you read, mark up the text. Save your work to *myNotebook*.
- Highlight details
- Add notes and questions
- Add new words to *myWordList*

Text in FOCUS THE GOLDEN APPLE

IN THE HIGH and far-off days when men were heroes and walked with the gods, Peleus, king of the Myrmidons, took for his wife a sea nymph called Thetis, Thetis of the Silver Feet. Many guests came to their wedding feast, and among the mortal guests came all the gods of high Olympus.

But as they sat feasting, one who had not been invited was suddenly in their midst: Eris, the goddess of discord,[1] had been left out because wherever she went she took trouble with

[1] **discord** (dĭs′kôrd′): disagreement; tension or strife.

Close Read Screencasts

 Close Read

Modeled Discussions

Have students click the *Close Read* icon in their eBook to access two screencasts in which readers discuss and annotate the following key passages:

- lines 76–89, the judgment of Paris
- lines 334–340, the nine-year war

As a class, view and discuss the videos. Then, have students pair up to do an independent close read of an additional passage—Achilles' quarrel with Agamemnon (lines 388–395).

Describe Stories: RL 1, RL 3

Myth (LINES 17–35)

Explain to students that in Greek mythology, gods and goddesses possess superhuman abilities, but that they also have very human emotions and shortcomings. Explain that their human qualities often result in arguments or conflicts between them.

B **CITE TEXT EVIDENCE** Ask students to reread lines 17–35 and identify the conflict that arises between Hera, Athene, and Aphrodite and how it advances the plot. *(Each goddess believes that the apple inscribed "To the fairest" is rightfully hers; they take this quarrel home with them, and other gods get involved.)* Ask them to tell how this conflict shows how the gods are like mortal humans. *(Possible responses: They argue bitterly over small things; they are vain, envious, and vengeful.)*

C **CITE TEXT EVIDENCE** Ask students to review lines 32–35 and describe how the text helps them understand the gods' actions and explain plot events. *(The author says that the quarrel between the gods went on for what seemed to a human to be a long time. However, even though the quarrel had been going on long enough for a human child to grow into an adult, it did not seem long to the gods because they "do not know time as mortals know it.")*

---

her; yet here she was, all the same, and in her blackest mood,
10 to avenge the insult.

All she did—it seemed a small thing—was to toss down on the table a golden apple. Then she breathed upon the guests once, and vanished.

The apple lay gleaming among the piled fruits and the brimming wine cups; and bending close to look at it, everyone could see the words "To the fairest" traced on its side.

Then the three greatest of the goddesses each claimed that it was hers. Hera claimed it as wife to Zeus, the All-father, and queen of all the gods. Athene claimed that she had the better
20 right, for the beauty of wisdom such as hers surpassed all else. Aphrodite only smiled, and asked who had a better claim to beauty's prize than the goddess of beauty herself.

B They fell to arguing among themselves; the argument became a quarrel, and the quarrel grew more and more bitter, and each called upon the assembled guests to judge between them. But the other guests refused, for they knew well enough that, whichever goddess they chose to receive the golden apple, they would make enemies of the other two.

In the end, the three took the quarrel home with them to
30 Olympus. The other gods took sides, some with one and some with another, and the ill will between them dragged on for a long while. More than long enough in the world of men for a child born when the quarrel first began, to grow to manhood **C** and become a warrior or a herdsman. But the immortal gods do not know time as mortals know it.

Now on the northeast coast of the Aegean Sea, there was a city of men. Troy was its name, a great city surrounded by strong walls, and standing on a hill hard by the shore. It had grown rich on the tolls that its kings demanded from
40 merchant ships passing up the nearby straits[2] to the Black Sea cornlands and down again. Priam, who was now king, was lord of wide realms and long-maned horses, and he had many sons about his hearth. And when the quarrel about the golden apple was still raw and new, a last son was born to him and his wife Queen Hecuba, and they called him Paris.

There should have been great rejoicing, but while Hecuba still carried the babe within her, the soothsayers[3] had foretold

---

[2] **strait** (strāt): a narrow channel of water that joins two larger bodies of water.
[3] **soothsayer** (sōōth´sā´ər): someone who claims to be able to predict the future.

English Language Support

Express and Justify Opinions Read lines 11–28 aloud and explain that authors include details so readers can form opinions about characters. Readers can use text details to justify, or support, opinions.

- Work with students to express and justify an opinion about Eris. Give them these sentence frames: I think that Eris feels that she has to/can (*cause trouble*). Eris is (*angry/hurt*) because the text says (*she wasn't invited*).
- Have pairs justify two opinions about the gods discussed in lines

11–28. Encourage them to use modal expressions such as *maybe/probably, can/could,* or *must.* Remind them to refer to specific details to support their ideas.

- Have a small group discuss the characters mentioned in lines 11–28. Ask students to form and justify their opinions about the characters. Challenge them to use terms such as *probably/certainly/definitely, should/would, might,* and *in my opinion* as they express their ideas. Remind them to provide textual evidence to support their opinions.

that she would give birth to a firebrand[4] that should burn down Troy. And so, when he was born and named, the king bade a servant carry him out into the wilderness and leave him to die. The servant did as he was bid; but a herdsman searching for a missing calf found the babe and brought him up as his own.

The boy grew tall and strong and beautiful, the swiftest runner and the best archer in all the country around. So his boyhood passed among the oak woods and the high hill-pastures that rose toward Mount Ida. And there he met and fell in love with a wood nymph called Oenone, who loved him in return. She had the gift of being able to heal the wounds of mortal men, no matter how sorely they were hurt.

Among the oak woods they lived together and were happy—until one day the three jealous goddesses, still quarreling about the golden apple, chanced to look down from Olympus, and saw the beautiful young man herding his cattle on the slopes of Mount Ida. They knew, for the gods know all things, that he was the son of Priam, king of Troy, though he himself did not know it yet; but the thought came to them that he would not know who they were, and therefore he would not be afraid to judge between them. They were growing somewhat **weary** of the argument by then.

So they tossed the apple down to him, and Paris put up his hands and caught it. After it the three came down, landing before him so lightly that their feet did not bend the mountain grasses, and bade him choose between them, which was the fairest and had best right to the prize he held in his hand.

First Athene, in her gleaming armor, fixed him with sword-gray eyes and promised him supreme wisdom if he would name her.

Then Hera, in her royal robes as queen of heaven, promised him vast wealth and power and honor if he awarded her the prize.

Lastly, Aphrodite drew near, her eyes as blue as deep-sea water, her hair like spun gold wreathed around her head, and, smiling honey-sweet, whispered that she would give him a wife as fair as herself if he tossed the apple to her.

weary
(wîr´ē) *adj.* If you are growing *weary*, you are getting tired of something, either physically or mentally.

Close Read

---
[4] **firebrand** (fīr´brănd´): a person who creates trouble or leads a revolt.

APPLYING ACADEMIC VOCABULARY

occur	period

THINK-PAIR-SHARE Have students turn to a partner to discuss the following questions. Guide students to include the academic vocabulary words *occur* and *period* in their responses. Ask volunteers to share their responses with the class.

- What **occurs** as a result of a particular character's choice or action?
- What **occurred** during the **period** of time in which the Greeks stayed on the beaches at Troy?

CLOSE READ

Describe Stories:
Myth (LINES 61–75)

RL 1,
RL 3

Tell students that a common element in myths involves interactions between gods and mortals. Explain that these interactions can be either positive or negative.

D CITE TEXT EVIDENCE Ask students to reread lines 61–75 and explain why the three goddesses chose to interact with Paris. *(Lines 69–70: They are "weary" of their argument and want him to settle it.)* Then, ask them whether they think this interaction might have a positive or negative outcome. *(Possible response: The outcome will probably be negative because, regardless of who he chooses, the goddesses who are not chosen will be angry and probably vengeful.)*

English Language Support

Prior to answering the questions, have students work in pairs to choral read lines 61–75. Encourage them to define terms that they find difficult either using context clues or a dictionary before answering these questions.

- Why do the goddesses want Paris to end their fight? *(They are tired, or weary, of the problem.)*
- Will Paris choose the fairest of the goddesses? What will most likely happen if he does? *(Yes, Paris will choose because he does not know about the fight. Two of the goddesses will be unhappy when he chooses.)*

CRITICAL VOCABULARY

weary: The author uses the word *weary* to describe how the goddesses feel about their argument.

ASK STUDENTS to tell why the goddesses might be feeling weary. *(The argument has been going on for a long time, and there seems to be no good way to settle it.)*

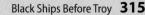

Determine Theme

RL 2

(LINES 86–94)

Tell students that a **theme** is a message about life or human nature that the writer shares with the reader. Explain that a theme is usually not stated directly in the text, so readers must figure it out for themselves. One way to determine a myth's theme is to **summarize,** or retell, important plot events.

E **ASK STUDENTS** to review lines 86–94, and have them summarize Paris's choice and the outcome of it. *(Possible response: Paris chooses Aphrodite as the fairest. She is very pleased by this, but Hera and Athene are angry with both him and Aphrodite.)* Then, ask students to suggest what themes, or messages about life, this might have taught the ancient Greeks. *(Possible responses: Men are often swayed by beauty; you cannot please all the gods; it is not a good idea to anger the gods.)*

English Language Support

Reread lines 86–94 with students and then work with them to write a summary on the board. Help students identify themes with questions such as

- Why does Paris chooses Aphrodite? *(She is beautiful.)*
- What does this tell you about the message the author might be giving about men? *(Men's choices can be affected by beauty.)*

And Paris forgot the other two with their offers of wisdom and power, forgot also, for that moment, dark-haired Oenone in the shadowed oak woods; and he gave the golden apple to Aphrodite.

E 90 Then Athene and Hera were angry with him for refusing them the prize, just as the wedding guests had known that they would be; and both of them were angry with Aphrodite. But Aphrodite was well content, and set about keeping her promise to the herdsman who was a king's son.

She put a certain thought into the heads of some of King Priam's men, so that they came cattle-raiding at the full of the moon and drove off Paris' big beautiful herd-bull, who was lord of all his cattle. Then Paris left the hills and came down into Troy, seeking his bull. And there Hecuba, his mother,

English Language Support

Write Summaries Explain to students that writing a summary can help them understand a text better. It is helpful to write short summaries as they read a text. Tell students that a summary, or retelling, needs to
- identify the topic or subject
- tell main ideas and important details
- give no opinion
- be clear, organized, and short

- Reread lines 95–106 with students and support them in writing notes about what happens when Aphrodite helps Paris. Write a brief summary of the plot action together.

- Have students work in pairs to take notes about lines 95–106 before writing a summary. Remind them to keep the summary short and write in complete sentences.

- Ask students to work independently to take notes on lines 95–106. Then have them write a summary of the action, using complete and concise sentences.

100 chanced to see him, and knew by his likeness to his brothers
and by something in her own heart that he was the son she
had thought dead and lost to her in his babyhood. She wept
for joy and brought him before the king; and seeing him living
and so good to look upon, all men forgot the prophecy, and
Priam welcomed him into the family and gave him a house of
his own, like each of the other Trojan princes.

There he lived whenever he would, but at other times he
would be away back to the oak woods of Mount Ida, to his
love Oenone.

110 And so things went on happily enough for a while.

But meantime, across the Aegean Sea, another wedding
had taken place, the marriage of King Menelaus of Sparta
to the Princess Helen, whom men called Helen of the Fair
Cheeks, the most beautiful of all mortal women. Her beauty
was famous throughout the kingdoms of Greece, and many
kings and princes had wished to marry her, among them
Odysseus, whose kingdom was the rocky island of Ithaca.

Her father would have none of them, but gave her to
Menelaus. Yet, because he feared trouble between her suitors
120 at a later time, he caused them all to swear that they would
stand with her husband for her sake, if ever he had need
of them. And between Helen and Odysseus, who married
her cousin Penelope and loved her well, there was a lasting
friendship that stood her in good stead when she had sore
need of a friend, years afterward.

Even beyond the farthest bounds of Greece, the fame
of Helen's beauty traveled, until it came at last to Troy, as
Aphrodite had known that it would. And Paris no sooner
heard of her than he determined to go and see for himself if
130 she was indeed as fair as men said. Oenone wept and begged
him to stay with her; but he paid no heed, and his feet came
no more up the track to her woodland cave. If Paris wanted
a thing, then he must have it; so he begged a ship from his
father, and he and his companions set out.

All the length of the Aegean Sea was before them, and the
winds blew them often from their true course. But they came
at last to their landfall, and ran the ship up the beach and
climbed the long hill tracks that brought them to the fortress-
palace of King Menelaus.

CLOSE READ

Describe Stories:
Myth (LINES 126–134)

RL 1,
RL 3

Tell students that, like fictional stories, myths include
story elements such as setting, characters, and
conflict. Explain that paying attention to a character's
traits and how he or she responds to plot events will
help them describe myths.

F **CITE TEXT EVIDENCE** Ask students to review
lines 126–134 and describe what Paris's actions tell
readers about his character. *(Possible responses: Even
though he has a faithful, beautiful partner in Oenone,
Paris is tempted by tales of Helen's beauty and decides
to journey to see her. This tells readers that Paris is easily
swayed by the idea of beauty. In lines 133–134, the text
says that if Paris wanted something, "he must have it,"
which tells readers that he is not a deep thinker, but
headstrong and willful.)*

English Language Support

Understand Cohesion Display lines 126–134. Read
the lines aloud with students following along. Ask
students to identify terms that show how the ideas
and events are linked in this paragraph. Highlight
the connecting and transitional words that students
provide. *(Possible responses: even beyond, until, no
sooner, indeed, paid no heed, if...then, so)* Explain that
understanding how ideas are connected can help
students understand the plot events and characters.

Strategies for Annotation   🖊 📋 *Annotate it!*

Describe Stories: Myth

RL 1,
RL 3

Share these strategies for guided or independent analysis:
- Highlight in yellow phrases that tell about Paris's character.
- Highlight in green actions that Paris takes.
- Review your annotations. On a note, describe Paris's strengths and
  weaknesses based on his actions.

Aphrodite had known that it would. And Paris no sooner

heard of her than he determined to go and see for hims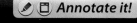

if she was indeed as fair as men said. Oenone wept and

him to stay with her; but he paid no heed, and his feet came

no more up the track to her woodland cave. If Paris wanted

a thing, then he must have it; so he begged a ship from his father,

selfish,
determined

**RL 1,
RL 3**

Describe Stories:
Myth (LINES 146–163)

Tell students that myths often involve a hero's journey, quest, or battle. Explain that heroes are often leaders or warriors who possess admirable qualities.

G **CITE TEXT EVIDENCE** Ask students to reread lines 146–163 and tell how they know whether Paris is being honest with King Menelaus about the reasons for his journey. How is this important to the plot? *(Paris isn't being honest; he flatters the king but does not tell the real motivation for his journey, which readers know is to meet Helen. This is important because Paris's hiding of his fascination with Helen will anger the king and probably have harmful results.)* Ask students why the ancient Greeks might have seen Paris as a hero. *(Possible responses: Paris is headstrong and willful, but he is also ambitious and determined, and those qualities might have been admirable to the ancient Greeks. The heroes, gods, and goddesses had strengths and weaknesses, just as human beings do.)*

English Language Support

Improve Reading Fluency Have students work with a partner to read lines 155–175. Review that when they read the text aloud, they will be telling a story and should vary the volume and pace of their reading to match the mood of the story. In addition, they should try to use facial expressions to match the flow of the story. Encourage students to provide feedback about their partner's volume and pace of reading, discussing the mood created by the text.

---

140 Slaves met them, as they met all strangers, in the outer court, and led them in to wash off the salt and the dust of the long journey. And presently, clad in fresh clothes, they were standing before the king in his great hall, where the fire burned on the raised hearth in the center and the king's favorite hounds lay sprawled about his feet.

"Welcome to you, strangers," said Menelaus. "Tell me now who you are and where you come from, and what brings you to my hall."

"I am a king's son, Paris by name, from Troy, far across the 150 sea," Paris told him. "And I come because the wish is on me to see distant places, and the fame of Menelaus has reached our shores, as a great king and a generous host to strangers."

"Sit then, and eat, for you must be way-weary with such far traveling," said the king.

And when they were seated, meat and fruit, and wine in golden cups were brought in and set before them. And while they ate and talked with their host, telling the adventures of their journey, Helen the queen came in from the women's quarters, two of her maidens following, one carrying her baby 160 daughter, one carrying her ivory spindle and distaff[5] laden with wool of the deepest violet color. And she sat down on the far side of the fire, the women's side, and began to spin. And as she spun, she listened to the stranger's tales of his journeying.

And in little snatched glances their eyes went to each other through the fronding[6] hearth-smoke. And Paris saw that Menelaus' queen was fairer even than the stories told, golden as a corn-stalk and sweet as wild honey. And Helen saw, above all things, that the stranger prince was young. Menelaus had been her father's choice, not hers, and though their marriage 170 was happy enough, he was much older than she was, with the first gray hairs already in his beard. There was no gray in the gold of Paris' beard, and his eyes were bright and there was laughter at the corners of his mouth. Her heart quickened as she looked at him, and once, still spinning, she snapped the violet thread.

---

[5] **distaff** (dĭs′tăf′): a staff that holds the unspun flax or wool from which the spinner draws thread when spinning by hand.

[6] **fronding** (frŏnd′ĭng): getting wispy; starting to look like the leaf of a fern, which is called a frond.

English Language Support

Modify to Add Details Display lines 146–148. Point out *hall* and ask a volunteer to read the first definition from a dictionary. Ask students if this definition fits the text. Explain that *hall* has multiple meanings. Ask volunteers to read aloud the other definitions and decide on the meaning that best fits the text. *(large room or building for gatherings)* Have students discuss other halls. *(study hall, town/city hall, community hall)*

• Work with individual students to expand the sentence in lines 146–148 with an adverb, an adverb phrase, or a prepositional

phrase that adds information about the place.

• Have pairs expand the sentence in lines 146–148 with an adverbial that adds a detail about the place. Then challenge them to write a sentence using a different meaning of *hall* with a prepositional phrase that adds a detail about the place, time, manner, or cause mentioned in the sentence.

For many days Paris and his companions remained the guests of King Menelaus, and soon it was not enough for Paris to look at the queen. Poor Oenone was quite forgotten, and he did not know how to go away leaving Helen of the Fair
180 Cheeks behind.

So the days went by, and the prince and the queen walked together through the cool olive gardens and under the white-flowered almond trees of the palace; and he sat at her feet while she spun her violet wool, and sang her the songs of his own people.

And then one day the king rode out hunting. Paris made an excuse not to ride with him, and he and his companions remained behind. And when they were alone together, walking in the silvery shade of the olives while his
190 companions and her maidens amused themselves at a little distance, Paris told the queen that it was for sight of her that he had come so far, and that now he had seen her, he loved her to his heart's core and could not live without her.

"You should not have told me this," said Helen. "For I am another man's wife. And because you have told me it will be the worse for me when you go away and must leave me behind."

"Honey-sweet," said Paris, "my ship is in the bay; come with me now, while the king, your husband, is away from
200 home. For we belong together, you and I, like two slips of a vine sprung from the same stock."

 And they talked together, on and on through the hot noontide with the crickets churring, he urging and she holding back. But he was Paris, who always got the things he wanted; and deep within her, her heart wanted the same thing.

And in the end she left her lord and her babe and her honor; and followed by his companions, with the maidens wailing and pleading behind them, he led her down the
210 mountain paths and through the passes to his ship waiting on the seashore.

So Paris had the bride that Aphrodite had promised him, and from that came all the sorrows that followed.

TEACH

CLOSE READ

Determine Theme   RL 2
(LINES 194–213)

Remind students that a theme is a message about life or human nature that the writer shares with the reader and that they can summarize plot events to help them determine a myth's theme.

H **ASK STUDENTS** to summarize the plot events in lines 194–213. *(Possible response: Paris's powers of persuasion finally convince Helen that they should be together, and she leaves her home and family to be with him.)*

English Language Support

Explain that a summary includes only the most important details in a text. Review lines 194–213 with students, clarifying any difficult terms and concepts. As you review, point out important ideas, such as that Paris is very persuasive. Then have pairs of students write a summary.

I **ASK STUDENTS** to review the phrase in line 213, "and from that came all the sorrows that followed." Ask them what theme about life or human behavior these events suggest. *(Possible responses: Poor choices can have far-reaching consequences; Sweet words can persuade another to make bad choices; The actions we take today have consequences for the future.)*

WHEN STUDENTS STRUGGLE . . .

To guide comprehension of plot events, have students work independently or with a partner to complete a sequence chart like the one shown. Then, have students use the chart to orally summarize the events.

LEVEL UP TUTORIALS For additional support, assign the following *Level Up* tutorial: **Plot: Sequence of Events**

Helen tells Paris she cannot be his because she is married.

Paris speaks sweetly to Helen to convince her that they belong together.

Determine Theme

RL 2

(LINES 237–249)

Tell students that readers can determine themes by thinking about the lessons a myth points out.

J **ASK STUDENTS** to summarize lines 237–249, telling what Thetis does and why. *(Possible response: She dips her infant son Achilles in the waters of the Styx so that he will not die in battle.)* Ask students to describe the outcome. *(She holds him by his heel, and that one area does not get protected.)* Then, have students compare this with how Paris's parents sent their infant son to the wilderness in order to avoid a prophecy. Ask students to suggest themes, or lessons, that these myths might have taught the ancient Greeks. *(Possible responses: One cannot change fate; It is useless to try to protect children from the future.)*

Make Inferences

RL 1

(LINES 245–249)

Explain to students that lessons from myths can be passed on from generation to generation.

K **CITE TEXT EVIDENCE** Ask students to explain what is meant when something is referred to as a person's "Achilles' heel" and tell how lines 245–249 explain this lesson or expression. *(The expression "Achilles' heel" refers to someone's weak spot or vulnerability; this text explains how this expression originated in this myth of Achilles being dipped in the river Styx for protection—everywhere except his heel.)*

English Language Support

Read lines 245–249 with students following along in their texts. Point out that the author does not introduce the term "Achilles heel" in the text. If the reader does not know the expression, then the reader will simply understand that Achilles had a weak spot on his heel. However, knowing the term can help students express ideas in speech or writing. Have students write a sentence using the term. *(Ali was a good student, but her Achilles' heel was history because she had a hard time remembering dates.)*

SHIP-GATHERING

WHEN MENELAUS returned from hunting and found his queen fled with the Trojan prince, the black grief and the red rage came upon him, and he sent word of the wrong done to him and a furious call for aid to his brother, black-bearded Agamemnon, who was High King over all the other kings of Greece.

220   And from golden Mycenae of the Lion Gate where Agamemnon sat in his great hall, the call went out for men and ships. To ancient Nestor of Pylos, to Thisbe, where the wild doves croon, to rocky Pytho, to Ajax the mighty, Lord of Salamis, and Diomedes of the Loud War Cry whose land was Argos of the many horses, to the cunning Odysseus among the harsh hills of Ithaca, even far south to Idomeneus of Crete, and many more.

And from Crete and Argos and Ithaca, from the mainland and the islands, the black ships put to sea, as the kings
230   gathered their men from the fields and the fishing and took up bows and spears for the keeping of their oath, to fetch back Helen of the Fair Cheeks and take vengeance upon Troy, whose prince had carried her away.

Agamemnon waited for them with his own ships in the harbor of Aulis; and when they had gathered to him there, the great fleet sailed for Troy.

But one of the war-leaders who should have been with them was lacking, and this was the way of it. Before ever Paris was born, Thetis of the Silver Feet had given a son to King
240   Peleus, and they called him Achilles. The gods had promised that if she dipped the babe in the Styx, which is one of the rivers of the underworld, the sacred water would proof him against death in battle. So, gladly she did as she was bidden, but dipping him headfirst in the dark and bitter flood, she held on to him by one foot. Thus her fingers, pressed about his heel, kept the waters from reaching that one spot. By the time she understood what she had done it was too late, for the thing could not be done again; so ever after she was afraid for her son, always afraid.
250   When he was old enough, his father sent him to Thessaly, with an older boy, Patroclus, for his companion, to Chiron, the wisest of all the Centaurs. And with the other boy, Chiron taught him to ride (on his own back) and trained him in all

English Language Support

Word Study Tell students that adding -s to most words is correct, as in *apple/apples*. Adding -es to words ending in s, sh, ch, x, or z as in *dish/dishes* is also common. Some words that end in f change the f to v as in *knife/knives*, some words change completely as in *child/children*, and some words stay the same as in *sheep/sheep*. Words that end in consonant + y usually drop the y and add -ies as in *country/countries*.

ASK STUDENTS to form plurals of the following: *arch, family, life, face, box, valley, hoof, deer, foot, sky.*

the warrior skills of sword and spear and bow, and in making the music of the lyre, until the time came for him to return to his father's court.

But when the High King's **summons** went out and the black ships were launched for war, his mother sent him secretly to the Isle of Scyros, begging King Lycomedes to
260 have him dressed as a maiden and hidden among his own daughters, so that he might be safe.

How it came about that Achilles agreed to this, no one knows. Maybe she cast some kind of spell on him, for love's sake. But there he remained among the princesses, while the ships gathered in the world outside.

But Thetis' loving plan failed after all, for, following the seaways eastward, part of the fleet put in to take on fresh water at Scyros, where the whisper was abroad that Prince Achilles was **concealed**.

270 King Lycomedes welcomed the warriors but denied all knowledge of the young prince. The leaders were desperate to find him, for Calchas, chief among the soothsayers who sailed with them, had said that they would not take Troy without him. Then Odysseus, who was not called the Resourceful for nothing, blackened his beard and eyebrows and put on the dress of a trader, turning his hair up under a seaman's red cap, and with a staff in one hand and a huge pack on his back went up to the palace.

When the girls heard that there was a trader in the
280 palace forecourt, out from the women's quarters they all came running, Achilles among them, veiled like the rest, to

summons
(sŭm′ənz) *n.* A *summons* is a call or a notice by an authority to appear somewhere or to do something.

conceal
(kən-sēl′) *v.* If you *conceal* something, you hide it and keep it from being found or seen.

Black Ships Before Troy **321**

TO CHALLENGE STUDENTS . . .

Describe Character Have students reread lines 250–256 and think about what they know about Achilles' character so far. Remind students to think about the fact that he is a royal prince from a kingdom that has promised allegiance to the High King Agamemnon.

ASK STUDENTS to tell why the author questions Achilles' agreement to being concealed as a maiden (lines 262–263). Why would a spell need to be cast on him in order for this to happen? Remind students to think about admirable traits that heroes in myths might have, such as courage, loyalty, and honesty, and why it is probable that Achilles is cast as a hero in this myth.

CLOSE READ

Describe Stories:
Myth (LINES 257–278)

RL 1,
RL 3

Explain to students that authors show the importance of characters in different ways.

ⓛ CITE TEXT EVIDENCE Ask students to reread lines 257–278 and tell why Achilles is important in the myth. *(Lines 273–274 say that Calchas, a soothsayer, "had said that [the fleet] would not take Troy without [Achilles].")* Then, have students describe how the author connects earlier descriptions of Achilles' life to the plot events. *(In lines 237–238, the author says that a leader was lacking from the fleet, "and this was the way of it." The story of Thetis and Achilles follows, which tells readers that Achilles will be important in some way.)*

English Language Support

Preview lines 257–274 with students. Have volunteers read portions of the text, pointing out that lines 273–274 explain why Achilles is important to the myth. Then help students turn back to lines 237–238 to show students that the author of the myth already hinted that Achilles would be important. Finally, read through the analyze text questions before asking students to answer them.

CRITICAL VOCABULARY

summons: The word *summons* is used to describe a call to prepare for war.

ASK STUDENTS to tell why the High King summoned warriors and soldiers for war. *(Possible response: He summoned them to prepare to set sail for Troy to battle to retrieve Helen.)*

conceal: The author uses the word *concealed* to tell about Achilles' whereabouts.

ASK STUDENTS to explain how and why Achilles was concealed. *(Possible response: His mother plotted with King Lycomedes to keep Achilles disguised and hidden among maidens because she was fearful that he would be killed in battle.)*

Describe Stories:
Myth (LINES 300–315)

RL 1,
RL 3

Remind students that heroes are often important characters in Greek myths. Point out that by examining the character traits of heroes in myths readers can get a deeper understanding of the culture of the ancient Greeks.

Ⓜ CITE TEXT EVIDENCE Ask students to reread lines 300–315, describe Achilles' decision and what it tells them about his character, and tell how it moves the story forward. *(Possible responses: Even though he has been disguised, Achilles cannot conceal his true nature as a warrior; he cares less about being safe than about making a name for himself. This establishes him as a hero and important character in the myth.)* Ask students what this tells them about what was valued by the ancient Greeks. *(Possible responses: Bravery and a willingness to fight seem to have been important; having a long, safe life did not mean much to young men.)*

English Language Support

Have students work with a partner to reread lines 300–315. Have one partner describe what Achilles' decision tells about his character. The other partner can explain how the decision moves the story forward. Together the partners can discuss what they think the ancient Greeks valued. Encourage partners to provide text evidence to support their ideas.

---

see him undo his pack. And when he had done so, each of them chose what she liked best: a wreath of gold, a necklace of amber, a pair of turquoise earrings blue as the sky, a skirt of embroidered scarlet silk, until they came to the bottom of the pack. And at the bottom of the pack lay a great sword of bronze, the hilt studded with golden nails. Then the last of the girls, still closely veiled, who had held back as though waiting all the while, swooped forward and caught it up, as one well used to the handling of such weapons. And at the familiar feel of it, the spell that his mother had set upon him dissolved away.

290

"This for me!" said Prince Achilles, pulling off his veil.

Then the kings and chieftains of the fleet greeted and rejoiced over him. They stripped off his girl's garments and dressed him in kilt and cloak as befitted a warrior, with his new sword slung at his side; and they sent him back to his father's court to claim the ships and the fighting men that were his by right, that he might add them to the fleet.

300

Ⓜ

His mother wept over him, saying, "I had hoped to keep you safe for the love I bear you. But now it must be for you to choose. If you bide here with me, you shall live long and happy. If you go forth now with the fighting men, you will make for yourself a name that shall last while men tell stories round the fire, even to the ending of the world. But you will not live to see the first gray hair in your beard, and you will come home no more to your father's hall."

"Short life and long fame for me," said Achilles, fingering his sword.

310

So his father gave him fifty ships, fully manned, and Patroclus to go with him for his friend and sword-companion. And his mother, weeping still, armed him in his father's armor; glorious war gear that Hephaestus, the smith of the gods, had made for him.

And he sailed to join the black ships on their way to Troy.

QUARREL WITH THE HIGH KING

Tʜᴇ ɢʀᴇᴇᴋs did not have smooth sailing. Storms beat them this way and that, and more than once they met with enemy fleets and had to fight them off. But at last they came in sight of the coast below Troy city.

Strategies for Annotation   ✎ 🗐 Annotate it!

Describe Stories: Myth

RL 1,
RL 3

Share these strategies for guided or independent analysis:

- Highlight in yellow phrases that tell about Thetis's character.
- Highlight in green actions that Thetis takes.
- Review your annotations. On a note, tell about Thetis's traits based on her actions.

His mother wept over him, saying, "I had hoped to keep you safe for the love I bear you. But now it must be for you to choose. . . ."

"Short life and long fame for me," said Achilles, fingering his sword. . . .

And his mother, weeping still, armed him in his father's armor; glorious war gear that Hephaestus, the smith of the gods, had

> loving, resigned, respectful of Achilles' choice

320 Then they made a race of it, the rowers quickening the oar beat, thrusting their ships through the water, each eager to come first to land. The race was won by the ship of Prince Protesilaus, but as the prince sprang ashore, an arrow from among the defenders took him in the throat and he dropped just above the tide line, the first of the Greeks to come ashore, the first man to die in the long war for Troy.

The rest followed him and quickly drove back the Trojan warriors, who were ill prepared for so great an enemy war-host. And when that day's sun went down, they were
330 masters of the coastwise dunes and reedbeds and rough grass that fringed the great plain of Troy.

They beached their ships, and built halls and huts in front of them to live in, so that in a while there was something like a seaport town. And in that town of turf and timber they lived while year after year of war went by.

Nine times the wild almonds flowered and fruited on the rocky slopes below the city. Nine times summer dried out the tamarisk scrub among the grave mounds of long-dead kings. The ships' timbers rotted, and the high fierce hopes that the
340 Greeks had brought with them grew weary and dull-edged.

They knew little of siege warfare. They did not seek to dig trenches round the city, nor to keep watch on the roads by which supplies and fighting men of allied countries might come in; nor did they try to break down the gates or scale the high walls. And the Trojans, ruled by an old king and a council of old men, remained for the most part within their city walls, or came out to skirmish[7] only a little way outside them, though Hector, their war-leader and foremost among the king's sons, would have attacked and stormed the Greek
350 camp if he had had his will.

But there were other, lesser cities along the coast that were easier prey; and the men of the black ships raided these and drove off their cattle for food and their horses for the chariots that they had built, and the fairest of their women for slaves.

On one of these raids far down the coast, when the almond trees were coming into flower for the tenth time, they captured and brought back two beautiful maidens, Chryseis and Briseis, among the spoils[8] of war. Chryseis was given to

---

[7] **skirmish** (skûr´mĭsh): to engage in a minor battle in war.
[8] **spoils** (spoilz): property taken from the losers by the winners of a battle or conflict.

Black Ships Before Troy **323**

CLOSE READ

Describe Stories:
Myth (LINES 327–350)

RL 1,
RL 2,
RL 3

Explain to students that to describe a myth they can identify the conflict and examine its resolution.

 CITE TEXT EVIDENCE Ask students to reread lines 327–350, summarize the conflict in this section, and tell how they know whether it is resolved. *(Possible response: The Greeks arrive to do battle with Troy, and they take over the coast. However, because they know "little of siege warfare," they spend nine years at the coast. The Trojans stay inside their city walls; this tells the reader that the conflict remains unresolved.)*

English Language Support

Have students work independently to write a summary of the conflict and resolution in lines 327–350. Tell them to reread the lines and take notes on the most important ideas and key words. Then have them use the notes to write their summaries. Remind them to edit their work to make their summaries clear, coherent, and concise.

WHEN STUDENTS STRUGGLE...

To guide comprehension of conflict and resolution, have students work independently or with a partner to complete a chart like the one shown to the right. Then, have students use the chart to discuss why the conflict does not get resolved.

LEVEL UP TUTORIALS For additional support, assign the following *Level Up* tutorials: **Myths, Legends, and Tales; Characters and Conflict**

Who is involved?	the Greek army and the Trojans
What is the conflict?	The Greeks want to battle the Trojans in order to reclaim Helen.
What happens?	
Is the conflict resolved? Why or why not?	

Describe Stories:

**RL 1,
RL 3**

Myth (LINES 388–400)

Remind students that to describe a myth they should note what the main characters are like and how they respond to plot events.

CITE TEXT EVIDENCE Ask students to reread lines 388–400, describe what they know about Achilles' character, and tell how this explains his conflict with King Agamemnon. *(Possible response: Achilles is young but "the proudest and hottest-hearted of all the Greek leaders." Achilles insults Agamemnon, calling him a "greedy coward" because he is proud and doesn't think he should lose Briseis just because Agamemnon is High King.)* Ask students to describe what Agamemnon's response tells them about whether the Greeks considered it wise to engage in a conflict with a king. *(Possible response: The High King's angered response, saying that Achilles is "no more than a prince among other princes," shows that although brave warriors were valued by the ancient Greeks they would be foolish to insult a king in this way.)*

CRITICAL VOCABULARY

despair: The author uses the word *despair* to describe the Greeks' feelings and behavior.

pestilence: The word *pestilence* is used to tell about a serious sickness that spreads among a group.

ASK STUDENTS why the Greeks might have felt despair when their camp was overtaken by a growing pestilence. *(Possible response: Seeing their comrades die from a terrible disease would make the soldiers fearful and feel great hopelessness.)*

Agamemnon, who as High King always received the richest of the plunder, while Briseis was awarded to Achilles, who had led the raid.

Chryseis' father, who was a priest of Apollo, the Sun God, followed and came to the Greek camp, begging for his daughter back again, and offering much gold for her ransom. But Agamemnon refused, and bade the old man be gone, with cruel insults. And there it seemed that the thing was ended.

But soon after, fever came upon the Greek camp. Many died, and the smoke of the death-fires hung day and night along the shore, and in **despair** the Greeks begged the soothsayer Calchas to tell them the cause of the evil. And Calchas watched the flight of birds and made patterns in the sand, and told them that Apollo, angry on behalf of his priest, was shooting arrows of **pestilence** into the camp from his silver bow; and that his anger would not be cooled until the maiden Chryseis was returned to her father.

On hearing this, Agamemnon fell into a great rage, and though the other leaders urged him to release the girl, he swore that if he did so, then he would have Briseis out from Achilles' hall in her place.

Then Achilles, who had grown to care for Briseis, would have drawn his sword to fight for her. But gray-eyed Athene, who was for the Greeks because Aphrodite was for Paris and the Trojans, put it into his mind that no man might fight the High King, and that all manner of evils, from defeat in battle to bad harvests, would come of it if he did. Even so, a bitter quarrel flared between them, though wise old Nestor tried to make peace.

Achilles, who despite his youth was the proudest and hottest-hearted of all the Greek leaders, called Agamemnon a greedy coward with the face of a dog and the heart of a deer. "It is small part you play in the fighting, but you take other men's prizes from them when the fighting is over, robbing them of the reward and the honor that is rightfully theirs—for this one reason, that you have the power to do it, because you are the High King!"

"I am the High King!" agreed Agamemnon, his face blackening as though a storm cloud gathered over it. "I have the power, even as you say, and let you not forget it! Also, as High King I have the right, and let you not forget that either, you who are no more than a prince among other princes!"

despair
(dĭ-spâr´) *n.* A complete loss of hope is called *despair*.

pestilence
(pĕs´tə-ləns) *n.* A *pestilence* is often a fatal illness or evil influence that spreads quickly to many people.

324 Collection 6

English Language Support

Use Nouns and Noun Phrases Explain to students that a noun phrase acts like a noun in a sentence. Write the sentence *Achilles liked sailing ships* on the board. Tell students that noun phrases can be built in various ways to add details about ideas, people, and things.

- Work with students to expand the sentence by adding a sensory adjective to the noun. For example, *Achilles liked sailing black ships*. Discuss how the adjective *black* helps the reader know more in the noun phrase *sailing black ships*.

- Have partners work to add details to the base sentence. Encourage them to add comparative or superlative adjectives or simple clauses. Remind students that clauses will have a subject and a verb. Have them underline each noun phrase.

- Have students work independently to write paragraphs about the attack on Troy. Encourage them to enrich their sentences with noun phrases containing comparative/superlative adjectives or clauses. Have them read their paragraphs aloud in a small group.

The quarrel roared on, despite all that the other leaders could do to stop it. And in the end it was Achilles who had the final word.

"Lord Agamemnon, you have dishonored me; and therefore now I swear on all the gods that I will fight for you no more! Nor will I take any part in this struggle against Troy until my honor is made good to me again!" And he strode out from the council gathering and went back to his own part of the camp, his own hall and his own black ships; and all the
410 men of his own country with him.

"I am the High King!"

Then Agamemnon, in a black and silent rage, caused Chryseis to be put into one of his ships, and cattle with her for a sacrifice to Apollo, and ordered Odysseus to take command of the ship and return the girl to her father. And as soon as the ship had sailed, he sent his heralds[9] to fetch Briseis from Achilles' hall and bring her to his own.

Achilles made no more attempt to resist, and stood by as though turned to stone while the girl was led weeping away. But when she was gone he went down to the cold seashore
420 and flung himself down upon the tide line and wept his heart away.

And his mother, Thetis of the Silver Feet, heard the voice of his furious grief from her home in the crystal palaces of

---

[9] **heralds** (hĕr´əldz): those who announce important news; messengers.

TEACH

CLOSE READ

Determine Theme   RL 2
(LINES 404–421)

Remind students that summarizing plot events can help them determine and describe a myth's themes.

P **ASK STUDENTS** to summarize the important plot events in lines 404–421. (*Achilles declares that he will no longer fight for King Agamemnon or in the battle for Troy until his honor is restored. Still insulted, the High King commands Odysseus to take Chryseis back to her father and orders that Briseis be brought to him. Achilles weeps at the seashore.*) Then, ask students what themes, or lessons, the ancient Greeks might have taken from this myth. (*Possible responses: It is not wise, even for a prince, to anger a king; It is important to make a stand against injustice, even if it means losing your station.*)

English Language Support

Display lines 404–421 and work with students to write a summary of the plot events. Remind students that a summary needs to include only the most important details. Then discuss the messages, or themes, that are contained in the myth so far. Ask students to explain what the Greeks were learning from this story.

FOR STUDENTS WITH DISABILITIES

Students may struggle to read a myth of this length and complexity. In addition to reading along with the text as they listen to the audio recording of the story in their eBooks, suggest that students work with a partner. Have them listen and read independently, pausing at the end of each section to review what they have learned about Achilles and the other characters. Some students may find it helpful to list all of the characters they encounter in the myth and make notes about how the characters are related to each other or what their title is in the myth.

Determine Meanings: Figurative Language

RL 1,
RL 4

(LINES 445–446)

Remind students that authors use imagery to help readers understand meaning in a story.

Q CITE TEXT EVIDENCE Ask students to reread lines 445–446, identify the simile, and tell how the simile helps them understand Achilles' feelings. *(The simile is "nursing his anger as though it were a red rose in his breast." This tells the reader that Achilles is still angry; he is keeping his anger alive, the way he might care for a red rose to keep it growing. The red rose also helps readers connect Achilles' anger with his love for Briseis, which makes his feelings of love and anger clear.)*

> **CRITICAL VOCABULARY**
>
> **brood**: The author uses the word *brooding* to describe Achilles after his argument with Agamemnon.
>
> **ASK STUDENTS** to tell whether it is probable that Achilles will get over his anger as he broods. *(Possible responses: Probably not; when someone "broods," he or she is not thinking in a positive way.)*

COLLABORATIVE DISCUSSION As they review events in the myth, have partners keep a list of the human occurrences and situations that the gods create or influence. Remind students to cite evidence from the text to support their ideas.

ASK STUDENTS to share any questions they generated in the course of reading and discussing the selection.

---

the sea, and she came up through the waters like a sea mist rising, no one seeing her except her son. And she sat down beside him and stroked his hair and his bowed shoulders and said, "What bitter grief is this? Tell me the darkness that is in your heart."

430 So, chokingly, Achilles told her what she asked; and in his grief and bitter fury, he demanded that she go to Zeus the Thunderer, chief of all the gods, and pray him for a Trojan victory that should make the High King feel the loss of his greatest captain and do him honor and beg for his return.

Thetis promised that she would do as he asked. But it could not be done at once, for the father of the gods was absent about some matter in the far-most part of his world, and it must wait for his return to Olympus.

So for twelve days Achilles remained by his ships, waiting and **brooding** on his wrongs. And Odysseus, having returned
440 Chryseis to her father with the proper sacrifices and prayers and purification, came again to the ship-strand, with the promise that Apollo was no longer set against them, and had lifted the plague-curse away.

But still Briseis wept in the hall of the High King, and Achilles sat among his ships, nursing his anger as though it were a red rose in his breast.

brood
(brood) *v.* If you *brood*, you are deep in thought, maybe worrying or feeling depressed about something.

Q

COLLABORATIVE DISCUSSION Gods and goddesses in Greek mythology often create or add to problems for mortals. With a partner, review the myth and discuss how gods and goddesses become involved in the lives of humans. Do they solve problems, or make them worse?

FOR STANDARD ENGLISH LEARNERS

Pronunciation Remind students that as they participate in their collaborative discussion, it is important to use the correct pronunciation of words so that their listeners will understand them. Some students may voice the initial /str/ sound as /skr/ as in *street/skreet*. List *strait* (line 40), *strong* (line 54), *stranger* (line 163), *struggle* (line 406), *strode* (line 407), *stroked* (line 426), and *strand* (line 441) on the board. Read each word aloud, emphasizing the /str/ sound. Have students echo your reading several times, and then ask them to work with a partner to use each word in a sentence that they might use in their discussion.

Describe Stories: Myth

RL 3

A **myth** is a traditional story told long ago in a particular culture. Myths were created as attempts to explain occurrences in nature, describe historical events, or act as a guide to social customs and human nature. Like fictional stories, myths have elements such as setting, characters, plot, conflict, and resolution. In addition, specific elements of myth often include:

- events in nature, such as the origin of the world and the seasons
- heroes, such as warriors or leaders who have admirable qualities
- gods and goddesses, who are immortal and have superhuman abilities but possess human emotions and shortcomings

Arguments or conflicts between two or more gods occur frequently in myths. Other characteristics might include a journey, quest, or battle, or a mortal's good or bad interaction with a god or goddess.

To analyze myths, ask questions such as the following:

- What is the conflict in the myth? Is it resolved? How?
- Who are the main characters? How do these characters change or respond as the plot moves toward resolution?
- Why was this myth important to the culture that created it?

Determine Theme

RL 2

A **theme** is a message or lesson about life or human nature from a story or myth. To determine and analyze a myth's theme, ask yourself these questions: *What is the important lesson the myth teaches? How is this message conveyed?*

Summarizing key events may also help you determine a myth's theme. To **summarize** plot, make a list of the important events. Here is a list of events from *Black Ships Before Troy*:

- A last son, Paris, is born to King Priam and Queen Hecuba.
- However, soothsayers have foretold that this son will burn down Troy.
- The king orders a servant to leave the baby in the wilderness.
- A herdsman finds the baby and raises Paris.

These events explain how the king thought he could avoid what had been foretold by leaving his son to die in the wilderness. His error points out this theme or message: *You can't change one's fate or destiny.*

As you analyze *Black Ships Before Troy*, look for elements of myth and use them to help you determine the theme or message.

TEACH

CLOSE READ

Describe Stories: Myth

RL 3

Help students understand that myths share elements found in fiction stories, such as setting, characters, and plot. Point out that for ancient cultures myths served many purposes, such as to explain how the world began and natural occurrences.

Point out that myths acted as guides for behavior for the people of ancient cultures. For example, the ancient Greeks believed that the proper worship of gods and goddesses would bring favorable results in broad areas, such as political power, as well as in everyday concerns, such as health, love, and farming.

Have students review the gods and goddesses who play a role in *Black Ships Before Troy*. Ask them to give examples that explain how the actions of the immortals have a direct influence on the lives of mortals.

Determine Theme

RL 2

Help students understand that a theme is a lesson or message about life and human nature that a myth shares. Clarify that a theme is usually stated in a complete sentence, such as the example *You can't change fate or destiny*. Point out that a myth may have multiple themes.

Have students practice summarizing plot events to determine key themes in *Black Ships Before Troy*. Invite volunteers to use complete sentences to describe lessons the events might have conveyed to the ancient Greeks.

Strategies for Annotation 🖊 📋 *Annotate it!*

Determine Theme

RL 2

Share these strategies for guided or independent analysis:

- Use a different color highlight to indicate key details about each important event.
- Review your annotations and think about an important lesson the ancient Greeks might have taken from the events.
- On a note, record a complete sentence that expresses the lesson, or theme.

Chryseis' father, who was a priest of Apollo, . . . came to the Greek camp, begging for his daughter back . . . Agamemnon refused, . . . soon after, fever came upon the Greek camp. Many died, . . . Apollo . . . was shooting arrows of pestilence into the camp . . . his anger would not be cooled until the maiden Chryseis was returned to her father.

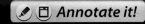

Do not anger a god with unjust acts.

PRACTICE & APPLY

Analyzing the Text

RL 1, RL 2,
RL 3, RL 5

Possible answers:

1. *When Eris, the goddess of discord, is not invited to a wedding, she plants a golden apple at the wedding feasts labeled "To the fairest." This event sets the stage for a longstanding argument between Hera, Athene, and Aphrodite. The myth might have been created to show people that engaging in a silly argument can have long-term consequences.*

2. *Elements of myth include goddesses who have human emotions and shortcomings, and an argument that develops among them. Their conflict leads to an interaction with a hero, Paris.*

3. *Paris is strong willed, ambitious, and bold. These traits help him accomplish his goals, but they are also weaknesses because he does not think about others or the consequences of his actions.*

4. *Paris convinces Helen to leave her husband, King Menelaus, for him. Menelaus's brother, Agamemnon, is the High King of Greece, and he calls on all Greek kings to join in battle against Troy, Paris's home. Soothsayers told Paris's parents that Paris would bring ruin to Troy, and this fortune appears to be coming true.*

5. *Mothers will do anything they can to protect their children; mothers cannot protect their children from everything; every person, no matter how strong, has at least one weakness.*

6. *In a raid, the Greeks steal two maidens to give to their kings. However, the father of Chryseis, one of the maidens, is a priest of the god Apollo, who, a soothsayer says, sends a plague on the Greek camp. This conflict might have been used to teach about the importance of honoring and respecting the gods.*

7. *Achilles' conflict is unresolved; as the myth ends, he sits for 12 days, feeling deeply insulted and angry. It seems likely that he will do something to get back at Agamemnon or that Zeus will intervene on his behalf.*

eBook *Annotate It!*

Analyzing the Text

RL 1, RL 2, RL 3,
RL 5, W 2a–b,
W 9a, W 10

Cite Text Evidence   Support your responses with evidence from the text.

1. **Summarize** Review lines 1–35. What events create the central conflict of the myth? Tell why this myth might have been created.

2. **Identify** Review lines 54–70. What elements of myth do you find?

3. **Infer** Reread lines 86–89 and lines 126–134. What words would you use to describe Paris' character? Tell whether you think these traits are strengths or weaknesses and why.

4. **Cause/Effect** Review lines 202–236. What happens to set a great battle in motion? Explain the connection between this event and the fortune told to Paris' parents.

5. **Interpret** Reread the story of Achilles in lines 237–249. What theme does it share about mothers? Tell what life lesson you feel it teaches about strength and weakness.

6. **Analyze** Review lines 355–375. Explain how this conflict might have taught an important lesson in the culture of the ancient Greeks.

7. **Predict** Review lines 411–446. Has the conflict Achilles faces been resolved? Tell how this might affect what happens in events to come.

PERFORMANCE TASK

Writing Activity: Analysis Several major events occur in *Black Ships Before Troy*. Choose one event to analyze, explaining how the plot unfolds and how the characters respond or change. Be sure to cite evidence from the text.

- First, summarize the key event and the conflict that takes place.

- Take notes on what the main characters are like and what they think and do.

- Use your summary and notes as you write your essay. Include evidence from the text to support your ideas.

Critical Vocabulary

L 4a, L 5b, L 6

weary	summons	conceal
despair	pestilence	brood

Practice and Apply Choose the correct response to answer each question.

1. Which of these would a group of **weary** toddlers be likely to do—play a wild game of tag or take a nap? Why?

2. Would a messenger be likely to **conceal** a **summons** from his king? Why or why not?

3. If a hiker experienced **despair** because she lost her supplies, would she rest and **brood** over her situation? Why or why not?

4. Would you go to a place where **pestilence** had spread? Why or why not?

Vocabulary Strategy: Cause-to-Effect Analogies

An **analogy** presents a relationship between pairs of words. Sometimes writers use analogies to explain unfamiliar ideas. A typical analogy begins with a pair of items that are related in some way. One common word relationship is cause to effect. **Cause-to-effect analogies** show a **cause,** something that happens, and the **effect,** something that happens as a result. Here is an example, displayed first as a sentence and then with special symbols:

> *Weary* is to *sleep* as *virus* is to *pestilence.*
>
> weary : sleep :: virus : pestilence

Both versions express a cause-to-effect analogy: *weary* and *virus* are the causes; *sleep* and *pestilence* are the effects. In the second version, the single colons stand for "is to" and the double colon stands for "as." Examining the full analogy helps you understand how the word pairs are related.

Practice and Apply Complete each cause-to-effect analogy by choosing the best answer.

1. drought : famine :: _____ : despair
   a. tragedy
   b. friendship

2. recklessness : _____ :: pain : discomfort
   a. safety
   b. accident

3. crime : imprisonment :: _____ : accomplishment
   a. completion
   b. perseverance

4. quarrel : discord :: _____ : merriment
   a. joking
   b. talking

PRACTICE & APPLY

Critical Vocabulary

L 4a, L 5b, L 6

Possible answers:

1. *They would be more likely to take a nap because they are tired.*

2. *Probably not; he would not hide the important message he had to deliver.*

3. *Probably not; if she were desperate, she would be more likely to keep moving than take a rest to fret.*

4. *Probably not, because I would not want to become ill or die.*

Vocabulary Strategy: Cause-to-Effect Analogies

1. *a. tragedy*

2. *b. accident*

3. *b. perseverance*

4. *a. joking*

English Language Support

Work with students to complete the Practice and Apply analogies. For each item, discuss the definition of each word. Then read each item and the possible answers with students echo reading the items from their texts. Discuss the correct answer, and review the cause and effect relationship between each side of the analogy.

Strategies for Annotation 🖊 📄 Annotate it!

Cause-to-Effect Analogies L 5b

Have students clarify the meaning of *discord* (line 7). Ask them to use their eBook annotation tools as follows:

- Look for a cause and an effect. Highlight *wedding* (a cause) in yellow. Underline *feasting* (an effect).
- Highlight the word *discord* in yellow.
- Look for an effect of discord. Underline the word *trouble*.
- On a note, decide whether the cause-to-effect analogies make sense. Use a dictionary to confirm the meaning of *discord*.

. . . Many guests came to their wedding feast, and among the mortal guests came all the gods of high Olympus.

But as they sat feasting, one who had not been invited was suddenly in their midst: Eris, the goddess of discord, had been left out because wherever she went she took trouble with her;

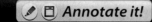

> Yes; wedding causes feasting; discord causes trouble.

PRACTICE & APPLY

Language Conventions: Spell Words Correctly

L 2b

Explain the two spelling rules with students and how a misspelled word can interrupt the flow of ideas for readers. Discuss the examples and provide additional ones. Have students add *-ing* and *-able* to the words *treat, measure, avoid,* and *adore.* Have them add *-ed* and *-er* to the words *carry, fasten, transform,* and *avenge.*

Answers:

1. *desirable*

2. *refused*

3. *lasting*

4. *welcoming*

5. *sailed*

6. *nervous*

7. *prepared*

English Language Support

Have students work independently to complete the Practice and Apply items. Tell them to copy each sentence on a sheet of paper before adding the correctly spelled combination of base word and suffix. Have them check their spellings with a partner.

Language Conventions: Spell Words Correctly

L 2b

Spelling words correctly is important if you want to communicate your ideas well. Misspelled words can confuse readers and weaken the ideas you're trying to express.

Some words change spelling when suffixes are added while other words do not. Here are some examples:

argue + -ing = arguing   surround + -ed = surrounded

It can be difficult to remember which words have spelling changes and which ones do not. Here are two rules that will help you when you add suffixes to words.

> Before adding a suffix beginning with a vowel or **y** to a word ending in silent **e,** drop the **e.**
>
> **amuse + -ing = amusing   love + -able = lovable**
>
> In most words ending with a consonant, simply add the suffix without changing the spelling of the base word.
>
> **demand + -ed = demanded   strong + -er = stronger**

As a writer, you don't want a misspelled word to interrupt or confuse your readers, so spelling words correctly is important!

Practice and Apply Complete each sentence by forming a new word from the base word and suffix in parentheses.

1. The golden apple was _____ to three goddesses. (desire + -able)

2. Paris _____ to give Athene or Hera the apple. (refuse + -ed)

3. Helen and Odysseus had a _____ friendship. (last + -ing)

4. King Priam is _____ Paris into his family. (welcome + -ing)

5. Achilles _____ to join the black ships on their way to Troy. (sail + -ed)

6. Thetis was _____ about Achilles going into battle. (nerve + -ous)

7. The Trojan warriors were not _____ for the Greeks. (prepare + -ed)

English Language Support

Use Affixes Tell students that since there are many exceptions to spelling rules, it is important to review the spelling of words with suffixes in a dictionary or with a partner.

- Work with students to add suffixes that start with consonants (*-s, -ment, -ly, -ful, -ness, -less,* and *-ship*) to these words: *friend, move, agree, weak,* and *mad.* Help students discover which suffixes can be added to each word. Point out that these words do not change their spelling before adding a suffix.

- Have partners add *-able, -ing, -ed, -ous* to the words *change,*

courage, and *notice.* Ask them what they discover about dropping the silent e in these words. (*It isn't always necessary.*) Then tell them to write three sentences about the myth using each word and appropriate affixes.

- Give students a list of suffixes including *-s, -es, -ed, -er, -ing, -tion, -ful, -ly, -ment, -ship, -ness, -ous,* and *-able.* Challenge them to use the suffixes correctly in a summary of why Achilles had an argument with Agamemnon. Have them review their summaries and the spelling of words with suffixes with a partner.

Understand Archaic Language

TEACH

Explain to students that if a story takes place in the distant past, an author might include language that was common long ago but is not often used in contemporary writing. Words, phrases, and expressions that were used long ago but are less commonly used today are called **archaic language.** Display these examples of archaic language from lines 74–75 in *Black Ships Before Troy*, underlining as shown:

> [The goddesses] bade him choose between them, which was the fairest and had best right to the prize he held in his hand.

Explain that in contemporary English, the sentence might read: *The goddesses invited him to choose who was the most beautiful and most deserved the prize he held in his hand.* Point out that archaic language feels somewhat formal because it is not the way most people write and talk today. Including archaic language in a story

- helps writers recreate a past era
- adds a tone that reflects the time the story is set
- makes a text sound authentic

Explain that readers can use context to help them understand the meaning of archaic language.

PRACTICE AND APPLY

Display the following examples from *Black Ships Before Troy*. Have students identify the archaic language used (see underlining). Then, have them replace the archaic language with contemporary language.

- **Lines 93–94:** But Aphrodite was well content, and set about keeping her promise to the herdsman who was a king's son. (*Possible responses: happy, satisfied; began, took action for*)
- **Lines 302–303:** "If you bide here with me, you shall live long and happy." (*Possible responses: stay here, live here, remain here*)
- **Lines 406–407:** "Nor will I take any part in this struggle against Troy until my honor is made good to me again!" (*Possible responses: my reputation is restored; you admit that you were wrong*)

Describe Stories: Myth

RETEACH

Review with students that a myth is a story told by a culture long ago and that myths might have been created to explain natural occurrences, describe historical events, or act as guides for behavior. Discuss that myths may include

- human characters, such as heroes, who have some admirable qualities
- immortal gods and goddesses, who may have superhuman abilities but behave much like humans
- arguments or conflicts between the gods
- a journey, quest, or battle
- interactions between gods and mortals

Assign small groups to review each section of *Black Ships Before Troy*: "The Golden Apple" (split into two parts), "Ship-Gathering," and "Quarrel with the High King." Ask each group to create a chart of the elements of myth they find in their section. Have students discuss their responses with a larger group.

 LEVEL UP TUTORIALS Assign the following *Level Up* tutorial: **Myths, Legends, and Tales**

INDEPENDENT READING

Students can apply these skills to another myth they may have read or are reading on their own. Invite students to share their ideas about the elements of myth with the class.

Medusa's Head

Greek Myth, retold by Olivia E. Coolidge

Why These Texts

Students may read a myth without being aware that it shares many similarities with a short story, such as its use of the fictional elements of setting, characters and a plot with a conflict and a resolution. Students may also not be aware that myths take shape around common themes and that these themes are similar in myths from many different cultures. With the help of the close-reading questions, students will analyze how the same character (Medusa) is treated in two different literary genres—a myth and a poem, noting similarities and differences.

Medusa

Poem by Agha Shahid Ali

Background Have students read the background and information about Olivia E. Coolidge and Agha Shahid Ali. Introduce the two texts by telling students that Coolidge is best known for her retelling of classical Greek myths for young people, having published her first book, *Greek Myths*, in 1949, at the age of 41, although she began writing as a child. Even though she is famous for her retelling of Greek myths, Coolidge is also known for her biographies of Lincoln, Gandhi, and other political figures.

SETTING A PURPOSE Ask students to pay close attention to the story of Medusa in both the Greek myth and the poem. How soon into the myth can students begin to make an inference about the theme?

Standards Support

- cite multiple pieces of textual evidence
- determine a theme and how it is conveyed through particular details
- describe how the plot of a myth unfolds in a series of episodes and how the characters respond or change as the plot moves toward a resolution
- summarize key elements of the plot to determine the theme

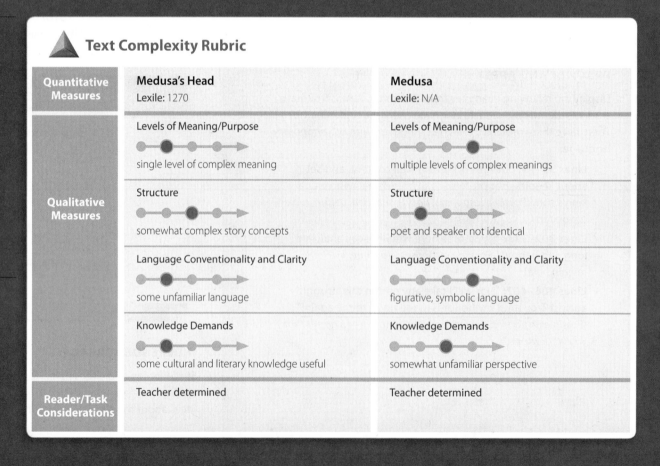

Text Complexity Rubric

	Medusa's Head Lexile: 1270	Medusa Lexile: N/A
Quantitative Measures		
Qualitative Measures	Levels of Meaning/Purpose single level of complex meaning	Levels of Meaning/Purpose multiple levels of complex meanings
	Structure somewhat complex story concepts	Structure poet and speaker not identical
	Language Conventionality and Clarity some unfamiliar language	Language Conventionality and Clarity figurative, symbolic language
	Knowledge Demands some cultural and literary knowledge useful	Knowledge Demands somewhat unfamiliar perspective
Reader/Task Considerations	Teacher determined	Teacher determined

Strategies for CLOSE READING

Determine Theme

Students should read the ancient Greek myth and the contemporary poem carefully all the way through. Close-reading questions at the bottom of the page will help them analyze the two works about Medusa. As they read the two selections, students should record comments or questions about the texts in the side margins.

WHEN STUDENTS STRUGGLE . . .

To help students understand the theme of a myth—an important message (or lesson) about life or human nature—have small groups summarize the main events in a chart such as the one shown as they analyze the myth.

CITE TEXT EVIDENCE For practice in tracing the rising action of a myth to its climax, have students summarize key events to help them determine the theme.

Medusa's Head

- Apollo's prophecy says King Acrisios will have a grandson who will kill him.
- Acrisios locks up his daughter Danae, but Zeus magically enters her room.
- Danae has a son, Perseus, and Acrisios casts the two of them into the sea in a sea chest.
- The gods help, and the chest is found by Dictys, who takes it to King Polydectes.
- Perseus grows up to be strong and handsome.
- King Polydectes fools Perseus into thinking he is getting married, knowing Perseus cannot buy a gift.
- Perseus offers to do anything Polydectes asks, and he is asked to slay the Gorgon Medusa and return with her head.
- Perseus calls on Athene, who will give him Hermes' sword and a shiny shield, warning him to turn his eyes away from the Gorgons so that their gaze will not turn him to stone, and to look at them only in the shield.
- Athene sends him to the sisters Phorcides, whose eye he steals, forcing them to tell him the way to the nymphs.
- Nymphs give him the hat of darkness, winged sandals, and a sack for Medusa's head.
- Perseus reaches the Gorgons' cave, lifts the sword, keeps his eyes on the shield, and kills Medusa, cutting off her head.

Theme: Bravery will be rewarded but cowardice punished.

Background According to Greek myth, Medusa was one of three beautiful sisters known as the Gorgons. The sisters were turned into monsters by Athene, the goddess of wisdom, who was angry at the destruction of one of her temples. Medusa was turned into a horrific creature with a gaping mouth, hypnotic eyes, and hair made of writhing snakes. Anyone who looked into Medusa's eyes was immediately turned to stone.

Medusa's Head

Retold by Olivia E. Coolidge

Medusa

By Agha Shahid Ali

Olivia E. Coolidge (1909–2006) was enjoying a perfectly normal childhood in London with a perfectly normal dislike for Greek literature when she twisted her ankle. For three months a cruel sprain kept her from going outside to play, so she read—and read. Soon she was reading Greek poetry and she made a shocking discovery: she loved it! Coolidge went on to write numerous books of Greek myths for young adults.

Agha Shahid Ali (1949–2001) was born in New Delhi, India, but he lived, studied, and taught in the United States for more than twenty-five years. Ali was a Kashmiri Muslim, but he identified himself as an American poet. Ali's poetry embraces multiple heritages (Hindu, Muslim, and Western) and crosses literary traditions. A joyful, brilliant poet, a man blessed with friends and honors, Ali died from a brain tumor at the age of 52.

101

1. **READ** ▶ As you read lines 1–37, begin to collect and cite text evidence.

- Circle what the oracle tells Acrisios.
- Summarize in the margin what Acrisios does to Danae.
- Underline the ways the gods help Danae.
- In the margin, explain Danae's behavior in lines 28–37.

Medusa's Head
Greek Myth retold by Olivia E. Coolidge

King Acrisios of Argos was a hard, selfish man. He hated his brother, Proitos, who later drove him from his kingdom and he cared nothing for his daughter, Danae. His whole heart was set on having a son who should succeed him, but since many years went by and still he had only the one daughter, he sent a message to the oracle of Apollo to ask whether he should have more children of his own. The answer of the oracle was terrible. Acrisios should have no son, but his daughter, Danae, would bear him a grandchild who should grow up to kill him. At these words Acrisios was beside himself with fear
A 10 and rage. Swearing that Danae should never have a child to murder him, he had a room built underground and lined all through with brass. Thither he conducted Danae and shut her up, bidding her spend the rest of her life alone.

Acrisios locks Danae in a sealed room.

It is possible to thwart the plans of mortal men, but never those of
B the gods. Zeus himself looked with pity at the unfortunate girl, and it is said he **descended** to her through the tiny hole that gave light and air to her chamber, pouring himself down into her lap in the form of a shower of gold.

descend:
come down

When word came to the king from those who brought food and
20 drink to his daughter that the girl was with child, Acrisios was angry and afraid. He would have liked best to murder both Danae and her infant son, but he did not dare for fear of the gods' anger at so hideous a crime. He made, therefore, a great chest of wood with bands of brass about it. Shutting up the girl and her baby inside, he cast them into the sea, thinking that they would either drown or starve.

Acrisios shuts Danae and her son in a wooden chest and throws it into the sea.

Again the gods came to the help of Danae, for they caused the planks of the chest to swell until they fitted tightly and let no water in.

The chest floated for some days and was cast up at last on an
30 island. There Dictys, a fisherman, found it and took Danae to his brother, Polydectes, who was king of the island. Danae was made a servant in the palace, yet before many years had passed, both Dictys and Polydectes had fallen in love with the silent, golden-haired girl. She in her heart preferred Dictys, yet since his brother was king, she did not dare to make her choice. Therefore she hung always over Perseus, pretending that mother love left her no room for any other, and year after year a silent frown would cross Polydectes' face as he saw her caress the child.

C At last, Perseus became a young man, handsome and strong beyond the common and a leader among the youths of the island,
40 though he was but the son of a poor servant. Then it seemed to Polydectes that if he could once get rid of Perseus, he could force Danae to become his wife, whether she would or not. Meanwhile, in order to lull the young man's suspicions, he pretended that he intended to marry a certain noble maiden and would collect a wedding gift for her. Now the custom was that this gift of the

Danae gives all her attention to Perseus to avoid having to marry Polydectes.

2. ◀ **REREAD** Reread lines 14–27. In what ways are the gods similar to humans? What superhuman powers do they have? Cite textual evidence in your response.

The gods in the story feel human emotions. For instance Zeus "looked with pity" on Danae after she is locked in her room. However, they are able to intervene in human affairs in superhuman ways, such as when Zeus takes the form of a "shower of gold."

3. **READ** ▶ As you read lines 38–81, continue to cite textual evidence.

- In lines 38–52, circle Perseus's qualities that suggest he may be a hero.
- In the margin, explain why Polydectes feels "satisfaction" (line 66).
- Underline the items Perseus will use on his journey. In the margin, summarize the steps Perseus must take to slay the Gorgon.

1. **READ AND CITE TEXT EVIDENCE** Explain to students that one way they can determine the theme of a myth is to summarize key events in the plot.

A **ASK STUDENTS** to read their margin notes to a partner and then write one response that best summarizes the action Acrisios takes against Danae, a key event in the development of the plot. *Students should cite specific textual evidence in lines 10–13 and 21–25 to summarize what Acrisios does to Danae to prevent the prophecy from coming true. First, he shuts her up in an underground room. Then, when she does have a son, he encloses them both in a locked wooden chest, which he throws into the sea, thinking they will starve or drown.*

Critical Vocabulary: descend (line 16) Have students share their definitions of *descend* and use it in a sentence.

2. **REREAD AND CITE TEXT EVIDENCE**

B **ASK STUDENTS** for examples of how the Greek gods show their human qualities as well as their supernatural strength and ability to transform themselves, which humans cannot do. *Students should cite evidence in lines 15–18 to highlight not only Zeus's human emotions (he feels "pity" for Danae) but also his superhuman powers (he can turn into a "shower of gold"). Gods can also intervene in human affairs in superhuman ways, as in saving Danae and her son (lines 26–27).*

3. **READ AND CITE TEXT EVIDENCE**

C **ASK STUDENTS** to show how Perseus has the qualities of a mythic hero in that he is handsome, brave, and strong, although of humble birth. *Students should cite details in lines 38–40 to show his heroic qualities, though he is the son of a servant.*

bridegroom to the bride was in part his own and in part put together from the marriage presents of his friends and relatives. All the young men, therefore, brought Polydectes a present, excepting Perseus, who was his servant's son and possessed nothing to bring. Then Polydectes

50 said to the others, "This young man owes me more than any of you, since I took him in and brought him up in my own house, and yet he gives me nothing."

Perseus answered in anger at the injustice of the charge, "I have nothing of my own, Polydectes, yet ask me what you will, and I will fetch it, for I owe you my life."

At this Polydectes smiled, for it was what he had intended, and he answered, "Fetch me, if this is your boast, the Gorgon's head."

Now the Gorgons, who lived far off on the shores of the ocean, were three fearful sisters with hands of brass, wings of gold, and

60 scales like a serpent. Two of them had scaly heads and tusks like the wild boar, but the third, Medusa, had the face of a beautiful woman with hair of writhing serpents, and so terrible was her expression that all who looked on it were immediately turned to stone. This much Perseus knew of the Gorgons, but of how to find or kill them, he had no idea. Nevertheless he had given his promise, and though he saw now the satisfaction of King Polydectes, he was bound to keep his word. In his perplexity he prayed to the wise goddess, Athene, who came to him in a vision and promised him her aid.

"First, you must go," she said, "to the sisters Phorcides, who will

70 tell you the way to the nymphs who guard the hat of darkness, the winged sandals, and the knapsack which can hold the Gorgon's head. Then I will give you a shield and my brother, Hermes, a sword which shall be made of adamant, the hardest rock. For nothing else can kill the Gorgon, since so venomous is her blood that a mortal sword when plunged in it is eaten away. But when you come to the Gorgons, invisible in your hat of darkness, turn your eyes away from them and look only on their reflection in your gleaming shield. Thus you may kill the monster without yourself being turned to stone. Pass her sisters by, for they are immortal, but smite off the head of Medusa

80 with the hair of writhing snakes. Then put it in your knapsack and return, and I will be with you."

(D)

The vision ended, and with the aid of Athene, Perseus set out on the long journey to seek the Phorcides. These live in a dim cavern in the far north, where nights and days are one and where the whole earth is overspread with perpetual twilight. There sat the three old women mumbling to one another, crouched in a dim heap together, for they had but one eye and one tooth between them which they passed from hand to hand. Perseus came quietly behind them, and as

90 they fumbled for the eye, he put his strong, brown hand next to one of the long, yellow ones, so that the old crone thought that it was her sister's and put the eye in it. There was a high scream of anger when they discovered the theft, and much clawing and groping in the dim recesses of the cavern. But they were helpless in their blindness and Perseus could laugh at them. At length for the price of their eye they told him how to reach the nymphs, and Perseus, laying the eye quickly in the hand of the nearest sister, fled as fast as he could before she could use it.

Again it was a far journey to the garden of the nymphs, where it is

100 always sunshine and the trees bear golden apples. But the nymphs are friends of the wise gods and hate the monsters of darkness and the spirits of anger and despair. Therefore, they received Perseus with rejoicing and put the hat of darkness on his head, while on his feet they bound the golden, winged sandals, which are those Hermes wears when he runs down the slanting sunbeams or races along the

The Phorcides help Perseus because they need their eye back.

The nymphs are friends with the gods, who are helping Perseus. They hate monsters, including the Gorgons.

4. ◀ REREAD Reread lines 53–68. What is heroic about the way Perseus responds to the request Polydectes makes? Support your answer with explicit textual evidence.

Even when Perseus realizes that Polydectes wants to send him away unjustly, he honors his word. He recognizes the challenge ahead and prays to Athene for help.

5. READ ▶ As you read lines 82–154, continue to cite textual evidence.

• In the margin, explain why the Phorcides and the nymphs help Perseus.

• Underline details that create concern for Perseus.

• Circle the text that may be the climax—the exciting point in a story where a conflict is about to be resolved.

Polydectes is satisfied because Perseus has left the island on a very dangerous mission.

1. Go to the sisters Phorcides.
2. Get the hat of darkness, winged sandals, and knapsack.
3. Take the shield from Athena and the sword from Hermes.
4. Kill the Gorgon while his face is turned away.

WHEN STUDENTS STRUGGLE . . .

To help students understand how the theme of a story or myth is a message (or lesson) about life or human nature, ask them to reread lines 38–81. Invite them to work with a small group to discuss how this section that introduces Perseus's quest gives insight into the theme of the myth.

FOR ELL STUDENTS Explain that a phrasal verb is followed by a preposition, which gives the verb another meaning, and that phrasal verbs may be difficult for ELL students to understand. Point out that several phrasal verbs are created from the verb *turn*. Tell students (or elicit) the meaning of *turn to (stone)* (line 63) and *turn (your eyes) away* (line 76). Turn to *means "to change into" and* turn away *means "to move in a different direction so as not to see something."* Ask students to use each phrasal verb in a sentence.

4. **REREAD AND CITE TEXT EVIDENCE** Explain that a mythic hero often goes on a quest (or journey) to accomplish a dangerous task.

(D) **ASK STUDENTS** to cite specific textual evidence to demonstrate the heroic way in which Perseus keeps his word to Polydectes. *Students should cite explicit evidence from lines 65–68 to show that despite the fact that Perseus realizes that the king is sending him away unjustly, he keeps his word to bring back the Gorgon's head. To help with the quest, he calls on Athene to help.*

5. **READ AND CITE TEXT EVIDENCE**

(E) **ASK STUDENTS** to tell at which point in the story the action rises to its highest point, and readers feel the most emotion. *Students should cite textual evidence from lines 139–141 to point out that this is the climax of the story, the point at which the conflict with the Gorgons is about to be resolved.*

"Their faces were neither snake nor woman, but part both . . ."

pathways of the wind. Next, Perseus put on his back the silver sack with the gleaming tassels of gold and flung across his shoulder the black-sheathed sword that was the gift of Hermes. On his left arm he fitted the shield that Athene gave, a gleaming silver shield like a mirror, plain without any marking. Then he sprang into the air and
110 ran, invisible like the rushing wind, far out over the white-capped sea, across the yellow sands of the eastern desert, over strange streams and towering mountains, until at last he came to the shores of the distant ocean which flowed round all the world.

There was a grey gorge of stone by the ocean's edge, where lay Medusa and her sisters sleeping in the dim depths of the rock. All up and down the cleft the stones took fantastic shapes of trees, beasts, birds, or serpents. Here and there a man who had looked on the terrible Medusa stood forever with horror on his face. Far over the twilit gorge Perseus **hovered** invisible, while he loosened the pale,
120 strange sword from its black sheath. Then with his face turned away and eyes on the silver shield he dropped, slow and silent as a falling leaf, down through the rocky cleft, twisting and turning past countless strange grey shapes, down from the bright sunlight into a chill, dim shadow echoing and re-echoing with the dashing of waves on the tumbled rocks beneath. There on the heaped stones lay the Gorgons sleeping together in the dimness, and even as he looked on them in the shield, Perseus felt stiff with horror at the sight.

F Two of the Gorgons lay sprawled together, shaped like women yet scaled from head to foot as serpents are. Instead of hands they had
130 gleaming claws like eagles, and their feet were dragons' feet. Skinny metallic wings like bats' wings hung from their shoulders. Their faces were neither snake nor woman, but part both, like faces in a nightmare. These two lay arm in arm and never stirred. Only the blue snakes still hissed and writhed round the pale, set face of Medusa, as

hover:
stay suspended in the air

106

though even in sleep she were troubled by an evil dream. She lay by herself, arms outstretched, face upwards, more beautiful and terrible than living man may bear. All the crimes and madnesses of the world rushed into Perseus' mind as he gazed at her image in the shield.
E Horror stiffened his arm as he hovered over her with his sword
140 uplifted. Then he shut his eyes to the vision and in the darkness struck.

There was a great cry and a hissing. Perseus groped for the head and seized it by the limp and snaky hair. Somehow he put it in his knapsack and was up and off, for at the dreadful scream the sister Gorgons had awakened. Now they were after him, their sharp claws grating against his silver shield. Perseus strained forward on the pathway of the wind like a runner, and behind him the two sisters came, smelling out the prey they could not see. Snakes darted from their girdles,[1] foam flew from their tusks, and the great wings beat the
150 air. Yet the winged sandals were even swifter than they, and Perseus fled like the hunted deer with the speed of desperation. Presently the horrible noise grew faint behind him, the hissing of snakes and the sound of the bat wings died away. At last the Gorgons could smell him no longer and returned home unavenged.

---
[1] **girdles:** belts.

6. **◀ REREAD** Reread lines 128–154. The resolution of a conflict may suggest a work's theme. What theme might be suggested by Perseus's triumph?

The resolution suggests that if you keep your word, act bravely, and obey the gods, you can triumph and achieve great things.

107

Critical Vocabulary: hover (line 119) Have students share their definitions of *hover*. What does the narrator mean by saying, "Far over the twilit gorge Perseus hovered invisible, while he loosened the pale, strange sword from its black sheath"? *The narrator means that while invisible, Perseus stays suspended in midair while he removes the unusual sword from its covering. Ask students to give examples of other things that hover, such as helicopters, and to create a sentence for each.*

6. **REREAD AND CITE TEXT EVIDENCE** Point out that the resolution of a conflict takes place after the climax and is part of the falling action of the plot.

F **ASK STUDENTS** to reread lines 128–154, paying close attention to lines 139–141, the climax of the story, and have them paraphrase how the conflict with the Gorgons is resolved. Then lead them to recognize that the resolution of the conflict begins with line 142, which signals the falling action in the second half of the story. Remind students that Perseus has performed a great feat. Ask students to consider the theme that might be represented by his triumphant success. *Students should be able to recognize that the resolution of the conflict suggests the theme that brave deeds will be rewarded.*

CLOSE READ
Notes

G By now Perseus was over the Lybian desert, and as the blood from the horrible head touched the sand, it changed to serpents, from which the snakes of Africa are descended.

H The storms of the Lybian desert blew against Perseus in clouds of eddying sand, until not even the divine sandals could hold him on his
160 course. Far out to sea he was blown, and then north. Finally, whirled around the heavens like a cloud of mist, he alighted in the distant west where the giant, Atlas, held up on his shoulders the heavens from the earth. There the weary giant, crushed under the load of centuries, begged Perseus to show him Medusa's head. Perseus uncovered for him the dreadful thing, and Atlas was changed to the mighty mountain whose rocks rear up to reach the sky near the gateway to the Atlantic. Perseus himself, returning eastwards and still battling with the wind, was driven south to the land of Ethiopia, where king Cepheus reigned with his wife, Cassiopeia.

170 As Perseus came wheeling in like a gull from the ocean, he saw a strange sight. Far out to sea the water was troubled, seething and boiling as though stirred by a great force moving in its depths. Huge, sullen waves were starting far out and washing inland over sunken trees and flooded houses. Many miles of land were under water, and as he sped over them, he saw the muddy sea lapping around the foot of a black, upstanding rock. Here on a ledge above the water's edge stood a young girl chained by the arms, lips parted, eyes open and staring, face white as her linen garment. She might have been a statue, so still she stood, while the light breeze fluttered her dress and stirred
180 her loosened hair. As Perseus looked at her and looked at the sea, the water began to boil again, and miles out a long, grey scaly back of vast length lifted itself above the flood. At that there was a shriek from a distant knoll where he could dimly see the forms of people, but the

7. **READ ▶** As you read lines 155–186, continue to cite text evidence.

- Circle the explanation of the origin of something found in nature.
- Underline what happens when Perseus shows Medusa's head to Atlas.
- Circle the author's description of the young girl in lines 170–186.

108

girl shrank a little and said nothing. Then Perseus, taking off the hat of darkness, alighted near the maiden to talk to her, and she, though nearly mad with terror, found words at last to tell him her tale.

I Her name was Andromeda, and she was the only child of the king and of his wife, Cassiopeia. Queen Cassiopeia was exceedingly beautiful, so that all people marveled at her. She herself was proud of
190 her dark eyes, her white, slender fingers, and her long black hair, so proud that she had been heard to boast that she was fairer even than the sea nymphs who are daughters of Nereus. At this Nereus in **wrath** stirred up Poseidon,[2] who came flooding in over the land, covering it far and wide. Not content with this he sent a vast monster from the dark depths of the bottomless sea to ravage the whole coast of Ethiopia. When the unfortunate king and queen had sought the advice of the oracle on how to appease the god, they had been ordered to sacrifice their only daughter to the sea monster Poseidon had sent. Not daring for their people's sake to disobey, they had chained her to
200 this rock, where she now awaited the beast who should devour her.

J Perseus comforted Andromeda as he stood by her on the rock, and she shrank closer against him while the great, grey back writhed its half-mile length slowly towards the land. Then bidding Andromeda hide her face, Perseus sprang once more into the air,

---

[2] **Poseidon:** in Greek mythology, the god of the seas.

wrath:

anger; fury

Andromeda's parents tied her to a rock as a sacrifice to the gods.

8. **◀ REREAD** Reread lines 158–169. Why does Atlas beg Perseus to show him Medusa's head? Cite explicit textual evidence in your response.

Atlas is "crushed under the load of centuries" from holding up the heavens. He wants to look at Medusa's head because he will not feel pain if he is turned to stone.

9. **READ ▶** As you read lines 187–212, continue to cite text evidence.

- Circle what Queen Cassiopeia does to make Nereus so angry.
- In the margin, summarize what has happened to Andromeda in lines 187–200.
- Underline what happens when Perseus shows Medusa's head to the sea monster.

109

---

7. **READ AND CITE TEXT EVIDENCE** Point out that myths explain how and why things in nature came to be.

G **ASK STUDENTS** to play close attention to lines 155–157 and 165–167 to explain how the ancient Greeks used this myth to account for how these things came to be in nature: the snakes in Africa and the mighty "mountain . . . near the gateway to the Atlantic." *Students should cite specific textual evidence in lines 155–157 and 165–167 to recognize that according to this Greek myth, while Perseus was flying over the Lybian desert, the blood from Medusa's head touched the sand and was changed into serpents, which is how the snakes of Africa came to be; when Perseus uncovered Medusa's head for the giant Atlas, who was holding up the heavens, Atlas was changed into the mighty Atlas Mountains, which still bear his name.*

8. **REREAD AND CITE TEXT EVIDENCE**

H **ASK STUDENTS** to draw an inference from lines 158–167 to suggest why the weary giant Atlas, who was holding up the heavens, may have pleaded with Perseus to show him the head of Medusa. *Students should infer that Atlas may have wanted to look at Medusa's head so that he can be turned to stone in order not to feel the heavy weight.*

9. **READ AND CITE TEXT EVIDENCE** .

I **ASK STUDENTS** to read their margin notes to a partner and write one response to summarize the events leading to Andromeda's being chained to a rock above the water's edge. *Students should cite specific textual evidence from lines 187–200 to summarize the events, beginning with Cassiopeia's insult to Nereus's daughters.*

Critical Vocabulary: wrath (line 192) Have students define *wrath* and use it in a sentence.

unveiling the dreadful head of dead Medusa to the monster which reared its dripping jaws yards high into the air. The mighty tail stiffened all of a sudden, the boiling of the water ceased, and only the gentle waves of the receding ocean lapped around a long, grey ridge of stone. Then Perseus freed Andromeda and restored her to her father

210 and beautiful mother. Thereafter with their consent he married her amid scenes of tremendous rejoicing, and with his bride set sail at last for the kingdom of Polydectes.

Polydectes had lost no time on the departure of Perseus. First he had begged Danae to become his wife, and then he had threatened her. Undoubtedly he would have got his way by force if Danae had not fled in terror to Dictys. The two took refuge at the altar of a temple whence Polydectes did not dare drag them away. So matters stood when Perseus returned. Polydectes was enraged to see him, for he had hoped at least that Danae's most powerful protector would never

220 return. But now, seeing him famous and with a king's daughter to wife, he could not contain himself. Openly he laughed at the tale of Perseus, saying that the hero had never killed the Gorgon, only pretended to, and that now he was claiming an honor he did not

> "You asked me for the Gorgon's head. Behold it!"

deserve. At this Perseus, enraged by the insult and by reports of his mother's persecution, said to him, "You asked me for the Gorgon's head. Behold it!" And with that he lifted it high, and Polydectes became stone.

Then Perseus left Dictys to be king of that island, but he himself went back to the Grecian mainland to seek out his grandfather,

230 Acrisios, who was once again king of Argos. First, however, he gave back to the gods the gifts they had given him. Hermes took back the golden sandals and the hat of darkness, for both are his. But Athene took Medusa's head, and she hung it on a fleece around her neck as part of her battle equipment, where it may be seen in statues and portraits of the warlike goddess.

Perseus took ship for Greece, but his fame had gone before him, and king Acrisios fled secretly from Argos in terror, since he remembered the prophecy and feared that Perseus had come to avenge the wrongs of Danae. The trembling old Acrisios took refuge

240 in Larissa, where it happened the king was holding a great athletic contest in honor of his dead father.

Heroes from all over Greece, among whom was Perseus, came to the games. As Perseus was competing at the discus throwing, he threw high into the air and far beyond the rest. A strong wind caught the discus as it spun so that it left the course marked out for it and was carried into the stands. People scrambled away to right and left.

---

10. ◀ REREAD   Reread lines 201–212. What is heroic about Perseus's rescue of Andromeda?

He saves Andromeda from her unjust punishment and preserves her parents' kingdom. He uses supernatural powers and Medusa's head to defeat a fearsome creature.

---

11. READ ▶   As you read lines 213–252, continue to cite textual evidence.

- Circle the resolution of the conflict between Perseus and Polydectes.
- Underline Perseus's action in lines 228–235 that shows his gratitude to the gods.
- In the margin, explain how the earlier prophecy of Apollo is fulfilled in lines 242–252.

---

10. REREAD AND CITE TEXT EVIDENCE

J ASK STUDENTS to cite specific textual evidence to illustrate how Perseus uses his intelligence, courage, strength, and supernatural powers to rescue Andromeda from Poseidon's sea monster. *Students should cite evidence from lines 203–209 to highlight how Perseus acts heroically to free Andromeda from her unjust fate by cleverly uncovering Medusa's head to turn the sea creature to stone; students should also cite evidence from lines 210–212 to show how he restores Andromeda to her parents, preserves her parents' kingdom, and marries the princess—all aspects of the mythic hero.*

11. READ AND CITE TEXT EVIDENCE

K ASK STUDENTS to work with a partner to write one response to state how Apollo's oracle is fulfilled, as Acrisios is killed by his grandson Perseus. *Students should cite specific textual evidence from lines 242–252 to show that Acrisios is killed by the discus Perseus throws at the athletic games, fulfilling the prophecy.*

WHEN STUDENTS STRUGGLE . . .

To help students understand how the theme—the message (or lesson) about life or human nature—can be determined in a myth, have students ask themselves these questions: *What is the lesson the myth teaches? How is this message conveyed by the characters' flaws, mistakes, or triumphs or by the action of the plot?* Invite students to work with a small group to discuss how students can infer the theme of this myth from Perseus's positive character traits and actions.

FOR ELL STUDENTS In order for students to understand this section in the falling action of the story, suggest that they use context clues to try to determine the meaning of these words and phrases: *Behold it!* (line 226), *battle equipment* (line 234), *athletic contest* (lines 240–241), *discus throwing* (line 243), *nimble* (line 247), *feeble* (line 248), and *prophecy* (line 249).

CLOSE READ
Notes

Though Perseus did not intend it, his discus kills Acrisios.

Only Acrisios was not nimble enough. The heavy weight fell full on his foot and crushed his toes, and at that the feeble old man, already weakened by his terrors, died from the shock. Thus the prophecy of 250 Apollo was fulfilled at last; Acrisios was killed by his grandson. Then Perseus came into his kingdom, where he reigned with Andromeda long and happily.

12. ◄ **REREAD AND DISCUSS** Reread lines 228–252. In a small group, discuss what is ironic, or unexpected, about Acrisios's death. Cite explicit textual evidence in your discussion.

SHORT RESPONSE

Cite Text Evidence What theme, or central idea about life, is expressed in this myth? Consider the way conflicts are resolved and the way characters behave. Review your reading notes and **cite text evidence** in your response.

The myth expresses the theme that bravery will be rewarded and cowardice will be punished. Perseus is sent on a dangerous mission to fetch the Gorgon's head. He did not know how to complete the mission but with the help of the gods he is able to escape harm and win the conflict. Perseus is also brave when he defeats a dangerous sea monster. He is rewarded when he takes Andromeda as his bride. On the other hand, characters such as Polydectes and Acrisios behave in a cowardly way and are punished. Polydectes mistreats and threatens Danae before going into hiding. He is punished when Perseus turns him to stone. Likewise, Acrisios flees from Argos to escape the fate the gods prophesized, but he is killed.

112

---

1. **READ** ▶ As you read lines 1–36 of the poem, collect and cite text evidence.

• Circle the questions Medusa asks.
• In lines 15–27, underline what Medusa threatens to do. In the margin, make an inference about her character.
• In the margin, summarize what happens in the last stanza.

Medusa
Poem by Agha Shahid Ali

B "I must be beautiful.
Or why would men be speechless
at my sight? I have populated the countryside
with animals of stone
5 and put nations painlessly to sleep.
I too was human, I who now live here
at the end of the world
with two aging sisters, spinsters
massaging poisons into our scalps
10 and sunning our ruffled snakes,

and dreading the night, when
under the warm stars
we recall men we have loved,
their gestures now forever refusing us.

A 15 Then why let anything remain
when whatever we loved
turned instantly to stone?
I am waiting for the Mediterranean
to see me: It will petrify.
20 And as caravans from Africa begin to cross it,
I will freeze their cargo of slaves.

Medusa is angry that she has been turned into a monster who cannot find love. In her anger, she wants revenge on the world.

113

---

12. **REREAD AND DISCUSS USING TEXT EVIDENCE**

L **ASK STUDENTS** to appoint a reporter for each group to cite specific textual evidence and line numbers to evaluate the effectiveness of the use of irony (or an unexpected situation) in the death of Acrisios. How does it fulfill the prophecy in an unexpected (and humorous) way? *Students should cite specific textual evidence from lines 242–252 to demonstrate the ironic situation implicit in the fact that Acrisios dies as a result of Perseus's throwing the discus, which lands on the feeble man's feet.*

SHORT RESPONSE

Cite Text Evidence Students should cite evidence from the text to support their view of the theme. Students should:

• explain the theme, or central idea about life.
• give reasons for their point of view.
• cite specific textual evidence to support their reasons.

1. **READ AND CITE TEXT EVIDENCE**

A **ASK STUDENTS** to read their margin notes to a partner and write one response that makes an inference about Medusa's character based on the threats she makes in lines 15–27. Point out that students should use what they already know about Medusa from the myth and combine it with specific evidence from the poem in order to make an inference about her character. *Students should cite explicit textual evidence from lines 15–27 to highlight how Medusa will use her power to turn anyone or anything that looks upon her to stone, so that she may seek her revenge upon the world for having turned her and her sisters into monsters whom no one can love.*

FOR ELL STUDENTS Point out that the word *to* (line 5) is a homophone, a word that sounds like another word but has a different meaning and spelling. Ask students to find and cite both homophones of *to* in the poem (lines 6 and 8).

Soon, soon, the sky will have eyes:
I will fossilize its dome into cracked blue,
I who am about to come
25 into God's full view
from the wrong side of the mirror
into which He gazes."

And so she dreams
till the sun-crimsoned shield
30 blinds her into nightmare;
her locks, failing from their roots,
crawl into rocks to die.
Perseus holds the sword above her neck.
Restless in her sleep, she,
35 for the last time, brushes back
the hissing curls from her forehead.

Perseus is about to slay Medusa, who has fallen asleep for the last time.

2. ◀ **REREAD AND DISCUSS** With a small group, discuss the way Medusa is presented in the poem. In what way does learning her thoughts and feelings affect your view of her? Cite text evidence in your discussion.

SHORT RESPONSE

Cite Text Evidence   How do "Medusa's Head" and "Medusa" differ in their presentation of Medusa? Review your reading notes, and be sure to **cite evidence from the text** in your response.

In "Medusa's Head," Medusa is a monster and Perseus is the hero who destroys her. We only see her briefly and we do not learn her thoughts and feelings. In "Medusa," the poet delves deeply into her character. We learn she is sad and angry about her curse and longs to be able to love again. We are more able to relate to Medusa in the poem because we learn her feelings.

114

2.   REREAD AND DISCUSS USING TEXT EVIDENCE

B **ASK STUDENTS** to appoint a reporter for each group to cite specific textual evidence and line numbers to discuss and evaluate the effectiveness of the way in which Medusa is presented in the poem. How do her human qualities of expressing her thoughts and feelings heighten the audience's emotions, enabling them to feel pity for her and influencing their point of view? *Students should cite evidence in lines 1–14 to describe her recollections, lines 15–27 to depict her anger and revenge, and lines 28–36 to portray her death at Perseus's hand.*

SHORT RESPONSE

Cite Text Evidence   Students should cite explicit evidence from the text to support their positions. Students should:

- explain how the two treatments of Medusa differ.
- give reasons for their point of view.
- cite evidence from the text to support their reasons.

TO CHALLENGE STUDENTS . . .

For more context, and a richer understanding of the gods and goddesses as well as the heroes and monsters of Greek mythology, students can view the video titled "Greek Gods" in their eBooks.

ASK STUDENTS to do some preliminary research to find out more information about Perseus, Medusa, or another Greek god, goddess, hero, or monster mentioned in the myth. Possible topics for their research report might be:

- further exploits of Perseus
- the Gorgons and other monsters in Greek mythology
- Greek gods and heroes

With the class, discuss these elements of a research report after students have chosen a topic.

- Plan Your Research
  - —Write questions about your topic.
  - —Research your topic and take notes.
  - —Organize your notes.
  - —Write an outline based on your notes.
- Write Your Report
  - —Keep your purpose and audience in mind.
  - —Write a first draft, revise your report, and proofread it.
  - —Reread your report and check that your bibliography is accurate.
- Publish and Share
  - —Make a final copy of your report.
  - —Publish and share it.

ASK STUDENTS what they hope to discover as they research their report. How is the information they find similar to yet different from the story and details shared by the myth and the poem about Medusa?

DIG DEEPER

1. With the class, return to Question 12, Reread and Discuss, in "Medusa's Head." Have students share the results of their discussion.

   ASK STUDENTS whether they were pleased with the outcome of their small-group discussions. Have each group share how it defined irony and what it identified as being unexpected about the death of Acrisios. What was ironic (and almost humorous) about the situation in which he died? Have each group cite the specific textual evidence it found to support its viewpoint.

   - Encourage students to tell whether there was any compelling evidence cited by group members holding a different opinion. If so, why didn't it sway the group?
   - How did the group resolve any differences of opinion?
   - After students have shared the results of their discussion, ask whether another group shared any ideas they wish they had thought of.

   ASK STUDENTS to return to their Short Response answer and to revise it based on the class discussion of the myth.

2. With the class, return to Question 2, Reread and Discuss, in the poem "Medusa." Have students share the results of their discussion.

   ASK STUDENTS whether they were pleased with the outcome of their small-group discussions. Have each group share its view concerning how Medusa is presented in the poem, and how knowing her thoughts and feelings influenced their point of view of her. What evidence did each group cite from the poem to support its viewpoint?

   - Encourage students to tell whether there was any covincing evidence cited by group members holding a different opinion. If so, why didn't it sway the group's point of view of Medusa in the poem? How did the group use conflict-resolution techniques to solve any disagreements?
   - After groups have shared the results of their discussion, ask whether another group shared any findings they wished they had brought to the table.

   ASK STUDENTS to return to their Short Response answer and to revise it based on the class discussion about the presentation of Medusa in the poem.

CLOSE READING NOTES

The Apple of Discord I

Poem by Kate Hovey

Why This Text?

Sometimes a poem is an interpretation of an old, well-known story, such as a myth. This lesson explores parody and how it can both entertain and encourage the reader to think about an old story in a new way.

Key Learning Objective: The student will be able to understand and identify the elements of a parody and learn to compare and contrast texts in different genres.

RL 1 Cite text evidence.

RL 2 Determine theme.

RL 4 Determine the meaning of words and phrases.

RL 5 Analyze structure.

RL 6 Explain how an author develops the point of view of the speaker.

RL 9 Compare and contrast texts in different genres.

RL 10 Read and comprehend poems.

SL 4 Present claims and findings logically to accentuate main ideas or themes; use appropriate eye contact, adequate volume, and clear pronunciation.

SL 6 Adapt speech to a variety of contexts and tasks.

▲ Text Complexity Rubric

Quantitative Measures	**The Apple of Discord I** Lexile: N/A
Qualitative Measures	**Levels of Meaning/Purpose** single level of complex meaning
	Structure poet and speaker not identical
	Language Conventionality and Clarity some unfamiliar language
	Knowledge Demands cultural and literary knowledge essential to understanding
Reader/Task Considerations	• Teacher determined • Vary by individual reader and type of text • See the Text X-Ray for suggested Reader/Task Considerations.

Meaning Making

Language Development

Effective Expression

Content Knowledge

Foundational Skills

English Language Support

Before teaching, use the Text X-Ray for an overview of the text's complexity. The Text X-Ray and the supports and scaffolds in the Teacher's Edition will help you guide students of different skill levels.

Text Complexity: Qualitative Measures

Levels of Meaning/Purpose

single level of complex meaning

Help students determine the meanings of words and phrases in a parody.

- Teacher's Edition side notes, pp. 332, 333
- English Language Support, p. 332
- Strategies for Annotation, p. 333
- Determine Meanings of Words and Phrases, p. 333

To reteach how to determine meaning of words and phrases, see

- Determine Meaning of Words and Phrases: Parody, p. 334a

 Use It! **Level Up Tutorials:** Tone

ZOOM IN ON **DETERMINING THEME** Explain that a parody makes fun of someone or something. Write "They claim/*I'm* the foul one!" (lines 26–27) on the board:

- Read the line aloud, emphasizing the italicized word. Ask students what tone is conveyed. Why does the speaker feel this way? *(She is angry to be blamed for the effects of her action.)*
- Ask students what idea this line mocks. *(The poet is making fun of Eris's unwillingness to accept any blame for the devastating Trojan War.)*

Structure

poet and speaker not identical

Help students compare and contrast a myth and a parody.

- Teacher's Edition side notes, pp. 331, 332, 333
- English Language Support, p. 331
- When Students Struggle, p. 332
- Compare and Contrast Genres, p. 333

To teach analyze symbols, see

- Analyze Language: Symbol, p. 334a

 Use It! **Level Up Tutorials:** Symbol

ZOOM IN ON **COMPARING AND CONTRASTING GENRES** Have students work in pairs to **compare** the poet's purpose in "The Apple of Discord I" with the author's purpose in the excerpt from *The Black Ships of Troy*. Guide their discussion with these questions:

- What does Eris reveal about herself in lines 13–26? *(She is as petty as the other gods.)* What is revealed about her in the myth? *(Very little; she just begins the conflict.)*
- *Discord* means "lack of agreement or tension." What idea about discord is in lines 28–40? Is this idea also shown in the myth? *(It has effects beyond the original fight. This is shown even more clearly in the myth as the conflict lasts for years.)*
- What is the poet's purpose in telling this story? Is it the same as or different from the author's? *(The poet's purpose is to look at the nature of discord. The author's purpose is to give background as to the cause of the Trojan War.)*

Language Conventionality and Clarity

some unfamiliar language

Support students' reading of the poem as well as their analysis of it through discussion and writing.

- Teacher's Edition side notes, p. 332
- English Language Support, p. 331

ZOOM IN ON **ANALYZING FIGURATIVE LANGUAGE** Poets often use **figurative language** to convey meaning or to help readers visualize an idea. Explain that sometimes single words are used figuratively; at other times, the poet may use a figure of speech such as a **simile**.

- Discuss the literal meaning of *hardheaded* (line 11). *(having a hard, as in unbreakable, skull)* Have students work together to explain the figurative meaning, using lines 11–12. *(stubborn, unwilling to learning new things)*
- Write the simile from lines 32–35 on the board. Discuss the idea brought out by comparing those who fight in the Trojan War to bulls being sacrificed. *(The speaker's view is that the men lose their lives for nothing.)*

Knowledge Demands

cultural and literary knowledge essential to understanding

Support English Learners in understanding ideas about the author and topic of the poem.

- Teacher's Edition Author note, p. 331

ZOOM IN ON **BUILDING CULTURAL AND HISTORICAL BACKGROUND** Explain that Eris was often considered the spirit of warfare. She is said to be the daughter of Nyx, or Night; her sisters are Nemesis, the goddess of vengeance; Apate, the goddess of deceit; Geras, the goddess of old age; and Philotes, the goddess of friendship. The last two seem harmless, but the ancient Greeks felt that fear of old age and unwise friendships often led to harmful behaviors.

Suggested Reader/Task Considerations

You might consider the following before assigning this poem to students.

- Do students have adequate familiarity with the genre to enable them to understand the parody?
- Will students need additional support to enable them to complete the Performance Task?

ZOOM IN ON **SUPPORTING COMPREHENSION**

- Tap students' prior knowledge of parodies by asking if they have seen movies that make fun of certain film genres, such as horror or teen movies. These films exaggerate the characteristics of the genres to create humor. Tell students to look for examples of exaggeration and humor as they read the poem.
- Have pairs prepare an argument agreeing or disagreeing with Eris's opinion. Meet with each pair to assess their organization and help them gather text evidence.

Kate Hovey Have students read the information about the author. Explain that Kate Hovey wrote an entire book of poems that tells the tale of the Trojan War, all from the viewpoint of the humans and gods who were a part of it. "The Apple of Discord I" is one of these poems, telling the story of the contest for a golden apple and its effects on this epic war.

SETTING A PURPOSE Direct students to use the Setting a Purpose prompt to focus their reading. Remind them to write down questions as they read.

Compare and Contrast Genres (LINES 1–10)

RL 1, RL 9

Explain to students that comparing texts in two different genres about the same story can help the reader gain a deeper understanding of each text. Recall the myth *Black Ships Before Troy* for students as needed.

Ⓐ **CITE TEXT EVIDENCE** Have a student or students reread the opening subhead and lines 1–10 aloud. Ask students how they know that this poem is a version of a myth. *(The subhead says the speaker is Eris, the Goddess of Discord; "Lofty Olympians" and "immortals" are clues that this poem is a version of a Greek myth.)*

Ⓑ **ASK STUDENTS** who the phrase "lesser immortals" refers to and how they know this. *(This line refers to Eris herself; she has been excluded from the wedding as "lesser immortals" have been; she is speaking in sarcasm and anger at the others for excluding her.)* Ask students to compare Eris's perspective to the perspective presented in *Black Ships Before Troy*. *(Possible responses: The myth is observant, unemotional; the poem is emotional and personal. In the myth, Eris was excluded because they thought she would make trouble; Eris thinks she was excluded because they think she is a "lesser immortal.")*

English Language Support

Explain that *immortal* means "not subject to death" and that gods/goddesses in the myths cannot die.

ASK STUDENTS to explain why Eris is angry even though she is an immortal goddess. *(She has less power than other gods, and these gods do not respect her.)*

Kate Hovey *first read the stories of Greek mythology in third grade and has been reading them ever since. Her interest in gods and goddesses grew during her childhood visits to the Getty Villa, a museum in Malibu, California, that was built to imitate an ancient Roman villa. The museum's collection of marble statues from the Greco-Roman period helped her imagine the ancient voices of the gods and goddesses that inspire her. Hovey is a metalsmith and mask-maker as well, using her arts of poetry, storytelling, and drama to bring the world of Greek mythology to life.*

The Apple of Discord I

Poem by Kate Hovey

SETTING A PURPOSE As you read, focus on how Eris compares herself to the other gods and goddesses.

Eris (Goddess of Discord) Speaks

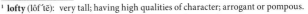

Lofty[1] Olympians
　like to exclude
lesser immortals
　who aren't imbued[2]
5　with the kind of power
　　they so admire.
　Still, I'm a goddess,
　　and I require
　certain courtesies,
10　　a little care and concern,

Ⓑ

Ⓐ

[1] **lofty** (lôf´tē): very tall; having high qualities of character; arrogant or pompous.
[2] **imbued** (ĭm-byōōd´): permeated; spreading or flowing throughout.

(tl) ©Jean Leeper Hoelsche/Kate Hovey; (cbg) ©Shutterstock; (inset) ©Blue Jean Images/Corbis

The Apple of Discord I **331**

English Language Support

Analyze Language Explain that a contraction is a short way of writing a word or words. An apostrophe takes the place of one or more letters. Write the contraction *isn't*. Tell students that *isn't* means "is not" and that an apostrophe takes the place of the letter *o*.

ASK STUDENTS to identify contractions and the words the contractions stand for as they read. *(aren't, line 4; I'm, lines 7 and 27; weren't, line 20).*

Read the first six lines. Then read the same lines with expanded contractions. Explain how the use of contractions improves the rhythm.

CLOSE READ

Determine Meanings: Tone (LINES 11–40)

RL 1, RL 4

Explain to students that a **parody** is an imitation of another work for the purpose of being humorous. Its language reveals the attitude the writer has about the subject. Sometimes a writer will exaggerate details about events or characters; sometimes he or she will tell the story from another character's point of view. Recall the myth *Black Ships Before Troy* with students.

C CITE TEXT EVIDENCE Ask students how they know that this poem is a parody. *(Possible responses: The poem shows another perspective on the myth by changing its viewpoint. Eris mocks the Olympian gods, calling them hypocrites; she says they should be embarrassed to squabble over the apple and describes them "tugging and pulling" like children.)*

English Language Support

Discuss who the "writer" of this poem is and what language shows how the writer feels about the gods. *(Kate Hovey, the poet, is writing for Eris, as if Eris were the writer. Eris feels contempt for the gods because they "squabble" over the apple, "sacrifice" people, and "let Troy burn.")*

Compare and Contrast Genres (LINES 11–40)

RL 9

Remind students that the myth and the poem both focus on Eris's actions at the sea queen's wedding.

D ASK STUDENTS to tell how the two texts are different and what the poem reveals that the myth does not. *(Possible responses: The myth is a story with setting, characters, plot, and conflict that explains why something happened. It is told from the third-person point of view. The poem is told from the point of view of one of the characters in that story who reveals her motivations for her actions.)*

COLLABORATIVE DISCUSSION Have students reread the poem and take notes that help them understand how Eris sees herself.

---

but the gods are hardheaded;
  they never learn.
So I came, uninvited,
  to the sea queen's wedding
15 and threw a gold apple
  far out on the spreading,
goddess-strewn lawn.
  Inscribed, "for the fairest,"
it caused a commotion—
20 weren't they embarrassed
to squabble that way?
  Hera, Athena,
and vain Aphrodite,
  tugging and pulling—
25 what high and mighty
  hypocrites![3] They claim
I'm the foul one!
They think they can blame
  my wedding surprise
30 for the horrors at Troy,
  when *they* are the guilty ones—
they who destroy,
  who sacrifice heroes,
Earth's glorious sons,
35 like bulls on an altar—
brave, innocent ones.
  To their lasting shame,
they let Troy burn.
  The gods are hardheaded;
40 they never learn.

COLLABORATIVE DISCUSSION How does Eris, the Goddess of Discord, see herself in relation to other gods and goddesses? Discuss your ideas with a partner, using evidence from the poem.

---

[3] **hypocrites** (hĭp′ə-krĭts′): people who pretend to have beliefs, feelings, or virtues that they actually do not have; falseness.

WHEN STUDENTS STRUGGLE . . .

As students analyze the myth and the poem, have them note similarities and differences and record the information in a chart as shown.

Myth	Poem	Both
third person	first person	gods and goddesses
adventure	parody	wedding

LEVEL UP TUTORIALS For additional support, assign the following *Level Up* tutorials: **Myths, Legends, and Tales; Tone**

Determine Meanings of Words and Phrases

RL 4

If a writer wants to make fun of a well-known story, he or she writes a parody of it. A **parody** is a humorous imitation of another writer's work. Usually a parody will:

- follow the form of the original text or story, but also might put a twist on the story and use a different form
- tell the story from a different character's point of view

Writers of parodies often add humor through exaggerated descriptions and double meanings of words and phrases. For example, in "The Apple of Discord I," when Eris describes the three goddesses as "high and mighty hypocrites," (lines 25–26) she is using figurative language that means the goddesses are arrogant and bossy. However, she also emphasizes the literal meanings of the words—the powerful goddesses live high atop Mount Olympus and they are, indeed, mighty.

As you analyze elements of parody in "The Apple of Discord I," think about these questions:

- How does the writer add a twist to or change the original story as told in *Black Ships Before Troy: The Story of The Iliad*? How does this add humor to the parody?
- How does the writer use language in a humorous way?

Compare and Contrast Genres

RL 9

When you compare and contrast a myth and a parody of the same myth, you analyze the characteristics of each text, how the events in each version are presented, and the techniques each author uses to achieve his or her purpose.

Ask these questions to compare and contrast a myth and a parody of the same myth:

- What is each author's purpose for writing?
- What elements of myth are found in each text?
- How is each author's presentation of events alike and different?
- How are characters portayed in each text? How are they alike and different?
- The author of the parody makes fun of the original work. What techniques does he or she use to accomplish this goal?

The Apple of Discord I   **333**

TEACH

CLOSE READ

Determine Meaning of Words and Phrases

RL 1, RL 4

Review the definition and information about parody. Tell students that paying attention to the details in a poem will help them understand a parody. Help them answer the questions as they analyze "The Apple of Discord I," and ask them to identify words and phrases in the poem that support their answers. Discuss the meaning that the speaker is trying to convey. *(Possible responses: The writer tells the story from the viewpoint of Eris. She makes fun of the gods and goddesses, minimizing her own actions and saying that if they weren't so "hardheaded" the war would not have happened. The language conveys childishness, pettiness, and immaturity in the goddesses.)*

Compare and Contrast Genres

RL 9

Tell students that when they compare and contrast, they tell how texts are alike and different. Guide students to answer the questions about the texts. *Possible responses:*

- *Author's purpose: myth explains causes of the Trojan War; poem approaches myth in a humorous way.*
- *Both explain an event and have gods and goddesses.*
- *Myth is third-person; poem is first-person.*
- *Characters are powerful, moody, and fierce in the myth, and hardheaded and arrogant in the poem.*
- *Eris makes fun of the gods, yet shows the same traits.*

Strategies for Annotation   ✏️ 🖥 *Annotate it!*

Determine Meanings of Words and Phrases

RL 4

Share these strategies for guided or independent analysis:

- Highlight in yellow words that have double meanings.
- Highlight in blue exaggerated descriptions.
- Use a note to explain what each highlighted example reveals.

Lofty Olympians

    like to exclude

[...]

    far out on the spreading,

goddess-strewn lawn.

mocking; creates humor

PRACTICE & APPLY

Analyzing the Text

RL 1, RL 2, RL 4, RL 5, RL 6, RL 9, RL 10

Possible answers:

1. *Eris calls the three goddesses "Lofty Olympians." The double meaning of "Lofty" in "Lofty Olympians" points out that gods live on high and that they think they are better than "lesser" goddesses like Eris.*

2. *Words and phrases like "commotion," "weren't they embarrassed," and "squabble" show that Eris finds the goddesses and their behavior ridiculous; they are also intended to show that she herself would never behave in such a lowly manner.*

3. *In the first part of the poem, Eris uses words such as embarrassed, squabble, tugging, and pulling. Her tone is mocking. In the second part, Eris's tone is harsh and critical with descriptions like "the horrors at Troy," "they who destroy, who sacrifice heroes," and "to their lasting shame."*

4. *The theme is that the gods and goddesses should not use humans to settle their disputes. The repeated statements of "the gods are hardheaded; they never learn" support the theme.*

5. *In both texts, the apple stands for how disagreement over a small, unimportant thing can lead to great conflict. In the myth, the apple is described as "a small thing," and the plot events show how it led to long-lasting battles and destruction. In the poem, Eris describes how the "commotion" caused by the apple led to the destruction of Troy and "Earth's glorious sons."*

6. *In the myth, Eris tosses the golden apple on a table. In the poem, she throws the apple on the grass. In the myth, the apple is inscribed with the words "to the fairest." In the poem, it is inscribed with the words "for the fairest." In both the myth and the poem, the goddesses fight over the apple, but in the myth, Eris is not mentioned after the wedding.*

 eBook *Annotate It!*

Analyzing the Text

RL 1, RL 2, RL 4, RL 5, RL 6, RL 9, RL 10, SL 4, SL 6

Cite Text Evidence Support your responses with evidence from the text.

1. **Infer** Reread lines 1–7. Eris describes herself as one of the "lesser immortals." What phrase does she use to describe the three goddesses? Tell why this description is humorous.

2. **Interpret** Reread lines 19–26. What words and phrases does Eris use to describe the three goddesses and their behavior? Explain what these word choices tell you about what she thinks of them, and how she sees herself.

3. **Analyze** Compare Eris' word choices in lines 1–27 with those in lines 28–40. As the poem progresses, how does Eris' tone change? Tell what language choices contribute to the change in tone.

4. **Infer** Review lines 1–40 of "The Apple of Discord I." What is the **theme,** or message about life, of the poem? What repeated statements help you infer the theme?

5. **Compare** A **symbol** is a person, place, or thing that stands for something else. In this poem and in *Black Ships Before Troy*, what is the symbol and what does it stand for? Do you think that the symbolic meaning is the same or different in the two texts? Cite evidence from both texts to support your ideas.

6. **Compare and Contrast** Review lines 1–94 of *Black Ships Before Troy.* Compare how the events in the myth are described with Eris' description of the events in "The Apple of Discord I." How are the descriptions alike? How are they different?

PERFORMANCE TASK

Speaking Activity: Argument "The Apple of Discord I" is told from the point of view of Eris, the Goddess of Discord. Do you agree with her that Hera, Aphrodite, and Athene are the ones responsible for the "horrors at Troy"? Give a speech that presents your opinion. Use facts and details from the poem to support it.

- Review the poem. Determine whether or not you agree with Eris.

- Write a statement that clearly presents your claim.
- Draft your speech, using evidence from the poem to support your claim.
- Practice your speech, using appropriate eye contact, adequate volume, and clear pronunciation.
- Present your ideas in a logical, organized way that helps listeners understand them.

PERFORMANCE TASK

SL 4, SL 6

Speaking Activity: Argument Direct students to

- introduce the topic and state their opinion
- use a graphic organizer, such as a hierarchy chart
- summarize, restating the most important reasons and evidence
- speak with adequate volume and clear pronunciation

Assign this performance task.

As students practice their speech, have them try speaking in front of a mirror or recording their reading and listening to it.

Analyze Language: Symbol

RL 4, RL 5

TEACH

Explain to students that a **symbol** is a person, a place, an object, or an activity that stands for something beyond itself. For example, the heart is often used as a symbol for love. Poets often use symbols as a way to add deeper meaning to their work. Tell students that analyzing the symbols in a poem can help them better understand the poem's meaning.

Explain that some symbols are universal, or they communicate meanings that most people understand. For example, a flag is a universal symbol for patriotism. Other symbols are unique to a specific piece of text. Tell them that in order to figure out a symbol in a text, readers must pay attention to objects, places, people, or activities that are described in great detail, or that are mentioned often in the language of the text.

Explain that a symbol can connect different parts of a text as well. Students must look at how the symbol first appears and then reappears throughout the text. Tracing a symbol throughout a text will show them how the symbol is used to introduce, illustrate, elaborate on, or develop ideas, events, and characters within the text. Looking for symbols can help them understand the overall structure and meaning of a text in a deeper way.

Review with students the symbol of the gold apple in "The Apple of Discord I." Ask:

- How does this symbol relate to what's happening in the story?
- What does this symbol mean to the characters?
- What might this symbol represent?

PRACTICE AND APPLY

Have students answer the questions to identify symbols in another poem of their choosing. Then, have them share their findings with a partner.

ENGLISH LANGUAGE SUPPORT

Support Opinions Have students work in a small group to read another poem of your choosing. Ask them to identify the symbols in the poem and discuss what the symbols represent. Encourage students to use sentence frames and questions such as *I think _____ because _____. I don't understand. Can you please repeat that?* in their discussion as they support their ideas.

Determine Meaning of Words and Phrases: Parody

RL 4, W 3a, W 4

RETEACH

Review that a **parody** is a humorous imitation of another work. Then, discuss the following features of a parody:

- follows the form of the original text or story
- adds a twist or changes the story
- tells the story from another point of view
- uses language in a humorous way

Guide students to interpret the parody of the poem "Twinkle, Twinkle, Little Star" from *Alice's Adventures In Wonderland*:

> Twinkle, Twinkle, Little Bat, / How I wonder what you're at: / Up above the world you fly / Like a tea tray in the sky.

Ask students what elements from the original poem are reflected in the parody and how the poet creates parody. *(Possible response: The parody follows the rhyme scheme and meter of the original but adds a twist by substituting the darkly humorous bat and tea tray for the shining star and the diamond.)*

 LEVEL UP TUTORIALS Assign the following *Level Up* tutorial: **Tone**

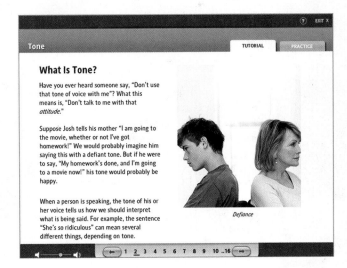

INDEPENDENT READING

Individuals or partners can analyze another parody of their choosing and share their analyses when finished. Then, have students write a parody of their own; partners can each write their own parody and then analyze each other's work.

Yeh-Shen: A Cinderella Story from China

Chinese Folk Tale by Ai-Ling Louie

Why This Text?

Many students have cherished memories of favorite folk tales. As students are exposed to traditional tales from all over the world, they realize that the stories they tell and the lessons they teach are universal. *Yeh-Shen*, from China, is one such tale.

Key Learning Objective: The student will be able to describe characteristics of folk tales, as well as analyze the use of foreshadowing.

RL 1 Cite text evidence; make inferences.
RL 2 Determine theme; provide a summary.
RL 3 Analyze story elements.
RL 4 Determine meaning of words and phrases.
RL 5 Analyze structure.
RL 9 Compare and contrast texts in different forms or genres.
W 3 Write narratives.
W 3a Engage and orient the reader.
W 3b Use narrative techniques.
W 3c Use transition words, phrases, and clauses.
W 3d Use precise words, descriptive details, and sensory language.
W 3e Provide a conclusion.
SL 1 Engage effectively in a range of collaborative discussions.
L 2b Spell correctly.
L 4a Use context as a clue to meaning.
L 4c Consult reference materials.
L 6 Acquire and use grade-appropriate academic words.

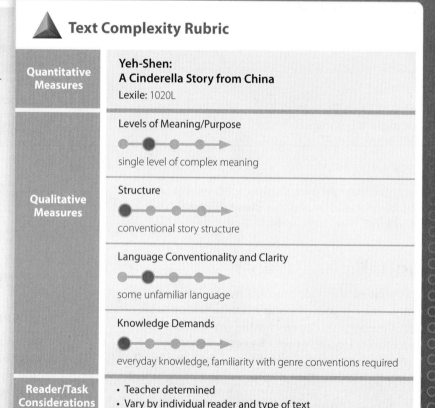

▲ Text Complexity Rubric

Quantitative Measures

Yeh-Shen: A Cinderella Story from China
Lexile: 1020L

Qualitative Measures

Levels of Meaning/Purpose

single level of complex meaning

Structure

conventional story structure

Language Conventionality and Clarity

some unfamiliar language

Knowledge Demands

everyday knowledge, familiarity with genre conventions required

Reader/Task Considerations

- Teacher determined
- Vary by individual reader and type of text
- See the Text X-Ray for suggested Reader/Task Considerations.

Meaning Making

Language Development

Effective Expression

Content Knowledge

Foundational Skills

TEXT X-RAY

English Language Support
Before teaching, use the Text X-Ray for an overview of the text's complexity. The Text X-Ray and the supports and scaffolds in the Teacher's Edition will help you guide students of different skill levels.

Text Complexity: Qualitative Measures

Levels of Meaning/Purpose

single level of complex meaning

Help students trace the use of foreshadowing in a folk tale.

- Teacher's Edition side notes, pp. 337, 338, 341
- English Language Support, p. 337
- Strategies for Annotation, p. 341
- Describe Stories: Foreshadowing, p. 341

To reteach foreshadowing, see

- Describe Stories: Foreshadowing, p. 344a

▶ *Use It!* **Level Up Tutorials:** Suspense and Foreshadowing

***ZOOM IN ON* TRACING FORESHADOWING** After students have read the folk tale once, ask them to find details in lines 121–177 that **foreshadow**, or hint, at the happy ending. Have students share their ideas with a partner before discussing them with the class. *(Possible response: (lines 124–126) The king is fascinated with the slipper and wants to find the woman to whom it belongs; (lines 156–160) the king notices Yeh-Shen's beauty and her tiny feet; (lines 171–174) Yeh-Shen changes when she puts the shoes back on; (lines 175–177) the king realizes he has found his true love.)*

Structure

conventional story structure

Help students describe the characteristics of a folk tale.

- Teacher's Edition side notes, pp. 335, 336, 339, 340, 341
- English Language Support, pp. 335, 336, 340
- When Students Struggle, p. 340
- Strategies for Annotation, p. 339
- Describe Stories: Folk Tales, p. 341

To teach how to summarize texts, see

- Summarize Text, p. 344a

▶ *Use It!* **Interactive Whiteboard Lesson:** Summarizing Text

***ZOOM IN ON* COMPARING AND CONTRASTING GENRES** Have student pairs use these sentence frames to discuss the characteristics of this **folk tale:**

- The main character is ___. *(Yeh-Shen)*
- The setting is ____. *(southern China in the very distant past)*
- The conflict is _____. *(that Yeh-Shen is treated badly by her stepmother)*
- One supernatural element is ____. *(the magical fish bones)*
- An important plot event is when Yeh-Shen goes to the festival ____. *(and loses her shoe)*
- The conflict is resolved when ____. *(the king finds Yeh-Shen, marries her, and takes her away)*
- An important theme is ____. *(goodness is rewarded, and bad deeds are punished)*

Language Conventionality and Clarity

some unfamiliar language

Teach unfamiliar vocabulary in context.

- Teacher's Edition Critical Vocabulary notes, pp. 336, 337, 338, 339, 343
- Applying Academic Vocabulary, p. 337
- Vocabulary Strategy: Using a Glossary, p. 343

Support students' reading and analysis of the selection.

- Teacher's Edition side notes, pp. 340, 344
- English Language Support, pp. 336, 342, 343, 344
- Language Conventions: Spell Words Correctly, p. 344

ZOOM IN ON **USING CONTEXT CLUES** Tell students that they can use **context clues** to help them figure out unfamiliar words. Write these words on the board and work with students to pick out clues to their meanings in the sentences around them. Then ask students pairs to write the definition for each.

- line 52: dwell *(keep talking or thinking about)*
- line 78: finery *(best clothes; dresses and jewelry)*
- line 157: harmony *(pleasing appearance; beauty)*
- line 179: fate: *(destiny; force that controls the future)*

Knowledge Demands

everyday knowledge, familiarity with genre conventions required

Support English Learners in understanding cultural background.

- Teacher's Edition Author note, p. 335
- English Language Support, p. 335

ZOOM IN ON **BUILDING CULTURAL BACKGROUND** Tell students that the Spring Festival (lines 68–71) is still celebrated by people in China and of Chinese descent. It is known as the Chinese New Year. To prepare, the house is cleaned, poems are pasted on doorways, and special foods are made. On the eve of the Chinese New Year, family members come home to eat dinner. In the past, fireworks were set off at midnight. The next day, children get gifts of money. For several days after the New Year, friends visit.

Suggested Reader/Task Considerations

You might consider the following before assigning this selection to students.

- Do students have the skills that will enable them to visualize action, character, and setting?
- Will the language and ideas within the text keep students interested and engaged?

ZOOM IN ON **SUPPORTING COMPREHENSION**

- Display lines 86–93. Work with students to highlight text that describes Yeh-Shen's appearance. Then ask them to draw what they see in their minds. Have them compare pictures with a partner.
- Read aloud lines 1–25 and have students predict what will happen next. Write their predictions on the board and have them read the rest of the paragraph independently to confirm their predictions. Use the same procedure to read the rest of the story.

Ai-Ling Louie Have students read the information about the author. Tell students that, as a child, Ai-Ling Louie heard many wonderful Chinese tales from her parents and their friends. She grew up loving books and libraries and eventually became a librarian herself. During her twenty-one years as a librarian, she noticed there were not many children's biographies of Asian Americans. As a result, she has begun a series called Amazing Asian Americans.

SETTING A PURPOSE Direct students to use the Setting a Purpose prompt to focus their reading. Have them write down similarities and differences they notice and any questions they have.

Describe Stories: RL 1, RL 3
Folk Tales (LINES 1–11)

Explain to students that **folk tales** are stories that have been told and retold for generations, and, like all stories, they have characters and a setting, the time and place in which the story takes place.

A CITE TEXT EVIDENCE Ask students to tell the setting of the story and how they know this. *(Southern China, in the "dim past" before the Ch'in and Han dynasties; lines 1–2)* Ask them what words they have read in fairy tales or other folk tales that establish the time period. *(Accept such phrases as "once upon a time" or "long ago and far away.")*

B ASK STUDENTS which two characters are introduced here and what similarities these characters have to two of the main characters in other versions of the Cinderella story they know. *(Yeh-Shen and her stepmother. Like Cinderella, Yeh-Shen is a lovely girl; like the evil stepmother in Cinderella, Yeh-Shen's stepmother is jealous of Yeh-Shen's good qualities; lines 8–11.)*

English Language Support

Understand Text Structure Explain to students that all stories have a **plot.** A plot is the sequence of events and has these parts:

- Exposition: the introduction of the basic story and characters
- Conflict: a problem that pushes the story action
- Rising Action: the story part when the conflict becomes bigger
- Climax: the part where there is the most action or conflict
- Falling Action: the time when the conflict is becoming smaller
- Resolution: the solution to the conflict

ASK STUDENTS to work with a partner to read the folk tale. Have them note where in the folk tale they think each plot element falls by listing line numbers. Invite them to share their ideas with the class.

Ai-Ling Louie (b. 1949) *grew up in the suburbs of New York City hearing stories from her parents and their friends. While working as a teacher and a children's librarian, Louie wrote her first book,* Yeh-Shen: A Cinderella Story from China, *a traditional folk tale passed down from her grandmother. The original story is one of the oldest written Cinderella stories in the world (A.D. 618–907), written several centuries before the first European Cinderella story (A.D. 1634, Italy). Now, Louie devotes her time to writing, family, and visiting schools to share stories, just as her family did for her.*

Yeh-Shen
A CINDERELLA STORY FROM CHINA

Chinese Folk Tale by Ai-Ling Louie

SETTING A PURPOSE As you read, pay attention to how the story of Yeh-Shen is similar to and different from familiar Cinderella stories that you know.

A   In the dim past, even before the Ch'in and the Han dynasties,[1] there lived a cave chief of southern China by the name of Wu. As was the custom in those days, Chief Wu had taken two wives. Each wife in their turn had presented Wu with a baby daughter. But one of the wives sickened and died, and not too many days after that Chief Wu took to his bed and died too.

Yeh-Shen, the little orphan, grew to girlhood in her stepmother's home. She was a bright child and lovely too, with skin as smooth as ivory and dark pools for eyes. Her stepmother was jealous of all this beauty and goodness, for her   B

10

---

[1] **Ch'in** (chĭn) **and the Han** (hän) **dynasties** (dī´nə-stēz): groups that held power in China. The Ch'in dynasty ruled from 221 to 206 B.C., and the Han dynasty ruled from 206 B.C. to A.D. 220.

CLOSE READ

Describe Stories: Folk Tales (LINES 12–20)

RL 1,
RL 3

Review with students that a **plot** is the series of events in a story, and it is usually centered on a **conflict,** or struggle, faced by the main character. Tell students that folk tales, too, have plots and conflicts.

C CITE TEXT EVIDENCE Have students reread lines 12–20 and find evidence of the conflict, or struggle, faced by Yeh-Shen. *(Lines 12–13: Yeh-Shen's stepmother gives her the hardest chores. Line 18: Her stepmother does not give Yeh-Shen enough food.)*

Explain to students that folk tales often include unrealistic or fantasy elements.

D ASK STUDENTS to find an example of an unrealistic or fantastic element in lines 12–20. *(Lines 14–17: Yeh-Shen feeds a fish that comes out of the water and waits for her.)*

English Language Support

Have students work in a small group to discuss why folk tales often include fantastic elements. Ask students to think about other folk tales they have read and what kind of characters and conflicts are often part of a folk tale. *(Possible responses: The characters in folk tales often have conflicts with characters who have control or power. The fantastic elements make it possible for the main characters to gain some power or control over their lives.)*

CRITICAL VOCABULARY

collapse: The word *collapsed* describes how Yeh-Shen's grief caused her to fall to the ground.

ASK STUDENTS how the word *collapsed* helps them to better understand Yeh-Shen's grief. *(The story says Yeh-Shen was "overcome with grief." The use of the word emphasizes her great sadness; she is so sad that she cannot control her body.)*

---

own daughter was not pretty at all. So in her displeasure, she gave poor Yeh-Shen the heaviest and most unpleasant chores.

C The only friend that Yeh-Shen had to her name was a fish she had caught and raised. It was a beautiful fish with golden eyes, and every day it would come out of the water and rest its head on the bank of the pond, waiting for Yeh-Shen to feed it. Stepmother gave Yeh-Shen little enough food for herself, but
20 the orphan child always found something to share with her fish, which grew to enormous size. **D**

Somehow the stepmother heard of this. She was terribly angry to discover that Yeh-Shen had kept a secret from her. She hurried down to the pond, but she was unable to see the fish, for Yeh-Shen's pet wisely hid itself. The stepmother, however, was a crafty woman, and she soon thought of a plan. She walked home and called out, "Yeh-Shen, go and collect some firewood. But wait! The neighbors might see you. Leave your filthy coat here!" The minute the girl was out of sight, her stepmother slipped on the coat herself and went down again
30 to the pond. This time the big fish saw Yeh-Shen's familiar jacket and heaved itself onto the bank, expecting to be fed. But the stepmother, having hidden a dagger in her sleeve, stabbed the fish, wrapped it in her garments, and took it home to cook for dinner.

When Yeh-Shen came to the pond that evening, she found her pet had disappeared. Overcome with grief, the girl **collapsed** on the ground and dropped her tears into the still waters of the pond.

"Ah, poor child!" a voice said.
40 Yeh-Shen sat up to find a very old man looking down at her. He wore the coarsest of clothes, and his hair flowed down over his shoulders.

"Kind uncle, who may you be?" Yeh-Shen asked.

"That is not important, my child. All you must know is that I have been sent to tell you of the wondrous powers of your fish."

"My fish, but sir . . ." The girl's eyes filled with tears, and she could not go on.

The old man sighed and said, "Yes, my child, your fish
50 is no longer alive, and I must tell you that your stepmother is once more the cause of your sorrow." Yeh-Shen gasped in horror, but the old man went on. "Let us not dwell on things that are past," he said, "for I have come bringing you a gift.

collapse
(kə-lăps´) *v.* If you *collapse*, you fall down suddenly.

English Language Support

Analyze Language Display lines 28–31. Underline *slipped* and explain that it has several meanings. Guide students to realize that the stepmother did not slide or trip on the coat; she *slipped* it on to wear it.

ASK STUDENTS to work with a partner to explain how the fish was fooled into leaving the water. Some students may find a cause-and-effect chart helpful in their thinking with the phrase *her stepmother slipped on the coat herself* in the cause column and the *big fish . . . heaved itself onto the bank* in the effect column.

(E) Now you must listen carefully to this: The bones of your fish are filled with a powerful spirit. Whenever you are in serious need, you must kneel before them and let them know your heart's desire. But do not waste their gifts."

Yeh-Shen wanted to ask the old sage[2] many more questions, but he rose to the sky before she could utter another word. With heavy heart, Yeh-Shen made her way to the dung heap to gather the remains of her friend.

Time went by, and Yeh-Shen, who was often left alone, took comfort in speaking to the bones of her fish. When she was hungry, which happened quite often, Yeh-Shen asked the bones for food. In this way, Yeh-Shen managed to live from day to day, but she lived in dread that her stepmother would discover her secret and take even that away from her.

So the time passed and spring came. Festival time was approaching: It was the busiest time of the year. Such cooking and cleaning and sewing there was to be done! (F) Yeh-Shen had hardly a moment's rest. At the spring festival young men and young women from the village hoped to meet and to choose whom they would marry. How Yeh-Shen longed to go! But her stepmother had other plans. She hoped to find a husband for her own daughter and did not want any man to see the beauteous Yeh-Shen first. When finally the holiday arrived, the stepmother and her daughter dressed themselves in their finery and filled their baskets with sweetmeats.[3] "You must remain at home now, and watch to see that no one steals fruit from our trees," her stepmother told Yeh-Shen, and then she departed for the **banquet** with her own daughter.

As soon as she was alone, Yeh-Shen went to speak to the bones of her fish. "Oh, dear friend," she said, kneeling before the precious bones, "I long to go to the festival, but I cannot show myself in these rags. Is there somewhere I could borrow clothes fit to wear to the feast?" At once she found herself dressed in a gown of azure blue,[4] with a cloak of kingfisher feathers draped around her shoulders. Best of all, on her tiny feet were the most beautiful slippers she had ever seen. They were woven of golden threads, in a pattern like the scales of a fish, and the **glistening** soles were made of solid gold. There

banquet

(băng'kwĭt) n. A *banquet* is a huge, elaborate feast with many kinds of food and drink.

glisten

(glĭs'ən) v. An object that *glistens* is sparkly and shiny.

[2] **sage** (sāj): a person respected for his or her wisdom, judgment, and experience.
[3] **sweetmeats** (swēt'mēts'): any kind of sweet food or delicacy.
[4] **azure blue** (ăzh'ər bloo): a light purplish blue.

Yeh-Shen: A Cinderella Story from China **337**

APPLYING ACADEMIC VOCABULARY

period	relevant	tradition

THINK-PAIR-SHARE Have students turn to a partner to discuss the following questions. Guide students to include the academic vocabulary words *period, relevant,* and *tradition* in their responses.

Ask volunteers to share their responses with the class.

- How does the time **period** in which this folk tale is set affect how the characters speak to one another?
- Does the time period make the story seem old fashioned and less **relevant** to modern readers, or does the **tradition** of folk tales continue to be important in modern culture?

CLOSE READ

Describe Stories: Foreshadowing
RL 1, RL 3, RL 5

(LINES 54–57; 71–76)

Explain to students that **foreshadowing** refers to hints a writer provides that suggest future events. These hints add suspense and excitement to a story and help develop the plot.

(E) **CITE TEXT EVIDENCE** Have students reread lines 54–57 and tell what words and phrases foreshadow possible future events. *(Possible responses: The old man's words "Whenever you are in serious need" suggest that difficult times are ahead for Yeh-Shen; "do not waste their gifts" hints that Yeh-Shen should use the bones' powers in helpful ways.)*

(F) **ASK STUDENTS** to reread lines 71–76. Ask what these lines foreshadow and how the foreshadowing helps to develop the plot. *(These lines foreshadow that someone, but maybe not the stepmother's daughter, will find a husband at the festival. Yeh-Shen's longing to go seems to foreshadow that somehow she will go.)*

English Language Support

Read lines 54–57 and 71–76 aloud, clarifying concepts as necessary. Work with students to identify instances of foreshadowing, modeling as necessary.

CRITICAL VOCABULARY

banquet: Yeh-Shen longs to go to the banquet.

ASK STUDENTS to tell why, based on the definition of the word, Yeh-Shen may be so eager to go to the banquet. *(Possible response: Yeh-Shen does not get enough food to eat or have any fun. At a banquet, there would be plenty of food and many people; Yeh-Shen might be able to find a husband there as well.)*

glisten: The soles of Yeh-Shen's shoes are made of solid gold, and they glisten.

ASK STUDENTS to name other things that could be described as glistening in the story. *(shiny jewelry, Yeh-Shen's dress, sunlight shining on the pond)*

Describe Stories: Foreshadowing (LINES 94–97)

RL 1,
RL 5

Remind students that authors use foreshadowing to give hints about future plot events.

G **CITE TEXT EVIDENCE** Have students explain the foreshadowing in lines 94–97 and tell how this scene affects the plot. *(The spirit warns Yeh-Shen not to lose her shoes; this highlights the importance of the shoes and hints that losing them might have unfortunate consequences. This foreshadowing helps create anticipation and suspense as the plot develops.)*

Make Inferences

RL 1

(LINES 103–110)

Tell students that they need to make **inferences,** or logical guesses based on text evidence and their own knowledge and experience, to understand parts of a story that are not directly stated.

H **CITE TEXT EVIDENCE** Have students reread lines 103–110 and find evidence to support an inference about why the spirit won't speak now. Remind them to combine the evidence with their own experiences to make the inference. *(Possible response: Yeh-Shen lost a slipper, which was all the spirit had asked her not to do. The spirit was probably disappointed that she had broken her promise. I know I get upset when someone breaks a promise to me.)*

CRITICAL VOCABULARY

entrance: The tiny slipper entranced the king.

ASK STUDENTS to identify context clues in lines 121–126 that help to clarify the meaning of *entranced.* ("more than happy," "marveled")

undaunted: The king's search for the owner of the shoe seems hopeless, but the king is undaunted.

ASK STUDENTS to discuss why the king might be undaunted by the odds against the search's success. *(He is determined; as king, he has many resources to aid his search; he may think the owner of such a marvelous thing must be marvelous herself.)*

was magic in the shoes, for they should have been quite heavy, yet when Yeh-Shen walked, her feet felt as light as air.

G "Be sure you do not lose your golden shoes," said the spirit of the bones. Yeh-Shen promised to be careful. Delighted with her transformation[5], she bid a fond farewell to the bones of her fish as she slipped off to join in the merrymaking.

100 That day Yeh-Shen turned many a head as she appeared at the feast. All around her people whispered, "Look at that beautiful girl! Who can she be?"

But above this, Stepsister was heard to say, "Mother, does she not resemble our Yeh-Shen?"

H Upon hearing this, Yeh-Shen jumped up and ran off before her stepsister could look closely at her. She raced down the mountainside, and in doing so, she lost one of her golden slippers. No sooner had the shoe fallen from her foot than all her fine clothes turned back to rags. Only one thing remained—a tiny golden shoe. Yeh-Shen hurried to the bones of her fish and returned the slipper, promising to find its 110 mate. But now the bones were silent. Sadly Yeh-Shen realized that she had lost her only friend. She hid the little shoe in her bedstraw, and went outside to cry. Leaning against a fruit tree, she sobbed and sobbed until she fell asleep.

The stepmother left the gathering to check on Yeh-Shen, but when she returned home she found the girl sound asleep, with her arms wrapped around a fruit tree. So thinking no more of her, the stepmother rejoined the party. Meantime, a villager had found the shoe. Recognizing its worth, he sold it to a merchant, who presented it in turn to the king of the 120 island kingdom of T'o Han.

The king was more than happy to accept the slipper as a gift. He was **entranced** by the tiny thing, which was shaped of the most precious of metals, yet which made no sound when touched to stone. The more he marveled at its beauty, the more determined he became to find the woman to whom the shoe belonged. A search was begun among the ladies of his own kingdom, but all who tried on the sandal found it impossibly small. **Undaunted**, the king ordered the search widened to include the cave women from the countryside where the 130 slipper had been found. Since he realized it would take many years for every woman to come to his island and test her

entrance
(ĕn-trăns´) *v.* To *entrance* is to fill with delight or wonder.

undaunted
(ŭn-dôn´tĭd) *adj.* An *undaunted* person is someone who is strongly courageous, not discouraged or disheartened.

---

[5] **transformation** (trăns´fər-mā´shən): a significant change in appearance or form, usually for the better.

TO CHALLENGE STUDENTS . . .

Analyze Point of View How would the story be different if it were told by a character in the story? Or if it were told by a news reporter at the time the story is taking place? Have students discuss what elements of the story would be different, which would remain the same, and how the descriptions of other characters in the story might change.

ASK STUDENTS to retell the story from a different point of view. Ask them to consider the stepmother, the stepsister, the old man, the fish, or a news reporter as the narrator for their retelling. Have partners or small groups work together and then share their retellings with the class.

foot in the slipper, the king thought of a way to get the right woman to come forward. He ordered the sandal placed in a pavilion[6] by the side of the road near where it had been found, and his herald announced that the shoe was to be returned to its original owner. Then from a nearby hiding place, the king and his men settled down to watch and wait for a woman with tiny feet to come and claim her slipper.

140   All that day the pavilion was crowded with cave women who had come to test a foot in the shoe. Yeh-Shen's stepmother and stepsister were among them, but not Yeh-Shen—they had told her to stay home. By day's end, although many women had eagerly tried to put on the slipper, it still had not been worn. Wearily, the king continued his vigil[7] into the night.

> ## All that day the pavilion was crowded with cave women who had come to test a foot in the shoe.

      It wasn't until the blackest part of night, while the moon hid behind a cloud, that Yeh-Shen dared to show her face at the pavilion, and even then she tiptoed **timidly** across the wide floor. Sinking down to her knees, the girl in rags
150   examined the tiny shoe. Only when she was sure that this was the missing mate to her own golden slipper did she dare pick it up. At last she could return both little shoes to the fish bones. Surely then her beloved spirit would speak to her again.
      Now the king's first thought, on seeing Yeh-Shen take the precious slipper, was to throw the girl into prison as a thief. But when she turned to leave, he caught a glimpse of her face.

timid
(tĭm´ĭd) *adj.* To act in a *timid* manner is to act shyly, fearfully, or hesitantly.

---
[6] **pavilion** (pə-vil´yən): a decorated tent.
[7] **vigil** (vĭj´əl): a time of watching, often during normal sleeping hours.

CLOSE READ

Describe Stories:
Folk Tales (LINES 146–153)

RL 1,
RL 3

Explain to students that characters in all stories have **traits,** or personal qualities, and **motivations,** or reasons why they do the things they do, that are revealed as the plot unfolds and the characters respond to challenges.

CITE TEXT EVIDENCE Have students reread lines 146–153 and describe how Yeh-Shen's traits are revealed through her actions. *(Yeh-Shen is brave. She goes out alone in the blackest part of night despite the danger; she is sorry for losing the shoe and longs for her beloved spirit to speak to her again.)* Ask students to describe other traits Yeh-Shen's actions have revealed about her. *(She has shown herself to be hard working, loving to those who show her kindness, and strong enough to defy her wicked stepmother and rebel against her forced isolation.)*

CRITICAL VOCABULARY

timid: Yeh-Shen is brave to go out alone at night, yet she is described as tiptoeing timidly across the floor of the king's pavilion.

ASK STUDENTS to explain why Yeh-Shen behaves timidly. *(She must act humble and be quiet. She is a peasant dressed in rags. If she were noticed, she would be taken for a thief and thrown into prison.)*

Strategies for Annotation   ✏️ 🖥 *Annotate it!*

Describe Stories: Folk Tales   RL 1, RL 3

Have students use their eBook annotation tools to analyze the text. Ask them to do the following:

- Highlight in yellow text clues that help in making inferences about Yeh-Shen's character.
- Underline words that help to reveal her motivation.
- Review your annotations, and jot down notes on the traits and motivations you infer.

    It wasn't until the <mark>blackest part of night</mark>, while the moon

hid behind a cloud, that <mark>Yeh-Shen dared to show her face</mark>

at the pavilion, . . . examined the tiny shoe. Only when she was sure

. . .did she dare pick it

up. <u>At last she could return both little shoes</u> to the fi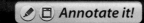

Surely then her beloved spirit would speak to her again.

> brave, determined, honest; wants her spirit friend back

Describe Stories: Folk Tales (LINES 157–177)

RL 3,
RL 5

Review with students that the **resolution** of a story's plot comes after the **climax,** the point of greatest excitement, when tension has eased and the story events are drawing to a close.

Ⓙ ASK STUDENTS to analyze and summarize how the climax of the story leads to the conflict in *Yeh-Shen* being resolved. *(The climax is Yeh-Shen returning to get the shoe, the king watching her, and letting her go. This scene leads to the king following Yeh-Shen home and asking her to put on the shoes. The magic of the bones works once again. The king falls in love, he and Yeh-Shen are married, and the conflict is resolved.)*

English Language Support

Write Summaries Work with students to gather information for their summaries. Read lines 157–177 aloud for students, asking them to write notes about the important words and ideas in the text. Then have students participate in the discussion about the climax of the story and how the conflict is resolved before writing their own summaries of the end of the story. Remind students to use their notes to help write concise and complete summaries with complete sentences.

COLLABORATIVE DISCUSSION Have students form small groups to discuss the similarities and differences between *Yeh-Shen* and other Cinderella stories with which they are familiar. To aid the discussion, ask groups to designate notetakers to create Venn diagrams, story maps, or comparison charts to record story data.

ASK STUDENTS to share any questions they generated in the course of reading and discussing the selection.

WHEN STUDENTS STRUGGLE . . .

Explain that one cause can have several effects. Have partners complete a chart like the one shown listing the events that result from Yeh-Shen's retrieval of the shoe. Discuss how none of the events would have happened if Yeh-Shen had not been motivated by her love of the spirit of her fish to take back her shoe.

At once the king was struck by the sweet harmony of her features, which seemed so out of keeping with the rags she wore. It was then that he took a closer look and noticed that she walked upon the tiniest feet he had ever seen.

160 With a wave of his hand, the king signaled that this tattered creature was to be allowed to depart with the golden slipper. Quietly, the king's men slipped off and followed her home.

Ⓙ All this time, Yeh-Shen was unaware of the excitement she had caused. She had made her way home and was about to hide both sandals in her bedding when there was a pounding at the door. Yeh-Shen went to see who it was—and found a king at her doorstep. She was very frightened at first, but 170 the king spoke to her in a kind voice and asked her to try the golden slippers on her feet. The maiden did as she was told, and as she stood in her golden shoes, her rags were transformed once more into the feathered cloak and beautiful azure gown.

Her loveliness made her seem a heavenly being, and the king suddenly knew in his heart that he had found his true love.

N ot long after this, Yeh-Shen was married to the king. But fate was not so gentle with her stepmother and stepsister. 180 Since they had been unkind to his beloved, the king would not permit Yeh-Shen to bring them to his palace. They remained in their cave home, where one day, it is said, they were crushed to death in a shower of flying stones.

COLLABORATIVE DISCUSSION With a small group, discuss how story elements, such as characters, setting, and plot events, in the story of Yeh-Shen and other Cinderella stories are alike and different.

CAUSE: Yeh-Shen retrieves her missing shoe.
EFFECTS:
• The king follows Yeh-Shen home.
• Yeh-Shen puts on the shoes and is transformed.
• The king falls in love with her, they marry, and they move to a palace.

LEVEL UP TUTORIALS For additional support, assign the following *Level Up* tutorial: **Suspense and Foreshadowing.**

Describe Stories: Folk Tales

A **folk tale** is a story that has been passed down from generation to generation by being told aloud. No matter what culture they come from, folk tales are alike in a number of ways.

- They are often set in the distant past.
- They may include humans and animals as characters, as well as superhuman beings that behave in ways that humans cannot.
- Story events may involve fantastic or supernatural occurrences that could not take place in the real world.
- A wise lesson or message about life is often presented.

Like other types of stories, folk tales have story elements such as setting, characters, plot, conflict, and resolution. As you analyze *Yeh-Shen,* ask:

- Who are the main characters? How does the central character change or respond as the story progresses?
- How would you summarize the conflict and main plot events? How is the conflict resolved?
- What important lesson or message does this folk tale share?

Describe Stories: Foreshadowing

Stories that are suspenseful are exciting to read. Foreshadowing is one way writers add suspense to a story. **Foreshadowing** is a hint that a writer provides to suggest that future events will take place in a story. It makes readers eager to find out what happens, creating suspense as the story unfolds.

When Yeh-Shen first meets a mysterious old man, he tells her how the spirit of a fish can provide help when she needs it. Then he warns her not to waste its gifts. This foreshadowing suggests to readers that a time may come when Yeh-Shen will not be able to turn to the fish's spirit for assistance.

As you analyze *Yeh-Shen,* look for examples of foreshadowing.

- Pay attention to warnings that characters share, references to danger, or unpleasant outcomes. Also note how the setting impacts the story.
- Use foreshadowing to make predictions about what might happen later on in the story.
- Follow the events as the story's plot unfolds to find out whether your predictions were accurate.

CLOSE READ

Describe Stories: Folk Tales

Help students understand that folk tales are passed down orally from generation to generation. Discuss story elements and the theme, or message or lesson about life that is usually part of a folk tale. As needed, describe together how the story unfolds.

Explain that students can focus on Yeh-Shen's responses to these challenges to help them analyze the theme of the story:

- mistreatment by her stepmother
- the loss of her pet fish
- the loss of the spirit bones

Describe Stories: Foreshadowing

Help students understand that foreshadowing adds excitement and suspense to a story. Foreshadowing can be subtle, and it takes a careful reader to recognize it. Remind students to be on the lookout for warnings, references to danger, or hints about outcomes of events yet to take place and how they contribute to the development of the plot. They can write down any predictions they make and check them with later story events.

Strategies for Annotation 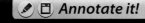 Annotate it!

Describe Stories: Foreshadowing

Share these strategies for guided or independent analysis:

- Highlight in yellow any words that seem to foreshadow, or hint at something yet to happen.
- Review your highlights. On a note, jot down what events you think the warning foreshadows.

> . . . "Let us not dwell on things that are past," he said, "for I have come bringing you a gift. Now you must listen carefully to this: The bones of your fish are filled with a powerful spirit. Whenever you are in serious need, you must kneel before them and let them know your heart's desire. But do not waste their gifts."

PRACTICE & APPLY

Analyzing the Text

RL 1, RL 2,
RL 3, RL 5,
RL 9

Possible answers:

1. *The story takes place long ago, "even before the Ch'in and Han dynasties"; the characters include humans and an unusual fish that Yeh-Shen becomes friends with.*

2. *The stepmother is sure that Yeh-Shen is keeping a secret from her. When she discovers the secret, she tricks Yeh-Shen's fish into coming out of the water and then kills it because she is cruel and wants to make Yeh-Shen unhappy.*

3. *The old man is similar to the fairy godmother in other Cinderella tales in that he helps Yeh-Shen in a time of difficulty. He is different in that he helps her just this one time by sharing the secret of the fish bones.*

4. *She is warned not to lose her golden shoes. This hint helps me predict that at some point Yeh-Shen will lose the shoes.*

5. *During the day, many try on the shoe, but the owner is not found. In the middle of the night, Yeh-Shen arrives and takes the shoe. Although she is dressed in rags, the king is struck by her beauty and lets her go home. He follows her and asks her to try on the shoes. She is transformed once again. They find true love and marry. These events lead to the conflict's resolution—Yeh-Shen leaves her home, no longer at the mercy of her stepmother's cruelty. Years later, the stepmother and stepsister, forbidden by the king to live in the palace, die a painful death.*

6. *Kindness and loyalty are rewarded. Yeh-Shen was kind to the fish, sharing her food with it even though she didn't have much. She risked imprisonment to retrieve the shoe because she wanted the spirit of her beloved fish to speak to her again. On the other hand, the stepmother, who was jealous of Yeh-Shen, did not miss an opportunity to inflict harm or punishment on Yeh-Shen. In the end, each person got what she deserved. Yeh-Shen's reward was happiness with the king, and the stepmother's reward was to continue to live in her cave home and eventually die a painful death.*

English Language Support

Use Nouns and Noun Phrases Explain to students that they can make their narrative more interesting by adding sensory adjectives to nouns. Work with students to write a sentence using adjectives. Underline and identify the noun phrase in the sentence. For example, *The girl made <u>steaming cocoa</u>.*

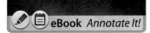

Analyzing the Text

RL 1, RL 2, RL 3,
RL 5, RL 9,
W 3a–e

Cite Text Evidence   Support your responses with evidence from the text.

1. **Identify** Review lines 1–20. What elements of folk tales can you identify in these lines?

2. **Cause/Effect** Reread lines 21–34. Describe what happens to the fish and explain why it happens.

3. **Compare** Review lines 39–61. A magic helper, like the old man, is sometimes found in folk tales. How is this magic helper similar to and different from magic helpers in other stories you know?

4. **Predict** Reread lines 82–97. What warning does Yeh-Shen receive from the spirit of the fish? Using this foreshadowing, what might you predict will happen?

5. **Summarize** Summarize the events that unfold in lines 139–183. How do they lead to the resolution of the story's conflict?

6. **Infer** What is the **theme,** or message about life, of *Yeh-Shen: A Cinderella Story from China?* Explain how the events in the story contribute to the theme.

PERFORMANCE TASK

Writing Activity: Narrative *Yeh-Shen* is one of the many versions of the tale of Cinderella. Write your own version of another popular tale.

- First, decide how your tale will be similar to and different from the original version.
- Use narrative techniques, such as dialogue and description, to present and develop plot events.

- Be sure you show how characters respond or change as the plot progresses.
- Include vivid sensory words and phrases to help readers "see" characters and events.
- End your story with a strong resolution to the plot and its conflict.

Assign this performance task.

PERFORMANCE TASK

W 3a-e

Writing Activity: Narrative Have students work independently. Direct them to
- review the characteristics of folk tales
- outline their stories before they begin writing—remember stories need a beginning, a middle, and an end as well as characters and a setting
- tell events in an order that makes sense
- try to include the element of foreshadowing

Critical Vocabulary

collapse	banquet	glisten
entrance	undaunted	timid

Practice and Apply Answer each question.

1. When have you been so tired you could have **collapsed**? Why?

2. When have you been to a **banquet**? What was it like?

3. When have you seen something **glisten**? Tell about it.

4. When have you been **entranced** by something? Tell about it.

5. When were you **undaunted** by a difficult task? What did you do?

6. Have you ever seen someone who was **timid**? Tell about it.

Vocabulary Strategy: Using a Glossary

A **glossary** is a list of specialized terms and their definitions. As with a dictionary, terms are arranged in alphabetical order. Sometimes a glossary includes pronunciation and syllabication for terms. A glossary is usually located at the back of a book. Most often, if a word is in boldface type in the text, you will find the term in the glossary. Glossaries can be useful when:

> you want to find more information about a term that is not defined
>
> you want to check the meaning of a word you infer from context
>
> you are studying for a test and want to review the meaning of key terms
>
> you do not have a dictionary available

Many textbooks include glossaries. Some, like this one, have more than one glossary. Each glossary includes terms in a particular category. In this textbook, for example, you will find glossaries for Academic Vocabulary, Critical Vocabulary, and Literary and Informational Terms.

Practice and Apply Use the glossaries at the end of this book to answer the questions.

1. Is *foreshadowing* the same thing as *suspense*? Explain your answer.

2. What words or phrases mean about the same thing as *undaunted*?

3. How are the syllables in *technician* divided?

4. How is *generalization* different from *conclusion*?

Yeh-Shen: A Cinderella Story from China **343**

PRACTICE & APPLY

Critical Vocabulary

Possible answers:

1. *After helping my cousins move into a new home, I **collapsed** at the end of the day.*

2. *I went to a wedding **banquet** last year. The decorations were fancy, and delicious food was served.*

3. *My father's car **glistened** after he waxed it.*

4. *When I visited the new Indian restaurant, I was **entranced** by the music and the delicious aromas.*

5. *Once, I had a paper to write and two tests to study for in one weekend. But I was **undaunted** and made a schedule, worked hard, and accomplished my goals.*

6. *There was a **timid** girl at the pool one day; she was having a hard time diving off the board.*

Vocabulary Strategy: Using a Glossary

Possible answers:

1. *They are not the same. Suspense is a growing feeling of tension and excitement and makes a reader curious to find out what happens. Foreshadowing creates suspense through hints that suggest what might happen.*

2. *not discouraged; brave*

3. *tech • ni • cian*

4. *A generalization is a broad statement that applies to a group or category of people, ideas, or things. A conclusion is a statement of belief based on evidence, experience, and reasoning.*

English Language Support

Condense Ideas Tell students that it is important to express their ideas clearly and concisely. Have them review their Performance Task narratives or another piece of writing for opportunities to condense ideas.

- Show students how to condense these sentences: *This is a Chinese folk tale about Yeh-Shen. Yeh-Shen married a king./This is a Chinese folk tale about Yeh-Shen who married a king.* Have students work with a partner to condense sentences in their writing.

- Challenge students to condense the ideas in these sentences: *Folk tales are stories. They have plots with characters. They often have foreshadowing and suspense.* Have them share their condensed sentences with the group.

- Review ways to condense ideas with embedded clauses and nominalization. Have students practice with these sentences before revising their own work. *The king asked the girl to try on the slipper. She did as she was told. The slippers fit and her rags turned to finery.* Discuss students' sentences.

Language Conventions: Spell Words Correctly

L 2b

Emphasize to students that misspellings can confuse readers, causing them to misread words and prevent them from understanding the writer's intent.

Display these sentences:

1. She bid a fond farewell to the bones of her fish as she ___ off to join in the merrymaking. *(slip; slipped)*

2. Leaning against a fruit tree, she ___ until she fell asleep. *(sob; sobbed)*

Give students the first word in parentheses and ask them to write the correct word to complete the sentence. Point out, as needed, that if they do not double the ending consonant, adding the *-ed* ending creates an unrecognizable word. Then, have students complete the Practice and Apply exercises independently.

Answers:

1. *hugged*

2. *planning*

3. *chopped*

4. *brimming*

5. *stripped*

6. *strumming*

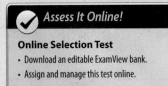

Assess It Online!

Online Selection Test
- Download an editable ExamView bank.
- Assign and manage this test online.

Language Conventions: Spell Words Correctly

L 2b

Spelling words correctly is important if you want to communicate your ideas well. Misspelled words can confuse readers and weaken the ideas you're trying to express.

You know that when you want to show that something is happening now or has happened in the past, you add *-ed* or *-ing* to the verb. Keep in mind, though, that for one-syllable words with a short vowel that end in a consonant, you double the consonant when you add *-ed* or *-ing*. Here are some examples:

| wrap | wrapped | hit | hitting | drag | dragging |

If you don't double the consonant when you add *-ed* or *-ing,* the word you form will have a long vowel sound and may be confusing to readers, especially if it is not a recognizable word.

The storm drains were *cloged* with leaves and branches.

Sometimes the misspelling will confuse a reader because it is a recognizable word, but it doesn't make sense in the sentence.

Megan froze as the *taping* at her window grew louder and more insistent.

As a writer, you don't want a misspelled word to interrupt or confuse your readers, so spelling words correctly is important!

Practice and Apply Write the past or present form of each verb in parentheses to complete each sentence.

1. At the airport, Meesha greeted her aunt and _____ her. (hug)

2. We were _____ to stop by the art museum if we had time. (plan)

3. Kevin sliced the tomatoes, and Gordon _____ the celery. (chop)

4. The student group was _____ with ideas for a holiday fair. (brim)

5. First, Ms. Chester _____ the old varnish from the bookshelves. (strip)

6. Clark waited in his room, idly _____ his guitar. (strum)

English Language Support

Use Affixes Introduce and practice some other rules that can help students use affixes successfully.

- Tell students that it is common to change the *y* to *i* before a vowel suffix such as *-ed, -es, -er, -est*. Have students practice with the words *study, dry,* and *cry,* noting which suffixes can be used. Then have them try to add *-ing,* and discuss this exception to the *y* to *i* rule before a vowel suffix.

- Have partners experiment with adding consonant suffixes (*-ful, -ly, -ment, -ness*) to words that end in *y* (*dry, happy, beauty, merry*). Ask

them what they discover about changing the *y* to *i* in these words. *(It isn't always the case.)* Then tell them to write three sentences about the tale, using each word and appropriate affixes. Have them share their sentences with a partner.

- Review the *y* rules above with students and then give them the suffixes *-s, -es, -ed, -er, -ing, -tion, -ful, -ly, -ment, -ship, -ness, -ous,* and *-able* and challenge them to use each suffix on at least one word in a brief retelling of *Yeh-Shen*. Have them review their summaries and the spelling of words with suffixes with a partner.

INTERACTIVE WHITEBOARD LESSON
Summarize Text

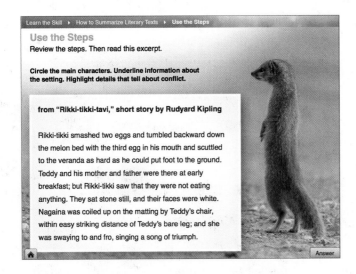

Learn the Skill ▸ How to Summarize Literary Texts ▸ **Use the Steps**

Use the Steps
Review the steps. Then read this excerpt.

Circle the main characters. Underline information about the setting. Highlight details that tell about conflict.

from "Rikki-tikki-tavi," short story by Rudyard Kipling

Rikki-tikki smashed two eggs and tumbled backward down the melon bed with the third egg in his mouth and scuttled to the veranda as hard as he could put foot to the ground. Teddy and his mother and father were there at early breakfast; but Rikki-tikki saw that they were not eating anything. They sat stone still, and their faces were white. Nagaina was coiled up on the matting by Teddy's chair, within easy striking distance of Teddy's bare leg; and she was swaying to and fro, singing a song of triumph.

Answer

TEACH

Explain to students that summarizing texts will help them write analyses and comparisons as well as their own narratives. Use the Interactive Whiteboard Lesson, teaching these steps:

- **Step 1: List the title, author, and text type.** Tell students that the original author of a folk tale may be unknown. Many versions of these tales are retellings by modern writers.
- **Step 2: Identify the main characters.** Remind students to also note minor characters as needed because they, like the old man in *Yeh-Shen*, often help to carry out the action of the story and reveal traits of the main character(s).
- **Step 3: Describe the setting.** Explain that the setting can include the geographical location, historical period, season, time of day, and culture.
- **Step 4: Identify the conflict.** Explain that conflict can be an external struggle against nature, a physical obstacle, or another character; an internal conflict that occurs within the main character; or both.

COLLABORATIVE DISCUSSION

After completing the Practice & Apply section of the whiteboard lesson, have students summarize *Yeh-Shen* and then discuss their summaries together.

INTERACTIVE LESSON Have students complete the tutorial in this lesson: **Participating in Collaborative Discussions**

Describe Stories: Foreshadowing

RETEACH

Review that foreshadowing occurs when a writer provides hints that suggest future events in a story. Examples of foreshadowing may include

- warnings
- hints about danger or trouble
- references to eagerly anticipated upcoming events, which may have unexpected results

With students, examine the passages from *Yeh-Shen* listed below to identify different forms of foreshadowing. Have students discuss what events are predicted by each.

- **Lines 11–13** *(Yeh-Shen's trouble with her stepmother)*
- **Lines 54–57** *(the fish's gifts of food and festival clothing, as well as Yeh-Shen's loss of the golden shoe)*
- **Lines 71–76** *(Yeh-Shen's longing to go to the festival)*
- **Lines 94–95** *(Yeh-Shen's loss of the golden shoe)*
- **Lines 124–126** *(the king's search for the owner of the shoe)*

LEVEL UP TUTORIALS Assign the following *Level Up* tutorial: **Suspense and Foreshadowing**

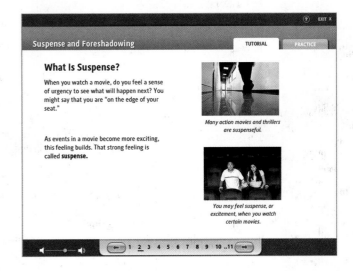

Suspense and Foreshadowing   TUTORIAL   PRACTICE

What Is Suspense?

When you watch a movie, do you feel a sense of urgency to see what will happen next? You might say that you are "on the edge of your seat."

Many action movies and thrillers are suspenseful.

As events in a movie become more exciting, this feeling builds. That strong feeling is called **suspense**.

You may feel suspense, or excitement, when you watch certain movies.

1 2 3 4 5 6 7 8 9 10 ..11

INDEPENDENT READING

Individual students can apply these skills to another selection in Collection 6 or to a short story or novel they may be reading on their own. After their analysis, have them share their ideas about suspense and foreshadowing with other students in the class.

ANCHOR TEXT

The Prince and the Pauper

Novel by Mark Twain   Dramatized by Joellen Bland

Why This Text?

Students encounter classic stories in a variety of formats and genres. This lesson explores a classic Mark Twain story adapted as a drama, examining it both as a story through its plot and as a play through the script and stage directions.

▶ **View It!**

Professional Development Podcast:
Text-Dependent Analysis

Key Learning Objective: The student will be able to describe the elements of drama in a play.

For practice and application:

Close Reader selections
The Prince and the Pauper
Novel Excerpt by Mark Twain
Drama by Joellen Bland
Graphic Story from Marvel Comics

RL 1 Cite textual evidence.
RL 2 Determine theme.
RL 3 Describe drama elements.
RL 4 Determine the meanings of words and phrases.
RL 5 Analyze structure.
RL 7 Compare and contrast the experience of reading a drama to listening to or viewing it.
SL 1 Engage effectively in a range of collaborative discussions.
SL 4 Present claims and findings; use appropriate eye contact, adequate volume, and clear pronunciation.
SL 6 Adapt speech to a variety of contexts and tasks.

 **Text Complexity Rubric**

	The Prince and the Pauper Lexile: N/A
Quantitative Measures	
Qualitative Measures	Levels of Meaning/Purpose
	single level of complex meaning
	Structure
	less familiar story structure
	Language Conventionality and Clarity
	some unfamiliar language
	Knowledge Demands
	some cultural and literary knowledge useful
Reader/Task Considerations	• Teacher determined • Vary by individual reader and type of text • See the Text X-Ray for suggested Reader/Task Considerations.

TEXT X-RAY

English Language Support Before teaching, use the Text X-Ray for an overview of the text's complexity. The Text X-Ray and the supports and scaffolds in the Teacher's Edition will help you guide students of different skill levels.

Meaning Making

Language Development

Effective Expression

Content Knowledge

Foundational Skills

Text Complexity: Qualitative Measures

Levels of Meaning/Purpose

single level of complex meaning

Help students use the elements of drama to understand character and theme.

- Teacher's Edition side notes, pp. 347, 348, 349, 350, 352, 356, 357, 359, 361
- English Language Support, pp. 345, 349, 350, 357
- Close Read Screencasts, p. 345
- Strategies for Annotation, p. 357

To reteach foreshadowing, see

- Describe Drama: Characterization, p. 362a

 Use It! **Interactive Whiteboard Lesson:** Character Development

ZOOM IN ON **ANALYZING MEANING** Remind students that the **dialogue**, or conversation, in a play is the key to understanding both **character** and **theme**. Have students work with a partner to reread lines 110–117 and 885–900. Then have them discuss what the passages show about the Prince and what the author is saying through his play, using these sentence frames:

- The Prince says only the clothes make him different from Tom because _____. *(it isn't how they look that counts but who they are inside)*
- The events in the play help the Prince understand _____. *(what life is like for the poor in his kingdom and how they are mistreated)*
- His words at the end show that the Prince is _____. *(wise and caring)*

Structure

less familiar story structure

Help students analyze the structure of a one-act play.

- Teacher's Edition side notes, pp. 346, 347, 350, 351, 353, 354, 355, 358, 361
- English Language Support, pp. 358, 360
- When Students Struggle, p. 350
- Strategies for Annotation, pp. 352, 361
- Describe Drama, p. 361

Text in FOCUS Reading Stage Directions

To reteach describing elements of drama, see

- Describe Elements of Drama, p. 362a

 Use It! **Level Up Tutorials:** Elements of Drama

ZOOM IN ON **ANALYZING STRUCTURE** Before students read the play, review the elements of drama. Display scene 2, lines 315–356.

- Remind students that a new **scene** indicates a change of **setting**, or place and time. Ask where and when this scene takes place. *(near Offal Court at night)*
- Point out that **stage directions**, in italicized text, describe scenery as well as characters' appearances, expressions, and actions. Ask students what the stage directions tell them about the Prince as the scene begins. *(The Prince is dirty and tired.)*

Language Conventionality and Clarity

some unfamiliar language

Teach unfamiliar vocabulary in context.

- Applying Academic Vocabulary, pp. 347, 358
- English Language Support, p. 346

Support students' reading and analysis of the selection through discussion and writing.

- Teacher's Edition side notes, p. 360
- English Language Support, pp. 351, 353, 355, 359, 360, 361, 362
- When Students Struggle, p. 354

ZOOM IN ON **UNDERSTANDING VERBAL HUMOR** Display lines 63–68. Highlight the verb forms *treat/treats* in the dialogue. Explain that the author uses the multiple meanings of *treat* to create humor.

- Have pairs of students look up *treat* in a dictionary and record the definitions related to how it is used in each sentence. *(The Prince means "how does your father behave toward you." Tom uses treats in the sense of giving someone something nice.)*
- Ask students to explain why Tom's use of the word in his response to the Prince is humorous. *(A beating is not something pleasant or thoughtful.)*

Knowledge Demands

some cultural and literary knowledge useful

Support English learners in understanding necessary background information.

- Teacher's Edition Background note, p. 345
- Content-Area Connection, p. 348

ZOOM IN ON **BUILDING BACKGROUND** Define and discuss these words related to the subject of the play:

- *subject* (line 38): one who is under the authority of another
- *heir* (line 228): person who will inherit a position or money or property
- *installed* (line 229): placed formally in a position
- *occasion of state* (line 250): an official ceremony or event
- *council* (line 390): group of advisors

Suggested Reader/Task Considerations

You might consider the following before assigning this play to students.

- Will students be able to recall details from previous scenes in order to understand the plot developments in later scenes?
- Do students have the ability to define multiple-meaning words using context clues?

ZOOM IN ON **SUPPORTING COMPREHENSION**

- After students have read each scene, have them work with a partner to write a summary of the events. Then have them make predictions about what might happen next.
- Tell students that many words in this play have more than one meaning. Model using context clues to define the word *manners* in line 32 as "socially correct way of acting." Then have pairs practice the strategy to define *manner* in line 39.

TEACH

CLOSE READ

Background Have students read the background and information about the author. Explain that even now Twain is one of America's most famous writers because of his style and humor. Twain, or Samuel Clemens as he was known then, had to quit school after completing only five grades; his father had died, and the 11-year-old Samuel needed to work to help support his mother and siblings. Through some of his writings, Twain reveals his ideas about society, about rich and poor, and about how people do and should treat each other.

SETTING A PURPOSE Direct students to use the Setting a Purpose question to focus their reading. Remind students to write down questions they have as they read.

English Language Support

Read Closely Read aloud the Setting a Purpose question with students following along in their books. Remind students that a **theme** is a message about life or human nature that the writer shares with the reader. Tell students that in order to determine the theme, it is important to think about the details in the text. Distribute a Cluster Diagram graphic organizer. Ask students to use the graphic organizer to take notes about the setting, characters' actions, feelings, and events as they read.

ASK STUDENTS to share their graphic organizers in small groups during reading. Have them use their notes to support their ideas about the themes in the play.

 Use It! INTERACTIVE GRAPHIC ORGANIZER Cluster Diagram

The Prince and the Pauper

Novel by Mark Twain Dramatized by Joellen Bland

Background *The historical novel* The Prince and the Pauper *was written by* **Mark Twain** *in 1882; it was his first attempt at historical fiction. The tale takes place in England in 1547, the year that Prince Edward, the nine-year-old son of King Henry VIII, was crowned King Edward VI.*

The novel has been adapted into stage, film, and even comic book versions. The adaptation you are about to read was written by **Joellen Bland**, *who has been writing scripted versions of classic stories for more than 30 years. This one-act play continues the tradition of this famous novel and its travels through American culture.*

Mark Twain (1835–1910) *is one of America's greatest and most beloved writers. His real name was Samuel Clemens, but he changed it when he began his writing career. Twain was born in Florida, Missouri. When he was four years old, he moved with his family to Hannibal, Missouri, a bustling town along the Mississippi River, where he lived until he was seventeen. Hannibal and the Mississippi River inspired many of Twain's most famous novels, including* The Adventures of Tom Sawyer (1876) *and* The Adventures of Huckleberry Finn (1885). *Twain wrote 28 books and many short stories, letters, and comic sketches, all for the enjoyment of readers for many decades to come.*

SETTING A PURPOSE As you read, pay attention to how the details of the setting, characters' actions, feelings, and events build and support the themes of the play.

(bg) ©Shutterstock; (tr) ©Heritage Images/Corbis; (b) © Alamy Images

---

Close Read Screencasts

Modeled Discussions

Have students click the *Close Read* icons in their eBooks to access two screencasts in which readers discuss and annotate the following key passages:

- the Prince is mistaken for a beggar (lines 142–156)
- the Prince is in the hands of thieves (lines 533–548)

As a class, view and discuss at least one of these videos. Then, have students work in pairs to do an independent close read of an additional passage in which the boys prove who they are (lines 834–853).

Describe Drama

RL 1,
RL 3,
RL 5

(CHARACTERS; LINES 1–19)

Explain to students that most plays have a **cast of characters,** or a list of the characters in the play, in the order in which they first appear in the play. Point out that the cast of characters has two purposes: (1) it shows how many and what kinds of actors are needed, and (2) it introduces the characters to the audience (both readers and watchers).

(A) CITE TEXT EVIDENCE Ask students to examine the cast of characters and tell what the details tell them about the play. *(Possible responses: The lords and ladies, King, Prince, and Villagers hint that the story takes place somewhere else or in the past. The Justice, Jailer, and young thief hint that someone gets in trouble.)*

Explain to students that plays are organized into acts and scenes.

(B) CITE TEXT EVIDENCE Ask students to locate the text that tells them what scene this is. *(Scene 1 head)* Then, ask students to page ahead and tell how many scenes and acts are in this play and how they know this. *(The play has eight scenes; there is a label/head for each one. The play has only one act; all eight scenes are part of this one act.)*

Explain to students that a play is made up mostly of dialogue between characters. To provide other information, playwrights include special passages, called **stage directions,** to tell when, where, and how the action takes place. Point out that the stage directions appear in slanted, or italic, type to distinguish them from the dialogue.

(C) ASK STUDENTS to reread lines 1–19 and explain how a director of a play might use these stage directions. How are the stage directions helpful to readers? *(A director would get ideas about costumes, stage sets, props, and so on. A reader is able to visualize the setting based on details about the time and place.)*

(A)

CHARACTERS

Edward, Prince of Wales	**Justice**
Tom Canty, the Pauper	**Constable**
Lord Hertford	**Jailer**
Lord St. John	**Sir Hugh Hendon**
King Henry VIII	**Two Prisoners**
Herald	**Two Guards**
Miles Hendon	**Three Pages**
John Canty, Tom's father	**Lords and Ladies**
Hugo, a young thief	**Villagers**
Two Women	

(B)

Scene 1

Time: *1547.*

(C) **Setting:** *Westminster Palace, England. Gates leading to courtyard are at right. Slightly to the left, off courtyard and inside gates, interior of palace anteroom[1] is visible. There is a couch with a rich robe draped on it, screen at rear, bellcord,* 10 *mirror, chairs, and a table with bowl of nuts, and a large golden seal on it. Piece of armor hangs on one wall. Exits are rear and downstage.*

At Curtain Rise: *Two Guards— one at right, one at left—stand in front of gates, and several* Villagers *hover nearby, straining to see into courtyard where* Prince *may be seen through fence, playing.* Two Women *enter right.*

---

[1] **anteroom** (ăn´tē-room´): an outer room that leads to another room and is often used as a waiting room.

20 **1st Woman.** I have walked all morning just to have a glimpse of Westminster Palace.

2nd Woman. Maybe if we can get near enough to the gates, we can have a glimpse of the young Prince. (Tom Canty, *dirty and ragged, comes out of crowd and steps close to gates.*)

Tom. I have always dreamed of 30 seeing a real Prince! (*Excited, he presses his nose against gates.*)

1st Guard. Mind your manners, you young beggar! (*Seizes* Tom *by collar and sends him sprawling into crowd.* Villagers *laugh, as* Tom *slowly gets to his feet.*)

Prince (*rushing to gates*). How dare you treat a poor subject of the King in such a manner! Open the gates 40 and let him in! (*As* Villagers *see* Prince, *they take off their hats and bow low.*)

©Shutterstock

English Language Support

Use Context to Determine Meaning Because of the setting, the play contains words that students may not have heard or read before. Read lines 13–19 aloud while students follow along in their texts. Underline the word *Guards.* Then ask what the guards are doing. Discuss the clues together and decide what a guard is. Ask a volunteer to confirm the definition in a dictionary.

ASK STUDENTS to work with a partner and use the same procedure to determine the meaning of *pages* (line 267) and *herald* (line 379).

Villagers (*shouting together*). Long live the Prince of Wales! (Guards *open gates and* Tom *slowly passes through, as if in a dream.*)

Prince (*to* Tom). You look tired, and you have been treated cruelly. I am Edward, Prince of Wales. What is your name?

50

Tom (*looking around in awe*). Tom Canty, Your Highness.

Prince. Come into the palace with me, Tom. (Prince *leads* Tom *into anteroom.* Villagers *pantomime conversation, and all but a few exit.*) Where do you live, Tom?

Tom. In the city, Your Highness, in Offal Court.

60

Prince. Offal Court? That is an odd name. Do you have parents?

Tom. Yes, Your Highness.

Prince. How does your father treat you?

Tom. If it please you, Your Highness, when I am not able to beg a penny for our supper, he treats me to beatings.

Prince (*shocked*). What! Beatings?

70 My father is not a calm man, but he does not beat me. (*looks at* Tom *thoughtfully*) You speak well and have an easy grace. Have you been schooled?

Tom. Very little, Your Highness. A good priest who shares our house in Offal Court has taught me from his books.

Prince. Do you have a pleasant life

80 in Offal Court?

Tom. Pleasant enough, Your Highness, save when I am hungry. We have Punch and Judy shows, and sometimes we lads have fights in the street.

Prince (*eagerly*). I should like that. Tell me more.

Tom. In summer, we run races and swim in the river, and we love to

90 wallow in the mud.

Prince (*sighing, wistfully*). If I could wear your clothes and play in the mud just once, with no one to forbid me, I think I could give up the crown!

Tom (*shaking his head*). And if I could wear your fine clothes just once, Your Highness . . .

Prince. Would you like that?

100 Come, then. We shall change places. You can take off your rags and put on my clothes—and I will put on yours. (*He leads* Tom *behind screen, and they return shortly, each wearing the other's clothes.*) Let's look at ourselves in this mirror. (*leads* Tom *to mirror*)

Tom. Oh, Your Highness, it is not proper for me to wear such clothes.

110 **Prince** (*excitedly, as he looks in mirror*). Heavens, do you not see it? We look like brothers! We have the same features and bearing.[2] If we went about together, dressed alike, there is no one who could say which is the Prince of Wales and which is Tom Canty!

---

[2] **features and bearing:** parts of the face and ways of standing or walking.

The Prince and the Pauper **347**

APPLYING ACADEMIC VOCABULARY

emphasize	occur

THINK-PAIR-SHARE Have students turn to a partner to discuss the following questions. Guide students to include the academic vocabulary words *emphasize* and *occur* in their responses. Ask volunteers to share their responses with the class.

- What has **occurred** so far in the play? Describe how the plot has unfolded.
- Why do Twain and the playwright **emphasize** certain characteristics of the boys and their lives?

CLOSE READ

Describe Drama (LINES 53–57)

RL 1, RL 3

Explain to students that stage directions appear in italic type and within parentheses in the midst of the dialogue, as needed.

D CITE TEXT EVIDENCE Ask students to tell what action is happening in lines 53–57 and how they know this. (*The Prince leads Tom into a room; the villagers talk, and most leave. The stage directions in the parentheses describe this action, in between the Prince's lines of dialogue.*) Then, ask students why the playwright would have the villagers "pantomime conversation" here. (*The focus is on the Prince and Tom. It would be natural for the villagers to talk about what they've just seen, but this would be distracting for the audience. So the instruction is only to pantomime—to look as if they are talking among themselves.*)

Text in FOCUS English Language Support

Reading Stage Directions (LINE 57)

Have students view the **Text in Focus** video on this page of their eBook to learn how to use stage directions to better understand the play's characters, setting, and action. Then have students use **Text in Focus Practice** to apply what they have learned.

Determine Meaning

RL 4

(LINES 58–61)

Tell students that Twain is known for using language to make a point. Explain that he has done something clever with the name of the place where Tom lives.

E ASK STUDENTS to tell what *offal* means, or to look up its meaning if they are uncertain. Ask what effect this word has on the text. (*The word* offal *means "the waste of by-product of a process." It is used most often to refer to the leftover trimmings and organs of a butchered animal. This is why the Prince thinks it is an odd name. Twain and Bland are making the point that Tom is very, very poor and that the city considers people who would live there basically leftovers or waste.*)

Describe Drama

RL 1,
RL 3,
RL 5

(LINES 121–129; 172–185)

Point out that both audience members and readers learn about characters in a play through the characters' actions and words.

F CITE TEXT EVIDENCE Have students tell what they learn about the Prince from his words and actions in lines 121–129. Tell students to cite the words and phrases they used to draw their conclusions. (*The Prince is caring; when he sees the bruise, he speaks "angrily" and says that the guard was "shameful and cruel." The Prince is also used to giving orders. Though he is being friendly and taking care of Tom, he says, "I command you!"*)

G CITE TEXT EVIDENCE Ask students to tell why Tom and Hertford act as they do in lines 172–185 and what this scene adds to the plot. (*Tom is afraid because he knows Hertford will not understand that the Prince switched clothes with Tom on purpose. Hertford is "puzzled and disturbed" because he is seeing Tom as the Prince and doesn't understand why the boy is acting like a beggar. This scene establishes the switching of identities that affects events to come.*)

Tom (*drawing back and rubbing his hand*). Your Highness, I am 120 frightened. . . .

Prince. Do not worry. (*seeing Tom rub his hand*) Is that a bruise on your hand?

Tom. Yes, but it is a slight thing, Your Highness.

Prince (*angrily*). It was shameful and cruel of that guard to strike you. Do not stir a step until I come back. I command you! (*He picks* 130 *up golden Seal of England[3] and carefully puts it into piece of armor. He then dashes out to gates.*) Open! Unbar the gates at once! (*2nd Guard opens gates, and as Prince runs out, in rags, 1st Guard seizes him, boxes him on the ear, and knocks him to the ground.*)

1st Guard. Take that, you little beggar, for the trouble you have 140 made for me with the Prince. (*Villagers roar with laughter.*)

Prince (*picking himself up, turning on Guard furiously*). I am Prince of Wales! You shall hang for laying your hand on me!

1st Guard (*presenting arms; mockingly*). I salute Your Gracious Highness! (*Then, angrily, 1st Guard shoves Prince roughly aside.*) Be 150 off, you mad bag of rags! (*Prince is surrounded by Villagers, who hustle him off.*)

---

[3] **Seal of England:** a device used to stamp a special design, usually a picture of the ruler, onto a document, thus indicating that it has royal approval.

Villagers (*ad lib,[4] as they exit, shouting*). Make way for His Royal Highness! Make way for the Prince of Wales! Hail to the Prince! (*etc.*)

Tom (*admiring himself in mirror*). If only the boys in Offal Court could see me! They will not believe me 160 when I tell them about this. (*looks around anxiously*) But where is the Prince? (*Looks cautiously into courtyard. Two Guards immediately snap to attention and salute. He quickly ducks back into anteroom as Lords Hertford and St. John enter at rear.*)

Hertford (*going toward Tom, then stopping and bowing low*). My 170 Lord, you look distressed. What is wrong?

Tom (*trembling*). Oh, I beg of you, be merciful. I am no Prince, but poor Tom Canty of Offal Court. Please let me see the Prince, and he will give my rags back to me and let me go unhurt. (*kneeling*) Please, be merciful and spare me!

Hertford (*puzzled and disturbed*). 180 Your Highness, on your knees? To me? (*bows quickly, then, aside to St. John*) The Prince has gone mad! We must inform the King. (*to Tom*) A moment, your Highness. (*Hertford and St. John exit rear.*)

Tom. Oh, there is no hope for me now. They will hang me for certain! (*Hertford and St. John re-enter, supporting King. Tom watches*

---

[4] **ad lib:** talk together about what is going on, but without an actual script.

CONTENT-AREA CONNECTION

History Tell students that Edward the VI was born on October 12, 1537 and died on July 6, 1553, just a few months before his sixteenth birthday. His mother died soon after he was born. He was the only living son of King Henry VIII and was therefore groomed to be king. However, from a very early age his health was poor. He was crowned in 1547 when he was only nine years old, after the death of his father.

Activity Have students work in pairs to investigate Edward the VI's family. Show students a family tree. Ask them to research the Tudor family and create a family tree that shows when each person was born, how and when he or she died, who his or her parents were, and any children the person had. Have students work in small groups to share how their information relates to details presented in the play.

190   *in awe as they help him to couch, where he sinks down wearily.*)

King (*beckoning* Tom *close to him*). Now, my son, Edward, my prince. What is this? Do you mean to deceive me, the King, your father, who loves you and treats you so kindly?

Tom (*dropping to his knees*). You are the King? Then I have no hope!

200   **King** (*stunned*). My child, you are not well. Do not break your father's old heart. Say you know me.

Tom. Yes, you are my lord the King, whom God preserve.

King. True, that is right. Now, you will not deny that you are Prince of Wales, as they say you did just a while ago?

Tom. I beg you, Your Grace,
210   believe me. I am the lowest of your subjects, being born a pauper, and it is by a great mistake that I am here. I am too young to die. Oh, please, spare me, sire!

King (*amazed*). Die? Do not talk so, my child. You shall not die.

Tom (*gratefully*). God save you, my king! And now, may I go?

King. Go? Where would you go?

220   **Tom.** Back to the alley where I was born and bred to misery.

King. My poor child, rest your head here. (*He holds* Tom's *head and pats his shoulder, then turns to* Hertford *and* St. John.) Alas, I am old and ill, and my son is mad. But this shall pass. Mad or sane, he is my heir and shall rule England. Tomorrow he shall be installed and
230   confirmed in his princely dignity! Bring the Great Seal!

The Prince and the Pauper **349**

(bg) ©Shutterstock; (fg) Frank Riccio

CLOSE READ

Describe Drama
RL 1,
RL 3,
RL 5

(LINES 198–216; 222–231)

Explain to students that here Tom meets the King for the first time. Remind students that the dialogue in a play moves the action of the play forward.

H **ASK STUDENTS** to describe how Tom responds to the King's presence. Why does he think he is going to die? (*Tom drops to his knees and speaks very respectfully to the King. Tom thinks he will be punished for pretending to be the Prince.*)

I **CITE TEXT EVIDENCE** Ask students to tell what the dialogue in these lines reveals about upcoming action. (*The King tells the Lords that "mad or sane," his son the Prince will rule England. The King is "old and ill," and his words seem to indicate that the Prince will become King very soon.*)

English Language Support

Explain that a reader can make an inference by combining details and prior knowledge to make logical guesses about what is happening. Often a reader will make an inference about something that the author does not state directly. Making inferences can help readers understand characters.

- Display lines 198–218 and work with students to find the clues that help the reader infer why Tom thinks he is going to die when he meets the King. (*"Then I have no hope!", "I am the lowest of your subjects . . . by a great mistake that I am here: "Oh, please, spare me sire!*) Discuss how the text leads the reader to understand that even though Tom is afraid of what the King will do, he tells the truth.

- Repeat the exercise with the question *"And now may I go?"* giving students time to discuss what they have learned about Tom's character.

TO CHALLENGE STUDENTS . . .

Analyze Tone and Structure Ask students to describe the tone of the scenes between the lords, Tom, and the King. As needed, help them see the exaggeration and comedy in these scenes. Discuss how it is rather unrealistic that no one would see that Tom and the Prince have switched places. Explain that Twain and Bland are using the exaggerated reactions of the characters to poke a little fun at these characters' inability to see beyond the clothes and situation to the actual people.

ASK STUDENTS to discuss why this exaggeration is important to the plot of the play and to look for other instances of it as they continue reading.

Describe Drama

RL 1,
RL 3,
RL 5

(LINES 239–260)

Point out to students that some stage directions tell what a character is doing. Others tell how a character's lines are to be delivered. Explain that stage directions can reveal emotions or plot points.

(J) CITE TEXT EVIDENCE Ask students what important things they learn about Tom and the King in lines 239–260. Have students cite words and phrases that show how they know and tell what this knowledge contributes to the plot. *(Tom is "trembling," so he is still a bit frightened of the King. Tom is also "resigned," which shows that he has probably given up trying to convince the King that he is not the Prince. The King stands "weakly," and is led off, which shows that he is ill and perhaps dying, which will be important to both Tom and the Prince as the plot unfolds.)*

Analyze Tone

RL 1,
RL 4

(LINES 263–280)

Explain to students that the playwright uses the actions and responses of the characters to create a little humor in this scene.

(K) CITE TEXT EVIDENCE Ask students to visualize the actions of the Pages in lines 263–280 and then tell how these actions and Tom's reaction create the tone of this scene. *(The Pages stop Tom from doing things and do them for him, which looks a little comical. The repeated phrase "does it for him" in the stage directions emphasizes the humor of these actions. Tom's comment, "I wonder that you do not try to breathe for me also!" is humorous, though he might say it in frustration. These interactions show that Tom is tired but is still very much himself and not the Prince.)*

English Language Support

Explain that writers use words to express **tone**, or their attitude or feelings about a subject or character. Read lines 263–280 with students following along. Ask volunteers to act out the scene and then work as a group to identify words that lend a humorous tone to the scene.

Hertford (*bowing low*). Please, Your Majesty, you took the Great Seal from the Chancellor two days ago to give to His Highness the Prince.

King. So I did. (*to* Tom) My child, tell me, where is the Great Seal?

(J) 240 **Tom** (*trembling*). Indeed, my lord, I do not know.

King. Ah, your affliction hangs heavily upon you. 'Tis no matter. You will remember later. Listen, carefully! (*gently, but firmly*) I command you to hide your affliction in all ways that be within your power. You shall deny to no one that you are the true prince, and if your memory should fail 250 you upon any occasion of state, you shall be advised by your uncle, the Lord Hertford.

Tom (*resigned*). The King has spoken. The King shall be obeyed.

King. And now, my child, I go to rest. (*He stands weakly, and* Hertford *leads him off, rear.*)

Tom (*wearily, to* St. John). May it please your lordship to let me 260 rest now?

St. John. So it please Your Highness, it is for you to command and us to obey. But it is wise that you rest, for this evening you must attend the Lord Mayor's banquet (K) in your honor. (*He pulls bellcord, and* Three Pages *enter and kneel before* Tom.)

Tom. Banquet? (*Terrified, he sits on* 270 *couch and reaches for cup of water,* but 1st Page *instantly seizes cup, drops on one knee, and serves it to him.* Tom *starts to take off his boots, but* 2nd Page *stops him and does it for him. He tries to remove his cape and gloves, and* 3rd Page *does it for him.*) I wonder that you do not try to breathe for me also! (*Lies down cautiously.* Pages *cover him with* 280 *robe, then back away and exit.*)

St. John (*to* Hertford, *as he enters*). Plainly, what do you think?

Hertford. Plainly, this. The King is near death, my nephew the Prince of Wales is clearly mad and will mount the throne mad. God protect England, for she will need it!

St. John. Does it not seem strange 290 that madness could so change his manner from what it used to be? It troubles me, his saying he is not the Prince.

Hertford. Peace, my lord! If he were an impostor and called himself Prince, that would be natural. But was there ever an impostor, who being called Prince by the King and court, denied it? 300 Never! This is the true Prince gone mad. And tonight all London shall honor him. (Hertford *and* St. John *exit.* Tom *sits up, looks around helplessly, then gets up.*)

Tom. I should have thought to order something to eat. (*sees bowl of nuts on table*) Ah! Here are some nuts! (*looks around, sees Great Seal in armor, takes it out, looks at it* 310 *curiously*) This will make a good

WHEN STUDENTS STRUGGLE . . .

To guide students' comprehension of the play's plot, have partners fill in a chart like the one shown for each scene. Direct students to pause after each scene, talk briefly about it, and agree on important notes to show in the chart.

SCENE 1	**Characters:** *Prince, Tom, Lords, King*
ACTION: Prince and Tom (pauper) change clothes and are mistaken for each other. Lords and King think the Prince has gone mad. Tom doesn't know what the Great Seal is or where it is. The king is not in good health.	
SCENE 2	**Characters:**
ACTION:	

nutcracker. (*He takes bowl of nuts, sits on couch and begins to crack nuts with Great Seal and eat them, as curtain falls.*)

Scene 2

Time: *Later that night.*

Setting: *A street in London, near Offal Court. Played before the curtain.*

320 **At Curtain Rise:** Prince *limps in, dirty and tousled. He looks around wearily. Several* Villagers *pass by, pushing against him.*

Prince. I have never seen this poor section of London. I must be near Offal Court. If I can only find it before I drop! (*John Canty steps out of crowd, seizes* Prince *roughly.*)

Canty. Out at this time of night, and I warrant you haven't brought 330 a farthing[5] home! If that is the case and I do not break all the bones in your miserable body, then I am not John Canty!

Prince (*eagerly*). Oh, are you his father?

Canty. *His* father? I am *your* father, and—

Prince. Take me to the palace at once, and your son will be 340 returned to you. The King, my father, will make you rich beyond your wildest dreams. Oh, save me, for I am indeed the Prince of Wales.

---
5 **farthing** (fär´thĭng): a former British coin worth one-fourth of a British penny.

Canty (*staring in amazement*). Gone stark mad! But mad or not, I'll soon find where the soft places lie in your bones. Come home! (*starts to drag* Prince *off*)

350 **Prince** (*struggling*). Let me go! I am the Prince of Wales, and the King shall have your life for this!

Canty (*angrily*). I'll take no more of your madness! (*raises stick to strike, but* Prince *struggles free and runs off, and* Canty *runs after him*)

Scene 3

Setting: *Same as Scene 1, with addition of dining table, set with dishes and goblets, on raised 360 platform. Throne-like chair is at head of table.*

At Curtain Rise: *A banquet is in progress.* Tom, *in royal robes, sits at head of table, with* Hertford *at his right and* St. John *at his left. Lords and* Ladies *sit around table eating and talking softly.*

Tom (*to* Hertford). What is this, my Lord? (*holds up a plate*)

370 **Hertford.** Lettuce and turnips, Your Highness.

Tom. Lettuce and turnips? I have never seen them before. Am I to eat them?

Hertford (*discreetly*). Yes, Your Highness, if you so desire. (Tom *begins to eat food with his fingers. Fanfare of trumpets is heard, and* Herald *enters, carrying scroll. All* 380 *turn to look.*)

The Prince and the Pauper **351**

TEACH

CLOSE READ

Describe Drama

RL 1, RL 3, RL 5

(LINES 315–322; 357–367)

Remind students that plays are organized into acts and scenes, and that this is a one-act play with several scenes.

L CITE TEXT EVIDENCE Ask students to tell when and where Scene 2 begins, how this is different from Scene 1, and how they know this. (*Scene 2 begins "Later that night," so it's the same day as Scene 1, but some hours have passed. Scene 1 ends in the palace; Scene 2 begins near Offal Court, which is where Tom Canty and his father live. The Time and Setting text tells where and when each scene takes place; Tom says in Scene 1 that he lives in Offal Court with his father.*) Ask students the meaning of the stage direction "Played before the curtain." (*This direction means that the scene is performed in front of the curtain.*)

M CITE TEXT EVIDENCE Have students tell what Scene 2 contributes to the plot and where and when Scene 3 begins. (*Scene 2 is a short "aside" to show how the Prince is getting along out in the world. In it, the Prince meets Tom's father and the identity switch is now complete; the King and now Tom's father have each been unable to identify their own son. Scene 3 takes us to the banquet at the palace where Tom was at the end of Scene 1; it is probably taking place at the same time as the Prince is found by Tom's father.*) You may also wish to point out to students that the short Scene 2, performed in front of the curtain, gives the stage crew time to set up the banquet table in the palace setting without an awkward delay in action.

English Language Support

Word Study Tell students that silent letter combinations can cause spelling and pronunciation errors. Point out the phrase *Scene 2* in the first column on page 351. Pronounce *scene* and have students repeat before asking which letter in *sc* is silent. (*c*) Write these words on the board and review the silent letter combinations by saying each example and having students echo the pronunciation. Circle the silent letter combinations.

• **silent b:** climb, debt, doubt, limb

• **silent h:** stomach, what, when, where

• **silent k:** knob, knife, knot, know, knee

• **silent c:** scent, science, scepter

• **silent w:** write, wrap, answer, sword

ASK STUDENTS to work with a partner to make word cards for the words on the board and other words they know with silent letter combinations. Have them write the silent letter on the front and some example words on the back. Ask students to use each word in a sentence and then say the sentence aloud, helping each other with pronunciation.

Describe Drama

RL 1,
RL 3,
RL 5

(LINES 381–401; 417–422)

N CITE TEXT EVIDENCE Ask students to identify the important event in this scene. *(the death of King Henry VIII, announced in lines 381–385)* Ask students whether the Prince knows of his father's death in lines 397–401 and how students know. *(No, he doesn't know yet; he did not hear the Herald's announcement because he is out at the gates, as noted in lines 394–396.)*

O ASK STUDENTS whether they think Miles Hendon will be an important character in the play and why they think this. *(Miles offers friendship to the Prince, and he protects him from the Villager who grabs him. He will probably be important because he is a good, caring person, and the Prince needs a friend right now.)*

P CITE TEXT EVIDENCE Ask students how the words and actions of the Herald contribute to the plot in this scene. *(The Herald announces the King's death to the people in the banquet hall and to the people at the gates; his actions connect Tom and the Prince to the news of the King's death.)*

Herald (*reading from scroll*). His Majesty, King Henry VIII, is dead! The King is dead! (*All rise and turn to Tom, who sits, stunned.*)

All (*together*). The King is dead. Long live the King! Long live Edward, King of England! (*All bow to Tom. Herald bows and exits.*)

Hertford (*to Tom*). Your Majesty, 390 we must call the council. Come, St. John. (*Hertford and St. John lead Tom off at rear. Lords and Ladies follow, talking among themselves. At gates, down right, Villagers enter and mill about. Prince enters right, pounds on gates and shouts.*)

Prince. Open the gates! I am the Prince of Wales! Open, I say! And though I am friendless with no 400 one to help me, I will not be driven from my ground.

Miles Hendon (*entering through crowd*). Though you be Prince or not, you are indeed a gallant lad and not friendless. Here I stand to prove it, and you might have a worse friend than Miles Hendon.

1st Villager. Tis another prince in disguise. Take the lad and dunk 410 him in the pond! (*He seizes Prince, but Miles strikes him with flat of his sword. Crowd, now angry, presses forward threateningly, when fanfare of trumpets is heard offstage. Herald, carrying scroll, enters up left at gates.*)

Herald. Make way for the King's messenger! (*reading from scroll*) His Majesty, King Henry VIII, 420 is dead! The King is dead! (*He exits right, repeating message, and Villagers stand in stunned silence.*)

Strategies for Annotation ✎ 🗐 Annotate it!

Describe Drama

RL 3

Share these strategies for guided or independent analysis:

- Highlight in yellow dialogue or stage directions that reveal important plot developments.
- Highlight in green dialogue or stage directions that reveal important responses or changes in a character.
- Review your annotations. On a note, write questions or important points you want to remember.

Miles Hendon (*entering through crowd*). Though you be P you are indeed a gallant lad and not friendless. Here I stand to prove it, . . .

Miles? important character?

1st Villager. Tis another prince in disguise. Take the lad and dunk him in the pond! (*He seizes Prince, but Miles strikes him with flat of his sword. . . . Herald, . . . enters . . . at gates.*)

Prince (*stunned*). The King is dead!

1st Villager (*shouting*). Long live Edward, King of England!

Villagers (*together*). Long live the King! (*shouting, ad lib*) Long live King Edward! Heaven protect
430 Edward, King of England! (*etc.*)

Miles (*taking* Prince *by the arm*). Come, lad, before the crowd remembers us. I have a room at the inn, and you can stay there. (*He hurries off with stunned Prince. Tom, led by Hertford, enters courtyard up rear. Villagers see them.*)

Villagers (*together*). Long live
440 King! (*They fall to their knees as curtains close.*)

Scene 4

Setting: Miles' *room at the inn. At right is table set with dishes and bowls of food, a chair at each side. At left is bed, with table and chair next to it, and a window. Candle is on table.*

At Curtain Rise: Miles *and* Prince *approach table.*

450 **Miles.** I have had a hot supper prepared. I'll bet you're hungry, lad.

Prince. Yes, I am. It's kind of you to let me stay with you, Miles. I am truly Edward, King of England, and you shall not go unrewarded. (*sits at table*)

Miles (*to himself*). First he called himself Prince, and now he is

460 King. Well, I will humor him. (*starts to sit*)

Prince (*angrily*). Stop! Would you sit in the presence of the King?

Miles (*surprised, standing up quickly*). I beg your pardon, Your Majesty. I was not thinking. (*Stares uncertainly at* Prince, *who sits at table, expectantly.* Miles *starts to uncover dishes of food, serves* Prince
470 *and fills glasses.*)

Prince. Miles, you have a gallant way about you. Are you nobly born?

Miles. My father is a baronet,[6] Your Majesty.

Prince. Then you must also be a baronet.

Miles (*shaking his head*). My father banished me from home
480 seven years ago, so I fought in the wars. I was taken prisoner, and I have spent the past seven years in prison. Now I am free, and I am returning home.

Prince. You have been shamefully wronged! But I will make things right for you. You have saved me from injury and possible death. Name your reward and if it be
490 within the compass of my royal power, it is yours.

Miles (*pausing briefly, then dropping to his knee*). Since Your Majesty is pleased to hold my simple duty worthy of reward,

---

6 **baronet** (băr´ə-nĭt): a rank of honor in Britain, below a baron and above a knight.

The Prince and the Pauper **353**

TEACH

CLOSE READ

Describe Drama
RL 1, RL 3
(LINES 460–470; 478–491)

Remind students that in a play readers learn about the characters from both dialogue and stage directions.

Q CITE TEXT EVIDENCE Have students describe how Miles' treatment of the Prince changes as he and the Prince share a meal. Tell students to cite dialogue and stage directions that support their answers. (*At first Miles is casual; he takes care of the Prince the way a kindly grown-up would care for a child. However, when the Prince speaks "angrily" as Miles "starts to sit," Miles stands up quickly and says, "I beg your pardon, Your Majesty." He then begins serving the Prince his dinner; he decides he must "humor" the Prince and go along with his claim that he is King.*)

R ASK STUDENTS what the Prince's responses to Miles' story reveal about him. Talk about whether the Prince's behavior in other situations fits with these responses. (*The Prince is kind and sympathetic to both Miles and Tom when he finds out they are being mistreated. In other situations, though, he is used to being waited on and to being spoken to respectfully by everyone, including grown-ups. That makes him seem a little less kind.*)

English Language Support

Use Verbs and Verb Phrases Remind students that it is important to consider tense as they answer questions about the text. Review conjugation for the pronouns *I, you, he/she/it, they,* and *we*. Have students echo your presentation of a simple sentence (e.g., *I speak, you speak . . .*). Tell students this is the present tense. They can use this tense in most of their answers. However, other tenses are also useful. Review the present progressive tense and the simple past with the same sentence (e.g., *I am speaking* or *I was speaking*). Have student pairs write sentences for each pronoun using the simple present, present progressive, and simple past tenses.

Describe Drama

RL 1,
RL 3,
RL 5

(LINE 533–561)

Remind students that the action in a play is described in both the dialogue and the stage directions.

Ⓢ CITE TEXT EVIDENCE Ask students to explain how the time of the action differs between Scenes 4 and 5 and how they know. *(The stage directions indicate that two weeks have passed.)* Ask students to examine the Prince's behavior in lines 545–561. How is it consistent with his previous behavior and attitudes? How is it different? Have students cite stage directions and dialogue to support their answers. *(The stage directions tell us that the Prince is being treated roughly, with Hugo "seizing Prince by the arm." The Prince's dialogue, in response, sounds like his usual self. He is outraged at his treatment and at the prospect of stealing. The Prince asserts his authority by refusing to cooperate with Hugo; he does not follow Hugo's instructions and simply "throws down bundle in disgust."* Then, ask students how Scenes 4 and 5 contribute to the development of the plot. *(Possible responses: Scene 4 tells Miles' story, which becomes important later. Scene 5 shows the effect both Canty and Miles have on the Prince and how the Prince is learning about the relationship between kings and subjects.)*

FOR STANDARD ENGLISH LEARNERS

Remind students that a play is intended to be performed and that when actors speak, they need to pay attention to their pronunciation and stress patterns so that listeners understand. Display lines 542–552. Read the lines aloud. Point out the words *today* (line 544) and *refuse* (line 551). Tell students that it is important to avoid stretching out the stress on the first part of these words. Read the words again, allowing students to hear the difference between *today/tooday* and *refuse/reefuse*. Have students choral read the lines, correcting their stress patterns as necessary.

I ask that I and my successors[7] may hold the privilege of sitting in the presence of the King.

500   **Prince** (*taking* Miles' *sword, tapping him lightly on each shoulder*). Rise and seat yourself. (*returns sword to* Miles, *then rises and goes over to bed*)

Miles (*rising*). He should have been born a king. He plays the part to a marvel! If I had not thought of this favor, I might have had to stand for weeks. (*sits down and begins to eat*)

510   **Prince.** Sir Miles, you will stand guard while I sleep? (*lies down and instantly falls asleep*)

Miles. Yes, Your Majesty. (*With a rueful look at his uneaten supper, he stands up.*) Poor little chap. I suppose his mind has been disordered with ill usage. (*covers* Prince *with his cape*) Well, I will be his friend and watch over him. (*Blows out candle, then yawns, sits* 520 *on chair next to bed, and falls asleep.* John Canty *and* Hugo *appear at window, peer around room, then enter cautiously through window. They lift the sleeping* Prince, *staring nervously at* Miles.)

Canty (*in loud whisper*). I swore the day he was born he would be a thief and a beggar, and I won't lose him now. Lead the way to the camp 530 Hugo! (Canty *and* Hugo *carry* Prince *off right, as* Miles *sleeps on and curtain falls.*)

---

7   **successors** (sək-sĕs´ərs): those, in sequence or line of succession, who have a right to property, to hold title or rank, or to hold the throne one after the other.

Scene 5

Time: *Two weeks later.*

Setting: *Country village street.*

Before Curtain Rise: Villagers *walk about.* Canty, Hugo, *and* Prince *enter.*

Canty. I will go in this direction. Hugo, keep my mad son with you, 540 and see that he doesn't escape again! (*exits*)

Hugo (*seizing* Prince *by the arm*). He won't escape! I'll see that he earns his bread today, or else!

Prince (*pulling away*). I will not beg with you, and I will not steal! I have suffered enough in this miserable company of thieves!

Hugo. You shall suffer more if 550 you do not do as I tell you! (*raises clenched fist at* Prince) Refuse if you dare! (Woman *enters, carrying wrapped bundle in a basket on her arm.*) Wait here until I come back. (Hugo *sneaks along after* Woman, *then snatches her bundle, runs back to* Prince, *and thrusts it into his arms.*) Run after me and call, "Stop, thief!" But be sure you lead her astray! (*Runs off.* Prince *throws* 560 *down bundle in disgust.*)

Woman. Help! Thief! Stop, thief! (*rushes at* Prince *and seizes him, just as several* Villagers *enter*) You little thief! What do you mean by robbing a poor woman? Somebody bring the constable! (Miles *enters and watches.*)

WHEN STUDENTS STRUGGLE . . .

Because of the time period of this play, the playwright uses some language that was common during the time period of the play's setting but that we do not hear often in modern times, such as *disordered with ill usage* (line 516). To guide students' comprehension of these words, pair students with a more proficient partner. Have students consult each other and work together, using context clues and a dictionary as needed, to determine the meaning of these old-fashioned words and phrases.

ASK STUDENTS to keep a list of the words and the meanings they discover to share with others later.

1st Villager (*grabbing* Prince). I'll teach him a lesson, the little villain!

570

Prince (*struggling*). Take your hands off me! I did not rob this woman!

Miles (*stepping out of crowd and pushing man back with the flat of his sword*). Let us proceed gently, my friends. This is a matter for the law.

Prince (*springing to* Miles' *side*). You have come just in time, Sir Miles. Carve this rabble to rags!

580

Miles. Speak softly. Trust in me and all shall go well.

Constable (*entering and reaching for* Prince). Come along, young rascal!

Miles. Gently, good friend. He shall go peaceably to the Justice.

Prince. I will not go before a Justice! I did not do this thing!

590

Miles (*taking him aside*). Sire, will you reject the laws of the realm, yet demand that your subjects respect them?

Prince (*calmer*). You are right, Sir Miles. Whatever the King requires a subject to suffer under the law, he will suffer himself while he holds the station of a subject. (Constable *leads them off right.* Villagers *follow. Curtain.*)

600

Scene 6

Setting: *Office of the Justice. A high bench is at center.*

At Curtain Rise: Justice *sits behind bench.* Constable *enters with* Miles *and* Prince, *followed by* Villagers. Woman *carries wrapped bundle.*

Constable (*to* Justice). A young thief, your worship, is accused of stealing a dressed pig from this poor woman.

610

Justice (*looking down at* Prince, *then* Woman). My good woman, are you absolutely certain this lad stole your pig?

Woman. It was none other than he, your worship.

Justice. Are there no witnesses to the contrary? (*All shake their heads.*) Then the lad stands convicted. (*to* Woman) What do you hold this property to be worth?

620

Woman. Three shillings and eight pence, your worship.

Justice (*leaning down to* Woman). Good woman, do you know that when one steals a thing above the value of thirteen pence, the law says he shall hang for it?

630

Woman (*upset*). Oh, what have I done? I would not hang the poor boy for the whole world! Save me from this, your worship. What can I do?

Justice (*gravely*). You may revise the value, since it is not yet written in the record.

CLOSE READ

Describe Drama
RL 3,
RL 5

(LINES 569–601)

Remind students that characters' actions affect plot events in a play just as they do in a story.

Ⓣ ASK STUDENTS to describe how the re-entry of Miles affects what is happening in the plot. Talk about how the Prince's and Miles' behavior fits with what readers know about them. (*Without Miles, the Prince was getting into deeper and deeper trouble. He wants Miles to behave as a servant or knight and "Carve this rabble to rags!" for him. With the calm advice of Miles, however, the Prince finally goes along with "Whatever the King requires." Miles continues to play along with the Prince by addressing him as "Sire," even though there is no evidence that Miles thinks he is anything other than an ordinary poor boy.*)

English Language Support

Condense Ideas Explain that writing concisely can help convey ideas more clearly. Some ways to condense ideas are to use clauses and nominalization. Provide and discuss these examples:

- The prince was in trouble. Miles was a friend and helpful. (*Possible answer: Miles helped the prince because he was in trouble.*)
- The villagers accused the prince of robbing a woman. The prince denied his guilt. (*Possible answer: The villagers' accusation of robbery was met with the prince's denial of guilt.*)

ASK STUDENTS to work independently to write sentences that describe Miles' impact on the plot in Scene 5. Then have them pair up to revise their sentences to be more precise and detailed.

English Language Support

Improve Reading Fluency Have students work with a partner to read Scene 6, lines 602–707. Model reading a portion of the dialogue as students follow along. Read expressively and place emphasis on lines and words based on the punctuation. Then discuss how you changed your voice, tone, and emphasis based on what you know about the setting of the play and the language in the dialogue. Then have students choose roles (noting that students should expect to have more than one role) and read the dialogue. Encourage students to provide feedback.

Describe Drama

RL 1,
RL 3

(LINES 638–661; 668–681)

Explain to students that they must pay close attention to the details of the plot in order to understand each character's motivation and actions.

 CITE TEXT EVIDENCE Ask students to explain why the woman changes the value of her pig to eight pence. *(The value of the stolen property determines the level of punishment of the thief. The woman doesn't want the boy to hang, so the Justice allows her to change the pig's value so the boy's punishment is not so severe.)* Why does the Constable do what he does? *(The Constable is looking for some cheap food. The woman has stated in court that the pig is worth eight pence, though it is worth much more; the Constable takes advantage of this, knowing that she can't make him pay more because he will tell the Justice, and the boy will hang.)*

V **ASK STUDENTS** to describe how Miles gets the best of the Constable, who has just gotten the best of the woman whose pig was stolen. What does this reveal about Miles? *(Miles cleverly threatens to turn the Constable in to the Justice for cheating the woman out of her pig. This shows a cunning side of Miles we haven't seen before.)* How does this advance the plot? *(The Constable allows the Prince to escape with Miles.)*

Woman. Then call the pig eight pence, your worship.

640 **Justice.** So be it. You may take your property and go. (Woman *starts off, and is followed by* Constable. Miles *follows them cautiously down right.*)

Constable (*stopping* Woman). Good woman, I will buy your pig from you. (*takes coins from pocket*) Here is eight pence.

Woman. Eight pence! It cost me three shillings and eight pence!

650 **Constable.** Indeed! Then come back before his worship and answer for this. The lad must hang!

Woman. No! No! Say no more. Give me the eight pence and hold your peace. (Constable *hands her coins and takes pig.* Woman *exits, angrily.* Miles *returns to bench.*)

Justice. The boy is sentenced to a fortnight[8] in the common jail. Take

660 him away, Constable! (Justice *exits.* Prince *gives* Miles *a nervous glance.*)

Miles (*following* Constable). Good sir, turn your back a moment and let the poor lad escape. He is innocent.

Constable (*outraged*). What? You say this to me? Sir, I arrest you in—

Miles. Do not be so hasty! (*slyly*) The pig you have purchased for

670 eight pence may cost you your neck, man.

Constable (*laughing nervously*). Ah, but I was merely jesting with the woman, sir.

Miles. Would the Justice think it a jest?

Constable. Good sir! The Justice has no more sympathy with a jest than a dead corpse! (*perplexed*)

680 Very well, I will turn my back and see nothing! But go quickly! (*exits*)

Miles (*to* Prince). Come, my liege.[9] We are free to go. And that band of thieves shall not set hands on you again, I swear it!

Prince (*wearily*). Can you believe, Sir Miles, that in the last fortnight, I, the King of England, have escaped from thieves and begged for food

690 on the road? I have slept in a barn with a calf! I have washed dishes in a peasant's kitchen, and narrowly escaped death. And not once in all my wanderings did I see a courier[10] searching for me! Is it no matter for commotion and distress that the head of state is gone?

Miles (*sadly, aside*). Still busy with his pathetic dream. (*to* Prince) It

700 is strange indeed, my liege. But come, I will take you to my father's home in Kent. We are not far away. There you may rest in a house with seventy rooms! Come, I am all impatience to be home again! (*They exit,* Miles *in cheerful spirits,* Prince *looking puzzled, as curtains close.*)

---

8 **fortnight:** 14 days; two weeks.

9 **my liege** (lēj): my lord.
10 **courier** (ko͝or´ē-ər): messenger.

FOR STANDARD ENGLISH LEARNERS

Pronunciation Some students may have difficult pronouncing words with final consonant clusters such *st, ld, nd, sk,* and *ft.* They may omit the final sound in the consonant cluster, e.g., I took a vocabulary tes' (test) in the morning. Write this sentence from lines 677–679, "The Justice has no more sympathy with a jest than a dead corpse." Read the sentence aloud, emphasizing the /st/ sound in *jest.* Have students echo your reading several times before having them discuss why the sentence about the Justice not finding a jest funny is humorous.

Scene 7

Setting: *Village jail. Bare stage, with barred window on one wall.*

710 **At Curtain Rise:** Two Prisoners, *in chains, are onstage. Jailer shoves* Miles *and* Prince, *in chains, onstage. They struggle and protest.*

Miles. But I tell you, I am Miles Hendon! My brother, Sir Hugh, has stolen my bride and my estate!

Jailer. Be silent! Impostor! Sir Hugh will see that you pay well for claiming to be his dead brother

720 and for assaulting him in his own house! *(exits)*

Miles *(sitting, with head in hands).* Oh, my dear Edith . . . now wife to my brother Hugh, against her will, and my poor father . . . dead!

1st Prisoner. At least you have your life, sir. I am sentenced to be hanged for killing a deer in the King's park.

730 **2nd Prisoner.** And I must hang for stealing a yard of cloth to dress my children.

Prince *(moved; to* Prisoners*).* When I mount my throne, you shall all be free. And the laws that have dishonored you shall be swept from the books. *(turning away)* Kings should go to school to learn their own laws and be merciful.

740 **1st Prisoner.** What does the lad mean? I have heard that the King is mad, but merciful.

2nd Prisoner. He is to be crowned at Westminster tomorrow.

Prince *(violently).* King? What King, good sir?

1st Prisoner. Why, we have only one, his most sacred majesty, King Edward the Sixth.

TEACH

CLOSE READ

Determine Theme RL 2

(LINES 738–739)

Ⓦ **ASK STUDENTS** to reread lines 738–739, summarize the events that have happened offstage between scenes, and explain a lesson that the Prince has learned. *(The Prince and Miles are in jail because Miles apparently attacked his brother, Hugh, when he discovered that their father is dead and that Hugh has married Miles' own wife. The Prince shows sympathy with the plight of Miles and the other prisoners, even though they have, technically, committed crimes; he has learned that "Kings should go to school to learn their own laws and be merciful.")*

English Language Support

Reread the Setting and lines 710–739 aloud with students following along. Model thinking about the action that has happened offstage and between scenes. Ask students the following questions and use their answers to help them explain orally a lesson the Prince has learned:

- How does what the jailer says in lines 717–721 help explain why Miles and the Prince are in prison? *(Miles is thought to be an impostor and impostors are jailed.)*
- What details have you gathered in your Cluster Diagram that support a lesson the Prince learned while he has been a pauper? *(Possible answers: Prince is almost dunked for asking to be let into the castle, Prince is nearly thrown in jail for a crime he didn't commit)*

Strategies for Annotation

Describe Drama RL 1, RL 3

Have students use their eBook annotation tools to analyze the text. Share these strategies for guided or independent analysis:

- Highlight in pink text that reveals the attitudes or nature of a character.
- Highlight in yellow text that shows actions or responses from other characters that affect the first character's thoughts, words, or actions.
- Add a note if or when characters' attitudes seem to change during the course of the play.

2nd Prisoner. And I must hang for stealing a yard of cloth to dress my children.

> Prince is more understanding.

Prince *(moved;* to Prisoners). When I mount my throne, you shall all be free. And the laws that have dishonored you shall be swept from the books. *(turning away)* Kings should go to school to learn their own laws and be merciful.

Describe Drama

RL 1,
RL 3,
RL 5

(LINES 796–811)

ⓧ CITE TEXT EVIDENCE Have students reread lines 796–811 and tell what important plot development occurs here. Discuss whether the Prince's and Tom's behavior are consistent with their previous behavior. Have students tell why the boys' behavior has been important to the plot before and why it continues to be important now. *(The Prince and Tom work together to try and sort out the identity switch. The Prince interrupts the royal procession and identifies himself as the King. This is the "I'm used to being waited on" Prince that we have seen glimpses of in the past. Tom immediately kneels, in keeping with his role as simply a subject of the King, a regular, humble citizen who has no desire to continue in this false role as royal heir. Both are continuing to act, as best they can, as their real selves, which has been true all along. Their behavior has pointed out how easily people are swayed by appearances and how unfair this can be. Their behavior, now that they are seen together, is finally forcing others to question their own mistaken ideas and work toward sorting out the identity issue together.)*

English Language Support

Analyze Language Before students work with a partner to analyze lines 796–811, read the lines aloud with students following along. Point out the phrase "enter into your own right again." Discuss the phrase with students, and tell them that the phrase helps show that Tom understood that he was not allowed, or did not have the right, to be crowned as King, while the prince did. Note to students, however, that if Tom did not say "I forbid it! He is the King!," the prince probably would have been dragged out. Discuss how Tom and the prince are both sure of who they are despite their change of clothing, while everyone around them based their judgment on how Tom and the prince were dressed.

---

750   **2nd Prisoner.** And whether he be mad or not, his praises are on all men's lips. He has saved many innocent lives, and now he means to destroy the cruelest laws that oppress the people.

     Prince (*turning away, shaking his head*). How can this be? Surely it is not that little beggar boy! (*Sir Hugh enters with* Jailer.)

760   **Sir Hugh.** Seize the impostor!

     Miles (*as Jailer pulls him to his feet*). Hugh, this has gone far enough!

     Sir Hugh. You will sit in the public stocks for two hours, and the boy would join you if he were not so young. See to it, jailer, and after two hours, you may release them. Meanwhile, I ride to London for the coronation![11] (*Sir Hugh exits*
770 *and* Miles *is hustled out by* Jailer.)

     Prince. Coronation! What does he mean? There can be no coronation without me! (*curtain falls*)

Scene 8

Time: *Coronation Day.*

Setting: *Outside gates of Westminster Abbey, played before curtain. Painted screen or flat at rear represents Abbey. Throne is in center. Bench is near it.*

780   **At Curtain Rise:** Lords *and* Ladies *crowd Abbey. Outside gates,* Guards

---

[11] **coronation** (kôr´ə-nā´shən): the act of crowning someone king or queen. In England, coronations usually take place at a large church in London called Westminster Abbey.

---

drive back cheering Villagers, *among them* Miles.

     Miles (*distraught*). I've lost him! Poor little chap! He has been swallowed up in the crowd! (*Fanfare of trumpets is heard, then silence.* Hertford, St. John, Lords *and* Ladies *enter slowly, in a*
790 *procession, followed by* Pages, *one of whom carries crown on a small cushion.* Tom *follows procession, looking about nervously. Suddenly,* Prince, *in rags, steps out from crowd, his hand raised.*)

     Prince. I forbid you to set the crown of England upon that head. I am the King!

     Hertford. Seize the little vagabond!

800   **Tom.** I forbid it! He is the King! (*kneels before* Prince) Oh, my lord the King, let poor Tom Canty be the first to say, "Put on your crown and enter into your own right again." (Hertford *and several* Lords *look closely at both boys.*)

     Hertford. This is strange indeed. (*to* Tom) By your favor, sir, I wish to ask certain questions of this lad.

810   **Prince.** I will answer truly whatever you may ask, my lord.

     Hertford. But if you have been well trained, you may answer my questions as well as our lord the King. I need a definite proof. (*thinks a moment*) Ah! Where lies

---

APPLYING ACADEMIC VOCABULARY

period	relevant

THINK-PAIR-SHARE Have students turn to a partner to discuss the following questions. Guide students to include the academic vocabulary words *period* and *relevant* in their responses. Ask volunteers to share their responses with the class.

- As the play has developed, what details are **relevant** to the plot and the characters?
- How is the **period** in which the play is set apparent from the various stage directions at the beginning of each scene?

the Great Seal of England? It has been missing for weeks, and only the true Prince of Wales can say where it lies.

Tom. Wait! Was the seal round and thick, with letters engraved on it? (*Hertford nods.*) I know where it is, but it was not I who put it there. The rightful King shall tell you. (*to Prince*) Think, my King, it was the very last thing you did that day before you rushed out of the palace wearing my rags.

Prince (*pausing*). I recall how we exchanged clothes, but have no recollection[12] of hiding the Great Seal.

Tom (*eagerly*). Remember when you saw the bruise on my hand, you ran to the door, but first you hid this thing you call the Seal.

Prince (*suddenly*). Ah! I remember! (*to St. John*) Go, my good St. John, and you shall find the Great Seal in the armor that hangs on the wall in my chamber. (*St. John hesitates, but at a nod from Tom, hurries off.*)

Tom (*pleased*). Right, my King! Now the scepter[13] of England is yours again. (*St. John returns in a moment with Great Seal.*)

All (*shouting*). Long live Edward, King of England! (*Tom takes off his cape and throws it over Prince's rags. Trumpet fanfare is heard.*)

St. John *takes crown and places it on* Prince. *All kneel.*)

Hertford. Let the small impostor be flung into the Tower!

Prince (*firmly*). I will not have it so. But for him, I would not have my crown. (*to Tom*) My poor boy, how was it that you could remember where I hid the Seal, when I could not?

Tom (*embarrassed*). I did not know what it was, my King, and I used it to . . . to crack nuts. (*All laugh, and* Tom *steps back.* Miles *steps forward, staring in amazement.*)

Miles. Is he really the King? Is he indeed the sovereign of England, and not the poor and friendless Tom o' Bedlam[14] I thought he was? (*He sinks down on bench.*) I wish I had a bag to hide my head in!

1st Guard (*rushing up to him*). Stand up, you mannerless clown! How dare you sit in the presence of the King!

Prince. Do not touch him! He is my trusty servant, Miles Hendon, who saved me from shame and possible death. For his service, he owns the right to sit in my presence.

Miles (*bowing, then kneeling*). Your Majesty!

Prince. Rise, Sir Miles. I command that Sir Hugh Hendon, who sits within this hall, be seized and put

---

[12] **recollection** (rĕk´ə-lĕk´shən): a memory or recalling to mind of something that happened before.

[13] **scepter** (sĕp´tər): a staff held by a king or queen as an emblem of authority.

[14] **Tom o' Bedlam:** an insane person, such as someone hospitalized at St. Mary of Bethlehem Hospital, or Bedlam Hospital, in London.

CLOSE READ

Describe Drama

RL 1, RL 3, RL 5

(LINES 817–851; 867–872)

Y CITE TEXT EVIDENCE Ask students why the Great Seal becomes important here. (*No one has been able to find the Great Seal; only the "true Prince of Wales" can say where it lies. Tom helps the Prince remember where he put it before he "rushed out of the palace wearing my rags." When it is found where the Prince says it will be, everyone believes that he is Edward, Prince of Wales, and now King of England.*)

Z ASK STUDENTS to describe how Miles reacts to the knowledge that the "mad" boy he has been helping really is the King. Why does he wish for a bag to hide his head in? (*Miles is stunned. He really thought he was helping an unfortunate, misguided boy. He asks for a bag because he is embarrassed to have been so informal and casual with the King.*)

English Language Support

Write Summaries Tell students that one way to increase their comprehension is to write summaries of important parts of the text. Have students use the information from the Cluster Diagram they have prepared (introduced on TE page 345), or review the text in order to write a summary of how the misunderstanding about the King is solved in Scene 8.

- Have students work with a partner to write three sentences that summarize the action in Scene 8. Remind them to write complete

sentences and to use their graphic organizer notes to help them remember key words and ideas.

- Ask students to work independently to write a concise summary of Scene 8 that has at least five sentences. Remind them to write complete sentences and to refer to their graphic organizer notes. Ask them to share their summaries in a small group and discuss how their summaries meet the criteria.

COLLABORATIVE DISCUSSION Before students break off into small groups, discuss possible themes as a class. Have volunteers suggest themes they think are present in the play. Then, with a list of themes generated, have small groups discuss whether each suggested theme is viable and, if so, what elements of the play support that theme. Explain that small groups should add any themes that are generated out of their focused discussions as well. Then, reconvene and ask groups to share the results of their discussion with the class.

ASK STUDENTS to share any questions they generated in the course of reading and discussing the selection.

English Language Support

Support Opinions Before students begin their discussion, provide the following sentence frames.

To gain and hold the floor:
In my opinion, the theme that is most important is_____. I know this because in lines_____ the text says _____.

To build or add on:
What I heard you say was _____. I also noticed that _____.

To support with agreement:
I think you are correct because _____.

To disagree with evidence:
I don't think the evidence supports your idea because the text says_____ in lines _____.

---

under lock and key until I have need of him. (*beckons to* Tom)

890 From what I have heard, Tom Canty, you have governed the realm with royal gentleness and mercy in my absence. Henceforth, you shall hold the honorable title of King's Ward! (Tom *kneels and kisses* Prince's *hand.*) And because I have suffered with the poorest of my subjects and felt the cruel force of unjust laws, I pledge myself to a

900 reign of mercy for all! (*All bow low, then rise.*)

All (*shouting*). Long live the King! Long live Edward, King of England! (*curtain*)

COLLABORATIVE DISCUSSION With a small group, identify themes you can take away from the play. Explain how different elements of the play support your ideas.

English Language Support

Read Closely Have students compare selections to strengthen their reading and comprehension skills.

- **First,** have students individually reread or skim "The Apple of Discord I," *Yeh-Shen,* and *The Prince and the Pauper,* taking notes and annotating as they review the texts. You might identify a specific aspect of each text for students to consider, such as the structure or the characters.
- **Then,** after students have finished reading, organize them into small "expert groups," assigning one text to each group. Have students discuss and compare notes and observations, agreeing on the information that is most important to share with anyone who has not analyzed their text.
- **Next,** have individual "experts" change groups, gathering into "jigsaw groups." Students in these groups will share with one another the information learned in their expert groups.
- **Finally,** reconvene the original expert groups, having members share any and all new or important information they may have learned in their jigsaw groups.

Describe Drama

A **drama,** or play, is a form of literature that is meant to be performed by actors in front of an audience. The author of a play is called a playwright or dramatist. In some ways, a drama is similar to a story.

A play is structured in the following way:

- A play is divided into **acts,** which are like chapters in a book. Each act can be divided into smaller sections, called scenes.
- A **scene** presents an episode of the plot and usually occurs at a single place and time. A play's plot unfolds in a series of episodes as it moves toward a resolution, similar to a story.

A short drama, like *The Prince and the Pauper,* may be presented as a **one-act play,** in which each episode of the plot is presented as one scene.

The written format of a play consists of these elements:

- A drama is written in the form of a **script**. A script usually includes a cast of characters, dialogue, and stage directions.
- A **cast of characters** is a list of all the characters in the play, often in order of appearance. This list is usually found at the beginning of the play and sometimes includes descriptions of the characters.
- In drama, **dialogue** (written conversation between two or more characters) and actions tell the story. Characters' dialogue reveals their thoughts, feelings, and traits as the plot moves forward.
- **Stage directions** are instructions in the text about how to perform the drama. Some stage directions tell about the scenery and setting. Other stage directions appear within the dialogue to explain to actors how to say or emphasize a line or speech, or to describe a physical action the character should perform.

Although a drama is similar to a story, one important difference is that a play is meant to be performed. Watching a play and reading a play are two different experiences. Think about this as you analyze *The Prince and the Pauper* or other dramas, using questions such as the following:

- How is the play structured? Is it divided into acts, or is it just one act? Why might the playwright have chosen this structure?
- What is the play's main conflict? How does the plot unfold, and how is the conflict resolved?
- Who are the main characters? How do I learn about what they are like and how they respond to events?
- How is the experience of reading a drama different from watching a live performance of it? In what ways does the script help me?

TEACH

CLOSE READ

Describe Drama

Guide students to understand the terms. Review the play with students, and have them locate the special elements of the play (the time and place information at the beginning of each scene as well as stage directions that describe characters' attitudes, movements, and so on) that would help actors and directors put on, or perform, the play.

Remind students that a play is a story that is presented in a different form. And, like every story, a play has a plot that involves a conflict. Guide students to identify the conflict in *The Prince and the Pauper.* Help students understand that this play's conflict stems from the mix-up of identities. As a result, there is conflict between Tom and the palace staff, and there is conflict between the Prince and John Canty and Hugo.

Discuss with students the elements that are different between a story, which is meant to be read or listened to, and a play, which is meant to be watched and listened to. Have students compare and contrast what they "see" and "hear" when they read to what they perceive when they listen or watch.

English Language Support

Have students work with a partner to write answers to the analysis questions in the Student Edition. Remind students to use line numbers from the play to help cite text evidence that supports their ideas.

Strategies for Annotation   🖋 🗐 Annotate it!

Describe Drama

Share these strategies for guided or independent analysis:

- Highlight in green dialogue and stage directions for the Prince that indicate his feelings.
- Review only the highlighted text.
- Make a note in your eBook wherever you notice a development or a change in the character.
- Unhighlight the Prince's text and then highlight Tom's text and repeat the exercise for Tom.

Prince (*rushing to gates*). How dare you treat a poor subject of the King in such a manner! Open the gates and let him in! (*As Villagers see Prince, they take off their hats and bow low.*) . . .

Prince (*to* Tom). You look tired, and you have been treated cruelly. I am Edward, Prince of Wales. What is your name?

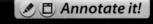

Prince is caring.

PRACTICE & APPLY

Analyzing the Text

RL 1, RL 2,
RL 3, RL 4,
RL 5, RL 7

Possible answers:

1. *The two main characters are Edward, the Prince of Wales, and Tom Canty, the pauper, a poor boy. Having invited Tom into the palace, the Prince decides they should switch clothes. Then, when he rushes out in Tom's clothes to reprimand a guard, Tom is at once seen as the Prince, and Prince Edward becomes a common village boy.*

2. *Tom is "terrified" in his role, while the Prince responds loudly and boldly. This reveals that Tom is fearful and afraid of getting into trouble, but the Prince is self-confident and used to being in charge.*

3. *The stage directions describe what the setting should look like and how Miles and the Prince react to each other. The Prince acts just as we would expect a Prince to act. Miles plays along and thereby wins the Prince's favor.*

4. *From the Jailer we learn that Miles has been taken to jail as an impostor and for assaulting Sir Hugh. From Miles, we learn that his father has died and that his brother has claimed the estate and Miles' wife as his own.*

5. *The Prince interrupts the ceremony to declare that he is the King, and Tom helps him prove it. In the end, the experience has not changed Tom much, but I think living as a commoner has opened the Prince's eyes, and he will be a better King because of it.*

6. *Aspects might include the switched identities, with possibilities for both humor and great confusion; characters with strong personalities; well-paced, exciting events; the contrast between the rich and powerful and the poor and powerless; and good opportunities for costumes and sets.*

 *eBook Annotate It!*

Analyzing the Text

RL 1, RL 2, RL 3,
RL 4, RL 5, RL 7,
SL 1, SL 4, SL 6

Cite Text Evidence   Support your responses with evidence from the text.

1. **Summarize** Review lines 29–137. Who are the two main characters? How would you describe the main conflict introduced in this scene?

2. **Compare** Compare how Tom responds to his new situation in Scene One, lines 157–280, with how the Prince behaves in Scene Two, lines 323–352. Do the boys react in similar or different ways? What do their words and behavior tell you about what they are like?

3. **Analyze** Review Scene Four, lines 442–532, in which Miles serves the Prince a meal. How are the stage directions helpful to readers?

4. **Analyze** Review lines 710–732 in Scene Seven. How does the dialogue help you understand what has happened to Miles?

5. **Draw Conclusions** Review lines 774–904 in Scene Eight. How is the play's conflict resolved? Think about the two main characters. Have either of them undergone any great changes? Why or why not?

6. **Synthesize** The play is based on a novel by Mark Twain. Think about the plot and characters. What aspects of the story make it well suited to a dramatic performance?

PERFORMANCE TASK

Speaking Activity: Dramatic Reading With a small group, rehearse and then perform a portion of the play. Then watch another group perform a portion of the play.

• Use the stage directions and what you know about the character to help you deliver your lines in a convincing way.

• When you rehearse and perform, work to use appropriate eye contact,

speak at an adequate volume, and pronounce words clearly.

• When you watch the performance, contrast it with what you "see" and "hear" when you read the text on your own.

• Share your ideas with your group, using examples from the text or the performance to support those ideas. Write a brief summary of your discussion.

Assign this performance task.

PERFORMANCE TASK

RL 7, SL 1,
SL 4, SL 6

Speaking Activity: Dramatic Reading Guide students to
• memorize their lines so that they can perform them confidently
• discuss stage directions and what they mean as a group
• after watching others' performances, share ideas about how the characters and action come to life during a dramatic reading in a way that they don't when reading the play silently

Describe Drama: Characterization

RL 3

TEACH

Explain to students that a playwright, just like a fiction writer, creates and develops characters. Each character has a mix of **traits,** or qualities, that make that character engaging. Writers want to create characters that are

- three-dimensional and complex, as in life
- distinct in personality or appearance
- engaging and easy to care about
- interesting because of what they say, do, or think
- capable of a range of emotions and actions

The way in which the writer creates and develops a character's traits is called **characterization.** Writers use different methods of characterization. A playwright develops a character and reveals that information through

- what the character says, does, or thinks
- what other characters say, do, or think about the character
- what the stage directions indicate about how the character looks, speaks, moves, or feels

Explain that students can look for important details and organize them into a character map according to the kind of information they provide. They can then use this information to make inferences about characters that are supported by the details in the play.

PRACTICE AND APPLY

Display lines 1–27 of *The Prince and the Pauper*. Have students examine the text to discover what they can about Tom Canty. Pose these questions:

- What does Tom's dialogue reveal about him?
- What does other people's dialogue reveal about Tom?
- What do the stage directions reveal about how Tom looks, how he speaks, or how he moves?

Have students repeat this exercise in Scene 2 to discover everything they can about Tom's father, John Canty. Remind students to think about all the different ways that writers reveal information about characters.

Then, have students or partners practice writing a character's part for a play. They can create a part for a character they read about in other stories in this collection or in previous collections. Remind students that they may need to include other characters in order to create a full portrait of their chosen characters. Have students share their character parts with the group.

Describe Elements of Drama

RL 1,
RL 3,
RL 5,
RL 7

RETEACH

Review with students that a play is a story written in a way that helps people act it out. Like a story, a play or drama has characters, a plot, dialogue, and action, usually divided into sections. Guide students to find examples of each of these elements in *The Prince and the Pauper* and to answer the questions:

- **Cast of characters:** What information does the cast of characters reveal? How is this different from a story?
- **Acts and scenes:** Explain the structure of plays. What elements are like a novel or a story?
- **Dialogue:** What does dialogue look like in a play's script? How is it different from dialogue in a story?
- **Stage directions:** Where do stage directions appear? What information do stage directions contain?

Next, choose scenes or sections of the play that were difficult for students, based on your observations during the lesson. Go through these selected scenes or sections together, identifying elements of drama and explaining the purpose of each one. Guide students to compare each element as it is used in stories and in dramas. Then, read each section or scene aloud with students.

 LEVEL UP TUTORIALS Assign the following *Level Up* tutorial: **Elements of Drama**

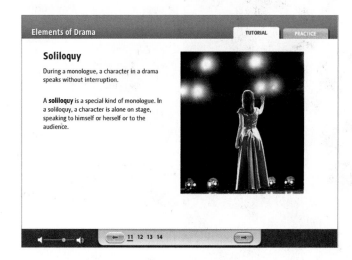

INDEPENDENT READING

Students can apply knowledge of the elements of drama and scripts. Ask students to read a play and then speak the parts aloud. Remind students of how reading it differs from hearing, seeing, or performing it.

The Prince and the Pauper

from the Novel by Mark Twain

The Prince and the Pauper

Dramatization by Joellen Bland

The Prince and the Pauper

Graphic Story by Marvel Comics

Why These Texts

Students can practice close reading by comparing versions of a scene from Mark Twain's novel with dramatic and graphic versions. With the help of the close-reading questions, students will analyze the excerpt in each of the three forms, compare them, and consider the advantages of one form over the other.

Background Have students read the background and the information about the authors. Tell them that they will read three versions of a scene from a novel by Mark Twain: Twain's version; a dramatization by Joellen Bland; and a Marvel Comics graphic version. In a previous chapter, two boys are born on the same day. One is rich, one is poor. One is wanted, one is not.

SETTING A PURPOSE Ask students to pay attention to similarities and differences between the prince and the pauper. How are they presented in each version of the scene?

Standards Support

- cite textual evidence
- describe how characters change as the plot moves forward
- analyze how a scene contributes to the development of the plot
- compare and contrast different versions of a scene

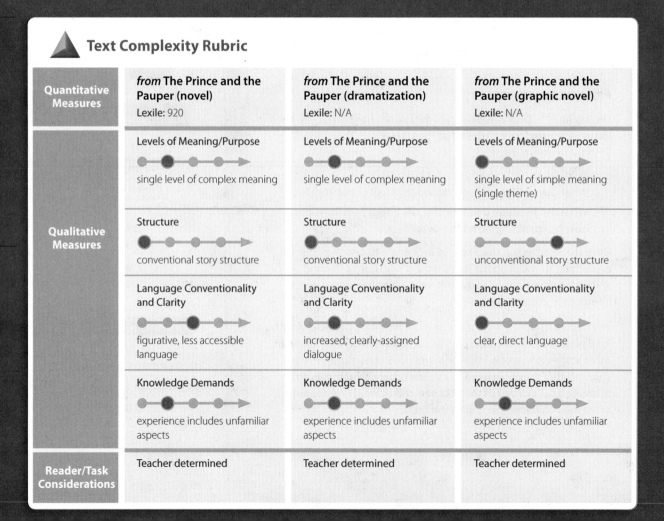

Text Complexity Rubric

	from The Prince and the Pauper (novel) Lexile: 920	*from* The Prince and the Pauper (dramatization) Lexile: N/A	*from* The Prince and the Pauper (graphic novel) Lexile: N/A
Quantitative Measures			
Qualitative Measures	Levels of Meaning/Purpose single level of complex meaning	Levels of Meaning/Purpose single level of complex meaning	Levels of Meaning/Purpose single level of simple meaning (single theme)
	Structure conventional story structure	Structure conventional story structure	Structure unconventional story structure
	Language Conventionality and Clarity figurative, less accessible language	Language Conventionality and Clarity increased, clearly-assigned dialogue	Language Conventionality and Clarity clear, direct language
	Knowledge Demands experience includes unfamiliar aspects	Knowledge Demands experience includes unfamiliar aspects	Knowledge Demands experience includes unfamiliar aspects
Reader/Task Considerations	Teacher determined	Teacher determined	Teacher determined

Strategies for CLOSE READING

Compare Versions of a Text

Students should read all three versions of this scene carefully all the way through. Close-reading questions at the bottom of the page will help them focus on a thorough analysis of the texts. As they read, students should jot down comments or questions about the texts in the side margins.

WHEN STUDENTS STRUGGLE . . .

To help students compare three versions of "The Prince and the Pauper," have them work in a small group to fill out charts, such as the ones shown below, as they analyze the texts.

CITE TEXT EVIDENCE For practice comparing and contrasting versions of a story, ask students to cite evidence of similarities and differences in each version of the scene. Also, ask students to describe *how* each version presents information about the characters.

Novel Version	
How do you learn about the characters? *The characters are described in the text.*	
One similarity between the prince and the pauper: They have "the same eyes, the same voice and manner, the same form and stature, the same face and countenance."	*One difference between the prince and the pauper: The pauper dressed "in his rags," whereas the prince's "clothing was all of lovely silks and satins."*

Dramatic Version	
How do you learn about the characters? *through dialogue and stage directions*	
One similarity between the prince and the pauper: They both would like to "play in the mud."	*One difference: Sometimes the pauper is "hungry," but the prince's palace has a "bowl of nuts."*

Graphic Version	
How do you learn about the characters? *from pictures as well as words*	
One similarity between the prince and the pauper: They look like twins.	*One difference: The guard treats the pauper roughly, but he follows the orders of the prince.*

Background Mark Twain *(1835–1910) is probably America's most celebrated humorist. Born Samuel L. Clemens in Hannibal, Missouri, Twain wrote a number of classic novels including* The Prince and the Pauper. *You are about to read three versions of a scene from* The Prince and the Pauper: *an excerpt from Twain's novel, a dramatization by* **Joellen Bland,** *and a graphic story by* **Marvel Comics.** *In the scene that follows, a poor boy named Tom Canty hopes to catch a glimpse of Edward Tudor, the Prince of Wales.*

COMPARING VERSIONS OF
The Prince and the Pauper

CLOSE READ
Notes

1. **READ ▶** As you read lines 1–45, begin to collect text evidence.
   - In the margin, explain what "the desire of Tom's soul" is (line 5).
   - Underline details that describe the boy who Tom sees.
   - Circle phrases that show the prince's kindness to Tom.

Tom's Meeting with the Prince.
from the Novel by Mark Twain

Tom got up hungry, and sauntered hungry away, but with his thoughts busy with the shadowy splendours of his night's dreams. He idled down a quiet, lovely road, past the great cardinal's stately palace, toward a far more mighty and **majestic** palace beyond—Westminster. Was the desire of his soul to be satisfied at last? Here, indeed, was a king's palace. Might he not hope to see a prince now—a prince of flesh and blood, if Heaven were willing?

Poor little Tom, in his rags, approached, and was moving slowly and timidly past the sentinels, with a beating heart and a rising hope, when all at once he caught sight through the golden bars of a spectacle that almost made him shout for joy. Within was a comely boy, tanned and brown with sturdy outdoor sports and exercises, whose clothing was all of lovely silks and satins, shining with jewels; at his hip a little jewelled sword and dagger; dainty buskins[1] on his feet, with red heels;

10 Ⓐ

[1] **buskin:** thick-soled laced boot that reaches to the calf.

majestic:
impressive; amazing

The desire of Tom's soul is to see a prince in person.

115

---

1. **READ AND CITE TEXT EVIDENCE**

Ⓐ **ASK STUDENTS** to use their marked text as evidence and describe the prince. *Students should cite underlined text in lines 11–17 as evidence of the prince's wealthy appearance and circled text in lines 28–32, 38, 40–41, and 43–44 as evidence of his kindness.*

Critical Vocabulary: majestic (line 4) Have students determine the meaning of *majestic* as it is used here. Ask students to compare *majestic* and the related word *grand*. What connotations does *majestic* have that *grand* does not? Why might Twain have chosen to use *majestic* to describe the palace? *The word* majestic *has to do with royalty (a king may be called "His Majesty"), and the palace is the home of the royal family.*

and on his head a jaunty crimson cap, with drooping plumes fastened with a great sparkling gem. Several gorgeous gentlemen stood near—his servants, without a doubt. Oh! He was a prince—a prince, a living prince, a real prince—without the shadow of a question; and the prayer of the pauper-boy's heart was answered at last.

20   Tom's breath came quick and short with excitement, and his eyes grew big with wonder and delight. Everything gave way in his mind instantly to one desire: that was to get close to the prince, and have a good, devouring look at him. Before he knew what he was about, he had his face against the gate-bars. The next instant one of the soldiers snatched him rudely away, and sent him spinning among the gaping crowd of country gawks and London idlers. The soldier said,—

"Mind thy manners, thou young beggar!"

The crowd jeered and laughed; but the young prince sprang to the gate with his face flushed, and his eyes flashing with indignation, and
30   cried out,—

B   "How dar'st thou use a poor lad like that? How dar'st thou use the King my father's meanest subject so? Open the gates, and let him in!"

You should have seen that fickle crowd snatch off their hats then. You should have heard them cheer, and shout, "Long live the Prince of Wales!"

The soldiers presented arms with their halberds,[2] opened the gates, and presented again as the little Prince of Poverty passed in, in his fluttering rags, to join hands with the Prince of Limitless Plenty.

[2] **halberd:** a weapon that resembles a battle-ax.

---

2.   ◀ REREAD   Reread lines 27–41. What does the prince's treatment of Tom reveal about his character? Cite text evidence in your response.

The prince invites Tom into the palace after scolding the guard, which suggests he is fair and humble.

3.   READ ▶   As you read lines 46–111, continue to cite text evidence.

- Underline the questions the prince asks Tom.
- In the margin, describe the prince's reaction to what Tom says in lines 57–64.
- Circle the prince's reactions to Tom's description of home in lines 79–111. In the margin, paraphrase what the prince says in lines 102–105.

116

Edward Tudor said—
40   "Thou lookest tired and hungry: thou'st been treated ill. Come with me."

Edward took Tom to a rich apartment in the palace, which he called his cabinet. By his command a repast was brought such as Tom had never encountered before except in books. The prince sat near by, and asked questions while Tom ate.

"What is thy name, lad?"

"Tom Canty, an' it please thee, sir."

"'Tis an odd one. Where dost live?"

"In the city, please thee, sir. Offal[3] Court, out of Pudding Lane."

50   "Offal Court! Truly 'tis another odd one. Hast parents?"

"Parents have I, sir, and a grand-dam likewise that is but indifferently precious to me, God forgive me if it be offence to say it—also twin sisters, Nan and Bet."

"Then is thy grand-dam not over kind to thee, I take it?"

"Neither to any other is she, so please your worship."

"Doth she mistreat thee?"

"There be times that she stayeth her hand, being asleep or overcome with drink; but when she hath her judgment clear again, she maketh it up to me with goodly beatings."

60   A fierce look came into the little prince's eyes, and he cried out—

"What! Beatings?"

"Oh, indeed, yes, please you, sir."

"*Beatings*!—and thou so frail and little. Is thy father kind to thee?"

"Not more than Gammer Canty, sir."

"Fathers be alike, mayhap. Mine hath not a doll's temper. He smiteth with a heavy hand, yet spareth me: he spareth me not always with his tongue, though, sooth to say. How doth thy mother use thee?"

"She is good, sir, and giveth me neither sorrow nor pain of any
70   sort. And Nan and Bet are like to her in this."

"How old be these?"

"Fifteen, an' it please you, sir."

"Thou speakest well; thou hast an easy grace in it. Art learned?"

"I know not if I am or not, sir. The good priest that is called Father Andrew taught me, of his kindness, from his books."

"Know'st thou the Latin?"

[3] **Offal:** waste or garbage.

The prince becomes angry and upset when Tom says he is beaten at home.

117

---

2.   **REREAD AND CITE TEXT EVIDENCE**

B   **ASK STUDENTS** to cite evidence to support their analysis of the prince's character. *Students should cite evidence that the prince scolds the guard and demands that he allow Tom to enter the palace (lines 31–32). From that evidence they may infer that the prince is fair and kind.*

3.   **READ AND CITE TEXT EVIDENCE**

C   **ASK STUDENTS** to read aloud their description of the prince's reaction to a partner. Have partners work together to find the best evidence to support their descriptions. Have them revise their descriptions if needed. *Students should cite evidence from lines 60–63 to show that the prince becomes angry and upset when Tom says he is beaten at home.*

FOR ELL STUDENTS Students may struggle with some of the vocabulary on this page. Have them work in small groups to discuss the meanings of *thou'st, repast, dost, grand-dam, stayeth, maketh, mayhap, smiteth, sooth, speakest.* Remind them to use context clues to determine the meanings of these words.

"But scantly, sir, I doubt."

"Tell me of thy Offal Court. Hast thou a pleasant life there?"

80 "In truth, yes, so please you, sir, save when one is hungry. There be Punch-and-Judy[4] shows, and monkeys—oh such antic creatures! and so bravely dressed!—and there be plays wherein they that play shout and fight till all are slain, and 'tis so fine to see, and costeth but a farthing[5]—albeit 'tis main hard to get the farthing, please your worship."

"Tell me more."

"We lads of Offal Court do strive against each other with the cudgel, like to the fashion of the 'prentices, sometimes."

The prince's eyes flashed. Said he—

"Marry, that would not I mislike. Tell me more."

90 "We strive in races, sir, to see who of us shall be fleetest."

"That would I like also. Speak on."

"In summer, sir, we wade and swim in the canals and in the river, and each doth duck his neighbour, and splatter him with water, and dive and shout and tumble and—"

"'Twould be worth my father's kingdom but to enjoy it once! Prithee go on."

"We dance and sing about the Maypole in Cheapside; we play in the sand, each covering his neighbour up; and times we make mud pastry—oh the lovely mud, it hath not its like for delightfulness in all

100 the world!—we do fairly wallow in the mud, sir, saving your worship's presence."

---

[4] **Punch-and-Judy show:** traditional puppet show. The puppets are Mr. Punch and his wife Judy, who get into comical fights.
[5] **farthing:** a former British coin worth one-fourth of a penny.

---

4. ◀ **REREAD AND DISCUSS** Reread lines 78–111. In a small group, discuss which elements of Tom's life most appeal to the prince. Cite text evidence in your discussion.

5. **READ** ▶ As you read lines 112–156, continue to cite textual evidence.

   • Underline what the boys realize after they switch clothes.
   • Circle what the prince sees on Tom's hand. In the margin, explain the Prince's reaction.
   • In the margin, explain what happens in lines 139–156.

"Oh, prithee, say no more, 'tis glorious! If that I could but clothe me in raiment like to thine, and strip my feet, and revel in the mud once, just once, with none to rebuke me or forbid, meseemeth I could forego the crown!"

"And if that I could clothe me once, sweet sir, as thou art clad—just once—"

"Oho, would'st like it? Then so shall it be. Doff thy rags, and don these splendours, lad! It is a brief happiness, but will be not less keen

110 for that. We will have it while we may, and change again before any come to molest."

A few minutes later the little Prince of Wales was garlanded with Tom's fluttering odds and ends, and the little Prince of Pauperdom was tricked out in the **gaudy** plumage of royalty. The two went and stood side by side before a great mirror, and lo, a miracle: there did not seem to have been any change made! They stared at each other, then at the glass, then at each other again. At last the puzzled princeling said—

"What dost thou make of this?"

120 "Ah, good your worship, require me not to answer. It is not meet that one of my degree should utter the thing."

"Then will I utter it. Thou hast the same hair, the same eyes, the same voice and manner, the same form and stature, the same face and countenance that I bear. Fared we forth naked, there is none could say which was you, and which the Prince of Wales. And, now that I am clothed as thou wert clothed, it seemeth I should be able the more nearly to feel as thou didst when the brute soldier—Hark ye, is not this a bruise upon your hand?"

"Yes; but it is a slight thing, and your worship knoweth that the

130 poor man-at-arms—"

"Peace! It was a shameful thing and a cruel!" cried the little prince, stamping his bare foot. "If the King—Stir not a step till I come again! It is a command!"

In a moment he had snatched up and put away an article of national importance that lay upon a table, and was out at the door and flying through the palace grounds in his bannered rags, with a hot face and glowing eyes. As soon as he reached the great gate, he seized the bars, and tried to shake them, shouting—

"Open! Unbar the gates!"

The prince would consider giving up his crown if he could dress and play like Tom one time.

gaudy:
flashy; tacky

The prince sympathizes with Tom, especially now that he is wearing his clothes. The prince sets off to scold the guard for giving Tom a bruise.

---

4. REREAD AND DISCUSS USING TEXT EVIDENCE

D **ASK STUDENTS** to appoint a reporter for each group to cite specific evidence and line numbers to support their conclusions about which elements of Tom's life most appeal to the prince. *Students should cite evidence that the prince would like to fight, race, swim, dance, and wallow in the mud.*

5. READ AND CITE TEXT EVIDENCE

E **ASK STUDENTS** to cite text evidence to support their explanation of what happens in lines 131–156. *Students should cite evidence that the prince is angry: "stamping his bare foot" (line 132), "glowing eyes" (line 137). He is wearing Tom's rags (line 136), and the soldier struck him, "a sounding box on the ear" (line 142), having mistaken him for Tom, "'thou beggar's spawn,'" (line 144). The guard tosses the prince out of the palace (lines 152–153), saying, "'Be off, thou crazy rubbish!'"*

Critical Vocabulary: gaudy (line 114) Have students determine the meaning of *gaudy* as it is used here. Is *gaudy* a compliment? What does this word choice tell you about the narrator's attitude toward the characters?

FOR ELL STUDENTS Point out to students that *tricked out* (line 114) has nothing to do with playing tricks. It means "adorned, extravagantly dressed up."

The guard strikes the prince and throws him out of the palace, thinking he is Tom.

140   The soldier that had maltreated Tom obeyed promptly; and as the prince burst through the portal, half-smothered with royal wrath, the soldier fetched him a sounding box on the ear that sent him whirling to the roadway, and said—

"Take that, thou beggar's spawn, for what thou got'st me from his Highness!"

The crowd roared with laughter. The prince picked himself out of the mud, and made fiercely at the sentry, shouting—

"I am the Prince of Wales, my person is sacred; and thou shalt hang for laying thy hand upon me!"

150   The soldier brought his halberd to a present-arms and said **mockingly**—

mockingly:
in an insulting manner; rudely

"I salute your gracious Highness." Then angrily—"Be off, thou crazy rubbish!"

Here the jeering crowd closed round the poor little prince, and hustled him far down the road, hooting him, and shouting—

"Way for his Royal Highness! Way for the Prince of Wales!"

---

6. **◄ REREAD** Reread lines 122–156. How does Tom and the prince's discovery help you understand what happens after the prince leaves Tom? Support your answer with explicit textual evidence.

It explains why the soldier and the crowd treat him badly. They think he is Tom, and again they delight in the mistreatment of a pauper.

SHORT RESPONSE

Cite Text Evidence Why might the prince want to trade places with Tom? Think about what you know of the prince's character. Review your reading notes and be sure to **cite text evidence** in your response.

The prince is very kind. He is interested in knowing what Tom's life is like—he probably does not have a chance to enjoy being a boy the way Tom does. The prince wants to know what life is like outside the palace—it is not something he experiences, and he realizes that it is the way most people live. He also might want to better understand his future subjects.

120

---

1. **READ ▶** As you read the introductory text and lines 1–25, begin to collect and cite text evidence.

- Underline details in the setting that suggest royalty.
- Underline stage directions that describe Tom's appearance and behavior.
- Circle the prince's dialogue. In the margin, explain what his response to events tells you about him.

from The Prince and the Pauper
Dramatization by Joellen Bland

CHARACTERS

Edward, Prince of Wales   **Two Guards**
Tom Canty, the Pauper   **Villagers**
Two Women

Ⓐ **Time:** *1547.*
Setting: *Westminster Palace, England. Gates leading to courtyard are at right. Slightly to the left, off courtyard and inside gates,* **interior** *of palace anteroom[1] is visible. There is a couch with a rich robe draped on it, screen at rear, bellcord, mirror, chairs, and a table with bowl of nuts, and a large golden seal on it. Piece of armor hangs on one wall. Exits are rear and downstage.*

interior:
inside

Scene One

At Curtain Rise. *Two Guards—one at right, one at left—stand in front of gates, several* Villagers *hover nearby, straining to see into courtyard where* Prince *may be seen through fence, playing. Two Women enter right.*

1st Woman. I have walked all morning just to have a glimpse of Westminster Palace.

2nd Woman. Maybe if we can get near enough to the gates, we can have a glimpse of the young Prince. (Tom Canty, *dirty and ragged, comes out of crowd and steps close to gates.*)

10 **Tom.** I have always dreamed of seeing a real prince! (*Excited, he*
Ⓑ *presses his nose against gates.*)

---

[1] **anteroom:** an outer room that leads to an inner room and is often used as a waiting room.

121

---

6. **REREAD AND CITE TEXT EVIDENCE**

Ⓕ **ASK STUDENTS** to read their response aloud to a partner. Then have partners work together to identify the best evidence. *Answers will vary. Students should cite lines 122–125 as evidence that Tom and the prince look identical, which explains why the soldier treats the prince badly in lines 140–156.*

Critical Vocabulary: mockingly (line 151) Have students model how the word *mockingly* describes the soldier's tone.

SHORT RESPONSE

Cite Text Evidence Students should:

- provide a text-based analysis of the prince.
- infer the prince's motivations.
- cite textual evidence to support their response.

---

1. **READ AND CITE TEXT EVIDENCE**

Ⓐ **ASK STUDENTS** to explain how they decided which details in the setting suggest royalty. *Students should have underlined these details that suggest the opulence of living in a palace: "Westminster Palace, England. Gates leading to courtyard," "interior of palace anteroom is visible," "couch with a rich robe draped on it," "large golden seal," and "piece of armor."*

Critical Vocabulary: interior (Setting) Ask students to explain why the word *interior* is used to describe the setting. *Students might say that it helps explain the layout of the palace.*

The prince has respect for every one of his countrymen.

1st Guard. Mind your manners, you young beggar! (*Seizes* Tom *by collar and sends him sprawling into crowd. Villagers* laugh, as Tom *slowly gets to his feet.*)

Prince (*rushing to gates*). How dare you treat a poor subject of the King in such a manner! Open the gates and let him in! (*As* Villagers *see* Prince, *they take off their hats and bow low.*)

Villagers (*shouting together*). Long live the Prince of Wales! (Guards *open gates and* Tom *slowly passes through, as if in a dream.*)

20 **Prince** (*to* Tom). You look tired, and you have been treated cruelly. I am Edward, Prince of Wales. What is your name?

Tom (*looking around in awe*). Tom Canty, Your Highness.

Prince. Come into the palace with me, Tom. (Prince *leads* Tom *into anteroom. Villagers* pantomime conversation, and all but a few exit.*) Where do you live, Tom?

Tom. In the city, Your Highness, in Offal Court.

Prince. Offal Court? That's an odd name. Do you have parents?

Tom. Yes, Your Highness.

Prince. How does your father treat you?

30 **Tom.** If it please you, Your Highness, when I am not able to beg a penny for our supper, he treats me to beatings.

Prince (*shocked*). What! Beatings? My father is not a calm man, but he does not beat me. (*looks at* Tom *thoughtfully*) You speak well and have an easy grace. Have you been schooled?

Tom. Very little, Your Highness. A good priest who shares our house in Offal Court has taught me from his books.

---

2. ◀ REREAD   Reread lines 8–22. In what ways do the stage directions help you understand Tom's character? Cite text evidence in your response.

When he "presses his nose" against the gates and looks "around in awe" we learn he is eager to see the prince and impressed by royalty.

3. READ ▶   As you read lines 26–48, continue to cite textual evidence.

• Underline what Tom tells the prince about life at Offal Court.
• Circle the stage direction that describes the prince's reaction when he learns that Tom's father hits him.
• In the margin, explain what each character wants.

122

Prince. Do you have a pleasant life in Offal Court?

Tom. Pleasant enough, Your Highness, save when I am hungry. We have Punch and Judy shows, and sometimes we lads have fights in the 40 street.

Prince (*eagerly*). I should like that. Tell me more.

Tom. In summer, we run races and swim in the river, and we love to wallow in the mud.

Prince (*sighing*, *wistfully*). If I could wear your clothes and play in the mud just once, with no one to forbid me, I think I could give up the crown!

Tom (*shaking his head*). And if I could wear your fine clothes just once, Your Highness . . .

Prince. Would you like that? Come, then. We shall change places. You 50 can take off your rags and put on my clothes—and I will put on yours. (*He leads* Tom *behind screen, and they return shortly, each wearing the other's clothes.*) Let's look at ourselves in this mirror. (*leads* Tom *to mirror*)

Tom. Oh, Your Highness, it is not proper for me to wear such clothes.

Prince (*excitedly, as he looks in the mirror*). Heavens, do you not see it? We look like brothers! We have the same features and bearing.² If we went about together, dressed alike, there is no one who could say which is the Prince of Wales and which is Tom Canty!

Tom (*drawing back and rubbing his hand*). Your Highness, I am 60 frightened. . . .

Prince. Do not worry. (*seeing* Tom *rub his hand*) Is that a bruise on your hand?

Tom. Yes, but it is slight thing, Your Highness.

Prince (*angrily*). It was shameful and cruel of that guard to strike you. Do not stir a step until I come back. I command you! (*He picks up the golden Seal of England³ and carefully puts it into a piece of armor. He then dashes out to gates.*) Open! Unbar the gates at once! (2nd Guard

---

² **features and bearing:** parts of the face and ways of standing and walking.
³ **Seal of England:** a device used to stamp a special design, usually a picture of the ruler, onto a document, thus indicating that it has royal approval.

---

wistfully:
longingly

The prince would love to play in the mud without worry like Tom does. Tom wishes he could wear the prince's clothes.

Tom is afraid of appearing disrespectful by dressing like the prince.

---

4. READ ▶   As you read lines 49–79, continue to cite textual evidence.

• In the margin, explain why Tom is "frightened" (line 60).
• Circle how the guards and villagers treat the prince when he leaves the palace in Tom's clothes.

123

---

2. **REREAD AND CITE TEXT EVIDENCE**

B **ASK STUDENTS** to cite evidence to support their explanation of how the stage directions help them understand Tom's character. *Students should cite "presses his nose against gates" (line 11) and "looking around in awe" (line 22).*

3. **READ AND CITE TEXT EVIDENCE**

C **ASK STUDENTS** to cite text evidence to support their explanation of what Tom and the prince each want. *Students should cite evidence that the prince would love to play in the mud from lines 44–45. They should cite evidence that Tom would like to wear the prince's clothes from lines 47–48.*

4. **READ AND CITE TEXT EVIDENCE**

D **ASK STUDENTS** to use their circled text to explain how the prince is treated differently by the guards and the villagers when he is wearing Tom's clothes. *Students should cite circled text in lines 68–69, 74–77, and 78–79, and explain that the guards and villagers are cruel when they do not recognize the prince.*

Critical Vocabulary: wistfully (line 44) Ask students to explain how the word *wistfully* helps them understand why the prince sighs.

FOR ELL STUDENTS Explain to students that a Punch and Judy show (line 39) is a hand-puppet show featuring a violent man, Punch, and his wife, Judy. Despite the violence, the puppet shows are comedy.

D opens gates, and *as* Prince *runs out, in rags,* 1st Guard *seizes him, boxes him on the ear, and knocks him to the ground.*)

70 **1st Guard.** Take that, you little beggar, for the trouble you have made for me with the Prince. (Villagers *roar with laughter.*)

Prince (*picking himself up, turning on* Guard *furiously*). I am Prince of Wales! You shall hang for laying your hand on me!

1st Guard (*presenting arms; mockingly*). I salute Your Gracious Highness! (*then, angrily,* 1st Guard *shoves* Prince *roughly aside.*) Be off, you mad bag of rags! (Prince *is surrounded by* Villagers, *who hustle him off.*)

E **Villagers** (*ad lib, as they exit, shouting*). Make way for His Royal Highness! Make way for the Prince of Wales! Hail to the Prince! (*Etc.*)

5. ◀ **REREAD AND DISCUSS** Reread lines 1–79. In a small group, discuss how the plot unfolds to create a conflict at the end of this scene. Cite explicit textual evidence in your discussion.

SHORT RESPONSE

Cite Text Evidence How do the stage directions and the dialogue help you understand the characters of Tom and the prince? Be sure to **cite text evidence** in your response.

Tom has a hard life (he is "dirty and ragged"), but he is eager and excited to encounter royalty ("looking around in awe"). The Prince has a good heart ("How dare you treat a poor subject") and reacts against injustice ("shocked"). The stage directions allow the reader to visualize how each person acts ("rushing to gates"). The dialogue also reveals each person's character. For example, the prince shows his kindness ("Open the gates and let him in!") and Tom shows his humility ("And if I could wear your fine clothes just once").

124

1. **READ** ▶ As you read the first two pages of the graphic story, begin to collect and cite textual evidence.
   - Underline Tom's feelings about the palace and the prince.
   - Circle text that shows the prince's character.

from **The Prince and the Pauper**
Graphic Story by Marvel Comics

125

---

5. REREAD AND DISCUSS USING TEXT EVIDENCE

E **ASK STUDENTS** to be prepared to share the results of their discussion with the class. Have them appoint a reporter for each group. *Students should cite evidence of Tom's curiosity (lines 10–11), the prince's kindness (lines 20–21), and the two boys' appearance (lines 55–56).*

SHORT RESPONSE

Cite Text Evidence Student responses will vary, but they should cite evidence from the text to support their explanation. Students should:

- explain how stage directions give insight into Tom and the prince.
- explain how dialogue gives insight into Tom and the prince.
- cite textual evidence to support their response.

1. READ AND CITE TEXT EVIDENCE

A **ASK STUDENTS** to use their marked text to describe how Tom feels about the palace and the prince. *Students should underline text in the fourth panel: "Was the desire of his soul to be satisfied at last?" and explain that Tom wants very much to see the prince. They should underline text in the fifth panel: "a spectacle that almost made him shout for joy," and explain that Tom is happy to see the prince.*

The jagged outlines show forceful expression—the prince is outraged.

I strike you because you got me in trouble with the prince. Now go away!

2. ◀ REREAD Reread the page above. How do the illustrations convey that the boys look alike? Circle illustrations that help you recognize their similarities.

The illustrations show that the boys have similar facial features. They also appear to be the same height and have the same build. The boys are frequently drawn side by side so that we can see that they are very much alike.

3. READ ▶ As you read this page, continue to cite textual evidence.
• Circle the dialogue that is shown with jagged outlines. In the margin, explain why the artist has used these outlines.
• In the margin, paraphrase what the guard says to the prince.
• Circle the prince's facial expression in the last panel.

126

127

2. **REREAD AND CITE TEXT EVIDENCE**

Ⓑ ASK STUDENTS which illustrations they circled and what similarities they noticed in those illustrations. *Students may indicate that the oval illustration and the illustration at the right in the bottom row show that the boys have similar facial features, hair, and similar builds. They should conclude that the boys are drawn side by side so that readers can see that they look very much alike.*

FOR ELL STUDENTS The word *duck* has several meanings. As a noun it can describe a water bird and as a verb it can mean "to lower or to evade." In this context, though, it means "to push under water."

3. **READ AND CITE TEXT EVIDENCE**

Ⓒ ASK STUDENTS to use their marked text as evidence and describe the feelings the prince experiences on this page. *Students should circle the jagged speech bubble in panel 1 on this page. They should explain that this shows that the prince is angry. They should see that the prince looks stunned when the guard abuses him. They should circle the prince's expression in the last panel, and explain that he is feeling sad and afraid.*

4. **◄ REREAD AND DISCUSS** The only time we see the prince's reaction to being thrown out is in the graphic story. In a small group, discuss how learning the prince's reaction impacts your perception of events.

SHORT RESPONSE

Cite Text Evidence Analyze the way you learn about Tom and the prince's similarities in the three versions of the story. Which version was most effective? Review your reading notes and **cite text evidence** in your response.

Possible response: It is easy to see what the characters are feeling in a graphic story. Tom looks longingly through the bars, and is happy to see the prince. The prince is very upset when the guard hits him as he leaves the palace. It is apparent that the two boys are identical, and that they strike up an immediate friendship. The speech bubbles show if they are shouting and are upset. In the final panel, the prince realizes what life is like for a pauper, as he is brutally beaten by his own guard.

128

---

4. **REREAD AND DISCUSS USING TEXT EVIDENCE** Have students review the ending of each version.

Ⓓ ASK STUDENTS to cite text evidence to support their analysis of how learning the prince's reaction impacts the reader's perception of events. *Students should cite the final panel as evidence that the prince is sad and afraid. They may say that this ending is sadder than the other two.*

SHORT RESPONSE

Cite Text Evidence Student responses will vary, but they should cite evidence from the text to support their analysis. Students should:

- analyze characterizations in all three versions.
- determine which version most effectively showed the similarities between Tom and the prince.
- cite textual evidence to support their response.

TO CHALLENGE STUDENTS . . .

Students will benefit from comparing and contrasting the experience of reading a drama to hearing it read aloud as a reader's theater performance or seeing it acted out. First, invite students to reread Joellen Bland's dramatization of *The Prince and the Pauper,* paying special attention to what they "see" or "hear" in their minds as they are reading. Then, work with students to prepare a performance of the script.

Assign students the parts of Prince Edward, Tom Canty, Two Women, Two Guards, and Villagers. You may also assign a stage director to read the stage directions. For more historical context, students may research the Tudor period of British history, and Prince Edward VI. Students may set the stage with simple props or designs that evoke the period of the scene.

ASK STUDENTS in the audience to contrast what they "see" and "hear" in their minds when they are reading the text to what they perceive when they listen or watch. After the performance, discuss as a class the differences between reading a drama and seeing or hearing it.

DIG DEEPER

1. With the class, return to novel excerpt Question 6, Reread, on page 120. Have students share their responses.

   ASK STUDENTS to cite the text evidence that led to their understanding of what happens after the prince leaves Tom.

   - Ask students what Tom and the prince discover in lines 122–125. *Students should say that Tom and the prince discover that they look alike.*
   - Have students cite text that shows that Tom and the prince look alike. *Students may identify "none could say which was you, and which the Prince of Wales" (lines 124–125).*
   - Have students cite text that shows that the prince left Tom. *Students may cite lines 134–136, "In a moment he…was out at the door and flying through the palace grounds…."*
   - Have students paraphrase what happens after the prince leaves Tom. *Possible answer: The prince demands that the soldier who bullied Tom unbar the gate. The prince thinks he is going to yell at the soldier, but instead the soldier hits him, and the villagers laugh at him. Then the soldier kicks the prince off the palace grounds.*
   - Ask students why the soldier did not recognize the prince. *The prince looked exactly like Tom, once he was wearing Tom's clothes.*

2. With the class, return to drama Question 5, Reread and Discuss, on page 124. Have students share their responses.

   ASK STUDENTS whether they were satisfied with the outcome of their small-group discussions. Have each group share their conclusions about how the plot unfolds to create a conflict at the end of the scene. What evidence did the group cite in the discussion?

   - Ask students to share personal insights that were not reported with the conclusions of the group. What evidence supported their personal conclusions?
   - As a class, draft a written response to Question 5 that is composed of the most compelling conclusions reported by groups and individuals. Demonstrate how to support conclusions with evidence from the text.

   ASK STUDENTS to return to their Short Response answer and revise it based on the class discussion.

CLOSE READING NOTES

The Role of Myths in Ancient Greece
from Greek Mythology

Essay by Simone Payment

Why This Text?

Understanding the role of myths in one culture can help students understand myths from other cultures. This lesson provides a basic understanding of the characters in Greek mythology that will help students understand allusions to these characters when encountered in conversation and literature.

View It!

Professional Development Podcast:

Text-Dependent Analysis

Key Learning Objective: The student will be able to analyze structure and cite textual evidence.

RI 1 Cite textual evidence.

RI 2 Determine central idea and details; provide a summary.

RI 3 Analyze text elements.

RI 5 Analyze structure.

RI 7 Integrate information presented in different media and formats.

SL 1 Engage effectively in a range of collaborative discussions.

SL 1a Come to discussions prepared.

SL 1b Follow rules for discussions, set goals, and define individual roles.

SL 1c Pose and respond to questions.

SL 1d Review key ideas and demonstrate understanding of multiple perspectives.

L 2a Use punctuation to set off nonrestrictive/parenthetical elements.

L 4a Use context as a clue to meaning.

L 4b Use Greek or Latin affixes and roots as clues to meaning.

L 6 Acquire and use academic and domain-specific vocabulary.

 Text Complexity Rubric

Quantitative Measures	**The Role of Myths in Ancient Greece *from* Greek Mythology** Lexile: 970L
Qualitative Measures	**Levels of Meaning/Purpose** single purpose, explicitly stated
	Structure clearly stated, sequential organization of main ideas and details
	Language Conventionality and Clarity some unfamiliar, academic, or domain-specific words
	Knowledge Demands some specialized knowledge required
Reader/Task Considerations	• Teacher determined • Vary by individual reader and type of text • See the Text X-Ray for suggested Reader/Task Considerations.

English Language Support Before teaching, use the Text X-Ray for an overview of the text's complexity. The Text X-Ray and the supports and scaffolds in the Teacher's Edition will help you guide students of different skill levels.

Meaning Making

Language Development

Effective Expression

Content Knowledge

Foundational Skills

Text Complexity: Qualitative Measures

Levels of Meaning/Purpose

single purpose, explicitly stated

Help students cite evidence in support of their ideas.

- Teacher's Edition side notes, pp. 364, 366, 369
- English Language Support, pp. 366, 369
- Strategies for Annotation, p. 367
- Cite Evidence, p. 369

ZOOM IN ON **CITING EVIDENCE** Remind students that when they **cite evidence**, they identify phrases and sentences in a text that support an idea. Write this statement on the board: *Eventually, bards began to write down the myths in the form of a long poem.* Then display lines 114–125.

- Ask students to find evidence in the paragraph that supports the main idea on the board.
- Then have them write a summary using the main idea and evidence on the board. Remind them to use words and expressions, such as *for example, also,* and *in addition*.

Structure

clearly stated, sequential organization of main ideas and details

Help students analyze the structure of an essay, identifying central ideas and supporting details.

- Teacher's Edition side notes, pp. 363, 365, 366, 367, 368, 369
- English Language Support, p. 363
- When Students Struggle, p. 368
- Strategies for Annotation, p. 369
- Analyze Structure, p. 369

To reteach how to analyze structure, see

- Analyze Structure, p. 372a

 Use It! **Level Up Tutorials:** Main Idea and Supporting Details; Reading for Details

ZOOM IN ON **ANALYZING STRUCTURE** Read aloud the headings in the essay. Explain that a heading signals that a new **central idea** will be developed. The words in the heading often give readers a clue to the central idea.

- Have students reread lines 62–89, focusing on the central idea. Ask them to write down a possible heading for this central idea. Have them prepare to defend their ideas by identifying supporting details.
- Ask students to share their headings with the class. Together decide which one best reflects the central idea of these lines. *(Possible response: Myths, Central to Greek Life, History, and Culture)*

Language Conventionality and Clarity

some unfamiliar, academic, or domain-specific words

Teach unfamiliar vocabulary in context.

- Teacher's Edition Critical Vocabulary notes, pp. 364, 365, 367, 371
- Applying Academic Vocabulary, p. 364
- English Language Support, p. 371
- Strategies for Annotation, p. 371
- Vocabulary Strategy: Latin Roots, p. 371

Support reading and analysis of the selection.

- Teacher's Edition side notes, pp. 368, 372
- English Language Support, pp. 363, 364, 365, 368, 372
- Language Conventions: Parentheses, p. 372

ZOOM IN ON **IDENTIFYING ROOTS** Explain that the Critical Vocabulary words in this selection have Latin or Greek roots. Ask students to work with a partner to look these words up in a dictionary: *monumental (monument), dialect, isolate, immortal (mortal)*. Ask students to identify the root of each word, using the form in parentheses as needed; explain whether the root is Latin or Greek; and discuss how the meaning of the root relates to the meaning of the word as it is understood today. Invite pairs to share what they have learned about each word's origin.

Knowledge Demands

some specialized knowledge required

Support English Learners in understanding ideas about the author and topic of the essay.

- Teacher's Edition Author note, p. 363

ZOOM IN ON **BUILDING LITERARY BACKGROUND** Give students information about characters mentioned in the essay.

- Arachne is mentioned in lines 79–81. The mortal Arachne insulted the gods by weaving a tapestry that showed them misbehaving. Arachne realized her mistake and hanged herself. Athena brought her back to life as a spider so that she could weave all day.
- Poseidon is named in line 85. He is the god of the sea and second-most powerful god.
- Zeus and Aphrodite are mentioned in line 145. Zeus is the king of the gods and Aphrodite is the goddess of love.

Suggested Reader/Task Considerations

You might consider the following before assigning this essay to students.

- Are students familiar enough with the topic to understand the essay?
- Will students be able to comprehend the author's main ideas?

ZOOM IN ON **SUPPORTING COMPREHENSION**

- Display a web diagram with "Greek myths" in the center. Write students' ideas about myths in the web. Explain that the essay shows why myths were important to the ancient Greeks and why they are also part of our culture.
- Have students listen to the audio recording of the essay. After each paragraph, have them work with a partner to identify the main idea.

TEACH

CLOSE READ

Simone Payment Have students read the information about the author. Explain that this essay is an excerpt from Simone Payment's larger work *Greek Mythology*. If students enjoy this selection, suggest that they explore the larger work to learn more about Greek myths and what tales tell us about ourselves and our world.

SETTING A PURPOSE Direct students to use the Setting a Purpose prompt to focus their reading. Remind students to write down questions they have as they read.

Analyze Structure

RI 1,
RI 5,
RI 6

(LINES 1–14)

Explain to students that an **essay** is a short work of nonfiction that deals with a single subject. Point out that an essay usually begins with an introduction.

Ⓐ CITE TEXT EVIDENCE Ask students to reread lines 1–7 and tell its purpose, citing words and phrases to support their idea. (*These lines introduce and define myths as "stories that have been passed down through the ages" and "tales of gods and goddesses, monsters, and adventure." They explain that myths are ancient stories that are still enjoyed today.*)

Ⓑ ASK STUDENTS how lines 1–7 help set up the text that follows in lines 8–14. (*The discussion of myths leads to the subject of classical Greece, which readers need to learn about in order to understand the role of myths in that culture.*)

English Language Support

Have students look through their text and share what they notice about how the text is organized. (*It has paragraphs that are separated by heads.*) Explain that the structure, or the way that the essay is organized, helps the reader understand what the author is discussing. Then read aloud the first paragraph with students following along in their books.

ASK STUDENTS to describe why the author included this paragraph. (*to introduce the topic of the essay*) Help students describe what the first paragraph explains about myths before they answer the questions with a partner.

Simone Payment *has college degrees in both psychology and education. She has taught elementary school, worked in book publishing, and worked for a health care company. Payment is the author of dozens of books for children and young adults. She has written biographies of both historical and contemporary characters. She has also written nonfiction books about a wide variety of subjects, including Greek mythology, the pony express, famous movie monsters, and robotics.*

The Role of Myths in Ancient Greece
from Greek Mythology

Essay by Simone Payment

SETTING A PURPOSE As you read, focus on the origin of myths and on understanding the relevance of myths in ancient Greek culture.

Ⓐ Many cultures have stories that have been passed down through the ages. These stories—called myths—are tales of gods and goddesses, monsters, and adventure. The myths from ancient Greece may be the best known of all cultures' mythologies, and perhaps the most exciting. The myths of the Greeks, which have been told for thousands of years, are still enjoyed today.

What we call classical Greece (from the sixth to the fourth centuries BC) gave future civilizations more than just stories.
10 The ancient Greeks made huge contributions to modern culture in Greece and elsewhere. In fact, ancient Greece is often called the cradle of Western civilization. This is because so much of modern life is based on contributions from the Greeks. The United States current system of government, democracy, came from Greek civilization. The Olympics Ⓑ

(c) ©Heritage Images/Corbis

The Role of Myths in Ancient Greece **363**

English Language Support

Condense Ideas Explain that the definition of *myth* is provided in two sentences in lines 1–3 and that combining the sentences will create a more precise definition.

- Reread lines 1–3 aloud. Work with students to create a detailed definition from the two sentences.
- Have students combine the sentences independently, using embedded clauses or nominalization to create a precise definition.

Cite Evidence (LINES 26–34)   RI 1, RI 2

Explain to students that each paragraph in an essay adds to the information about the topic.

Ⓒ CITE TEXT EVIDENCE Ask students to reread lines 26–34 and summarize the information. Remind students to cite evidence from the text to support the summary. *(Each city-state had its own mythology because citizens from one city-state didn't usually visit citizens from another city-state. Details: forests, mountains, and distance separated city-states; people often lived their whole lives in their own city-state)*

CRITICAL VOCABULARY

revolutionary: Greek thinkers made revolutionary discoveries.

ASK STUDENTS what recent changes in our world they might consider revolutionary. *(Answers may vary but should contain the idea of a complete and/or sudden change. Possibilities include the Internet, cell phones, Skype, and so on.)*

dialect: Dialects spoken in each city-state varied.

ASK STUDENTS why different dialects would affect the spread of myths. *(Answers will vary but should include the idea of regional language variations, such as pronunciation, grammar, or vocabulary, making it hard for people to understand one another and their stories.)*

immortal: The Greeks believed the gods and goddesses were immortal.

ASK STUDENTS if they can think of anything in the natural world that is immortal. Why or why not? *(Nothing in the natural world is immortal. All living things must die, though some things, such as trees, live much, much longer than other things.)*

English Language Support

Culturally Responsive Instruction Lead a class discussion about how the dialects in Greece helped create a barrier to the sharing of myths.

ASK STUDENTS to share ideas about the difficulty of language barriers and ways to overcome them.

---

began in ancient Greece. Great Greek thinkers made **revolutionary** discoveries in astronomy, biology, and medicine. Ancient Greeks also wrote stories and plays that are still read and performed today. Their art and architecture also
20 live on in modern times.

Ancient Greece was not in the exact location where Greece is today. It included parts of what are now Turkey and Italy. There were dense forests and steep, rocky cliffs along the coast. Inland, there were snow-covered mountains. Many islands dotted the Aegean Sea off the eastern coast of Greece.

In the earliest days of Greece, the country was divided into small, individually governed areas called city-states. City-states were often separated by forests or mountains and were far apart, and the **dialects** spoken in each city-state
30 varied. Because of these barriers, people did not travel much, so city-states did not frequently interact. If you were born in a particular city-state, you would usually live there your whole life. As a result, each city-state had its own myths that most residents knew and told over and over again.

Starting in the fourth century BC, Alexander the Great (the king of Macedon, a part of Greece) began invading other countries. His successes brought Greeks together politically. Some city-states began to work together, sometimes against a common enemy. By that time, they also shared a
40 common language. People began to travel and move to other city-states. They also began to travel outside of Greece. This travel helped spread Greek myths around the country and to other countries.

Everyday life was not always easy in ancient Greece. People did not live as long as they do now. Life was more difficult, with no modern conveniences such as heat or running water. People had to kill animals and farm for food. The hardships in their daily lives led the ancient Greeks to look to their gods and goddesses for help. They believed that the **immortal**
50 gods and goddesses had a great deal of power. The gods and goddesses could be helpful to humans if the humans showed them the proper respect. To show respect to the gods and goddesses, Greeks worshipped at their local temples. They wanted to stay in good favor with the higher powers for fear that they might be punished. They also believed that the gods and goddesses might punish not just them but their whole community.

revolutionary
(rĕv´ə-lōō´shə-nĕr´ē) *adj.* Something that is *revolutionary* causes important and sometimes sudden changes in a situation.

dialect
(dī´ə-lĕkt´) *n.* A *dialect* is a regional language variation, characterized by differences in pronunciation, grammar, or vocabulary.

immortal
(ĭ-môr´tl) *adj.* If someone or something is *immortal*, it will never die.

APPLYING ACADEMIC VOCABULARY

emphasize	period	tradition

THINK-PAIR-SHARE Have students turn to a partner to discuss the following questions. Guide students to include the academic vocabulary words *emphasize, period,* and *tradition* in their responses. Ask volunteers to share their responses with the class.

- Why does the author **emphasize** the **traditions** of ancient Greece?
- How can a myth hold clues to the **period** and culture during which it was created?

In addition to regular visits to local temples, Greeks also held special festivals to honor specific gods or goddesses. Each
60 god and goddess worshipped by the Greeks played a specific role in life.

The word "myth" comes from the Greek word *mythos*, which literally means "story." However myths were much more than simple stories to the Greeks. They were an important part of Greek life. They were passed from person to person and from generation to generation.

Myths tell several types of stories. Some are tales of adventure based on actual events. For example, Homer's *The Iliad* is based on the Trojan War, a ten-year war between the
70 Greeks and the people of the Turkish city of Troy.

Myths were more than just accounts of exciting occurrences. They also told stories about such **monumental** events as the creation of human beings. In ancient Greece, there was no one text, such as the Bible or the Koran, to explain everything about a particular religion's view of the world. Instead, myths served the purpose of providing answers.

Myths also taught important lessons. For example, they might have warned against being too proud. One version of
80 the Greek myth of Arachne tells how Arachne was turned into a spider for bragging about her weaving skills.

The ancient Greeks also created myths to help them make sense of natural phenomena[1] that they could explain in no other way. For example, the Greeks did not understand why earthquakes occurred. A story about the god Poseidon punishing his enemies by shaking the ground underneath them offered Greeks an answer. Poseidon was also believed to control the sea. His changing moods could explain why the sea was calm one day and stormy the next.

monumental
(mŏn´yə-mĕn´tl) *adj.*
A *monumental* event is one that is of outstanding significance.

Different Cultures, Similar Myths

90 If you study ancient cultures, you can see that many of them have myths. Myths are often similar from culture to culture. This is most likely because there are certain qualities of life that are important or meaningful to people everywhere.

---

[1] **phenomena** (fĭ-nŏm´ə-nə): occurrences, circumstances, or facts that can be perceived by the senses.

CLOSE READ

Analyze Structure

RI 1, RI 2, RI 5

(LINES 67–89)

Explain to students that essays usually have a **pattern of organization,** which is the way that the ideas and information are arranged and presented. Tell students that one common pattern of organization is by central (main) idea and supporting details. Remind students that the **central (main) idea** is the most important idea, and the **supporting details** are words, details, and phrases that support that idea.

D **CITE TEXT EVIDENCE** Have students reread lines 67–89 and identify this section's central idea. (*Myths tell several types of stories.*) Ask students to explain how each paragraph in this section supports this central idea. (*Each paragraph describes a different type of myth: tales of adventures in lines 67–70; myths that explain events in lines 71–77; myths that teach lessons in lines 78–81; myths that make sense of natural phenomenon in lines 82–89.*)

CRITICAL VOCABULARY

monumental: Greek myths told stories about monumental events, such as the creation of human beings.

ASK STUDENTS to explain why they think myths addressed monumental events. (*Ancient Greeks did not have much scientific information about the natural world. They wanted explanations for these large, or monumental, questions they had about where people came from or how the world began.*)

English Language Support

Express Opinions Write this sentence starter on the board, "A myth written about the time we live in _____." Clarify that students will be writing about what a myth about today would be like. Remind them to use their imaginations and to look back at lines 1–89 to justify their opinions with evidence from the text.

• Coach individual students through the process of completing a sentence with the sentence starter. Encourage them to use the modal expressions *can* and *has to*. Have them read their sentences to each other in small groups.

• Have students write several sentences voicing their opinion about a modern-day myth using the modal expressions *maybe/probably, can/could,* or *must*. Have them share their writing and discuss their ideas in small groups.

• Ask students to write an opinion paragraph about a modern-day myth using expressions such as *should/would, might,* and *probably/ certainly/definitely* and the phrase *in my opinion*. Tell students to include information from the text to support their ideas.

CLOSE READ

Cite Evidence (LINES 94–102)   RI 1, RI 2

Explain to students that some informational paragraphs support the central idea by focusing on a single example. Often in these paragraphs, the single example will be developed in considerable depth, over two or more sentences. Other examples, if provided at all, are less well developed.

 CITE TEXT EVIDENCE Have students reread lines 94–102 and identify the central idea of the paragraph. *(It is the first sentence: "Each culture creates myths that reflect its beliefs, which are often a result of its circumstances.")* Ask what examples and details the author gives to support the central idea. *(The first example is geography. This example is supported by the information about Mount Olympus being "known as the home of the gods in Greek mythology." Another example is that a culture personalizes its myths based on what is important to that culture.)*

English Language Support

Display lines 94–102. Review the meaning of *circumstances*, "a condition related to the culture." Read the text aloud and point out the phrase *for example*. Tell students that the author included this phrase to help the reader understand how ideas are connected in the paragraph. Then have volunteers identify the central idea of the paragraph and the examples and details the author provides to support it.

Integrate Information   RI 7

(PHOTO AND CAPTION)

Remind students that they can integrate information in the text with information presented in visuals, such as photos and captions.

 ASK STUDENTS to tell how the photo and its caption support and add to the information in the text. *(The photo shows the geography of Greece and in particular Mount Olympus; the caption adds the detail that the gods and goddesses, known as Olympians because they lived on Olympus, were said to have claimed the mountain after winning a war.)*

Mount Olympus is the highest mountain in Greece. It is regarded as the home of gods and goddesses in Greek mythology. The gods and goddesses were known as Olympians who, according to myth, claimed the mountain after winning a war. As a result, Mount Olympus became a symbol of ancient cultural development in Greece.

Each culture creates myths that reflect its beliefs, which are often a result of its circumstances. For example, myths may be influenced by the geography of the country in which a civilization lives. Mount Olympus, a towering, snow-covered mountain in Greece, became known as the home of the gods in Greek mythology. The top of the mountain was so high
100   and so unreachable to the Greeks that they said the gods and goddesses must live there. Myths are also personalized by what is important to a particular country or culture.

©Panos Karas/Shutterstock

TO CHALLENGE STUDENTS . . .

Interpret Literature How might myths created in today's world be different than or the same as myths that were created in ancient Greece? What creates the need for myths in a culture, and do those conditions exist in the modern world? Is it simply a love of good stories, or is it something different?

ASK STUDENTS to discuss these questions with a partner or small group. Remind students to think about the reasons for creating myths, how myths spread from place to place, and how different cultures tend to create similar myths that still reflect a culture's particular beliefs. Have students share their ideas with the class.

How Myths Spread

Many of the Greek myths were based on people and events from even earlier times. In the very early days of Greece (about 2000 BC), Greeks had huge fleets of ships and attacked neighboring countries. About 1,000 years later, Greece had entered a less heroic era. People were poor and life was hard, so they told stories of a more exciting time. Men called bards (poets or story-tellers) would memorize the stories and then
110 travel around the countryside, telling these tales. During the time when each city-state was **isolated** from the others, stories varied. Bards might change the story slightly, adding their own exciting details.

Eventually, myths were written down in a format similar to a poem. Some of the myths, when written down, were up to 1,000 lines long. Homer (circa² eighth or ninth century BC) was one of the most famous bards. He wrote two landmark works, *The Iliad* and *The Odyssey. The Iliad* tells the story of the Trojan War. *The Odyssey* tells the many adventures of
120 the Greek hero Odysseus. Two other famous written myths are *Theogony* and *Works and Days* by Hesiod (circa 800 BC). *Theogony* is the story of the creation of the gods. *Works and Days* offers advice on how to farm or on which days to do certain things, like cut your fingernails. Also included in *Works and Days* are myths, such as the story of Pandora.

Greeks heard myths at an early age. Elders³ would tell the stories to young children. Sometimes the stories were used as warnings to get children to behave. Young children also learned about myths at school, although in most places in
130 ancient Greece, only boys went to school.

Adults heard myths at social gatherings and informal meetings. Myths were also recited as a part of rituals at religious temples. In addition, bards might tell myths—or even sing them—for wealthy people or kings. The theater was an important part of Greek life, and sometimes choirs would perform myths as plays.

isolate
(ī´sə-lāt´) *v.* To *isolate* something is to set it apart or separate it from others.

---

² **circa** (sûr´kə): in approximately; about or around the specified time.
³ **elders** (ĕl´dərz): older, influential members of a family, tribe, or community.

CLOSE READ

Analyze Structure
RI 1, RI 5

(LINES 103–113)

Explain to students that authors use text features such as headings as part of the structure, or pattern of organization of their writing.

G ASK STUDENTS what information they expect to find in this section of the text. *(The head is "How Myths Spread," so this information should be about different ways that myths spread throughout Greece and perhaps to other parts of the world.)*

H CITE TEXT EVIDENCE Ask students how lines 103–113 develop the section "How Myths Spread." Have students identify the central idea and cite words and phrases that support their responses. *(These lines tell how myths began and one way they spread in ancient Greece. The central idea is that myths began when life in Greece became less exciting and people started telling stories about exciting events of the past. Poets or storytellers, called bards, would memorize these exciting stories and travel around telling them to others. This was one way myths spread.)*

CRITICAL VOCABULARY

isolate: The Greek city-states were once isolated from each other.

ASK STUDENTS to tell how being isolated affected the stories of each Greek city-state. *(When the city-states were isolated, stories varied because bards added their own exciting details, improving the story as they told it each time.)*

Strategies for Annotation

Cite Evidence
RI 1, RI 2, RI 5

Have students reread lines 126–130. Tell them to use their eBook annotation tools to do the following:

- Highlight in yellow the central idea.
- Underline details that support the central idea.
- On a note, tell how this paragraph fits into the overall structure of the essay.

Greeks heard myths at an early age. Elders would tell the stories to young children. Sometimes the stories were used as warnings to get children to behave. Young children also learned about myths at school, although in most places in ancient Greece, only boys went to school.

tells another way myths spread

CLOSE READ

Analyze Structure

RI 1,
RI 2,
RI 5

(LINES 137–152)

Remind students that looking for central ideas and details in a work can help them better understand a text. Explain that sometimes they need to analyze layers of information in order to understand a work's structure.

CITE TEXT EVIDENCE Have students identify the central idea in lines 137–152. *(There are several ways we have learned about Greek myths.)* Then, ask students to identify two basic details that support this central idea. *(One way we learn about myths is through written works; another way is through artwork.)* Finally, ask students to cite examples that support each way we know about Greek myths. *(Examples for written works include books and plays. Examples for artwork include sculptures, paintings, mosaics, vases, and coins.)* Then, have students tell how these lines illustrate the structure of this text.

COLLABORATIVE DISCUSSION Have students review the essay one section at a time, listing their ideas and evidence as they review each section. When partners complete their review, have all pairs share their ideas with the group.

ASK STUDENTS to share any questions they generated in the course of reading and discussing this selection.

English Language Support

Support Opinions Remind students that in their discussion they will need to support their ideas with evidence from the essay. Provide the following sentence frames to help them express their ideas.

To support an idea:
Please look at line(s) _____, on page _____ because that text supports my idea that _____.

To disagree kindly:
I think you made an interesting comment, but _____.

To agree with a restatement:
I like your comment because you said _____.

How Do We Know About Greek Myths?

Greek myths have been passed down for thousands of years. There are several ways we have learned about them. One is through written works, such as books or plays, that were
140 created by later cultures based on stories from ancient Greece. These works have survived and are still enjoyed today. We have also learned about ancient Greek myths through artwork such as sculptures and paintings. The Greeks sometimes told their myths in the form of art, for example creating a sculpture of Zeus or a painting of Aphrodite. Sometimes they made mosaics[4] depicting important myths. They also decorated vases and other containers with stories of their heroes, heroines, gods, and goddesses. Even Greek coins were often decorated with images from myths. Many Greek
150 sculptures still exist today in museums. We can even see some floor mosaics in their original locations. Hopefully, these relics[5] will be preserved for years to come.

COLLABORATIVE DISCUSSION With a partner, discuss ways myths were important to the ancient Greeks and why myths are still relevant today. Cite evidence from the text to support your ideas.

---

[4] **mosaics** (mō-zā´ĭks): pictures or decorative designs made of small colored pieces of tile or stone, set into a surface.

[5] **relics** (rĕl´ĭks): things that have lasted over time, especially those objects or customs whose original culture has disappeared.

WHEN STUDENTS STRUGGLE . . .

Have students create a chart of the information in lines 137–152 like the one shown to help them understand the organization of the information.

> **CENTRAL IDEA:** *We have learned about myths in several ways.*

> **DETAIL 1:** *through written works*
> *Examples: books, plays*

> **DETAIL 2:** *through artwork*
> *Examples: sculptures, paintings, mosaics, vases, coins*

Analyze Structure

RI 5

A **pattern of organization** is the way ideas and information are arranged in a nonfiction text. One common pattern of organization authors use is **central (main) idea and supporting details**. The **central**, or most important, **idea** is supported by **details**, words, phrases, or sentences that tell more about the central idea.

If you look at lines 94–102 in "The Role of Myths," you can tell that the first sentence of the paragraph expresses the central idea that each culture creates myths that reflect its beliefs. The sentences that follow give details about how the geography of ancient Greece helped shape these beliefs.

Questions such as the following will help you analyze the central idea and supporting details as a pattern of organization:

- For an individual paragraph: What is the central idea? How are the details arranged to tell more about the central idea?
- For sections under headings: What central idea does the author discuss in this section? How do details add more information?
- How does a section or paragraph fit into the overall structure of the text? How does it help develop the writer's ideas?

Cite Evidence

RI 1

When you analyze a text, you examine it carefully for a reason, such as to figure out its structure, to determine an author's point of view, or to see how well a writer presents and supports a claim.

To support your analysis of a text, you need to **cite textual evidence**. This means that you have to identify specific pieces of relevant information from the text to support your ideas. When you cite evidence, you show that your analysis connects to the text in a logical way. Keep in mind these points:

- The evidence needs to clearly support your analysis or idea. For example, if you are analyzing how geography helped form Greek mythology in "The Role of Myths," you might cite evidence that includes information from lines 26–34.
- Whether you are presenting your analysis orally or in written form, it is a good idea to use linking words and phrases, such as *for example, because,* or *this shows.* Linking words and phrases help emphasize to readers or listeners how your idea is connected to the text.
- If in your writing you quote directly from the text to cite evidence for your ideas, set off the quoted material with quotation marks.

TEACH

CLOSE READ

Analyze Structure

RI 1,
RI 2,
RI 5

Discuss the terms and the levels of development within one paragraph, one section, and the essay as a whole. Have volunteers identify the central, or main, idea of the essay and one or two supporting details. Then, discuss the central idea of one of the sections, along with its supporting details. Finally, take a close look at one paragraph, having volunteers once again identify the central idea and supporting details. Then, ask students how the paragraph develops the overall ideas of the essay.

Cite Evidence

RI 1

Discuss the definition of the phrase *cite textual evidence* as provided in the lesson. Then, ask volunteers to make an assertion about the essay and support that assertion by citing evidence within the text. Repeat the exercise with another student and a different assertion.

English Language Support

Use Linking Words Review that it is important to use linking words and phrases to support ideas. Have students work in pairs to write an idea about the text and then cite text evidence with sentences that include linking words such as *first, next, at the same time, for example, in the first place, as a result,* or *on the other hand.*

Strategies for Annotation 🖍 🗐 *Annotate it!*

Analyze Structure

RI 2,
RI 5

Share these strategies for guided or independent analysis:

- Highlight in yellow the central idea within one paragraph.
- Underline supporting and explanatory details.
- Write a sentence describing how the paragraph contributes to the overall structure and development of ideas in the essay.

Starting in the fourth century BC, Alexander the Great (the king of Macedon, a part of Greece) began invading other countries. His successes brought Greeks together politically. Some city-states began to work together, . . . shared a common language. People began to travel. . . . This travel helped spread Greek myths around the country and to other countries.

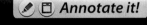

explains one way Greek myths spread

PRACTICE & APPLY

Analyzing the Text

RI 1, RI 2,
RI 3, RI 5

Possible answers:

1. *The central idea is that classical Greece passed on more than stories; details include that Greece is often referred to as "the cradle of Western civilization" and information about contributions the ancient Greeks made to Western civilization in government and in the arts and sciences.*

2. *The central idea is that ancient Greece was made up of city-states. Details include that different dialects and geographical barriers kept people from traveling very much, so each city-state wrote and knew just their own myths. The next two paragraphs follow the same pattern of organization because they begin with a central idea and include details that tell more about it.*

3. *I would describe Poseidon as powerful, passionate, and vengeful; the text says that he controlled the seas and caused earthquakes, that he punished his enemies, and that his moods often changed from one day to the next.*

4. *They "heard myths at an early age" and in school; myths were shared "at social gatherings and informal meetings" and by traveling bards; myths were used in religious ceremonies and performed as theater.*

5. *Homer wrote* The Iliad *and* The Odyssey, *both of which tell about the Trojan War and the adventures of the Greek hero Odysseus. Hesiod wrote a myth about the creation of the gods and a book about everyday tasks that also included myths. The Greeks recorded their myths in artwork such as sculpture, paintings, mosaics, and architecture that can still be seen today.*

6. *Each subheading is a clue to the central idea of each section, and each paragraph contains a central idea that supports the subheading. This organization is logical and clear; it makes the important ideas pretty easy to identify.*

FOR STANDARD ENGLISH LEARNERS

Remind students that clear pronunciation is important when they share their ideas. Review the pronunciations of /ch/ and /sh/ with the words *unreachable* (line 100), *children* (line 127), *hardships* (line 47), *worshipped* (line 53), and *punished* (line 55). Read each sentence containing the word, asking students to echo read using their texts. Then ask students to repeat the words containing the /ch/ and /sh/ sounds correcting their pronunciation as necessary.

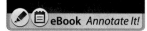 eBook *Annotate It!*

Analyzing the Text

RI 1, RI 2, RI 3,
RI 5, SL 1a–d

Cite Text Evidence   Support your responses with evidence from the text.

1. **Identify**   Review lines 8–20. Identify the central idea in this paragraph. What details support the central idea?

2. **Identify Patterns**   Reread lines 26–57. What is the central idea of the first paragraph, and what details tell more about it? Tell whether the next two paragraphs follow a similar pattern of organization.

3. **Draw Conclusions**   Reread lines 82–89. Based on what you learn in this paragraph, how would you describe the character or personality of the god Poseidon?

4. **Cite Evidence**   Review lines 103–136 in the section "How Myths Spread." Identify evidence that supports the conclusion that myths were intertwined with every part of the lives of the ancient Greeks.

5. **Cite Evidence**   Review lines 114–152. Cite evidence to support the conclusion that myths helped to preserve Greek culture.

6. **Evaluate**   How does the author's use of **subheadings,** or titles that indicate the beginning of a new topic, contribute to the pattern of organization used in "The Role of Myths in Ancient Greece"? Tell whether you think this pattern of organization is effective and why.

PERFORMANCE TASK

Speaking Activity: Discussion With a small group, have a discussion about the purpose of myths and how they influenced ancient Greek culture.

- As a group, decide on questions your group will attempt to answer.
- Pick group moderators who will keep track of the questions and make sure that all members have opportunities to share ideas.

- Have group members review the text and prepare ideas and details to answer the questions.
- During the discussion, listen to ideas closely and respectfully. Find opportunities to share additional information or perspectives.
- Review key ideas together and demonstrate understanding through shared reflection and paraphrasing.

Assign this
performance task.

PERFORMANCE TASK

SL 1a–d

Speaking Activity: Discussion Guide each group as they complete their discussion plans. Remind them to

- appoint someone to take notes during the discussion
- follow discussion rules and set goals and deadlines
- use appropriate eye contact, volume, and clear pronunciation as they share their ideas.

Critical Vocabulary

revolutionary	dialect	immortal
monumental	isolate	

Practice and Apply Answer each question.

1. Which vocabulary word goes with *speak*? Why?
2. Which vocabulary word goes with *task* or *significant*? Why?
3. Which vocabulary word goes with *change* and *radical*? Why?
4. Which vocabulary word goes with *alone*? Why?
5. Which vocabulary word goes with *live forever*? Why?

Vocabulary Strategy: Latin Roots

Sometimes you can figure out the meaning of an unfamiliar word by examining its root. A **root** is a word part that contains the core meaning of the word. For example, *volut-* comes from a Latin root that can mean "turn" or "roll." You can find this root in the vocabulary word *revolutionary* and use the meaning of the root to figure out that *revolutionary* describes a major change, or turn, in thinking.

Another way to use Latin roots to help you determine the meaning of an unfamiliar word is to think of other words that include the same root and create a word family. Then you can think over the related meanings of the words in that family to help you arrive at a meaning for the unfamiliar word.

Practice and Apply Complete a word web like the one shown with other words that share the roots *volut-* and *volv-*. Tell how the meanings of the words are related.

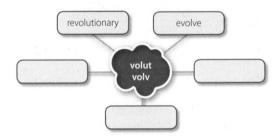

PRACTICE & APPLY

Critical Vocabulary

Possible answers:

1. *dialect*
2. *monumental*
3. *revolutionary*
4. *isolate*
5. *immortal*

Explanations of answers should include a clear understanding of the meaning of each word.

Vocabulary Strategy: Latin Roots

Possible answers:

revolution, revolve, evolution, evolutionary, revolt, involve, volume

Explanations of answers should include a clear understanding of the meaning of each word.

English Language Support

Before students complete the activity on Latin Roots, work as a group to brainstorm possible words to include in the web. As students propose words, have volunteers look up the words in a dictionary to confirm that they each have *volut-* or *volv-* as a root. Then have students work in pairs to write explanations of how the meanings of the words are related. Remind them to use a dictionary to help them define the words and to write in complete sentences.

Strategies for Annotation 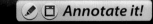 Annotate it!

Latin Roots

Have students use their eBook annotation tools to do the following:

- Highlight the word *revolutionary* on line 17.
- Use what you know about the Latin root *volut* to make a guess at the word's meaning.
- Confirm the meaning in a dictionary.
- Make a note that shows other words that contain the same root.

began in ancient Greece. Great Greek thinkers made revolutionary discoveries in astronomy, biology, and medicine. Ancient Greeks also wrote stories and plays that are still read and performed today. Their art and architecture also live on in modern times.

> revolt, evolve, involve

Language Conventions: Parentheses

L 2a

Explain to students that the chart shows just some of the ways parentheses can be used. Invite volunteers to come up with familiar examples for each category. Have students discuss the effect of parentheses in a sentence and how that effect is different from the effect that commas have in a sentence. Ask how writers might decide whether to use parentheses or commas to set off information within a sentence.

Answers:

1. *Gloria introduced us to Lily (I think her last name is Nicholls) at the party this weekend.*

2. *Paris (often called the City of Lights) is one of the world's most popular tourist destinations.*

3. *The reception will be held at the Hubbard Hotel (west of Marlborough Avenue) on Saturday from one to five o'clock.*

4. *Mr. Martinez (Gina's uncle) will be picking us up at the airport.*

5. *Players must hold a minimum of three (3) cards at all times.*

6. *Available to all residents of Pine Grove, the library (open every day except Monday) offers a wealth of reading materials in all formats.*

English Language Support

After students have completed the activity, explain that it is important to make sure that the text they put in parentheses is not part of the sentence grammatically.

ASK STUDENTS to practice recognizing the correct structure by rewriting the Practice and Apply sentences without the material in parentheses. Tell them to read each sentence aloud to make sure that it still makes sense.

English Language Support

Connect Ideas Remind students that parentheses are one way to connect or clarify ideas in a sentence. Have students practice joining ideas by combining these phrases to make sentences.

- it was snowing/Mr. Martinez rode (didn't ride) his bike to work
- Gloria drives to work/highways are important/people don't like to pay for repairs
- Alex's car was broken/he had (didn't have) enough money to buy a new one

- Work with students to create compound sentences with the phrases using *and, but,* or *so.* Have them chorally read each written sentence.

- Have students work in pairs to write sentences that include the phrases listed. They should add words or phrases to give reasons for something happening in the sentence. Remind them that *even though* or *although* can be used to start a clause that explains why something happened when the rest of the sentence makes it seem as if it wouldn't happen.

Language Conventions: Parentheses

L 2a

Parentheses are punctuation marks that are used to set off useful but less important information in a sentence. Here's an example from "The Role of Myths in Ancient Greece":

> **What we call classical Greece (from the sixth to the fourth centuries BC) gave future civilizations more than just stories.**

The information within the parentheses clarifies what the author calls "classical Greece," but it is of less importance than the rest of the information in the sentence.

Here are some reasons you might use parentheses:

> To enclose information that is related but not of primary importance:
> *The movie (we all loved it) runs about ninety minutes.*
>
> To enclose directions or other information that explains something:
> *Sam's Shoe Store (at the Cherry Mall) is having a storewide sale.*
>
> To repeat numbers or figures to ensure accuracy:
> *The cost of the service will be three hundred dollars ($300) a month.*

Use parentheses so that information you want to include but that is not of great importance doesn't interrupt the flow of a sentence.

Practice and Apply For each sentence, write the word or words that should be in parentheses.

1. Gloria introduced us to Lily I think her last name is Nicholls at the party this weekend.

2. Paris often called the City of Lights is one of the world's most popular tourist destinations.

3. The reception will be held at the Hubbard Hotel west of Marlborough Avenue on Saturday from one to five o'clock.

4. Mr. Martinez Gina's uncle will be picking us up at the airport.

5. Players must hold a minimum of three 3 cards at all times.

6. Available to all residents of Pine Grove, the library open every day except Monday offers a wealth of reading materials in all formats.

Generate Discussion Questions

TEACH

Explain to students that an important part of participating in discussions is being able to ask and answer questions. Tell students that asking good questions will help them not only in discussions but also when doing research and planning writing projects.

Point out that some questions are better than others for creating good discussions.

- **Closed questions** will have short answers, such as simple facts or yes and no answers. These questions do not yield good discussions.
- **Open questions** require a long answer and often begin with the words *how* or *why*. These questions usually create good discussions and ideas for additional questions and discussion.

Explain to students that they can improve their questions by using specific types of question stems. Review the examples below with students.

What is the main idea of . . . ?
What is the cause (effect) of . . . ?
What is a new example of . . . ?
What if . . . ?
Explain why . . .   Explain how . . .
How does . . . affect . . . ?
How does this relate to . . . ?
What conclusions can we draw about . . . ?
What is the difference between . . . and . . . ?
How are . . . and . . . similar?
How would I use . . . to . . . ?
What are the strengths and weaknesses of . . . ?
What is the best . . . and why?

PRACTICE AND APPLY

Have small groups or partners work together to formulate questions. Assign a topic or have students choose their own. Ask students to create charts of their questions to share and discuss with the class. Have students keep their charts to help them with Performance Tasks and other activities as needed.

 INTERACTIVE LESSON Have students complete the tutorials in this lesson: **Participating in Collaborative Discussions.**

Analyzing Structure

RETEACH

Review the terms *pattern of organization, central (main) idea,* and *supporting details*. Point out that most essays, such as "The Role of Myths in Ancient Greece," have a clear structure in which a pattern of organization can be identified and analyzed.

Have small groups work together and analyze the sections of "The Role of Myths in Ancient Greece." Ask each group member to independently break the section down into its central idea and details, using a Spider Map, and share his or her ideas with the group.

- **Lines 44–57**, everyday life in ancient Greece
- **Lines 62–89**, what myths are

Once individual students have their analyses, have groups compare individual results and discuss any differences. Then, have the whole class come together to discuss how these sections of text develop the author's ideas and fit into the overall structure of the essay.

 LEVEL UP TUTORIALS Assign one or more of the following *Level Up* tutorials: **Main Idea and Supporting Details; Reading for Details**

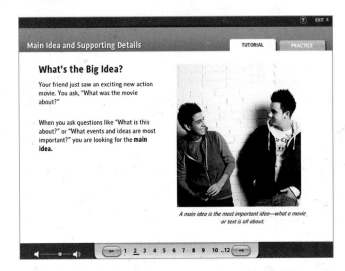

INDEPENDENT READING

Students can complete an analysis of the essay or apply the skill to another informational text. Have students record central ideas and details. Have them share their analyses with other students.

 INTERACTIVE GRAPHIC ORGANIZER Students can use a **Spider Map** to organize information.

WHAT TALES TELL

The FYI site provides links to online articles from a variety of magazines and newspapers. Help students choose a few articles to read to further their exploration of the topic What Tales Tell.

NOVELWISE

Students can unlock the power of novels with this unique resource. Help students read through longer works with these tips:

- Find a Book
- Before You Read
- As You Read
- After You Read

Each book includes introductory material, worksheets, graphic organizers, and discussion guides.

ADDITIONAL TEXTS BY COLLECTION

Suggest students read the following:

- "The Walrus and the Carpenter" by Lewis Carroll
- "Meeting at Night" by Robert Browning

Have students take turns reading the poems aloud. Then have them analyze the poems for theme, symbols, and tone. How does the language used in each contribute to the mood and setting?

NONFICTION CONNECTIONS

Suggest that students increase their reading of informational texts. The nonfiction connections include

- speeches
- diaries
- true-life accounts
- newspaper articles
- political cartoons

Creating an Independent Reading Program

OPPORTUNITIES FOR SOCIAL INTERACTION

Discussing books with classmates allows students to share what they know and to learn about other books.

- Give students time for small group discussions. Have them show the book, give the title and author, and then summarize it.
- If students read the same book, have them sit together and take turns reading aloud and discussing paragraphs or pages that made an impression on them.
- If students read different books on a similar topic, have them compare and contrast the books. One student should act as moderator to make sure everyone has an opportunity to share.
- At the end of the discussions, students should say whether they'd recommend their books. Set aside space in your class library to call out the books they think others will like.

WRITING IN RESPONSE TO BOOKS AND TEXTS READ

Writing in response to texts gives students the opportunity to think more deeply about the text.

- Before group discussions, allow time for students to write notes about the book they'd like to present.
- After the group discussions, encourage students to write a book review. Additionally, they can draw posters or bookmarks that can be posted to a class bulletin board alongside the review.
- Suggest students retell the book they read in a different format, such as a graphic novel, a dramatic presentation, or a limerick.
- Throughout the school year, ask students to compare books they are reading and others they have read. What characters or genres are they drawn to? Do they read about people and topics that have relevance to what they do in or outside of school?

Participate in a Collaborative Discussion

W 9 Draw evidence from literary or informational texts.

SL 1a–d Engage effectively in a collaborative discussion.

SL 3 Delineate a speaker's argument, claims, and attitude toward the subject.

Myths and tales are not always strictly entertaining; they might also be written to teach a lesson about life. Look back at *Black Ships Before Troy* and the other texts in the collection. What lessons about life do they express? Do these texts convey their ideas effectively? Consider the way the texts in this collection teach a lesson. Then, discuss your ideas in a panel discussion, citing evidence to support your ideas.

An effective participant in a panel discussion

- prepares by reading and studying all required material
- synthesizes, or combines, information to make a clear, logical, and well-defended generalization
- refers to quotations, specific examples, and other text evidence to support ideas on the topic
- responds thoughtfully and politely to other panel members
- evaluates other panel members' contributions, distinguishing claims that are supported with reasons and evidence from those that are not

Mentor Text See how this excerpt from "The Role of Myths in Ancient Greece" uses a specific example to support an idea.

> " Myths also taught important lessons. For example, they might have warned against being too proud. One version of the Greek myth of Arachne tells how Arachne was turned into a spider for bragging about her weaving skills. "

myNotebook

Use the annotation tools in your eBook to find evidence to support your ideas. Save each piece of evidence to your notebook.

ACADEMIC VOCABULARY

As you participate in your panel discussion, be sure to use the academic vocabulary words.

emphasize

occur

period

relevant

tradition

PLAN

Get Organized Work with your classmates to prepare for the discussion.

- Join a group of four classmates and begin to define individual roles. Select one student to be the moderator for your discussion. A moderator helps the discussion run smoothly.

PERFORMANCE TASK A

PARTICIPATE IN A COLLABORATIVE DISCUSSION

W 9, SL 1a–d, SL 3

Introduce students to the Performance Task by reading the introductory paragraph with them and reviewing the criteria for what makes an effective participant in a collaborative discussion. Remind students that effective discussion participants use text evidence to support their own ideas and to respond to the ideas of classmates.

PLAN

GET ORGANIZED

As groups organize their panels and select the texts they'll discuss, they should consider what generalizations they might make about each text's lessons. Remind students that the role of the moderator will be to ask thought-provoking questions and to elicit well-supported responses.

English Language Support

Plan a Collaborative Discussion Remind students that their collaborative discussions must draw upon evidence from three collection texts to support broad conclusions about the lessons that the texts convey. To help each group choose the texts it will discuss, have two members review one half of the collection texts and two members review the other half. Instruct students to write brief summaries of their assigned texts and then use the following sentence frames to share their thoughts: [Title] is about ___.

A lesson about life that this text suggests is _____.

Text evidence that helps readers infer this lesson includes _____.

I think we [should/should not] discuss this text because _____.

After students select texts for discussion, they can use these conversations to help them choose roles and collect evidence.

PERFORMANCE TASK A

English Language Support

Summarize Evidence Tell students that it is important to gather sufficient evidence because they will not have time to flip through the text to collect information during the discussion. Advise students to prepare notes that summarize or paraphrase the text evidence that supports their answer to each question. Quotations from the text should be brief and should clearly support their points.

PRODUCE

WRITE AND PRACTICE

Suggest that students make their outlines as thorough and detailed as possible to include adequate and relevant support for their key points. Remind students that their outlines will serve as a general road map they can refer to during the discussion, but they may not have time to present every piece of evidence.

English Language Support

Support Opinions Explain that to participate effectively in the discussion students should clearly state their position. Suggest that they begin such statements with "I think that . . ." or "I agree with your point, but . . ." Remind students to use transitional words to link ideas. Have them practice by stating their position and then using a transitional word or phrase to introduce supporting evidence.

- Choose three collection texts that you will use to discuss the way literature can teach a lesson about life. Each student who is not the moderator will be the expert on one of these texts. Decide which student will focus on which text.
- Create a schedule that shows the order in which members of the panel will speak and for how long. It will be the moderator's job to keep the discussion on schedule.
- Set rules regarding appropriate times for the moderator or the audience to ask questions.

Gather Evidence Work individually to analyze your assigned text. Gather evidence that you will use to discuss the way your text can teach a lesson about life. Ask yourself these questions as you take notes:

- What important lesson do the conflict and the resolution of the story suggest?
- What does the main character learn over the course of the story?
- What values or qualities are discussed in the text? What details and examples from the text support these values and qualities?
- What generalization, or broad conclusion, can you make about the way literature can teach a lesson about life?

During this time, the moderator should make a list of relevant questions to be asked during the discussion.

Interactive Lessons
To help you gather evidence, complete the following lesson:
• Participating in Collaborative Discussions: Introduction

PRODUCE

Write and Practice Work with your group to outline your ideas about your assigned text. Then practice with your group.

- State a clear generalization about the ways literature teaches a lesson about life.
- Write several main ideas that support your generalization. Each idea should relate to your generalization of the text.
- Review your evidence. Match each piece of evidence with the main idea it supports. Provide clear examples.
- Present your ideas to your group. The moderator can ask you questions about your ideas and examples, preparing you to "think on your feet" during the real discussion.

WriteSmart

Outline your ideas in *my*WriteSmart. Focus on getting your ideas down, rather than perfecting your choice of language.

Interactive Lessons
To help you gather evidence, complete the following lesson:
• Using Textual Evidence: Writing an Outline

English Language Support

Prepare to Practice and Present Advise students to organize their outlines in a way that lets them find information quickly to make a point or answer a question. Also emphasize that they become familiar enough with their topic to speak directly to the panel and to the audience, glancing at their outlines only as needed. Note that in a collaborative discussion, precise language and verbal and nonverbal techniques can

help participants engage and inform their audience. Before students practice, suggest the following strategies as they review their outlines:

- Make sure your ideas and evidence are ordered logically. Highlight your strongest pieces of evidence to help you find them easily.
- Circle any words that you're not sure how to pronounce. Consult a dictionary to confirm the pronunciation.

- If you are the moderator, decide how you will introduce and conclude the panel discussion. Write a statement that tells the audience the topic of the discussion and its format. Write notes for a concluding statement. Be prepared to change your remarks based on new ideas that come up in your discussion.

REVISE

REVISE

Reinforce Your Ideas Based on the practice session and the rubric on the following page, make changes to your outline. Consider the following questions:

- Were you able to defend your generalization? If not, revise your statement so it reflects your main ideas and evidence.
- Were you able to answer the moderator's questions clearly and without hesitation?
- Did the moderator's questions help you see your topic in a new way? If so, add elaboration and detail to your outline that you can share during the actual discussion.

✓ my WriteSmart

Have your partner or a group of peers review your outline in *my*WriteSmart. Ask your reviewers to note any evidence that does not support your ideas about the way literature can teach a lesson about life.

Interactive Lessons
To help you revise your outline, complete the following lesson:
- Participating in Collaborative Discussions: Listening and Responding

REINFORCE YOUR IDEAS

Tell students to provide specific feedback on how group members might improve their responses. Encourage students to simplify each response and express their ideas clearly and concisely.

FOR STANDARD ENGLISH LEARNERS

Use Formal English Encourage students to use formal English in their discussions. Remind them to pay special attention to subject-verb agreement as they respond to fellow panel members. Use the following examples to review differences in agreement between formal and informal English: *he say/he says, she be/she is, both is/both are.*

PRESENT

PRESENT

Have the Discussion Present your panel discussion before the rest of the class. Have your outline at hand for your discussion.

- Have the moderator introduce the topic, the panelists, and the basic format for the discussion. The moderator will then ask the first question and keep the discussion moving.
- Look briefly at your outline to remind you of your main points, but speak directly to the panel and to the audience.
- Listen carefully to what speakers say so you can give an appropriate response.
- Keep a respectful tone toward your fellow panel members, even when you disagree with their ideas.
- After the discussion, the moderator can invite audience members to ask questions.
- After the question period, the moderator can summarize the discussion and thank the panelists for their participation.

Summarize Write a summary of the main points from your discussion. Then explain whether the discussion made you rethink your generalization, and why.

HAVE THE DISCUSSION

When presenting, panelists should speak loudly and clearly and remember to maintain eye contact with the moderator, other panelists, and audience members when addressing them. When not speaking, panelists should model good listening behavior and direct their full attention to each speaker.

Collection Performance Task A **375**

FOR STUDENTS WITH DISABILITIES

Videotape the Discussion Give groups the option of videotaping their discussions. Students can then use the recordings to review and critique their performance.

WHEN STUDENTS STRUGGLE...

Practice Speaking Techniques Provide an opportunity to view a video of a model discussion before students deliver their own summaries. Pause the video intermittently to point out strong speaking techniques. Note examples of effective eye contact, facial expressions, gestures, voice modulation, and inflection. Then have students practice these techniques to emphasize important points in their discussions.

USE THE SCORING RUBRIC

Let audience members use the rubric to evaluate discussion panelists. Assign one student to score the performance of a specific panelist. Students should use the language of the rubric to explain the reasons for the score they gave.

REFLECT ON THE PROCESS

Explain that taking the time to reflect on the preparation for and engagement in their discussions will help students prepare for future assignments. Ask students to think about the insights they gained from their discussion. Then have them answer the following questions:

- What were your strongest pieces of evidence?
- How did you elaborate on and respond to questions and comments from other panelists?
- What nonverbal elements did you use effectively in your discussion?

PERFORMANCE TASK A RUBRIC
PANEL DISCUSSION

	Ideas and Evidence	Organization	Language
4	• The panelist clearly states a valid generalization and supports it with strong ideas, relevant reasons and well-chosen evidence from the texts. • The panel member carefully evaluates others' evidence and reasoning and responds with insightful comments and questions. • The panelist synthesizes the analysis of the texts to help listeners understand the generalization.	• The panelist's remarks are based on a well-organized outline of supporting ideas and evidence. • The panelist concludes with a statement that supports the main generalization and includes the ideas that have emerged from the discussion.	• The panelist adapts speech to the context of the discussion, using appropriately formal English to discuss texts and ideas. • The panelist quotes accurately from the texts to support ideas. • The panel member keeps a polite and thoughtful tone throughout the discussion.
3	• The panelist states a generalization and supports it with ideas, reasons and evidence from the texts. • The panel member evaluates others' evidence and reasoning and responds with appropriate comments and questions. • The panelist synthesizes some ideas and links to the generalization.	• The panelist's remarks are based on an outline that identifies supporting ideas and evidence. • The panelist concludes with a statement that supports the main generalization.	• The panelist uses mostly formal English to discuss texts and ideas. • The panelist mostly quotes accurately from the texts to support ideas. • The panel member keeps a polite and thoughtful tone throughout most of the discussion.
2	• The panelist states a reasonably clear generalization and supports it with some ideas, reasons and evidence. • The panel member's response to others' comments shows limited evaluation of the evidence and reasoning. • The panelist does not synthesize ideas but simply repeats the generalization in a vague way.	• The panelist's remarks reflect an outline that does not organize supporting ideas and evidence effectively. • The panelist makes a weak concluding statement that does little to support the generalization.	• The panelist uses some formal English to discuss texts and ideas. • The panelist's quotations and examples sometimes do not accurately reflect the texts. • The panel member occasionally forgets to keep a polite and thoughtful tone.
1	• The panelist's generalization is unclear; ideas, reasons and evidence are not coherent. • The panel member does not evaluate others' evidence and reasoning. • The panelist does not synthesize ideas.	• The panelist does not follow an outline that organizes supporting ideas and evidence. • The panelist's remarks lack any kind of conclusion or summary.	• The panelist uses informal English and/or slang, resulting in a lack of clarity. • The panelist's quotations and examples do not accurately reflect the texts. • The panel member does not keep a polite tone.

TO CHALLENGE STUDENTS . . .

Gather Additional Evidence Challenge students to look for additional details, examples, and quotations that relate to the insights gained from their discussions. Encourage them to gather additional information from resources outside of the collection texts. Ask students to add a section to their discussion summaries that reflect on this new evidence.

Interactive Lessons

To help you complete this task, use
- *Writing Narratives*
- *Writing as a Process*
- *Giving a Presentation*

Write and Produce a Play

The play *The Prince and the Pauper*, based on the novel of the same name, brings a classic story to life through dialogue and action. Now you will adapt another selection (or part of a selection) in this collection as a play. Then you will perform the play for an audience.

RL 7 Compare and contrast the experience of reading to listening or viewing.
W 3a–e Write narratives.
W 4 Produce clear and coherent writing.
W 5 Develop and strengthen writing.
SL 4 Present claims and findings.
SL 6 Adapt speech to a variety of contexts and tasks.

A successful play

- establishes a situation with background information about characters and setting
- develops a plot that has a clear beginning, middle, and end
- includes stage directions and a cast of characters
- uses dialogue and stage directions to develop events, characters, and to convey mood and tone
- is structured in acts and scenes
- is formatted in a consistent style so that dialogue and stage directions are easy to follow

Mentor Text Notice how the dialogue is used in the following speech from *The Prince and the Pauper* to develop the plot.

> **Prince.** Would you like that? Come, then. We shall change places. You can take off your rags and put on my clothes—and I will put on yours.

myNotebook

Use the annotation tools in your eBook to mark up key details that you might want to include. Save each detail to your notebook.

PLAN

Choose a Selection Review the selections in the collection. Choose a story or a part of a story you think could be rewritten into an entertaining play.

Organize Your Ideas Note elements, such as setting, mood, events, and dialogue, that are important to the plot.

Consider Your Purpose and Audience Who will watch your play? What techniques will you use to help the audience relate to the characters and events?

ACADEMIC VOCABULARY

As you write your play, be sure to use the academic vocabulary words.

emphasize
occur
period
relevant
tradition

PERFORMANCE TASK B

WRITE AND PRODUCE A PLAY

RL 7, W 3a–e, W 4, W 5, W 6, SL 6

Introduce students to the Performance Task by reading the introductory paragraph with them and reviewing the criteria for what makes a good play. Remind students that plays, like good stories, often revolve around strong characters and a central problem. Students may produce their plays in connection with their music or art studies. Coordinate with other teachers as appropriate.

PLAN

ORGANIZE YOUR IDEAS

Once students have chosen their selection and reviewed its details carefully, they can begin organizing their plays. In addition to noting setting, mood, dialogue, and events, have students create a character grid to help them develop their characters. Explain to students that a character grid is a chart that provides information about the main characters. It contains the following information for each character: name, gender, age, strength, and weakness.

English Language Support

Write and Produce a Play Review the differences between a drama and a story, using examples from the drama and novel excerpts of *The Prince and the Pauper* in the Close Reader. Then have students review the collection texts with a partner. Ask pairs to discuss how the following points might affect each text's adaptation into the format of a play. Students can use their conversations to help them choose texts to adapt.

- *Dialogue:* Plays rely on dialogue to move the plot forward. However, a play may also have a narrator that describes action.

- *Structuring a story into scenes:* A scene might end with a completed action, a change of location, or a change in point of view.
- *Stage Directions:* Descriptions of characters or setting can be adapted into stage directions.
- *Plot:* If only part of a text is adapted, the plot must still make sense to the audience. Leave out any events that only make sense in the context of the complete story.

PRODUCE

DRAFT YOUR SCRIPT

Remind students to organize their play into acts and scenes. Examining the events they plan to include can help students do this. Are there several short scenes or a few long scenes? Is there a change of setting? Help students use their notes to help them answer these questions.

LANGUAGE CONVENTIONS

Use Verbs and Verb Phrases Point out the differences in tense between the verb phrases in the last sentence of Miles' speech. *(simple past, past perfect)* Guide students to understand how this shows that Miles was taken prisoner in the past and spent the time since then in prison. Encourage students to use verb phrases in their drafts to clearly show when actions took place.

English Language Support

Use Verb Phrases Ask students to identify the helping verbs and the main verbs in Miles' speech. *(main: taken, spent; helping: was, have)* Then have students work in pairs to look for places where they could add verb phrases to dialogue in their drafts.

WHEN STUDENTS STRUGGLE . . .

Create a Storyboard If students have trouble organizing their plays, suggest that they work with partners to list the setting, main characters, and plot events. Then have partners discuss how to divide the plot events into scenes using simple storyboards. Students might ask: *Which characters will be in each scene? What will they talk about? What do they do?*

PRODUCE

myWriteSmart

Write your rough draft in *my*WriteSmart. Focus on getting your ideas down, rather than perfecting your choice of language.

Draft Your Script Review your notes. Use *The Prince and the Pauper* as a guide for formatting your script as you write.

- List characters in the order that they first appear in the play.
- Use stage directions at the beginning of your script to provide background about the story, characters, and setting.
- Divide your script into acts to distinguish the introduction, middle, and conclusion of your play. Use scenes within the acts to show events that occur at different places and times.
- Describe the tone, or attitude, of the characters through dialogue and stage directions that describe vocal delivery, facial expressions, and body language.
- Convey the mood of the play through dialogue and through stage directions that describe sights and sounds.
- If the story you choose to adapt is written from the third-person point of view, you may want to use a narrator. The narrator can explain some of the plot events.
- Write the script in the present tense. The events are happening as the play is being performed. The way the characters speak in your script should mimic the way they speak in the story.

Interactive Lessons
To help you draft your script, complete the following lessons in **Writing Narratives:**
- Narrative Structure
- Point of View and Characters

Language Conventions: Verbs and Verb Phrases

A **verb** expresses an action, a condition, or state of being. A **verb phrase** combines a helping verb and a main verb. Because the action in a play is conveyed mainly through dialogue and stage directions, it is important to use precise verbs and verb phrases. Notice how verbs and verb phrases are used in this excerpt.

> **Miles.** *(shaking his head).* My father banished me from home seven years ago, so I fought in the wars. I was taken prisoner and I have spent the past seven years in prison. . . .

Stage the Play You will need to choose and design a space in which to perform the play. Ask yourself these questions:

- What costumes and scenery will you use for the setting?
- What images and sounds will you use to convey the mood?
- How will actors move on stage?

English Language Support

Structure a Play Review the terms that students will use in their scripts. Ask them to identify examples of each term in *The Prince and the Pauper*.
act: a major division of a play.
scene: a section within an act of a play. Events in a scene usually occur at a single place and time.
cast of characters: a list of all the roles in a play that appears at the beginning the script; the list may include a brief description of the characters.
stage directions: instructions in the script that provide information about characters or setting.

Review Your Script

Have your partner or group of peers review the draft of your play. Use the following chart to revise it.

Questions	Tips	Revision Techniques
Does my play include a list of characters, in the order that they first appear?	**Highlight** the cast of characters.	**Add** a list of the cast, if necessary. **Reorder** the list so that the characters are in the correct order.
Do the stage directions introduce the story and setting, develop characters, and convey a clear mood and tone?	**Highlight** the stage directions throughout the play.	**Add** stage directions, if necessary, or add more detail. **Add** or **revise** words and phrases to reflect the mood and tone.
Do I use precise verbs and verb phrases in my dialogue and stage directions to describe the action?	**Underline** verbs and verb phrases in dialogue and stage directions.	**Replace** verbs that do not adequately develop the characters or describe the action.
Do I include acts and scenes that show how the plot progresses from the beginning, middle, and end?	**Highlight** each act and scene. **Underline** the beginning, middle, and conclusion of the play.	**Add** acts and scenes, if necessary, to divide the stages of the plot and explain plot events.

Rehearse Your Play Choose actors for your play and spend time rehearsing it.

- Practice how the actors will say their lines and move on stage.
- Focus one rehearsal on technical aspects, such as lighting, sounds, and any changes needed to the stage.
- Conduct a dress rehearsal with actors in full costume.

PRESENT

Perform Your Play Finalize your script, and perform your play for the class. You might record your play and post it on a personal or school website. After you watch the play, compare and contrast the experience of reading the original story with viewing the play.

PERFORMANCE TASK B

REVISE

REVIEW YOUR SCRIPT

As students use the revision chart to evaluate their drafts, remind them to model their scripts on *The Prince and the Pauper*. Have partners or groups discuss whether their scripts' explain action clearly. If not, students can decide whether to add or revise dialogue or stage directions.

PRESENT

PERFORM YOUR PLAY

Students can record their plays and post them on a personal or school website. Have students try several different angles when recording to find the one that best captures the action. Remind students to compare watching the play to reading the original story after they view each performance.

FOR STANDARD ENGLISH LEARNERS

Adapt Speech Remind students of the differences between formal speech and informal conversation. As they practice their lines, encourage students to pay special attention to words containing the final consonant sequences -ft, -sk, sp, and -pt and to make sure they pronounce the final letters. Speaking slowly and clearly can help them focus on following the rules of standard English pronunciation.

FOR STUDENTS WITH DISABILITIES

Practice a Staged Reading Have students rehearse the play with scripts in hand. Tell them to read through the play once without worrying about stage movement, focusing on only lines, tone, and cues. Then have them incorporate movement and any stage directions related to their positions on stage. Explain that they can mark the stage with tape to help them remember where to go before or after they deliver an important line.

PERFORMANCE TASK B

USE THE SCORING RUBRIC

Assign three students to score each play, with one student focusing on each of the three rubric categories. Ask students to write a brief explanation of the reasons for their score.

REFLECT ON THE PROCESS

Tell students that taking the time to think about how they wrote and produced their plays will help them with other writing tasks. Ask students to think about how their play compares to the text they adapted it from. Then ask them the following questions.

- Which character had the most interesting things to say? Why do you think so?
- How well did you adapt the plot of the original text?
- Did writing and producing a play help you better understand how dialogue can move a plot forward?

PERFORMANCE TASK B RUBRIC
PLAY

	Ideas and Evidence	Organization	Language
4	• All of the characters in the cast are listed in the order in which they first appear in the play. • The play has a clear beginning, middle, and end. • The play's setting is clearly described. • Scene changes occur smoothly and at the right time. • Descriptive dialogue and details help introduce and develop the conflict, characters, and setting.	• The script is organized into acts and scenes effectively; the sequence of events is clear. • Stage directions concisely connect acts and scenes.	• Vivid sensory details reveal the setting, characters, and action. • Dialogue is sharp, clear, and actively moves the plot forward. • Stage directions are clear and direct. • Spelling, capitalization, and punctuation are correct. • Grammar and usage are correct.
3	• The cast of characters is included but does not list the characters in the order in which they first appear in the play. • The play contains a clear beginning, middle, or ending, but not all three. • The play has a specific location, but it is not clearly defined. • Most, but not all, scene changes occur smoothly and at the right time. • Descriptive dialogue and details help tell the story, but main events could be more vividly portrayed.	• The script is organized into acts and scenes, but the sequence of events is confusing at times. • Stage directions mostly connect acts and scenes.	• More sensory details are needed to keep the action moving. • Dialogue is unclear in parts but moves the plot forward. • Stage directions are sometimes unclear. • Some spelling, capitalization, and punctuation mistakes occur. • Some grammar and usage errors, but the writer's ideas are still clear.
2	• The cast of characters only includes the main characters in the play. • The beginning is a little unclear and is not always focused on the main character or conflict. • The setting is described, but details are not relevant. • Scene changes are rough or not timed well. • Descriptive dialogue and details are missing; main events are inadequately portrayed.	• The script generally lacks act and/or scene organization; too many or too few events confuse the plot. • Stage directions are distracting.	• Sensory details do not advance the plot. • Dialogue is mostly unclear, random, or missing. • Stage directions are generally unclear. • Several spelling and capitalization mistakes occur, and punctuation is inconsistent. • Grammar and usage are incorrect in many places.
1	• The cast of characters is missing. • The beginning does not establish the subject of the story. • The play's setting is not described. • Scene changes do not occur at the right time. • Descriptive details and dialogue are unrelated or missing.	• The script lacks acts and/or scenes; a sequence of events is missing. • Stage directions are missing.	• Sensory details are rarely or never used. • Dialogue is unclear or missing. • Stage directions are missing. • Spelling, capitalization, and punctuation are incorrect throughout. • Grammar and usage errors change the meaning of the writer's ideas.

TO CHALLENGE STUDENTS...

Advertise the Play Challenge students to create a poster or a theatrical trailer to advertise their plays. Encourage them to present the most engaging aspects of their plays to attract a wide audience.

TEACHER NOTE:

The page numbers to the left indicate pages in the Student Edition. Except for the entries below, the page numbers in the Student Edition and Teacher's Edition correspond.

Writing an Argument

Many of the Performance Tasks in this book ask you to craft an argument in which you support your ideas with text evidence. Any argument you write should include the following sections and characteristics.

Introduction

Clearly state your **claim**—the point your argument makes. As needed, provide context or background information to help readers understand your position. Note the most common opposing views as a way to distinguish and clarify your ideas. From the very beginning, make it clear for readers why your claim is strong; consider providing an overview of your reasons or a quotation that emphasizes your view in your introduction.

EXAMPLES

vague claim: We need more bike lanes.	**precise claim:** The city should provide more bike lanes. Several of the city's thorough-fares are dangerous for cyclists because the roadways don't provide designated safe areas for bikers to ride in.
not distinguished from opposing view: Many people think riding a bike is unsafe.	**distinguished from opposing view:** While some people consider bike lanes a distraction for car drivers, cyclists have never caused an auto accident when they were in their own lane.
confusing relation-ship of ideas: People love to bike. Fewer cars on the road is better.	**clear relationship of ideas:** By providing cyclists with dedi-cated space on roads, the city is ensuring that riders can travel safely.

Development of Claims

The body of your argument must provide strong, logical reasons for your claim and must support those reasons with relevant evidence. A **reason** tells why your claim is valid; **evidence** provides specific examples that illustrate a reason. In the process of developing your claim you should also refute **counterclaims,** or opposing views, with equally strong reasons and evidence. To demonstrate that you have thoroughly considered your view, look at both the strengths and limitations of your claim and opposing claims. The goal is not to undercut your argument, but rather to answer your readers' potential objections to it. Be sure, too, to consider how much your audience may already know about your topic in order to avoid boring or confusing readers.

EXAMPLES

claim lacking reasons: Bike lanes are important because people would use them and they would help the environment.	**claim developed by reasons:** By providing bike lanes, more cyclists will feel comfortable riding on city streets and will opt to ride their bikes rather than drive their cars. With fewer cars on the roads, the city's pollution will improve as less green-house gases will be omitted.
omission of limita-tions: People who oppose this idea and who hate to exercise admit there is no downside to adding bike lanes to city streets.	**fair discussion of limitations:** We should not forget to include safety precautions. All bike lanes should be clearly marked, and it should be mandatory that all cyclists wear helmets when riding on city streets.

continued

inattention to audience's knowledge: Bikes made with cromoly or aluminum frames are safe to ride on porous asphalt pavements.	awareness of audience's knowledge: Those unfamiliar with biking should know that most bike accidents in urban environments happen in cities that don't have dedicated bike lanes.

Links Among Ideas

Even the strongest reasons and evidence will fail to sway readers if it is unclear how the reasons and evidence relate to the central claim of an argument. Make the connections clear for your readers, using transitional words and phrases as a bridge between ideas.

EXAMPLES

transitional word linking claim and reason: All residents will benefit from more bike lanes on city streets. First, with fewer cars on the road, the city's traffic conditions will improve, as will its air pollution.

transitional phrase linking reason and evidence: Biking on city streets in dedicated bike lanes would reduce rush hour traffic. In fact, several cities with bike lanes on every street report that with more people biking to work and less of them driving, rush hour traffic is a thing of the past.

Appropriate Style and Tone

An effective argument is most often written in a direct and formal style. The style and tone you choose in an argument should not be an afterthought—the way you express your argument can either drive home your ideas or detract from them. Even as you argue in favor of your viewpoint, take care to remain objective in tone.

EXAMPLES

informal style: Because bike lanes on city streets benefit all residents, even those who don't own a bike, the city should pay for the lanes' construction with tax dollars.	formal style: Because bike lanes help all residents by reducing the chances of bike and auto accidents and reducing traffic and air pollution, the city should provide funding for the project.
biased tone: There is no logical reason to oppose more bike lanes on city streets.	objective tone: Arguments against this plan have not been as compelling as the statistics and evidence provided by cities that have bike lanes.

Conclusion

Your conclusion may range from a sentence to a full paragraph, but it must wrap up your argument in a satisfying way; a conclusion that sounds tacked-on helps your argument no more than providing no conclusion at all. A strong conclusion is a logical extension of the argument you have presented. It carries forth your ideas through an inference, question, quotation, or challenge.

EXAMPLES

inference: Support for a safe and healthy city comes from our government leaders.

question: Don't all residents want to live in a city that promotes health and wellness and is committed to lessening pollution?

quotation: After Chicago installed its first two-way bike route with dedicated traffic signals, Mayor Rahm Emauel said ". . . having bike lanes is important to the quality of life in Chicago."

challenge: Having dedicated bike lanes on city roads demonstrates the city's commitment to the health and safety of its residents and sets it apart from other towns that lack such facilities.

Writing an Informative Essay

W 2a-f, W 4

Most of the Performance Tasks in this book ask you to write informational or explanatory texts in which you present a topic and examine it thoughtfully through a well-organized analysis of relevant content. Any informative or explanatory text that you create should include the following parts and features.

Introduction

Develop a strong **thesis statement**. That is, clearly state your **topic** and the **organizational framework** through which you will connect or **distinguish** elements of your topic. For example, you might state that your text will compare ideas, examine causes and effects, or explore a problem and its solutions.

EXAMPLES

Topic: animal adoptions
Sample Thesis Statements

Compare-contrast: When deciding whether to adopt an animal from a shelter or buy one from a breeder, consider the satisfaction of rescuing a dog in addition to the differences in cost.

Cause-effect: Because of these tough economic times, many dog owners can't afford their pets and are having to surrender their dogs to shelters, which are experiencing a worsening canine overpopulation problem.

Problem-solution: If more people would adopt from shelters instead of purchasing from breeders, space in shelters could be freed up to save the 5 million dogs in the United States currently in need of good homes.

Clarifying the organizational framework up front will help you organize the body of your text, come up with **headings** you can use to guide your readers, and identify **graphics** that you may need to clarify information. For example, if you compare and contrast the procedures and costs when adopting a pet from a shelter versus buying one from a breeder, you might create a chart like the one shown to guide your writing. You could include the same chart in your paper as a graphic for readers. The row or column headings serve as natural paragraph headings.

	Shelter Adoptions	Breeder Adoptions
Procedures	Extensive background checks required of potential owners; spaying/neutering animal required within 30 days of adoption	No necessary verification of name and address or criminal background; spaying/neutering animal not mandatory
Costs	Typically between $50–$100, which may include the animal's spaying/neutering	Usually $3,000 or more for a specific breed; spaying/neutering costs extra, typically $150 or more

Development of the Topic

In the body of your text, flesh out the organizational framework you established in your introduction with strong supporting paragraphs. Include only support directly relevant to your topic. Don't rely on a single source, and make sure the sources you do use are reputable and current. The table that follows illustrates types of support you might use to develop aspects of your topic. It also shows how transitions link text sections, create cohesion, and clarify the relationships among ideas.

Types of Support in Explanatory/ Informative Texts	Uses of Transitions in Explanatory/ Informative Texts
Facts and examples: One cause of over-crowding in animal shelters is economic hardship; *for example, when home foreclosures increase, the populations of animal shelters also rise.*	*One cause* signals the shift from the introduction to the body text in a cause-and-effect essay. *For example* introduces the support for the cause being cited.
Concrete details: On the other hand, while it is sad for dogs to be surrendered to a shelter, *it is better than letting the dog loose on the streets or chaining the dog outside with no food.*	*On the other hand* transitions the reader from one point of comparison to another in a compare-contrast essay.
Statistics: *Turn to the Humane Society of the United States if you doubt the scope of the problem.* Each year more than 5 million dogs are abandoned on the streets or given up by owners to shelters.	The entire transitional sentence introduces the part of a problem-solution essay that demonstrates the existence of a problem.

Style and Tone

Use formal English to establish your credibility as a source of information. To project authority, use the language of the domain, or field, that you are writing about. However, be sure to define unfamiliar terms to avoid using jargon your audience may not know. Provide extended definitions when your audience is likely to have limited knowledge of the topic.

Using quotations from reputable sources can also give your text authority; be sure to credit the source of quoted material. In general, keep the tone objective, avoiding slang or biased expressions.

Informal, jargon-filled, biased language: Backyard breeders only care about themselves and value money over life. They have no regard for an animal's welfare, and they reuse these dogs over and over again for breeding purposes until the dog dies. The puppies are treated even worse, raised in deplorable conditions, malnourished, and given no medical attention.

Extended definition in formal style and objective tone: Of the more than 50 million dogs in the United States, more than two-thirds come from "backyard breeders." A backyard breeder, as defined by the Humane Society of the United States, "breeds dogs for quick sales, with or without adequate care for the dogs' or puppies' health and seldom requires pre-sale testing for diseases and/or genetic abnormalities in the dogs and puppies."

Conclusion

Wrap up your essay with a concluding statement or section that sums up or extends the information in your essay.

EXAMPLES

Articulate implications: If people continue to support backyard breeders, this country's homeless dog problem will never be remedied. People need to support shelters so that owners can be found for all of the 5 million dogs in need of new homes. Otherwise, this dog overpopulation crisis will continue.

Emphasize significance: The number of dogs waiting to die in shelters will only keep increasing if people do not start adopting dogs from shelters. By adopting from a shelter and not buying from a breeder, you help free up space in the shelter so another homeless dog can be rescued.

Writing a Narrative

When you are writing a fictional tale, an autobiographical incident, or a firsthand biography, you write in the narrative mode. That means telling a story with a beginning, a climax, and a conclusion. Though there are important differences between fictional and nonfiction narratives, you use similar processes to develop them.

Identify a Problem, Situation, or Observation

For a nonfiction narrative, think about a problem you have dealt with or an observation you've made about your life. For fiction, try to invent a problem or situation that can unfold in interesting ways.

EXAMPLES

Problem (nonfiction)	As a vegetarian, I find it almost impossible to find healthy foods to eat when traveling.
Situation (fiction)	Tommy, the new kid at school, has been experiencing bullying by several of his classmates, who mock his Texas accent.

Establish a Point of View

Decide who will tell your story. If you are writing a reflective essay about an important experience or person in your own life, you will be the narrator of the events you relate. If you are writing a work of fiction, you can choose to create a first-person narrator or tell the story from the third-person point of view. In that case, the narrator can focus on one character or reveal the thoughts and feelings of all the characters. The examples show the differences between first- and third-person narrator.

First-person narrator (nonfiction)	At the airport, at gas stations, and at most hotels, I have had a hard time finding foods that are not made with animal products. It seems that most items are loaded with meats, cheeses, and oils.

Third-person narrator (fiction)	Tommy's first day at his new school was brutal. The kids made fun of the way he talked, imitating him mercilessly. At lunch, a group of boys taunted Tommy by calling him names, and one boy even threw food at him.

Gather Details

To make real or imaginary experiences come alive on the page, you will need to use narrative techniques like description and dialogue. The questions in the left column in the chart that follows can help you search your memory or imagination for the details that will form the basis of your narrative. You don't have to respond in full sentences, but try to capture the sights, sounds, and feelings that will bring your narrative to life.

Who, What, When, Where?	Narrative Techniques
People: Who are the people or characters involved in the experience? What did they look like? What did they do? What did they say?	**Description:** Tommy moved from Texas to New York, and he loves wearing cowboy boots and flannel shirts to school. Jason, who sits behind Tommy in English class, is always laughing at Tommy's clothes and Texas accent. Jason said loudly, "Doesn't that guy look like he should be at a rodeo?" Tommy turned around and said, "Why thank you. I take that as a compliment because rodeos are really cool!"

Experience: What led up to or caused the event? What is the main event in the experience? What happened as a result of the event?	**Description:** After my dad's heart attack, he needed to change the way he ate and eliminate animal products and fats from his diet. My dad began to eat a diet of vegetables, fruits, and whole grains. To show our support, my mom and I also adopted a vegetarian diet.
Places: When and where did the events take place? What were the sights, sounds, and smells of this place?	**Description:** I was sitting by my dad's hospital bed. The room was dark except for the glow of street lights that flickered through the window blinds. The only sound was the rattling hum of my dad's respirator.

Sequence Events

Before you begin writing, list the key events of the experience or story in chronological, or time, order. Place a star next to the point of highest tension—for example, the point at which a key decision determines the outcome of events. In fiction, this point is called the climax, but a gripping nonfiction narrative will also have a climactic event.

To build suspense—the uncertainty a reader feels about what will happen next—you'll want to think about the pacing or rhythm of your narrative. Consider disrupting the chronological order of events by beginning at the end, then starting over. Or interrupt the forward flow of events with a flashback, which takes the reader to an earlier point in the narrative.

Another way to build suspense is with multiple plot lines. For example, the personal narrative about the father who has a heart attack involves a second plot line in which the father and his family eat better in an effort to avoid health complications like heart disease. Both plot lines intersect when the father gets out of the hospital and makes a commitment to be healthier, enlisting his family's support.

Use Vivid Language

As you revise, make an effort to use vivid language. Use precise words and phrases to describe feelings and action. Use telling details to show, rather than directly state, what a character is like. Use sensory language that lets readers see, feel, hear, smell, and taste what you or your characters experienced.

First Draft	Revision
My dad's newfound appreciation for life was contagious, inspiring me to do things I had never done before.	Walking outside for the first time since his heart attack, my dad breathed in, exhaling to say, "I will make healthier choices for myself and inspire my family to eat well."
As I walked around the airport food court, I looked through each restaurant's menu and could not find one healthy entree.	Hamburgers, French fries, sodas—nothing on the restaurants' menus was healthy; everything was ladened with animal fat.
As Tommy walked along the hallway, he could see something dripping down the front of his locker.	Tommy could feel his face get hotter, anger boiling up as he approached his locker. It was covered with garbage.

Conclusion

At the conclusion of the narrative, you or your narrator will reflect on the meaning of the events. The conclusion should follow logically from the climactic moment of the narrative. The narrator of a personal narrative usually reflects on the significance of the experience—the lessons learned or the legacy left.

EXAMPLES

As my dad rounds the corner, I see him approaching the marathon's finish line. I raise a sign that says, "Dad! We Are Proud of You!" and yell out his name. He waves and glides by, crossing the finish line. After losing over 60 pounds, my dad is not the same as he was in that hospital bed a year ago. He is a new man.

Conducting Research

The Performance Tasks in this book will require you to complete research projects related to the texts you've read in the collections. Whether the topic is stated in a Performance Task or is one you generate, the following information will guide you through your research project.

Focus Your Research and Formulate a Question

Some topics for a research project can be effectively covered in three pages; others require an entire book for a thorough treatment. Begin by developing a topic that is neither too narrow nor too broad for the time frame of the assignment. Also check your school and local libraries and databases to help you determine how to choose your topic. If there's too little information, you'll need to broaden your focus; if there's too much, you'll need to limit it.

With a topic in hand, formulate a research question; it will keep you on track as you conduct your research. A good research question cannot be answered in a single word. It should be open-ended. It should require investigation. You can also develop related research questions to explore your topic in more depth.

EXAMPLES

Possible topics for *Titanic*	The ship *Titanic*—too broad *Titanic's* captain Edward Smith—too narrow Settings and events—fact or fiction?
Possible research question	To what extent are the circumstances involving *Titanic's* sinking based on fact?

Related questions	Is it true that *Titanic* sank because its captain ignored warnings of icebergs and forged ahead instead of taking a different route? Was it because the Irish did not properly build the ship to withstand the impact from an ice field? Were the testimonies from employees at Harland & Wolfe, the architecture firm that constructed the ship, more credible than accounts from ship captains who confirmed they had sent messages to *Titanic* about seeing masses of ice in the Atlantic?

Locate and Evaluate Sources

To find answers to your research question, you'll need to investigate primary and secondary sources, whether in print or digital formats. **Primary sources** contain original, firsthand information, such as diaries, autobiographies, interviews, speeches, and eyewitness accounts. **Secondary sources** provide other people's versions of primary sources in encyclopedias, newspaper and magazine articles, biographies, and documentaries.

Your search for sources begins at the library and on the World Wide Web. Use **advanced search features** to help you find things quickly. Add a minus sign (–) before a word that should not appear in your results. Use an asterisk (*) in place of unknown words. List the name and location of each possible source, adding comments about its potential usefulness. Assessing, or evaluating, your sources is an important step in the research process. Your goal is to use sources that are credible, or reliable and trustworthy.

Criteria for Assessing Sources	
Relevance: It covers the target aspect of my topic.	• How will the source be useful in answering my research question?
Accuracy: It includes information that can be verified by more than one authoritative source.	• Is the information up-to-date? Are the facts accurate? How can I verify them? • What qualifies the author to write about this topic? Is he or she an authority?
Objectivity: It presents multiple viewpoints on the topic.	• What, if any, biases can I detect? Does the writer favor one view of the topic?

Incorporate and Cite Source Material

When you draft your research project, you'll need to include material from your sources. This material can be **direct quotations, summaries,** or **paraphrases** of the original source material. Two well-known **style manuals** provide information on how to cite a range of print and digital sources: the *MLA Handbook for Writers of Research Papers* (published by the Modern Language Association) and Kate L. Turabian's *A Manual for Writers* (published by The University of Chicago Press). Both style manuals provide a wealth of information about conducting, formatting, drafting, and presenting your research, including guidelines for citing sources within the text (called parenthetical citations) and preparing the list of Works Cited, as well as correct use of the mechanics of writing. Your teacher will indicate which style manual you should use. The following examples use the format in the *MLA Handbook.*

Any material from sources must be completely documented, or you will commit **plagiarism,** the unauthorized use of someone else's words or ideas. Plagiarism is not honest. As you take notes for your research project, be sure to keep complete information about your sources so that you can cite them correctly in the body of your paper. This applies to all sources, whether print or digital. Having complete information

will also enable you to prepare the list of Works Cited. The list of Works Cited, which concludes your research project, provides author, title, and publication information for both print and digital sources. The following pages show the *MLA Handbook's* Works Cited citation formats for a variety of sources.

EXAMPLES

Direct quotation [The writer] is citing a quote from the British Broadcasting Corporation (BBC) on *Titanic's* sinking.]	In a BBC news report, "*Titanic:* Sinking the Myths," journalist Paul Louden-Brown reports that ". . . little thought was given to how a ship, 852 feet in length, might . . . avoid collision with an iceberg."
Summary [The writer is summarizing the BBC news report's conclusion on the sinking of *Titanic.*]	*Titanic's* captain failed the ship's crew and passengers by not heeding iceberg warnings and not slowing down *Titanic* when ice was reported to be in the ship's path. The captain also allowed lifeboats to leave the ship partially full, causing hundreds more passengers to die.
Paraphrase [The writer is paraphrasing, in his own words, facts asserted in the BBC report, as well as transcripts from the 1912 U.S. Senate hearings on the *Titanic's* sinking.]	The *Titanic* disaster is a reminder of how weak mankind is compared to the forces of nature, and how the mistakes of those in charge, *Titanic's* captain in this instance, can put people in grave danger and cause them to die. The first lifeboat to leave the ship's side had a capacity of 40 but only carried 12 people.

MLA Citation Guidelines

Today, you can find free websites that generate ready-made citations for research papers, using the information you provide. Such sites have some time-saving advantages when you're developing a Works Cited list. However, you should always check your citations carefully before you turn in your final paper. If you are following MLA style, use these guidelines to evaluate and finalize your work.

Books

One author

Lastname, Firstname. *Title of Book*. City of Publication: Publisher, Year of Publication. Medium of Publication.

Two authors or editors

Lastname, Firstname, and Firstname Lastname. *Title of Book*. City of Publication: Publisher, Year of Publication. Medium of Publication.

Three authors

Lastname, Firstname, Firstname Lastname, and Firstname Lastname. *Title of Book*. City of Publication: Publisher, Year of Publication. Medium of Publication.

Four or more authors

The abbreviation *et al.* means "and others." Use *et al.* instead of listing all the authors.

Lastname, Firstname, et al. *Title of Book*. City of Publication: Publisher, Year of Publication. Medium of Publication.

No author given

Title of Book. City of Publication: Publisher, Year of Publication. Medium of Publication.

An author and a translator

Lastname, Firstname. *Title of Book*. Trans. Firstname Lastname. City of Publication: Publisher, Year of Publication. Medium of Publication.

An author, a translator, and an editor

Lastname, Firstname. *Title of Book*. Trans. Firstname Lastname. Ed. Firstname Lastname. City of Publication: Publisher, Year of Publication. Medium of Publication.

Parts of Books

An introduction, a preface, a foreword, or an afterword written by someone other than the author(s) of a work

Lastname, Firstname. Part of Book. *Title of Book*. By Author of book's Firstname Lastname. City of Publication: Publisher, Year of Publication. Page span. Medium of Publication.

A poem, a short story, an essay, or a chapter in a collection of works by one author

Lastname, Firstname. "Title of Piece." *Title of Book*. Ed. Firstname Lastname. City of Publication: Publisher, Year of Publication. Page span. Medium of Publication.

A poem, a short story, an essay, or a chapter in an anthology of works by several authors

Lastname, Firstname. "Title of Piece." *Title of Book*. Ed. Firstname Lastname. City of Publication: Publisher, Year of Publication. Page range. Medium of Publication.

Magazines, Newspapers, and Encyclopedias

An article in a newspaper

Lastname, Firstname. "Title of Article." *Title of Book Periodical* Day Month Year: pages. Medium of Publication.

An article in a magazine

Lastname, Firstname. "Title of Article." *Title of Book Periodical* Day Month Year: pages. Medium of Publication.

An article in an encyclopedia

"Title of Article." *Title of Encyclopedia*. Year ed. Medium of Publication.

Miscellaneous Nonprint Sources

An interview

Lastname, Firstname. Personal interview. Day Month Year.

A video recording

Title of Recording. Producer, Year. Medium of Publication.

Electronic Publications

A CD-ROM

"Title of Piece." *Title of CD*. Year ed. City of Publication: Publisher, Year of Publication. CD-ROM.

A document from an Internet site

Entries for online sources should contain as much information as available.

Lastname, Firstname. "*Title of Piece*." Information on what the site is. Year. Web. Day Month Year (when accessed).

Participating in a Collaborative Discussion

Often, class activities, including the Performance Tasks in this book, will require you to work collaboratively with classmates. Whether your group will analyze a work of literature or try to solve a community problem, use the following guidelines to ensure a productive discussion.

Prepare for the Discussion

A productive discussion is one in which all the participants bring useful information and ideas to share. If your group will discuss a short story the class read, first re-read and annotate a copy of the story. Your annotations will help you quickly locate evidence to support your points. Participants in a discussion about an important issue should first research the issue and bring notes or information sources that will help guide the group. If you disagree with a point made by another group member, your case will be stronger if you back it up with specific evidence from your sources.

EXAMPLES

> **disagreeing without evidence:** I don't think Mark Twain is relevant today because people would rather learn about current events through social media.
>
> **providing evidence for disagreement:** I disagree that author Mark Twain, who addresses important cultural topics through works of fiction, is relevant today. With so much information about current events readily available on the Internet and on social media sites, kids don't want to take the time to read a book to learn about social issues. They would rather get their news and commentary immediately from the Web and read a story's comments section to see how others feel about the topic. Plus, Twain's humor is more satirical than kids today are used to. Kids prefer humor that is more blunt.

Set Ground Rules

The rules your group needs will depend on what your group is expected to accomplish. A discussion of themes in a poem will be unlikely to produce a simple consensus; however, a discussion aimed at developing a solution to a problem should result in one strong proposal that all group members can support. Answer the following questions to set ground rules that fit your group's purpose:

- What will this group produce? A range of ideas, a single decision, a plan of action, or something else?
- How much time is available? How much of that time should be allotted to each part of the discussion (presenting ideas, summarizing or voting on final ideas, creating a product such as a written analysis or speech)?
- What roles need to be assigned within the group? Do we need a leader, a note-taker, a timekeeper, or other specific roles?
- What is the best way to synthesize our group's ideas? Should we take a vote, list group members as "for" or "against" in a chart, or use some other method to reach a consensus or sum up the results of the discussion?

Move the Discussion Forward

Everyone in the group should be actively involved in synthesizing ideas. To make sure this happens, ask questions that draw out ideas, especially from less-talkative members of the group. If an idea or statement is confusing, try to paraphrase it, or ask the speaker to explain more about it. If you disagree with a statement, say so politely and explain in detail why you disagree.

SAMPLE DISCUSSION

HEIDI: David, how do you feel about Mark Twain's relevance today? We would love to hear your thoughts.	*Question draws out quiet member*
DAVID: On one hand, I think Twain's stories are inspirational and students should read them to learn about issues of the past. But who wants to take time to read a book when you can use the Internet and get the information immediately?	*Response relates discussion to larger ideas*
KIM: I think students should be required to spend time reading a book and cultivating their own opinions rather than being persuaded by radical discussions on the Internet.	*Question challenges David's conclusion*
MATT: Yes, students should form their own opinions, but we are in an age when speed is king. People want to know about the news almost before it happens, and they want to discuss social issues without having to read a long book.	*Response elaborates on ideas*
MOLLY: Evidence has shown that when students rely on the Internet to get information instead of reading and thinking about ideas first, they don't learn how to think on their own or how to organize their ideas into cohesive arguments. The Internet seems to take away their ability to think critically and independently.	*Paraphrases idea and challenges it further based on evidence*

Respond to Ideas

In a diverse group, everyone may have a different perspective on the topic under discussion, and that's a good thing. Consider what everyone has to say, and don't resist changing your view if other group members provide convincing evidence for theirs. If, instead, you feel more strongly than ever about your view, don't hesitate to say so and provide

reasons related to what those with opposing views have said. Before wrapping up the discussion, try to sum up the points on which your group agrees and disagrees.

SAMPLE DISCUSSION

MOLLY: We have a little time before class ends. Can we come to an agreement?	*Molly and Heidi try to summarize points of agreement*
HEIDI: I think the main points to vote on are: Is the Internet the best source for commentary or does reading books by authors like Twain help cultivate students' own ideas about social issues? What do you guys think?	
MATT: I still think today's students want quick answers about social issues. They want to use the Internet for research. Reading long books is something my parents would do. We are different; we were raised on the Internet.	*Matt maintains his position*
HEIDI: I am leaning toward thinking that books and the Internet can work together. You can read a book and form your own opinions. Then you can go on the Internet and see what others are saying about similar topics.	*Heidi and David qualify their views based on what they have heard*
DAVID: I agree with Heidi. Why can't books and the Internet both be useful but for different reasons? Books allow you to dig deep into a topic, whereas the Internet gives you an instant outlet to see what others think.	
KIM: I'm with David and Heidi. I think students should read a book first and then investigate what others are saying on the Internet.	*Kim supports her position by making a new connection*

Debating an Issue

SL 3, SL 4

The selection and collection Performance Tasks in this text will direct you to engage in debates about issues relating to the selections you are reading. Use the guidelines that follow to have a productive and balanced argument about both sides of an issue.

The Structure of a Formal Debate

In a debate, two teams compete to win the support of the audience about an issue. In a **formal debate,** two teams, each with two members, present their arguments on a given proposition or policy statement. One team argues for the proposition or statement and the other team argues against it. Each debater must consider the proposition closely and must research both sides of it. To argue convincingly either for or against a proposition, a debater must be familiar with both sides of the issue.

Plan the Debate

The purpose of a debate is to allow participants and audience members to consider both sides of an issue. Use these planning suggestions to hold a balanced and productive debate.

- **Identify Debate Teams** Form groups of six members based on the issues that the Performance Tasks include. Three members of the team will argue for the affirmative side of the issue—that is, they support the issue. The other three members will argue for the negative side of the issue—that is, they do not support the issue.
- **Appoint a Moderator** The moderator will present the topic and goals of the debate, keep track of the time, and introduce and thank the participants.
- **Research and Prepare Notes** Search the texts you've read as well as print and online sources for valid reasons and evidence to support your team's claim. As with argument, be sure to anticipate possible opposing claims and compile evidence to counter those claims. You will use notes from your research during the debate.
- **Assign Debate Roles** One team member will introduce the team's claim and supporting evidence. Another team member will respond to questions and opposing

claims in an exchange with a member of the opposing team. The last member will present a strong closing argument.

Hold the Debate

A formal debate is not a shouting match—rather, a well-run debate is an excellent forum for participants to express their viewpoints, build on others' ideas, and have a thoughtful, well-reasoned exchange of ideas. The moderator will begin by stating the topic or issue and introducing the participants. Participants should follow the moderator's instructions concerning whose turn it is to speak and how much time each speaker has.

Speaker	Role	Time
Affirmative Speaker 1	Present the claim and supporting evidence for the affirmative ("pro") side of the argument.	5 minutes
Negative Speaker 1	Ask probing questions that will prompt the other team to address flaws in the argument.	3 minutes
Affirmative Speaker 2	Respond to the questions posed by the opposing team and counter any concerns.	3 minutes
Negative Speaker 2	Present the claim and supporting evidence for the negative ("con") side of the argument.	5 minutes

continued

Speaker	Role	Time
Affirmative Speaker 3	Summarize the claim and evidence for the affirmative side and explain why your reasoning is more valid.	3 minutes
Negative Speaker 3	Summarize the claim and evidence for the negative side and explain why your reasoning is more valid.	3 minutes

FORMAL DEBATE FORMAT

Evaluate the Debate

Use the following guidelines to evaluate a team in a debate.

- Did the team prove that the issue is significant? How thorough was the analysis?
- How well did the team effectively argue that you should support its affirmative or negative side of the proposition or issue?
- How effectively did the team present reasons and evidence, including evidence from the texts, to support the proposition?
- How effectively did the team rebut, or respond to, arguments made by the opposing team?
- Did the speakers maintain eye contact and speak at an appropriate rate and volume?
- Did the speakers observe proper debate etiquette—that is, did they follow the moderator's instructions, stay within their allotted time limits, and treat their opponents respectfully?

Reading Informational Texts: Patterns of Organization

Reading any type of writing is easier once you recognize how it is organized. Writers usually arrange ideas and information in ways that best show how they are related. There are several common patterns of organization:

- main idea and supporting details
- chronological order
- cause-effect organization
- compare-and-contrast organization
- problem-solution order

Writers try to present their arguments in ways that will help readers follow their reasoning and accept their viewpoints.

1. Main Idea and Supporting Details

Main idea and supporting details is a basic pattern of organization in which a central idea about a topic is supported by details. The **main idea** is the most important idea about a topic that a particular text or paragraph conveys. **Supporting details** are words, phrases, or sentences that tell more about the main idea. The main idea may be directly stated at the beginning and then followed by supporting details, or it may merely be implied by the supporting details. It may also be stated after it has been implied by supporting details.

Strategies for Reading

- To find a stated main idea in a paragraph, identify the paragraph's topic. The topic is what the paragraph is about and can usually be summed up in one or two words. The word, or synonyms of it, will usually appear throughout the paragraph. Headings and subheadings are also clues to the topics of paragraphs.
- Ask: What is the topic sentence? The topic sentence states the most important idea, message, or information the paragraph conveys about this topic. It is often the first sentence in a paragraph; however, it may appear at the end.
- To find an implied main idea, ask yourself: Whom or what did I just read about? What do the details suggest about the topic?
- Formulate a sentence stating this idea and add it to the paragraph. Does your sentence express the main idea?

Notice how the main idea is expressed in each of the following models.

Model:
Main idea as the first sentence

> Technology consists of all the ways in which people apply knowledge, tools, and inventions to meet their needs. Technology dates back to early humans. At least 2 million years ago, people made stone tools for cutting. Around 1,500 BC, early humans also made carrying bags, stone hand axes, awls (tools for piercing holes in leather or wood), and drills.

Main idea — (first sentence)
Supporting details

Model:
Main idea as the last sentence

> In time, humans developed more complex tools, such as hunting bows made of wood. They learned to make flint spearheads and metal tools. Early humans used tools to hunt and butcher animals and to construct simple forms of shelter. Technology—these new tools—gave humans more control over their environment and set the stage for a more settled way of life.

Supporting details
Main idea

Model:
Implied main idea

Prehistoric art exists in Africa, Asia, Europe, Australia, and the Americas. Cave paintings thousands of years old show lively images of bulls, stallions, and bison. Prehistoric jewelry and figurines also have been found. Early humans may have worn these items. Other items may have had religious meaning.

> **Implied main idea:** Early humans created art and art objects for many purposes.

Strategies for Reading

- Look in the text for headings and subheadings that may indicate a chronological pattern of organization, such as *Early Life* or *The Later Years.*
- Look for words and phrases that identify times, such as *in a year, three weeks later, in* AD *79,* and *the next day.*
- Look for words that signal order, such as *first, afterward, then, during,* and *finally,* to see how events or steps are related.
- Note that a paragraph or passage in which ideas and information are arranged chronologically will have several words or phrases that indicate time order, not just one.
- Ask yourself: Are the events in the paragraph or passage presented in time order?

Notice the words and phrases that signal time in the first two paragraphs of the following model.

PRACTICE AND APPLY POSSIBLE ANSWERS

1. *Paragraph 1: Main Idea: Yellow is the best color to paint a room with few windows, or with windows that admit little sunlight.*
   Paragraph 2: Main Idea: Musical instruments come in a variety of shapes.

2. *Paragraph 1: stated*
   Paragraph 2: implied

Practice and Apply

Read each paragraph, and then do the following:

1. Identify the main idea in the paragraph, using one of the strategies discussed on the previous page.
2. Identify whether the main idea is stated or implied in the paragraph.

Yellow is the best color to paint a room with few windows, or with windows that admit little sunlight. Yellow is a light color, so it will make the room seem larger and will relieve the darkness. Yellow paint will also make it seem as if the sun is always shining, even on a rainy day. Finally, yellow will add warmth to the room.

The trombone is the only instrument with a long slide that the player moves back and forth to play different pitches. Flutes and piccolos have perfectly straight tubes; all other wind instruments have tubes that taper and end in bell shapes. The French horn is distinctive for its curved, curled shape and its bell that points backward.

2. Chronological Order

Chronological order is the arrangement of events in the order in which they happen. This type of organization is used in short stories and novels, historical writing, biographies, and autobiographies. To show the order of events, writers use order words, such as *before, after, next,* and *later,* and time words and phrases that identify specific times of day, days of the week, and dates, such as *the next morning, Friday,* and *on June 6, 2009.*

The great Chinese teacher Confucius was born in 551 BC. His father died when he was three years old. Although Confucius came from a very poor family, he studied hard and became well-educated.

> **Events**

> **Time phrase**

By the time he was 15, in 536 BC, Confucius's heart was set on learning. In his 30s, Confucius started his teaching career. He later became one of the most important teachers in history. One of his teachings was that people should treat each other the way they would like to be treated. His teachings still seem wise after 2,500 years.

When Confucius died in 479 BC, he had many followers. About 100 years later, one of his followers, Mencius, began spreading Confucius's ideas. Mencius extended these ideas and added some of his own. He taught that people are basically good and that everyone has equal value. For that reason, he believed that rulers are no better than their subjects. A good king, he said, must treat his people well.

PRACTICE AND APPLY
POSSIBLE ANSWERS

1. *By the time; In his 30s; When; 100 years later; After*

2. *Born in 551 BC; father died when he was three years old; started his teaching career in his 30s; died in 479 BC.*

3. *The timeline should contain all the events listed in step 2, in correct chronological order.*

After Mencius died in 289 BC, Hsun-tzu carried on Confucius' teachings. Hsun-tzu lived from about 300 to 230 BC. He did not agree with Mencius that people were basically good. Instead, he taught that human nature was evil. He did believe that education and strong laws and governments could help people become good. Some people say that Hsun-tzu's teachings about strong government later helped the dictator Shih Huang Ti to conquer China and set up the Ch'in Dynasty in 221 BC.

Order word

Practice and Apply

Reread the preceding model and then do the following:

1. List at least four words or phrases in the last three paragraphs that indicate time or order.

2. List all the events in Confucius's life that are mentioned in the model.

3. Create a timeline, beginning with Confucius's birth and ending in 479 BC, that shows all the events you listed for step 2.

3. Cause-Effect Organization

Cause-effect organization is a pattern of organization that shows the relationships between events, ideas, and trends. Cause-effect relationships may be directly stated or merely implied by the order in which the information is presented. Writers often use the cause-effect pattern in historical and scientific writing. Cause-effect relationships may have several forms.

One cause with one effect

Cause	Effect

One cause with multiple effects

Cause	Effect
	Effect

Multiple causes with a single effect

Cause	
	Effect
Cause	

A chain of causes and effects

Effect	Effect	Cause ▶	Effect

Strategies for Reading

- Look for headings and subheadings that indicate a cause-effect pattern of organization, such as "Effects of Hurricanes."
- To find the effect or effects, read to answer the question "What happened?"
- To find the cause or causes, read to answer the question "Why did it happen?"
- Look for words and phrases that help you identify specific relationships between events, such as *because, since, had the effect of, led to, as a result, resulted in, for that reason, due to, therefore, if . . . then,* and *consequently.*
- Look closely at each cause-effect relationship. Do not assume that because one event happened before another, the first event caused the second event.
- Use graphic organizers like the diagrams shown to record cause-effect relationships as you read.

Notice the words that signal causes and effects in the following model.

Model:
Watch Out for Mosquitoes

If you spend any time outdoors in the summer, at some point you will probably find yourself covered with mosquito bites. Mosquitoes can transmit serious diseases such as yellow fever, encephalitis, and malaria. Usually, though, mosquito bites just cause people to develop raised, red bumps that itch.

This is what happens. Female mosquitoes need blood to nourish their eggs. Consequently, they zero in on living things whose blood they can suck. Once they find a likely victim, the attack begins.

Cause
Effect
Cause
Signal word
Effect

This attack is not really a bite, since a mosquito isn't able to open her jaws. Instead, she punctures the victim's skin with sharp stylets inside her mouth. The mosquito's saliva then flows into these puncture wounds. Because the saliva keeps the victim's blood from clotting, the mosquito can drink her fill.

Meanwhile, the mosquito's saliva causes the person to have an allergic reaction. As a result, the person develops the itchy swelling we call a mosquito bite. Ironically, if the mosquito finishes eating before the victim slaps her or brushes her off, there will be less saliva left in the skin. Therefore, the redness and itching will not be so severe.

Practice and Apply

1. Make a graphic organizer like the sample illustrated on page R18 to show the chain of causes and effects described in the text.
2. List three words or phrases that the writer uses to signal cause-effect relationships in the last two paragraphs.

4. Compare-and-Contrast Organization

Compare-and-contrast organization is a pattern of organization that provides a way to look at similarities and differences in two or more subjects. A writer may use this pattern of organization to compare the important points or characteristics of two or more subjects. These points or characteristics are called **points of comparison.** The compare-and-contrast pattern of organization may be developed in either of two ways:

Point-by-point organization—The writer discusses one point of comparison for both subjects, then goes on to the next point.

Subject-by-subject organization—The writer covers all points of comparison for one subject and then all points of comparison for the next subject.

Strategies for Reading

- Look in the text for headings, subheadings, and sentences that may suggest a compare-

and-contrast pattern of organization, such as "Plants Share Many Characteristics," to help you identify where similarities and differences are addressed.

- To find similarities, look for words and phrases such as *like, similarly, both, all, every, also,* and *in the same way.*
- To find differences, look for words and phrases such as *unlike, but, on the other hand, more, less, in contrast,* and *however.*
- Use a graphic organizer, such as a Venn diagram or a compare-and-contrast chart, to record points of comparison and similarities and differences.

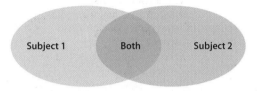

	Subject 1	Subject 2
Point 1		
Point 2		
Point 3		

Read the following models. As you read, use the signal words and phrases to identify the similarities and differences between the subjects and how the details are organized in each text.

Model 1
Pass the Bread, Please

There are as many varieties of bread as there are countries. Two kinds that you can enjoy today—from Paris, France, to Paris, Texas, and from Cairo, Illinois, to Cairo, Egypt—are the baguette and the bagel. Both baguettes and bagels are made from the same basic ingredients, which may include flour, water, yeast, butter, eggs, and salt. Different methods are used to prepare them, however. In each case, bakers first mix the dough, knead it, and leave it to rise. Unlike baguettes, though, bagels are boiled in water before they are

Comparison word

Subjects

Contrast word

Reading Informational Texts **R19**

PRACTICE AND APPLY POSSIBLE ANSWERS

1. *Chain of causes and effects: Mosquitos need food > zero in on living things > puncture skin > saliva flows into skin > causes allergic reaction > person develops itchy swelling*

2. *Then; Because; As a result; therefore*

PRACTICE AND APPLY
POSSIBLE ANSWERS

1. *Model 1: organized point by point*
   Model 2: organized by subject

2. *Model 1: on the other hand; in contrast*
   Model 2: unlike; different

3. *Model 1: the shape of bagels and baguettes; the ways in which they are made*
   Model 2: the type of people who like cats and dogs; the care needed by cats and dogs

4. *Venn diagrams will vary but should follow the model shown on page R19. A sample Venn diagram of Model 1 is shown.*

- *Baguettes are thin and long.*
- *Baguettes are soft in the center and have a crisp crust.*

- *Both are made from the same ingredients.*

- *Bagels are shaped like rings.*
- *Bagels are heavy and chewy.*

---

baked. This process makes them heavy and chewy and gives them a very light crust. Baguettes, on the other hand, are soft in the center and have a crisp, crunchy crust.

Another difference between the two types of bread is their shape. The word *baguette* means "wand" or "stick" in French. That describes what the bread looks like, too. Baguettes are thin and usually about two feet long. In some places, you can find shorter and fatter versions as well.

The bagel, in contrast, is shaped like a ring. Some legends say that it was originally created to honor a Polish king. It was made to look like a stirrup as a symbol of his victories in battle on horseback. Although all bagels are round, their size can vary greatly. You can choose from minibagels that are only a couple of inches in diameter to larger bagels six inches or more across.

Standard baguettes and bagels are both made from white flour. Nowadays, you can choose from a whole universe of variations, however. Baguettes come in sourdough, rye, or whole-wheat varieties.

Bagels come in all those varieties, too. In addition, though, they are available in flavors ranging from apple and blueberry to spinach and tomato. Inside, you might find raisins, nuts, or even chocolate chips. And they might be topped with poppy seeds, sunflower seeds, or sesame seeds.

So the next time you get a craving for crispy, light bread, try a baguette. But for chewy bread with tasty flavors and fillings, choose a bagel.

Model 2
What Kind of Person Are You?

There are definitely two types of people in the world—cat people and dog people. About the only thing they share is the fact that they like pets. Aside from that, they are as different as the pets they favor. Comparing these pets might help you figure out what kind of person you are.

Subjects

Comparison word

Contrast word

Cat people tend to be very independent. They don't like to be controlled or to control anything else. So they don't want an animal that needs a lot of attention. Cats are their perfect pets since they almost take care of themselves.

You can leave cats alone for days at a time. Just set out bowls of food and water, and they will eat and drink only what they want.

Cats also groom themselves without your help. They can be quite affectionate, but only on their own terms. A cat will snuggle with you—when and if it feels like it.

Dog people, on the other hand, enjoy feeling needed and don't mind having a pet that is more dependent. Dogs definitely are dependent.

Contrast words and phrases

Unlike cats, dogs need a lot of attention daily. They can't be left alone for more than several hours because they have to be fed and walked regularly. You can't just leave food out for them, because they'll eat it all at once. Dogs also generally need a lot of interaction with people. Many of them seem to think their only purpose in life is to please their owners.

As different as cats and dogs are, the good news is that there are plenty of each to go around.

Refer to the preceding models to answer the following questions:

1. Which model is organized by subject? Which model is organized by points of comparison?
2. Identify two words or phrases in each model that signal a compare-and-contrast pattern of organization.
3. List two points that the writer of each model compares and contrasts.
4. For one of the two models, use a Venn diagram or a compare-and-contrast chart to identify two or more points of comparison and the similarities and differences shown.

5. Problem-Solution Order

Problem-solution order is a pattern of organization in which a problem is stated and analyzed and then one or more solutions are proposed and examined. This pattern of organization is often used in persuasive writing, where an author expresses a specific viewpoint, such as in editorials or proposals.

Strategies for Reading

- Look for an explanation of the problem in the first or second paragraph.
- Look for words, such as *problem* and *reason,* that may signal an explanation of the problem.
- To find the solution, ask: What suggestion does the writer offer to solve the problem?
- Look for words, such as *propose, conclude,* and *answer,* that may signal a solution.

Model

It happened again last night. Two cars collided at the corner of West Avenue and Beach Street. This is the sixth accident that has taken place at that intersection in the past year. Luckily, no one has been seriously injured or killed so far. But we need to do something before it's too late. How many crashes do there have to be before we make the streets safer for everyone?

This intersection is so dangerous because West Avenue bends around just before it crosses Beach Street. This means that drivers or cyclists aren't able to see traffic approaching on West Avenue until they're entering the intersection. They have to just take their chances and hope they make it to the other side. Too many times, they don't.

One action that would help solve this problem would be to put a stoplight at the intersection. This would allow drivers and cyclists to move safely through the intersection in both directions. It would also slow traffic down and force people to pay more attention to their driving. Although it would cost the community some money to put in the stoplight, think how much it would save in car repairs, personal injuries, and possibly even lives.

Here's what you can do to help solve this problem. First, talk to your friends and neighbors about it. Then, go to the village hall and sign the petition!

Reread the model and then answer the following questions:

1. According to the model, what is the cause of the problem?
2. What solution does the writer offer? What words are a clue?

RI 3,
RI 5

PRACTICE AND APPLY POSSIBLE ANSWERS

1. *Cause: Drivers cannot see other cars or people at the intersection because of a bend in the road.*
2. *Solution: a stoplight*
   Possible clues: we need to do something; one action that would help solve; solve this problem

PRACTICE AND APPLY POSSIBLE ANSWERS

Students should create a chart similar to the one on page R22. The chart should include details similar to the ones below.

Claim: *This school needs a swimming pool.*
Reasons: *Learning to swim can save your life; swimming can keep you healthy.*
Evidence: *Swimming is one of the few activities that won't harm the body but can improve circulation, breathing and mobility.*
Counterargument: *Kids can swim at the local health club; however most kids can't afford it, and even if they can, they won't have time between homework, classes, and jobs.*

Reading Arguments

1. Analyzing an Argument

A **persuasive text** is writing that tries to sway its readers' feelings, beliefs, or actions. It typically makes use of an argument and persuasive devices, or tricks. An **argument** is a logical appeal that consists of the following elements:

- A **claim** is the writer's position on an issue or problem. It usually reflects the writer's viewpoint, or attitude, on the issue.
- **Support** consists of the reasons and evidence given to support a claim.
- **Reasons** are declarations made to justify an action, decision, or belief. For example, "I carry an umbrella *because it rains so often.*"
- **Evidence** can be facts, expert opinions, examples, or other details that back up a reason or a claim. For example, "This week, it has rained every day!" (fact)
- A **counterargument** is an argument made to answer likely objections.

Claim	We get too much homework.
Reason	We have no time for other activities.
Evidence	We had to quit Eagle Scouts.
Counter-argument	Students do need to do a certain amount of homework to learn, but the amount we get is more than necessary. It's overwhelming.

Practice and Apply

Use a chart like the one shown to identify the claim, reasons, evidence, and counterargument in the following editorial.

Our School Needs to Get in the Swim
by Maria Lopez

This school needs a swimming pool. Swimming is an important life skill and one of the best forms of exercise there is. It is one of the few activities that won't harm the body and can actually improve circulation,

breathing, and mobility. I believe it is the responsibility of the school to provide this essential part of students' lifelong education.

The school's mission is to educate the whole person—mind and body—and to prepare students to be productive citizens. In addition to our academic subjects, we are taught how to eat right and budget our money. But we don't learn the water safety skills that could someday save our lives.

The community and school board obviously don't feel the same way about this issue as I do, however. They repeatedly have refused to fund the building of a pool. In the opinion of one board member, "Students can take swimming lessons at the local health club." Other school officials think that the school has more important needs, such as repairing the sagging gym floor.

In my opinion, these reasons are not valid. First, most students cannot afford swimming lessons at the health club. Even those who have the money don't have the time. They're busy with homework and other activities during the school year and have to work or go to summer school during vacation.

I agree that the gym floor should be replaced, but I believe that educational needs should come first. Even if knowing how to swim never saves your life, it can improve its quality. Isn't that what an education is all about?

2. Recognizing Persuasive Techniques

Persuasive texts typically rely on more than just the **logical appeal** of an argument to be convincing. They also rely on ethical and emotional appeals and other **persuasive techniques**—devices that can convince you to adopt a position or take an action.

Ethical appeals establish a writer's credibility and trustworthiness with an audience. When a writer links a claim to a widely accepted value, the writer not only gains moral support for that claim but also establishes him- or herself as a reputable person readers can trust. For example, with the following appeal the writer reminds readers of a value they should accept and aligns himself with the reader: "Most of us think it's important to be informed about current events, but we don't spend much time reading newspapers."

The chart shown here explains several other methods of persuasion.

Persuasive Technique	Example
Appeals by Association	
Bandwagon appeal Suggests that a person should believe or do something because "everyone else" does	Don't be the last person in town to be connected to Neighbor Net.
Testimonial Relies on endorsements from well-known people or satisfied customers	Start your day with the vitamins recommended by four out of five doctors— Superstrength Vigorvites.
Snob appeal Taps into people's desire to be special or part of an elite group	You deserve to eat like a king. Join the distinguished diners at Marco's Palace.
Appeal to loyalty Relies on people's affiliation with a particular group	Show your support for the community by marching in our local parade!
Emotional Appeals	
Appeals to pity, fear, or vanity Use strong feelings, rather than facts, to persuade	If you don't see a dentist regularly, your teeth will rot.

Practice and Apply

Identify the persuasive techniques used in this model.

Learn While You Sleep

Join the increasing number of with-it people who are making every hour of their day—and night—count. No matter whether they're awake or asleep, they keep going, growing, and improving themselves every minute. Impossible? Not according to college basketball superstar Jordan Navarro, whose grade-point average went from 2.5 to 4.0 after just one month

on the program. "As amazing as it sounds, my free-throw average shot up, too," he said. Stop wasting time and start becoming the smart and effective person you always dreamed of being. Just call 555-ZZ-LEARN and sign up right now.

3. Analyzing Logic and Reasoning

While persuasive techniques may sway you to side with a writer, they should not be enough to convince you that an argument is sound. To determine the soundness of an argument, you really need to examine the argument's claim and support and the logic or reasoning that links them. To do this, identify the writer's mode of reasoning.

The Inductive Mode of Reasoning

When a person adds up evidence to arrive at a general idea, or generalization, that person is using **inductive reasoning.** Here is an example.

Evidence

Fact 1 Allison's eyes swell and she has trouble breathing when she's around cats.

Fact 2 Roses make her sister Lucy sneeze.

Fact 3 Max gets an allergic reaction from nuts.

Generalization

People can be allergic to animals, plants, and foods.

Strategies for Determining the Soundness of Inductive Reasoning

Ask yourself the following questions to evaluate inductive reasoning.

- **Is the evidence valid?** Inaccurate facts can lead to false conclusions.
- **Does the conclusion follow logically from the evidence?** From the facts listed, the conclusion that *all* animals, plants, and foods cause allergic reactions would be too broad.
- **Is the evidence drawn from a large enough sample?** These three facts are enough to support the generalization. However, if you wanted to support a conclusion that most people are allergic to something, you would need a much larger sample.

RI 4, RI 5

PRACTICE AND APPLY POSSIBLE ANSWERS

Persuasive techniques: bandwagon appeal, testimonial, snob appeal, appeal to vanity

PRACTICE AND APPLY
POSSIBLE ANSWERS

deductive reasoning

PRACTICE AND APPLY
POSSIBLE ANSWERS

The last three sentences contain unsupported inferences. There is insufficient evidence to support the inference that it is gym class that makes the writer's cousin healthy or that physical education alone would make the students at the writer's school healthy. There is no evidence to support the inference that physical education classes would help students get along better.

The Deductive Mode of Reasoning

When a person starts with a generally accepted idea and then applies it to a situation or problem in order to reach a conclusion, that person is using **deductive reasoning.** Here's an example.

Many people are allergic to animals.	Generally accepted idea
Allison's eyes swell up and she has trouble breathing when she's around cats.	Specific situation
Allison is allergic to cats.	Conclusion

Strategies for Determining the Soundness of Deductive Reasoning

Ask yourself the following questions to evaluate deductive reasoning.

- **What is the generally accepted idea or generalization that the conclusion is based on?** Writers don't always state their general idea. So you may need to begin your evaluation by identifying it.
- **Is the generally accepted idea or generalization something you know is true and agree with?** Sometimes it isn't. Be sure to consider whether you think it is really true.
- **Is the conclusion valid?** To be valid, the conclusion must be the only logical one you can reach by applying the general idea to the specific situation. Here is an example of flawed deductive reasoning.

Many people are allergic to animals.	Generally accepted idea
Allison's eyes are swollen and she's having trouble breathing.	Specific situation
Allison is allergic to cats.	Conclusion

While the general idea is true, there is no evidence present in this situation to suggest that Allison's symptoms are the result of an allergy to any animal.

Identify the mode of reasoning used here.

I was doing my homework in my room last night when the light went out. Going into the hall, I saw that the kitchen lights were still on. That told me the problem was just in my room. The lamp was still plugged in, so I put in a new light bulb. Luckily, that worked.

Unsupported Inferences

An **inference** is a guess that is based on evidence and, usually, some sort of prior knowledge.

An **unsupported inference** is a guess that is not adequately supported by the evidence that has been provided.

See whether you can spot the unsupported inference in the following paragraph.

Model

My pediatrician says, "When children exercise, they establish a positive pattern for the rest of their lives." That was true for my mom. She danced as a child and now does aerobics as an adult. Clearly, children who exercise regularly are likely to become adults who exercise regularly. They are also more likely to get involved in aerobics classes as adults.

If you guessed that the last sentence in the model was an unsupported inference, you would be right. Although the writer's mother went on to take aerobics classes as an adult, there is certainly not enough evidence present to back up the last statement.

Identify the unsupported inferences in the following text. Give reasons for your answers.

A good education should include physical fitness classes. The exercise that children get in gym class helps make them strong. It also helps them establish the healthy habit of exercising. My cousin's gym classes have made her the healthy girl she is today. I am sure that we would be healthy, too, if we had physical education at school. We would also get along better.

Identifying Faulty Reasoning

Have you ever heard or read an argument that struck you as being wrong or faulty but been unable to say just why? If so, chances are good that the argument was based on a **logical fallacy,** or an error in logic. Becoming familiar with common fallacies will give you a better chance of detecting their presence and explaining precisely why an argument is unconvincing. This chart identifies errors in logic that most often find their way into arguments.

Type of Fallacy	Definition	Example
Circular reasoning	Supporting a statement by simply repeating it in different words	I forgot my lunch because **I didn't remember to bring it.**
Either/or fallacy	A statement that suggests that there are only two choices available in a situation that really offers more than two options	**Either** you get an A in English this year **or** you'll get an F.
Oversimplification	An explanation of a complex situation or problem as if it were much simpler than it is	**Just be a good listener** and you'll have lots of friends.
Overgeneralization	A generalization that is too broad. You can often recognize overgeneralizations by the use of words such as *all, everyone, every time, anything, no one,* and *none.*	I **always** say the wrong thing.
Hasty generalization	A conclusion drawn from too little evidence or from evidence that is biased	**We all must have done badly on the test,** because Ms. Chen looked angry at the beginning of class today.
Stereotyping	A dangerous type of overgeneralization. Stereotypes are broad statements about people on the basis of their gender, ethnicity, race, or political, social, professional, or religious group.	**Boys** are better at sports than **girls** are.
Attacking the person or name-calling	An attempt to discredit an idea by attacking the person or group associated with it	Only **immature** people like animated movies.
Evading the issue	Responding to an objection with arguments and evidence that do not address its central point	I didn't tell you I broke the statue, **but you said you never liked it anyway.**
False cause	The mistake of assuming that because one event occurred after another event in time, the first event caused the second one	Ellie studied really hard for the test, **so the teacher cancelled it.**

PRACTICE AND APPLY ANSWERS

Circular Reasoning: *My parents can't understand me because they just don't get it. ("Can't understand" and "just don't get it" mean the same thing.)*

Attacking the person/Stereotyping: *Adults are like robots . . .*

Overgeneralization: *All my friends are allowed . . .*

Oversimplification: *Why? Because that's how my parents were raised.*

Either/or fallacy: *If I can't stay up later, I'll lose all my friends.*

Hasty generalization: *I'll never understand, because I'll never have kids.*

Look for examples of logical fallacies in the following argument. Identify each one and explain why you identified it as such.

My parents can't understand me because they just don't get it. Adults are like robots and just keep doing things the way they were taught. For example, all my friends are allowed to stay up as late as they want on weekends, but I have to be in bed by 9:00. Why? Because that's how my parents were raised. I've tried to explain to them that if I can't stay up later, I'll lose all my friends. They just say I'll understand when I'm a parent. Well, I guess I'll never understand, because I'll never have kids.

4. Evaluating Persuasive Texts

Learning how to evaluate persuasive texts and identify bias and propaganda will help you become more selective when doing research or just trying to stay informed.

Strategies for Identifying Bias

Bias is an inclination for or against a particular opinion or viewpoint. Journalists usually try to keep their personal biases from affecting their writing, but sometimes a bias shows up anyway. Here are some of the most common signs of bias.

- Presenting just one way of looking at an issue or topic
- The absence of key information
- Stacking more evidence on one side of the argument than the other
- Treating weak or unproven evidence as valid and important
- Using **loaded language,** or words with strongly positive or negative connotations

EXAMPLE

This movie insults my intelligence. It was so ridiculous that I walked out before it was done. (*Insults* and *ridiculous* have very negative connotations.)

Strategies for Identifying Propaganda

Propaganda is any form of communication that is so distorted that it conveys false or misleading information. When a text includes more than one of the following, it is probably propaganda.

- Signs of **bias,** such as the absence of key information
- Inflammatory images that make powerful **emotional appeals**
- **Logical fallacies,** such as name-calling, false cause, and the either/or fallacy
- Lots of **ethical appeals,** or attempts to make readers feel that they and the writer(s) of the text share the same values

EXAMPLE

I care about you people. He doesn't. His voting record shows that he really only cares about rich businessmen. (The candidate does not mention that he voted exactly the same way as his opponent did on the issues.)

Strategies for Evaluating Evidence

Use the questions below to critically evaluate evidence in persuasive texts.

- **Are the facts presented verifiable?** Facts can be proven by eyewitness accounts, authoritative sources, experts, or research.
- **Are the opinions well informed?** Any opinions offered as support should come from experts on the topic or eyewitnesses to the event.
- **Is the evidence sufficient?** Sufficient evidence leaves no reasonable questions unanswered. If a choice is offered, background for making the choice is provided. If taking a side is called for, all sides of the issue are presented.
- **Is the evidence relevant?** The evidence should come from sources that the text's intended audience respects and regards as suitable. For example, in a report for scientists, evidence should come from scientific journals, experts in the field, and experiments rather than a casual poll of friends, a personal experience, or an expert in some unrelated field.

Read the argument below. Identify the facts, opinions, and elements of bias.

Lewis Middle School doesn't care about students' needs. I know the school board voted to remove our lockers so we can't hide dangerous items there. We don't deserve this lack of respect and suspicion, though. The lockers gave us a place to store our books, jackets, lunches, and other gear when we weren't using them. It's not fair to make us haul our stuff around all day. After all, my textbooks alone weigh over 70 pounds—as much as I do. Would you board members want to carry me around on your back all day?

Strategies for Determining a Strong Argument

Make sure that all or most of the following statements are true.

- The argument presents a claim or thesis.
- The claim is connected to its support by a general principle that most readers would readily agree with. Valid general principle: *People are responsible for treating others with kindness.* Invalid general principle: *People are responsible for making other people happy.*
- The reasons make sense.
- The reasons are presented in a logical and effective order.
- The claim and all reasons are adequately supported by sound evidence.
- The evidence is adequate, accurate, and appropriate.
- The logic is sound. There are no instances of faulty reasoning.
- The argument offers counterarguments to address possible reader concerns and counterclaims.

Use the preceding criteria to evaluate the strength of the following proposal.

Model

Summary of Proposal

I propose that the town put trash containers at bus stops, train stations, playgrounds, parks, beaches, and all other public areas.

Need

The community is littered with paper, food and drink containers, and other garbage. This situation doesn't make us feel good about ourselves or where we live.

Proposed Solution

Making trash containers available in places where people gather will help create a cleaner environment and restore our pride in our community.

Everybody would be willing to throw their bottles, cans, newspapers, gum wrappers, bags, and other garbage in a container if there was one available. Most people aren't willing to carry their trash with them until they find a proper place to throw it, however. Many citizens are such slobs that they won't even walk across the street to throw something away rather than just dropping it on the ground.

I know that installing these trash containers will cost money. Workers also will have to be paid to empty them regularly. Another objection might be that kids sometimes overturn trash containers or enjoy rolling them around.

These objections are ridiculous, though. None of us really believe that having a clean, pleasant community wouldn't be worth the few dollars this would cost. And a simple—and cheap—way to prevent kids from playing with the containers would be to chain them to a pole or fence.

Either the town council votes to approve this proposal and put it into effect right away, or the members should be voted out of office.

RI 4, RI 5, RI 8

PRACTICE AND APPLY ANSWERS

Facts: The school board voted to remove lockers. The lockers gave us a place to store our books. My textbooks alone weigh over 70 pounds . . .
Opinions: Lewis Middle School doesn't care about students' needs. We don't deserve this suspicion. It's not fair.
Elements of bias: loaded language (doesn't care, not fair, suspicion, lack of respect)

RI 2, RI 4, RI 5, RI 6, RI 8

PRACTICE AND APPLY ANSWERS

Evaluations will vary. Students should identify the claim in the proposal and determine whether the reasons make sense and are supported by sound evidence. Students should decide if bias or faulty reasoning weakens the proposal. Students should also determine whether the proposal offers counterarguments.

Grammar

Writing that has a lot of mistakes can confuse or even annoy a reader. Punctuation errors in a letter might lead to a miscommunication or delay a reply. A sentence fragment might lower your grade on an essay. Paying attention to grammar, punctuation, and capitalization rules can make your writing clearer and easier to read.

Quick Reference: Parts of Speech

Part of Speech	Function	Examples
Noun	names a person, a place, a thing, an idea, a quality, or an action	
Common	serves as a general name, or a name common to an entire group	subway, fog, puzzle, tollbooth
Proper	names a specific, one-of-a-kind person, place, or thing	Mrs. Price, Pompeii, China, Meg
Singular	refers to a single person, place, thing, or idea	onion, waterfall, lamb, sofa
Plural	refers to more than one person, place, thing, or idea	dreams, commercials, men, tortillas
Concrete	names something that can be perceived by the senses	jacket, teacher, caterpillar, aroma
Abstract	names something that cannot be perceived by the senses	friendship, opportunities, fear, stubbornness
Compound	expresses a single idea through a combination of two or more words	jump rope, paycheck, dragonfly, sandpaper
Collective	refers to a group of people or things	colony, family, clan, flock
Possessive	shows who or what owns something	Mama's, Tito's, children's, waitresses'
Pronoun	takes the place of a noun or another pronoun	
Personal	refers to the person making a statement, the person(s) being addressed, or the person(s) or thing(s) the statement is about	I, me, my, mine, we, us, our, ours, you, your, yours, she, he, it, her, him, hers, his, its, they, them, their, theirs
Reflexive	follows a verb or preposition and refers to a preceding noun or pronoun	myself, yourself, herself, himself, itself, ourselves, yourselves, themselves
Intensive	emphasizes a noun or another pronoun	(same as reflexives)
Demonstrative	points to one or more specific persons or things	this, that, these, those

continued

Part of Speech	Function	Examples
Interrogative	signals a question	who, whom, whose, which, what
Indefinite	refers to one or more persons or things not specifically mentioned	both, all, most, many, anyone, everybody, several, none, some
Relative	introduces an adjective clause by relating it to a word in the clause	who, whom, whose, which, that
Verb	expresses an action, a condition, or a state of being	
Action	tells what the subject does or did, physically or mentally	run, reaches, listened, consider, decides, dreamed
Linking	connects the subject to something that identifies or describes it	am, is, are, was, were, sound, taste, appear, feel, become, remain, seem
Auxiliary	precedes the main verb in a verb phrase	be, have, do, can, could, will, would, may, might
Transitive	directs the action toward someone or something; always has an object	The storm **sank** the ship.
Intransitive	does not direct the action toward someone or something; does not have an object	The ship **sank.**
Adjective	modifies a noun or pronoun	**strong** women, **two** epics, **enough** time
Adverb	modifies a verb, an adjective, or another adverb	walked **out, really** funny, **far** away
Preposition	relates one word to another word	at, by, for, from, in, of, on, to, with
Conjunction	joins words or word groups	
Coordinating	joins words or word groups used the same way	and, but, or, for, so, yet, nor
Correlative	used as a pair to join words or word groups used the same way	both . . . and, either . . . or, neither . . . nor
Subordinating	introduces a clause that cannot stand by itself as a complete sentence	although, after, as, before, because, when, if, unless
Interjection	expresses emotion	wow, ouch, hurrah

Quick Reference: The Sentence and Its Parts

The diagrams that follow will give you a brief review of the essentials of a sentence and some of its parts.

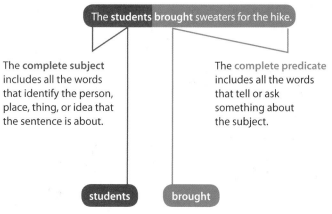

The **students brought** sweaters for the hike.

The **complete subject** includes all the words that identify the person, place, thing, or idea that the sentence is about.

The **complete predicate** includes all the words that tell or ask something about the subject.

students

brought

The **simple subject** tells exactly whom or what the sentence is about. It may be one word or a group of words, but it does not include modifiers.

The **simple predicate** or **verb,** tells what the subject does or is. It may be one word or several, but it does not include modifiers.

Every word in a sentence is part of a complete subject or a complete predicate.

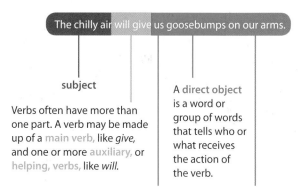

The chilly air will give us goosebumps on our arms.

subject

Verbs often have more than one part. A verb may be made up of a main verb, like *give,* and one or more auxiliary, or helping, verbs, like *will.*

A **direct object** is a word or group of words that tells who or what receives the action of the verb.

An **indirect object** is a word or group of words that tells to whom or for whom or to what or for what the verb's action is performed. A sentence can have an indirect object only if it has a direct object. The indirect object always comes before the direct object.

A **prepositional phrase** consists of a preposition, its object, and any modifiers of the object. In this phrase, *on* is the preposition, *arms* is the object, and *our* modifies *arms.*

Quick Reference: Punctuation

Mark	Function	Examples
End Marks period, question mark, exclamation point	ends a sentence	We can start now. When would you like to leave? What a fantastic hit!
period	follows an initial or abbreviation **Exception**: postal abbreviations of states	Mrs. Dorothy Parker, Apple Inc., C. P. Cavafy, P.M., lb., oz., Blvd., Dr., NE (Nebraska), NV (Nevada)

period	follows a number or letter in an outline
	or a list
		I. Volcanoes
		  A. Central-vent
		    1. Shield

Comma	separates parts of a compound sentence	I had never disliked poetry, but now I really love it.
	separates items in a series	She is brave, loyal, and kind.
	separates adjectives of equal rank that modify the same noun	The slow, easy route is best.
	sets off a term of address	Maria, how can I help you? You must do something, soldier.
	sets off a parenthetical expression	Hard workers, as you know, don't quit. I'm not a quitter, believe me.
	sets off an introductory word, phrase, or dependent clause	Yes, I forgot my key. At the begin- ning of the day, I feel fresh. While she was out, I was here. Having finished my chores, I went out.
	sets off a nonessential phrase or clause	Ed Pawn, the captain of the chess team, won. Ed Pawn, who is the captain, won. The two leading runners, sprinting toward the finish line, finished in a tie.
	sets off parts of dates and addresses	Mail it by May 14, 2010, to the Hauptman Company, 321 Market Street, Memphis, Tennessee.
	separates words to avoid confusion	By noon, time had run out. What the minister does, does matter. While cooking, Jim burned his hand.

Mark	Function	Examples
Semicolon	separates items in a series that contain commas	We spent the first week of summer vacation in Chicago, Illinois; the second week in St. Louis, Missouri; and the third week in Albany, New York.
	separates parts of a compound sentence that are not joined by a coordinating conjunction	The last shall be first; the first shall be last. I read the Bible; however, I have not memorized it.
	separates parts of a compound sentence when the parts contain commas	After I ran out of money, I called my parents; but only my sister was home, unfortunately.
Colon	introduces a list	The names we wrote were the following: Dana, John, and Will.
	introduces a long quotation	Abraham Lincoln wrote: "Four score and seven years ago, our fathers brought forth on this continent a new nation. . . ."
	follows the salutation of a business letter	To Whom It May Concern: Dear Leonard Atole:
	separates certain numbers	1:28 P.M., Genesis 2:5
Dash	indicates an abrupt break in thought	I was thinking of my mother—who is arriving tomorrow— just as you walked in.
Parentheses	enclose less important material	It was so unlike him (John is always on time) that I began to worry. The last World Series game (did you see it?) was fun.
Hyphen	joins parts of a compound adjective before a noun	That's a not-so-happy face.
	joins parts of a compound with *all-*, *ex-*, *self-*, or *-elect*	The ex-firefighter helped rescue him. Our president-elect is self-conscious.
	joins parts of a compound number (to ninety-nine)	My bicycle wheel has twenty-six spokes.
	joins parts of a fraction	My cup is one-third full.
	joins a prefix to a word beginning with a capital letter	Were your grandparents born post-World War II? The mid-April snowstorm surprised everyone.
	indicates that a word is divided at the end of a line	How could you have any reason-able expectations of getting a new computer?

continued

Mark	Function	Examples
Apostrophe	used with *s* to form the possessive of a noun or an indefinite pronoun	my friend's book, my friends' books, anyone's guess, somebody else's problem
	replaces one or more omitted letters in a contraction or numbers in a date	don't (omitted *o*), he'd (omitted *woul*), the class of '99 (omitted *19*)
	used with *s* to form the plural of a letter	I had two A's on my report card.
Quotation Marks	set off a speaker's exact words	Sara said, "I'm finally ready." "I'm ready," Sara said, "finally." Did Sara say, "I'm ready"? Sara said, "I'm ready!"
	set off the title of a story, an article, a short poem, an essay, a song, or a chapter	I like Salisbury's "The Ravine" and Frost's "The Road Not Taken." I like Blake Shelton's "Over You."
Ellipses	replace material omitted from a quotation	"Early one morning, Mrs. Bunnin wobbled into the classroom lugging a large cardboard box. . . . Robert was at his desk scribbling a ballpoint tattoo . . . on the tops of his knuckles."
Italics	indicate the title of a book, a play, a magazine, a long poem, an opera, a film, or a TV series, or the name of a ship	*Colin Powell: Military Leader*, *The Prince and the Pauper*, *Time*, *After the Hurricane*, *The Marriage of Figaro*, *Hatchet*, *American Idol*, *Titanic*

Quick Reference: Capitalization

Category	Examples
People and Titles	
Names and initials of people	Maya Angelou, **W.E.B.** DuBois
Titles used before a name	Mrs. Price, Scoutmaster Brenkman
Deities and members of religious groups	Jesus, Allah, Buddha, Zeus, Baptists
Names of ethnic and national groups	Hispanics, Jews, African Americans
Geographical Names	
Cities, states, countries, continents	Philadelphia, Kansas, Japan, Europe
Regions, bodies of water, mountains	the South, Lake Baikal, Mount Everest
Geographic features, parks	Great Basin, Yellowstone National Park
Streets and roads, planets	318 East Sutton Drive, Charles Court, Jupiter, Mars
Organizations, Events, Etc.	
Companies, organizations, teams	Ford Motor Company, Boy Scouts of America, St. Louis Cardinals
Buildings, bridges, monuments	Empire State Building, Eads Bridge, Washington Monument
Documents, awards	Declaration of Independence, Stanley Cup
Special named events	Mardi Gras, World Series
Government bodies, historical periods and events	U.S. Senate, House of Representatives, Middle Ages, Vietnam War
Days and months, holidays	Thursday, March, Thanksgiving, Labor Day
Specific cars, boats, trains, planes	Porsche, *Carpathia*, *Southwest Chief*, Concorde
Proper Adjectives	
Adjectives formed from proper nouns	French cooking, Spanish omelet, Edwardian age
First Words and the Pronoun *I*	
First word in a sentence or quotation	This is it. He said, "Let's go." I have it.
First word of a sentence in parentheses that is not within another sentence	The spelling rules are covered in another section. (Consult that section for more information.)
First words in the salutation and closing of a letter	Dear Madam, Very truly yours,
First word, last word, and all important words in a title	"Alone in the Nets," *Under the Royal Palms*

1 Nouns

A **noun** is a word used to name a person, a place, a thing, an idea, a quality, or an action. Nouns can be classified in several ways.

For more information on different types of nouns, see **Quick Reference: Parts of Speech,** page R28.

1.1 COMMON NOUNS

Common nouns are general names, common to entire groups.

1.2 PROPER NOUNS

Proper nouns name specific, one-of-a-kind people, places, and things.

Common	Proper
volcano, student, country, president	Mount Vesuvius, June, China, President Cleveland

For more information, see **Quick Reference: Capitalization,** page R34.

1.3 SINGULAR AND PLURAL NOUNS

A noun may take a singular or a plural form, depending on whether it names a single person, place, thing, or idea or more than one. Make sure you use appropriate spellings when forming plurals.

Singular	Plural
walrus, bully, lagoon, goose	walruses, bullies, lagoons, geese

For more information, see **Forming Plural Nouns,** page R58.

1.4 POSSESSIVE NOUNS

A **possessive noun** shows who or what owns something.

For more information, see **Forming Possessives,** page R58.

2 Pronouns

A **pronoun** is a word that is used in place of a noun or another pronoun. The word or word group to which the pronoun refers is called its **antecedent.**

2.1 PERSONAL PRONOUNS

Personal pronouns change their form to express person, number, gender, and case. The forms of these pronouns are shown in the following chart.

	Nominative	Objective	Possessive
Singular			
First Person	I	me	my, mine
Second Person	you	you	your, yours
Third Person	she, he, it	her, him, it	her, hers, his, its
Plural			
First Person	we	us	our, ours
Second Person	you	you	your, yours
Third Person	they	them	their, theirs

2.2 AGREEMENT WITH ANTECEDENT

Pronouns should agree with their antecedents in number, gender, and person.

If an antecedent is singular, use a singular pronoun.

> EXAMPLE: That **poem** was fun to read. *It rhymed.*

If an antecedent is plural, use a plural pronoun.

> EXAMPLES: *Poets choose their words carefully.*
> *I like **poems,** but Mischa doesn't care for them.*

The gender of a pronoun must be the same as the gender of its antecedent.

> EXAMPLE: *Eve Merriam's creativity makes her poems easy to remember.*

The person of the pronoun must be the same as the person of its antecedent. As the chart in Section 2.1 shows, a pronoun

L 1a

GRAMMAR PRACTICE ANSWERS

1. *her*
2. *I*
3. *their*
4. *they*
5. *my*

L 1a

GRAMMAR PRACTICE ANSWERS

1. *he*
2. *her*
3. *their*
4. *We*
5. *I*

---

can be in first-person, second-person, or third-person form.

EXAMPLES: *We each have our favorite poets.*

Grammar Practice

Rewrite each sentence so that the underlined pronoun agrees with its antecedent.

1. The speaker in Maya Angelou's poem "Life Doesn't Frighten Me" talks about <u>their</u> fears.
2. When I read this poem, <u>we</u> felt braver already.
3. Scary things lose <u>its</u> power.
4. Even frogs and snakes don't seem as bad as <u>you</u> usually do.
5. I want to know how to be unafraid in <u>her</u> life.

2.3 PRONOUN FORMS

Personal pronouns change form to show how they function in sentences. The three forms are the subject form, the object form, and the possessive form. For examples of these pronouns, see the chart in Section 2.1.

A **subject pronoun** is used as a subject in a sentence.

EXAMPLES: *Steven is my brother. He is the best player on the team.*

Also use the subject form when the pronoun follows a linking verb.

EXAMPLE: *The girl in the closet was she.*

An **object pronoun** is used as a direct object, an indirect object, or the object of a preposition.

SUBJECT   OBJECT
They locked her in it.
            OBJECT OF PREPOSITION

A **possessive pronoun** shows ownership. The pronouns *mine, yours, hers, his, its, ours,* and *theirs* can be used in place of nouns.

EXAMPLE: *The cat is mine.*

The pronouns *my, your, her, his, its, our,* and *their* are used before nouns.

EXAMPLE: *I found her keys on the floor.*

WATCH OUT! Many spelling errors can be avoided if you watch out for *its* and *their.* Don't confuse the possessive pronoun *its* with the contraction *it's,* meaning "it is" or "it has." The homonyms *they're* (a contraction of *they are*) and *there* ("in that place") are often mistakenly used for *their.*

TIP To decide which pronoun to use in a comparison, such as "He tells better tales than (*I* or *me*)," fill in the missing word(s): *He tells better tales than I tell.*

Grammar Practice

Write the correct pronoun form to complete each sentence.

1. When (he, him) is done with the book, I will give it to you.
2. Mary is going to invite (her, she) to go rollerskating.
3. My friends have lost (their, they) tickets.
4. (We, Us) can cook vegetables on the grill tonight, or we can make a salad.
5. (I, Me) sent an e-mail earlier today to my aunt.

2.4 REFLEXIVE AND INTENSIVE PRONOUNS

These pronouns are formed by adding *-self* or *-selves* to certain personal pronouns. Their forms are the same, and they differ only in how they are used.

A **reflexive pronoun** follows a verb or preposition and reflects back on an earlier noun or pronoun.

EXAMPLES: *He likes himself too much. She is now herself again.*

Intensive pronouns intensify or emphasize the nouns or pronouns to which they refer.

EXAMPLES: *They themselves will educate their children.*

You yourself did it.

WATCH OUT! Avoid using *hisself* or *theirselves.* Standard English does not include these forms.

> NONSTANDARD: *The children congratulated theirselves.*
>
> STANDARD: *The children congratulated themselves.*

2.5 DEMONSTRATIVE PRONOUNS

Demonstrative pronouns point out things and persons near and far.

	Singular	Plural
Near	this	these
Far	that	those

2.6 INDEFINITE PRONOUNS

Indefinite pronouns do not refer to specific persons or things and usually have no antecedents. The chart shows some commonly used indefinite pronouns.

Singular	Plural	Singular or Plural	
another	both	all	none
anybody	few	any	some
no one	many	more	most
neither			

TIP Indefinite pronouns that end in *one, body,* or *thing* are always singular.

> INCORRECT: *Did everybody play their part well?*

If the indefinite pronoun might refer to either a male or a female, *his or her* may be used to refer to it, or the sentence may be rewritten.

> CORRECT: *Did everybody play his or her part well? Did all the students play their parts well?*

2.7 INTERROGATIVE PRONOUNS

An **interrogative pronoun** tells a reader or listener that a question is coming. The interrogative pronouns are *who, whom, whose, which,* and *what.*

> EXAMPLES: *Who is going to rehearse with you?*
> *From whom did you receive the script?*

TIP *Who* is used as a subject; *whom* is used as an object. To find out which pronoun you need to use in a question, change the question to a statement.

> QUESTION: *(Who/Whom) did you meet there?*
>
> STATEMENT: *You met (?) there.*

Since the verb has a subject (*you*), the needed word must be the object form, *whom.*

> EXAMPLE: *Whom did you meet there?*

WATCH OUT! A special problem arises when you use an interrupter, such as *do you think,* within a question.

> EXAMPLE: *(Who/Whom) do you think will win?*

If you eliminate the interrupter, it is clear that the word you need is *who.*

2.8 RELATIVE PRONOUNS

Relative pronouns relate, or connect, adjective clauses to the words they modify in sentences. The noun or pronoun that a relative clause modifies is the antecedent of the relative pronoun. Here are the relative pronouns and their uses.

	Subject	Object	Possessive
Person	who	whom	whose
Thing	which	which	whose
Thing/ Person	that	that	whose

Often, short sentences with related ideas can be combined by using a relative pronoun to create a more effective sentence.

> SHORT SENTENCE: *Lucy is an accountant.*
>
> RELATED SENTENCE: *She helped us do our taxes.*
>
> COMBINED SENTENCE: *Lucy is an accountant who helped us do our taxes.*

GRAMMAR PRACTICE ANSWERS

1. *who*
2. *me*
3. *whom*
4. *We*
5. *she*

GRAMMAR PRACTICE ANSWERS

1. *The teacher was speaking to Maggie, and Maggie looked unhappy.*
2. *High winds developed and trapped mountain climbers in their tents.*
3. *Although Matt likes working at a donut shop, he doesn't eat donuts.*
4. *When the pitcher was set on the glass-topped table, the table broke.*
5. *They unloaded the clothes from the boxes and then threw away the boxes.*

Grammar Practice

Write the correct form of each incorrect pronoun.

1. John is a car salesman whom helped me buy a new automobile.
2. The pitcher threw the ball to I.
3. To who should I address this letter?
4. Us love the sea.
5. Betty is as smart as her is.

2.9 PRONOUN REFERENCE PROBLEMS

You should always be able to identify the word a pronoun refers to. Avoid problems by rewriting sentences.

An **indefinite reference** occurs when the pronoun *it, you,* or *they* does not clearly refer to a specific antecedent.

> UNCLEAR: *They told me how the story ended, and it was annoying.*
>
> CLEAR: *They told me how the story ended, and I was annoyed.*

A **general reference** occurs when the pronoun *it, this, that, which,* or *such* is used to refer to a general idea rather than a specific antecedent.

> UNCLEAR: *I'd rather not know what happens. That keeps me interested.*
>
> CLEAR: *I'd rather not know what happens. Not knowing keeps me interested.*

Ambiguous means "having more than one possible meaning." An **ambiguous reference** occurs when a pronoun could refer to two or more antecedents.

> UNCLEAR: *Jan told Danielle that she would read her story aloud.*
>
> CLEAR: *Jan told Danielle that she would read Danielle's story aloud.*

Grammar Practice

Rewrite the following sentences to correct indefinite, ambiguous, and general pronoun references.

1. The teacher was speaking to Maggie, and she looked unhappy.
2. High winds developed. This trapped mountain climbers in their tents.

3. Although Matt likes working at a donut shop, he doesn't eat them.
4. The pitcher was set on the glass-topped table and it broke.
5. They unloaded the clothes from the boxes and then threw them away.

3 Verbs

A **verb** is a word that expresses an action, a condition, or a state of being.

For more information, see **Quick Reference: Parts of Speech,** page R28.

3.1 ACTION VERBS

Action verbs express mental or physical activity.

> EXAMPLE: *Lucy ran several miles every day.*

3.2 LINKING VERBS

Linking verbs join subjects with words or phrases that rename or describe them.

> EXAMPLE: *After a few months, her shoes were worn out.*

3.3 PRINCIPAL PARTS

Action and linking verbs typically have four principal parts, which are used to form verb tenses. The principal parts are the **present,** the **present participle,** the **past,** and the **past participle.**

Action verbs and some linking verbs also fall into two categories: regular and irregular. A **regular verb** is a verb that forms its past and past participle by adding *-ed* or *-d* to the present form.

Present	Present Participle	Past	Past Participle
jump	(is) jumping	jumped	(has) jumped
solve	(is) solving	solved	(has) solved
grab	(is) grabbing	grabbed	(has) grabbed
carry	(is) carrying	carried	(has) carried

An **irregular verb** is a verb that forms its past and past participle in some other way than by adding *–ed* or *–d* to the present form.

Present	Present Participle	Past	Past Participle
begin	(is) beginning	began	(has) begun
break	(is) breaking	broke	(has) broken
go	(is) going	went	(has) gone

3.4 VERB TENSE

The **tense** of a verb indicates the time of the action or the state of being. An action or state of being can occur in the present, the past, or the future. There are six tenses, each expressing a different range of time.

The **present tense** expresses an action or state that is happening at the present time, occurs regularly, or is constant or generally true. Use the present part.

> NOW: *This apple is rotten.*
> REGULAR: *I eat an apple every day.*
> GENERAL: *Apples are round.*

The **past tense** expresses an action that began and ended in the past. Use the past part.

> EXAMPLE: *They settled the argument.*

The **future tense** expresses an action or state that will occur. Use *shall* or *will* with the present part.

> EXAMPLE: *You will understand someday.*

The **present perfect tense** expresses an action or state that (1) was completed at an indefinite time in the past or (2) began in the past and continues into the present. Use *have* or *has* with the past participle.

> EXAMPLE: *These buildings have existed for centuries.*

The **past perfect tense** expresses an action in the past that came before another action in the past. Use *had* with the past participle.

> EXAMPLE: *I had told you, but you forgot.*

The **future perfect tense** expresses an action in the future that will be completed before another action in the future. Use *shall have* or *will have* with the past participle.

> EXAMPLE: *She will have found the note by the time I get home.*

TIP A past-tense form of an irregular verb is not used with an auxiliary, or helping, verb, but a past-participle main irregular verb is always used with an auxiliary verb.

> INCORRECT: *He has did that too many times.* (*Did* is the past-tense form of an irregular verb and shouldn't be used with *has*.)
> INCORRECT: *He done that too many times.* (*Done* is the past participle of an irregular verb and shouldn't be used without an auxiliary verb.)
> CORRECT: *He has done that too many times.*

3.5 PROGRESSIVE FORMS

The progressive forms of the six tenses show ongoing actions. Use forms of *be* with the present participles of verbs.

> PRESENT PROGRESSIVE: *Angelo is taking the test.*
> PAST PROGRESSIVE: *Angelo was taking the test.*
> FUTURE PROGRESSIVE: *Angelo will be taking the test.*
> PRESENT PERFECT PROGRESSIVE: *Angelo has been taking the test.*
> PAST PERFECT PROGRESSIVE: *Angelo had been taking the test.*
> FUTURE PERFECT PROGRESSIVE: *Angelo will have been taking the test.*

WATCH OUT! Do not shift from tense to tense needlessly. Watch out for these special cases:

- In most compound sentences and in sentences with compound predicates, keep the tenses the same.

> INCORRECT: *She smiled and shake his hand.*
> CORRECT: *She smiled and shook his hand.*

Grammar **R39**

GRAMMAR PRACTICE ANSWERS

1. *became—past, was—past*
2. *changed—past*
3. *had been—past perfect, had—past*
4. *is—present*
5. *will remember—future*

GRAMMAR PRACTICE ANSWERS

1. *wrote*
2. *learned*
3. *had forgotten*
4. *did*
5. *had begun*

- If one past action happens before another, do shift tenses.

  INCORRECT: *He remembered what he studied.*

  CORRECT: *He remembered what he had studied.*

Grammar Practice

Rewrite each sentence using a form of the verb(s) in parentheses. Identify each form that you use.

1. Helen Keller (become) blind and deaf before she (be) two.
2. A wonderful teacher (change) her life.
3. Anne Sullivan (be) almost blind before she (have) an operation.
4. Even now, Keller (be) an inspiration to everyone with a disability.
5. People (remember) both Helen and her teacher for years to come.

Rewrite each sentence to correct an error in tense.

1. Helen Keller writes a book about her life.
2. She described how she learns to understand language.
3. She felt like she knew it once and forgotten it.
4. Anne Sullivan was a determined teacher and does not give up.
5. Helen had began a life of learning.

3.6 ACTIVE AND PASSIVE VOICE

The voice of a verb tells whether its subject performs or receives the action expressed by the verb. When the subject performs the action, the verb is in the **active voice.** When the subject is the receiver of the action, the verb is in the **passive voice.**

Compare these two sentences:

ACTIVE: *Nancy Wood wrote "Animal Wisdom."*

PASSIVE: *"Animal Wisdom" was written by Nancy Wood.*

To form the passive voice, use a form of ***be*** with the past participle of the verb.

WATCH OUT! Use the passive voice sparingly. It can make writing awkward and less direct.

AWKWARD: *"Animal Wisdom" is a poem that was written by Nancy Wood.*

BETTER: *Nancy Wood wrote the poem "Animal Wisdom."*

There are occasions when you will choose to use the passive voice because:

- you want to emphasize the receiver: ***The king was shot.***
- the doer is unknown: ***My books were stolen.***
- the doer is unimportant: ***French is spoken here.***

4 Modifiers

Modifiers are words or groups of words that change or limit the meanings of other words. Adjectives and adverbs are common modifiers.

4.1 ADJECTIVES

Adjectives modify nouns and pronouns by telling which one, what kind, how many, or how much.

WHICH ONE: *this, that, these, those*
EXAMPLE: *This poem moves along quickly.*

WHAT KIND: *square, dirty, fast, regular*
EXAMPLE: *Fast runners make baseball exciting.*

HOW MANY: *some, few, both, thousands*
EXAMPLE: *Thousands of fans cheer in the stands.*

HOW MUCH: *more, less, enough, as much*
EXAMPLE: *I had more fun watching the game than I expected.*

4.2 PREDICATE ADJECTIVES

Most adjectives come before the nouns they modify, as in the examples above. A **predicate adjective,** however, follows a linking verb and describes the subject.

EXAMPLE: *Baseball players are strong.*

Be especially careful to use adjectives (not adverbs) after such linking verbs as *look, feel, grow, taste,* and *smell.*

> EXAMPLE: *Exercising feels good.*

4.3 ADVERBS

Adverbs modify verbs, adjectives, and other adverbs by telling where, when, how, or to what extent.

> WHERE: *The children played outside.*
>
> WHEN: *The author spoke yesterday.*
>
> HOW: *We walked slowly behind the leader.*
>
> TO WHAT EXTENT: *He worked very hard.*

Adverbs may occur in many places in sentences, both before and after the words they modify.

> EXAMPLE: *Suddenly the wind shifted.*
>
> *The wind suddenly shifted.*
>
> *The wind shifted suddenly.*

4.4 ADJECTIVE OR ADVERB?

Many adverbs are formed by adding *–ly* to adjectives.

> EXAMPLES: *sweet, sweetly; gentle, gently*

However, *–ly* added to a noun will usually yield an adjective.

> EXAMPLES: *friend, friendly; woman, womanly*

4.5 COMPARISON OF MODIFIERS

Modifiers can be used to compare two or more things. The form of a modifier shows the degree of comparison. Both adjectives and adverbs have **comparative** and **superlative forms.**

The **comparative form** is used to compare two things, groups, or actions.

> EXAMPLES: *Today's weather is hotter than yesterday's.*
>
> *The boy got tired more quickly than his sister did.*

The **superlative form** is used to compare more than two things, groups, or actions.

> EXAMPLES: *This has been the hottest month ever recorded.*

Older people were most affected by the heat.

4.6 REGULAR COMPARISONS

Most one-syllable and some two-syllable adjectives and adverbs have comparatives and superlatives formed by adding *-er* and *-est.* All three-syllable and most two-syllable modifiers have comparatives and superlatives formed with *more* or *most.*

Modifier	Comparative	Superlative
messy	messier	messiest
quick	quicker	quickest
wild	wilder	wildest
tired	more tired	most tired
often	more often	most often

WATCH OUT! Note that spelling changes must sometimes be made to form the comparatives and superlatives of modifiers.

> AWKWARD: *friendly, friendlier* (Change *y* to *i* and add the ending.)
>
> *sad, sadder* (Double the final consonant and add the ending.)

4.7 IRREGULAR COMPARISONS

Some commonly used modifiers have irregular comparative and superlative forms. They are listed in the following chart. You may wish to memorize them.

Modifier	Comparative	Superlative
good	better	best
bad	worse	more
far	farther *or* further	farthest *or* furthest
little	less *or* lesser	least
many	more	most
well	better	best
much	more	most

GRAMMAR PRACTICE ANSWERS

1. *bad*
2. *worst*
3. *any*
4. *well*
5. *more*

4.8 PROBLEMS WITH MODIFIERS

Study the tips that follow to avoid common mistakes.

Farther and Further Use *farther* for distances; use *further* for everything else.

Double Comparisons Make a comparison by using *-er/-est* or by using *more/most*. Using *-er* with *more* or using *-est* with *most* is incorrect.

> INCORRECT: *I like her more better than she likes me.*

> CORRECT: *I like her better than she likes me.*

Illogical Comparisons An illogical or confusing comparison occurs when two unrelated things are compared or when something is compared with itself. The word *other* or the word *else* should be used when comparing an individual member to the rest of a group.

> ILLOGICAL: *I like "A Voice" more than any poem.*
> (implies that "A Voice" isn't a poem)

> LOGICAL: *I like "A Voice" more than any other poem.*
> (identifies that "A Voice" is a poem)

Bad vs. Badly *Bad,* always an adjective, is used before a noun or after a linking verb. *Badly,* always an adverb, never modifies a noun. Be sure to use the right form after a linking verb.

> INCORRECT: *I felt badly that I missed the game.*

> CORRECT: *I felt bad that I missed the game.*

Good vs. Well *Good* is always an adjective. It is used before a noun or after a linking verb. *Well* is often an adverb meaning "expertly" or "properly." *Well* can also be used as an adjective after a linking verb when it means "in good health."

> INCORRECT: *I wrote my essay good.*

> CORRECT: *I wrote my essay well.*

> CORRECT: *I didn't feel well when I wrote it, though.*

Double Negatives If you add a negative word to a sentence that is already negative, the result will be an error known as a double negative. When using *not* or *-n't* with a verb, use *any-* words, such as *anybody* or *anything,* rather than *no-* words, such as *nobody* or *nothing,* later in the sentence.

> INCORRECT: *The teacher didn't like nobody's paper.*

> CORRECT: *The teacher didn't like anybody's paper.*

Using *hardly, barely,* or *scarcely* after a negative word is also incorrect.

> INCORRECT: *My friends couldn't hardly catch up.*

> CORRECT: *My friends could hardly catch up.*

Misplaced Modifiers Sometimes a modifier is placed so far away from the word it modifies that the intended meaning of the sentence is unclear. Prepositional phrases and participial phrases are often misplaced. Place modifiers as close as possible to the words they modify.

> MISPLACED: *We found the child in the park who was missing.*

> CLEARER: *We found the child who was missing in the park.* (The child was missing, not the park.)

Dangling Modifiers Sometimes a modifier doesn't appear to modify any word in a sentence. Most dangling modifiers are participial phrases or infinitive phrases.

> DANGLING: *Looking out the window, his brother was seen driving by.*

> CLEARER: *Looking out the window, Josh saw his brother driving by.*

Grammar Practice

Choose the correct word from each pair in parentheses.

1. According to my neighbor, squirrels are a (bad, badly) problem in the area.
2. The (worst, worse) time of the year to go to India is in the summer.
3. The boy didn't have (any, no) interest in playing baseball.

4. Molly sings really (good, well), though.
5. Tom was (more, most) daring than any other boy scout on the trip.

Grammar Practice

Rewrite each sentence that contains a misplaced or dangling modifier. Write "correct" if the sentence is written correctly.

1. Coyotes know how to survive in the wild.
2. Hunting their prey, we have seen them in the forest.
3. Looking out the window, a coyote was seen in the yard.
4. My brother and I found books about coyotes at the library.
5. We learned that wolves are their natural enemies reading about them.

5 The Sentence and Its Parts

A **sentence** is a group of words used to express a complete thought. A complete sentence has a subject and a predicate.

For more information, see **Quick Reference: The Sentence and Its Parts,** page R30.

5.1 KINDS OF SENTENCES

There are four basic types of sentences.

Type	Definition	Example
Declarative	states a fact, a wish, an intent, or a feeling	Salisbury writes about young people.
Interrogative	asks a question	Have you read "The Ravine"?
Imperative	gives a command or direction	Find a copy.
Exclamatory	expresses strong feeling or excitement	It's really suspenseful!

5.2 COMPOUND SUBJECTS AND PREDICATES

A compound subject consists of two or more subjects that share the same verb. They are typically joined by the coordinating conjunction *and* or *or.*

> EXAMPLE: *A short story or novel will keep you interested.*

A compound predicate consists of two or more predicates that share the same subject. They too are usually joined by a coordinating conjunction such as *and, but,* or *or.*

> EXAMPLE: *The class finished all the poetry but did not read the short stories.*

5.3 COMPLEMENTS

A **complement** is a word or group of words that completes the meaning of a sentence. Some sentences contain only a subject and a verb. Most sentences, however, require additional words placed after the verb to complete the meaning of the sentence. There are three kinds of complements: direct objects, indirect objects, and subject complements.

Direct objects are words or word groups that receive the action of action verbs. A direct object answers the question *what* or *who.*

> EXAMPLES: *Daria caught the ball.* (Caught what?)
> *She tagged the runner.* (Tagged who?)

Indirect objects tell to whom or what or for whom or what the actions of verbs are performed. Indirect objects come before direct objects. In the examples that follow, the indirect objects are highlighted.

> EXAMPLES: *The audience gave us a standing ovation.* (Gave to whom?)
> *We offered the newspaper an interview.*
> (Offered to what?)

Subject complements come after linking verbs and identify or describe the subjects. A subject complement that names or identifies a subject is called a **predicate nominative.** Predicate

GRAMMAR PRACTICE ANSWERS

1. *correct*
2. *We have seen them hunting their prey in the forest.*
3. *While looking out the window, we saw a coyote in the yard.*
4. *correct*
5. *While reading about them, we learned that wolves are their natural enemies.*

nominatives include **predicate nouns** and **predicate pronouns.**

> EXAMPLES: *The students were happy campers. The best actor in the play is he.*

A subject complement that describes a subject is called a **predicate adjective.**

> EXAMPLE: *The coach seemed thrilled.*

6 Phrases

A **phrase** is a group of related words that does not contain a subject and a predicate but functions in a sentence as a single part of speech.

6.1 PREPOSITIONAL PHRASES

A **prepositional phrase** is a phrase that consists of a preposition, its object, and any modifiers of the object. Prepositional phrases that modify nouns or pronouns are called **adjective phrases.** Prepositional phrases that modify verbs, adjectives, or adverbs are **adverb phrases.**

> ADJECTIVE PHRASE: *The central character of the story is a villain.*

> ADVERB PHRASE: *He reveals his nature in the first scene.*

6.2 APPOSITIVES AND APPOSITIVE PHRASES

An **appositive** is a noun or pronoun that identifies or renames another noun or pronoun. An **appositive phrase** includes an appositive and modifiers of it. An appositive usually follows the noun or pronoun it identifies.

An appositive can be either **essential** or **nonessential.** An **essential appositive** provides information that is needed to identify what is referred to by the preceding noun or pronoun.

> EXAMPLE: *Longfellow's poem is about the American patriot Paul Revere.*

A **nonessential appositive** adds extra information about a noun or pronoun whose meaning is already clear. Nonessential appositives and appositive phrases are set off with commas.

> EXAMPLE: *The story, a poem, has historical inaccuracies.*

7 Verbals and Verbal Phrases

A **verbal** is a verb form that is used as a noun, an adjective, or an adverb. A **verbal phrase** consists of a verbal along with its modifiers and complements. There are three kinds of verbals: infinitives, participles, and gerunds.

7.1 INFINITIVES AND INFINITIVE PHRASES

An **infinitive** is a verb form that usually begins with *to* and functions as a noun, an adjective, or an adverb. An **infinitive phrase** consists of an infinitive plus its modifiers and complements.

> NOUN: *To be happy is not easy.* (subject)
> *I want to have fun.* (direct object)
>
> *My hope is to enjoy every day.* (predicate nominative)
>
> ADJECTIVE: *That's a goal to be proud of.* (adjective modifying goal)
>
> ADVERB: *I'll work to achieve it.* (adverb modifying work)

Because *to,* the sign of the infinitive, precedes infinitives, it is usually easy to recognize them. However, sometimes *to* may be omitted.

> EXAMPLE: *No one can help me [to] achieve my goal.*

7.2 PARTICIPLES AND PARTICIPIAL PHRASES

A **participle** is a verb form that functions as an adjective. Like adjectives, participles modify nouns and pronouns. Most participles are present-participle forms ending in *-ing,* or past-participle forms ending in *-ed* or *-en.* In the examples below, the participles are highlighted.

> MODIFYING A NOUN: *The waxed floor was sticky.*
>
> MODIFYING A PRONOUN: *Sighing, she mopped up the mess.*

Participial phrases are participles with all their modifiers and complements.

MODIFYING A NOUN: *The girls working on the project are very energetic.*

MODIFYING A PRONOUN: *Having finished his work, he took a nap.*

7.3 DANGLING AND MISPLACED PARTICIPLES

A participle or participial phrase should be placed as close as possible to the word that it modifies. Otherwise the meaning of the sentence may not be clear.

MISPLACED: *The boys were looking for squirrels searching the trees.*

CLEARER: *The boys searching the trees were looking for squirrels.*

A participle or participial phrase that does not clearly modify anything in a sentence is called a **dangling participle.** A dangling participle causes confusion because it appears to modify a word that it cannot sensibly modify. Correct a dangling participle by providing a word for the participle to modify.

DANGLING: *Waiting for the show to start, the phone rang.* (The phone wasn't waiting.)

CLEARER: *Waiting for the show to start, I heard the phone ring.*

7.4 GERUNDS AND GERUND PHRASES

A **gerund** is a verb form ending in *-ing* that functions as a noun. Gerunds may perform any function nouns perform.

SUBJECT: *Cooking is a good way to relax.*

DIRECT OBJECT: *I enjoy cooking.*

INDIRECT OBJECT: *They should give cooking a chance.*

SUBJECT COMPLEMENT: *My favorite pastime is cooking.*

OBJECT OF PREPOSITION: *A love of cooking runs in the family.*

Gerund phrases are gerunds with all their modifiers and complements.

SUBJECT: *Depending on luck never got me far.*

OBJECT OF PREPOSITION: *I will finish before leaving the office.*

APPOSITIVE: *Her hobby, training horses, finally led to a career.*

Grammar Practice

Rewrite each sentence, adding the type of phrase shown in parentheses.

1. "Fine?" is by Margaret Peterson Haddix. (appositive phrase)
2. Bailey suffered from a migraine headache. (infinitive phrase)
3. Bailey had an MRI. (prepositional phrase)
4. The pediatric wing is full. (gerund phrase)
5. Bailey's mom leaves the hospital. (participial phrase)

8 Clauses

A **clause** is a group of words that contains a subject and a predicate. A sentence may contain one clause or more than one. The sentence in the following example contains two clauses. The subject and verb in each clause are highlighted.

EXAMPLE: *Some students like to play sports, but others prefer to play music.*

There are two kinds of clauses: independent clauses and subordinate clauses.

8.1 INDEPENDENT AND SUBORDINATE CLAUSES

An independent clause expresses a complete thought and can stand alone as a sentence.

INDEPENDENT CLAUSE: *I read "The Banana Tree."*

A sentence may contain more than one independent clause.

EXAMPLE: *I read it once, and I liked it.*

In the preceding example, the coordinating conjunction *and* joins two independent clauses.

For more information, see **Coordinating Conjunctions**, page R29.

A **subordinate (dependent) clause** cannot stand alone as a sentence because it does not express a complete thought.

GRAMMAR PRACTICE ANSWERS

1. *"Fine?," a short story, is by Margaret Peterson Haddix.*
2. *Bailey suffered from a migraine headache, to her dismay.*
3. *Bailey had an MRI at the hospital.*
4. *Waiting for treatment is difficult when the pediatric wing is full.*
5. *Worried about her daughter, Bailey's mom leaves the hospital.*

L1

GRAMMAR PRACTICE ANSWERS

1. *IC*
2. *SC*
3. *SC*
4. *IC*
5. *IC*

L1

GRAMMAR PRACTICE ANSWERS

1. *S*
2. *CD*
3. *S*
4. *S*
5. *S*
6. *S*

By itself, a subordinate clause is a sentence fragment. It needs an independent clause to complete its meaning. Most subordinate clauses are introduced by words such as *after, although, because, if, that, when,* and *while.*

> SUBORDINATE CLAUSE: *Because they worked hard.*

A subordinate clause can be joined to an independent clause to make a sentence that expresses a complete thought. In the following example, the subordinate clause explains why the students did well on the test.

> EXAMPLE: *The students did well on the test because they worked hard.*

Grammar Practice

Identify the underlined group of words in each sentence as either an independent clause (*IC*) or a subordinate clause (*SC*).

1. He stopped at the library before he came home.
2. You have to arrive early if you want to get a front row seat.
3. She bought a ticket when she boarded the train.
4. I finished my homework while you were gone.
5. Because the test was long, the teacher gave the students extra time to finish it.

9 The Structure of Sentences

When classified by their structure, there are four kinds of sentences: simple, compound, complex, and compound-complex.

9.1 SIMPLE SENTENCES

A **simple sentence** is a sentence that has one independent clause and no subordinate clauses. Even a simple sentence can include many details.

> EXAMPLES: *Chloe looked for the train. Seth drove to the station in an old red pickup truck.*

A simple sentence may contain a compound subject or a compound verb. A compound subject is made up of two or more subjects that share the same verb. A compound verb is made up of two or more verbs that have the same subject.

> EXAMPLES: *Seth and Chloe drove to the station.* (compound subject)
> *They waved and shouted as the train pulled in.* (compound verb)

9.2 COMPOUND SENTENCES

A **compound sentence** consists of two or more independent clauses. The clauses in compound sentences are joined with commas and coordinating conjunctions (*and, but, or, nor, yet, for, so*) or with semicolons. Like simple sentences, compound sentences do not contain any subordinate clauses.

> EXAMPLES: *We all get older, but not everyone gets wiser.*
> *Some young people don't want to grow up; others grow up too quickly.*

WATCH OUT! Do not confuse compound sentences with simple sentences that have compound parts.

> EXAMPLE: *Books and clothes were scattered all over her room.*

Here, the conjunction *and* is used to join the parts of a compound subject, not the clauses in a compound sentence.

Grammar Practice

Identify each sentence as simple (*S*) or compound (*CD*).

1. Justin and his dad loved bikes.
2. They had their garage set up like a bike shop; they worked there all the time.
3. Justin bought a couple of old bikes and fixed them up.
4. He decided to donate them to a homeless shelter.
5. Many people offered him their old bikes for free.
6. Last year, Justin fixed 250 bikes and gave them all away.

9.3 COMPLEX SENTENCES

A **complex sentence** consists of one independent clause and one or more subordinate clauses. Most subordinate clauses start with words such as *when, until, who, where, because,* and *so that.*

> EXAMPLES: *While I eat my breakfast, I often wonder what I'll be like in ten years. When I think about the future, I see a canvas that has nothing on it.*

Grammar Practice

Write these sentences on a sheet of paper. Underline each independent clause once and each subordinate clause twice.

1. Although the Foster Grandparent Program is more than 40 years old, many people do not know about it.
2. This program was established so that children with special needs could get extra attention.
3. Anyone can volunteer who is at least 60 years old and meets other requirements.
4. After a volunteer is trained, he or she works 15 to 40 hours a week.
5. Foster grandparents often help with homework so that the children can improve in school.
6. Since this program was founded in 1965, there have been foster grandparent projects in all 50 states.

9.4 COMPOUND-COMPLEX SENTENCES

A **compound-complex** sentence contains two or more independent clauses and one or more subordinate clauses. Compound-complex sentences are both compound and complex. If you start with a compound sentence, all you need to do to form a compound-complex sentence is add a subordinate clause.

> COMPOUND: *All the students knew the answer, yet they were too shy to volunteer.*
>
> COMPOUND–COMPLEX: *All the students knew the answer that their teacher expected, yet they were too shy to volunteer.*

Grammar Practice

Identify each sentence as compound (*CD*), complex (*C*), or compound-complex (*CC*).

1. In 1998, a hurricane swept through Central America, where it hit Honduras and Nicaragua especially hard.
2. Hurricane Mitch was one of the strongest storms ever in this region; it caused great destruction.
3. People on the coast tried to flee to higher ground, but flooding and mudslides made escape difficult.
4. More than 9,000 people were killed, and crops and roads were wiped out.
5. TV images of homeless and hungry people touched many Americans, who responded generously.
6. They donated money and supplies, which were flown to the region.
7. Volunteers helped clear roads so that supplies could get to villages that needed them.
8. Charity groups distributed food and safe drinking water, and they handed out sleeping bags and mosquito nets, which were needed in the tropical climate.
9. Medical volunteers treated people who desperately needed care.
10. Other volunteers rebuilt homes, and they helped restore the farm economy so that people could earn a living again.

10 Writing Complete Sentences

Remember, a sentence is a group of words that expresses a complete thought. In writing that you wish to share with a reader, try to avoid both sentence fragments and run-on sentences.

10.1 CORRECTING FRAGMENTS

A **sentence fragment** is a group of words that is only part of a sentence. It does not express a complete thought and may be confusing to a reader or listener. A sentence fragment may be lacking a subject, a predicate, or both.

L 1

GRAMMAR PRACTICE ANSWERS

1. *Although the Foster Grandparent Program is more than 40 years old, many people do not know about it.*
2. *This program was established so that children with special needs could get extra attention.*
3. *Anyone can volunteer who is at least 60 years old and meets other requirements.*
4. *After a volunteer is trained, he or she works 15 to 40 hours a week.*
5. *Foster grandparents often help with homework so that the children can improve in school.*
6. *Since this program was founded in 1965, there have been foster grandparent projects in all 50 states.*

L 1

GRAMMAR PRACTICE ANSWERS

1. *C*
2. *CD*
3. *CD*
4. *CD*
5. *C*
6. *C*
7. *C*
8. *CC*
9. *C*
10. *CC*

FRAGMENT: *Didn't care about sports.* (no subject)

CORRECTED: *The lawyer didn't care about sports.*

FRAGMENT: *Her middle-school son.* (no predicate)

CORRECTED: *Her middle-school son played on the soccer team.*

FRAGMENT: *Before every game.* (neither subject nor predicate)

CORRECTED: *Before every game, he tried to teach his mom the rules.*

In your writing, fragments may be a result of haste or incorrect punctuation. Sometimes fixing a fragment will be a matter of attaching it to a preceding or following sentence.

FRAGMENT: *She made an effort. But just couldn't make sense of the game.*

CORRECTED: *She made an effort but just couldn't make sense of the game.*

10.2 CORRECTING RUN-ON SENTENCES

A **run-on sentence** is made up of two or more sentences written as though they were one. Some run-ons have no punctuation within them. Others may have only commas where conjunctions or stronger punctuation marks are necessary. Use your judgment in correcting run-on sentences, as you have choices. You can change a run-on to two sentences if the thoughts are not closely connected. If the thoughts are closely related, you can keep the run-on as one sentence by adding a semicolon or a conjunction.

RUN–ON: *Most parents watched the game his mother read a book instead.*

MAKE TWO SENTENCES: *Most parents watched the game. His mother read a book instead.*

RUN–ON: *Most parents watched the game they played sports themselves.*

USE A SEMICOLON: *Most parents watched the game; they played sports themselves.*

ADD A CONJUNCTION: *Most parents watched the game since they played sports themselves.*

WATCH OUT! When you form compound sentences, make sure you use appropriate punctuation: a comma before a coordinating conjunction, a semicolon when there is no coordinating conjunction. A very common mistake is to use a comma without a conjunction or instead of a semicolon. This error is called a **comma splice.**

INCORRECT: *He finished the job, he left the village.*

CORRECT: *He finished the job, and he left the village.*

11 Subject-Verb Agreement

The subject and verb in a clause must agree in number. Agreement means that if the subject is singular, the verb is also singular, and if the subject is plural, the verb is also plural.

11.1 BASIC AGREEMENT

Fortunately, agreement between subjects and verbs in English is simple. Most verbs show the difference between singular and plural only in the third person of the present tense. In the present tense, the third-person singular form ends in *-s.*

Present-Tense Verb Forms	
Singular	**Plural**
I sleep	we sleep
you sleep	you sleep
she, he, it sleeps	they sleep

11.2 AGREEMENT WITH *BE*

The verb *be* presents special problems in agreement, because this verb does not follow the usual verb patterns.

Forms of *Be*			
Present Tense		**Past Tense**	
Singular	**Plural**	**Singular**	**Plural**
I am	we are	I was	we were
you are	you are	you were	you were
she, he, it is	they are	she, he, it was	they were

11.3 WORDS BETWEEN SUBJECT AND VERB

A verb agrees only with its subject. When words come between a subject and a verb, ignore them when considering proper agreement. Identify the subject and make sure the verb agrees with it.

> **EXAMPLES:** *The poem I read describes a moose.*
> *The moose in the poem searches for a place where he belongs.*

11.4 AGREEMENT WITH COMPOUND SUBJECTS

Use plural verbs with most compound subjects joined by the word *and.*

> **EXAMPLE:** *My father and his friends play chess every day.*

To confirm that you need a plural verb, you could substitute the plural pronoun *they* for *my father and his friends.*

If a compound subject is thought of as a unit, use a singular verb. Test this by substituting the singular pronoun *it.*

> **EXAMPLE:** *A bagel and cream cheese [it] is my usual breakfast.*

Use a singular verb with a compound subject that is preceded by *each, every,* or *many a.*

> **EXAMPLES:** *Each novel and short story seems grounded in personal experience.*

When the parts of a compound subject are joined by *or, nor,* or the correlative conjunctions *either . . . or* or *neither . . . nor,* make the verb agree with the noun or pronoun nearest the verb.

> **EXAMPLES:** *Cookies or ice cream is my favorite dessert.*
> *Either Cheryl or her parents are being invited. Neither ice storms nor snow is predicted today.*

11.5 PERSONAL PRONOUNS AS SUBJECTS

When using a personal pronoun as a subject, make sure to match it with the correct form of the verb **be.** (See the chart in Section 11.2.) Note especially that the pronoun *you* takes the forms *are* and *were,* regardless of whether it is singular or plural.

WATCH OUT! *You is* and *you was* are nonstandard forms and should be avoided in writing and speaking. *We was* and *they was* are also forms to be avoided.

> **INCORRECT:** *You was a good student.*
> **CORRECT:** *You were a good student.*
> **INCORRECT:** *They was starting a new school.*
> **CORRECT:** *They were starting a new school.*

11.6 INDEFINITE PRONOUNS AS SUBJECTS

Some indefinite pronouns are always singular; some are always plural.

Singular Indefinite Pronouns			
another	either	neither	one
anybody	everybody	nobody	somebody
anyone	everyone	no one	someone
anything	everything	nothing	something
each	much		

> **EXAMPLES:** *Each of the writers was given an award.*
> *Somebody in the room upstairs is sleeping.*

Plural Indefinite Pronouns			
both	few	many	several

> **EXAMPLES:** *Many of the books in our library are not in circulation.*
> *Few have been returned recently.*

Still other indefinite pronouns may be either singular or plural.

Singular or Plural Indefinite Pronouns		
all	more	none
any	most	some

The number of the indefinite pronoun *any* or *none* often depends on the intended meaning.

> EXAMPLES: *Any of these stories has an important message.* (any one story)
> *Any of these stories have important messages.* (all of the many stories)

The indefinite pronouns *all, some, more, most,* and *none* are singular when they refer to quantities or parts of things. They are plural when they refer to numbers of individual things. Context will usually give a clue.

> EXAMPLES: *All of the flour is gone.* (referring to a quantity)
> *All of the flowers are gone.* (referring to individual items)

11.7 INVERTED SENTENCES

A sentence in which the subject follows the verb is called an **inverted sentence.** A subject can follow a verb or part of a verb phrase in a question; a sentence beginning with *here* or *there*; or a sentence in which an adjective, an adverb, or a phrase is placed first.

> EXAMPLES: *Here comes the scariest part.*
> *There goes the hero with a flashlight.*
> *Then, into the room rushes a big black cat!*

> **TIP** To check subject-verb agreement in some inverted sentences, place the subject before the verb. For example, change *There are many people* to *Many people are there.*

11.8 SENTENCES WITH PREDICATE NOMINATIVES

In a sentence containing a predicate noun (nominative), the verb should agree with the subject, not the predicate noun.

> EXAMPLES: *Josh's jokes are a source of laughter.* (*Jokes* is the subject—not *source*—and it takes the plural verb *are.*)
> *One source of laughter is Josh's jokes.* (The subject is *source*—not *jokes*—and it takes the singular verb *is.*)

11.9 *DON'T* AND *DOESN'T* AS AUXILIARY VERBS

The auxiliary verb *doesn't* is used with singular subjects and with the personal pronouns *she, he,* and *it.* The auxiliary verb *don't* is used with plural subjects and with the personal pronouns *I, we, you,* and *they.*

> SINGULAR: *The humor doesn't escape us.*
> *Doesn't the limerick about Dougal MacDougal make you laugh?*

> PLURAL: *We don't usually forget such funny images.*
> *Don't people like to recite limericks?*

11.10 COLLECTIVE NOUNS AS SUBJECTS

Collective nouns are singular nouns that name groups of persons or things. *Team,* for example, is a collective name of a group of individuals. A collective noun takes a singular verb when the group acts as a single unit. It takes a plural verb when the members of the group act separately.

> EXAMPLES: *The class creates a bulletin board of limericks.* (The class as a whole creates the board.)
> *The faculty enjoy teaching poetry.* (The individual members enjoy teaching poetry.)

11.11 RELATIVE PRONOUNS AS SUBJECTS

When the relative pronoun *who, which,* or *that* is used as a subject in an adjective clause, the verb in the clause must agree in number with the antecedent of the pronoun.

> SINGULAR: *The myth from ancient Greece that interests me most is "The Apple of Discord I."*

The antecedent of the relative pronoun *that* is the singular *myth*; therefore, *that* is singular and must take the singular verb *interests.*

PLURAL: *James Berry and Sandra Cisneros are writers who publish short stories.*

The antecedent of the relative pronoun **who** is the plural subject **writers.** Therefore **who** is plural, and it takes the plural verb **publish.**

Grammar Practice

Locate the subject of each verb in parentheses in the sentences below. Then choose the correct verb form.

1. George Graham Vest's "Tribute to a Dog" (describes, describe) the friend-ship and loyalty canines show humans.

2. Stories about a dog (is, are) touching.

3. Besides dogs, few animals (has, have) an innate desire to please humans.

4. Many traits specific to dogs (bring, brings) their owners happiness.

5. No matter if the owner is rich or poor, a dog, and all canines for that matter, (acts, act) with love and devotion.

6. There (is, are) countless reasons to own a dog.

7. A dog's unselfishness (endears, endear) it to its owner.

8. (Doesn't, Don't) a dog offer its owner constant affection and guardianship?

9. A man's dog (stands, stand) by him in prosperity and in poverty.

10. A dog (guards, guard) his master as if the owner was a prince.

GRAMMAR PRACTICE ANSWERS

1. *describes*
2. *are*
3. *have*
4. *bring*
5. *act*
6. *are*
7. *endears*
8. *Doesn't*
9. *stands*
10. *guards*

Vocabulary and Spelling

The key to becoming an independent reader is to develop a tool kit of vocabulary strategies. By learning and practicing the strategies, you'll know what to do when you encounter unfamiliar words while reading. You'll also know how to refine the words you use for different situations—personal, school, and work.

Being a good speller is important when communicating your ideas in writing. Learning basic spelling rules and checking your spelling in a dictionary will help you spell words that you may not use frequently.

1 Using Context Clues

The context of a word is made up of the punctuation marks, words, sentences, and paragraphs that surround the word. A word's context can give you important clues about its meaning.

1.1 GENERAL CONTEXT

Sometimes you need to determine the meaning of an unfamiliar word by reading all the information in a passage.

> *Kevin set out the broom, a dustpan, and three trash bags before beginning the monumental task of cleaning his room.*

You can figure out from the context that *monumental* means "huge."

1.2 SPECIFIC CONTEXT CLUES

Sometimes writers help you understand the meanings of words by providing specific clues such as those shown in the chart. When reading content area materials, use word, sentence, and paragraph clues to help you figure out meanings.

1.3 IDIOMS, SLANG, AND FIGURATIVE LANGUAGE

Use context clues to figure out the meanings of idioms, slang, and figurative language.

An **idiom** is an expression whose overall meaning differs from the meaning of the individual words.

> *The mosquitos drove us crazy on our hike. (Drove us crazy means "irritated.")*

Slang is informal language that features made-up words and ordinary words that are used to mean something different from their meanings in formal English.

> *That's a really cool backpack you're wearing. (Cool means "excellent.")*

Figurative language is language that communicates meaning beyond the literal meaning of the words.

> *Like a plunging horse, my car kicked up dirt, moved ahead quickly, and made a loud noise when I hit the gas. (Kicked up dirt, moved ahead, and made a loud noise describe a plunging horse.)*

Specific Context Clues		
Type of Clue	**Key Words/ Phrases**	**Example**
Definition or restatement of the meaning of the word	or, which is, that is, in other words, also known as, also called	In 1909, a French inventor flew a *monoplane*, or a **single-winged plane.**
Example following an unfamiliar word	such as, like, as if, for example, especially, including	The stunt pilot performed *acrobatics*, such as **dives and wing-walking.**

continued

Type of Clue	Key Words/ Phrases	Example
Comparison with a more familiar word or concept	as, like, also, similar to, in the same way, likewise	The doctor prescribed a *bland* diet, similar to the **rice and potatoes** he was already eating.
Contrast with a familiar word or experience	unlike, but, however, although, on the other hand, on the contrary	The moon will *diminish* at the end of the month; however it will **grow** during the first part of the month.
Cause-and-effect relationship in which one term is familiar	because, since, when, consequently, as a result, therefore	Because their general was *valiant*, the soldiers **showed courage** in battle.

2 Analyzing Word Structure

Many words can be broken into smaller parts. These word parts include base words, roots, prefixes, and suffixes.

2.1 BASE WORDS

A **base word** is a word part that by itself is also a word. Other words or word parts can be added to base words to form new words.

2.2 ROOTS

A **root** is a word part that contains the core meaning of the word. Many English words contain roots that come from older languages such as Greek and Latin. Knowing the meanings of a word's root can help you determine the word's meaning.

Root	Meaning	Example
auto (Greek)	self, same	**auto**mobile
hydr (Greek)	water	**hydr**ant
cent (Latin)	hundred	**cent**ury
circ (Latin)	ring	**circ**le
port (Latin)	carry	**port**able

2.3 PREFIXES

A **prefix** is a word part attached to the beginning of a word. Most prefixes come from Greek, Latin, or Old English (OE).

Prefix	Meaning	Example
dis- (Latin)	not	**dis**honest
auto- (Greek)	self, same	**auto**biography
un- (OE)	the opposite of, not	**un**happy
re- (Latin)	carry, back	**re**pay

2.4 SUFFIXES

A **suffix** is a word part that appears at the end of a root or base word to form a new word. Some suffixes do not change word meaning. These suffixes are:

- added to nouns to change the number of persons or objects
- added to verbs to change the tense
- added to modifiers to change the degree of comparison

Suffix	Meaning	Example
-s, -es	to change the number of a noun	lock + s = locks
-d, -ed, -ing	to change verb tense	stew + ed = stewed
-er, -est	to indicate comparison in modifiers	mild + er = milder soft + est = softest

PRACTICE AND APPLY ANSWERS

Sentences will vary.

Other suffixes can be added to the root or base to change the word's meaning. These suffixes can also determine a word's part of speech.

Suffix	Meaning	Example
-ion (Latin)	process of	operation
-able (Latin)	capable of	readable
-ize (Greek)	to cause or become	legalize

Strategies for Understanding New Words

- If you recognize elements—prefix, suffix, root, or base—of a word, you may be able to guess its meaning by analyzing one or two elements.
- Think about the way the word is used in the sentence. Use the context and the word parts to make a logical guess about the word's meaning.
- Look in a dictionary to see if you are correct.

3 Understanding Word Origins

3.1 ETYMOLOGIES

Etymologies show the origin and historical development of a word. When you study a word's history and origin, you can find out when, where, and how the word came to be.

> **em•per•or** (ĕm′pər-ər) *n.* **1.** The male ruler of an empire. **2a.** The emperor butterfly. **b.** The emperor moth. [Middle English emperour, from Old French *empereor*, from Latin imperātor, from *imperāre*, to command: *in-*, *in*; see EN-¹ + *parāre*, to prepare.]

3.2 WORD FAMILIES

Words that have the same root make up a word family and have related meanings. The following chart shows a common Greek root and a common Latin root. Notice how the meanings of the example words are related to the meanings of their roots.

Latin Root	*man:* "hand"
English	**manual** by hand **manage** handle **manuscript** document written by hand

Greek Root	*phon:* "sound"
English	**telephone** an instrument that transmits sound **phonograph** machine that reproduces sound **phonetic** representing sounds of speech

3.3 FOREIGN WORDS IN ENGLISH

The English language includes words from other languages, such as French, Dutch, Spanish, Italian, and Chinese. Many words have stayed the way they were in their original language.

French	Dutch	Spanish	Italian
ballet	boss	canyon	diva
vague	caboose	rodeo	cupola
mirage	dock	bronco	spaghetti

Practice and Apply

Look up the origin and meaning of each word listed in the preceding chart. Then use each word in a sentence.

4 Synonyms and Antonyms

4.1 SYNONYMS

A **synonym** is a word with a meaning similar to that of another word. You can find synonyms in a thesaurus or a dictionary. In a dictionary, synonyms are often given as part of the definition of a word. The following word pairs are synonyms:

satisfy/please   occasionally/sometimes

rob/steal   schedule/agenda

4.2 ANTONYMS

An **antonym** is a word with a meaning opposite that of another word. The following word pairs are antonyms.

accurate/incorrect   similar/different

fresh/stale   unusual/ordinary

5 Denotation and Connotation

5.1 DENOTATION

A word's dictionary meaning is called its **denotation.** For example, the denotation of the word *thin* is "having little flesh; spare; lean."

5.2 CONNOTATION

The images or feelings you connect to a word add a finer shade of meaning, called **connotation.** The connation of a word goes beyond its basic dictionary definition. Writers use connotations of words to communicate positive or negative feelings.

Positive	Negative
slender	scrawny
thrifty	cheap
young	immature

Make sure you understand the denotation and connotation of a word when you read it or use it in your writing.

6 Analogies

An **analogy** is a comparison between two things that are similar in some way but are otherwise not alike. Analogies are sometimes used in writing when unfamiliar subjects or ideas are explained in terms of familiar ones. Analogies often appear on tests as well. In an analogy problem, the analogy is expressed using two groups of words. The relationship between the first pair of words is the same as the relationship between the second pair of words. Some analogy problems are expressed like this:

in love **:** hate **::** war **:** _____

a. soldier **b.** peace **c.** battle **d.** argument

Follow these steps to determine the correct answer:

- Read the problem as "*Love* is to *hate* as *war* is to . . . ."
- Ask yourself how the words *love* and *hate* are related. (*Love* and *hate* are antonyms.)
- Ask yourself which answer choice is an antonym of *war*. (*Peace* is an antonym of *war,* therefore **peace** is the best answer.)

7 Homonyms, Homographs, and Homophones

7.1 HOMONYMS

Homonyms are words that have the same spelling and sound but have different meanings.

> *The snake shed its skin in the shed behind the house.*

Shed can mean "to lose by natural process," but an identically spelled word means "a small structure."

Sometimes only one of the meanings of a homonym may be familiar to you. Use context clues to help you figure out the meaning of an unfamiliar word.

7.2 HOMOGRAPHS

Homographs are words that are spelled the same but have different meanings and origins. Some are also pronounced differently, as in these examples:

> *Please close the door.* (klōz)

> *That was a close call.* (klōs)

If you see a word used in a way that is unfamiliar to you, check a dictionary to see if it is a homograph.

7.3 HOMOPHONES

Homophones are words that sound alike but have different meanings and spellings. The following homophones are frequently misused:

it's/its   they're/their/there

to/too/two   stationary/stationery

Many misused homophones are pronouns and contractions. Whenever you are unsure whether to write *your* or *you're* and *who's* or *whose,* ask yourself if you mean *you are* and *who is/has.* If you do, write the contraction. For other homophones, such as *fair* and *fare,* use the meaning of the word to help you decide which one to use.

8   Words with Multiple Meanings

Over time, some words have acquired additional meanings that are based on the original meaning.

> *I had to be replaced in the cast of the play because of the cast on my arm.*

These two uses of cast have different meanings, but both of them have the same origin. You will find all the meanings of cast listed in one entry in the dictionary. Context can also help you figure out the meaning of the word.

9   Specialized Vocabulary

Specialized vocabulary is a group of terms suited to a particular field of study or work. For example, science, mathematics, and history all have their own technical or specialized vocabularies. To figure out specialized terms, you can use context clues and reference sources, such as dictionaries on specific subjects, atlases, or manuals.

10   Using Reference Sources

10.1   DICTIONARIES

A **general dictionary** will tell you not only a word's definitions but also its pronunciation, syllabication, parts of speech, history, and origin.

①   **②**   **③**

tan·gi·ble (tăn′jə-bəl) *adj.* **1a.** Discernible by the touch; palpable. **b.** Possible to touch. **c.** Possible to be treated as fact; **④** real or concrete. **2.** Possible to understand or realize. **3.** *Law* That can be valued monetarily. **⑤** [Late Latin *tangibilis,* from Latin *tangere,* to touch.]

①	Entry word syllabication
②	Pronunciation
③	Part of speech
④	Definitions
⑤	Etymology

A **specialized dictionary** focuses on terms related to a particular field of study or work. Use a dictionary to check the spelling of any word you are unsure of in your reading.

10.2   THESAURI

A **thesaurus** (plural, *thesauri*) is a dictionary of synonyms. A thesaurus can be especially helpful when you find yourself using the same modifiers over and over again.

10.3   SYNONYM FINDERS

A **synonym finder** is often included in wordprocessing software. It enables you to highlight a word and be shown a display of its synonyms.

10.4   GLOSSARIES

A **glossary** is a list of specialized terms and their definitions. It is often found in the back of a book and sometimes includes pronunciations. Many textbooks contain glossaries. In fact, this textbook has three glossaries: the **Glossary of Literary and Informational Terms,** the **Glossary of Academic Vocabulary,** and the **Glossary of Critical Vocabulary.** Use these glossaries to help you understand how terms are used in this textbook.

11 Spelling Rules

11.1 WORDS ENDING IN A SILENT *E*

Before adding a suffix beginning with a vowel or *y* to a word ending in a silent *e,* drop the *e* (with some exceptions).

amaze + -ing = amazing

love + -able = lovable

create + -ed = created

nerve + -ous = nervous

Exceptions: *change + -able = changeable; courage + -ous = courageous*

When adding a suffix beginning with a consonant to a word ending in a silent *e,* keep the *e* (with some exceptions).

late + -ly = lately

spite + -ful = spiteful

noise + -less = noiseless

state + -ment = statement

Exceptions: *truly, argument, ninth, wholly, awful,* and *others*

When a suffix beginning with *a* or *o* is added to a word with a final silent *e,* the final *e* is usually retained if it is preceded by a soft *c* or a soft *g.*

bridge + -able = bridgeable

peace + -able = peaceable

outrage + -ous = outrageous

advantage + -ous = advantageous

When a suffix beginning with a vowel is added to words ending in *ee* or *oe,* the final, silent *e* is retained.

agree + -ing = agreeing

free + -ing = freeing

hoe + -ing = hoeing

see + -ing = seeing

11.2 WORDS ENDING IN *Y*

Before adding most suffixes to a word that ends in *y* preceded by a consonant, change the *y* to *i.*

easy + -est = easiest

crazy + -est = craziest

silly + -ness = silliness

marry + -age = marriage

Exceptions: *dryness, shyness,* and *slyness*

However, when you add *-ing,* the *y* does not change.

empty + -ed = emptied   but

empty + -ing = emptying

When adding a suffix to a word that ends in *y* preceded by a vowel, the *y* usually does not change.

play + -er = player

employ + -ed = employed

coy + -ness = coyness

pay + -able = payable

11.3 WORDS ENDING IN A CONSONANT

In one-syllable words that end in one consonant preceded by one short vowel, double the final consonant before adding a suffix beginning with a vowel, such as *-ed* or *-ing.* These are sometimes called 1+1+1 words.

dip + -ed = dipped

set + -ing = setting

slim + -est = slimmest

fit + -er = fitter

The rule does not apply to words of one syllable that end in a consonant preceded by two vowels.

feel + -ing = feeling

peel + -ed = peeled

reap + -ed = reaped

loot + -ed = looted

In words of more than one syllable, double the final consonant when (1) the word ends with one consonant preceded by one vowel and (2) when the word is accented on the last syllable.

be•gin´   per•mit´   re•fer´

In the following examples, note that in the new words formed with suffixes, the accent remains on the same syllable.

be•gin´ + -ing = be•gin´ning = beginning

per•mit´ + -ed = per•mit´ted = permitted

Exceptions: In some words with more than one syllable, though the accent remains on the same syllable when a suffix is added, the final consonant is nevertheless not doubled, as in the following examples.

tra′vel + er = tra′vel•er = traveler

mar′ket + er = mar′ket•er = marketer

In the following examples, the accent does not remain on the same syllable; thus, the final consonant is not doubled:

re•fer′ + -ence = ref′er•ence = reference

con•fer′ + -ence = con′fer•ence = conference

11.4 PREFIXES AND SUFFIXES

When adding a prefix to a word, do not change the spelling of the base word. When a prefix creates a double letter, keep both letters.

dis- + approve = disapprove

re- + build = rebuild

ir- + regular = irregular

mis- + spell = misspell

anti- + trust = antitrust

il- + logical = illogical

When adding **-ly** to a word ending in **l,** keep both **l's.** When adding **-ness** to a word ending in **n,** keep both **n's.**

careful + -ly = carefully

sudden + -ness = suddenness

final + -ly = finally

thin + -ness = thinness

11.5 FORMING PLURAL NOUNS

To form the plural of most nouns, just add **-s.**

prizes   dreams   circles   stations

For most singular nouns ending in **o,** add **-s.**

solos halos studios photos pianos

For a few nouns ending in **o,** add **-es.**

heroes tomatoes potatoes echoes

When a singular noun ends in **s, sh, ch, x,** or **z,** add **-es.**

waitresses	**brushes ditches**
axes	**buzzes**

When a singular noun ends in **y** with a consonant before it, change the **y** to **i** and add **-es.**

army—armies	**candy—candies**
baby—babies	**diary—diaries**
ferry—ferries	**conspiracy—conspiracies**

When a vowel (**a, e, i, o, u**) comes before the **y,** just add **-s.**

boy—boys	**way—ways**
array—arrays	**alloy—alloys**
weekday—weekdays	**jockey—jockeys**

For most nouns ending in **f** or **fe,** change the **f** to **v** and add **-es** or **-s.**

life—lives	**loaf—loaves**
calf—calves	**knife—knives**
thief—thieves	**shelf—shelves**

For some nouns ending in **f,** add **-s** to make the plural.

roofs   chiefs   reefs   beliefs

Some nouns have the same form for both singular and plural.

deer   sheep   moose   salmon   trout

For some nouns, the plural is formed in a special way.

man—men	**goose—geese**
ox—oxen	**woman—women**
mouse—mice	**child—children**

For a compound noun written as one word, form the plural by changing the last word in the compound to its plural form.

stepchild—stepchildren   firefly—fireflies

If a compound noun is written as a hyphenated word or as two separate words, change the most important word to the plural form.

brother-in-law—brothers-in-law

life jacket—life jackets

11.6 FORMING POSSESSIVES

If a noun is singular, add **'s.**

mother—my mother's car

Ross—Ross's desk

Exception: An apostrophe alone is used to indicate the possessive case with the names Jesus and Moses and with certain names in classical mythology (such as Zeus).

If a noun is plural and ends with **s,** add an apostrophe.

parents—my parents' car

the Santinis—the Santinis' house

If a noun is plural but does not end in **s,** add **'s.**

> **people—the people's choice**
>
> **women—the women's coats**

11.7 SPECIAL SPELLING PROBLEMS

Only one English word ends in **-sede:** supersede. Three words end in **-ceed: exceed, proceed,** and **succeed.** All other verbs ending in the sound "seed" are spelled with **-cede.**

> **concede   precede   recede   secede**

In words with **ie** or **ei,** when the sound is long **e** (as in **she**), the word is spelled **ie** except after **c** (with some exceptions).

i before *e*	thief	relieve	field
	piece	grieve	pier
except after *c*	conceit	perceive	ceiling
	receive	receipt	
Exceptions:	either	neither	weird
	leisure	seize	

11.8 USING A SPELL CHECKER

Most computer word processing programs have spell checkers to catch misspellings. Most computer spell checkers do not correct errors automatically. Instead, they stop at a word and highlight it. Sometimes the highlighted word may not be misspelled; it may be that the program's dictionary does not include the word. Keep in mind that spell checkers will identify only misspelled words, not misused words. For example, if you used **their** when you meant to use **there,** a spelling checker will not catch the error.

12 Commonly Confused Words

Words	Definitions	Examples
accept/except	The verb *accept* means "to receive" or "to believe." *Except* is usually a preposition meaning "excluding."	Did the teacher **accept** your report? Everyone smiled for the photographer **except** Jody.
advice/advise	*Advise* is a verb. *Advice* is a noun naming that which an *adviser* gives.	I **advise** you to take that job. Whom should I ask for **advice**?
affect/effect	As a verb, *affect* means "to influence." *Effect* as a verb means "to cause." If you want a noun, you will almost always want *effect.*	How deeply did the news **affect** him? The students tried to **effect** a change in school policy. What **effect** did the acidic soil produce in the plants?
all ready/already	*All ready* is an adjective meaning "fully ready." *Already* is an adverb meaning "before" or "by this time."	He was **all ready** to go at noon. I have **already** seen that movie.
desert/dessert	*Desert* (dĕz´ərt) means "a dry, sandy, barren region." *Desert* (dĭ-zûrt´) means "to abandon." *Dessert* (dĭ-zûrt´) is a sweet, such as cake.	The Sahara, in North Africa, is the world's largest **desert.** The night guard did not **desert** his post. Alison's favorite **dessert** is chocolate cake.

continued

Words	Definitions	Examples
among/between	*Between* is used when you are speaking of only two things. *Among* is used for three or more.	**Between** ice cream and sherbet, I prefer the latter. Gary Soto is **among** my favorite authors.
bring/take	*Bring* is used to denote motion toward a speaker or place. *Take* is used to denote motion away from such a person or place.	**Bring** the books over here, and I will **take** them to the library.
fewer/less	*Fewer* refers to the number of separate, countable units. *Less* refers to bulk quantity.	We have **less** literature and **fewer** selections in this year's curriculum.
leave/let	*Leave* means "to allow something to remain behind." *Let* means "to permit."	The librarian will **leave** some books on display but will not **let** us borrow any.
lie/lay	To *lie* is "to rest or recline." It does not take an object. *Lay* always takes an object.	Rover loves to **lie** in the sun. We always **lay** some bones next to him.
loose/lose	*Loose* (lo͞os) means "free, not restrained." *Lose* (lo͞oz) means "to misplace" or "to fail to find."	Who turned the horses **loose**? I hope we won't **lose** any of them.
passed/past	*Passed* is the past tense of *pass* and means "went by." *Past* is an adjective that means "of a former time." *Past* is also a noun that means "time gone by."	We **passed** through the Florida Keys during our vacation. My **past** experiences have taught me to set my alarm. Ebenezer Scrooge is a character who relives his **past**.
than/then	Use *than* in making comparisons. Use *then* on all other occasions.	Ramon is stronger **than** Mark. Cut the grass and **then** trim the hedges.
two/too/to	*Two* is the number. *Too* is an adverb meaning "also" or "very." Use *to* before a verb or as a preposition.	Meg had **to** go **to** town, **too**. We had **too** much reading **to** do. **Two** chapters is **too** many.
their/there/they're	*Their* means "belonging to them." *There* means "in that place." *They're* is the contraction for "they are."	**There** is a movie playing at 9 P.M. **They're** going to see it with me. Sakara and Jessica drove away in **their** car after the movie.

Glossary of Literary and Informational Terms

Act An act is a major division within a play, similar to a chapter in a book. Each act may be further divided into smaller sections, called scenes. Plays can have as many as five acts, or as few as one.

Adventure Story An adventure story is a literary work in which action is the main element. An **adventure novel** usually focuses on a main character who is on a mission and faces many challenges and choices.

Alliteration Alliteration is the repetition of consonant sounds at the beginning of words. Note the repetition of the *d* sound in this line: The *d*aring boy *d*ove into the *d*eep sea.

Allusion An allusion is a reference to a famous person, place, event, or work of literature.

Almanac *See* Reference Works.

Analogy An analogy is a comparison between two things that are alike in some way. Often, writers use analogies to explain unfamiliar subjects or ideas in terms of familiar ones.
See also Metaphor; Simile.

Anecdote An anecdote is a short account of an event that is usually intended to entertain or make a point.

Antagonist The antagonist is a force working against the protagonist, or main character, in a story, play, or novel. The antagonist is usually another character but can be a force of nature, society itself, or an internal force within the main character.
See also Protagonist.

Appeal to Authority An appeal to authority is an attempt to persuade an audience by making reference to people who are experts on a subject.

Argument An argument is speaking or writing that expresses a position on a problem and supports it with reasons and evidence. An argument often anticipates and answers objections that opponents might raise.
See also Claim; Counterargument; Evidence.

Assonance Assonance is the repetition of vowel sounds within nonrhyming words. An example of assonance is the repetition of the o͞o sound in the following line: Do you like blue?

Assumption An assumption is an opinion or belief that is taken for granted. It can be about a specific situation, a person, or the world in general. Assumptions are often unstated.

Audience The audience of a piece of writing is the group of readers that the writer is addressing. A writer considers his or her audience when deciding on a subject, a purpose, a tone, and a style in which to write.

Author's Message An author's message is the main idea or theme of a particular work.
See also Main Idea; Theme.

Author's Perspective An author's perspective is the combination of ideas, values, feelings, and beliefs that influences the way the writer looks at a topic. **Tone,** or attitude, often reveals an author's perspective.
See also Author's Purpose; Tone.

Author's Position An author's position is his or her opinion on an issue or topic.
See also Claim.

Author's Purpose A writer usually writes for one or more of these purposes: to express thoughts or feelings, to inform or explain, to persuade, or to entertain.
See also Author's Perspective.

Autobiography An autobiography is a writer's account of his or her own life. In almost every case, it is told from the first-person point of view. An autobiography focuses on the most important events and people in the writer's life over a period of time.
See also Memoir; Personal Narrative.

Ballad A ballad is a type of narrative poem that tells a story and was originally meant to be sung or recited. Because it tells a story, a ballad has a setting, a plot, and characters. **Folk ballads** were composed orally and handed down by word of mouth from generation to generation.

Bias In a piece of writing, the author's bias is the side of an issue that he or she favors. Words with extremely positive or negative connotations are often a signal of an author's bias.

Bibliography A bibliography is a list of related books and other materials used to write a text. Bibliographies can be good sources for further study on a subject.

See also Works Consulted.

Biography A biography is the true account of a person's life, written by another person. As such, biographies are usually told from a third-person point of view. The writer of a biography—a **biographer**—usually researches his or her subject in order to present accurate information. The best biographers strive for honesty and balance in their accounts of their subjects' lives.

Career Development Documents These documents include written business communications such as business letters, e-mails, and memos. In general, business correspondence is brief, to the point, clear, courteous, and professional.

Cast of Characters In the script of a play, a cast of characters is a list of all the characters in the play, usually in order of appearance. It may include a brief description of each character.

Cause and Effect Two events are related by cause and effect when one event brings about, or causes, the other. The event that happens first is the **cause**; the one that follows is the **effect.** Cause and effect is also a way of organizing an entire piece of writing. It helps writers show the relationships between events or ideas.

Character Characters are the people, animals, or imaginary creatures who take part in the action of a work of literature. Like real people, characters display certain qualities, or **character traits,** that develop and change over time, and they usually have **motivations,** or reasons, for their behaviors.

> **Main character:** Main characters are the most important characters in literary works. Generally, the plot of a short story focuses on one main character, but a novel may have several main characters.

> **Minor characters:** The less important characters in a literary work are known as minor characters. The story is not centered on them, but they help carry out the action of the story and help the reader learn more about the main character.

> **Dynamic character:** A dynamic character is one who undergoes important changes as a plot unfolds. The changes occur because of the character's actions and experiences in the story. The changes are usually internal and may be good or bad. Main characters are usually, though not always, dynamic.

> **Static character:** A static character is one who remains the same throughout a story. The character may experience events and interact with other characters, but he or she is not changed because of them.

See also Characterization; Character Traits.

Character Development Characters that change during a story are said to undergo character development. Any character can change, but main characters usually develop the most.

See also Character: Dynamic Character.

Characterization The way a writer creates and develops characters is known as characterization. There are four basic methods of characterization.

- The writer may make direct comments about a character through the voice of the narrator.
- The writer may describe the character's physical appearance.
- The writer may present the character's own thoughts, speech, and actions.
- The writer may present the thoughts, speech, and actions of other characters.

See also Character; Character Traits.

Character Traits Character traits are the qualities shown by a character. Traits may be physical (tall) or expressions of personality (confidence). Writers reveal the traits of their characters through methods of characterization. Sometimes writers directly state a character's traits, but more often readers need to infer traits from a character's words, actions, thoughts, appearance, and relationships. Examples of words that describe traits include *brave, considerate,* and *rude.*

Chronological Order Chronological order is the arrangement of events in their order of occurrence. This type of organization is used in fictional narratives and in historical writing, biography, and autobiography.

Citation Writers of reports and arguments that include quotations or research information document their sources using a citation method such as footnotes or endnotes.

See also Works Cited.

Claim In an argument, a claim is the writer's position on an issue or problem. Although an argument focuses on supporting one claim, a writer may make more than one claim in a text.

Clarify Clarifying is a reading strategy that helps readers understand or make clear what they are reading. Readers usually clarify by rereading, reading aloud, or discussing.

Classification Classification is a pattern of organization in which objects, ideas, and/or information are presented in groups, or classes, based on common characteristics.

Cliché A cliché is an overused expression. "Better late than never" and "hard as nails" are common examples. Good writers generally avoid clichés unless they are using them in dialogue to indicate something about a character's personality.

Climax The climax stage is the point of greatest interest in a story or play. The climax usually occurs toward the end of a story, after the reader has understood the **conflict** and become emotionally involved with the characters. At the climax, the conflict is resolved and the outcome of the plot usually becomes clear.

See also Plot.

Comedy A comedy is a dramatic work that is light and often humorous in tone, usually ending happily with a peaceful resolution of the main conflict.

Compare and Contrast To compare and contrast is to identify the similarities and differences of two or more subjects. Compare and contrast is also a pattern of organizing an entire piece of writing.

See also Pattern of Organization.

Conclusion A conclusion is a statement of belief based on evidence, experience, and reasoning. A valid conclusion is one that logically follows from the facts or statements upon which it is based.

Conflict A conflict is a struggle between opposing forces. Almost every story has a main conflict—a conflict that is the story's focus. An **external conflict** involves a character who struggles against a force outside him- or herself, such as nature, a physical obstacle, or another character. An **internal conflict** is one that occurs within a character. For example, a character with an internal conflict might struggle with fear.

See also Plot.

Connect Connecting is a reader's process of relating the content of a text to his or her own knowledge and experience.

Connotation A word's connotations are the ideas and feelings associated with the word, as opposed to its dictionary definition. For example, the word *bread,* in addition to its basic meaning ("a baked food made from flour and other ingredients"), has connotations of life and general nourishment.

See also Denotation.

Consumer Documents Consumer documents are printed materials that accompany products and services. They usually provide information about the use, care, operation, or assembly of the product or service they accompany. Some common consumer documents are applications, contracts, warranties, manuals, instructions, labels, brochures, and schedules.

Context Clues When you encounter an unfamiliar word, you can often use context clues to understand it. Context clues are the words or phrases surrounding the word that provide hints about the word's meaning.

Counterargument A counterargument is an argument made to oppose another argument. A good argument anticipates opposing viewpoints and provides counterarguments to disprove them.

Couplet A couplet is a rhymed pair of lines. A couplet may be written in any rhythmic pattern.

For example, Follow your heart's desire/And good things may transpire.

See also Rhyme; Stanza.

Credibility Credibility is the believability or trustworthiness of a source and the information it provides.

Critical Essay *See* Essay.

Critical Review A critical review is an evaluation or critique by a reviewer, or critic. Types of reviews include film reviews, book reviews, music reviews, and art show reviews.

Cultural Values Cultural values are the behaviors that a society expects from its people.

Database A database is a collection of information that can be quickly and easily accessed and searched and from which information can be easily retrieved. It is frequently presented in an electronic format.

Debate A debate is an organized exchange of opinions on an issue. In school settings, debate is usually a formal contest in which two opposing teams defend and attack a proposition.

See also Argument.

Deductive Reasoning Deductive reasoning is a way of thinking that begins with a generalization, presents a specific situation, and then moves forward with facts and evidence toward a logical conclusion. The following passage has a deductive argument embedded in it: "All students in the math class must take the quiz on Friday. Since Lana is in the class, she had better show up." This deductive argument can be broken down as follows: generalization—All students in the math class must take the quiz on Friday; specific situation—Lana is a student in the math class; conclusion—Therefore, Lana must take the math quiz.

Denotation A word's denotation is its dictionary definition.

See also Connotation.

Description Description is writing that helps a reader to picture events, objects, and characters. To create descriptions, writers often use **imagery**—words and phrases that appeal to the reader's senses.

Dialect A dialect is a form of a language that is spoken in a particular place or by a particular group of people. Dialects may feature unique pronunciations, vocabulary, and grammar.

Dialogue Dialogue is written conversation between two or more characters. Writers use dialogue to bring characters to life and to give readers insights into the characters' qualities, traits, and reactions to other characters. In fiction, dialogue is usually set off with quotation marks. In drama, stories are told primarily through dialogue.

Diary A diary is a daily record of a writer's thoughts, experiences, and feelings. As such, it is a type of autobiographical writing. A **journal** is another term for a diary.

Dictionary *See* Reference Works.

Domain-Specific Vocabulary Domain-specific vocabulary includes terms and expressions used in a particular field, or domain. For example, the terms in this glossary are from the domain of language arts.

Drama A drama, or play, is a form of literature meant to be performed by actors in front of an audience. In a drama, the characters' dialogue and actions tell the story. The written form of a drama is called a script. A script usually includes dialogue, a cast of characters, and stage directions that give instructions about performing the drama. The person who writes the drama is known as the playwright or dramatist.

Draw Conclusions To draw a conclusion is to make a judgment or arrive at a belief based on evidence, experience, and reasoning.

Editorial An editorial is an opinion piece that usually appears on the editorial page of a newspaper or as part of a news broadcast. The editorial section of the newspaper presents opinions rather than objective news reports.

See also Op/Ed Piece.

Either/Or Fallacy An either/or fallacy is a statement that suggests that there are only two choices available in a situation when in fact there are more than two.

Emotional Appeal An emotional appeal is a message that creates strong feelings in order to make a point. An appeal to fear is a message that taps into people's fear of losing their safety or security. An appeal to pity is a message that taps into people's sympathy and compassion for others to build support for an idea, a cause, or a proposed action. An appeal to vanity is a message that attempts to persuade by tapping into people's desire to feel good about themselves.

Encyclopedia *See* Reference Works.

Epic Poem An epic poem is a long narrative poem about the adventures of a hero whose actions reflect the ideals and values of a nation or a group of people.

Essay An essay is a short work of nonfiction that deals with a single subject. There are many types of essays. An **informative essay** presents or explains information and ideas. An **argumentative essay** attempts to convince the reader to adopt a certain viewpoint. A **critical essay** evaluates a situation or a work of art. A **personal essay** usually reflects the writer's experiences, feelings, and personality.

See also Argument.

Ethical Appeal In an ethical appeal, a writer links a claim to a widely accepted value in order to gain moral support for the claim. The appeal also creates an image of the writer as a trustworthy, moral person.

Evaluate To evaluate is to examine something carefully and to judge its value or worth. A reader can evaluate the actions of a particular character, for example. A reader can also form opinions about the value of an entire work.

Evidence Evidence is a specific piece of information that supports a claim. Evidence can take the form of a fact, a quotation, an example, a statistic, or a personal experience, among other things.

Exaggeration An extreme overstatement of an idea is called an exaggeration. It is often used for purposes of emphasis or humor.

Exposition Exposition is the first stage of a typical story plot. The exposition provides important background information and introduces the setting and the important

characters. The conflict the characters face may also be introduced in the exposition, or it may be introduced later, in the rising action.

See also Plot.

External Conflict *See* Conflict.

Fable A fable is a brief tale told to illustrate a moral or teach a lesson. Often the moral of a fable appears in a distinct and memorable statement near the tale's beginning or end.

See also Moral.

Fact Versus Opinion A **fact** is a statement that can be proved, or verified. An opinion, on the other hand, is a statement that cannot be proved because it expresses a person's beliefs, feelings, or thoughts.

See also Generalization; Inference.

Fallacious Reasoning Reasoning that includes errors in logic or fallacies.

Fallacy A fallacy is an error of reasoning. Typically, a fallacy is based on an incorrect inference or a misuse of evidence.

See also Either/Or Fallacy; Logical Appeal; Overgeneralization.

Falling Action The falling action is the stage of the plot in which the story begins to draw to a close. The falling action comes after the **climax** and before the **resolution,** also called denouement. Events in the falling action show the results of the important decision or action that happened at the climax. Tension eases as the falling action begins; however, the final outcome of the story is not yet fully worked out at this stage.

See also Climax; Plot.

Fantasy Fantasy is a type of fiction that is highly imaginative and portrays events, settings, or characters that are unrealistic. The setting might be a nonexistent world, the plot might involve magic or the supernatural, and the characters might have superhuman powers.

Faulty Reasoning *See* Fallacy.

Feature Article A feature article is an article in a newspaper or magazine about a topic of human interest or lifestyles.

Fiction Fiction is prose writing that tells an imaginary story. The writer of a short story or novel might invent all the events and characters or might base parts of the story on real people and events. The basic elements of fiction are plot, character, setting, and theme. Different types of fiction include realistic fiction, historical fiction, science fiction, and fantasy.

See also Novel; Novella; Short Story.

Figurative Language In figurative language, words are used in an imaginative way to express ideas that are not literally true. "Megan has a bee in her bonnet" is an example of figurative language. The sentence does not mean that Megan is wearing a bonnet, nor that there is an actual bee in it. Instead, it means that Megan is angry or upset about something. Figurative language is used for comparison, emphasis, and emotional effect.

See also Metaphor; Onomatopoeia; Personification; Simile.

First-Person Point of View *See* Point of View.

Flashback In a literary work, a flashback is an interruption of the action to present events that took place at an earlier time. A flashback provides information that can help a reader better understand a character's current situation.

Folklore The traditions, customs, and stories that are passed down within a culture are known as its folklore. Folklore includes various types of literature, such as legends, folk tales, myths, trickster tales, and fables.

See also Fable; Folk Tale; Myth.

Folk Tale A folk tale is a story that has been passed down from generation to generation by word of mouth. Folk tales may be set in the distant past and involve supernatural events. The characters in them may be animals, people, or superhuman beings.

Foreshadowing Foreshadowing occurs when a writer provides hints that suggest future events in a story. Foreshadowing creates suspense and makes readers eager to find out what will happen.

Form The structure or organization of a written work is often called its form. The form of a poem includes the arrangement of its words and lines on the page.

Free Verse Poetry without regular patterns of rhyme and rhythm is called free verse. Some poets use free verse to capture the sounds and rhythms of ordinary speech.

See also Rhyme, Rhythm.

Generalization A generalization is a broad statement about a class or category of people, ideas, or things based on a study of, or a belief about, only some of its members.

See also Overgeneralization; Stereotyping.

Genre The term *genre* refers to a category in which a work of literature is classified. The major genres in literature are fiction, nonfiction, poetry, and drama.

Government Publications Government publications are documents produced by government organizations. Pamphlets, brochures, and reports are just some of the many forms these publications take. Government publications can be good resources for a wide variety of topics.

Graphic Aid A graphic aid is a text feature that is printed, handwritten, or drawn. Charts, diagrams, graphs, photographs, maps, and captions are examples of graphic aids.

Graphic Organizer A graphic organizer is a "word picture"—a visual illustration of a verbal statement—that helps a reader understand a text. Charts, tables, webs, and diagrams can all be graphic organizers. Graphic organizers and graphic aids can look the same. However, graphic organizers and graphic aids do differ in how they are used. Graphic aids help deliver important information to students using a text. Graphic organizers are actually created by students themselves. They help students understand the text or organize information.

Haiku Haiku is a form of Japanese poetry in which 17 syllables are arranged in three lines of 5, 7, and 5 syllables. The rules of haiku are strict. In addition to following the syllabic count, the poet must create a clear picture that will evoke a strong emotional response in the reader. Nature is a particularly important source of inspiration for Japanese haiku poets, and details from nature are often the subjects of their poems.

Hero A hero is a main character or protagonist in a story. They are typically courageous, strong, honorable, and intelligent. They are protectors of society who hold back the forces of evil and fight to make the world a better place. In modern literature, a hero may simply be the most important character in a story. Such a hero is often an ordinary person with ordinary problems.

Historical Document Historical documents are writings that have played a significant role in human events. The Declaration of Independence, for example, is a historical document.

Historical Fiction A short story or a novel can be called historical fiction when it is set in the past and includes real places and real events of historical importance.

How-To Book A how-to book explains how to do something—usually an activity, a sport, or a household project.

Humor Humor is a quality that provokes laughter or amusement. Writers create humor through exaggeration, amusing descriptions, irony, and witty and insightful dialogue.

Idiom An idiom is an expression that has a meaning different from the meaning of its individual words. For example, "to let the cat out of the bag" is an idiom meaning "to reveal a secret or surprise."

Imagery Imagery consists of words and phrases that appeal to a reader's five senses. Writers use sensory details to help the reader imagine how things look, feel, smell, sound, and taste.

Implied Main Idea *See* Main Idea.

Index The index of a book is an alphabetized list of important topics covered in the book and the page numbers on which they can be found. An index can be used to quickly find specific information about a topic.

Inductive Reasoning Inductive reasoning is the process of logical reasoning that starts with observations, examples, and facts and moves on to a general conclusion or principle.

Inference An inference is a logical guess that is made based on facts and one's own knowledge and experience.

Informational Text Informational text is writing that provides factual information. Examples include news reports, a science textbook, and lab reports. Informational text also includes literary nonfiction, such as personal essays, opinion pieces, speeches, biographies, and historical accounts.

Informative Essay *See* Essay.

Internal Conflict *See* Conflict.

Internet The Internet is a global, interconnected system of computer networks that allows for communication through e-mail, listservs, and the World Wide Web. The Internet connects computers and computer users throughout the world.

Interview An interview is a conversation conducted by a writer or reporter in which facts or statements are elicited from another person, recorded, and then broadcast or published.

Irony Irony is a contrast between what is expected and what actually exists or happens. Exaggeration and sarcasm are techniques writers use to express irony.

Journal A journal is a periodical publication used by legal, medical, and other professional organizations. The term may also be used to refer to a diary or daily record.
See Diary.

Legend A legend is a story handed down from the past about a specific person, usually someone of heroic accomplishments. Legends usually have some basis in historical fact.

Limerick A limerick is a short, humorous poem made up of five lines. It usually has the rhyme scheme *aabba,* created by two rhyming couplets followed by a fifth line that rhymes with the first couplet. A limerick typically has a sing-song rhythm.

Literary Nonfiction *See* Narrative Nonfiction.

Loaded Language Loaded language consists of words with strongly positive or negative connotations intended to influence a reader's or listener's attitude.

Logical Appeal A logical appeal is a way of writing or speaking that relies on logic and facts. It appeals to people's reasoning or intellect rather than to their values or emotions. Flawed logical appeals—that is, errors in reasoning—are called logical fallacies.

See also Fallacy.

Logical Argument A logical argument is an argument in which the logical relationship between the support and claim is sound.

Lyric Poetry Lyric poetry is poetry that presents the personal thoughts and feelings of a single speaker. Most poems, other than narrative poems, are lyric poems. Lyric poetry can be in a variety of forms and cover many subjects, from love and death to everyday experiences.

Main Character *See* Character.

Main Idea The main idea, or central idea, is the most important idea about a topic that a writer or speaker conveys. It can be the central idea of an entire work or of just a paragraph. Often, the main idea of a paragraph is expressed in a topic sentence. However, a main idea may just be implied, or suggested, by details. A main idea is typically supported by details.

Make Inferences *See* Inference.

Memoir A memoir is a form of autobiographical writing in which a writer shares his or her personal experiences and observations of important events or people. Often informal in tone, memoirs usually give readers information about a particular person or period of time in the writer's life. In contrast, autobiographies focus on many important people and events in the writer's life over a long period of time.

See also Autobiography; Personal Narrative.

Metaphor A metaphor is a comparison of two things that are basically unlike but have some qualities in common. Unlike a simile, a metaphor does not contain the words *like* or *as.*

See also Figurative Language; Simile.

Meter In poetry, meter is the regular pattern of stressed (´) and unstressed (˘) syllables. Although poems have rhythm, not all poems have regular meter. Each unit of meter is known as a **foot** and is made up of one stressed syllable and one or two unstressed syllables.

See also Rhythm.

Minor Character *See* Character.

Monitor Monitoring is the strategy of checking your comprehension as you read and modifying the strategies you are using to suit your needs. Monitoring often includes the following strategies: questioning, clarifying, visualizing, predicting, connecting, and rereading.

Mood Mood is the feeling or atmosphere that a writer creates for the reader. Descriptive words, imagery, and figurative language all influence the mood of a work.

Moral A moral is a lesson that a story teaches. A moral is often stated at the end of a fable.

See also Fable.

Motivation Motivation is the reason why a character acts, feels, or thinks in a certain way. A character may have more than one motivation for his or her actions. Understanding these motivations helps readers get to know the character.

Myth A myth is a traditional story that attempts to answer basic questions about human nature, origins of the world, mysteries of nature, and social customs.

Narrative Writing that tells a story is called a narrative. The events in a narrative may be real or imagined. Autobiographies and biographies are narratives that deal with real people or events. Fictional narratives include short stories, fables, myths, and novels. A narrative may also be in the form of a poem.

See also Autobiography; Biography; Personal Narrative.

Narrative Nonfiction Narrative nonfiction is writing that reads much like fiction, except that the characters, setting, and plot are real rather than imaginary. Narrative nonfiction includes autobiographies, biographies, and memoirs.

Narrative Poetry Poetry that tells a story is called narrative poetry. Like fiction, a narrative poem contains characters, a setting, and a plot. It might also contain such elements of poetry as rhyme, rhythm, imagery, and figurative language.

Narrator The narrator is the voice that tells a story. Sometimes the narrator is a character in the story. At other times, the narrator is an outside voice created by the writer. The narrator is not the same as the writer.

See also Point of View.

News Article A news article is writing that reports on a recent event. In newspapers, news articles are usually brief and to the point, presenting the most important facts first, followed by more detailed information.

Nonfiction Nonfiction is writing that tells about real people, places, and events. Unlike fiction, nonfiction is mainly written to convey factual information. Nonfiction includes a wide range of writing—newspaper articles, letters, essays, biographies, movie reviews, speeches, true-life adventure stories, advertising, and more.

Novel A novel is a long work of fiction. Like a short story, a novel is the product of a writer's imagination. Because a novel is considerably longer than a short story, a novelist can develop the characters and story line more thoroughly.

See also Fiction.

Novella A novella is a work of fiction that is longer than a short story but shorter than a novel. Due to its shorter length, a novella generally includes fewer characters and a less complex plot than a novel.

See also Fiction; Novel; Short Story.

Ode An ode is a type of lyric poem that deals with serious themes, such as justice, truth, or beauty.

Onomatopoeia Onomatopoeia is the use of words whose sounds echo their meanings, such as *buzz, whisper, gargle,* and *murmur.*

Op/Ed Piece An op/ed piece is an opinion piece that typically appears opposite ("op") the editorial page of a newspaper. Unlike editorials,

op/ed pieces are written and submitted by readers.

Oral Literature Oral literature, or the oral tradition, consists of stories that have been passed down by word of mouth from generation to generation. Oral literature includes folk tales, legends, and myths. In more recent times, some examples of oral literature have been written down or recorded so that the stories can be preserved.

Organization *See* Pattern of Organization.

Overgeneralization An overgeneralization is a statement that is too broad to be accurate. You can often recognize overgeneralizations by the appearance of words and phrases such as *all, everyone, every time, any, anything, no one,* or *none.* An example is "None of the city's workers really cares about keeping the environment clean." In all probability, there are many exceptions. The writer can't possibly know the feelings of every city worker.

Overview An overview is a short summary of a story, a speech, or an essay.

Paraphrase Paraphrasing is the restating of information in one's own words.

See also Summarize.

Parody A parody is a humorous imitation of another writer's work. Parodies can take the form of fiction, drama, or poetry. Jon Scieszka's "The True Story of the Three Little Pigs" is an example of a parody.

Pattern of Organization The term *pattern of organization* refers to the way ideas and information are arranged and organized. Patterns of organization include cause and effect, chronological, compare and contrast, classification, and problem-solution, among others.

See also Cause and Effect; Chronological Order; Classification; Compare and Contrast; Problem-Solution Order; Sequential Order.

Periodical A periodical is a magazine or another type of publication that is issued on a regular basis.

Personal Narrative A short essay told as a story in the first-person point of view. A personal narrative usually reflects the writer's experiences, feelings, and personality.

See also Autobiography; Memoir.

Personification The giving of human qualities to an animal, object, or idea is known as personification.

See also Figurative Language.

Persuasion Persuasion is the art of swaying others' feelings, beliefs, or actions. Persuasion normally appeals to both the mind and the emotions of readers.

See also Appeal to Authority; Emotional Appeal; Ethical Appeal; Loaded Language; Logical Appeal.

Play *See* Drama.

Playwright *See* Drama.

Plot The series of events in a story is called the plot. The plot usually centers on a **conflict**, or struggle, faced by the main character. The action that the characters take to solve the problem builds toward a **climax** in the story. At this point, or shortly afterward, the problem is solved and the story ends. Most story plots have five stages: exposition, rising action, climax, falling action, and resolution.

See also Climax; Conflict; Exposition; Falling Action; Rising Action.

Poetry Poetry is a type of literature in which words are carefully chosen and arranged to create certain effects. Poets use a variety of sound devices, imagery, and figurative language to express emotions and ideas.

See also Alliteration; Assonance; Ballad; Free Verse; Imagery; Meter; Narrative Poetry; Rhyme; Rhythm; Stanza.

Point of View Point of view refers to how a writer chooses to narrate a story. When a story is told from the **first-person** point of view, the narrator is a character in the story and uses first-person pronouns, such as *I, me,* and *we.* In a story told from the **third-person** point of view, the narrator is not a character in the story. A writer's choice of narrator affects the information readers receive.

See also Narrator.

Predict Predicting is a reading strategy that involves using text clues to make a reasonable guess about what will happen next in a story.

Primary Source *See* Sources.

Prior Knowledge Prior knowledge is the knowledge a reader already possesses about a topic. This information might come from personal experiences, expert accounts, books, films, or other sources.

Problem-Solution Order Problem-solution order is a pattern of organization in which a problem is stated and analyzed and then one or more solutions are proposed and examined.

Prop The word *prop,* originally an abbreviation of the word *property,* refers to any physical object that is used in a drama.

Propaganda Propaganda is any form of communication that is so distorted that it conveys false or misleading information to advance a specific belief or cause.

Prose The word *prose* refers to all forms of writing that are not in verse form. The term may be used to describe very different forms of writing, such as short stories and essays.

Protagonist A protagonist is the main character in a story, play, or novel. The protagonist is involved in the main conflict of the story. Usually, the protagonist undergoes changes as the plot runs its course.

Public Document Public documents are documents that were written for the public to provide information that is of public interest or concern. They include government documents, speeches, signs, and rules and regulations. Most public documents use text features, such as graphics, headers, or captions, to make sure readers can easily understand the information they communicate.

See also Government Publications.

Pun A pun is a play on words based on similar senses of two or more words, or on various meanings of the same word. A pun is usually made for humorous effect. For example, the fisherman was fired for playing hooky.

Radio Play A radio play is a drama that is written specifically to be broadcast over the radio. Because the audience is not meant to see a radio play, sound effects are often used to help listeners imagine the setting and the action. The stage directions in the play's script indicate the sound effects.

Realistic Fiction Realistic fiction is fiction that is set in the real, modern world. The characters behave like real people and use human abilities to cope with modern life's problems and conflicts.

Recurring Theme *See* Theme.

Reference Work Reference works are sources that contain facts and background information on a wide range of subjects. Most reference works are good sources of reliable information because they have been reviewed by experts. The following are some common reference works: encyclopedias, dictionaries, thesauri, almanacs, atlases, and directories.

Refrain A refrain is one or more lines repeated in each stanza of a poem.

Repetition Repetition is a technique in which a sound, word, phrase, or line is repeated for emphasis or unity. Repetition often helps to reinforce meaning and create an appealing rhythm.

See also Alliteration; Refrain; Sound Devices.

Resolution *See* Falling Action.

Review *See* Critical Review.

Rhetorical Question Rhetorical questions are those that have such obvious answers that they do not require a reply. Writers often use them to suggest that their claim is so obvious that everyone should agree with it.

Rhyme Rhyme is the repetition of sounds at the end of words. Words rhyme when their accented vowels and the letters that follow have identical sounds. *Pig* and *dig* rhyme, as do *reaching* and *teaching.* The most common type of rhyme in poetry is called **end rhyme,** in which rhyming words come at the ends of lines. Rhyme that occurs within a line of poetry is called **internal rhyme.**

Rhyme Scheme A rhyme scheme is a pattern of end rhymes in a poem. A rhyme scheme is noted by assigning a letter of the alphabet,

beginning with *a,* to each line. Lines that rhyme are given the same letter.

Rhythm Rhythm is the musical quality created by the alternation of stressed and unstressed syllables in a line of poetry. Poets use rhythm to emphasize ideas and to create moods. Devices such as alliteration, rhyme, and assonance often contribute to creating rhythm.

See also Meter.

Rising Action The rising action is the stage of the plot that develops the **conflict,** or struggle. During this stage, events occur that make the conflict more complicated. The events in the rising action build toward a **climax,** or turning point.

See also Plot.

Scanning Scanning is the process used to search through a text for a particular fact or piece of information. When you scan, you sweep your eyes across a page, looking for key words that may lead you to the information you want.

Scene In drama, the action is often divided into acts and scenes. Each scene presents an episode of the play's plot and typically occurs at a single place and time.

See also Act.

Scenery Scenery is a painted backdrop or other structures used to create the setting for a play.

Science Fiction Science fiction is fiction in which a writer explores unexpected possibilities of the past or the future, combining scientific information with his or her creative imagination. Most science fiction writers create believable worlds, although some create fantasy worlds that have familiar elements.

See also Fantasy.

Scope Scope refers to a work's focus. For example, an article about Austin, Texas, that focuses on the city's history, economy, and residents has a broad scope. An article that focuses only on the restaurants in Austin has a narrower scope.

Script The text of a play, film, or broadcast is called a script.

Secondary Source *See* Source.

Sensory Details Sensory details are words and phrases that appeal to the reader's senses of sight, hearing, touch, smell, and taste.

See also Imagery.

Sequential Order Sequential order is a pattern of organization that shows the order of steps or stages in a process.

Setting The setting of a story, poem, or play is the time and place of the action. Sometimes the setting is clear and well-defined. At other times, it is left to the reader's imagination. Elements of setting include geographic location, historical period (past, present, or future), season, time of day, and culture.

Setting a Purpose The process of establishing specific reasons for reading a text is called setting a purpose. Readers can look at a text's title, headings, and illustrations to guess what it might be about. They can then use these guesses to figure out what they want to learn from reading the text.

Short Story A short story is a work of fiction that centers on a single idea and can be read in one sitting. Generally, a short story has one main conflict that involves the characters and keeps the story moving.

See also Fiction.

Sidebar A sidebar is additional information set in a box alongside or within a news or feature article. Popular magazines often make use of sidebars.

Signal Words In a text, signal words are words and phrases that help show how events or ideas are related. Some common examples of signal words are *and, but, however, nevertheless, therefore,* and *in addition.*

Simile A simile is a figure of speech that makes a comparison between two unlike things using the words *like* or *as.*

See also Figurative Language; Metaphor.

Sound Devices Sound devices are ways of using words for the sound qualities they create. Sound devices can help convey meaning and mood in a writer's work. Some common sound devices include **alliteration, assonance,** meter, onomatopoeia, repetition, rhyme, and rhythm.

See also Alliteration; Assonance; Meter; Onomatopoeia; Repetition; Rhyme; Rhythm.

Source A source is anything that supplies information. **Primary sources** are materials created by people who witnessed or took part in the event they supply information about. Letters, diaries, autobiographies, and eyewitness accounts are primary sources. **Secondary sources** are those made by people who were not directly involved in the event or even present when it occurred. Encyclopedias, textbooks, biographies, and most news articles are secondary sources.

Speaker In poetry the speaker is the voice that "talks" to the reader, similar to the narrator in fiction. The speaker is not necessarily the poet.

Speech A speech is a talk or public address. The purpose of a speech may be to entertain, to explain, to persuade, to inspire, or any combination of these purposes.

Stage Directions In the script of a play, the instructions to the actors, director, and stage crew are called the stage directions. Stage directions might suggest scenery, lighting, sound effects, and ways for actors to move and speak. Stage directions often appear in parentheses and in italic type.

Stanza A stanza is a group of two or more lines that form a unit in a poem. Each stanza may have the same number of lines, or the number of lines may vary.

See also Couplet; Form; Poetry.

Stereotype In literature, characters who are defined by a single trait are known as stereotypes. Such characters do not usually demonstrate the complexities of real people. Familiar stereotypes in popular literature include the absent-minded professor and the busybody.

Stereotyping Stereotyping is a dangerous type of overgeneralization. It can lead to unfair judgments of people based on their ethnic background, beliefs, practices, or physical appearance.

Structure The structure of a work of literature is the way in which it is put together. In poetry, structure involves the arrangement of words and lines to produce a desired effect. One structural unit in poetry is the stanza. In prose, structure involves the arrangement of such elements as sentences, paragraphs, and events. **Sentence structure** refers to the length and types of sentences used in a work.

Style A style is a manner of writing. It involves how something is said rather than what is said.

Subject The subject of a literary work is its focus or topic. In an autobiography, for example, the subject is the life of the person telling the story. Subject differs from **theme** in that theme is a deeper meaning, whereas the subject is the main situation or set of facts described by the text.

Summarize To summarize is to briefly retell the main ideas of a piece of writing in one's own words.

See also Paraphrase.

Support Support is any information that helps to prove a claim.

Supporting Detail *See* Main Idea.

Surprise Ending A surprise ending is an unexpected plot twist at the end of a story. The surprise may be a sudden turn in the action or a piece of information that gives a different perspective to the entire story.

Suspense Suspense is a feeling of growing tension and excitement experienced by a reader. Suspense makes a reader curious about the outcome of a story or an event within a story. A writer creates suspense by raising questions in the reader's mind. The use of **foreshadowing** is one way that writers create suspense.

See also Foreshadowing.

Symbol A symbol is a person, a place, an object, an animal, or an activity that stands for something beyond itself. For example, a flag is a colored piece of cloth that stands for a country. A white dove is a bird that represents peace.

Synthesize To synthesize information means to take individual pieces of information and combine them in order to gain a better understanding of a subject.

Tall Tale A tall tale is a humorously exaggerated story about impossible events, often involving the supernatural abilities of the main character. Stories about folk heroes such as Pecos Bill and Paul Bunyan are typical tall tales.

Teleplay A teleplay is a play written for television. In a teleplay, scenes can change quickly and dramatically. The camera can focus the viewer's attention on specific actions. The camera directions in teleplays are much like the stage directions in stage plays.

Text Feature Text features are elements of a text, such as boldface type, headers, captions, and subheadings, that help organize and call attention to important information. Italic type, bulleted or numbered lists, sidebars, and graphic aids such as charts, tables, timelines, illustrations, and photographs are also considered text features.

Theme A theme is a message about life or human nature that the writer shares with the reader. In many cases, readers must infer the writer's message. One way to infer a theme is to note the lessons learned by the main characters.

  Recurring themes: Themes found in a variety of works. For example, authors from different backgrounds might express similar themes having to do with the importance of family values.

  Universal themes: Themes that are found throughout the literature of all time periods. For example, Cinderella stories contain a universal theme relating to goodness being rewarded.

See also Moral.

Thesaurus *See* Reference Works.

Thesis Statement A thesis statement, or controlling idea, is the main proposition that a writer attempts to support in a piece of writing.

Third-Person Point of View *See* Point of View.

Title The title of a piece of writing is the name that is attached to it. A title often refers to an important aspect of the work.

Tone The tone of a literary work expresses the writer's attitude toward his or her subject. Words such as *angry, sad,* and *humorous* can be used to describe different tones.

See also Author's Perspective.

Topic Sentence The topic sentence of a paragraph states the paragraph's main idea. All other sentences in the paragraph provide supporting details.

Tragedy A tragedy is a dramatic work that presents the downfall of a character or characters. The events in a tragic plot are set in motion by a decision that is often an error in judgment on the part of the hero. Events are linked in a cause-and-effect relationship and lead to a disastrous conclusion, usually death.

Traits *See* Character.

Treatment The way a topic is handled in a work is referred to as its treatment. Treatment includes the form the writing takes as well as the writer's purpose and tone.

Turning Point *See* Climax.

Universal Theme *See* Theme.

Unsupported Inference A guess that may seem logical but that is not supported by facts.

Visualize Visualizing is the process of forming a mental picture based on written or spoken information.

Voice The term *voice* refers to a writer's unique use of language that allows a reader to "hear" a human personality in the writer's work. Elements of style that contribute to a writer's voice can reveal much about the author's personality, beliefs, and attitudes.

Website A website is a collection of "pages" on the World Wide Web that usually covers a specific subject. Linked pages are accessed by clicking hyperlinks or menus, which send the user from page to page within a website. Websites are created by companies, organizations, educational institutions, government agencies, the military, and individuals.

Word Choice The success of any writing depends on the writer's choice of words. Words not only communicate ideas but also help describe events, characters, settings, and so on. Word choice can make a writer's work sound formal or informal, serious or humorous. A writer must choose words carefully depending on the goal of the piece of writing. For example, a writer working on a science article would probably use technical, formal words; a writer trying to establish the setting in a short story would probably use more descriptive words. Word choice is sometimes referred to as diction.

See also Style.

Workplace Document Workplace documents are materials that are produced or used within a work setting, usually to aid in the functioning of the workplace. They include job applications, office memos, training manuals, job descriptions, and sales reports. Many functional workplace documents include helpful text features, such as graphics, headers, and captions.

Works Cited The term *works cited* refers to a list of all the works a writer has referred to in his or her text. This list often includes not only books and articles but also Internet sources.

Works Consulted The term *works consulted* refers to a list of all the works a writer consulted in order to create his or her text. It is not limited just to those works cited in the text.

See also Bibliography.

Using the Glossary

This glossary is an alphabetical list of vocabulary words found in the selections in this book. Use this glossary just as you would a dictionary—to determine the meanings, parts of speech, pronunciation, and syllabication of words. (Some technical, foreign, and more obscure words in this book are not listed here but are defined for you in the footnotes that accompany many of the selections.)

Many words in the English language have more than one meaning. This glossary gives the meanings that apply to the words as they are used in the selections in this book. Words closely related in form and meaning are listed together in one entry (for instance, *consumption* and *consume*), and the definition is given for the first form.

The following abbreviations are used to identify parts of speech of words:

adj. adjective   *adv.* adverb   *n.* noun   *v.* verb

Each word's pronunciation is given in parentheses. A guide to the pronunciation symbols appears in the Pronunciation Key below. The stress marks in the Pronunciation Key are used to indicate the force given to each syllable in a word. They can also help you determine where words are divided into syllables.

For more information about the words in this glossary or for information about words not listed here, consult a dictionary.

Pronunciation Key

Symbol	Examples	Symbol	Examples	Symbol	Examples
ă	pat	m	mum	ûr	urge, term, firm, word, heard
ā	pay	n	no, sudden* (sud'n)		
ä	father	ng	thing	v	valve
âr	care	ŏ	pot	w	with
b	bib	ō	toe	y	yes
ch	church	ô	caught, paw	z	zebra, xylem
d	deed, milled	oi	noise	zh	vision, pleasure, garage
ĕ	pet	ŏŏ	took	ə	about, item, edible, gallop, circus
ē	bee	ōō	boot		
f	fife, phase, rough	ŏŏr	lure	ər	butter
g	gag	ôr	core		
h	hat	ou	out		
hw	which	p	pop		
ĭ	pit	r	roar		
ī	pie, by	s	sauce		
îr	pier	sh	ship, dish		
j	judge	t	tight, stopped		
k	kick, cat, pique	th	thin		
l	lid, needle* (nēd'l)	*th*	this		
		ŭ	cut		

Sounds in Foreign Words

Symbol	Examples
KH	*German* ich, ach; *Scottish* loch
N	*French*, bon (bôn)
œ	*French* feu, œuf; *German* schön
ü	*French* tu; *German* uber

*In English the consonants *l* and *n* often constitute complete syllables by themselves.

Stress Marks

The relevant emphasis with which the syllables of a word or phrase are spoken, called stress, is indicated in three different ways. The strongest, or primary, stress is marked with a bold mark (´). An intermediate, or secondary, level of stress is marked with a similar but lighter mark (´). The weakest stress is unmarked. Words of one syllable show no stress mark.

Glossary of Academic Vocabulary

achieve (ə-chēv′) *v.* to perform or carry out with success; accomplish

appropriate (ə-prō′prē-ĭt) *adj.* suitable or acceptable for a particular situation, person, place, or condition

authority (ə-thôr′ĭ-tē) *n.* an accepted source, such as a person or text, of expert information or advice

benefit (bĕn′ə-fĭt) *n.* something that provides help or improves something else

circumstance (sûr′kəm-stăns′) *n.* a condition or fact that affects an event

consequence (kŏn′sĭ-kwĕns′) *n.* something that logically or naturally follows from an action or condition

constraint (kən-strānt′) *n.* something or someone that limits or restricts another's actions

distinct (dĭ-stĭngkt′) *adj.* easy to tell apart from others; not alike

emphasize (ĕm′fə-sīz′) *v.* to give something special importance or attention

environment (ĕn-vī′rən-mənt) *n.* surroundings; the conditions that surround someone or something

evident (ĕv′ĭ-dənt) *adj.* easily seen or understood; obvious

factor (făk′tər) *n.* someone or something that has an affect on an event, a process, or a situation

illustrate (ĭl′ə-strāt′) *v.* to show, or clarify, by examples or comparing

impact (ĭm′păkt′) *n.* something striking against another; also, the effect or impression of one thing on another

indicate (ĭn′dĭ-kāt′) *tr.v.* to point out; also, to serve as a sign or symbol of something

individual (ĭn′də-vĭj′ōo-əl) *n.* a single human being apart from a society or community

injure (ĭn′jər) *tr.v.* to hurt or cause damage

instance (ĭn′stəns) *n.* an example that is cited to prove or disprove a claim or illustrate a point

justify (jŭs′tə-fī′) *v.* to demonstrate or prove to be just, right, reasonable, or valid

legal (lē′gəl) *adj.* permitted by law; of, related to, or concerned with law

occur (ə-kûr′) *v.* to take place; happen

outcome (out′kŭm′) *n.* a natural result or consequence

period (pîr′ē-əd) *n.* a particular length of time, often referring to a specific time in history or in a culture

principle (prĭn′sə-pəl) *n.* a rule or standard, especially of good behavior

relevant (rĕl′ə-vənt) *adj.* important to, connected to, or significant to an issue, event, or person in some way

respond (rĭ-spŏnd′) *v.* to make a reply; answer

significant (sĭg-nĭf′ĭ-kənt) *adj.* meaningful; important

similar (sĭm′ə-lər) *adj.* alike in appearance or nature, though not identical; having features that are the same

specific (spĭ-sĭf′ĭk) *adj.* concerned with a particular thing; also, precise or exact

tradition (trə-dĭsh′ən) *n.* the passing down of various elements of a culture from generation to generation; a custom

Glossary of Critical Vocabulary

activate (ăk′tə-vāt′) *v.* To *activate* something means to cause it to start working.

aggression (ə-grĕsh′ən) *n.* Angry, violent behavior or action is called *aggression*.

alley (ăl′ē) *n.* An *alley* is a narrow street or passage behind or between city buildings.

allure (ə-lŏŏr′) *n.* An *allure* is a power of attraction, an ability to interest or entice others.

ambush (ăm′bŏŏsh) *v.* Some animals *ambush* their prey by hiding and then attacking as the prey comes near them.

amiable (ā′mē-ə-bəl) *adj.* To be *amiable* is to be good-natured and friendly.

antibiotic (ăn′tĭ-bī-ŏt′ĭk) *n.* An *antibiotic* is a drug used in medicine to kill bacteria and to cure infections.

aptitude (ăp′tĭ-tōōd′) *n.* An *aptitude* for something is an ability to easily and quickly learn how to do it.

attribute (ə-trĭb′yōōt) *tr.v.* If you *attribute* something to a person, thing, or event, you believe that they cause it or have it.

banquet (băng′kwĭt) *n.* A *banquet* is a huge, elaborate feast with many kinds of food and drink.

bore (bôr) *v.* (past tense of *bear*) If you say a person *bore* something, you mean they carried it or had it on them; it is visible in some way.

brood (brōōd) *v.* If you *brood*, you are deep in thought, maybe worrying or feeling depressed about something.

cascade (kăs-kād′) *v.* Something that can *cascade* will fall, pour, or rush in stages, like a waterfall over steep rocks.

claustrophobic (klô′strə-fō′bĭk) *adj.* A *claustrophobic* place feels uncomfortably closed or crowded.

collapse (kə-lăps′) *v.* If you *collapse*, you fall down suddenly.

complexity (kəm-plĕk′sĭ-tē) *n. Complexity* is the state of having many different parts that are connected in a tangled or layered way.

conceal (kən-sēl′) *v.* If you *conceal* something, you hide it and keep it from being found or seen.

confidence (kŏn′fĭ-dəns) *n.* A person who has *confidence* believes in his or her abilities or ideas.

conscientious (kŏn′shē-ĕn′shəs) *adj.* If someone is *conscientious,* that person is very careful and thorough.

criticize (krĭt′ĭ-sīz′) *v.* To *criticize* is to tell someone what you think is wrong with them.

degradation (dĕg′rə-dā′shən) *n.* Damage done to something in nature, by weather or water for example, is called *degradation*.

despair (dĭ-spâr′) *n.* Feeling defeated, with a complete loss of hope, is called *despair*.

dialect (dī′ə-lĕkt′) *n.* A *dialect* is a regional language variation, characterized by differences in pronunciation, grammar, or vocabulary.

dictate (dĭk′tāt′) *v.* To *dictate* something is to require it to be done or decided.

distract (dĭ-străkt′) *v.* To *distract* is to pull attention away from something or someone.

eavesdrop (ēvz′drŏp′) *intr.v.* To *eavesdrop* is to listen secretly to others′ private conversations.

embrace (ĕm-brās′) *n.* An *embrace* is a hug or encirclement, showing acceptance.

emphatic (ĕm-făt′ĭk) *adj.* If something is *emphatic,* it is expressed in a definite and forceful way.

entrance (ĕn-trăns′) *v.* To *entrance* is to fill with delight or wonder.

evolve (ĭ-vŏlv′) *v.* When animals and plants *evolve,* they gradually change and develop into different forms.

exotic (ĭg-zŏt′ĭk) *adj.* Something that is *exotic* is from another part of the world.

foil (foil) *tr.v.* If you *foil* someone, you stop that person from being successful at something.

gauge (gāj) *tr.v.* To *gauge* something is to measure it or judge it, as in to make an estimate.

glisten (glĭs´ən) *v.* An object that *glistens* is sparkly and shiny.

gnarly (när´lē) *adj.* Something that is *gnarly* has many knots and bumpy areas on its surface.

grimace (grĭm´ĭs) *v.* If you *grimace*, you twist your face in an unattractive way because you are unhappy, disgusted, or in pain.

immaturity (ĭm´ə-työor´ĭ-tē) *n.* *Immaturity* is the state of not being fully developed or grown.

immortal (ĭ-môr´tl) *adj.* If someone or something is *immortal*, it will never die.

inconsistency (ĭn´kən-sĭs´tən-sē) *n.* If something shows *inconsistency*, it does not always behave or respond the same way every time.

indignity (ĭn-dĭg´nĭ-tē) *n.* An *indignity* is something that offends, insults, or injures one's pride or dignity.

indomitable (ĭn-dŏm´ĭ-tə-bəl) *adj.* Something or someone that is *indomitable* is unable to be tamed or defeated.

indulge (ĭn-dŭlj´) *v.* If you *indulge* in something, you allow yourself to do or have something you want.

intercept (in´tər-sĕpt´) *v.* To *intercept* is to stop or interrupt something.

invisible (ĭn-vĭz´ə-bəl) *adj.* If something is *invisible*, you cannot see it.

isolate (ī´sə-lāt´) *v.* To *isolate* something is to set it apart or separate it from others.

jar (jär) *n.* A *jar* can be a jolt or shock, as well as a harsh, scraping sound.

knot (nŏt) *n.* A *knot* is a unit of speed used by ships. One knot is equal to one nautical mile, or about 1.85 kilometers per hour.

lament (lə-mĕnt) *v.* If you *lament*, you are wailing or crying as a way of expressing grief.

lethargy (lĕth´ər-jē) *n.* In a state of *lethargy*, a person experiences drowsiness, inactivity, and a lack of energy.

linger (lĭng´gər) *v.* To *linger* means to leave slowly and reluctantly, not wanting to go.

magnitude (măg´nĭ-tōod´) *n.* *Magnitude* is a measure of the amount of energy released by an earthquake.

malice (măl´ĭs) *n.* *Malice* is a desire to harm others or to see someone suffer.

mandate (măn´dāt´) *n.* A *mandate* is an authoritative command or instruction.

menagerie (mə-năj´ə-rē) *n.* A *menagerie* is a collection of live wild animals, often kept for showing to the public.

mock (mŏk) *v.* To *mock* someone is to treat them with scorn or contempt.

monumental (mŏn´yə-mĕn´tl) *adj.* A *monumental* event is one that is of outstanding significance.

mope (mōp) *intr.v.* To *mope* is to be gloomy, miserable, and not interested in anything.

morbid (môr´bĭd) *adj.* A *morbid* quality or feeling is one that is unhealthy or unwholesome, like an illness or disease.

ominous (ŏm´ə-nəs) *adj.* Something that is *ominous* is frightening or threatening.

perseverance (pûr´sə-vîr´əns) *n.* To have *perseverance* is to stay focused on a plan, a belief, or a purpose.

pestilence (pĕs´tə-ləns) *n.* A *pestilence* is often a fatal illness or evil influence that spreads quickly to many people.

phenomenon (fĭ-nŏm´ə-nŏn´) *n.* A *phenomenon* is an unusual or remarkable fact or event.

plummet (plŭm´ĭt) *v.* If you *plummet*, you fall straight down, suddenly and steeply.

poised (poizd) *adj.* To be *poised* means to be calm and assured, showing balanced feeling and action.

precarious (prĭ-kâr´ē-əs) *adj.* If something is done in a *precarious* manner, it is done in a dangerously unstable or insecure way.

precipice (prĕs´ə-pĭs) *n.* A *precipice* is an overhanging or extremely steep area of rock.

predator (prĕd´ə-tər) *n.* A *predator* is an animal that survives by eating other animals.

prestigious (prĕ-stē´jəs) *adj.* If something is *prestigious,* it has a greater level of people's respect or honor than others like it.

priority (prī-ôr´ĭ-tē) *n.* A *priority* is the thing that is most important to a person in a particular situation or relationship.

prosperity (prŏ-spĕr´ĭ-tē) *n. Prosperity* means having success, particularly having enough money.

raggedy (răg´ĭ-dē) *adj.* Something that is *raggedy* is worn out, torn, or frayed.

rattle (răt´l) *v.* If you hear something *rattle,* it is making short, fast knocking sounds as it moves.

recoil (rĭ-koil´) *intr. v.* To *recoil* from something is to shrink back, as if in fear.

regulate (rĕg´yə-lāt´) *v.* If you *regulate* something, you control or direct it according to a rule, principle, or law.

reminisce (rĕm´ə-nĭs´) *v.* When you *reminisce,* you remember past experiences or events.

repress (rĭ-prĕs´) *v.* If you *repress* something, you hold it back or try to stop it from happening.

resentment (rĭ-zĕnt´mənt) *n.* If you feel *resentment,* you feel anger or irritation.

revolutionary (rĕv´ə-lōō´shə-nĕr´ē) *adj.* Something that is *revolutionary* causes important and sometimes sudden changes in a situation.

rivulet (rĭv´yə-lĭt) *n.* A *rivulet* is a small brook or stream.

rupture (rŭp´chər) *v.* To *rupture* means to break open or burst.

serene (sə-rēn´) *adj.* If you are *serene,* you are calm and unflustered.

shudder (shŭd´ər) *n.* A *shudder* is a strong shiver or tremor.

stake (stāk) *n.* A *stake* is something that can be gained or lost in a situation, such as money, food, or life.

stealthily (stĕl´thə-lē) *adv.* To do something *stealthily* means doing it quietly and secretly so no one notices.

summons (sŭm´ənz) *n.* A *summons* is a call or a notice by an authority to appear somewhere or to do something.

surfeit (sûr´fĭt) *n.* A *surfeit* is an excessive amount of something, such as food or drink.

technician (tĕk-nĭsh´ən) *n.* A *technician* is a person who does skilled practical work using specific equipment.

timid (tĭm´ĭd) *adj.* To act in a *timid* manner is to act shyly, fearfully, or hesitantly.

traumatize (trô´mə-tīz´, trou´-) *tr.v.* To *traumatize* means to upset or shock someone, causing emotional and mental pain.

treacherous (trĕch´ər-əs) *adj.* A *treacherous* person is untrustworthy and likely to betray others.

trigger (trĭg´ər) *v.* To *trigger* something means to cause it to begin.

turbulence (tûr´byə-ləns) *n.* In flying, *turbulence* is an interruption in the flow of wind that causes planes to rise, fall, or sway in a rough way.

undaunted (ŭn-dôn´tĭd) *adj.* An *undaunted* person is someone who is strongly courageous, not discouraged or disheartened.

venture (vĕn´chər) *n.* A *venture* is a dangerous, daring, or poorly planned task or activity.

vigil (vĭj´əl) *n.* A *vigil* is an act or a time of watching, often during normal sleeping hours.

wallop (wŏl´əp) *v.* To *wallop* is to hit or strike with a hard blow.

weary (wîr´ē) *adj.* If you are growing *weary,* you are getting tired of something, either physically or mentally.

Index of Skills

Key:

Teacher's Edition page numbers and subject entries are printed in **boldface** type.
Subject entries and page references that apply to both the Student Edition and the Teacher's Edition appear in lightface type.
There is no content from the Close Reader in this index.

third-person, **18, 19, 20,** 33, **222a,** 266, R6, R70
    third-person limited, 33
    third-person omniscient, **22, 26, 27, 28,** 33
    unreliable narrator, 78, 79, 81
predicates, of sentences. *See* sentences
predict, R70
prefixes, 49, R53, R58
prepositions, R29
primary sources. *See* sources
prior knowledge, **2a, 72a, 138a, 210a, 252a, 312a,** R70
problem-solution order, R21, R70
pronouns, 50, 116, 156, R35
    antecedents, agreement with 116, 156, 270, R35
    demonstrative, R28, R37
    indefinite, R29, R37
    intensive, 92, R28, R36
    interrogative, R29, R37
    object, 50, R36
    objective case, 50, R36
    personal, 58, R28, R35
    plural, 50, 58, R35
    point of view and, **222a**
    possessive, 58, R36
    predicate, R43
    reference problems, R38
    reflexive, R28, R36
    relative, 98, R29, R37
    shifts in pronoun person, 156, R38
    singular, 50, 58, R35
    subject, 50, R36
    subjective case, 50
    who and whom, 98, R37
propaganda, R26, R70
prose, R70
protagonists, R70
public documents, R70
punctuation, **157,** R31–R33
    apostrophes, R33
    capitalization, 128, 184, R34
    colons, R32
    commas, 36, R31
    dashes, 36, R32
    ellipses, R33
    exclamation points, R31
    hyphens, R32
    parentheses, 372, R32
    periods, R31
    question marks, R31
    quotation marks, R33
    semicolons, R32
puns, R70
purpose of media, 61
Purpose, Setting a, 3, 17, 37, 41, 51, 59, 73, 93, 99, 105, 117, 139, 157, 171, 185, 197, 211, 223, 233, 241, 253, 271, 281, 285, 293, 313, 331, 335, 345, 363, R72

Q

quotation marks, 42
quotations, 266, 301

R

radio plays, R70
realistic fiction, R70

reasoning, 116a
    deductive, R24, R64
    faulty, R25
    inductive, R23, R67
    reasons as support of argument, **93,** 95, 226, R22
recurring themes, R70
reference work, R71
refrains, 291, R71
relative pronouns, 98, R29, R37
repetition, **6, 7, 37,** 39, **40a, 45, 160,** R71
rereading
    to analyze author's choices, 194, 220, 229, 334
    to analyze characters, 220, 238, 328
    to analyze plot, 278, 280
    to analyze tone of a text, 194, 246
    to cite evidence, 14
    to compare and contrast, 165, 246, 278
    to draw conclusions about an author's purpose, 56
    to evaluate a poem's structure, 40, 165, 168
    to evaluate suspense, 34
    to find context clues, 15
    to identify and analyze personification, 182
    to identify author's purpose, 114
    to identify cause-and-effect relationships, 48, 342
    to identify counterarguments, 96, 226, 230
    to identify imagery, 104
    to identify main idea and details of a text, 55, 126
    to identify metaphors, 246
    to identify patterns of text structure, 370
    to identify point of view, 90
    to identify similes, 238, 246
    to infer, 278
    to interpret theme, 328
    to predict what will happen in a text, 342
    to summarize, 154
    to summarize evidence, 96, 226, 229
    to understand multiple-meaning words in context, 97
research, conducting, 67–68, 133–134, R8–R9
research questions, 186, 191
resolution, of a plot, **32,** 33, 64, R71
response to literature, 40, 63–66
review, critical, R64
rhetorical question, R71
rhyme, **40a, 281,** 283, R71
rhyme scheme, **37,** 39, **40a, 281,** 283, R71
rhythm, **170a, 292a,** R71
rising action, of a plot, **21,** 33, 64, R71
roots, word parts, R53

S

scanning, R71
scenery, R71
scenes, 361, R71
science fiction, R71
science writing, 105 –112
scripts, 361, R71
secondary sources. *See* sources

sensory details, **25, 31, 235,** R71
sensory language, 104a
sentences
    agreement, subject-verb, R48–R51
    complements in, R43
    complex, 68, 309, R47
    compound, 68, 309, R46
    compound-complex, R47
    declarative, R43
    definitions of, R43
    diagrams of, R30
    exclamatory, R43
    fragments, R47
    imperative, R43
    interrogative, R43
    inverted, R50
    objects of, R30, R43
    predicates of, R30, R43
    prepositional phrases in, R30
    run-on, R48
    simple, R46
    structure of, **58a, 196a, 240a,** R30, R46
    subjects of, R30, R43
    varying patterns of, **273,** 280
    verbs, R30
    writing complete, R47–R48
sequence, 261
sequential order, R71
setting, 13, **217, 292a,** R72
Setting a Purpose. *See* Purpose, Setting a
short stories, 3–12, 17–32, 63–65, 73–88, 171–180, 211–218, 233–236, 271–276, R72
sidebars, 42
signal words, R72
significant, 138, **159, 172, 198**
similes, **9, 142, 176,** 221, 238, **242,** 245, **246b,** R72
situational irony, 92a
slang, R52
sound bites, 301
sound devices, R72
sound elements, **60,** 61. *See also* media elements and techniques
sources, R72
    autobiographies, 267, R61
    biographies, 267, R62
    citing, R9
    diaries, 267
    direct quotations, R9
    encyclopedias, 267, R64
    evaluating, **302a**
    experts, 301
    eyewitness accounts, 267
    footage, 301
    letters, 267
    locating and evaluating, R8
    news articles, 267, 301
    newscasts, 301
    paraphrase, 103, R69
    primary, 199, **200b, 264,** 267, R70
    quotations, 301
    secondary, **264,** 267, R71
    textbooks, 267
    witnesses, 301
speakers, **37,** 39, **40a, 242, 243,** 245, 283, R72

speaking activity
    argument, 334
    discussions, 96, 154, 238, 284, 370, **373–376**
    dramatic readings, 362
    response to literature, 40
    speeches, 93–94, R72
specialized vocabulary, 195
speeches, 93–94, R72
    persuasive, 95
spelling. *See also* Vocabulary and Spelling
    commonly confused words, 232, R59–R60
    plural nouns, R58
    possessives, R58
    prefixes, R58
    rules, 330, 344, R57–R59
    special problems, R59
    spell checker, R59
    suffixes, R58
    words correctly, 232, 330, 344, R57–R60
    words ending in a consonant, R57
    words ending in a silent *e,* R57
    words ending in a *y,* R57
spondee, 170a
stage directions. *See* drama
stanza, **104a, 166.** *See also* poetry; poetic elements and devices
statistics, 55
stereotype, R72
stills, **60,** 61, **62b**
story elements
    character development, **6,** 13, **16a,** R62
    character motivation, 13, R62
    character responses, **73, 74, 76, 78, 80, 81, 82, 84, 86, 88,** 89, **233, 234, 235**
    characters, **3, 4, 5, 7, 8, 9, 10, 11,** 13, **13,** 89, **276,** R62
    character traits, 13, R62
    climax, 33, 64
    conflict, **16a,** 33, 34, **212, 213, 215, 216,** 219, R63
    exposition, 33, 64, R65
    external conflict, 219, R65
    falling action, 33, 64, R65
    flashbacks, **274,** 277, R66
    foreshadowing, 341, R66
    internal conflict, 219, R67
    irony, 89, R67
    metaphors, 221, 245, R68
    mood, 277, R68
    plot, 33, 64, 89, R70
    points of view, 33, 64, 89, R70
    protagonists, R70
    resolution, 33, 64, R71
    rising action, 33, 64, R71
    settings, 13, R72
    similes, 221, 238, 245, R72
    speakers, 39, 245, 283, R72
    style, 56, 70, 193, 237, R72
    suspense, 33, R73
    symbols, 219, 283, 334, R73
    themes, 219, 283, 327, R73
Standard English Learners, For, 3, 28, 62, 65, 68, 112, 131, 134, 159, 178, 203, 206, 207, 220, 221, 238, 248, 257, 278, 305, 309, 326, 354, 356, 370, 375, 378, 379

Index of Titles and Authors

Key:

Authors and titles that appear in the Student Edition are in lightface type.
Authors and titles that appear in the Close Reader are in **boldface** type.
Names of authors who appear in both the Student Edition and the Close Reader are lightface.
For these authors, Student Edition page references are lightface and Close Reader page references are **boldface**.

Student Edition Acknowledgments

Excerpt from "After the Hurricane" by Rita Williams-Garcia from *Free? Stories About Human Rights* by Amnesty International. Text copyright © 2009 by Rita Williams-Garcia. Reprinted by permission of Rita Williams-Garcia.

Excerpt from *The American Heritage Dictionary of the English Language, Fifth Edition.* Text copyright © 2011 by Houghton Mifflin Harcourt. Adapted and reprinted by permission of Houghton Mifflin Harcourt Publishing Company.

Excerpt from *Animal Snoops: The Wondrous World of Wildlife Spies* by Peter Christie. Text copyright © 2010 by Peter Christie. Reprinted by permission of Annick Press, Ltd. All rights reserved.

"Animal Wisdom" from *Sacred Fire* by Nancy Wood. Text copyright © 1998 by Nancy Wood. Reprinted by permission of Nancy Wood.

"The Apple of Discord I" from *Voices of the Trojan War* by Kate Hovey. Text copyright © 2004 by Kate Hovey. Reprinted by permission of Margaret K. McElderry Books, an imprint of Simon & Schuster Children's Publishing Division, and Kate Hovey.

"The Banana Tree" from *A Thief in the Village and Other Stories* by James Berry. Text copyright © 1987 by James Berry. Reprinted by permission of Penguin Books Ltd. and Peters Fraser & Dunlop (www.petersfraserdunlop.com) on behalf of James Berry.

Excerpt from *Black Ships Before Troy: The Story of the Iliad* by Rosemary Sutcliffe. Originally published by Frances Lincoln, Ltd., 1993. Text copyright © 1993 by Anthony Lawton. Reprinted by permission of Delacorte Press, a division of Random House, Inc. and Frances Lincoln, Ltd. Any third party use of this material, outside of this publication, is prohibited. Interested parties must apply directly to Random House, Inc. for permission.

Excerpt from *Colin Powell: Military Leader* by Warren Brown. Text copyright © 1992 by Chelsea House Publishers, a division of Main Line Book Co. Reprinted by permission of Chelsea House Publishers.

"Eleven" from *Woman Hollering Creek and Other Stories* by Sandra Cisneros. Text copyright © 1991 by Sandra Cisneros. Published by Vintage Books, a division of Random House, Inc. Reprinted by permission of Susan Bergholz Literary Services, New York, NY and Lamy, NM and Bloomsbury. All Rights Reserved.

"Fears and Phobias" from *kidshealth.org.* Text copyright © 1995-2012 by The Nemours Foundation/KidsHealth®. Reprinted by permission of The Nemours Foundation.

"Fine?" by Margaret Peterson Haddix from *On the Edge: Stories at the Brink* edited by Lois Duncan. Text copyright © 2000 by Margaret Peterson Haddix. Reprinted by permission of Adams Literary.

"The First Day of School" from *The Happy Marriage and Other Stories* by R.V. Cassill. Text copyright © 1966 by R.V. Cassill. Reprinted by permission of R.V. Cassill.

Excerpt from *Greek Mythology* by Simone Payment. Text copyright © 2006 by The Rosen Publishing Group, Inc. Reprinted by permission of The Rosen Publishing Group, Inc.

Excerpt from *How Smart Are Animals?* by Dorothy Hinshaw Patent. Text copyright © 1990 by Dorothy Hinshaw Patent. Reprinted by permission of Houghton Mifflin Harcourt Publishing Company.

"In the Spotlight" from *Stuff that Scares Your Pants Off* by Glenn Murphy. Text copyright © 2011 by Glenn Murphy. Reprinted by permission of Roaring Brook Press, an imprint of Macmillan Children's Publishing Group.

Excerpt from *It Worked for Me: In Life and Leadership* by Colin Powell with Tony Kolz. Text copyright © 2012 by Colin Powell. Reprinted by permission of HarperCollins Publishers.

"The Last Wolf" by Mary TallMountain. Text copyright © 1994 by the TallMountain Estate. Reprinted by permission of the TallMountain Estate. All rights reserved.

"Let People Own Exotic Animals" by Zuzana Kukol from *USA Today,* March 3, 2003. Text copyright © 2003 by Gannet. Reprinted by permission of PARS International on behalf of USA Today. All Rights Reserved.

"Life Doesn't Frighten Me" from *And Still I Rise* by Maya Angelou. Text copyright © 1978 by Maya Angelou. Reprinted by permission of Random House, Inc. and Virago, an imprint of Little, Brown Book Group. Any third party use of this material, outside of this publication, is prohibited. Interested parties must apply directly to Random House, Inc. for permission.

"Mammoth Shakes and Waves, Disaster in 12 Countries" from *Disasters: Natural and Man-Made Catastrophes Through the Centuries* by Brenda Guiberson. Text copyright © 2010 by Brenda Guiberson. Reprinted by permission of Macmillan Children's Publishing Group.

"The Midnight Ride of Paul Revere" by Henry Wadsworth Longfellow, read by c-david cotrill, sound editing by Shaelyn Hall. Text copyright © 2011 by The Funny Farm Studios. Reprinted by permission of Ron Hall/Evans-Hall, Inc.

Excerpt from "My Wonder Horse" from *Tierra Amarilla: Stories of New Mexico* by Sabine Ulibarrí, translated by Thelma Campbell Nason. Text and English translation copyright © 1971 by University of New Mexico Press. Reprinted by permission of University of New Mexico Press and the Estate of Sabine Ulibarrí.

Excerpt from *A Night to Remember* by Walter Lord. Text copyright © 1955, 1983 by Walter Lord. Reprinted by permission of Henry Holt and Company, LLC.

"On Doomed Flight, Passengers Vowed to Perish Fighting" by Jodi Wilgoren and Edward Wong from *The New York Times,* September 13, 2001. Text copyright © 2001 by The New York Times. Reprinted by permission of PARS International on behalf of The New York Times. All Rights Reserved.

"The Prince and the Pauper" by Mark Twain, adapted by Joellen Bland, in *Plays, The Drama Magazine for Young People* © 2012 and *Stage Plays from the Classics* © 1987. Text copyright © 1987 by Joellen Bland. Reprinted by permission of Plays/Sterling Partners, Inc. Performance rights must be obtained in writing from the publisher.

"The Ravine" by Graham Salisbury from *On the Edge: Stories at the Brink* edited by Lois Duncan. Text copyright © 2000 by Graham Salisbury. Reprinted by permission of Jennifer Flannery Literary Agency.

"The Road Not Taken" from *Mountain Interval* by Robert Frost. Text copyright © 1916 by Henry Holt and Company, LLC. Reprinted by permission of Henry Holt and Company, LLC.

"A Voice" from *Communion* by Pat Mora. Text copyright © 1991 by Arte Público Press - University of Houston. Reprinted by permission of Arte Público Press - University of Houston.

"Watcher (After Katrina, 2005)" from *Beyond Katrina: A Meditation on the Mississippi Gulf Coast* by Natasha Trethewey. Text copyright © 2010 by Natasha Trethewey. Reprinted by permission of the University of Georgia Press.

"Wild Animals Aren't Pets" from *USA Today,* October 20, 2011. Text copyright © 2011 by Gannett. Reprinted by permission of PARS International on behalf of USA Today. All Rights Reserved.

"Words Like Freedom" from *The Collected Works of Langston Hughes* by Langston Hughes, edited by Arnold Rampersad with David Roessel. Text copyright © 1994 by the Estate of Langston Hughes. Reprinted by permission of Random House, Inc. and Harold Ober Associates Inc. as given by Random House. Any third party use of this material, outside of this publication, is prohibited. Interested parties must apply directly to Random House, Inc. for permission.

Yeh-Shen: Cinderella Story from China retold by Ai-Ling Louie. Text copyright © 1982 by Ai-Ling Louie. Reprinted by permission of Philomel Books, a division of Penguin Group (USA) Inc. and McIntosh & Otis, Inc.

Close Reader Acknowledgments

Excerpt from *The Bat Scientists,* retitled "Bats!" by Mary Kay Carson. Text copyright © 2010 by Mary Kay Carson. Reprinted by permission of Houghton Mifflin Harcourt Publishing Company.

"Community Hero: Chief Wilma Mankiller" by Susannah Abbey from www.myhero.com. Text copyright © 2010 by The My Hero Project, Inc. Reprinted by permission of The My Hero Project, Inc.

Excerpt from *The Discovery of the Titanic* by Dr. Robert D. Ballard with Rich Archbold. Text copyright © 1987, 1989 by Ballard & Family. Reprinted by permission of Madison Press Books.

Excerpt from *Every Day Is a Good Day: Reflections by Contemporary Indigenous Women,* retitled "from Every Day Is a New Day" by Wilma Mankiller. Text copyright © 2004, 2011 by Wilma Mankiller. Reprinted by permission of Fulcrum Publishing.

"Face Your Fears," retitled "Face Your Fears: Choking Under Pressure Is Every Athlete's Worst Nightmare" by Dana Hudepohl from *Sports Illustrated for Women,* February 12, 2001. Text copyright © 2001 by CNN/Sports Illustrated. Reprinted by permission of CNN/Sports Illustrated.

"Face Your Fears and Scare the Phobia Out of Your Brain" by Jason Koebler from www.usnews.com, May 21, 2012. Text copyright © 2012 by U.S. News & World Report LP. Reprinted by permission of U.S. News & World Report LP.

Excerpt from *The Jumping Tree* by René Saldaña Jr. Text copyright © 2001 by René Saldaña Jr. Reprinted by permission of Random House, Inc.

"The Light—Ah! The Light" from *Eureka! Poems About Inventors* by Joyce Sidman. Text copyright © 2002 by Joyce Sidman. Reprinted by permission of Lerner Publishing Group.

"Medusa" from *A Nostalgist's Map of America: Poems* by Agha Shahid Ali. Text copyright © 1992 by Agha Shahid Ali. Reprinted by permission of W.W. Norton & Company.

"Medusa's Head" from *Greek Myths* by Olivia E. Coolidge. Text copyright © 1949, renewed 1977 by Olivia E. Coolidge. Reprinted by permission of Houghton Mifflin Harcourt Publishing Company.

"*Moby-Duck* Book Review" by David Holahan, from www.csmonitor.com, April 5, 2011. Text copyright © 2011 by David Holahan. Reprinted by permission of David Holahan.

"On the Titanic, Defined by What They Wore" by Guy Trebay from *The New York Times,* April 11, 2012, www.nytimes.com. Text copyright © 2012 by The New York Times Company. Reprinted by permission of PARS International on behalf of The New York Times.

"The Pod" by Maureen Crane Wartski from *Boy's Life* Magazine, August 2012. Text copyright © 2012 by Maureen Crane Wartski. Published by the Boy Scouts of America. Reprinted by permission of Maureen Crane Wartski.

"The Prince and the Pauper" by Mark Twain, adapted by Joellen Bland from *Stage Plays from the Classics.* Text copyright © 1987, 2000, 2005 by *PLAYS,* The Drama Magazine for Young People/Sterling Partners, Inc. Reprinted by permission of Kalmbach Publishing Company.

Excerpt from *Stan Lee Presents The Prince and the Pauper by Mark Twain.* Copyright © 1978 by Marvel Characters, Inc. Reprinted by permission of Marvel Entertainment.

"There Will Come Soft Rains" by Ray Bradbury. Text copyright © 1950 by the Crowell-Collier Publishing Company, renewed 1977 by Ray Bradbury. Reprinted by permission of Don Congdon Associates, Inc.

"What Do Fish Have to Do with Anything?" from *What Do Fish Have to Do With Anything?* by Avi. Text Copyright © 1997 by Avi. Reprinted by permission of Candlewick Press, Somerville, MA and Brandt & Hochman Literary Agents, Inc.